Microsoft®
SQL Server® 2012
Bible

Microsoft® SQL Server® 2012 BIBLE

Adam Jorgensen

Patrick LeBlanc

Jose Chinchilla

Jorge Segarra

Aaron Nelson

John Wiley & Sons, Inc.

Microsoft® SQL Server® 2012 Bible

Published by
John Wiley & Sons, Inc.
10475 Crosspoint Boulevard
Indianapolis, IN 46256
www.wiley.com

Copyright © 2012 by John Wiley & Sons, Inc., Indianapolis, Indiana

Published simultaneously in Canada

ISBN: 978-1-118-10687-7

ISBN: 978-1-118-28217-5 (ebk)

ISBN: 978-1-118-28386-8 (ebk)

ISBN: 978-1-118-28682-1 (ebk)

Manufactured in the United States of America

10 9 8 7 6 5 4 3 2 1

For general information on our other products and services please contact our Customer Care Department within the United States at (877) 762-2974, outside the United States at (317) 572-3993 or fax (317) 572-4002.

Wiley also publishes its books in a variety of electronic formats and by print-on-demand. Not all content that is available in standard print versions of this book may appear or be packaged in all book formats. If you have purchased a version of this book that did not include media that is referenced by or accompanies a standard print version, you may request this media by visiting http://booksupport.wiley.com. For more information about Wiley products, visit us at www.wiley.com.

Library of Congress Control Number: 2012941788

This book is dedicated to my Lord and Savior, Jesus Christ, who has blessed me with a family and fiancé, who are always my biggest supporters.
-- Adam Jorgensen

To my precious wife, Madeline, for her unconditional love and support for my career and passion for SQL Server and Business Intelligence technologies. To my two princesses, Sofia and Stephanie, for making me understand everyday how beautiful and fun life is.
-- Jose Chinchilla

To my wife, Jessica, whose love, patience, and abundant supply of caffeine helped make this book a reality.
-- Jorge Segarra

About the Authors

Adam Jorgensen (www.adamjorgensen.com), lead author for this edition of the SQL Server 2012 Bible, is the president of Pragmatic Works Consulting (www.pragmaticworks.com); a director for the Professional Association of SQL Server (PASS) (www.sqlpass.org); a SQL Server MVP; and a well-known speaker, author, and executive mentor. His focus is on helping companies realize their full potential by using their data in ways they may not have previously imagined. Adam is involved in the community, delivering more than 75 community sessions per year. He is based in Jacksonville, FL, and has written and contributed to five previous books on SQL Server, analytics, and SharePoint. Adam rewrote or updated the following chapters: 1, 53, 54, and 57.

Jose Chinchilla is a Microsoft Certified Professional with dual MCITP certifications on SQL Server Database Administration and Business Intelligence Development. His career focus has been in Database Modeling, Data Warehouse and ETL Architecture, OLAP Cube Development, Master Data Management, and Data Quality Frameworks. He is the founder and CEO of Agile Bay, Inc., and serves as president of the Tampa Bay Business Intelligence User Group. Jose is a frequent speaker, avid networker, syndicated blogger (www.sqljoe.com), and social networker and can be reached via twitter under the @SQLJoe handle or LinkedIn at www.linkedin.com/in/josechinchilla. He rewrote or updated the following chapters: 3, 24, 25, 29, 32, 33, 43, 58, and 59.

Patrick LeBlanc, former SQL Server MVP, is currently a SQL Server and BI Technical Specialist for Microsoft. He has worked as a SQL Server DBA for the past 9 years. His experience includes working in the educational, advertising, mortgage, medical, and financial industries. He is also the founder of TSQLScripts.com, SQLLunch.com, and the president of the Baton Rouge Area SQL Server User Group. Patrick rewrote or updated the following chapters: 6, 7, 8, 10, 11, 12, 28, 48, 49, and 51.

Aaron Nelson is a SQL Server Architect with more than 10 years' experience in architecture, Business Intelligence, development, and performance tuning. He has the distinction of being a second-generation DBA, having learned the family business at his father's knee. Aaron is the chapter leader for the PowerShell Virtual Chapter of PASS and volunteers for Atlanta MDF, the Atlanta PowerShell User Group, and SQL Saturday. He blogs at http://sqlvariant.com and can be found on Twitter as @SQLvariant. He loves walking on the beach, winding people up, and falling out of kayaks with his beautiful daughter, Dorothy. When Aaron is not busy traveling to PASS or Microsoft events, he can usually be found somewhere near Atlanta, GA. Aaron rewrote or updated the following chapters: 9, 30, 36, 37, 38, 41, and 42.

Jorge Segarra is currently a DBA consultant for Pragmatic Works and a SQL Server MVP. He also authored *SQL Server 2008 Pro Policy-Based Management* (APress, 2010). Jorge has been an active member of the SQL Server community for the last few years and is a regular presenter at events such as webinars, user groups, SQLSaturdays, SQLRally, and PASS Summit. He founded SQL University, a free community-based resource aimed at teaching people SQL Server from the ground up. SQL University can be found online at http://sqluniversity.org. Jorge also blogs at his own site http://sqlchicken.com and can be found on Twitter as @sqlchicken. He rewrote or updated the following chapters: 4, 5, 19, 20, 21, 22, 23, 26, 27, and 50.

About the Contributors

Tim Chapman is a Dedicated Support Engineer in Premier Field Engineering at Microsoft where he specializes in database architecture and performance tuning. Before coming to Microsoft, Tim Chapman was a database architect for a large financial institution and a consultant for many years. Tim enjoys blogging, teaching and speaking at PASS events, and participated in writing the second SQL Server MVP Deep Dives book. Tim graduated with a bachelor's degree in Information Systems from Indiana University. Tim rewrote or updated chapters 39, 40, 44, 45, 46, and 47.

Audrey Hammonds is a database developer, blogger, presenter, and writer. Fifteen years ago, she volunteered to join a newly formed database team so that she could stop writing COBOL. (And she never wrote COBOL again.) Audrey is convinced that the world would be a better place if people would stop, relax, enjoy the view, and normalize their data. She's the wife of Jeremy; mom of Chase and Gavin; and adoptive mother to her cats, Bela, Elmindreda, and Aviendha. She blogs at http://datachix.com and is based in Atlanta, Georgia. Audrey rewrote or updated the following chapters: 2, 16, 17, and 18.

Scott Klein is a Technical Evangelist for Microsoft, focusing on Windows Azure SQL Database (formerly known as SQL Azure). He has over 20 years working with SQL Server, and he caught the cloud vision when he was introduced to the Azure platform. Scott's background includes co-owning an Azure consulting business and providing consulting services to companies large and small. He speaks frequently at conferences world-wide as well as community events, such as SQL Saturday events and local user groups. Scott has authored a half-dozen books for both Wrox and APress, and co-authored the book *Professional SQL Azure* (APress, 2010). Scott is also the founder of the South Florida Geek Golf charity golf tournament, which has helped raise thousands of dollars for charities across South Florida, even though he can't play golf at all. As much as he loves SQL Server and Windows Azure, Scott also enjoys spending time with his family and looks forward to getting back to real camping in the Pacific Northwest. Scott rewrote or updated the following chapters: 13, 14, 15, and 31.

David Liebman is a developer specializing in .Net, SQL, and SSRS development for more than 5 of the 18 years he has spent in the IT industry, working for some big companies in financial, healthcare, and insurance sectors. Dave has written some custom reporting solutions and web applications for large companies in the Tampa Bay area using .NET, SSRS, and SQL. He is currently a senior developer at AgileThought located in Tampa, FL. Dave rewrote or updated the content in the following chapters: 34 and 35.

Julie Smith has spent the last 12 years moving data using various tools, mostly with SQL Server 2000–2012. She is an MCTS in SQL Server 2008 BI, and a Business Intelligence Consultant at Innovative Architects in Atlanta, GA. She is a co-founder of http://Datachix.com, where she can be reached. With the help of MGT (Mountain Dew, Gummy Bears, and Tic Tacs), she revised and updated the following chapters: 52, 55, and 56. She dedicates her effort on this book to her husband, Ken.

About the Technical Editors

 Kathi Kellenberger is a Senior Consultant with Pragmatic Works. She enjoys speaking and writing about SQL Server and has worked with SQL Server since 1997. In her spare time, Kathi enjoys spending time with friends and family, running, and singing.

 Bradley Schact is a consultant at Pragmatic Works in Jacksonville, FL and an author on the book *SharePoint 2010 Business Intelligence 24-Hour Trainer* (Wrox, 2012). Bradley has experience on many parts of the Microsoft BI platform. He frequently speaks at events like SQL Saturday, Code Camp, SQL Lunch, and SQL Server User Groups.

 Mark Stacey founded Pragmatic Works South Africa, the first Pragmatic Works international franchise, and works tirelessly to cross the business/technical boundaries in Business Intelligence, working in both Sharepoint and SQL.

Credits

Executive Editor
Robert Elliott

Senior Project Editor
Ami Frank Sullivan

Technical Editors
Kathi Kellenberger
Wendy Pastrick
Mark Stacey
Bradley Schact

Production Editor
Kathleen Wisor

Copy Editor
Apostrophe Editing Services

Editorial Manager
Mary Beth Wakefield

Freelancer Editorial Manager
Rosemarie Graham

Associate Director of Marketing
David Mayhew

Marketing Manager
Ashley Zurcher

Business Manager
Amy Knies

Production Manager
Tim Tate

Vice President and Executive Group Publisher
Richard Swadley

Vice President and Executive Publisher
Neil Edde

Associate Publisher
Jim Minatel

Project Coordinator, Cover
Katie Crocker

Proofreader
Nancy Carrasco

Indexer
Robert Swanson

Cover Image
© Aleksandar Velasevic / iStockPhoto

Cover Designer
Ryan Sneed

Acknowledgments

From Adam Jorgensen:

Thank you to my team at Pragmatic Works, who are always a big part of any project like this and continue to give me the passion to see them through. I would also like to thank my furry children, Lady and Mac, for their "dogged" persistence in keeping me awake for late nights of writing. Thank you especially to the SQL Community; my fellow MVP's; and all of you who have attended a SQL Saturday, other PASS event, spoke at a user group, or just got involved. You are the reason we have such a vibrant community, the best in technology. Keep it up; your passion and curiosity drives all of us further every day.

I want to thank my incredible author and tech editing teams. This team of community experts and professionals worked very hard to take a great book and re-invent it in the spirit of the changing landscape that we are witnessing. There were so many new features, focuses, messages, and opportunities to change the way we think, do business, and provide insight that we needed an amazing team of folks. They put up with my cat herding and hit "most" of their deadlines. Their passion for the community is tremendous, and it shines throughout this book. Thank you all from the bottom of my heart. You readers are about to see why this book was such a labor of love! A special thanks to Bob and Ami over at Wiley for their support and effort in getting this title completed. What a great team!

From Jose Chinchilla:

Many thanks to the team that put together this book for keeping us in line with our due dates. Thanks to my lovely family for allowing me to borrow precious time from them in order to fulfill my writing and community commitments. I also want to thank Nicholas Cain for his expert contribution to the SQL Clustering Chapter and to Michael Wells for his SQL Server deployment automation PowerShell scripts that are part of his Codeplex project named SPADE.

From Aaron Nelson:

Thank you to my parents, Michael & Julia Nelson. Thanks to my daughter, Dorothy Nelson, for being patient during this project. Finally, thank you to my Atlanta SQL Community members that helped me make this happen: Audrey Hammonds, Julie Smith, Rob Volk, and Tim Radney.

Acknowledgments

From Jorge Segarra:

First and foremost I'd like to thank my wife. There's no way I would've been able to get through the long nights and weekends without her. To our amazing editors, Ami Sullivan and Robert Elliott, and the rest of the folks at Wrox/Wiley: Your tireless efforts and ability to herd A.D.D.-afflicted cats is astounding and appreciated. Thanks to Adam Jorgensen for giving me and the rest of this author team the opportunity to write on this title.

To my fellow authoring team, Adam Jorgensen, Patrick LeBlanc, Aaron Nelson, Julie Smith, Jose Chinchilla, Audrey Hammonds, Tim Chapman, and David Liebman: Thank you all for your tireless work and contributions. To the authors of the previous edition: Paul Nielsen, Mary Chipman, Scott Klein, Uttam Parui, Jacob Sebastian, Allen White, and Michael White — this book builds on the foundation you all laid down, so thank you.

One of the greatest things about being involved with SQL Server is the community around it. It really is a like a big family, a SQLFamily! I'd love to name everyone here I've met (and haven't met yet!) at events or online, but I'd run out of room. Special thanks to Pam Shaw for introducing me to the community and giving me my first speaking opportunity.

Finally, huge thanks to the folks at Microsoft for putting together such an amazing product! SQL Server has grown by leaps and bounds over the years and this release is by far the most exciting. In addition to the product team, special thanks to the SQL Server MVP community, of which I'm honored and privileged to be a part.

Contents

Contents

Contents

Contents

Part IX: Business Intelligence

Introduction

Welcome to the *SQL Server 2012 Bible*. SQL Server is an incredible database product that offers an excellent mix of performance, reliability, ease of administration, and new architectural options, yet enables the developer or DBA to control minute details. SQL Server is a dream system for a database developer.

If there's a theme to SQL Server 2012, it's this: enterprise-level excellence. SQL Server 2012 opens several new possibilities to design more scalable and powerful systems. The first goal of this book is to share with you the pleasure of working with SQL Server.

Like all books in the Bible series, you can expect to find both hands-on tutorials and real-world practical applications, as well as reference and background information that provide a context for what you are learning. However, to cover every minute detail of every command of this complex product would consume thousands of pages, so it is the second goal of this book to provide a concise yet comprehensive guide to SQL Server 2012. By the time you have completed the *SQL Server 2012 Bible*, you will be well prepared to develop and manage your SQL Server 2012 database and BI environment.

Some of you are repeat readers of this series (thanks!) and are familiar with the approach from the previous *SQL Server* Bibles. Even though you might be familiar with this approach, you will find several new features in this edition, including the following:

- A What's New sidebar in most chapters presents a timeline of the features so that you can envision the progression.
- Expanded chapters on Business Intelligence.
- The concepts on T-SQL focusing on the best and most useful areas, while making room for more examples.
- New features such as Always On, performance tuning tools, and items like column store indexing.
- All the newest features from T-SQL to the engine to BI, which broaden the reach of this title.

Who Should Read This Book

There are five distinct roles in the SQL Server space:

- Data architect/data modeler
- Database developer

- Database administrator
- Business Intelligence (BI) developer
- PTO performance tuning and optimization expert

This book has been carefully planned to address each of these roles.

Whether you are a database developer or a database administrator, whether you are just starting out or have one year of experience or five, this book contains material that will be useful to you.

Although the book is targeted at intermediate-level database professionals, each chapter begins with the assumption that you've never seen the topic before and then progresses through the subject, presenting the information that makes a difference.

At the higher end of the spectrum, the book pushes the intermediate professional into certain advanced areas in which it makes the most sense. For example, you can find advanced material on T-SQL queries, index strategies, and data architecture.

How This Book Is Organized

SQL Server is a huge product with dozens of technologies and interrelated features. Just organizing a book of this scope is a daunting task.

A book of this size and scope must also be approachable as both a cover-to-cover read and a reference book. The nine parts of this book are organized by job role, project flow, and skills progression:

Part I: Laying the Foundations

Part II: Building Databases and Working with Data

Part III: Advanced T-SQL Data Types and Querying Techniques

Part IV: Programming with T-SQL

Part V: Enterprise Data Management

Part VI: Securing Your SQL Server

Part VII: Monitoring and Auditing

Part VIII: Performance Tuning and Optimization

Part IX: Business Intelligence

SQL Server Books Online

This book is not a rehash of Books Online and doesn't pretend to replace Books Online. We avoid listing the complete syntax of every command — there's little value in reprinting Books Online.

Instead, this book shows you what you need to know to get the most out of SQL Server so that you can learn from the author's and co-authors' experience.

You can find each feature explained as if we are friends — you have a new job that requires a specific feature you're unfamiliar with, and you ask us to get you up-to-speed with what matters most.

The chapters contain critical concepts, real-world examples, and best practices.

Conventions and Features

This book contains several different organizational and typographical features designed to help you get the most from the information.

Tips, Notes, Cautions, and Cross-References

Whenever the authors want to bring something important to your attention, the information appears in a Caution, Tip, or Note.

> **CAUTION**
>
> This information is important and is set off in a separate paragraph. Cautions provide information about things to watch out for, whether simply inconvenient or potentially hazardous to your data or systems.

> **TIP**
>
> Tips generally provide information that can make your work simpler — special shortcuts or methods for doing something easier than the norm. You will often find the relevant .sys files listed in a tip.

> **NOTE**
>
> Notes provide additional, ancillary information that is helpful, but somewhat outside of the current presentation of information.

 Cross-references provide a roadmap to related content, be it on the web, another chapter in this book, or another book.

What's New and Best Practice Sidebars

Two sidebar features are specific to this book: the What's New sidebars and the Best Practice sidebars.

What's New with SQL Server Feature

Whenever possible and practical, a sidebar will be included that highlights the relevant new features covered in the chapter. Often, these sidebars also alert you to which features have been eliminated and which are deprecated. Usually, these sidebars are placed near the beginning of the chapter.

Best Practice

This book is based on the real-life experiences of SQL Server developers and administrators. To enable you to benefit from all that experience, the best practices have been pulled out in sidebar form wherever and whenever they apply.

Where to Go from Here

There's a whole world of SQL Server. Dig in. Explore. Play with SQL Server. Try out new ideas, and post questions in the Wrox forums (monitored by the author team) if you have questions or discover something cool. You can find the forums at www.wrox.com.

Come to a conference or user group where the authors are speaking. They would love to meet you in person and sign your book. You can learn where and when on SQLSaturday.com and SQLPASS.org.

With a topic as large as SQL Server and a community this strong, a lot of resources are available. But there's a lot of hubris around SQL Server, too; for recommended additional resources and SQL Server books, check the book's website.

Part I

Laying the Foundations

IN THIS PART

The World of SQL Server

IN THIS CHAPTER

Understanding SQL Server History and Overview

Understanding SQL Server Components and Tools

Understanding Notable Features in SQL 2012

What's New with SQL Server 2012?

SQL Server 2012 represents another tremendous accomplishment for the Microsoft data platform organization. A number of new features in this release drive performance and scalability to new heights. A large focus is on speed of data access, ease and flexibility of integration, and capability of visualization. These are all strategic areas in which Microsoft has focused on to add value since SQL Server 2005.

SQL Server History

SQL Server has grown considerably over the past two decades from its early roots with Sybase.

In 1989, Microsoft, Sybase, and Ashton-Tate jointly released **SQL Server 1.0.** The product was based on Sybase SQL Server 3.0 for UNIX and VMS.

SQL Server 4.2.1 for Windows NT released in 1993. Microsoft began making changes to the code.

SQL Server 6.0 (code named SQL 95) released in 1995. In 1996, the 6.5 upgrade (Hydra) was released in 1996. It included the first version of Enterprise Manager (StarFighter I) and SQL Server Agent (StarFighter II.)

SQL Server 7.0 (Sphinx), released in 1999 and was a full rewrite of the database engine by Microsoft. From a code sense, this was the first Microsoft SQL Server. SQL Server 7 also included English Query (Argo), OLAP Services (Plato), Replication, Database Design and Query tools (DaVinci), and Full-Text Search (aptly code named Babylon). Data Transformation Services (DTS) was introduced.

SQL Server 2000 (Shiloh) 32-bit, version 8, introduced SQL Server to the enterprise with clustering, better performance, and OLAP. It supported XML through three different XML add-on packs. It added user-defined functions, indexed views, clustering support, OLAP, Distributed Partition Views, and improved Replication. SQL Server 2000 64-bit version for Intel Itanium (Liberty) released in 2003, along with the first version of Reporting Services (Rosetta) and Data Mining tools (Aurum). DTS becomes powerful and gained in popularity. Northwind joined Pubs as the sample database.

SQL Server 2005 (Yukon), version 9, was another rewrite of the database engine and pushed SQL Server further into the enterprise space. In 2005, a ton of new features and technologies were added including Service Broker, Notification Services, CLR, XQuery and XML data types, and SQLOS. T-SQL gained try-catch, and the system tables were replaced with Dynamic Management Views. Management Studio replaced Enterprise Manager and Query Analyzer. DTS was replaced by Integration Services. English Query was removed, and stored procedure debugging was moved from the DBA interface to Visual Studio. AdventureWorks and AdventureWorksDW replaced Northwind and Pubs as the sample database. SQL Server 2005 supported 32-bit, 64x, and Itanium CPUs. Steve Ballmer publically vowed to never again make customers wait 5 years between releases and to return to a 2-to-3-year release cycle.

SQL Server 2008 (Katmai), version 10, is a natural evolution of SQL Server adding Policy-Based Management, Data Compression, Resource Governor, and new beyond relational data types. Notification Services went the way of English Query. T-SQL finally has date and time data types, table-valued parameters, the debugger returns, and Management Studio gets IntelliSense.

SQL Server 2008R2, version 10.5, is a release mostly focused on new business intelligence features and SharePoint 2010 supportability. The list of major new work and code in the SQL Server 2005 and 2008/R2 releases have been fully covered in previous editions, but the high points would be SQLCLR (this was the integration of another long-term strategy project); XML support; Service Broker; and Integration Services, which is all ground up code. Microsoft formed a new team built on the original members of the DTS team, adding in some C++, hardware, AS and COM+ folks, and Report Builder. Additional features to support SharePoint 2010 functionality and other major releases are also critically important. Now you have SQL 2012; so look at where this new release can carry you forward.

SQL Server in the Database Market

SQL Server's position in the database market has consistently grown over time. This section discusses some of the primary competition to SQL Server, and what makes SQL a strong choice for data management, business intelligence, and cloud computing along with the strength of the SQL Server community.

SQL Server's Competition

SQL Server competes primarily with two other major database platforms, Oracle and IBM's DB2. Both of these products have existed for longer than SQL Server, but the last four releases of SQL Server have brought them closer together. They are adding features that SQL has had for years and vice versa. Many of the scalability improvements added since SQL 2005 have been directly focused on overtaking the performance and other qualities of these products. Microsoft has succeeded in these releases in besting benchmarks set by many other products both in the relational database platforms as well as in data integration, analytics, and reporting. These improvements, along with the strongest integrated ecosystem, including cloud (Windows Azure SQL Database), portal (SharePoint 2010), and business intelligence make SQL Server the market leader.

Strength of Community

SQL Server has one of the strongest communities of any technology platform. There are many websites, blogs, and community contributors that make up a great ecosystem of support. Some great avenues to get involved with include the following:

- PASS (Professional Association of SQL Server) `SQLPASS.org`
- SQL Saturday events — `SQLSaturday.com`
- `SQLServerCentral.com`
- `BIDN.com`
- `MSSQLTips.com`
- `SQLServerPedia.com`
- `Twitter.com` — #SQLHelp

Many of these are started and operated by Microsoft SQL Server MVPs and companies focused on SQL Server, education, and mentoring.

SQL Server Components

SQL Server is composed of the database engine, services, business intelligence tools, and other items including cloud functionality. This section outlines the major components and tools you need to become familiar with as you begin to explore this platform.

Database Engine

The SQL Server *Database Engine*, sometimes called the *relational engine*, is the core of SQL Server. It is the component that handles all the relational database work. SQL is a descriptive language, meaning that SQL describes only the question to the engine; the engine takes over from there.

Within the relational engine are several key processes and components, including the following:

- The *Algebrizer* checks the syntax and transforms a query to an internal representation used by the following components.

  - SQL Server's *Query Optimizer* determines how to best process the query based on the costs of different types of query-execution operations. The estimated and actual query-execution plans may be viewed graphically, or in XML, using Management Studio or SQL Profiler.

  - The *Query Engine*, or *Query Processor* executes the queries according to the plan generated by the Query Optimizer.

  - The *Storage Engine* works for the Query Engine and handles the actual reading and writing to and from the disk.

  - The *Buffer Manager* analyzes the data pages used and prefetches data from the data file(s) into memory, thus reducing the dependency on disk I/O performance.

  - The *Checkpoint* process writes dirty data pages (modified pages) from memory to the data file.

  - The *Resource* Monitor optimizes the query plan cache by responding to memory pressure and intelligently removing older query plans from the cache.

  - The *Lock Manager* dynamically manages the scope of locks to balance the number of required locks with the size of the lock.

  - SQL Server eats resources for lunch, and for this reason it needs direct control of the available resources (memory, threads, I/O request, and so on). Simply leaving the resource management to Windows isn't sophisticated enough for SQL Server. SQL Server includes its own OS layer, called *SQLOS*, which manages all its internal resources.

SQL Server 2012 supports installation of many instances of the relational engine on a physical server. Although they share some components, each instance functions as a complete separate installation of SQL Server.

Services

The following components are client processes for SQL Server used to control, or communicate with, SQL Server.

SQL Server Agent

The Server Agent is an optional process that, when running, executes SQL jobs and handles other automated tasks. It can be configured to automatically run when the system boots or may be started from the SQL Server Configuration Manager or the Management Studio's Object Explorer.

Database Mail

The Database Mail component enables SQL Server to send mail to an external mailbox through SMTP. Mail may be generated from multiple sources within SQL Server, including T-SQL code, jobs, alerts, Integration Services, and maintenance plans.

Microsoft Distributed Transaction Coordinator (MSDTC)

The Distributed Transaction Coordinator is a process that handles dual-phase commits for transactions that span multiple SQL Servers. DTC can be started from within Windows' Computer Administration/Services. If the application regularly uses distributed transactions, you should start DTC when the operating system starts.

Business Intelligence

Business intelligence (BI) is the name given to the discipline and tools that enable the management of data for the purpose of analysis, exploration, reporting, mining, and visualization. Although aspects of BI appear in many applications, the BI approach and toolset provide a rich and robust environment to understand data and trends.

SQL Server provides a great toolset to build BI applications, which explains Microsoft's continued gains in the growing BI market. SQL Server includes three services designed for BI: Integration Services (IS, sometimes called SSIS for SQL Server Integration Services), Reporting Services (RS), and Analysis Services (AS). Development for all three services can be done using the new SQL Server Data Tools, which is the new combining of Business Intelligence Development Studio and database development into a new environment in Visual Studio.

SSIS

Integration Services moves data among nearly any types of data sources and is SQL Server's Extract-Transform-Load (ETL) tool. IS uses a graphical tool to define how data can be moved from one connection to another connection. IS packages have the flexibility to either copy data column for column or perform complex transformations, lookups, and exception handling during the data move. IS is extremely useful during data conversions, collecting data from many dissimilar data sources, or gathering for data warehousing data that can be analyzed using Analysis Services.

IS has many advantages over using custom programming or T-SQL to move and transform data; chief among these are speed and traceability. If you have experience with other databases but are new to SQL Server, this is one of the tools that will impress you. If any other company were marketing SSIS, it would be the flagship product, but instead it's bundled inside SQL Server without much fanfare and at no extra charge. Be sure to find the time to explore IS.

SSAS

The Analysis Services service hosts two key components of the BI toolset: Online Analytical Processing (OLAP) hosts multidimensional databases where data is stored in cubes, whereas Data Mining provides methods to analyze datasets for nonobvious patterns in the data.

OLAP

Building cubes in a multidimensional database provides a fast, pre-interpreted, flexible analysis environment. Robust calculations can be included in a cube for later query and reporting, going a long way toward the "one version of the truth" that is so elusive in many organizations. Results can be used as the basis for reports, but the most powerful uses involve the interactive data exploration using tools such as Excel pivot tables or similar query and analysis applications. Tables and charts that summarize billions of rows can be generated in seconds, allowing users to understand the data in ways they never thought possible.

Although relational databases in SQL Server are queried using T-SQL, cubes are queried using the Multidimensional Expressions (MDX), a set-based query language tailored to retrieving multidimensional data. (See Figure 1-1.) This enables relatively easy custom application development in addition to standard analysis and reporting tools.

FIGURE 1-1

Example of MDX query in Analysis Services.

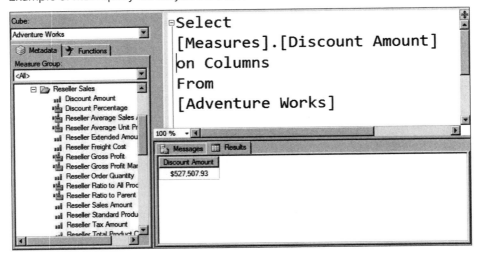

Data Mining

Viewing data from cubes or even relational queries can reveal the obvious trends and correlations in a dataset, but data mining can expose the nonobvious ones. The robust set of mining algorithms enables tasks such as finding associations, forecasting, and classifying cases into groups. When a model is trained on an existing set of data, it can predict new cases that occur, for example, predicting the most profitable customers to spend scarce advertising dollars on or estimating expected component failure rates based on its characteristics.

SSRS

Reporting Services (RS) for SQL Server 2012 is a full-featured, web-based, managed reporting solution. RS reports can be exported to PDF, Excel, or other formats with a single click and are easy to build and customize.

Reports are defined graphically or programmatically and stored as `.rdl` files in the RS databases in SQL Server. They can be scheduled to be pre-created and cached for users, e-mailed to users, or generated by users on-the-fly with parameters. Reporting Services is bundled with SQL Server so there are no end-user licensing issues. It's essentially free; although most DBAs place it on its own dedicated server for better performance. There is new functionality in SSRS 2012 with the addition of Power View. This is a SharePoint integrated feature that provides for rich drag and drop visualization and data exploration. It is one of the hottest new features in SQL 2012.

Tools and Add-Ons

SQL Server 2012 retains most of the UI feel of SQL Server 2008, with a few significant enhancements.

SQL Server Management Studio

Management Studio is a Visual Studio–esque integrated environment that's used by database administrators and database developers. At its core is the visual Object Explorer complete with filters and the capability to browse all the SQL Server servers (database engine, Analysis Services, Reporting Services, and so on). Management Studio's Query Editor is an excellent way to work with raw T-SQL code, and it's integrated with the Solution Explorer to manage projects. Although the interface can look crowded (see Figure 1-2), the windows are easily configurable and can auto-hide.

SQL Server Configuration Manager

This tool is used to start and stop any server, set the start-up options, and configure the connectivity. It may be launched from the Start menu or from Management Studio. It can show you all the services and servers running on a particular server.

FIGURE 1-2

SQL Server Management Studio Query Interface.

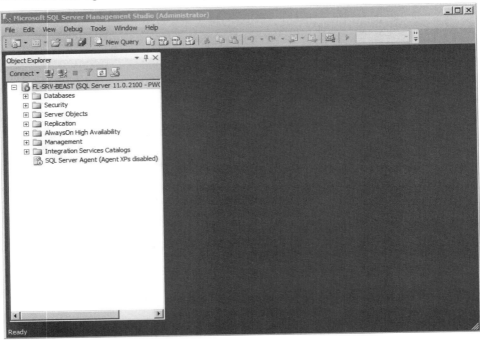

SQL Profiler/Trace/Extended Events

SQL Server has the capability to expose a trace of selected events and data points. The server-side trace has nearly no load on the server. SQL Profiler is the UI for viewing traces in real time (with some performance cost) or viewing saved Trace files. Profiler is great for debugging an application or tuning the database. Profiler is being deprecated in favor of extended events. This will enable a deeper level of tracing with a decreased load on the server overall . This feature is continually enhanced and grown by support for other features such as Reporting services, Analysis Services, etc.

Performance Monitor

Although Profiler records large sets of details concerning SQL traffic and SQL Server events, Performance Monitor is a visual window into the current status of the selected performance counters. Performance Monitor is found within Windows's administrative tools. When SQL Server is installed, it adds a ton of useful performance counters to Performance Monitor. It's enough to make a network administrator jealous.

Database Engine Tuning Advisor

The Database Engine Tuning Advisor analyzes a batch of queries (from Profiler) and recommends index and partition modifications for performance. The scope of changes it can recommend is configurable, and the changes may be applied in part or in whole at the time of the analysis or later. The features of DBTA have been significantly enhanced in this newest version.

Command-Line Utilities

You can use various command-line utilities to execute SQL code (sqlcmd) or perform bulk copy program (bcp) from the DOS prompt or a command-line scheduler. Integration Services and SQL Server Agent have rendered these tools somewhat obsolete, but in the spirit of extreme flexibility, Microsoft still includes them.

Management Studio has a mode that enables you to use the Query Editor as if it were the command-line utility sqlcmd.

Online Resources

The SQL Server documentation team did an excellent job with Books Online (BOL) — SQL Server's mega help on steroids. The articles tend to be complete and include several examples. The indexing method provides a short list of applicable articles. BOL may be opened from Management Studio or directly from the Start menu.

BOL is well integrated with the primary interfaces. Selecting a keyword within Management Studio's Query Editor and pressing F1 launches BOL to the selected keyword. The Enterprise Manager help buttons can also launch the correct BOL topic.

Management Studio also includes a dynamic Help window that automatically tracks the cursor and presents help for the current keyword.

Searching returns both online and local MSDN articles. In addition, BOL searches the Codezone Community for relevant articles.

The Community Menu and Developer Center both launch web pages that enable users to ask a question or learn more about SQL Server.

CodePlex.com

If you haven't discovered CodePlex.com, allow me to introduce it to you. CodePlex.com is Microsoft's site for open source code. That's where you can find AdventureWorks, the official sample database for SQL Server 2012, along with AdventureWorksLT (a smaller version for AdventureWorks) and AdventureWorksDW (the BI companion to AdventureWorks).

Editions of SQL Server 2012

The edition layout of SQL Server has changed again with this release to align closer with the way organizations use the product. Following are three main editions:

- **Enterprise:** This edition focused on mission critical applications and data warehousing.
- **Business intelligence:** This new edition has premium corporate features and self-service business intelligence features. If your environment is truly mission critical however, this may be missing some key features you might want. The key is to leverage this edition on your BI servers and use Enterprise where needed.
- **Standard:** This edition remains to support basic database capabilities including reporting and analytics.

You may wonder about the previous editions and how to move from what you have to the new plan. Following is a breakdown of deprecated editions and where the features now reside.

- **Datacenter:** Its features are now available in Enterprise Edition.
- **Workgroup:** Standard will become your edition for basic database needs.
- **Standard for small business:** Standard becomes your sole edition for basic database needs.

Notable SQL Server 2012 Enhancements

SQL 2012 has added many areas to its ecosystem. This includes new appliances, integration with "Big Data," and connectors that leverage this technology as sources and destinations for analytics. Reference architectures have been improved and are released with improvements for SQL 2012. New features that add incredible performance boosts make these architectures a major weapon in return on investment (ROI) for many organizations.

Many of the important features that have been added to SQL Server 2012 fall into several categories, including the following:

- **Availability Enhancements**
  - AlwaysOn Failover Cluster instances
  - AlwaysOn Availability Groups
  - Online operations
- **Manageability Enhancements**
  - SQL Server Management Studio enhancements
  - Contained databases
  - Data-Tier Applications

- Windows PowerShell
- Database Tuning Advisor enhancements
- New Dynamic Management Views and Functions
- **Programmability Enhancements**
  - FileTables
  - Statistical Semantic Search functionality
  - Full-Text Search improvements
  - New and improved Spatial features
  - Metadata discovery and Execute Statement metadata support
  - Sequence Objects
  - THROW statement
  - 14 new T-SQL functions
  - Extended Events enhancements and more
- **Security Enhancements**
  - Enhanced Provisioning during setup
  - New permissions levels
  - New role management
  - Significant SQL Audit enhancements
  - Improved Hashing algorithms
- **Scalability and Performance Enhancements**
  - ColumnStore Indexes and Velocity
  - Online Index operation support for x(max) columns
  - Partition support increased to 15,000
- **Business Intelligence Features**
  - New Data Cleansing Components
  - Improved usability for SSIS and new deployment functionality
  - Master Data functionality has been significantly enhanced
  - New exciting features for Power Pivot
  - Power View data exploration and visualization
  - Tabular Models in SSAS
  - Expanded Extended Events throughout the BI ecosystem

These enhancements are discussed in detail through the upcoming chapters. More exciting details to come!

Summary

SQL Server 2012 has created many new opportunities for building some incredible scalable and high-performance applications and solutions. Many improvements have been added for availability performance, configuration, intelligence and insight, and cloud functionality. This book covers all these new features, how to use them, and how to best leverage them for your organization.

Data Architecture

IN THIS CHAPTER

Understanding Pragmatic Data Architecture

Evaluating Six Objectives of Information Architecture

Designing a Performance Framework

Using Advanced Scalability Options

You can tell by looking at a building whether there's elegance to the architecture, but architecture is more than just good looks. Architecture brings together materials, foundations, and standards. In the same way, data architecture is the study to define what a good database is and how you can build a good database. That's why data architecture is more than just data modeling, more than just server configuration, and more than just a collection of tips and tricks.

Data architecture is the overarching design of the database, how the database should be developed and implemented, and how it interacts with other software. In this sense, data architecture can be related to the architecture of a home, a factory, or a skyscraper. Data architecture is defined by the *Information Architecture Principle* and the six attributes by which every database can be measured.

Enterprise data architecture extends the basic ideas of designing a single database to include designing which types of databases serve which needs within the organization; how those databases share resources; and how they communicate with one another and other software. In this sense, enterprise data architecture is community planning or zoning, and is concerned with applying the best database meta-patterns (for example, relational OTLP database, object-oriented database, and multidimensional) to an organization's various needs.

What's New with Data Architecture in SQL Server 2012

SQL Server 2012 introduces a couple of new features that the data architect will want to be familiar with and leverage while designing a data storage solution. These include:

- **Columnstore indexes**: allows data in the index to be stored in a columnar format rather than traditional rowstore format, which provides the potential for vastly reduced query times for large-scale databases. More information about columnstore indexes can be found in Chapter 45, "Indexing Strategies".

- **Data Quality Services (DQS)**: enables you to build a knowledge base that supports data quality analysis, cleansing, and standardization.

Information Architecture Principle

For any complex endeavor, there is value in beginning with a common principle to drive designs, procedures, and decisions. A credible principle is understandable, robust, complete, consistent, and stable. When an overarching principle is agreed upon, conflicting opinions can be objectively measured, and standards can be decided upon that support the principle.

The Information Architecture Principle encompasses the three main areas of information management: database design and development, enterprise data center management, and business intelligence analysis.

> *Information Architecture Principle: Information is an organizational asset, and, according to its value and scope, must be organized, inventoried, secured, and made readily available in a usable format for daily operations and analysis by individuals, groups, and processes, both today and in the future.*

Unpacking this principle reveals several practical implications. There should be a known inventory of information, including its location, source, sensitivity, present and future value, and current owner. Although most organizational information is stored in IT databases, uninventoried critical data is often found scattered throughout the organization in desktop databases, spreadsheets, scraps of papers, and Post-it notes, and (the most dangerous of all) inside the head of key employees.

Just as the value of physical assets varies from asset to asset and over time, the value of information is also variable and so must be assessed. Information value may be high for an individual or department, but less valuable to the organization as a whole; information that is critical today might be meaningless in a month; or information that may seem insignificant individually might become critical for organizational planning when aggregated.

If the data is to be made readily available in the future, then current designs must be flexible enough to avoid locking the data in a rigid, but brittle, database.

Database Objectives

Based on the Information Architecture Principle, every database can be architected or evaluated by six interdependent database objectives. Four of these objectives are primarily a function of design, development, and implementation: *usability*, *extensibility*, *data integrity*, and *performance*. *Availability* and *security* are more a function of implementation than design.

With sufficient design effort and a clear goal to meet all six objectives, it is fully possible to design and develop an elegant database that does just that. No database architecture is going to be 100 percent perfect, but with an early focus on design and fundamental principles, you can go a long way toward creating a database that can grow along with your organization.

You can measure each objective on a continuum. The data architect is responsible to inform the organization about these six objectives, including the cost associated with meeting each objective, the risk of failing to meet the objective, and the recommended level for each objective.

It's the organization's privilege to then prioritize the objectives compared with the relative cost.

Usability

The usability of a data store (the architectural term for a database) involves the completeness of meeting the organization's requirements; the suitability of the design for its intended purpose; the effectiveness of the format of data available to applications; the robustness of the database; and the ease of extracting information (by programmers and power users). The most common reason why a database is less than usable is an overly complex or inappropriate design.

Usability is enabled in the design by ensuring the following:

- A thorough and well-documented understanding of the organizational requirements
- Life-cycle planning of software features
- Selecting the correct meta-pattern (for example, transactional and dimensional) for the data store
- Normalization and correct handling of optional data
- Simplicity of design
- A well-defined abstraction layer

Extensibility

The Information Architecture Principle states that the information must be readily available today and in the future, which requires the database to be *extensible* and able to be easily adapted to meet new requirements. The concepts of data integrity, performance, and availability are all mature and well understood by the computer science and IT professions. With enough time and resources, you can design a data architecture that meets the objective of extensibility. The trick is to make sure that your entire organization understands that the resource investment is not only important, but also absolutely necessary to good data architecture. There are many databases that fell victim to the curse of not enough time and too few resources. These are usually the ones that can't grow and adapt to new business requirements or organizational change well. Extensibility is incorporated into the design as follows:

- Normalization and correct handling of optional data.
- Generalization of entities when designing the schema.
- Data-driven designs that not only model the obvious data (for example, orders and customers), but also enable the organization to store the behavioral patterns, or process flow.
- A well-defined abstraction layer that decouples the database from all client access, including client apps, middle tiers, ETL, and reports.
- Extensibility is also closely related to simplicity. Complexity breeds complexity and inhibits adaptation. Remember, a simple solution is easy to understand and adopt, and ultimately, easy to adjust later.

Data Integrity

The ability to ensure that persisted data can be retrieved without error is central to the Information Architecture Principle, and it was the first major problem tackled by the database world. Without data integrity, a query's answer cannot be guaranteed to be correct; consequently, there's not much point in availability or performance. Data integrity can be defined in multiple ways:

- **Entity integrity**: Involves the structure (primary key and its attributes) of the entity. If the primary key is unique and all attributes are scalar and fully dependent on the primary key, then the integrity of the entity is good. In the physical schema, the table's primary key enforces entity integrity.
- **Domain integrity**: Ensures that only valid data is permitted in the attribute. A domain is a set of possible values for an attribute, such as integers, bit values, or characters. Nullability (whether a null value is valid for an attribute) is also a part of domain integrity. In the physical schema, the data type and nullability of the row enforce domain integrity.
- **Referential integrity**: Refers to the domain integrity of foreign keys. Domain integrity means that if an attribute has a value, then that value must be in the

domain. In the case of the foreign key, the domain is the list of values in the related primary key. Referential integrity, therefore, is not an issue of the integrity of the primary key but of the foreign key.

■ **Transactional integrity:** Ensures that every logical unit of work, such as inserting 100 rows or updating 1,000 rows, is executed as a single transaction. The quality of a database product is measured by its transactions' adherence to the *ACID* properties: *atomic* — all or nothing; *consistent* — the database begins and ends the transaction in a consistent state; *isolated* — one transaction does not affect another transaction; and *durable* — once committed always committed.

In addition to these four generally accepted definitions of data integrity, user-defined data integrity should be considered as well:

■ User-defined integrity means that the data meets the organization's requirements with simple business rules, such as a restriction to a domain and limiting the list of valid data entries. Check constraints are commonly used to enforce these rules in the physical schema.

■ Complex business rules limit the list of valid data based on some condition. For example, certain tours may require a medical waiver. Implementing these rules in the physical schema generally requires stored procedures or triggers.

■ Some data-integrity concerns can't be checked by constraints or triggers. Invalid, incomplete, or questionable data may pass all the standard data-integrity checks. For example, an order without any order detail rows is not a valid order, but no SQL constraint or trigger traps such an order. The abstraction layer can assist with this problem, and SQL queries can locate incomplete orders and help to identify other less measurable data-integrity issues, including wrong data, incomplete data, questionable data, and inconsistent data.

Integrity is established in the design by ensuring the following:

■ A thorough and well-documented understanding of the organizational requirements

■ Normalization and correct handling of optional data

■ A well-defined abstraction layer

■ Data quality unit testing using a well-defined and understood set of test data

■ Metadata and data audit trails documenting the source and veracity of the data, including updates

Performance/Scalability

Presenting readily usable information is a key aspect of the Information Architecture Principle. Although the database industry has achieved a high degree of performance, the ability to scale that performance to large databases is still an area of competition between database engine vendors.

Performance is enabled in the database design and development by ensuring the following:

- A well-designed schema with normalization and generalization, and correct handling of optional data
- Set-based queries implemented within a well-defined abstraction layer
- A sound indexing strategy, including careful selection of clustered and nonclustered indexes
- Tight, fast transactions that reduce locking and blocking
- Partitioning, which is useful for advanced scalability

Availability

The availability of information refers to the information's accessibility when required regarding uptime, locations, and the availability of the data for future analysis. Disaster recovery, redundancy, archiving, and network delivery all affect availability.

Availability is strengthened by the following:

- Quality, redundant hardware
- SQL Server's high-availability features
- Proper DBA procedures regarding data backup and backup storage
- Disaster recovery planning

Security

The sixth database objective based on the Information Architecture Principle is security. For any organizational asset, the level of security must be secured depending on its value and sensitivity.

Security is enforced by the following:

- Physical security and restricted access of the data center
- Defensively coding against SQL injection
- Appropriate operating system security
- Reducing the surface area of SQL Server to only those services and features required
- Identifying and documenting ownership of the data
- Granting access according to the principle of least privilege, which is the concept that users should have only the minimum access rights required to perform necessary functions within the database
- Cryptography — data encryption of live databases, backups, and data warehouses
- Metadata and data audit trails documenting the source and veracity of the data, including updates

Planning Data Stores

The enterprise data architect helps an organization plan the most effective use of information throughout the organization. An organization's data store configuration (see Figure 2-1) includes multiple types of data stores, as illustrated in the following figure, each with a specific purpose:

- *Operational databases*, or *online transaction processing (OLTP) databases* collect first-generation transactional data that is essential to the day-to-day operation of the organization and unique to the organization. An organization might have an operational data store to serve each unit or function within it. Regardless of the organization's size, an organization with a singly focused purpose may have only one operational database.

- For performance, operational stores are tuned for a balance of data retrieval and updates, so indexes and locking are key concerns. Because these databases receive first-generation data, they are subject to data update anomalies and benefit from normalization.

FIGURE 2-1

Data store types and their typical relationships

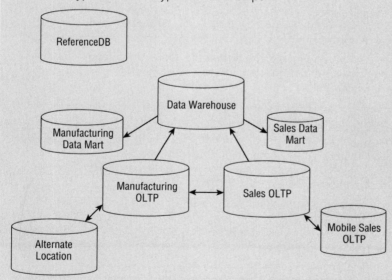

- *Caching data stores*, sometime called *reporting databases*, are optional read-only copies of all or part of an operational database. An organization might have multiple caching data stores to deliver data throughout the organization. Caching data stores might use SQL Server replication or log shipping to populate the database and are tuned for high-performance data retrieval.

Continues

continued

- *Reference data stores* are primarily read-only and store generic data required by the organization but which seldom changes — similar to the reference section of the library. Examples of reference data might be unit of measure conversion factors or ISO country codes. A reference data store is tuned for high-performance data retrieval.

- *Data warehouses* collect large amounts of data from multiple data stores across the entire enterprise using an *extract-transform-load (ETL)* process to convert the data from the various formats and schema into a common format, designed for ease of data retrieval. Data warehouses also serve as the archival location, storing historical data and releasing some of the data load from the operational data stores. The data is also pre-aggregated, making research and reporting easier, thereby improving the accessibility of information and reducing errors.

- Because the primary task of a data warehouse is data retrieval and analysis, the data-integrity concerns presented with an operational data store don't apply. Data warehouses are designed for fast retrieval and are not normalized like master data stores. They are generally designed using a basic star schema or snowflake design. Locks generally aren't an issue, and the indexing is applied without adversely affecting inserts or updates.

- The analysis process usually involves more than just SQL queries and uses data cubes that consolidate gigabytes of data into dynamic pivot tables. *Business intelligence (BI)* is the combination of the ETL process, the data warehouse data store, and the acts to create and browse cubes.

- A common data warehouse is essential to ensure that the entire organization researches the same data set and achieves the same result for the same query — a critical aspect of the Sarbanes-Oxley Act and other regulatory requirements.

- *Data marts* are subsets of the data warehouse with pre-aggregated data organized specifically to serve the needs of one organizational group or one data domain.

- *Master data store*, or *master data management (MDM)*, refers to the data warehouse that combines the data from throughout the organization. The primary purpose of the master data store is to provide a single version of the truth for organizations with a complex set of data stores and multiple data warehouses.

- Data Quality Services (DQS) refers to the SQL Server instance feature that consists of three SQL Server catalogs with data-quality functionality and storage. The purpose of this feature is to enable you to build a knowledge base to support data quality tasks.

 Chapter 51, "Business Intelligence Database Design," discusses star schemas and snowflake designs used in data warehousing.

Smart Database Design

More than a few databases do not adhere to the principles of information architecture, and as a result, fail to meet organization's needs. In nearly every case, the root cause of the failure was the database design. It was too complex, too clumsy, or just plain inadequate. The side effects of a poor database design include poorly written code because developers work around, not with, the database schema; poor performance because the database engine is dealing with improperly structured data; and an inflexible model that can't grow with the organization it is supposed to support. The bottom line is that good database design makes life easier for anyone who touches the database. The database schema is the foundation of the database project; and an elegant, simple database design outperforms a complex database both for the development process and the final performance of the database application. This is the basic idea behind the Smart Database Design.

Database System

A database system is a complex system, which consists of multiple components that interact with one another. The performance of one component affects the performance of other components and thus the entire system. Stated another way, the design of one component can set up other components and the whole system to either work well together or to frustrate those trying to make the system work.

Every database system contains four broad technologies or components: the database, the server platform, the maintenance jobs, and the client's data access code, as shown in Figure 2-2. Each component affects the overall performance of the database system:

- The *server environment* is the physical hardware configuration (CPUs, memory, disk spindles, and I/O bus), the operating system, and the SQL Server instance configuration, which together provide the working environment for the database. The server environment is typically optimized by balancing the CPUs, memory, and I/O, and identifying and eliminating bottlenecks.

- The database *maintenance jobs* are the steps that keep the database running optimally (index defragmentation, DBCC integrity checks, and maintaining index statistics).

- The *client application* is the collection of data access layers, middle tiers, front-end applications, ETL (extract, transform, and load) scripts, report queries, or SQL Server Integration Services (SSIS) packages that access the database. These cannot only affect the user's perception of database performance, but can also reduce the overall performance of the database system.

- Finally, the *database* component includes everything within the data file: the physical schema, T-SQL code (queries, stored procedures, user-defined functions [UDFs], and views), indexes, and data.

All four database components must function well together to produce a high-performance database system; if one of the components is weak, then the database system will fail or perform poorly.

However, of these four components, the database is the most difficult component to design and the one that drives the design of the other three components. For example, the database workload determines the hardware requirements. Maintenance jobs and data access code are both designed around the database; and an overly complex database can complicate both the maintenance jobs and the data access code.

FIGURE 2-2

Smart Database Design is the premise that an elegant *physical schema* makes the data intuitively obvious and enables writing great set-based *queries* that respond well to *indexing*. This in turn creates short, tight transactions, which improves *concurrency* and *scalability*, while reducing the aggregate workload of the database. This flow from layer to layer becomes a methodology for designing and optimizing databases.

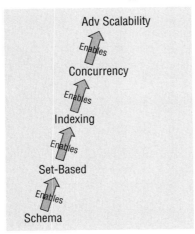

Physical Schema

The base layer of Smart Database Design is the database's physical schema. The physical schema includes the database's tables, columns, primary and foreign keys, and constraints. Basically, the "physical" schema is what the server creates when you run Data Definition Language (DDL) commands. Designing an elegant, high-performance physical schema typically involves a team effort and requires numerous design iterations and reviews.

Well-designed physical schemas avoid over-complexity by generalizing similar types of objects, thereby creating a schema with fewer entities. While designing the physical schema, make the data obvious to the developer and easy to query. The prime consideration when converting the logical database design into a physical schema is how much work is required for a query to navigate the data structures while maintaining a correctly normalized design. Not only is the schema then a joy to use, but it also makes it easier to code against, reducing the chance of data integrity errors caused by faulty queries.

Conversely, a poorly designed (either non-normalized or overly complex) physical schema encourages developers to write iterative code, code that uses temporary buckets to manipulate data, or code that will be difficult to debug or maintain.

Agile Modeling

Agile development is popular for good reasons. It gets the job done quickly and often produces a better result than traditional methods. Agile development also fits well with database design and development.

The traditional *waterfall process* steps through four project phases: requirements gathering, design, development, and implementation. Although this method may work well for some endeavors, when creating software, the users often don't know what they want until they see it, which pushes discovery beyond the requirements gathering phase and into the development phase.

Agile development addresses this problem by replacing the single long waterfall with numerous short cycles or iterations. Each iteration builds out a working model that can be tested and enables users to play with the software and further discover their needs. When users see rapid progress and trust that new features can be added, they become more willing to allow features to be planned into the life cycle of the software, instead of insisting that every feature be implemented in the next version.

A project might consist of a dozen of these tight iterations; and with each iteration, more features are fleshed out in the database and code. The principle of extensibility, mentioned earlier in this chapter, is highlighted by an agile development process; as you cycle through iterations, an extensible database absorbs new business requirements with less refactoring. Frankly, this is how requirements evolve. You never know everything up front, so plan for and embrace the idea that your database needs to evolve along with the rest of the project. This might include time built into your schedule for design refactoring, aligning database design tasks with iterative application coding cycles, or deferring design decisions until requirements become more robust.

Set-Based Queries

SQL Server is designed to handle data in sets. SQL is a declarative language, meaning that the SQL query describes the problem, and the Query Optimizer generates an execution plan to resolve the problem as a set.

Iterative T-SQL code is code that acts upon data one row at a time instead of as a set. It is typically implemented via cursors and forces the database engine to perform thousands of wasteful single-row operations, instead of handling the problem in one larger, more efficient set. The performance cost of these single-row operations is huge. Depending on the task, SQL cursors perform about half as well as set-based code, and the performance differential grows with the size of the data. This is why set-based queries, based on an obvious physical schema, are so critical to database performance.

A good physical schema and set-based queries set up the database for excellent indexing, further improving the performance of the query (refer to Figure 2-2).

However, queries cannot overcome the errors of a poor physical schema and won't solve the performance issues of poorly written code. It's simply impossible to fix a clumsy database design by throwing code at it. Poor database designs tend to require extra code, which performs poorly and is difficult to maintain. Unfortunately, poorly designed databases also tend to have code that is tightly coupled (refers directly to tables), instead of code that accesses the database's abstraction layer (stored procedures and views). This makes it harder to refactor the database.

Indexing

An index is an organized pointer used to locate information in a larger collection. An index is only useful when it matches the needs of a question. In this case, it becomes the short-cut between a question and the right answer. The key is to design the fewest number of shortcuts between the right questions and the right answers.

A sound indexing strategy identifies a handful of queries that represent 90 percent of the workload and, with judicious use of clustered indexes and covering indexes, solves the queries without expensive lookup operations.

An elegant physical schema, well-written set-based queries, and excellent indexing reduce transaction duration, which implicitly improves concurrency and sets up the database for scalability.

Nevertheless, indexes cannot overcome the performance difficulties of iterative code. Poorly written SQL code that returns unnecessary columns is difficult to index and will likely not take advantage of covering indexes. Moreover, it's difficult to properly index an overly complex or non-normalized physical schema.

Concurrency

SQL Server, as an ACID-compliant database engine, supports transactions that are atomic, consistent, isolated, and durable. Whether the transaction is a single statement or an explicit transaction within BEGIN TRAN...COMMIT TRAN statements, locks are typically used to prevent one transaction from seeing another transaction's uncommitted data. Transaction isolation is great for data integrity, but locking and blocking hurt performance.

Multi-user concurrency can be tuned by limiting the extraneous code within logical transactions, setting the transaction isolation level no higher than required, and keeping trigger code to a minimum.

 Chapter 47, "Managing Transactions, Locking, and Blocking," provides an excellent overview of the different transaction isolation levels available in SQL Server 2012.

A database with an excellent physical schema, well-written set-based queries, and the right set of indexes will have tight transactions and perform well with multiple users.

When a poorly designed database displays symptoms of locking and blocking issues, transaction isolation level tuning only partially alleviates the problem. The sources of the concurrency issue are the long transactions and additional workload caused by the poor database schema, lack of set-based queries, or missing indexes. Concurrency tuning cannot overcome the deficiencies of a poor database design.

Advanced Scalability

With each release, Microsoft has consistently enhanced SQL Server for the enterprise. These technologies can enhance the scalability of heavy transaction databases.

The Resource Governor can restrict the resources available for different sets of queries, enabling the server to maintain the service-level agreement (SLA) for some queries at the expense of other less critical queries.

Indexed views were introduced in SQL Server 2000. They actually materialize the view as a clustered index and can enable queries to select from joined data without hitting the joined tables, or to pre-aggregate data. In effect, an indexed view is a custom covering index that can cover across multiple tables.

Partitioned tables can automatically segment data across multiple filegroups, which can serve as an auto-archive device. By reducing the size of the active data partition, the requirements for maintaining the data, such as defragging the indexes, are also reduced.

Service Broker can collect transactional data and process it after the fact, thereby providing an "over time" load leveling as it spreads a 5-second peak load over a 1-minute execution without delaying the calling transaction.

Column store indexes, introduced in SQL Server 2012, are column-based indexes (rather than traditional row-based indexes) that can greatly improve query speed in certain database environments.

 Chapter 45, "Indexing Strategies," covers column-based indexes in more depth.

Although these high-scalability features can extend the scalability of a well-designed database, they are limited in their ability to add performance to a poorly designed database, and they cannot overcome long transactions caused by a lack of indexes, iterative code, or all the multiple other problems caused by an overly complex database design.

The database component is the principle factor determining the overall monetary cost of the database. A well-designed database minimizes hardware costs, simplifies data access code and maintenance jobs, and significantly lowers both the initial and the total cost of the database system.

A Performance Framework

By describing the dependencies between the schema, queries, indexing, transactions, and scalability, Smart Database Design is a framework for performance.

The key to mastering Smart Database Design is to understand the interaction, or cause-and-effect relationship, between these hierarchical layers (schema, queries, indexing, and concurrency). Each layer enables the next layer; conversely, no layer can overcome deficiencies in lower layers. The practical application of Smart Database Design takes advantage of these dependencies when developing or optimizing a database by employing the right best practices within each layer to support the next layer.

Reducing the aggregate workload of the database component has a positive effect on the rest of the database system. An efficient database component reduces the performance requirements of the server platform, increasing capacity. Maintenance jobs are easier to plan and also execute faster when the database component is designed well. There is less client access code to write and the code that needs to be written is easier to write and maintain. The result is an overall database system that's simpler to maintain, cheaper to run, easier to connect to from the data access layer, and that scales beautifully.

Although it's not a perfect analogy, picturing a water fountain on a hot summer day can help demonstrate how shorter transactions improve overall database performance. If everyone takes a small, quick sip from the fountain, then no queue forms; but as soon as someone fills up a liter-sized bottle, others begin to wait. Regardless of the amount of hardware resources available to a database, time is finite, and the greatest performance gain is obtained by eliminating the excess work of wastefully long transactions. Striving for database design excellence is a smart business move with an excellent estimated return on investment (ROI). Further, early investment in thoughtful database design can pay huge dividends in saved development and maintenance time. In the long term, it's far cheaper to design the database correctly than to throw money or labor at project overruns or hardware upgrades.

The cause-and-effect relationship between the layers helps diagnose performance problems as well. When a system is experiencing locking and blocking problems, the cause is likely found in the indexing or query layers. These issues can be caused by poorly written code. However, the root cause isn't always the code; it is often the overly complex, antinormalized database design that is driving the developers to write horrid code.

The bottom line? Designing an elegant database schema is the first step to maximize the performance of the overall database system while reducing costs.

Issues and Objections

There are some objections to the Smart Database Design framework addressed here. Some say that buying more hardware is the best way to improve performance. Although this is a viable and sometimes necessary solution, it can mask underlying data architecture issues that will probably crop up later. Performance problems tend to grow exponentially as DB size grows, whereas hardware performance grows more or less linearly over time. You can almost predict when the "best" hardware available no longer suffices to get acceptable performance. Sometimes companies spend incredible amounts to upgrade their hardware and see little or no improvement because the bottleneck is the transaction locking and blocking and poor code. Sometimes, a faster CPU only waits faster. Strategically, reducing the workload is cheaper than increasing the capacity of the hardware.

Some argue that they would like to apply Smart Database Design but can't because the database is a third-party database, and they can't modify the schema or the code. True, for most third-party products, the database schema and queries are not open for optimization, and this can be frustrating if the database needs optimization. However, most vendors are interested in improving their product and keeping their clients happy. (Both clients and vendors have contracted with the author to help identify areas of opportunity and suggest solutions for the next revision.)

Some say they'd like to apply Smart Database Design, but they can't because any change to the schema would break hundreds of other objects. It's true — databases without abstraction layers are expensive to alter. An abstraction layer decouples the database from the client applications, making it possible to change the database component without affecting the client applications. In the absence of a well-designed abstraction layer, the first step toward gaining system performance is to create one. As expensive as it may seem to refactor the database and every application so that all communications go through an abstraction layer, the cost of not doing so could be that IT can't respond to the organization's needs, forcing the company to outsource or develop wasteful extra databases. At the worst, the failure of the database to be extensible could force the end of the organization.

In both the case of the third-party database and the lack of abstraction, it's still a good idea to optimize at the lowest level possible and then move up the layers. However, the best performance gains are made when you can start optimizing at the lowest level of the database component, the physical schema.

Summary

This chapter presented the concept of the Information Architecture Principle, unpacked the six database objectives, and then discussed the Smart Database Design, showing the dependencies between the layers and how each layer enables the next layer.

In a chapter packed with ideas, the following are key take-aways:

- The database architect position should be equally involved in the enterprise-level design and the project-level designs.

- You can measure any database design or implementation using six database objectives: usability, extensibility, data integrity, performance, availability, and security. These objectives don't need to compete — you can design an elegant database that meets all six objectives.

- Early investment in database design is worth it; it can save development and maintenance cost later.

- Extensibility is the most expensive database objective to correct after the fact. A database incapable of absorbing organizational changes and new requirements elegantly will evolve into an unmaintainable mess. Smart Database Design is the premise that an elegant *physical schema* makes the data intuitively obvious and enables writing great set-based *queries* that respond well to *indexing*. This in turn creates short, tight transactions, which improves *concurrency* and *scalability* while reducing the aggregate workload of the database. This flow from layer to layer becomes a methodology for designing and optimizing databases.

- Reducing the aggregate workload of the database has a longer-term positive effect than buying more hardware.

From this overview of data architecture, the next chapter digs deeper into the concepts and patterns of relational database design, which are critical for usability, extensibility, data integrity, and performance.

Installing SQL Server

IN THIS CHAPTER

Preparing for a SQL Server 2012 Installation

Selecting the SQL Server 2012 Edition

Understanding Licensing Differences of SQL Server 2012

Understanding the Installation Process

The installation process for SQL Server 2012 is straightforward and relatively simple with the new included tools and resources that help you plan and assess your SQL Server 2012 deployment, whether it is a new installation, an upgrade, or a migration from another database system.

A successful SQL Server 2012 installation depends in great part on a good amount of planning ahead to ensure it satisfies both SQL Server 2012 requirements and your specific environment needs. Having a good plan can not only save you time and money, but it also can ensure that your database systems can adequately perform and scale as your business grows. Some of the most important considerations that need to be defined prior to installing SQL Server 2012 include the following:

- Hardware
- Operating System
- Collation
- Edition
- Licensing
- Service Accounts

Defining hardware requirements is part science and part art. You must know your current hardware needs and also anticipate future hardware needs. Following are some important questions and baselines that can help you determine hardware requirements:

- How much average utilization of your server resources, such as memory, processor, and storage, does your database server experience now during low, medium, and high workloads?
- Are excessive processor, memory, or disk waits over extended periods of time reported?
- What is the resource utilization trend for the last 12 months?

- What is the expected growth in workload for the next 12 to 24 months?
- What is your availability and disaster recovery service-level agreement (SLA)?

The answers to these questions are important to gain a better understanding of your hardware needs and to plan accordingly. You need to invest the time to capture these baseline utilization metrics and statistics. Chapter 43, "Management Data Warehouse," discusses how to configure Master Data Warehouse (MDW) to capture these and many other important resource utilization trends and statistics for SQL Server 2012.

What's New with Installation in SQL Server 2012

SQL Server 2012 installation introduces a few changes in the options and features available, including the following:

- **Analysis Services mode**: During the installation process you are now prompted to choose the deployment mode of Analysis Services, Tabular or Multidimensional mode.
- **Reporting Services for SharePoint and binaries**: The option to install Reporting Services for SharePoint is now separate than Reporting Services Native Mode. A separate option to install only the Reporting Services binaries for SharePoint is also available.
- **AlwaysOn Availability Groups**: This option enables the new High Availability feature in SQL Server 2012 that allows to failover a group of databases together.

Preparing the Server

Before you initiate the SQL Server 2012 installation process there are several pre-installation tasks that need to be completed to guarantee a successful SQL Server 2012 deployment. Some of the pre-installation tasks include verifying that the hardware, software, and network configurations are optimal to deploy SQL Server 2012 as well as having a good understanding of the SQL Server 2012 editions and the hardware and feature limitations imposed on each edition.

This section discusses planning and design considerations for a successful SQL Server 2012 deployment.

Hardware and Software Requirements

An important step to define hardware requirements is to make sure all the minimum hardware, software, and operating system requirements are met for a successful SQL Server 2012 installation. This step is critical in order to pass hardware validation checks during installation process and to ensure that performance and response time requirements are met. Table 3-1 lists the minimum hardware, software, and operating system requirements.

TABLE 3-1 Minimum Hardware Requirements

Component	Requirement
Processor	64-bit installations: Speed: 1.4 Ghz or higher AMD Opteron, Athlon 64, Intel Pentium IV, Xeon with Intel EM64T support 32-bit installations: Speed: 1.0 Ghz or higher Pentium III compatible
Memory	1GB (512MB Express Edition)
Storage	Installer: 4.0GB Database Engine Services: 986MB Integration Services: 304MB Analysis Services: 517MB Master Data Services: 243MB Reporting Services (Native Mode): 1022MB Reporting Services (SharePoint Integrated Mode): 129MB Management Tools (Complete): 1551MB Business Intelligence Development Studio: 2145MB
Operating System	64-bit and 32-bit (WOW64) Windows Server 2008 R2 SP1 Windows Server 2008 SP2 Windows 7 SP1 Windows Vista SP2
Framework	NET Framework 3.5 SP1 NET Framework 4 1 SQL Server Native Client SQL Server Setup support files

Proper Patching

SQL Server 2012 requires that the operating system and software components are updated to the proper service pack level. Table 3-2 lists the required service pack and the corresponding download link.

TABLE 3-2 Operating System and Software Patches

Component	Requirement	Download Link
Windows Server 2008 Windows Vista	Service Pack 2	http:// technet.microsoft.com/en-us/dd727510
Windows Server 2008 R2 Windows 7	Service Pack 1	www.microsoft.com/download/en/details.aspx?id=5842
.NET Framework 3.5	Service Pack 1	www.microsoft.com/download/en/details.aspx?id=22

Firewalls

As part of the deployment process, Database Administrators need to work along with Network Administrators to ensure that network firewalls are configured to allow inbound and outbound traffic to the SQL Server instance. If a network firewall is not properly configured, connections to SQL Server instances and related services will be blocked. Table 3-3 lists the default ports for common SQL Server 2012 Services.

TABLE 3-3 **Default Ports for Common SQL Server 2012 Services**

Service	Description	Port
SQL Server Database Services	Default Instance	TCP 1433
	Dedicated Admin Connection	TCP 1434
SQL Server Analysis Services	Default Instance	TCP 2383
SQL Server Integration Services	Default	TCP 135
SQL Server Reporting Services	Non-SSL (http://)	TCP 80
	SSL (https://)	TCP 443
SQL Server Service Broker	Default	TCP 4022
SQL Server Browser Service	Default	UDP 1434 TCP 2382

Selecting the Edition

Selecting the right SQL Server Edition is another important consideration in the deployment plan because some editions have feature limitations and hardware support restrictions, while other editions are geared toward more specialized workloads.. The three main editions of SQL Server 2012 include Standard Edition, Business Intelligence Edition, and Enterprise Edition. SQL Server 2012 editions can be categorized as follows:

- Core Editions:
  - Enterprise
  - Business Intelligence
  - Standard
- Specialized Editions:
  - Developer
- Free Editions:
  - Express
  - Express LocalDB
  - Compact

> **NOTE**
>
> Data Center Edition and Workgroup Edition are no longer available in SQL Server 2012. Web Edition is only available through hosting providers such as Amazon Web Services and Rackspace.

The core editions of SQL Server 2012 are the three main editions that can be licensed for production, testing, Q.A., and U.A.T. environments.

> **NOTE**
>
> Core editions is a categorization of the three main editions and must not be confused with Server Core installations. New in SQL Server 2012, you can install SQL Server on Windows Server 2008 R2 SP1 Server Core. For more information on SQL Server 2012 installations on Windows Server Core please refer to `http://msdn.microsoft.com/en-us/library/hh231669.aspx`

The Developer Edition of SQL Server 2012 is a specialized license intended for development purposes only and cannot be used in production environments. The free editions of SQL Server 2012 are light-weight versions of SQL Server intended for learning, developing, and redistributing with small applications.

With each new release of SQL Server, new features are introduced and some existing features get shuffled around between editions. Understanding the available features for each edition is key in deploying the right edition that suits your needs. For a complete list of features supported by each edition please refer to `http://msdn.microsoft.com/en-us/library/cc645993(v=SQL.110).aspx`.

In SQL Server 2012, additional features have been added to support highly scalable and highly available database environments as well as additional tools to support Enterprise Information Management. Some of these new features include the following:

- Column-store indexes
- Always-on Availability Groups
- Distributed Replay
- Data Quality Services
- Analysis Services xVelocity Engine (formerly known as Vertipaq)
- Windows Server Core Installation Support

Edition Differences

Several differences exist between SQL Server 2012 editions ranging from database size limitations to the number of supported processors and the maximum supported memory. Several features such as partitioning, encryption, compression, and some advanced indexing options are also a key difference between SQL Server 2012 editions.

- **Enterprise Edition**: SQL Server 2012 Enterprise Edition provides the highest level of scalability for large mission-critical application workloads. It provides support for the highest amount of memory and number of processors than any other edition to support an organization's entire consolidated and virtualized database infrastructure. Enterprise Edition includes several powerful tools for complex data analytics, large data warehouses, and end-to-end Business Intelligence solutions.

- **Standard Edition**: SQL Server 2012 Standard Edition is tailored for small to mid-sized organizations, capable of providing reliable data management and essential Business Intelligence capabilities.

- **Parallel Data Warehouse**: SQL Server 2012 Parallel Data Warehouse is a highly scalable appliance-based data warehouse solution. Parallel Data Warehouse provides cost-effective performance through a massively parallel processing (MPP) architecture that enables an organization to easily scale from terabytes of data to a petabyte range of data.

- **Web Edition**: SQL Server 2012 Web Edition is a cost-effective database solution to support web applications, websites, and web services. It is only available through hosting providers such as Amazon and Rackspace.

- **Developer Edition**: SQL Server 2012 Developer Edition includes all the functionality of Enterprise Edition for development, test, and demonstration purposes. It is not intended for production environments. You can purchase Developer Edition licenses for approximately $50. It is the most cost-effective way for developers to develop and test all the features available in SQL Server 2012.

- **Evaluation Edition**: SQL Server 2012 Evaluation Edition is a free 180-day trial license of SQL Server 2012 with all the functionality of Enterprise Edition. You can download the 180-day Evaluation Edition of SQL Server 2012 at www.microsoft .com/sqlserver/en/us/get-sql-server/try-it.aspx.

- **Express Edition**: SQL Server 2012 Express Edition is a free redistributable edition ideal for learning, managing, and developing small database applications. SQL Server 2012 Express Edition is limited to 10GB of storage per database.

- **Express LocalDB Edition**: SQL Server 2012 Express LocalDBEdition is a new, free, lightweight version of Express Edition that has a fast zero configuration installation and fewer prerequisites. It runs in user mode and includes all features found in Express Edition.

- **Compact Edition**: SQL Server 2012 Compact Edition is a free redistributable edition that can be embedded in mobile devices, desktops, and web clients.

Downgrading Later

A good SQL Server 2012 deployment plan eliminates the possibility of having to undo, redo, or make major changes to the configuration of a SQL Server installation. It some cases, you may be forced to change an existing installation to a different edition or version of SQL Server.

Downgrading Between SQL Server Editions

Suppose a new corporate IT licensing policy mandates that all middle-tiered database applications need to be SQL Server Standard Edition, in which case you may find yourself needing to downgrade an existing Enterprise Edition of SQL Server to the Standard Edition.

Downgrading from a higher-tier SQL Server 2012 edition to a lower-tier SQL Server edition, such as from the Enterprise Edition to the Standard Edition, is only possible by performing an uninstallation of SQL Server. The process requires you to install the lower-tier SQL Server edition after you uninstall the higher-tier SQL Server Edition.

You can re-attach or restore user databases from a database backup to the lower-tier SQL Server edition. User databases with higher-tier SQL Server edition specific features enabled cannot be attached or restored to a lower-tier SQL Server edition. For example, a database created in SQL Server 2012 Enterprise Edition that uses Enterprise Edition features, such as Table Partitioning or Transparent Data Encryption (TDE), cannot be restored or attached to the SQL Server 2012 Standard Edition without first disabling these edition-specific features.

To find out edition-specific features applied to a database, you can query the dynamic management view [sys].[dm_db_persisted_sku_features]. For example, the following T-SQL script queries edition-specific features applied to the SQL Server 2012 AdventureWorks2012 database:

```
SELECT [feature_name]
FROM [AdventureWorks2012].[sys].[dm_db_persisted_sku_features]
```

The [sys].[dm_db_persisted_sku_features] dynamic management view may return rows containing any of the following Enterprise or Developer Edition features:

- Compression
- Partitioning
- Transparent Data Encryption
- Change Capture

If no edition-specific features have been enabled in the user database, the [sys].[dm_db_persisted_sku_features] dynamic management view does not return any rows.

Downgrading Between SQL Server Versions

In some cases you may need to downgrade between a newer version of SQL Server back to a previous version. For example, a SQL Server version upgrade of an application's back-end database instance may have exposed bugs in the application that now force you to downgrade back to the previous SQL Server version.

You can downgrade from SQL Server 2012 to previous versions of SQL Server by following the same uninstallation process as previously mentioned. On the other hand, you can no longer attach or restore user databases created or attached to an older version of SQL Server to a SQL Server 2012 instance.

Setting the compatibility mode of a database attached to a SQL Server 2012 instance to a lower compatibility level does not mean you can attach or restore this database to an older version of SQL Server. The capability of setting a database at a lower compatibility level is provided for backward compatibility as a temporary step to support legacy code.

For example, a database attached to a SQL Server 2012 instance and set in compatibility mode level 90, enables you to run code compatible with SQL Server 2005, but you cannot restore this database to a SQL Server 2005 instance. Table 3-4 shows the database compatibility levels and corresponding SQL Server Version.

TABLE 3-4   SQL Server Database Compatibility Levels

SQL Server Version	Database Compatibility Level
SQL Server 6	60
SQL Server 6.5	65
SQL Server 7	70
SQL Server 2000	80
SQL Server 2005	90
SQL Server 2008	100
SQL Server 2008R2	100
SQL Server 2012	110

SQL Server 2012 supports only databases at compatibility levels 90, 100, and 110, meaning it supports databases going back to SQL Server 2005 only.

To identify the compatibility level of a specific SQL Server database, you can query the master.sys.sysdatabases table as follows:

```
SELECT cmptlevel
FROM   master.sys.sysdatabases
WHERE name='AdventureWorks2012'
```

All databases attached or restored to a newer version of a SQL Server instance upgrade automatically to the database version number that the newer SQL Server instance supports. In the case of SQL Server 2012, all databases created, attached, or restored in a SQL Server 2012 instance convert to database version number 700.

As you see, database compatibility levels are not the same as database version numbers. Perhaps Paul Randal described it best when he explained it this way: The database version number is an internal number associated with a specific structure of a database's system tables containing metadata about various objects such as tables, columns, indexes, allocations, and details about the relational and physical structure of the database.

Table 3-5 lists the database version number and the corresponding SQL Server version.

TABLE 3-5   SQL Server Database Version Numbers

SQL Server Version	Database Version Number
SQL Server 7	515
SQL Server 2000	539
SQL Server 2005	611
SQL Server 2005 SP2 + (vardecimal enabled)	612
SQL Server 2008	661
SQL Server 2008R2	665
SQL Server 2012	700

To identify the version number of a specific SQL Server database, you can query the
`master.sys.sysdatabases` table as follows

```
SELECT version
FROM   master.sys.sysdatabases
WHERE name='AdventureWorks2012'
```

Upgrading Later

Selecting the right SQL Server Edition upfront allows you to accommodate for future needs
as your business grows. Many organizations choose to deploy a SQL Server Edition that contains the features that meet the minimum requirements for their environment and upgrade
to a different edition as additional features are needed.

Deploying the SQL Server 2012 edition that satisfies the minimum functionality
requirements initially is a cost-effective way to manage licensing costs. You can upgrade
all editions of SQL Server 2012 except for the Compact Edition to higher tier SQL Server
editions. For example, you can upgrade Express, Web, and Workgroup editions to Standard,
Enterprise, or Data Center editions. You can upgrade the Standard Edition to only the
Enterprise or Data Center editions.

The upfront savings in licensing costs may justify the decision to install a lower or mid-tier
SQL Server 2012 edition such as the Standard Edition. However, you also need to consider
downstream effects on budget, time, and resources when the need to upgrade to a higher
tier SQL Server Edition arises. Some of the factors that might require a higher tier SQL
Server Edition upgrade include implementing more robust mechanisms for disaster recovery, high availability efforts, and scaling out as workloads increase.

For this reason, some organizations deploy higher tier SQL Server editions such as Enterprise,
which allows them to scale up and scale out when necessary both for performance and availability purposes, without having to undergo an environment upgrade process.

Licensing Differences

The SQL Server 2012 release introduces significant changes to the licensing model than previous versions. The two licensing options, Server + CAL (Client Access License) and socket-based are still offered. The major differences revolve around the way processing power is licensed for the core-based licensing option and the licensing options available for each edition.

Core-Based Licensing

As discussed previously in this chapter, under the "Selecting the Edition" section, the main editions of SQL Server 2012 have been reduced to three: "Enterprise, Business Intelligence and Standard Editions". Only Enterprise and Standard Editions of SQL Server 2012 are available for core-based licensing.

In previous releases of SQL Server, core-based licensing was based on the number of physical processors and was independent of the number of cores. With SQL Server 2012, each of the processor cores requires licensing. For example, to license a SQL Server 2008R2 Enterprise server with two quad-core processors, only two processor licenses were required, one for each physical processor. This type of licensing was referred to as per-socket licensing since it was based on the number of physical processors occupying a processor socket in the motherboard.

To license this same server running SQL Server 2012 Enterprise, licensing for eight cores is now required since each processor has four cores for a total of eight cores.

Core-based licenses are sold in two-core packs with a minimum of 4 core licenses required for each physical processor. This means that at a minimum you need to purchase two of these two-core packs for each physical processor occupying a processor socket. Table 3-6 provides the licensing matrix for different processor core configurations.

TABLE 3-6   Licensing Matrix for Different Processor Core Configurations

Cores	Two-Core Packs Required	Total Licensed Cores
1	2	4
2	2	4
3	2	4
4	2	4
6	3	6
8	4	8
12	6	12
16	8	16

The number of two-core packs listed in the second column of Table 3-6, is the number of two-core packs required for each physical processor. As you may notice, even if you license a single or dual core processor, you still have to buy enough two-core packs to license the minimum of four cores. With this four-core minimum license per physical processor requirement of SQL Server 2012, it makes more sense to have a single four-core processor than two dual-core processors.

Server + CAL Licensing

Server + CAL Licensing for SQL Server 20120 is only available for the Standard and Business Intelligence Editions. Users need a CAL that is the same version or newer than the version of the licensed SQL Server they need to access. A SQL Server 2012 CAL can be used to access multiple licensed SQL Servers, including SQL Server 2012 Standard and Business Intelligence Editions. These new CALs can also be used for previous versions of SQL Server, including the Enterprise Editions of 2008 and 2008R2, for which the Server + CAL licensing model was still available.

Virtual Machine Licensing

Virtual machine licensing of SQL Server 2012 can be done in one of three ways:

1. **Individual VM core licensing:** Each individual virtual machine requires a core license for each allocated virtual processor. There is a minimum of four core licenses required for each virtual machine. This licensing model of virtual machines can be very costly, as multiple virtual machines with only one or two allocated virtual processors would still require four core licenses each.

2. **Individual VM Server + CAL licensing:** Only SQL Server 2012 Standard and Business Intelligence Edition can be licensed using the Server + Cal licensing model. Each individual VM requires a Server license, and a CAL is needed for each user that connects to a licensed server. This type of licensing is great for applications with a small number of users.

3. **Host server or server farm core licensing:** The total number of cores available on a host server or server farm can be licensed to maximize virtualization capabilities and take advantage of full computing power. To fully license a host server or server farm, Enterprise Edition core licenses along with Software Assurance are required. This type of licensing allows for an unlimited number of virtual machines and allows dynamic provisioning and de-provisioning of virtual processors.

For more details on SQL Server 2012 licensing options and how to transition to the new licensing models refer to the SQL Server 2012 Licensing Datasheet at `http://www.microsoft.com/sqlserver/en/us/get-sql-server/how-to-buy.aspx`.

The Installation Process

As in previous versions, you can install SQL Server 2012 services with a graphical user interface: the Installation Center. Unattended and automated deployments are also possible using the Command Line and PowerShell.

You can install all the SQL Server 2012 services by following the installation wizards launched from the Installation Center. Some of the services and features that can be installed using Installation Center include Database Services, Integration Services (SSIS), Analysis Services (SSAS), Reporting Services (SSRS), Master Data Services (MDS), and Data Quality Services (DQS). Additionally, management and development tools such as SQL Server Management Studio (SSMS) and SQL Server Data Tools (formerly BIDS) can be installed through Installation Center. Additional settings and configurations may be necessary after the core installation process completes.

The scope of this chapter includes the installation process of a SQL Server 2012 standalone Database Engine instance.

SQL Server 2012 Installation Center

The Installation Center provides a graphical user interface that groups common installation tasks and resources in seven logical sections:

- Planning
- Installation
- Maintenance
- Tools
- Resources
- Advanced
- Options

To launch the Installation Center, locate and execute the Setup.exe application in your installation media. Figure 3-1 shows the Installation Center.

The initial section of the Installation Center is the Planning section. The Planning section provides shortcuts to important documentation, links, and applications that facilitate a successful SQL Server installation, upgrade, or migration.

The installation section provides shortcuts to launch the following installation wizards:

- New SQL Server standalone installation or add features to an existing installation.
- New SQL Server failover cluster installation.
- Add a node to a SQL Server failover cluster.
- Upgrade from SQL Server 2005, SQL Server 2008, or SQL Server 2008 R2.
- Search for product updates.

FIGURE 3-1

SQL Server 2012 Installation Center.

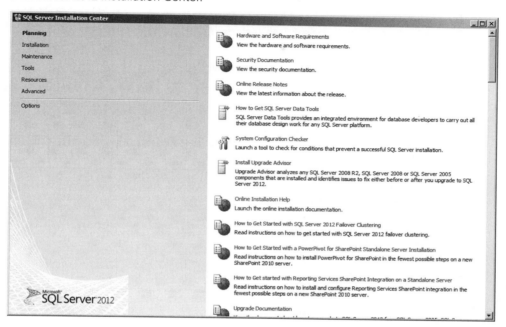

The Maintenance section provides shortcuts to do an edition upgrade, and to repair and update an existing SQL Server installation. It also allows you to remove a node from an existing SQL Server failover cluster.

The Tools section provides shortcuts to the following four tools:

- System Configuration Checker
- Installed SQL Server features discovery report
- Microsoft Assessment and Planning (MAP) Toolkit for SQL Server
- PowerPivot Configuration Tool

The Resources section provides shortcuts to SQL Server 2012 documentation, product registration, and community resources such as blogs, forums, Books on Line, License Agreement, and Microsoft Privacy Statement.

The Advanced section provides shortcuts to additional installation, configuration and deployment tasks including:

- Install based on a configuration file
- Advanced cluster preparation
- Advanced cluster completion

- Image preparation of a standalone instance of SQL Server
- Image completion of a prepared standalone instance of SQL Server

The Options section allows you to specify the architecture of SQL Server 2012 to install, either 32-bit or 64-bit processor architecture. Additionally it allows you to specify the location of the SQL Server installation media.

Installing SQL Server 2012 Through the Installation Center

The Installation Center is perhaps the easiest and most common way to install and modify any SQL Server installation. To initiate the installation of a new SQL Server 2012 stand-alone instance trough the Installation Center, follow these steps:

1. From the Installation Center, select the Installation tab, as shown in Figure 3-2.

FIGURE 3-2

Installation section.

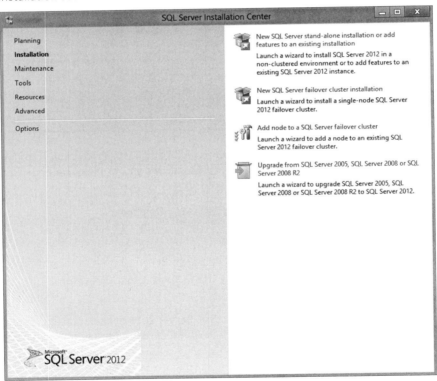

2. Select the New SQL Server StandAlone Installation or Add Features to an Existing Installation option. The first step in the SQL Server 2012 setup process involves examining the server using the System Configuration Checker for conditions that prevent a successful SQL Server installation. The System Configuration Checker runs a series of tests known as the Setup Support Rules that confirm the following:

- The computer that Microsoft SQL Server is installed on is not pending a reboot.
- The Windows Management Instrumentation (WMI) service is running and is accessible.
- The registry keys are consistent and can be used for a SQL Server installation.
- The pathname to the installation media is not too long.
- The product installation is compatible with the operating system.

The No-Reboot package is installed.

> **NOTE**
>
> You can find the complete list and description of the Setup Support Rules at `http://go.microsoft.com/fwlink/?LinkId=194954.`

3. If you detect any problems, they must first be corrected before the installation process can continue. After the test completes, you may see the results by selecting the Show Details button, or you can review a more detailed HTML report by selecting the View Detailed Report link, as shown in Figure 3-3.

FIGURE 3-3

SQL Server 2012 Setup Support Rules results.

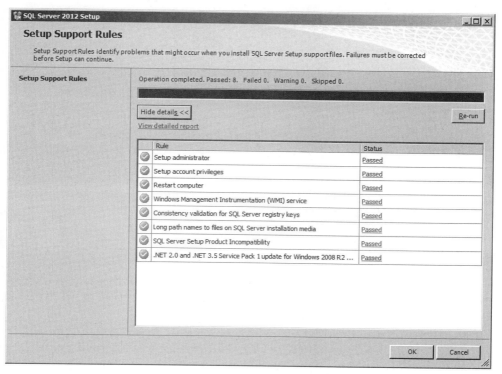

45

4. After reviewing the results, click the OK button. If you perform the installation on a server with access to the Internet, the Setup Wizard can check for product updates. If updates are found they display, as shown in Figure 3-4.

FIGURE 3-4

Product updates.

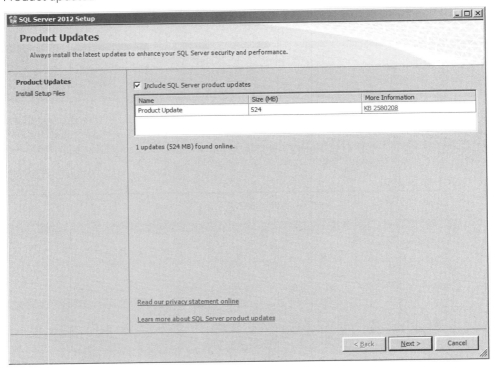

TIP

You should include all product updates in the installation process because they may include critical performance and security fixes and enhancements.

5. After reviewing the product updates list, click the Next button. The Setup Wizard launches the System Configuration Checker one more time to run the Setup Support

Rules test to identify any condition that might prevent the installation of the SQL Server setup support files. If you detect any problems, they must first be corrected before the installation process can continue. After the test completes, you may see the results by selecting the Show Details button, or you can review a more detailed HTML report by selecting the View Detailed Report link, as shown in Figure 3-5.

FIGURE 3-5

SQL Server 2012 Setup Support Rules results.

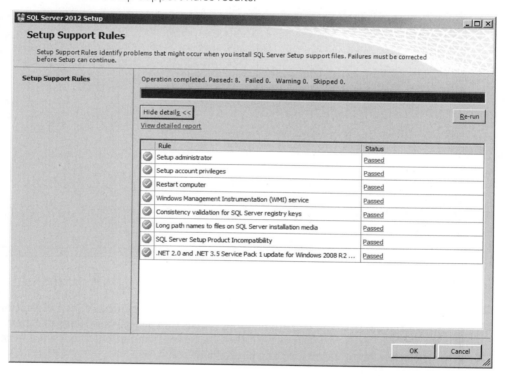

6. After reviewing the results, click the Next button. The next screen displays the Product Key validation. In this screen you can enter the SQL Server 25-character key assigned to your organization as part of a licensing agreement with Microsoft or from the certificate of authenticity or product packaging. You may also specify a free edition such as Evaluation or Express Edition. Figure 3-6 shows the Product Key screen.

FIGURE 3-6

Product Key screen.

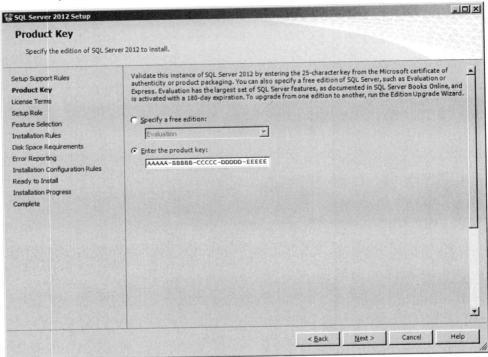

7. After entering the product key or specifying a free edition, click the Next button. In the next screen, you are required to read and accept the Microsoft Software and License Terms to continue with the SQL Server installation. Check the I Accept the License Terms check box, and click the Next button.

8. In the next screen, select the option SQL Server Feature Installation, and click the Next button. Figure 3-7 shows the options available to install SQL Server features.

9. The next screen enables you to select the features you want to include in the SQL Server installation. Select Database Engine Service and Management Tools Basic.

You may change the installation paths for the shared featured directory in this screen as well. After you select the features to install, click the Next button. Figure 3-8 shows the feature selection list and shared feature directory default paths.

FIGURE 3-7

Setup Role screen with SQL Server feature selection options.

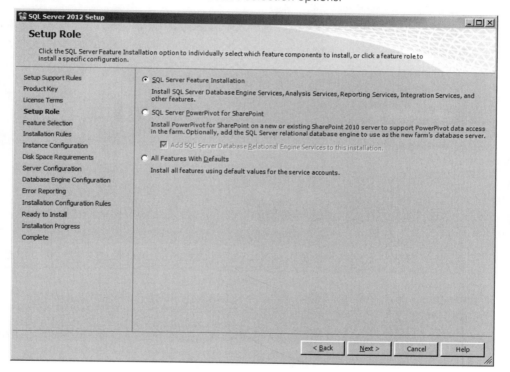

10. The Installation Rules screen opens. In this screen, installation rules are tested to make sure that the installation process is not blocked. After the test completes you may see the results by clicking the Show Details button. Click the Next button.

FIGURE 3-8

Feature selection list.

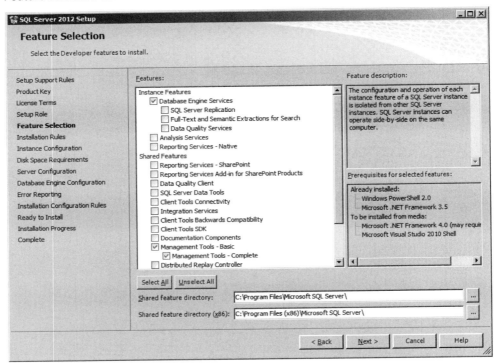

11. After reviewing the results, click the Next button. The next screen allows you to specify the name, instance `id` and `root` directory of the SQL Server instance. If there are other SQL Server instances installed, they appear in the Installed Instances section, as shown in Figure 3-9.

> **TIP**
> It is highly recommended that you use separate Active Directory domain accounts as startup service accounts for each SQL Server service. Each of these accounts should have minimum permission required.

FIGURE 3-9

Instance configuration.

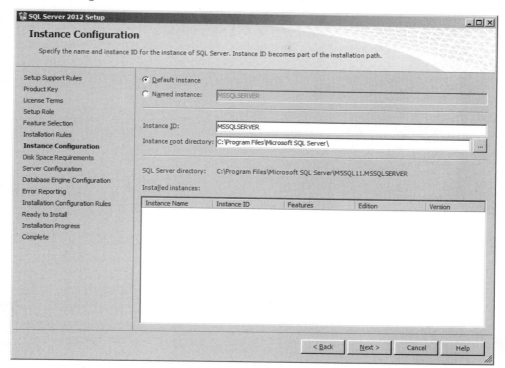

12. Click the Next button. The Setup Wizard evaluates current disk space available and calculates required disk space to install selected components. The Disk Space Requirements screen provides a breakdown of available and required disk space, as seen in Figure 3-10.

13. Click the Next button. The next screen enables you to specify service accounts and collation configuration. You can use individual accounts and startup types to start each service, as shown in Figure 3-11.

FIGURE 3-10

Disk Requirements.

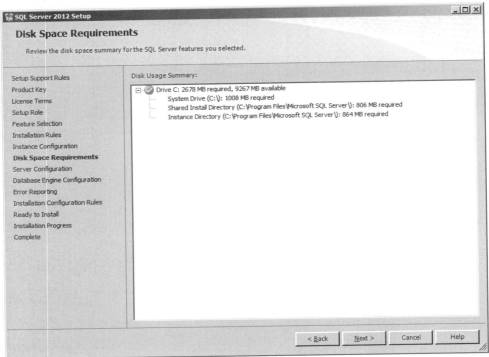

14. Click the Next button. The Database Engine Configuration screen opens. In this screen you can define some of the most critical configurations in the setup process, such as:

    ■ User authentication mode

    ■ SQL Server Administrators

    ■ Data, log, and backup file default directories

    ■ Filestream configuration

15. Click the Add Current User to add your Windows login to the sysadmin role. You may add additional Windows users to the sysadmin role by clicking the Add button.

Figure 3-12 shows the Database Engine Configuration options.

FIGURE 3-11

Service Accounts.

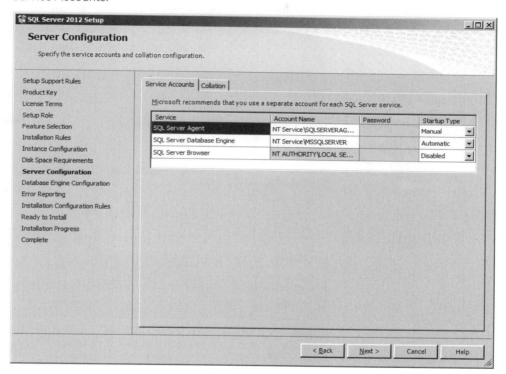

FIGURE 3-12

Database Engine Configuration.

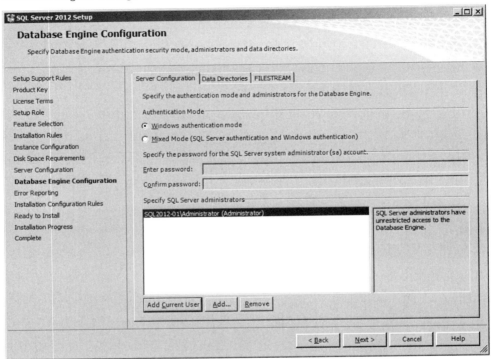

16. Click the Next button. The next screen enables you to opt-in to send Windows and SQL Server Error Reports to Microsoft or a corporate report server.

17. Click the Next button. The Setup Wizard runs the Installation Configuration Rules step to determine if specific components are missing or installed that might prevent the installation process to complete. If there are any problems detected, they must first be corrected before the installation process can continue. After the test completes, you may see the results by selecting the Show Details button, or a more detailed HTML report can be reviewed by selecting the View Detailed Report link below the Show Details button.

18. After reviewing the results, click the Next button. At this point, the Setup Wizard has gathered all the necessary information to install the SQL Server 2012 features selected. The next screen provides a summary of all configurations provided, as shown in Figure 3-13.

FIGURE 3-13

Ready to Install the configuration summary.

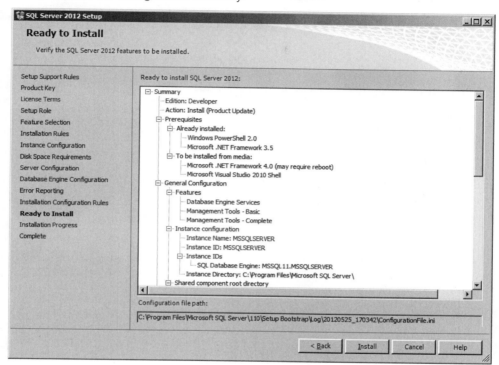

19. After reviewing the configuration summary, click the Install button. The installation process starts.

20. When the installation process completes, the Setup Wizard displays the list of selected features with the corresponding installation status, errors, or additional required configuration steps, as shown in Figure 3-14.

21. After reviewing the installation results, click the Close button to close the SQL Server 2012 Setup wizard. At this point you have completed the steps necessary to install a SQL Server 2012 Database Services instance.

To verify that SQL Server 2012 Database Services has been installed successfully, open SQL Server Management Studio (SSMS) and connect to the Database Engine.

FIGURE 3-14

Installation results.

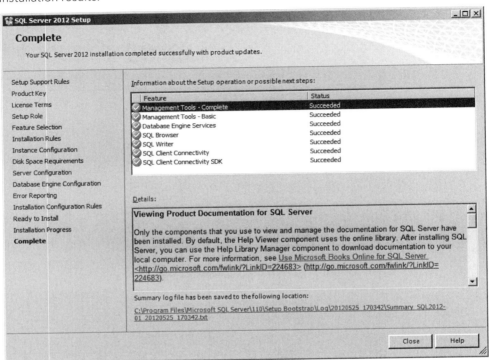

If SQL Server 2012 Database Services were installed as the default instance, you can connect via SQL Server Management Studio (SSMS) by providing the computer name or IP address where the SQL Server 2012 instance was installed. If you connect within the computer where the SQL Server instance was installed, you can connect using localhost, (local), or "." in the server name field.

If SQL Server 2012 Database Services were not installed as the default instance, then you need to provide the server name in the form of servername\instancename or IPaddress\ servername. In addition, you could provide the server name as localhost\instancename, or .\instancename.

Default versus Named Instances

A SQL Server instance that is not installed as the default instance is a *named instance*. There can be only one SQL Server instance installed as the default instance per computer. There can be many SQL Server instances installed as named instances in a single computer. A default SQL Server instance is not required. You can have one or more named instances in a computer but no default instance.

Installing SQL Server 2012 Through the Command Line

In addition to installing SQL Server using the Setup Wizard as shown in the first part of this chapter, SQL Server can also be installed via the command line. Command-line installations of SQL Server enable you to install, upgrade, or remove SQL Server instances with little or no user interaction by specifying silent, basic, or full user interface.

Every option available in the graphical user interface using the Setup Wizard can also be configured via command-line parameters. Sixty-eight parameters are available when running Setup.exe from the command line to configure SQL Server features and services. You can find the complete list of command line parameters at `http://msdn.microsoft .com/en-us/library/ms144259(v=SQL.110).aspx`.

Table 3-7 lists commonly used parameters for SQL Server Engine Services command-line installations.

TABLE 3-7 Commonly Used SQL Server 2012 Setup Command Line Parameters

Parameter	Description
/Q	Optional. Specifies to run Setup in quiet mode for unattended installations.
/QS	Optional. Specifies to run Setup and show progress through the UI. No input is accepted or errors displayed.
/UIMODE	Optional. Specifies whether to display only essential dialog boxes during Setup.

Continues

3

TABLE 3-7   *(continued)*

Parameter	Description
/ACTION	Required. Specifies a workflow. Supported values: Install, Uninstall, or Upgrade.
/IACCEPTSQLSERVERLICENSETERMS	Required. Accepts licensing terms.
/UPDATEENABLED	Optional. Specifies whether to look for product updates. Supported values: `true` and `false` or 1 and 0.
/UPDATESOURCE	Optional. Specifies location of product updates. Supported values: MU to search the Microsoft Update server, a folder path, a relative path, or a UNC share.
/CONFIGURATIONFILE	Optional. Specifies a configuration file to be used.
/ERRORREPORTING	Optional. Specifies error reporting opt-in option to Microsoft or a corporate report server. Supported values: 1 = enabled; 0 = disabled.
/FEATURES or /ROLE	Required. Specifies components to install or specifies a predetermined configuration known as the setup role.
/INSTALLSHAREDDIR	Optional. Specifies a nondefault installation directory for 64-bit shared components.
/INSTANCEDIR	Optional. Specifies a nondefault installation directory for instance-specific components.
/INSTANCEID	Optional. Specifies a nondefault instance id.
/INSTANCENAME	Required. Specifies an instance name.
/PID	Optional. Specifies product key for the edition to be installed. If not specified, the Evaluation edition is installed.
/INSTALLSQLDATADIR	Optional. Specifies the directory for SQL Server data (.mdf) files.
/SECURITYMODE	Optional. Specifies security mode for SQL Server. Default value: Windows-only authentication. Supported value: SQL.
/SAPWD	Required if /SECURITYMODE=SQL. Specifies sa SQL Server account password.

Parameter	Description
/SQLUSERDBLOGDIR	Optional. Specifies directory for SQL Server log files (*.ldf).
/SQLTEMPDBDIR	Optional. Specifies directory for SQL Server tempdb data file.
/SQLTEMPDBLOGDIR	Optional. Specifies directory for SQL Server tempdb log file.
/SQLBACKUPDIR	Optional. Specifies directory for SQL Server backup files (*.bak, *.trn).
/SQLCOLLATION	Optional. Specifies collation settings.
/SQLSVCACCOUNT	Required. Specifies the startup account for the SQL Server service.
/SQLSVCPASSWORD	Required. Specifies the password for the SQL Server service account.
/SQLSVCSTARTUPTYPE	Optional. Specifies the startup mode of the SQL Server service. Supported values: Automatic, Manual, and Disabled.
/SQLSYSADMINACCOUNTS	Required. Specifies accounts to be added to the sysadmin role.

Only a handful of these command-line parameters are required to complete a SQL Server 2012 installation. Errors may generate for required configuration options if no value is specified for the corresponding parameter. For some parameters, default values are automatically set when a value is not explicitly defined. You can use the following script to install a standalone SQL Server 2012 instance with all Database Services components:

```
Setup.exe /q /ACTION=Install /FEATURES=SQL /INSTANCENAME=MSSQLSERVER
/SQLSVCACCOUNT="<<DomainName\UserName>" /
SQLSVCPASSWORD="<MyPassword>"
/SQLSYSADMINACCOUNTS="<DomainName\UserName>" /AGTSVCACCOUNT="NT
AUTHORITY\Network
  Service" /IACCEPTSQLSERVERLICENSETERMS
```

Command-line installations can also use configuration files to reduce the number of command-line parameters and standardize SQL Server deployments. Configuration files are created during the installation process using the SQL Server installation wizard. The path where the configuration file is specified in the bottom section of the Ready to Install screen as shown in Figure 3-13, under the "Installing SQL Server 2012 Through the Installation Center" section.

Use the following script to execute an unattended installation of SQL Server:

```
Setup.exe /ConfigurationFile="<MyConfigurationFile.INI>"
```

Installing SQL Server 2012 Through PowerShell

You can also use PowerShell to perform unattended installs. Simple PowerShell scripts can be written to execute SQL Server 2012 Setup through its command-line interface. For example, you can execute the command-line script used in the previous section from the command line as follows:

```
$cmd = "d:\setup.exe /ACTION=install /Q /INSTANCENAME="MSSQLSERVER"
/IACCEPTSQLSERVERLICENSETERMS
/FEATURES=SQLENGINE,SSMS
/SQLSYSADMINACCOUNTS="YourDomain\Administrators";
Invoke-Expression -command $cmd | out-null;
```

More complex PowerShell scripts can be written for larger SQL Server 2012 deployments. A common approach is the use of PowerShell functions that accept the setup parameters necessary to perform unattended installations. These PowerShell functions are then executed in batches or inside a process that loops through a list of server names with corresponding parameters.

For example, a PowerShell function can be saved in a PowerShell script file and called along with setup parameters to perform a large scale unattended deployment of SQL Server 2012. Listing 3-1 provides an example of a PowerShell function that you can use for SQL Server 2012 unattended installations.

LISTING 3-1   Install-Sql2012.ps1

The PowerShell function contained in the Install-SQL2012.ps1 script file (included in the downloads on this book's website www.wiley.com/go/sql2012bible) is as follows:

```
Function Install-Sql2012
{
param
(
[Parameter(Position=0,Mandatory=$false)] [string] $Path,
[Parameter(Position=1,Mandatory=$false)] [string] $InstanceName =
"MSSQLSERVER",
[Parameter(Position=2,Mandatory=$false)] [string] $ServiceAccount,
[Parameter(Position=3,Mandatory=$false)] [string] $ServicePassword,
[Parameter(Position=4,Mandatory=$false)] [string] $SaPassword,
   [Parameter(Position=5,Mandatory=$false)] [string] $LicenseKey,
[Parameter(Position=6,Mandatory=$false)] [string] $SqlCollation =
  "SQL_Latin1_General_CP1_CI_AS",
[Parameter(Position=7,Mandatory=$false)] [switch] $NoTcp,
[Parameter(Position=8,Mandatory=$false)] [switch] $NoNamedPipes
)
#Build the setup command using the install mode
if ($Path -eq $null -or $Path -eq "")
{
#No path means that the setup is in the same folder
```

```
$command = 'setup.exe /Action="Install"'
}
else
{
#Ensure that the path ends with a backslash
if(!$Path.EndsWith("\"))
{$Path += "\"
}
$command = $path + 'setup.exe /Action="Install"'
}
#Accept the license agreement - required for command line installs
$command += ' /IACCEPTSQLSERVERLICENSETERMS'
#Use the QuietSimple mode (progress bar, but not interactive)
$command += ' /QS'
#Set the features to be installed
$command += ' /FEATURES=SQLENGINE,CONN,BC,SSMS,ADV_SSMS'
#Set the Instance Name
$command += (' /INSTANCENAME="{0}"' -f $InstanceName)
#Set License Key only if a value was provided,
#else install Evaluation edition
if ($LicenseKey -ne $null -and $LicenseKey -ne "")
{
$command += (' /PID="{0}"' -f $LicenseKey)
}
#Check to see if a service account was specified
if ($ServiceAccount -ne $null -and $ServiceAccount -ne "")
{
#Set the database engine service account
$command += (' /SQLSVCACCOUNT="{0}" /SQLSVCPASSWORD="{1}"
/SQLSVCSTARTUPTYPE="Automatic"' -f
$ServiceAccount, $ServicePassword)
#Set the SQL Agent service account
$command += (' /AGTSVCACCOUNT="{0}" /AGTSVCPASSWORD="{1}"
 /AGTSVCSTARTUPTYPE="Automatic"' -f
$ServiceAccount, $ServicePassword)
}
else
{
#Set the database engine service account to Local System
$command += ' /SQLSVCACCOUNT="NT AUTHORITY\SYSTEM"
/SQLSVCSTARTUPTYPE="Automatic"'
#Set the SQL Agent service account to Local System
$command += ' /AGTSVCACCOUNT="NT AUTHORITY\SYSTEM"
 /AGTSVCSTARTUPTYPE="Automatic"'
}
#Set the server in SQL authentication mode if SA password was provided
if ($SaPassword -ne $null -and $SaPassword -ne "")
{
$command += (' /SECURITYMODE="SQL" /SAPWD="{0}"' -f $SaPassword)
```

Continues

3

LISTING 3-1   *(continued)*

```
}
#Add current user as SysAdmin
$command += (' /SQLSYSADMINACCOUNTS="{0}"' -f
  [Security.Principal.WindowsIdentity]::GetCurrent().Name)
#Set the database collation
$command += (' /SQLCOLLATION="{0}"' -f $SqlCollation)
#Enable/Disable the TCP Protocol
if ($NoTcp)
{
$command += ' /TCPENABLED="0"'
}
else
{
$command += ' /TCPENABLED="1"'
}
#Enable/Disable the Named Pipes Protocol
if ($NoNamedPipes)
{
$command += ' /NPENABLED="0"'
}
else
{
$command += ' /NPENABLED="1"'
}
if ($PSBoundParameters['Debug'])
{
Write-Output $command
}
else
{
Invoke-Expression $command
}
}
```

After you download Listing 3-1 from the companion website, save it to a folder, for example c:\scripts. Because this is a file that you download from the Internet, you may be required to right-click the file and unblock it. When downloaded, execute this function by following these steps.

1. Launch the PowerShell command line with elevated Administrator privileges by right-clicking the PowerShell executable and selecting Run as Administrator. The PowerShell command line opens.

2. Verify that you can run and load unsigned PowerShell scripts and files. In the PowerShell command line, type **get-executionpolicy** to verify the current execution policy. If it is not set to RemoteSigned, you need to change it to this value by executing the following command:

```
Set-ExecutionPolicy RemoteSigned
```

3. Next, load the PowerShell function in the script file by executing the following command:

```
. c:\scripts\Install-Sql2012.ps1
```

Notice the . and blank space before the script file path. The . and blank space is a required character to dot-source the script file.

4. Verify that the function has been loaded by issuing the following command:

```
get-command Install-Sql2012
```

A single row is returned showing CommandType Function and Name Install-Sql2012.

5. At this point you are ready to invoke the PowerShell function you just loaded. Invoke the Install-Sql2012 as follows:

```
Install-Sql2012 -Param1 Param1Value -Param2 Param2Value
```

For example, the following command invokes the Install-Sql2012 function and sets the SQL Server service account and password along with the Instance Name and initiates a SQL Server 2012 installation.

```
Install-Sql2012 -Path d:\ -ServiceAccount "winserver\Administrator"
-ServicePassword "P@ssword"
-SaPassword "P@ssword"
-InstanceName "MyInstanceName"
```

> **NOTE**
> The SQL Server 2012 installation path may differ depending on your installation media.

Figure 3-15 shows the PowerShell command-line window with the steps necessary to invoke the Install-Sql2012 function.

> **NOTE**
> A community-based project called SPADE that automates SQL Server installations using PowerShell is available for download at Codeplex.com. For more information about this project visit http://sqlspade.codeplex.com/.

3

FIGURE 3-15

PowerShell command line.

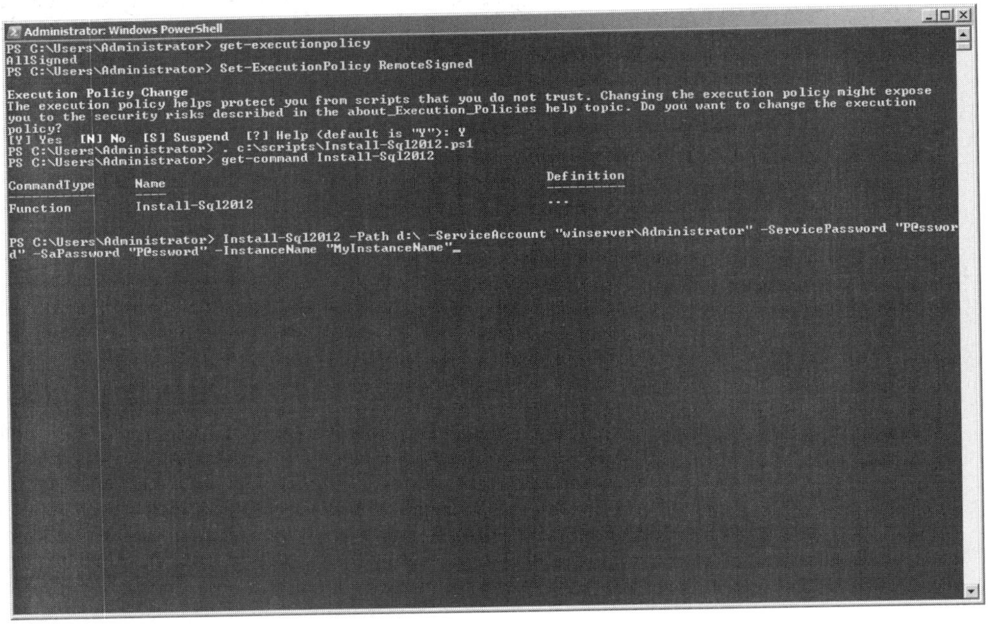

Post Installation Tasks

After SQL Server 2012 is installed, additional settings need to be configured and tasks need to be completed to have a production-ready server. Some of these settings are geared toward fine-tuning the SQL Server instance for optimal performance. Other settings and tasks are geared toward securing, auditing, and monitoring the SQL Server instance.

Memory

Two important server property settings include maximum and minimum server memory. By default, SQL Server is configured with a minimum memory of 0MB and a maximum memory of 2147483647MB (2TB), as shown in Figure 3-16.

The consequences of leaving the default values for these two settings is sometimes misunderstood and often overlooked. The minimum server memory setting specifies the amount of memory that will not be released back to the operating system by SQL Server when allocated. In other words, SQL Server holds on to this minimum amount of memory even if it is no longer needed.

FIGURE 3-16

Default minimum and maximum memory settings.

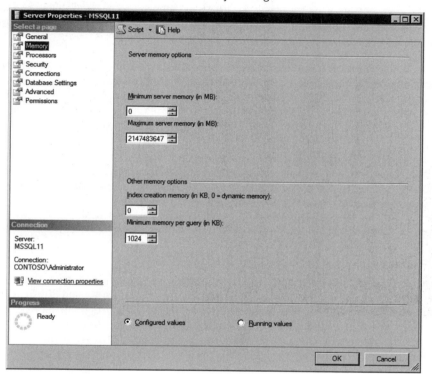

Misconception

A common misconception is that SQL Server immediately allocates up to this minimum amount of memory upon startup. Instead, SQL Server allocates memory only as it is required and may or may not reach the minimum server memory value specified.

The minimum server memory setting does not need to be changed unless the operating system constantly requests memory resources for other applications sharing the same memory space. You want to avoid having to release too much memory to the operating system and potentially starve a SQL Server instance from memory.

On the other hand, the maximum server memory setting limits the maximum amount of memory a SQL Server instance can allocate. A value set too high can potentially starve an operating system from memory resources. The maximum server memory value should not equal or exceed the total amount of server memory available. This value should be at least 1GB less than the total server memory.

Additional SQL Server settings such as processor affinity, parallelism thresholds, login auditing, and network packet size may need to be configured depending on your environment requirements. You can configure the most commonly used SQL Server settings and properties using SQL Server Management Studio (SSMS). You can access the complete set of configuration options using the sp_configure System Stored Procedure.

 Visit http://msdn.microsoft.com/en-us/library/ms189631(v=SQL.110).aspx for a complete list and description of all available SQL Server configuration options available through the sp_configure System Stored Procedure, a and a complete list and description of SQL Server properties available through SQL Server Management Studio (SSMS).

Chapter 4, "Client Connectivity," covers SQL Server configurations in more detail.

TCP/IP Ports

As discussed earlier in this chapter in the "Firewalls" section, default instances of SQL Server use default TCP/IP port 1433 to communicate with clients. Named SQL Server instances on the other hand are dynamically assigned TCP/IP ports upon service startup. For hacking prevention and firewall configuration purposes, you may need to change default ports and control the port numbers over which named SQL Server instances communicate.

SQL Server 2012 includes a tool called SQL Server Configuration Manager to manage SQL Server services and their related network configurations. The SQL Server Configuration Manager can be found under Microsoft SQL Server 2012 ⇨ Configuration Tools folder in the Start Menu. Figure 3-17 shows the TCP/IP Properties dialog box in SQL Server Configuration Manager where the default 1433 port can be changed.

Best Practices Analyzer (BPA)

The Microsoft SQL Server 2012 Best Practices Analyzer (BPA) is a free diagnostic tool that gathers information about installed SQL Server 2012 instances, determines if the configurations align to recommended best practices, outlines settings that do not align to these recommendations, indicates potential problems, and recommends solutions.

BPA can help you identify potential issues about your SQL Server 2012 installation. It is always best to catch configuration issues before a server goes into production to avoid unplanned downtime.

You can download the Best Practices Analyzer for SQL Server 2012 at `www.microsoft .com/en-us/download/details.aspx?id=29302`.

FIGURE 3-17

SQL Server Configuration Manager.

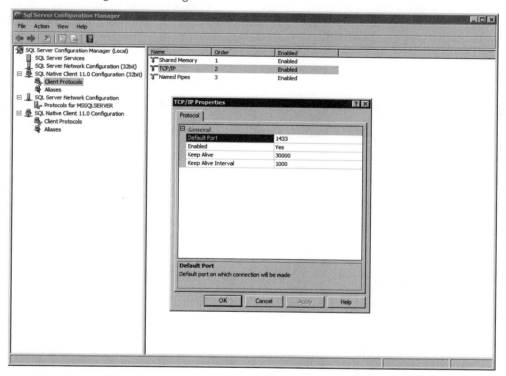

Patches

After a freshly installed SQL Server instance, it is always recommended to review available updates. SQL Server updates may be available in the form of hotfixes, cumulative updates, and service packs. To avoid negatively impacting your applications, all updates need to be reviewed carefully before they are applied. It is not recommended to enable automatic updates on production SQL Server instances. All updates should be tested in a controlled testing environment before they are applied in production.

Other updates, on the other hand, may be critical security fixes against newly discovered threats such as software worms and other vulnerabilities.

Monitoring

Being on top of what's going on in your SQL Server instances is one of the most important job functions of database administrators. With so many areas to monitor including resource utilization, performance, availability, critical events, errors, jobs, and so on, you must implement a monitoring framework to capture real-time metrics and keep the history of them to analyze trends and patterns.

SQL Server 2012 includes real-time monitoring through the Activity Monitor that can be launched from SQL Server Management Studio (SSMS). In addition, SQL Server 2012 comes packed with a performance metric collection and monitoring framework called Management Data Warehouse that can help you keep track of you environment along with some of the included performance dashboards. For more details on how to implement the Management Data Warehouse refer to Chapter 43.

Other tools and features included with SQL Server 2012, such as SQL Server Profiler, Extended Events, and Dynamic Management Views (DMVs), can help you uncover details of running processes and pinpoint issues. You can also use Microsoft products such as System Center Operations Manager (SCOM) and other third-party tools to monitor SQL Server 2012 instances. For more details on Performance Monitoring, refer to Part 7, "Monitoring and Auditing."

Model Database

The model database is a system database that serves as a template for all user databases. On creation, every user database inherits database objects from the model database including database options, such as recovery model, database initial size, and autogrowth settings, permissions, roles, tables, functions, stored procedures, and so on.

Modifying the model database ensures that all user databases have a standardized set of database objects when they are created, which can greatly simplify manual processes.

Summary

Installing SQL Server 2012 requires planning to ensure a successful installation. Some of the planning requires checking for minimum hardware and software requirements, proper software patching, and proper configuration of firewalls and network devices.

You must have a good understanding of the features and limitations of each edition of SQL Server 2012 to avoid unnecessary upgrade or downgrade tasks.

In this chapter you learned about the changes in the licensing model of SQL Server 2012, primarily in the shift of socket-based licensing to core-based licensing.

You also learned that SQL Server 2012 can be installed through the Installation Center, command line, or PowerShell, and that post-installation tasks, such as setting minimum and maximum memory settings, are necessary to prevent SQL Server from overtaking all the memory resources and at the same time securing a minimum amount for itself.

3

Client Connectivity

IN THIS CHAPTER

Enabling Server Connectivity

Using SQL Native Client's Development Features

Understanding Client Software Connectivity

SQL Server follows Microsoft's philosophy of "secure by default" and reduces the surface area of the application. The initial installation enables local access only and no network connections for express and developer additions. (That is, remote client applications cannot connect.)

 Chapter 3, "Installing SQL Server" discusses SQL Server surface area configuration as part of the installation process.

The Server Configuration Manager tool installed with SQL Server can nearly always communicate with SQL Server, so you can configure the server connectivity options and open the server up for network access. The connectivity relies on open paths between the client and server machines. As Windows Server by default comes with a firewall enabled, there will often be issues.

With network access allowed on the SQL Server, SQL Server provides clients with a new means to access functionality and features through the SQL Server Native Client (SNAC).

Before getting into the SNAC, you must enable network access for the new server.

What's New in SQL Server Native Client 11.0

Listed here are the significant new features in the SQL Server Native Client 11.0.

- Support for LocalDB.
- Metadata Discovery ensures that column or parameter metadata returned from a query is identical or compatible with the metadata format specified before the query was executed.
- UTF-16 Support.
- Asynchronous Execution on connection-related operations.
- C Data Type Extensibility.
- Deprecation announcement of SNAC OLE DB provider.

Enabling Server Connectivity

When initially installed, SQL Server enables the Shared Memory protocol and disables the remaining protocols. This provides the greatest default security because only applications running locally to the SQL Server can connect.

To broaden SQL Server availability, you must allow additional network protocols on the server.

 Chapter 19, "Configuring SQL Server," discusses SQL Server configuration in detail.

Server Configuration Manager

SQL Server Configuration Manager is a tool to manage the services associated with SQL Server, to configure the network protocols used by SQL Server, and to manage the network connectivity configuration from SQL Server client computers.

Network protocols define the common set of rules and formats that computers and applications use when communicating with one another. Table 4-1 lists the protocols available in SQL Server.

TABLE 4-1 Three Available Protocols for SQL Server

Protocol	Description
Shared Memory	This is an in-memory protocol and thus is only suitable for applications running on the same machine as the SQL Server.
Named Pipes	This is an interprocess communications protocol (IPC) that enables a process to communicate with another process, possibly running on a different computer, through the use of shared memory. This protocol typically works well in small and fast local area networks because it generates additional network traffic during use. In larger and slower networks, TCP/IP works better.
TCP/IP	Transmission Control Protocol/Internet Protocol (TCP/IP), is widely used today. TCP guarantees the delivery and order of the information sent between computers, while IP defines the format or structure of the data sent. TCP/IP also contains advanced security features that make it attractive to security-sensitive organizations and users. This protocol works well in larger networks and slower networks.

The Server Configuration Manager enables for these various protocols to be enabled, disabled, and configured as appropriate for the operational environment. You can launch the utility from the Start menu by selecting Start ⇨ All Programs ⇨ Microsoft SQL Server

2012 ⇨ Configuration Tools ⇨ SQL Server Configuration Manager. The Server Configuration Manager presents a list of all the available protocols and communication options, as shown in Figure 4-1.

FIGURE 4-1

The SQL Server Configuration Manager establishes the connectivity protocols used by SQL Server to communicate with clients.

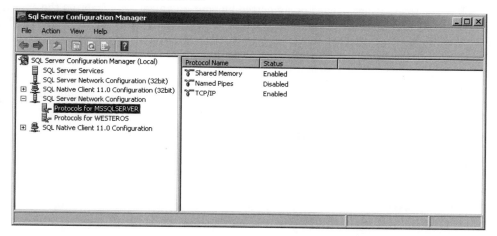

All TCP/IP communications are performed over a specified port. There are well-known ports such as HTTP (port 80), FTP (port 21), and SSL (port 443). By default, SQL Server communicates over port 1433 when using TCP/IP. If communications are performed through a firewall, this could cause the communication to be blocked. Port 1433 must be opened in a firewall for communications to be possible.

You can also change the port number for instances of SQL Server. In this way, you can map instances to specific TCP/IP ports. When you do this, ensure that there is an opening in the firewall for any ports that you need.

SQL Native Client Connectivity (SNAC)

The SQL Native Client connectivity is managed through the same Server Configuration Manager. SNAC installations can initially default the network protocols to enabling Shared Memory, TCP/IP, and Named Pipes.

SNAC also adds support for large User Defined Types (UDT). This enables developers to create custom types that are any arbitrary size. In addition, SNAC supports table value parameters. Table-valued parameters are declared by using user-defined table types. You can use table-valued parameters to send multiple rows of data to a T-SQL statement or a routine, such as a stored procedure or function, without creating a temporary table or many parameters.

There is a SNAC OLEDB provider, which gives much better performance in certain circumstances; however, it is being deprecated from the SQL Server product in lieu of ODBC providers instead. For more details on this shift, see the sidebar later in this chapter.

If SNAC access is not needed or supported by your organization, disabling the appropriate network protocols can reduce your security risks (surface area). You can enable and disable these protocols from the SQL Server Configuration Manager as shown in Figure 4-2.

FIGURE 4-2

The SQL Server Configuration Manager view for SQL Native Client Configuration Client Protocols.

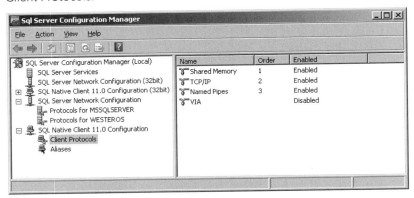

SQL Server Native Client Features

The development community gains access to the new features of SQL Server 2012 through the SQL Server Native Client (SNAC). If the new features are not needed and managed code is a requirement for data access, ADO.NET can suffice. Although a detailed examination of the features is beyond the scope of this chapter, a summary of each is provided.

> **NOTE**
>
> ADO.NET is an umbrella label applied to the .NET functionality that supports connections to a variety of data sources. Classes within this library supply the programmatic capability to create, maintain, dispose of, and execute actions against a database.

SQL Server Native Client OLE DB Provider Being Deprecated

The SQL Server Native Client OLE DB Provider is being deprecated in SQL Server 2012 and will no longer be available in future releases. Please note that only the SQL Server Native Client OLEDB Provider is being deprecated at this time and other OLE DB providers will still be supported until an official announcement is made on their respective deprecations.

The reasoning behind this move is to align with the industry for using ODBC as the standard for native relational data access. This shift not only allows for universal cross-application compatibility, but this allows developers to concentrate on one set of APIs for all their native client applications. This means that if you're developing for standalone SQL Server and Windows Azure SQL Database, or porting applications to Windows Azure for the first time, it's all built on the same API so the development transition is seamless.

For more detailed information on this transition see this Technet article: `http://technet.microsoft.com/en-us/library/hh510181`

Chapter 3 provides details about SQL Server installation requirements.

Native Client Support for LocalDB

SQL Server 2012 introduced Microsoft SQL Server Express LocalDB, a lightweight execution mode of SQL Server Express that allows developers to connect to a SQL Server Engine to write and test Transact-SQL code without the hassle of having to manage a full instance of SQL Server.

Metadata Discovery

Thanks to updates to metadata discovery in SQL Server 2012, applications using SQL Server Native Client will now get back column or parameter metadata from a query execution identical to or compatible with the metadata format you specified.

When developing applications that use the SQL Server Native Client while connected to an earlier version of SQL Server, the metadata discovery functionality corresponds to the version of the server.

High-Availability/Disaster Recovery Support

When a database connection is established to a SQL Server 2012 server, the failover partner is automatically identified in a mirrored scenario. This information is used by SNAC to transparently connect to the failover partner if the principal server fails. The failover

4

partner's identity can also be supplied as an optional parameter in the database connection string using the `Failover_Partner` keyword.

Additionally, you can also use SNAC to take advantage of the new AlwaysOn Availability Groups feature built on the mirroring technology. Applications using SNAC can connect to the primary replica of a given availability group either via a network name or connection strings much like you do with mirroring.

Applications connecting to an availability group using SQL Server Native Client can connect using an availability group listener, which is a virtual network name for the availability group. This concept should be familiar if you've ever set up a cluster and had to configure a virtual name for the cluster. For more information on setting up and interacting with AlwaysOn Availability Groups see Chapter 27, "Database Mirroring."

> **NOTE**
>
> If the connection to the principal server fails for a transaction, and if a transaction is involved, it will be rolled back. The connection must be closed and reopened to access the failover partner, and then any data work must be reapplied. The failover connection is automatic as long as the failover partner's identity is a part of the connection object supplied from either the connection string or a prior successful connection to the server before it went down.

 Chapter 28, "Replicating Data," details another tool used in disaster recovery setups or copying and distributing data and database objects across servers.

Improved Date/Time Support

SQL Server 2008 introduced the distinct date and time data types. These distinct data types provide much more flexibility for application developers when dealing with date and time types.

The distinct time type offers precision accurate up to 100 nanoseconds. This precision can be accessed via new types in SNAC: `DBTYPE_DBTIME2` for OLE DB providers and `SQL_SS_TIME2` for ODBC providers. If an application is written to use time with no fractional seconds, you can use time(0) columns. Precision of this magnitude can be extremely useful in process control and manufacturing applications that require that level of precision.

Other time-related support available is the ability to use date-time values with timezone information. This feature is supported through the use of `DBTYPE_DBTIMESTAMPOFFSET` for OLE DB and `SS_TIMESTAMPOFFSET` for ODBC types.

Accessing Diagnostic Information in the Extended Events Log

Another new feature in SNAC 11 is that data access tracing has been updated to make it easier to get diagnostic information about connection failures from the connectivity ring buffer and application performance information from the extended events log. Using data access tracing is outside the scope of this book, but if you would like to learn more about this feature, check out this technical article from Microsoft: `http://msdn.microsoft` `.com/en-us/library/cc765421(SQL.100).aspx`.

In SQL Server 2012, connection operations via the SQL Server Native Client will generate a client connection ID. If connectivity fails, you can access the connectivity ring buffer and find the `ClientConnectionID` field to get diagnostic information about the session and the connection failure. For more detailed examples on how you can leverage this feature, see the Technet article: `http://technet.microsoft.com/en-us/library/` `hh213095`.

> **NOTE**
> Data access tracing is intended only for troubleshooting and diagnostic purposes and may not be suitable for auditing or security purposes.

ODBC Features

With SQL Server 2012, Microsoft has made a radical shift on its stance with regard to ODBC. As of this release, they have decided to push ODBC as the primary method of connectivity and will be deprecating OLEDB in future releases, although it's still available in SQL 2012. In this release, the SQL Server Native Client OLE DB provider is the first of the OLE DB providers that will be deprecated and will not be available in the next release of SQL Server; however, it will be supported for the life cycle of SQL Server 2012.

As for the ODBC provider itself, three new features were added to the ODBC support, which were also added to the standard ODBC in the Windows 7 SDK:

- Asynchronous execution on connection-related operations
- C Data Type Extensibility
- Calling `SQLGetData` with a small buffer multiple times to retrieve a large parameter value

Multiple Active Result Sets (MARS)

SQL Server 2012 provides support for having multiple active SQL statements on the same connection. This capability includes being able to interleave reading from multiple result sets and being able to execute additional commands while a result set is open.

Microsoft guidelines for applications using MARS include the following:

- Result sets should be short-lived per SQL statement.
- If a result set is long-lived or large, then server cursors should be used.
- Always read to the end of the results and use API/property calls to change connection properties.

> **NOTE**
> By default, MARS functionality is not enabled. Turn it on by using a connection string value — MarsConn for the OLE DB provider and Mars_Connection for the ODBC provider.

XML Data Types

Much like the current VarChar data type that persists variable character values, a new XML data type persists XML documents and fragments. This type is available for variable declarations within stored procedures, parameter declarations, and return types and conversions.

User-Defined Types

These types are defined using .NET Common Language Runtime (CLR) code. This would include the popular C# and VB.NET languages. The data itself is exposed as fields and properties, with the behavior being exposed through the class methods.

Large Value Types

Three new data types have been introduced to handle values up to $2 \wedge 31\text{-}1$ bytes long. This includes variables, thus allowing for text values in excess of the old 8K limit. The data types and their corresponding old types are listed in Table 4-2.

TABLE 4-2 SQL Server 2012 Large Values Types

Large Data Types	Prior Data Types
varchar(max)	Text
nvarchar(max)	Ntext
varbinary(max)	Image

FILESTREAM Support

FILESTREAM is a feature that was introduced in SQL Server 2008 that allows you to store and access large binary values, either through SQL Server or by direct access to the Windows file system. Large binary values are considered any values larger than 2 gigabytes (GB). This feature allows SQL Server-based applications to store and manipulate unstructured data, such as images and documents, on the file system.

Handling Expired Passwords

This feature of SQL Server 2012 enables users to change their expired password at the client without the intervention of an administrator.

A user's password may be changed in any of the following ways:

- Programmatically changing the password such that both the old and new passwords are provided in the connection string
- A prompt via the user interface to change the password prior to expiration
- A prompt via the user interface to change the password after expiration

Best Practice

If the old and new passwords are supplied on the connection string, then ensure that this information has not been persisted in some external file. Instead, build it dynamically to mitigate any security concerns.

Snapshot Isolation

The snapshot isolation feature enhances concurrency and improves performance by avoiding reader-writer blocking.

Snapshot isolation relies on the row versioning feature. A transaction begins when the BeginTransaction call is made but is not assigned a sequence transaction number until the first T-SQL statement is executed. The temporary logical copies used to support row versioning are stored in tempdb.

NOTE

If tempdb does not have enough space for the version store, then various features and operations, such as triggers, MARS, indexing, client executed T-SQL, and row versioning will fail, so ensure that tempdb has more than enough space for anticipated uses.

Summary

SQL Server Configuration Manager provides the server and SQL Native Client protocol management.

SQL Server 2012 supports new features that enrich the client and programmatic data experience. Developers access these new features through the SQL Server Native Client (SNAC) and can now enhance the user experience by improving metadata discovery, improving access to diagnostic information through extended events logs, and offering better user interface response with asynchronous calls and ODBC connection improvements. In addition, stability increases significantly with the use of mirrored servers, AlwaysOn Availability Groups, and other useful features.

SQL Server Management and Development Tools

IN THIS CHAPTER

Exploring a UI Worthy of SQL Server 2012

Navigating SQL Server's Objects

Organizing Projects

Being Productive with Query Editor

Using SQL Snippets

SQL Server's primary user interface is SQL Server Management Studio (SSMS), a powerful set of tools within a Visual Studio shell that enables the developer or DBA to develop database projects and manage SQL Server with either a GUI interface or T-SQL code. For business intelligence (BI) work with Integration Services, Reporting Services, and Analysis Services, a companion tool is available called SQL Server Data Tools.

Like many things in life, Management Studio's greatest strength is also its greatest weakness. The number of tasks, tree nodes, and tools within the studios can overwhelm the new user. The windows can dock, float, or become tabbed, so the interface can appear cluttered without any sense of order.

However, when the individual pages are understood, and the interface options mastered, the studios are flexible, and you can configure interfaces to meet the specific needs of any database task.

Much of using Management Studio is obvious to experienced IT professionals, and subsequent chapters in this book explain how to accomplish tasks using Management Studio, so every feature or menu item isn't explained in this chapter. Instead, this chapter is a navigational guide to the landscape, pointing out the more interesting features along the way.

> **TIP**
>
> Management Studio is backward compatible, so you can use it to manage SQL Server 2008 R2, SQL Server 2008, and SQL Server 2005 servers. It's SMO-based so some features may work with SQL Server 2000, but it's not guaranteed to be compatible.

A common misconception among new SQL Server DBAs is that Management Studio is SQL Server. It's not. Management Studio is a front-end client tool used to manage SQL Server and develop databases. Typically, Management Studio is run on a workstation and connects to the actual server. Management Studio sends T-SQL commands to SQL Server, or uses SQL Management Objects (SMOs), just like any other client application. It also inspects SQL Server and presents the data and configuration for viewing.

 It's interesting to watch the commands sent by Management Studio to SQL Server. Although Management Studio can generate a script for nearly every action, you can view the actual traffic between SQL Server and its clients using SQL Profiler, which is discussed in Chapter 38, "Using Profiler and SQL Trace."

What's New with Management Studio in SQL 2012

SQL Server 2012's Management Studio is a continuing evolution of SQL Server 2008's Management Studio. Since SQL Server 2005, the SQL Server Management Studio has been using the Visual Studio shell for 2005 and 2008, respectively. SQL Server 2012's SSMS uses the Visual Studio 2010 bringing with it a new look, feel, and a few nice feature enhancements. There are quite a few enhancements to SQL Server Management Studio including:

- Transact-SQL code snippets, templates you can use as starting points for building batches and scripts.
- Transact-SQL Surround with snippets, templates you can use to surround T-SQL statements in BEGIN, IF, or WHILE blocks.
- Transact-SQL debugger support for instances running SQL Server 2005 Service Pack 2 (SP2) or later.
- The Watch window and Quick Watch now support Transact-SQL expressions.
- Point-in-time restore visual timeline that allows you to quickly and easily identify a feasible point in time as a target time for a database restore.
- New Page Restore interface allows you to check database pages for corruption and to restore selected corrupt pages from a database backup and subsequent log backups.
- New nodes or node organization (for AlwaysOn/High Availability and SSIS DB) in Object Explorer navigation.

Organizing the Interface

Management Studio includes a wide variety of functionality organized into thirteen tools, which you can open from the View menu, from the standard toolbar, or from the associated hotkey:

- **Object Explorer (F8):** Used for administering and developing SQL Server database objects. The Object Explorer Details page presents a list of objects under the selected node.
- **Registered Servers (Ctrl+Alt+G):** Used to manage the connections to multiple SQL Server engines ranging from SQL Server 2005 all the way up to SQL Server 2012.

You can register database engines, Analysis Services, Report Servers, SQL Server Express, SQL Server Express LocalDB, and Integration Services servers.

- **Utility Explorer:** Opens the Utility Explorer dashboard. Allows you to create a Utility Control Point (UCP) and enroll instances and monitor health states of those servers at a holistic level.

- **Template Explorer (Ctrl+Alt+T):** Used to create and manage T-SQL code templates.

- **Solution Explorer (Ctrl+Alt+L):** Organizes projects and manages source code control.

- **Properties window (F4):** Displays properties for the selected object.

- **Bookmarks window (Ctrl+K, Ctrl+W):** Lists current bookmarks from within the Query Editor.

- **Web Browser (Ctrl+Alt+R):** Used by the Query Editor to display XML or HTML results.

- **Output window (Ctrl+Alt+O):** Displays messages from Management Studio's integrated development tools.

- **Query Editor:** The descendant of SQL Server 2000's Query Analyzer, the Query Editor is used to create, edit, and execute T-SQL batches. Query Editor may be opened from the File ⇨ New menu by opening an existing query file (assuming you have the .sql file extension associated with Management Studio), by clicking the New Query toolbar button, or by launching a query script from an object in Object Explorer.

- **Toolbox (Ctrl+Alt+X):** Used to hold tools for some tasks.

- **Error List (Ctrl+\, Ctrl+E):** Lists multiple errors.

- **Task List (Ctrl+Alt+K):** Tracks tasks for solutions.

The most commonly used tools — Query Editor, Object Explorer, Template Explorer, and Properties windows — are available on the standard toolbar.

 This chapter primarily discusses Management Studio because it's used with the Relational Engine, but Management Studio is used with the Business Intelligence (BI) tools as well. Part 9, "Business Intelligence ," covers the BI tools.

Window Placement

Using the Visual Studio look and feel, most windows may float, be docked, be part of a tabbed window, or be hidden off to one side. The exception is the Query Editor, which shares the center window: the document window. Here multiple documents are presented using tabs to select a document.

You can change any window's mode by right-clicking the window's title bar, and selecting the down arrow on the right side of a docked window or from the Window menu. In addition, grabbing a window and moving it to the wanted location can also change the window's mode. Following are the available options by either dragging the tool's window or using the tool context menu:

- Setting the mode to **floating** instantly removes the window from Management Studio's window. A floating window behaves like a nonmodal dialog box.

- Setting the mode to **tabbed** immediately moves the window to a tabbed document location in the center of Management Studio, adding it as a tab to any existing documents already in the location. In effect, this makes the tool appear to become a tab in the Query Editor. Dragging a tab to a side location creates a new tabbed document. Any location (center, right left, top, bottom) can hold several tabbed tools or documents. The center document location displays the tabs on the top of the documents; the other locations display the tabs at the bottom.

- A tabbed document area can hold more documents than there is space to display the tabs. You can view the hidden tabs in two ways. Control + tab opens the active tools window and scrolls through the open files, or the Active File arrow in the upper right corner of the tabbed document area opens a drop-down list of the tabs.

- While a **dockable** window is being moved, Management Studio displays several blue docking indicators. Dropping a window on the arrow docks it in the selected location. Dropping the window on the center blue spot adds the window to the center location as a tabbed document. See Figure 5-1.

TIP

When dropping a window onto the arrow, make sure the cursor has to be over the arrow, or it won't work.

FIGURE 5-1

Moving a floating Window in Management Studio presents several drop points. The shaded area indicates where the dropped window will be placed.

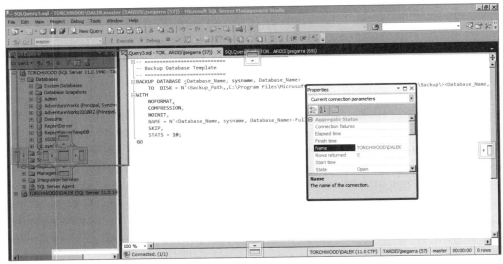

■ Opening several windows can keep the tools right at hand, but unless you have a mega monitor (a 24" widescreen works well!), the windows will likely use too much real estate. One solution is *auto-hiding* any docked window that you want out of the way until the window's tab is clicked. To auto-hide a window toggle the pin icon in the window's title bar. When the pin is vertical, the window stays open. When the window is unpinned, the window auto-hides. An auto-hidden window must be pinned back to normal before its mode can be changed to floating or tabbed. You might find that you accidentally open the hidden tab so much that you avoid auto-hiding windows. Or you might find the feature useful.

> **TIP**
>
> Ctrl+Tab displays all windows and documents. You can click a window or document with the Ctrl key still depressed to select it. You can also use the arrow keys with the Ctrl key still depressed and release Ctrl when the window you need is selected. One press of Ctrl+Tab selects the most recently selected document. Repeatedly pressing Ctrl+Tab cycles though all the documents in the center location.

To reset Management Studio to its default configuration (Object Explorer, Tabbed Documents, Property Window) use the Window ➪ Reset Window Layout menu command. Fortunately, this command does not reset any custom toolbar modifications.

To hide all the docked windows and keep only the tabbed documents in the center visible, use the Window ➪ Auto Hide All menu command.

The flexible positioning of the windows means you can configure the interface to give you access to the tools in whatever way makes you the most comfortable and productive. You might tend to close every window but the Query Editor and work with multiple scripts using the vertical split panes, as shown in Figure 5-2.

The Context Menu

In keeping with the Microsoft Windows interface standards, the context menu (accessed via right-click) is the primary means to select actions or view properties throughout Management Studio. The context menu for most object types includes submenus for new objects and tasks. These are the workhorse menus within Management Studio.

> **TIP**
>
> Add -nosplash to your SQL Server Management Studio shortcuts to improve startup time. To do this, right-click your SSMS shortcut (on your desktop, Start menu or taskbar) and go to Properties. In the Target window, add -nosplash after the quotes.

5

FIGURE 5-2

Although Management Studio can be configured with multiple windows, this is a common configuration for doing development work: Object Explorer Details for searches and Query Editor for script-style coding in the tabbed view, with a little Object Explorer on the side.

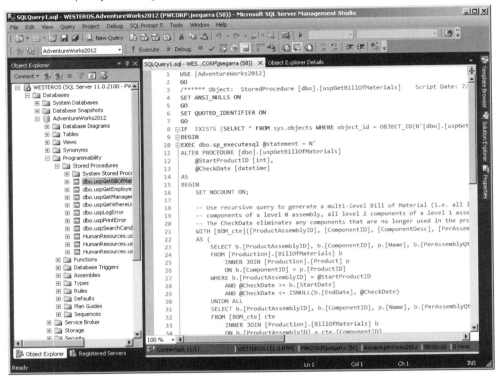

Registered Servers

Registered Servers is an optional built-in feature; if you manage only one or a few SQL Servers, Registered Servers offers little benefit. If, however, you are responsible for many SQL Servers, or if you simply want an organized way to manage your registered instances, this is the right place to take control.

Using Registered Servers, you can maintain connection information for connections to the Database Engine, Analysis Services, Reporting Services, SQL Server Mobile Edition Databases, and Integration Services. The toolbar at the top of Registered Services enables selection among the types of services.

Managing Servers

Servers are easily registered using the context menu and supplying the Properties page with the server name, authentication, and maybe the connection information. One key benefit of registering a server is that it can be given an alias, or Registered Server Name, in the Properties page, which is great if you're a DBA managing dozens of servers or instances with cryptic server names.

After a server is registered, you can easily select a server, and using the context menu, connect to it with Object Explorer or Query Editor. Although this is a good thing, the server aliases don't propagate to the Object Explorer, which can lead to confusion. The workaround is to keep the Object Explorer free from all other connections except those currently in use.

You can also use the Server context menu, as shown in Figure 5-3, to connect to the server with Object Explorer or Query Editor, or apply Policies. Other tasks include starting and stopping the service, and opening the registration's Properties page.

To share your registered server list, or move from one SSMS installation to another, export and import the server configurations using the Context menu ⇨ Tasks ⇨ Import/Export.

FIGURE 5-3

Registered Servers is the tool used to manage multiple servers. Here, we see the context menu showing how to manage service control remotely on your servers.

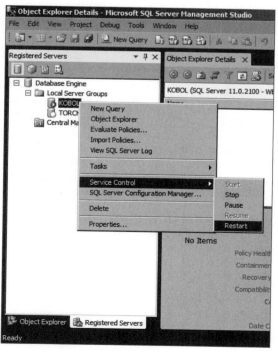

5

Server Groups

Within the Registered Servers tree, servers may be organized by server groups. This not only organizes the servers, but enables new group actions as well.

- **Local Server Groups**: Stores the connection information in the local file system. Think of these as Management Studio groups. The tree in Registered Servers flows from the service (i.e. Database Engine), to Local Server Groups, to Server Group (if you've created any), and finally to the registered server itself. Registering servers locally allows you to register servers using both Windows and SQL Server authentication.

- **Central Management Server**: Central Management Server functions just like Local Server Group registrations except that the connection information for registered servers is stored in the msdb database of the designated Central Management Server. The other notable difference is that server registrations under a Central Management Server can only use Windows authentication to register.

The server group (local or Central Management Servers) context menu includes the same Object Explorer, Query Editor, and Policy commands as registered servers. When a query/command/policy is executed at the root level of the registered servers, they apply to all servers and groups below it. However, when these commands are executed from a specific group, they apply only to all servers in the group or groups nested below the selected group.

- **Object Explorer**: Opens Object Explorer and connects to every server in the Server Group or groups nested below it.

- **New Query**: Opens a new query window with a connection to the group instead of a connection to the server. T-SQL commands can then be submitted to every server simultaneously. The Query Editor merges (or "unions") the results from every server and adds two columns, server name and login, to indicate which server returned each row as seen in Figure 5-4. The columns and whether results are merged or returned in separate result sets can be configured in Tools ⇨ Options ⇨ Query Results ⇨ SQL Server ⇨ MultiServer Results, or Query Editor context menu ⇨ Results ⇨ MultiServer. Messages now include the server name and login with each message.

- **Policy-Based Management Policies**: May be applied to every server in the group or groups.

FIGURE 5-4

Multi-server results in Management Studio.

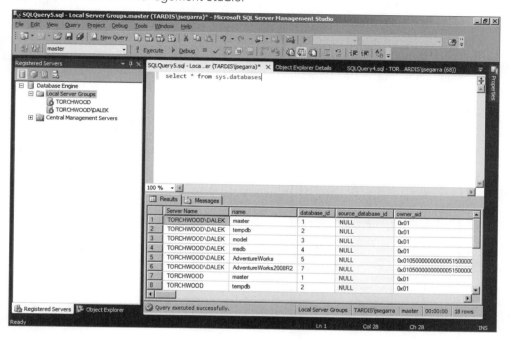

 Management Studio is not the only way to submit T-SQL scripts to SQL Server. For details on running the command-line interface, SQLCmd, refer to Chapter 22, "Maintaining the Database."

Object Explorer

Object Explorer offers a well-organized view of the world of SQL Server. The top level of the tree lists the connected servers. Object Explorer can connect to a server regardless of whether the server is known by Registered Servers. The server icon color indicates whether the server is running.

5

Navigating the Tree

In keeping with the Explorer metaphor, Object Explorer (see Figure 5-5) is a hierarchical, expandable view of the objects available within the connected servers.

Each Database Engine server node includes Databases, Security, Server Objects, Replication, AlwaysOn High Availability, Management, Integration Services Catalogs, and SQL Server Agent. Most of the tree structure is fixed, but additional nodes are added as objects are created within the server.

FIGURE 5-5

Object Explorer's tree structure invites you to explore the various components of SQL Server management and development.

The Databases node contains all the server's databases. When you right-click on a database, the context menu includes a host of options and commands. Under each database are standard nodes (see Figure 5-5), which manage the following database objects:

- **Database Diagrams:** Illustrates several tables and their relationships. A database may contain multiple diagrams, and each diagram does not need to display all the tables. This makes it easy to organize large databases into modular diagrams.

- **Tables:** Used to create and modify the design of tables, view and edit the contents of tables, and work with the tables' indexes, permissions, and publications. Triggers, stored procedures that respond to data-modification operations (insert, update, and delete), may be created and edited here.
- **Views:** Stored SQL statements are listed, created, and edited, and the results viewed, from this node.
- **Synonyms:** Alternative names for SQL Server database objects.
- **Programmability:** A large section that includes most of the development objects, stored procedures, functions, database triggers, assemblies, types, rules, defaults, Plan Guides and Sequences.
- **Service Broker:** Used to view and create Server broker objects, such as message types, contracts, queues, services, routes, remote service bindings, and broker priorities. You can now quickly create Service Broker applications using pre-defined templates. These code templates are presented when you right-click any node under Service Broker and choose to create a new item of that grouping's type.
- **Storage:** Used to manage nonstandard storage, such as full-text search and table partition schemes and functions, Full Text Stoplists, and Search Property Lists.
- **Security:** Used to manage security at the database level.

The Security node is used to manage server-wide security:

- **Logins:** Server-level authentication of logins.
- **Server Roles:** Predefined security roles. You can now also create your own custom server-lever roles.
- **Credentials:** Lists credentials.
- **Cryptographic Providers:** Used for advanced data encryption.
- **Audits:** Part of SQL Audit, collects data from Extended Events.
- **Server Audit Specifications:** Defines a SQL Audit for a server-level audit.
- **Server Objects:** Holds server-wide items:
  - **Backup Devices:** Organizes tapes and files for backup operations.
  - **Endpoints:** HTTP endpoints used by database mirroring, service broker, SOAP, and T-SQL.
  - **Linked Servers:** Lists predefined server credentials for distributed queries.
  - **Triggers:** Contains server level DDL triggers.

Replication is used to set up and monitor replication:

- **Local Publications:** Lists publications available from this server.
- **Local Subscriptions:** Lists subscriptions this server subscribes to from other servers.

The AlwaysOn High Availability node contains information about AlwaysOn Availability Groups.

5

- **Availability Groups:** Lists the Availability Groups configured on this server. This node will only appear if the AlwaysOn feature is enabled on the server instance.

The Management node contains several server-wide administration tools:

- **Policy Management:** Creates and manages Policy-Based Management policies.
- **Data Collection:** Defines data collection points for SQL Server's Management Data Warehouse.
- **Resource Governor:** Controls Enterprise Edition's CPU and Memory Resource Governor.
- **Extended Events:** Set up and monitor Extended Events sessions.
- **Maintenance Plans:** Create and manage Maintenance Plans.
- **SQL Server Logs:** SQL Server creates a new log with every restart of the service; view them here.
- **Database Mail:** Configures and monitors Database Mail.
- **Distributed Transaction Coordinator:** Manages DTC for transactions involving multiple servers.
- **Legacy:** Contains deprecated objects such as older database maintenance plans.

Integration Services Catalogs contains the SSISDB catalog, which contains the objects needed to work with Integration Services (SSIS) projects.

- **SSISDB:** Stores objects needed for working with Integration Services such as projects, packages, parameters, environments, and operational history.

The final node links to SQL Server Agent tools (if SQL Server Agent is running):

- **Jobs:** Control SQL Server Agent Jobs.
- **Job Activity Monitor:** View Job Activity.
- **Alerts:** Configure SQL Server Agent Alerts.
- **Operators:** Set up SQL Server Agent Operators.
- **Proxies:** Manage SQL Server Agent external.
- **Error Logs:** View SQL Server Error Logs.

> **CAUTION**
>
> Because Management Studio and SQL Server are communicating as client and server, the two processes are not always in sync. Changes on the server are often not immediately reflected in Management Studio unless Management Studio is refreshed, which is why nearly every tool has a Refresh icon, and Refresh is in nearly every context menu.

Filtering Object Explorer

Some databases are huge. To ease navigating these objects, Microsoft has included a filter for portions of the tree that include user-defined objects, such as tables or views. The Filter icon is in the toolbar at the top of the Object Explorer. The icon is enabled only when the top node for a type of user-defined object is selected. For example, to filter the tables, select the tree node, and then click the Filter icon, or right-click to open the tree's context menu, and select Filter ⇨ Filter Settings.

The Filter Settings dialog box enables you to filter the object by name, schema, owner, or creation date. To remove the filter, use the same context menu, or open the Filter Settings dialog box and choose Clear Filter. The filter accepts only single values for each parameter; boolean operators are not permitted.

Object Explorer Details

The Object Explorer Details page offers lots of useful information at a glance, such as recovery model, containment type, compatibility level, collation, database owner, and much, much more. You can open the Object Explorer Details page by going to View ⇨ Object Explorer Details or just press the F7 key.

- Object Explorer Details has dozens of additional columns that may be added to the grid. Right-click the grid headers to select additional columns.
- The columns can be rearranged and the rows sorted by any column.
- Data can be selected (highlighted) and copied to the clipboard (Ctrl+C) in a tabbed format with header columns — perfect for pasting into Excel and graphing.
- The pane below the grid displays several properties depending on the size of the pane.

The Object Explorer Details Search is one of the best kept secrets of SQL Server.

- If Object Explorer is at the server node level, the Object Explorer Details Search searches every object in the server.
- If Object Explorer is at any node at or under the database node level, it searches the current database.
- The Object Explorer Details page is rather object type generic and so is its context menu. The best solution is to use the synchronize toolbar button or context menu command to quickly jump to the object in Object Explorer.
- If the Back button in Object Explorer Detail returns to search results, it automatically reexecutes the search to be sure the list is as up-to-date as possible.

5

The Table Designer

Creating a new table, or modifying the design of an existing table, is easy with the Table Designer. The Table Designer, as shown in Figure 5-6, is similar to MS Access and other database design tool interfaces.

Create a new table by selecting the table node in the tree and then selecting New Table from the context menu. You can alter the design of existing tables by selecting the table, right-clicking, and selecting Design from the context menu.

FIGURE 5-6

Using the Table Designer tool, you can create tables or edit their designs.

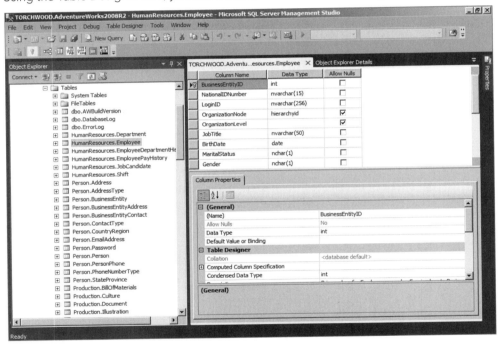

You can individually select and edit columns in the top pane. The column properties for the selected column are listed in the bottom pane. You can open dialog boxes for modifying foreign keys and indexes using the Table Designer menu or toolbar.

Although you may prefer Query Editor to the GUI tools, the Table Designer page is a clean, straightforward UI that generates scripts for every modification. Open the Property window as well, because some table properties are visible only there.

Chapter 7, "Relational Database Design and Creating the Physical Database," covers the logical design of tables and columns. The realities of implementing the logical design, and how to script tables using DDL, are discussed in Chapter 2, "Data Architecture."

Building Database Diagrams

The Database Diagram tool takes the Table Designer up a notch by adding custom table design views (see Figure 5-7) and a multitable view of the foreign-key relationships. The Database Diagram tool has its own node under each database. Each database may contain multiple diagrams, which makes working with large databases easier because each module, or schema, of the database may be represented by a diagram.

FIGURE 5-7

The AdventureWorks database relationships viewed with the Database Diagram tool.

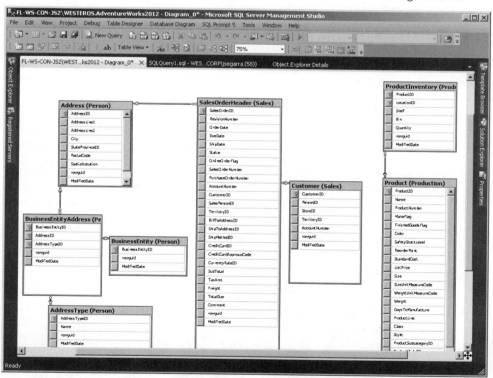

Sometimes the Database Diagram tool is useful to visually explore the schemas of large databases. Unfortunately, the Database Diagram tool suffers from a few clumsy issues.

- It makes sense to create a separate diagram for each section of a large database, and databases can be organized by schemas (as AdventureWorks is).

- Previous versions of the Database Diagram tool were not schema aware, however, the SQL Server 2012 version is and now displays the table schema in parentheses after the table name.

- There's no way to select all the tables of a schema and add them to the diagram as a set from the Object Explorer tree. The Object Explorer does not permit selecting multiple tables. The Object Explorer Details page enables multiple table selection but does not permit dragging the tables to the design. Even worse, the Add Table dialog box in the Database Diagram tool does not sort by the table's schema.

- The Add Related Tables option on the table's context menu helps solve this problem.

- Relationship lines have the frustrating tendency to become pretzels when tables or lines are moved.

Best Practice

If your goal is to print the database diagram, be sure to check the page breaks and arrange the tables first, or you might end up wasting a lot of paper. To view the page breaks, use the tool's context menu or the Database Diagram menu.

The Query Designer

The Query Designer is a popular tool for data retrieval and modification, even though it's not the easiest tool to find within Management Studio. You can open it three ways:

- Using the Object Explorer, select a table. Using the context menu, choose Edit Top 200 Rows. This opens the Query Designer, showing the return from a select top (200) query in the results pane. You can now open the other panes using the Query Designer menu or the toolbar.

- When using the Query Editor, use the Query Designer button on the toolbar, use the Query ⇨ Design Query in Editor menu command, or use the Query Editor's own context menu.

- When you open the Query Designer from the Query Editor, it's a modal dialog box, and the results pane is disabled.

Tip

If editing 200 rows, or viewing 1,000 rows, seems like too many (or not enough) for your application, you can edit those values in the Options ⇨ SQL Server Object Explorer ⇨ Command tab.

Unlike other query tools that alternate between a graphic view, a SQL text view, and the query results, Management Studio's Query Designer simultaneously displays multiple panes (see Figure 5-8), as selected with the view buttons in the toolbar:

- **Diagram pane:** You can add multiple tables or views to the query and join them together in this graphic representation of the SELECT statement's FROM clause.

- **Grid pane:** Lists the columns displayed, filtered, or sorted.
- **SQL pane:** You can enter or edit the raw SQL SELECT statement in this pane.
- **Results pane:** When the query is executed with the Run button (!), the results are captured in the results pane. If the results are left untouched for too long, Management Studio requests permission to close the connection.

TIP

A cool feature in Management Studio is the capability to create and graphically join derived tables within Query Designer's Diagram pane.

FIGURE 5-8

Object Explorer's Query Designer.

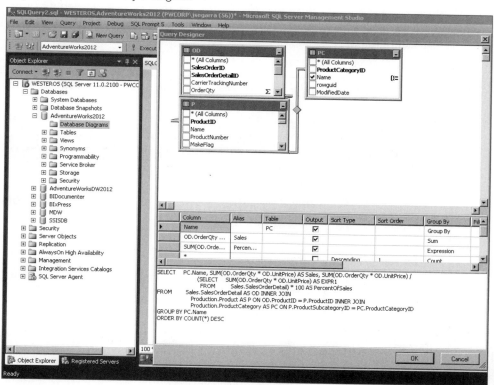

The Query Designer can perform *Data Manipulation Language (DML)* queries — (SELECT, INSERT, UPDATE, DELETE) besides SELECT. The Change Type drop-down list in the Query Designer toolbar offers to change the query from a default select query to an Insert Results, Insert Values, Update, Delete, or Make Table query.

However, the Query Designer is no substitute for the Query Editor. Unlike Query Editor, it cannot perform batches or non-DML commands. Nor can it execute SQL statements using F5. Table and column names can't be dragged from the Object Explorer to the SQL pane.

You can use the Query Designer to edit data directly in the results pane — a quick-and-dirty way to correct or mock up data.

Navigating the Query Designer should feel familiar to experienced Windows users. Although Books Online lists several pages of keyboard shortcuts, most are standard Windows navigation commands. The one worth mentioning here is Ctrl+0, which enters a NULL into the result pane.

Object Explorer Reports

No section on Object Explorer would be complete without mentioning the dozens of great reports hidden within, one of which is shown in Figure 5-9. You can find these reports in the context menus of server, database, and security ⇨ login nodes. While all reports aren't listed here, they're an excellent resource and one of the most underused features of Management Studio.

FIGURE 5-9

The server or database standard reports are a great way to quickly investigate your SQL Server.

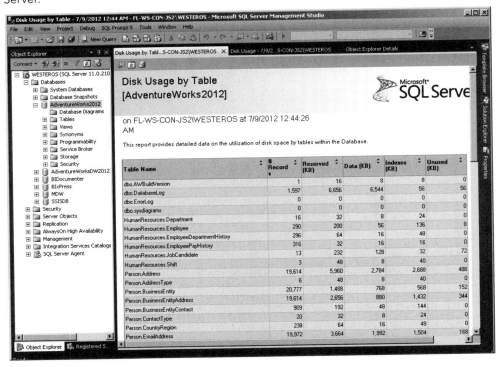

You can install custom reports in any Object Explorer node by placing the report definition file in the following directory:

```
...\Documents and Settings\{user}\Documents\SQL Server Management
Studio\Custom Reports
```

For more details see `http://msdn.microsoft.com/en-us/library/ bb153684(v=SQL.110).aspx`.

Using the Query Editor

With SQL Server 2005, the Query Editor carried on the legacy of SQL Server's Query Analyzer as the primary UI for database developers. In SQL Server 2008 and 2008R2, that experienced was enhanced and evolved. Now, with SQL Server 2012 it's an absolutely awesome product to work with!

Opening a Query Connecting to a Server

The Query Editor can maintain multiple open query documents and connections within the tabbed document area. Different queries may be connected as different users, which is useful for testing security. And the Query Editor can open and work with a `.sql` file even when not connected to a server.

When Query Editor first opens, it prompts for an initial login. To make further connections, use the File ➪ New Connection menu command.

The New Query toolbar button opens a new Query Editor document. There's some intelligence in how it selects the current database for the new query. If the Object Explorer has focus before the New Query button is pressed, the new query connects to Object Explorer's currently selected database. If the Query Editor has focus, the new query opens to the same database as the Query Editor's current query.

You can also switch a query's connection to another server using the Query ➪ Connection menu, the Change Connection toolbar button, or the Query Editor's context menu.

The query tab displays the most it can of the current SQL Server and database merged with the filename.

> **TIP**
>
> In some extreme cases, if SQL Server appears to not accept new connections, SQL Server listens on a dedicated port for a special diagnostic connection and tries to make a connection. A Dedicated Administrator Connection (DAC) is only possible if you are a member of the server's sysadmin role. To attempt a DAC connection using Query Editor, connect to the server with a prefix of `admin:` before the server name. For example, my servers' name is Torchwood, so connecting to it as `admin:torchwood` opens a DAC connection. DAC connections are also possible using the SQLCMD utility. For more about the DAC connection, see Chapter 22.

5

> **TIP**
>
> You can set Query Editor's connection bar's (at the bottom of the Query Editor) display color per connected server. This is a great visual cue. You can set the development server to green and the production server to red. When connecting to a server, open the connection dialog's options, and select Use Custom Color to set the color for that server.

Opening a .sql File

You can open a saved query batch file in multiple ways, and a huge trap you want to avoid follows:

- If Management Studio is not open, double-clicking a .sql file in Windows File Explorer launches Management Studio, prompts you for a connection, and opens the file. Here's the gotcha: If you select multiple .sql files in Windows File Explorer and open them as a group, Windows launches a separate instance of Management Studio for each file — not a good thing. You end up running several copies of Management Studio.

- If Management Studio is already open, double-clicking opens the file or selected files into a Query Editor document. Each file prompts you for a connection.

- Multiple .sql files may be dragged from Widows File Explorer and dropped on Management Studio. Each file opens a Query Editor after prompting for a connection.

- The most recently viewed files are listed in the Files ⇨ Recent Files menu. Selecting a file opens it in the Query Editor.

- The File ⇨ File Open menu or toolbar command opens a dialog box to select one or more files.

Real-World Developing with the Query Editor

With the release of SQL Server 2012, SQL Server Data Tools should be the preferred development environment for all developers. If you wish to stick to developing within Management Studio, here are some tips for using the Query Editor as a developer.

- View multiple scripts at the same time in Query Editor by right- clicking one of the documents and selecting New Vertical Tab Group. The selected document is the one that becomes the new tab to the right.

- Liberally use bookmarks to save points in the script to which you'll need to refer back. For example, I'll bookmark a table's DDL code, and the CRUD stored procedures for that table, while I'm working on the stored procedures.

- Begin every script with use *database* and set nocount on. (Chapter 16, "Programming with T-SQL," covers these commands.) Every script ends with use tempdb. That way if you run all the scripts, no script stays in the user database, and the initial create script can easily drop and re-create the database.

- You can drag and drop column names from the Object Explorer tree onto the query window. This allows you to quickly pick and choose specific columns for a query without having to manually type out each column name.

- If the default size of the text is too small, hold down the Ctrl key and use your mouse scroll wheel to increase/decrease the size of the font.

- When more documents exist than can display as tabs, the easy way to select the correct tab is to use the Active Documents drop-down list, at the far right of the Query Editor next to the close document X button. This is also the best way to see if a script is still executing, but it does sometimes reorder the tabs.

- If there's an error in the script, double-clicking the error message jumps to a spot near the error.

- Use uppercase for all reserved words in the outer query, and then use PascalCase (sometimes called CamelCase) for user-defined objects and reserved words in subqueries.

- IntelliSense Rocks! 'Nuff said.

- Use code outlining to collapse large sections of code. The Code Outliner can collapse multiline statements.

- IntelliSense and Code Outlining can be turned off in Tools ⇨ Options ⇨ Text Editor ⇨ Transact-SQL ⇨ Advanced.

- Dragging the folder named Columns (listed under a table in the Object Explorer) onto the query window will automatically list out all the columns in comma-delimited order. This can be a great time saver if you're trying to pick and choose specific columns for a query and don't want to manually type out each column's name.

- The Query Editor provides a quick visual indicator of lines that have been edited. The Track Changes Indicator displays a thin yellow bar to the left of the line if the text is modified and a green bar if that change has been saved.

- Use the SQLCMD toolbar button or Query ⇨ SQLCMD Mode menu command to switch the editor to work with SQLCMD utility scripts.

- While working with T-SQL code in Query Editor, you can get Books On Line (BOL) keyword help by pressing F1.

- The new SQL Snippets feature is awesome! It's a quick way to generate T-SQL code. You can access this using the keyboard shortcut Ctrl+K,Ctrl+X, or right-clicking the Query Editor window and selecting Insert Snippet. You can also assign keyboard shortcuts for your favorite code snippets!

TIP

Out-of-the- box, Management Studio's Query Editor does not provide automatic formatting of T-SQL. Some free websites enable you to submit a SQL statement and will format the code. But consider using a third-party tool like SQL Prompt from Red Gate, highly recommended. If you don't want to purchase a third-party tool there are also free websites like `http://format-sql.com` that allow you to copy/paste code and have it formatted for you.

5

Shortcuts and Bookmarks

Bookmarks are a great way to navigate large scripts. You can set bookmarks manually or automatically using the Find command. Bookmarks work with double control key combinations. For example, holding down the Ctrl key and pressing K and then N moves you to the next bookmark. The Ctrl+K keys also control some of the other editing commands, such as commenting code. You can also control bookmarks using the Edit ➪ Bookmarks menu or the bookmark next and previous toolbar buttons. Table 6-1 lists useful shortcuts.

TABLE 6-1 Useful Query Editor Shortcuts

Shortcut	Description
Ctrl+Shift+R	Refreshes IntelliSense
Ctrl+K, Ctrl +K	Adds or removes a bookmark
Ctrl+K, Ctrl +A	Enables all bookmarks
Ctrl+K, Ctrl +N	Moves to the next bookmark
Ctrl+K, Ctrl +P	Moves to the previous bookmark
Ctrl+K, Ctrl +L	Clears all bookmarks
Ctrl+K, Ctrl +C	Comments the selection
Ctrl+K, Ctrl +U	Uncomments the selection
Ctrl+K, Ctrl +W	Opens the Bookmark Window
Ctrl+K, Ctrl +X	Inserts Code Snippet
Ctrl+K, Ctrl+S	Inserts Code Snippet to surround code with

The Bookmark Window displays a list of all bookmarks and offers tools to control bookmarks, navigate bookmarks, and even to change the name of a bookmark.

Bookmarks are lost if the file is simply saved as a .sql file; however, if the query is saved within a solution in the Solution Explorer, bookmarks are saved from session to session.

Query Options

When a batch is sent from Query Editor to SQL Server, it has several query option settings that go with the batch. The defaults for these settings can be set in Tools ➪ Options ➪ Query Execution ➪ SQL Server. The current query options can be viewed or changed in Query ➪ Query Options, as shown in Figure 5-10.

Executing SQL Batches

As a developer's tool, the Query Editor is designed to execute T-SQL batches, which are collections of multiple T-SQL statements. To submit a batch to SQL Server for processing, use

Query ⇨ Execute Query, click the Run Query toolbar button, use the F5 key, or press Ctrl+E. Because batches tend to be long, and it's often preferable to execute a single T-SQL command or a portion of the batch for testing or stepping through the code, the SQL Server team provides you with a convenient feature. If no text is highlighted, the entire batch executes. If text is highlighted, only that text executes.

FIGURE 5-10

You can view and set Advanced and ASNI query options using the Query Options dialog. This view shows the Advanced Query Options.

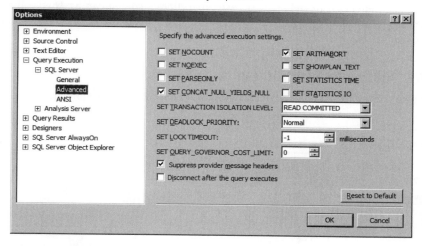

Chapter 16, "Programming with T-SQL," discusses this more, but technically, when Query Editor sends the script to SQL Server, it breaks it up into smaller batches separated by the Batch Separator — go.

It's worth pointing out that the Parse Query menu command and toolbar button checks only the SQL code. It does not check object names (tables, columns, stored procedures, and so on). This actually is a feature, not a bug. By not including the object name–checking in the syntax check, SQL Server permits batches that create objects and then reference them.

The T-SQL batch executes within the context of a current database. The current database displays and may be changed, within the database combo box in the toolbar.

Results!

The results of the query display in the bottom pane, along with the Messages tab, and optionally the Client Statistics, or Query Execution Plan tabs. The Results tab format may be either text or grid; you can switch using Ctrl+T or Ctrl+D, respectively. The new format will be applied to the next batch execution.

Alternatively, the results can display in another tab, instead of at the bottom of the query document. In Tools ⇨ Options, use the Query Results ⇨ SQL Server ⇨ Results to Grid tab, or in the context menu in the query window select the Results tab, and choose the Display Results in a Separate Tab option.

Another useful Result option is to play the Windows default beep sound file when a query completes. This can be set only in the Tools ⇨ Options ⇨ Query Results tab.

SQL Server 2000's Query Editor had a toolbar button to open or close the result pane. It disappeared with SQL Server 2005, but Ctrl+R still toggles the Query Editor Results Pane. And the command is still in the Customize Toolbar dialog, so you can fix the toolbar if you want. It's called the Show Results Pane, and it's not in the Query category where you'd expect to find it, but hiding in the Window category.

Viewing Query Execution Plans

One of Query Editor's most significant features is its capability to graphically view query execution plans (see Figure 5-11).

FIGURE 5-11

Query Editor's capability to graphically display the execution plan of a query is perhaps its most useful feature.

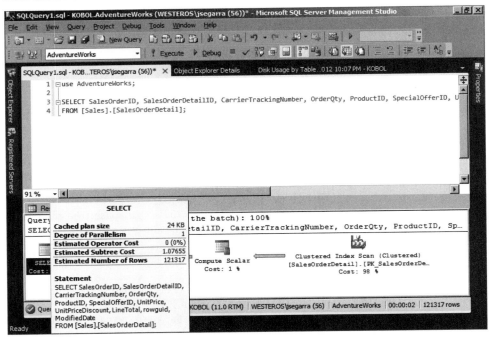

What makes the query execution plans even more important is that SQL is a descriptive language, so it doesn't tell the Query Optimizer exactly how to get the data, but only which data to retrieve. Although some performance tuning can be applied to the way the query is stated, most of the tuning is accomplished by adjusting the indexes, which greatly affects how the Query Optimizer can compile the query. The query execution plan reveals how SQL Server optimizes the query, takes advantage of indexes, pulls data from other data sources, and performs joins. Reading the query execution plans and understanding their interaction with the database schema and indexes is both a science and an art.

 Chapter 44, "Interpreting Query Execution Plans," includes a full discussion on reading the query execution plan.

Query Editor can display either an estimated query execution plan prior to executing the query or the actual plan after the query is run. Both display very similar plans; the major differences (beside the wait) is that the actual plan can display both the estimated and actual row counts for each operation, whereas the estimated query execution plan knows about only the estimated rows counts.

In addition to the query execution plan, the Query Editor can display the client statistics, which is a quick way to see the server execution times for the batch. (Although Profiler is a much better tool for detail work.) Enable Include Client Statistics using the Query menu or toolbar to add this tab to the results.

Using the Solution Explorer

The optional Solution Explorer enables you to organize files and connections within *solutions*, which then contain *projects*, similar to the Solution Explorer in Visual Studio. You don't need to use it; File ➪ Open and Save works well without Solution Explorer, but if you work on several database projects, you may find that Solution Explorer helps keep your life organized — or at least your code organized. You can find the Solution Explorer in the View menu, and you can add the Solution Explorer icon to the Standard toolbar using the Customize toolbar.

To use the Solution Explorer for managing query scripts, use the Solution Explorer context menu to create a new project. This creates the nodes and directories for the files. When the project exists, use it to create new queries.

Other than simply organizing your project, the Solution Explorer offers two practical benefits. First, if queries are saved within a solution, bookmarks are retained. Secondly, the Solution Explorer can be used with source control.

Getting a Jumpstart on Code with Templates and Code Snippets

Management Studio templates and Code Snippets are useful because they provide a starting point when programming new types of code, and they help make the code consistent.

Using Templates

To use a template, open the Template Explorer, select a template, and double-click it. This opens a new query in the Query Editor using code from the template.

You can also drag a template from the Template Explorer to an open Query and deposit the template code into the query.

The new query likely includes several template parameters. Rather than edit these in text, you can use a dialog box using the Query ⇨ Specify Values for Template Parameters (Ctrl+Shift+M). The dialog box has an entry for every parameter and automatically fills in the parameters within the query. If you make an error, the only way to go back is to undo each parameter change (Ctrl+Z).

Using Code Snippets

Code Snippets is a new feature to SQL Server 2012. Unlike templates, however, Code Snippets do create template parameters for you.

To activate Code Snippets, in the Query Editor window, you can either right-click the window and select Insert Snippet from the context menu, or you can use the keyboard shortcut Ctrl+K, Ctrl+X. This brings up the Code Snippet window, which enables you to choose the code snippet of your choosing via a drop-down menu. Simply double-click the options you want, and SSMS generates the T-SQL code accordingly.

Summary

Management Studio's Object Explorer and Query Editor are the two primary DBA and developer interfaces for SQL Server. Mastering the navigation of both these tools is vital to your success with SQL Server.

Following are a few key takeaways:

- Management Studio can be visually intimidating — so many windows. Close any window not needed for the task at hand. Remove the distractions and get the job done.

- Registered Servers can be useful if you have lots of servers to manage or if you want to easily query groups of your servers simultaneously.

- Management Studio offers a scalable experience. The accidental DBA can use the wizards and GUI, whereas the master DBA can work with raw T-SQL, PowerShell, DMVs, and wait states.

- The Query Editor is the place where T-SQL happens. Take the time to master its little features, such as bookmarks, to get the most out of SQL Server.

- IntelliSense takes some getting used to. But when it's mastered, it's great.

5

Part II

Building Databases and Working with Data

IN THIS PART

Introducing Basic Query Flow

IN THIS CHAPTER

Using Understanding Query Flow

Using FROM Clause Data Source

Using WHERE conditions

Using Columns, Starts, Aliases, and Expressions

Ordering the Result Set

Using SELECT Distinct

Using TOP()

S tructured Query Language (SQL), or more specifically Transact SQL (T-SQL) for SQL Server, is the romance language of data. Extracting or querying the single correct answer from giga-bytes of relational data can seem overwhelming. This is until you master the logical flow of the query.

One of the first points to understand is that SQL is a *declarative* language. This means that the SQL query logically describes the question to the SQL Query Optimizer, which then determines the best method to physically execute the query. This method of execution is the query execution plan. As covered in the next eight chapters, you can often construct the query in many ways, but you can optimize each method to the same query execution plan. However, in some cases, queries that produce the same result set may use different execution plans. As a result, you can express the SQL query in the way that is most comprehensible and the easiest to maintain. In some cases, one method may be more efficient and faster than the other.

SQL queries aren't limited to the SELECT command. The four Data Manipulation Language (DML) commands, SELECT, INSERT, UPDATE, and DELETE, are sometimes taught as four separate and distinct commands. However, think of queries as a single structural method of manipulating data; in other words, use the four commands as four verbs, using each with the full power and flexibility of the SQL.

In addition to SQL queries' elegance and flexibility, coining and executing SQL queries are not limited to one graphical user interface. Many SQL developers who came up through the ranks from Microsoft

Access and who have built queries using only the query interface available in Access are amazed when they understand the enormous power and capabilities of the full SQL query language.

This chapter builds a single table query structure and establishes the logical query execution order critical for developing basic or advanced queries. With this foundation in place, the rest of Part II, "Building Databases and Working with Data," develops the basic SELECT into the most elegant, flexible, and powerful command in all of computing.

Understanding Query Flow

You can think about query flow in four different ways. The first is to imagine the query using a logical flow. Some developers, on the other hand, think through a query visually using the layout of SQL Server Management Studio's Query Designer. The third approach is to syntactically view the query . You can view the query in a specific fixed order: SELECT – FROM – WHERE – GROUP BY – HAVING – ORDER BY. Finally, to illustrate the declarative nature of SQL, the fourth way to think about the query flow — the actual physical execution of the query — is to execute in the most efficient order depending on the data mix and the available indexes.

Syntactical Flow of the Query Statement

In its basic form, the SELECT statement tells SQL Server what data to retrieve, including which columns, rows, and tables to pull from, and how to sort the data. The order of the clauses in the SELECT statement are significant; however, they process in an order different from how they are syntactically specified, which this chapter discusses later.

Following is an abbreviated syntax for the SELECT command:

```
SELECT
  [DISTINCT] [TOP (n)] *, columns, or expressions
  [FROM data source(s)]
    [JOIN data source
      ON condition] (may include multiple joins)
  [WHERE conditions]
  [GROUP BY columns]
  [HAVING conditions]
  [ORDER BY Columns];
```

The SELECT statement begins with a list of columns or expressions. You need at least one expression — everything else is optional. An integer, scalar function, or a string value encapsulated in single quotes can represent the expression. The simplest possible valid SELECT statement is as follows:

```
SELECT 1;
```

If you do not supply a FROM clause, SQL Server returns a single row with values. (Oracle requires a FROM DUAL to accomplish the same thing.)

When you include the FROM portion of the SELECT statement, it assembles all the data sources into a result set, which the rest of the SELECT statement uses. You can represent these data sources in many ways. This chapter represents them only as tables. Within the FROM clause, you can reference multiple tables by using one of several types of joins.

The WHERE clause acts upon the record set assembled by the FROM clause to filter certain rows based upon conditions. You can specify several conditions in the WHERE clause. This chapter discusses some of these conditions later.

Aggregate functions perform summation-type operations across the data set. The GROUP BY clause can group the larger data set into smaller data sets based on the columns specified in the GROUP BY clause. The aggregate functions are then performed on the new smaller groups of data. You can restrict the results of the aggregation using the HAVING clause.

Finally, the ORDER BY clause determines the sort order of the result set. You can sort the data in ascending or descending order based on one or more columns in the list of columns from the SELECT statement. If you do not specify a sort order, the default is ascending.

A Graphical View of the Query Statement

SQL Server Management Studio includes two basic methods to construct and submit queries: Query Designer and Query Editor. Query Designer offers a graphical method to build a query, whereas Query Editor is an excellent tool for writing SQL code or ad hoc data retrieval because there are no graphics to get in the way, and the developer can work as close to the SQL code as possible. Even further, limiting yourself to the Query Designer may limit your ability to fully understand the SQL programming language and how to debug any potential errors you may encounter.

From SQL Server's point of view, it doesn't matter where the query originates; each statement is evaluated and processed as a SQL statement.

When selecting data using the Query Designer, you can enter the SQL statements as raw code in the third pane, as shown in Figure 6-1. The bottom pane displays the results in Grid mode or Text mode and displays any messages. The Object Browser presents a tree of all the objects in SQL Server, as well as templates for creating new objects with code.

> **TIP**
> If you select text in the Query Editor, then only the highlighted text is submitted to SQL Server when you press the Execute command button or the F5 key. This is an excellent way to test single SQL statements or portions of SQL code.

> **TIP**
> Although it may vary depending on the user account settings, the default database is probably the master database. Be sure to change to the appropriate user database using the database selector combo box in the toolbar, or the USE database command.
>
> The best solution is to change the user's default database to a user database and avoid master altogether.

FIGURE 6-1

Use the Query Designer to graphically create queries.

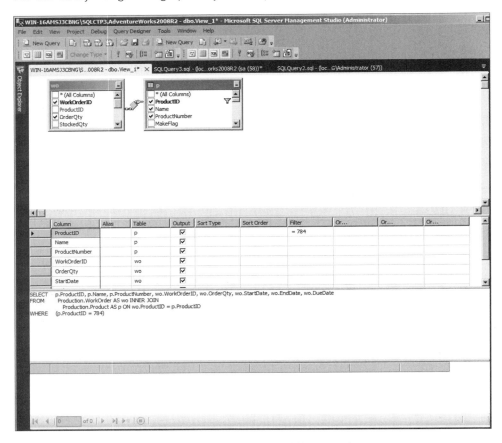

Logical Flow of the Query Statement

The best way to think through a SQL DML statement is to walk through the query's logical flow (see Figure 6-2). Because SQL is a declarative language, the logical flow may or may not be the actual physical flow that SQL Server's query processor uses to execute the query. Nor is the logical flow the same as the query syntax. Regardless, think through a query in the following order.

FIGURE 6-2

A simplified view of the logical flow of the query showing how data moves through the major clauses of the SQL select command.

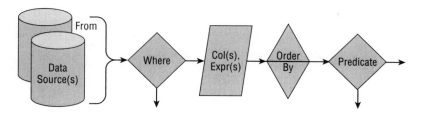

Following is a more detailed explanation of the logical flow of the query. *Every* step except step 4 is optional:

1. **[From]:** The query begins by assembling the initial set of data, as specified in the FROM portion of the SELECT statement. (Chapter 9, "Merging Data with Joins, Subqueries, and CTEs," discusses how to build even the most complex FROM clauses.)

2. **[Where]:** The filter process is actually the WHERE clause, selecting only those rows that meet the criteria.

3. **[Aggregations]:** SQL can optionally perform aggregations on the data set, such as finding the average, grouping the data by values in a column, and filtering the groups (see Chapter 10, "Aggregating, Windowing, and Ranking Data").

4. **Column Expressions:** The SELECT list is processed, and any expressions are calculated (covered in Chapter 8, "Data Types, Expressions, and Scalar Functions").

5. **[Order By]:** The resulting rows are sorted according to the ORDER BY clause, which can be ascending or descending. The default sort order is ascending.

6. **[Over]:** Windowing and ranking functions can provide a separately ordered view of the results with additional aggregate functions.

7. **[Distinct]:** Any duplicate rows are eliminated from the result set.

8. **[Top]:** After the rows are selected, the calculations are performed, and the data is sorted into the wanted order, SQL can restrict the output to the top few rows.

9. **[Insert, Update, Delete]:** The final logical step of the query is to apply the data modification action to the results of the query. These three verbs are explained in Chapter 12, "Modifying Data in SQL Server."

10. **[Output]:** The inserted and deleted virtual tables (normally only used with a trigger) can be selected and returned to the client, inserted into a table, or serve as a data source to an outer query.

11. **[Union]:** The results of multiple queries can be stacked or combined using a union command (see Chapter 9).

As more complexity has been added to the SQL SELECT command over the years, how to think through the logical flow has also become more complex. In various sources, you can find minor differences in how SQL professionals view the logical flow. That's OK — it's just a way to think through a query.

As you begin to think in terms of the SQL SELECT statement, rather than in terms of the graphical user interface, understanding the flow of SELECT and how to read the query execution plan can help you think through and develop difficult queries.

Physical Flow of the Query Statement

SQL Server can take the SELECT statement and develop an optimized query execution plan, which may not be in the execution order you would guess (see Figure 6-3). The indexes available to the SQL Server Query Optimizer also affect the query execution plan, as explained in Chapter 45, "Indexing Strategies."

FIGURE 6-3

The physical execution plan is different from the syntactical order, or logical understanding, of the query.

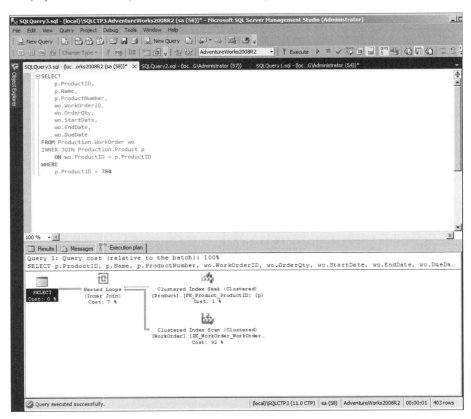

The rest of this chapter walks through the logical order of the basic query.

FROM Clause Data Sources

The first logical component of a typical SQL SELECT statement is the FROM clause. In a simple SQL SELECT statement, the FROM clause contains a single table. However, the FROM clause can also combine data from multiple sources and multiple types of data sources. The maximum number of tables that may be accessed within a single SQL SELECT statement is 256.

The FROM clause is the foundation of the rest of the SQL statement. For a table column to be in the output, accessed in the WHERE conditions, or in the ORDER BY, it must be in the FROM clause.

Possible Data Sources

SQL is extremely flexible and can accept data from 10 distinctly different types of data sources within the FROM clause:

- Local **SQL Server tables**.
- **Subqueries** serving as derived tables, also called *subselects* or *in-line views* (see Chapter 9). Common table expressions (CTEs) are functionally similar to subqueries but may be referenced multiple times within the query.
- You can reference **views** or stored SELECT statements within the FROM clause as if they were tables. Chapter 11, "Projecting Data through Views," discusses views.
- **Table-valued user-defined functions** return rows and columns. See Chapter 18, "Building User- Defined Functions," for more information.
- **Distributed data sources** pull in data from other SQL Server databases, other SQL Servers, other database platforms (for example, Microsoft Access, Oracle, and Foxpro), or applications (for example, Excel) using openquery() and other distributed functions, as detailed in Chapter 15, "Executing Distributed Queries."
- **Full-text** search can return data sets with information about which rows contain certain words.
- **Pivot** creates a crosstab within the FROM clause and is covered in Chapter 10.
- **XML** data sources using XQuery, as discussed in Chapter 14, "Using XML Data."
- **Row constructors** build hard-coded rows using the values() clause, as covered in Chapter 9.
- **Inserted and deleted** virtual tables from an insert, update, or delete can be passed to an outer query in the form of a subquery using the output clause.

The output clause is covered in Chapter 12. Consuming the output clause as a subquery is demonstrated in Chapter 9.

The FROM clause can merge data from multiple sources using several types of joins, as described in detail in Chapter 9.

Table Aliases

You can assign a data source a *table alias* within the FROM clause. When the data source has an alias, you must refer to it by this new name. In some cases the data source must have an alias. The following code accesses the Person table but refers to it within the query as table P:

```
-- From Table [AS] Table Alias
USE AdventureWorks;
SELECT
P.LastName,P.FirstName
   FROM Person.Person AS P;
```

In some cases the data source must have an alias. For example, when writing a query that has a subquery as the source, you must specify an alias. The following code accesses a subquery that has an alias of SQ.

```
--From Subquery [AS] Alias
USE AdventureWorks
SELECT
SQL.LastName, SQL.FirstName
FROM
(
        SELECT LastName, FirstName from Person.Person
) AS SQL;
```

Best Practice

Using the keyword AS to assign an alias to a column or data source is optional and is commonly ignored. However, this practice leads to errors in the query, as seen regularly in SQL Server newsgroups. As a rule, always include the AS keyword.

NOTE

In SQL, the USE command specifies the current database. It's the code version of selecting a database from the toolbar in Management Studio.

[Table Name]

If the name of a database object, such as a table or column name, conflicts with a SQL reserved keyword, you can let SQL know that it's the name of an object by placing it inside square brackets. The square brackets are specific to SQL Server and not part of the ANSI SQL standard. For example, if you have a database (DB1) that contains a table named [Order] you would be required to place the table name inside square brackets. The following code illustrates this:

```
USE DB1;
SELECT OrderID, OrderDate
  FROM [Order];
```

Although it's an incredibly poor practice to include spaces within the names of database objects, it is possible nevertheless. If this is the case, square brackets are required when specifying the database object. Again, assuming you work in database DB1 and it contains a table name Order Details, you would query the table using the following code:

```
USE DB1;
SELECT OrderID, ProductID, Quantity
  FROM [Order Details];
```

> **CAUTION**
>
> The collation of the database determines its character set and sort order, but it can also affect object names within SQL statements. If the collation is case-sensitive, then the object names must be case-sensitive as well. For example, with a case-sensitive collation, a table created with the name Person is different from person or PERSON. As a result, when referencing these objects in queries, you must adhere to any case-sensitivity specified for that object name.

Fully Qualified Names

The full and proper name for a table is not just the table name but a *fully qualified name*, sometimes informally referred to as the *four-part name*:

```
Server.Database.Schema.Table
```

If the table is in the current database, then the server and database name are not required, so when SQL Server developers talk about a qualified table name, they usually mean a two-part table name:

```
Schema.Table
```

Best Practice

Using the two-part name, (that is, the schema and object name) is sufficient and the best practice. Including the server and database name would restrict moving code from one server to another (for example, from development to production). The following code shows an example of using a two-part name:

```
USE DB1;

SELECT * FROM dbo.[Order]
```

In addition to writing cleaner code, using the qualified name has two specific benefits:

- The same table may exist in multiple schemas. If this is the case, then the schema selected is based on the user's default schema. Qualifying the name avoids accidentally using the wrong table.
- Qualified table names are required for the Query Engine to reuse the query execution plan, which is important for performance.

 For more about schemas, scope, and permission issues, see Chapter 32, "Authentication Types in SQL Server," and Chapter 33, "Authorizing Securables." Query plan reuse is discussed in Chapter 46, "Maximizing Query Plan Reuse."

WHERE Conditions

The WHERE conditions filter the output of the FROM clause and restrict the returned rows in the result set. The conditions can refer to the data within the tables, expressions, built-in SQL Server scalar functions, other queries, or user-defined functions. The WHERE conditions can also use several possible comparison operators and wildcards, as listed in Table 6-1. In addition, you can combine multiple WHERE conditions using Boolean AND, OR, and NOT operators.

Best Practice

To improve the performance of a client/server database, let the database engine do the work of restricting the rows returned, rather than make the client application wade through unnecessary data.

TABLE 6-1 **Standard Comparison Operators**

Description	Operator	Example
Equals	=	Quantity = 12
Greater than	>	Quantity > 12
Greater than or equal to	>=	Quantity >= 12
Less than	<	Quantity < 12
Less than or equal to	<=	Quantity<= 12
Not equal to	<> , !=	Quantity <> 12 , Quantity != 12
Not less than	!<	Quantity !< 12
Not greater than	!>	Quantity !> 12

CAUTION

The comparison operators that include an exclamation point are not ANSI standard SQL. <> is portable; ! = is not.

In addition to the standard comparison operators, which are no doubt familiar, SQL provides four special comparison operators: BETWEEN, IN, LIKE, and IS. The first three are explained in this section. Testing for nulls using the IS keyword and handling nulls are explained in Chapter 8.

Best Practice

The best way to find a thing is to look for it, rather than to first eliminate everything it isn't. It's easier to locate a business in a city than it is to prove that the business doesn't exist. The same is true of database searches. Proving that a row meets a condition is faster than first eliminating every row that doesn't meet that condition. In general (but not always), restating a negative WHERE condition as a positive condition improves performance.

Using the BETWEEN Search Condition

The BETWEEN search condition tests for values within a range. The range can be deceiving, however, because it is inclusive. For example, BETWEEN 1 and 10 would be true for 1 and 10. When using the BETWEEN search condition, the first condition must be less than the latter value because in actuality, the BETWEEN search condition is shorthand for "greater than or equal to the first value, and less than or equal to the second value."

In this example, the BETWEEN selects all the work orders with a quantity greater than 9 and less than 20:

```
USE AdventureWorks;

SELECT WorkOrderID
  FROM Production.WorkOrder
    WHERE OrderQty BETWEEN 10 and 19
```

> **CAUTION**
>
> The BETWEEN search condition is commonly used with dates. However, BETWEEN without a time looks for the beginning of the final day, or with a time rounds up the final millisecond to possibly include 12:00:00.000 of the next day. The solution is to use the following:
>
> ```
> WHERE Col >= StartDay AND Col < Ending Day + 1
> ```
>
> For example,
>
> ```
> WHERE SalesDate >= '6/1/2008' AND SalesDate < '7/1/2008'
> ```

 There's actually quite a lot to consider when working with dates, which is covered in Chapter 8.

Comparing with a List

The WHERE condition can compare the test value against the values in a list using IN, SOME, ANY, or ALL. Each operator can also be mixed with a NOT to reverse the condition.

Algebra Actually Is Useful

As much fun as algebra class was, although you thought algebra might improve your logical minds, few of you believe you would actually use algebra in your chosen profession.

Enter the SQL WHERE clause.

Here's the problem: If you apply a function to the test column in the WHERE clause, then SQL Server is forced to calculate that function on every row before it can filter the WHERE clause. This is a sure setup for "Gee, I don't know, it worked OK on my notebook" syndrome.

For a simple example, assume there's an index on Col1. The following WHERE clause generates an unnecessary scan, reading every row, as every column is modified and then compared to 130:

```
SELECT Col2, Col3
  FROM table
  WHERE Col11 + 30 = 130;
```

Algebra to the rescue. Somehow figure out a way to move that function to the parameter on the right side of the = and off the column, so that the column on the left side is unencumbered by any calculation or functions:

```
SELECT Col2, Col3
  FROM table
  WHERE Col11 = 130 - 30;
```

Now SQL Server can evaluate `130 - 30` and perform a blazingly fast index seek on the rows with `100` in Col11. Although this is a simple example, the principle is true. How you write your `WHERE` clauses has a significant effect on the performance of your queries.

This is only a small taste of the Query Optimizer and whether `WHERE` clause expressions are searchable arguments, known as *sargs*. Reading query execution plans and tuning queries and indexes are covered in greater detail in Chapters 44, "Interpreting Query Execution Plans." and 45, "Indexing Strategies."

`SOME` and `ANY` search conditions are functionally similar to `IN` — all are `true` if any value in the list is `true` — with three significant differences:

- `SOME` and `ANY` require a subquery. A list of literal values won't do.
- `SOME` and `ANY` are used with a mathematical operator (`=`, `>`, `<`, `=>`, etc.).
- `IN`, `SOME`, and `ANY` function differently when used with a `NOT` condition.

The `AND` search condition also requires a `true` subquery and returns a `true` when the search condition is `true` for every value in the list.

 IN, SOME, ANY, and ALL are revisited in Chapter 9. This chapter focuses on IN with a literal list.

`IN` is similar to the `EQUALS` comparison operator because it searches for an exact match from a list. If the value is in the list, then the comparison is `true`. For instance, if you query the StateProvince table in the AdventureWorks database providing a list of state or province codes similar to the following:

```
USE AdventureWork;
SELECT Name
  FROM Person.StateProvince
  WHERE StateProvinceCode IN ('NC', 'WV');
```

Result:

```
Name
-----------
North Carolina
West Virginia
```

Effectively, the IN search condition is the equivalent of multiple EQUALS comparisons ORed together:

```
USE AdventureWorks;
SELECT Name
  FROM Person.StateProvince
  WHERE StateProvinceCode = 'NC'
    OR StateProvinceCode = 'WV';
```

Result:

```
Name
-----------
North Carolina
West Virginia
```

The IN operator may also search for a value in a list of columns. The following example searches for the text 'Ken in either the FirstName and LastName columns:

```
USE AdventureWorks;
SELECT FirstName, LastName
  FROM Person.Person
  WHERE 'Ken' IN (FirstName, LastName)
```

Result:

```
FirstName    LastName
----------------------
Ken          Kwok
Ken          Meyer
Ken          Myer
Ken          Myer
Ken          Sanchez
Ken          Sanchez
```

You can combine the IN operator with NOT to exclude certain rows. For example, WHERE NOT IN ('NC', 'WV') would return all rows except those in North Carolina and West Virginia:

```
USE AdventureWorks;
SELECT StateProvinceCode
  FROM Person.StateProvince
  WHERE StateProvinceCode NOT IN ('NC', 'WV');
```

Abbreviated Result:

```
StateProviceCode
-----------
AB
AK
```

```
AL
AR
AS
AS
. . .
```

It's difficult to prove a negative, especially when a `null` value is involved. Because the meaning of `null` is "unknown," the value being searched for could be in the list. The following code sample demonstrates how a `null` in the list makes it impossible to prove that `'A'` is not in the list:

```
SELECT 'IN' WHERE 'A' NOT IN ('B',NULL);
```

There's no result because the unknown `null` value might simply be an "A." Because SQL can't logically prove that "A" is not in the list, the `WHERE` clause returns a `false`. Anytime a `NOT IN` condition is mixed with a `null` in the list, every row will be evaluated as `false`.

Using the LIKE Search Condition

The `LIKE` search condition uses wildcards to search for patterns within a string. The wildcards, however, are different from the MS-DOS wildcards with which you may be familiar. Table 6-2 shows both the SQL and MS-DOS wildcards.

TABLE 6-2   SQL Wildcards

Description	SQL Wildcard	MS-DOS Wildcard	Example
Any number (zero or more) of arbitrary characters	%	*	'Able' LIKE 'A%'
One arbitrary character	_	?	'Able' LIKE 'Abl_'
One of the enclosed characters	[ ]	n/a	'a' LIKE '[a-g]'
			'a' LIKE '[abcdefg]'
Match not in range of characters	[ᵌ]	n/a	'a' LIKE '[ᵌw-z]'
			'a' LIKE '[ᵌwxyz] '

The next query uses the `LIKE` search condition to locate all products that begin with `'Chain'` optionally followed by any number of characters:

```
USE AdventureWorks;
SELECT Name
FROM Production.Product
WHERE
      Name LIKE 'Chain%'
```

Result:

```
Name
------------------
Chain
Chain Stays
Chainring
Chainring Bolts
Chainring Nut
```

The following query finds any StateProvince name beginning with a letter between d and f, inclusive:

```
USE AdventureWorks;
SELECT Name
   FROM Person.StateProvince
   WHERE Name LIKE  '[d-f]%';
```

Result:

```
Name
--------------------------------------------------
Delaware
District of Columbia
Dordogne
Drome
England
Essonne
Eure
Eure et Loir
Finistere
Florida
France
```

The two possible methods for searching for a pattern that contains a wildcard are to either enclose the wildcard in square brackets or put an escape character before it. The trick to the latter workaround is that the escape character is defined within the LIKE expression.

When using the LIKE operator, be aware that the database collation's sort order determines both case-sensitivity and the sort order for the range of characters. You can optionally use the keyword COLLATE to specify the collation sort order used by the LIKE operator.

Best Practice

Although the LIKE operator can be useful, it can also cause a performance hit. Indexes are based on the beginning of a column, not on phrases in the middle of the column. If you find that the application requires frequent use of the LIKE operator, you should enable full-text indexing — a powerful indexing method that can even take into consideration weighted words and variations of inflections and can return the result set in table form for joining.

Multiple WHERE Conditions

You can combine multiple WHERE conditions within the WHERE clause using the Boolean logical operators: AND, OR, and NOT. As with the mathematical operators of multiplication and division, an order of precedence exists with the Boolean logical operators: NOT comes first, then AND, and then OR:

```
USE AdventureWorks;
SELECT ProductID, Name
FROM Production.Product
WHERE
        Name LIKE 'Chain%'
OR
        ProductID BETWEEN 320 AND 324
AND
        Name Like '%s%';
```

Result:

```
ProductID      Name
-----------    --------------------
952            Chain
324            Chain Stays
322            Chainring
320            Chainring Bolts
321            Chainring Nut
```

With parentheses, the result of the query is radically changed:

```
USE AdventureWorks;
SELECT ProductID, Name
FROM Production.Product
WHERE
(
        Name LIKE 'Chain%'
OR
        ProductID BETWEEN 320 AND 324
)
AND
        Name Like '%s%';
```

Result:

```
ProductID       Name
--------------  --------------------
324             Chain Stays
320             Chainring Bolts
```

Although the two preceding queries are similar, in the first query the natural order of precedence for Boolean operators caused the AND to be evaluated before the OR. The OR included the Chains in the results.

The second query used parentheses to explicitly dictate the order of the Boolean operators. The OR collected the Chains and products with a ProductID of 952, 324, 322, 320, 321, or 323. This list was then ANDed with products that included the letter g in their names. Only products 320 and 324 passed both of those tests.

Best Practice

When coding complex Boolean or mathematical expressions, explicitly stating your intentions with parentheses and detailed comments reduces misunderstandings and errors based on false assumptions.

SELECT ... WHERE

Surprisingly, using the WHERE clause in a SELECT statement does not require the use of a FROM clause or any data source reference. A SELECT statement without a FROM clause returns a single row that includes any expressions in the SELECT's column list.

A WHERE clause on a nontable SELECT statement serves as a restriction to the entire SELECT statement. If the WHERE condition is true, the SELECT statement functions as expected:

```
SELECT 'abc' AS col
  WHERE 1>0;
```

Result:

```
col
----
abc
 (1 row(s) affected)
```

If the WHERE condition is false, the SELECT statement still executes but it returns zero rows:

```
SELECT 'abc' AS col WHERE 1<0;
```

Result:

```
col
----
```

(0 row(s) affected)Columns, Stars, Aliases, and Expressions

The title of this section may read like a bad tabloid headline, but in all seriousness it means that the SQL SELECT statement returns columns in the order in which you list them in the SELECT statement. The column may be any expression or any column in the FROM clause.

Following the FROM clause and the WHERE clause, the next logical step in the query is the list of returned expressions.

The Star

The *, commonly called "star," is a special wildcard that includes all columns in their table order. If the query pulls from multiple tables, the * includes all columns from every table. Alternatively, tablename.* includes only the columns from the named table. Also, if you alias any tables in the FROM clause, you can return a complete column list of a specific example by using table alias.*.

Aliases

The name of the column in the underlying table becomes the name of the column in the result set. Optionally, you can change the column name using a column alias.

Expressions and constants have a blank column heading in the result set unless an alias is provided.

The AS keyword is optional, but just as with a table alias, using it is a good practice that improves the readability of the code and helps prevent errors.

To use an alias that's identical to a SQL Server keyword or that includes a space, enclose the alias in square brackets, single quotes, or double quotes. Although the square brackets are not technically required if the alias is the same as an object name (that is, table or column name), you an explicitly specify that the alias is not a keyword.

The following code demonstrates adding aliases to columns:

```
USE AdventureWorks;
SELECT
        Name AS ProductName,
        'abc',
        SellStartDate + 365 OneYearSellStartDate
FROM Production.Product;
```

Result:

```
ProductName                            OneYearSaleStartDate
-------------------------  ----  ------------------------
Adjustable Race            abc   2003-06-01 00:00:00.000
Bearing Ball               abc   2003-06-01 00:00:00.000
BB Ball Bearing            abc   2003-06-01 00:00:00.000
. . .
```

The first column's name is changed from `Name` to `ProductName` by means of an alias. The second column is an expression without an alias, so it has no column name. A better practice is to name expression columns using an alias, as demonstrated in the third column.

Accidental aliases are a common source of errors. Take a careful look at the next query:

```
USE AdventureWorks;
SELECT
        Name
        'abc',
        SellStartDate + 365 OneYearSellStartDate
FROM Production.Product;
```

Result:

```
abc                        OneYearSaleStartDate
-------------------------  ------------------------
Adjustable Race            2003-06-01 00:00:00.000
Bearing Ball               2003-06-01 00:00:00.000
BB Ball Bearing            2003-06-01 00:00:00.000...
```

The second column isn't `abc` as in the previous query. Instead, because of a missing comma, the `'abc'` in the query became an accidental alias for the first column.

What's Wrong with Select *?

For some developers, using SELECT * is common practice. However, this method of programming can pose a few challenges. If you talk to five SQL Server DBAs, it is likely that you get five different reasons not to use the SELECT *. On the other hand, if you talk to five SQL developers, they might give you five different reasons to use SELECT *. Basically you should avoid using it for several reasons, but if you are ever faced with the challenge of validating, here are a few reasons why:

- It is a waste of resources. In most cases more data is returned than needed.
- If you use a SELECT * in your query, how do you build a covering index to satisfy the needs of the query?
- Adding a column to the table could potentially break the application.

These are only a few, but there are many more and they all are valid. Just a quick Internet search should reveal a list that provides enough ammunition for any DBA.

Qualified Columns

A common problem with queries is that column names are duplicated in multiple tables. Including the column in the select list by column names alone can cause an "ambiguous column name" error. Basically, SQL Server complains that it doesn't know which column you refer to. Even if they contain the same exact data, SQL Server must know which column to select.

```
CREATE TABLE t1 (col1 INT);
CREATE TABLE t2 (col1 INT);

SELECT col1
  FROM t1
    CROSS JOIN t2;
```

Result:

```
Msg 209, Level 16, State 1, Line 2
Ambiguous column name 'col1'.
```

The solution, of course, is to qualify the column name by including the table:

```
SELECT t1.col1
  FROM t1
    CROSS JOIN t2;
```

 Chapter 8 details how to build expressions that you can use as columns or in several other places within the SELECT statement.

Ordering the Result Set

Logically, relational data should always be considered an unordered list. The primary key's purpose is to uniquely identify the row, not sort the table. SQL Server usually returns the data in the order of the primary key (because that's probably the clustered index), but there's no logical guarantee of that order. The only correct way to sort the results is with an ORDER BY clause.

SQL can sort by multiple columns, and the sort columns don't have to be columns that are returned by the SELECT, so there's a lot of flexibility in how you can specify the columns. Using Management Studio's Query Designer, you can create the ORDER BY by selecting the sort order for the column, as shown in Figure 6-4.

FIGURE 6-4

Within Management Studio's Query Designer, you can define the sort order and sort type in the column pane. The `TOP()` predicate is set for the Query Designer inside the query's Properties page.

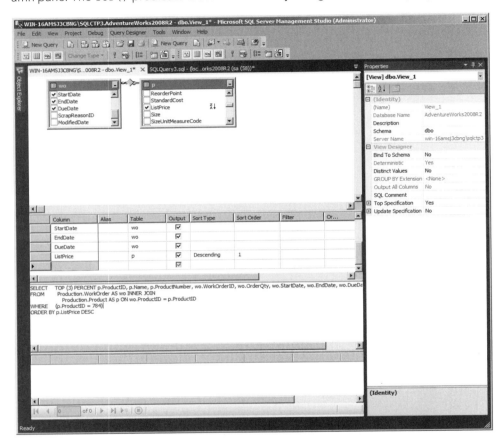

Although there is not a limit on the number of columns that you can specify in the `ORDER BY` clause of the select statement, an internal operation exists that indirectly enforces a limit. During a sort operation, a worktable see Chapter 44, "Interpreting Query Execution Plans" is created. This worktable has a maximum row size of 8060 bytes. As a result, this limits the total size of the columns specified in an `ORDER BY` clause.

Specifying the ORDER BY Using Column Names

The best way to sort the result set is to completely spell out the `ORDER BY` columns:

```
USE AdventureWorks;

SELECT FirstName, LastName
```

```
       FROM Person.Person

   ORDER BY LastName, FirstName;
```
Result:
```
   FirstName      LastName
   ------------   ------------------
   Syed           Abbas
   Catherine      Abel
   Kim            Abercrombie
   . . .
```

> **NOTE**
> ORDER BY and the order of columns in the select list are completely independent.

Specifying the ORDER BY Using Expressions

In the case of sorting by an expression, you can repeat the entire expression in the ORDER BY clause. This does not cause a performance hit because the SQL Server Query Optimizer is smart enough to avoid recomputing the expression:

```
SELECT
LastName + ', ' + FirstName AS FullName
  FROM Person.Person
  ORDER BY LastName + ', ' + FirstName;
```

Result:
```
   FullName
   ----------------------
   Abbas, Syed
   Abel, Catherine
   Abercrombie, Kim
   . . .
```

Using an expression in the ORDER BY clause can solve some headaches. For example, some database developers store product titles in two columns: One column includes the full title, and the duplicate column stores the title stripped of the leading "The." In terms of performance, such denormalization might be a good idea, but using a case expression within the ORDER BY clause correctly sorts without duplicating the title. (Chapter 8 covers the full syntax for the CASE expression.)

The AdventureWorks sample database includes a list of Product Descriptions. If the Description includes a leading "This," then the CASE expression removes it from the data and passes to the ORDER BY:

```
USE AdventureWorks;
SELECT Description, LEN(Description) AS TextLength
```

```
FROM Production.ProductDescription
WHERE
    Description LIKE 'Replacement%'
ORDER BY
CASE
    WHEN LEFT(Description, 5) = 'This '
    THEN Stuff(Description, 1, 5, '')
ELSE
    Description
END;
```

Result:

```
Description                                                 TextLength
---------------------------------                           ----------
Replacement mountain wheel for entry-level rider.                   49
Replacement mountain wheel for entry-level rider.                   49
Replacement mountain wheel for the casual to serious rider.         59
Replacement mountain wheel for the casual to serious rider.         59
Replacement rear mountain wheel for entry-level rider.              54
Replacement rear mountain wheel for the casual to serious rider.    64
Replacement rear wheel for entry-level cyclist.                     47
Replacement road front wheel for entry-level cyclist.               53
Replacement road rear wheel for entry-level cyclist.                52
. . .
```

Specifying the ORDER BY Using Column Aliases

Alternatively, you can use a column alias to specify the columns used in the ORDER BY clause. This is the preferred method for sorting by an expression because it makes the code easier to read. This example sorts in descending order, rather than the default ascending order:

```
USE AdventureWorks
SELECT LastName + ', ' + FirstName as FullName
  FROM Person.Person
    ORDER BY FullName DESC;
```

Result:

```
FullName
------------
Zwilling, Michael
Zwilling, Michael
Zukowski, Jake
Zugelder, Judy
Zubaty, Patricia
Zubaty, Carla
Zimprich, Karin
. . .
```

An alias is allowed in the ORDER BY clause but not the WHERE clause because the WHERE clause is logically executed prior to processing columns and expressions. The ORDER BY clause follows the assembling of the columns and aliases, so it can use column aliases.

Using the Column Ordinal Position

You can use the ordinal number of the column (column position number) to indicate the ORDER BY columns, but don't do this. If the select columns are changed or their order changes, the sort order also changes.

One case for which it's not necessarily a horrid practice to use the ordinal number to specify the sort is for complex union queries (see Chapter 9).

The following query demonstrates sorting by ordinal position:

```
USE AdventureWorks
SELECT LastName + ', ' + FirstName as FullName
  FROM Person.Person
  ORDER BY 1;
```

Result:

```
FullName
----------------------
Abbas, Syed
Abel, Catherine
Abercrombie, Kim
. . .
```

ORDER BY and Collation

SQL Server's collation order is vital to sorting data. In addition to determining the alphabet, the collation order also determines whether accents, case, and other alphabet properties are considered in the sort order. For example, if the collation is case-sensitive, then the uppercase letters are sorted before the lowercase letters. The following function reports the installed collation options and the current collation server property:

```
SELECT * FROM fn_helpcollations();
```

Result:

```
name                     description
--------------------     --------------------------
Albanian_BIN             Albanian, binary sort
Albanian_CI_AI           Albanian, case-insensitive,
                         accent-insensitive,
                         kanatype-insensitive, width-insensitive
Albanian_CI_AI_WS        Albanian, case-insensitive,
                         accent-insensitive,
```

```
                              kanatype-insensitive, width-sensitive
   . . .
SQL_Latin1_General_CP1_CI_AI
                              Latin1-General, case-insensitive,
                              accent-insensitive,
                              kanatype-insensitive, width-insensitive
                              for Unicode Data, SQL Server Sort Order
                              54 on Code Page 1252 for non-Unicode
                              Data
   . . .
```

The following query reports the current server collation:

```
SELECT SERVERPROPERTY('Collation') AS ServerCollation;
```

Result:

```
ServerCollation
-----------------------
SQL_Latin1_General_CP1_CI_AS
```

Although the server collation setting is determined during setup, you can set the colla-tion property for a database or a column using the COLLATE keyword. The following code changes the AdventureWorks database collation so that it becomes case-sensitive:

```
CREATE DATABASE CollateChange
  GO
  ALTER DATABASE CollateChange
  COLLATE SQL_Latin1_General_CP1_CS_AS;
  GO
  SELECT DATABASEPROPERTYEX('CollateChange','Collation')
  AS DatabaseCollation;
```

Result:

```
DatabaseCollation
-----------------------------------
SQL_Latin1_General_CP1_CS_AS
```

Not only can SQL Server set the collation at the server, database, and column levels, colla-tion can even be set at the individual query level. The following query sorts according to the Danish collation, without regard to case or accents:

```
Use AdventureWorks
SELECT *
  FROM Production.Product
  ORDER BY Name
    COLLATE Danish_Norwegian_CI_AI;
```

Not all queries need to be sorted, but for those that do, the ORDER BY clause combined with the many possible collations yields tremendous flexibility in sorting the result set.

Terminating the Statement

ANSI SQL uses a semicolon to terminate a statement. Although it's been there as an option for several versions, code with semicolons was unheard of in the SQL Server community until recently. SQL Server 2005 began requiring it for some commands. Therefore, following are the rules about semicolons.

When semicolons are required:

- At the end of the statement preceding a common table expression (CTE)
- At the end of a MERGE statement

When not to use a semicolon:

- Between the END TRY and BEGIN CATCH.
- Between the IF condition and the BEGIN.
- Don't mix GO and the semicolon on the same line.

Select Distinct

The first predicate option in the SELECT command is the keyword DISTINCT, which eliminates duplicate rows from the result set of the query. The duplications are based only on the output columns, not the underlying tables. The opposite of DISTINCT is ALL. Because ALL is the default, it is typically not included.

The following example demonstrates the difference between DISTINCT and ALL. Joins are explained in Chapter 9 but here the JOIN between product and salesorderdetails generates a row each time a product is sold as part of an order. Because this select statement returns only the productname column, it's a perfect example of duplicate rows for the DISTINCT predicate:

```
USE AdventureWorks;
SELECT ALL p.Name
FROM Production.Product p
INNER JOIN Sales.SalesOrderDetail so
      ON p.ProductID = so.ProductID
```

Result:

```
Name
----------------------------------------------------
Sport-100 Helmet, Red
Sport-100 Helmet, Red
Sport-100 Helmet, Red
Sport-100 Helmet, Red
Sport-100 Helmet, Red
Sport-100 Helmet, Red
Sport-100 Helmet, Red
```

```
Sport-100 Helmet, Red
Sport-100 Helmet, Red
Sport-100 Helmet, Red
Sport-100 Helmet, Red
Sport-100 Helmet, Red
. . .
```

With the DISTINCT predicate:

```
USE AdventureWorks;
SELECT DISTINCT p.Name
FROM Production.Product p
INNER JOIN Sales.SalesOrderDetail so
    ON p.ProductID = so.ProductID;
```

Result:

```
Name
---------------------------------
Sport-100 Helmet, Red
Sport-100 Helmet, Black
Mountain Bike Socks, M
Mountain Bike Socks, L
Sport-100 Helmet, Blue
AWC Logo Cap
Long-Sleeve Logo Jersey, S
. . .
```

Whereas the first query returned 121,317 rows, the DISTINCT predicate in the second query eliminated the duplicate rows and returned only 266 unique rows.

CAUTION

SQL Server's DISTINCT is different from MS Access' distinctrow, which eliminates duplicates based on data in the source tables, not duplicates in the result set of the query.

Select DISTINCT functions as though a GROUP BY clause (see Chapter 10) exists on every output column.

Of course, using DISTINCT is based on the query's requirements, so there may be no choice; just be aware that depending on the size and mix of the data, there may be a performance impact.

TOP ()

By definition, SELECT works with sets of data. Sometimes, however, it's only the first few rows from the set that are of interest. For these situations, SQL Server includes several ways to filter the results and find the top rows.

As mentioned earlier, SQL Server returns all the rows from the SELECT statement by default. The optional TOP() predicate tells SQL Server to return only a few rows (either a fixed number or a percentage) based upon the options specified (refer to Figure 6-4). A variable can be passed to TOP().

TOP() works hand-in-hand with ORDER BY. It's the ORDER BY clause that determines which rows are first. If the SELECT statement does not have an ORDER BY clause, then the TOP() predicate still works by returning an unordered sampling of the result set.

The AdventureWorks sample database is a good place to test the TOP() predicate. The following query finds the top 3 percent of product prices in the Product table. The Product lists all products and their corresponding prices:

```
USE AdventureWorks;
SELECT TOP(3) PERCENT
        ProductNumber, Name, ListPrice, SellStartDate
FROM Production.Product
ORDER BY ListPrice DESC
```

Result:

```
ProductNumber   Name                    ListPrice    SellStartDate
-------------   --------------------    ----------   -----------------------
BK-R93R-62      Road-150 Red, 62        3578.27      2005-07-01 00:00:00.000
BK-R93R-44      Road-150 Red, 44        3578.27      2005-07-01 00:00:00.000
BK-R93R-48      Road-150 Red, 48        3578.27      2005-07-01 00:00:00.000
BK-R93R-52      Road-150 Red, 52        3578.27      2005-07-01 00:00:00.000
BK-R93R-56      Road-150 Red, 56        3578.27      2005-07-01 00:00:00.000
BK-M82S-38      Mountain-100 Silver, 38 3399.99      2005-07-01 00:00:00.000
BK-M82S-42      Mountain-100 Silver, 42 3399.99      2005-07-01 00:00:00.000
BK-M82S-44      Mountain-100 Silver, 44 3399.99      2005-07-01 00:00:00.000
BK-M82S-48      Mountain-100 Silver, 48 3399.99      2005-07-01 00:00:00.000
BK-M82B-38      Mountain-100 Black, 38  3374.99      2005-07-01 00:00:00.000
BK-M82B-42      Mountain-100 Black, 42  3374.99      2005-07-01 00:00:00.000
BK-M82B-44      Mountain-100 Black, 44  3374.99      2005-07-01 00:00:00.000
BK-M82B-48      Mountain-100 Black, 48  3374.99      2005-07-01 00:00:00.000
BK-R89R-44      Road-250 Red, 44        2443.35      2006-07-01 00:00:00.000
BK-R89R-48      Road-250 Red, 48        2443.35      2006-07-01 00:00:00.000
BK-R89R-52      Road-250 Red, 52        2443.35      2006-07-01 00:00:00.000
```

The next query locates the six lowest prices in the product table:

```
USE AdventureWorks;
SELECT TOP(6)
```

```
        ProductNumber, Name, ListPrice,
          CONVERT(VARCHAR(10),SellStartDate,1) SellStartDate
   FROM Production.Product
   ORDER BY ListPrice DESC
```

Result:

ProductNumber	Name	ListPrice	SellStartDate
BK-R93R-62	Road-150 Red, 62	3578.27	07/01/05
BK-R93R-44	Road-150 Red, 44	3578.27	07/01/05
BK-R93R-48	Road-150 Red, 48	3578.27	07/01/05
BK-R93R-52	Road-150 Red, 52	3578.27	07/01/05
BK-R93R-56	Road-150 Red, 56	3578.27	07/01/05
BK-M82S-38	Mountain-100 Silver, 38	3399.99	07/01/05

The query looks clean and the result looks good, but unfortunately it's wrong. If you look at the raw data sorted by price, you can actually see five rows with a price of 3578.27 and four rows with a price of 3399.33. The WITH TIES option solves this problem, as described in the following section.

Best Practice

By the nature of the formatting, computer-generated data tends to appear correct. Unit testing the query against a set of data with known results is the only way to check its quality.

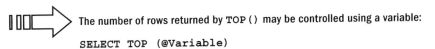

The number of rows returned by TOP () may be controlled using a variable:

```
SELECT TOP (@Variable)
```

For more details about using variables, turn to Chapter 16, "Programming with T-SQL."

The WITH TIES Option

The WITH TIES option is important to the TOP() predicate. It enables the last place to include multiple rows if those rows have equal values in the columns used in the ORDER BY clause. The following version of the preceding query includes the WITH TIES option and correctly results in five rows from a TOP 6 predicate:

```
USE AdventureWorks;
SELECT TOP(6) WITH TIES
        ProductNumber, Name, ListPrice,
          CONVERT(VARCHAR(10),SellStartDate,1) SellStartDate
```

```
FROM Production.Product
ORDER BY ListPrice DESC
```

Result:

```
ProductNumber    Name                     ListPrice     SellStartDate
-------------    --------------------     ---------     -------------
BK-R93R-62       Road-150 Red, 62         3578.27       07/01/05
BK-R93R-44       Road-150 Red, 44         3578.27       07/01/05
BK-R93R-48       Road-150 Red, 48         3578.27       07/01/05
BK-R93R-52       Road-150 Red, 52         3578.27       07/01/05
BK-R93R-56       Road-150 Red, 56         3578.27       07/01/05
BK-M82S-38       Mountain-100 Silver, 38  3399.99       07/01/05
BK-M82S-38       Mountain-100 Silver, 38  3399.99       07/01/05
BK-M82S-38       Mountain-100 Silver, 38  3399.99       07/01/05
BK-M82S-38       Mountain-100 Silver, 38  3399.99       07/01/05
```

NOTE

If you move from Access to SQL Server, be aware that Access, by default, automatically adds the `WITH TIES` option to the `TOP()` predicate.

NOTE

An alternative to `TOP()` is the `SET ROWCOUNT` command, which limits any DML command to affecting only *n* number of rows until it's turned off with `SET ROWCOUNT 0`. The issue is that `ROWCOUNT` isn't portable either, and it's been deprecated for `INSERT`, `UPDATE`, and `DELETE` in SQL Server 2008.

Selecting a Random Row

There are times when you need a single random row. You can use this technique when populating a table with random names.

Using the `TOP(1)` predicate returns a single row, and sorting the result set by `newid()` randomizes the sort. Together they return a random row each time the query executes.

There is a performance cost to using `TOP(1)` and `newid()`. SQL Server has to add a `uniqueidentifier` to every row and then sort by the `uniqueidentifier`. An elegant solution is to add a `tablesample` option to the table when randomly selecting a single row from a large table. `Tablesample` works by randomly selecting pages within the table and then returning every row from those pages from the `FROM` clause:

```
USE AdventureWorks;
SELECT TOP(1) LastName
  FROM Person.Person TableSample (10 Percent)
  ORDER BY NewID();
```

Summary

The simple SELECT command has a wealth of power and flexibility.

The key to understanding the SQL query is understanding that the query is declarative — you only phrase a question. The Query Optimizer determines how to execute the query, so SQL enables some flexibility in the development style of the query.

Following are a few of the key points from this chapter:

- Think through the query in the logical flow of the query, not the syntax flow for the query.
- The FROM clause can assemble data from ten different types of data sources. Think creatively about where you can find data for your query.
- Never use SELECT *.
- Aliases are a good thing, and always use the AS.
- Be intentional about the WHERE clause. Use parentheses. Keep the expressions away from the source column.
- Never trust the sort order to the physical order of the data on the disk. If the data needs to be sorted, then use an ORDER BY.

From this introduction, the next eight chapters incrementally add more advanced features that augment the power of SELECT: incorporating complex expressions, multiple types of joins, subqueries, and groupings.

Welcome to the set-based power of SQL.

Relational Database Design and Creating the Physical Database Schema

IN THIS CHAPTER

There are some musicians who can hear a song and then play it; most people don't have that ability. Most can feel the rhythm, but have to work through the chords and figure them out almost mathematically before they can play anything but a simple piece. To most, building chords and chord progressions is like drawing geometric patterns on the guitar neck using the frets and strings.

Music theory encompasses the scales, chords, and progressions used to make music. Every melody, harmony, rhythm, and song draws from music theory. For some musicians there's just a feeling that the song sounds right. For those who make music their profession, they understand the theory behind why a song feels right. Great musicians have both the feel and the theory in their music.

Designing databases is similar to playing music. Databases are designed by combining the right patterns to correctly model a specific solution to a problem. Normalization is the theory that shapes the design. There's both the mathematic theory of relational algebra and the intuitive feel of an elegant database.

Designing databases is both science and art.

Database Basics

The purpose of a database is to store the information required by an organization. Any means of collecting and organizing data is a database. Prior to the Information Age, information was primarily stored on cards, in file folders, or in ledger books. Before the adding machine, offices employed dozens of workers who spent all day adding columns of numbers and double-checking the math of others. The job title of those who had that exciting career was *computer*.

Author's Note

Welcome to the second of three chapters that deal with database design. Although they're spread out in the table of contents, they weave a consistent theme that good design yields great performance:

- Chapter 2 provides an overview of data architecture.
- Partitioning the physical layer is covered in Chapter 49, "Partitioning."
- Designing data warehouses for business intelligence is covered in Chapter 51, "Business Intelligence Database Design."

There's more to this chapter than the standard "Intro to Normalization." This chapter draws on the lessons that have been learned over many years.

This chapter covers a book's worth of material, but concisely summarizes the main ideas. The chapter opens with an introduction to database design terms and concepts. Then the same concept is presented from three perspectives: first, with the common patterns, then with a custom Layered Design concept, and lastly with the normal forms. Each of these ideas is easier to comprehend after you understand the other two, so if you have the time, read the chapter twice to get the most out of it.

As the number crunching began to be handled by digital machines, human labor, rather than being eliminated, shifted to other tasks. Analysts, programmers, managers, and IT staff have replaced the human "computers" of days gone by.

Benefits of a Digital Database

The Information Age and the relational database brought several measurable benefits to organizations:

- Increased data consistency and better enforcement of business rules
- Improved sharing of data, especially across distances
- Improved ability to search for and retrieve information
- Improved generation of comprehensive reports
- Improved ability to analyze data trends

The general theme is that a computer database originally didn't save time in the entry of data, but rather in the retrieval of data and in the quality of the data retrieved. However, with automated data collection in manufacturing, bar codes in retailing, databases sharing more data, and consumers placing their own orders on the Internet, the effort required to enter the data has also decreased.

> **NOTE**
>
> This chapter presents the relational database design principles and patterns used to develop operational, or online transaction processing (OLTP), databases.
>
> Some of the relational principles and patterns may apply to other types of databases, but databases not used for first-generation data (such as most BI, reporting databases, data warehouses, or reference data stores) do not necessarily benefit from normalization.
>
> In this chapter, the term "database" exclusively refers to a relational, OLTP-style database.

Tables, Rows, Columns

A relational database collects related, or common, data in a single list. For example, all the product information may be listed in one table and all the customers in another table.

A table appears similar to a spreadsheet and is constructed of columns and rows. The appeal (and the curse) of the spreadsheet is its informal development style, which makes it easy to modify and add to as the design matures. Managers tend to store critical information in spreadsheets, and many databases started as informal spreadsheets.

In both a spreadsheet and a database table, each row is an item in the list and each column is a specific piece of data concerning that item, so each cell should contain a single piece of data about a single item.

Whereas a spreadsheet tends to be free-flowing and loose in its design, database tables should be consistent in terms of the meaning of the data in a column. Because row and column consistency is important to a database table, the design of the table is critical.

Over the years, different development styles have referred to these concepts with various different terms, as listed in Table 7-1.

TABLE 7-1 Comparing Database Terms

Development Style	List of Common Items	Item in the List	Piece of Information in the List
Legacy software	File	Record	Field
Spreadsheet	Spreadsheet/worksheet/named range	Row	Column/cell
Relational algebra/logical design	Entity, or relation	Tuple (rhymes with couple)	Attribute
SQL DDL design	Table	Row	Column
Object-oriented design	Class	Object instance	Property

SQL Server developers generally refer to database elements as tables, rows, and columns when discussing the SQL Data Definition Language (DDL) layer or physical schema and sometimes use the terms entity, tuple, and attribute when discussing the logical design. The rest of this book uses the SQL terms (table, row, and column), but this chapter is devoted to the theory behind the design, so the relational algebra terms (entity, tuple, and attribute) are also used.

Database Design Phases

Traditionally, data modeling has been split into two phases: the logical design and the physical design. However, after spending countless hours designing relation databases and listening to several lectures on database design the authors are convinced that there are three phases to database design. To avoid confusion with the traditional terms, they are defined as follows:

- **Conceptual model:** The first phase digests the organizational requirements and identifies the entities, their attributes, and their relationships. During this phase every opportunity should be taken to collect any information that may have or has any relevance to the project.

  The conceptual diagram model is great for understanding, communicating, and verifying the organization's requirements. The diagramming method should be easily understood by all the stakeholders — the subject-matter experts, development team, and management. Visio or some similar diagramming tool can assist to provide a visual aspect to the conceptual model.

  At this layer, the design is implementation-independent: It could end up on Oracle, SQL Server, or even Access. Some designers refer to this as the "logical model."

- **SQL DDL Layer:** This phase concentrates on performance without losing the fidelity of the logical model as it applies the design to a specific version of a database engine — SQL Server 2012, for example, generating the DDL for the actual tables, keys, and attributes. Typically, the SQL DDL Layer generalizes some entities and replaces some natural keys with surrogate computer-generated keys.

  Typically, database developers realize the need for additional tables (entities) and their corresponding attributes and keys. As a result, the SQL DDL layer might look different than the conceptual model.

- **Physical layer:** The implementation phase considers how the data will be physically stored on the disk subsystems using indexes, partitioning, and materialized views. Changes made to this layer won't affect how the data is accessed, only how it's stored on the disk.

  The physical layer ranges from simple, for small databases (under 20Gb), to complex, with multiple files and filegroups, indexed views, and data routing partitions.

This chapter focuses on designing the conceptual model, with a brief look at normalization followed by a repertoire of database patterns.

CAUTION

Implementing a database without working through the SQL DLL Layer design phase is a certain path to a poorly performing database. Many database purists didn't care to learn SQL Server implement conceptual designs only to blame SQL Server for the horrible performance.

Normalization

In 1970, Dr. Edgar F. Codd published "A Relational Model of Data for Large Shared Data Bank" and became the father of the relational database. During the 1970s Codd wrote a series of papers that defined the concept of database normalization. He wrote his famous "Codd's 12 Rules" in 1985 to define what constitutes a relational database and to defend the relational database from software vendors who were falsely claiming to be relational. Since that time, others have amended and refined the concept of normalization.

The primary purpose of *normalization* is to improve the data integrity of the database by reducing or eliminating modification anomalies that can occur when the same fact is stored in multiple locations within the database. In other words, the process of normalization attempts to reduce redundant data that causes unnecessary updates.

Duplicate data raises all sorts of interesting problems for inserts, updates, and deletes. For example, if the product name is stored in the order detail table, and the product name is edited, should every order details' row be updated? If so, is there a mechanism to ensure that the edit to the product name propagates down to every duplicate entry of the product name? If data is stored in multiple locations, is it safe to read just one of those locations without double-checking other locations? Normalization prevents these kinds of modification anomalies.

In addition to the primary goal of consistency and data integrity, several other good reasons to normalize an OLTP relational database exist:

- **Performance:** Duplicate data requires extra code to perform extra writes, maintain consistency, and manipulate data into a set when reading data. Addressing the aforementioned issues is even more problematic when dealing with large highly transactional databases. Imagine a 2-terabyte database that averages approximately 30K transactions per second. Moreover, assume that the database is the back end for a large retail store. If a change were made to one product or item, that change would need to be propagated across every table that referenced that product. This could be tens or even hundreds of tables, resulting in a 10–15 percent system performance degradation.

  Normalization also reduces locking contention and improves multiple-user concurrency because you need fewer updates.

- **Development costs:** Although it may take longer to design a normalized database, it's easier to work with a normalized database, and it reduces development costs.

- **Usability**: By placing columns in the correct table, it's easier to understand the database and easier to write correct queries.

- **Extensibility**: A non-normalized database is often more complex and therefore more difficult to modify. This can be directly attributed to the distribution of the redundant data across several tables within the database.

The Three "Rules of One"

Normalization is well defined as normalized forms — specific issues that address specific potential errors in the design. (There's a whole section on normal forms later in this chapter.) Therefore, when designing databases, you should implement normalization design principles from the onset. This approach can help minimize design errors and produce a highly stable and performing database.

You should follow three rules known as the "Rules of One," when designing a database. One type of item is represented by one entity (table). The key to designing a schema that avoids update anomalies is to ensure that each single fact in real life is modeled by a single data point in the database. Three principles define a single data point:

- One group of similar things is represented by one entity (table).
- One thing is represented by one tuple (row).
- One descriptive fact about the thing is represented by one attribute (column).

Learn these three simple rules to help you design a properly normalized database.

Identifying Entities

The first step to designing a database conceptual diagram is to identify the entities (tables). Because any entity represents only one type of thing, it takes several entities together to represent an entire process or organization.

Entities are usually discovered from several sources:

- Examining existing documents (order forms, registration forms, patient files, and reports)
- Interviews with subject-matter experts
- Diagramming the process flow

At this early stage the goal is to simply collect a list of possible entities and their facts. Some of the entities will be obvious nouns, such as customers, products, flights, materials, and machines.

Other entities will be verbs: shipping, processing, assembling parts to build a product. Verbs may be entities, or they may indicate a relationship between two entities.

The goal is to simply collect all the possible entities and their attributes. At this early stage, it's also useful to document as many known relationships as possible, even if those relationships will be edited several times.

Generalization

Normalization has a reputation of creating complex and unwieldy databases. It's true that some database schemas are far too complex, but normalization, by itself, isn't the root cause.

The difference between elegant databases that are a joy to query and overly complex designs that make you want to polish your resume is the data modeler's view of entities.

When identifying entities, there's a continuum, as illustrated in Figure 7-1, ranging from a broad all-inclusive view to a specific, narrow definition of the entity.

FIGURE 7-1

You can identify entities along a continuum, from overly generalized with a single table, to overly specific with too many tables.

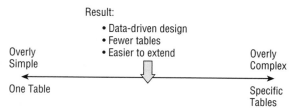

The overly simple view groups together entities that are different types of things, for example, storing machines, products, and processes in the single entity. This approach might risk data integrity for two reasons. First, it's difficult to enforce referential integrity (foreign key constraints) because the primary key attempts to represent multiple types of items. Second, these designs tend to merge entities with different attributes, which means that many of the attributes (columns) won't apply to various rows and will simply be left null. Many nullable columns means the data will probably be sparsely filled and inconsistent.

At the other extreme, the overly specific view segments entities that could be represented by a single entity into multiple entities, for example, splitting different types of subassemblies and finished products into multiple different entities. This type of design risks flexibility and usability:

- The additional tables create additional work at every layer of the software.

- Database relationships become more complex because what could have been a single relationship are now multiple relationships. For example, instead of relating an assembly process between any part, the assembly relationship must now relate with multiple types of parts.

- The database has now hard-coded the specific types of similar entities, making it difficult to add another similar type of entity. Using the manufacturing example again, if there's an entity for every type of subassembly, adding another type of subassembly means changes at every level of the software.

- Coining a query to extract the proper set of data to meet reporting requirements is now difficult and sometimes a daunting task due to the sheer number of tables that are needed to fulfill the requirement.

The sweet spot in the middle generalizes, or combines, similar entities into single entities. This approach creates a more flexible and elegant database design that is easier to query and extend:

- Look for entities with similar attributes, or entities that share some attributes.

- Look for types of entities that might have an additional similar entity added in the future.

- Look for entities that might be summarized together in reports.

When designing a generalized entity, two techniques are essential:

- Use a lookup entity to organize the types of entities. For the manufacturing example, a `subassemblytype` attribute would serve the purpose of organizing the parts by subassembly type. Typically, this would be a foreign key to a `subassemblytype` entity.

- Typically, the different entity types that could be generalized together do have some differences — which is why a purist view would want to segment them. Employing the supertype/subtype (discussed in the "Data Design Patterns" section) solves this dilemma perfectly.

Although generalization sounds like denormalization — it's not. When generalizing, it's critical that the entities comply with all the rules of normalization.

Generalized databases tend to be data-driven, have fewer tables, and are easier to extend. For example, an advertising company allowed the application architect to develop the database. As a result, writing a query that returned customer information (first name, last name, address, phone, city, state, and so on) required accessing more than 40 tables in one query. o mitigate the problem, the developer wrote a process that transformed and loaded the data into a database that contained one-third of the number of tables as the original. The same customer query could be written against the new database only requiring the need of 10 tables. For which database would you rather write a stored procedure?

On the other hand, be careful when merging entities because they actually do share a root meaning in the data. Don't merge unlike entities just to save programming. The result will be more complex programming.

Best Practice

Granted, knowing when to generalize and when to segment can be an art form and requires a repertoire of database experience, but generalization is the buffer against database over-complexity; and
consciously working at understanding generalization is the key to becoming an excellent data modeler.

Primary Keys

Perhaps the most important concept of an entity (table) is that it has a primary key — an
attribute or set of attributes that can be used to uniquely identify the tuple (row). Every
entity must have a primary key; without a primary key, it's not a valid entity.

By definition, a primary key must be unique and must have a value (not null). The simplest primary key is identified by a single column. For example, a database may contain an
employee table (entity) whose primary key could be the employees' Social Security number
or a system-generated employee identifier.

For some entities, there might be multiple possible primary keys to choose from: employee
number, driver's license number, national ID number (ssn). In this case, all the potential
primary keys are known as *candidate keys*. Candidate keys that are not selected as the primary key are then known as *alternate keys*. It's important to document all the candidate
keys because later, at the SQL DLL layer, they need unique constraints.

At the conceptual diagramming phase, a primary key might be obvious — an employee
number, an automobile VIN number, a state or region name — but often there is no clearly
recognizable uniquely identifying value for each item in reality. That's OK because that
problem can be solved later during the SQL DLL layer.

Foreign Keys

When two entities (tables) relate to one another, one entity is typically the primary entity,
and the other entity is the secondary entity.

The connection between the two entities is made by replicating the primary key from the
primary entity in the secondary entity. The duplicated attributes in the secondary entity
are known as a *foreign key*. Informally this type of relationship is sometimes called a parent-child relationship.

Enforcing the foreign key is referred to as *referential integrity*. This type of integrity ensures
that values in the secondary table are contained within the primary table. By applying referential integrity to your database, you assist in yielding accurate and valid result sets.

The classic example of a primary key and foreign key relationship is the *order* and *order
details* relationship. Each order item (primary entity) can have multiple order detail rows
(secondary entity). The order's primary key is duplicated in the order detail entity, providing the link between the two entities, as shown in Figure 7-2.

FIGURE 7-2

A one-to-many relationship consists of a primary entity and a secondary entity. The secondary entity's foreign key points to the primary entity's primary key. In this case, the Sales.SalesOrderDetail's SalesOrderID is the foreign key that relates to Sales .SalesOrderHeader's primary key.

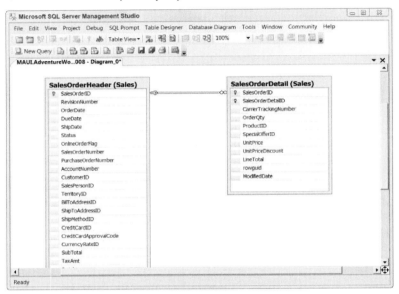

If the database was not properly normalized, you would see the order information for a specific order repeated for each order detail associated with that order. You can see several examples of primary keys and foreign keys in the "Data Design Patterns" section later in this chapter.

Cardinality

The cardinality of the relationship describes the number of tuples (rows) on each side of the relationship. Either side of the relationship may be restricted to allow zero, one, or multiple tuples.

The type of key enforces the restriction of multiple tuples. Primary keys are by definition unique and enforce the single-tuple restriction, whereas foreign keys permit multiple tuples.

There are several possible cardinality combinations, as shown in Table 7-2. Within this section, each of the cardinality possibilities is examined in detail.

TABLE 7-2 Common Relationship Cardinalities

Relationship Type	First Entity's Key	Second Entity's Key
One-to-one	Primary entity–primary key–single tuple	Primary entity–primary key–single tuple
One-to-many	Primary entity–primary key–single tuple	Secondary entity–foreign key–multiple tuples
Many-to-many	Multiple tuples	Multiple tuples

Optionality

The second property of the relationship is its *optionality*. The difference between an optional relationship and a mandatory relationship is critical to the data integrity of the database.

Some relationships are mandatory, or strong. These secondary tuples (rows) require that the foreign key point to a primary key. The secondary tuple would be incomplete or meaningless without the primary entity. For the following examples, it's critical that the relationship be enforced:

- An order-line item without an order is meaningless.
- An order without a customer is invalid.

In the AdventureWorks2012 `sample` database, a `salesorderdetail` without an associated product is a useless detail. Conversely, some relationships are optional, or weak. The secondary tuple can stand alone without the primary tuple. The object in reality that is represented by the secondary tuple would exist with or without the primary tuple. For example:

- A customer is valid with or without a discount code.
- In the `AdventureWorks2012` sample database, an order may or may not have a sales person. Whether or not the order points to a valid tuple in the sales person entity, it's still a valid order.

Some database developers prefer to avoid optional relationships, so they design all relationships as mandatory, and point tuples that wouldn't need a foreign key value to a surrogate tuple in the primary table. For example, rather than allow nulls in the discount attribute for customers without discounts, a "no discount" tuple is inserted into the `discount` entity, and every customer without a discount points to that tuple.

There are two reasons to avoid surrogate null tuples (pointing to a "no discount" tuple): The design adds work when work isn't required (additional inserts and foreign key checks), and it's easier to locate a tuple without the relationship by selecting `where column is not null`. The null value is a standard and useful design element. Ignoring the benefits of nullability creates additional work for both the developer and the database.

From a purist's point of view, a benefit of using the surrogate null tuple is that the "no discount" is explicit and a null value can then actually mean unknown or missing, rather than "no discount."

Some rare situations call for a complex optionality based on a condition. Depending on a rule, the relationship must be enforced, for example:

- If an organization sometimes sells ad hoc items that are not in the item entity, the relationship may, depending on the item, be considered optional. The orderdetail entity can use two attributes for the item. If the ItemID attribute is used, it must point to a valid item entity primary key.

- However, if the NonStandardItemDescription attribute is used instead, the ItemID attribute is left null.

- A check constraint ensures that for each row, either the ItemID or NonStandardItemDescription is null.

How the optionality is implemented is up to the SQL DDL Layer. The only purpose of the conceptual design layer is to model the organization's objects, their relationships, and their business rules.

 The AdventureWorks2012 database can be downloaded from http://msftdbprodsamples .codeplex.com/releases/view/55330.

Data-Model Diagramming

Data modelers use several methods to graphically work out their data models. The Chen ER diagramming method is popular, and Visio Professional includes it and five others. Information Engineering — E/R Diagramming, is rather simple, easy to understand and explain, and works well on a whiteboard, as shown in Figure 7-3. The cardinality of the relationship is indicated by a single line or by three lines (crow's feet). If the relationship is optional, a circle is placed near the foreign key.

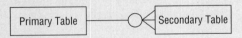

FIGURE 7-3
A simple method for diagramming logical schemas.

Another benefit of this simple diagramming method is that it doesn't require an advanced version of Visio. Visio is OK as a starting point, but it doesn't give you a nice life cycle like a dedicated modeling tool. There are several more powerful tools, but it's actually a personal preference.

Data Design Patterns

Design is all about building something new by combining existing concepts or items using patterns. The same is true for database design. The building blocks are tables, rows, and columns, and the patterns are one-to-many, many-to-many, and others. This section explains these patterns.

When the entities — nouns and verbs — are organized, the next step is to determine the relationships among the objects. Each relationship connects two entities using their primary and foreign keys.

Clients or business analysts should describe the common relationships between the objects using terms such as *includes*, *has*, or *contains*. For example, a customer may place (has) many orders. An order may include (contains) many items. An item may be on many orders.

Based on these relationship descriptions, you can choose the best data design pattern.

One-to-Many Pattern

By far the most common relationship is a one-to-many relationship; this is the classic parent-child relationship. Several tuples (rows) in the secondary entity relate to a single tuple in the primary entity. The relationship is between the primary entity's primary key and the secondary entity's foreign key, as illustrated in the following examples:

- In the AdventureWorks2012 sample database, each productsubcategory may contain several products. Each product belongs to only one productsubcategory, so the relationship is modeled as one productsubcategory relating to multiple products. The relationship is made between the ProductSubCategories primary key and the Products entity's ProductSubcategoryID foreign key, as diagrammed in Figure 7-4. Each Product's foreign key attribute contains a copy of its SubCategories's primary key.

- Each customer may place multiple orders. Although each order has its own unique SalesOrderID primary key, the SalesOrder Header entity also has a foreign key attribute that contains the CustomerID of the customer who placed the order. The SalesOrderHeader entity may have several tuples with the same CustomerID that defines the relationship as one-to-many.

FIGURE 7-4

The one-to-many relationship relates zero to many tuples (rows) in the secondary entity to a single tuple in the primary entity.

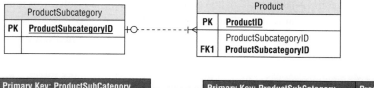

One-to-One Pattern

At the conceptual diagram layer, one-to-one relationships are quite rare. Typically, one-to-one relationships are used in the SQL physical layer to partition the data for some performance or security reason.

One-to-one relationships connect two entities with primary keys at both entities. Because a primary key must be unique, each side of the relationship is restricted to one tuple.

For example, a Contact entity can store general information about various contacts at a company. However, additional employee information may be stored in a separate entity, as shown in Figure 7-5. Although security can be applied on a per-attribute basis, or a view can project selected attributes, many organizations choose to model sensitive information as two one-to-one entities.

FIGURE 7-5

This one-to-one relationship partitions contact data, segmenting additional employee information into a separate entity.

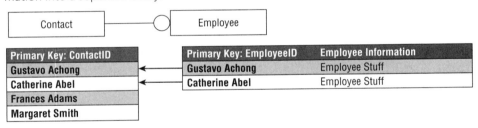

Many-to-Many Pattern

In a many-to-many relationship, both sides may relate to multiple tuples (rows) on the other side of the relationship. The many-to-many relationship is common in reality, as shown in the following examples:

- The classic example is members and groups. A member may belong to multiple groups, and a group may have multiple members.

- In a typical sales system, an order may contain multiple products, and each product may be sold on multiple orders.

- In the AdventureWorks2012 sample database, a product may qualify for several special offers, and each special offer may have several qualified products.

In a conceptual diagram, the many-to-many relationship can be diagramed by signifying multiple cardinality at each side of the relationship, as shown in Figure 7-6.

FIGURE 7-6

The many-to-many logical model shows multiple tuples on both ends of the relationship.

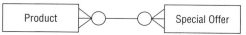

Many-to-many relationships are nearly always optional. For example, the many products-to-many special offers relationship is optional because the product and the special offer are each valid without the other.

The one-to-one and the one-to-many relationship can typically be constructed from items within an organization that users can describe and understand. That's not always the case with many-to-many relationships.

To implement a many-to-many relationship in SQL DDL, a third table, called an *associative table* (sometimes called a *junction table*) is used, which artificially creates two one-to-many relationships between the two entities (see Figure 7-7).

FIGURE 7-7

The many-to-many implementation adds an associative table to create artificial one-to-many relationships for both tables.

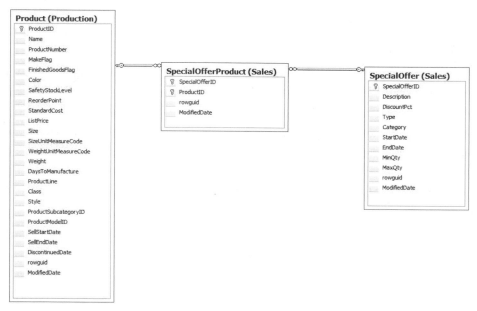

Figure 7-8 shows the associative entity with data to illustrate how it has a foreign key to each of the two many-to-many primary entities. This enables each primary entity to assume a one-to-many relationship with the other entity.

FIGURE 7-8

In the associative entity (SpecialOfferProduct), each special offer can be represented multiple times, which creates an artificial one-specialoffer-to-many-product relationship. Likewise, each product can be listed multiple times in the associative entity, creating a one-product-to-many-special relationship.

In some cases the subject-matter experts can readily recognize the associated table:

- In the case of the many orders to many products example, the associative entity is the order details entity.
- A class may have many students, and each student may attend many classes. The associative entity would be recognized as the registration entity.

In other cases an organization might understand that the relationship is a many-to-many relationship, but there's no term to describe the relationship. In this case, the associative entity is still required to resolve the many-to-many relationship — just don't discuss it with the subject-matter experts.

Typically, additional facts and attributes describe the many-to-many relationship. These attributes belong in the associative entity. For example:

- In the case of the many orders to many products example, the associative entity (order details entity) would include the quantity and sales price attributes.
- In the members and groups example, the member_groups associative entity might include the datejoined and status attributes.

When designing attributes for associative entities, it's extremely critical that every attribute actually describe only the many-to-many relationship and not one of the primary entities. For example, including a product name describes the product entity and not the many orders to many products relationship.

Supertype/Subtype Pattern

One design pattern that's not used often enough is the supertype/subtype pattern. The supertype/subtype pattern is also perfectly suited to modeling an object-oriented design in a relational database. For the application this model provides advantages that may not be realized with the traditional relational database design patters. However, because this model has the potential to increase the number of tables by several times, writing queries for reporting purposes could become an arduous task. Figure 7-9 provides a detail illustration of this method.

FIGURE 7-9

The supertype/subtype pattern uses an optional one-to-one relationship that relates a primary key to a primary key.

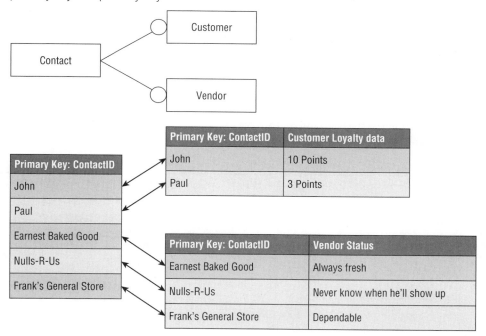

The supertype/subtype relationship leverages the one-to-one relationship to connect one supertype entity with one or more subtype entities. This extends the supertype entity with what appears to be flexible attributes.

The textbook example is a database that needs to store multiple types of contacts. All contacts have basic contact data such as name, location, phone number, and so on. Some contacts are customers with customer attributes (credit limits, loyalty programs, and so on). Some contacts are vendors with vendor-specific data.

Although you can use separate entities for customers and vendors, an alternative design is to use a single `Contact` entity (the supertype) to hold every contact, regardless of their type, and the attributes common to every type (probably just the name and contact attributes). Separate entities (the subtypes) hold the attributes unique to customers and vendors. A customer would have a tuple (row) in the contact and the customer entities. A vendor would have tuples in both the contact and vendor entities. All three entities share the same primary key (refer to Figure 7-9).

Sometime data modelers who use the supertype/subtype pattern add a `type` attribute in the supertype entity, so it's easy to quickly determine the type by searching the subtypes. This works well but it restricts the tuples to a single subtype.

Without the `type` attribute, you can allow tuples to belong to multiple subtypes. Sometimes, this is referred to as allowing the supertype to have multiple roles. In the contact example, multiple roles (for example, a contact who is both an employee and customer) could mean the tuple has data in the supertype entity (for example, contact entity) and each role subtype entity (for example, employee and customer entities).

Domain Integrity Lookup Pattern

The domain integrity lookup pattern, informally called the lookup table pattern, is common in production databases. This pattern serves to only limit the valid options for an attribute, as illustrated in Figure 7-10.

FIGURE 7-10

The domain integrity lookup pattern uses a foreign key to ensure that only valid data is entered into the attribute.

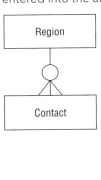

Primary Key: RegionID	Region Description
CO	Colorado
NC	North Carolina
NY	New York

Primary Key: ContactID	Foreign Key: RegionID
John	NC
Paul	CO
Earnest Baked Good	CO
Nulls-R-Us	NY
Frank's General Store	NC

The classic example is the state, or region, lookup entity. Unless the organization regularly deals with several states as clients, the state lookup entity serves only to ensure that the state attributes in other entities are correctly entered. Its only purpose is data consistency.

Recursive Pattern

A recursive relationship pattern (sometimes called a *self-referencing*, *unary*, or *self-join* relationship) is one that relates back to itself. In reality, these relationships are quite common:

- An organizational chart represents a person reporting to another person.
- A bill of materials details how a material is constructed from other materials.

 Chapter 13, "Working with Hierarchies," deals specifically with modeling and querying recursive relationships within SQL Server 2012.

To use the standard organization chart as an example, each tuple in the employee entity represents one employee. Each employee reports to a supervisor who is also listed in the employee entity. The ReportsToID foreign key points to the supervisor's primary key.

Because EmployeeID is a primary key and ReportsToID is a foreign key, the relationship cardinality is one-to-many, as shown in Figure 7-11. One manager may have several direct reports, but each employee may have only one manager.

FIGURE 7-11

The reflexive, or recursive, relationship is a one-to-many relationship between two tuples of the same entity.

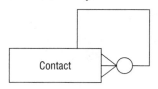

Primary Key: ContactID	Foreign Key: Reports ToID
Ken Sánchez	<NULL>
Jean Trenary	Ken Sánchez
Stephanie Conroy	Jean Trenary
François Ajenstat	Jean Trenary
Dan Wilson	Jean Trenary

A bill of materials is a more complex form of the recursive pattern because a part may be built from several source parts, and the part may be used to build several parts in the next step of the manufacturing process, as illustrated in Figure 7-12.

FIGURE 7-12

The conceptual diagram of a many-to-many recursive relationship shows multiple cardinality at each end of the relationship.

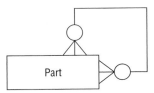

An associative entity is required to resolve the many-to-many relationship between the component parts being used and the part being assembled. Figure 7-13 illustrates the BoM (bill of materials) associative entity that has two foreign keys that both point to the Part entity. The first foreign key points to the part being built. The second foreign key points to the source parts.

Part A is constructed from two parts (a Thing1 and a bolt) and is used in the assembly of two parts (Widget and SuperWidget).

FIGURE 7-13

The physical implementation of the many-to-many reflexive relationship must include an associative entity to resolve the many-to-many relationship, just like the many-to-many two-entity relationship.

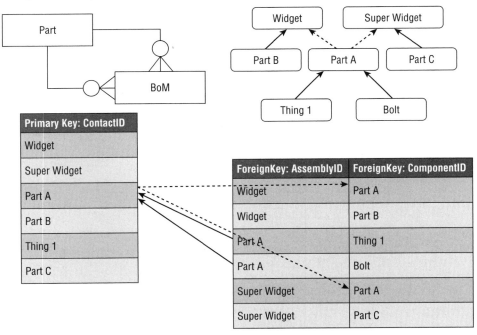

Entity-Value Pairs Pattern

Entity -value pairs pattern, also known as the *entity-attribute-value (EAV) pattern*, sometimes called the *generic pattern* or *property bag/property table pattern*, illustrated in Figure 7-14, is another database design pattern often used by data modelers. This is not a popular design pattern, but in some cases it lends itself well to the problem you are attempting to solve.

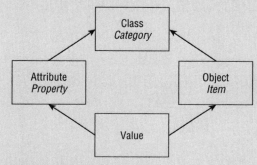

FIGURE 7-14
The entity-values pairs pattern is a simple design with only four tables: class/type, attribute/column, object/item, and value. The value table stores every value for every attribute for every item — one long list.

This design can be popular when applications require dynamic attributes. Sometimes it's used as an Object Oriented (OO) DBMS physical design within an RDBMS product. It's also gaining popularity with cloud databases.

At first blush, the entity-value pairs pattern is attractive, novel, and appealing. It offers unlimited logical design alterations without any physical schema changes — the ultimate flexible extensible design.

But there are problems — many problems:

- The entity-value pairs pattern lacks data integrity — specifically, data typing. The data type is the most basic data constraint. The basic entity-value pairs pattern stores every value in a single nvarchar or sql_variant column and ignores data typing. One option not recommended is to create a value table for each data type. Although this adds data typing, it certainly complicates the code.

- It's difficult to query the entity-value pairs pattern, and there are two solutions. The most common method is hard-coding .NET code to extract and normalize the data. Another option is to code-gen a table-valued UDF or crosstab view for each class/type to extract the data and return a normalized data set. This has the advantage of being usable in normal SQL queries, but performance and inserts/updates remain difficult. Either solution defeats the dynamic goal of the pattern.

- Perhaps the greatest complaint against the entity-value pairs pattern is that it's nearly impossible to enforce referential integrity.

..

Database Design Layers

Every database can be visualized as three layers: domain integrity (lookup) layer, business visible layer, and supporting layer, as shown in Figure 7-15.

Visualizing the database as three layers can be useful when designing the conceptual diagram and coding the SQL DLL implementation.

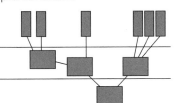

- Domain Integrity
  - Look up tables
- Business Entities (Visible)
  - Objects the user can describe
- Supporting Entities
  - Associative tables

While you are designing the conceptual diagram, visualizing the database as three layers can help organize the entities and clarify the design. When the database design moves into the SQL DDL implementation phase, the database design layers become critical in optimizing the primary keys for performance.

The center layer contains those entities that the client or subject-matter expert would readily recognize and understand. These are the main work tables that contain working data such as transaction, account, or contact information. When a user enters data on a daily basis, these are the tables hit by the insert and update. You can refer to this layer as the *visible layer* or the *business entity layer*.

Above the business entity layer is the domain integrity layer. This top layer has the entities used for validating foreign key values. These tables may or may not be recognizable by the subject-matter expert or a typical end user. The key point is that they are used only to maintain the list of what's legal for a foreign key, and they are rarely updated after initially populated.

Below the visible layer live the tables that are a mystery to the end user — associative tables used to materialize a many-to-many logical relationship are a perfect example of a supporting table. Like the visible layer, these tables are often heavily updated.

Normal Forms

Taking a detailed look at the normal forms moves this chapter into a more formal study of relational database design.

Contrary to popular opinion, the forms are not a progressive methodology, but they do represent a progressive level of compliance. Technically, you can't be in 2NF until 1NF has been met.

Don't plan to design an entity and move it through a first normal form to a second normal form, and so on. Each normal form is simply a different type of data integrity fault to be avoided.

First Normal Form (1NF)

The first normalized form means the data is in an entity format, such that the following three conditions are met:

- **Every unit of data is represented within scalar attributes**. A scalar value is a value "capable of being represented by a point on a scale," according to Merriam-Webster.

   Every attribute must contain one unit of data, and each unit of data must fill one attribute. Designs that embed multiple pieces of information within an attribute violate the first normal form. Likewise, if multiple attributes must be combined in some way to determine a single unit of data, the attribute design is incomplete.

- **All data must be represented in unique attributes**. Each attribute must have a unique name and a unique purpose. An entity should have no repeating attributes. If the attributes repeat, or the entity is wide, the object is too broadly designed.

   A design that repeats attributes, such as an order entity that includes item1, item2, and item3 attributes to hold multiple line items, violates the first normal form.

- **All data must be represented within unique tuples**. If the entity design requires or permits duplicate tuples, that design violates the first normal form.

   If the design requires multiple tuples to represent a single item, or multiple items are represented by a single tuple, the table violates first normal form.

For an example of the first normal form in action, assume that you have a listing of customers and each customer can have multiple phone numbers. Table 7-3 shows customer data in a model that violates the first normal form. The repeating phone number attribute is not unique.

TABLE 7-3   Violating the First Normal Form

Customer	PhoneNumber1	PhoneNumber2	PhoneNumber2
John Doe	111 111 1111	222 222 2222	
Jane Smith	333 333 3333	444 444 4444	
Luke Phillips	555 555 5555		

To redesign the data model so that it complies with the first normal form, resolve the repeating group of phone number attributes into a single unique attribute, as shown in Table 7-4, and then move any multiple values to a unique tuple. The Customer entity contains a unique tuple for each customer, and the PhoneNumber entity's CustomerID refers to the primary key in the Customer entity.

TABLE 7-4   **Conforming to the First Normal Form**

PhoneNumber Entity		CustomerEntity	
CustomerID(FK)	PhoneNumber	CustomerID (PK)	Name
1	111 111 1111	1	John Doe
1	222 222 2222	2	Jane Smith
2	333 333 3333Excess Inventory	3	Luke Phillips
2	444 444 4444		
3	555 555 5555		

Another example of a data structure that desperately needs to adhere to the first normal form is a corporate product code that embeds the department, model, color, size, and so forth within the code. I've even seen product codes that were so complex they included digits to signify the syntax for the following digits.

In a theoretical sense, this type of design is wrong because the attribute isn't a scalar value. In practical terms, it has the following problems:

- Using a digit or two for each data element means that the database will soon run out of possible data values.
- Databases don't index based on the internal values of a string, so searches require scanning the entire table and parsing each value.
- Business rules are difficult to code and enforce.

Entities with nonscalar attributes need to be completely redesigned so that each individual data attribute has its own attribute. Smart keys may be useful for humans, but it is best if it is generated by combining data from the tables.

Second Normal Form (2NF)

The second normal form ensures that each attribute describes the entity. It's a dependency issue. Does the attribute depend on, or describe, the item identified by the primary key?

If the entity's primary key is a single value, this isn't too difficult. Composite primary keys can sometimes get into trouble with the second normal form if the attributes aren't dependent on every attribute in the primary key. If an attribute depends on one of the primary key attributes but not the other that is a partial dependency, which violates the second normal form.

For example, assume a database contains the table RegionalOfficeStore, whose primary key was a composite key including RegionalOfficeID and StoreID. Adding the regional phone number to the data model would violate the second normal form, as shown in Table 7-5. Because the primary key (PK) is a composite of both RegionalOffice and Store, and that the phone number is a permanent phone number for the regional office, a phone number isn't assigned for each store.

TABLE 7-5   Violating the Second Normal Form

PK-RegionalOffice	PK-Store	RegionalOffice PhoneNumber
Southeast	Store One	828-555-1212
Southeast	Store Two	828-555-1212
North	Store Three	828-555-1213
North	Store Four	828-555-1213
Northwest	Store Five	828-555-1214
Northwest	Store Six	828-555-1215

The problem with this design is that the phone number is an attribute of the regional office but not the store, so the `PhoneNumber` attribute is only partially dependent on the entity's primary key.

An obvious practical problem with this design is that updating the phone number requires either updating multiple tuples or risking having two phone numbers for the same phone.

The solution is to remove the partially dependent attribute from the entity with the composite keys, and create an entity with a unique primary key for the store as shown in Table 7-6. This new entity is then an appropriate location for the dependent attribute.

TABLE 7-6   Conforming to the Second Normal Form

Store Entity		Regional Office Entity	
PK-Regional Office	PK-Store	PK-Regional Office	PhoneNumber
Southeast	Store One	Southeast	828-555-1212
Southeast	Store Two	North	828-555-1213
North	Store Three	Northwest	828-555-1214
North	Store Four		
Northwest	Store Five		
Northwest	Store Six		

The `PhoneNumber` attribute is now fully dependent on the entity's primary key. Each phone number is stored in only one location, and no partial dependencies exist.

Third Normal Form (3NF)

The third normal form checks for transitive dependencies. A *transitive dependency* is similar to a partial dependency in that they both refer to attributes that are not fully dependent on a primary key. A dependency is transient when `attribute1` is dependent on `attribute2`, which is dependent on the primary key.

The second normal form is violated when an attribute depends on part of the key. The third normal form is violated when the attribute does depend on the key but also depends on another non-key attribute.

The key phrase when describing the third normal form is that every attribute *"must provide a fact about the key, the whole key, and nothing but the key."*

Just as with the second normal form, the third normal form is resolved by moving the non-dependent attribute to a new entity.

Continuing with the Regional Office Store example, assume that a manager is assigned to each region. The `Regional Manager` attribute belongs in the `Regional Office` entity; but it is a violation of the third normal form if other information describing the manager is stored in the regional office, as shown in Table 7-7.

TABLE 7-7   Violating the Third Normal Form

Regional Office Entity			
RegionalOfficePK	**RegionalOfficePhoneNumber**	**LManager**	**DateofHire**
Southeast	1-828-555-1212	Jeff Davis	5/1/99
North	1-828-555-1213	Ken Frank	4/15/97
Northwest	1-828-555-1214	Dab Smith	7/7/2001

The `DateofHire` describes the manager not the region, so the hire-date attribute is not directly dependent on the `RegionalOffice` entity's primary key. The `DateOfHire`'s dependency is transitive — it describes the key and a non-key attribute — in that it goes through the `Manager` attribute.

Creating a `Manager` entity and moving its attributes to the new entity resolves the violation of the third normal form and cleans up the logical design, as demonstrated in Table 7-8.

TABLE 7-8   Conforming to the Third Normal Form

Regional Office Entity		Manager Entity	
RegionalOfficePK	**Manager**	**ManagerPK**	**DateofHire**
Southeast	Jeff Davis	Jeff Davis	5/1/99
North	Ken Frank	Ken Frank	4/15/97
Northwest	Dab Smith	Dab Smith	7/7/2001

Best Practice

If the entity has a good primary key and every attribute is scalar and fully dependent on the primary key, the logical design is in the third normal form. Most database designs stop at the third normal form.

The additional forms prevent problems with more complex logical designs. If you tend to work with mind-bending modeling problems and develop creative solutions, understanding the advanced forms can prove useful.

The Boyce-Codd Normal Form (BCNF)

The Boyce-Codd normal form occurs between the third and fourth normal forms, and it handles a problem with an entity that has multiple candidate keys. One of the candidate keys is chosen as the primary key, and the others become alternative keys. For example, a person might be uniquely identified by his or her Social Security number (ssn), employee number, and driver's license number. If the ssn is the primary key, the employee number and driver's license number are the alternative keys.

The Boyce-Codd normal form simply stipulates that in such a case every attribute must describe every candidate key. If an attribute describes one of the candidate keys but not another candidate key, the entity violates BCNF.

Fourth Normal Form (4NF)

The fourth normal form deals with problems created by complex composite primary keys. If two independent attributes are brought together to form a primary key along with a third attribute, but the two attributes don't uniquely identify the entity without the third attribute, the design violates the 4NF. For example, assume the following conditions:

1. Regional Office and the regional office's Manager were used as a composite primary key.
2. A Store and the Manager were brought together as a primary key.
3. Because both used a manager all three were combined into a single entity.

The preceding example violates the fourth normal form.

The fourth normal form is used to help identify entities that should be split into separate entities. Usually this is only an issue if large composite primary keys have brought too many disparate objects into a single entity.

Fifth Normal Form (5NF)

The fifth normal form provides the method for designing complex relationships that involve multiple (three or more) entities. A *three-way* or *ternary* relationship, if properly designed, is in the fifth normal form. The cardinality of any of the relationships could be one or many. What makes it a ternary relationship is the number of related entities.

As an example of a ternary relationship, consider a manufacturing process that involves an operator, a machine, and a bill of materials. From one point of view, this could be an operation entity with three foreign keys. Alternatively, it could be thought of as a ternary relationship with additional attributes.

Just like a two-entity many-to-many relationship, a ternary relationship requires a resolution entity in the physical schema design to resolve the many-to-many relationship into multiple artificial one-to-many relationships; but in this case the resolution entity has three or more foreign keys.

In such a complex relationship, the fifth normal form requires that each entity, if separated from the ternary relationship, remains a proper entity without any loss of data.

It's commonly stated that a third normal form is enough. Boyce-Codd, fourth, and fifth normal forms may be complex, but violating them can cause severe problems. It's not a matter of more entities versus fewer entities; it's a matter of properly aligned attributes and keys.

Strategy Considerations

When you have finalized all the design patterns that will be used throughout your database, a pivotal decision about the physical location of each table (entity) must be made. Following are three schools of thought:

Store all tables in one database and one schema.

Store subject-specific tables in separate databases.

Store subject-specific tables in one database and separate schemas.

Traditionally, most database designers using SQL Server have followed the pattern to store each table in the same database under the dbo schema. However, this approach does limit the scalability of the database. Deciding whether to store the tables in the same database with different schemas or in different databases affects the scalability and flexibility of the database.

When to Separate into Different Databases

If you anticipate the need to scale you database, you may need to consider storing related tables in separate databases. For example, you may have tables specific to Human Resources and another set of tables specific to Sales. In the Human Resources database you may store Employee information. On the other hand, you may track orders and products in the Sales database.

This approach lends itself directly to scalability and flexibility. If all the objects for a particular database were all contained within one database and the need to move a specific set of objects to a different server arose, how would this be handled? If the related tables were stored in individual databases, moving the tables would require only backing up and restoring the database to the new server.

In addition to scalability, different databases enable you to secure objects based on their location. Security can be aligned directly with the specific databases. For example, if there were a group of individuals that needed permission to Human Resource information and not sales information, you can quickly specify security in that database holistically instead of identifying each individual table and granting permissions for each object.

When to Use Which Schema

Separating tables into different schemas is similar to locating the objects in separate databases. From the DBA's perspective, managing security is simpler. Security can be applied at a schema level as opposed to an object level, and the objects will be grouped according to the schema they are assigned.

Further, if you need to move the tables to another database, you can quickly identify and move the tables based on the schema. However, this requires a little more effort than the aforementioned approach to store in separate databases. You need to either back up the individual tables and move them or script the tables and then copy the data from one location to the next.

Summary

Smart database design, covered in Chapter 2, "Data Architecture," showed why the database physical schema is critical to the database's performance. This chapter looked at the theory behind the logical correctness of the database design and the many patterns used to assemble a database schema.

- The three phases in database design are the conceptual (diagramming) phase, the SQL DDL (create table) phase, and the physical layer (partition and file location) phase. Databases designed with only the conceptual phase perform poorly.

- Normalization can be summed up as the three "Rules of One": one group of items = one table; one item = one row; and one fact = one column.

- Generalization is the buffer against normalization over-complexity.

Data Types, Expressions, and Scalar Functions

IN THIS CHAPTER

Data Types

Working with Expressions and Scalar Functions

Using Logic Within a Query

Working with Nulls, Strings, and Dates

Imagine you had a large pile of LEGO bricks that all fit each other. You could construct elaborate buildings, boats, trucks, and so on. If you do a quick search on the Internet, you can find large and complex LEGO constructions. The interconnectivity of this unique set of LEGOs makes them flexible. In the same way, the interconnectivity of SQL expressions and functions makes Transact-SQL (T-SQL) one of the most flexible and powerful database querying languages.

Expressions can retrieve data from a subquery, handle complex logic, convert data types, and manipulate data. If the secret to being a competent SQL database developer is mastering SQL queries, wielding expressions and scalar functions are definitely in the arsenal.

An *expression* is any combination of constants, functions, or formulas that returns a single value. Expressions may be as simple as a hard-coded number, or as complex as a case expression that includes several formulas and functions.

Expressions may be employed in several places within the SQL syntax. Nearly anywhere a value may be used, an expression may be used instead. This includes column values, JOIN ON clauses, WHERE and HAVING clauses, and ORDER BY columns. Expressions can't be substituted for object names, such as table names or column names.

Data Types

Now you may be wondering, data types, isn't this section all about expressions and functions? You are correct. However, before discussing those important aspects of T-SQL, here's a quick overview of the various data types available in SQL Server. Understanding these different types are pivotal when it comes to building expressions and using the scalar functions in an effective and efficient manner.

Character Data Types

SQL Server supports several character data types, as listed in Table 8-1.

TABLE 8-1 **Character Data Types**

Data Type	Description	Size in Bytes
Char(n)	Fixed-length character data up to 8,000 characters long using collation character set	Defined length * 1 byte
Nchar(n)	Unicode fixed-length character data	Defined length * 2 bytes
VarChar(n)	Variable-length character data up to 8,000 characters long using collation character set	1 byte per character
VarChar(max)	Variable-length character data up to 2GB in length using collation character set	1 byte per character
nVarChar(n)	Unicode variable-length character data up to 8,000 characters long using collation character set	2 bytes per character
nVarChar(max)	Unicode variable-length character data up to 2GB in length using collation character set	2 bytes per character
Text	Variable-length character data up to 2,147,483,647 characters in length *Warning: Deprecated*	1 byte per character
nText	Unicode variable-length character data up to 1,073,741,823 characters in length *Warning: Deprecated*	2 bytes per character
Sysname	A Microsoft user-defined data type used for table and column names that is the equivalent of nvarchar(128)	2 bytes per character

Unicode data types are useful for storing multilingual data. The cost, however, is the doubled size. Some developers use nvarchar for all their character-based columns, whereas others avoid it at all costs. You should use Unicode data when the database might use foreign languages; otherwise, use char, varchar, or text.

Numeric Data Types

SQL Server supports several numeric data types, as listed in Table 8-2.

TABLE 8-2 Numeric Data Types

Data Type	Description	Size in Bytes
Bit	1 or 0	1 bit
Tinyint	Integers from 0 to 255	1 byte
Smallint	Integers from −32,768 to 32,767	2 bytes
Int	Integers from −2,147,483,648 to 2,147,483,647	4 bytes
Bigint	Integers from −$2^{3}63$ to $2^{3}63$-1	8 bytes
Decimal or Numeric	Fixed-precision numbers up to −$10^{3}38$ + 1	Varies according to length
Money	Numbers from −$2^{3}63$ to $2^{3}63$, accuracy to one ten-thousandths (.0001)	8 bytes
SmallMoney	Numbers from −214,748.3648 through +214,748.3647, accuracy to ten thousandths (.0001)	4 bytes
Float	Floating-point numbers ranging from −1.79E + 308 through 1.79E + 308, depending on the bit precision	4 or 8 bytes
Real	Float with 24-bit precision	4 bytes

Best Practice

When working with monetary values, be careful with the data type. Using float or real data types for money causes rounding errors. The data types money and smallmoney are accurate to one hundredth of a U.S. penny. For some monetary values, the client may request precision only to the penny, in which case decimal is the more appropriate data type.

Date/Time Data Types

Traditionally, SQL Server stores both the date and the time in a single column using the datetime and smalldatetime data types, as described in Table 8-3.

8

TABLE 8-3 **Date/Time Data Types**

Data Type	Description	Size in Bytes
Datetime	Date and time values from January 1, 1553 (beginning of the Julian calendar) through December 31, 9999, accurate to 3 milliseconds	8 bytes
Smalldatetime	Date and time values from January 1, 1900 through June 6, 2079, accurate to 1 minute	4 bytes
DateTime2()	Date and time values January 1, 0001 through December 31, 9999 (Gregorian calendar), variable accuracy from .01 seconds to 100 nanoseconds	6–8 bytes depending on precision
Date	Date and time values January 1, 0001 through December 31, 9999 (Gregorian calendar)	3 bytes
Time(2)	Time values, variable accuracy from .01 seconds to 100 nanoseconds	3–5 bytes depending on precision
Datetimeoffset	Date and time values January 1, 0001 through December 31, 9999 (Gregorian calendar), variable accuracy from .01 seconds to 100 nanoseconds, includes embedded time zone	8–10 bytes depending on precision

> **CAUTION**
>
> Some programmers (non-DBAs) choose character data types for date columns. This can cause a horrid conversion mess. Use the ISDATE() function to sort through the bad data.

Other Data Types

Other data types, as shown in Table 8-4, fulfill the needs created by unique values, binary large objects, and variant data.

TABLE 8-4 **Other Data Types**

Data Type	Description	Size in Bytes
Timestamp or Rowversion	Database-wide unique random value generated with every update based on the transaction log LSN value	8 bytes
Uniqueidentifier	System-generated 16-byte value	16 bytes
Binary(n)	Fixed-length data up to 8,000 bytes	Defined length
VarBinary(max)	Fixed-length data up to 8,000 bytes	Defined length

VarBinary	Variable-length binary data up to 8,000 bytes	Bytes used
Image	Variable-length binary data up to 2,147,483,647 bytes: *Warning: Deprecated*	Bytes used
Sql_variant	Can store any data type up to 2,147,483,647 bytes	Depends on data type and length

Building Expressions

You can construct SQL expressions from a nearly limitless list of constants, variables, operators, and functions, as detailed in Table 8-5.

TABLE 8-5   Building Expressions

Expression Components	Examples
Numeric constants	1, 2, 3, -17, -100
String literals	'LastName', 'Employee: ', 'Lifes Great!'
Dates	'1/30/1980', 'January 30, 1980', '19800130'
Mathematical operators (in order of precedence)	*, /, % (remainder), +, -
String operator (concatenation)	+
Bitwise operators (in order of precedence)	not, and &, or |, exclusive or
Columns	LastName, PrimaryKeyID

Case expressions	CASE Column1
	
	    WHEN 1 THEN 'on'
	
	      ELSE 'off'
	
	END AS Status

Subqueries	(Select 3)
User-defined variables	@MyVariable
System functions	@@Error
Scalar functions	GetDate(), Radians()
User-defined functions	dbo.MyUDF()

> **NOTE**
>
> The syntax of SQL keywords is not case-sensitive. The convention is to use keywords in all uppercase, all lowercase, camel case, etc. Regardless of the method you choose, that is the method that should be adopted throughout the entire database. This convention is not required, but it does improve the readability of the query.
>
> Depending on the collation setting of the server or database, database, table, and column names, and even the data itself, might be case-sensitive.

One thing that should be noted is the use of @, which is part of the variable declaration. Whenever, you declare a variable that will be used in an expression, stored procedure, or function you must prefix it with an @ symbol.

Chapter 9, "Merging Data with Joins, Subqueries, and CTEs," covers subqueries. Chapter 18, "Building User-Defined Functions," covers user-defined functions.

Operators

Although the meaning of many of these expression constants, operators, and expressions is obvious and common to other programming languages, a few deserve special mention.

The *division* mathematical operator (/) is a common source of errors when integers are divided because there is an implicit truncation of values. For instance, 17/9 gives a result of 1; although, it is almost 2 (which 18/9 would yield). If you are interested in obtaining a true decimal value, simply modify the query to this, 17/9, and your result will be 1.888888. Simply adding a decimal to one of the values in the expression tells SQL server to return a more precise value.

The *modulo* mathematical operator (%) returns only the remainder of the division. The `floor()` and `ceiling()` mathematical functions, which return the integer rounded down or up, respectively, are related to it. The `floor()` function is the SQL Server equivalent of the BASIC `int()` function:

```
SELECT 15%4 AS Modulo,
  FLOOR(1.25) AS [Floor], CEILING(1.25) AS [Ceiling];
```

Result:

```
Modulo       Floor   Ceiling
-----------  -----   -------
3            1       2
```

The + operator is used for both mathematical expressions and string concatenation. This operator is different from the Visual Basic symbol for string concatenation, the ampersand (&):

```
SELECT 123 + 456 AS Addition,
```

```
       'abc' + 'defg' AS Concatenation;
```

Result:

```
Addition        Concatenation
----------      ------------------
579             abcdefg
```

Data from table columns and string literals may be concatenated to return custom data:

```
. . .
USE AdventureWorks
GO
SELECT 'Product: '+ Name as Product
FROM Production.Product
```

Result:

```
Proudct
----------------
Product: Adjustable Race
Product: All-Purpose Bike Stand
Product: AWC Logo Cap
. . .
```

One thing to note is that if you are concatenating integers and strings, you must cast or convert the integer to a string.

Bitwise Operators

The *bitwise* operators are useful for binary manipulation. These aren't typically used in transactional databases, but they can prove useful for certain metadata operations. For example, one way to determine which columns were updated in a trigger (code that is executed as the result of a data insert, update, or delete, as covered in Chapter 18) is to inspect the columns_updated() function, which returns a binary representation of those columns. The trigger code can test columns_updated() using bitwise operations and respond to updates on a column-by-column basis. Developers often use this operator when they try to implement a change detection process but want to know only when certain columns are changed. Of course, there are more elegant solutions, but in some specific cases, this may be a viable option.

Boolean bit operators (and, or, and not) are the basic building blocks of digital electronics and binary programming. Whereas digital-electronic boolean gates operate on single bits, these bitwise operators work across every bit of the integer family data type (int, smallint, tinyint, and bit) values.

Boolean and

A boolean and (represented by the ampersand character, &) returns a value of true only if both inputs are true (or 1 for mathematical bit operations). If either or both are false (or 0 for mathematical bit operations), then the and will return a value of 1, as follows:

```
SELECT 1 & 1;
Result:
1
```

Another and example:

```
SELECT 1 & 0;
Result:
0
```

"And"ing two integers is illustrated as follows:

```
decimal 3 = binary 011
decimal 5 = binary 101
3 AND 5
decimal 1 = binary 001
```

```
SELECT 3 & 5;
Result:
1
```

Boolean or

The boolean OR operator, the vertical pipe character (|), returns true if either input is true:

```
SELECT 1 | 1;
Result:
1
```

The following SELECT statement combines a set (true or 1) and a cleared (false or 0) bit using the bitwise or operator:SELECT 1 | 0;

```
Result:
1
```

ORing two integers can be illustrated as follows:

```
decimal 3 = binary 011
decimal 5 = binary 101
3 OR 5
decimal  7 = binary 111
```

```
SELECT 3 | 5;
Result:
7
```

Boolean exclusive or

The exclusive or (XOR) bitwise operator, the carat (ɔ), returns a value of true if either input is true, but not if both are true. The operator is shown here:

```
SELECT 1ɔ1;
Result:
0
```

A set bit XORed with a cleared bit results in a set bit:

```
SELECT 1ɔ0;
Result:
1
```

XORing two integers can be illustrated as follows:

```
decimal 3 = binary 011
decimal 5 = binary 101
3 OR 5
decimal  6 = binary 110
```

Bitwise not

The last bitwise operator, denoted by the tilde (~), is a bitwise NOT function. This bitwise "not" is a little different. The "not" performs a logical bit reversal for every bit in the expression. The result depends on the data length of the expression. For example, the bitwise "not" of a set bit is a cleared bit:

```
DECLARE @A BIT;
SET @A = 1;
SELECT (~)@A;
Result:
0
```

The bitwise "not" is not suitable for use with boolean expressions such as IF conditions. The following code, for example, is invalid:

```
USE AdventureWorks
SELECT * FROM Production.Product WHERE < (1=1);
```

The "not" operator also serves as the *one's complement* operator. The system known as one's complement can be used to represent negative numbers. The one's complement form of a negative binary number is the bitwise NOT applied to it — the complement of its positive counterpart.

Case Expressions

SQL Server's CASE expression is a flexible and excellent means of building dynamic expressions. If you're a programmer, no doubt you use the case command in other languages. The SQL CASE expression, however, is different. It's not used for programmatic flow of control, but rather to logically determine the value of an expression based on a condition.

Best Practice

When programmers write procedural code, it's often because part of the formula changes depending on the data. To a procedural mind-set, the best way to handle this is to loop through the rows and use multiple IF statements to branch to the correct formula. However, using a CASE expression to handle the various calculations and executing the entire operation in a single query enable SQL Server to optimize the process and make it *dramatically* faster.

Because the case expression returns an expression, it may be used anywhere in the SQL DML statement (SELECT, INSERT, UPDATE, DELETE) where an expression may be used, including column expressions, join conditions, WHERE conditions, having conditions, in the ORDER BY, or even embedded in a longer expression. A case expression can even be used mid-expression to create a dynamic formula — very powerful.

The CASE statement has two forms, simple and searched, described in the following sections.

Simple Case

With the simple CASE, the variable is presented first, and then each test condition is listed. However, this version of CASE is limited in that it can perform only equal comparisons. The CASE expression sequentially checks the WHEN conditions and returns the THEN value of the first true WHEN condition.

In the following example, based on the AdventureWorks database, the SalariedFlag in the Employee table is set to true for salaried employees and false for those employees that are not salaried. The CASE expression compares the value in the SalariedFlag column with each possible bit setting and returns the character string 'Exempt' or 'Non-Exempt' based on the bit setting:

```
USE AdventureWorks
GO
SELECT
    FirstName+' '+LastName EmployeeName,
    CASE SalariedFlag
            WHEN 1 THEN 'Exempt'
            WHEN 0 THEN 'Non-Exempt'
    END SalaryType
FROM HumanResources.Employee e
INNER JOIN Person.Person p
    ON e.BusinessEntityID = p.BusinessEntityID
```

Result:

```
EmployeeName        SalaryType
Ken Sánchez         Exempt
Terri Duffy         Exempt
```

```
Roberto Tamburello      Exempt
Rob Walters             Non-Exempt
```

The CASE expression concludes with an end and an alias. In this example, the CASE expression evaluates the SalariedFlag column but produces the SalaryType column in the SQL SELECT result set.

Be careful if you use NULL in a simple CASE. This translates literally to "=NULL" and not to "IS NULL". You can get unintended results if you are not careful.

Boolean Case

The boolean form of case (called the searched case in BOL) is more flexible than the simple form in that each individual case has its own boolean expression. Therefore, not only can each WHEN condition include comparisons other than =, but the comparison may also reference different columns:

```
SELECT
  CASE
    WHEN 1<0 THEN 'Reality is gone.'
    WHEN CURRENT_TIMESTAMP = '20161221'
      THEN 'Patrick gets his driver''s license.'
    WHEN 1>0 THEN 'Life is normal.'
  END AS RealityCheck;
```

Following is the result of the query when executed on Patrick's sixteenth birthday:

```
RealityCheck
---------------------------------
Patrick gets his driver's license.
```

As with the simple case, the first true WHEN condition halts evaluation of the case and returns the THEN value. In this case (a pun!), if 1 is ever less than 0, then the RealityCheck case accurately reports 'reality is gone'. (When the author's son turns 16, the RealityCheck will again accurately warn of his legal driving status.) If neither of these conditions is true, and 1 is still greater than 0, then all is well with reality and 'Life is normal'.

The point of the preceding code is that the searched CASE expression offers more flexibility than the simple CASE. This example mixed various conditional checks (<,=,>), and differing data was checked by the WHEN clause.

The boolean CASE expression can handle complex conditions, including boolean AND and OR operators. The following code sample uses a batch to set up the CASE expression (including T-SQL variables, which are explained in Chapter 16, "Programming with T-SQL"), and the CASE includes an AND and a BETWEEN operator:

```
DECLARE @b INT, @q INT;

SET @b = 2007;
```

8

```
SET @q = 25;

SELECT CASE
    WHEN @b = 2007 AND @q BETWEEN 10 AND 30 THEN 1
    ELSE NULL
END AS Test;
```

Result:

```
Test
---------
1
```

New SQL Server 2012 Logical Functions

SQL Server 2012 introduces two new logical functions, IIF and CHOOSE.

The IIF Function

The IIF function is a shorthand version for the CASE statement. The syntax for the IIF function is as follows:

```
IIF(boolean_expression, true_value, false_value)
```

The function behaves exactly as it does in Microsoft Excel. If the boolean expression evaluates to true, the first value is return, and if it evaluates to false, the second value is returned. The following script illustrates the use of the function:

```
SELECT IIF(1=1, 'True', 'False') Condition
Result
Condition
------------
True
```

The Choose Function

The CHOOSE function is also a logical operator, but it behaves in a somewhat different manner. CHOOSE is similar to an index in an array, assuming the array is a list of arguments. The syntax for the CHOOSE function is as follows:

```
CHOOSE(index, val_1, val_2 [, val_n])
```

Index is a 1-based integer that acts as the index into the list of values. The corresponding values are the list of values that will be searched. The following script illustrates the use of the function:

```
SELECT CHOOSE(3, 'Lions', 'Tigers', 'Bears') Chosen
```

Result:

```
Chosen
-----------
Bears
```

If you supply an integer value outside the bounds of the arry, NULL value is returned.

Working with Nulls

The relational database model represents missing data using null. Technically, null means "value absent," and it's commonly understood to mean "unknown." In practice, null can indicate that the data has not yet been entered into the database or that the column does not apply to the particular row.

Because null values are unknown, the result of any expression that includes null will also have a value that is unknown. If the contents of a bank account are unknown, and its funds are included in a portfolio, then the total value of the portfolio is also unknown. The same concept is true in SQL, as the following code demonstrates.

```
SELECT 1 + NULL;
Result:
NULL
```

Because nulls have such a devastating effect on expressions, some developers detest the use of nulls. They develop their databases so that nulls are never permitted, and column defaults supply surrogate nulls (blank, 0, or 'n/a') instead.

Other database developers argue that an unknown value should be represented by a zero or a blank just to make coding easier. Nulls are valuable in a database because they provide a consistent method to identify missing data. And regardless of how missing data is represented in the database, certain types of queries often produce nulls in the results, so it's worthwhile to write code that checks for nulls and handles them appropriately.

> **NOTE**
>
> An advantage to using nulls is that SQL Server's `AVG()` and `COUNT(column)` aggregate functions automatically exclude nulls from the calculation. If you use a surrogate null (for example, some IT shops use 0 or −999 to represent missing numeric data), then every aggregate query must filter out the surrogate null or the results will be less than accurate. In addition to the aforementioned advantages, you must also consider the fact that NULL does not consume any space. As a result, if you have a very large table it would be more beneficial to store all NULLS instead of inserting a default value.

Testing for Null

Because null represents a missing value, there is no way to know whether a null is equal or unequal to a given value, or even to another null. Returning to the bank account example, if the balance of account 123 is missing and the balance of account 234 is missing, then it's logically impossible to say whether the two accounts have an equal or unequal balance.

Consider this simple test that proves that null does not equal null:

```
IF NULL
= NULL
  SELECT '=';
ELSE
  SELECT '<> ';
```

Result:

```
<>
```

Because the = and <> operators can't check for nulls, SQL includes two special operators, IS and IS NOT, to test for equivalence to special values, as follows:

```
WHERE Expression IS NULL
```

Repeating the simple test, the IS search operator works as advertised:

```
IF NULL
IS NULL
  SELECT 'Is';
ELSE
  SELECT 'Is Not';
```

Result:

```
Is
```

The IS search condition may be used in the SELECT statement's WHERE clause to locate rows with null values. Most of the AdventureWorks people in the Persons table do not have a middle name in the database. The following query retrieves only those people with a null in the MiddleName column:

```
USE AdventureWorks
GO
SELECT FirstName, MiddleName, LastName
FROM Person.Person
WHERE
     MiddleName IS NULL
ORDER BY
     LastName,
     FirstName
```

Result:

```
FirstName         MiddleName        LastName
- - - - - - - - - - -    - - - - - - - - - - -    - - - - - - - - - - -
Kim               NULL              Abercrombie
Kim               NULL              Abercrombie
Sam               NULL              Abolrous
Humberto          NULL              Acevedo
  . . .
```

The IS operator may be combined with NOT to test for the presence of a value by restricting the result set to those rows where MiddleName is not null:

```
USE AdventureWorks
GO
SELECT FirstName, MiddleName, LastName
FROM Person.Person
WHERE
     MiddleName IS NOT NULL
ORDER BY
     LastName,
     FirstName
```

Result:

```
FirstName      MiddleName    LastName
----------     ----------    ---------...
Syed           E             Abbas
Catherine      R.            Abel
Kim            B             Abercrombie
Hazem          E             Abolrous
```

Handling Nulls

When you supply data to reports, to end users, or to some applications, a null value is less than welcome. Often a null must be converted to a valid value so that the data may be understood, or so the expression won't fail.

Nulls require special handling when used within expressions, and SQL includes a few functions designed specifically to handle nulls. ISNULL() and COALESCE() convert nulls to usable values, and NULLIF() creates a null if the specified condition is met.

Using the COALESCE() Function

COALESCE() is not used as often as it could (some would say *should*) be, perhaps because it's not well known. It's a cool function. COALESCE() accepts a list of expressions or columns and returns the first non-null value, as follows:

```
COALESCE(expression, expression, …)
```

COALESCE() is derived from the Latin words *co + alescre*, which mean to unite toward a common end, to grow together, or to bring opposing sides together for a common good. The SQL keyword, however, is derived from the alternate meaning of the term: "to arise from the combination of distinct elements." In a sense, the COALESCE() function brings together multiple, differing values of unknown usefulness, and from them emerges a single valid value.

Functionally, COALESCE() is the same as the following case expression:

```
CASE
   WHEN expression1 IS NOT NULL THEN expression1
   WHEN expression2 IS NOT NULL THEN expression2
   WHEN expression3 IS NOT NULL THEN expression3
   . . .
   ELSE NULL
END
```

The following code sample demonstrates the COALESCE() function returning the first non-null value. In this case, it's 1 + 2:

```
SELECT COALESCE(NULL, 1+NULL, 1+2, 'abc');
```

Result:

```
3
```

COALESCE() is excellent for merging messy data. For example, when a table has partial data in several columns, the COALESCE() function can help pull the data together. For example, assume that a client had collected names and addresses from several databases and applications into a single table called TempSalesContact. The contact name and company name made it into the proper columns, but some addresses were in Address1, some were in Address2, and some were in Address3. Some rows had the second line of the address in Address2. If the address columns had an address, then the SalesNote was a real note. In many cases, however, the addresses were in the SalesNote column. Here's the code to extract the address from such a mess:

```
SELECT COALESCE(
       Address1 + STR(13) + STR(10) + Address2,
       Address1,
       Address2,
       Address3,
       SalesNote) AS NewAddress
   FROM TempSalesContacts;
```

For each row in the TempSalesContacts table, the COALESCE() function searches through the listed columns and returns the first non-null value. The first expression returns a value only if there's a value in both Address1 and Address2 because a value concatenated with a null produces a null. Therefore, if a two-line address exists, then it will be returned. Otherwise, a one-line address in Address1, Address2, or Address3 will be returned. Failing those options, the SalesNote column will be returned. Of course, the result from such a messy source table still needs to be manually scanned and verified.

Using the ISNULL() Function

The most common null-handling function is ISNULL(), which is different from the IS NULL search condition. This function accepts a single expression and a substitution value. If the source is not equal to null, then the ISNULL() function passes the value on. However, if the source is null, then the second parameter is substituted for the null, as follows:

```
ISNULL(source_expression, replacement_value)
```

Functionally, ISNULL() is similar to the following case expression:

```
CASE
  WHEN source_expression IS NULL THEN replacement_value
  ELSE source_expression
END
```

The following code sample builds on the preceding queries by substituting the string ('NONE') for a null for people without a middlename:

```
USE AdventureWorks
GO
SELECT
     FirstName,
     ISNULL(MiddleName, 'None') MiddleName,
     LastName
FROM Person.Person
```

Result:

```
FirstName      MiddleName      LastName
-----------    -------------   ------------
Syed           E               Abbas
Catherine      R.              Abel
Kim            None            Abercrombie
. . .
```

If the row has a value in the Nickname column, then that value is passed through the ISNULL() function untouched. However, if the nickname is null for a row, then the null is handled by the ISNULL() function and converted to the value none.

CAUTION

The ISNULL() function is specific to T-SQL, whereas NULLIF() is ANSI standard SQL.

Using the NULLIF() Function

Sometimes a null should be created in place of surrogate null values. If a database is polluted with n/a, blank, or – values where it should contain nulls, then you can use the NULLIF() function to replace the inconsistent values with nulls and clean the database.

The NULLIF() function accepts two parameters. If they are equal, then it returns a null; otherwise, it returns the first parameter. Functionally, NULLIF() is the same as the following case expression:

```
CASE
  WHEN Expression1 = Expression2 THEN NULL
  ELSE Expression1
END
```

The following code converts any blanks in the `MiddleName` column into nulls. The first statement updates one of the rows to a blank for testing purposes:

```
USE AdventureWorks
UPDATE Person.Person
SET MiddleName = ''
WHERE LastName = 'Abbas'

SELECT LastName, FirstName,
    CASE MiddleName
    WHEN '' THEN 'blank'
        ELSE MiddleName
        END AS MiddleName,
        NULLIF(MiddleName, '') as MiddleNameNullIf
FROM Person.Person
WHERE LastName IN ('Abbas', 'Abel')
ORDER BY LastName, FirstName;
```

Result:

LastName	FirstName	MiddleName	MiddleNameNullIf
Abbas	Syed	blank	NULL
Abel	Catherine	R.	R.
Abercrombie	Kim	NULL	NULL

The third column uses a case expression to expose the blank value as "blank," and indeed the `NULLIF()` function converts the blank value to a null in the fourth column. To test the other null possibilities, Catherine's MiddleName was not affected by the `NULLIF()` function, and Kim's null MiddleName value is still in place.

A common use of `NULLIF()` prevents divide-by-zero errors. The following expression generates an error if the variable b is zero:

```
a / b « Error if b is 0, otherwise a normal division result
```

However, you can use `NULLIF()` such that if the value of the b variable is 0, it results in a `NULL` instead of an error, as follows:

```
a / NULLIF(b,0) « NULL result if b is 0,
    otherwise a normal division result
```

Now with a 0 as the result instead of an error, you can use `COALESCE()` to replace it with something more usable if needed.

Scalar Functions

Scalar functions return a single value. They are commonly used in expressions within the `SELECT`, `WHERE`, `ORDER BY`, `GROUP`, and `HAVING` clauses, or T-SQL code. SQL Server includes dozens of functions. This section describes some useful functions.

Best Practice

Performance is as much a part of the data-schema design as it is a part of the query. Plan to store the data in the way that it will be searched by a WHERE condition, rather than depend on manipulating the data with functions at query time. Although using a function in an expression in a result-set column may be unavoidable, using a function in a WHERE condition forces the function to be calculated for every row. In addition, another bottleneck is created because using a function in a WHERE clause makes it impossible for the Query Optimizer to use an index seek — it has to use a scan instead, resulting in much more I/O.

User Information Functions

In a client/server environment, it's good to know who the client is. Toward that end, the following four functions are useful, especially for gathering audit information:

- USER_NAME(): Returns the name of the current user as he or she is known to the database. When a user is granted access to a database, a username that is different from the server login name may be assigned. The results are affected by an EXECUTE AS command, in which case the username shown is that of the impersonated user.

- SUSER_SNAME(): Returns the login name by which the user was authenticated to SQL Server. If the user was authenticated as a member of a Windows user group, then this function still returns the user's Windows login name. The results are affected by an EXECUTE AS command, in which case the username shown is that of the impersonated user.

- HOST_NAME(): Returns the name of the user's workstation.

- APP_NAME(): Returns the name of the application (if set by the application itself) connected to SQL Server, as follows:

```
SELECT
  USER_NAME() AS 'User',
  SUSER_SNAME() AS 'Login',
  HOST_NAME() AS 'Workstation',
  APP_NAME() AS 'Application';
```

Result:

```
User     Login               Workstation     Application
-------  ----------------    -----------     ------------------
Dbo      Demo\Administrator  WIN-V7B3M53ERC1 Management Studio
```

Date and Time Functions

Databases must often work with date and time data, and SQL Server includes several useful functions for that. SQL Server stores both the data and the time in a single data type. It also has types for date only, time only, and zone-aware times.

T-SQL includes several functions to return the current date and time:

- `GetDate()`: Returns the current server date and time to the nearest 3 1/3 milliseconds, rounded to the nearest value.
- `CURRENT_TIMESTAMP`: The same as `GETDATE()` except ANSI standard.
- `GetUTCDate()`: Returns the current server date converted to Greenwich mean time (also known as UTC time) to the nearest 3 milliseconds. This is extremely useful for companies that cross time boundaries.
- `SysDateTime()`: Returns the current server date and time to the nearest hundred nanoseconds.
- `SysUTCDateTime()`: Returns the current server date converted to Greenwich mean time to the nearest hundred nanoseconds.
- `SYSDATETIMEOFFSET()`: Returns a `DateTimeOffset` value that contains the date and time of the computer on which the instance of SQL Server is running. The time zone offset is included.
- `ToDateTimeOffset()`: Returns a `DateTimeOffset` type.

The following four SQL Server date-time functions handle extracting or working with a specific portion of the date or time stored within a datetime column:

- `DATEADD(date portion, number, date)`: Returns a new value after adding the number
- `DATEDIFF(date portion, start date, end date)`: Returns the count of the date portion boundaries
- `DateName(date portion, date)`: Returns the proper name for the selected portion of the datetime value or its ordinal number if the selected portion has no name (the portions for `DateName()` and `DatePart()` are listed in Table 8-6):

```
SELECT DATENAME(year, CURRENT_TIMESTAMP) AS 'Year';
```

Result:

```
Year
--------
2009
```

TABLE 8-6   DateTime Portions Used by Date Functions

Portion	Abbreviation
Year	yy, yyyy
quarter	qq, q
month	mm, m
dayofyear	dy, d

day	dd, d
week	wk, ww
weekday	dw
hour	hh
minute	mi, n
second	ss, s
millisecond	ms
microsecond	mcs
nanosecond	ns
TZoffset	tz

This code gets the month and weekday name:

```
select DATENAME(MONTH,CURRENT_TIMESTAMP) as "Month",
    DATENAME(WEEKDAY,CURRENT_TIMESTAMP) As "Day"
```

Result:

```
Month      Day
--------   -----------
February   Tuesday
```

This code gets the month and weekday name and displays the results in Italian:

```
Set language Italian
select DATENAME(MONTH,CURRENT_TIMESTAMP) as "Month",
    DATENAME(WEEKDAY,CURRENT_TIMESTAMP) As "Day"
```

Result:

```
Month      Day
--------   -----------
Febbraio   Martedi
```

 For more information about `datetime`, `datetime2`, **and other data types, refer to Chapter 2, "Data Architecture."**

The following code example retrieves the proper names of some of the portions of the order date using the `DateName()` function:

```
USE ADVENTUREWORKS
GO
SELECT OrderDate,
    DATENAME(yy,OrderDate) AS [Year],
    DATENAME(mm,OrderDate) AS [Month],
    DATENAME(dd,OrderDate) AS [Day],
    DATENAME(weekday, OrderDate) AS Today
```

```
FROM Sales.SalesOrderHeader
```

Result:

OrderDate	Year	Month	Day	OrderDay
2005-07-01 00:00:00.000	2005	July	1	Friday

> **NOTE**
> There are two supported types: `DateTime` and `DateTime2` were introduced in 2008. `DateTime2` represents time to a much finer granularity, within 100 nanoseconds.

The `DatePart(date portion, date)` returns the ordinal number of the selected portion of the datetime value. The following example retrieves the day of the year and the day of the week as integers:

```
SELECT DATEPART(dayofyear, CURRENT_TIMESTAMP) AS DayCount;
```

Result:

```
DayCount
-----------
122
```

```
SELECT DATEPART(weekday, CURRENT_TIMESTAMP) AS DayWeek;
```

Result:

```
DayWeek
-----------
3
```

An easy way to obtain just the date, stripping off the time, is to use a couple of string functions:

```
SELECT CONVERT(char(10), CURRENT_TIMESTAMP, 112) AS "DateTime";
```

- `DateAdd(DATE PORTION, AMOUNT, BEGINNING DATE)` and `DateDiff(DATE PORTION, BEGINNING DATE, ENDING DATE)`: Performs addition and subtraction on datetime data, which databases often need to do. The `DATEDIFF()` and the `DATEADD()` functions are designed expressly for this purpose. The `DATEDIFF()` doesn't look at the complete date, only the date part being extracted:

```
select DATEDIFF(year,'september 4 2008','november 10 2009')
```

Result:

```
1
select DATEDIFF(month,'september 4 2008','november 10 2009')
2
```

The following query calculates the number of years and days that my wife, Karlyn, and I have been married:

```
SELECT
    DATEDIFF(yy,'6/28/1997', CURRENT_TIMESTAMP) AS MarriedYears,
    DATEDIFF(dd,'6/28/1997', CURRENT_TIMESTAMP) AS MarriedDays;
```

Result:

```
MarriedYears      MarriedDays
------------      -----------
15                5411
```

The next query adds 100 hours to the current millisecond:

```
SELECT DATEADD(hh,100, CURRENT_TIMESTAMP) AS [100HoursFromNow];
```

Result:

```
100HoursFromNow
-----------------------
2009-11-21 18:42:03.507
```

The following query is based on the AdventureWorks sample database and calculates the number of days between the order and ship dates for a customer's order, using the DateDiff() function:

```
USE ADVENTUREWORKS
GO
SELECT
    p.FirstName +' '+p.LastName CustomerName,
    DateDiff(dd,OrderDate, ShipDate ) DaysDiff
FROM Sales.SalesOrderHeader soh
INNER JOIN Sales.Customer c
    on soh.CustomerID = c.CustomerID
INNER JOIN Person.Person p
    ON c.PersonID = p.BusinessEntityID
```

Because the function is in a column expression, it is calculated for each row in the result set:

```
CustomerName      DaysDiff
-------------      ----------
James Hendergart  7
Takiko Collins    7
Jauna Elson       7
. . .
```

The ToDateTimeOffset(expression, time_zone) returns a DateTimeOffset value.

The following example gets the date and time for a given time zone:

```
SELECT TODATETIMEOFFSET(CURRENT_TIMESTAMP,'-07:00');
```

Result:

```
2009-11-05 11:24:15.490 -07:00
```

8

New SQL 2012 Functions

This section discusses functions new to SQL Server 2012. You can take a look at the functions and then see the results of some queries.

The `EOMonth(start_date, month_to_add)` returns a datetime2(7) value. The value returned is the last date of the month for the specified start date. If the optional value month to add is provided, the function adds that number of months to the start date and the last date for the resulting month is returned.

The following example returns the last date of the month for the given start date.

```
SELECT EOMONTH ( '5/26/1972') AS Result;
```

Result:

```
---------
1972-05-31 00:00:00.0000000
```

In addition to this new function, six new date time functions get date and time values from their parts. The following section details each function and provides a sample script.

The `DateFromParts(year, month, day)` function returns a Date value based on the given values. The following example returns a date value:

```
SELECT DateFromParts(1972, 5, 26) As Result;
```

The `DateTime2FromParts(year, month, day, hour, minute, seconds, fractions, precision)` function returns a `DateTime2` value based on the given values. The following example returns a datetime2 value:

```
SELECT DateTime2FromParts(1972, 5, 26, 5, 12, 59, 5, 3) As Results;
```

The result of the fraction argument is dependent upon the value provided for the precision. If the precision is set to 7, then the fraction represents 100 nanoseconds. If the precision is set to 3, then the fraction represents a millisecond. Finally, if the precision is zero, you must set the fraction to zero; otherwise, an error will be returned.

The `DateTimeFromParts(year, month, day, hour, minute, seconds, milliseconds)` function returns a `DateTime` value based on the given values. The following example returns a datetime value:

```
SELECT DateTimeFromParts(1972, 5, 26, 5, 12, 59, 100) As Results;
```

The `DateTimeOffSetFromParts(year, month, day, hour, minute, seconds, fractions, hour_offset, minute_offset, precision)` function returns a `DateTimeOffset` value based on the given values. The following example returns a datetimeoffset value:

```
SELECT DateTimeOffSetFromParts(1972, 5, 26, 5, 12, 59, 0, 12, 0, 7)
As Results;
```

Using the offset values, you can represent time zone offsets. However, you must provide both offsets if you plan to use these values. If one is supplied without the other, the function raises an error.

The `SmallDateTimeFromParts`(year, month, day, hour, minute) function returns a `DateTime` value based on the given values. The following example returns a `datetime` value:

```
SELECT SmallDateTimeFromParts(1972, 5, 26, 5, 12) As Results
```

The `TimeFromParts`(hour, minute, seconds, fractions, precision) function returns a `Time` value based on the given values. The following example returns a `datetime` value:

```
SELECT TimeFromParts(5, 12, 47, 3, 7) As Results
```

The precision and fractions' values follow the same rules as the `DateTime2FromParts` function.

If any arguments for any of the aforementioned functions are invalid an error will be raised. Also, if a null value is supplied for any of the values, a null value is returned.

String Functions

Like most modern programming languages, T-SQL includes many string-manipulation functions:

- `SUBSTRING(string, starting position, length)`
- `STUFF(string, insertion position, delete count, string inserted)`
- `CHARINDEX(search string, string, starting position)`
- `PATINDEX(pattern, string)`
- `RIGHT(string, count)` and `Left(string, count)`
- `LEN(string)`
- `RTRIM(string)` and `LTrim(string)`
- `UPPER(string)` and `Lower(string)`:
- `REPLACE(string, string)`:
- `dbo.pTitleCase (source, search, replace)`

SUBSTRING (string, starting position, length)

Substring function returns a portion of a string. The first parameter is the string; the second parameter is the beginning position of the substring to be extracted; and the third parameter is the length of the string extracted:

```
SELECT SUBSTRING('abcdefg', 3, 2);
```

Result:

```
cd
```

STUFF (string, insertion position, delete count, string inserted)

The STUFF() function inserts one string into another string. The inserted string may delete a specified number of characters as it is inserted:

```
SELECT STUFF('abcdefg', 3, 2, '123');
```

Result:

```
ab123efg
```

The following code sample uses nested STUFF() functions to format a U.S. Social Security number:

```
SELECT STUFF(STUFF('123456789', 4, 0, '-'), 7, 0, '-');
```

Result:

```
123-45-6789
```

CHARINDEX (search string, string, starting position)

CHARDINDEX returns the character position of a string within a string. The third argument is optional and rarely used in practice. It defaults to 1.

```
SELECT CHARINDEX('c', 'abcdefg', 1);
```

Result:

```
3
```

The user-defined function dbo.pTitleCase() later in this section uses CHARINDEX() to locate the spaces separating words.

PATINDEX(pattern, string)

PATINDEX searches for a pattern, which may include wildcards, within a string. The following code locates the first position of either a c or a d in the string:

```
SELECT PATINDEX('%[cd]%', 'abdcdefg');
```

Result:

```
3
```

RIGHT (string, count) and LEFT (string, count)

RIGHT and LEFT Returns the rightmost or leftmost part of a string:

```
SELECT LEFT('LeBlanc',2) AS  [Left] ,
  RIGHT('LeBlanc',2) AS [Right];
```

Result:

```
Left      Right
-----     ----
Le        nc
```

LEN (string)

LEN returns the length of a string:

```
SELECT LEN('Supercalifragilisticexpialidocious') AS [Len];
```

Result:

```
Len
-----------
34
```

RTRIM(string) and LTRIM(string)

RTRIM(string) and LTrim(string) remove leading or trailing spaces. Although it's difficult to see in print, the three leading and trailing spaces are removed from the following string. They are often used together as RTRIM(LTRIM(string). The column-header lines are adjusted with the remaining spaces to illustrate the functions:

```
SELECT RTRIM('   middle earth   ') AS [RTrim],
  LTRIM('   middle earth   ') AS [LTrim];
```

Result:

```
RTrim                  LTrim
---------------        ---------------
middle earth           middle earth
```

UPPER(string) and LOWER(string):

UPPER and LOWER convert the entire string to uppercase or lowercase. There's not much to know about these two functions:

```
SELECT UPPER('one TWO tHrEe') AS UpperCase,
  LOWER('one TWO tHrEe') AS LowerCase;
```

Result:

```
UpperCase              LowerCase
-------------          -------------
ONE TWO THREE          one two three
```

REPLACE (string, string)

The Replace() function operates as a global search and replace within a string. Using REPLACE() within an update DML command can quickly fix problems in the data, such as removing extra tabs or correcting string patterns. The following code sample adds apostrophes to the Name column in the AdventureWorks database's Product table:

```
-- Create test case by modifying one product's name.
USE AdventureWorks
GO
UPDATE Production.Product
SET
     Name = 'Chain Stay''s'
WHERE
     Name = 'Chain Stays'

SELECT
Name,
        REPLACE(Name, '''', '') Replaced
FROM Production.Product
WHERE
        ProductID = 324
```

Result:

```
Name                 Replaced
-------------        ------------
Chain Stay's         Adams
```

To demonstrate the REPLACE() function using an update command, the next query actually changes the data in place and removes any apostrophes:

```
USE AdventureWorks
GO
UPDATE Production.Product
SET
     Name = REPLACE(Name, '''', '')
WHERE
        ProductID = 324

SELECT ProductID,
       Name
FROM Production.Product
WHERE
        ProductID = 324
```

Result:

```
Name
- - - - - - - - - - - - - - - - - - - - - - - - - - - - - - - - - - - - - - - -
Chain Stays
```

> **NOTE**
>
> When working with string literals, it's generally difficult to insert a quote into the string without ending the string and causing a syntax error. SQL Server handles this situation by accepting two single quotes and converting them into one single quote within the string:
>
> 'Life''s Great!' is interpreted as Life's Great!

dbo.pTitleCase (source, search, replace)

T-SQL lacks a function to convert text to title case (first letter of each word in uppercase, and the remainder in lowercase). Therefore, the following user-defined function accomplishes that task:

```sql
CREATE FUNCTION dbo.pTitleCase (
  @StrIn NVARCHAR(MAX))
RETURNS NVARCHAR(MAX)
AS
  BEGIN;
    DECLARE
      @StrOut NVARCHAR(MAX),
      @CurrentPosition INT,
      @NextSpace INT,
      @CurrentWord NVARCHAR(MAX),
      @StrLen INT,
      @LastWord BIT;

    SET @NextSpace = 1;
    SET @CurrentPosition = 1;
    SET @StrOut = '';
    SET @StrLen = LEN(@StrIn);
    SET @LastWord = 0;

    WHILE @LastWord = 0
      BEGIN;
        SET @NextSpace =
          CHARINDEX(' ', @StrIn, @CurrentPosition + 1);
        IF  @NextSpace = 0 -- no more spaces found
          BEGIN;
            SET @NextSpace = @StrLen;
            SET @LastWord = 1;
          END;
```

```
        SET @CurrentWord =
          UPPER(SUBSTRING(@StrIn, @CurrentPosition, 1));
        SET @CurrentWord = @CurrentWord +
          LOWER(SUBSTRING(@StrIn, @CurrentPosition+1,
                @NextSpace - @CurrentPosition));
        SET @StrOut = @StrOut + @CurrentWord;
        SET @CurrentPosition = @NextSpace + 1;
    END;
  RETURN @StrOut;
END;
```

Running a user-defined function requires including the owner name in the function name:

```
SELECT dbo.pTitleCase('one TWO tHrEe') AS TitleCase;
```

Result:

```
TitleCase
-----------------------
One Two Three
```

> **NOTE**
>
> The dbo.pTitleCase function does not take into consideration surnames with nonstandard capitalization, such as McDonald, VanCamp, or de Jonge. It would be inadequate to hard-code a list of exceptions. Perhaps the best solution is to store a list of exception phrases (Mc, Van, de, and so on) in an easily updatable list.

New SQL Server 2012 String Functions

SQL Server 2012 introduces two new string functions, CONCAT and FORMAT.

The CONCAT Function

The CONCAT function combines two or more strings into a single string:

```
SELECT CONCAT('Patrick ','LeBlanc') Results;
```

Result:

```
Results
---------------
Patrick LeBlanc
```

The function requires a minimum of two arguments. It will implicitly convert all values to a string, and NULL values are converted to an empty string:

```
SELECT CONCAT(NULL, 'Patrick ', 1, ' LeBlanc') Results;
```

Results:

```
Results
---------------------------
Patrick 1 LeBlanc
```

The FORMAT Function

The FORMAT function, as the name states, returns a formatted value:

```
DECLARE @myMoney decimal(5,2) = 10.52;
SELECT FORMAT(@myMoney, 'C', 'en-US');
```

Result:

```
MyMoney
---------------------------
$10.52
```

The first argument can be an explicit value or a parameter, which is the value that will be formatted. The second is a .NET format string. In the above example C was used to format the value to currency. The final, which is optional, is the language. If it is not provided the default language will be used.

Soundex Functions

Soundex is a phonetic pattern-matching system created for the American census. Franklin Roosevelt directed the United States Bureau of Archives to develop a method of cataloguing the population that could handle variations in the spelling of similar surnames. Margaret K. Odell and Robert C. Russell developed Soundex and were awarded U.S. patents 1261167 (1918) and 1435663 (1922) for their efforts. The census filing card for each household was then filed under the Soundex method. Soundex has been applied to every census since and has been post-applied to census records back to 1880.

The purpose of Soundex is to sort similar-sounding names together, which is useful for dealing with contact information in a database application. For example, if I call a phone bank and give them my name (LeBlanc), they invariably spell it "LaBlanc" in the contact lookup form, but if the database uses Soundex properly, then I'll still be in the search-result list box.

For more information concerning Soundex and its history, refer to the following websites:

- www.nara.gov/genealogy/coding.html
- www.amberskyline.com/treasuremaps/uscensus.html
- www.bluepoof.com/soundex/

Here's how Soundex works. The first letter of a name is stored as the letter, and the following Soundex phonetic sounds are stored according to the following code:

1 = B, F, P, V

2 = C, G, J, K, Q, S, X, Z

3 = D, T

4 = L

5 = M, N

6 = R

Double letters with the same Soundex code, A, E, I, O, U, H, W, Y, and some prefixes, are disregarded. Therefore, "LeBlanc" becomes "L145" via the following method:

1. The L is stored.

2. The e is disregarded.

3. The b sound is stored as the Soundex code 1.

4. The l is stored as the Soundex code 4.

5. The a is disregarded.

6. The n is stored as the Soundex code 5.

7. The c is ignored.

By boiling them down to a few consonant sounds, Soundex assigns "LeBlanc," "LeBlank" and "LaBlanc" the same code: N145.

Following are additional Soundex name examples:

- Brown = B650 (r = 6, n = 5)
- Jeffers = J162 (ff = 1, r = 6, s = 2)
- Letterman = L365 (tt = 3, r = 6, m = 5)
- Nicholson = N242 (c = 2, l = 4, s = 2)
- Nickols = N242 (c = 2, l = 4, s = 2)

SQL Server includes two Soundex-related functions, SOUNDEX() and DIFFERENCE().

Using the SOUNDEX() Function

The SOUNDEX(string) function calculates the Soundex code for a string as follows:

```
SELECT SOUNDEX('LeBlanc') AS LeBlanc,
   SOUNDEX('LaBlanc) AS LaBlanc,
   SOUNDEX(LeBlank) AS LeBlank;
```

Result:

```
LeBlanc    LaBlanc    LeBlank
--------   -------    --------
L145       L145       L145
```

You can add Soundex searches to a database in two ways. The simplest method is to add the SOUNDEX() function within the WHERE clause, as follows:

```
USE AdventureWorks
GO
SELECT LastName, FirstName
FROM Person.Person
WHERE
        SOUNDEX('Andersen') = SOUNDEX(LastName)
```

Scrolling through the result reveals three distinct last names: Andersen, Anderson, and Atrim. This is because they each have a SOUNDEX value of A536.

Although this implementation has the smallest impact on the data schema, it can cause performance issues as the data size grows because the SOUNDEX() function must execute for every row in the database, and an index on the name column (if any) cannot be used with an efficient seek operation, but only with a much more expensive scan. A faster variation of this first implementation method pretests for names with the same first letter, thus enabling SQL Server to use any indexes to narrow the search, so fewer rows must be read, and the SOUNDEX() function must be performed only for rows selected by the index:

```
USE AdventureWorks
GO
SELECT LastName, FirstName
FROM Person.Person
WHERE
        SOUNDEX('Andersen') = SOUNDEX(LastName) and LastName LIKE 'A%'
```

The second implementation method is to write the Soundex value in a column and index it with a nonclustered index. Because the Soundex value for each row is calculated during the write, the SOUNDEX() function does not need to be called for every row read by the SELECT statement. This is a recommended method for a database application that heavily depends on Soundex for contact searches. With that in place, search for a row, or all the matching rows, because the stored Soundex code is extremely fast. You can use a similar query to the following, assuming the new column is named SoundexCode:

To accomplish this you could add a new column to the Person table in the AdventureWorks data. The column could be a persisted calculated column, so it is automatically calculated for every insert and kept updated with every update.

```
USE AdventureWorks
GO

SELECT LastName, FirstName, SoundexCode
  FROM Person.Person
  WHERE SoundexCode = 'A536';
```

Result:

```
LastName        FirstName          SoundexCode
------------    --------------     -----------
Andersen        Alejandro          A536
Andersen        Alicia             A536
. . .
```

Using the DIFFERENCE() Soundex Function

The second SQL Server Soundex function, DIFFERENCE(), returns the Soundex difference between two strings in the form of a ranking from 1 to 4, with 4 representing a perfect Soundex match:

```
USE AdventureWorks2008
GO

SELECT
     LastName,
     DIFFERENCE('LeBlanc', LastName) NameSearch
FROM Person.Person
ORDER BY DIFFERENCE('LeBlanc', LastName)  DESC
```

Result:

```
LastName          NameSearch
-------------     -----------
Kobylinski        3
Shabalin          3
Slattengren       2
Slaven            2
. . .
```

The advantage of the DIFFERENCE() function is that it broadens the search beyond the first letters. The problem with the function is that it wants to calculate the

Soundex value for both parameters, which prevents it from taking advantage of pre-stored Soundex values.

Data-Type Conversion Functions

Converting data from one data type to another data type is often handled automatically by SQL Server. Many of those conversions are implicit, or automatic.

Explicit conversions require a CAST() or CONVERT() function:

- CAST(Input as data type): The ANSI standard SQL means to convert from one data type to another. Even when the conversion can be performed implicitly by SQL Server, using the CAST() function forces the wanted data type.

  CAST() is actually programmed slightly differently than a standard function. Rather than separate the two parameters with a comma (as most functions do), the data passed to the CAST() function is followed by the as keyword and the requested output data type:

  ```
  SELECT CAST('Away' AS NVARCHAR(5)) AS 'Tom Hanks'
  ```

Result:

```
TOM HANKS
---------
AWAY
```

Another example:

```
SELECT CAST(123 AS NVARCHAR(15)) AS Int2String
```

Result:

```
INT2STRING
--------------
123
```

- CONVERT(datatype, expression, style): Returns a value converted to a different data type with optional formatting. The first parameter of this non-ANSI SQL function is the wanted data type to be applied to the expression:

  ```
  CONVERT (data type, expression[, style])
  ```

The style parameter usually refers to the optional date styles listed in Table 8-7. The style is applied to the output during conversion from datetime to a character-based data type, or to the input during conversion from text to datetime. Generally, the one- or two-digit style provides a two-digit year, and its three-digit counterpart provides a four-digit year. For example, style 1 provides 01/01/03, whereas style 101 provides 01/01/2003. The styles marked with an asterisk (*) in Table 8-7 are the exceptions to this rule.

SQL Server also provides numeric formatting styles, but numeric formatting is typically the task of the user interface, not the database.

TABLE 8-7   Convert Function Date Styles

Style	Description	Format
0/100*	Default	mon dd yyyy hh:miAM (or PM)
1/101	USA	mm/dd/yy
2/102	ANSI	yy.mm.dd
3/103	British/French	dd/mm/yy
4/104	German	dd.mm.yy
5/105	Italian	dd-mm-yy
6/106	—	dd mon yy
7/107	—	mon dd, yy
8/108	—	hh:mm:ss
9 or 109*	Default+milliseconds	mon dd yyyy hh:mi:ss:mmmAM (or PM)
10 or 110	USA	mm-dd-yy
11 or 111	Japan	yy/mm/dd
12 or 112	ISO	yymmdd
13 or 113*	Europe default+milliseconds	dd mon yyyy hh:mm:ss:mmm (24h)
14 or 114	—	hh:mi:ss:mmm (24h)
20 or 120*	ODBC canonical	yyyy-mm-dd hh:mi:ss (24h)
21 or 121*	ODBC canonical + milliseconds	yyyy-mm-dd hh:mi:ss.mmm (24h)
126	ISO8601 for XML use	yyyy-mm-dd Thh:mm:ss:mmm (no spaces)
127	ISO8601 with time zone Z	yyyy-mm-ddThh:mi:ss.mmmZ
130	Kuwaiti	dd mon yyyy hh:mi:ss:mmmAM (or PM)
131	Kuwaiti	dd/mm/yy hh:mi:ss:mmmAM (or PM)

* Both styles return dates with centuries.

Best Practice

In a clean client/server design, the server provides the data in an internal format, and the client application formats the data as required by the user. Unformatted data is more independent than formatted data and can be used by more applications.

The following code demonstrates the CONVERT() function:

```
SELECT  CURRENT_TIMESTAMP AS RawDate,
    CONVERT (NVARCHAR(25), CURRENT_TIMESTAMP, 100) AS Date100,
    CONVERT (NVARCHAR(25), CURRENT_TIMESTAMP, 1) AS Date1;
```

Result:

```
RawDate                            Date100                    Date1
--------------------------         ----------------------     ----------
2009-11-17 10:27:27.413            Nov 17 2001 10:27AM        11/17/01
```

An additional data-type conversion function provides a fast way to move data between text and numeric. STR(number, length, decimal): returns a string from a number:

```
SELECT STR(123,6,2) AS [Str];
```

Result:

```
Str
-----
123.00
```

SQL Server 2012 introduces three new built-in conversion functions. Two of the three are completely new to SQL Server, whereas the third is a slight modification of an existing function.

The Parse(string_value as data_type using culture) and Try_Parse(string_value as data_type using culture) are similar for what values they expect and what is returned. The following scripts are samples of how to use both functions:

```
SELECT PARSE('123' AS INT) AS Parsed
```

Result:

```
Parsed
---------
123

SELECT TRY_PARSE('123' AS DATETIME) TryParse
```

Result:

```
TryParse
----------
NULL
```

The string_value in both functions represents the formatted value to be parsed into the specified data type. The values can be parsed only into Numeric and Date/Time data types. The culture, which is optional, represents various SQL Server languages. The following script illustrates how to execute the Try_Parse function using the culture function:

```
SELECT TRY_PARSE('Monday, 13 December 2010' AS datetime2 using
'en-US') AS Result
```

Result:

```
Result
--------------------
2010-12-13 00:00:00.0000000
```

The difference between the two functions is that when using the Parse function if the conversion fails, an error is raised. However, if you use the Try_Parse function, a null value is returned.

The last conversion introduced in SQL Server 2011 is `Try_Convert(data type, expression style)`. This function is the counterpart to the existing Convert function just as the `Try_Parse` is to Parse. When using the `Try_Convert` if the conversion fails, it returns a null value. The following script illustrates how to execute the `Try_Convert` function:

```
SELECT TRY_CONVERT(DATE,'19720526', 112) Results
```

Result:

```
Results
-----------
1972-05-26
```

Server Environment Information

System functions return information about the current environment. This section covers the two more commonly used system functions.

`DB_NAME()`: Returns the name of the current database, as shown in the following example:

```
SELECT CURRENT_TIMESTAMP AS [Date],
  DB_NAME() AS [Database];
```

Result:

```
Date                        Database
------------------------    -------
2009-11-15 18:38:50.250     CHA2
```

`SERVERPROPERTY()`: Several useful pieces of information about the server may be determined from this function, including the following:

- **Collation:** The collation type
- **Edition:** Enterprise, Developer, Standard, and so on
- **EngineEdition:** 2 = Standard, 3 = Enterprise, 4 = Express

- **InstanceName:** Null if the default instance
- **ProductVersion:** The version number of SQL Server
- **ProductLevel:** "RTM" for the initial release-to-manufacturing version, "SP*n*" for service packs (*n* is the service pack number), and "CTP" for Community Technology Preview versions
- **ServerName:** The full server and instance name

For example, the following code returns SQL Server engine edition and version information for my current instance of SQL Server:

```
SELECT
SERVERPROPERTY ('ServerName') AS ServerName,
SERVERPROPERTY ('Edition') AS Edition,
SERVERPROPERTY ('ProductVersion') AS 'ProductVersion',
SERVERPROPERTY ('ProductLevel') AS ProductLevel;
```

Result:

```
ServerName                    Edition              ProductVersion ProductLevel
----------- --------------    --------------       -------------  ------------
WIN-V7B3M53ERC1\DENALICTP3    Developer Edition (64-bit)          11.0.1422.17RTM
```

Summary

Chapter 7, "Relational Database Design and Creating the Physical Database Schema," introduced the basic SELECT statement and query flow. This chapter expanded the concept with expressions and calculations that can be inserted in several places within the query, significantly improving its flexibility. In subsequent chapters, you see how expressions can receive data from subqueries and user-defined functions, further increasing the power of the query.

Chapter 9, "Merging Data with Joins, Subqueries, and CTEs," continues the progression of adding capability to the query by joining data from multiple data sources.

8

Merging Data with Joins, Subqueries, and CTEs

Relational databases, by their nature, segment data into several narrow, but long, tables. Seldom does looking at a single table provide meaningful data. Therefore, merging data from multiple tables is an important task for SQL developers. The theory behind merging data sets is *relational algebra*, as defined by E. F. Codd in 1970.

Relational algebra consists of eight relational operators:

- **Restrict:** Returns the rows that meet a certain criterion
- **Project:** Returns selected columns, or calculated data, from a data set
- **Product:** Relational multiplication that returns all possible combinations of data between two data sets
- **Union:** Relational addition and subtraction that merges two tables vertically by stacking one table above another table and lining up the columns

- **Intersection**: Returns the rows common to two data sets
- **Difference**: Returns the rows unique to one data set
- **Join**: Returns the horizontal merger of two tables, matching up rows based on common data
- **Divide**: The inverse of relational multiplication, returns rows in one data set that match every row in a corresponding data set

In addition, as a method to accomplish relational algebra, SQL has implemented the following:

- **Subqueries**: Similar to a join but more flexible; the results of the subquery are used in place of an expression, list, or data set within an outer query.

In the formal language of relational algebra:

- A table, or data set, is a *relation* or *entity*.
- A row is a *tuple*.
- A column is an *attribute*.

However, this chapter uses the common terms of table, row, and column.

Relational theory is now thirty-something and has become better defined over the years as database vendors compete with extensions, and database theorists further define the problem of representing reality within a data structure. However, E. F. Codd's original work is still the foundation of relational database design and implementation.

SQL's real power is its capability to mix and match multiple methods of selecting data. It's this skill in fluidly assembling a complex query in code to accomplish what can't be easily done with GUI tools that differentiates SQL gurus from the wannabes. You must study embedded simple and correlated subqueries, derived tables, and common table expressions, and then apply these query components to solve complex relational problems such as relational division.

> **NOTE**
> To give credit where credit is due, much of this chapter is based on the work of E. F. Codd and C. J. Date.

Joins work with more than just tables. As listed in Chapter 6, "Introducing Basic Query Flow," data sources include local SQL Server tables, subqueries/CTEs, views, table-valued user-defined functions, distributed data sources (other database tables), full-text search results, and XQueries.

The reason for writing set-based queries is more than just writing elegant code. Set-based queries scale extremely well.

Using Joins

In relational algebra, a *join* is the multiplication of two data sets followed by a restriction of the result so that only the intersection of the two data sets is returned. The whole purpose of the join is to horizontally merge two data sets and produce a new result set from the combination by matching rows in one data source to rows in the other data source, as shown in Figure 9-1. This section explains the various types of joins and how to use them to select data.

FIGURE 9-1

A join merges rows from one data set with rows from another data set, creating a new set of rows that includes columns from both. The code, 101, is common to Smith and order number 1 and merges the two original rows into a single result row.

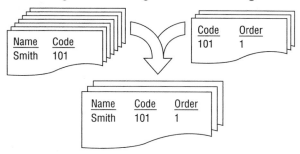

By merging the data using the join, the rest of the SQL SELECT statement, including the column expressions, aggregate groupings, and WHERE clause conditions, can access any of the columns or rows from the joined tables. These capabilities are the core and power of SQL.

Joins are based on the idea of intersecting data sets. As shown in Figure 9-2, a relational join deals with two sets of data that have common values, and it's these common values that define how the tables intersect.

FIGURE 9-2

Relational joins are based on the overlap, or common intersection, of two data sets.

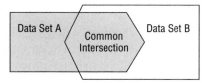

The intersection simply represents that some common column can connect a row from the first data set to data in the second data set. The common values are typically a primary key and a foreign key, such as these examples from the `AdventureWorksLT2012` sample database. All tables listed are from the `SalesLT` schema:

- `CustomerID` between the `Customer` and `CustomerAddress` tables
- `SalesOrderID` between the `SalesOrderHeader` and `SalesOrderDetail` tables
- `ProductID` between the `Product` and `SalesOrderDetail` tables

SQL includes many types of joins that determine how the rows are selected from the different sides of the intersection. Table 9-1 lists the join types. (Each is explained in more detail later in this section.)

TABLE 9-1 Join Types

Join Type	Query Designer Symbol	Definition
Inner join		Includes only matching rows
Left outer join		Includes all rows from the left table regardless of whether a match exists, and matching rows from the right table
Right outer join		Includes all the rows from the right table regardless of whether a match exists, and matching rows from the left table
Full outer join		Includes all the rows from both tables regardless of whether a match exists
Θ (theta) join		Matches rows using a nonequal condition — the symbol shows the actual theta condition (<, >, <=, >=, <>)
Cross join	No join connection	Produces a Cartesian product — a match between each row in data source one with each row from data source two without any conditions or restrictions

> **NOTE**
> This chapter uses the AdventureWorksLT2012 sample database, which is available for download from `http://msftdbprodsamples.codeplex.com/releases/view/55330`

Inner Joins

The *inner join* is by far the most common join. It's also referred to as a *common join* and was originally called a *natural join* by E. F. Codd. The inner join returns only those rows that represent a match between the two data sets. An inner join is well named because it extracts only data from the inner portion of the intersection of the two overlapping data sets, as shown in Figure 9-3.

FIGURE 9-3

The inner join includes only those rows from each side of the join that are contained within the intersection of the two data sources.

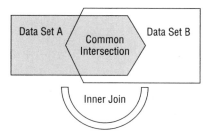

Creating Inner Joins

Using T- SQL code, joins are specified within the FROM portion of the SELECT statement. The keyword JOIN identifies the second table, and the ON clause defines the common ground between the two tables. The default type of join is an inner join, so the keyword INNER is optional. For clarity, however, you should always include it:

```
SELECT *
  FROM Table1
    [INNER] JOIN Table2
      ON Table1.column = Table2.column;
```

Because joins pull together data from two data sets, it makes sense that SQL needs to know how to match up rows from those sets. SQL Server merges the rows by matching a value common to both tables. Typically, a primary key value from one table is matched with a foreign key value from the secondary table; however, tables can be related by columns that are not defined as keys. As long as the data types are compatible, a join can be performed. Whenever a row from the first table matches a row from the second table, the two rows are merged into a new row containing data from both tables.

The following code sample joins the SalesLT.RetailSales (secondary) and SalesLT .Customer (primary) tables from the AdventureWorksLT2012 sample database. The ON clause specifies the common data:

```
USE AdventureWorksLT2012;

SELECT CST.CompanyName, SOH.TotalDue
  FROM SalesLT.Customer CST
 INNER JOIN SalesLT.SalesOrderHeader SOH
    ON CST.CustomerID = SOH. CustomerID
```

The query begins with the Customer table. For every Customer row, SQL Server attempts to identify matching SalesOrderHeader rows by comparing the CustomerID columns in both tables. The `Customer` table rows and `SalesOrderHeader` table rows that match merge into a new result:

```
CompanyName                             TotalDue
------------------------------------    ------------
Professional Sales and Service          43962.7901
Remarkable Bike Store                   7330.8972
Bulk Discount Store                     98138.2131
Coalition Bike Company                  2669.3183
Futuristic Bikes                        272.6468
Channel Outlet                          608.1766
Aerobic Exercise Company                2361.6403
Vigorous Sports Store                   1170.5376
Thrilling Bike Tours                    15275.1977
Extreme Riding Supplies                 63686.2708
Action Bicycle Specialists              119960.824
Central Bicycle Specialists             43.0437
The Bicycle Accessories Company         117.7276
Riding Cycles                           86222.8072
Good Toys                               972.785
Paints and Solvents Company             14017.9083
Closest Bicycle Store                   39531.6085
Many Bikes Store                        81834.9826
Instruments and Parts Company           70698.9922
Trailblazing Sports                     45992.3665
Eastside Department Store               92663.5609
Sports Products Store                   3673.3249
Discount Tours                          3293.7761
Tachometers and Accessories             2228.0566
Essential Bike Works                    45.1995
Engineered Bike Systems                 3754.9733
Transport Bikes                         665.4251
Metropolitan Bicycle Supply             108597.9536
West Side Mart                          87.0851
Thrifty Parts and Sales                 1261.444
Sports Store                            2711.4098
Nearby Cycle Shop                       42452.6519
```

Number of Rows Returned

It is rare that an inner join returns all the rows from all tables. The preceding query has 32 rows in the `SalesLT.SalesOrderHeader` table, which is the number of rows returned in the query. However, 847 rows are in the `SalesLT.Customer` table, but only 32 rows in the `SalesLT.Customer` table matched on the CustomerID column to the rows in the `SalesLT.SalesOrderHeader` table. Depending on the number of matching rows from each data source and the type of join, you can decrease or increase the final number of rows in the result set.

To see how joins can alter the number of rows returned, look at the following query. First, create some data in the `tempdb` by executing the following SQL:

```
USE tempdb;

CREATE TABLE [dbo].[Customer](
[CustomerID] [int] NOT NULL,
[LastName] [varchar](50) NOT NULL);

INSERT INTO Customer(CustomerID, LastName)
VALUES(101, 'Smith'),
(102, 'Adams'),
(103, 'Reagan'),
(104, 'Franklin'),
(105, 'Dowdry')


CREATE TABLE [dbo].[SalesOrder](
[OrderNumber] [varchar](50) NOT NULL,
[CustomerID] [int] NOT NULL);

INSERT INTO SalesOrder (OrderNumber, CustomerID  )
VALUES( '1',101),
( '2',101),
( '3',102),
( '4',102),
( '5',103),
( '6',105),
( '7',105)
```

The initial row count of `Customer` is 5, yet when the customers are matched with their orders, the row count changes to 7. The following code compares the two queries and their respective results side-by-side:

```
USE tempdb;

SELECT CustomerID , LastName       SELECT cst.CustomerID , OrderNumber
from Customer;                        FROM SalesOrder so
                                        INNER JOIN Customer cst
                                      ON so.CustomerID = cst.CustomerID;
```

Results from both queries:

```
CustomerID    LastName             CustomerID    OrderNumber
-----------   --------             -----------   -----------
101           Smith          ----→ 101           1
                             ----→ 101           2
102           Adams          ----→ 102           3
                             ----→ 102           4
```

CustomerID	LastName	CustomerID	OrderNumber
103	Reagan	103	5
104	Franklin		
105	Dowdry	105	6
		105	7

Joins can appear to multiply rows. If a row on one side of the join matches with several rows on the other side of the join, the result includes a row for every match. In the preceding query, some customers (Smith, Adams, Reagan, and Dowdry) are listed multiple times because they have multiple orders.

Joins also eliminate rows. Franklin (104) has no matching orders and therefore is eliminated in the join set.

Multiple Data Source Joins

As some of the examples have already demonstrated, a SELECT statement isn't limited to one or two data sources (tables, views, CTEs, subqueries, and so on); a SQL Server SELECT statement may refer to up to 256 data sources. That's a lot of joins.

Because SQL is a declarative language, the order of the data sources is not important for inner joins. (The query optimizer decides the best order to actually process the query based on the indexes available and the data in the tables.) Multiple joins may be combined in multiple paths, or even circular patterns (A joins B joins C joins A) — a large white board and a consistent development style can pay off.

The following query (first shown in Figure 9-5 and then worked out in code) answers the question, "Who purchased a crankset from AdventureWorks?" The answer must involve five tables from AdventureWorks2012LT:

- The ProductCategory table for finding all ProductCategoryIDs that are classified as Cranksets.
- The Product table for the set of specific ProductIDs that are touring bikes. Their rows match on ProductCategoryID to the previous set.
- The SalesOrderDetail table for the set of SalesOrderIDs that contained one of the touring bike products (one of the ProductIDs found in the preceding set).
- The SalesOrderHeader table for the set of CustomerIDs that contain the preceding set of SalesOrderIDs.
- The Customer table for the set of Customers (CompanyName) that matches the set of CustomerIDs found in SalesOrderHeader.

The following SQL SELECT statement begins with the "who" portion of the question and specifies the join tables and conditions as it works through the required tables. The WHERE clause restricts the ProductCategory table rows and yet affects the customers selected:

```
USE AdventureWorksLT2012;

SELECT cst.CompanyName, prod.Name ProductName
  FROM SalesLT.Customer cst
 INNER JOIN SalesLT.SalesOrderHeader soh
    ON cst.CustomerID = soh. CustomerID
 INNER JOIN SalesLT.SalesOrderDetail sod
    ON soh.SalesOrderID = sod.SalesOrderID
 INNER JOIN SalesLT.Product prod
    ON sod.ProductID = prod.ProductID
 INNER JOIN SalesLT.ProductCategory pc
    ON prod.ProductCategoryID = pc.ProductCategoryID
 WHERE pc.Name = 'Cranksets'
 ORDER BY cst.CompanyName, prod.Name;
```

Result:

```
CompanyName                          ProductName
---------------------------------    -------------------------
Instruments and Parts Company          HL Crankset
Instruments and Parts Company          LL Crankset
Metropolitan Bicycle Supply            HL Crankset
Metropolitan Bicycle Supply            LL Crankset
Professional Sales and Service         HL Crankset
Trailblazing Sports                    HL Crankset
Trailblazing Sports                    LL Crankset
```

Three companies appear multiple times because they purchased two types of Cranksets.

> **NOTE**
>
> Joins are not limited to primary and foreign keys. The join can match a row in one data source with a row in another data source using any column, as long as the columns share compatible data types and the data matches.

Following is a summary of the main points about inner joins:

- They match only rows with a common value.
- The order of the data sources is unimportant.
- They can appear to multiply rows.
- Newer ANSI 92 style is the best way to write them.

Outer Joins

Whereas an inner join contains only the intersection of the two data sets, an *outer join* extends the inner join by adding the nonmatching data from the left or right data set, as shown in Figure 9-4.

Outer joins solve a significant problem for many queries by including all the data regardless of a match. The common customer-order query demonstrates this problem well. If the requirement is to build a query that lists all customers plus their recent orders, only an outer join can retrieve every customer whether or not the customer has placed an order. An inner join between customers and orders would miss every customer who did not place a recent order.

> **CAUTION**
>
> Depending on the nullability of the keys and the presence of rows on both sides of the join, it's easy to write a query that misses rows from one side or the other of the join. This error might occur in third-party ISV application code. To avoid this data integrity error, know your schema well and always unit test your queries against a small data set with known answers.

FIGURE 9-4

An outer join includes not only rows from the two data sources with a match, but also unmatched rows from outside the intersection.

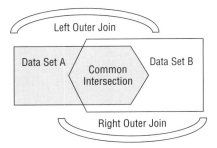

Some of the data in the result set produced by an outer join looks just like the data from an inner join. Data is in columns that come from each of the data sources, but any rows from the outer-join table that do not have a match in the other side of the join return data only from the outer-join table. In this case, columns from the other data source have null values.

T-SQL Code and Outer Joins

In SQL code, an outer join is declared by the keywords LEFT OUTER or RIGHT OUTER before the JOIN (technically, the keyword OUTER is optional):

```
SELECT *
  FROM Table1
    LEFT|RIGHT [OUTER] JOIN Table2
      ON Table1.column = Table2.column;
```

> **NOTE**
>
> Several keywords (such as INNER, OUTER, or AS) in SQL are optional or may be abbreviated (such as PROC for PROCEDURE). Although most developers omit the optional syntax, explicitly stating the intent by spelling out the full syntax improves the readability of the code.

There's no trick to telling the difference between left and right outer joins. In code, left or right refers to the table that is included regardless of the match. The outer-join table (sometimes called the *driving table*) is typically listed first, so left outer joins are more common than right outer joins. Any confusion between left and right outer joins is probably caused by the use of graphical-query tools to build joins because left and right refers to the table's listing in the SQL text, and the tables' positions in the graphical-query tool are moot.

Best Practice

When coding outer joins, always order your data sources so that you can write left outer joins. Don't use right outer joins, and never mix left outer joins and right outer joins.

To modify the previous customer-sales order query so that it returns all contacts regardless of any orders, changing the join type from inner to left outer is all that's required, as follows:

```
USE AdventureWorksLT2012;

SELECT CST.CompanyName, SOH.TotalDue
  FROM SalesLT.Customer CST
  LEFT OUTER JOIN SalesLT.SalesOrderHeader SOH
    ON CST.CustomerID = SOH.CustomerID
  ORDER BY CST.CompanyName;
```

The left outer join includes all rows from the `Customer` table and matching rows from the `SalesOrderHeader` table. The abbreviated result of the query is as follows:

```
CompanyName                             TotalDue
-------------------------------------   --------------------
A Bike Store                            NULL
A Bike Store                            NULL
A Cycle Shop                            NULL
A Great Bicycle Company                 NULL
A Great Bicycle Company                 NULL
A Typical Bike Shop                     NULL
A Typical Bike Shop                     NULL
Acceptable Sales & Service              NULL
Acceptable Sales & Service              NULL
Action Bicycle Specialists              119960.824
```

Because all the companies except for Action Bicycle Specialists in this sample set do not have corresponding rows in the `SalesOrderHeader` table, the columns from the `SalesOrderHeader` table return a null for those rows.

Having said that, SQL Server supports backward compatibility, so if the database compatibility level is set to 80 (SQL Server 2000), the ANSI 82 style outer joins still work.

Full Outer Joins

A *full outer join* returns all the data from both data sets regardless of the intersection, as shown in Figure 9-5. It is functionally the same as taking the results from a left outer join and the results from a right outer join, and unioning them together. (Unions are explained later in this chapter.)

FIGURE 9-5

The full outer join returns all the data from both data sets, matching the rows where it can and presenting NULL when it cannot.

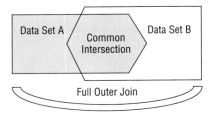

In real life, referential integrity reduces the need for a full outer join because every row from the secondary table should have a match in the primary table (depending on the optionality of the foreign key), so left outer joins are typically sufficient. Full outer joins are most useful for cleaning up data that has not had the benefit of clean constraints to filter out bad data.

The following example is a mock-up of such a situation and compares the full outer join with an inner and a left outer join. Table `Customer2` is the primary table. Table `SalesOrder2` is a secondary table with a foreign key that refers to `Customer2`. No foreign key constraint exists, so there may be some nonmatches for the outer join to find:

```
USE tempdb
GO

CREATE TABLE dbo.Customer2 (
CustomerID INT ,
LastName VARCHAR(50)
);


CREATE TABLE dbo.SalesOrder2 (
OrderNumber VARCHAR(15),
CustomerID INT
);
```

The sample data includes rows that would normally break referential integrity. The following batch inserts the six sample data rows:

```
INSERT Customer2(CustomerID,LastName)
VALUES(101, 'Smith'),
(102, 'Adams'),
(103, 'Reagan');

INSERT SalesOrder2 (OrderNumber ,CustomerID  )
VALUES( '1',102),
( '2',104),
( '3',105);
```

An inner join between table Customer2 and table SalesOrder2 returns only one matching row:

```
SELECT c.CustomerID, c.LastName , so.OrderNumber
  FROM dbo.Customer2 c
    INNER JOIN dbo.SalesOrder2 so
      ON c.CustomerID = so.CustomerID;
```

Result:

```
CustomerID        LastName       OrderNumber
--------------    ------------   ----------------
102               Adams          1
```

A left outer join extends the inner join and includes the rows from table Customer2 without a match:

```
SELECT c.CustomerID, c.LastName , so.OrderNumber
 FROM dbo.Customer2 c
    LEFT OUTER JOIN dbo.SalesOrder2 so
      ON c.CustomerID = so.CustomerID;
```

All the rows are now returned from table Customer2, but two rows are still missing from table SalesOrder2:

```
CustomerID        LastName       OrderNumber
--------------    ------------   ----------------
101               Smith          NULL
102               Adams          1
103               Reagan         NULL
```

A full outer join retrieves every row from both tables, regardless of a match between the tables:

```
SELECT c.CustomerID, c.LastName , so.OrderNumber
  FROM dbo.Customer2 c
    FULL OUTER JOIN dbo.SalesOrder2 so
      ON c.CustomerID = so.CustomerID;
```

All the order numbers from the `SalesOrder2` table are now listed along with every row from `Customer2`:

```
CustomerID        LastName   OrderNumber
---------------   ----------  ----------------
101               Smith      NULL
102               Adams      1
103               Reagan     NULL
NULL              NULL       2
NULL              NULL       3
```

As this example shows, full outer joins are an excellent tool for finding all the data, even bad data. Set difference queries, explored later in this chapter, build on outer joins to zero in on bad data.

Placing the Conditions Within Outer Joins

When working with inner joins, a condition has the same effect whether it's in the JOIN clause or the WHERE clause, but that's not the case with outer joins:

- When the condition is in the JOIN clause, SQL Server includes all rows from the outer table and then uses the condition to include rows from the second table.
- When the restriction is placed in the WHERE clause, the join is performed, and then the WHERE clause is applied to the joined rows.

The following two queries demonstrate the effect of the placement of the condition.

In the first query, the left outer join includes all rows from `Customer2` and then joins those rows from `SalesOrder2` where `CustomerID` is equal in both tables and `LastName`'s value is `Adams`. The result is all the rows from `Customer2` and rows from `SalesOrder2` that meet both join restrictions:

```
SELECT c.CustomerID, c.LastName , so.OrderNumber
  FROM dbo.Customer2 c
    LEFT OUTER JOIN dbo.SalesOrder2 so
      ON c.CustomerID = so.CustomerID
        AND c.LastName = 'Adams';
```

Result:

```
CustomerID        LastName     OrderNumber
---------------   ------------  ------------
101               Smith        NULL
102               Adams        1
103               Reagan       NULL
```

The second query first performs the left outer join, producing the same three rows as the previous query but without the AND condition. The WHERE clause then restricts that result to those rows where `LastName` is equal to `Adams`. The net effect is the same as when an inner join was used (but it might take more execution time):

```
SELECT c.CustomerID, c.LastName , so.OrderNumber
  FROM dbo.Customer2 c
    LEFT OUTER JOIN dbo.SalesOrder2 so
      ON c.CustomerID = so.CustomerID

WHERE c.LastName = 'Adams';
```

Result:

```
CustomerID          LastName          OrderNumber
---------------     ------------      ------------
102                 Adams             1
```

Multiple Outer Joins

Coding a query with multiple outer joins can be tricky. Typically, the order of data sources in the FROM clause doesn't matter, but here it does. The key is to code them in a sequential chain. If you are tasked with providing a result that contains all customers, any orders they may have placed, and any corresponding shipping details for those orders, think through it this way:

1. Grab all the customers regardless of whether they've placed any orders.
2. Then grab all the orders regardless of whether they've shipped.
3. Then grab all the ship details.

When chaining multiple outer joins, stick to left outer joins because mixing left and right outer joins quickly becomes confusing. Be sure to unit test the query with a small sample set of data to ensure that the outer join chain is correct.

Self-Joins

A *self-join* is a join that refers back to the same table. This type of unary relationship is often used to extract data from a *reflexive* (also called a *recursive*) relationship, such as organizational charts (employee to boss). Think of a self-join as a table joined with a temporary copy of itself.

To set up some sample data, use the following code:

```
USE tempdb;

CREATE TABLE dbo.Employee (
EmployeeID  int PRIMARY KEY,
EmployeeName  varchar(30),
```

9

```
MgrID   int FOREIGN KEY REFERENCES Employee(EmployeeID));

INSERT INTO dbo.Employee
VALUES(1, 'Janet Jones', NULL),
(2, 'Tom Smith', 1),
(3, 'Ted Adams', 2),
(4, 'Mary Thomas', 2),
(5, 'Jack Jones', 2),
(6, 'Anita Kidder', 3),
(7, 'William Owens', 3),
(8, 'Sean Watson', 4),
(9, 'Brenda Jackson', 5),
(10, 'Frank Johnson', 5)
```

The `Employee` sample table uses a self-join between an Employee and his manager, as shown in the database diagram in Figure 9-6. The managers are also employees, of course, and are listed in the same table. They link back to their managers, and so on, until the top of the hierarchy is reached when there is a NULL value in the `MgrID` column. The sample database is populated with three levels that can be used for sample queries.

FIGURE 9-6

The database diagram of the Employee table shows the self-referencing foreign key relationship.

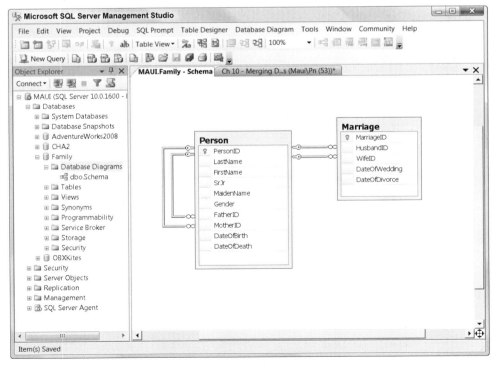

The key to constructing a self-join is to include a second reference to the table using a table alias. When the table is available twice to the SELECT statement, the self-join functions much like any other join. In the following example, the dbo.Employee table is referenced using the table alias Mgr.

Switching to the sample data, the following query reveals all employees and their corresponding managers:

```
SELECT  Mgr.EmployeeName MgrName, Mgr.EmployeeID EmpIDMgr,
Emp.EmployeeName , Emp.EmployeeID
FROM dbo.Employee Emp JOIN dbo.Employee Mgr
ON Emp.MgrID = Mgr.EmployeeID;
```

The results shown here illustrate the relationship:

```
MgrName              EmpIDMgr   EmployeeName         EmployeeID
-------------------  ---------  -----------------    ----------
Janet Jones          1          Tom Smith            2
Tom Smith            2          Ted Adams            3
Tom Smith            2          Mary Thomas          4
Tom Smith            2          Jack Jones           5
Ted Adams            3          Anita Kidder         6
Ted Adams            3          William Owens        7
Mary Thomas          4          Sean Watson          8
Jack Jones           5          Brenda Jackson       9
Jack Jones           5          Frank Johnson        10
```

Cross Joins

The *cross join*, which is an *unrestricted join*, is a pure relational algebra multiplication of the two source tables. Without a join condition restricting the result set, the result set includes every possible combination of rows from the data sources. Each row in data set one is matched with every row in data set two — for example, if the first data source has 5 rows and the second data source has 4 rows, a cross join between them would result in 20 rows. This type of result set is referred to as a *Cartesian Product*.

Using the Customer2/SalesOrder2 sample tables, you can construct a cross join in Management Studio by omitting the join condition between the two tables, as shown in Figure 9-7.

In code, this type of join is specified by the keywords CROSS JOIN and the lack of an ON condition:

```
SELECT Customer2.CustomerID,
       Customer2.LastName,
       SalesOrder2.OrderNumber
  FROM Customer2 CROSS JOIN
       SalesOrder2;
```

9

FIGURE 9-7

A graphical representation of a cross join is simply two tables without a join condition.

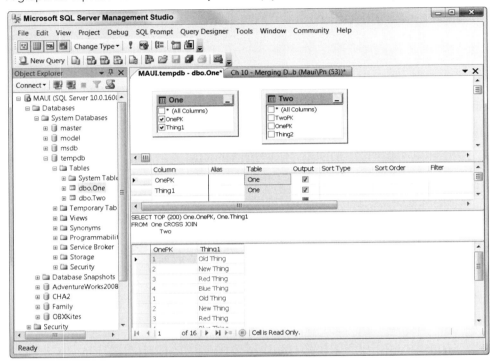

The result of a join without restriction is that every row in table `Customer2` matches with every row from table `SalesOrder2`:

```
CustomerID   LastName              OrderNumber
-----------  -------------------   ---------------
101          Smith                 1
102          Adams                 1
103          Reagan                1
101          Smith                 2
102          Adams                 2
103          Reagan                2
101          Smith                 3
102          Adams                 3
103          Reagan                3
```

Exotic Joins

Nearly all joins are based on a condition of equality between the primary key of a primary table and the foreign key of a secondary table, which is why the inner join is sometimes called an *equi-join*. Although it's commonplace to base a join on a single equal condition, it is not a requirement. The condition between the two columns is not necessarily equal, nor is the join limited to one condition.

The ON condition of the JOIN behaves much like a WHERE condition, restricting the product of the two joined data sets. WHERE-clause conditions may be flexible and powerful, and the same is true of join conditions. This understanding of the ON condition enables the use of two powerful techniques: Θ (theta) joins and *multiple-condition joins*.

Multiple-Condition Joins

If a join is nothing more than a condition between two data sets, it makes sense that multiple conditions are possible at the join. Multiple-condition joins and Θ joins go hand-in-hand. Without the ability to use multiple-condition joins, Θ joins would be of little value.

If the database schema uses natural primary keys, there are probably tables with composite primary keys, which means queries must use multiple-condition joins.

> **NOTE**
>
> A composite key is a primary key made up of more than one column. A natural key is a primary key made up of meaningful business data rather than an arbitrary sequence number (IDENTITY). Because it can be difficult to find a consistently unique value in business data, composite keys are common when natural keys are used.

Join conditions can refer to any table in the FROM clause, enabling interesting three-way joins:

```
FROM A
  INNER JOIN B
    ON A.col = B.col
  INNER JOIN C
    ON B.col = C.col
    AND A.col = C.col;
```

The first query in the previous section, "Placing the Conditions Within Outer Joins," was a multiple-condition join.

Θ (theta) Joins

A theta join (depicted throughout as Θ) is a join based on a nonequal on condition. In relational theory, conditional operators (=, >, <, >=, <=, <>) are called Θ operators. Although the equals condition is technically a Θ operator, it is commonly used, so only joins with conditions other than equal are referred to as Θ joins.

The Θ condition may be set within Management Studio's Query Designer using the join Properties dialog (refer to Figure 9-7).

Now that this chapter has covered the basics of how to join tables in SQL Server and how the syntax of your join criteria can affect how many results you receive, it's time to cover combining data from multiple queries and subquerying.

Set Difference Queries

A query type that's useful for analyzing the correlation between two data sets is a *set difference* query, sometimes called a *left* (or *right*) *anti-semi join*, which finds the difference between the two data sets based on the conditions of the join. In relational algebra terms, it removes the divisor from the dividend, leaving the difference. This type of query is the inverse of an inner join. Informally, it's called a *find unmatched rows* query.

Set difference queries are great for locating out-of-place data or data that doesn't match, such as rows that are in data set one but not in data set two (see Figure 9-8).

FIGURE 9-8

The set difference query finds data outside the intersection of the two data sets.

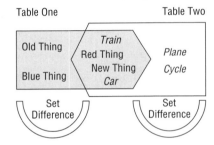

Left Set Difference Query

A *left set difference query* finds all the rows on the left side of the join without a match on the right side of the joins.

Using the `Customer2` and `SalesOrder2` sample tables, the following query locates all rows in `Customer2` without a match in table `SalesOrder2`, removing set two (the divisor) from set one (the dividend). The result is the rows from set one that do not have a match in set two.

The outer join already includes the rows outside the intersection, so to construct a set difference query, use an `OUTER JOIN` with an `IS NULL` restriction on the second data set's primary key. This returns all the rows from `Customer2` that do not have a match in table `SalesOrder2`:

```
USE tempdb;

SELECT c.CustomerID, c.LastName, so.OrderNumber
```

```
     FROM dbo.Customer2 c
     LEFT OUTER JOIN dbo.SalesOrder2 so    ON c.CustomerID = so.Customer
ID WHERE so.OrderNumber IS NULL;
```

Customer2's difference follows:

```
CustomerID     LastName              OrderNumber
----------     ----------------      ----------------
101            Smith                 NULL
103            Reagan                NULL
```

Full Set Difference Queries

You can use a modified version of this technique to clean up bad data during conversions. A *full set difference query* is the logical opposite of an inner join. It identifies all rows outside the intersection from either data set by combining a full outer join with a WHERE restriction that accepts only nulls in either primary key:

```
SELECT c2.CustomerID c2CustomerID, so2.CustomerID so2CustomerID
  FROM dbo.Customer2 c2
  FULL OUTER JOIN dbo.SalesOrder2 so2
    ON c2.CustomerID = so2.CustomerID
 WHERE c2.CustomerID IS NULL
    OR so2.CustomerID IS NULL;
```

The result is every row without a match in the sample tables:

```
c2CustomerID so2CustomerID
------------ -------------
101          NULL
103          NULL
NULL         104
NULL         105
```

Using the result, the bad data can either be remediated or removed.

Using Unions

The UNION operation is different from a join. In relational algebra terms, a union is addition, whereas a join is multiplication. Instead of extending a row horizontally as a join would, the union stacks multiple result sets into a single long table, as shown in Figure 9-9.

FIGURE 9-9

A union vertically appends the result of one SELECT statement to the result of another SELECT statement.

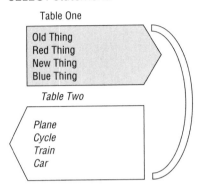

Table One

Old Thing
Red Thing
New Thing
Blue Thing

Table Two

Plane
Cycle
Train
Car

Unions come in three basic flavors: union, intersect union, and difference (or except) union.

Union [All]

The most common type of union by far is the UNION ALL query, which simply adds the individual SELECT's results.

In the following UNION query, the CustomerIDs from Customer2 and the CustomerIDs from SalesOrder2 are appended together into a single list. The first SELECT sets up the overall result, so it supplies the result set column headers. Each individual SELECT generates a result set for the UNION operation, so each SELECT's individual WHERE clause filters data for that SELECT. The final SELECT's ORDER BY then serves as the ORDER BY for the entire unioned results set. The ORDER BY must refer to the columns by either the first SELECT's column names or by the ordinal position of the column:

```
SELECT CustomerID, 'Customer2 - Source' as Source
  FROM dbo.Customer2
UNION ALL
SELECT CustomerID, 'SalesOrder2 - Source'
  FROM dbo.SalesOrder2
 ORDER BY 1;
```

The resulting record set uses the column names from the first SELECT statement:

```
CustomerID  Source
----------  --------------------
101         Customer2 - Source
102         Customer2 - Source
102         SalesOrder2 - Source
```

```
CustomerID   Source
----------   -------------------
103          Customer2 - Source
104          SalesOrder2 - Source
105          SalesOrder2 - Source
```

When constructing unions, you need to understand a few rules:

- UNION returns a distinct list set of values after the included result sets are combined. UNION ALL returns all rows from each result set, regardless of whether duplicates exist.

- Every SELECT must have the same number of columns, and each column must have a compatible data type with the corresponding columns in the other queries.

- The column names, or aliases, are determined by the first SELECT.

- The ORDER BY clause sorts the results of all the SELECTs and must go on the last SELECT, but it uses the column names from the first SELECT.

- Expressions may be added to the SELECT statements to identify the source of the row so long as the column is added to every SELECT.

- The union may be used as part of a SELECT into (a form of the insert verb covered in Chapter 12, "Modifying Data in SQL Server"), but the INTO keyword must go in the first SELECT statement.

Unions aren't limited to two tables. As long as the total number of tables referenced by a query is 256 or fewer, SQL Server handles the load.

Intersection Union

An *intersection union* finds the rows common to both data sets. An inner join finds common rows horizontally, whereas an intersection union finds common rows vertically.

```
SELECT CustomerID
  FROM dbo.Customer2
INTERSECT
SELECT CustomerID
  FROM dbo.SalesOrder2
ORDER BY 1;
```

Result:

```
CustomerID
----------
102
```

An intersection union query is similar to an inner join. The inner join merges the rows horizontally, whereas the intersect union stacks the rows vertically. The intersect must match every column to be included in the result. A twist, however, is that the intersect sees null values as equal and accepts the rows with nulls.

Difference Union/Except

The *difference union* is the union equivalent of the set difference query — it find rows in one data source that are not in the other data source.

SQL Server uses the ANSI Standard keyword EXCEPT to execute a difference union:

```
SELECT CustomerID
  FROM dbo.Customer2
EXCEPT
SELECT CustomerID
  FROM dbo.SalesOrder2
ORDER BY 1;
```

Result:

```
CustomerID
-----------
101
103
```

Whereas a set difference query is interested only in the join conditions (typically the primary and foreign keys) and joins the rows horizontally, a difference union EXCEPT query looks at the entire row (or more specifically, all the columns that participate in the union's SELECT statements).

Now that you know how to combine sets of data, it's time to introduce subqueries into sets. Subqueries come in many different flavors, and while they all have their strengths and weaknesses, none perform well 100 percent of the time. It's important to not only know the different types of subqueries, but also to frequently check to make sure the subquery you picked originally is still the best choice as you increase the scope of what your query is doing. Just because a nested subquery starts out running just as quickly as a CTE for a given query, doesn't mean that it will continue to outperform that CTE as the logic and aggregates become more complex.

Subqueries

A *subquery* is an embedded SQL statement within an outer query. The subquery provides an answer to the outer query in the form of a scalar value, a list of values, or a data set and may be substituted for an expression, list, or table, respectively, within the outer query. Traditionally, a subquery may contain only a SELECT query and not a data-modification query, which explains why subqueries are sometimes referred to as *subselects*.

Three basic forms are possible when building a subquery, depending on the data needs and your favored syntax:

- **Simple subquery:** The simple subquery can be a standalone query and can run by itself. It is executed once, with the result passed to the outer query. Simple subqueries are constructed as normal SELECT queries and placed within parentheses.

- **Common table expression (CTE):** CTEs are a syntactical variation of the simple subquery, similar to a view, which defines the subquery at the beginning of the query using the WITH command. The CTE can then be accessed multiple times within the main query as if it were a view or derived table.

- **Correlated subquery:** This is similar to a simple subquery except that it references at least one column in the outer query, so it cannot run independently. Conceptually, the outer query runs first, and the correlated subquery runs once for every row in the outer query. Physically, the Query Optimizer might generate a more efficient plan.

Simple Subqueries

Simple subqueries are executed in the following order:

1. The simple subquery is executed once.
2. The results are passed to the outer query.
3. The outer query is executed once.

The most basic simple subquery returns a single (scalar) value, which is then used as an expression in the outer query, as follows:

```
SELECT (SELECT 3) AS SubqueryValue;
```

Result:

```
SubqueryValue
-------------
3
```

The subquery (SELECT 3) returns a single value of 3, which is passed to the outer SELECT statement. The outer SELECT statement is then executed as if it were the following:

```
SELECT 3 AS SubqueryValue;
```

Of course, a subquery with only hard-coded values is of little use. Generally, a simple subquery fetches data from a table, for example:

```
USE AdventureWorksLT2012;

SELECT pd.Name as ProductName
  FROM SalesLT.Product pd
 WHERE ProductCategoryID
   IN (Select ProductCategoryID
         FROM SalesLT.ProductCategory
         Where Name = 'Cranksets');
```

To execute this query, SQL Server first evaluates the subquery and returns a value to the outer query:

```
SELECT ProductCategoryID
  FROM SalesLT.ProductCategory
 WHERE Name = 'Cranksets';
```

Result:

```
ProductCategoryID
--------------------
12
```

The outer query then executes as if it were the following:

```
SELECT Name as ProductName
  FROM SalesLT.Product
 WHERE ProductCategoryID
   = 12
```

Result:

```
ProductName
--------------
LL Crankset
ML Crankset
HL Crankset
```

Best Practice

Use a join to pull data from two data sources that can be filtered or manipulated as a whole after the join. If the data must be manipulated prior to the join, try a derived table subquery.

Common Table Expressions

The common table expression (CTE) defines what could be considered a temporary view, which can be referenced just like a view in the same query. Because CTEs may be used in the same ways that simple subqueries are used and they compile exactly like a simple subquery, they are included in the simple subquery heading and show example code CTEs alongside simple subqueries.

The CTE uses the WITH clause, which defines the CTE. Inside the WITH clause is the name, column aliases, and SQL code for the CTE subquery. The main query can then reference the CTE as a data source:

```
WITH CTEName (Column aliases)
AS (Simple Subquery)
SELECT...
  FROM CTEName;
```

The following example is the exact same query as the preceding subquery, only in CTE format. The name of the CTE is CTEQuery. It returns the ProductCategoryID column and uses the exact SELECT statement as the preceding simple subquery:

```
WITH CTEQuery (ProductCategoryID)
  AS (Select ProductCategoryID
        from SalesLT.ProductCategory
        Where Name = 'Cranksets')
```

(A CTE by itself is an incomplete SQL statement. If you try to run the preceding code, a syntax error occurs.)

After the CTE has been defined in the WITH clause, the main portion of the query can reference the CTE using its name as if the CTE were any other table source, such as a table or a view. Following is the complete example, including the CTE and the main query:

```
WITH CTEQuery (ProductCategoryID)
  AS (Select ProductCategoryID
        from SalesLT.ProductCategory
        Where Name = 'Cranksets')
SELECT Name as ProductName
  FROM SalesLT.Product p
    INNER JOIN CTEQuery c
       ON p.ProductCategoryID = c.ProductCategoryID;
```

To include multiple CTEs within the same query, define the CTEs in sequence prior to the main query separated by a comma:

```
WITH
  CTE1Name (column names)
    AS (Simple Subquery),
  CTE2Name (column names)
    AS (Simple Subquery)
```

9

```
SELECT...
  FROM CTE1Name
    INNER JOIN CTE2Name
      ON . . .
```

Although CTEs may include complex queries, they come with two key restrictions:

- CTEs may not be nested. A CTE may not include another CTE.
- The CTE definition may not refer to the referencing query (the one that comes immediately after the CTE). However, a CTE may reference any CTE defined before it if multiple CTEs are defined and comma-separated.

 A CTE is actually just a different syntax for a simple subquery used as a derived table, with one key exception: CTEs can recursively refer to the same table during runtime using a UNION ALL. For more details on using CTEs for hierarchies, turn to Chapter 13, "Working with Hierarchies."

Using Scalar Subqueries

If the subquery returns a single value, it may then be used anywhere inside the SELECT statement where an expression might be used, including column expressions, JOIN conditions, WHERE conditions, or HAVING conditions.

Normal operators (+, =, between, and so on) work with single values returned from a subquery; data-type conversion using the CAST() or CONVERT() functions may be required, however.

The example in the last section used a subquery within a WHERE condition. The following sample query uses a subquery within a column expression to calculate the total sales:

```
SELECT pc.Name as ProductCategoryName ,
     SUM(OrderQty * UnitPrice) AS Sales
  FROM SalesLT.SalesOrderDetail AS sod
    INNER JOIN SalesLT.Product AS pd
      ON sod.ProductID = pd.ProductID
    INNER JOIN SalesLT.ProductCategory AS pc
      ON pd.ProductCategoryID = pc.ProductCategoryID
  GROUP BY pc.Name
  ORDER BY Count(*) DESC;
```

The subquery, SELECT SUM(OrderQty * UnitPrice) from SalesLT .SalesOrderDetail, returns one value: 714002.9136. This number represents all sales in the entire table. The abbreviated result lists the product categories and sales amount:

```
ProductCategoryName    Sales
--------------------   -------------
Touring Bikes          221081.9622
Mountain Bikes         173085.846
```

```
Road Bikes          185513.0436
Mountain Frames     54949.602
Jerseys             7094.1662
Pedals              2996.496
Road Frames         24346.584
. . .
```

Be cautious of overusing scalar subqueries. Because they must execute for each row returned by the main query, a large result set that includes a scalar subquery can result in poor performance.

Using Subqueries as Lists

One common use of subqueries is to provide a list to an IN operator. In this scenario, a single column is returned from the subquery with one or more values contained in it. The IN operator returns a value of true if the column value is found anywhere in the list supplied by the subquery.

A list subquery serves as a dynamic means to generate the WHERE ... IN condition list:

```
SELECT FirstName, LastName
  FROM dbo.Contact
 WHERE Region IN (Subquery that returns a list of states);
```

Nested Subqueries

Subqueries can be nested, and just as the simple subquery can execute before the outer main query, nested subqueries execute from the inside out. The most inner subquery executes first, passing its results up to the next most inner subquery and then executes it. This pattern repeats until the final outer query executes.

```
SELECT Name as ProductName
  FROM SalesLT.Product
 WHERE ProductID IN
    (SELECT ProductID
      FROM SalesLT.SalesOrderDetail
     WHERE SalesOrderID IN
     (SELECT SalesOrderID  -- Find the Orders with vests
       FROM SalesLT.SalesOrderDetail
      WHERE ProductID IN
        (SELECT ProductID
          FROM SalesLT.Product
         WHERE ProductCategoryID =
            -- 1. Find the Vests category
            (Select ProductCategoryID
              FROM SalesLT.ProductCategory
             Where Name = 'Vests' ) ) ) );
```

9

Using Subqueries as Tables

In the same way that you can use a view in the place of a table within the FROM clause of a SELECT statement, a subquery in the form of a *derived table* can replace a table, provided the subquery has an alias. This technique is powerful and is often used to break a difficult query problem down into smaller bite-size chunks.

A derived table solution is quite useful when you need to aggregate data before querying for the result set:

```
SELECT P1.Name,
       a.ProductID ,
       a.ProductTotal ,
       a.ModifiedDate
  FROM SalesLT.Product p1
  JOIN (SELECT sod.ProductID,
               SUM(sod.LineTotal) AS 'ProductTotal',
               sod.ModifiedDate
          FROM SalesLT.SalesOrderDetail sod
          JOIN SalesLT.Product p
            ON sod.ProductID = p.ProductID
          JOIN SalesLT.ProductCategory pc
            ON p.ProductCategoryID = pc.ProductCategoryID
         WHERE pc.Name = 'Vests'
         GROUP BY sod.ProductID, sod.ModifiedDate
       ) a
    ON p1.ProductID = a.ProductID
```

 For more information about aggregate functions and the GROUP BY keyword, see Chapter 10, "Aggregating, Windowing, and Ranking Data."

All, Some, and Any

Though not as popular as IN, three other options are worth examining when using a subquery in a WHERE clause. Each provides a twist on how items in the subquery are matched with the WHERE clause's test value. ALL must be true for every value. SOME and ANY, which are equivalent keywords, must be true for some of the values in the subquery.

The next query demonstrates a simple ALL subquery. In this case, select returns true if 1 is less than every value in the subquery:

```
SELECT 'True' as 'AllTest'
  WHERE 1 < ALL
    (SELECT a
       FROM
         (VALUES
           (2),
           (3),
```

```
                                (5),
                                (7),
                                (9)
                          ) AS ValuesTable(a)
                );
```

Result:

```
AllTest
--------------
True
```

Row-Value Constructors

The previous sample uses a feature introduced in SQL Server 2008, row-value constructors. This structure enables you to hard-code values as a result set. `ValuesTable` is a derived table, but there is no `SELECT`. Instead, the `VALUES` clause was used to specify the contents of the table.

Be careful with the `ALL` condition if the subquery might return a `null`. A `null` value in the subquery results forces the `ALL` to return a `false` because it's impossible to prove that the test is `true` for every value in the subquery if one of those values is unknown.

In this query, the last value is changed from a 9 to `null`, and the query no longer returns true:

```
SELECT 'True' AS 'AllTest'
   WHERE 1 < ALL
     (SELECT a
        FROM
            (VALUES
               (2),
               (3),
               (5),
               (7),
               (null)
            ) AS ValuesTable(a)
     );
```

Result (empty result set):

```
AllTest
--------------
```

The `SOME` and `ANY` conditional tests return `true` if the condition is met for any values in the subquery result set. For example:

```
SELECT 'True' as 'SomeTest'
```

```
WHERE 5 = SOME
  (SELECT a
     FROM
        (VALUES
           (2),
           (3),
           (5),
           (7),
           (9)
        ) AS MyTable(a)
  );
```

Result:

```
SomeTest
--------------
True
```

The ANY and SOME conditions are similar to the IN condition. In fact = ANY and = SOME are exactly like IN. ANY and SOME conditions have the extra functionality to testing for other conditional tests such as <, <=, >, =>, and <>.

Correlated Subqueries

Correlated subqueries sound impressive, but they actually aren't. They are used in the same ways that simple subqueries are used; the difference being that correlated subqueries reference columns in the outer query. They do this by referencing the name or alias of a table in the outer query, to reference the outer query. This capability to limit the subquery by the outer query makes these queries flexible. Because correlated subqueries can reference the outer query, they are especially useful for complex WHERE conditions.

Correlating in the WHERE Clause

The capability to reference the outer query also means that correlated subqueries won't run by themselves because the reference to the outer query would cause the query to fail. The logical execution order follows:

1. The outer query is executed once.
2. The subquery is executed once for every row in the outer query, substituting the values from the outer query into each execution of the subquery.
3. The subquery's results are integrated into the result set.

If the outer query returns 100 rows, SQL Server executes the logical equivalent of 101 queries — one for the outer query and one subquery for every row returned by the outer query. In practice, the SQL Server Query Optimizer tries to come up with a plan that is more efficient than this. To explore correlated subqueries, the next query, based on the AdventureWorksLT2012 sample database, uses one to compare list prices to average prices of items in a product category.

The query asks, "Which products have a list price that is less than the average sale price for all items in a product category?" The query uses a correlated subquery to determine the average sales price of items in a product category. The subquery is executed for every row in the Product table, using the outer query's named range, p, to reference the outer query. If a ProductCategoryID match exists for that row, the ListPrice for the ProductID is compared to the calculated average price. If the ListPrice is less than the average price sold, the condition is true and the row is accepted into the result set:

```
SELECT p.ProductID , p.ProductCategoryID , p.Name
  FROM SalesLT.Product p
 WHERE ListPrice <
 (SELECT
     SUM(OrderQty * UnitPrice) /Sum(sod.OrderQty)
 AS AveragePricePerItemInCategory
  FROM SalesLT.SalesOrderDetail AS sod
    INNER JOIN SalesLT.Product AS pd
      ON sod.ProductID = pd.ProductID
    INNER JOIN SalesLT.ProductCategory AS pc
      ON pd.ProductCategoryID = pc.ProductCategoryID
     WHERE pc.ProductCategoryID = p.ProductCategoryID
  GROUP BY pc.Name) ;
```

Result:

ProductID	ProductCategoryID	ProductName	ListPrice
722	18	LL Road Frame - Black, 58	337.22
723	18	LL Road Frame - Black, 60	337.22
724	18	LL Road Frame - Black, 62	337.22
725	18	LL Road Frame - Red, 44	337.22
726	18	LL Road Frame - Red, 48	337.22
727	18	LL Road Frame - Red, 52	337.22
728	18	LL Road Frame - Red, 58	337.22
729	18	LL Road Frame - Red, 60	337.22
730	18	LL Road Frame - Red, 62	337.22
736	18	LL Road Frame - Black, 44	337.22
737	18	LL Road Frame - Black, 48	337.22
738	18	LL Road Frame - Black, 52	337.22
759	6	Road-650 Red, 58	782.99
760	6	Road-650 Red, 60	782.99

Correlating a Derived Table Using Apply

In a WHERE clause, a subquery can be correlated, referring up to the outer query. However, a derived table subquery in the FROM clause is not allowed to reference the outer query if it is part of a JOIN. However, the CROSS APPLY or OUTER APPLY method of including a subquery in the FROM clause enables you to pass data from the outer query into the derived table subquery.

First, set up some sample data:

```
USE tempdb;

CREATE TABLE TableA (ID INT);

INSERT INTO TableA(ID)
VALUES (1),(2);

CREATE TABLE TableB (ID INT);

INSERT INTO TableB(ID)
VALUES (1),(3);
```

The following query uses a CROSS APPLY to pass every row from the outer query to the derived table subquery. The subquery then filters its rows to those that match IDs. The CROSS APPLY returns every row from the outer query that had a match in the subquery. Functionally, it's the equivalent to an inner join between TableA and TableB:

```
SELECT B.ID AS Bid, A.ID AS Aid
  FROM TableB AS B
    CROSS APPLY
      (Select ID from TableA
         where TableA.ID = B.ID) AS A;
```

Result:

```
Bid         Aid
----------- -----------
1           1
```

The next query uses the same derived table subquery but changes to an OUTER APPLY to include all rows from the outer query. This query is the same as a left outer join between TableA and TableB:

```
SELECT B.ID AS Bid, A.ID AS Aid
  FROM TableB AS B
    OUTER APPLY
      (Select ID  from TableA
         where TableA.ID = B.ID) AS A;
```

Result:

```
ID          ID
----------- -----------
1           1
3           NULL
```

Summary

Merging data is the heart of SQL, and it shows in the depth of relational algebra as well as the power and flexibility of SQL. From natural joins to exotic joins, SQL is excellent at selecting sets of data from multiple sources.

The challenge for the SQL Server database developer is to master the theory of relational algebra and the many T-SQL techniques to effectively manipulate the data.

Manipulating data with SELECT is one of the core benefits of SQL Server. Although joins are the most natural method to work with relational data, subqueries are an effective tool for manipulating and querying data as well.

This chapter established the foundation for working with SQL, covering the SELECT statement, expressions, joins, unions, subqueries, and CTEs.

9

Aggregating, Windowing, and Ranking Data

IN THIS CHAPTER

Understanding Basic Aggregations

Using SQL Server Aggregation Functions

Customizing Aggregation Sets

Understanding Windowing

Ranking Functions

Information is the foundation of most organizational decisions. In its raw form, that data is meaningless and offers little value to an information wonk or data analyst; not until the data is summarized or grouped is it considered useful information. Although summarization and analysis can certainly be performed with other tools, such as Reporting Services, Analysis Services, PowerPivot, or an external tool such as SAS, SQL is a set-based language, and a fair amount of summarizing and grouping can be performed well within the SQL SELECT statement.

SQL excels at calculating sums, max values, and averages for the entire data set or for segments of data. In addition, the product of SQL queries can be as simple as a table to a complex pivot table that includes subtotals and totals. In this chapter you explore different ways to group, gather, and summarize data within SQL Server.

Aggregating Data

When a T-SQL query is written that includes an aggregate function, it returns a single row of computed summarized values or values grouped by other columns in the query. More complex aggregate queries can slice the selected rows into subsets and then summarize every subset. Types of aggregate calculations range from totaling the data to performing basic statistical operations. In the logical order of the SQL query, the aggregate functions (indicated by the Summing function in the diagram) occur following the FROM clause and the WHERE filters. This means that the data can be assembled and filtered prior to being summarized without needing to use a subquery; although, sometimes a subquery is still needed to build more complex aggregate queries.

Basic Aggregations

SQL includes a set of *aggregate functions*, listed in Table 10-1, which you can use as expressions in the SELECT statement to return summary data.

TABLE 10-1 **Basic Aggregate Functions**

Aggregate Function	Data Type Supported	Description
sum()	Numeric	Totals all the non-null values in the column.
avg()	Numeric	Averages all the non-null values in the column. The result has the same data type as the input, so the input is often converted to a higher precision, such as avg(cast col as float).
min()	Numeric, string, datetime	Returns the smallest number or the first datetime or the first string according to the current collation from the column.
max()	Numeric, string, datetime	Returns the largest number or the last datetime or the last string according to the current collation from the column.
Count [_big] (*)	Any data type (row-based)	Performs a simple count of all the rows in the result set up to 2,147,483,647. The count_big() variation uses the bigint data type and can handle up to 2^63-1 rows.
Count [_big] ([distinct] column)	Any data type (row-based)	Performs a simple count of all the rows with non-null values in the column in the result set up to 2,147,483,647. The distinct option eliminates duplicate rows. Does not count blobs.
Var	float	Returns the statistical variance of non-null values of a numeric expression.

Aggregate Function	Data Type Supported	Description
StDev	Float	Returns the statistical standard deviation of all non-null values of a numeric expression.
Checksum_Agg	Int	Returns the checksum value of all non-values of an integer expression.

The simplest aggregate query would be to summarize a single value in a table. Instead of returning the actual rows from the table, the query returns a summary row. In the following query the summary row is a count of all rows in the Sales.SalesOrderHeader table from the AdventureWorks database:

```
USE AdventureWorks;


SELECT COUNT(*) AS NumRows
    FROM Sales.SalesOrderHeader;
```
Result:

```
NumRows
-----------
31465
```

Because aggregate functions are expressions, their results have null column names. In some cases null columns names cause problems for applications and other types of data access clients. Therefore, a best practice is to use an alias to name the column in the results.

Because SQL now returns information from a set, rather than building a record set of rows, as soon as a query includes an aggregate function, every column (in the column list, in the expression, or in the ORDER BY) must participate in an aggregate function. This makes sense because if a query returned the total number of order sales, then it could not return a single order number on the summary row.

As mentioned (refer to Table 10-1), T-SQL also includes an array of mathematical aggregate functions. The following query demonstrates the use of the SUM(), AVG(), MIN(), and MAX() functions on the TotalDue column of the Sales.SalesOrderHeader table in the AdventureWorks database:

```
USE AdventureWorks;

SELECT
    SUM(TotalDue) AS [SUM],
    AVG(TotalDue) AS [AVG],
    MIN(TotalDue) AS [MIN],
    MAX(TotalDue) AS [MAX]
```

10

```
FROM Sales.SalesOrderHeader
```

Results:

Sum	Avg	Min	Max
123216786.1159	3915.9951	1.5183	187487.825

Aggregates, Averages, and Nulls

Aggregate functions ignore nulls, which creates a special situation when calculating averages. A SUM() or AVG() aggregate function does not error out on a null, but simply skips the row with a null. For this reason, a SUM()/COUNT(*) calculation may provide a different result from an AVG() function. The COUNT(*) function includes every row, whereas the AVG() function might divide using a smaller count of rows.

To test this behavior, the next query uses two methods to calculate the average amount, and each method generates a different result:

```
USE AdventureWorks;

ALTER TABLE Sales.SalesPersonQuotaHistory
    ALTER COLUMN SalesQuota money null
GO

UPDATE Sales.SalesPersonQuotaHistory
SET SalesQuota = NULL
WHERE BusinessEntityID = 274
AND QuotaDate = '2005-07-01 00:00:00.000'
SELECT
    AVG(SalesQuota) AS [Avg Function],
    SUM(SalesQuota) /COUNT(*) AS [Manual AVG]
FROM Sales.SalesPersonQuotaHistory
```

Result:

Avg Function	Manual AVG
590654.3209	587030.6748

```
Warning: Null value is eliminated by an aggregate or other
        SET operation.
```

The first column performs the standard AVG() aggregate function and divides the sum of the amount (95686000) by the number of rows with a non-null value for the amount (162).

The SUM(AMOUNT)/COUNT(*) calculation in column two actually divides 95686000 by the total number of rows in the table (163), yielding a different answer.

Grouping Within a Result Set

Aggregate functions are all well and good, but how often do you need a total for an entire table? Most aggregate requirements include a date range, department, type of sale, region, or the like. That presents a problem. If the only tool to restrict the aggregate function were the WHERE clause, then database developers would waste hours replicating the same query, or writing a lot of dynamic SQL queries and the code to execute the aggregate queries in sequence.

Fortunately, aggregate functions are complemented by the GROUP BY function, which automatically partitions the data set into subsets based on the values in certain columns. When the data set is divided into subgroups, the aggregate functions are performed on each subgroup.

Simple Groupings

Using the GROUP BY clause to complement the aggregate functions provides the ability to include descriptive columns to the result. For example, in the following query the GROUP BY clause is included in the query to slice the data by Country or Region Code:

```
USE AdventureWorks;

SELECT
    st.CountryRegionCode,
    SUM(TotalDue) TotalSalesDue
FROM Sales.SalesOrderHeader soh
INNER JOIN Sales.SalesTerritory st
    ON soh.TerritoryID = st.TerritoryID
GROUP BY
    st.CountryRegionCode
```

Result:

```
CountryRegionCode TotalSalesDue
----------------- ---------------------
AU                11814376.0952
CA                18398929.188
DE                5479819.5755
FR                8119749.346
GB                8574048.7082
US                70829863.203
```

The first column of this query returns the CountryRegionCode column. Although this column does not have an aggregate function, it still participates within the aggregate because that's the column by which the query is grouped. It may therefore be included in the result set because, by definition, there can be only a single country or region code value in each group. Each row in the result set summarizes one country or region code, and the aggregate functions now calculate total sales due for each country or region code.

SQL is not limited to grouping by a column. You can group by an expression, but the exact same expression must be used in the SELECT list, not the individual columns used to generate the expression.

Nor is SQL limited to grouping by a single column or expression. Grouping by multiple columns and expressions is quite common. The following query is an example of grouping by one expression that calculates the year number and the country or region code:

10

```
USE AdventureWorks;

SELECT
    Year(DueDate) DueYear,st.[Group],
    SUM(TotalDue) TotalSalesAmount
FROM Sales.SalesOrderHeader soh
INNER JOIN Sales.SalesTerritory st
    ON soh.TerritoryID = st.TerritoryID
GROUP BY
    Year(DueDate) ,st.[Group]
ORDER BY Year(DueDate)
Result:
DueYear     Group               TotalSalesAmount
----------- ------------------- ----------------------
2005        Europe              726467.4426
2005        North America       10304264.4596
2005        Pacific             1353785.5482
2006        Europe              3686361.9651
2006        North America       28468091.6318
2006        Pacific             2388704.7024
2007        Europe              9954422.8419
2007        North America       32492706.9613
2007        Pacific             4232931.026
2008        Europe              7806365.3801
2008        North America       17963729.3383
2008        Pacific             3838954.8186
```

> **NOTE**
> For the purposes of a GROUP BY, null values are considered equal to other nulls and are grouped together into a single result row.

Grouping Sets

Normally, SQL Server groups by every unique combination of values in every column listed in the GROUP BY clause. The ability of grouping sets is a variation of what was introduced in SQL Server 2008. With grouping sets, a summation row is generated for each unique value in each set. You can think of grouping sets as executing several GROUP BY queries (one for each grouping set) and then combining, or unioning, the results.

For example, the following two queries produce the same result. The first query uses two GROUP BY queries which are combined into one result set using a UNION; the second query uses the new grouping set feature:

```
USE AdventureWorks;

SELECT
```

```
        NULL AS DueYear,
        st.[Group],
        SUM(TotalDue) TotalSalesAmount
FROM Sales.SalesOrderHeader soh
INNER JOIN Sales.SalesTerritory st
    ON soh.TerritoryID = st.TerritoryID
GROUP BY
    st.[Group]
UNION
SELECT
Year(DueDate) DueYear,
    NULL [Group],
        SUM(TotalDue) TotalSalesAmount
FROM Sales.SalesOrderHeader soh
INNER JOIN Sales.SalesTerritory st
    ON soh.TerritoryID = st.TerritoryID
GROUP BY
    Year(DueDate)


SELECT
    Year(DueDate) DueYear,st.[Group],
        SUM(TotalDue) TotalSalesAmount
FROM Sales.SalesOrderHeader soh
INNER JOIN Sales.SalesTerritory st
    ON soh.TerritoryID = st.TerritoryID
GROUP BY
    GROUPING SETS(
    Year(DueDate) ,st.[Group])
```

Result (same for both queries):

```
DueYear       Group            TotalSalesAmount
-----------   ---------------  ----------------------
NULL          Europe           2173617.6297
NULL          North America    89228792.391
NULL          Pacific          11814376.0952
2005          NULL             12384517.4504
2006          NULL             34543158.2993
2007          NULL             46680060.8292
2008          NULL             9609049.537
```

The `Grouping Sets` syntax is considerably more simple and precise. It provides the ability to directly specify the needed aggregations.

Filtering Grouped Results

When combined with grouping, filtering can be a problem. Are the row restrictions applied before the GROUP BY or after the GROUP BY? Some databases use nested queries to properly filter before or after the GROUP BY. SQL, however, uses the HAVING clause to filter the groups. At the beginning of this chapter, you saw the simplified order of the SQL SELECT statement's execution. A more complete order is as follows:

1. The FROM clause assembles the data from the data sources.
2. The WHERE clause restricts the rows based on the conditions.
3. The GROUP BY clause assembles subsets of data.
4. Aggregate functions are calculated.
5. The HAVING clause filters the subsets of data.
6. Any remaining expressions are calculated.
7. The ORDER BY sorts the results.

The following query removes from the analysis any grouping having a sum of greater than or equal to 10 million:

```
SELECT
    st.CountryRegionCode,
    SUM(TotalDue) TotalSalesAmount
FROM Sales.SalesOrderHeader soh
INNER JOIN Sales.SalesTerritory st
    ON soh.TerritoryID = st.TerritoryID
GROUP BY
    st.CountryRegionCode
HAVING SUM(TotalDue) > 10000000
```

Result :

```
CountryRegionCode  TotalSalesAmount
-----------------  --------------------
AU                 11814376.0952
CA                 18398929.188
US                 70829863.203
```

Without the HAVING clause, all Countries or Regions will be included in the results.

Windowing and Ranking

T-SQLs windowing and ranking function provides developers with the ability to shed new light on the same old data. Windowing as it relates to SQL Server is not related in any way to Microsoft Windows. Instead, it refers to ways of working with subsets of data. Windowing, using the OVER() clause, provides a new perspective of the data. The ranking functions use the new perspective to provide additional ways for manipulating the data.

Although these two methods are similar to aggregating data, they should be thought of as a different technique and technology. This is because they work within an independent sort order separate from the query's sort order.

Windowing

As previously stated, windowing in a T-SQL query creates a new perspective of the data. Even though windowing and ranking are placed together in the T-SQL syntax, the window must be established prior to the ranking functions.

The OVER() Clause

The OVER() clause creates a new window on the data. Consider it as a new perspective, or independent ordering of the rows, which may or may not be the same as the sort order of the ORDER BY clause. In a way, the windowing capability creates an alternative flow to the query with its own sort order and ranking functions.

The complete syntax is OVER(ORDER BY columns). The columns may be any available column or expression, just like the ORDER BY clause; but unlike the ORDER BY clause, the OVER() clause won't accept a column ordinal position, for example, 1, 2. Also, like the ORDER BY clause, it can be ascending (asc), the default, or descending (desc); and it can be sorted by multiple columns.

The window's sort order can take advantage of indexes and can be fast, even if the sort order is different from the main query's sort order.

In the following query, the OVER() clause creates a separate view to the data sorted by ShipDate (ignore the ROW_NUMBER() function for now):

```
USE AdventureWorks
GO
SELECT
    ROW_NUMBER() OVER(Order By ShipDate) AS RowNumber,
        PurchaseOrderID,
        ShipDate
FROM Purchasing.PurchaseOrderHeader
WHERE EmployeeID = 259
ORDER BY RowNumber
```

Result (abbreviated; the ShipDate does not include time information, so the results might vary within a given date):

```
RowNumber              PurchaseOrderID ShipDate
-------------------- --------------- ------------------------
1                      9               2006-01-23 00:00:00.000
2                      19              2006-01-24 00:00:00.000
3                      29              2006-02-17 00:00:00.000
```

4	49	2006-03-01 00:00:00.000
5	59	2006-03-05 00:00:00.000
6	69	2006-03-06 00:00:00.000
7	79	2006-03-21 00:00:00.000

SQL Server 2012 introduced several new arguments that you can use with the OVER() clause. Varying combinations of the new arguments assist T-SQL in limiting the rows with a partition. The section "New T-SQL Features in SQL Server 2012," later in this chapter explains all arguments and illustrates their uses.

Partitioning Within the Window

The OVER() clause normally creates a single sort order, but it can divide the windowed data into partitions, which are similar to groups in an aggregate GROUP BY query. This is dramatically powerful because the ranking functions can restart with every partition.

The next query example uses the OVER() clause to create a sort order of the query results by ShipDate, and then partitions the data by YEAR() and MONTH().The syntax is the opposite of the logical flow. The PARTITION BY goes before the ORDER BY within the OVER() clause:

```
USE AdventureWorks
GO
SELECT
        ROW_NUMBER()
            OVER(
                PARTITION BY YEAR(ShipDate), Month(ShipDate)
                Order By ShipDate
            )
        AS RowNumber,
        PurchaseOrderID,
        ShipDate
FROM Purchasing.PurchaseOrderHeader
WHERE EmployeeID = 259
ORDER BY RowNumber
```

Result (abbreviated):

RowNumber	PurchaseOrderID	ShipDate
1	9	2006-01-23 00:00:00.000
2	19	2006-01-24 00:00:00.000
1	29	2006-02-17 00:00:00.000
1	49	2006-03-01 00:00:00.000
2	59	2006-03-05 00:00:00.000
3	69	2006-03-06 00:00:00.000
4	79	2006-03-21 00:00:00.000

As expected, the windowed sort (in this case, the RowNumber column) restarts with every new month.

Ranking Functions

The windowing capability (the OVER() clause) by itself doesn't create any query output columns; that's where the *ranking functions* come into play:

- row_number
- rank
- dense_rank
- ntile

Just to be explicit, the ranking functions all require the windowing function. These functions add a rank to each row of the subset of data. The ranking of the rows depends on which function that is specified.

You can use all the normal aggregate functions — SUM(), MIN(), MAX(), COUNT(*), and so on — as ranking functions.

Row number() Function

The ROW_NUMBER() function generates an on-the-fly auto-incrementing integer according to the sort order of the OVER() clause. It's similar to Oracle's RowNum column.

The row number function simply numbers the rows in the query result; there's absolutely no correlation with any physical address or absolute row number. This is important because in a relational database, row position, number, and order have no meaning. It also means that as rows are added or deleted from the underlying data source, the row numbers for the query results will change. In addition, if there are sets of rows with the same values in all ordering columns, then their order is undefined, so their row numbers may change between two executions even if the underlying data does not change.

One common practical use of the ROW_NUMBER() function is to filter by the row number values for pagination. For example, a query that easily produces rows 21–40 would be useful for returning the second page of data for a web page. Just be aware that the rows in the pages may change — typically, this grabs data from a temp table.

It would seem that the natural way to build a row number pagination query would be to simply add the OVER() clause and ROW_NUMBER() function to the WHERE clause:

```
USE AdventureWorks
GO
SELECT
    ROW_NUMBER() OVER(ORDER BY PurchaseOrderID, ShipDate)
        AS RowNumber,
        PurchaseOrderID,
        ShipDate
FROM Purchasing.PurchaseOrderHeader
```

10

```
WHERE EmployeeID = 259 AND ROW_NUMBER() OVER(ORDER BY
    PurchaseOrderID,
    ShipDate)
BETWEEN 21 AND 40
ORDER BY RowNumber
```

Result:

```
Msg 4108, Level 15, State 1, Line 4
Windowed functions can only appear in the SELECT or ORDER BY clauses.
```

Because the WHERE clause occurs early in the query processing — often in the query operation that actually reads the data from the data source — and the OVER() clause occurs late in the query processing, the WHERE clause doesn't yet know about the windowed sort of the data or the ranking function. The WHERE clause can't possibly filter by the generated row number.

There is a simple solution: Embed the windowing and ranking functionality in a subquery or common table expression:

```
USE AdventureWorks
GO
WITH Results
AS
(
    SELECT
        ROW_NUMBER() OVER(ORDER BY PurchaseOrderID, ShipDate)
            AS RowNumber,
        PurchaseOrderID,
        ShipDate
    FROM Purchasing.PurchaseOrderHeader
)
SELECT *
FROM Results
WHERE RowNumber BETWEEN 21 AND 40
```

Result:

```
RowNumber              PurchaseOrderID ShipDate
---------------------  --------------- ------------------------
21                     21              2006-01-24 00:00:00.000
22                     22              2006-01-24 00:00:00.000
23                     23              2006-01-24 00:00:00.000
24                     24              2006-01-24 00:00:00.000
25                     25              2006-01-24 00:00:00.000
26                     26              2006-01-24 00:00:00.000
27                     27              2006-01-24 00:00:00.000
28                     28              2006-01-24 00:00:00.000
29                     29              2006-02-17 00:00:00.000
30                     30              2006-02-17 00:00:00.000
31                     31              2006-02-17 00:00:00.000
```

32	32	2006-02-17 00:00:00.000
33	33	2006-02-25 00:00:00.000
34	34	2006-02-25 00:00:00.000
35	35	2006-02-25 00:00:00.000
36	36	2006-02-25 00:00:00.000
37	37	2006-02-25 00:00:00.000
38	38	2006-02-25 00:00:00.000
39	39	2006-02-25 00:00:00.000
40	40	2006-02-25 00:00:00.000

The second query in this chapter, in the "Partitioning Within the Window" section, showed how grouping the sort order of the window generated row numbers that started over with every new partition.

SQL Server 2012 introduces two new arguments, OFFSET and FETCH, to the ORDER BY clause that further simplifies paging in T-SQL. Although they are two operators, they must be used together for paging to correctly work. The following query illustrates their use:

```
USE AdventureWorks
GO
SELECT
    ROW_NUMBER() OVER(ORDER BY PurchaseOrderID, ShipDate) AS RowNumber,
    PurchaseOrderID,
    ShipDate
FROM Purchasing.PurchaseOrderHeader
ORDER BY RowNumber
OFFSET 20 ROWS
FETCH NEXT 20 ROWS ONLY
```

Result:

RowNumber	PurchaseOrderID	ShipDate
21	21	2006-01-24 00:00:00.000
22	22	2006-01-24 00:00:00.000
23	23	2006-01-24 00:00:00.000
24	24	2006-01-24 00:00:00.000
25	25	2006-01-24 00:00:00.000
26	26	2006-01-24 00:00:00.000
27	27	2006-01-24 00:00:00.000
28	28	2006-01-24 00:00:00.000
29	29	2006-02-17 00:00:00.000
30	30	2006-02-17 00:00:00.000
31	31	2006-02-17 00:00:00.000
32	32	2006-02-17 00:00:00.000
33	33	2006-02-25 00:00:00.000
34	34	2006-02-25 00:00:00.000
35	35	2006-02-25 00:00:00.000
36	36	2006-02-25 00:00:00.000

10

37	37	2006-02-25 00:00:00.000
38	38	2006-02-25 00:00:00.000
39	39	2006-02-25 00:00:00.000
40	40	2006-02-25 00:00:00.000

The results are the same as the previous query. However, the need for a subquery or common table expression has been removed. Using OFFSET and FETCH as a paging mechanism requires running the query only once for each page. In the above query the OFFSET clause specifies the number of rows to skip before the results of the query is returned. The FETCH clause specifies the number of rows to return after the OFFSET.

RANK() and DENSE_RANK() Functions

The RANK() and DENSE_RANK() functions return values as if the rows were competing according to the windowed sort order. Any ties are grouped together with the same ranked value. For example, if Frank and Jim both tied for third place, then they would both receive a RANK() value of 3.

Using sales data from AdventureWorks, there are ties for least sold products, which makes it a good table to play with RANK() and DENSE_RANK(). ProductID's 943 and 911 tie for third place and ProductID's 927 and 898 tie for fourth or fifth place depending on how ties are counted:

```
-- Least Sold Products:
USE AdventureWorks
GO

SELECT ProductID, COUNT(*) as [Count]
  FROM Sales.SalesOrderDetail
  GROUP BY ProductID
  ORDER BY COUNT(*);
```

Result (abbreviated):

```
ProductID   count
----------- -----------
897         2
942         5
943         6
911         6
927         9
898         9
744         13
903         14
...
```

Examining the sales data using windowing and the RANK() function returns the ranking values:

```
USE AdventureWorks
GO

SELECT ProductID, SalesCount,
    RANK() OVER (ORDER BY SalesCount) as [Rank],
    DENSE_RANK() OVER(Order By SalesCount) as [DenseRank]
  FROM (SELECT ProductID, COUNT(*) as SalesCount
        FROM Sales.SalesOrderDetail
        GROUP BY ProductID
      ) AS Q
    ORDER BY [Rank];
```

Result (abbreviated):

ProductID	SalesCount	Rank	DenseRank
897	2	1	1
942	5	2	2
943	6	3	3
911	6	3	3
927	9	5	4
898	9	5	4
744	13	7	5
903	14	8	6
...			

This example perfectly demonstrates the difference between RANK() and DENSE_RANK(). RANK() counts each tie as a ranked row. In this example, Product IDs 943 and 911 both tie for third place but consume the third and fourth row in the ranking, placing ProductID 927 in fifth place.

DENSE_RANK() handles ties differently. Tied rows consume only a single value in the ranking, so the next rank is the next place in the ranking order. No ranks are skipped. In the previous query, ProductID 927 is in fourth place using DENSE_RANK().

Just as with the ROW_NUMBER() function, you can use RANK() and DENSE_RANK() with a partitioned OVER() clause. You could partition the previous example by product category to rank product sales with each category.

Ntile() Function

The fourth ranking function organizes the rows into *n* number of groups, called *tiles*, and returns the tile number. For example, if the result set has 10 rows, then NTILE(5) would split the 10 rows into five equally sized tiles with 2 rows in each tile in the order of the OVER() clause's ORDER BY.

If the number of rows is not evenly divisible by the number of tiles, then the tiles get the extra row. For example, for 74 rows and 10 tiles, the first 4 tiles get 8 rows each, and tiles

5 through 10 get 7 rows each. This can skew the results for smaller data sets. For example, 15 rows into 10 tiles would place 10 rows in the lower 5 tiles and only place 5 tiles in the upper 5 tiles. But for larger data sets — splitting a few hundred rows into 100 tiles, for example — it works great.

This rule also applies if there are fewer rows than tiles. The rows are not spread across all tiles; instead, the tiles are filled until the rows are consumed. For example, if five rows are split using NTILE(10), the result set would not use tiles 1, 3, 5, 7, and 9, but instead show tiles 1, 2, 3, 4, and 5.

A common real-world example of NTILE() is the percentile scoring used in college entrance exams.

The following query first calculates the AdventureWorks products' sales quantity in the subquery. The outer query then uses the OVER() clause to sort by the sales count, and the NTILE(100) to calculate the percentile according to the sales count:

```
USE AdventureWorks
GO

SELECT ProductID, SalesCount,
    NTILE(100) OVER (ORDER BY SalesCount) as Percentile
  FROM (SELECT ProductID, COUNT(*) as SalesCount
          FROM Sales.SalesOrderDetail
          GROUP BY ProductID
        ) AS Q
  ORDER BY Percentile DESC;
```

Result (abbreviated):

```
ProductID    SalesCount   Percentile
-----------  -----------  --------------------
712          3382         100
870          4688         100
921          3095         99
873          3354         99
707          3083         98
711          3090         98
922          2376         97
...
830          33           5
888          39           5
902          20           4
950          28           4
946          30           4
744          13           3
903          14           3
919          16           3
```

911	6	2
927	9	2
898	9	2
897	2	1
942	5	1
943	6	1

Like the other three ranking functions, you can use NTILE() with a partitioned OVER() clause. Similar to the ranking example, you could partition the previous example by product category to generate percentiles within each category.

Aggregate Functions

SQL query functions all fit together like a magnificent puzzle. A fine example is how windowing can use not only the four ranking functions — ROW_NUMBER(), RANK(), DENSE_RANK(), and NTILE() — but also the standard aggregate functions: COUNT(*), MIN(), MAX(), and so on.

Usually the aggregate functions fit well within a normal aggregate query; however, following is an example of using the SUM() aggregate function in a window to calculate the total sales order count for each product subcategory. Using that result from the window, you can calculate the percentage of sales orders for each product within its subcategory:

```
USE AdventureWorks
GO

SELECT ProductID, Product,  SalesCount,
  NTILE(100) OVER (ORDER BY SalesCount)  as Percentile,
  SubCat,
  CAST(CAST(SalesCount AS NUMERIC(9,2))
    / SUM(SalesCount) OVER(Partition BY SubCat)
    * 100 AS NUMERIC (4,1)) AS SubPer
  FROM (SELECT P.ProductID, P.[Name] AS Product,
         PSC.Name AS SubCat, COUNT(*) as SalesCount
         FROM Sales.SalesOrderDetail AS SOD
           JOIN Production.Product AS P
             ON SOD.ProductID = P.ProductID
           JOIN Production.ProductSubcategory PSC
             ON P.ProductSubcategoryID = PSC.ProductSubcategoryID
         GROUP BY PSC.Name, P.[Name], P.ProductID
       ) Q
  ORDER BY Percentile DESC
```

10

Result (abbreviated):

```
Product
      ID Product                 SalesCount  Percentile SubCat               SubPer
------- ----------------------- ----------- ---------- ----------------    ------
   870  Water Bottle - 30 oz.    4688        100        Bottles and Cages 55.6
   712  AWC Logo Cap             3382        100        Caps              100.0
   921  Mountain Tire Tube       3095        99         Tires and Tubes    17.7
   873  Patch Kit/8 Patches      3354        99         Tires and Tubes    19.2
   707  Sport-100 Helmet, Red    3083        98         Helmets            33.6
   711  Sport-100 Helmet, Blue   3090        98         Helmets            33.7
   708  Sport-100 Helmet, Black  3007        97         Helmets            32.8
   922  Road Tire Tube           2376        97         Tires and Tubes    13.6
   878  Fender Set - Mountain    2121        96         Fenders           100.0
   871  Mountain Bottle Cage     2025        96         Bottles and Cages 24.0
   ...
```

New T-SQL Features in SQL Server 2012

As mentioned earlier, SQL Server 2012 introduced several new arguments, listed in Table 10-2, that you can use with the OVER() clause. Most of the arguments are dependent upon one or the other and cannot be independently used. As a result, each argument is discussed in detail, and then sample queries illustrating their use are provided.

TABLE 10-2 **New OVER() Clause Arguments**

Argument	Description
ROWS/RANGE	Limits the rows within a partition for the current row.
BETWEEN	Used with ROWS or RANGE to specify starting and ending boundary points of the window.
CURRENT ROW	Specifies the starting or ending point of the window as the current row when used with ROWS or the current value when used with RANGE.
UNBOUNDED PRECEDING	Specifies that the window starts at the first row of the partition. Can only be used as a starting point.
UNBOUNDED FOLLOWING	Specifics that the window ends at the last row of the partition. Can only be used as an ending point.

The following query couples the ROWS and UNBOUNDED PRECEDING arguments to create a cumulative total of the specified salesperson's Sales for a particular year:

```
USE AdventureWorks
GO

SELECT
    sp.FirstName,
    sp.LastName,
    Year(soh.OrderDate) OrderYear,
```

```
        soh.TotalDue,
        SUM(soh.TotalDue) OVER
            (ORDER BY sp.FirstName ROWS  UNBOUNDED PRECEDING)
                CumulativeTotal
FROM Sales.SalesOrderHeader soh
INNER JOIN Sales.vSalesPerson sp
    ON soh.SalesPersonID = sp.BusinessEntityID
WHERE
        soh.SalesPersonID IN (274) AND
        soh.OrderDate BETWEEN '1/1/2005' AND '12/31/2005'
```

Results:

```
FirstName   LastName  OrderYear    TotalDue     CumulativeTotal
----------  --------  -----------  -----------  ----------------
Stephen     Jiang     2005         23130.2957   23130.2957
Stephen     Jiang     2005         2297.0332    25427.3289
Stephen     Jiang     2005         4723.1073    30150.4362
Stephen     Jiang     2005         2417.4793    32567.9155
```

In the preceding query the UNBOUND PRECEDING argument tells the query engine to continually aggregate the Total Due column until the end of the set. The same results are returned if the query is slightly changed to the following:

```
USE AdventureWorks
GO

SELECT
    sp.FirstName,
    sp.LastName,
    Year(soh.OrderDate) OrderYear,
    soh.TotalDue,
    SUM(soh.TotalDue) OVER
        (ORDER BY sp.FirstName ROWS BETWEEN CURRENT ROW AND UNBOUNDED
            FOLLOWING) CumulativeTotal
FROM Sales.SalesOrderHeader soh
INNER JOIN Sales.vSalesPerson sp
    ON soh.SalesPersonID = sp.BusinessEntityID
WHERE
        soh.SalesPersonID IN (274) AND
        soh.OrderDate BETWEEN '1/1/2005' AND '12/31/2005'
```

The preceding example illustrates the use of ROWS and BETWEEN together to physically limit the results of the cumulative total by a range that starts at the current row and ends at the end of the set. The end of the set is specified by the UNBOUNDED FOLLOWING argument.

Previous and Current Row

The true value in the new OVER() arguments is their capability to access previous and next rows. The following query introduces an additional modification to the PRECEDING argument that was defined earlier:

```
USE AdventureWorks
GO

WITH YearlyCountryRegionSales
AS
(
    SELECT
        [Group] AS CtryReg,
        Year(soh.OrderDate) OrYr,
        SUM(TotalDue) TotalDueYTD
    FROM Sales.SalesOrderHeader soh
    INNER JOIN Sales.SalesTerritory st
    ON soh.TerritoryID = st.TerritoryID
    GROUP BY
        [Group], Year(soh.OrderDate)
)
SELECT
    CtryReg,
    OrYr,
    TotalDueYTD CurrentYearTotals,
    SUM(TotalDueYTD)
        OVER( PARTITION BY CtryReg ORDER BY OrYr
            ROWS BETWEEN 1 PRECEDING AND CURRENT ROW ) - TotalDueYTD
    PreviousYearTotals,
            SUM(TotalDueYTD)
        OVER( PARTITION BY CtryReg ORDER BY OrYr
            ROWS BETWEEN CURRENT ROW AND 1 FOLLOWING) - TotalDueYTD
    NextYearTotals
    FROM YearlyCountryRegionSales
```

Results:

```
CtryReg         OrYr  CurrentYearTotals PreviousYearTotals NextYearTotals
-------         ----  ----------------- ------------------ ----------------
Europe          2005  784491.6708       0.00               3713564.3139
Europe          2006  3713564.3139      784491.6708        10120806.8258
Europe          2007  10120806.8258     3713564.3139       7554754.8192
Europe          2008  7554754.8192      10120806.8258      0.00
North America   2005  10462261.7812     0.00               28369799.2827
North America   2006  28369799.2827     10462261.7812      32737387.8837
North America   2007  32737387.8837     28369799.2827      17659343.4434
North America   2008  17659343.4434     32737387.8837      0.00
Pacific         2005  1446497.1744      0.00               2380484.8387
Pacific         2006  2380484.8387      1446497.1744       4313294.8365
Pacific         2007  4313294.8365      2380484.8387       3674099.2456
Pacific         2008  3674099.2456      4313294.8365       0.00
```

As seen in the preceding results, the PreviousYearTotals column represents the value of the previous year totals, and the NextYearTotals column represents the value of the following year's total.This is accomplished by replacing UNBOUNDED in the OVER() clause with a positive integer value. Instead of aggregating the value to the end of the set, the integer specifies the number of rows or values to precede or follow the current row. In other words, add the value of the next n row(s) or the previous n row(s) to the current row, where n represents the number of rows to aggregate with the current row. To finalize accessing the previous or next row, simply subtract the value of the current row from the product of the over() clause, and this yields the expected results.

Summary

SQL Server excels in aggregate functions, with the proverbial rich suite of features, and it is capable of calculating sums and aggregates to suit nearly any need. From the simple COUNT() aggregate function to the complex dynamic crosstab query and the new PIVOT command, these query methods enable you to create powerful data analysis queries for impressive reports. The most important points to remember about aggregation are as follows:

- Aggregate queries generate a single summary row, so every column must be an aggregate function.

- No performance difference exists between COUNT(*) and COUNT(pk).

- Aggregate functions, such as COUNT(column) and AVG(column), ignore nulls, which can be a good thing, and a reason why nulls make life easier for the database developer.

- GROUP BY queries divide the data source into several segmented data sets and then generate a summary row for each group. For GROUP BY queries, the GROUP BY columns can and should be in the column list.

- In the logical flow of the query, the GROUP BY occurs after the FROM clause and the WHERE clause, so when coding the query, get the data properly selected and then add the GROUP BY.

- Complex aggregations (for example, nested aggregations) often require CTEs or subqueries. Design the query from the inside out — that is, design the aggregate subquery first and then add the outer query.

- The OVER() clause generates the sort order for the ranking functions.

- The new T-SQL functions extend the existing capabilities of the Windowing and Ranking functions.

10

Projecting Data Through Views

A *view* is the saved text of a T-SQL SELECT statement that may be referenced as a data source within a query, similar to how a subquery can be used as a data source—no more, no less. A view cannot be executed by itself; it must be used within a query.

Views are sometimes described as "virtual tables." This isn't an accurate description because all views do not store any data. Views that are indexed are materialized and actually store data. If they are not indexed, they are like any other SQL query; views merely refer to the data stored in tables.

With this in mind, you need to fully understand how views work, the pros and cons of using views, and the best place to use views within your project architecture.

Why Use Views?

Although several opinions exist for the use of views, ranging from total abstinence to overuse, the Information Architecture Principle (from Chapter 2, "Data Architecture") serves as a guide for their most appropriate use. The principle states that "information ... must be ... made readily available in a usable format for daily operations and analysis by individuals, groups, and processes ..."

Presenting data in a more useable format is precisely what views do best.

Based on the premise that views are best used to increase data integrity and for ease of writing ad hoc queries, and not as a central part of a production application, following are some ideas for building ad hoc query views:

- Use views to denormalize or flatten complex joins and hide any surrogate keys used to link data within the database schema. A well-designed view invites the user to get right to the data of interest.

- Save complex aggregate queries as views. Even power users appreciate a well-crafted aggregate query saved as a view.

Best Practice

Views are an important part of the abstraction puzzle; be intentional in their use. Some developers are enamored with views and use them as the primary abstraction layer for their databases. They create layers of nested views or stored procedures that refer to views. This practice serves no valid purpose, creates confusion, and requires needless overhead.

Data within a normalized database is rarely organized in a readily available format. Building ad hoc queries that extract the correct information from a normalized database is a challenge for most end users. A well-written view can hide the complexity of the underlying data structures and present the correct data to the user. The following is a list of best practices that could be used when creating your views.

- Plan generic, but standard, naming conventions for all views and column aliases.

- Use aliases to change cryptic column names to recognizable column names. Just as the SELECT statement can use column or table aliases to modify the names of columns or tables, these features may be used within a view to present a more readable recordset to the user.

- Include only the columns of interest to the user. When columns that don't concern users are left out of the view, the view is easier to query. The columns included in the view are called *projected columns*, meaning they project only the selected data from the entire underlying tables.

- Plan generic, dynamic views that will have long, useful lives. Single-purpose views quickly become obsolete and clutter the database. Build the view with the intention that it will be used with a WHERE clause to select a subset of data. The view should return all the rows if the user does not supply a WHERE restriction. For example, the vEventList view returns all the events; the user should include a WHERE clause to select the local events, or the events in a certain month.

- If a view is needed to return a restricted set of data, such as the next month's events, then the view should calculate the next month so that it can continue to function over time. Hard-coding values such as a month number or name would be poor practice.

- If the view selects data from a range, then consider writing it as a user-defined function (see Chapter 18, "Building User-Defined Functions"), which can accept parameters.

- Consolidate data from across a complex environment. Queries that need to collect data across multiple servers are simplified by encapsulating the union of data from multiple servers within a view. This is one case in which basing several reports, and even stored procedures, on a single view improves the stability, integrity, and maintainability of the system.

- Typically views are created for specific purposes or for a specific group or department within an organization. To group the views together in an attempt to ease maintainability, you may assign them to a specific schema. For example, you have a set of views that have been created specifically for reporting. Those views could all be included as part of a Reporting Schema.

Using Views for Column-Level Security

One of the basic relational operators is projection—the capability to expose specific columns. One primary advantage of views is their natural capacity to project a predefined set of columns. Here is where theory becomes practical. A view can project columns on a need-to-know basis and hide sensitive, irrelevant, or confusing columns for the purpose of the view (for example, payroll and credit card data).

SQL Server supports column-level security, and it's a powerful feature. The problem is that ad hoc queries made by users who don't understand the schema well often run into security errors. You should implement SQL Server column-level security, and then also use views to shield users from ever encountering the security. Grant users read permission from only the views, and restrict access to the physical tables (see Chapter 33, "Authorizing Securables").

Some databases use only views for column-level security without any SQL Server–enforced security. This is woefully inadequate and will surely be penalized by any serious security audit.

The goal when developing views is two-fold: to enable users to get to the data easily and to protect the data from the users. By building views that provide the correct data, you can prevent erroneous or inaccurate queries and misinterpretation.

NOTE

Other advanced forms of views exist.

Distributed partition views, or *federated databases*, divide large tables across multiple smaller tables or separate servers to improve performance. The partitioned view then spans the multiple tables or servers, thus sharing the query load across more disk spindles. (See Chapter 49, "Partitioning.")

Indexed views are a powerful feature that actually materializes the data, storing the results of the view in a clustered index on disk, so in this sense it's not a pure view. Like any view, it can select data from multiple data sources. Think of the indexed view as a covering index but with greater control — you can include data from multiple data sources, and you don't need to include the clustered index keys. The index may then be referenced when executing queries, regardless of whether the view is in the query, so the name is slightly confusing. (See Chapter 45, "Indexing Strategies.")

 Because designing an indexed view is more like designing an indexing structure than creating a view, Chapter 45, "Indexing Strategies," includes indexed views.

The Basic View

Using SQL Server Management Studio, views may be created, modified, executed, and included within other queries, using either the Query Designer or the DDL code within the Query Editor.

Creating Views Using the Query Designer

Because a view is nothing more than a saved T-SQL SELECT statement, the creation of a view begins with a working SELECT statement. Any SELECT statement, as long as it's a valid SELECT statement (with a few minor exceptions), can be cut and pasted from nearly any other tool into the view designer.

Within SQL Server Management Studio, views are listed in their own node under each database.

The New View command in the context menu launches the Query Designer in a mode that creates views, as shown in Figure 11-1.

FIGURE 11-1

Creating a view in Management Studio's Query Designer.

The View Designer mode functions within Management Studio's Query Designer, which is also used to query tables. You can display or edit the actual T-SQL code for the view in the

SQL pane. You can add columns to the view by using the Diagram pane, the Grid pane, or the SQL pane. The Add Table feature, available in the context menu or toolbar, can add tables, other views, synonyms, and table-valued functions.

You can add tables or other views to the new view by dragging them to the Diagram pane from the Object Explorer or using the Add Table context menu option.

You can use a toolbar button and a context menu item to add a derived table to the view, but all it does is slightly modify the FROM clause to create a placeholder for the subquery. Then you need to manually enter the SQL for the subquery in the SQL pane.

The Verify SQL Syntax button in the toolbar verifies only the T-SQL syntax; it does not verify the names of tables, views, or columns in the SELECT statement. As a result, the Query Designer may report the syntax of the query as correct, but when you try to create the view, it may fail.

To test the view's SELECT statement within Query Designer, use the Execute SQL button, F5, or CTRL+R. This runs the SELECT statement by itself, without creating the view.

The Save toolbar button actually runs the script to create the view in the database. The view must be a valid, error-free SELECT statement to be saved.

 For more details on using the Query Designer, refer to Chapter 5, "SQL Server Management and Development Tools."

After the view is created, you can perform several tasks on the view using Object Explorer's view context menu:

- **Design the view**: Opens the Query Designer tool with the view's SELECT statement.
- **Select top 1000 rows**: Opens the Query Editor with a SELECT statement referencing the view. You can modify the number of selected rows in Management Studio's options.
- **Edit top 200 rows**: Opens the Query Designer with a SELECT statement referencing the view, with only the results pane visible, and executes the view.
- **Script View as**: Management Studio can script the DDL statements to CREATE, ALTER, or DROP the view, as well as sample DML statements referencing the view.
- **View dependencies**: This option is important because views, by definition, reference other data sources and are often referenced themselves.
- **Policies**: Apply and manage policy-based management policies for the view.
- **Rename/Delete the view**: To rename or drop the view, select it and press Rename or Delete, respectively.
- **Properties**: Opens the properties dialog with pages for security permissions and extended properties.

Double-clicking the view opens its subnodes: columns, triggers (instead of tasks), indexes (indexed views), and statistics.

Creating Views with DDL Code

You can manage views using the Query Editor by executing SQL scripts with the *Data Definition Language (DDL)* commands: CREATE, ALTER, and DROP. Even though the designer may seem like an easy tool to use when creating and modifying views, you should consider using a query editor as the primary tool for tool editing. The basic syntax for creating a view follows:

```
CREATE VIEW schemaname.ViewName [(Column aliases)]
AS
SQL Select Statement;
```

For example, to create the view vEmployeeList in code, the following command would be executed in a query window:

```
USE AdventureWorks2008R2
Go

CREATE VIEW dbo.vEmployeeList
AS
   SELECT P.BusinessEntityID, P.Title, P.LastName,
        P.FirstName, E.JobTitle
      FROM Person.Person P
        INNER JOIN HumanResources.Employee E
          ON P.BusinessEntityID = E.BusinessEntityID
```

As with creating any object, the CREATE command must be the only command in the batch.

> **NOTE**
>
> Although I'm generally opposed to Hungarian notation (tblTablename, intIntegerColumn, and so on) for database objects, I prefer to preface views with a lowercase v or vw, simply to keep them separate in data source listings, but, to be honest, most database developers do not preface views with a v. You should also avoid using SELECT* in views. This is because if the number of columns change or the data type or sizes change, using SELECT* could cause problems for those applications that consume the views.

The view name must be unique in the database. Attempting to create a view with a name shared by any other object generates an error.

Executing Views

Technically, you cannot execute a view by itself. A view can only patiently wait to be referenced by a SQL query.

A query (SELECT, INSERT, UPDATE, DELETE, or MERGE) can include the view as a data source, and that query can be executed. As illustrated in Figure 11-2, a view is useful only as a data source within a query. You can think of a view as nothing more than a placeholder for a saved SELECT statement.

FIGURE 11-2

When the query that references a view is submitted to SQL Server, the query parser picks the query apart and replaces the name of the view with the view's SELECT statement.

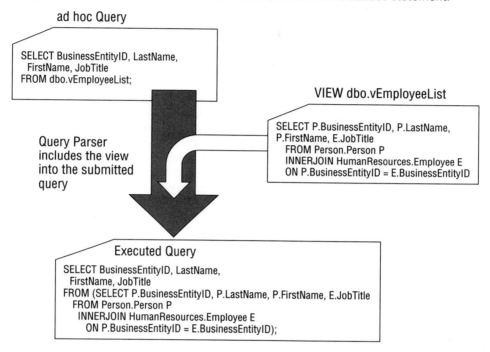

ad hoc Query

```
SELECT BusinessEntityID, LastName,
    FirstName, JobTitle
FROM dbo.vEmployeeList;
```

Query Parser includes the view into the submitted query

VIEW dbo.vEmployeeList

```
SELECT P.BusinessEntityID, P.LastName,
P.FirstName, E.JobTitle
    FROM Person.Person P
    INNERJOIN HumanResources.Employee E
    ON P.BusinessEntityID = E.BusinessEntityID
```

Executed Query

```
SELECT BusinessEntityID, LastName,
    FirstName, JobTitle
FROM (SELECT P.BusinessEntityID, P.LastName, P.FirstName, E.JobTitle
    FROM Person.Person P
    INNERJOIN HumanResources.Employee E
    ON P.BusinessEntityID = E.BusinessEntityID);
```

The following SELECT statement references the vEmployeeList view:

```
SELECT BusinessEntityID, LastName, FirstName, JobTitle
    FROM dbo.vEmployeeList
ORDER BY BusinessEntityID
```

Result (abbreviated):

```
BusinessEntityID LastName     FirstName   JobTitle
---------------- ------------ ----------- -----------------------
1                Sánchez      Ken         Chief Executive Officer
2                Duffy        Terri       Vice President of Engineering
3                Tamburello   Roberto     Engineering Manager
4                Walters      Rob         Senior Tool Designer
```

When views are referenced from ad hoc queries, a WHERE condition is typically added to filter the data from the view:

```
SELECT BusinessEntityID, LastName, FirstName, JobTitle
```

```
FROM dbo.vEmployeeList
WHERE JobTitle = 'Database Administrator';
```

Result:

```
BusinessEntityID LastName     FirstName   JobTitle
---------------- -----------  ----------- ----------------------------
270              Ajenstat     Françoi     Database Administrator
271              Wilson       Dan         Database Administrator
```

Altering and Dropping a View

It's likely that you need to change the view's SELECT statement at some point in time. After you create a view, you can easily edit the SELECT statement by using the ALTER command. Altering the view changes the saved SELECT statement while keeping any properties and security settings in place. This is preferable to dropping the view, losing all the security settings and properties, and then re-creating the view.

The ALTER command supplies a new SELECT statement for the view:

```
ALTER SchemaName.ViewName
AS
[SELECT Statement];
```

Management Studio can automatically generate an ALTER statement from an existing view. In Object Explorer, select the view, and then choose Script View As ➪ Alter To ➪ New Query Editor Window from the context menu.

If you no longer need the view, you can completely erase it from the database using the DROP command:

```
DROP VIEW SchemaName.ViewName;
```

A view could also be deleted using Management Studio. In the Object Explorer, select the view, and then choose Delete from the context menu.

Within a script intended to be executed several times, use the following code to drop and re-create the view:

```
IF OBJECT_ID('vEmployeeList') IS NOT NULL
   DROP VIEW dbo.vEmployeeList
Go
CREATE VIEW SchemaName.ViewName
AS
[SELECT Statement];
```

Just to reiterate, views don't contain any data, so there's no danger that dropping a view causes any data loss. However, applications, reports, and other objects might depend on the view, and dropping the view might break something else. For more about viewing dependencies within SQL Server, see the section "Nesting Views" later in this chapter.

A Broader Point of View

The basic mechanics to create a view and select data from the view are straightforward, but views have their own particular nuances—topics such as sorting data, updating data through a view, and nesting views several levels deep. This section examines views from a broader point of view.

Column Aliases

The column aliases option is rarely used. With syntax similar to the column list for a common table expression, the view's column list renames every output column just as if every column had those alias names in the SELECT statement. The view's column list names override any column names or column aliases in the view's SELECT statement.

The following query alters the vEmployeeList view so that the result columns become ID, Last, First, and Job:

```
ALTER VIEW dbo.vEmployeeList (
ID, Last, First, Job)
AS
  SELECT P.BusinessEntityID,
      P.LastName, P.FirstName, E.JobTitle
    FROM Person.Person P
      INNER JOIN HumanResources.Employee E
        ON P.BusinessEntityID = E.BusinessEntityID
GO

SELECT *
  FROM dbo.vEmployeeList
ORDER BY ID
```

Result (abbreviated):

```
ID              Last          First       Job
--------------------  -----------   -----------------------------
1               Sánchez       Ken         Chief Executive Officer
2               Duffy         Terri       Vice President of Engineering
3               Tamburello    Roberto     Engineering Manager
4               Walters       Rob         Senior Tool Designer
```

ORDER BY and Views

Views serve as data sources for other queries and do not support sorting the data within the view. To sort data from a view, include the ORDER BY clause in the query referencing the view. For example, the following code selects data from the vEmployeeList view and orders it by LastName, FirstName. The ORDER BY clause is not a part of vEmployeeList, but it is applied to the view by the executing SQL statement:

```
SELECT *
  FROM dbo.vEmployeeList
  ORDER BY LastName, FirstName
```

Result:

```
BusinessEntityID LastName      FirstName   JobTitle
---------------- -----------   ---------   ------------------------
     285         Abbas         Syed        Pacific Sales Manager
      38         Abercrombie   Kim         Production Technician - WC60
     211         Abolrous      Hazem       Quality Assurance Manager
     121         Ackerman      Pilar       Shipping and Receiving
                                           Supervisor
```

If the view includes a TOP predicate, then the view is allowed to include an ORDER BY—without the ORDER BY, the TOP would be meaningless. However, this ORDER BY clause serves *only* to define which rows qualify for the TOP predicate. The only way to logically guarantee sorted results is to define the ORDER BY clause in the executing query.

> **WARNING**
>
> SQL Server 2000, and some service packs of SQL Server 2005, had a bug (yes, let's call it a bug) in the Query Optimizer that would enable an ORDER BY in a view using a top 100 percent predicate. This behavior was never documented or officially supported. However, in SQL Server 2008, this error was corrected and the TOP 100 percent with an ORDER BY trick does not sort the result.
>
> A source of confusion is that Management Studio's Query Designer enables views to have sorted columns, and it adds the TOP 100 percent trick to the view. That is a SQL Server 2008 "bug."

View Restrictions

Although a view can contain nearly any valid SELECT statement, a few basic restrictions do apply:

- Views may not include the SELECT INTO option that creates a new table from the selected columns. SELECT INTO fails if the table already exists and it does not return any data, so it's not a valid view:

```
SELECT * INTO Table
```

- Views may not refer to a temporary table (one with a # in the name) or a table variable (preceded with an @) because these types of tables are transient.

- The OPTION clause, which gives table or query hints for the entire query, is not allowed.

- The tablesample table option, which can randomly select pages, is not allowed within a view.

- Views may not contain compute or compute by columns. Instead, use standard aggregate functions and groupings. (Compute and compute by are obsolete and are included for backward compatibility only.)

Nesting Views

Because a view is nothing more than a SELECT statement, and a SELECT statement may reference any data source, views may reference other views. Views referred to by other views are sometimes called *nested views*.

The following view uses vEmployeeList and adds a WHERE clause to restrict the results to the smartest and best-looking employees:

```
CREATE VIEW dbo.vEmployeeListDBA
AS
   SELECT BusinessEntityID, LastName, FirstName, JobTitle
      FROM dbo.vEmployeeList AS vE
      WHERE JobTitle = 'Database Administrator';
```

In this example, the view vEmployeeList is nested within vEmployeeListDBA. Another way to express the relationship is to say that vEmployeeListDBA depends on vEmployeeList.

You can easily view dependencies from other objects in SQL Server using Object Explorer's view context menu ⇨ View Dependencies. Figure 11-3 shows the Object Dependencies dialog for a nested view.

You can see FROM code dependencies using the function sys.dm_sql_referencing_ entities(). For example, the following query would indicate whether any other SQL Server object referenced vEmployeeList:

```
SELECT *
  FROM sys.dm_sql_referencing_entities
      ('dbo.vEmployeeList, 'Object')
```

Best Practice

Although there may be a good reason for nesting views to support power users who build ad hoc queries, I don't recommend nesting views as a general practice. They're just too difficult to diagnose and maintain. I've seen development shops that build their production abstraction layer with nested views several layers deep.

 For other options to nesting subselects within outer queries, see Chapter 9, "Merging Data with Joins, Subqueries, and CTE's."

FIGURE 11-3

The dependency chain for nested views is easily seen in the Object Dependencies dialog. Here, the vEmployeeListDBA includes the nested view vEmployeeList, which in turn is based on the Employee table, and so on.

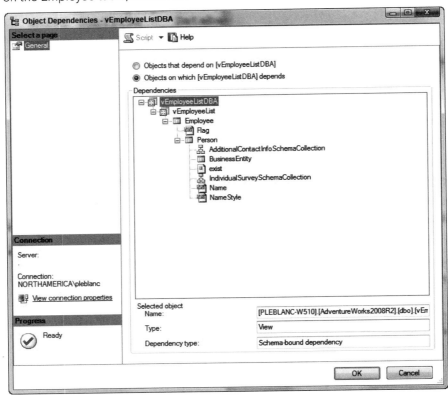

Updating Through Views

One of the main complaints concerning views is that unless the view is a simple single table view, it's difficult to update the underlying data through the view. Although the SQL Server Query Optimizer can update through some complex views, some hard-and-fast limitations exist.

Best Practice

Designing an application around updatable views is not recommended. Views are best used as an abstraction layer for ad hoc queries and reports, not for power users to update data, and certainly not for forms, websites, or client applications to update the database.

Any of the following factors may cause a view to be non-updatable:

- Only one table may be updated. If the view includes joins, then the UPDATE statement that references the view must change columns in only one table.

- Aggregate functions or GROUP BY in the view can cause the view to be non-updatable. SQL Server couldn't possibly determine which of the summarized rows should be updated.

- If the view includes a subquery as a derived table, and any columns from the subquery are exposed as output from the view, then the view is not updatable. However, aggregates are permitted in a subquery used as a derived table, so long as any columns from the aggregate subquery are not in the output columns of the view.

- If the view includes the WITH CHECK OPTION, the INSERT or UPDATE operation must meet the view's WHERE clause conditions.

NOTE
Of course, the other standard potential difficulties with updating and inserting data still apply.

 One way to work around non-updatable views is to build an INSTEAD OF trigger that inspects the modified data and then performs a legal UPDATE operation based on that data. Chapter 18 explains how to create an INSTEAD OF trigger.

Views and Performance

Views add a level of abstraction that offers an effective method for data access and ad-hoc queries for end-users, but sometimes views are perceived as having poor performance.

Several factors contribute to this:

- Views are often used by power users who submit ad hoc SQL. In earlier versions of SQL Server, ad hoc SQL didn't perform as well as stored procedures.

- Views are often used by power users who use front-end UI applications to select and browse data. Some of these applications opened the connections and held locks, causing all sorts of performance problems.

- Views are often used by power users who find useful data in a view and then build new views on top of views. These nested views might result in a complex view several layers deep that kills performance, whereas the top-level view appears to be a simple, easy view.

Let me put the myth to rest: Well-written views will perform well. The reason to limit views to ad hoc queries and reports isn't for performance, but for extensibility and control.

Alternatives to Views

Besides views, SQL Server offers several technologies to build an abstraction layer around the data. Stored procedures are generally a first choice when exposing any data to the outside world. User-defined functions offer several benefits, and inline table-valued user-defined functions are similar to views but with parameters. Chapter 17, "Developing Stored Procedures," and Chapter 18 discuss the aforementioned topics at length.

If you use views to support ad hoc queries, as I suggest you do, you may also want to explore providing Analysis Services cubes for those users who need to perform complex explorations of the data. Cubes *pre-aggregate*, or summarize, the data along multiple dimensions. The user may then browse the cube and compare the different data dimensions. For the developer, providing one cube can often eliminate several queries or reports.

Chapter 53, "Building Multidimensional Cubes with Analysis Services and MDX," explains how to create cubes.

Locking Down the View

Views are designed to control access to data. Several options protect the data or the view.

The WITH CHECK OPTION causes the WHERE clause of the view to check the data being inserted or updated through the view in addition to the data being retrieved. In a sense, it makes the WHERE clause a two-way restriction.

The WITH CHECK OPTION is useful when the view should limit inserts and updates with the same restrictions applied to the WHERE clause.

Unchecked Data

To understand the need for the WITH CHECK OPTION, you must first understand how views function without the CHECK OPTION. The following view generates a list of Product SubCategories for the Bikes Product Category:

```
USE AdventureWorks2008R2
GO
CREATE view vComponentsProductSubCats
AS
SELECT
    ProductCategoryID,
    Name ProductSubCategory
FROM Production.ProductSubcategory
WHERE ProductCategoryID = 1;
GO
SELECT ProductCategoryID, ProductSubCategory FROM
```

```
     dbo.vComponentsProductSubCats
Results:
ProductCategoryID    ProductSubCatgory
------------------   --------------------
1                    Mountain Bikes
1                    Road Bikes
1                    Touring Bikes
```

If someone adds a Bike Pedal Accessory and inserts using the view without the CHECK OPTION, the INSERT is permitted.

```
INSERT INTO vComponentsProductSubCats(ProductCategoryID,
    ProductSubCategory)
VALUES(2, 'Bike Pedal');
(1 row(s) affected)
```

The INSERT worked, and the new row is in the database, but the row is not visible through the view because the WHERE clause of the view filters out the inserted row. This phenomenon is called *disappearing rows*:

```
SELECT ProductCategoryID, ProductSubCategory FROM
    dbo.vComponentsProductSubCats
Results:
ProductCategoryID    SProductSubCatgory
-----------------    --------------------
1                    Mountain Bikes
1                    Road Bikes
1                    Touring Bikes
```

If the purpose of the view were to give users that managed the Bikes Subcategories access to those subcategories alone, then the view failed. Although they can see only the Bike Subcategories, they successfully modified another Categories Product Subcategories. The WITH CHECK OPTION would have prevented this fault.

Protecting the Data

A view with a WHERE clause and the WITH CHECK OPTION can protect the data from undesired inserts and updates.

The following code can back out the previous INSERT and redo the same scenario, but this time the view includes the WITH CHECK OPTION:

```
DELETE FROM Production.ProductSubcategory
    WHERE Name = 'Bike Pedal';
GO
USE AdventureWorks2008R2
GO
ALTER view vComponentsProductSubCats
AS
```

```
SELECT
    ProductCategoryID,
    Name ProductSubCategory
FROM Production.ProductSubcategory
WHERE ProductCategoryID = 1;
    WITH CHECK OPTION;
go
INSERT INTO vComponentsProductSubCats(ProductCategoryID,
    ProductSubCategory)
VALUES(2, 'Bike Pedal');


Server: Msg 550, Level 16, State 1, Line 1
The attempted insert or update failed because the target view either
specifies WITH CHECK OPTION or spans a view that specifies WITH CHECK
OPTION and one or more rows resulting from the operation did not
Qualify under the CHECK OPTION constraint.
The statement has been terminated.
```

This time the INSERT failed and the error message attributed the cause to the
WITH CHECK OPTION in the view, which is exactly the wanted effect.

Some developers employ views and the WITH CHECK OPTION as a way to provide row-level
security—a technique called *horizontally positioned views*. As in the subcategory view example, they create a view for each subcategory and then give users security permission to the
view that pertains to them. Although this method does achieve row-level security, it also
has a high maintenance cost.

 For the application, row-level security can be designed using user-access tables and stored procedures,
as demonstrated in Chapter 35, "Row Level Security," but views can help enforce row-level security for
ad hoc queries.

Within Management Studio's View Designer, you can enforce the WITH CHECK OPTION
within the View Properties form. Actually two properties must be enabled. The first is Update
Using View Rules, which prohibits Management Studio and MDAC from decoding the view and
directly accessing the underlying tables. Only when Update Using View Rules is enabled can
the second option, WITH CHECK OPTION, be enabled. To access the properties of a view from
the View Designer, either use the F4 key or on the menu choose Views ➪ Properties Window.
Expand the Update Specification Property and set both of its properties to Yes.

Protecting the View

Three options protect views from data schema changes and prying eyes. These options are
simply added to the CREATE command and applied to the view, in much the same way that
the WITH CHECK OPTION is applied.

Database code is fragile and tends to break when the underlying data structure changes.
Because views are nothing more than stored SELECT queries, changes to the referenced
tables may break the view.

Creating a view with schema binding locks the underlying tables to the view and prevents changes, as demonstrated in the following code sample:

```
Use AdventureWorks2012
go
CREATE TABLE dbo.Test (
    [Name] NVARCHAR(50)
    );
go

CREATE VIEW dbo.vTest
WITH SCHEMABINDING
AS
SELECT [Name] FROM dbo.Test;
go

use AdventureWorks2012
go
ALTER TABLE Test
    ALTER COLUMN [Name] NVARCHAR(100);
```

Result:

```
Msg 5074, Level 16, State 1, Line 1
The object 'vTest' is dependent on column 'Name'.
Msg 4922, Level 16, State 9, Line 1
ALTER TABLE ALTER COLUMN Name failed because one
or more objects access this column.
```

Some restrictions apply to the creation of schema-bound views. The SELECT statement must include the schema name for any referenced objects, and SELECT * (all columns) is not permitted. (But that last requirement shouldn't bother anyone who follows best practices.)

Within Management Studio's View Designer, the WITH SCHEMA BINDING option can be enabled within the View Properties page.

When the schema underlying a view that is not schema bound does change, it likely breaks the view. If this happens, to repair the view, either re-create it or run the sp_ refreshview system stored procedure.

Encrypting the View's SELECT Statement

The WITH ENCRYPTION option is another security feature. When views or stored procedures are created, the text can be retrieved through the sys.sql_modules and sys .syscomments system views. The code is therefore available for viewing. The view may contain a WHERE condition that should be kept confidential, or there may be some other reason for encrypting the code. The WITH ENCRYPTION option encrypts the code in the system tables, hides the code from sys.sql_modules and sys.syscomments, and prevents anyone from viewing the original code.

In the following code example, the text of the view is inspected within `sys.sql_modules`, the view is encrypted, and `sys.sql_modules` is again inspected (as expected, the `SELECT` statement for the view is then no longer readable):

```
SELECT definition
    FROM sys.sql_modules
    WHERE object_id = OBJECT_ID(N'dbo.vTest');
```

The result is the text of the vText view:

```
definition
---------------------------
CREATE VIEW vTest
WITH SCHEMABINDING
AS
SELECT [Name] FROM dbo.Test;
```

The following `ALTER` command rebuilds the view `WITH ENCRYPTION`:

```
ALTER VIEW vTest
WITH ENCRYPTION
AS
SELECT [Name] FROM dbo.Test;
```

Be careful with this option. When the code is encrypted, Management Studio can no longer produce a script to alter the view and instead generates this message:

```
/****** Encrypted object is not transferable,
and script cannot be generated. ******/
```

In addition, be aware that the encryption affects replication. An encrypted view cannot be published.

Application Metadata

The front-end application or data access layer may request schema information, called *metadata*, along with the data when querying SQL Server. Typically, SQL Server returns schema information for the underlying tables, but the `WITH VIEW METADATA` option tells SQL Server to return schema information about the view, rather than the tables referenced by the view. This prohibits someone from learning about the table's schema and is useful when the view's purpose is to hide sensitive columns.

Using SQL Synonyms

Views are sometimes employed to hide cryptic database schema names. Synonyms are similar to views, but they are more limited. Whereas views can project columns, assign column aliases, and build data using joins and subqueries, synonyms can assign only alternative names to tables, views, and stored procedures.

Use synonyms primarily to simplify complex object names, particularly with lengthy schema names. A synonym can change HumanResources.vEmployeeDepartmentHistory into EmpHist. Which would you rather type 100 times? The following script illustrates how to create the EmpHist synonym:

```
CREATE SYNONYM EmpHist
FOR HumanResources.vEmployeeDepartmentHistory;
```

Synonyms are part of the SQL standard and are used frequently by Oracle DBAs. Oracle includes both private and public synonyms. SQL Server synonyms are only public. Even though they were introduced to SQL Server with version 2005, I've seen little acceptance or use of synonyms in the SQL community.

Schemas enhance security and help prevent SQL injection attacks.

The hacker needs to guess the schema name as well as the table name. Little Bobby Tables (a standard DBA joke: http://xkcd.com/327/) would need to know myschema .students. Giving the table myschema.students an easy-to-guess synonym would defeat the purpose of using the schema as a mechanism to prevent SQL injection.

You can manage synonyms using Object Explorer, or CREATE and DROP DDL commands.

Summary

Views are nothing more than stored T-SQL SELECT queries. There's no magic in a view. You can save any valid SELECT statement as a view, including subqueries, complex joins, and aggregate functions.

Views are great for simplifying a complex schema and presenting a more useful picture of the data for power users writing ad hoc queries and reports. Views can simplify complex aggregate queries and hide nasty joins. Any well-planned abstraction layer should include views. Be careful not to push the view too far. Don't expect to sort data in a view, and don't make views the pillar of the front-end application or website. However, for those who detest views, a view is infinitely better than an ad hoc SQL statement that directly hits a table without any abstraction layer.

The previous chapters have discussed retrieving data using the powerful SELECT statement. Views store the SELECT statement for ad hoc queries. The next chapter continues the discussion of SELECT, extending its power by adding data modification verbs.

Modifying Data In SQL Server

IN THIS CHAPTER

Inserting Data From Expressions, Other Result Sets, and Stored Procedures

Updating and Deleting Data

Mastering the Merge Command

Exposing Inserted and Deleted Tables to the Dml

Things change. Life moves on. Because the purpose of a database is to accurately represent reality, the data must change along with reality. For SQL programmers, that means inserting, updating, and deleting rows — using the basic data manipulation language (DML) commands. However, these operations aren't limited to writing single rows of data. Working with SQL means thinking in terms of data sets. The process to modify data with SQL draws on the entire range of SQL Server data-retrieval capabilities — the powerful SELECT, joins, full-text searches, subqueries, and views.

This chapter is all about modifying data within SQL Server using the INSERT, UPDATE, DELETE, and MERGE SQL commands. Modifying data raises issues that you need to address, or at least consider. Inserting surrogate primary keys requires special methods. Table constraints may interfere with the data modification. Referential integrity demands that some DELETE operations cascade to other related tables. This chapter can help you understand these concerns and offer some ways to deal with them. Because these potential obstacles affect INSERT, UPDATE, MERGE, and, to some degree, DELETE, they are addressed in their own sections after the sections devoted to the individual commands.

The ACID database properties (atomic, consistent, isolated, and durable) are critical to the modification of data. For many databases, SQL Server's default transactional control is sufficient. However, misapplied transaction locking and blocking represents one of the top four causes of poor performance. Chapter 47, "Managing Transactions, Locking, and Blocking," digs into SQL Server's architecture and explains how data modifications occur within transactions to meet the ACID requirements, and how SQL Server manages data locks.

Best Practice

The SQL INSERT, UPDATE, DELETE, and MERGE commands are actually verb extensions of the basic SELECT command. The full potential of the SELECT command lies within each data-modification operation. Even when modifying data, you should think in terms of sets, rather than single rows.

Data-modification commands may be submitted to SQL Server from any one of several interfaces. This chapter is concerned more with the strategy and use of the INSERT, UPDATE, DELETE, and MERGE commands than with the interface used to submit a given command to SQL Server.

SQL Server Management Studio offers two interfaces for submitting SQL commands: Query Designer and Query Editor. If you like a visual UI, then Query Designer may work for a while, but you should migrate to Query Editor to enjoy the richness of T-SQL. You probably can do all your development work exclusively in Query Editor. Even though the Query Designer offers a very intuitive UI it may present unseen challenges that could result in invalid or incorrect data.

 For more details on using Management Studio's Query Designer and Query Editor, see Chapter 5, "SQL Server Management and Development Tools."

Inserting Data

SQL offers six forms of INSERT and SELECT/INTO as the primary methods to insert data (as shown in Table 12-1). The most basic method simply inserts a row of data, whereas the most complex builds a data set from a complex SELECT statement and creates a table from the result.

TABLE 12-1   Insert Forms

Insert Form	Description
INSERT/VALUES	Inserts one or more rows of values; commonly used to insert data from a user interface
INSERT/SELECT	Inserts a result set; commonly used to manipulate sets of data
INSERT/EXEC	Inserts the results of a stored procedure; used for complex data manipulation
INSERT/DEFAULT VALUES	Creates a new row with all defaults; used for pre-populating pigeonhole data rows
SELECT/INTO	Creates a new table from the result set of a SELECT statement
MERGE	Combines inserting, updating, and deleting data in a single statement

Each of these `INSERT` forms is useful for a unique task, often depending on the source of the data being inserted.

 SQL Server complements the SQL `INSERT` commands with other tools to aid in moving large amounts of data or performing complex data conversions. The venerable Bulk Copy Wizard and the Copy Database Wizard are introduced in Chapter 23, "Transferring Databases." The Copy Database Wizard actually creates a simple Integration Services package. Chapter 52, "Building, Deploying, and Managing ETL Workflows in Integration Services," details Integration Services, a powerful tool that can move and manipulate large sets of data between/among nearly any data sources.

When inserting new data, if the table has surrogate keys, then primary key values must be generated to identify the new rows. Although identity columns and GUIDs both make excellent primary keys, each requires special handling during the insertion of rows. This section describes how to create identity-column values and GUIDs.

12

Inserting Simple Rows of Values

The simplest and most direct method to insert data is the `INSERT...VALUES` method. Until SQL Server 2008, `INSERT...VALUES` was limited to inserting a single row, but SQL Server is now compliant with the ANSI standard and can include row constructors — inserting multiple rows in a single `INSERT...VALUES` statement:

```
INSERT [INTO] schema.table [(columns, ...)]
   VALUES (value,...), (value,..., ... ;
```

Building an `INSERT...VALUES` statement is mostly straightforward, although you do have a few options. The `INTO` keyword is optional and is commonly ignored. The key to building an `INSERT` statement is getting the columns correctly listed and ensuring that the data type of the value is valid for the inserted column.

When the values are inserted into a new row, each value corresponds to an insert column. The insert columns may be in any order — the order of the columns within the table is irrelevant — as long as the insert columns and the value columns in the SQL `INSERT` command are in the same order.

 As with every chapter that includes code, the file `Ch 12 - Modifying Data.sql` on www `.SQLServerBible.com` contains all the sample code for this chapter.

Before any data can be inserted, first start by running the following script:

```
Use AdventureWorks
GO
CREATE TABLE dbo.[Address]
(
      AddressID int identity(1,1)
```

```
                        CONSTRAINT PK_Address_AddressID PRIMARY KEY,
              Address1 varchar(75) NOT NULL,
              City varchar(75) NOT NULL,
              State char(3) NOT NULL,
              County varchar(50) NULL,
              PostalCode varchar(10)
       )
```

Now that a table is created, execute the following INSERT commands, which reference the columns in varying order, inserting one row and then multiple rows:

```
Use AdventureWorks
Go
INSERT INTO dbo.Address(City, State, Address1, PostalCode)
VALUES('Houston', 'TX', '1411 Mesa Road', 77016);

INSERT INTO dbo.Address(City, State, Address1, County, PostalCode)
VALUES('Baton Rouge', 'LA', '444 Perkins Road', 'East Baton Rouge',
    70808), ('Chicago', 'IL', '8765 Buttonwood Walk', 'Cook', 60429);
```

The following SELECT command verifies the insert:

```
Use AdventureWorks
go
SELECT AddressID, City, State, Address1, County, PostalCode
FROM dbo.Address;
```

Result (your result may differ depending on the data loaded into the database):

```
AddressID City        State Address1              County            PostalCode
--------- ----------- ----- -------------------- ------------- ---------
1         Houston      TX    1411 Mesa Road        NULL              77016
2         Baton Rouge  LA    444 Perkins Road      East Baton Rouge 70808
3         Chicago      IL    8765 Buttonwood Walk  Cook              60429
```

Not every column in the table must be listed, but if a column appears, then a value must be available for the INSERT command. The first INSERT statement in the previous sample code omitted the County column. The INSERT operation worked nonetheless and inserted a NULL into the omitted column.

If the County column had a default constraint, then the default value would have been inserted instead of the NULL. When a column has both no default and a NOT NULL constraint, and no value is provided in the INSERT statement, the INSERT operation fails.

You can explicitly force the INSERT of a default without knowing the default value. If the keyword DEFAULT is provided in the value-column list, then SQL Server stores the default value for the column. This is a good practice because it documents the intention of the code, rather than leaving the code blank and assuming the default. The insert-column list is required when using row constructors to insert multiple rows.

Explicitly listing the columns is a good idea. It prevents an error if the table schema changes, and it helps document the insert. However, the insert-column list is optional. In this case, the values are inserted into the table according to the order of the columns in the table (ignoring an identity column). It's critical that every table column receive valid data from the value list. Omitting a column in the value list causes the INSERT operation to fail.

You learned earlier that when the columns are explicitly listed within the INSERT... VALUES command, an identity column can't receive a value. Similarly, the identity column is also ignored in the value list when the columns are assumed. The rest of the values are in the same order as the columns of the Guide table, as follows:

```
Use AdventureWorks
go
INSERT INTO dbo.Address
VALUES('3333 Pike Street', 'Seattle', 'WA','Pike', '23674');
```

To view the inserted data, the following SELECT command pulls data from the Guide table:

```
Use AdventureWorks
go
SELECT AddressID, City, State, Address1, County, PostalCode
FROM dbo.Address;
```

Result:

```
AddressID  City         State  address1              County            PostalCode
---------- ----------   -----  --------------------  ----------------  ----------
1          Houston      TX     1411 Mesa Road        NULL              77016
2          Baton Rouge  LA     444 Perkins Road      East Baton Rouge  70808
3          Chicago      IL     8765 Buttonwood Walk  Cook              60429
5          Seattle      WA     3333 Pike Street      Pike              23674
```

However, if you wanted to insert data into the identity column you could use the SET IDENTITY_INSERT keywords. The syntax is as follows:

```
Use AdventureWorks
Go
SET IDENTITY_INSERT dbo.Address ON
INSERT INTO dbo.Address(AddressID, Address1, City, State, County,
    PostalCode)
VALUES(999,'444 Our Way', 'Detroit', 'MI','Pike', '66666');
SET IDENTITY_INSERT dbo.Address OFF
```

After running the insert, if you select the data from the table you will see a new row with the AddressID of 999.

So far in the sample code, values have been hard-coded string literals. Alternatively, the value could be returned from an expression. This is useful when a data type requires conversion, or when data needs to be altered, calculated, or concatenated:

```
Use AdventureWorks
Go
INSERT INTO dbo.Address
VALUES('99934'+' Orange Ct', 'Memphis', 'TN','Vols', '74944');
```

The next SELECT statement verifies the insert:

```
Use AdventureWorks
go
SELECT AddressID, City, State, Address1, County, PostalCode
FROM dbo.Address;
```

Result:

AddressID	City	State	address1	County	PostalCode
1	Houston	TX	1411 Mesa Road	NULL	77016
2	Baton Rouge	LA	444 Perkins Road	East Baton Rouge	70808
3	Chicago	IL	8765 Buttonwood Walk	Cook	60429
5	Seattle	WA	3333 Pike Street	Pike	23674
6	Memphis	TN	99934 Orange Ct	Vols	74944

When the data to be inserted, usually in the form of variables sent from the user interface, is known, inserting using the INSERT...VALUES form is the best insert method.

Typically, to reference values from a data source, the INSERT...SELECT is used, but an INSERT...VALUES can include a scalar subquery as one of the values.

 The topic of subqueries is discussed in detail in Chapter 9, Merging Data with Joins, Subqueries, and CTEs.

Inserting a Result Set from Select

You can move and massage data from one result set into a table by means of the INSERT...SELECT statement. The real power of this method is that the SELECT command can pull data from nearly anywhere and reshape it to fit the current needs. It's this flexibility that the INSERT...SELECT statement exploits. Because SELECT can return an infinite number of rows, this form can insert an infinite number of rows.

Of course, the full power of the SELECT can generate rows for the insert. A simplified form of the syntax follows:

```
INSERT [INTO] schema.Table [(columns, …)]
    SELECT columns
```

```
FROM data sources
[WHERE conditions];
```

As with the INSERT...VALUES statement, the data columns must line up, and the data types must be valid. If the optional insert columns are ignored, then every table column (except an identity column) must be populated in the table order.

The following code sample uses the AdventureWorks database. It selects the first 10 California addresses from the Address table and inserts them into the Address table created in tempdb. All the columns are pulled directly from the table, while the county is a string literal (the Address table is specified by means of a three-part name, database .schema.table):

```
use AdventureWorks
go
INSERT INTO Address
SELECT TOP(10)
      AddressLine1, City, sp.StateProvinceCode, 'Sunshine', PostalCode
FROM Person.Address a
INNER JOIN Person.StateProvince sp
      ON a.StateProvinceID = sp.StateProvinceID
WHERE
      sp.Name = 'California';
```

To verify the insert, the following SELECT statement reads the data from the Address table:

```
Use AdventureWorks
go
SELECT AddressID, City, State,
Address1, County, PostalCode
FROM dbo.Address;
```

Result:

```
City          State address1                  County             PostalCode
-----------   ----- ------------------------  -----------------  ----------
Houston       TX    1411 Mesa Road            NULL               77016
Baton Rouge   LA    444 Perkins Road          East Baton Rouge   70808
Chicago       IL    8765 Buttonwood Walk      Cook               60429
Seattle       WA    3333 Pike Street          Pike               23674
Memphis       TN    99934 Orange Ct           Vols               74944
Los Angeles   CA    1 Smiling Tree Court      Sunshine           90012
Berkeley      CA    1002 N. Spoonwood Court   Sunshine           94704
Colma         CA    1005 Fremont Street       Sunshine           94014
Mill Valley   CA    1005 Matterhorn Ct.       Sunshine           94941
Bellflower    CA    1006 Deercreek Ln         Sunshine           90706
Torrance      CA    1006 Deercreek Ln         Sunshine           90505
El Cajon      CA    1007 Cardinet Dr.         Sunshine           92020
```

```
Burbank      CA     1008 Lydia Lane          Sunshine        91502
Berkeley     CA     1011 Yolanda Circle      Sunshine        94704
Burbank      CA     1016 Park Avenue         Sunshine        91502
```

The key to using the INSERT/SELECT statement is selecting the correct result set. It's a good idea to run the SELECT statement by itself to test the result set prior to executing the insert. Measure twice, cut once.

Inserting the Result Set from a Stored Procedure

The INSERT...EXEC form of the INSERT operation pulls data from a stored procedure and inserts it into a table. Behind these inserts are the full capabilities of T-SQL. The basic function is the same as that of the other insert forms. The columns must line up between the INSERT columns and the stored-procedure result set. Following is the basic syntax of the INSERT...EXEC command:

```
INSERT [INTO] schema.Table [(Columns)]
    EXEC StoredProcedure Parameters;
```

Be careful, though, because stored procedures can easily return multiple record sets, in which case the INSERT attempts to pull data from each of the result sets, and the columns from every result set must line up with the insert columns.

 For more about programming stored procedures, refer to Chapter 17, "Developing Stored Procedures."

The following code sample builds a stored procedure that returns 10 Arizona addresses from the Address table in the AdventureWorks database. When the stored procedure is in place, the sample code performs the INSERT...EXEC statement:

```
use tempdb
go
IF(OBJECT_ID('ListAZAddresses')) IS NOT NULL
      DROP PROC ListAZAddresses
GO
CREATE PROC ListAZAddresses
AS
SELECT --TOP(10)
    AddressLine1, City, sp.StateProvinceCode, 'Sunshine', PostalCode
FROM Person.Address a
INNER JOIN Person.StateProvince sp
    ON a.StateProvinceID = sp.StateProvinceID
WHERE
    sp.Name = 'Arizona';
```

To insert the results set of the stored procedure execution into the Address table use the following:

```
USE AdventureWorks
Go
```

```
INSERT INTO Address
Exec ListAZAddresses;
```

To verify the insert, the following SELECT statement reads the data from the Address table:

```
USE AdventureWorks
GO
SELECT AddressID, City, State,
Address1, County, PostalCode
FROM dbo.Address
WHERE
        State = 'AZ';
```

Result (abbreviated):

```
AddressLine1                   City          StateProvinceCode County   PostalCode
--------------------------     ----------    ---------------   -------- ----------
137 Lancelot Dr                Phoenix       AZ                Sunshine 85004
25250 N 90th St                Scottsdale    AZ                Sunshine 85257
253731 West Bell Road          Surprise      AZ                Sunshine 85374
2551 East Warner Road          Gilbert       AZ                Sunshine 85233
3294 Buena Vista               Lemon Grove   AZ                Sunshine 85284
4584 Hamiliton Ave.            Chandler      AZ                Sunshine 85225
6441 Co Road                   Lemon Grove   AZ                Sunshine 85252
6500 East Grant Road           Tucson        AZ                Sunshine 85701
7656 Ramsey Circle             Chandler      AZ                Sunshine 85225
7709 West Virginia Avenue      Phoenix       AZ                Sunshine 85004
7750 E Marching Rd             Scottsdale    AZ                Sunshine 85257
870 N. 54th Ave.               Chandler      AZ                Sunshine 85225
9228 Via Del Sol               Phoenix       AZ                Sunshine 85004
9980 S Alma School Road        Chandler      AZ                Sunshine 85225
. . .
```

INSERT/EXEC does require more work than INSERT...VALUES or INSERT/SELECT, but because the stored procedure can contain complex logic, it's the most powerful of the three.

In addition to inserting the results of a stored procedure execution into a physical table, you can also insert into variable tables, which can be seen in the following script:

```
declare @address TABLE
(

        Address1 varchar(25) NOT NULL,
        City varchar(13) NOT NULL,
        StateAbbrev char(3) NOT NULL,
        County varchar(10) NULL,
        PostalCode varchar(10)
)
insert into @address
exec ListAZAddresses

select * from @address
```

Results:

Address1	City	StateAbbrev	County	PostalCode
137 Lancelot Dr	Phoenix	AZ	Sunshine	85004
25250 N 90th St	Scottsdale	AZ	Sunshine	85257
253731 West Bell Road	Surprise	AZ	Sunshine	85374
2551 East Warner Road	Gilbert	AZ	Sunshine	85233
3294 Buena Vista	Lemon Grove	AZ	Sunshine	85284
4584 Hamiliton Ave.	Chandler	AZ	Sunshine	85225
6441 Co Road	Lemon Grove	AZ	Sunshine	85252
6500 East Grant Road	Tucson	AZ	Sunshine	85701
7656 Ramsey Circle	Chandler	AZ	Sunshine	85225
7709 West Virginia Avenue	Phoenix	AZ	Sunshine	85004
7750 E Marching Rd	Scottsdale	AZ	Sunshine	85257
870 N. 54th Ave.	Chandler	AZ	Sunshine	85225
9228 Via Del Sol	Phoenix	AZ	Sunshine	85004
9980 S Alma School Road	Chandler	AZ	Sunshine	85225
Arcadia Crossing	Phoenix	AZ	Sunshine	85004
Factory Stores Of America	Mesa	AZ	Sunshine	85201
Factory Stores/tucson	Tucson	AZ	Sunshine	85701
Prime Outlets	Phoenix	AZ	Sunshine	85004

Creating a Default Row

SQL includes a special form of the INSERT command that creates a single new row with only default values. The only parameter of the new row is the table name. Data and column names are not required. The syntax is simple, as shown here:

```
INSERT schema.Table DEFAULT VALUES;
```

I have never used this form of INSERT in any real-world applications. It could be used to create "pigeon hole" rows with only keys and null values, but I don't recommend that design.

Creating a Table While Inserting Data

The last method to insert data is a variation on the SELECT command. The INTO select option takes the results of a SELECT statement and creates a new table containing the results. SELECT...INTO is often used during data conversions and within utilities that must dynamically work with a variety of source-table structures. The full syntax includes every SELECT option. Following is an abbreviated syntax to highlight the function of the INTO option:

```
SELECT Columns
   INTO   NewTable
   FROM DataSources
   [WHERE conditions];
```

The data structure of the newly created table might be less of an exact replication of the original table structure than expected because the new table structure is based on a combination of the original table and the result set of the SELECT statement. String lengths and numerical digit lengths may change. If the SELECT...INTO command pulls data from only one table and the SELECT statement contains no data-type conversion functions, then there's a good chance that the table columns and null settings will remain intact. However, keys, constraints, and indexes will be lost.

SELECT...INTO is a bulk-logged operation, similar to BULK INSERT and BULK COPY. Bulk-logged operations may enable SQL Server to quickly move data into tables by minimally recording the bulk-logged operations to the transaction log (depending on the database's recovery model). Therefore, the database options and recovery model affect SELECT...INTO and the other bulk-logged operations.

 For more about BULK INSERT and BULK COPY, refer to Chapter 16, "Programming with T-SQL." For details on recovery models, refer to Chapter 21, "Backup and Recovery Planning."

The following code sample demonstrates the SELECT/INTO command as it creates the new table PersonList by extracting data from Person table in the AdventureWorks database (some results abridged):

```
USE AdventureWorks;

-- sample code for setting the bulk-logged behavior
ALTER DATABASE AdventureWorks SET RECOVERY BULK_LOGGED;

-- the select/into statement

Use AdventureWorks
GO
SELECT BusinessEntityID, LastName, FirstName
INTO PersonList
FROM Person.Person
ORDER BY
     LastName, FirstName;
...
```

The following insert adds a new row to test the identity column created by the SELECT/INTO:

```
INSERT PersonList (BusinessEntityID, LastName, FirstName)
  VALUES(99999,'LeBlanc', 'Patrick');
```

To view the data inserted using the SELECT/INTO command and the row that was just added with the INSERT...VALUES command, the following SELECT statement extracts data from the PersonList table:

```
SELECT * FROM PersonList
```

Results:

```
BusinessEntityID LastName        FirstName
---------------- -------------   --------
285              Abbas           Syed
293              Abel            Catherine
295              Abercrombie     Kim
2170             Abercrombie     Kim
38               Abercrombie     Kim
211              Abolrous        Hazem
2357             Abolrous        Sam
```

I recommend that you manually build tables, or at least carefully check the data structures created by SELECT/INTO.

SELECT/INTO can serve many useful functions:

- If zero rows are selected from a table, then SELECT/INTO creates a new table with only the data schema (although with the limitations listed earlier).
- If SELECT reorders the columns, or includes the cast() function, then the new table retains the data within a modified data schema.
- When combined with a UNION query, SELECT/INTO can vertically combine data from multiple tables. The INTO goes in the first SELECT statement of a UNION query.
- SELECT/INTO is especially useful for denormalizing tables. The SELECT statement can pull from multiple tables and create a new flat-file table.

> **CAUTION**
> There's one caveat concerning SELECT/INTO and development style: The SELECT/INTO statement should not replace the use of joins or views. When the new table is created, it's a snapshot in time — a second copy of the data. Databases containing multiple copies of old data sets are a sure sign of trouble. If you need to denormalize data for ad hoc analysis, or to pass to a user, then creating a view is likely a better alternative.

Updating Data

SQL's UPDATE command is an incredibly powerful tool. What used to take dozens of lines of code with multiple nested loops now takes a single statement. Even better, SQL is not a true language — it's a declarative language. The SQL code is describing to the Query Optimizer only what you want to do. The Query Optimizer then develops a cost-based, optimized query execution plan to accomplish the task. It determines which tables to fetch and in which order, how to merge the joins, and which indexes to use. It does this based on several factors, including the current data-population statistics, the indexes available, how they relate to the data population within the table, and table sizes. The Query Optimizer even considers current CPU performance, memory capacity, and hard-drive performance when designing the plan. Writing code to perform the update row-by-row could never result in that level of optimization.

Updating a Single Table

The UPDATE command in SQL is straightforward and simple. It can update one column of one row in a table, or every column in every row in the updated table, but the optional FROM clause enables that table to be part of a complete complex data source with all the power of the SQL SELECT.

Following is how the UPDATE command works:

```
UPDATE schema.Table
  SET column = expression,
    column = value…
  [FROM  data sources]
  [WHERE conditions];
```

The UPDATE command can update multiple rows but only one table. The SET keyword is used to modify data in any column in the table to a new value. The new value can be a hard-coded string literal, a variable, an expression, or even another column from the data sources listed in the FROM portion of the SQL UPDATE statement.

 For a comprehensive list of expression possibilities, see Chapter 8, "Data Types, Expressions, and Scalar Functions."

The WHERE clause is vital to any UPDATE statement. Without it, the entire table is updated. If a WHERE clause is present, then only the rows not filtered out by the WHERE clause are updated. Be sure to check and double-check the WHERE clause. Again, measure twice, cut once. Remember, there is not an undo command.

The following sample UPDATE resembles a typical real-life operation, altering the value of one column for a single row. The best way to perform a single-row update is to filter the UPDATE operation by referencing the primary key:

```
USE AdventureWorks;
UPDATE dbo.Address
SET Address1 = '1970 Napa Court'
WHERE AddressID = 1
```

The following SELECT statement confirms the preceding UPDATE command:

```
Use AdventureWorks
go
SELECT AddressID, Address1
  FROM dbo.Address
  WHERE AddressID = 1;
```

Result:

```
AddressID  Address1
----------  -------------
1           1970 Napa Court
```

Performing Global Search and Replace

Cleaning up bad data is a common database developer task. Fortunately, SQL includes a REPLACE() function, which when combined with the UPDATE command can serve as a global search and replace. You can use this to remove extra tabs from data.

In the following example, which references the AdventureWorks sample database, every occurrence of 'Sun' in the County column is updated to 'Dark':

```
Use AdventureWorks
Go
UPDATE Address
SET County = REPLACE(County, 'Sun', 'Dark')
WHERE County LIKE '%Shine';
```

The following SELECT statement examines the result of the REPLACE() function:

```
Select County from Address
WHERE County LIKE '%Shine';
```

Result (abbreviated):

```
County
---------
Darkshine
Darkshine
Darkshine
Darkshine
. . .
```

Referencing Multiple Tables While Updating Data

A more powerful function of the SQL UPDATE command is setting a column to an expression that can refer to the same column, other columns, or even other tables.

Although expressions are certainly available within a single-table update, expressions often need to reference data outside the updated table. The optional FROM clause enables joins between the table being updated and other data sources. Only one table can be updated, but when the table is joined to the corresponding rows from the joined tables, the data from the other columns is available within the UPDATE expressions.

One way to envision the FROM clause is to picture the joins merging all the tables into a new super-wide result set. Then the rest of the SQL statement sees only that new result set. Although that is what's happening in the FROM clause, the actual UPDATE operation is functioning not on the new result set, but only on the declared UPDATE table.

The following queries first adds the HasPurchased column to the Customer table in the AdventureWork table; then the next query uses the FROM clause to access the Customer and SalesOrderHeader tables. The JOIN limits the query to only those customer rows that have placed orders. The UPDATE command updates only the Customer table:

```
use AdventureWorks
go

ALTER TABLE Sales.Customer
ADD HasPurchased bit;

UPDATE Sales.Customer
SET HasPurchased = 1
FROM Sales.Customer c
INNER JOIN Sales.SalesOrderHeader soh
        ON c.CustomerID = soh.CustomerID
```

CAUTION

The UPDATE FROM syntax is a T-SQL extension and not standard ANSI SQL 92. If the database will possibly be ported to another database platform in the future, then use a subquery to select the correct rows:

```
USE AdventureWorks
go
UPDATE Sales.Customer
SET HasPurchased = 1
FROM Sales.Customer c
WHERE CustomerID IN (SELECT CustomerID FROM Sales.SalesOrderHeader)
```

For a real-life example, suppose all employees will soon be granted a generous across-the-board raise (OK, so it's not a real-life example) based on department, length of service in the position, performance rating, and length of time with the company. If the percentage for each department is stored in the Department table, SQL can adjust the salary for every employee with a single UPDATE statement by joining the Employee table with the Department table and pulling the Department raise factor from the joined table. Assume the formula is as follows:

```
2 + (((Years in Company * .1) + (Months in Position * .02)
+ ((PerformanceFactor * .5 ) if over 2))
 * Department RaiseFactor)
```

The sample code sets up the scenario by creating a couple of tables and populating them with test data:

```
USE AdventureWorks

CREATE TABLE dbo.Dept (
   DeptID INT IDENTITY
            NOT NULL
            PRIMARY KEY,
   DeptName VARCHAR(50) NOT NULL,
   RaiseFactor NUMERIC(4, 2)
   )

CREATE  TABLE dbo.Employee (
   EmployeeID INT IDENTITY
                NOT NULL
                PRIMARY KEY,
   DeptID INT FOREIGN KEY REFERENCES Dept,
   LastName VARCHAR(50) NOT NULL,
   FirstName VARCHAR(50) NOT NULL,
   Salary NUMERIC(9,2) NOT NULL,
   PerformanceRating NUMERIC(4,2) NOT NULL,
   DateHire DATE NOT NULL,
   DatePosition DATE NOT NULL
   )

INSERT dbo.Dept (DeptName, RaiseFactor)
  VALUES ('Engineering', 1.2),
         ('Sales', .8),
         ('IT', 2.5),
         ('Manufacturing', 1.0) ;

INSERT dbo.Employee (DeptID, LastName, FirstName,
       Salary, PerformanceRating, DateHire, DatePosition)
  VALUES (1, 'Smith', 'Sam', 54000, 2.0, '19970101', '19970101'),
         (1, 'Nelson', 'Slim', 78000, 1.5, '19970101', '19970101'),
         (2, 'Ball', 'Sally', 45000, 3.5, '19990202', '19990202'),
         (2, 'Kelly', 'Jeff', 85000, 2.4, '20020625', '20020625'),
         (3, 'Guelzow', 'Jo', 120000, 4.0, '19991205', '19991205'),
         (3, 'Ander', 'Missy', 95000, 1.8, '19980201', '19980201'),
         (4, 'Reagan', 'Sam', 75000, 2.9, '20051215', '20051215'),
         (4, 'Adams', 'Hank', 34000, 3.2, '20080501', '20080501');
```

When developing complex queries, work from the inside out. The first step performs the date math; it selects the data required for the raise calculation, assuming June 25, 2012 is the effective date of the raise, and ensures the performance rating won't count if it's only 1:

```
SELECT EmployeeID, Salary,
   CAST(CAST(DATEDIFF(d, DateHire, '20120625')
   AS DECIMAL(7, 2)) / 365.25 AS INT)
      AS YrsCo,
CAST(CAST(DATEDIFF(d, DatePosition, '20120625')
      AS DECIMAL(7, 2)) / 365.25
      * 12 AS INT)
      AS MoPos,
   CASE WHEN Employee.PerformanceRating >= 2
         THEN Employee.PerformanceRating
         ELSE 0
   END AS Perf,
   Dept.RaiseFactor
  FROM dbo.Employee
   JOIN dbo.Dept
     ON Employee.DeptID = Dept.DeptID
```

Result:

```
EmployeeID  Salary     YrsCo       MoPos        Perf    RaiseFactor
----------- -------    ----------  ----------   ------  -----------
1           54000.00   15          185          2.00    1.20
2           78000.00   15          185          0.00    1.20
3           45000.00   13          160          3.50    0.80
4           85000.00   10          120          2.40    0.80
5           120000.00  12          150          4.00    2.50
6           95000.00   14          172          0.00    2.50
7           75000.00   6           78           2.90    1.00
8           34000.00   4           49           3.20    1.00
```

The next step in developing this query is to add the raise calculation. The simplest way to see the calculation is to pull the values already generated from a subquery:

```
SELECT EmployeeID,  Salary,
     (2 + ((YearsCompany * .1) + (MonthPosition * .02)
     + (Performance * .5)) * RaiseFactor) / 100 AS EmpRaise
  FROM (SELECT EmployeeID, FirstName, LastName, Salary,
            CAST(CAST(DATEDIFF(d, DateHire, '20120625') AS
            DECIMAL(7, 2)) / 365.25 AS INT) AS YearsCompany,
            CAST(CAST(DATEDIFF(d, DatePosition, '20120625') AS
            DECIMAL(7, 2)) / 365.25 * 12 AS INT) AS MonthPosition,
            CASE WHEN Employee.PerformanceRating >= 2
               THEN Employee.PerformanceRating
               ELSE 0
            END AS Performance, Dept.RaiseFactor
          FROM dbo.Employee
           JOIN dbo.Dept
             ON Employee.DeptID = Dept.DeptID) AS SubQuery
```

Result:

```
EmployeeID  Salary       EmpRaise
----------- ------------ ----------------
1           54000.00     0.082160000
2           78000.00     0.070160000
3           45000.00     0.061840000
4           85000.00     0.048640000
5           120000.00    0.149500000
6           95000.00     0.115500000
7           75000.00     0.046900000
8           34000.00     0.039600000
```

The last query was relatively easy to read, but there's no logical reason for the subquery. The query could be rewritten combining the date calculations and the case expression into the raise formula:

```
SELECT EmployeeID, Salary,
    (2 +
    -- years with company
    + ((CAST(CAST(DATEDIFF(d, DateHire, '20120625')
        AS DECIMAL(7, 2)) / 365.25 AS INT) * .1)
    -- months in position
    + (CAST(CAST(DATEDIFF(d, DatePosition, '20120625')
        AS DECIMAL(7, 2)) / 365.25 * 12 AS INT) * .02)
    -- Performance Rating minimum
    + (CASE WHEN Employee.PerformanceRating >= 2
            THEN Employee.PerformanceRating
          ELSE 0
      END * .5))
    -- Raise Factor
    * RaiseFactor) / 100 AS EmpRaise
  FROM dbo.Employee
    JOIN dbo.Dept
      ON Employee.DeptID = Dept.DeptID
```

It's easy to verify that this query gets the same result, but which is the better query? From a performance perspective, both queries generate the exact same query execution plan. When considering maintenance and readability, you should probably go with the second query carefully formatted and commented.

The final step is to convert the query into an UPDATE command. The hard part is already done — it just needs the UPDATE verb at the front of the query:

```
UPDATE Employee

SET Salary = Salary *
    (1 + ((2
    -- years with company
    + ((CAST(CAST(DATEDIFF(d, DateHire, '20120625')
```

```
            AS DECIMAL(7, 2)) / 365.25 AS INT) * .1)
     -- months in position
   + (CAST(CAST(DATEDIFF(d, DatePosition, '20120625')
          AS DECIMAL(7, 2)) / 365.25 * 12 AS INT) * .02)
     -- Performance Rating minimum
   + (CASE WHEN Employee.PerformanceRating >= 2
             THEN Employee.PerformanceRating
           ELSE 0
       END * .5))
     -- Raise Factor
      * RaiseFactor) / 100 ))
  FROM dbo.Employee
    JOIN dbo.Dept
      ON Employee.DeptID = Dept.DeptID
```

A quick check of the data confirms that the update was successful:

```
SELECT FirstName, LastName, Salary
  FROM dbo.Employee
```

Result:

```
FirstName     LastName        Salary
-----------   -------------   ----------
Sam           Smith           59097.60
Slim          Nelson          84427.20
Sally         Ball            48150.00
Jeff          Kelly           89828.00
Jo            Guelzow         141000.00
Missy         Anderson        108395.00
Sam           Reagan          79207.50
Hank          Adams           35603.20
```

The final step of the exercise is to clean up the sample tables:

```
DROP TABLE dbo.Employee, dbo.Dept;
```

This sample code pulls together techniques from many of the previous chapters: creating and dropping tables, CASE expressions, joins, and date scalar functions, not to mention the inserts and updates from this chapter. The example is long because it demonstrates more than just the UPDATE statement. It also shows the typical process of developing a complex UPDATE, which includes the following:

1. **Check the available data:** The first SELECT joins employee and dept and lists all the columns required for the formula.

2. **Test the formula:** The second SELECT is based on the initial SELECT and assembles the formula from the required rows. From this data, a couple of rows can be hand-tested against the specs, and the formula verified.

3. **Perform the update:** After the formula is constructed and verified, the formula is edited into an UPDATE statement and executed.

The SQL UPDATE command *is* powerful. The terribly complex record sets and nested loops that were painfully slow and error-prone have been replaced with UPDATE statements and creative joins that worked well. As a result, execution times have been reduced from hours to a few seconds.

Deleting Data

The DELETE command is dangerously simple. In its basic form, it deletes all the rows from a table. Because the DELETE command is a row-based operation, it doesn't require specifying any column names. The first FROM is optional, as are the second FROM and the WHERE conditions. However, although the WHERE clause is optional, it is the primary subject of concern when you use the DELETE command. Following is an abbreviated syntax for the DELETE command:

```
DELETE [FROM] schema.Table
  [FROM data sources]
  [WHERE condition(s)];
```

Everything is optional except the actual DELETE command and the table name. The following command would delete all data from the Address table — no questions asked and no second chances:

```
DELETE
  FROM AdventureWorks.dbo.Address1;
```

SQL Server has no inherent UNDO command. When a transaction is committed, that's it. That's why the WHERE clause is so important when you're deleting.

By far, the most common use of the DELETE command is to delete a single row. The primary key is usually the means to select the row:

```
USE AdventureWorks;
DELETE FROM dbo.Address
  WHERE AddressID = 1;
```

If you wanted to completely remove data from a table, the TRUNCATE option is available:

```
TRUNCATE TABLE dbo.Address
```

CAUTION

Please be careful when executing a TRUNCATE statement. It removes all data from a table and there is not an UNDO in SQL Server.

Referencing Multiple Data Sources While Deleting

You can use two techniques for referencing multiple data sources while deleting rows: the double FROM clause and subqueries.

The UPDATE command uses the FROM clause to join the updated table with other tables for more flexible row selection. The DELETE command can use the exact same technique. When using this method, the first optional FROM can make it look confusing. To improve readability and consistency, you can omit the first FROM in your code.

For example, the following DELETE statement ignores the first FROM clause and uses the second FROM clause to join Product with ProductCategory so that the WHERE clause can filter the DELETE based on the ProductCategoryName. This query creates the dbo. Product table then removes all jerseys from the Product table:

```
USE AdventureWorks;
SELECT *
INTO dbo.Product
FROM Production.Product

DELETE dbo.Product
FROM dbo.Product p
INNER JOIN Production.ProductSubcategory s
    ON p.ProductSubcategoryID = s.ProductSubcategoryID
WHERE s.Name = 'Jerseys'
```

The second method looks more complicated at first glance, but it's ANSI standard and the preferred method. A correlated subquery actually selects the rows to be deleted, and the DELETE command just picks up those rows for the DELETE operation. It's a clean query:

```
DELETE FROM dbo.Product
  WHERE EXISTS
    (SELECT *
      FROM Production.ProductSubcategory AS ps
      WHERE ps.ProductSubcategoryID = Product.ProductSubcategoryID
        AND ps.Name = 'Jerseys');
```

In terms of performance, both methods generate the exact same query execution plan.

> **CAUTION**
>
> As with the UPDATE command's FROM clause, the DELETE command's second FROM clause is not an ANSI SQL standard. If portability is important to your project, then use a subquery to reference additional tables.

Cascading Deletes

Referential integrity (RI) refers to the idea that no secondary row foreign key should point to a primary row primary key unless that primary row exists. This means that an attempt to delete a primary row can fail if a foreign-key value somewhere points to that primary row.

 For more information about referential integrity and when to use it, turn to Chapter 7, "Relational Database Design and Creating the Physical Database Schema," and Chapter 2, "Data Architecture."

When correctly implemented, referential integrity blocks any delete operation that would result in a foreign key value without a corresponding primary key value. The way around this is to first delete the secondary rows that point to the primary row, and then delete the primary row. This technique is called a *cascading delete*. In a complex database schema, the cascade might bounce down several levels before working its way back up to the original row being deleted.

You can implement a cascading delete in two ways: manually with triggers or automatically with *declared referential integrity (DRI)* via foreign keys.

Manually implementing cascading deletes is a lot of work. Triggers are significantly slower than foreign keys (which are checked as part of the query execution plan), and trigger-based cascading deletes usually also handle the foreign key checks. Although this was commonplace a decade ago, today trigger-based cascading deletes are rare and might be needed only with a complex nonstandard foreign key design that includes business rules in the foreign key. If you do that, then you're either new at this or very, very good.

Fortunately, SQL Server offers cascading deletes as a function of the foreign key. Cascading deletes may be enabled via Management Studio, in the Foreign Key Relationship dialog, or in SQL code.

The following script drops an existing foreign key relationship between the `HumanResource.JobCandidate` and the `HumanResources.Employee` tables in the `AdventureWorks` database. Next it adds a new foreign key between the table setting the cascade delete option for referential integrity. The `ON DELETE CASCADE` foreign-key option is what actually specifies the cascade action:

```
USE [AdventureWorks]
GO
ALTER TABLE [HumanResources].[JobCandidate]
    DROP CONSTRAINT [FK_JobCandidate_Employee_BusinessEntityID]
GO

ALTER TABLE [HumanResources].[JobCandidate]
    WITH CHECK ADD  CONSTRAINT [FK_JobCandidate_Employee_BusinessEntityID]
        FOREIGN KEY([BusinessEntityID])
```

```
            REFERENCES [HumanResources].[Employee] ([BusinessEntityID])
                  ON DELETE CASCADE
     GO
```

As a caution, cascading deletes, or even referential integrity, are not suitable for every relationship. It depends on the permanence of the secondary row. If deleting the primary row makes the secondary row moot or meaningless, then cascading the delete makes good sense; but if the secondary row is still a valid row after the primary row is deleted, then referential integrity and cascading deletes would cause the database to break its representation of reality.

Alternatives to Physically Deleting Data

Some database developers choose to completely avoid deleting data. Instead, they build systems to remove the data from the user's view while retaining the data for safekeeping like dBase did. This can be done in several different ways:

- A logical-delete bit flag, or nullable MomentDeleted column is added to each row. The bit flag is set to zero by default. When the row is deleted it is set to 1, marking the row as logically deleted. The MomentDeleted is a datetime column that is null initially. When the row is deleted the column is updated to the date and time of the delete. This makes deleting or restoring a single row a straightforward matter of setting or clearing a bit. However, because a relational database involves multiple related tables, there's more work to it than that. All queries must check the logical-delete flag and filter out logically deleted rows. This means that a bit column (with extremely poor selectivity) is probably an important index for every query. Although SQL Server's filtered indexes are a perfect fit, it's still a performance killer.

- The cascading logical deletes method is complex to code and difficult to maintain. This is a case of complexity breeding complexity, so the authors no longer recommend this method.

- Another alternative to physically deleting rows is to archive the deleted rows in an archive or audit table. This method is best implemented by an INSTEAD OF trigger that copies the data to the alternative location and then physically deletes the rows from the production database. This method offers several advantages. Data is physically removed from the database, so there's no need to artificially modify SELECT queries or index on a bit column. Physically removing the data enables SQL Server referential integrity to remain in effect. In addition, the database is not burdened with unnecessary data. Retrieving archived data remains relatively straightforward and can be easily accomplished with a view that selects data from the archive location.

 Chapter 42, "SQL Audit," details how to automatically generate the audit system discussed here that stores, views, and recovers deleted rows.

Merging Data

An *upsert* operation is a logical combination of an insert and an update. If the data isn't already in the table, the upsert inserts the data; if the data is already in the table, then the upsert updates with the differences. Ignoring for a moment the MERGE command in SQL Server, you can code an upsert operation with T-SQL in a few ways:

- The most common method is to attempt to locate the data with an IF EXISTS; if the row is found, UPDATE; otherwise INSERT.

- If the most common use case is that the row exists and the UPDATE is needed, then the best method is to do the update; if @@RowCount = 0, then the row was new, and the insert should be performed.

- If the overwhelming use case is that the row would be new to the database, then TRY to INSERT the new row; if a unique index blocked the INSERT and fired an error, then CATCH the error and UPDATE instead.

All three methods are potentially obsolete with the new MERGE command. The MERGE command is well done by Microsoft — it solves a complex problem with a clean syntax and good performance.

First, it's called "merge" because it does more than an upsert. Upsert inserts or updates only; merge can be directed to insert, update, and delete all in one command.

In a nutshell, MERGE sets up a join between the source table and the target table and can then perform operations based on matches between the two tables.

To walk through a merge scenario, the following example sets up an airline flight check-in scenario. The main work table is FlightPassengers, which holds data about reservations. It's updated as travelers check in, and by the time the flight takes off, it has the actual final passenger list and seat assignments. In the sample scenario, four passengers are scheduled to fly SQL Server Airlines flight 2008 (Denver to Seattle) on March 1, 2008. Poor Jerry, he has a middle seat on the last row of the plane — the row that doesn't recline:

```
USE AdventureWorks;

-- Merge Target Table
CREATE TABLE
FlightPassengers
  (
    FlightID INT NOT NULL
                IDENTITY
                PRIMARY KEY,
    LastName VARCHAR(50) NOT NULL,
    FirstName VARCHAR(50) NOT NULL,
    FlightCode CHAR(6) NOT NULL,
    FlightDate DATE NOT NULL,
```

```
   Seat CHAR(3) NOT NULL
   );

INSERT FlightPassengers
          (LastName, FirstName, FlightCode, FlightDate, Seat)
    VALUES ('LeBlanc, 'Patrick, 'SS2008', '20090301', '9F'),
           ('Jenkins', 'Sue', 'SS2008', '20090301', '7A'),
           ('Smith', 'Sam', 'SS2008', '20090301', '19A'),
           ('Nixon', 'Jerry', 'SS2008', '20090301', '29B');
```

The day of the flight, the check-in counter records all the passengers as they arrive, and their seat assignments, in the CheckIn table. One passenger doesn't show, a new passenger buys a ticket, and Jerry decides today is a good day to burn an upgrade coupon:

```
-- Merge Source table
CREATE TABLE
CheckIn
 (
   LastName VARCHAR(50),
   FirstName VARCHAR(50),
   FlightCode CHAR(6),
   FlightDate DATE,
   Seat CHAR(3)
   );

INSERT
CheckIn
 (LastName, FirstName, FlightCode, FlightDate, Seat)
    VALUES ('LeBlanc, 'Patrick, 'SS2008', '20090301', '9F'),
           ('Jenkins', 'Sue', 'SS2008', '20090301', '7A'),
           ('Nixon', 'Jerry', 'SS2008', '20090301', '2A'),
           ('Anderson', 'Missy', 'SS2008', '20090301', '4B');
```

Before the MERGE command is executed, the next three queries look for differences in the data. The first set-difference query returns any no-show passengers. A LEFT OUTER JOIN between the FlightPassengers and CheckIn tables finds every passenger with a reservation joined with their CheckIn row if the row is available. If no CheckIn row is found, then the LEFT OUTER JOIN fills in the CheckIn column with nulls. Filtering for the null returns only those passengers who made a reservation but didn't make the flight:

```
-- NoShows
SELECT F.FirstName + ' ' + F.LastName AS Passenger, F.Seat
  FROM FlightPassengers AS F

LEFT OUTER JOIN
 CheckIn AS C
     ON C.LastName = F.LastName
        AND C.FirstName = F.FirstName
        AND C.FlightCode = F.FlightCode
```

```
                   AND C.FlightDate = F.FlightDate
       WHERE
   C.LastName IS NULL
```

Result:

```
Passenger                    Seat
-------------------------    -------
Sam Smith                    19A
```

The walk-up check-in query uses a LEFT OUTER JOIN and an IS NULL in the
WHERE clause to locate any passengers who are in the CheckIn table but not in the
FlightPassenger table:

```
-- Walk Up CheckIn
SELECT C.FirstName + ' ' + C.LastName AS Passenger, C.Seat
  FROM CheckIn AS C

LEFT OUTER JOIN
 FlightPassengers AS F
      ON C.LastName = F.LastName
         AND C.FirstName = F.FirstName
         AND C.FlightCode = F.FlightCode
         AND C.FlightDate = F.FlightDate
     WHERE
   F.LastName IS NULL
```

Result:

```
Passenger                    Seat
-------------------------    -------
Missy Anderson               4B
```

The last difference query lists any seat changes, including Jerry's upgrade to first class.
This query uses an inner join because it's searching for passengers who both had previous
seat assignments and now are boarding with a seat assignment. The query compares the
seat columns from the FlightPassenger and CheckIn tables using a not equal comparison, which finds any passengers with a different seat than previously assigned. Go Jerry!

```
-- Seat Changes
SELECT C.FirstName + ' ' + C.LastName AS Passenger, F.Seat AS
    'previous seat', C.Seat AS 'final seat'
  FROM CheckIn AS C
    INNER JOIN FlightPassengers AS F
      ON C.LastName = F.LastName
         AND C.FirstName = F.FirstName
         AND C.FlightCode = F.FlightCode
         AND C.FlightDate = F.FlightDate
         AND C.Seat <> F.Seat
   WHERE F.Seat IS NOT NULL
```

Result:

```
Passenger                        previous seat   final seat
----------------------------     -------------   ----------
Jerry Nixon                      29B             2A
```

CAUTION

For another explanation of set difference queries, flip to Chapter 9, "Merging Data with Joins, Subqueries, and CTEs."

With the scenario's data in place and verified with set-difference queries, it's time to merge the check-in data into the FlightPassenger table.

The first section of the merge query identifies the target and source tables and how they relate. Following the table definition, there's an optional clause for each match combination, as shown in this simplified syntax:

```
MERGE TargetTable
  USING SourceTable
    ON join conditions
[WHEN Matched
   THEN DML]
[WHEN NOT MATCHED BY TARGET
   THEN DML]
[WHEN NOT MATCHED BY SOURCE
   THEN DML]
```

Applying the MERGE command to the airline check-in scenario, there's an appropriate action for each match combination:

- If the row is in both FlightPassengers (the target) and CheckIn (the source), then the target is updated with the CheckIn table's seat column.

- If the row is present in CheckIn (the source) but there's no match in FlightPassenger (the target), then the row from CheckIn is inserted into FlightPassenger. The data from the source table is gathered by the INSERT command using INSERT...VALUES.

- If the row is present in FlightPassenger (the target), but there's no match in CheckIn (the source), then the row is deleted from FlightPassenger. The DELETE command deletes from the target and does not require a WHERE clause because the rows are filtered by the MERGE command.

Following is the complete working MERGE command for the scenario:

```
MERGE FlightPassengers F

USING CheckIn C
```

```
    ON C.LastName = F.LastName
       AND C.FirstName = F.FirstName
       AND C.FlightCode = F.FlightCode
       AND C.FlightDate = F.FlightDate
WHEN Matched
THEN UPDATE
               SET F.Seat = C.Seat
WHEN NOT MATCHED BY TARGET
       THEN INSERT (FirstName, LastName, FlightCode, FlightDate, Seat)
               VALUES (FirstName, LastName, FlightCode, FlightDate, Seat)
WHEN NOT MATCHED BY SOURCE
  THEN DELETE ;
```

The next query looks at the results of the MERGE command, returning the finalized passenger list for SQL Server Airlines flight 2008:

```
SELECT FlightID, FirstName, LastName, FlightCode, FlightDate, Seat
  FROM FlightPassengers
```

Result:

```
FlightID    FirstName    LastName    FlightCode    FlightDate  Seat
----------  -----------  ----------  ------------  ----------  ----
1           Patrick      LeBlanc     SS2008        2009-03-01  9F
2           Sue          Jenkins     SS2008        2009-03-01  7A
4           Jerry        Nixon       SS2008        2009-03-01  2A
5           Missy        Anderson    SS2008        2009-03-01  4B
```

MERGE has a few specific rules:

- It must be terminated by a semicolon.
- The rows must match one-to-one. One-to-many matches are not permitted.
- The join conditions must be deterministic, meaning they are repeatable.

Returning Modified Data

SQL Server can optionally return the modified data as a data set for further use. This can be useful to perform more work on the modified data, or to return the data to the front-end application to eliminate an extra round-trip to the server.

The OUTPUT clause can access the inserted and deleted virtual tables, as well as any data source referenced in the FROM clause, to select the data to be returned. Normally used only by triggers, inserted and deleted virtual tables contain the before and after views to the transaction. The deleted virtual table stores the old data, and the inserted virtual table stores the newly inserted or updated data.

For more examples of the inserted and deleted table, turn to Chapter 18, "Building User-Defined Functions."

Returning Data from an Insert

The INSERT command makes the inserted virtual table available. The following example, taken from earlier in this chapter, has been edited to include the OUTPUT clause. The inserted virtual table has a picture of the new data being inserted and returns the data:

```
USE AdventureWorks
GO
INSERT INTO PersonList
OUTPUT Inserted.*
VALUES(77777, 'Jane', 'Doe');
```

Result:

```
BusinessEntityID    LastName       FirstName
----------------    -------------  --------------
7777                Jane           Doe
```

Best Practice

An excellent application of the OUTPUT clause within an INSERT is returning the values of newly created surrogate keys. The identity_scope() function returns the last single identity inserted, but it can't return a set of new identity values. There is no function to return the GUID value just created by a newsequentialid() default. However, the OUTPUT clause returns sets of new surrogate keys regardless of their data type. You can almost think of the INSERT...OUTPUT as a scope_GUID() function or a set-based scope_identity().

Returning Data from an Update

The OUTPUT clause also works with updates and can return the before and after picture of the data. In this example, the deleted virtual table is used to grab the original value, whereas the inserted virtual table stores the new updated value. Only the Qualifications column is returned:

```
use AdventureWorks;
UPDATE PersonList
SET FirstName = 'Jane', LastName = 'Doe'
OUTPUT Deleted.FirstName OldFirstName,Deleted.LastName OldLastName,
Inserted.FirstName NewFirstName, Inserted.LastName NewLastName
WHERE BusinessEntityID = 77777
```

Result:

```
OldFirstName      OldLastName       NewFirstName    NewLastName
----------------  ----------------  --------------- ---------------
Doe               Jane              Jane            Doe
```

Returning Data from a Delete

When deleting data, only the deleted table has any useful data to return:

```
Use AdventureWorks
Go
DELETE FROM PersonList
OUTPUT DELETED.*
WHERE BusinessEntityID = 77777
```

Result:

```
BusinessEntityID LastName      FirstName
---------------- ------------  --------------
77777            Doe           Jane
```

Returning Data from a Merge

The MERGE command can return data using the OUTPUT clause as well. A twist is that the MERGE command adds a column, $action, to identify whether the row was inserted, updated, or deleted from the target table. The next query adds the OUTPUT clause to the previous MERGE command:

```
MERGE FlightPassengers F
  USING CheckIn C
  ON C.LastName = F.LastName
    AND C.FirstName = F.FirstName
    AND C.FlightCode = F.FlightCode
    AND C.FlightDate = F.FlightDate
  WHEN MATCHED
    THEN UPDATE
        SET F.Seat = C.Seat
  WHEN NOT MATCHED BY TARGET
    THEN INSERT (FirstName, LastName, FlightCode, FlightDate, Seat)
        VALUES (FirstName, LastName, FlightCode, FlightDate, Seat)
  WHEN NOT MATCHED BY SOURCE
    THEN DELETE
OUTPUT
    deleted.FlightID, deleted.LastName, Deleted.Seat,
$action,
    inserted.FlightID, inserted.LastName, inserted.Seat ;
```

Result:

```
FlightID   LastName   Seat    $action   FlightID   LastName   Seat
---------  ---------  -----   --------  ---------  ---------  ----
NULL       NULL       NULL    INSERT    5          Anderson   4B
1          LeBlanc    9F      UPDATE    1          LeBlanc    9F
2          Jenkins    7A      UPDATE    2          Jenkins    7A
3          Smith      2A      DELETE    NULL       NULL       NULL
4          Nixon      29B     UPDATE    4          Nixon      2A
```

Returning Data into a Table

For T-SQL developers, the OUTPUT clause can return the data for use within a batch or stored procedure. The data is received into a user table, temp table, or table variable, which must already have been created. Although the syntax may seem similar to the INSERT...INTO syntax, it actually functions differently.

In the following example, the OUTPUT clause passes the results to a @DeletedPerson table variable:

```
DECLARE @DeletedPerson TABLE (
  BusinessEntityID INT NOT NULL PRIMARY KEY,
  LastName VARCHAR(50) NOT NULL,
  FirstName VARCHAR(50) NOT NULL
  );

DELETE dbo.PersonList
  OUTPUT Deleted.BusinessEntityID, Deleted.LastName,
         Deleted.FirstName
  INTO @DeletedPerson
  WHERE BusinessEntityID = 2;
```

Interim result:

```
(1 row(s) affected)
```

Continuing the batch...

```
SELECT BusinessEntityID, LastName, FirstName FROM @DeletePerson;
```

Result:

```
(1 row(s) affected)
BusinessEntityID LastName    FirstName
---------------- ----------- ------------
64               Zwilling    Michael
```

 An advance use of the OUTPUT clause, called *composable DML*, passes the output data to an outer query, which can then be used in an INSERT command. For more details, refer to Chapter 9, "Merging Data with Joins, Subqueries, and CTEs."

Summary

Data retrieval and data modification are primary tasks of a database application. This chapter examined the workhorse INSERT, UPDATE, DELETE, and MERGE DML commands and described how you can use them to manipulate data.

Key points in this chapter include the following:

- There are multiple formats for the INSERT command depending on the data's source: INSERT...VALUES, INSERT...SELECT, INSERT...EXEC, and INSERT...DEFAULT.
- INSERT...VALUES now has row constructors to insert multiple rows with a single INSERT.
- INSERT...INTO creates a new table and then inserts the results into the new table.
- UPDATE always updates only a single table, but it can use an optional FROM clause to reference other data sources.
- Using DELETE without a WHERE clause is dangerous.
- Using UPDATE without a WHERE clause is dangerous.
- The new MERGE command pulls data from a source table and inserts, updates, or deletes in the target table depending on the match conditions.
- INSERT, UPDATE, DELETE, and MERGE can all include an optional OUTPUT clause that can select data from the query or the virtual inserted and deleted tables. The result of the OUTPUT clause can be passed to the client, inserted into a table, or passed to an outer query.

This chapter explained data modifications assuming all goes well, but several conditions and situations can conspire to block the INSERT, UPDATE, DELETE, or MERGE. The next chapter looks at the dark side of data modification and what can go wrong.

Part III

Advanced T-SQL Data Types and Querying Techniques

IN THIS PART

Working with Hierarchies

Ever since there have been databases, there has been a need to fit nonrelational data in the databases. Anyone can quickly put together a list of this type of data, but one of the most often used and the subject of this chapter is hierarchical data. Included in this type of hierarchical data are organizational charts, genealogical data, manufacturing data (Bill of Material), and even Object-Oriented class inheritance. This list could go on as well, but the problem is that there hasn't been a decent solution for solving hierarchical data within the walls of a relational database.

Hierarchical data is defined as data items related to each other by their hierarchical relationship. OK, easy enough; but if you look at the underlying structure of any type of hierarchical data, the problems that surface when working with this type of data are evident. How do you traverse a hierarchy tree? How do you easily look at ancestor or descendant data? How do you manipulate the hierarchical tree?

The basis for hierarchical data is its storage. What is the proper structure and format for storing hierarchical data? Many things have been tried over the years, and even the sample AdventureWorks database implements its own flavor of hierarchical data when tracking managers and employees. SQL Server 2005 implemented the Common Table Expression (CTE), which included the recursive query, which enabled traversing hierarchical data much easier. But you still needed to implement the solution yourself.

The great thing is that wonderful enhancements have been made in the area of supporting hierarchical data in a relational database. SQL Server 2008 introduced the Hierarchy data type, which helps many of the problems of storing and querying hierarchical information. However, it is still hierarchical data; data that doesn't easily lend itself to relational format in a relational database.

There are three main approaches and techniques for working with hierarchical data:

- HierarchyID
- Adjacency List
- Materialized Path

This chapter primarily focuses on the HierarchyID data type because it is relatively new, and there is still much to be learned about it. This chapter briefly discusses other options such as Material Path, XML, and CTEs.

The examples for this chapter are taken from the AdventureWorks database for SQL Server 2012, which can be downloaded from Codeplex here:

`http://msftdbprodsamples.codeplex.com/releases/view/55330`

HierarchyID

The `HierarchyID` data type was introduced in SQL Server 2008 with the intention to provide and solve the problems surrounding working with hierarchical data. As a quick background, the `HierarchyID` data type is a CLR data type, but enabling the CLR to use the `HierarchyID` data type is not needed.

The following query joins the `HumanResources.Employee` table with the `Person.Person` table, including the column `OrganizationNode` as one of the columns returned in the query.

```
SELECT   TOP 25
         e.BusinessEntityID AS BusEntID,
         e.OrganizationNode AS OrgNode,
         e.OrganizationLevel AS OrgLevel,
         p.FirstName + ' ' + p.LastName AS 'Name'
FROM   HumanResources.Employee e
INNER JOIN Person.Person p ON e.BusinessEntityID = p.BusinessEntityID
```

In the following results, notice the data returned in the OrgNode column. The OrganizationNode column in the `HumanResources.Employee` table is a `HierarchyID` data type. In its raw form, it is simply hex data.

BusEntID	OrgNode	OrgLevel	Name
1	0x	0	Ken Sánchez
2	0x58	1	Terri Duffy
3	0x5AC0	2	Roberto Tamburello
4	0x5AD6	3	Rob Walters
5	0x5ADA	3	Gail Erickson
6	0x5ADE	3	Jossef Goldberg
7	0x5AE1	3	Dylan Miller
8	0x5AE158	4	Diane Margheim
9	0x5AE168	4	Gigi Matthew
10	0x5AE178	4	Michael Raheem
11	0x5AE3	3	Ovidiu Cracium
12	0x5AE358	4	Thierry D'Hers

13	0x5AE368	4	Janice Galvin
14	0x5AE5	3	Michael Sullivan
15	0x5AE7	3	Sharon Salavaria
16	0x68	1	David Bradley
17	0x6AC0	2	Kevin Brown
18	0x6B40	2	John Wood
19	0x6BC0	2	Mary Dempsey
20	0x6C20	2	Wanida Benshoof
21	0x6C60	2	Terry Eminhizer
22	0x6CA0	2	Sariya Harnpadoungsataya
23	0x6CE0	2	Mary Gibson
24	0x6D10	2	Jill Williams
25	0x78	1	James Hamilton

In its raw form, the HierarchyID data type doesn't tell you anything. What you can do is use the ToString() method to convert the data from hex to text.

```
SELECT    TOP 25
        e.BusinessEntityID AS BusEntID,
        e.OrganizationNode AS OrgNode,
        e.OrganizationNode.ToString() AS 'Hierarchy',
        e.OrganizationLevel AS OrgLevel,
        p.FirstName + ' ' + p.LastName AS 'Name'
FROM   HumanResources.Employee e
INNER JOIN Person.Person p ON e.BusinessEntityID = p.BusinessEntityID
```

The third column now looks much like the materialized path pattern. You know the materialized path pattern well. You deal with it every day when you work with directory structures (such as in Windows Explorer).

BusEntID	OrgNode	HierarchyID	OrgLevel	Name
1	0x	/	0	Ken Sánchez
2	0x58	/1/	1	Terri Duffy
3	0x5AC0	/1/1/	2	Roberto Tamburello
4	0x5AD6	/1/1/1/	3	Rob Walters
5	0x5ADA	/1/1/2/	3	Gail Erickson
6	0x5ADE	/1/1/3/	3	Jossef Goldberg
7	0x5AE1	/1/1/4/	3	Dylan Miller
8	0x5AE158	/1/1/4/1/	4	Diane Margheim
9	0x5AE168	/1/1/4/2/	4	Gigi Matthew
10	0x5AE178	/1/1/4/3/	4	Michael Raheem
11	0x5AE3	/1/1/5/	3	Ovidiu Cracium
12	0x5AE358	/1/1/5/1/	4	Thierry D'Hers
13	0x5AE368	/1/1/5/2/	4	Janice Galvin
14	0x5AE5	/1/1/6/	3	Michael Sullivan
15	0x5AE7	/1/1/7/	3	Sharon Salavaria
16	0x68	/2/	1	David Bradley

17	0x6AC0	/2/1/	2	Kevin Brown
18	0x6B40	/2/2/	2	John Wood
19	0x6BC0	/2/3/	2	Mary Dempsey
20	0x6C20	/2/4/	2	Wanida Benshoof
21	0x6C60	/2/5/	2	Terry Eminhizer
22	0x6CA0	/2/6/	2	Sariya Harnpadoungsataya
23	0x6CE0	/2/7/	2	Mary Gibson
24	0x6D10	/2/8/	2	Jill Williams
25	0x78	/3/	1	James Hamilton

The results in column 3 are a denormalized representation of the complete ancestry and hierarchy, but unlike the materialized path pattern, the HierarchyID data type stores the relative node position.

Select a Single Node

The HierarchyID makes it easy to filter the data type in the WHERE clause to return single rows by using the text form of the data:

```
SELECT    TOP 25
          e.BusinessEntityID AS BusEntID,
          p.FirstName + ' ' + p.LastName AS 'Name',
          e.JobTitle
FROM   HumanResources.Employee e
INNER JOIN Person.Person p ON e.BusinessEntityID = p.BusinessEntityID
WHERE e.OrganizationNode = '/3/3/'
```

What makes this nice is that the conversion was implicit, in that you didn't need to use the ToString() method to convert the data to text form.

```
BusEntID  Name             JobTitle
-------   -----------      ----------------

222       A. Scott Wright  Master Scheduler
```

Searching for Ancestors

Searching for ancestors is made easy with the HierarchyID data type via the use of the IsDescendantOf() method. This method tests specified nodes to determine if those nodes are a descendant of another node. The IsDescendantOf() method returns true if nodes are found.

The following example is a two-step process. The first SELECT statement gets the HierarchyID for a given employee (in this case, A. Scott Wright). Because the variable is of type HierarchyID, you can easily apply the IsDescendantOf() method in the second SELECT statement, which is what is applied in the fourth column.

```
DECLARE @EmpNode HierarchyID

SELECT @EmpNode = OrganizationNode
FROM HumanResources.Employee
WHERE OrganizationNode = '/3/3/'

SELECT    e.BusinessEntityID AS BusEntID,
       p.FirstName + ' ' + p.LastName AS 'Name',
       e.JobTitle,
       @EmpNode.IsDescendantOf(OrganizationNode)
FROM   HumanResources.Employee e
INNER JOIN Person.Person p ON e.BusinessEntityID = p.BusinessEntityID
WHERE @EmpNode.IsDescendantOf(OrganizationNode) = 1
```

The results, shown next, show the three descendant nodes, and in the fourth column you can tell by the value of 1 that they are a descendant of A. Scott Wright.

BusEntID	Name	JobTitle	No column name)
1	Ken Sánchez	Chief Executive Officer	1
25	James Hamilton	Vice President of Production	1
222	A. Scott Wright	Master Scheduler	1

Performing a Subtree Search

If you flip the IsDescendantOf() method around, you can search a subtree to locate all descendants of the specified node. You can start to see the flexibility in these examples in that the IsDescendantOf() method can be used with a column as well as a HierarchyID variable. This example varies from the previous in that the HierarchyID variable is used as a parameter of the IsDescendantOf() method.

In this example, you grab the HierarchyID of the Information Services Manager and use that to return the descendants of that HierarchyID.

```
DECLARE @EmpNode HierarchyID

SELECT @EmpNode = OrganizationNode
FROM HumanResources.Employee
WHERE OrganizationNode = '/5/'

SELECT e.BusinessEntityID AS BusEntID,
       p.FirstName + ' ' + p.LastName AS 'Name',
       e.OrganizationNode.ToString() AS 'Hierarchy',
       e.OrganizationLevel
FROM   HumanResources.Employee e
INNER JOIN Person.Person p ON e.BusinessEntityID = p.BusinessEntityID
WHERE    OrganizationNode.IsDescendantOf(@EmpNode) = 1
```

13

What you see is that the results show everyone who is a descendant of the root /5/ HierarchyID.

BusEntID	Name	Hierarchy	OrganizationLevel
263	Jean Trenary	/5/	1
264	Stephanie Conroy	/5/1/	2
291	Gustavo Achong	/5/1/	2
265	Ashvini Sharma	/5/1/1/	3
266	Peter Connelly	/5/1/2/	3
267	Karen Berg	/5/2/	2
268	Ramesh Meyyappan	/5/3/	2
269	Dan Bacon	/5/4/	2
270	François Ajenstat	/5/5/	2
271	Dan Wilson	/5/6/	2
272	Janaina Bueno	/5/7/	2

Inserting New Nodes

Now that you have an idea of how to query the HierarchyID data type, how do you modify it? What if you need to insert some nodes? To insert a node you can simply use the GetDescendant() method, which returns a child node of the parent node.

How does the GetDescendant() method help you? The GetDescendant() method takes two parameters, which can be either NULL or the hierarchyid of a child of the current node. Because you already have the current node from the first SELECT statement, simply pass NULL for both parameters informing the GetDescendant() method that you want to insert this new node as a descendant of that node.

```
DECLARE @Manager hierarchyid

SELECT @Manager = OrganizationNode
FROM HumanResources.Employee
WHERE OrganizationNode = '/5/'

INSERT HumanResources.Employee (BusinessEntityID, NationalIDNumber,
LoginID, OrganizationNode,
JobTitle, BirthDate, MaritalStatus, Gender, HireDate, SalariedFlag,
VacationHours, SickLeaveHours, CurrentFlag)
VALUES
(291, '8675309', 'adventure-works\Gustav0', @Manager.GetDescendant
(NULL, NULL),
'Rock Star DBA', '09/15/1966', 'M', 'M', '06/15/2001', 1,
99, 20, 1) ;
```

You can now rerun the query from earlier and see that indeed you have a new record of Gustavo Achong, who just happens to be a Rock Star DBA, who is now a descendant of the Information Services Manager.

```
DECLARE @EmpNode HierarchyID
```

```
SELECT @EmpNode = OrganizationNode
FROM HumanResources.Employee
WHERE OrganizationNode = '/5/'

SELECT e.BusinessEntityID AS BusEntID,
       p.FirstName + ' ' + p.LastName AS 'Name',
       e.OrganizationNode.ToString() AS 'Hierarchy',
       e.OrganizationLevel,
       e.JobTitle
FROM  HumanResources.Employee e
INNER JOIN Person.Person p ON e.BusinessEntityID = p.BusinessEntityID
WHERE     OrganizationNode.IsDescendantOf(@EmpNode) = 1
```

BusEntID	Name	Hierarchy	OrganizationLevel	JobTitle
263	Jean Trenary	/5/	1	Information Services Manager
264	Stephanie Conroy	/5/1/	2	Network Manager
265	Ashvini Sharma	/5/1/1/	3	Network Administrator
266	Peter Connelly	/5/1/2/	3	Network Administrator
267	Karen Berg	/5/2/	2	Application Specialist
268	Ramesh Meyyappan	/5/3/	2	Application Specialist
269	Dan Bacon	/5/4/	2	Application Specialist
270	François Ajenstat	/5/5/	2	Database Administrator
271	Dan Wilson	/5/6/	2	Database Administrator
272	Janaina Bueno	/5/7/	2	Application Specialist
291	Gustavo Achong	/5/1/	2	Rock Star DBA

A few methods of the hierarchyid data type have been discussed, but there are a few more, plus it is a good idea to index the hierarchyid data type, which is discussed next.

HierarchyID Methods

The hierarchyid data type includes several methods that easily and quickly help to navigate hierarchical data. You saw some examples of the IsDescendantOf method, which validate the existence of a descendant of a parent. The IsDescendantOf method returns true if the specified node is a descendant of parent.

The GetAncestor() method accepts an argument for the level you try to return and returns the hierarchyid representing the nth ancestor of the current level. In this example, use the GetAncestors() method to return the first level ancestors of the hierarchyid returned in the first SELECT statement.

```
DECLARE @CurrentEmployee hierarchyid

SELECT @CurrentEmployee = OrganizationNode
FROM HumanResources.Employee
WHERE OrganizationNode = '/5/'

SELECT OrganizationNode.ToString() AS 'Hierarchy',
       p.FirstName + ' ' + p.LastName AS 'Name',
       e.OrganizationLevel,
       e.JobTitle
FROM   HumanResources.Employee e
INNER JOIN Person.Person p ON e.BusinessEntityID = p.BusinessEntityID
WHERE OrganizationNode.GetAncestor(1) = @CurrentEmployee
```

Hierarchy	Name	OrganizationLevel	JobTitle
/5/1/	Stephanie Conroy	2	Network Manager
/5/2/	Karen Berg	2	Application Specialist
/5/3/	Ramesh Meyyappan	2	Application Specialist
/5/4/	Dan Bacon	2	Application Specialist
/5/5/	François Ajenstat	2	Database Administrator
/5/6/	Dan Wilson	2	Database Administrator
/5/7/	Janaina Bueno	2	Application Specialist
/5/1/	Gustavo Achong	2	Rock Star DBA

By changing the parameter value, you can change the results. In the following example the parameter value changes from 1 to 2 to return the second-level hierarchy.

```
DECLARE @CurrentEmployee hierarchyid

SELECT @CurrentEmployee = OrganizationNode
FROM HumanResources.Employee
WHERE OrganizationNode = '/5/'

SELECT OrganizationNode.ToString() AS 'Hierarchy',
       p.FirstName + ' ' + p.LastName AS 'Name',
       e.OrganizationLevel,
       e.JobTitle
FROM HumanResources.Employee e
INNER JOIN Person.Person p ON e.BusinessEntityID = p.BusinessEntityID
WHERE OrganizationNode.GetAncestor(2) = @CurrentEmployee
```

Hierarchy	Name	OrganizationLevel	JobTitle
/5/1/1/	Ashvini Sharma	3	Network Administrator
/5/1/2/	Peter Connelly	3	Network Administrator

One of the difficulties when dealing with hierarchical data is that as it grows it can become more difficult to determine where the members are in the hierarchy. This is where the GetLevel() method comes in, which returns the value of how many levels down each row is in the hierarchy.

The following code uses the GetLevel() method as the second column in the SELECT query to return the levels down each row in the hierarchy.

```
SELECT OrganizationNode.ToString() AS 'Hierarchy',
       OrganizationNode.GetLevel() AS EmpLevel,
       p.FirstName + ' ' + p.LastName AS 'Name',
       e.JobTitle
FROM HumanResources.Employee e
INNER JOIN Person.Person p ON e.BusinessEntityID = p.BusinessEntityID
GO
```

Hierarchy	EmpLevel	Name	JobTitle
/	0	Ken Sánchez	Chief Executive Officer
/1/	1	Terri Duffy	Vice President of Engineering
/1/1/	2	Roberto Tamburello	Engineering Manager
/1/1/1/	3	Rob Walters	Senior Tool Designer
/1/1/2/	3	Gail Erickson	Design Engineer
/1/1/3/	3	Jossef Goldberg	Design Engineer
/1/1/4/	3	Dylan Miller	Research and Development Manager
/1/1/4/1/	4	Diane Margheim	Research and Development Engineer
/1/1/4/2/	4	Gigi Matthew	Research and Development Engineer
/1/1/4/3/	4	Michael Raheem	Research and Development Manager
/1/1/5/	3	Ovidiu Cracium	Senior Tool Designer
/1/1/5/1/	4	Thierry D'Hers	Tool Designer
/1/1/5/2/	4	Janice Galvin	Tool Designer
/1/1/6/	3	Michael Sullivan	Senior Design Engineer
/1/1/7/	3	Sharon Salavaria	Design Engineer
/2/	1	David Bradley	Marketing Manager
/2/1/	2	Kevin Brown	Marketing Assistant
/2/2/	2	John Wood	Marketing Specialist
/2/3/	2	Mary Dempsey	Marketing Assistant
/2/4/	2	Wanida Benshoof	Marketing Assistant
/2/5/	2	Terry Eminhizer	Marketing Specialist
/2/6/	2	Sariya Harnpadoungsataya	Marketing Specialist
/2/7/	2	Mary Gibson	Marketing Specialist
/2/8/	2	Jill Williams	Marketing Specialist
/3/	1	James Hamilton	Vice President of Production
/3/1/	2	Peter Krebs	Production Control Manager
/3/1/1/	3	Jo Brown	Production Supervisor - WC60

Indexing Strategies

There are two approaches when needing to index hierarchical data, and the index you apply depends on which approach you take:

- Depth-first
- Breadth-first

In a depth-first approach, rows in a subtree are stored near each other. For example, employee records are stored near their managers' record. In a breadth-first approach, rows for each level in the hierarchy are stored together. For example, managers and their direct reports are stored near each other.

Thus, in a depth-first approach the index is applied so that all nodes in the subtree of a node are colocated. Depth-first indexes are efficient for queries about the subtree, such as "Find all files in this folder and its subfolders."

```
CREATE UNIQUE INDEX OrgNode_Depth_First
ON HumanResources.Employee(OrganizationNode) ;
GO
```

In a breadth-first index all direct children of a node are colocated. Breadth-first indexes are efficient for queries about immediate children, such as "Find all employees who report directly to this manager."

```
CREATE CLUSTERED INDEX OrgNode_Breadth_First
ON HumanResources.Employee(OrganizationLevel) ;
GO
```

Whether to have depth-first, breadth-first, or both, and which to make the clustering key (if any), depends on the relative importance of the above types of queries, and the relative importance of SELECT versus DML operations.

Hierarchical Data Alternatives

Although the hierarchyid is a great way to work hierarchical data, you can use alternatives where the hierarchyid is not available. Plenty of alternative methods exist, but a couple of the more popular methods are CTEs and XML.

Recursive CTE

Common Table Expression (CTE) was introduced in SQL Server 2005 as an alternative to derived tables and an expansion of temporary results sets. A CTE is defined within the execution scope of a single SELECT, INSERT, UPDATE, and DELETE statement. Much like a derived table, a CTE is not stored as an object and lasts only for the duration of the query.

CTEs can be self-referencing, enabling it to be referenced multiple times in the same query. Because it is self-referencing, it therefore creates recursion, thus a recursive CTE. A recursive CTE is one in which an initial CTE is repeatedly executed to return subsets of data until the complete result set is returned.

A recursive CTE is a common use for querying and returning hierarchical data. An example of this is the `HumanResources.Employee` table in which there are two columns; `EmployeeID` and `ManagerID`. The following query shows the structure of a recursive CTE by returning a hierarchical list of employees. The list starts with the highest ranking employee.

This example comes from the SQL Server 2005 AdventureWorks database because, as mentioned earlier, the Hierarchyid data type was introduced in SQL Server 2008. Thus, in order to illustrate hierarchical data "pre" hierarchy id, the use of an earlier version of the AdventureWorks database is necessary.

```
WITH DirectReports(ManagerID, EmployeeID, Title, EmployeeLevel) AS
(
    SELECT ManagerID, EmployeeID, Title, 0 AS EmployeeLevel
    FROM HumanResources.Employee
    WHERE ManagerID IS NULL
    UNION ALL
    SELECT e.ManagerID, e.EmployeeID, e.Title, EmployeeLevel + 1
    FROM HumanResources.Employee AS e
        INNER JOIN DirectReports AS d
        ON e.ManagerID = d.EmployeeID
)
SELECT ManagerID, EmployeeID, Title, EmployeeLevel
FROM DirectReports
ORDER BY ManagerID;
GO
```

ManagerID	EmployeeID	Title	EmployeeLevel
NULL	109	Chief Executive Officer	0
3	4	Senior Tool Designer	3
3	9	Design Engineer	3
3	11	Design Engineer	3
3	158	Research and Development Manager	3
3	263	Senior Tool Designer	3
3	267	Senior Design Engineer	3
3	270	Design Engineer	3
6	2	Marketing Assistant	2
6	46	Marketing Specialist	2
6	106	Marketing Specialist	2
6	119	Marketing Specialist	2
6	203	Marketing Specialist	2

6	269	Marketing Assistant	2
6	271	Marketing Specialist	2
6	272	Marketing Assistant	2
7	37	Production Technician - WC60	4
7	76	Production Technician - WC60	4
7	84	Production Technician - WC60	4
7	122	Production Technician - WC60	4
7	156	Production Technician - WC60	4
7	194	Production Technician - WC60	4
12	3	Engineering Manager	2
14	29	Production Technician - WC50	4
14	67	Production Technician - WC50	4

XML

Per the SQL Server documentation, an XML document is a tree, and thus a single XML data type instance can represent a complete hierarchy. In fact, when creating an XML index in SQL Server, hierarchyid values are used to represent the position in the hierarchy internally.

I know this chapter discusses the Hierarchyid in SQL Server, but it should be noted that there are indeed times when using the XML data type to store hierarchical information is more efficient. However, in order for XML to claim superiority you need to ensure the following:

- The entire hierarchy is always stored and retrieved.

- The hierarchy data is consumed in XML format by the retrieving application.

- Predicate searches are very limited, and these searches are not performance dependent.

For example, we could have a table which looks like the following:

```
CREATE TABLE OrgXML
(
    OrgID int,
    OrgData xml
)
```

Thus, our data would look something like this:

```
OrgID       OrgData
1           <ManagerID id= ""><EmployeeID id= " 109" /></ManagerID>
1           <ManagerID id= "3"><EmployeeID id= "4" /></ManagerID>
1           <ManagerID id= "6"><EmployeeID id= "2" /></ManagerID>
1           <ManagerID id= "7"><EmployeeID id= "37" /></ManagerID>
1           <ManagerID id= "12"><EmployeeID id= "3" /></ManagerID>
```

It would be nice to have the ability to query the hierarchyid data and return it as an XML document, but unfortunately, right now, it is not possible. You should see that capability in the future, but not now.

Although you can't write a simple query to retrieve XML from `hierarchyid` data, there are other options, , but they require a lot of work. There are two ways to compose XML from the hierarchyid; by looping through the hierarchy structure or by using recursive CTE to generate a list of nodes and their corresponding hierarchy. Depending on the amount of data and your hierarchy structure, the two different methods will differ in performance.

Peter DeBetta did a write-up on the two different approaches and his findings in speed and performance, so I'm not going to rehash them here. However, you can find the blog post at `http://sqlblog.com/blogs/peter_debetta/archive/2010/02/17/` `converting-hierarchyid-to-xml-in-t-sql.aspx`.

Summary

The hierarchyid has been around for a few years now, and it really hasn't changed much since it was first introduced. Its purpose is simply to represent positions within a hierarchy, but the key to understanding the hierarchyid data type is understanding that it does not automatically represent a hierarchy tree. Instead, it is up to the application to generate and assign the appropriate hierarchy values. The trick is to do this is a way that reflects the relationships between the rows accurately.

This chapter covered the data type methods that provide efficient querying of the hierarchyid data type. However, you also looked briefly at a well-known alternative to the hierarchyid data type, XML. XML has been around for a lot longer than the hierarchyid and has roots deep into describing and shaping data, such as hierarchies.

Unfortunately, the two don't quite mesh yet, meaning that you can't query the hierarchyid and simply return a nicely shaped XML document. Regardless, the hierarchyid is an excellent method for storing hierarchical data, and with the supported methods makes is much more efficient and a performant solution over XML.

13

Using XML Data

The ability to process XML in SQL Server began with SQL Server 2000. Since then, many wonderful and significant changes and enhancements have been added to SQL Server to make working with and processing XML easier and more efficient.

With SQL Server 2005, Microsoft added the XML data type and other great XML features, such as support for XML data type methods and using XML as a variable and parameter. SQL Server 2008 and SQL Server 2008 R2 added even more support, such as support for the `let` clause of the FLWOR operations.

Although there haven't been any major enhancements to XML in Denali, working with XML is and always will be crucial in nearly every environment. It should be obvious that Microsoft is embracing XML all the way because you can see XML used in nearly every aspect. For example, SQL Server Reporting Services report definitions are actually just XML documents. SQL Server Integration Services packages are XML documents and support XML configuration files. And there is a lot more.

This chapter covers some of the major areas to work with XML, including the XML data type in both column form and variable form. It also talks about the methods used to query XML, and follows that up by discussing the FOR XML clause, which is used to turn tabular data into many different formats of XML. The chapter finishes by discussing XQuery, a language designed to query XML, and the related FLWOR operations, which provide query and transformation capabilities against XML documents.

What's New with XML in SQL Server 2012

SQL Server 2012 didn't add any new XML features or enhancements except for adding support for the new collation option "SC", or "supplementary characters." This new option identifies whether a collation is UTF-16 aware, and as such means that support for the collation options has been added in the SQL Types XML schema and other locations where SQL Server exposes, or consumes, information in an XML context.

With this addition, the XML schema version has been updated to 1.2 and now exposes a new global attribute called supplementaryCharacters.

This new global attribute can now be found in a few catalog views (sys.xml_schema_components, sys.xml_schema_attributes, and sys.xml_schema_component_placements), and pre-populated in the built-in sys.xml_schemas_collection catalog view.

More information on the Supplementary Characters can be found at http://msdn.microsoft.com/en-us/library/ms180942(v=SQL.110).aspx.

The XML Data Type

Working with XML can be broken into three main categories:

- Generating XML
- Querying XML
- Validating XML

Prior to SQL Server 2008, it was the responsibility of the application layer to produce the XML, and there was no consistent or defined way to produce the XML. Typically, it would use the XML API functions available in the programming languages to produce the desired XML, and if you have done it, it wasn't easy.

Luckily, XML started gaining acceptance, and developers saw more and more need to produce and consume XML. Developers started to see the benefit of XML, and today you see it all over in websites that produce RSS or ATOM feeds. And you can't forget XML and (WCF, Windows Communication Foundation) web services, which generate XML documents containing information to be exchanged.

SQL Server 2000 was a great first step into supporting XML with support for the T-SQL FOR XML clause. The FOR XML clause transforms the results of a T-SQL query into an XML stream. This was a huge benefit for developers who no longer needed to build XML documents in their applications. In subsequent releases Microsoft made great improvements to the FOR XML clause to make it easier to produce XML, and you see how the FOR XML clause works later in the chapter.

Querying XML wasn't a walk in the park either, in the beginning. The same XML API's that were used to produce XML were used to query the XML. This caused a lot of overhead in any application that produced or consumed XML. Something better was needed, and the answer came with SQL Server 2000 in the form of the OPENXML function. The OPENXML function requires a three-step process, using a couple of system stored procedures to prepare an XML document handle and then another to release the handle, while calling OPENXML in between to obtain the result set.

Because of the way OPENXML was implemented (a function call between two system stored procedure calls) it made it difficult in some circumstances to implement. For example, you could not use it in set-based operations, and this is what SQL Server excels at!

Luckily, SQL Server 2005 came to the rescue with the XML data type which enables you to store complete XML documents or XML fragments. Included with the XML data type was support for XQuery, a language specifically designed to query XML documents. This functionality alone makes the OPENXML clause nearly obsolete because using XQuery is more lightweight, more powerful, and much easier to use. It also does not have the limitations of the OPENXML function.

However, even though later versions of SQL Server came with better support for producing and querying XML, protecting and ensuring the validity of the XML can't be left behind. Any production application should include a robust validation process to information being exchanged, and even more so when exchanging XML data simply because the chances of invalid values are much greater.

For example, an application passing the value "thirty" to the @age parameter of a stored procedure (@age INT) would receive a conversion error immediately as SQL Server would perform an implicit data type validation.

XML, however, is different. SQL Server can't detect an error in an XML document. For example, given the element "<Employee age="too old to code" />", the @age attribute is not associated with a data type, and SQL Server simply does not know how to validate it.

The solution is the support for schemas, included with SQL Server 2005. Schema Definition Language (XSD) is a language specifically used to describe and validate XML documents. The validation is based on structure and format rules, providing the ability to validate an XML document against the schema.

Starting with SQL Server 2005, SQL Server supports XML Schemas via XML Schema Collection objects, and you learn more about schemas and schema collections shortly. The great thing is that you can apply schemas to an XML data type column, a variable, and a parameter. By applying schemas, you can provide a more stringent validation of XML to help many of the validation scenarios you might find when dealing with non-XML data, such as the following:

14

- Elements in your XML need to follow a certain order (FirstName must proceed LastName).
- Dealing with optional or mandatory elements.
- Validation of data types (for example, age is an integer).
- Enforcing specific formats of data (for example, Social Security numbers formatted as 999-99-9999).
- Ensuring elements appear only once.

The ability to apply a schema to an XML document is called "typing" your XML. You learn about typed versus untyped XML shortly. But enough blabbering. Let's start working with some data.

The examples throughout this chapter use the following code to help explain and illustrate how to create, query, and validate XML. Open Microsoft SQL Server Management Studio and create a new database. Open a new query window and execute the following code against your new database.

```
IF EXISTS (SELECT * FROM sys.objects WHERE object_id =
    OBJECT_ID(N'[dbo].[Customer]') AND type in (N'U'))
DROP TABLE [dbo].[Customer]
GO

IF EXISTS (SELECT * FROM sys.objects WHERE object_id =
    OBJECT_ID(N'[dbo].[Item]') AND type in (N'U'))
DROP TABLE [dbo].[Item]
GO

IF EXISTS (SELECT * FROM sys.objects WHERE object_id =
    OBJECT_ID(N'[dbo].[Orders]') AND type in (N'U'))
DROP TABLE [dbo].[Orders]
GO

IF EXISTS (SELECT * FROM sys.objects WHERE object_id =
    OBJECT_ID(N'[dbo].[OrderDetail]') AND type in (N'U'))
DROP TABLE [dbo].[OrderDetail]
GO

IF EXISTS (SELECT * FROM sys.objects WHERE object_id =
    OBJECT_ID(N'[dbo].[ItemInfo]') AND type in (N'U'))
DROP TABLE [dbo].[ItemInfo]
GO

/****** Object:  Table [dbo].[Customer] ******/
SET ANSI_NULLS ON
GO
SET QUOTED_IDENTIFIER ON
```

```
GO
CREATE TABLE [dbo].[Customer](
        [CustomerID] [int] IDENTITY(1,1) NOT NULL,
        [Name] [nvarchar](50) NULL,
        [Address] [nvarchar](50) NULL,
        [City] [nvarchar](50) NULL,
        [State] [nvarchar](50) NULL,
        [ZipCode] [nvarchar](50) NULL,
        [Phone] [nvarchar](50) NULL,
CONSTRAINT [PK_Customer] PRIMARY KEY CLUSTERED
(
        [CustomerID] ASC
)WITH (PAD_INDEX  = OFF, STATISTICS_NORECOMPUTE  = OFF, IGNORE_DUP_KEY = OFF,
 ALLOW_ROW_LOCKS  = ON, ALLOW_PAGE_LOCKS  = ON) ON [PRIMARY]
) ON [PRIMARY]
GO
SET IDENTITY_INSERT [dbo].[Customer] ON
INSERT [dbo].[Customer] ([CustomerID], [Name], [Address], [City], [State],
  [ZipCode], [Phone])
VALUES (1, N'Scott', N'555 Main St.', N'Palm Beach', N'FL', N'33333', N'555-555-
5555')
INSERT [dbo].[Customer] ([CustomerID], [Name], [Address], [City], [State],
  [ZipCode], [Phone])
VALUES (2, N'Adam', N'111 Works St.', N'Jax', N'FL', N'34343', N'444-444-4444')
INSERT [dbo].[Customer] ([CustomerID], [Name], [Address], [City], [State],
  [ZipCode], [Phone])
VALUES (3, N'John', N'123 Pike Blvd', N'Seattle', N'WA', N'98989', N'999-999-
9999')
SET IDENTITY_INSERT [dbo].[Customer] OFF


/****** Object:  Table [dbo].[Item] ******/
SET ANSI_NULLS ON
GO
SET QUOTED_IDENTIFIER ON
GO
CREATE TABLE [dbo].[Item](
        [ItemID] [int] IDENTITY(1,1) NOT NULL,
        [ItemNumber] [nvarchar](50) NULL,
        [ItemDescription] [nvarchar](50) NULL,
CONSTRAINT [PK_Item] PRIMARY KEY CLUSTERED
(
        [ItemID] ASC
)WITH (PAD_INDEX  = OFF, STATISTICS_NORECOMPUTE  = OFF, IGNORE_DUP_KEY = OFF,
ALLOW_ROW_LOCKS  = ON, ALLOW_PAGE_LOCKS  = ON) ON [PRIMARY]
) ON [PRIMARY]
GO
SET IDENTITY_INSERT [dbo].[Item] ON
```

14

```
INSERT [dbo].[Item] ([ItemID], [ItemNumber], [ItemDescription])
    VALUES (1, N'V001', N'Verizon Windows Phone 7')
INSERT [dbo].[Item] ([ItemID], [ItemNumber], [ItemDescription])
    VALUES (2, N'A017', N'Alienware MX 17')
INSERT [dbo].[Item] ([ItemID], [ItemNumber], [ItemDescription])
    VALUES (3, N'P002', N'Peters Pea Shooter 3000')
SET IDENTITY_INSERT [dbo].[Item] OFF


/****** Object:  Table [dbo].[Orders] ******/
SET ANSI_NULLS ON
GO
SET QUOTED_IDENTIFIER ON
GO
CREATE TABLE [dbo].[Orders](
        [OrderID] [int] IDENTITY(1,1) NOT NULL,
        [CustomerID] [int] NOT NULL,
        [OrderNumber] [nvarchar](50) NULL,
        [OrderDate] [datetime] NULL,
CONSTRAINT [PK_Orders] PRIMARY KEY CLUSTERED
(
        [OrderID] ASC
)WITH (PAD_INDEX  = OFF, STATISTICS_NORECOMPUTE  = OFF, IGNORE_DUP_KEY = OFF,
 ALLOW_ROW_LOCKS  = ON, ALLOW_PAGE_LOCKS  = ON) ON [PRIMARY]
) ON [PRIMARY]
GO
SET IDENTITY_INSERT [dbo].[Orders] ON
INSERT [dbo].[Orders] ([OrderID], [CustomerID], [OrderNumber], [OrderDate])
    VALUES (1, 1, N'10001', '6/15/2011')
INSERT [dbo].[Orders] ([OrderID], [CustomerID], [OrderNumber], [OrderDate])
    VALUES (2, 2, N'10002', '6/16/2011')
INSERT [dbo].[Orders] ([OrderID], [CustomerID], [OrderNumber], [OrderDate])
    VALUES (3, 1, N'10003', '6/17/2011')
INSERT [dbo].[Orders] ([OrderID], [CustomerID], [OrderNumber], [OrderDate])
    VALUES (4, 2, N'10004', '6/18/2011')
SET IDENTITY_INSERT [dbo].[Orders] OFF


/****** Object:  Table [dbo].[OrderDetail] ******/
SET ANSI_NULLS ON
GO
SET QUOTED_IDENTIFIER ON
GO
CREATE TABLE [dbo].[OrderDetail](
        [OrderDetailID] [int] IDENTITY(1,1) NOT NULL,
        [OrderID] [int] NULL,
        [ItemID] [int] NULL,
        [Quantity] [int] NULL,
        [Price] [money] NULL,
CONSTRAINT [PK_OrderDetail] PRIMARY KEY CLUSTERED
```

```
(
        [OrderDetailID] ASC
)WITH (PAD_INDEX  = OFF, STATISTICS_NORECOMPUTE  = OFF, IGNORE_DUP_KEY = OFF,
ALLOW_ROW_LOCKS  = ON, ALLOW_PAGE_LOCKS  = ON) ON [PRIMARY]
) ON [PRIMARY]
GO
SET IDENTITY_INSERT [dbo].[OrderDetail] ON
INSERT [dbo].[OrderDetail] ([OrderDetailID], [OrderID], [ItemID], [Quantity],
[Price])
 VALUES (1, 1, 1, 1, 299.9900)
INSERT [dbo].[OrderDetail] ([OrderDetailID], [OrderID], [ItemID], [Quantity],
[Price])
 VALUES (2, 2, 2, 1, 2999.9900)
INSERT [dbo].[OrderDetail] ([OrderDetailID], [OrderID], [ItemID], [Quantity],
[Price])
VALUES (3, 1, 1, 5, 1499.9500)
INSERT [dbo].[OrderDetail] ([OrderDetailID], [OrderID], [ItemID], [Quantity],
[Price])
VALUES (4, 2, 3, 2, 3.9900)

SET IDENTITY_INSERT [dbo].[OrderDetail] OFF


/****** Object:  Table [dbo].[ItemInfo] ******/
SET ANSI_NULLS ON
GO
SET QUOTED_IDENTIFIER ON
GO
CREATE TABLE [dbo].[ItemInfo](
        [OrderID] [int] NOT NULL,
        [ItemData] [xml] NULL
) ON [PRIMARY]
GO
```

Nothing was inserted into the ItemInfo table. That is because you can use that table to insert and update XML. Before starting, however, spend a few minutes to talk about typed versus untyped XML.

Typed versus Untyped XML

The difference between typed and untyped XML is simply the process to apply a schema to the XML. For example, you can create columns, variables, and parameters of type XML without applying a schema. These instances are untyped. Applying an XML schema makes the XML instances typed.

Now look at an example. In the following code, an XML data type variable called @var is declared, and an XML fragment is then assigned the variable. That variable is then used to insert the XML fragment into the ItemInfo table. The next statement assigns a different XML fragment to the XML data type variable and inserts it into the ItemInfo table.

```
DECLARE @var xml
```

```
SET @var =
'<Root>
      <Junk1>Some Junk</Junk1>
      <Junk2>Some More Junk</Junk2>
      <Junk3>Even More Junk</Junk3>
      <Junk4>Too Much Junk</Junk4>
</Root>'

INSERT INTO ItemInfo (OrderID, ItemData)
VALUES (1, @var)

SET @var =
'<Vendor Name="Fast Freddys Five Finger Discount" Address="No Specific Location"
    Phone="" Description="All conversations should start with pssssst,
buddy...." />'

INSERT INTO ItemInfo (OrderID, ItemData)
VALUES (2, @var)
GO
```

Although this is doable, two important and critical questions should pop into mind:

- How do you validate the XML?
- How do you query the XML?

What this simple example illustrates is that allowing any format of XML into a column makes it difficult to validate and even more difficult to query it. For example, suppose you allow anyone to insert any format of XML into an XML column. This is unmanageable, and has a negative impact on performance.

Typing XML offers several benefits, the most important being that the validation constraints are always respected, and the content of the XML can always be valid as per the schema. Thus, SQL Servers' query optimizer will always know the structure of the XML, including data types, and can then generate a more optimized query plan to query the XML.

With that, now consider how to create and apply XML schemas and use them to validate XML.

XML Schemas

As mentioned earlier, XML validation is accomplished through the schemas, or XML Schema Definition language. The XSD language is a specific language used to validate XML documents (and fragments).

An XML schema "describes" the structure of an XML document and various constraints on the data in the document. An XML schema is itself an XML document using the XSD language to describe the XML document structure, and if you are not familiar with the XSD language, it can take some time to get used to.

The great thing is that you don't need to learn a new language because Microsoft has created a nifty little tool to generate the schema for you based on the XML you want to validate. Walk through an example.

Open up your favorite text editor (Notepad works just fine) and type in the following XML:

```
<Order OrderID="1">
    <Item>
        <ItemNumber>V001</ItemNumber>
        <Quantity>1</Quantity>
        <Price>299.99</Price>
    </Item>
</Order>
```

Save the text file as orderxml.xml. With the XML document created, you can use a nifty little tool to create the schema based on the XML document you just created. The tool is called the XML Schema Definition Tool (XSD.exe go figure) and generates XML schema or even Common Language Runtime (CLR) classes from XDR, XML, and XML files. You can find this tool in the following location:

```
C:\Program Files (x86)\Microsoft SDKs\Windows\v7.0A\Bin\x64
```

Open a command prompt, and navigate the preceding directory. The syntax for creating the schema is simple:

```
Xsd.exe filename.xml /outputdirectory /parameters
```

To create the schema, you need to pass the path to the file you previously created, and the path and name of the new XSD schema you want to create. You can optionally supply a number of parameters.

In your command prompt, type the following (assuming you saved your XML file in C:\Temp):

```
Xsd.exe c:\temp\orderxml.xml /outputdir:c:\temp
```

When specifying the output directory, you need to specify only the directory, as shown in the preceding code. If you leave off the actual name of the file, it uses the name of the XML file as the name of the XSD file.

Press the Enter key after you have typed it in, and quickly you notice a new file in the same directory as your XML file. Open the orderxml.xsd file to look at its contents. Intricate syntax isn't covered here, but what you see is the validation of your XML, and this is what you create your XML Schema Collection from.

So, copy all the contents of the orderxml.xsd file to the clipboard, and create a new query window in SQL Server Management Studio, pasting in the contents of the clipboard. To create the XML Schema Collection, you simply need to add the CREATE XML SCHEMA COLLECTION statement to the beginning of the schema, as shown here:

14

```
CREATE XML SCHEMA COLLECTION OrderInfoSchemaCollection AS
N'<?xml version="1.0" encoding="utf-16"?>
<xs:schema id="NewDataSet" xmlns="" xmlns:xs="http://www.w3.org/2001/XMLSchema"
xmlns:msdata="urn:schemas-microsoft-com:xml-msdata">
  <xs:element name="Order">
    <xs:complexType>
      <xs:sequence>
        <xs:element name="Item" minOccurs="0" maxOccurs="unbounded">
          <xs:complexType>
            <xs:sequence>
              <xs:element name="ItemNumber" type="xs:string" minOccurs="0" />
              <xs:element name="Quantity" type="xs:string" minOccurs="0" />
              <xs:element name="Price" type="xs:string" minOccurs="0" />
            </xs:sequence>
          </xs:complexType>
        </xs:element>
      </xs:sequence>
      <xs:attribute name="OrderID" type="xs:string" />
    </xs:complexType>
  </xs:element>
  <xs:element name="NewDataSet" msdata:IsDataSet="true"
msdata:UseCurrentLocale="true">
    <xs:complexType>
      <xs:choice minOccurs="0" maxOccurs="unbounded">
        <xs:element ref="Order" />
      </xs:choice>
    </xs:complexType>
  </xs:element>
</xs:schema>' ;
```

Now execute the statement to create the schema collection. A schema is just like any other object in SQL Server, such as a table or stored procedure. It is an actual object. However, even though it is created, it still needs to be applied to the XML column of the ItemInfo table. So, type in the following syntax to alter the ItemData column of the ItemInfo table.

```
/* Apply it to the table/columns */
ALTER TABLE ItemInfo
ALTER COLUMN ItemData xml (OrderInfoSchemaCollection)
GO
```

It didn't work, and you received an error. The error you received is not because the schema is invalid but because the two XML fragments inserted earlier can't be validated by the schema. Remember that you built the schema from an XML document, and that document is much different from the XML fragments used earlier.

So, you need to delete the records in the ItemInfo table.

```
DELETE FROM ItemInfo
GO
```

Now go back and execute the ALTER statement again, and when applied successfully, try to insert some XML. First, try some bogus data.

```
/* Fail */
DECLARE @var xml

SET @var =
'<Root>
     <Junk1>Some Junk</Junk1>
     <Junk2>Some More Junk</Junk2>
     <Junk3>Even More Junk</Junk3>
     <Junk4>Too Much Junk</Junk4>
</Root>'

INSERT INTO ItemInfo (OrderID, ItemData)
VALUES (1, @var)
```

The preceding code will fail because the XML does not match, or fails to be validated against the XML schema. The XML is not valid. So try some valid XML.

```
/* Succeed */

DECLARE @var xml

SET @var =
'<Order OrderID="1">
    <Item>
        <ItemNumber>V001</ItemNumber>
        <Quantity>1</Quantity>
        <Price>299.99</Price>
    </Item>
</Order>'

INSERT INTO ItemInfo (OrderID, ItemData)
VALUES (1, @var)

SET @var =
'<Order OrderID="2">
    <Item>
        <ItemNumber>A017</ItemNumber>
        <Quantity>1</Quantity>
        <Price>2999.99</Price>
    </Item>
```

```
</Order>'

INSERT INTO ItemInfo (OrderID, ItemData)
VALUES (2, @var)

GO
```

The preceding statement executes successfully because the XML is successfully validated against the schema and therefore is inserted into the ItemData column.

XML Columns and Variables

We have seen through the previous examples how to use the XML data type in both columns and variables. You created a table with an XML data type column, created an XSD schema, and from that created an XML Schema Collection and applied the schema collection to the table. If you have everything created beforehand, you can apply the schema collection during the creation of the table:

```
DROP TABLE ItemInfo
GO
CREATE TABLE [dbo].[ItemInfo](
        [OrderID] [int] NOT NULL,
        [ItemData] [xml](CONTENT [dbo].[OrderInfoSchemaCollection]) NULL
) ON [PRIMARY]

GO
```

You can also apply the schema collection with an XML variable:

```
DECLARE @var xml (OrderInfoSchemaCollection)

SET @var =
'<Root>
        <Junk1>Some Junk</Junk1>
        <Junk2>Some More Junk</Junk2>
        <Junk3>Even More Junk</Junk3>
        <Junk4>Too Much Junk</Junk4>
</Root>'

SELECT @var
```

Now obviously the preceding statement fails because the XML is invalid, but the next statement succeeds:

```
DECLARE @var xml (OrderInfoSchemaCollection)

SET @var =
```

```
'<Order OrderID="1">
    <Item>
        <ItemNumber>V001</ItemNumber>
        <Quantity>1</Quantity>
        <Price>299.99</Price>
    </Item>
</Order>'

SELECT @var
```

It is also possible to initialize an XML variable from the results of a FOR XML query:

```
DECLARE @var xml

SET @var = (SELECT OrderID FROM Orders FOR XML AUTO)

SELECT @var
```

You can also initialize XML variables a number of ways, such as by static XML strings, from another XML variable, or from the return value of a function.

XML Parameters and Return Values

Both typed and untyped XML parameters can be passed to a stored procedure as INPUT as well as OUTPUT parameters. XML parameters can even be used as arguments, including as return values of scalar functions or the results of a table-valued function.

The following example illustrates how to use the XML data type as an input parameter to a stored procedure:

```
CREATE PROCEDURE SampleProc
(
  @var xml
)
AS
        SELECT @var

EXEC SampleProc '<Root>
        <Junk1>Some Junk</Junk1>
        <Junk2>Some More Junk</Junk2>
        <Junk3>Even More Junk</Junk3>
        <Junk4>Too Much Junk</Junk4>
</Root>'
```

The following example illustrates how to apply an XML schema to an input parameter. The first EXEC statement fails while the second succeeds because the second XML fragment passes validation.

```
CREATE PROCEDURE SampleProc2
(
  @var xml (OrderInfoSchemaCollection)
)
AS
        SELECT @var

EXEC SampleProc2 '<Root>
        <Junk1>Some Junk</Junk1>
        <Junk2>Some More Junk</Junk2>
        <Junk3>Even More Junk</Junk3>
        <Junk4>Too Much Junk</Junk4>
</Root>'


EXEC SampleProc2 '
<Order OrderID="1">
    <Item>
        <ItemNumber>V001</ItemNumber>
        <Quantity>1</Quantity>
        <Price>299.99</Price>
    </Item>
</Order>'
```

When a function returns an XML data type value, XML data type methods can be directly called on the return value:

```
CREATE FUNCTION XMLFunc
(
  @var int
) RETURNS xml
AS
BEGIN
    DECLARE @val xml
    SET @val = (SELECT OrderID, CustomerID
                FROM Orders
                WHERE OrderID = @var
                FOR XML PATH(''), ROOT('OrderInfo'))
    RETURN @val
END
GO
SELECT dbo.XMLFunc(1).value('(OrderInfo/CustomerID)[1]', 'INT')
  as customer
```

The previous example is a nice segue into the next session discussing the XML data type methods.

XML Data Type Methods

The XML data type supports a number of methods providing various operations on the XML document. An operation on an XML document is applied to one or more elements or attributes at a specific location. To perform an operation, the location of the specific element needs to be specified.

Common operations on XML documents typically involve reading values from elements or attributes, querying for information, or making modifications to the XML document by inserting, updating, or deleting elements or attributes.

This section begins with an overview of the XPath language to provide a foundation in which to cover the methods.

XPath

XPath is an expression language that provides quick and efficient processing of values and the locating of XML elements and attributes in an XML document. It also allows for easy navigation through an XML tree.

The concept is that each element and attribute has a unique "path," for example:

```
<Items>
    <ItemNumber>1234</ItemNumber>
    <ItemNumber>2345</ItemNumber>
</Items>
```

In the preceding code, the path to the first ItemNumber element is /Items/ItemNumber[1], and the path to the second ItemNumber element is /Items/ItemNumber[2]. Each element and attribute within an XML document can be uniquely identified and processed using an XPath expression.

All the XML data type methods accept XPath expressions to specify the target element or attribute on which the given operation is performed.

XPath is a language used to create expressions that can address parts of an XML document. It can also be used to manipulate numbers and strings, and can match a set of nodes in an XML document. As such, we can use XPath to identify nodes in an XML document based on their type, name, and values.

value()

The value() method is the most useful of the methods, providing the ability to retrieve scalar values from an XML document as relational columns. The value() method takes an

XQuery expression and evaluates the expression to a single node. During the process the results are cast to the specified SQL Server data type and returned. The following example illustrates this using an XML variable.

```
DECLARE @var xml
SET @var = '<Order OrderID="1">
    <Item>
        <ItemNumber>V001</ItemNumber>
        <Quantity>1</Quantity>
        <Price>299.99</Price>
    </Item>
</Order>'

SELECT @var.value('(Order/@OrderID)[1]', 'INT') as orderid,
@var.value('(Order/Item/ItemNumber)[1]', 'NVARCHAR(50)') as itemnumber
```

The following example illustrates the same functionality but directly queries an XML data type column.
```
SELECT ItemData.value('(Order/@OrderID)[1]', 'INT') as orderid,
ItemData.value('(Order/Item/ItemNumber)[1]', 'NVARCHAR(50)') as itemnumber
FROM ItemInfo
```

nodes()

Suppose you want to return the values from nodes that match a specific expression. The nodes() method returns a rowset representation of the XML document. An XQuery operation can be performed on each node returned by the nodes() method.

```
DECLARE @var xml
SET @var = '
<Item>
    <ItemNumber>V001</ItemNumber>
    <ItemNumber>A017</ItemNumber>
    <ItemNumber>P002</ItemNumber>
</Item>'

SELECT var.value('.','NVARCHAR(10)') as ItemNumber
FROM @var.nodes('/Item/ItemNumber')  o(var)
```

The following example illustrates the same functionality but directly queries an XML data type column.

```
SELECT OrderID,
ItemData.value('(Order/Item/ItemNumber)[1]', 'NVARCHAR(50)') as itemnumber
FROM ItemInfo
CROSS APPLY ItemData.nodes('/Order/Item') o(x)
```

The question from the preceding example is why CROSS APPLY is used. When working with XML columns, multiple XML documents are processed in a single batch. The CROSS APPLY operator helps with this processing.

exist()

The exist() method checks for the existence of a specified element or attribute specified in the XPath expression. The following example uses the exist() method to filter rows that have a specific item number:

```
SELECT OrderID
FROM ItemInfo
WHERE ItemData.exist('Order/Item/ItemNumber = "A017"') = 1
```

The exist() method returns true (1) if an element or attribute exists in the XML document that is specified in the XPath expression.

query() and modify()

The query() method takes an XQuery expression and evaluates it to a list of XML elements that can be accessed and processed further. The modify() method is used to modify XML documents, either insert, update, and delete operations on elements or attributes.

These methods are discussed in more detail when discussing the FLWOR operations and data modification later in the chapter.

FOR XML

Up until now you have talked about how to query XML, either a document or fragment, and return tabular data. The FOR XML clause does the reverse, meaning it takes tabular data and returns XML.

The FOR XML clause is a rowset aggregation function that returns a one-row, one-column result set containing an NVARCHAR(MAX) value. Several directives can be applied to the FOR XML clause, which provides different control and structure over the resulting XML. This section discusses the FOR XML clause and the different directives that can be applied.

> **NOTE**
> Before discussing the modes, you need to understand that the XMLDATA directive to the FOR XML options has been deprecated in SQL Server 2012. In its place you should use XSD generation when using the RAW and AUTO modes.

14

Auto

The AUTO directive is the easiest of the directives to use in which to generate XML output from results specified in the SELECT statement. Although it is certainly the easiest of the directives to use, it doesn't provide a lot of control over the resulting structure of the XML output.

The key to the AUTO directive is in its name, in that it "automatically" names the elements and hierarchies based on table and column names, any aliases used, and joins in the query.

For example, the following code illustrates a simple FOR XML AUTO clause:

```
SELECT CustomerID, OrderNumber, OrderDate
FROM Orders
FOR XML AUTO
```

The results show that the element name is taken from the table in which the data comes from.

```
<Orders CustomerID="1" OrderNumber="10001" OrderDate="2011-06-15T00:00:00" />
<Orders CustomerID="2" OrderNumber="10002" OrderDate="2011-06-16T00:00:00" />
<Orders CustomerID="1" OrderNumber="10003" OrderDate="2011-06-17T00:00:00" />
<Orders CustomerID="2" OrderNumber="10004" OrderDate="2011-06-18T00:00:00" />
```

You can change the name of the element by aliasing the table name in the query:

```
SELECT CustomerID, OrderNumber, OrderDate
FROM Orders o
FOR XML AUTO

/*
<o CustomerID="1" OrderNumber="10001" OrderDate="2011-06-15T00:00:00" />
<o CustomerID="2" OrderNumber="10002" OrderDate="2011-06-16T00:00:00" />
<o CustomerID="1" OrderNumber="10003" OrderDate="2011-06-17T00:00:00" />
<o CustomerID="2" OrderNumber="10004" OrderDate="2011-06-18T00:00:00" />
*/
```

The two previous examples produced XML fragments, not documents. A valid XML document can have only a single top-level node. You can add that by using the ROOT directive and specifying the name of the element:

```
SELECT CustomerID, OrderNumber, OrderDate
FROM Orders
FOR XML AUTO, ROOT('TodaysOrders')

/*
<TodaysOrders>
  <Orders CustomerID="1" OrderNumber="10001" OrderDate="2011-06-15T00:00:00" />
  <Orders CustomerID="2" OrderNumber="10002" OrderDate="2011-06-16T00:00:00" />
  <Orders CustomerID="1" OrderNumber="10003" OrderDate="2011-06-17T00:00:00" />
  <Orders CustomerID="2" OrderNumber="10004" OrderDate="2011-06-18T00:00:00" />
</TodaysOrders>
*/
```

The XML AUTO clause is also smart enough to generate hierarchical XML based on queries that use joins:

```
SELECT o.OrderNumber, o.OrderDate, c.Name
FROM Orders o
INNER JOIN Customer c ON o.CustomerID = c.CustomerID
FOR XML AUTO

/*
<o OrderNumber="10001" OrderDate="2011-06-15T00:00:00">
  <c Name="Scott" />
</o>
<o OrderNumber="10002" OrderDate="2011-06-16T00:00:00">
  <c Name="Adam" />
</o>
<o OrderNumber="10003" OrderDate="2011-06-17T00:00:00">
  <c Name="Scott" />
</o>
<o OrderNumber="10004" OrderDate="2011-06-18T00:00:00">
  <c Name="Adam" />
</o>
*/
```

The AUTO clause works by generating elements for each row in which values are created as attributes. You can take the previous query and apply the ELEMENTS directive to it to turn the attributes into elements:

```
SELECT o.OrderNumber, o.OrderDate, c.Name
FROM Orders o
INNER JOIN Customer c ON o.CustomerID = c.CustomerID
FOR XML AUTO, ELEMENTS

/*
<o>
  <OrderNumber>10001</OrderNumber>
  <OrderDate>2011-06-15T00:00:00</OrderDate>
  <c>
    <Name>Scott</Name>
  </c>
</o>
<o>
  <OrderNumber>10002</OrderNumber>
  <OrderDate>2011-06-16T00:00:00</OrderDate>
  <c>
    <Name>Adam</Name>
  </c>
</o>
<o>
```

14

```
    <OrderNumber>10003</OrderNumber>
    <OrderDate>2011-06-17T00:00:00</OrderDate>
    <c>
      <Name>Scott</Name>
    </c>
  </o>
  <o>
    <OrderNumber>10004</OrderNumber>
    <OrderDate>2011-06-18T00:00:00</OrderDate>
    <c>
      <Name>Adam</Name>
    </c>
  </o>
*/
```

Although the previous query works, the problem is no one knows what c and o are. XML is all about describing the data, so remove the alias on the customer and rename the Orders alias to [Order].

```
SELECT [Order].OrderNumber, [Order].OrderDate, Customer.Name
FROM Orders [Order]
INNER JOIN Customer ON [Order].CustomerID = Customer.CustomerID
FOR XML AUTO, ELEMENTS
```

Now the XML is more readable.

```
<Order>
  <OrderNumber>10001</OrderNumber>
  <OrderDate>2011-06-15T00:00:00</OrderDate>
  <Customer>
    <Name>Scott</Name>
  </Customer>
</Order>
<Order>
  <OrderNumber>10002</OrderNumber>
  <OrderDate>2011-06-16T00:00:00</OrderDate>
  <Customer>
    <Name>Adam</Name>
  </Customer>
</Order>
<Order>
  <OrderNumber>10003</OrderNumber>
  <OrderDate>2011-06-17T00:00:00</OrderDate>
  <Customer>
    <Name>Scott</Name>
  </Customer>
</Order>
<Order>
  <OrderNumber>10004</OrderNumber>
  <OrderDate>2011-06-18T00:00:00</OrderDate>
```

```
    <Customer>
      <Name>Adam</Name>
    </Customer>
  </Order>
```

Raw

FOR XML RAW is similar to FOR XML AUTO but with several differences. First, FOR XML AUTO does not enable you to alter the name of the elements in the resulting XML. Also, as you saw in the previous section, FOR XML AUTO names the elements after the name of the table or alias.

For example, the following code illustrates a simple FOR XML RAW clause:

```
SELECT CustomerID, OrderNumber, OrderDate
FROM Orders
FOR XML RAW

/*
<row CustomerID="1" OrderNumber="10001" OrderDate="2011-06-15T00:00:00" />
<row CustomerID="2" OrderNumber="10002" OrderDate="2011-06-16T00:00:00" />
<row CustomerID="1" OrderNumber="10003" OrderDate="2011-06-17T00:00:00" />
<row CustomerID="2" OrderNumber="10004" OrderDate="2011-06-18T00:00:00" />
*/
```

By default, FOR XML RAW generates elements named <row> but enables you to rename it if you want via an optional element name of the RAW directive:

```
SELECT CustomerID, OrderNumber, OrderDate
FROM Orders
FOR XML RAW('Order')

/*
<Order CustomerID="1" OrderNumber="10001" OrderDate="2011-06-15T00:00:00" />
<Order CustomerID="2" OrderNumber="10002" OrderDate="2011-06-16T00:00:00" />
<Order CustomerID="1" OrderNumber="10003" OrderDate="2011-06-17T00:00:00" />
<Order CustomerID="2" OrderNumber="10004" OrderDate="2011-06-18T00:00:00" />
*/
```

In the following example, notice that table names in the query are both aliased, but because no name is specified in the RAW directive, each row is still named <row>.

```
SELECT o.OrderNumber, o.OrderDate, c.Name
FROM Orders o
INNER JOIN Customer c ON o.CustomerID = c.CustomerID
FOR XML RAW

/*
<row OrderNumber="10001" OrderDate="2011-06-15T00:00:00" Name="Scott" />
<row OrderNumber="10002" OrderDate="2011-06-16T00:00:00" Name="Adam" />
```

```
<row OrderNumber="10003" OrderDate="2011-06-17T00:00:00" Name="Scott" />
<row OrderNumber="10004" OrderDate="2011-06-18T00:00:00" Name="Adam" />
*/
```

The RAW directive also enables you to specify an optional ROOT directive (similar to the AUTO directive), which generates a root element with the specified name.

```
SELECT o.OrderNumber, o.OrderDate, c.Name
FROM Orders o
INNER JOIN Customer c ON o.CustomerID = c.CustomerID
FOR XML RAW('Order'), ROOT('Orders')

/*
<Orders>
  <Order OrderNumber="10001" OrderDate="2011-06-15T00:00:00" Name="Scott" />
  <Order OrderNumber="10002" OrderDate="2011-06-16T00:00:00" Name="Adam" />
  <Order OrderNumber="10003" OrderDate="2011-06-17T00:00:00" Name="Scott" />
  <Order OrderNumber="10004" OrderDate="2011-06-18T00:00:00" Name="Adam" />
</Orders>
/*
```

If you specify the ROOT directive without including a name for the ROOT element, a top-level root element named <root> generates.

The RAW directive also accepts the ELEMENTS directive:

```
SELECT o.OrderNumber, o.OrderDate, c.Name
FROM Orders o
INNER JOIN Customer c ON o.CustomerID = c.CustomerID
FOR XML RAW('Order'), ROOT('Orders'), ELEMENTS

/*
<Orders>
  <Order>
    <OrderNumber>10001</OrderNumber>
    <OrderDate>2011-06-15T00:00:00</OrderDate>
    <Name>Scott</Name>
  </Order>
  <Order>
    <OrderNumber>10002</OrderNumber>
    <OrderDate>2011-06-16T00:00:00</OrderDate>
    <Name>Adam</Name>
  </Order>
  <Order>
    <OrderNumber>10003</OrderNumber>
    <OrderDate>2011-06-17T00:00:00</OrderDate>
    <Name>Scott</Name>
  </Order>
  <Order>
    <OrderNumber>10004</OrderNumber>
    <OrderDate>2011-06-18T00:00:00</OrderDate>
```

```
    <Name>Adam</Name>
  </Order>
</Orders>
/*
```

Explicit

The EXPLICIT directive of the FOR XML clause is the most powerful of the directives and provides the most control over the resulting structure of the XML. It is, however, the most difficult to figure out and understand simply because it is so complicated.

The EXPLICIT directive requires two columns in each row: Tag and Parent. The resulting data should be structured in a way that represents a hierarchical relationship between the Tag rows and the Parent rows.

Because of the complexity of the EXPLICIT directive, SQL Server 2005 introduced the PATH directive, which provides the same control over resulting XML without the headache of the syntax. Thus, you can bypass the EXPLICIT directive and go straight to the PATH directive. If you would like more information using the EXPLICIT directive, you can find information at http://msdn.microsoft.com/en-us/library/ms189068.aspx.

Path

The PATH directive was introduced in SQL Server 2005 as an alternative over the EXPLICIT directive. The PATH directive is just as powerful as the EXPLICIT directive, but it is as simple to use as the AUTO and RAW directives.

On the surface, the PATH directive may not seem powerful, but it shines and shows its supremacy when dealing with more complex XML structures, such as in working with a multilevel hierarchy.

The following is an example of how easy the PATH directive is used with several levels of hierarchy.

```
SELECT
        o.OrderNumber AS '@OrderNumber',
        c.Name AS 'Customer/@Name',
        i.ItemNumber AS 'LineItems/Item/@ItemNo',
        od.Quantity AS 'LineItems/Item/@Qty'
FROM Orders o
INNER JOIN Customer c on o.customerID = c.customerid
INNER JOIN OrderDetail od on od.OrderID = o.OrderID
INNER JOIN Item i on i.ItemID = od.ItemID
FOR XML PATH('Order'), ROOT('Orders')
```

You can see in the query how easy it is to specify the values are attributes while including multiple joins and the resulting XML.

```
/*
<Orders>
  <Order OrderNumber="10001">
    <Customer Name="Scott" />
    <LineItems>
      <Item ItemNo="V001" Qty="1" />
    </LineItems>
  </Order>
  <Order OrderNumber="10002">
    <Customer Name="Adam" />
    <LineItems>
      <Item ItemNo="A017" Qty="1" />
    </LineItems>
  </Order>
  <Order OrderNumber="10001">
    <Customer Name="Scott" />
    <LineItems>
      <Item ItemNo="V001" Qty="5" />
    </LineItems>
  </Order>
  <Order OrderNumber="10002">
    <Customer Name="Adam" />
    <LineItems>
      <Item ItemNo="P002" Qty="2" />
    </LineItems>  </Order>
</Orders>
/*
```

To produce these same results using the EXPLICIT directive would have taken three times the amount of code. The power of the PATH directive comes from the ability to generate deep hierarchies based on simply the column name. For example, the column name LineItems/ Item/@Qty creates an Item element with a Qty attribute under the LineItems element.

The PATH directive also supports a number of special characters to produce different XML formatting requirements. For example, you can create elements that have a text value as well as attributes simply by naming a column with an asterisk (*):

```
SELECT CustomerID AS '@customerid', OrderNumber AS '*'
FROM Orders
FOR XML PATH('Order'), ROOT('Orders')

/*
<Orders>
  <Order customerid="1">10001</Order>
  <Order customerid="2">10002</Order>
  <Order customerid="1">10003</Order>
  <Order customerid="2">10004</Order>
</Orders>
*/
```

Similar results can be achieved by using special column name indicators such as data() and text(). For example, you can use the data() indicator to create a list of values separated by spaces. They key here is to make the PATH name empty.

```
SELECT ItemNumber AS 'data()'
FROM Item
FOR XML PATH(''), ROOT('Items')

/*
<Items>V001 A017 P002</Items>
*/
```

The text() indicator can produce a similar string but without spaces (also using an empty PATH name).

```
SELECT ItemNumber AS 'text()'
FROM Item
FOR XML PATH(''), ROOT('Items')

/*
<Items>V001A017P002</Items>
*/
```

Lastly, you can add comments to your XML by applying the comments() indicator; although you still need to use the FOR XML PATH directive:

```
SELECT 'Order Number' AS 'comment()',
OrderNumber,
'CustomerID' AS 'comment()',
CustomerID
FROM Orders WHERE OrderID = 1
FOR XML PATH(''), ROOT

/*
<Items>V001A017P002</Items>
<root>
  <!--Order Number-->
  <OrderNumber>10001</OrderNumber>
  <!--CustomerID-->
  <CustomerID>1</CustomerID>
</root>
*/
```

XQuery and FLWOR Operations

XQuery is a language that provides the ability to query structured and semi-structured XML data. XQuery is based on the existing XPath query language but includes added support for improved iteration, sorting results, and XML construction.

You have seen XQuery used throughout this chapter; for example, the query() method of the XML data type methods implements a subset of the XQuery specifications.

The real muscle of XQuery comes with the FLWOR operation. FLWOR stands for FOR LET WHERE ORDER BY and RETURN.

The following example is an example of a basic FLWOR query using for and return:

```
DECLARE @var xml
SET @var = '
<Item>
        <ItemNumber>V001</ItemNumber>
        <ItemNumber>A017</ItemNumber>
</Item>
'

SELECT @var.query('for $item in Item/ItemNumber return $item')

/*
<ItemNumber>V001</ItemNumber>
<ItemNumber>A017</ItemNumber>
*/
```

where and order by can be specified to filter and sort the output:

```
DECLARE @var xml
SET @var = '
<Item>
        <ItemNumber>1010</ItemNumber>
        <ItemNumber>1009</ItemNumber>
        <ItemNumber>1008</ItemNumber>
        <ItemNumber>1007</ItemNumber>
        <ItemNumber>1006</ItemNumber>
        <ItemNumber>1005</ItemNumber>
        <ItemNumber>1004</ItemNumber>
        <ItemNumber>1003</ItemNumber>
        <ItemNumber>1002</ItemNumber>
        <ItemNumber>1001</ItemNumber>
</Item>
'

SELECT @var.query('
        for $item in Item/ItemNumber
        where $item[.>"1005"]
        order by $item
        return $item')

<ItemNumber>1006</ItemNumber>
<ItemNumber>1007</ItemNumber>
```

```
<ItemNumber>1008</ItemNumber>
<ItemNumber>1009</ItemNumber>
<ItemNumber>1010</ItemNumber>
```

The where clause filters the XQuery expression for item numbers greater than 1005, and the order by clause orders the nodes in ascending order.

Summary

Anyone reading this book that remembers trying to use XML with SQL Server 2000 should also remember how much of a pain it was to work with (XML, not SQL Server). There was no XML data type in SQL Server then, but XML was quickly gaining popularity. Anyone remember XHTML?

To the rescue comes SQL Server 2005 with the wonderful XML data type and the ability to work with XML natively. While it wasn't perfect (FOR XML EXPLICIT, ugh) and the performance wasn't great, it was FAR better than what you were working with previously.

Over the years improvements have been made and performance increased to make it a solid way to store and work with XML documents and fragments in SQL Server. However, as mentioned at the beginning of this chapter, very little was added to SQL Server 2012 for the XML data type, but that doesn't mean it isn't valuable.

This chapter covered the XML data type and its associated methods and syntax. You also spent considerable time discussing XQuery and the FLWOR statements used to easily and efficiently query XML as well as the FOR XML clause to format the shape of resulting XML when querying TDS data.

14

Executing Distributed Queries

Data is everywhere. Even within the walls of a company, you never find data in the same place. As the amount of data increases within an organization, the need to access that data using distributed methods becomes even more critical. With SQL Server, getting to and querying distributed data is not a problem; SQL Server can access data from a plethora of data sources.

SQL Server provides several methods for accessing data from many different external data sources from a source location. This chapter discusses the methods for accessing and querying distributed data.

Distributed Query Overview

Several methods exist for querying data from different distributed data sources, ranging from linking servers to developing and executing distributed queries. The most common method is to use Linked Servers, or to link to an external data source, whereas a similar practice to develop and execute distributed queries is also common.

In this section you will look at the concept of linking to external data sources such as Microsoft Excel and other SQL Server instances using Linked Servers.

Connecting to External Data

Connecting to external data is the first step in working with distributed queries. First consider connecting to physical servers using linked servers to assist in your distributed query exploration.

Linking to an external data source is nothing more than configuring the name of the linked server, along with the necessary login information. After you supply this information, you can access data from the linked server.

Linking is a one-way configuration between two servers. For example, if Server A links to Server B, then Server A knows how to access and log in to Server B. As far as Server B is concerned, Server A is just another user.

Linked Servers is not a new concept; it has been around for a while. Linking a server is not the same as registering a server in SQL Server Management Studio (SSMS). Management Studio communicates only with the servers as a client application and provides the ability to do the server *linking*, different from *registering* a server in Management Studio. Linking the servers enables SQL Server Instance A to communicate directly with SQL Server Instance B.

You can establish links in two ways: through code or through SQL Server Management Studio. Using T-SQL code to link servers has the added advantage of repeatability in case a rebuild is necessary. Obviously rebuilding the links via code requires more steps but provides the flexibility and repeatability developers look for. OK, yes, you *could* create the link in Management Studio and then script the link, but honestly, that's cheating.

Linking a server goes far beyond just linking to SQL Server instances. A linked server can be a SQL Server or any other data source with either an OLE DB provider or ODBC driver. Distributed queries can select data and modify it depending on the features of the provider or driver. SQL Server queries can reference external data by referring to the preconfigured linked server or specifying the link in the query code. You will see some examples of that later.

By physically linking the servers in Management Studio, declaring the link becomes administrative rather than developmental. Queries can easily refer to a named link without the worry of location or the security concerns. Queries that use linked servers are more portable and easier to maintain simply because if the linked database moves to a new server, a simple creation of the new link in Management Studio is all that you need, and the queries can work without any modification.

Linking to External Data Sources

To understand how linking works, first take a look how it works within the same server. Most of you have written queries that pull data from one database while connected to another on the same server. A SQL Server query may access another database on the same server by referring to the remote object in the other database, such as a table or stored procedure, using the three parts of the four-part name:

```
Server.Database.Schema.Object
```

When the database is on the same server, the server name is optional. If the objects are in the dbo schema, then you can assume the dbo schema is as follows:

```
SELECT FirstName, LastName FROM AdventureWorks.dbo.Contact
```

You can also assume the schema to be dbo and ignore it by leaving the schema empty:

```
SELECT FirstName, LastName FROM AdventureWorks..Contact
```

However, if the objects are not in the dbo schema, then you must use the appropriate schema:

```
SELECT FirstName, LastName FROM AdventureWorks.Person.Contact
```

Querying on the same server is easy, but now take this up a notch and link to an external source.

Linking to SQL Server with Management Studio

A link to another SQL Server can be established by means of SQL Server Management Studio, or if you prefer, via code. In SSMS, linked servers are listed under the Server Objects node in the Object Explorer window. To add a linked server, right mouse click the Linked Server node and select New Linked Server from the context menu, which opens the New Linked Server dialog (see Figure 15-2).

FIGURE 15-1

New Linked Server Dialog.

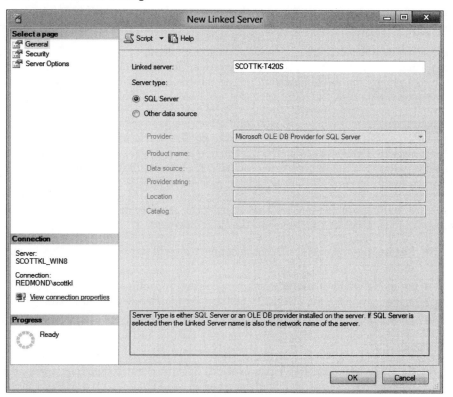

This dialog has three pages; General, Security, and Server Options. These pages define the properties of the server you are linking to.

General Page

The General page is where the linked server and server type are specified. In the Linked Server textbox, enter the name of the external SQL Server and select the SQL Server button for the Server Type. For named SQL Server instances, enter the instance name as *server\instance*.

SQL Server 2012 can link to a SQL Server 7 and later. If you want to link to SQL Server 6.5, you need to use an ODBC driver.

Security Page

The Security page is a page that should not be overlooked. The purpose of using linked servers is to provide users with the ability to run queries that access data from other data sources. You definitely want your data to be secure, so requiring users to authenticate is required.

For linked servers, authentication is achieved via login mappings. If the users are local users whose logins are not mapped, authentication is done by setting the default behavior.

The login mapping works by either passing the user along to the external source without translating the login name (if the Impersonate option is checked), or by translating a user's login to a remote login and password (if the Impersonate option is not checked). It should go without saying that the login specified must be a valid login on the external server.

The list on this page is where you map local server logins to remote server logins. The local login specifies the login that can connect to the linked server using either Windows or SQL authentication. If you want to pass the username and password from the local login to the linked server, select the Impersonate checkbox. The Remote User and Password fields in the list allow you to map users (and their associated passwords) not defined in the local login field.

There are four connection options that specify the security context that are used when connecting the original SQL Server to the linked server:

- **Not be made:** Specifies that the connection will not be made for logins not defined in the list
- **Be made without using a security context:** Specifies that the connection will be made without using a security context for logins not defined in the list
- **Be made using the login's current security context:** Specifies that the connection will be made using the current security context of the login for logins defined in the list
- **Be made using this security context:** Specifies that a connection will be made using the login and password specified in the Remote login and With password boxes

In a domain environment where users are connecting by using their domain credentials, selecting the third option, "Be made using the login's current security context" is the best practice. If connected to the local server using Windows authentication, your Windows credentials will be used to connect to the remote server. However, if you are connecting to the local server using SQL authentication, the login name and password will be used to connect to the remote server.

Server Options Page

The Server Options page contains optional settings for changing the default characteristics of the linked server, such as connection and query timeout, enabling or disabling distributed query access for the linked server, or enabling RPC to and from the linked server.

Linking to SQL Server via T-SQL

As you saw in the previous section, SQL Server Management Studio handles the connection and login information in a single location. The other option is to establish the connection via T-SQL and use separate T-SQL commands to handle the connection information and the login information.

The process to establish a Linked Server via T-SQL is done through the `sp_addlinkedserver` system stored procedure. If you connect to another SQL Server, the syntax for using this stored procedure is simple: Pass two parameters, the server name and server product:

```
EXEC sp_addlinkedserver @server='', @srvproduct='SQL Server'
```

This command doesn't actually establish the link. It simply records information that SQL Server can use to establish the link at a later time. Also this command doesn't check to see whether the server with the supplied name even exists or is accessible.

Now do a quick example in which two SQL Server instances exist; SQL Server 2012 and SQL Server 2008 R2. The SQL Server 2008 R2 SQL Server has a database called AdventureWorks, and this example will link the SQL Server 2008 R2 server to SQL Server 2012. Open a query window on the SQL Server 2012 box and execute the following:

```
EXEC sp_addlinkedserver @server='AvalonDev', @srvproduct='SQL Server'
GO
SELECT * FROM AvalonDev.AdventureWorks.Person.Contact
```

The first line of code creates a linked server to the development box. This is the same as using the UI in SQL Server Management Studio to create a linked server. If I execute that line of code individually and then look at my Linked Server node in Management Studio, I would see a new linked server called AvalonDev in the list.

The second line executes a query against that link server. This query executes, but the question is, will you get data back? The answer here is No. Why? Because the XML data type is not supported in distributed queries. So, change the last line to the following and re-execute the last line:

```
SELECT * FROM AvalonDev.AdventureWorks.HumanResources.Employee
```

Partial results of the query are shown here:

```
EmployeeID      NationalIDNumber      ContactID
----------      ----------------      ---------
1               14417807              1209
2               253022876             1030
```

You can also link to another SQL Server instance using a linked server name other than the actual SQL Server instance name. To do this, simply add a couple of additional parameters: the `provider` and `datasrc` parameters. When connecting to a SQL Server instance, the provider value must be:

```
EXEC sp_addlinkedserver @server='ScottsDev',
    @srvproduct='',
    @provider='SQLNCLI',
    @datasrc = 'AvalonDev'
GO
SELECT * FROM AvalonDev.AdventureWorks.HumanResources.Employee
```

Executing these lines of code produces the same results as the previous example, but you also see another linked server called `ScottsDev` listed in the Linked Servers node in Management Studio.

Dropping Linked Servers

You can drop linked servers via the `sp_dropserver` system stored procedure:

```
EXEC sp_dropserver @server='ScottsDev'
```

In addition, you can right-click the wanted linked server in SQL Server Management Studio and select `Delete` from the context menu.

Distributed Security and Logins

In Management Studio, you can break down the security issue into two parts: login mapping and what to do with nonmapped logins. T-SQL uses the `sp_addlinkedsrvlogin` system stored procedure to handle both, as follows:

```
EXEC sp_addlinkedsrvlogin
    @rmtsrvname='rmtsrvname',
    @useself='useself',
    @locallogin='locallogin',
    @rmtuser='rmtuser',
    @rmtpassword='rmtpassword'
```

If the linked server were added using T-SQL instead of Management Studio, the security option for nonmapped logins is already configured to use the login's current security context. If the @logicallogin is null, the setting applies to all nonmapped users. The @useself option is the same as the Impersonate option within the New Linked Server dialog in SQL Server Management Studio.

The @useself parameter expects a true/false/null value because this parameter determines whether to connect to the remote server by impersonating local logins or explicitly submitting a login and password. The default value is true. A value of true specifies that logins use their own credentials to connect to the remote server. The @rmtuser and @rmtpassword arguments will be ignored when the statement is executed. A value of false specifies that the @rmtuser and @rmtpassword arguments connect to the remote server specified for the @locallogin.

The following example calls the sp_addlinkedsrvlogin system stored procedure to enable the AvalonDev\Tester login to access the AvalonDev server as the sa user with the password P@$$w0rd.

```
EXEC sp_addlinkedsrvlogin
    @rmtsrvname='AvalonDev',
    @useself='FALSE',
    @locallogin='AvalonDev\Scott',
    @rmtuser='sa',
    @rmtpassword='P@$$w0rd'
```

The following example sets all nonmapped users to connect using their own security context. (This is the recommended option.) The local user is null, so this linked server login applies to all nonmapped users. The @useself option is not specified, so the default setting, true, applies here. This causes the users to use the local security context. This is the default setting, so you need this code if you want to return to the default setting:

```
EXEC sp_addlinkedsrvlogin
    @rmtsrvname='AvalonDev'
```

This next example prevents all nonmapped users from executing distributed queries. The second parameter, @useself, is set to false and the corresponding user login and password are left as null:

```
EXEC sp_addlinkedsrvlogin
    @rmtsrvname='AvalonDev', @useself='false'
```

If you want to remove a mapped login, simply use the sp_droplinkedsrvlogin system stored procedure:

```
EXEC sp_droplinkedsrvlogin
    @rmtsrvname='AvalonDev', @locallogin='AvalonDev\Scott'
```

To remove all nonmapped users' default mappings, run the same drop stored procedure, but this time specify null as the local login:

```
EXEC sp_droplinkedsrvlogin
    @rmtsrvname='AvalonDev', @locallogin=NULL
```

15

Linking to Non-SQL Server Data Sources

You have spent quite a bit of time considering linking to external SQL Server data sources but rarely is all the information you need stored in SQL Server. Frequently, you need to query data from data sources, such as Excel, Access, or other database systems such as Oracle.

Getting access to that data, however, depends on the availability and the features of the ODBC drivers and the OLE DB providers. SQL Server uses OLE DB for the external data, and SQL Server includes several OLE DB providers.

Setting up a linked server to a non-SQL Server data source is similar to a SQL Server link. A data source (location) and possibly a provider string to supply additional information is essentially all you need. Table 15-1 lists some of the more common data sources and their settings.

TABLE 15-1 Common External Data Sources

Data Source	Provider Name	Use in Four-Part Names	Use in Pass-Through Queries and Commands	Use in INSERT, UPDATE, or DELETE	Use in Distributed Transactions
SQL Server	SQLNCLI	Yes	Yes	Yes	Yes
ODBC	MSDASQL	Yes	Yes	Yes	Yes
Access	Microsoft.Jet.OLEDB.4.0	Yes	Yes	Yes	No
Excel	Microsoft.Jet.OLEDB.4.0	Yes	Yes	Yes	No
Oracle	OraOLEDB.Oracle	Yes	Yes	Yes	Yes
File System	MSIDXS	No	Yes	No	No
DB2	DB2OLEDB	Yes	Yes	Yes	Yes
Exchange		No	Yes	No	No

In this section, you link to an Excel spreadsheet to get data and then link to an Access database.

Linking to Excel

With Microsoft Excel, each spreadsheet page and named range appears as a table when accessed from an external data provider. Within Excel, you can create a named range in several ways. The easiest way to create a named range is to highlight the range of cells you want to define as a "table," and then when highlighted, enter the name of the range in the space above the A1 cell, as shown in Figure 15-2.

FIGURE 15-2

Creating a Named Range.

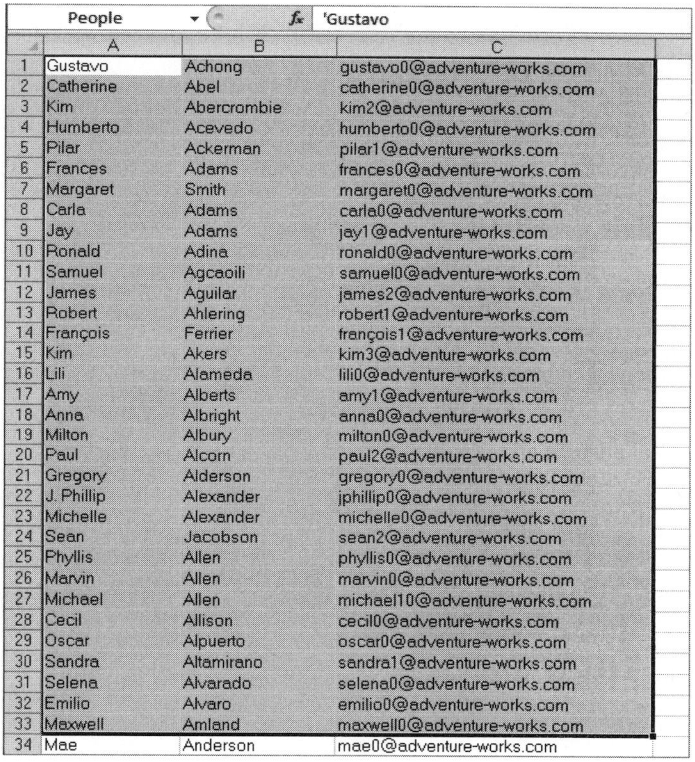

People | 'Gustavo

	A	B	C
1	Gustavo	Achong	gustavo0@adventure-works.com
2	Catherine	Abel	catherine0@adventure-works.com
3	Kim	Abercrombie	kim2@adventure-works.com
4	Humberto	Acevedo	humberto0@adventure-works.com
5	Pilar	Ackerman	pilar1@adventure-works.com
6	Frances	Adams	frances0@adventure-works.com
7	Margaret	Smith	margaret0@adventure-works.com
8	Carla	Adams	carla0@adventure-works.com
9	Jay	Adams	jay1@adventure-works.com
10	Ronald	Adina	ronald0@adventure-works.com
11	Samuel	Agcaoili	samuel0@adventure-works.com
12	James	Aguilar	james2@adventure-works.com
13	Robert	Ahlering	robert1@adventure-works.com
14	François	Ferrier	françois1@adventure-works.com
15	Kim	Akers	kim3@adventure-works.com
16	Lili	Alameda	lili0@adventure-works.com
17	Amy	Alberts	amy1@adventure-works.com
18	Anna	Albright	anna0@adventure-works.com
19	Milton	Albury	milton0@adventure-works.com
20	Paul	Alcorn	paul2@adventure-works.com
21	Gregory	Alderson	gregory0@adventure-works.com
22	J. Phillip	Alexander	jphillip0@adventure-works.com
23	Michelle	Alexander	michelle0@adventure-works.com
24	Sean	Jacobson	sean2@adventure-works.com
25	Phyllis	Allen	phyllis0@adventure-works.com
26	Marvin	Allen	marvin0@adventure-works.com
27	Michael	Allen	michael10@adventure-works.com
28	Cecil	Allison	cecil0@adventure-works.com
29	Oscar	Alpuerto	oscar0@adventure-works.com
30	Sandra	Altamirano	sandra1@adventure-works.com
31	Selena	Alvarado	selena0@adventure-works.com
32	Emilio	Alvaro	emilio0@adventure-works.com
33	Maxwell	Amland	maxwell0@adventure-works.com
34	Mae	Anderson	mae0@adventure-works.com

The code samples used in this section are from a spreadsheet included on the website for this book. The spreadsheet contains a single page taken from the Person. Contact table from the AdventureWorks SQL Server database. The range defined in the spreadsheet includes a first name column, a last name column, and an e-mail address. The spreadsheet is called AdvetureWorksContacts, and the range is called People.

The following example sets up the Excel spreadsheet as a linked server:

```
exec sp_addlinkedserver
    @server='AdventureWorksContacts',
    @srvproduct = 'Jet 4.0',
    @provider='Microsoft.Jet.OLEBDB.4.0',
    @datasrc='D:\Projects\Wiley\SQL Server 2011 Bible\
AdventureWorksContacts.xls',
    @provstr='Excel 5.0'
```

15

With the link to the spreadsheet defined, you can now query the specific range just as you would query a normal table, as follows:

```
SELECT * FROM AdventureWorksContacts...People
```

Partial results of the query are shown here:

```
FirstName     LastName      EmailAddress
---------     --------      ------------
Gustavo       Achong        gustavo0@adventure-works.com
Catherine     Abel          catherine0@adventure-works.com
Kim           Abercrombie   kim2@adventure-works.com
Humberto      Acevedo       humberto0@adventure-works.com
Pilar         Ackerman      pilar1@adventure-works.com
```

Excel spreadsheets are not multiuser spreadsheets. SQL Server can't perform a distributed query that accesses an Excel spreadsheet while that spreadsheet is open in Excel.

Now take a look at linking to Microsoft Access.

Linking to Access

SQL Server links easily to Microsoft Access, using the OLE DB Jet provider to connect to Jet data sources and execute queries. Because Access is a database, there are no special steps for preparing an Access data for linking as there is for Excel (creating named ranges). Every Access table appears as a table under the Linked Servers node in Management Studio.

For this example, use the sample NWind Access database from the Microsoft MSDN site, which the download materials for this book also include.

The following example links the NWind.mdb Access database to SQL Server so that you can retrieve data:

```
exec sp_addlinkedserver
    @server='Nwind',
    @srvproduct = 'Access 2003',
    @provider='Microsoft.Jet.OLEDB.4.0',
    @datasrc='D:\Projects\Wiley\SQL Server 2011 Bible\Nwind.mdb'
```

With the Access database linked, you can execute queries, such as the following:

```
SELECT * FROM Nwind...Customers
```

Partial results of the query are shown here:

```
Customer ID   Company Name          Contact Name
-----------   ------------          ------------
ALFKI         Alfreds Futterkiste   Maria Anders
ANATR         Ana Trujillo Empa     Ana Trujillo
ANTON         Antonio Moeno Taquiria Antonio Moreno
```

```
AROUT      Around the Horn          Thomas Hardy
BERGS      Berglunds snabbkop       Christina Berglund
BLAUS      Blauer See Delikatessen  Hanna Moos
```

Developing Distributed Queries

After you establish the link to the external data source (whether it's via Linked Servers in Management Studio or via T-SQL), SQL Server can reference the external data using standard queries. Querying external data is as simple as using the four available basic syntax methods, depending on the link setup.

As you saw earlier, you can query a data source using the four-part name if it is a local server, or you can use the four-part name using the OpenQuery() pass-through if it is an external data source.

For Ad Hoc queries (in which the Link is declared in the query), look at a couple of built-in T-SQL functions that provide remote access to data from OLE DB data sources:

- OPENDATASOURCE(): Provides ad hoc connection information as part of a four-part name without using a linked server name
- OPENROWSET(): Includes the connection information necessary to access remote data from an OLE DB data source

In this section you look at how to use these two functions to execute distributed queries both locally and in a pass-through fashion.

Distributed Queries and SSMS

SQL Server Management Studio doesn't contain a graphical way to executing distributed queries, and it isn't possible to drag a linked server or remote table into the query designer. You can, however, enter the distributed query manually then execute it. It is also possible to drag the name of the linked server from Object Explorer to a query window.

Distributed Views

Views are saved T-SQL SELECT statements and are very useful for ad hoc queries and preventing user access directly to the underlying table. They are also good, however, for distributing queries. Wrapping a distributed query inside a view allows users and developers alike the ability to execute distributed queries when they are unfamiliar with the different methods for executing distributed queries.

Local Distributed Queries

A local-distributed query sounds like an oxymoron, but it is far from it. A local distributed query is a query in which the external data is pulled into the local SQL Server

15

and processed. These types of queries are often called T-SQL distributed queries simply because the queries use T-SQL syntax.

Local distributed queries use the four-part name discussed earlier if the data is on another SQL Server. For example, you can use the four-part name in any SELECT or data modification query:

```
SELECT BusinessEntityID, NationalIDNumber, LoginID
FROM AvalongDev.AdventureWorks2012.HumanResources.Employee
```

Following are the partial results of the query:

```
EmployeeID     NationalIDNumber     LoginID
----------     ----------------     ---------
1              14417807             adventure-works\ken0
2              253022876            adventure-works\terri0
3              509647174            adventure-works\roberto0
4              112457891            adventure-works\rob0
5              480168528            adventure-works\gail0
```

When performing DML operations as a distributed query, you must substitute either the four-part name or a distributed query function for the table name. The following example uses the four-part name as the source for an INSERT statement against the same AdventureWorks database.

```
INSERT Contact(Name)
SELECT [First Name]
FROM AdventureWorksContacts...People
```

You can also do the same with updates:

```
UPDATE AvalonDev.AdventureWorks.Person.Contact
SET Title = 'Geek'
WHERE ContactID = 5
```

OpenDataSource()

Using the OpenDatasource() function is equivalent to using a four-part name to access a linked server, except that the OpenDatasource() function defines the link within the function instead of referencing a predefined linked server. Although defining the link in code bypasses the linked server requirement, if the link location changes, the change can affect every query that uses the OpenDatasource() function. The OpenDatasource() also does not accept variables as parameters.

The basic OpenDatasource() syntax is quite simple:

```
OPENDATASOURCE(provider_name, init_string)
```

The OpenDatasource() function is substituted for a server in the four-part name and may be used with any DML statement. However, there is more to it than this. The init string is a delimited string containing several parameters. The parameters depend on the type of data source but include the data source, location, extended properties, execution timeout, username and password, and catalog. The `init` string must define the entire external data-source connection and security context within the function. You do not need to use quotes, but avoid the common mistake of mixing the commas and semicolons in the `OpenDatasource()` function.

The following example is a relatively simple example that illustrates how to use the `OpenDatasource()` to connect to another SQL Server instance:

```
SELECT EmployeeID,NationalIDNumber, LoginID
FROM OPENDATASOURCE(
    'SQLOLEDB',
    'Data Source=AvalonDev;User ID=Scott;Password=P@$$W0rd'
).AdventureWorks.HumanResources.Employee
```

What about non-SQL data sources? No problem there. The following example illustrates how to use the `OpenDatasource()` against an Access database:

```
SELECT EmployeeID,NationalIDNumber, ContactID
FROM OPENDATASOURCE(
    'Microsoft.Jet.OLEDB.4.0',
    'Data Source= D:\Projects\Wiley\SQL Server 2011 Bible\Nwind.mdb'
)...Customers
```

You can also use the `OpenDatasource()` to perform DML operations as well, as shown in the following example:

```
UPDATE OpenDatasource(
    'Microsoft.Jet.OLEDB.4.0',
    'Data Source= D:\Projects\Wiley\SQL Server 2011 Bible\Nwind.mdb'
)...Employee
SET Title = 'Geek'
WHERE EmployeeID = 5
```

The same applies to an Excel worksheet:

```
UPDATE OpenDatasource(
    'Microsoft.Jet.OLEDB.4.0',
    'Data Source= D:\Projects\Wiley\SQL Server 2011 Bible\
AdventureWorksContacts.xls;
    Extended Properties=Excel 5.0'
)...People
SET LastName = 'Abelito'
WHERE FirstName = 'Catherine'
```

To verify your changes, execute the following query:

```
SELECT *
FROM OpenDatasource(
    'Microsoft.Jet.OLEDB.4.0',
    'Data Source= D:\Projects\Wiley\SQL Server 2011 Bible\
AdventureWorksContacts.xls;
```

15

```
      Extended Properties=Excel 5.0'
)...People
SET FirstName = 'Catherine'
```

Pass-Through Distributed Queries

A pass-through query executes at the external data source and returns the results to the calling SQL Server. The primary reason to use a pass-through query is to reduce the amount of data passed from the server and the client. Instead of pulling 1 million rows into SQL Server so that it can use only a fraction of them, it may be easier to select just the rows it needs from the external data source.

A pass-through query must use the query syntax of the external source. For example, if the external data source is Oracle, you must use the PL/SQL in the pass-through query.

In the case of a pass-through query that modifies data, the remote data type determines whether you locally or remotely perform the update:

- When another SQL Server is updated, the remote SQL Server performs the update.
- When non-SQL Server data is updated, the data providers determine where to perform the update.

Two forms of local distributed queries exist: one for linked servers and one for external data sources defined in the query. Likewise, two forms of explicitly declaring pass-through distributed queries exist as well; OpenQuery() uses an established linked server, and OpenRowSet() declares the link within the query.

The key to using pass-through queries, when using SQL Server as the external data source, is understanding how they execute and how to construct the query for optimal performance. Depending on the FROM and WHERE clauses, SQL Server attempts to pass as much of the query as possible to the external SQL Server to improve performance.

OpenQuery()

The OpenQuery() function uses a linked server, so it is certainly the easiest to develop and use. You can also use it within DML statements as a table, requiring only two parameters: the name of the linked server and the pass-through query.

The following illustrates a simple example using the OpenQuery() function to query an external SQL Server instance.

```
SELECT *
FROM OPENQUERY(AvalonDev, 'SELECT * FROM Person.Contact WHERE
ContactID = 1')
```

The OpenQuery() function requires a low amount of processing by SQL Server. In the previous example, exactly one row was returned to SQL Server. The engine executes the WHERE clause as it reads from the database.

The following example illustrates the same but against the Excel spreadsheet used in earlier examples:

```
SELECT *
FROM OPENQUERY(AdventureWorksContacts, 'SELECT * FROM People WHERE
LastName = "Brown"');
```

Here again, the remote scan returned the necessary rows (in this case 3).

OK, a quick UPDATE example — for DML executions, the exact rows requiring the update return to SQL Server where the update takes place. The results are written back to the external data source.

```
UPDATE OPENQUERY(
    AdventureWorksContacts,
    'SELECT * FROM People WHERE LastName = "Brown"')
SET LastName = 'Browns';
```

The great thing about the OpenQuery() function is that it handles changes in server configuration without requiring any changes to the code.

OpenRowSet()

The OpenRowSet() function is the pass-through counterpart to the OpenDataSet() function. Both require the remote data source to be fully specified in the distributed query, but the OpenRowSet() function adds a parameter to specify the pass-through query.

```
SELECT [First Name], [Last Name]
FROM OPENROWSET(
    'Microsoft.Jet.OLEDB.4.0',
    'D:\Projects\Wiley\SQL Server 2011 Bible\Nwind.mdb',
    'SELECT * FROM Employees');
```

Updates operate the same way:

```
UPDATE OPENROWSET(
    'Microsoft.Jet.OLEDB.4.0',
    'D:\Projects\Wiley\SQL Server 2011 Bible\Nwind.mdb',
    'SELECT * FROM Employees WHERE [Employee ID] = 5')
SET Title = 'Geek';
```

Using Distributed Transactions

Transactions are key to data integrity — that goes without saying. If the logical unit of work includes modifying data outside the local SQL Server, standard transactions cannot handle the atomicity of the transaction. If a distributed transaction fails during the processing of the operation, how is it handled? Who is responsible for handling that error and execution?

A mechanism must be in place to roll back the partial work; otherwise, a partial transaction would be recorded and the database left in an inconsistent state. This cannot happen.

15

Distributed Transaction Coordinator

The responsibility of handling distributed transactions falls on the shoulders of the Microsoft Distributed Transaction Coordinator (DTC). SQL Server uses the DTC to handle server transactions, commits, and rollbacks. The DTC uses a two-phase commit for multiple server transactions. This two-phase commit ensures that every server is available and handling the transactions by performing the following, and highly necessary, steps:

1. Each server is sent a "prepare to commit" message.

2. Each server performs the first phase of the commit, ensuring it can commit the transaction.

3. Each server replies when it finishes preparing for the commit.

4. Only after every participating server positively responds to the "prepare to commit" message is the actual commit message sent to each server.

It should go without saying that the DTC is needed only when DML operations are required. If the unit of work involves reading only, you do not need the DTC.

Developing Distributed Transactions

Distributed transactions are not that different from normal local SQL Server transactions, except for a few minor extensions to the syntax:

```
SET xact_abort ON;
BEGIN DISTRIBUTED TRANSACTION
```

In case of an error, the xact_abort connection option can cause the current transaction, not the current T-SQL statement, to roll back. You need the xact_abort ON option for any distributed transactions accessing a remote SQL Server, including most other OLE DB connections.

The BEGIN DISTRIBUTED TRANSACTION command first determines if the DTC service is available, but the command is not strictly required. If a transaction begins with BEGIN TRAN, the transaction escalates to a distributed transaction, and DTC is checked as soon as the distributed query executes.

That doesn't mean you shouldn't include the BEGIN DISTRIBUTED TRANSACTION command. It is a good practice to include the command so that DTC is checked at the beginning of the transaction.

How does it work? The following example illustrates distributed transactions between two different instances: a local instance and a linked server instance:

```
SET xact_abort ON
BEGIN DISTRIBUTED TRANSACTION

UPDATE Person.Contact
```

```
SET LastName = 'Klein'
WHERE ContactID = 55

UPDATE AvalonDev.AdventureWorks.Person.Contact
SET LastName = 'Klein'
WHERE ContactID = 55

COMMIT TRANSACTION
```

There is a difference between rolling back a local transaction and a DTC transaction. Rolling back a nested SQL Server local transaction rolls back all the pending transactions. DTC uses true nested transactions, and rolling back a DTC transaction can roll back only the current transaction.

Monitoring Distributed Transactions

The Distributed Transaction Coordinator (see Figure 15-3) is a completely separate service than SQL Server, and thus can be viewed from within the Windows operating system via the Component Services application.

FIGURE 15-3

Distributed Transaction Coordinator.

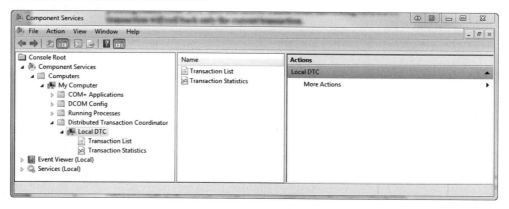

Performance Consideration

In the beginning of this chapter, the following statement was made: "With SQL Server, getting to and querying distributed data is not a problem; SQL Server can access data from a plethora of data sources. SQL Server provides several methods for accessing data from many different external data sources from a source location." Yet, you cannot simply rely on distributed queries alone to solve complex application performance concerns.

This section, therefore, looks at several options for improving database and application performance. Although SQL Server does as much of the query optimization as it can, there still remain areas where the design and development decision can have a huge impact on query performance.

Optimizing Distributed Queries

As SQL developers the responsibility to write optimal performing queries falls upon you. With tools and utilities such as SQL Server Profiler and Execution Plans, there is no excuse for writing bad queries. This also goes for distributed queries.

However, SQL Server also steps in and performs two types of optimization specific to distributed queries:

- OLE DB SQL Command providers used for remote query execution
- OLE DB Index providers allowing indexed access

The next sections briefly cover each of these.

Remote Query Execution

SQL Server can delegate as much of the elevation of a distributed query to the SQL Command provider as possible. The key here is the use of an OLE DB provider, in that, the OLE DB provider is considered a SQL Command provider if the OLE DB provider supports the Command object and all associated interfaces. The OLE DB provider must all meet syntax criteria, including the support of ISO at an entry level or higher to support ODBC at the Core level or higher.

This plays an important role on how remote queries are executed. SQL queries that access only the remote tables stored in the data source of the provider are extracted from the original distributed query and executed against the provider. This extraction is crucial because it reduces the number of rows returned from the provider and allows the provider to use its own indexes in any query evaluation.

SQL Server doesn't stop at query extraction to improve performance. SQL Server considers different aspects of the environment to determine how much of the original distributed query is handed off to the SQL Command Provider:

- SQL Command provider dialect level
- Collation compatibility

What are dialect levels? Specifically, they are SQL Server, ISO Entry Level, ODBC core, and Jet. SQL Server delegates query operations only if they are supported by the specific dialect level. The highest level is SQL Server. The lowest level is Jet. The higher the dialect level, the more operations SQL Server can delegate to the provider. Each dialect level is a superset of the lower levels. Thus, if an operation is delegated to a particular level, it can also be delegated to all the higher levels.

Collations also play an important role in distributed queries. SQL Server supports multiple collations, and collations can differ even at the column level. Each character value has an associated collation property. For distributed queries all character data is defined by the character set and sort order of the local instance of SQL Server. Thus, for distributed queries, SQL Server can interpret the collation property of the character data of both the local SQL Server instance and the remote data source and treat them accordingly.

For example, SQL Server can use the collation properties to determine the proper comparison and ordering operations and apply the same rules for converting, comparing, and ordering for local columns.

Indexed Access

The important thing to remember about indexed access is that SQL Server can use execution strategies that include using the indexes of the Index provider to evaluate predicates and perform the necessary sorting operations against remote tables. However, to enable indexed access against a provider, the `IndexAsAccessPath` provider option must be set.

Sharding and Federations

The concept of Database Sharding has been gaining popularity over the past several years, due to the enormous growth in transaction volume and the size of business application databases.

Database Sharding is a "shared-nothing" partitioning scheme for large databases across a number of servers, enabling new levels of database performance and scalability achievable. If you think of broken glass, you can get the concept of sharding — breaking your database down into smaller chunks called shards and spreading those across a number of distributed servers.

Microsoft has taken this concept and implemented a sharding/partitioning strategy called Federations, which will soon be available in Azure SQL Database. This is not a chapter on Azure SQL Database (see Chapter 31, "Managing Data in Windows Azure SQL Database" for more information), the concept of partitioning or sharding your data does not apply only to Azure SQL Database or cloud databases. You can use these techniques and technologies with on-premises databases as well.

You must understand when it's appropriate to shard your database; the decision to do so should not be taken lightly because it adds an additional level of complexity to your application. For certain scenarios the benefits of database scale out can be huge. This is particularly true for applications that require massive throughput.

You can use many different approaches to scale out your databases. You need to determine the right strategy because it can directly impact the complexity and performance of your solution. For example, you might have a scenario in which you have a workload for a single application spread across multiple databases with the need for your application to dynamically determine which database to connect to for a given query and the ability to combine

15

the result sets. For some scenarios, especially for Independent Software Vendors (ISVs) a much simpler strategy may be to assign all customers their own database, removing the need to allow for queries across multiple databases.

When using a scale-out database strategy, you get the added resources of each of the machines processing your workload. Having one 10GB database is not the same as having 10 1GB databases. When you have 10 1GB databases, you have distributed your workload over many more machines, which is particularly important for high throughput.

Summary

Distributed Queries and linked servers have been around for quite some time in SQL Server, and while nothing has changed with linked servers in SQL Server 2012, knowing how to execute distributed queries and how to improve distributed query performance is always good to know.

This chapter also covered linking to external data sources, such as Excel and Access, simply because not all external data will come from SQL Server. Being able to access and query data from multiple different data sources is crucial in today's environments.

Part IV

Programming with T-SQL

Programming with T-SQL

S tandard SQL Data Manipulation Language (DML) commands — SELECT, INSERT, UPDATE, and DELETE — modify or return only data. SQL DML lacks both the programming structure to develop procedures and algorithms, and the database-specific commands to control and tune the server. To compensate, each full-featured database product must complement the SQL standard with some proprietary SQL language extension.

Transact-SQL, better known as T-SQL, is Microsoft's implementation of ANSI SQL plus its proprietary collection of extensions to SQL. The purpose of T-SQL is to provide a set of procedural and administrative tools for the development of a transactional database. You can use these tools in several different ways within a SQL Server client/server application:

- T-SQL is used within expressions as part of DML commands (INSERT, UPDATE, and DELETE) submitted by the client process.
- It is used within blocks of code submitted to SQL Server from a client as a batch or script.
- T-SQL functions are used as expressions within check constraints.
- T-SQL code is used within batches of code that have been packaged within SQL Server as stored procedures, functions, or triggers.

Truth be told, this book has been covering T-SQL programming since Chapter 6, "Introducing Basic Query Flow." The DML commands are the heart of T-SQL. This chapter merely adds the programmatic elements required to develop server-side procedural code. The language features explained in this chapter are the foundation for developing stored procedures, user-defined functions, and triggers.

Transact-SQL Fundamentals

T-SQL is designed to add structure to the handling of sets of data. Because of this, it does not provide several language features that application development needs. If you do a lot of application programming development, you'll find that T-SQL is in many ways the exact opposite of how you think when programming in VB, C#, Java, or any other structured development language.

Best Practice

SQL Server 2005 added the capability to create stored procedures, functions, and triggers using .NET and the common language runtime (CLR). Nevertheless, T-SQL is the native language of SQL Server and remains the best choice for any data-oriented task.

T-SQL Batches

A *query* is a single SQL DML statement, and a *batch* is a collection of one or more T-SQL statements. The entire collection is sent to SQL Server from the front-end application as a single unit of code.

SQL Server parses the entire batch as a unit. Any syntax error will cause the entire batch to fail, meaning that none of the batch executes. However, the parsing does not check any object names or schemas because a schema may change by the time the statement executes.

Terminating a Batch

A SQL script file or a Query Analyzer window may contain multiple batches. If this is the case, a batch-separator keyword terminates each batch. By default, the batch-separator keyword is GO (similar to how the Start button is used to shut down Windows). The batch-separator keyword must be the only keyword in the line. You can add a comment after the GO.

The batch separator is actually a function of SQL Server Management Studio and SQLCMD, not SQL Server. It can be modified in the Query Execution page by selecting Tools ⇨ Options, but it isn't recommended that you create a custom batch separator (at least not for your friends).

Because the GO batch terminator tells Management Studio's Query Editor to send the batch to the connected SQL Server, it can be used to submit the batch multiple times. The following script demonstrates this poor man's cursor:

```
PRINT 'I'm a batch.';
go 5 -- will execute 5 times
```

Result:

```
Beginning execution loop
I'm a batch.
I'm a batch.
I'm a batch.
I'm a batch.
I'm a batch.
Batch execution completed 5 times.
```

Terminating a batch kills all local variables, temporary tables, and cursors created by that batch.

DDL Commands

Some T-SQL DDL commands, such as CREATE PROCEDURE, are required to be the only command in the batch. Long scripts that create several objects often include numerous GO batch terminators. Because SQL Server evaluates syntax by the batch, using GO throughout a long script also helps locate syntax errors.

Switching Databases

Interactively, the current database is indicated in the Query Editor toolbar and can be changed there. In code, the current database is selected with the USE command. You can insert USE within a batch to specify the database from that point on:

```
USE AdventureWorks2012;
```

It's a good practice to explicitly specify the correct database with the USE command, rather than assume that the user will select the correct database prior to running the script.

Executing Batches

A batch can be executed in several ways:

- A complete SQL script (including all the batches in the script) may be executed by opening the .sql file with SQL Server Management Studio's SQL Editor and pressing F5, clicking the! Execute toolbar button, or selecting Query ⇨ Execute.

- Selected T-SQL statements may be executed within SQL Server Management Studio's SQL Editor by highlighting those statements and pressing F5, clicking the! Execute toolbar button, or selecting Query ⇨ Execute.

- An application can submit a T-SQL batch using ADO or ODBC for execution.

- A SQL script may be executed by running the SQLCMD command-line utility and passing the SQL script file as a parameter.

 A SQL script may be executed through PowerShell. Please refer to Chapter 30, "Configuring and Managing SQL Server with PowerShell," for more information.

T-SQL Formatting

Throughout this book, T-SQL code has been formatted for readability; this section specifies the details of formatting T-SQL code.

Statement Termination

The ANSI SQL standard is to place a semicolon (;) at the end of each command to terminate it. When programming T-SQL, the semicolon is optional. Most other database products (including Access) do require semicolons.

There are a few rules about using the semicolon:

- Don't place one after an END TRY.
- Don't place one after an IF or WHILE condition.
- You must place one before any CTE if it is not the first statement in the batch.
- Don't place one after BEGIN.
- A statement terminator is required following a MERGE command.

> **NOTE**
>
> As of SQL Server 2012, not terminating a SQL statement with a semicolon has been deprecated. This means that in a future version of SQL Server, all T-SQL will *require* a semicolon terminator.

Line Continuation

T-SQL commands, by their nature, tend to be long. One author has written production queries with multiple joins and subqueries that were a few pages long. It's nice that T-SQL ignores spaces and end-of-line returns. This smart feature means that long lines can be continued without a special line-continuation character, which makes T-SQL code significantly more readable.

Comments

T-SQL accepts both simple comments and bracketed comments within the same batch. The simple comment begins with two hyphens and concludes with an end-of-line:

```
-- This is a simple comment
```

Simple comments may be embedded within a single SQL command:

```
SELECT Name, ProductID    -- selects the columns
  FROM Production.Product         -- the source table
   WHERE Name LIKE 'Hex%'; -- the row restriction
```

Management Studio's Query Editor can apply or remove simple comments to all selected lines. Select either Edit ➪ Advanced ➪ Comment Selection (Ctrl+K, Ctrl+C) or Edit ➪ Advanced ➪ Uncomment Selection (Ctrl+K, Ctrl+U), respectively.

Bracketed comments begin with /* and conclude with */. These comments are useful for commenting out a block of lines such as a code header or large test query:

```
/*
Product Table INSERT
Version 1.0
May 15, 2012
*/
```

A benefit of bracketed comments is that a large multiline query within the comments may be selected and executed without altering the comments.

Working with Variables

Every language requires variables to temporarily store values in memory. T-SQL variables are created with the DECLARE command. The DECLARE command is followed by the variable name and data type. The available data types are similar to those used to create tables, with the addition of the table and cursor. The deprecated text, ntext, and image data types are only available for table columns, and not for variables. Multiple comma-separated variables can be declared with a single DECLARE command.

Variable Default and Scope

The scope, or application and duration, of the variable extends only to the current batch. Newly declared variables default to NULL and must be initialized if you want them to have a value in an expression. Remember that NULL added to a value yields NULL.

The following script creates two test variables and demonstrates their initial value and scope. The entire script is a single execution, even though it's technically two batches (separated by a GO), so the results of the three SELECT statements appear at the conclusion of the script:

```
DECLARE   @Test INT ,
          @TestTwo NVARCHAR(25);
SELECT @Test, @TestTwo;

SET @Test = 1;
SET @TestTwo = 'a value';
SELECT @Test, @TestTwo ;

GO

SELECT @Test AS BatchTwo, @TestTwo;
```

Result of the entire script:

```
---------- ------------------------
NULL       NULL

(1 row(s) affected)


---------- ------------------------
1          a value

(1 row(s) affected)

Msg 137, Level 15, State 2, Line 2
Must declare the scalar variable "@Test".
```

The first SELECT returns two NULL values. After the variables have been initialized, they properly return the sample values. When the batch concludes (due to the GO terminator), so do the variables. Error message 137 is the result of the final SELECT statement.

Variables are local in scope and do not extend to other batches or called stored procedures.

Using the Set and Select Commands

Both the SET command and the SELECT command can assign the value of an expression to a variable. The main difference between the two is that a SELECT can retrieve data from a data source (for example, table, subquery, or view) and can include the other SELECT clauses as well (for example, FROM, WHERE), whereas a SET is limited to retrieving data from expressions. Both SET and SELECT can include functions. Use the simpler SET command when you need to assign only a function result or constant to a variable and don't need the Query Optimizer to consider a data source. Additionally, SET can only set the value of one variable, while multiple variable values may be set with a single SELECT statement.

A detailed exception to the preceding paragraph is when a SET command uses a scalar subquery that accesses a data source. This is a best practice if you want to ensure that the variable is set to NULL if no rows qualify, and that you get an error if more than one row qualifies.

Of course, a SELECT statement may retrieve multiple columns. Each column may be assigned to a variable. If the SELECT statement retrieves multiple rows, then the values from the last row are stored in the variables. No error will be reported.

The following SQL batch creates two variables and initializes one of them. The SELECT statement will retrieve multiple rows, ordered by ProductID. The ProductID and the ProductName of the last product returned by the SELECT will be stored in the variables:

```
USE AdventureWorks2012;
GO

DECLARE @ProductID int,
```

```
    @ProductName varchar(25);

SET @ProductID = 782;
SELECT
    @ProductID = ProductID,
    @ProductName = Name
FROM Production.Product
ORDER BY ProductID;

SELECT @ProductID as ProductID, @ProductName as ProductName;
```

Result:

```
ProductID    ProductName
-----------  -------------------------
999          Road-750 Black, 52
```

CAUTION

The preceding code demonstrates a common coding mistake. Never use a SELECT to populate a variable unless
you're sure that it will return only a single row.

If no rows are returned from the SELECT statement, the SELECT does not affect the variables. In the following query, there is no product with a ProductID of 999, so the SELECT
statement does not affect either variable:

```
USE AdventureWorks2012;
GO

DECLARE @ProductID int,
    @ProductName varchar(25);

SET @ProductID = 999;
SELECT
    @ProductID = ProductID,
    @ProductName = Name
FROM Production.Product
WHERE ProductID = 1000;

SELECT @ProductID as ProductID, @ProductName as ProductName;
```

The final SELECT statement reports the value of @ProductID and @ProductName, and
indeed they are still 999 and NULL, respectively. The first SELECT did not alter its value:

```
ProductID    ProductName
-----------  -------------------------
999          NULL
```

Incrementing Variables

T-SQL has the increment variable feature, which saves a few keystrokes when coding and certainly looks cleaner and more modern.

The basic idea is that an operation and equals sign will perform that function on the variable. For example, the code

```
SET @x += 5;
```

is the logical equivalent of

```
SET @x = @x + 5
```

The next short script walks through addition, subtraction, and multiplication using the new variable increment feature:

```
DECLARE @x INT = 1

SET @x += 5
SELECT @x

SET @x -=3
SELECT @x

SET @x *= 2
SELECT @x
```

Result (of whole batch):

```
-----------
6

-----------
3

-----------
6
```

Conditional Select

Because the SELECT statement includes a WHERE clause, the following syntax works well, although those not familiar with it may be confused:

```
SELECT @Variable = expression WHERE BooleanExpression;
```

The WHERE clause functions as a conditional IF statement. If the boolean expression is true, then the SELECT takes place. If not, the SELECT is performed, but the @Variable is not altered in any way because the SELECT command has no effect.

Using Variables within SQL Queries

Another feature of T-SQL is that variables may be used with SQL queries without having to build any complex dynamic SQL strings to concatenate the variables into the code. Dynamic SQL still has its place, but the single value can simply be modified with a variable.

Anywhere an expression can be used within a SQL query, a variable may be used in its place. The following code demonstrates using a variable in a WHERE clause:

```
USE AdventureWorks2012;

DECLARE @ProductID int = 999;

SELECT Name
  FROM Production.Product
  WHERE ProductID = @ProductID;
```

Result:

```
Name
--------------------------------------------------
Road-750 Black, 52
```

Debugging T-SQL

When a syntax error is found, the Query Editor displays the error and the line number of the error within the batch. Double-clicking on the error message places the cursor near the offending line.

Often the error won't occur at the exact word that is reported as the error. The error location reported simply reflects how far SQL Server's parser got before it detected the error. Usually the actual error is somewhere just before or after the reported error. Nevertheless, the error messages are generally close.

Multiple Assignment Variables

A *multiple assignment variable,* sometimes called an *aggregate concatenation*, is a fascinating method that appends a variable to itself using a SELECT statement and a subquery.

This section demonstrates a real-world use of multiple assignment variables, but because it's an unusual use of the SELECT statement, here it is in its basic form:

```
SELECT @variable = @variable + d.column
  FROM datasource d;
```

Each row from the derived table is appended to the variable, changing the vertical column in the underlying table into a horizontal list.

This type of data retrieval is quite common. Often a vertical list of values is better reported as a single comma-delimited horizontal list than as a subreport or another subheading level several inches long. A short horizontal list is more readable and saves space.

The following example builds a list of departments in the AdventureWorks2012 sample database from the HumanResources.Department table:

```
USE AdventureWorks2012;

DECLARE @MAV varchar(max)

SELECT @MAV = Coalesce(@MAV + ', '+ d.Name, d.Name)
  FROM (
        SELECT Name
        FROM HumanResources.Department
        )
ORDER BY d.Name;

SELECT @MAV;
```

Result (line breaks added for readability):

```
------------------------------------------------------------------
Document Control, Engineering, Executive, Facilities and Maintenance,
Finance, Human Resources, Information Services, Marketing, Production,
Production Control, Purchasing, Quality Assurance, Research and
Development, Sales, Shipping and Receiving, Tool Design
```

Using COALESCE

If you're not familiar with COALESCE, it's a worthy part of T-SQL to learn. It evaluates each comma-separated value immediately following the keyword, using the first one it encounters that doesn't have a NULL value. It is quite similar to ISNULL, but is able to evaluate more than two items. In the above case, it is checking the value of @MAV + ', '+d.Name, and if it is NULL, will use the next value, d.Name. This means that in this particular case, the string that is built will start out with a department name rather than a leading comma (because @MAV will start out as NULL), and all subsequent assignments of this variable will have the concatenated comma, thus allowing COALESCE to use the first item in the list.

The problem with multiple assignment variables is that Microsoft is vague about their behavior. The order of the denormalized data isn't guaranteed, but queries do seem to respond to the ORDER BY clause. It's not documented in Books Online, but it has been documented in Microsoft Knowledge Base article 287515. It performs well, but be cautious about using it when the result is order-dependent.

An alternative method to denormalize a list is the XML PATH method:

```
SELECT [text()] = Name + ','
  FROM (
            SELECT DISTINCT Name
            FROM HumanResources.Department) d
  ORDER BY Name
  FOR XML PATH('');
```

 For more details on XML, see Chapter 14, "Using XML Data."

Procedural Flow

At first glance, it appears that T-SQL is weak in procedural-flow options. Although it's less rich than some other languages, it suffices. The data-handling boolean extensions — such as EXISTS, IN, and CASE — offset the limitations of IF and WHILE.

Using If for Conditional T-SQL

This is your grandfather's IF. The T-SQL IF command determines the execution of *only* the next single statement — one IF, one command. In addition, there's no THEN and no END IF command to terminate the IF block:

```
IF Condition
  Statement;
```

In the following script, the IF condition should return a false, preventing the next command from executing:

```
IF 1 = 0

PRINT 'Line One';
PRINT 'Line Two';
```

Result:

```
Line Two
```

> **NOTE**
>
> The IF statement is not followed by a semicolon; in fact, a semicolon causes an error. That's because the IF statement is actually a prefix for the following statement; the two are compiled as a single statement.

Using Begin/End to Conditionally Execute Multiple Statements

An IF command that can control only a single command is less than useful. However, a BEGIN/END block can make multiple commands appear to the IF command as the next single command:

```
IF Condition
   Begin;
      Multiple lines;
   End;
```

Using If exists() as an Existence-Based Condition

While the IF command may seem limited, the condition clause can include several powerful SQL features similar to a WHERE clause, such as IF EXISTS() and IF...IN().

The IF EXISTS() structure uses the presence of any rows returned from a SQL SELECT statement as a condition. Because it looks for any row, the SELECT statement should select all columns (*). This method is faster than checking an @@rowcount >0 condition because the total number of rows isn't required. As soon as a single row satisfies the IF EXISTS(), the query can move on.

The following example script uses the IF EXISTS() technique to process orders only if any open orders exist:

```
USE AdventureWorks2012;
  IF EXISTS
     (
     SELECT * FROM Production.ProductInventory WHERE Quantity = 0
     )
  BEGIN;
     PRINT 'Replenish Inventory';
  END;
```

There is effectively no difference between SELECT * or selecting a column. However, selecting all columns enables SQL Server to select the best column from an index and might, in some situations, be slightly faster.

Using Nested If for Complex Query Flow

More complex query flow can be achieved by nesting IF statements. You can do this when dropping tables in a database setup script; checking first for the existence of the table and then nesting IF statements below that to check for and drop dependent objects like indexes and foreign keys before dropping the table you were after in the first place.

The following example creates two tables, one with a foreign key relationship to the other and a single index on the main table. In the first IF statement, you attempt to drop dbo.MainTable. This fails because the object has dependencies that need to be handled first. In the second IF, you nest IF statements to first check for the existence of dbo.MainTable, and if it does exist, drop the dependent objects prior to issuing the DROP TABLE dbo.MainTable command.

```
USE AdventureWorks2012;
GO

CREATE TABLE dbo.MainTable(
```

```
    PKColumn int PRIMARY KEY,
    ColumnA int);

CREATE TABLE dbo.FKTable(
    FKColumn int PRIMARY KEY REFERENCES dbo.MainTable(PKColumn),
    ColumnB int);

CREATE INDEX MainTableIndex ON dbo.MainTable(PKColumn);

--This statement will fail
IF EXISTS (SELECT OBJECT_ID('dbo.MainTable') FROM sys.objects)
BEGIN
    DROP TABLE dbo.MainTable;
END;

--This statement will succeed
IF EXISTS (SELECT OBJECT_ID('dbo.MainTable') FROM sys.objects)
BEGIN
    IF EXISTS (SELECT OBJECT_ID('dbo.FKTable') from sys.objects)
      BEGIN
        DROP TABLE dbo.FKTable;
    END

    IF EXISTS (SELECT OBJECT_ID('dbo.MainTableIndex') FROM sys.objects)
      BEGIN
        DROP INDEX MainTableIndex
          ON dbo.MainTable;
    END

    DROP TABLE dbo.MainTable;
END;
```

Using If/Else to Execute an Alternative Statement

The optional ELSE command defines code that is executed only when the IF condition is false. Like IF, ELSE controls only the next single command or BEGIN/END block:

```
IF Condition
Single line or begin/end block of code;
ELSE
Single line or begin/end block of code;
```

Looping with WHILE

The WHILE command is used to loop through code while a condition is still true. Just like the IF command, the WHILE command determines the execution of only the following single T-SQL command. To control a full block of commands, you should use BEGIN/END.

Some looping methods differ in the timing of the conditional test. The T-SQL WHILE works in the following order:

1. The WHILE command tests the condition. If the condition is true, WHILE executes the following command or block of code; if not, it skips the following command or block of code and moves on.

2. When the following command or block of code is complete, flow of control is returned to the WHILE command.

The following short script demonstrates using the WHILE command to perform a loop:

```
DECLARE @Temp INT;
SET @Temp = 0;

WHILE @Temp < 3
  BEGIN;
    PRINT 'tested condition' + STR(@Temp);
    SET @Temp = @Temp + 1;
  END;
```

Result:

```
tested condition        0
tested condition        1
tested condition        2
```

The CONTINUE and BREAK commands enhance the WHILE command for more complex loops. The CONTINUE command immediately jumps back to the WHILE command. The condition is tested as normal.

The BREAK command immediately exits the loop and continues with the script as if the WHILE condition was false. The following pseudocode (not intended to actually run) demonstrates the BREAK command:

```
CREATE PROCEDURE MyLife()
AS
WHILE Not @@Eyes2blurry = 1
  BEGIN;
    EXEC Eat;
    INSERT INTO Book(Words)
      FROM Brain(Words)
      WHERE Brain.Thoughts
        IN('Make sense', 'Good Code', 'Best Practice');
    IF @Firefly = 'On'
      BREAK;
  END;
```

Using Goto to Move to a Label

Before you associate the T-SQL GOTO command with bad memories of 1970s-style spaghetti-BASIC, this GOTO command is limited to jumping to a label within the same batch or procedure and is rarely used for anything other than jumping to an error handler at the close of the batch or procedure. Although this is syntactically correct, and you're likely to see it quite a bit in legacy code, GOTO should be avoided if possible. It's a brute force way to control query flow, and most likely, there is a more elegant way to move the script along.

The label is created by placing a colon after the label name:

```
LabelName:
```

The following code sample uses the GOTO command to branch to the ErrorHandler: label, bypassing the 'more code':

```
GOTO ErrorHandler;
Print 'more code';
ErrorHandler:
Print 'Logging the error';
```

Result:

```
Logging the error
```

Examining SQL Server with Code

One of the benefits of using SQL Server is the cool interface it offers to develop and administer the database. Management Studio is great for graphically exploring a database; T-SQL code, although more complex, exposes even more detail within a programmer's environment.

Dynamic Management Objects

Introduced in SQL Server 2005, dynamic management objects (DMOs) offer a powerful view into the structure of SQL Server and the databases, as well as the current SQL Server status (memory, IO, and so on).

As an example of using DMOs, the next query looks at three DMOs concerning objects and primary keys:

```
USE AdventureWorks2012;
GO

SELECT s.NAME + '.' + o2.NAME AS 'Table', pk.NAME AS 'Primary Key'
  FROM sys.key_constraints AS pk
    JOIN sys.objects AS o
      ON pk.OBJECT_ID = o.OBJECT_ID
    JOIN sys.objects AS o2
      ON o.parent_object_id = o2.OBJECT_ID
    JOIN sys.schemas AS s
      ON o2.schema_id = s.schema_id;
```

Result:

```
Table                      Primary Key
------------------------   -------------------------------------
dbo.ErrorLog               PK_ErrorLog_ErrorLogID
Person.Address             PK_Address_AddressID
Person.AddressType         PK_AddressType_AddressTypeID
dbo.AWBuildVersion         PK_AWBuildVersion_SystemInformationID
Production.BillOfMaterials PK_BillOfMaterials_BillOfMaterialsID
Production.Document        UQ__Document__F73921F793071A63
Person.BusinessEntity      PK_BusinessEntity_BusinessEntityID
```

sp_help

Sp_help, and its variations, return information regarding the server, database, objects, connections, and more. The basic sp_help lists the available objects in the current database; the other variations provide detailed information about the various objects or settings.

Adding an object name as a parameter to sp_help returns additional appropriate information about the object:

```
USE AdventureWorks2012;
GO

sp_help 'Production.Product';
```

The result here is nine data sets of information about the Production.Product table:

- Name, creation date, and owner
- Columns
- Identity columns
- Row GUID columns
- FileGroup location
- Indexes
- Constraints
- Foreign Key references
- View references

System Functions

A system function, sometimes called a global variable, returns information about the current system or connection status.

System functions can't be created. There's a fixed set of system functions, all beginning with two @ signs. (The more significant ones are listed in Table 16-1.) The most commonly used global variables are @@NestLevel, @@Rowcount, @@ServerName, and @@Version. The system functions are being replaced by DMO information.

TABLE 16-1 **System Functions**

System Function	Returns	Scope
@@DateFirst	The day of the week currently set as the first day of the week; 1 represents Monday, 2 represents Tuesday, and so on. For example, if Sunday is the first day of the week, @@DateFirst returns a 7.	Connection
@@Error	The error value for the last T-SQL statement executed.	Connection
@@Fetch_Status	The row status from the last cursor fetch command.	Connection
@@LangID	The language ID used by the current connection.	Connection
@@Language	The language, by name, used by the current connection.	Connection
@@Lock_TimeOut	The lock timeout setting for the current connection.	Connection
@@Nestlevel	Current number of nested stored procedures.	Connection
@@ProcID	The stored procedure identifier for the current stored procedure. This can be used with sys .objects to determine the name of the current stored procedure, as follows: SELECT name FROM sys.objects WHERE object_id = @@ProcID;	Connection
@@RowCount	Number of rows returned by the last T-SQL statement.	Connection
@@ServerName	Name of the current server.	Server
@@ServiceName	SQL Server's Windows service name.	Server
@@SPID	The current connection's server-process identifier — the ID for the connection.	Connection
@@TranCount	Number of active transactions for the current connection.	Connection
@@Version	SQL Server edition, version, and service pack.	Server

Temporary Tables and Table Variables

Temporary tables and table variables play a different role from standard user tables. By their temporary nature, these objects are useful as a vehicle for passing data between objects or as a short-term scratch-pad table intended for temporary work.

Local Temporary Tables

A temporary table is created the same way as a standard user-defined table, except the temporary table must have a pound, or hash, sign (#) preceding its name. Temporary tables are actually created on the disk in `tempdb`:

```
CREATE TABLE #ProductTemp (
  ProductID INT PRIMARY KEY
  );
```

A temporary table has a short life. When the batch or stored procedure that created it ends, the temporary table is dropped. If the table is created during an interactive session (such as a Query Editor window), it survives only until the end of that session. Of course, a temporary table can also be manually dropped within the batch. However, a temporary table may have many characteristics of a permanent table, including primary keys and clustered and nonclustered indexes.

The scope of a temporary table is also limited. Only the connection that created the local temporary table can see it. Even if a thousand users create temporary tables with the same name, each user sees only his temporary table. The temporary table is created in `tempdb` with a unique name that combines the assigned table name and the connection identifier. Most objects can have names up to 128 characters in length, but temporary tables are limited to 116 so that the last 12 characters can make the name unique. To demonstrate the unique name, the following code finds all the temporary tables beginning with #Pro stored in `tempdb.sys.objects`:

```
SELECT name
  FROM tempdb.sys.objects
  WHERE name LIKE '#Pro%';
```

Result (shortened to save space; the real value is 128 characters wide):

```
name
-------------------------------------------------------------
#ProductTemp_____00000000002D
```

Despite the long name in `sys.objects`, SQL queries still reference any temporary tables with the original name.

Global Temporary Tables

Global temporary tables are similar to local temporary tables but they have a broader scope. All users can reference a global temporary table, and the life of the table extends until the session that created the table disconnects.

To create a global temporary table, begin the table name with two pound signs, for example, ##*TableName*. The following code sample tests to determine whether the global temporary table exists and creates one if it doesn't:

```
IF NOT EXISTS(
  SELECT * FROM tempdb.sys.objects
    WHERE name = '##TempWork')
CREATE TABLE ##TempWork(
  PK INT PRIMARY KEY,
  Col1 INT
  );
```

NOTE

There are a few benefits of global temporary tables and many drawbacks. Application code that depends on the existence of a global temporary table can get tripped up if it doesn't exist or tries to create one that already exists. If you create global temporary tables, consider whether that data would be better stored in a permanent table in your database.

When a temporary table is required, it's likely used for a work in progress. Another alternative is to simply create a standard user table in `tempdb`. Every time the SQL Server is restarted, it dumps and rebuilds `tempdb`, effectively clearing the alternative temporary worktable.

Table Variables

Table variables are similar to temporary tables. The main difference, besides syntax, is that table variables have the same scope and life as a local variable. They are seen only by the batch, procedure, or function that creates them. To be seen by called stored procedures, the table variables must be passed in as table-valued parameters, and then they are read-only in the called routine.

The life span of a table variable is also much shorter than a temp table. Table variables cease to exist when the batch, procedure, or function concludes. Table variables have a few additional limitations:

- Table variables may not be created by means of the `select * into` or `insert into @tablename exec` table syntax.
- Table variables are limited in their allowable constraints: No foreign keys are allowed. Primary keys, defaults, nulls, check constraints, and unique constraints are OK.
- Table variables may not have any dependent objects, such as triggers or foreign keys.

Table variables are declared as variables, rather than created with SQL DDL statements. When a table variable is referenced with a SQL query, the table is used as a normal table but named as a variable. The following script must be executed as a single batch or it will fail:

```
DECLARE @WorkTable TABLE (
  PK INT PRIMARY KEY,
  Col1 INT NOT NULL);

INSERT INTO @WorkTable (PK, Col1)
  VALUES ( 1, 101);

SELECT PK, Col1
  FROM @WorkTable;
```

Result:

```
PK          Col1
----------- -----------
            101
```

Memory versus Disk; Temp Tables versus Table Variables

A common SQL myth is that table variables are stored in memory. They're not. They exist in tempdb just like a temporary table. However, the life span of a table variable (as well as that of most temporary tables) is such that it's extremely unlikely that it would actually be written to disk. The truth is that the table variable lives in tempdb pages in memory.

So if the difference isn't memory versus disk, how do you choose between using a temp table or a table variable? Size and scope.

Rule of thumb: If the temp space will hold more than approximately 250 rows, then go with a temp table; otherwise choose a table variable. The reason is because temp tables have the overhead of statistics, whereas table variables do not. This means that for more data, the temp table's statistics can help the Query Optimizer choose the best plan. Of course, you always must consider the overhead of maintaining the statistics.

Table variables don't have statistics, so they save on the overhead; but without statistics, the Query Optimizer always assumes the table variable will result in one row and may therefore choose a poor plan if the table variable contains a lot of data.

Scope is the other consideration. If the temp space must be visible and updatable by called routines, then you need to choose a temp table.

What's New in T-SQL for 2012

New features and enhancements in SQL Server 2012 are highlighted throughout this book. However, there are a few items that deserve a mention within this chapter.

Debugging Enhancements

Debugging within SQL Server Management Studio has historically been an exercise in frustration. With SQL Server 2012, you now have the ability to set conditional breakpoints, hit count thresholds, and import and export the breakpoints to an XML file for portability. In addition, you may now fully customize the keyboard for debug mode.

Metadata Discovery

Two new enhancements, delivered via system stored procedures and functionally equivalent dynamic management objects (DMO), provide metadata about what the result set will be when a T-SQL batch is executed.

Sys.dm_exec_describe_first_result_set

The DMO sys.dm_exec_describe_first_result_set returns metadata for the first possible result set of the Transact-SQL batch. The metadata provided is similar to what you might see if you query sys.objects. The huge advantage is that it evaluates all columns in the query, consolidating object metadata into one result set. The system stored procedure sp_describe_first_result_set provides the same information. Simply pass the T-SQL batch to the DMO, along with any parameters and their data types, as well as the browse_information_mode parameter.

```
SELECT *
FROM sys.dm_exec_describe_first_result_set
    (N'TSQL', N'Parameters', 0);
```

The following example returns three rows of metadata from ProductCategory, ProductSubCategory, and Product, respectively.

```
USE AdventureWorks2012;
GO

SELECT *
FROM sys.dm_exec_describe_first_result_set
    (N'SELECT c.Name, s.Name, p.Name
        FROM Production.ProductCategory c
          JOIN Production.ProductSubcategory s
            ON c.ProductCategoryID = s.ProductCategoryID
          JOIN Production.Product p
            ON s.ProductSubcategoryID = p.ProductSubcategoryID
```

```
      WHERE c.ProductCategoryID = @ProductCategoryID',
   N'@ProductCategoryID int',
   0);
```

Sys.dm_exec_describe_first_result_set_for_object

In addition passing a T-SQL batch to a DMO to get result metadata, you may pass a stored procedure or trigger to sys.dm_exec_describe_first_result_set_for_object.

```
SELECT *
FROM sys.dm_exec_describe_first_result_set_for_object
   (OBJECT_ID(N'dbo.uspGetEmployeeManagers'), 0)
```

Sp_describe_undeclared_parameters

This system stored procedure wins the SQL Server 2012 prize for most difficult to understand name. Basically, you can pass in a T-SQL batch and zero or more of the parameters included in the batch. Whatever you don't declare, you'll be returned the metadata for those parameters. It's best to see an example.

```
sp_describe_undeclared_parameters
 N'SELECT c.Name, s.Name, p.Name
   FROM Production.ProductCategory c
     JOIN Production.ProductSubcategory s
       ON c.ProductCategoryID = s.ProductCategoryID
     JOIN Production.Product p
       ON s.ProductSubcategoryID = p.ProductSubcategoryID
     WHERE c.ProductCategoryID = @ProductCategoryID
       AND s.ProductSubcategoryID = @ProductSubcategoryID',
     N'@ProductCategoryID int';

parameter_ordinal name
---------------- ---------------------------
1                @ProductSubCategoryID
. . .
```

Because the parameter @ProductSubCategoryID wasn't passed into the system stored procedure, the metadata that is returned is for this parameter.

Offset and Fetch

Paging on a website looks so simple. You perform a search for your favorite widget. There are 118 results returned. The first 20 are shown, with the ability to go to the next page if you want to see more. If the results paging was done in T-SQL prior to SQL Server 2012, the backend code is likely ugly. Microsoft has made this task much simpler by providing OFFSET and FETCH in SQL Server 2012. It is integrated into the ORDER BY clause and allows you to specify where to start returning rows (OFFSET) and how many rows to return (FETCH).

```
USE AdventureWorks2012;
GO

SELECT DepartmentID, Name
FROM HumanResources.Department
ORDER BY DepartmentID
  OFFSET 2 ROWS
  FETCH NEXT 5 ROWS ONLY;
```

Result:

```
DepartmentID Name
------------ --------------------------
3            Sales
4            Marketing
5            Purchasing
6            Research and Development
7            Production
```

This is quite powerful and allows results paging to be handled server-side rather than client-side as it has traditionally been done. If you need to return all rows but want to break them into individual pages with a given number of rows per page, the following example should do just that for you.

```
DECLARE @StartRow int = 1,
  @RowsPerPage int = 4

WHILE (SELECT count(*) FROM HumanResources.Department) >= @StartRow
BEGIN;
  SELECT DepartmentID, Name
  FROM HumanResources.Department
  ORDER BY DepartmentID
    OFFSET @StartRow -1 ROWS
    FETCH NEXT @RowsPerPage ROWS ONLY;

  SET @StartRow = @StartRow + @RowsPerPage;
END;
```

Results (partial):

```
DepartmentID Name
------------ --------------------------
1            Engineering
2            Tool Design
3            Sales
4            Marketing
```

```
DepartmentID Name
------------ -------------------------
5            Purchasing
6            Research and Development
7            Production
8            Production Control

DepartmentID Name
------------ -------------------------
9            Human Resources
10           Finance
...
```

One key point to note is that when you page your results in this manner, the entire query is run each time the WHILE condition is met. Meaning, if you have one million rows and you fetch five rows at a time, you'll execute the query 200,000 times. The OFFSET and FETCH conditions are applied after the full result set has been returned from the server.

This is an abbreviated list of new features in SQL Server 2012. Throughout this book, you'll see the application of new features and functionality that you can apply to your environment.

Error Handling

If you've never encountered an error in T-SQL, you're better than most people. For everyone else, error handling is a critical and often overlooked component of T-SQL programming.

Of course, all robust programming languages provide some method for trapping, logging, and handling errors. In this area, T-SQL has a sad history, but it's made significant progress over the last couple of releases.

There are two distinctly different ways to code error handling with SQL Server:

- Legacy error handling is how it's been done since the beginning of SQL Server, using @@error to see the error status of the previous SQL statement.
- Try/catch was introduced in SQL Server 2005, bringing SQL Server into the 21st century. I highly recommend taking this approach.

Legacy Error Handling

Historically, T-SQL error handling has been tedious at best. I'd prefer to not even include this legacy method of handling errors, but you'll see it in old code, so it must be covered.

What's New with Error Handling?

SQL Server 2005 introduced TRY...CATCH. SQL Server 2012 rounds out that functionality (and aligns you with .NET) by introducing THROW. Now, instead of RAISERROR, you have the ability to THROW an error, which is covered it in the TRY...CATCH section.

The basic error information system functions, such as @@error and @@rowcount, contain the status for the previous T-SQL command in the code. This means that the legacy method of error handling must examine T-SQL's system functions and handle the error after each SQL statement that might potentially encounter an error.

@@error System Function

The @@error system function contains the integer error code for the previous T-SQL statement. A 0 indicates success.

The difficulty is that @@error, unlike other languages that hold the last error in a variable until another error occurs, is updated for every command, so even testing its value updates it.

The following code sample attempts to update the primary key to a value, but it has a foreign key constraint on it. This generates an error. The @ErrorMsg parameter is set to @@error, and then @@error and @ErrorMsg are both sent to PRINT commands. The second PRINT for @ErrorNumber contains the error number, but the first PRINT command returns 0. This is because the successful SET command cleared the @@Error value.

```
DECLARE @ErrorNumber nvarchar(1000);

UPDATE HumanResources.Employee
  SET BusinessEntityID = 30000
  WHERE BusinessEntityID = 2;

SET @ErrorNumber = @@Error

PRINT @@error;

PRINT @ErrorNumber;
Result:
Msg 547, Level 16, State 0, Line 3
The UPDATE statement conflicted with the REFERENCE constraint
"FK_EmployeeDepartmentHistory_Employee_BusinessEntityID". The
 conflict occurred in database "AdventureWorks2012", table
"HumanResources.EmployeeDepartmentHistory", column 'BusinessEntityID'.
The statement has been terminated.
0
547
```

This example illustrates both the problem and solution for @@error. If you want to capture this value, set it to a local variable immediately after the statement you want to capture the error for.

@@rowcount System Function

Another way to determine whether the query was a success is to check the number of rows affected. Even if no error was generated, it's possible that the data didn't match and the operation failed, which might indicate a data, logic, or business rule problem. The `@@rowCount` system function is useful for checking the effectiveness of the query.

The reset issue that affects `@@error` also affects `@@rowcount`.

The following batch uses `@@rowcount` to check for rows updated. The failure results from the incorrect WHERE clause condition. No row with DepartmentID = 100 exists. `@@rowcount` is used to detect the query failure:

```
USE AdventureWorks2012;
GO

UPDATE HumanResources.Department
  SET Name = 'Ministry of Silly Walks'
  WHERE DepartmentID = 100;

IF @@rowCount = 0
  BEGIN
    -- error handling code
    PRINT 'no rows affected'
  END;
```

Result:

```
no rows affected
```

To capture both the `@@error` and the `@@rowcount` functions, use a SELECT statement with two variables:

```
SELECT @err = @@error, @rcount = @@rowcount
```

Raiserror

To return custom error messages to the calling procedure or front-end application, you can use the RAISERROR command. It has four useful features:

- Specifies the severity level
- Dynamically modifies the error message
- Uses serverwide stored messages
- May optionally log the error to the event log

The syntax for RAISERROR includes parameters for the severity level, state (seldom used), and message-string arguments:

```
RAISERROR (
  message or number, severity, state, optional arguments
  ) WITH LOG;
```

Error Severity

Windows has established standard error-severity codes, listed in Table 16-2. The other severity codes are reserved for Microsoft's use. In any case, the severity code you'll use for your RAISERROR will almost always be 16.

TABLE 16-2 Available Severity Codes

Severity Code	Description
10	Status message: Does not raise an error but returns a message, such as a PRINT statement.
11–13	No special meaning.
14	Informational message.
15	Warning message: Something may be wrong.
16	Critical error: The procedure failed.

Adding Variable Parameters to Messages

The error message can be a fixed-string message or the error number of a stored message. Either type can work with optional arguments.

The arguments are substituted for placeholders within the error message. Although several types and options are possible, two useful placeholders are %s for a string and %i for a signed integer. The following example uses one string argument:

```
RAISERROR ('Unable to update %s.', 14, 1, 'Customer');
```

Result:

```
Msg 50000, Level 14, State 1, Line 1
Unable to update Customer.
```

Stored Messages

The RAISERROR command can also pull a message from the sys.messages system view. Message numbers 1–50,000 are reserved for Microsoft. Higher message numbers are available for user-defined messages. The benefit to use stored messages is that all messages are forced to become consistent and numbered.

Note that with sys.messages stored messages, the message-number scheme is server-wide. If two vendors, or two databases, use overlapping messages, then no division exists between databases, and there's no solution beyond recoding all the error handling on one of the projects. The second issue is that when migrating a database to a new server, the messages must also be moved.

The sys.messages table includes columns for the message_id, text, severity, and whether the error should be logged. However, the severity of the RAISERROR command is used instead of the severity from the sys.messages table, so sys.messages .severity is moot.

To manage messages in code, use the sp_addmessage system stored procedure:

```
EXEC sp_addmessage 50001, 16, 'Unable to update %s';
```

For database projects that may be deployed in multiple languages, the optional @lang parameter can be used to specify the language for the error message.

If the message already exists, then a replace parameter must be added to the system stored procedure call, as follows:

```
EXEC sp_addmessage 50001, 16,
  'Update error on %s', @replace = 'replace';
```

To view the existing custom messages, select from the sys.messages system view:

```
SELECT *
  FROM sys.messages
  WHERE message_id > 50000;
```

Result:

```
message_id  language_id severity is_event_logged text
----------- ----------- -------- --------------- ------------------
50001       1033        16       0               Unable to update %s
```

To move messages between servers, do one of the following:

- Save the script that was originally used to load the messages.

- Use the following query to generate a script that adds the messages:

```
SELECT 'EXEC sp_addmessage, '
   + CAST(message_id AS VARCHAR(7))
   + ', ' + CAST(severity AS VARCHAR(2))
   + ', ''' + [text] + ''';'
  FROM sys.messages
  WHERE message_id > 50000;
```

Result:

```
--------------------------------------------------------------
EXEC sp_addmessage, 50001, 16, 'Unable to update %s';
```

To drop a message, use the sp_dropmessage system stored procedure with the error number:

```
EXEC sp_dropmessage 50001;
```

Logging the Error

Another advantage to using the RAISERROR command is that it can log the error to the Windows Application event log and the SQL Server event log.

To specify that an event should be logged from the RAISERROR command, add the WITH LOG option:

```
RAISERROR ('Unable to update %s.', 14, 1, 'Customer')
   WITH LOG
```

Result:

```
Server: Msg 50000, Level 14, State 1, Line 1
Unable to update Customer.
```

To view errors in the Application event log (see Figure 16-1), select Control Panel ⇨ System and Security ⇨ Administrative Tools ⇨ Event Viewer. An Event Viewer is also located in Control Panel ⇨ Administrative Tools.

FIGURE 16-1

A SQL Server RAISERROR error in the Windows Application event log. Notice that the server and database name are embedded in the error data.

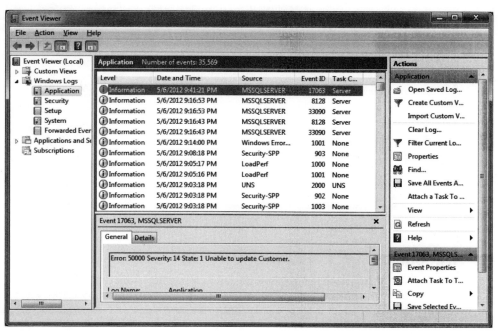

SQL Server Log

SQL Server also maintains a series of log files. Each time SQL Server starts, it creates a new log file. Six archived copies of the last log files are retained, for a total of seven log files. Management Studio's Object Explorer in the Management ⇨ SQL Server Logs node lists the logs. Double-clicking a log opens SQL Server's cool Log File Viewer, as shown in Figure 16-2. It's worth exploring because it has a filter and search capabilities.

FIGURE 16-2

Viewing an error in the SQL Server log using Management Studio.

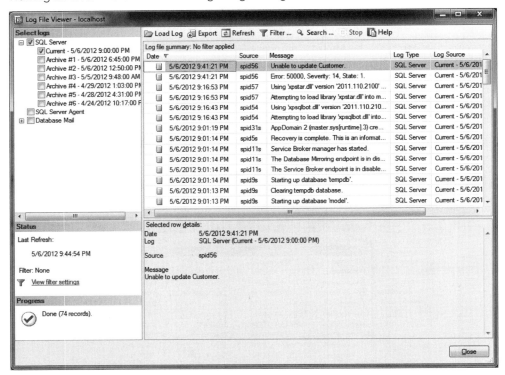

Try...Catch

TRY...CATCH is a standard method to trap and handle errors that .NET programmers have enjoyed for years. The basic idea is that if SQL Server encounters any errors when it tries to execute a block of code, it stops execution of the TRY block and immediately jumps to the CATCH block to handle the error:

```
BEGIN TRY
    <SQL code>;
END TRY
BEGIN CATCH
    <error handling code>;
END CATCH;
```

If the TRY block of code executes without any error, then the CATCH code is never executed, and execution resumes after the CATCH block:

```
BEGIN TRY
    SELECT 'Try One';
    RAISERROR('Simulated Error', 16, 1);
    Select 'Try Two';
END TRY
BEGIN CATCH
    SELECT 'Catch Block';
END CATCH;
SELECT 'Post Try';
```

Result:

```
---------
Try One


------------
Catch Block


-----------
Post Try


(1 row(s) affected)
```

Walking through this example, SQL Server executes the TRY block until the RAISERROR's simulated error, which sends the execution down to the CATCH block. The entire CATCH block is executed. Following execution of the CATCH block, execution continues with the next statement, SELECT 'Post Try'.

NOTE
The T-SQL compiler treats the END TRY ... BEGIN CATCH combination as a single contiguous command. Any other statements, a batch terminator (go), or a statement terminator (;) between these two commands, causes an untrapped error. END TRY must be followed immediately by a BEGIN CATCH.

Catch Block

When an error does occur, the best way to trap and handle it is in the CATCH blocks. Within the CATCH block, you want to do the following:

1. If the batch uses logical transactions (BEGIN TRAN/COMMIT TRAN), then, depending on the error and situation, the error handler might need to roll back the transaction. If this is the case, rolling back the transaction is recommended as the first action so that any locks the transaction might be holding are released.

2. If the error is one that the stored procedure logic detects, and it's not a SQL Server error, then raise the error message so that the user or front-end application is informed.

3. Optionally, log the error to an error table.

4. Terminate the batch. If it's a stored procedure, user-defined function, or trigger, then terminate it with a RETURN command.

When an error occurs in the TRY block and execution is passed to the CATCH block, the error information is also passed to the CATCH block. At this point, you have two options. You may use the RAISERROR functionality that has been available in SQL Server for quite some time, or you may use the new THROW command introduced in SQL Server 2012. First, walk through the traditional RAISERROR functionality, and then look at THROW.

RAISERROR

RAISERROR enables you to examine the details of the error using the error functions listed in Table 16-3. These functions are designed specifically for the CATCH block. Outside a CATCH block, they always return a null value.

TABLE 16-3 Catch Functions

Error Function	Returns
Error_Message()	The text of the error message
Error_Number()	The number of the error
Error_Procedure()	The name of the stored procedure or trigger in which the error occurred
Error_Severity()	The severity of the error
Error_State()	The state of the error
Error_Line()	The line number within the batch or stored procedure that generated the error
Xact_State()	Whether the transaction can be committed (see Chapter 47)

These CATCH functions retain the error information of the error that fired the CATCH block. They may be called multiple times and still retain the error information.

The following sample demonstrates a CATCH block using the CATCH functions and a RAISERROR to report the error to the client. The contents of the error functions are passed to variables so a custom error string can be assembled for the RAISERROR:

```
BEGIN CATCH

    DECLARE
        @Error_Severity INT,
        @Error_State INT,
        @Error_Number INT,
        @Error_Line INT,
        @Error_Message VARCHAR(245);

    SELECT
        @Error_Severity = ERROR_SEVERITY(),
        @Error_State = ERROR_STATE(),
        @Error_Number = ERROR_NUMBER(),
        @Error_Line = ERROR_LINE(),
        @Error_Message = ERROR_MESSAGE();

    RAISERROR ('Msg %d, Line %d: %s',
        @Error_Severity,
        @Error_State,
        @Error_Number,
        @Error_Line,
        @Error_Message);

    SELECT @Error_Number;

END CATCH;
```

Throw

The information captured by a THROW is quite similar to RAISERROR and can largely be configured, with the exception of severity level, which will always be 16. In its simplest form, THROW looks like the following example, where 50001 represents the error number, 'Thrown Error Message' represents the error message, and 1 represents the error state.

```
THROW 50001, 'Thrown Error Message', 1;
```

If custom error information is not needed, the keyword THROW can be included in the CATCH block without any provided parameters.

```
BEGIN TRY
    SELECT 1/0;
```

```
END TRY

BEGIN CATCH
   THROW;
END CATCH;
```

Result:

```
Msg 8134, Level 16, State 1, Line 3
Divide by zero error encountered.
```

Finally, if you want to migrate from RAISERROR to THROW but have invested a lot of time and effort into populating sys.messages with meaningful error information, don't fret. The FORMATMESSAGE statement enables you to THROW customized error messages contained in sys.messages.

```
USE AdventureWorks2012;
GO

IF NOT EXISTS (SELECT * FROM sys.messages WHERE message_id = 50003)
BEGIN
   EXECUTE sp_addmessage 50003, 16, 'Custom message for sys.messages';
END
GO

DECLARE @Message nvarchar(2000);

SELECT @Message = FORMATMESSAGE(50003);

BEGIN TRY
   INSERT INTO Person.BusinessEntity
      (BusinessEntityID, rowguid, ModifiedDate)
   VALUES(1, newid(), getdate());
END TRY

BEGIN CATCH
   THROW 50003, @Message, 1;
END CATCH;
```

Result:

```
Msg 50003, Level 16, State 1, Line 12
Custom message courtesy of sys.messages
```

Table 16-4 breaks down the primary differences between RAISERROR and THROW.

TABLE 16-4 **Differences between RAISERROR and THROW**

RAISERROR	THROW
A `msg_id` passed to RAISERROR must be contained in `sys.messages`.	`Error_number` parameter does not need to exist in `sys.messages`.
`Msg_str` parameter may contain `printf` formatting styles.	Message parameter does not accept `printf` styles.
`Severity` parameter specifies error severity.	No severity parameter; always set to 16.

Nested Try/Catch and Rethrown Errors

Any error can bubble up through every layer of stored procedures until it's caught by a try/catch block or it reaches the client. Visualizing the call stack — the stack of procedures that have executed or called other stored procedures — it's possible for lower level, or nested, stored procedures to use this principle to send, or rethrow, errors to higher-level stored procedures in the call stack.

TRY/CATCH blocks can easily be nested even if the nesting is unintentional. If one stored procedure calls another stored procedure and both procedures are well written, with TRY/CATCH blocks, then not only are the stored procedures nested, but the TRY/CATCH blocks are nested, too.

In the following example, the TopProc executes, or calls, the CalledProc. A divide by zero error in CalledProc causes the code to jump to the CATCH block. The CATCH block issues a THROW.

The TopProc receives the error that was raised by the CalledProc. It sees the error as any other type of error and therefore jumps down to its CATCH block. The THROW in the TopProc is executed, and it too raises an error. This time the raised error is seen by the client, in this case Management Studio:

```
CREATE PROC TopProc
AS
BEGIN TRY
  EXEC CalledProc
END TRY
BEGIN CATCH
  THROW 50001, 'TopProc Raiserror',1
END CATCH

GO

CREATE PROC CalledProc
```

```
AS
BEGIN TRY
  SELECT 3/0
END TRY
BEGIN CATCH
  THROW 50002,'CalledProc Raiserror',1
END CATCH

Go

EXEC TopProc
```

Result:

```
Msg 50001, Level 16, State 1, Procedure TopProc, Line 7
TopProc Raiserror
```

T-SQL Fatal Errors

If T-SQL encounters a fatal error, then the batch immediately aborts without giving you the opportunity to test @@Error, handle the error, or correct the situation.

Fatal errors are rare enough that they shouldn't pose much of a problem. Generally, if the code works once, then it should continue to work unless the schema is changed or SQL Server is reconfigured. The most common fatal errors are those caused by the following:

- Data-type incompatibilities
- Unavailable SQL Server resources
- SQL Server advanced settings that are incompatible with certain tasks
- Missing objects or misspelled object names

For a list of most of the fatal error messages, run the following query:

```
SELECT message_id, severity, language_id, text
  FROM master.sys.messages
  WHERE language_id = 1033    -- US English
  AND severity >= 19
  ORDER BY severity, message_id;
```

Try...Catch does a good job of handling typical day-to-day user errors, such as constraint-violation errors. Nevertheless, to be safe, front-end application developers should also include error-handling code in their programs.

Bulk Operations

Often, DBAs need to load copious amounts of data quickly — whether it's a nightly data load or a conversion from comma-delimited text files. When a few hundred megabytes of data need to get into SQL Server in a limited time frame, a bulk operation is the way to get the heavy lifting done.

XML's popularity may be growing, but its file sizes seem to be growing even faster. XML's data tags add significant bloat to a data file, sometimes quadrupling the file size or more. For large files, IT organizations are sticking with CSV (also known as comma-delimited) files. For these old standby files, the best way to insert that data is using a bulk operation.

In SQL Server, bulk operations pump data directly to the data file according to the following models:

- **Simple recovery model:** The transaction log is used for current transactions only.

- **Bulk-logged recovery model:** The bulk operation transaction bypasses the log, but then the entire bulk operation's data is still written to the log. One complication with bulk-logged recovery is that if bulk operations are undertaken, point-in-time recovery is not possible for the time period covered by the transaction log. To regain point-in-time recovery, the log must be backed up. As extent allocations are logged for bulk operations, a log backup after bulk operations can contain *all* the pages from extents that have been added, which results in a large transaction log backup.

- **Full recovery model:** In a full recovery model, bulk operations are not performed; the engine does full logging of inserts. To restart the transaction log recoverability process, following the bulk operation, perform a complete backup, and restart the transaction logs.

 For more details on recovery models and how to set them, see Chapter 21, "Backup and Recovery Planning." Details on the transaction log are covered in Chapter 47, "Managing Transactions, Locking, and Blocking."

Technically, the SELECT INTO syntax is also a bulk-logged operation, and it too bypasses the transaction log. SELECT INTO creates a table from the results of a SELECT statement; it is discussed in Chapter 12, "Modifying Data in SQL Server."

Bulk insert operations are normally one step of an extract-transform-load (ETL) nightly process. Although developing these ETL processes in T-SQL is perfectly acceptable, Integration Services is a strong alternative and includes bulk operations. For more details about developing Integration Services solutions, see Chapter 52, "Building, Deploying, and Managing ETL Workflows in Integration Services."

Bulk operations can be performed with a command prompt using bcp (a command-prompt utility to copy data to and from SQL Server), within T-SQL using the BULK INSERT command or using Integration Services.

Bulk Insert

You can use the BULK INSERT command within any T-SQL script or stored procedure to import data into SQL Server. The parameters of the command specify the table receiving the data, the location of the source file, and the options.

To test the BULK INSERT command, use the Address.csv file that's part of the build script to load the AdventureWorks2012 sample database. You can find it at http://msftdbprodsamples.codeplex.com/releases/view/55330 and it is called AdventureWorks 2012 OLTP Script.

The following batch bulk inserts from the Address.csv file in the AdventureWorks OLTP directory into the AWAddress table:

```
Use Tempdb;

DROP TABLE AWAddressStaging;
CREATE TABLE AWAddressStaging (
  ID INT,
  Address NVARCHAR(500),
  City    NVARCHAR(500),
  Region NVARCHAR(500),
  PostalCode NVARCHAR(500),
  SpatialLocation nvarchar(500),
  GUID NVARCHAR(500),
  Updated DATETIME
  );

BULK INSERT AWAddressStaging
FROM
 'C:\Program Files\Microsoft SQL Server\110\Tools\Samples
   \AdventureWorks OLTP\Address.csv'
  WITH (FIRSTROW = 1,ROWTERMINATOR ='\n');
```

The first thing to understand about BULK INSERT is that every column from the source table is simply inserted directly into the destination table using a one-to-one mapping. The first column from the source file is dumped into the first column of the destination table. Each column lines up. If there are too many columns in the destination table, then it will fail. However, if there are not enough columns in the destination table, then BULK INSERT will work, as the extra data is placed into the bit bucket and simply discarded.

Best Practice

Because BULK INSERT is dependent on the column position of both the source file and the destination table, it is best practice to use a view as an abstraction layer between the BULK INSERT command and the table. If the structure of either the source file or the destination table is altered, then modifying the view can keep the BULK INSERT running without having to change the other object's structure.

Another best practice is to BULK INSERT the data into a staging table, check the data, and then perform the rest of the transformations as you merge the data into the permanent tables. As long as you don't mind copying the data twice, this works well.

Bulk Insert Options

In practice, you probably need to use some options when using BULK INSERT:

- **Field Terminator:** Specifies the character used to delimit or separate columns in the source file. The default, of course, is a comma, but the pipe character (|) can be used in production.

- **Row Terminator:** Specifies the character that ends a row in the source file. "\n" means end of row and is the typical setting. However, files from mainframes or other systems sometimes don't use a clean end of line. In these cases, use a hex editor to view the actual end of line characters and specify the row terminator in hex. For example, a hex value of 0A is coded as follows:

```
ROWTERMINATOR = '0x0A'
```

- **FirstRow:** Useful when specifying whether the incoming file has column headers. If the file does have column headers, then use this option to indicate that the first row of data is actually the second row of the file.

- **TabLock:** Places an exclusive lock on the entire table and saves SQL Server the trouble of having to lock the table's data pages being created. This option can dramatically improve performance, but at the cost of blocking data readers during the bulk insert. If the bulk insert is part of an ETL into a staging table, then there's no problem, but if it's a bulk insert into a production system with potential users selecting data, then this might not be a good idea. Multiple bulk-import streams can potentially block each other. To prevent this, SQL Server provides a special internal lock, called a bulk-update (BU) lock. To get a BU lock, you need to specify the TABLOCK option with each bulk-import stream without blocking other bulk-import streams.

- **Rows per Batch:** Tells SQL Server to insert *n* number of rows in a single batch, rather than the entire file. Tweaking the batch size can improve performance. Beginning with 100 and then experimenting to find the best size for the particular set of data works best. This helps performance because the logging is done less often. Too many rows, however, often exceed memory cache and may create waits. Often, 2,000 rows is the best number.

- **Max Errors:** Specifies how many rows can fail before the bulk insert fails. Depending on the business requirement for the data, you may need to set this to zero.

- **The Errorfile:** Option that points to a file that can collect any rows not accepted by the BULK INSERT operation. This is a great idea and should be used with every BULK INSERT command in production.

Other options, which you may never need in production include Check_Constraints, CodePage, DataFileType, Fire_Triggers, KeepIdentity, KeepNulls, Kilobytes_per_batch, and Order. (The best practice of bulk inserting into a staging table and then performing the ETL merge into the permanent tables makes these commands less useful.)

> **TIP**
>
> `BULK INSERT` handles columns in the order they appear in the source comma-delimited file, and the columns must be in the same order in the receiving SQL table. Bulk inserting into a view provides a data abstraction layer so that any changes in column order won't break the `BULK INSERT` code.

When developing a `BULK INSERT` statement, it's generally useful to open the source file using Excel and examine the data. Excel often reformats data, so it's best not to save files in Excel. Sorting the data by the columns can help find data formatting anomalies.

BCP

Bcp, short for bulk copy program, is a command-line variation of bulk operations. Bcp differs from `BULK INSERT` in that it is command-line executed and can import or export data. It uses many of the same options as `BULK INSERT`. The basic syntax is as follows:

```
BCP destination table  direction datafile options
```

For the destination, use the server name along with the complete three-part name (server and database.schema.object). For a complete listing of the syntax, just type **bcp** at the command prompt.

Because this is an external program, it needs authorization to connect to SQL Server. You have two options: Use the `-P` password option and hard-code your password into the batch file script, or omit the `-P`, in which case it prompts for a password. Neither is a good option. You can also use integrated security, which is usually considered the best practice.

> **NOTE**
>
> For straightforward ETL operations, use T-SQL and `BULK INSERT`. For complex ETL loads, Integration Services is great. You might have little use for automating ETL processes using DOS batch scripts and bcp, although PowerShell may be an option to consider.

Summary

T-SQL extends the SQL query with a set of procedural commands. Although it's not the most advanced programming language, T-SQL gets the job done. You can use T-SQL batch commands in expressions or packaged as stored procedures, user-defined functions, or triggers.

Following are a few key points to remember from this chapter:

- The batch terminator, GO, is only a Query Editor command, and it can send the batch multiple times when followed by a number.
- Ctrl+K+C converts the current lines to comments, and Ctrl+K+U uncomments the lines.

- ■ `IF` controls only execution of the next line, unless it is followed by a `BEGIN...END` block.

- ■ Variables can be incremented with `+=`.

- ■ If the temporary space needs to hold more than 250 rows, then use a temp table; otherwise, use a table variable.

Chapter 17 moves into the next important step in T-SQL programming, stored procedures. This is where you take advantage of your knowledge of flow-control and make your procedures flexible and powerful.

Developing Stored Procedures

IN THIS CHAPTER

S tored procedures are a way to store and reuse T-SQL code within the SQL Server Database Engine. The procedure is stored as an object within SQL Server, and when created, can be modified and executed with simple T-SQL commands. The mechanics of using stored procedures are straightforward, but they are powerful. From a basic SELECT statement to a multi-statement, parameterized process, stored procedures enable you to define and control interaction with data. Stored procedures offer some compelling benefits:

- **Consistency:** A stored procedure encapsulates one or more T-SQL statements, enabling it to be executed consistently across different areas of a system.

- **Maintainability:** Stored procedures are maintainable because they are modular and independent of the application or tool that they're called from. Complex logic within a stored procedure can be modified with little to no impact on the application that calls it.

- **Security:** Using stored procedures provides security benefits on two fronts: database and application. From a database perspective, the stored procedure is an object. This means that the ability to execute the procedure can be granted to specific users or groups. From an application perspective, stored procedures provide an opportunity to validate input to a T-SQL process before it is executed.

- **Performance:** Stored procedure execution is a server-side process. This means that no matter how complex the procedure, only one statement is sent over the network. An application that has embedded T-SQL code might have to use multiple round trips to the server to achieve the same result.

The Performance Myth

Many DBAs and developers, especially those who worked with SQL Server prior to SQL Server 2000 will say that stored procedures provide a performance benefit because the execution plan is cached and stored for reuse. The phrase "precompiled" might also come up. This is no longer true. As of SQL Server 2000, all execution plans are cached, regardless of whether they're the result of inline T-SQL or a stored procedure call. The name of the cache area was changed from Procedure Cache to Plan Cache with SQL Server 2000 to properly reflect what was actually happening. There are some performance benefits to stored procedures, but a cached execution plan is no longer one of them.

Many different philosophies exist on the appropriate use of stored procedures, but they all come down to two basic ideas: dumb stored procedures versus smart stored procedures. Organizational policy and team coding standards might dictate in advance how stored procedures are implemented, but it is worth looking at these two approaches.

Some organizations require that all T-SQL called by an application must be encapsulated within a stored procedure. This results in a high number of stored procedures, many consisting of basic Create, Retrieve, Update, and Delete (CRUD) operations. These are "dumb" stored procedures. On the other hand, some organizations implement a stored procedure only when a process calls for multiple T-SQL statements, multiple result sets, complex processing, or parameterization. These are "smart" stored procedures. The goals of both approaches are similar: maintainability, security, performance, and consistency. Depending on how an organization and its application is structured and built, either approach may be appropriate. The key is consistency. Decide upfront how to implement stored procedures and stick to it.

Managing Stored Procedures

The actual management of stored procedures is simple compared to the logic within them. When you know the basic facts and syntax, managing stored procedures shouldn't present any problems.

All code samples use the AdventureWorks2012 database, available at `http://msftdbprodsamples.codeplex.com/`.

Create, Alter, and Drop

Adding, modifying, and removing a stored procedure within the database is a straightforward process. You can use three basic Data Definition Language (DDL) commands: CREATE, ALTER, and DROP.

Create

The CREATE statement must be the first statement in a batch, and the termination of the batch ends the stored procedure definition. In other words, everything between the CREATE PROCEDURE statement and the next batch terminator is considered part of the stored procedure definition. In SQL Server Management Studio (SSMS), the default batch terminator is the word GO. When creating a stored procedure, consider a few best practices:

- Never use sp_ to prefix the name of a stored procedure. These are reserved for system stored procedures, covered later in this chapter.

- Use a standard prefix for the stored procedure name, such as usp, Proc, p, and so on. The prefix helps identify an object as a stored procedure when reviewing and troubleshooting code.

- Always use a two-part naming convention, schema.objectname, when creating stored procedures. This ensures that the stored procedure is added to the appropriate schema.

- Use descriptive names for stored procedures. When there are hundreds, if not thousands, of stored procedures in the database, it helps to have a name that describes what the stored procedure does.

- Implement error handling in stored procedures. Syntax and logic errors should be gracefully handled, with meaningful information sent back to the calling application.

 For more information on how to implement error handling, refer to Chapter 16, "Programming with T-SQL."

The following example creates a basic stored procedure that selects the contents of the Sales.Currency table from the AdventureWorks2012 database.

```
USE AdventureWorks2012
GO

CREATE PROCEDURE Sales.uspGetCurrencyInformation

AS

SELECT CurrencyCode, Name
FROM Sales.Currency;

GO
```

Alter

The ALTER statement modifies the stored procedure. The benefit of choosing to alter a stored procedure rather than drop and re-create it is that the procedure is never removed from the server. All object permissions are retained after an ALTER, whereas a DROP and CREATE results in lost permissions.

```
USE AdventureWorks2012
GO

ALTER PROCEDURE Sales.uspGetCurrencyInformation

AS

SELECT CurrencyCode, Name, ModifiedDate
FROM Sales.Currency;

GO
```

Drop

The DROP statement removes the stored procedure from the server. It is a good idea to maintain stored procedure code in some sort of version control system in addition to the database engine. Accidentally dropping a stored procedure without having a way to easily retrieve it can create time-consuming work.

```
DROP PROCEDURE Sales.uspGetCurrencyInformation;
```

Viewing Stored Procedures

After a stored procedure has been created, you can view the code within the database engine in a few ways.

SQL Server Management Studio (SSMS) GUI

The first option is to use the SQL Server Management Studio (SSMS) graphical user interface.

1. From SQL Server Management Studio, open the Object Explorer by clicking F8 or by going to the View menu and selecting Object Explorer.

2. Within Object Explorer, click Connect, and provide connection information for the server where you created the stored procedure.

3. Expand the Databases folder, then the Database the stored procedure was created in, and then the Programmability Folder. From here, there is a Stored Procedures folder. Expand this folder, and the stored procedure should be visible. If it is not, right-click and select Refresh.

4. Right-click the stored procedure, and mouse-over Script Stored Procedure As. The submenu should display, enabling you to select CREATE To. The options include New Query Editor Window, File, Clipboard, and Agent Job. Choosing New Query Editor Window adds a new query tab to SSMS with the stored procedure code scripted in it.

EXECUTE sp_HelpText

The second option for viewing a stored procedure is to execute a system stored procedure called sp_helptext. The stored procedure code is visible from a system view called sys

`.syscomments`. `Sp_helptext` retrieves the stored procedure code and returns it as the result set.

```
EXECUTE sp_helptext 'Sales.uspGetCurrencyInformation'
```

Query sys.sql_modules

The third option is to query the `sys.sql_modules` system view.

```
USE AdventureWorks2012;
GO

SELECT definition
FROM sys.sql_modules
WHERE object_id = (OBJECT_ID
(
N'Sales.uspGetCurrencyInformation')
   );
```

Use OBJECT_DEFINITION

The fourth option is to use the `OBJECT_DEFINITION` built-in function with the `OBJECT_ID` built-in function.

```
USE AdventureWorks2012;
GO

SELECT OBJECT_DEFINITION (OBJECT_ID
(
N'AdventureWorks2012Sales.uspGetCurrencyInformation')
   );
```

> **TIP**
>
> Because the stored procedure code is stored as multiple rows in the database metadata, it is easier to read the returned code if the results are returned as text rather than as a grid. To change this setting, use the Query menu in SSMS. There is a Results To option, and the options are Results to Grid, Results to Text, and Results to File. Choose Results to Text; then execute `sp_helptext`, query `sys.sql_modules`, or call `OBJECT_DEFINITION`. Alternatively, you can use keyboard shortcut Ctrl+T to change the results to text format.

Encrypting Stored Procedure Code

You can encrypt stored procedure code so that the text of the code is not visible by any of the means previously described. Encrypting stored procedures is not a common practice, and there are some serious drawbacks, such as the inability to publish an encrypted stored procedure as part of SQL Server replication. There needs to be a compelling and carefully considered justification for encrypting a stored procedure. One implementation in which this approach might be seen is in third-party software. Vendors might try to protect proprietary formulas or logic using stored procedure encryption.

```
USE AdventureWorks2012
GO

ALTER PROCEDURE Sales.uspGetCurrencyInformation
WITH ENCRYPTION
AS

SELECT CurrencyCode, Name, ModifiedDate
FROM Sales.Currency;

GO
```

A user with proper object permissions can still execute encrypted stored procedures; however, the text of the code is not accessible to the user.

Executing Stored Procedures

You can call a stored procedure in three ways:

```
Sales.uspGetCurrencyInformation;
EXECUTE Sales.uspGetCurrencyInformation;
EXEC Sales.uspGetCurrencyInformation;
```

If the stored procedure call is the first statement in a batch, the EXECUTE (or the abbreviated EXEC) is not required. If the stored procedure call is not the first statement in a batch, the EXECUTE or EXEC command is required. It is a good practice to always use EXECUTE or EXEC in case code is reordered later and so that it is obvious to a developer or DBA that a stored procedure is being executed.

WITH RESULT SETS

SQL Server 2012 introduces a new clause called WITH RESULT SETS. This enables one or more result sets to be explicitly defined as part of the EXECUTE command. The "Returning Data from Stored Procedures" section covers this feature.

Executing Remote Stored Procedures

Two methods exist for calling a stored procedure located on another server: a four-part name reference and a distributed query. Both methods require that the remote server be a linked server. Stored procedures may only be remotely called; they may not be remotely created.

The remote stored procedure may be executed by means of the four-part name:

```
EXECUTE Server.Database.Schema.StoredProcedureName;
```

Alternatively, you can use the `OpenQuery()` function to call a remote stored procedure:

```
OpenQuery(LinkedServerName, 'EXECUTE Schema.StoredProcedureName');
```

As with any other distributed query, the Distributed Transaction Coordinator service must be running if the transaction updates data on more than one server.

System Stored Procedures

SQL Server provides many stored procedures used for administrative tasks and to gather information about the database or server. Each of these system stored procedures is pre-fixed with `sp_`, and is the reason why you should never name a user-defined stored proce-dure with a `sp_` prefix.

There is a wealth of information and functionality within these system stored procedures. Check out Books Online for documentation and use cases.

Passing Data to Stored Procedures

The characteristic of a stored procedure that makes it a powerful option for code reuse is parameterization. Stored procedures can be defined so that they accept input parameters. The `Sales.uspGetCurrencyInformation` procedure created in the previous section returned all rows from `Sales.Currency`. An input parameter can specify which rows should be returned or can completely change the logic of the stored procedure based on how it is coded.

As of SQL Server 2005, the number of parameters that can be specified for a single stored procedure is 2,100.

Input Parameters

Input parameters are a way to provide external information to a stored procedure. You can add input parameters that pass data to the stored procedure by listing the parameters after the procedure name in the `CREATE PROCEDURE` command. Each parameter must begin with an @ sign and becomes a local variable within the procedure. Like local variables, the parameters must be defined with valid data types. When the stored procedure is called, every parameter value must be included (unless the parameter has a default value).

The following code sample creates a stored procedure that returns a single currency type. The `@CurrencyCode` parameter can accept a character value with a length of up to three characters. The value assigned to the parameter during stored procedure execution is available within the procedure as the local variable `@CurrencyCode` in the `WHERE` clause of the query:

```
USE AdventureWorks2012
```

```
GO

CREATE PROCEDURE Sales.uspGetCurrencyInformation

@CurrencyCode char(3)

AS

SELECT CurrencyCode, Name
FROM Sales.Currency
WHERE CurrencyCode = @CurrencyCode;

GO

EXECUTE Sales.uspGetCurrencyInformation @CurrencyCode = 'USD';
GO

CurrencyCode Name
------------ --------------------------------------------------
USD          US Dollar
```

Specifying Parameter Values

You can pass parameter values during stored procedure execution in two ways: named parameter values and positional parameter values.

Named Parameter Values

When the stored procedure is executed, you can pass parameters as a set of comma-delimited name-value pairs. The syntax follows:

```
EXECUTE Sales.uspGetCurrencyInformation @CurrencyCode = 'USD';
```

When you pass parameters using this method, the order of the provided parameter values does not matter.

Positional Parameter Values

When you create a stored procedure, the input parameters are defined in a specific order. During stored procedure execution, if values are not provided as a collection of name-value pairs, the position of the parameter values becomes the method by which the stored procedure knows how to assign the variable values within the stored procedure.

```
EXECUTE Sales.uspGetCurrencyInformation 'USD';
```

Default Parameter Values

A value must be provided for every defined parameter during a stored procedure call. However, default values can be supplied as part of the stored procedure definition. In the absence of a supplied input parameter value, the default value will be used. If a value is provided during execution, the default is overridden. A default value is defined as part of the input parameter definition; simply place "= *default value*" after the input parameter information.

```
USE AdventureWorks2012
GO

ALTER PROCEDURE Sales.uspGetCurrencyInformation

@CurrencyCode char(3) = 'USD'

AS

SELECT CurrencyCode, Name
FROM Sales.Currency
WHERE CurrencyCode = @CurrencyCode;

GO
```

Now that a default parameter value is defined, there are two ways to tell the stored procedure to use the default value. The first is by not passing any information to the stored procedure:

```
EXECUTE Sales.uspGetCurrencyInformation;
```

The second method is to use the DEFAULT keyword during the stored procedure call. This can come in handy if multiple input parameters are required, but only some of them should use the default value:

```
EXECUTE Sales.uspGetCurrencyInformation @CurrencyCode = DEFAULT;
EXECUTE Sales.uspGetCurrencyInformation DEFAULT;
```

All the preceding stored procedures produce the same result set because the default value for @CurrencyCode is USD.

```
CurrencyCode Name
------------ ----------------------------------------------------
USD          US Dollar
```

Providing Lists and Tables as Input Parameters to Stored Procedures

One of the most common challenges a developer can encounter when implementing stored procedures is how to pass multiple values into a stored procedure with a single input parameter. Multiple options are available, and the most common approaches are covered here.

Providing a List as an Input Parameter

Two methods to pass a list as an input parameter are shown here. The first method is to construct a string that is suitable for an IN clause, and the second is to pass a list that is then turned into a table that can be included in a table join.

If a list will be passed into the stored procedure using a string, you must use Dynamic SQL to construct the T-SQL statement so that it can concatenate the string while maintaining correct syntax. This approach adds some complexity to the stored procedure and uses the `sp_executesql` system stored procedure to execute the query.

```
USE AdventureWorks2012
GO

CREATE PROCEDURE Sales.uspGetCurrencyRate

@CurrencyRateIDList varchar(50)

AS

DECLARE @SQLString nvarchar(1000)

SET @SQLString = N'
SELECT CurrencyRateID, CurrencyRateDate, FromCurrencyCode,
ToCurrencyCode, AverageRate, EndOfDayRate
FROM Sales.CurrencyRate
WHERE CurrencyRateID in ('+@CurrencyRateIDList+');'

EXECUTE sp_executesql @SQLString;

GO

EXECUTE Sales.uspGetCurrencyRate @CurrencyRateIDList = '1, 4, 6, 7';
```

The previous example passed in a list of integers and required no special formatting of the input parameter string. However, when a list of strings is passed into a stored procedure, the required string formatting becomes more complex.

```
CREATE PROCEDURE Sales.uspGetCurrencyInformation

@CurrencyCodeList varchar(200) = 'USD'

AS

DECLARE @SQLString nvarchar(1000)

SET @SQLString = N'
SELECT CurrencyCode, Name
FROM Sales.Currency
WHERE CurrencyCode in ('+@CurrencyCodeList+');'

EXECUTE sp_executesql @SQLString;

GO

EXECUTE Sales.uspGetCurrencyInformation
    @CurrencyCodeList = '''USD'', ''AUD'', ''CAD'', ''MXN''';
```

The string value must be assigned to the input parameter as a single value, but when it is concatenated into the Dynamic SQL, it must be recognized as a list of strings. This means that each individual string value must be wrapped in two single tick marks (") rather than one, and the entire list must be qualified with a single tick mark ('). This can create a headache for a developer who tries to call the stored procedure. Luckily, there is more than one approach available to pass a list into a stored procedure as an input parameter. Another option is to use an XML data type.

XML can be intimidating for someone who hasn't used it before, but after a comfort level is achieved with using this flexible data type, the value of XML becomes apparent. In the next example, a list is passed in XML format, an XML document is prepared using the system stored procedure sp_xml_preparedocument, and then the contents of the XML document are inserted into an internal table variable using the OPENXML function. It sounds confusing, but it is actually an efficient way to pass a list to a stored procedure.

17

 For more information on working with XML, see Chapter 14, "Using XML Data."

```
CREATE PROCEDURE Sales.uspGetCurrencyInformationXML

@XMLList varchar(1000)

AS

DECLARE @XMLDocHandle int
DECLARE @CurrencyCodeTable table
(
CurrencyCode char(3)
)

EXECUTE sp_xml_preparedocument @XMLDocHandle OUTPUT, @XMLList;

INSERT INTO @CurrencyCodeTable(CurrencyCode)
SELECT CurrencyCode
FROM OPENXML (@XMLDocHandle, '/ROOT/Currency',1)
    WITH (
        CurrencyCode   char(3)
        );

SELECT c.CurrencyCode, c.Name, c.ModifiedDate
FROM Sales.Currency        c
JOIN @CurrencyCodeTable tvp
ON c.CurrencyCode = tvp.CurrencyCode;

EXECUTE sp_xml_removedocument @XMLDocHandle

GO

--Execute the stored procedure, passing in XML
```

```
EXECUTE Sales.uspGetCurrencyInformationXML @XMLList ='
<ROOT>
  <Currency CurrencyCode="USD"> </Currency>
  <Currency CurrencyCode="AUD"> </Currency>
  <Currency CurrencyCode="CAD"> </Currency>
  <Currency CurrencyCode="MXN"> </Currency>
</ROOT>';
GO
```

The beauty of using XML to pass a list of values as an input parameter is that it isn't much of a leap to pass a table (or array) to a stored procedure using the same method. The next example expands on the XML data type concept and enables you to create a two-column table variable from the passed XML data.

Providing a Table as an Input Parameter

Using an XML data type to pass multiple values to a stored procedure using a single input parameter means that you can pass an entire table into the stored procedure.

```
CREATE PROCEDURE Sales.uspGetCurrencyRatesXML

  @XMLList varchar(1000)
 ,@CurrencyRateDate datetime

AS

DECLARE @XMLDocHandle int
DECLARE @CurrencyCodeTable table
(
 FromCurrencyCode char(3)
,ToCurrencyCode char(3)
)

EXECUTE sp_xml_preparedocument @XMLDocHandle OUTPUT, @XMLlist;

INSERT INTO @CurrencyCodeTable(FromCurrencyCode, ToCurrencyCode)
SELECT FromCurrencyCode, ToCurrencyCode
FROM OPENXML (@XMLDocHandle, '/ROOT/CurrencyList',1)
        WITH (
                FromCurrencyCode char(3)
                ,ToCurrencyCode char(3)
                );

SELECT cr.CurrencyRateID, cr.FromCurrencyCode,
cr.ToCurrencyCode, cr.AverageRate,
cr.EndOfDayRate, cr.CurrencyRateDate
FROM Sales.CurrencyRate cr
   JOIN @CurrencyCodeTable tvp
      ON cr.FromCurrencyCode = tvp.FromCurrencyCode
        AND cr.ToCurrencyCode = tvp.ToCurrencyCode
WHERE CurrencyRateDate = @CurrencyRateDate;
```

```
EXECUTE sp_xml_removedocument @XMLDocHandle;

GO

--Execute the stored procedure
EXECUTE Sales.uspGetCurrencyRatesXML @XMLList ='
<ROOT>
  <CurrencyList FromCurrencyCode="USD" ToCurrencyCode="AUD"> </CurrencyList>
  <CurrencyList FromCurrencyCode="USD" ToCurrencyCode="EUR"> </CurrencyList>
  <CurrencyList FromCurrencyCode="USD" ToCurrencyCode="GBP"> </CurrencyList>
  <CurrencyList FromCurrencyCode="USD" ToCurrencyCode="MXN"> </CurrencyList>
</ROOT>', @CurrencyRateDate = '2005-07-14';
```

The second option to provide a table as an input parameter is to use a table-valued parameter. On the surface this seems like the obvious choice, but consider a couple of requirements:

1. To pass a table-valued parameter as an input parameter to a stored procedure, it must first be defined as a user-defined table type.

2. When the user-defined table type is specified as an input parameter during stored procedure creation, it must be defined as READONLY.

The first step to passing a table-valued parameter as an input parameter is to create a user-defined table type.

```
CREATE TYPE CurrencyCodeListType as TABLE
(
 FromCurrencyCode char(3)
,ToCurrencyCode char(3)
);
GO
```

After you create the user-defined table type , it can be used as the data type for the input parameter in the stored procedure definition.

```
CREATE PROCEDURE Sales.uspGetCurrencyRatesUDT

 @CurrencyCodeTable as CurrencyCodeListType READONLY
,@CurrencyRateDate date

AS

SELECT cr.CurrencyRateID, cr.FromCurrencyCode,
cr.ToCurrencyCode, cr.AverageRate,
cr.EndOfDayRate, cr.CurrencyRateDate
FROM Sales.CurrencyRate cr
   JOIN @CurrencyCodeTable tvp
      ON cr.FromCurrencyCode = tvp.FromCurrencyCode
        AND cr.ToCurrencyCode = tvp.ToCurrencyCode
```

```
            WHERE CurrencyRateDate = @CurrencyRateDate;

            GO
```

To execute the stored procedure, a table-valued parameter needs to be declared and then populated. Then, it can be assigned to the input parameter during stored procedure execution.

```
       DECLARE @CurrencyCodeTVP as CurrencyCodeListType

       INSERT INTO @CurrencyCodeTVP(FromCurrencyCode, ToCurrencyCode)
       VALUES
       ('USD', 'AUD'),
       ('USD', 'GBP'),
       ('USD', 'CAD'),
       ('USD', 'MXN');

       EXECUTE Sales.uspGetCurrencyRatesUDT
          @CurrencyCodeTable = @CurrencyCodeTVP,
          @CurrencyRateDate = '2005-07-14';
```

All the preceding examples illustrate one key point about stored procedures. Passing a list or a table into a stored procedure creates additional complexity and forethought to make it work. Take the calling application into consideration, and if at all possible, discuss the different options with the development team. What works well for one application might be inelegant for another.

Returning Data from Stored Procedures

The previous section covered how to get data into a stored procedure. This section addresses how to get the data back out. SQL Server provides five means to return data from a stored procedure. You can use any combination of these options in a single stored procedure.

- **Output parameters**: Scalar data can be returned from a stored procedure with output variables.
- **RETURN**: A single integer value can be returned from a stored procedure with a RETURN statement.
- **Result sets**: A stored procedure can return data via one or more SELECT statements.
- RAISERROR **or** THROW: Informational or error messages can be returned to the calling application via RAISERROR or THROW.
- **Table population**: A table can be populated as part of stored procedure processing and then queried after execution.

Best Practice

With every operation that affects data, SQL Server, by default, also sends a message stating the number of rows affected or returned. In most cases, this information is not used by the calling application and is just extra information (and an extra server round trip). You can eliminate this message and improve performance by using SET NOCOUNT ON at the beginning of a stored procedure definition.

```
CREATE PROCEDURE schema.StoredProcedureName

AS

SET NOCOUNT ON;
...
```

Output Parameters

Output parameters enable a stored procedure to return data to the calling application. The keyword OUTPUT is required both when the procedure is created and when it is called. Within the stored procedure, the output parameter appears as a local variable, just like an input parameter. Although output parameters are typically used solely for output, they are actually two-way parameters. When the stored procedure concludes, its current value is passed to the calling application.

Best Practice

Output parameters are useful for returning single units of data when a whole record set is not required. For returning single values, an output parameter can perform better than returning the data as a result set.

In the calling application, a local variable must have been created to receive the value of the output parameter. This can be illustrated within SQL Server Management Studio (SSMS).

1. CREATE the stored procedure Sales.uspGetCurrencyName with the OUTPUT parameter @CurrencyName.

2. DECLARE the local variable @CurrencyNameOutput to receive the output parameter.

3. EXECUTE the stored procedure, assigning the output parameter the value of @CurrencyNameOutput, which is NULL until it has been initialized.

4. During stored procedure execution, the output parameter is assigned a value via the SELECT statement based on the value of the input parameter @CurrencyCode.

5. The stored procedure completes and execution is passed back to SSMS. The value of the output parameter is received by the local variable @CurrencyCodeOutput.

6. The PRINT command sends the value of the local variable to the Messages tab of SSMS.

This is the stored procedure:

```
USE AdventureWorks2012USE AdventureWorks2012
GO

CREATE PROCEDURE Sales.uspGetCurrencyName

 @CurrencyCode char(3)
,@CurrencyName varchar(50) OUTPUT

AS

SELECT @CurrencyName = Name
FROM Sales.Currency
WHERE CurrencyCode = @CurrencyCode;

GO


This is the calling batch within SSMS:
DECLARE @CurrencyNameOutput varchar(50);

EXECUTE Sales.uspGetCurrencyName
    @CurrencyCode = 'USD',
    @CurrencyName = @CurrencyNameOutput OUTPUT;

PRINT @CurrencyNameOutput;
GO
```

Using the RETURN Command

A RETURN command unconditionally terminates the procedure and returns an integer value to the calling batch or application. Technically, a RETURN can be used with any batch process, but it can return a value only from a stored procedure or a function. The most common use of a RETURN command is to report success or failure of the process with a single integer value. Common convention is to assign 0 to success and some other value to failure. However, RETURN can be used by a calling application for any purpose that suits an integer-based return code. The important consideration is that the database and application is consistent in the use of RETURN.

If the RETURN code needs to be captured, the syntax for executing the stored procedure is slightly different than what has been seen so far in the examples.

```
EXECUTE @LocalVariable = schema.uspStoredProcedureName;
```

The following example alters the stored procedure created to illustrate output parameters and checks to see whether the output parameter is NULL. If so, it assigns a RETURN code of 1; if not, a RETURN code of 0 is assigned.

```
USE AdventureWorks2012
GO

ALTER PROCEDURE Sales.uspGetCurrencyName

 @CurrencyCode char(3)
,@CurrencyName varchar(50) OUTPUT

AS

SELECT @CurrencyName = Name
FROM Sales.Currency
WHERE CurrencyCode = @CurrencyCode;

IF @CurrencyName IS NULL
 BEGIN
    RETURN 1;
 END;
ELSE
 BEGIN
    RETURN 0;
 END;

GO

--Receive a RETURN code of 0
DECLARE @CurrencyNameOutput varchar(50);
DECLARE @ReturnCode int;

EXECUTE @ReturnCode = Sales.uspGetCurrencyName
    @CurrencyCode = 'USD',
    @CurrencyName = @CurrencyNameOutput OUTPUT;

PRINT @CurrencyNameOutput;
PRINT @ReturnCode;
GO

--Receive a RETURN code of 1
DECLARE @CurrencyNameOutput varchar(50);
DECLARE @ReturnCode int;

EXECUTE @ReturnCode = Sales.uspGetCurrencyName
    @CurrencyCode = 'USA',
```

```
        @CurrencyName = @CurrencyNameOutput OUTPUT;

PRINT @CurrencyNameOutput;
PRINT @ReturnCode;
GO
```

Result Sets

The easiest way to see the output of a stored procedure is with a result set. When a result set is created within a stored procedure, it is returned to the calling application. This stored procedure returns a single result set, containing all the rows in Sales.Currency.

```
USE AdventureWorks2012
GO

CREATE PROCEDURE Sales.uspGetCurrencyTable

AS

SELECT CurrencyCode, Name
FROM Sales.Currency;
GO

EXECUTE Sales.uspGetCurrencyTable;
```

WITH RESULT SETS

With the release of SQL Server 2012, there is a new option called WITH RESULT SETS. This feature allows the EXECUTE statement to define the structure of one or more result sets that are returned by a stored procedure. Assume that for a single currency code, the calling application expects two result sets: currency code information and currency rate information. This can be defined cleanly with this approach.

The stored procedure makes no reference to the result set definition. Because the EXECUTE statement defines the result sets, this means that a calling application can define results in different ways based on the context of the procedure call.

```
USE AdventureWorks2012
GO

CREATE PROCEDURE Sales.uspGetCurrencyInfoAndDetail

 @CurrencyCode char(3)
,@CurrencyRateDate date

AS

--Header Information
SELECT CurrencyCode, Name
```

```
FROM Sales.Currency
WHERE CurrencyCode = @CurrencyCode;

--Detail Information
SELECT FromCurrencyCode, ToCurrencyCode,
AverageRate, EndOfDayRate, CurrencyRateDate
FROM Sales.CurrencyRate
WHERE FromCurrencyCode = @CurrencyCode
  AND CurrencyRateDate = @CurrencyRateDate;

GO

--Execute the stored procedure
EXECUTE Sales.uspGetCurrencyInfoAndDetail
   @CurrencyCode = 'USD',
   @CurrencyRateDate = '2007-07-14'
WITH RESULT SETS
(
    ( [Currency Code] char(3)
     , [Currency Name] varchar(50)
    )
    ,                   -- Separate each defined result set with a comma
    ( [From Currency] char(3)
     , [To Currency] char(3)
     , [Average Rate] numeric(7,4)
     , [End of Day Rate] numeric(7,4)
     , [Currency As-Of Date] date
    )
);
```

WITH RESULT SETS enables the EXECUTE statement to define column names and data types. All columns returned by the stored procedure must be defined in the WITH RESULT SETS definition, and assigned data types must be compatible with the data types of the returned columns.

INSERT...EXECUTE

One variation on the concept of result sets is to pass data directly from a stored procedure to a table. This is known as an INSERT...EXECUTE. The following example inserts the results of the stored procedure directly into a new table in AdventureWorks2012.

```
USE AdventureWorks2012
GO

--Create New Table
CREATE TABLE Sales.NewCurrency
(
 CurrencyCode char(3)
,Name varchar(50)
```

```
);
GO

--Create Procedure
CREATE PROCEDURE Sales.uspInsertNewCurrency

@CurrencyCode char(3)

AS

SELECT CurrencyCode, Name
FROM Sales.Currency
WHERE CurrencyCode = @CurrencyCode;
GO

--INSERT... EXECUTE into Sales.NewCurrency
INSERT Sales.NewCurrency(CurrencyCode, Name)
EXECUTE Sales.uspInsertNewCurrency @CurrencyCode = 'CAD';

--View the contents of Sales.NewCurrency
SELECT CurrencyCode, Name
FROM Sales.NewCurrency;
```

`INSERT...EXECUTE` can be used with a permanent table, a table variable, or a temporary table.

Path and Scope of Returning Data

Any stored procedure has five possible methods to return data (SELECT, OUTPUT parameters, RETURN, RAISERROR/THROW, and table population). Deciding which method is right for a given stored procedure depends on the quantity and purpose of the data to be returned and the scope of the method used to return the data. The return scope for the five methods is as follows:

- Selected record sets are passed to the calling stored procedure. If the calling stored procedure consumes the result set (for example, INSERT...EXECUTE) the result set ends there. If the calling stored procedure does not consume the result set, it is passed up to the next calling stored procedure or client.

- RETURN values and OUTPUT parameters are all passed to local variables in the immediate calling procedure or application within SQL Server.

- RAISERROR is passed to the calling stored procedure and continues to bubble up until it is trapped by a TRY...CATCH or it reaches the client application.

If SQL Server Management Studio (SSMS) executes a batch that calls stored procedure A, which then calls stored procedure B, procedure B can pass data back to procedure A or to the client application in multiple ways, as illustrated in Figure 17-1.

FIGURE 17-1

Possible ways for stored procedures to pass data.

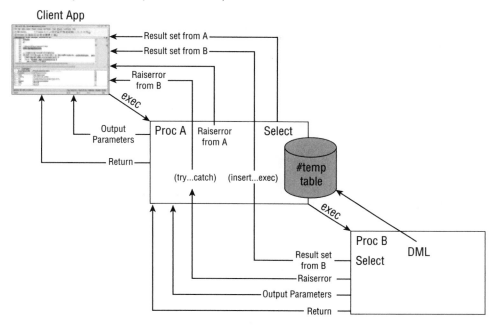

Nested Stored Procedures and Manageability

Stored procedures that call other stored procedures give you the ability to modularize and reuse your code, resulting in cleaner, more consistent processing. But be careful; getting carried away with nesting stored procedures might leave you with a headache if you ever need to troubleshoot a procedure that is buried multiple levels under the called procedure. Take advantage of SQL Server 2012's ability to pass data between stored procedures, but balance that with the need for simple, easy to troubleshoot code.

Summary

Stored procedures are a powerful way to implement reuse and consistency in an application. Data processed by a stored procedure can be used in various ways and is a great option for everything from returning the results of a basic SELECT statement to performing complex calculations. Parameterization is the key benefit of a stored procedure, enabling a single procedure to return different data based on the value of the passed parameters.

Building User-Defined Functions

IN THIS CHAPTER

Creating Scalar Functions

Replacing Views with Inline Table-valued Functions

Using Complex Code within Multistatement, Table-valued Functions to Generate a Result Set

SQL Server 2000 introduced user-defined functions (UDFs), and adoption throughout the SQL Server community has, quite frankly, been spotty. In some cases, overuse and improper application of UDFs has given them a bad reputation as a performance killer. In other cases, UDFs have been implemented as a way to repeatedly enforce complex business rules through function logic, and co-exist peacefully with other T-SQL programming constructs. Your experience with functions will depend largely on your understanding of how they execute, their impact on performance, and when to use them. Functions can be a useful tool in your T-SQL toolbox when applied judiciously and thoughtfully.

Before digging into the different types of UDFs, consider the basics of what a function is. A UDF is a routine that accepts parameters, performs an action, and returns the result of that action. The result is either a scalar (single) value or a table, depending on how the function is defined.

The benefits of UDFs include:

- UDFs can embed complex logic within a query. UDFs can create new functions for complex expressions.
- They can be used within the FROM clause of a SELECT statement or an expression, and they can be schema-bound. In addition, user-defined functions can accept parameters. UDFs can help enforce consistency and reusability when a complex calculation must be applied throughout an application.

The chief argument against developing with user-defined functions has to do with potential performance issues if they're misused. Any function, user-defined or system, that must be executed for every row in a WHERE clause will cripple performance.

User-defined functions come in three distinct types (as shown in Figure 18-1). Management Studio groups inline table-valued functions together with multi-statement:

- Scalar functions that return a single value
- Inline table-valued functions similar to views
- Multi-statement, table-valued functions that build a result set with code

FIGURE 18-1

Management Studio's Object Explorer lists all the user-defined functions within a database, organized by table-valued and scalar-valued functions.

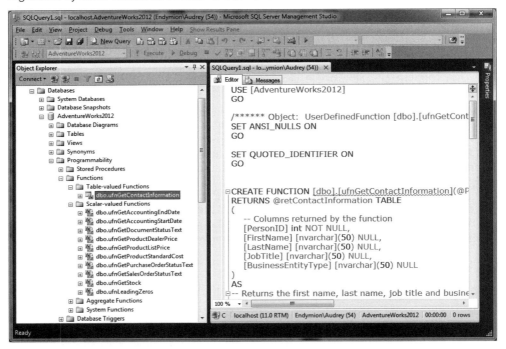

What's New with UDFs in SQL Server 2012

User-defined functions haven't gained any new functionality with SQL Server 2012. However, there is one deprecated feature of table-valued functions in SQL Server 2012. The indirect application of table hints to an invocation of a multi-statement, table-valued function through a view will be removed in a future version of SQL Server.

NOTE

If you'd like to see the metadata associated with UDFs in your database, the system view `sys.sqlmodules` provides an alternative to Management Studio.

```
USE AdventureWorks2012;
GO
SELECT definition, type
FROM sys.sql_modules AS m
JOIN sys.objects AS o ON m.object_id = o.object_id
    AND type IN ('FN', 'IF', 'TF');
GO
```

Scalar Functions

A *scalar function* is one that returns a single, specific value. The function can accept multiple parameters, perform a calculation, and then return a single value. For example, a scalar function could accept three parameters, perform a calculation, and return the answer.

Within the code of a scalar function, the value is passed back through the function by means of a RETURN command. Every possible codepath in the user-defined function should conclude with a RETURN command.

Scalar user-defined functions may be used within any expressions in SQL Server, even expressions within check constraints (although this isn't recommended practice).

Understanding Limitations

The scalar function must be deterministic, meaning it must repeatedly return the same value for the same input parameters. For this reason, nondeterministic functions — such as newid() and rand() — are not allowed within scalar functions. User-defined scalar functions are not permitted to update the database, call stored procedures, or call DBCC commands, with the single exception that they may update table variables. They cannot return binary large object (BLOB) data such as text, ntext, timestamp, and image data-type variables, nor can scalar functions return table variables or cursor data types. For error handling, UDFs may not include TRY...CATCH or RAISERROR.

A user-defined function may call other user-defined functions nesting up to 32 levels deep, or it can call itself recursively up to 32 levels deep before it blows up. However, this limitation is academic. Nesting functions can have serious performance implications; avoid this if at all possible.

Creating a Scalar Function

User-defined functions are created, altered, or dropped with the same DDL commands used for other objects; although the syntax is slightly different to allow for the return value:

```
CREATE FUNCTION FunctionName (InputParameters)
RETURNS DataType
AS
BEGIN;
  Code;
  RETURN Expression;
END;
```

The input parameters include a data-type definition and may optionally include a default value similar to stored procedure parameters (parameter = default). Function parameters differ from stored procedure parameters in that even if the default is wanted, the parameter is still required to call the function. Parameters with defaults don't become optional parameters. To request the default when calling the function, pass the keyword DEFAULT to the function.

The following user-defined scalar function performs a simple mathematical function. The second parameter includes a default value:

```
CREATE FUNCTION dbo.ufnCalculateQuotient
  (@Numerator numeric(5,2),
  @Denominator numeric(5,2)= 1.0)
RETURNS numeric(5,2)
AS
BEGIN;
  RETURN @Numerator/@Denominator;
END;
GO

SELECT dbo.ufnCalculateQuotient(12.1,7.45),
       dbo.ufnCalculateQuotient (7.0,DEFAULT);
```

Result:

```
----------- -----------
1.62        7.00
```

For a more complex scalar user-defined function, the ufnGetOrderTotalByProduct function created in the AdventureWorks2012 sample database returns the total number of orders for each product. Because the task returns a single value, calculating the total number of orders is a prime candidate for a scalar user-defined function. As a function, it can be plugged into any query, whereas a stored procedure is more difficult to use as a building block in other code.

```
USE AdventureWorks2012;
```

```
GO

CREATE FUNCTION dbo.ufnGetOrderTotalByProduct(@ProductID int)
RETURNS int
AS
BEGIN
    DECLARE @OrderTotal int;

    SELECT @OrderTotal = sum(sod.OrderQty)
    FROM Production.Product p
      JOIN Sales.SalesOrderDetail sod
        ON p.ProductID = sod.ProductID
    WHERE p.ProductID = @ProductID
    GROUP BY p.ProductID;

    RETURN @OrderTotal;
END;
GO
```

Calling a Scalar Function

Scalar functions may be used anywhere within any expression that accepts a single value.
User-defined scalar functions must always be called by means of at least a two-part name
(owner.name). The following script demonstrates calling the ufnGetOrderTotalByProduct
function within AdventureWorks2012. In this case, you ask for the order total for each
ProductID in the Production.Product table. You could pass a single value into the scalar
function as in the previous example, but the scalar function enables you to do something a
little more complex. You can use the ProductID from the table you're querying as the
parameter value for the UDF. This means that the UDF will be called once per ProductID
returned by the query.

```
USE AdventureWorks2012;
GO

SELECT p.Name, dbo.ufnGetOrderTotalByProduct(p.ProductID) as OrderTotal
FROM Production.Product p
ORDER BY OrderTotal DESC;
```

Partial result set:

```
Name                                               OrderTotal
-------------------------------------------------- -----------
AWC Logo Cap                                       8311
Water Bottle - 30 oz.                              6815
Sport-100 Helmet, Blue                             6743
Long-Sleeve Logo Jersey, L                         6592
Sport-100 Helmet, Black                            6532
Sport-100 Helmet, Red                              6266
Classic Vest, S                                    4247
...
```

18

Inline Table-Valued Functions

The second type of user-defined function, the inline table-valued function, is similar to a view. Both are wrapped for a stored SELECT statement. An inline table-valued user-defined function retains the benefits of a view, and adds parameters. As with a view, if the SELECT statement is updatable, then the function is also updatable.

Creating an Inline Table-Valued Function

The inline table-valued user-defined function has no BEGIN/END body. Instead, the SELECT statement is returned as a virtual table:

```
CREATE FUNCTION FunctionName (InputParameters)
RETURNS Table
AS
RETURN (Select Statement);
```

The following inline table-valued function is similar to ufnGetOrderTotalByProduct, but instead of returning a single order total for a supplied product, it returns a set that includes product name and order total for a provided product category.

```
CREATE FUNCTION
  dbo.ufnGetOrderTotalByProductCategory(@ProductCategoryID int)
RETURNS TABLE
AS
RETURN
    (
    SELECT p.ProductID, p.Name, sum(sod.OrderQty) as TotalOrders
    FROM Production.Product p
      JOIN Sales.SalesOrderDetail sod
        ON p.ProductID = sod.ProductID
      JOIN Production.ProductSubcategory s
        ON p.ProductSubcategoryID = s.ProductSubcategoryID
      JOIN Production.ProductCategory c
        ON s.ProductCategoryID = c.ProductCategoryID
    WHERE c.ProductCategoryID = @ProductCategoryID
    GROUP BY p.ProductID, p.Name
    );
GO
```

Calling an Inline Table-Valued Function

To retrieve data through dbo.ufnGetOrderTotalByProductCategory, call the function within the FROM portion of a SELECT statement:

```
SELECT ProductID, Name, TotalOrders
FROM dbo.ufnGetOrderTotalByProductCategory(1)
ORDER BY TotalOrders DESC;
```

Result (abridged):

```
ProductID    Name                            TotalOrders
-----------  ------------------------------  -----------
   756       Road-450 Red, 44                346
   779       Mountain-200 Silver, 38         2394
   971       Touring-2000 Blue, 50           322
   965       Touring-3000 Yellow, 62         844
   762       Road-650 Red, 44                2254
   793       Road-250 Black, 44              1642
   750       Road-150 Red, 44                437
   . . .
```

Using Parameters

An advantage of inline table-valued functions over views is the function's capability to include parameters within the precompiled SELECT statement. Views, conversely, do not include parameters, and restricting the result at run time is typically achieved by adding a WHERE clause to the SELECT statement that calls the view.

The following examples compare adding a restriction to the view to using a function parameter. The following view returns the total quantity ordered for all products:

```
USE AdventureWorks2012;
GO

CREATE VIEW dbo.vwProductOrderTotals

AS

    SELECT p.ProductID, p.Name, sum(sod.OrderQty) as TotalOrders
    FROM Production.Product p
      JOIN Sales.SalesOrderDetail sod
        ON p.ProductID = sod.ProductID
    GROUP BY p.ProductID, p.Name;
```

To retrieve the order total for a single product, the calling SELECT statement adds a WHERE clause restriction when calling the view:

```
SELECT *
FROM dbo.vwProductOrderTotals
WHERE ProductID = 782;
```

Result:

```
ProductID    Name                     TotalOrders
-----------  -----------------------  -----------
   782       Mountain-200 Black, 38   2977
```

18

SQL Server internally creates a new SQL statement from dbo.vwProductOrderTotals and the calling SELECT statement's WHERE clause restriction and then generates a query execution plan.

In contrast, a function allows the restriction to be passed as a parameter to the SELECT statement:

```
CREATE FUNCTION dbo.ufnProductOrderTotals (@ProductID nvarchar(100))
RETURNS TABLE
AS
    RETURN
    (
     SELECT p.ProductID, p.Name, sum(sod.OrderQty) as TotalOrders
     FROM Production.Product p
       JOIN Sales.SalesOrderDetail sod
         ON p.ProductID = sod.ProductID
     WHERE p.ProductID = @ProductID
     GROUP BY p.ProductID, p.Name
    );
```

To return the order total for a single product, pass the product ID into the function as a parameter value:

```
SELECT ProductID, Name, TotalOrders
FROM dbo.ufnProductOrderTotals(782);
```

Result:

```
ProductID    Name                     TotalOrders
-----------  -----------------------  -----------
782          Mountain-200 Black, 38   2977
```

Correlated User-Defined Functions

The APPLY command may be used with a table-valued user-defined function so that the UDF accepts a different parameter value for each corresponding row being processed by the main query.

APPLY was introduced in SQL Server 2005 and greatly increases the flexibility of T-SQL and especially the implementation of user-defined functions. The APPLY command has two forms. The most common form, the CROSS APPLY, operates much like an inner join. The CROSS APPLY command joins data from the main query with any table-valued data sets from the user-defined function. If no data is returned from the UDF, then the row from the main query is also not returned, as shown in the following example:

```
SELECT t.Name, t.TotalOrders
FROM Production.Product p
```

```
    CROSS APPLY dbo.ufnProductOrderTotals(p.ProductID) t
ORDER BY t.TotalOrders DESC;
```

Result:

```
Name                                               TotalOrders
-------------------------------------------------  -----------
AWC Logo Cap                                       8311
Water Bottle - 30 oz.                              6815
Sport-100 Helmet, Blue                             6743
Long-Sleeve Logo Jersey, L                         6592
Sport-100 Helmet, Black                            6532
Sport-100 Helmet, Red                              6266
Classic Vest, S                                    4247
. . .
```

The second form, the OUTER APPLY command, operates much like a left outer join. With this usage, rows from the main query are included in the result set regardless of whether the virtual table returned by the user-defined function is empty.

Best Practice

The scalar function dbo.ufnGetOrderTotalByProduct and the inline table-valued function dbo.ufnProductOrderTotals can produce the same result set. So what's different? The scalar function fires once per row, whereas the inline table valued function is treated by the query optimizer much like a view. There is a growing school of thought that because of this treatment by the query optimizer, it is highly preferable to use inline table-valued functions instead of scalar functions wherever possible.

18

Creating Functions with Schema Binding

All three types of user-defined functions may be created with the significant added benefit of schema binding. Views may be schema bound; in this way, UDFs are like views — both can be schema bound. This is one reason why you might choose a UDF over a stored procedure because stored procedures cannot be schema bound.

Schema binding prevents the altering or dropping of any object on which the function depends. If a schema-bound function references TableA, then columns may be added to TableA, but no existing columns can be altered or dropped, and neither can the table itself.

 Although it is true that stored procedures cannot be schema bound, there is a new feature in SQL Server 2012 called Result Sets that can guarantee the structure of the returned results at run time. Check out Chapter 16, "Programming with T-SQL" for more information.

To create a function with schema binding, add the option after `RETURNS` and before `AS` during function creation, as shown here:

```
CREATE FUNCTION FunctionName (Input Parameters)
RETURNS DataType
WITH SCHEMA BINDING
AS
BEGIN;
   Code;
   RETURNS Expression;
END;
```

Schema binding not only alerts the developer that the change may affect an object, it also prevents the change. To remove schema binding so that changes can be made, `ALTER` the function so that schema binding is no longer included.

Multistatement Table-Valued Functions

The multistatement table-valued, user-defined function combines the scalar function's capability to contain complex code with the inline table-valued function's capability to return a result set. This type of function creates a table variable and then populates it within code. The table is then passed back from the function so that it may be used within `SELECT` statements. From a query optimizer standpoint, it is treated much like an external call, like joining a stored procedure's result set to a table using `OPENQUERY`.

The primary benefit of the multistatement table-valued, user-defined function is that complex result sets may be generated within code and then easily used with a `SELECT` statement. This enables you to build complex logic into a query and solve problems that would otherwise be difficult to solve without a cursor.

The `APPLY` command may be used with multistatement table-valued, user-defined functions in the same way that it's used with inline user-defined functions.

Creating a Multistatement Table-Valued Function

The syntax to create the multistatement table-valued function is similar to that of the scalar user-defined function:

```
CREATE FUNCTION FunctionName (InputParamenters)
RETURNS @TableName TABLE (Columns)
AS
BEGIN;
   Code to populate table variable
   RETURN;
END;
```

The following process builds a multistatement table-valued, user-defined function that returns a basic result set:

1. The function first creates a table variable called @ProductList within the CREATE FUNCTION header.

2. Within the body of the function, two INSERT statements populate the @ProductList table variable.

3. When the function completes execution, the @ProductList table variable is passed back as the output of the function.

The dbo.ufnGetProductsAndOrderTotals function returns every product in the Production.Product table and the order total for each product:

```
USE AdventureWorks2012;
GO

CREATE FUNCTION dbo.ufnGetProductsAndOrderTotals()
RETURNS @ProductList TABLE
    (ProductID int,
     ProductName nvarchar(100),
     TotalOrders int)
AS
BEGIN;
    INSERT @ProductList(ProductID, ProductName)
    SELECT ProductID, Name
    FROM Production.Product;

    UPDATE pl
    SET TotalOrders =
     (SELECT sum(sod.OrderQty)
      FROM @ProductList ipl
       JOIN Sales.SalesOrderDetail sod
         ON ipl.ProductID = sod.ProductID
      WHERE ipl.ProductID = pl.ProductID)
    FROM @ProductList pl;

    RETURN;
END;
```

Calling the Function

To execute the function, refer to it within the FROM portion of a SELECT statement. The following code retrieves the result from the dbo.ufnGetProductsAndOrderTotals function:

```
SELECT ProductID, ProductName, TotalOrders
FROM dbo.ufnGetProductsAndOrderTotals()
ORDER BY TotalOrders DESC;
```

Result:

```
ProductID    ProductName                          TotalOrders
-----------  -----------------------------------  -----------
712          AWC Logo Cap                         8311
870          Water Bottle - 30 oz.                6815
711          Sport-100 Helmet, Blue               6743
715          Long-Sleeve Logo Jersey, L           6592
708          Sport-100 Helmet, Black              6532
707          Sport-100 Helmet, Red                6266
864          Classic Vest, S                      4247
...
```

CAUTION

Multistatement table-valued, user-defined functions use `tempdb` to pass the table variable to the calling query. For many applications this is not a concern, but for high-transaction applications, it could pose a performance problem. Consider incorporating the code directly into the calling stored procedure.

Best Practices with User-Defined Functions

Although user-defined functions add flexibility to your T-SQL options, there are some serious performance drawbacks to the improper application of them. They are not a standard replacement for subqueries, views, or stored procedures. In some cases, the user-defined function provides benefits that make a strong case for its use, such as parameterization or reusability. The trick is to use them properly.

Maximizing Performance

From a query optimizer perspective, different types of user-defined functions are handled differently. You've probably noticed that the examples provided for each of the three types of UDF, scalar, inline, and table-valued, all produced essentially the same result set. This was by design so that you could illustrate that in quite a few cases; you can define your function as any one of the three types. If you choose to use a user-defined function to encapsulate your query logic, follow these basic guidelines:

- Choose inline table-valued functions over multistatement table-valued functions whenever possible.

- Even if it looks like you need a scalar function, write it as an inline table-valued function; avoid scalar functions wherever possible.

- If you need a multistatement table-valued function, check to see if a stored procedure might be the appropriate solution. This might require a broader look at query structure, but it's worth taking the time to do it.

Using Consistent Naming Conventions

There are few things more frustrating than trying to troubleshoot a query and not knowing that what you're looking at is a user-defined function. Make sure to create a naming convention of some sort for all user-defined functions. Name prefixes seem to be the most commonly adopted method to achieve this. If you want to go a step further, make your prefix indicate whether the UDF is a scalar, inline table-valued, or mutistatement table-valued function. It will make your T-SQL easier to read and to troubleshoot. For example, an inline table-valued function that returns the average monthly sales per product category might be named `ifn_AvgMonthlySalesPerCategory` or `udfAvgMonthlySalesPerCategory`.

Summary

User-defined functions expand the capabilities of SQL Server objects and open a world of flexibility within expressions and the `SELECT` statement.

The big ideas from this chapter follow:

- Scalar user-defined functions return a single value and must be deterministic.
- Inline table-valued user-defined functions are similar to views and return the results of a single `SELECT` statement.
- Multistatement, table-valued, user-defined functions use code to populate a table variable, which is then returned.
- The `APPLY` function can be used to pass data to an inline table-valued UDF or a multistatement, table-valued UDF from the outer query, similar to how a correlated subquery can receive data from the outer query.

T-SQL code can be packaged in stored procedures, user-defined functions, and triggers. The next chapter delves into stored procedures.

18

Part V

Enterprise Data Management

IN THIS PART

Configuring SQL Server

S QL Server has a plethora of configuration options. The difficulty in mastering them lies in the fact that they are spread across three levels:

- Server-level options generally configure how the server works with hardware and determine the database defaults.
- Database-level options determine the behavior of the database and set the connection-level defaults.
- Connection-level options determine the current behaviors within the connection or current procedure.

Several of the configuration options overlap or simply set the default for the level immediately below. This chapter pulls these three configuration levels into a single unified understanding of how they relate to and affect each other. This chapter does not cover all SQL Server configuration options but covers most of the important ones. If you are a SQL Server beginner, you may find that some of the configuration options are advanced, and you may not immediately need them.

Setting the Options

Whether you choose to adjust the properties from SQL Server Management Studio's graphical tool or from code is completely up to you, but not every property is available from Management Studio using the graphical interface. Although the graphical interface has the advantages of being easy to use and walks you through easy-to-understand dialogs that prompt for the possible options in a pick and choose format, it lacks the repeatability of a T-SQL script run as a query.

> **TIP**
> To view miscellaneous information about the computer system while configuring SQL Server, query the `sys.dm_os_sys_info` dynamic management view.

New in SQL Server 2012 Configuration

SQL Server 2012 brings many security enhancements for configuration, specifically for service accounts and permissions:

- BUILTIN\administrators and Local System NT (NT Authority\SYSTEM) are no longer automatically provisioned in the sysadmin fixed server role on initial install.
- Setup now offers default accounts for SQL Server services whenever possible.
- Support for Managed Service Accounts and Virtual Accounts when installed on Windows 7 or Windows Server 2008 R2.
- Protection of operating services under a per-service SID now extended to all operating systems.

Additionally there are quite a few major changes in regards to SQL Server Setup:

- Datacenter Edition, which was introduced in SQL Server 2008 R2, is no longer available as a SQL Server 2012 edition. It's functionality has been replaced by the Enterprise Edition.
- New edition: SQL Server Business Intelligence edition — this edition delivers business intelligence-centric features such as Data Quality Services, Integration Services, Master Data Services, PowerPivot for SharePoint, Power View, StreamInsight Standard Edition.
- Service Pack 1 is the minimum requirement for Windows 7 and Windows Server 2008 R2 operating systems.
- Data Quality Services can now be installed using SQL Server setup.
- Product Update — Integrates the latest product updates with the main product installation so that the main product and its applicable updates are installed at the same time.
- Support for installing SQL Server 2012 on Windows Server 2008 R2 Server Core SP1.
- SQL Server Data Tools (formerly called Business Intelligence Development Studio) — IDE for building solutions for the Business Intelligence components: Analysis Services, Reporting Services, and Integration Services.
- Support for mutli-subnet clustering configurations.
- Support for SMB file shares as a storage option.
- Local disk is now a supported storage option for `tempdb` for SQL Server failover cluster installations.
- Dropped support for Itanium.

For full details regarding these changes, go to `http://msdn.microsoft.com/en-us/library/cc645578(v=sql.110).aspx`.

Configuring the Server

The server-level configuration options control server-wide settings, such as how SQL Server interacts with hardware, how it multithreads within Windows, and whether triggers are permitted to fire other triggers. When configuring the server, keep in mind the goals of configuration: consistency and performance.

Graphically, many of the server options may be configured within the Server Properties page, which you can open by right-clicking a server in the console tree and choosing Properties from the Context menu. The General tab in Management Studio's SQL Server Properties dialog box (see Figure 19-1) reports the versions and environment of the server.

FIGURE 19-1

The General tab of Management Studio's Server Properties dialog.

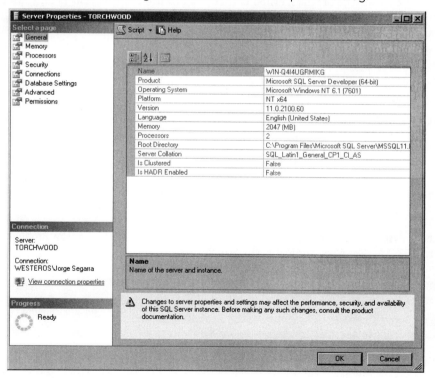

The same information is available to code. For example, the version may be identified with the @@VERSION global variable:

```
select @@VERSION;
```

Result:

```
Microsoft SQL Server 2012 - 11.0.2100.60 (X64)
        Feb 10 2012 19:39:15
        Copyright (c) Microsoft Corporation
        Developer Edition (64-bit) on Windows NT 6.1 <X64>
(Build 7601: Service Pack 1) (Hypervisor) (Build 7601: Service Pack 1)
```

The first line of the preceding result has the product version of SQL Server. In this example, the SQL Server product version is 11.0.2100.60. The last line of the result can be confusing. The last line reports the edition of SQL Server. In this example, it is SQL Server 2012 Developer Edition. However the service pack reported in the last line is the Windows service pack level and not SQL Server service pack level. In this example, it is SP1 for Windows Server 2008 R2. That is one of the reasons why not to use the SELECT @@VERSION command. Instead you can use the SERVERPROPERTY system function to determine the information. The advantage of this method is that you can use the function as an expression within a SELECT statement. The following example uses the SERVERPROPERTY function to return the SQL Server product version, product level, and edition.

```
SELECT
SERVERPROPERTY('ProductVersion') AS ProductVersion,
SERVERPROPERTY('ProductLevel') AS ProductLevel,
SERVERPROPERTY('Edition') AS Edition;
```

Result:

```
ProductVersion      ProductLevel    Edition
--------------      ------------    --------
11.0.2100.60        RTM             Developer Edition (64-bit)
```

In the preceding result, the ProductVersion indicates the SQL Server product version number. The ProductLevel indicates the SQL Server product level. If a SQL Server service pack is installed, the product level also indicates the service pack level. For example, if you run the previous command against your SQL Server 2005 SP3 instance, the ProductLevel returns SP3. The Edition indicates the SQL Server edition.

> **NOTE**
> Many of the configuration properties do not take effect until SQL Server is restarted. For this reason, the General tab in the SQL Server Properties (Configure) dialog box displays the current running values.

Within code, many of the server properties are set by means of the sp_configure system stored procedure. When executed without any parameters, this procedure reports the current settings, as in the following code (with word-wrap adjusted to fit on the page):

```
EXEC sp_configure;
```

Result:

name	minimum	maximum	config_value	run_value
allow updates	0	1	0	0
backup compression default	0	1	0	0
clr enabled	0	1	0	0
cross db ownership chaining	0	1	0	0
default language	0	9999	0	0
FILESTREAM access level	0	2	2	2
max text repl size (B)	-1	2147483647	65536	65536
nested triggers	0	1	1	1
remote access	0	1	1	1
remote admin connections	0	1	0	0
remote login timeout (s)	0	2147483647	20	20
remote proc trans	0	1	0	0
remote query timeout (s)	0	2147483647	600	600
server trigger recursion	0	1	1	1
show advanced options	0	1	0	0
user options	0	32767	0	0

> **NOTE**
>
> You can always discover the minimum and maximum values for a particular configuration option by running the `sp_configure` command with the option, but without any value. For example, run:
>
> ```
> EXEC sp_configure 'remote login timeout';
> ```
> and you discover that the `remote login timeout` configuration option can have any value in the range of 0 to 2,147,483,647.

The extended stored procedure, `xp_msver`, reports additional server and environment properties:

```
EXEC xp_msver;
```

Result:

Index	Name	Internal_Value	Character_Value
1	ProductName	NULL	Microsoft SQL Server
2	ProductVersion	655360	11.0.2100.6
3	Language	1033	English (United States)
4	Platform	NULL	NT INTEL X64
5	Comments	NULL	SQL
6	CompanyName	NULL	Microsoft Corporation
7	FileDescription	NULL	SQL Server Windows NT
8	FileVersion	NULL	2011.0110.2100.060 ((SQL11_RTM).120210-1917)
9	InternalName	NULL	SQLSERVR

19

10	LegalCopyright	NULL	Microsoft Corp. All rights reserved.
11	LegalTrademarks	NULL	Microsoft SQL Server is a registered trademark of Microsoft Corporation.
12	OriginalFilename	NULL	SQLSERVR.EXE
13	PrivateBuild	NULL	NULL
14	SpecialBuild	116588544	NULL
15	WindowsVersion	393281542	6.1 (7601)
16	ProcessorCount	1	1
17	ProcessorActiveMask	1	00000001
18	ProcessorType	586	PROCESSOR_INTEL_PENTIUM
19	PhysicalMemory	2046	2046 (2145845248)
20	Product ID	NULL	NULL

> **NOTE**
> The information returned by `sp_configure` is settable, but the information returned by `xp_msver` is not.

Configuring the Database

The database-level options configure the current database's behavior regarding ANSI compatibility and recovery.

Most database options can be set in Management Studio within the Database Properties page, which you can find by right-clicking a database in the console tree and choosing Properties from the context menu. Figure 19-2 shows the Options tab.

The database configuration options can be set using T-SQL `ALTER DATABASE SET` options. The following example sets the AdventureWorks database to single user mode to obtain exclusive access.

```
ALTER DATABASE AdventureWorks SET SINGLE_USER;
```

View database configuration options using the `sys.databases` catalog view or the `DATABASEPROPERTYEX()` function. The following example returns all the database properties of the AdventureWorks database:

```
SELECT * FROM sys.databases WHERE name = 'AdventureWorks';
```

> **NOTE**
> Do not use the `sp_dboption` system stored procedure because this has been removed in SQL Server 2012.

FIGURE 19-2

Use Management Studio's Database Properties Options tab to configure the most common database properties.

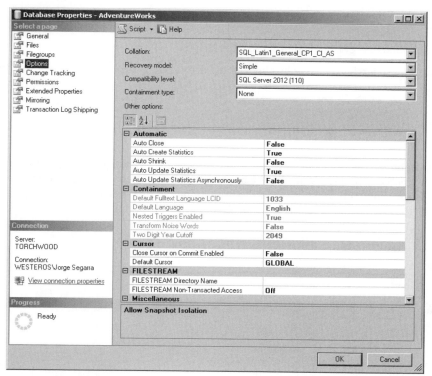

Configuring the Connection

Many of the connection-level options configure ANSI compatibility or specific connection-performance options.

Connection-level options are limited in scope. If the option is set within an interactive session, then the setting is in force until it's changed or the session ends. If the option is set within a stored procedure, then the setting persists only for the life of that stored procedure.

The connection-level options are typically configured by means of the SET command. The following code configures how SQL Server handles nulls within this current session:

```
SET ANSI_NULLS OFF;
```

Result:

```
Command(s) completed successfully.
```

Connection properties can also be checked by means of the SessionProperty() function:

```
Select SESSIONPROPERTY ('ANSI_NULLS');
```

Result:

```
0
```

Management Studio enables you to set several query properties. You can review and set these properties for current queries by clicking the Query menu and then Query Options. For all future connections, review and set the properties by clicking the Tools menu and then Options. Figure 19-3 shows an example of the ANSI settings that SQL Server uses to run the queries.

FIGURE 19-3

The ANSI settings that SQL Server uses to run your queries.

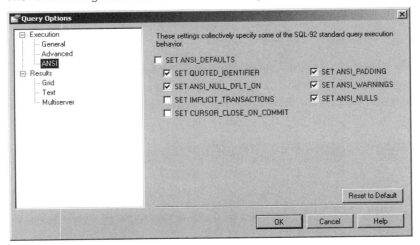

> **TIP**
>
> To view current settings of connection-level options, query the sys.dm_exec_connections dynamic management view.

Surface Area Configuration Facets

In SQL Server 2005 you were introduced to the Surface Area Configuration Wizard. This simple wizard enabled you to quickly lock down common security attack vectors in SQL Server.

When 2008 was released, that wizard was then replaced by the functionality of Policy-Based Management. The Surface Area Configuration Wizard's tasks were then made into facets within Policy-Based Management. You can use these facets to create policies that dictate the status of the various features previously controlled by the Surface Area Configuration Wizard, as shown in Figure 19-4. You can learn more about creating and evaluating policies in Chapter 20, "Policy-Based Management."

FIGURE 19-4

The Surface Area Configuration facet exposes properties that enable you to allow or disallow features.

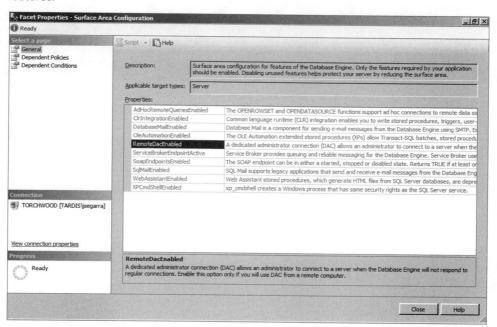

Configuration Options

Because so many similar configuration options are controlled by different commands and at different levels (server, database, connection), this section organizes the configuration options by topic, rather than by command or level.

Displaying the Advanced Options

As with many operations, displaying advanced options can be achieved using several methods. One method is to query the sys.configurations catalog view as shown here:

```
SELECT   name, minimum, maximum, value, value_in_use
FROM     sys.configurations
WHERE    is_advanced = 1
ORDER BY name;
```

The preceding example displays all the SQL Server advanced options. To display all the options, comment out the WHERE clause. Another method to display the advanced options is to turn on the show advanced options configuration using the following code:

```
EXEC sp_configure 'show advanced options', 1;
RECONFIGURE;
```

> **NOTE**
>
> After a configuration setting is changed with sp_configure, the RECONFIGURE command causes the changes to take effect. If you don't run RECONFIGURE, then the config_value field still shows the change, but the change won't appear in the run_value field, even if you restart the service. Some configuration changes take effect only after SQL Server is restarted.

After you set the advanced option display on, you can use the sp_configure command to display a list of all the options.

```
EXEC sp_configure;
```

Result (with advanced options enabled):

name	minimum	maximum	config_value	run_value
access check cache bucket count	0	16384	0	0
access check cache quota	0	2147483647	0	0
Ad Hoc Distributed Queries	0	1	0	0
affinity I/O mask	-2147483648	2147483647	0	0
affinity64 I/O mask	-2147483648	2147483647	0	0
affinity mask	-2147483648	2147483647	0	0
affinity64 mask	-2147483648	2147483647	0	0
Agent XPs	0	1	1	1
allow updates	0	1	0	0
awe enabled	0	1	0	0
backup compression default	0	1	0	0
blocked process threshold (s)	0	86400	0	0
c2 audit mode	0	1	0	0
clr enabled	0	1	0	0
common criteria compliance enabled	0	1	0	0

cost threshold for parallelism	0	32767	5	5
cross db ownership chaining	0	1	0	0
cursor threshold	-1	2147483647	-1	-1
Database Mail XPs	0	1	0	0
default full-text language	0	2147483647	1033	1033
default language	0	9999	0	0
default trace enabled	0	1	1	1
disallow results from triggers	0	1	0	0
EKM provider enabled	0	1	0	0
FILESTREAM access level	0	2	2	2
fill factor (%)	0	100	0	0
ft crawl bandwidth (max)	0	32767	100	100
ft crawl bandwidth (min)	0	32767	0	0
ft notify bandwidth (max)	0	32767	100	100
ft notify bandwidth (min)	0	32767	0	0
index create memory (KB)	704	2147483647	0	0
in-doubt xact resolution	0	2	0	0
lightweight pooling	0	1	0	0
locks	5000	2147483647	0	0
max degree of parallelism	0	64	0	0
max full-text crawl range	0	256	4	4
max server memory (MB)	16	2147483647	2147483647	
				2147483647
max text repl size (B)	-1	2147483647	65536	65536
max worker threads	128	32767	0	0
media retention	0	365	0	0
min memory per query (KB)	512	2147483647	1024	1024
min server memory (MB)	0	2147483647	0	0
nested triggers	0	1	1	1
network packet size (B)	512	32767	4096	4096
Ole Automation Procedures	0	1	0	0
open objects	0	2147483647	0	0
optimize for ad hoc workloads	0	1	0	0
PH timeout (s)	1	3600	60	60
precompute rank	0	1	0	0
priority boost	0	1	0	0
query governor cost limit	0	2147483647	0	0
query wait (s)	-1	2147483647	-1	-1
recovery interval (min)	0	32767	0	0
remote access	0	1	1	1
remote admin connections	0	1	0	0
remote login timeout (s)	0	2147483647	20	20
remote proc trans	0	1	0	0
remote query timeout (s)	0	2147483647	600	600
Replication XPs	0	1	0	0
scan for startup procs	0	1	0	0
server trigger recursion	0	1	1	1
set working set size	0	1	0	0
show advanced options	0	1	1	1
SMO and DMO XPs	0	1	1	1

19

```
SQL Mail XPs                     0        1        0         0
transform noise words           0        1        0         0
two digit year cutoff        1753     9999     2049      2049
user connections                0    32767        0         0
user options                    0    32767        0         0
xp_cmdshell                     0        1        0         0
```

> **NOTE**
> The key difference between the previous two methods to display advanced options is that the sys
> .configurations catalog view displays only the configurations. The show advanced options configura-
> tion not only controls the display of advanced options through sp_configure system stored procedure, but it also
> controls whether these advanced options can be changed.

Start/Stop Configuration Properties

The startup configuration properties, described in Table 19-1, control how SQL Server and the processes are launched.

TABLE 19-1 **Start/Stop Configuration Properties**

Property	Level*	Graphic Control	Code Option
AutoStart SQL Server	S	Configuration Manager or Services Console	–
AutoStart SQL Server Agent	S	Configuration Manager or Services Console	–
AutoStart MS DTC	S	Services Console	–
Scan for startup procs	S	–	EXEC sp_configure 'scan for startup procs'

* The configuration level refers to server, database, or connection.

Startup Parameters

You use the startup parameters with the SQL Server services. The startup parameters are passed as parameters to the SQL Server program when the SQL Server service is started. Although you can add startup parameters from Services console, it's highly recommend that you use the SQL Server Configuration Manager, as shown in Figure 19-5. One of the main reasons has to do with minimizing downtime. Configuration Manager enables you to add startup parameters with the SQL Server service still running. You can restart the service during a maintenance window and minimize downtime. Also, Configuration manager is the only method for SQL Server failover clustering instance because it is a cluster-aware tool, and services console is not.

FIGURE 19-5

Add startup parameters to the SQL Server service to change its behavior.

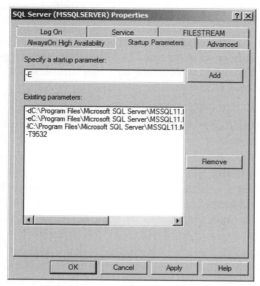

To add the startup parameters in SQL Server Configuration Manager, follow these steps:

1. Open SQL Server Configuration Manager from Start ➪ Programs ➪ Microsoft SQL Server 2012 ➪ Configuration Tools ➪ SQL Server Configuration Manager.
2. Under SQL Server Configuration Manager, click SQL Server Services.
3. Right-click the SQL Server service (on the right side) on which you want to add startup parameters, and select the Startup Parameters tab.
4. Add parameters individually in the text box, and click the Add button (refer to Figure 19-5).

In addition to the standard master database-location parameters, two parameters are particularly useful:

- -m: Starts SQL Server in single-user mode. This is required to restore the master database.
- -f: Starts up with a minimal configuration.

Additional startup parameters are as follows:

- -d: Includes the full path of the master database file, with no spaces between the d and the path.
- -l: Includes the full path of the master database log file, with no spaces between the l and the path.
- -e: Includes the full path of the SQL Server error log file, with no spaces between the e and the path.

- -c: Starts SQL Server so that it is not running as a Windows service.
- -x: Enables maximum performance by disabling monitoring features. Because the monitoring features are disabled, your ability to troubleshoot performance and functional problems is greatly reduced.
- -g: Specifies virtual memory (in MB) available to SQL Server for memory allocations within the SQL Server process, but outside the SQL Server memory pool (extended procedure .dll files, OLE DB providers referenced by distributed queries, and automation objects referenced in Transact-SQL statements).
- -n: Disables logging to the Windows application log.
- -s: Starts a named instance of SQL Server. The instance name follows directly after the s, with no spaces in between.
- -Ttrace#: Enables trace-specific flags by trace flag number. Refer to SQL Server 2012 Books Online topic "Trace Flags" for documented trace flags. Using trace flags for an extended period of time is not recommended. Use trace flags for troubleshooting SQL Server issues and remove them when the issue is resolved. Also, never use undocumented trace flags because they can cause more damage than they can provide assistance with any issue.
- -h: Assuming your hardware enables you to add physical memory without restarting the server, use this option to enable SQL Server to immediately begin using the hot add memory. This is only available on the SQL Server Enterprise Edition and can be used on 64-bit SQL Server and 32-bit SQL Server with AWE enabled.

Startup Stored Procedures

You can figure SQL Server to scan for a startup stored procedure every time the SQL Server starts — similar to how Microsoft DOS operating systems scan for the autoexec.bat file when they boot up. All the startup procedures need to be in the master database, but there is no limit on the number of startup procedures. The key is to remember that each startup procedure consumes one worker thread while executing it. To mark an existing stored procedure to execute automatically when SQL Server starts, use the sp_procoption system stored procedure as follows:

```
EXEC sp_procoption @ProcName = 'ExistingSP',
        @OptionName = 'startup',
        @OptionValue = 'on';
```

You use the same sp_procoption system stored procedure to stop a stored procedure from executing at SQL Server startup as follows:

```
EXEC sp_procoption @ProcName = 'ExistingSP',
        @OptionName = 'startup',
        @OptionValue = 'off';
```

Although you can individually mark a stored procedure for automatic execution at SQL Server startup, you can further control the execution of all the startup stored procedures by using the scan for startup procs configuration option. If this option is set to 1, SQL Server scans for and runs all stored procedures marked for automatic execution at startup. An example of a use case for a startup stored procedure would be if you have an expensive query that takes a long time to run at first execution. By using a startup stored procedure to execute this query at startup, it pushes the data into memory for quick access for subsequent requests. It should be noted that while this is a way to "warm the cache" with data, this particular method should be used carefully. While in theory it's possible to do this for multiple tables, you may find yourself pushing the physical resources (i.e. memory) fairly quickly or accidently pushing other items you've loaded out of cache if you're not careful.

The default value of this option is 0, which skips automatic execution of startup stored procedures. The scan for startup procs configuration option is automatically set to 1 when you execute sp_procoption to mark the first stored procedure for automatic execution and is set to 0 when you unmark the last stored procedure for automatic execution. Use the following code to skip automatic execution for all startup stored procedures:

```
EXEC sp_configure 'scan for startup procs', 0;
RECONFIGURE;
```

Memory-Configuration Properties

SQL Server can either dynamically request memory from the operating system or consume a fixed amount of memory. You can configure these settings on the SQL Server Properties Memory tab, as shown in Figure 19-6, or from code by means of the sp_configure stored procedure.

FIGURE 19-6

Memory tab of Management Studio's SQL Server Properties dialog.

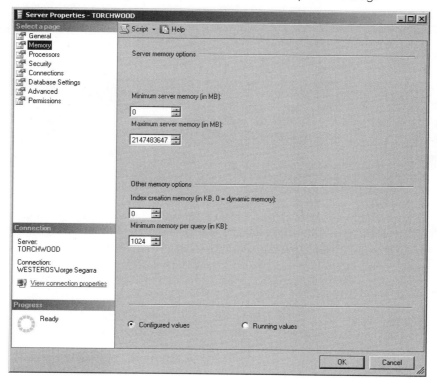

The memory-configuration properties, listed in Table 19-2, control how SQL Server uses and allocates memory.

TABLE 19-2   **Memory-Configuration Properties**

Property	Level*	Graphic Control	Code Option
Dynamic Memory Minimum	S	Management Studio	`EXEC sp_configure 'min server memory'`
Dynamic Memory Maximum	S	Management Studio	`EXEC sp_configure 'max server memory'`
Fixed Memory Size	S	Management Studio	`EXEC sp_configure 'min server memory' and EXEC sp_configure 'max server memory'`
Minimum Query Memory	S	Management Studio	`EXEC sp_configure 'min memory per query'`
Query Wait	S	Management Studio	`EXEC sp_configure 'query wait'`
AWE Enabled	S	Management Studio	`EXEC sp_configure 'AWE Enabled'`
Index Create Memory	S	Management Studio	`EXEC sp_configure 'index create memory'`

* The configuration level refers to server, database, or connection.

> **NOTE**
>
> The configuration options `set working set size`, `open objects`, and `locks` are still present in the `sp_configure` stored procedure, but their functionality was removed in SQL Server 2008 and is unavailable in Microsoft SQL Server 2012. These options have no effect. Do not use these options in new development work because they may be removed in future SQL Server versions.

Dynamic Memory

If SQL Server is set to dynamically use memory, then SQL Server's memory can grow or be reduced as needed within the minimum and maximum constraints based on the physical memory available and the workload. SQL Server tries to maintain its requirement of 64MB and 128MB for the 32-bit and 64-bit versions respectively. The goal is to have enough memory available while avoiding Windows needing to swap pages from memory to the virtual-memory support file (`pagefile.sys`).

The minimum-memory property prohibits SQL Server from reducing memory below a certain point and hurting performance, but it does not guarantee that SQL Server will immediately allocate the minimum amount of memory at startup. The minimum simply means that when SQL Server memory has reached that point, it will not reduce memory below it.

The maximum-memory setting prevents SQL Server from growing to the point where it contends with the operating system, or other applications, for memory. If the maximum is set too low, then performance suffers.

> **NOTE**
>
> In SQL Server 2012, all memory allocations by SQL Server components will now observe the "max server memory" configuration option. In previous versions only the 8K allocations were limited by the "max server memory" configuration option. Allocations larger than 8K weren't constrained.

Multiple SQL Server instances do not cooperate when requiring memory. In servers with multiple instances, it's highly possible for two busy instances to contend for memory and for one to become memory-starved. Reducing the maximum-memory property for each instance can prevent this from happening.

From T-SQL code, the minimum- and maximum-memory properties are set by means of the sp_configure system stored procedure. It's an advanced option, so it can be changed only if the show advanced options property is on:

```
EXEC sp_configure 'show advanced options', 1;
RECONFIGURE;
```

> **NOTE**
>
> show advanced options needs to be turned on only if it is not already turned on. After it is turned on, you can change the advanced options and then reset it to the default value of 0.

The following code sets the min-memory configuration to 1GB:

```
EXEC sp_configure 'min server memory', 1024;
RECONFIGURE;
```

Result:

```
Configuration option 'min server memory (MB)'
    changed from 0 to 1024.
Run the RECONFIGURE statement to install.
```

The following code sets the max-memory configuration to 4GB:

```
EXEC sp_configure 'max server memory', 4096;
RECONFIGURE;
```

Result:

```
Configuration option 'max server memory (MB)'
    changed from 2147483647 to 4096.
Run the RECONFIGURE statement to install.
```

19

Fixed Memory

Instead of dynamically consuming memory, you can configure SQL Server to request a fixed amount of memory from the operating system. To set a fixed amount of memory from code, set the minimum- and maximum-memory properties to the same value. The following code sets the SQL Server memory to a fixed memory of 6144MB.

```
EXEC sp_configure 'show advanced options', 1;
RECONFIGURE;
EXEC sp_configure 'min server memory', 6144;
RECONFIGURE;
EXEC sp_configure 'max server memory', 6144;
RECONFIGURE;
```

Although calculating memory cost, polling the environment, and requesting memory may seem as if they would require overhead, you aren't likely to see any performance gains from switching from dynamic to fixed memory. The primary purpose of using fixed memory is to configure a dedicated SQL Server computer to use a fixed amount of memory after the value is reached.

Minimum Query Memory

At times, the SQL Server team amazes me with the level of detailed control it passes to DBAs. SQL Server can allocate the required memory for each query as needed. The `min memory per query` option sets the minimum threshold for the memory (KB) used by each query. Although increasing this property to a value higher than the default 1MB may provide slightly better performance for some queries, there is no reason to override SQL Server automatic memory control and risk causing a memory shortage. If you insist on doing so, here's how to do it. The following code increases the minimum query memory to 2MB:

```
EXEC sp_configure 'show advanced options', 1;
RECONFIGURE;
EXEC sp_configure 'min memory per query', 2048;
RECONFIGURE;
```

Query Wait

If the memory is unavailable to execute a large query, SQL Server waits for the estimated amount of time necessary to execute the query times 25 and then times out.

Usually you do not need to change the `query wait` option, but if you have a valid reason to change this option, you can either use Management Studio or T-SQL-code. In Management Studio, you can set the `query wait` option by entering the value in the query wait box on the Server Properties Advanced tab (see Figure 19-9 later in this chapter).

The following code specifies that every query either starts executing within 20 seconds or times out.

```
EXEC sp_configure 'show advanced options', 1;
RECONFIGURE;
EXEC sp_configure 'query wait', 20;
RECONFIGURE;
```

To revert to the default wait time of the estimated execution time times 25, you must specify the query wait time as -1.

AWE-Enabled

On 32-bit operation systems, SQL Server is normally restricted to the standard 2GB physical-memory limit (or 3GB if /3GB switch is used in boot.ini). On 64-bit operation systems, the awe enabled option is ignored, even though it is present in the sp_configure stored procedure.

SQL Server x86 Standard, Enterprise, and Developer Editions, when running on Windows Server 2003 or 2008 Enterprise or Datacenter Editions, can use up to 64GB of physical memory by configuring SQL Server to address the Address Windowing Extensions (AWE) API. The AWE-enabled property turns on AWE memory addressing within SQL Server.

```
EXEC sp_configure 'show advanced options', 1;
RECONFIGURE;
EXEC sp_configure 'awe enabled', 1;
RECONFIGURE;
```

> **NOTE**
>
> In SQL Server 2012, Address Windowing Extensions (AWE) has been deprecated.

> **NOTE**
>
> The Windows privilege LOCK PAGES IN MEMORY must be granted to the SQL Server service account before enabling awe. A system administrator can use the Windows Group Policy tool (gpedit.msc) to enable this privilege for the SQL Server service account.

> **NOTE**
>
> The SQL Server instance must be restarted for the awe enabled option to take effect. If the awe enabled option is configured successfully, then the SQL Server Error Log includes an Address Windowing Extensions Enabled message when the SQL Server restarts.

Index Create Memory

The amount of memory SQL Server uses to perform sorts when creating an index is generally self-configuring. However, you can control it by using sp_configure to hard-code a certain memory footprint (KB) for index creation. For example, the following code sets the memory used to create an index to 8MB:

```
EXEC sp_configure 'show advanced options', 1;
RECONFIGURE;
EXEC sp_configure 'index create memory', 8096;
RECONFIGURE;
```

> **NOTE**
>
> Index create memory option is self-configuring and usually works without additional adjustments. The option to modify index creation memory is an advanced option and should only be changed by an experienced database administrator or certified SQL Server technician.

Processor-Configuration Properties

You can use the processor-configuration properties (listed in Table 19-3) to control how SQL Server uses multiprocessor computers.

TABLE 19-3 Processor-Configuration Properties

Property	Level*	Graphic Control	Code Option
Processors Used	S	Management Studio	EXEC sp_configure 'affinity mask'
Maximum Worker Threads	S	Management Studio	EXEC sp_configure 'max worker threads'
Boost SQL Server Priority on Windows	S	Management Studio	EXEC sp_configure 'priority boost'
Use Windows NT Fibers	S	Management Studio	EXEC sp_configure 'lightweight pooling'
Number of processors for parallel execution of queries	S	Management Studio	EXEC sp_configure 'max degree of parallelism'
Minimum query plan threshold for parallel execution	S	Management Studio	EXEC sp_configure 'cost threshold for parallelism'

* The configuration level refers to server, database, or connection.

The Processors tab (see Figure 19-7) of the SQL Server Properties page determines how SQL Server uses multiprocessor computers. Most of these options are moot in a single-processor server.

Processor Affinity

In a multi-CPU server, the operating system can move processes to CPUs as the load requires. The SQL Server processor affinity, or the relationship between a task and a CPU, can be configured on a per-CPU basis. By enabling the affinity between SQL Server and a CPU, you make that CPU available to SQL Server, but it is not dedicated to SQL Server. Therefore, although a CPU can't be forced to run SQL Server, it can be segmented from SQL Server.

FIGURE 19-7

The Processors tab shows the processors available on the system and enables you to set how SQL Server uses them.

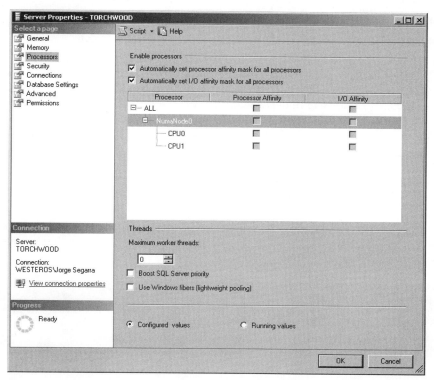

SQL Server supports processor affinity by means of two affinity mask configuration options: `affinity mask` (also referred to as CPU affinity mask) and `affinity I/O mask`. The `affinity mask` configuration option enables you to specify which CPUs on a multiprocessor computer are to be used to run threads from SQL Server. The `affinity I/O mask` configuration option enables you to specify which CPUs are configured to run SQL Server threads related to I/O operations. These two configuration options give you the ability to allocate particular CPUs for disk IO processing and particular CPUs for nondisk-related CPU requirements.

The affinity mask is a bitmap in which the rightmost bit specifies the lowest-order CPU(0), the next rightmost bit specifies the next lowest-order CPU(1), and so on. A 1-byte (8 bits) mask covers 8 CPUs in a multiprocessor server, a 2-byte mask covers up to 16 CPUs, a 3-byte mask covers up to 24 CPUs, and a 4-byte mask covers up to 32 CPUs. A 1 bit specifies that the corresponding CPU is allocated and a 0 bit specifies that the corresponding CPU is not allocated.

When you configure the affinity mask option, you must use it with an affinity I/O mask. Enabling the same CPU for both affinity mask and affinity I/O mask configuration options is not recommended because doing so will cause contention on the CPU for both resources. The bit corresponding to each CPU should be one of the following:

- 0 for both `affinity mask` and `affinity I/O mask` options
- 1 for `affinity mask` and 0 for `affinity I/O mask` option
- 0 for `affinity mask` and 1 for `affinity I/O mask` option

As an example, say on a 8-CPU system, you want to allocate CPUs 0, 1, 2, and 3 for processing SQL Server threads, CPUs 4 and 5 for disk I/O processing, and CPUs 6 and 7 for other non-SQL Server activities. This means the last 4 bits will be one for the `affinity mask` bitmap (00001111) that is 15 in decimal and the fifth and sixth bits will be one for the `affinity I/O mask` (00110000) that is 48 in decimal.

```
EXEC sp_configure 'show advanced options', 1;
RECONFIGURE;
EXEC sp_configure 'affinity mask', 15;
RECONFIGURE;
EXEC sp_configure 'affinity I/O mask', 48;
RECONFIGURE;
```

The affinity mask setting takes effect immediately without requiring a restart of the SQL Server service whereas the `affinity I/O mask` setting takes effect only after restarting the SQL Server service.

> **NOTE**
> The default value of 0 for the `affinity mask` option indicates that all the processors on the server are available for processing SQL Server threads. The default value of 0 for the `affinity I/O mask` option indicates that any CPUs that are eligible to process SQL Server threads are available for disk I/O processing.

> **NOTE**
> The affinity mask feature will be removed in a future version of Microsoft SQL Server. It is advised that you do not use this feature in new development work.

In Management Studio, processor affinity is configured by means of the check boxes on the Server Properties Processors tab (refer to Figure 19-7).

```
EXEC sp_configure 'show advanced options', 1;
RECONFIGURE;
GO
EXEC sp_configure 'affinity mask', 3;
RECONFIGURE;
```

> **NOTE**
> Affinity support for SQL Servers with 33 to 64 processors is available only on 64-bit SQL Servers and requires the additional use of `affinity64 mask` and `affinity64 I/O mask` configuration options.

Max Worker Threads

SQL Server is a multithreaded application, meaning that it can execute on multiple processors concurrently for increased performance. Multithreaded applications also enable more efficient use of a single processor because this enables another task to execute while a task waits for a process that doesn't use the CPU to finish. The threads are designed as follows:

- A thread for each network connection.
- A thread to handle database checkpoints.
- Multiple threads to handle user requests. When SQL Server handles a small number of connections, a single thread is assigned to each connection. However, as the number of connections grows, a pool of threads handles the connections more efficiently.

Depending on the number of connections and the percentage of time those connections are active (versus idle), making the number of worker threads less than the number of connections can force connection pooling, conserve memory, and improve performance.

In Management Studio, the `max worker threads` option is set by typing or selecting a value in the Maximum worker Threads box on the Server Properties Processor tab (refer to Figure 19-7 earlier in the chapter).

From code, the maximum number of worker threads is set by means of the `sp_configure` stored procedure and the `max worker threads` option. For example, the following code sets the `max worker threads` to 128.

```
EXEC sp_configure 'show advanced options', 1;
RECONFIGURE;
EXEC sp_configure 'max worker threads', 128;
RECONFIGURE;
```

SQL Server service must be restarted for the `max worker threads` setting to take effect.

Best Practice

On SQL Server 2008 and SQL Server 2012, the default value of 0 for the `max worker threads` property provides the best performance of SQL Server. This default value indicates that SQL Server automatically determines the correct number of active worker threads based on user requests.

If you do need to change the default value, it is not recommend to set the `max worker threads` option to a small value because that may prevent enough threads from servicing incoming client requests in a timely manner and could lead to "thread starvation." However, do not set the `max worker threads` option to a large value because that can waste memory because each active thread consumes 512KB on 32-bit servers and up to 4MB on 64-bit servers.

19

Priority Boost

Different processes in Windows operate at different priority levels, ranging from 0 to 31. The highest priorities are executed first and are reserved for the operating-system processes. Typically, Windows scheduling priority-level settings for applications are 4 (low), 7 (normal), 13 (high), and 24 (real time). By default, SQL Server installs with a Windows scheduling priority level of 7. The default value of `priority boost` gives SQL Server enough CPU resources without adversely affecting other applications.

Best Practice

In almost all cases, it is recommended to leave the `priority boost` option to the default value of 0. Raising the priority of SQL Server may drain essential operating system and networking functions and thereby result in a poorly performing SQL Server; in some cases it may even result in a SQL Server shutdown. If you do change the priority boost from 0 to 1, then be sure to test it thoroughly and evaluate all other performance tuning opportunities first.

If you still insist on changing the `priority boost` configuration option, you can either use Management Studio or T-SQL-code. In Management Studio, `priority boost` is set to 1 by checking the Boost SQL Server priority check box in the Server Properties Processor tab (refer to Figure 19-7 earlier in this chapter).

Using T-SQL-code, the following command can set the `priority boost` option to 1. This sets the Windows scheduling priority level to 13 (high).

```
EXEC sp_configure 'show advanced options', 1;
RECONFIGURE;
EXEC sp_configure 'priority boost', 1;
RECONFIGURE;
```

SQL Server service must be restarted for the `priority boost` option to take effect.

Lightweight Pooling

You can use the `lightweight pooling` option for servers with multiprocessing servers to reduce the overhead of frequently switching processes among the CPUs.

Best Practice

For most SQL Servers the default value of 0 for the `lightweight pooling` configuration option gives the best performance. In fact, changing the value from 0 to 1 may result in decreased performance. If you do change the `lightweight pooling` option to 1, then be sure to test it thoroughly and evaluate all other performance tuning opportunities first.

If you still insist on changing the value of the `lightweight pooling` option, you can either use Management Studio or T-SQL-code. In Management Studio, `lightweight pooling` can be set to 1 (default is 0) by checking the Use Windows fibers (lightweight pooling) check box on the Server Properties Processor tab (refer to Figure 19-7 earlier in this chapter).

In code, to set the `lightweight pooling` option:

```
EXEC sp_configure 'show advanced options', 1;
RECONFIGURE;
EXEC sp_configure 'lightweight pooling', 1;
RECONFIGURE;
```

SQL Server service must be restarted for the `lightweight pooling` option to take effect.

CAUTION

The need for the `lightweight pooling` option is reduced by improved context switching in Microsoft Windows Server 2003 and 2008.

The `lightweight pooling` and `clr enabled` configuration options are mutually exclusive. You can use one of the two options: `lightweight pooling` or `clr enabled`. If you disable CLR, features that rely on it (such as hierarchy data type, replication and Policy-Based Management) will not work properly.

Parallelism

On a multiprocessor server, SQL Server detects the best number of processors that can be used to run a single statement for each parallel plan. The `max degree of parallelism` configuration option can be used to limit the number of processors to use in a parallel plan execution.

SQL Server's query optimizer is a cost-based optimizer, which means it chooses a plan that returns the results in a reasonable amount of time with a reasonable resource cost. SQL Server always considers a serial plan first. If this serial plan costs less than the `cost threshold for parallelism` value, then no parallel plan is generated. The `cost threshold for parallelism` option refers to the cost of the query in seconds on a specific hardware configuration. If the cheapest serial plan costs more than the `cost threshold for parallelism`, then a parallel plan is produced. The parallel plan cost is compared with the serial plan cost, and the cheaper one is chosen.

Complex queries benefit the most from parallelism because generating a parallel query execution plan, synchronizing the parallel query, and terminating the query all require additional overhead. To determine whether a query uses parallelism, view the query execution plan in Management Studio. A symbol shows the merger of different parallel query execution threads.

> **NOTE**
> The default value of the `max degree of parallelism` option is 0, which tells SQL Server to use all the available processors.

In Management Studio, you can set the `max degree of parallelism` option by entering the maximum number of processors to use in a parallel plan in the Max Degree of Parallelism box on the Server Properties Advanced tab (refer to Figure 19-10 later in the chapter).

The following code sets the `max degree of parallelism` option to 4.

```
EXEC sp_configure 'show advanced options', 1;
RECONFIGURE;
GO
EXEC sp_configure 'max degree of parallelism', 4;
RECONFIGURE;
```

Best Practice

The default value of 0 for the `max degree of parallelism` option works well for SQL Servers that have up to 8 processors. The performance of the SQL Server can actually degrade if more than 8 processors are used in a parallel plan. It is recommended to change the `max degree of parallelism` option on SQL Servers that have more than 8 processors from the default value of 0 to 8 or less. For servers that have NUMA configured, the `max degree of parallelism` option should not exceed the number of CPUs that are assigned to each NUMA node.

For servers that have hyperthreading enabled, the `max degree of parallelism` option should not exceed the number of physical processors.

Although a parallel query execution plan can be much faster, there is a point at which the parallel query execution becomes inefficient and can even extend the execution time. For example, parallel queries performing small joins and aggregations on small data sets might be inefficient. Also, due to different degrees of parallelism chosen at execution time, response times for one query can be different depending on resource availability such as CPU and memory.

Many people recommend setting the max degree of parallelism option to 1 for OLTP workloads. This can be a misleading over-generalization that folks who are not familiar with the topic might blindly follow. Certain applications need the max degree of parallelism option set to 1. For example, the max degree of parallelism option is set to 1 during the configuration of BizTalk Server for the SQL Server instances that host the BizTalk Server MessageBox databases. As per BizTalk's documentation, changing this to anything other than 1 can have a significant negative impact on the BizTalk Server stored procedures and performance. With this in mind, it is recommended to check with your application vendor for any best practices for the max degree of parallelism option. If you cannot contact the vendor or it is an in-house built application, you may want to test with different values of the max degree of parallelism option to see which value gives the maximum performance gains.

If you find that setting the max degree of parallelism option to 1 or any low value works best for your workload, it is recommended to change the option back to 0 (or 8 if you have more than 8 CPUs) when you perform database maintenance tasks such as index creation, index rebuild, and checkdb because this can speed up these tasks if they can leverage more CPUs. You can change the max degree of parallelism option without the need to restart SQL Server.

Although these server-tuning options can affect performance, performance begins with the database schema, queries, and indexes. No amount of server tuning can overcome poor design and development.

A safer alternative than simply enabling the max degree of parallelism setting at the instance level, is to make use of the MAXDOP query hint. This, however, requires a deep understanding of what the query needs and how it behaves. Query hints should be used with caution and tested extensively.

You need to do extensive testing with your workloads to find the configuration that works best for your particular setup. For more information on this topic, check out Adam Machanic's blog on the matter: http://sqlblogs.com/adam_machanic/parallelism/

> **NOTE**
>
> The default value of the cost threshold for parallelism option works well for most SQL Servers. Change the default value only after performing thorough testing and considering other performance tuning opportunities.

19

However, if you insist on changing the default value of the cost threshold for parallelism option, then you can either use Management Studio or T-SQL code. In Management Studio, the cost threshold for parallelism option can be set by entering the desired value in the Cost Threshold for Parallelism box on the Server Properties Advanced tab (refer to Figure 19-10 later in the chapter).

The following code sets the cost threshold for parallelism option to 30 seconds.

```
EXEC sp_configure 'show advanced options', 1;
RECONFIGURE;
EXEC sp_configure 'cost threshold for parallelism', 30;
RECONFIGURE;
```

Security-Configuration Properties

The security-configuration properties, as shown in Table 19-4, control the security features of SQL Server.

TABLE 19-4 Security-Configuration Properties

Property	Level*	Graphic Control	Code Option
Server Authentication Mode	S	Management Studio	-
Security Audit Level	S	Management Studio	-
C2 Audit Tracing	S	Management Studio	`EXEC sp_configure 'c2 audit mode'`
Common Criteria Compliance	S		`EXEC sp_configure 'common criteria compliance enabled'`
Cross Database Ownership Chaining	S D	Management Studio	`EXEC sp_configure 'cross db ownership chaining'` `ALTER DATABASE xxx SET DB_CHAINING {ON	OFF}`

* The configuration level refers to server, database, or connection.

The same security-configuration options established during the installation are again presented in the Security tab of the Server Properties page (see Figure 19-8), so the configuration may be adjusted after installation.

Server Authentication Mode

The server authentication modes are exactly the same as presented during the SQL Server installation. Following are two server authentication modes:

- **Windows Authentication mode:** This uses Windows Authentication to validate connections.
- **SQL Server and Windows Authentication mode:** This uses both SQL and Windows Authentication to validate connections.

> **NOTE**
>
> During installation, if you select SQL Server and Windows Authentication mode, you are prompted for an sa password. When you select Windows Authentication mode, the sa account gets a random strong password, unknown to the user. When you change to SQL Server and Windows Authentication mode, the sa account is disabled. You need to enable the sa account and then change the sa password to use the account (refer to Figure 19-8).

FIGURE 19-8

Security tab of Management Studio's SQL Server Properties dialog.

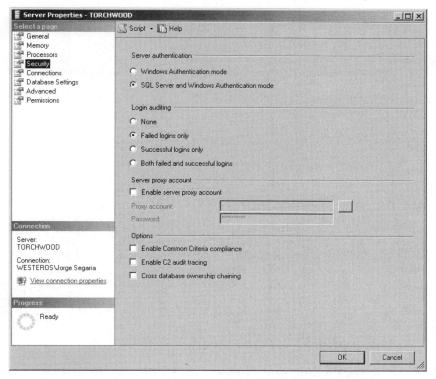

Security-Audit Level

The login auditing options configure the level of user-login auditing performed by SQL Server. You can choose one of the following four login auditing options (refer to Figure 19-8):

- None
- Failed logins only
- Successful logins only
- Both failed and successful logins

Based on the setting, SQL Server records every successful or failed user login attempt to the Windows application log and the SQL Server log. SQL Server service must be restarted for the login auditing options to take effect.

C2 Audit Tracing

C2 auditing is a U.S. government standard for monitoring database security. SQL Server supports C2 auditing. To configure SQL Server for C2 auditing, enable the c2 audit mode option. Enabling the `c2 audit mode` option configures the SQL Server to all security related events. You can find all the events by browsing through them in SQL Server Profiler.

In Management Studio, the `c2 audit mode` option can be turned on by selecting the Enable C2 Audit Tracing box in the Server Properties Security tab (refer to Figure 19-8).

In code, to turn on the `c2 audit mode` option, do the following:

```
EXEC sp_configure 'show advanced options', 1;
RECONFIGURE;
EXEC sp_configure 'c2 audit mode', 1;
RECONFIGURE;
```

SQL Server service must be restarted for the `c2 audit mode` option to take effect.

The C2 auditing mode has been superseded by Common Criteria Compliance. Common Criteria Compliance can be enabled only by code using the sp_configure system stored procedure:

```
EXEC sp_configure 'show advanced options', 1;
RECONFIGURE;
EXEC sp_configure 'common criteria compliance enabled', 1;
RECONFIGURE;
```

SQL Server service must be restarted for the `common criteria compliance enabled` option to take effect.

 In addition to enabling the option, you also must download and run a script from the Microsoft SQL Server Common Criteria website at `www.microsoft.com/sqlserver/en/us/common-criteria.aspx`.

Cross Database Ownership Chaining

By default, all database objects such as table, view, and stored procedure have owners. When an object references another object, an ownership chain is formed. When the same user owns the source object and the target object, SQL Server checks permission on the source objects and not on the target objects.

Cross-database ownership chaining occurs when the source object depends on objects in another database. Cross-database ownership chaining works in the same way as ownership chaining in a database, except that an unbroken ownership chain is based on all the object owners being mapped to the same login account. If your application uses more than one database and it calls objects from one database based on objects in another database, then cross database chaining is used. If the source object in the source database and the target object in the target database are owned by the same login, SQL Server does not check permissions on the target objects.

The `cross db ownership chaining` option enables control of the cross database ownership chaining for all databases. By default, the `cross db ownership chaining` option is turned off (0). This is good because it ensures maximum security. If you turn this option on (1), database owners and members of the `db_ddladmin` or the `db_owners` database roles can create objects owned by other users. These objects can potentially target objects in other databases. This means you must fully trust these users with data in all databases.

> **TIP**
>
> In Management Studio, you can turn on cross database ownership chaining by checking the Cross Database Ownership Chaining option on the Server Properties Security tab (refer to Figure 19-8).
>
> In code, to turn on cross database ownership chaining, do the following:
>
> ```
> EXEC sp_configure 'cross db ownership chaining', 1;
> RECONFIGURE;
> ```
>
> When you turn off (0) the `cross db ownership chaining` option , you can control cross database ownership chaining at the database level with the `SET DB_CHAINING` option of the `ALTER DATABASE` command.

 For more information about locking down SQL Server's security, refer to the chapters in Part 6, "Securing Your SQL Server."

Connection-Configuration Properties

The connection-configuration properties, as shown in Table 19-5, can set connection options in SQL Server.

TABLE 19-5 **Connection-Configuration Properties**

Property	Level*	Graphic Control	Code Option
Max Concurrent User Connections	S	Management Studio	EXEC sp_configure 'user connections'
Query Cost Governor	CS	Management Studio	EXEC sp_configure 'query governor cost limit' SET QUERY_GOVERNOR_COST_LIMIT 15
Permit Remote Server Connections	S	Management Studio	EXEC sp_configure 'remote access'

Continues

TABLE 19-5 *(continued)*

Property	Level*	Graphic Control	Code Option
Remote Login Timeout	S	Management Studio	EXEC sp_configure 'remote login timeout'
Remote Query Timeout	S	Management Studio	EXEC sp_configure 'remote query timeout'
Enforce DTC	S	Management Studio	EXEC sp_configure 'remote proc trans'
Network Packet Size	S	Management Studio	EXEC sp_configure 'network packet size'

* The configuration level refers to server, database, or connection.

The Server Properties Connections tab (refer to Figure 19-9) sets connection-level properties, including defaults, number of connections permitted, and timeout settings.

FIGURE 19-9

Connections tab of Management Studio's SQL Server Properties dialog.

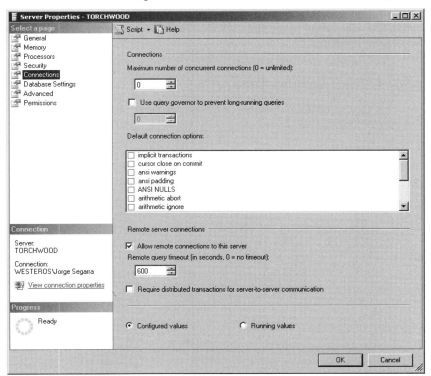

Maximum Concurrent User Connections

The user connections option can specify the maximum number of simultaneous user connections allowed on SQL Server. This option is a self-configuring option and SQL Server automatically adjusts the maximum number of user connections as needed, up to a maximum of 32,767 user connections.

> **NOTE**
>
> The default for the user connections option is zero, which means that unlimited user connections are allowed. For most SQL Servers, the default value for the user connections option works best. If you do set this option, do not set the value too high because each connection has overhead regardless of whether the connection is used. However, do not set the user connections option to a small value, such as 1 or 2, because this may prevent administrators from connecting to administer the SQL Server. However, the Dedicated Admin Connection can always connect.

The maximum concurrent user connections option should probably not be set to a given number of users because applications often open several connections to SQL Server. For example, ODBC- and ADO-based applications open a connection for every connection object in code — possibly as many as one for every form, list box, or combo box. Access tends to open at least two connections.

In Management Studio, the user connections configuration option can be set by typing a value from 0 through 32767 in the Max Number of Concurrent Connections box on the Server Properties Connections tab (refer to Figure 19-9).

The following code sets the maximum number of user connections to 10240:

```
EXEC sp_configure 'show advanced options', 1;
RECONFIGURE;
GO
EXEC sp_configure 'user connections', 10240;
RECONFIGURE;
```

SQL Server service must be restarted for the user connections option to take effect.

To determine the maximum number of simultaneous user connections allowed on a SQL Server instance using code, examine the value in the @@ MAX_CONNECTIONS global variable. The number returned is not the actual number of connections nor is it the configured value; it is the maximum number allowed:

```
SELECT @@MAX_CONNECTIONS;
```

Result:

```
-----------
32767
```

Query Governor Cost Limit

In the same way that a small gas-engine governor controls the top speed of the engine, the query governor limits the queries that SQL Server can run according to the estimated query cost on a specific hardware configuration. If a user submits a query that exceeds the limit set by the query governor, then SQL Server does not execute the query. By default, the query governor cost limit option is set to 0. This value enables all queries to execute, no matter how long they take.

> **NOTE**
> The query governor cost limit option does not abort queries with an estimated duration of less than the limit but a longer actual duration.

In Management Studio, the `query governor cost limit` configuration option can be set by typing the limit in the Use Query Governor to Prevent Long-Running Queries box on the Server Properties Connections tab (refer to Figure 19-9).

The following code sets the `query governor cost limit` to 300 seconds for the entire server:

```
EXEC sp_configure 'show advanced options', 1;
RECONFIGURE;
EXEC sp_configure 'query governor cost limit', 300;
RECONFIGURE;
```

In code, the query governor can also be changed for the current connection. The following code overrides the currently configured `query governor cost limit` value for the current connection and sets it to 15 seconds:

```
SET QUERY_GOVERNOR_COST_LIMIT 15;
```

> **TIP**
> Use the `query governor cost limit` option to stop long-running queries before they start and thereby help prevent system resources from being consumed by these long-running queries.

Remote Access

The `remote access` option enables running local stored procedures from remote servers or remote stored procedures from the local server. By default, the `remote access` option is enabled.

> **NOTE**
> The `remote access` option applies only to servers added using `sp_addserver` and is included for backward compatibility.
>
> Using this feature is not recommended because it will be removed in the next version of Microsoft SQL Server. Use the `sp_addlinkedserver` feature instead.

To disallow `remote access`, uncheck the Allow Remote Connections to This Server check box in Management Studio on the Server Properties Connections tab (refer to Figure 19-9) or set the `remote access` option to 0 in code:

```
EXEC sp_configure 'remote access', 0;
RECONFIGURE;
```

SQL Server service must be restarted for the remote access option to take effect.

Remote Login Timeout

The remote login timeout configuration option specifies the number of seconds to wait before returning from a failed attempt to connect to a remote SQL Server. The default value for remote login timeout is 20 seconds.

In Management Studio, you can set the remote login timeout option by entering the new timeout in seconds in the Remote Login Timeout box on the Server Properties Advanced tab (refer to Figure 19-10).

The following code changes the default value of 20 to 30:

```
EXEC sp_configure 'remote login timeout', 30;
RECONFIGURE;
```

NOTE

To cause an indefinite wait, you can change the value for the remote login timeout option to 0.

Remote Query Timeout

The remote query timeout option sets the number of seconds SQL Server waits on a remote query before assuming it failed and generating a timeout error. The default value of 600 seconds (10 minutes) seems sufficient for executing a remote query:

```
EXEC sp_configure 'remote query timeout', 600;
RECONFIGURE;
```

In Management Studio, you can set the remote query timeout option by entering the desired time in the Remote Query Timeout (in Seconds, 0 = No Timeout) box on the Server Properties Connections tab (refer to Figure 19-9).

Enforce DTC

When updating multiple servers within a transaction (logical unit of work), SQL Server can enforce dual-phase commits using Microsoft Distributed Transaction Coordinator.

From code, the Enforce DTC property is enabled by setting the remote proc trans option to 1:

```
EXEC sp_configure 'remote proc trans', 1;
RECONFIGURE;
```

In Management Studio, you can set the remote proc trans option by checking the Require Distributed Transactions for Server-to-Server Communication box on the Server Properties Connections tab (refer to Figure 19-10).

> **NOTE**
>
> Don't use this feature in new development work because it will likely be removed in the next version of Microsoft SQL Server. Plan to modify applications that currently use this feature.
>
> Use the `sp_addlinkedserver` feature instead.

 Transactions are explained in Chapter 47, "Managing Transactions, Locking, and Blocking."

Network-Packet Size

Packets are blocks of information sent over the network to transfer requests that results between clients and servers. You can change the network-packet size from its default of 4KB by using the `network packet size` option. However, the network-packet size should rarely need reconfiguring. Consider this property a fine-tuning tool and use it only when the data passed tends to greatly exceed the default size, such as large text or image data.

In Management Studio, you can set the `network packet size` option by entering the new size (in bytes) in the Network Packet Size box on the Server Properties Advanced tab (refer to Figure 19-10).

The following code sets the network-packet size to 2KB:

```
EXEC sp_configure 'network packet size', 2048;
RECONFIGURE;
```

> **TIP**
>
> The `sys.dm_exec_connections` dynamic management view contains information about the network-packet size (column named `net_packet_size`) used for information and data transfer.

Advanced Server-Configuration Properties

The advanced server-configuration properties, as shown in Table 19-6, enable you to set advanced SQL Server configuration options.

TABLE 19-6 Advanced Server-Configuration Properties

Property	Level*	Graphic Control	Code Option
FILESTREAM Access Level	S	Management Studio	`EXEC sp_configure 'FILESTREAM access level'`
Extensible Key Management	S	-	`EXEC sp_configure 'EKM provider enabled'`

Property	Level*	Graphic Control	Code Option
Default Full-text Language	S	Management Studio	`EXEC sp_configure 'default full-text language'`
Default Language	S	Management Studio	`EXEC sp_configure 'default language'`
Two-Digit Year Cutoff	S	Management Studio	`EXEC sp_configure 'two digit year cutoff'`
Max Text Replication Size	S	Management Studio	`EXEC sp_configure 'max text repl size'`

* The configuration level refers to server, database, or connection.

The Advanced tab of Management Studio's Server Properties page (see Figure 19-10) is used to view or modify the advanced server settings.

FIGURE 19-10

Advanced tab of Management Studio's SQL Server Properties dialog.

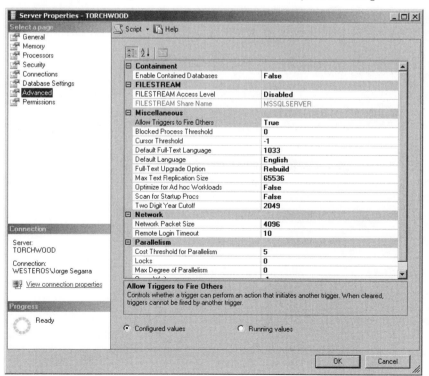

FILESTREAM Access Level

SQL Server 2008 introduced a new feature called FILESTREAM that enables you to store structured data in the database and associated unstructured (that is, BLOB) data such as text documents, images, and videos directly in the NTFS file system. By default, FILESTREAM is not enabled. Before you can start using FILESTREAM, you must enable FILESTREAM. You can enable FILESTREAM during the SQL Server 2011 installation in the Database Engine Configuration page of the setup. You can also enable the FILESTREAM feature after the installation using the SQL Server Configuration Manager as follows:

- Open SQL Server Configuration Manager from Start ⇨ Programs ⇨ Microsoft SQL Server 2012 ⇨ Configuration Tools ⇨ SQL Server Configuration Manager.

- Under SQL Server Configuration Manager, click SQL Server Services.

- Right-click the SQL Server service (on the right side) on which you want to enable FILESTREAM and select Properties.

- Click the FILESTREAM tab (see Figure 19-11) and select the Enabled FILESTREAM for Transact-SQL Access check box.

FIGURE 19-11

Enabling FILESTREAM feature using SQL Server Configuration Manager.

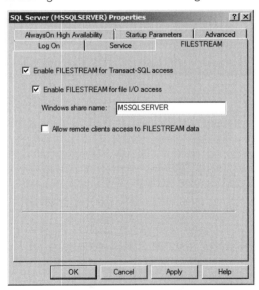

- If you want to read and write FILESTREAM data from Windows, select the Enable FILESTREAM for File I/O Access check box. Enter the name of the Windows share in which the FILESTREAM data will be stored in the Windows Share Name box.

- If you want to allow remote clients to access the FILESTREAM data stored on this share, select the Allow Remote Clients to Have Streaming Access to the FILESTREAM Data check box.
- Click Apply.

After enabling FILESTREAM during setup or by using SQL Server Configuration Manager, the next step is to configure it in SQL Server using the `FILESTREAM_access_level` configuration option. Following are the possible FILESTREAM access settings:

- **0**: Disables FILESTREAM support for this SQL Server instance
- **1**: Enables FILESTREAM for Transact-SQL access only
- **2**: Enables FILESTREAM for Transact-SQL and Win32 streaming access

The following example configures FILESTREAM for both Transact-SQL and Win32 streaming access.

```
EXEC sp_configure 'filestream_access_level', 2;
RECONFIGURE;
```

Extensible Key Management

The *Extensible Key Management (EKM)* feature in SQL Server 2012 enables third-party EKM and hardware security module vendors to register their devices in SQL Server. This capability makes it possible for DBAs to use third-party EKM products along with SQL Server's built-in encryption.

> **NOTE**
>
> The EKM feature is available only on the Enterprise, Developer, and Evaluation edition of SQL Server 2012. Trying to allow this option on other editions can result in an error. By default, the EKM feature is 0 (OFF) for all editions.

To turn the EKM feature ON in code, do the following:

```
EXEC sp_configure 'show advanced options', 1;
RECONFIGURE;
EXEC sp_configure 'EKM provider enabled', 1;
RECONFIGURE;
```

Default Full-Text Language

The default language for full-text index columns can be set using the `default full-text language` configuration option. Linguistic analysis of full-text indexed data is dependent on the language of the data.

> **NOTE**
>
> The default value for the `default full-text language` option is the language of the SQL Server instance. Also, the default value set by this option applies only when no language is indicated in the `CREATE` or `ALTER FULLTEXT INDEX` statement.

In Management Studio, you can set the `default full-text language` configuration option by specifying the local identifier (`lcid`) for the language you want, as listed in the `sys.fulltext_languages` table in the Default Full-Text Language box on the Server Properties Advanced tab (refer to Figure 19-10).

The following example sets the `default full-text language` option to US English using T-SQL code:

```
EXEC sp_configure 'show advanced options', 1;
RECONFIGURE;
EXEC sp_configure 'default full-text language', 1033;
RECONFIGURE;
```

In this case, the value of `1033` refers to US English. You need to change this value only when you need to support something other than the default system language.

 Many of the language settings in SQL Server rely on a *locale identifier* (*LCID*). You can find a list of common LCID values at `http://msdn.microsoft.com/en-us/goglobal/bb964664.aspx`.

Default Language

The default language for all newly created logins can be set in Management Studio as well as in code using the `default language` configuration option. The default language is used for messages from the server and formatting dates. It can be overridden by the `CREATE LOGIN` or `ALTER LOGIN` statements.

In Management Studio, set the `default language` configuration option by selecting the language from the Default Language drop-down list on the Server Properties Advanced tab (refer to Figure 19-10).

From code, you can set the `default language` configuration option by specifying the unique language id of the language you want, as listed in the `sys.syslanguages` table. For example, to set the default language to British English, first query the sys.syslanguages table to get the language id for British English. Then use the language id in the code:

```
EXEC sp_configure 'default language', 23;
RECONFIGURE;
```

> **NOTE**
> The language for a session can be changed during the session through the `SET LANGUAGE` statement.

Two-Digit-Year Cutoff

The two-digit-year cutoff converts a two-digit year to a four-digit year based on the values supplied. The default time span for SQL Server is 1950–2049, which represents a cutoff year of 2049. If the two-digit year falls on or after the first value (default 50), then it is interpreted as being in the twentieth century. If it falls on or before the second value (default 49), then it is interpreted as being in the twenty-first century. For example, 01/01/69 is interpreted as 01/01/1969, and 01/01/14 is interpreted as 01/01/2014.

In Management Studio, you can set the two digit year cutoff configuration option by specifying an integer that represents the cutoff year in the Two Digit Year Cutoff box in the Server Properties Advanced tab (refer to Figure 19-10).

The following code sets the two digit year cutoff to 2041:

```
EXEC sp_configure 'show advanced options', 1;
RECONFIGURE;
EXEC sp_configure 'two digit year cutoff', 2041;
RECONFIGURE;
```

Best Practice

Use four-digit date formats to avoid ambiguity with dates.

To maintain backward compatibility, leave the default setting for the two digit year cutoff configuration option.

Max Text Replication Size

By default, text or image data greater than 65536 bytes (64KB) cannot be added to a replicated column or captured column. The max text repl size option applies to transactional replication and the Change Data Capture feature. This option does not apply to snapshot and merge replication. The maximum size of 65536 bytes is configurable using the max text repl size configuration option.

In Management Studio, you can set the max text repl size configuration option by specifying maximum size in the Max Text Replication Size box in the Server Properties Advanced tab (refer to Figure 19-10).

The following code sets the max text repl size to 131072 (128KB):

```
EXEC sp_configure 'max text repl size', 131072;
RECONFIGURE;
```

 The details of replication and change data capture are discussed in Chapter 28, "Replicating Data" and Chapter 41, "Data Change Tracking and Capture," respectively.

Configuring Database Auto Options

Five database-configuration options determine the automatic behaviors of SQL Server databases (see Table 19-7). In Management Studio, they are all set in the Options tab of the Database Properties page (refer to Figure 19-2).

TABLE 19-7 **Index-Configuration Properties**

Property	Level*	Graphic Control	Code Option
Auto Close	D	Management Studio	`ALTER DATABASE <DB Name> SET auto_close`
Auto Shrink	D	Management Studio	`ALTER DATABASE <DB Name> SET auto_shrink`
Auto Create Statistics	D	Management Studio	`ALTER DATABASE <DB NAME> SET auto_create_statistics`
Auto Update Statistics	D	Management Studio	`ALTER DATABASE <DB NAME> SET auto_update_statistics`
Auto Update Statistics Asynchronously	D	Management Studio	`ALTER DATABASE <DB Name> SET auto_update_statistics_async`

* The configuration level refers to server, database, or connection.

Auto Close

Auto close directs SQL Server to release all database resources (cached data pages, compiled stored procedures, and saved query execution plans) when all users exit the database and all processes are complete. This frees memory for other databases. Although this option can slightly improve performance for other databases, reloading the database can take longer, as will recompiling the procedures and recalculating the query execution plans, after the database is again opened by a SQL Server when a user accesses the database again.

If the database is used regularly, do not enable auto close. If the database is used occasionally, then auto close might be appropriate to save memory.

> **CAUTION**
> Many front-end client applications repeatedly open and close a connection to SQL Server. Setting auto close ON in this type of environment is a sure way to kill SQL Server performance.

Use the following to set `auto close` ON for the AdventureWorks2012 sample database in code:

```
ALTER DATABASE AdventureWorks2012 SET AUTO_CLOSE ON;
```

Best Practice

Do not set `auto_close` ON for production SQL Server databases. There may be situations in which you may have hundreds or even thousands of databases with archived data that are never all used at the same time. For these situations you may benefit from having `auto_close` on for some or even all databases. By default, `auto_close` is on only for SQL Server Express Edition and is off by default for all other editions.

Auto Shrink

If the database has more than 25 percent free space, then this option causes SQL Server to perform a data and log file shrink operation. This option also causes the transaction log to shrink after it's backed up.

Performing a file shrink is a costly operation because several pages must be moved within the file. Plus, it's probable that the files have to grow again later (another costly operation), causing file fragmentation at the OS level. This option also regularly checks the status of the data pages to determine whether they can be shrunk.

 Shrinking the data and transaction log files is discussed in detail in Chapter 21, "Backup and Recovery Planning."

To set the auto shrink option off for the AdventureWorks2012 sample database in code, do the following:

```
ALTER DATABASE AdventureWorks2012 SET AUTO_SHRINK OFF;
```

Best Practice

Use of `auto_shrink` can cause severe performance issues as it can cause index fragmentation as well disk fragmentation at the operating system level. It's generally best practice that you do not have this enabled on your databases. For more information on this topic, see Paul Randal's blog: www .sqlskills.com/blogs/paul/post/Auto-shrink-e28093-turn-it-OFF!.aspx.

Auto Create Statistics

Data-distribution statistics are a key factor in how the SQL Server Query Optimizer creates query execution plans. This option directs SQL Server to automatically create statistics for any columns for which statistics could be useful. The default for this option is set to ON.

To set auto create statistics on for the AdventureWorks2012 sample database in code, do the following:

```
ALTER DATABASE AdventureWorks2012 SET AUTO_CREATE_STATISTICS ON;
```

19

Auto Update Statistics

SQL Server's cost-based query optimizer uses statistics to choose the most efficient plan for retrieving or updating data. Hence, out-of-date data-distribution statistics aren't very useful. The AUTO_UPDATE_STATISTICS database option causes statistics to be recomputed every time a certain number of rows in the table changes. The default for this option is set to on, which is best practice and works for most environments. Based on the row changes, sometimes the statistics may be updated too frequently, other times too infrequently, and sometimes automatically updating the statistics may cause a delay just when you don't want it. To avoid these situations, you can disable the AUTO_UPDATE_STATISTICS database option and schedule jobs to recompute statistics during a low traffic or maintenance window. In some environments, DBAs schedule jobs to manually compute the statistics and keep the AUTO_UPDATE_STATISTICS option on as a failsafe measure in case many more rows change than they normally do. To set the auto update statistics option on for AdventureWorks2012 sample database in code, do the following:

```
ALTER DATABASE AdventureWorks2012 SET AUTO_UPDATE_STATISTICS ON;
```

Auto Update Statistics Asynchronously

When a query triggers an AUTO_UPDATE_STATISTICS event, the query waits until the updated statistics can be used. This can cause unpredictable query response times. Starting from SQL Server 2005, there is a database option called AUTO_UPDATE_STATISTICS_ASYNC that you can enable to asynchronously update the statistics. By default, this option is off. If the AUTO_UPDATE_STATISTICS_ASYNC database option is turned on, then SQL Server performs the automatic update of statistics in the background. The query that causes the automatic statistics does not need to wait for the statistics to be updated and proceeds with the old statistics. This may result in a less-efficient query plan, but the query response times are predictable. Queries that start after the statistics are updated use those statistics.

To set the auto update statistics asynchronous option on for the AdventureWorks2012 sample database in code, do the following:

```
ALTER DATABASE AdventureWorks2012 SET AUTO_UPDATE_STATISTICS_ASYNC ON;
```

> **NOTE**
>
> The AUTO_UPDATE_STATISTICS_ASYNC database option is dependent on the AUTO_UPDATE_STATISTICS option. Therefore, you need to ensure that the AUTO_UPDATE_STATISTICS option is ON and then enable the AUTO_UPDATE_STATISTICS_ASYNC option. Like any SQL Server configuration, you need to thoroughly test this option to see if your SQL Server applications benefit from this option.

 Query execution plans rely heavily on data-distribution statistics, which is covered in more detail in Chapter 45, "Indexing Strategies."

Cursor-Configuration Properties

The cursor-configuration properties, as shown in Table 19-8, are used to control cursor behavior in SQL Server.

TABLE 19-8 **Cursor-Configuration Properties**

Property	Level*	Graphic Control	Code Option
Cursor Threshold	S	Management Studio	`EXEC sp_configure 'cursor threshold'`
Cursor Close on Commit	SDC	Management Studio	`ALTER DATABASE <DB Name> SET cursor_close_on_commit`
Cursor Default	D	Management Studio	`ALTER DATABASE <DB Name> SET cursor_default`

* The configuration level refers to server, database, or connection.

> **TIP**
> To view information about the open cursors in various databases, query the `sys.dm_exec_cursors` dynamic management view.

Cursor Threshold

The `cursor threshold` property sets the number of rows in a cursor set before the cursor keysets are asynchronously generated. The query optimizer estimates the number of rows that will be returned from the result set. If the estimated number of rows is greater than the `cursor threshold`, then the cursor is asynchronously generated; if it is synchronously generated causing a delay, the query must wait until all rows are fetched. Every cursor keyset will be asynchronously generated if the `cursor threshold` property is set to 0.

The default of -1 causes all keysets to be synchronously generated, which is okay for smaller keysets. For larger cursor keysets, though, this may be a problem.

In Management Studio, you can set the `cursor threshold` option to the wanted value in the "Cursor Threshold box on the Server Properties Advanced tab (refer to Figure 19-10).

When you work with cursors, the following code permits synchronous cursor keysets for cursors of up to 10,000 rows:

```
EXEC sp_configure 'show advanced options', 1;
RECONFIGURE;
EXEC sp_configure 'cursor threshold', 10000;
RECONFIGURE;
```

19

Cursor Close on Commit

The cursor close on commit property closes an open cursor after a transaction is committed when set to on. If it is set to off (default), then cursors remain open across transactions until a close cursor statement is issued.

The cursor close on commit option can be set from Management Studio and code at server, database, and connection level. In Management Studio, the cursor close on commit option can be turned on at the following level:

- **Server level:** Checks the Cursor Close on Commit check box on the Server properties Connections tab (refer to Figure 19-9).
- **Database level:** Selects True for the Close Cursor on Commit Enabled box on the Database Properties Options tab (refer to Figure 19-2).
- **Connection level:** To set this property for current queries, click the Query menu ⇨ Query Options ⇨ Execution ⇨ ANSI, and check the Set Cursor Close on Commit check box. To set this property for all future connections, click the Tools menu ⇨ Options ⇨ Query Execution ⇨ ANSI, and check Set Cursor Close on Commit check box

To set cursor close on commit in code, do the following:

- **Server level:** Sets the option on for the server:

```
EXEC sp_configure 'user options', 4;
RECONFIGURE;
```

- **Database level:** Sets the option on for the AdventureWorks2012 sample database:

```
ALTER DATABASE AdventureWorks2012 SET CURSOR_CLOSE_ON_COMMIT ON;
```

- **Connection level:** Sets the option on for the current connection:

```
SET CURSOR_CLOSE_ON_COMMIT ON;
```

Cursor Default

This property makes each cursor local to the object that declared it when set to local. When it is set to global (default), the scope of the cursor can be extended outside the object that created it.

In Management Studio, you can set the cursor default option to the wanted scope in the Default Cursor box on the Database Properties Options tab (refer to Figure 19-2).To set the cursor default for the AdventureWorks2012 sample database to LOCAL in code, do the following:

```
ALTER DATABASE AdventureWorks2012 SET CURSOR_DEFAULT LOCAL;
```

SQL ANSI–Configuration Properties

The SQL ANSI–configuration properties, as shown in Table 19-9, are used to set ANSI behavior in SQL Server.

TABLE 19-9   SQL ANSI–Configuration Properties

Property	Level*	Graphic Control	Code Option
ANSI Defaults	C	Management Studio	`SET ANSI_DEFAULTS`
ANSI Null Behavior	SDC	Management Studio	`ALTER DATABASE <DB Name> SET ANSI_NULL_DFLT_OFF` `SET ANSI_NULL_DFLT_ON`
ANSI Nulls	SDC	Management Studio	`ALTER DATABASE <DB Name> SET ANSI_NULLS`
ANSI Padding	SDC	Management Studio	`ALTER DATABASE <DB Name> SET ANSI_PADDING`
ANSI Warnings	SDC	Management Studio	`ALTER DATABASE <DB Name> SET ANSI_WARNINGS`
Arithmetic Abort	SDC	Management Studio	`ALTER DATABASE <DB Name> SET arithabort`
Arithmetic Ignore	SC	-	`SET ARITHIGNORE`
Numeric Round Abort	SDC	Management Studio	`ALTER DATABASE <DB Name> SET NUMERIC_ROUNDABORT{ON	OFF}`
Null Concatenation	SDC	Management Studio	`ALTER DATABASE <DB Name> SET CONCAT_NULL_YIELDS_NULL`
Use Quoted Identifier	SD	Management Studio	`ALTER DATABASE <DB Name> SET QUOTED_IDENTIFIER`

* The configuration level refers to server, database, or connection.

The connection default properties (there are several) affect the environment of batches executed within a connection. Most of the connection properties change SQL Server behavior so that it complies with the ANSI standard. Because so few SQL Server installations modify these properties, it's much safer to modify them in code at the beginning of a batch than to set them at the server or database level.

For example, T-SQL requires a `begin transaction` to start a logical unit of work. Oracle assumes a `begin transaction` is at the beginning of every batch. If you prefer to work with implicit (nonstated) transactions, then you're safer setting the implicit transaction connection property at the beginning of your batch. For these reasons, you should leave the connection properties at the default values and set them in code if needed.

The SQL ANSI-configuration settings are set at three levels: server, database, and connection, as indicated in Table 19-9. The sp_configure system stored procedure has the User Options setting that enables manipulation of serverwide ANSI settings, and it works across databases. The `ALTER DATABASE` command can set the default database setting for ANSI. Connection level settings are set with the `SET` command and override the default database setting.

In Management Studio, the ANSI settings can be enabled (ON) at the following levels:

- **Server level:** Checks the ANSI setting check box in the Server properties Connections tab (refer to Figure 19-9).
- **Database level:** Checks the ANSI setting check box in the Database Properties Options tab (refer to Figure 19-2).
- **Connection level:** Click the Query menu ⇨ Query Options ⇨ Execution ⇨ ANSI, and check the ANSI setting check box.

> **NOTE**
>
> The `sp_dboption` procedure is no longer supported in this version of SQL Server. To set these options use the `ALTER DATABASE` command.
>
> You can change the default database setting for ANSI in the model system database and then the defaults change for all future databases.
>
> The database setting for ANSI overwrites the server setting, and the connection setting overwrites the server and database setting.

ANSI Defaults

SQL Server provides the SET ANSI_DEFAULTS command to manage a group of SQL Server settings. When SET ANSI_DEFAULTS is enabled, it enables the following settings (explained later in this section):

- SET ANSI_NULLS
- SET ANSI_NULL_DFLT_ON
- SET ANSI_PADDING
- SET ANSI_WARNINGS
- SET CURSOR_CLOSE_ON_COMMIT
- SET IMPLICIT_TRANSACTIONS
- SET QUOTED_IDENTIFIER

To set ANSI_DEFAULTS in code, do the following:

SET ANSI_DEFAULTS ON; ANSI Null Default

The ANSI_NULL_DEFAULT setting controls the default nullability. This setting is used when a NULL or NOT_NULL is not explicitly specified when creating a table. The default database setting for ANSI_NULL_DEFAULT is OFF.

To set the ANSI_NULL_DEFAULT option on for the AdventureWorks2012 sample database in code, do the following:

```
ALTER DATABASE AdventureWorks2012 SET ANSI_NULL_DEFAULT ON;
```

If the `ANSI_NULL_DEFAULT` option is not set at the database level, you can also set the nullability of new columns using the `SET ANSI_NULL_DFLT_ON` and `SET ANSI_NULL_DFLT_OFF` commands. `SET ANSI_NULL_DFLT_ON` can enable null values at the connection level:

```
SET ANSI_NULL_DFLT_ON ON;
```

`SET ANSI_NULL_DFLT_OFF` can be set to not enable null values at the connection level:

```
SET ANSI_NULL_DFLT_OFF ON;
```

To enable `ANSI_NULL_DFLT_ON` at the server level in code, do the following:

```
EXEC sp_configure 'user options', 1024;
RECONFIGURE;
```

To enable `ANSI_NULL_DFLT_OFF` at the server level in code, do the following:

```
EXEC sp_configure 'user options', 2048;
RECONFIGURE;
```

> **NOTE**
> Both `SET ANSI_NULL_DFLT_ON` and `SET ANSI_NULL_DFLT_OFF` commands cannot be set to ON at the same time. Either one can be ON and the other can be OFF or both can be OFF.

ANSI NULLs

The `ANSI_NULLS` connection setting can determine comparison evaluations. When set to ON, all comparisons to a null value evaluate to UNKNOWN. When set to OFF, the comparison to a null value evaluates to `true` if both values are NULL. The default database setting for `ANSI_NULLS` is OFF.

To enable `ANSI_NULLS` in code at the connection level, do the following:

```
SET ANSI_NULLS ON;
```

If `SET ANSI_NULLS` is not specified, then the settings of `ANSI_NULLS` of the current database apply. To enable `ANSI_NULLS` for the AdventureWorks2012 sample database in code, do the following:

```
ALTER DATABASE AdventureWorks2012 SET ANSI_NULLS ON;
```

To enable `ANSI_NULLS` at the server level in code, do the following:

```
EXEC sp_configure 'user options', 32;
RECONFIGURE;
```

> **NOTE**
> The `ANSI_NULLS` option is deprecated and will always be ON in a future version of SQL Server.

ANSI Padding

The `ANSI_PADDING` connection setting affects only newly created columns. When set to ON, data stored in char, varchar, binary, and varbinary data types retain any padded zeros to the left of variable binary numbers, and any padded spaces to the right or left of variable-length characters. When set to OFF, all leading and trailing blanks and zeros are trimmed. The default database setting for `ANSI_PADDING` is OFF.

To enable `ANSI_PADDING` in code at connection level, do the following:

```
SET ANSI_PADDING ON;
```

If `SET ANSI_PADDING` is not specified, then the settings of `ANSI_PADDING` of the current database applies. To enable `ANSI_PADDING` for the AdventureWorks2012 sample database in code, do the following:

```
ALTER DATABASE AdventureWorks2012 SET ANSI_PADDING ON;
```

To enable `ANSI_PADDING` at the server level in code, do the following:

```
EXEC sp_configure 'user options', 16;
RECONFIGURE;
```

> **NOTE**
>
> `ANSI_PADDING` option is deprecated and will always be ON in a future version of SQL Server.

ANSI Warnings

The `ANSI_WARNINGS` connection setting can handle ANSI errors and warnings such as arithmetic overflow, divide-by-zero, and null values appearing in aggregate functions. The default database setting for `ANSI_WARNINGS` is OFF. When this setting is OFF, no warnings are raised when null values appear in aggregate functions, and null values are returned when divide-by-zero occurs and overflow errors occur. When the setting is ON, query is aborted and errors are raised when arithmetic overflow errors and divide-by-zero occur.

To set `ANSI_WARNINGS` in code at connection level, do the following:

```
SET ANSI_WARNINGS ON;
```

If `SET ANSI_WARNINGS` is not specified, then the settings of `ANSI_WARNINGS` of the current database apply. To enable `ANSI_WARNINGS` for the AdventureWorks2012 sample database in code, do the following:

```
ALTER DATABASE AdventureWorks2012 SET ANSI_WARNINGS ON;
```

To enable `ANSI_WARNINGS` at the server level in code, do the following:

```
EXEC sp_configure 'user options', 8;
RECONFIGURE;
```

Arithmetic Abort

The ARITHABORT connection setting can handle query termination if an arithmetic error such as data overflow or divide-by-zero occurs. The default database setting for ARITHABORT is OFF.

What exactly is terminated also depends on the ANSI_WARNINGS setting. Table 19-10 explains the behavior based on the values of ANSI_WARNINGS and ARITHABORT.

TABLE 19-10 **ANSI_WARNINGS and ARITHABORT Behavior**

ARITHABORT	ANSI_WARNINGS	Behavior
ON	ON	Query is aborted.
ON	OFF	Batch is aborted or transaction is rolled back.
OFF	ON	Query is aborted.
OFF	OFF	No warning is raised and null is returned.

To set ARITHABORT in code at connection level, do the following:

```
SET ARITHABORT ON;
```

If ARITHABORT is not specified, then the settings of the current database apply. To enable ARITHABORT for the AdventureWorks2012 sample database in code, do the following:

```
ALTER DATABASE AdventureWorks2012 SET ARITHABORT ON;
```

To enable ARITHABORT at the server level in code, do the following:

```
EXEC sp_configure 'user options', 64;
RECONFIGURE;
```

Arithmetic Ignore

The ARITHIGNORE connection setting controls whether an error message is returned from arithmetic overflow or divide-by-zero errors. To abort the query, you need to use the ARITHABORT setting. Both ARITHABORT and ARITHIGNORE can be set to ON but ARITHABORT takes precedence over ARITHIGNORE. To set ARITHIGNORE in code, do the following:

```
SET ARITHIGNORE ON;
```

To enable ARITHIGNORE at the server level in code, do the following:

```
EXEC sp_configure 'user options', 128;
RECONFIGURE;
```

19

Numeric Round Abort

The NUMERIC_ROUNDABORT connection setting controls the behavior of numeric decimal-precision-rounding errors in process. When NUMERIC_ROUNDABORT is set to ON and ARITHABORT is set to ON, an error is generated, and no result is returned if the numeric-decimal precision is lost in an expression value. Loss of numeric-decimal precision can occur when a value with fixed precision is stored in a column or variable with less precision. If ARITHABORT is set to OFF and NUMERIC_ROUNDABORT is set to ON, warning is returned and null is returned. When NUMERIC_ROUNDABORT is set to OFF, the process proceeds without errors or warnings, and the result is rounded down to the precision of the object in which the number is stored. The default database setting for NUMERIC_ROUNDABORT is OFF.

To set NUMERIC_ROUNDABORT in code at the connection level, do the following:

```
SET NUMERIC_ROUNDABORT ON;
```

If NUMERIC_ROUNDABORT is not specified, then the settings of the current database apply. To enable NUMERIC_ROUNDABORT for the AdventureWorks2012 sample database in code, do the following:

```
ALTER DATABASE AdventureWorks2012 SET NUMERIC_ROUNDABORT ON;
```

To enable NUMERIC_ROUNDABORT at the server level in code, do the following:

```
EXEC sp_configure 'user options', 8192;
RECONFIGURE;
```

Concatenation Null Yields Null

The CONCAT_NULL_YIELDS_NULL setting controls the behavior of the result when concatenating a string with a null. When set to ON, any string concatenated with a null results in a null. When set to OFF, any string concatenated with a null results in the original string, ignoring the null. The default database setting for CONCAT_NULL_YIELDS_NULL is OFF.

To set CONCAT_NULL_YIELDS_NULL in code at the connection level, do the following:

```
SET CONCAT_NULL_YIELDS_NULL ON;
```

If CONCAT_NULL_YIELDS_NULL is not specified, then the settings of the current database apply. To enable CONCAT_NULL_YIELDS_NULL for the AdventureWorks2012 sample database in code, do the following:

```
ALTER DATABASE AdventureWorks2012 SET CONCAT_NULL_YIELDS_NULL ON;
```

To enable CONCAT_NULL_YIELDS_NULL at the server level in code, do the following:

```
EXEC sp_configure 'user options', 4096;
RECONFIGURE;
```

Use Quoted Identifier

The QUOTED_IDENTIFIER setting enables you to refer to an identifier, such as a column name, by enclosing it within double quotes. When set to ON, identifiers can be delimited by double quotation marks. When set to OFF, identifiers cannot be placed in quotation marks and must not be keywords. The default database setting for QUOTED_IDENTIFIER is OFF. To change the value to ON, use the following code.

To set QUOTED_IDENTIFIER in code at the connection level, do the following:

```
SET QUOTED_IDENTIFIER ON;
```

If QUOTED_IDENTIFIER is not specified, then the settings of the current database apply. To enable QUOTED_IDENTIFIER for the AdventureWorks2012 sample database in code, do the following:

```
ALTER DATABASE AdventureWorks2012 SET QUOTED_IDENTIFIER ON;
```

To enable QUOTED_IDENTIFIER at the server level in code, do the following:

```
EXEC sp_configure 'user options', 256;
RECONFIGURE;
```

> **NOTE**
> When dealing with indexes on computed columns and indexed views, four of these defaults (ANSI_NULLS, ANSI_PADDING, ANSI_WARNINGS, and QUOTED_IDENTIFIER) must be set to ON.

Trigger Configuration Properties

The trigger configuration properties, as shown in Table 19-11, control trigger behavior in SQL Server.

TABLE 19-11 **Trigger Configuration Properties**

Property	Level*	Graphic Control	Code Option
Allow Nested Triggers	S	Management Studio	EXEC sp_configure 'nested triggers'
Recursive Triggers	D	Management Studio	ALTER DATABASE <DB Name> SET recursive_triggers

* The configuration level refers to server, database, or connection.

Trigger behavior can be set at both the server and database levels.

Nested Triggers

A trigger is a small stored procedure executed on an `insert`, `update`, or `delete` operation on a table. Triggers are nested when a trigger performs an action that initiates another trigger, which can initiate another trigger, and so on. Triggers can be nested up to 32 levels. You can use the `nested triggers` server configuration option to control whether `AFTER` trigger can be nested triggers.

In Management Studio, you can set the `nested trigger` option by selecting True (default) or False in the Allow Triggers to Fire Others option on the Server Properties Advanced tab (refer to Figure 19-10).

To turn `nested triggers` `OFF` in code, do the following:

```
EXEC sp_configure 'nested triggers', 0;
RECONFIGURE;
```

> **NOTE**
> `INSTEAD OF` triggers can be nested regardless of the setting of this option.

Recursive Triggers

If the code in the trigger inserts, updates, or deletes the same table again, then the trigger causes itself to be executed again. Recursion can also occur if the code in the trigger fires and performs an action that causes a trigger on another table to fire. This second trigger performs an action that causes an update to occur on the original table, which causes the original trigger to fire again. Recursive behavior is enabled or disabled by the recursive trigger database option. By default, the `RECURSIVE_TRIGGERS` option is set to `off`.

In Management Studio, the recursive triggers option can be enabled by selecting True in the Recursive Triggers Enabled option in the Database Properties Options tab (refer to Figure 19-2).

To set the recursive triggers option on in the AdventureWorks2012 sample database in T-SQL code, do the following:

```
ALTER DATABASE AdventureWorks2012 SET RECURSIVE_TRIGGERS ON;
```

 The server property `nested triggers` and the database property `recursive triggers` are often confused with each other. Refer to Chapter 36, "Creating Triggers," for a complete explanation, including coverage of how triggers can call other triggers and how these properties control trigger behavior.

Database-State-Configuration Properties

The database-state-configuration properties, as shown in Table 19-12, are available in SQL Server. These configurations are mostly used when a DBA performs maintenance on the database.

TABLE 19-12 **Database-State-Configuration Properties**

Property	Level*	Graphic Control	Code Option
Database OffLine	D	Management Studio	ALTER DATABASE <DB Name> SET OFFLINE
Database OnLine	D	Management Studio	ALTER DATABASE <DB Name> SET ONLINE
EMERGENCY	D	-	ALTER DATABASE <DB Name> SET EMERGENCY
Read-Only	D	Management Studio	ALTER DATABASE <DB Name> SET READ_ONLY
Restricted Access — Members of db_owner, dbcreator, or sysadmin	D	Management Studio	ALTER DATABASE <DB Name> SET RESTRICTED_USER
Restricted Access — Single user	D	Management Studio	ALTER DATABASE <DB Name> SET SINGLE_USER
Multi User	D	Management Studio	ALTER DATABASE <DB Name> SET MULTI_USER
Compatibility Level	D	Management Studio	ALTER DATABASE <DB NAME> SET COMPATIBILITY_LEVEL

* The configuration level refers to server, database, or connection.

You can set the state of the database with the ALTER DATABASE command. The sp_dboption command has been removed in this version of SQL Server and can no longer be used.

Database-Access Level

The database-access-configuration options set the state of the database. When the database is offline, no access to the database is enabled.

To set the AdventureWorks2012 sample database to an OFFLINE state in code, do the following:

```
ALTER DATABASE AdventureWorks2012 SET OFFLINE;
```

To revert this change and make the AdventureWorks2012 database online and available in code, execute the following command:

```
ALTER DATABASE AdventureWorks2012 SET ONLINE;
```

19

You may encounter a situation in which the database is inaccessible and you do not have a backup. To access the database no matter what state things are, members of the sysadmin role can put the database in EMERGENCY mode. When in EMERGENCY mode, the database is in read-only mode and is accessible only by members of the sysadmin role. To put the AdventureWorks2012 sample database in EMERGENCY mode in code, execute the following command:

```
ALTER DATABASE AdventureWorks2012 SET EMERGENCY;
```

The READ_ONLY database-state settings enable only selects from the database. READ_ONLY cannot take effect if any users are in the database. To reset the database to a normal read-and-write state, the READ_WRITE database setting is used.

To set the AdventureWorks2012 sample database to a READ_ONLY state in code, do the following:

```
ALTER DATABASE AdventureWorks2012 SET READ_ONLY;
```

The restricted access database-state settings are also available. The three restricted access levels are single_user, restricted_user, and multi_user states. These settings control which users are allowed to access the database. The SINGLE_USER setting is appropriate when you do database maintenance. The RESTRICTED_USER setting enables database access only to users in the db_owner, dbcreator, and sysadmin roles. The MULTI_USER setting is used to set the database in the normal operating state.

To set the AdventureWorks2012 sample database to SINGLE_USER access in code, do the following:

```
ALTER DATABASE AdventureWorks2012 SET SINGLE_USER;
```

To revert this change and set the AdventureWorks2012 database access to MULTI_USER access in code, do the following:

```
ALTER DATABASE AdventureWorks2012 SET MULTI_USER;
```

Compatibility Level

In SQL Server, the database-compatibility level can be set to 90 (SQL Server 2005), 100 (SQL Server 2011) or 110 (SQL Server 2011). When a database is upgraded to SQL Server 2012 from any earlier version of SQL Server, the database retains its existing compatibility level. If the original compatibility level of the database is 80 (SQL Server 2000) or earlier, then the database automatically is set to the server's lowest compatibility mode, which is 90 (SQL Server 2005). Setting the database-compatibility level to a level lower than 110 may be necessary if you upgrade the Database Engine and still need to maintain the behavior of an earlier version of SQL Server.

> **NOTE**
> The compatibility level option does not provide full backward compatibility. It is mainly intended to enable new reserved words to be used in tables, and retain some (limited) changed behavior. Refer to SQL Server Books Online for a full overview.

To set the compatibility level of the AdventureWorks2012 sample database to 110 (SQL Server 2012) in code, do the following:

```
ALTER DATABASE AdventureWorks2012 SET COMPATIBILITY_LEVEL = 110;
```

> **TIP**
>
> To view the compatibility level of SQL Server, query the compatibility_level column in the `sys.databases` catalog view.

Recovery-Configuration Properties

The recovery-configuration properties, as shown in Table 19-13, are used to set recovery options in SQL Server.

TABLE 19-13 **Recovery-Configuration Properties**

Property	Level*	Graphic Control	Code Option
Recovery Model	D	Management Studio	ALTER DATABASE <DB Name> SET RECOVERY
PAGE VERIFY	D	Management Studio	ALTER DATABASE <DB Name> SET PAGE_VERIFY
Media Retention	S	Management Studio	EXEC sp_configure 'media retention'
Backup Compression	S	Management Studio	EXEC sp_configure 'backup compression default'
Recovery Interval	S	Management Studio	EXEC sp_configure 'recovery interval'

* The configuration level refers to server, database, or connection.

The recovery options determine how SQL Server handles transactions and the transaction log, and how the transaction log is backed up.

Recovery Model

SQL Server 2012 uses a recovery model to configure several settings that work together to control how the transaction log behaves regarding file growth and recovery possibilities. The three recovery model options are as follows:

- **Simple:** The transaction log contains only transactions that are not yet written to the data file. This option does not provide up-to-the-minute recovery.

- **Bulk-Logged:** The transaction log contains all DML operations, but bulk insert operations are only marked, not logged.
- **Full:** The transaction log contains all changes to the data file. This option provides the greatest recovery potential.

 Chapter 21 focuses on recovery planning and operations in detail.

You can set the recovery option in code with the ALTER DATABASE SET RECOVERY command.

In Management Studio, you can change the recovery model by selecting Simple, Bulk-logged, or Full in the Recovery Model drop-down list in the Database Properties Options tab (refer to Figure 19-2).

To set the recovery model AdventureWorks2012 sample database to Bulk-Logged in code, do the following:

```
ALTER DATABASE AdventureWorks2012 SET RECOVERY BULK_LOGGED;
```

Page Verify

Even though SQL Server works with 8KB data pages, the operating system I/O writes in 512-byte sectors. Therefore, a failure might occur in the middle of a data-page write, resulting in only some of the 512-byte sectors to be written to disk. This is known as a torn page. You can tell SQL Server to tell you if a torn page occurs by using the PAGE_VERIFY database option.

The PAGE_VERIFY database option can be set to one of the following values:

- CHECKSUM: This is the default level for PAGE_VERIFY. With this option, SQL Server calculates a checksum over the contents of each page and stores the value in the page header when a page is written to disk. When the page is read from disk, the checksum is recalculated and compared to the original checksum value.

- TORN_PAGE_DETECTION: This option instructs SQL Server to toggle a bit on each 512-byte sector with each write operation. If all the sectors were written to disk, then all the detection bits should be identical. If, on recovery, any of the bits are different, then SQL Server can detect the torn-page condition and mark the database as suspect.

- NONE: Database page writes do not generate a CHECKSUM or TORN_PAGE_ DETECTION value.

To change the PAGE_VERIFY option, you can either use Management Studio or T-SQL-code. In Management Studio, you can change PAGE_VERIFY by selecting CHECKSUM, TORN_ PAGE_DETECTION, or NULL in the Page Verify box on the Database Properties Options tab (refer to Figure 19-02).

Using T-SQL-code, you can use the following command to set the PAGE_VERIFY option for the AdventureWorks2012 sample database to TORN_PAGE_DETECTION:

```
ALTER DATABASE AdventureWorks2012 SET PAGE_VERIFY TORN_PAGE_DETECTION;
```

> **TIP**
>
> To view the page verification level of a database, query the page_verify_option_desc column in the sys.databases catalog view.

Media Retention

The media retention option sets the number of days to retain each backup set. The default value for media retention is 0 days. This option helps protect backups from being overwritten until the specified number of days has elapsed.

In Management Studio, you can set the media retention server configuration option by entering the number of days to retain each backup media in the Default Backup Media Retention (in Days) box on the Server Properties Database Settings tab (see Figure 19-12).

FIGURE 19-12

The Database Settings tab of Management Studio's Server Properties.

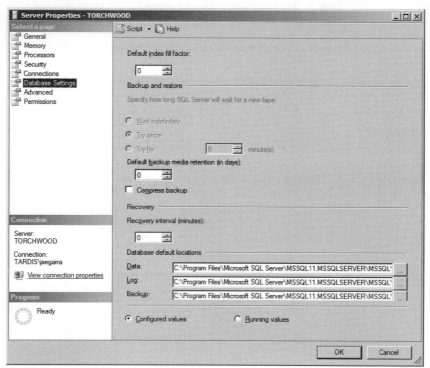

To set media retention to 10 days in code, do the following:

```
EXEC sp_configure 'show advanced options', 1;
RECONFIGURE;
EXEC sp_configure 'media retention', 10;
RECONFIGURE;
```

Backup Compression

Backup compression is a feature introduced in the SQL Server 2008 Enterprise Edition. Although initially introduced as an Enterprise Edition feature, starting with SQL Server 2008 R2 backup compression became supported by the Standard and all higher editions.

In Management Studio, to compress new backups by default set backup compression default by checking the Compress backup check box on the Server Properties Database Settings tab (refer to Figure 19-12).

To set backup compression default in code, do the following:

```
EXEC sp_configure 'backup compression default', 1
RECONFIGURE
```

> **NOTE**
> After installation, new backups are uncompressed by default. Backup compression can greatly reduce the backup sizes and backup/restore times. But this improvement is not free. Backup compression significantly increases the CPU usage that may impact other operations on the server. Hence, you should test this feature thoroughly to understand the pros and cons before implementing in your production SQL Server.

 For more information about backup compression, refer to the Chapter 21.

Recovery Interval

The recovery interval server configuration option controls when SQL Server issues checkpoints for each database. A checkpoint flushes dirty pages from the buffer cache of the database to disk. Checkpoints are done when SQL Server estimates that the recovery time will be longer than the specified recovery interval. The estimated duration applies only to the REDO (roll forward) phase of the recovery and not to the UNDO (roll backward) phase. The default value for this option is 0, which implies that this option is automatically configured by SQL Server.

Best Practice

Leave the recovery interval option to the default value of 0. If you do change the recovery interval, then be sure to test it thoroughly and evaluate all other performance tuning opportunities first.

If you insist on changing the recovery interval option, you can either use Management Studio or T-SQL-code. In Management Studio, you can set the `recovery interval` server configuration option by entering the maximum number of minutes per database to recover databases in the Recovery Interval (Minutes) box on the Server Properties Database Settings tab (refer to Figure 19-12).

Using T-SQL-code, the following command sets the `recovery interval` server configuration option to 5 minutes:

```
EXEC sp_configure 'show advanced options', '1';
RECONFIGURE;
EXEC sp_configure 'recovery interval', 5;
RECONFIGURE;
```

Summary

Configuration options are important for compatibility, performance tuning, and controlling the connection. The configuration options are set at the server, database, and connection level. Most of the options can be set from Management Studio and all can be configured with code.

Continuing with SQL Server administration tasks, the next chapter focuses on managing policies.

19

Policy Based Management

With the release of SQL Server 2008, database administrators everywhere were handed an absolute gift of power in the form of the Policy-Based Management feature. Do you think that statement is a little over the top? Consider this: In the past, IT departments everywhere spent a great deal of time and money creating official data policies and procedures. After going through all that time and effort, those policies were then placed into a document somewhere and more than likely ignored or forgotten ... that is until an auditor arrives and starts asking those questions everyone loves to answer.

Policy-Based Management (PBM) is a feature that enables those paper policies to finally be put into action with ease. With a few simple clicks, you can check the recovery model of all your databases. Want to see if a particular feature is enabled across your enterprise? You can create a policy for that. Would you like to enforce naming standards on new items created in your databases, such as stored procedures? You can do that! PBM is a powerful and flexible tool that should be part of every DBA's Toolbox.

So, with that introduction, what is PBM?

Traditionally, applying and enforcing server and database settings and configurations across multiple SQL Servers has been a mash-up of log books, checklists, jobs, DDL triggers, scripts, and good ideas on the white board that never actually were implemented.

PBM, changes all that by making policies *declarative* — during its early life, PBM was actually called Declarative Management Framework.

SQL is a declarative language, meaning that SQL commands don't state how the query should be solved. SQL describes the question, and the query optimizer figures out how to solve the query.

Similarly, PBM abstracts the management intent, meaning the policies, from the procedural implementation. As the DBA, you define what the system should be and then let SQL Server figure out how to achieve it. Policy checking can be automated, with the results logged, and in some cases even actively stop an action from occurring.

Defining Policies

Policies may be defined interactively in Management Studio, loaded in from XML, or defined with either T-SQL code or PowerShell with DMO.

What's New with PBM in SQL 2012

Policy-Based Management as a whole hasn't changed much since SQL Server 2008 R2, but there are 8 new facets available to you. The new facets for availability groups are the basis of the flexible failover polices you can configure for AlwaysOn Availability Groups, which you can read more about in Chapter 27 "Database Mirroring." The following list calls out the new facets in SQL Server 2012 and what properties they contain.

- **Availability Database**: Properties of databases in an availability group including their name, status and synchronization states
- **Availability Group**: Availability Group properties, such as health check timeouts, failure condition level, and name of the replica holding the role of primary in the group
- **Availability Group State**: State of the Availability Group
- **Availability Replica**: Properties of the Availability Replica object including operational state, quorum vote count, connection state and much more
- **Search Property List**: Properties of the Search Property Lists, used in Semantic Search
- **Sequence**: Properties of sequence objects
- **Database Replica State**: Properties of the physical database replicas participating in an availability group
- **Server Role**: Properties of the server role object

There are three types of PBM objects. In a sense they function as three levels, with Policies built from Conditions, which are built out of facets:

- **84 Facets**: Defined only by Microsoft, are collections of properties that represent a management dimension. For example, the Table facet has 34 specific properties that can be checked about a table. Examples of common facets include logins, a server, a linked server, or an index. Inside each facet are anywhere from a handful to dozens of properties, which can be referred to by a condition. (For a full list of the facets, see Table 20-1 later in this chapter.)

- **Conditions:** Defined by the DBA, based on one facet, are the anted states, or values, for facet properties. An example of a condition is to check that a database's Recovery mode must be set to Simple mode. Conditions can contain one or more clauses in them.

- **Policies:** Defined by the DBA, based on a single condition, declare how and upon what object (server, database, and so on) the condition should be enforced.

The UI for PBM is in Management Studio's Object Explorer under the Management node, as shown in Figure 20-1. For many other objects within Management Studio, you can access PBM features related to that object by selecting Facets from the object's context menu.

FIGURE 20-1

You can also evaluate policies directly against an object, Under the Management node PBM's policies, conditions, and facets in Object Explorer.

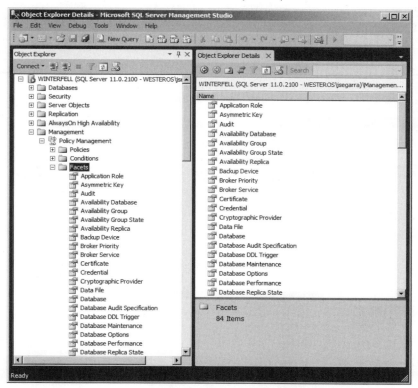

Management Facets

A brilliant-cut diamond has 58 facets. PBM has 84 management facets.. The easiest way to see all the facets is to open the Facets node under Management ⇨ Policy Management (refer to Figure 20-1).

20

In database design terminology, there's a many-to-many relationship between SQL Server object types and properties. For example, database facet properties apply only to databases, but the term facet can apply to 84 different types of SQL Server objects ranging from `ApplicationRoles` to `XmlSchemaCollections`, including databases.

The Facet collection is the associative table between SQL Server object types and properties.

You can open a facet by double-clicking the facet or by selecting the Properties option in its context menu. The Facet Properties dialog, as shown in Figure 20-2, has three pages:

- **General**: Describes the property, lists the type of SQL Server objects to which the facet properties may apply, and lists the facet's properties.
- **Dependent Policies**: Lists the policies that use any dependent conditions of the facet.
- **Dependent Conditions**: Lists the conditions that use any property from the facet.

FIGURE 20-2

The Facet Properties' General page lists of all the facet properties and their descriptions. In this case, it's showing the properties for the Database facet.

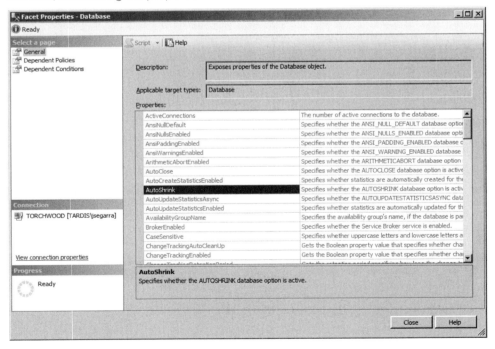

The last two pages are not without purpose. There may potentially be a large number of conditions and policies; the dependent policies and conditions pages are useful for quickly tracking down a condition or policy.

It's worth spending some time browsing the facets and exploring the properties of each facet available from the facet context menu.

The Object Explorer ➪ Management ➪ Policy Management ➪ Facets context menu also includes New Condition and New Policy. The only difference between these context menu items and New Condition under Conditions or New Policy under Policies is that when the new condition or policy is opened from the facet node, it preselects the facet in the drop-down selection box. This fact is worth noting because PBM is context-sensitive; meaning if you were to try and evaluate a policy on an object from a context menu on a specific object, such as a table, you will be presented only with the option to evaluate policies relating to that particular facet.

There's not much action just looking at facets because their purpose is to be evaluated by conditions. But you need to be intimately familiar with the breadth of facets and their properties to realize the types of policies that may be declared and enforced by SQL Server.

Because the facet collection is actually a many-to-many relationship between properties and object types, it makes sense that there should be a way to see all the facets and properties that apply to any given object. Indeed, every object in Object Explorer that can have PBM applied has a Facet menu option in its context menu. Open the View Facets dialog (shown in Figure 20-3) and it presents a drop-down box to select a facet from the list of facets that applies to the object, and a list of applicable properties. If the object is an example of what you want, the View Facets dialog can even export the current state to a new policy. Very cool.

Conditions

Conditions are the second step in the chain and provide the logical connection between facet properties and policies. Most of the key policy design decisions are made while creating conditions.

To begin building a new condition, use either the Management ➪ Policy Management ➪ Conditions context menu and choose New Condition or Object Explorer Management ➪ Policy Management ➪ Facets ➪ Database context menu.

You can open an existing condition by double-clicking the condition or by using the Property command in its context menu. A condition may have multiple expressions, but each condition is based on only one facet, so every property in all the expressions in a condition must belong to the same facet.

Condition expressions use facet properties in boolean expressions that can be evaluated as true or false. The expression consists of a facet property, a comparison operator (such as =, !=, in, not in, like, not like), and a value.

20

FIGURE 20-3

The View Facets dialog, opened from any object's context menu, presents a browsable UI of every facet and property that can apply to that type of object, and even can export a new policy to match the current object's settings.

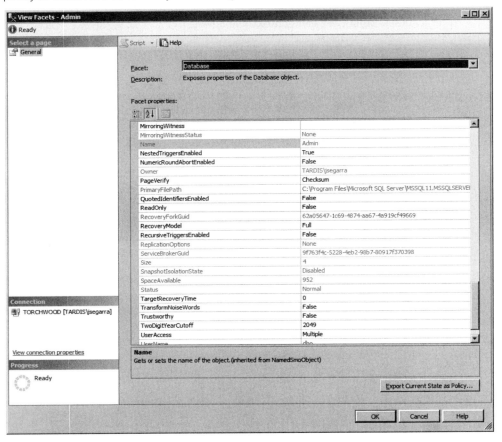

To construct a condition that tests a database's autoshrink property, the expression would use the database facet and the @AutoShrink property, as shown in Figure 20-4. In this case the full expression is:

```
@AutoShrink = False
```

Best Practice

Think of condition expressions as positive statements. Instead of thinking, "No database should be set to autoshrink," think "All databases should have autoshrink set to False."

FIGURE 20-4

This condition includes an expression that tests the Database Facet's @AutoShrink. The condition evaluates as True if @AutoShrink = False.

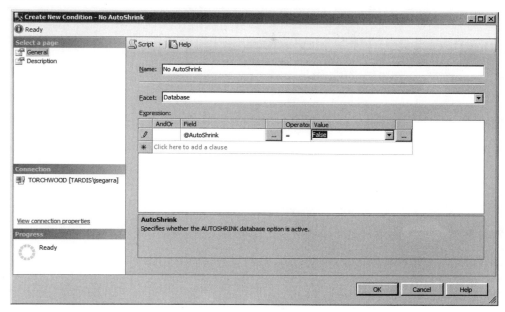

The ellipsis button under Field and Value opens the Advanced Edit dialog box, as shown in Figure 20-5. The Cell value is typically a property, function, or a literal value; however, it is possible to build more advanced expressions that reference DMV or system tables.

A condition may include multiple expressions, in which case the AndOr column defines how they are evaluated.

Best Practice

In the entire policy design scheme, the only place that enables multiples is designing multiple expressions within a single condition. Therefore, if every expression should indeed be tested, encapsulating multiple expressions in a single condition can reduce the number of conditions and policies.

The open condition's description page may be used to record a description of the condition, and the dependent policies page lists the policies based on the condition. After the condition is created, it may be enforced by one or more policies. To programmatically view the created conditions, query the dbo.syspolicy_conditions view in the MSDB database:

20

```
select * from msdb.dbo.syspolicy_conditions
```

FIGURE 20-5

Use the Advanced Edit dialog to create each side of the expression. In this case it shows the left side of the AutoShrink expression.

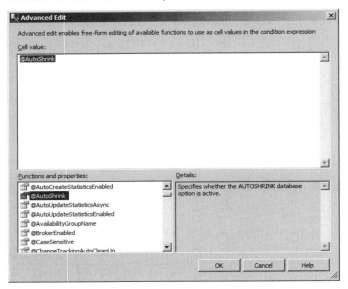

> **NOTE**
>
> To build advanced conditions that check factors other than the built-in facets, look into the `executeSQL` and `executeWMI` functions.

Creating Policies

If the facet property is the fact and the condition the brain, the policy is the muscle. Policies define how and where the condition is applied and enforced.

You can create a new policy using the New Policy menu item in Object Explorer's Management ⇨ Policy Management ⇨ Policies and then selecting the New Policy option from the context menu. Alternatively, you can go to the File menu, browse to the New submenu, and then select Policy from the list. The Create New Policy dialog, as shown in Figure 20-6, has a general page and a description page.

FIGURE 20-6

Viewing a Policy. This policy enforces the AutoShrink condition for every database on demand.

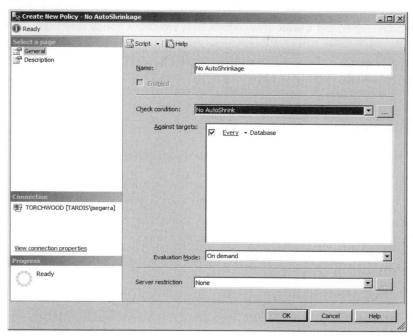

You can open an existing policy by double-clicking the policy or by using the Property command in its context menu.

The general page has four key selections. The first is the condition; a policy may check only a single condition. The ellipsis opens the condition.

The second selection, targets, defines which objects will be tested. The options vary depending on the type of object the facets apply to.

Evaluation mode is the third key selection. There are four Evaluation modes for a policy:

- **On Demand:** The policy is evaluated only manually. There's no schedule, automatic testing, or enforcement.
- **On Schedule:** The policy is evaluated and any violations are logged but not corrected.

- **On Change — Log Only:** The policy is evaluated when the facet is changed, and violations are logged.

- **On Change — Prevent:** The policy is evaluated when the facet is changed, and violations are rolled back. This action rolls back a violation only *after* the action has occurred; meaning a large transaction that violates a policy may take a long time to roll back changes.

Every facet may be set to On Demand or On Schedule, but On Change is limited. PBM relies on DDL eventing to do CheckOnChange, and not all objects support DDL eventing. The following query reports which Execution modes are available for which facets:

```
SELECT name as Facet,
    Max(CASE WHEN execution_mode & 0 = 0 Then 1 else 0 End)
        as 'On Demand',
    Max(CASE WHEN execution_mode & 4 = 4 Then 1 else 0 End)
        as 'On Schedule',
    Max(CASE WHEN execution_mode & 2 = 2 Then 1 else 0 End)
        as 'On Change Log Only',
    Max(CASE WHEN execution_mode & 1 = 1 Then 1 else 0 End)
        as 'On Change Prevent'
FROM msdb.dbo.syspolicy_management_facets
GROUP BY name
ORDER BY name
```

Result is shown in Table 20-1:

TABLE 20-1 **Facet Listing**

Facet	On Demand	On Schedule	On Change Log Only	On Change Prevent
ApplicationRole	1	1	1	1
AsymmetricKey	1	1	1	1
Audit	1	1	0	0
BackupDevice	1	1	0	0
BrokerPriority	1	1	0	0
BrokerService	1	1	0	0
Certificate	1	1	0	0
Computer	1	1	0	0
Credential	1	1	0	0
CryptographicProvider	1	1	0	0
Database	1	1	0	0
DatabaseAuditSpecification	1	1	0	0

Facet	On Demand	On Schedule	On Change Log Only	On Change Prevent
DatabaseDdlTrigger	1	1	0	0
DatabaseRole	1	1	1	1
DataFile	1	1	0	0
Default	1	1	0	0
DeployedDac	1	1	0	0
Endpoint	1	1	1	1
FileGroup	1	1	0	0
FullTextCatalog	1	1	0	0
FullTextIndex	1	1	0	0
FullTextStopList	1	1	0	0
IDatabaseMaintenanceFacet	1	1	0	0
IDatabaseOptions	1	1	1	0
IDatabasePerformanceFacet	1	1	0	0
IDatabaseSecurityFacet	1	1	0	0
IDataFilePerformanceFacet	1	1	0	0
ILogFilePerformanceFacet	1	1	0	0
ILoginOptions	1	1	1	1
IMultipartNameFacet	1	1	1	1
INameFacet	1	1	0	0
Index	1	1	0	0
IServerAuditFacet	1	1	0	0
IServerConfigurationFacet	1	1	1	0
IServerInformation	1	1	0	0
IServerPerformanceFacet	1	1	0	0
IServerProtocolSettingsFacet	1	1	0	0
IServerSecurityFacet	1	1	0	0
IServerSelectionFacet	1	0	0	0
IServerSettings	1	1	0	0
IServerSetupFacet	1	1	0	0
ISurfaceAreaConfigurationForAnalysisServer	1	0	0	0
ISurfaceAreaConfigurationForReportingServices	1	0	0	0
ISurfaceAreaFacet	1	1	1	0
ITableOptions	1	1	1	1

Continues

20

TABLE 20-1 *(continued)*

Facet	On Demand	On Schedule	On Change Log Only	On Change Prevent
IUserOptions	1	1	1	1
IViewOptions	1	1	1	1
LinkedServer	1	1	0	0
LogFile	1	1	0	0
Login	1	1	0	0
MessageType	1	1	0	0
PartitionFunction	1	1	0	0
PartitionScheme	1	1	0	0
PlanGuide	1	1	0	0
Processor	1	1	0	0
RemoteServiceBinding	1	1	0	0
ResourceGovernor	1	1	0	0
ResourcePool	1	1	1	1
Rule	1	1	0	0
Schema	1	1	1	1
SearchPropertyList	1	1	1	0
Sequence	1	1	1	1
Server	1	1	0	0
ServerAuditSpecification	1	1	0	0
ServerDdlTrigger	1	1	0	0
ServerRole	1	1	1	1
ServiceContract	1	1	0	0
ServiceQueue	1	1	0	0
ServiceRoute	1	1	0	0
Statistic	1	1	0	0
StoredProcedure	1	1	1	1
SymmetricKey	1	1	0	0
Synonym	1	1	0	0
Table	1	1	0	0
Trigger	1	1	0	0
User	1	1	0	0
UserDefinedAggregate	1	1	0	0

Facet	On Demand	On Schedule	On Change Log Only	On Change Prevent
UserDefinedDataType	1	1	0	0
UserDefinedFunction	1	1	1	1
UserDefinedTableType	1	1	0	0
UserDefinedType	1	1	0	0
Utility	1	1	0	0
View	1	1	0	0
Volume	1	1	0	0
WorkloadGroup	1	1	1	1
XmlSchemaCollection	1	1	0	0

The fourth key selection on the general page is Server Restriction. You can use this option to define the target servers based on criteria.

> **CAUTION**
> PBM generates DDL triggers that enforce the policy and roll back DDL operations that don't comply with the policy. Don't manually delete or edit these DDL triggers. Also, servers that use PBM must have nested triggers enabled.
> PBM also generates agent jobs for policy automation. They shouldn't be deleted either.

To programmatically view the created policies, query the `dbo.syspolicy_policies` view in the MSDB database:

```
select * from msdb.dbo.syspolicy_policies
```

You can export policies to XML and import them using the Policy context menu.

Evaluating Policies

Of course, policies would be purely academic if they never actually executed and evaluated any objects. Policies may be set for On Schedule, On Demand, On Change, or Log Only. Policies must be enabled using their context menu. On demand policies may not be enabled.

For policies set to On Demand, the policies may be evaluated for any object using the object's context menu ➪ Policies ➪ Evaluate. This opens the Evaluate Polices dialog for the object, as shown in Figure 20-7.

The outcome of the policy evaluations is displayed in the Evaluation Results page, as seen in Figure 20-8.

You can see the current state of any object for all policies regardless of their Execution mode by right-clicking on a policy and seeing the Enabled or Disabled options in the context menu.

Within the View Policies dialog, you can see the history for any policy evaluation for the object using the log viewer by clicking the view history link in the policy row. You can also see the policy evaluation in the Windows event log and the SQL Server event log.

To view a history of policy execution query use the following:

```
SELECT * FROM msdb.dbo.syspolicy_policy_execution_history_details;
```

To view exception query use the following:

```
SELECT * FROM msdb.dbo.syspolicy_policy_execution_history;
```

PBM health is also well integrated into Management Studio's object listings. The Object Explorer Details page has an optional column to display the Policy Health of any object.

FIGURE 20-7

All the policies that can be run on-demand for an object can be selected and evaluated using the Evaluate Polices dialog.

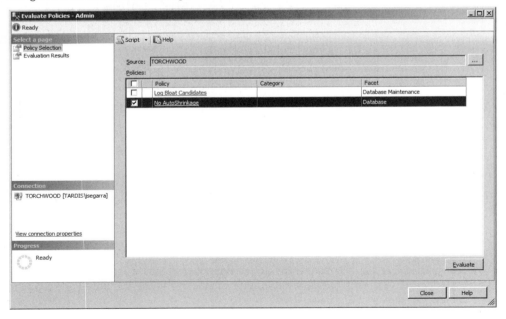

FIGURE 20-8

Here the Aesop database passes the No AutoShrinkage policy and declares to be in good health.

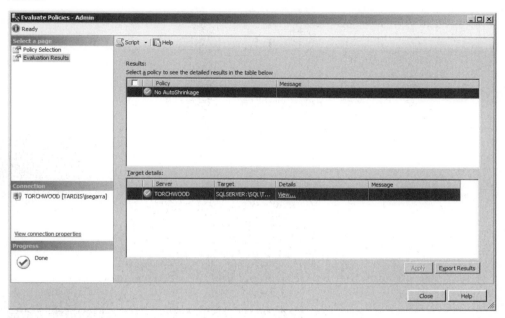

> **NOTE**
> PBM requires SQL Server Agent running on the central monitoring server. Be sure the SQL Server Agent service is set to start automatically and that its service account password won't expire.

Summary

Policies — if you're an operational DBA, they can change your world. IT database operations are more consistent, and your life should become smoother. Indeed, Policy-Based Management (PBM) is a completely new animal, and it will take some time to build up a set of good conditions and policies, but when it's all put together, it will have been worth it.

Chapter 21, "Backup and Recovery Planning," continues the thread of database administration with the nuts and bolts or backup and restore.

20

Backup and Recovery Planning

T he foundation for this book, the Information Architecture Principle (introduced in Chapter 2, "Data Architecture"), puts into words the reason why there must be a solid recovery plan:

Information is an organizational asset, and, according to its value and scope, must be organized, inventoried, secured, and made readily available in a usable format for daily operations and analysis by individuals, groups, and processes, both today and in the future.

It goes without writing that for information to be "readily available...both today and in the future," regardless of hardware failure, catastrophes, or accidental deletion, there must be a plan B.

Obviously, this is an imperfect world and bad things do happen to good people. Because you're bothering to read this chapter, it's true that performing backups isn't exciting. In some jobs excitement means trouble, and this is one of them. To a good DBA, being prepared for the worst means having a sound recovery plan that has been tested more than once.

Consistent with the flexibility found in other areas of SQL Server, you can perform a backup in multiple ways, each suited to a different purpose. SQL Server offers three recovery models, which help organize the backup options and simplify database administration.

This chapter discusses the concepts that support the recovery effort, which entails both backup and restoration. It seems foolish to study backup without also learning about how restoration completes the recovery.

Recovery planning is not an isolated topic. Transactional integrity is deeply involved in the theory behind a sound recovery plan. After you determine the recovery strategy, it's often implemented within maintenance plan (Chapter 22). Because recovery is actually a factor of availability, the high availability of log shipping (Chapter 26), database mirroring (Chapter 27), and failover clustering (Chapter 29) is also a factor in recovery planning.

Although backups tend to be boring, restores tend to occur when people are excited. For this reason, it makes sense to be as familiar with restoration as with backup. Without restoring a backup, there is no way to tell if the backup is good and can be used when it is needed.

What's New in SQL Server Recovery?

SQL Server 2012 offers an exciting, new high-availability and disaster recovery feature called AlwaysOn Availability Groups. AlwaysOn enables you to configure one or more databases into groups called Availability Groups. Each group enables you to fail over a set a user databases together. This feature is covered more in-depth in Chapter 27 "Database Mirroring."

Recovery Concepts

The concept of database recovery is based on the D in the transactional-integrity ACID properties — transactional *durability*. Durability means that a transaction, when committed, regardless of hardware failure, must be persistent.

SQL Server accomplishes transactional durability with a write-ahead transaction log. Every transaction is written to the transaction log prior to being written to the data file. This provides a few benefits to the recovery plan:

- The transaction log ensures that every transaction can be recovered up to the last moment before the server stopped.
- The transaction log permits backups while transactions are processed.
- The transaction log reduces the impact of a hardware failure because the transaction log and the data file may be placed on different disk subsystems.

The strategy of a recovery plan should be based on the organization's tolerance level, or *pain level*, for lost transactions. Recovery-plan tactics involve choosing among the various backup options, generating a backup schedule, and off-site storage.

SQL Server backup and recovery are flexible, offering three recovery models from which to choose. The transaction log can be configured, based on your recovery needs, according to one of the following recovery models:

- **Simple**: No transaction log backups.
- **Bulk-logged**: The bulk-logged recovery model minimally logs bulk operations, although fully logging other transactions.
- **Full**: All transactions are logged.

In addition, SQL Server offers the following backup options:

- **Full**: Complete backup of all data.

- **Differential**: Backup of all data pages modified since the last full backup.
- **Partial**: Backup of primary filegroup, every read/write filegroup, and any optionally specified read-only files.
- **Transaction log**: Backup of all transactions in the log.
- **File or filegroup**: Backup of all the data in the file or filegroup.
- **File differential**: Backup of all data pages modified since the last file or filegroup backup.
- **Copy-only**: Backup all the data without affecting the overall backup and restore procedures for the database. In other words this allows you to take a full backup of the database without breaking the existing backup chain.

> **NOTE**
> Backing up the database may not be the only critical backup you must perform. If the database-security scheme relies on SQL Server authentication, backing up the database users is important as well. In SQL Server 2012 another important feature, called Contained Databases, makes this user account management much easier.

SQL Server backups are flexible and can handle any backup-to-file ratio. A single backup instance can be spread across several backup files, creating a *backup set*. Conversely, a single backup set can contain multiple backup instances.

Restoration always begins with a full backup. Differential and transaction log backups then restore the transaction that occurred after the full backup.

Recovery Models

The recovery model configures SQL Server database settings to accomplish the type of recovery required for the database, as shown in Table 21-1. The key differences among the recovery models involve how the transaction log behaves and which data is logged.

TABLE 21-1   SQL Server Recovery Models

Recovery Model	Description	Transaction Atomicity	Transaction Durability	Bulk-Copy Operations (Select Into and Bulk Insert)
Simple	Transaction log is continuously truncated on checkpoints.	Yes	No, can restore only to the last full or differential backup.	Minimally logged — high performance

Continues

TABLE 21-1 *(continued)*

Recovery Model	Description	Transaction Atomicity	Transaction Durability	Bulk-Copy Operations (Select Into and Bulk Insert)
Bulk-Logged	Bulked operations are minimally logged, and all other transactions are fully logged. Minimal logging logs only the information required to recover the transaction but does not allow point-in-time recovery.	Yes	Maybe, can restore only to the last full or differential backup, or to the last trans-action-log backup if no bulk-copy operations have been performed.	Minimally logged — high performance
Full	All transactions are logged and stored until trans-action-log backup.	Yes	Yes, can restore up to the point of recovery.	Slower than simple or bulk-logged

Although the durability of the transaction is configurable, the transaction log is still used as a write-ahead transaction log to ensure that each transaction is atomic. In case of system failure, SQL uses the transaction log to roll back any uncommitted transactions and to complete any committed transactions.

Simple Recovery Model

The simple recovery model is suitable for databases that require that each transaction be atomic but not necessarily durable. The simple recovery model directs SQL Server to truncate, or empty, the transaction log on checkpoints. The transaction log keeps a transaction until it is confirmed in the data file, but after that point the space may be reused by another transaction in a round-robin style. This is the reason why a simple recovery model does not support a transaction log backup.

A simple recovery model has the benefit of keeping the transaction log small, at the cost of potentially losing all transactions since the last full or differential backup.

A recovery plan based on a simple recovery model might include performing full backups once a week and differential backups every weeknight, as shown in Figure 21-1. The full backup copies the entire database, and the differential backup copies all changes that have been made since the last full backup.

FIGURE 21-1

A typical recovery plan using the simple recovery model includes only full and differential backups.

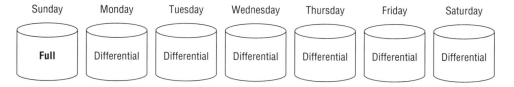

Simple Recovery Model
Sample Backup Plan

Sunday	Monday	Tuesday	Wednesday	Thursday	Friday	Saturday
Full	Differential	Differential	Differential	Differential	Differential	Differential

When restoring from a simple recovery plan:

1. Restore the most recent full backup.
2. Restore the most recent (optional) single differential backup.

Best Practice

Simple recovery is mostly used for test and development databases or databases containing mostly read-only data. Simple mode can, and often is, used for databases which you don't necessarily want or need to log large transactions such as a data warehouse. Simple recovery should not be used where loss of data since the last full or differential backup is unacceptable. In these cases, full recovery model is recommended. Full recovery model is also a requirement for Database Mirroring and Log Shipping. The bottom line is: Know your data, and plan your recovery plan accordingly with what the business can accept.

The Full Recovery Model

The full recovery model offers the most robust recovery plan. Under this model all transactions, including bulk-logged operations, are fully logged in the transaction log. Even system functions such as index creation are fully logged. The primary benefit of this model is that every committed transaction in the database can be restored right up to the point when failure occurred.

Best Practice

Use full recovery model for production user databases where data loss since last full or differential backup is unacceptable. Although it can run on a single drive system, the transaction log should be located on a fault-tolerant disk subsystem, physically separate from the data files, to ensure a high level of transactional durability.

The trade-off for this high level of transactional integrity is a certain amount of performance:

- Bulk-logged and select-into operations will be slower. If the database doesn't import data using these methods, this is a moot point.

- Depending on the database activities, the transaction log may be huge. You can control this by performing regularly scheduled transaction log backups. Also, if copious drive space is available, this too is a moot point.

- Backing up and restoring the transaction log can take longer than it does with the other recovery models. However, in a crisis, restoring all the data is likely more important than quickly restoring partial data.

The full recovery model can use all types of database backups. Figure 21-2 shows a typical backup schedule.

FIGURE 21-2

A sample recovery plan using the full recovery model, using full, differential, and transaction-log backups.

**Full Recovery Model
Sample Backup Plan**

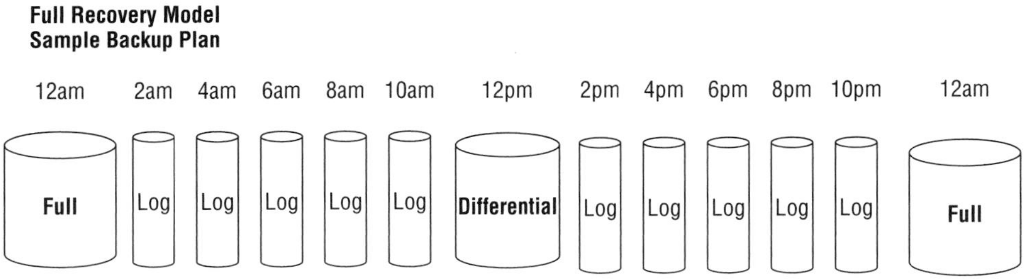

A sample full-recovery backup plan typically does a full database backup once or twice a week and differential backups every day or every other night. The transaction log is backed up throughout the day, from as little as two times a day to as often as every 15 minutes. Or you could do a daily full backup, with a differential backup every 6 hours and transaction log backups every 2 hours in between. The frequency of the transaction log backup is based around the maximum amount of acceptable data loss. For example, perform a transaction log backup every 15 minutes if you can afford to lose up to 15 minutes of data. You can mix and match options that make the most sense for your databases, your environment, and most importantly your resources (i.e. storage available for backup purposes).

To restore from the full-recovery model, do the following:

1. Perform a special kind of transaction log backup called a tail-log backup. This captures all the log records since the last transaction log backup and places the database in a restoring state.

> **NOTE**
>
> If the disk subsystem containing the transaction log is lost, the database is marked suspect by SQL Server, and it is not possible to back up the current transaction log. In this case, the best recovery option is to restore to the last transaction-log backup. Other reasons for a database being marked suspect would be that the database file itself has been removed or renamed.

2. Restore the most recent full backup.

3. Restore the most recent single differential backup, if one has been made since the last full backup.

4. Restore, in sequence, all the transaction-log backups made since the time of the last full or differential backup. If the last backup were a full backup, then restoring it is sufficient. If the last backup were a differential backup, you need to restore the most recent full backup before restoring the most recent differential.

The Management Studio restore form (discussed in the section "Performing the Restore with Management Studio" later in this chapter) automatically helps you choose the correct set of backups, so it's not as complicated as it sounds.

Bulk-Logged Recovery Model

The bulk-logged recovery model is similar to the full recovery model except that the following operations are minimally logged:

- Bulk import operations (BCP, BULK INSERT, and INSERT ... SELECT * FROM OPENROWSET (BULK...))
- SELECT INTO operations
- WRITETEXT and UPDATETEXT BLOB operations
- CREATE INDEX (including indexed views)
- ALTER INDEX REBUILD or DBCC DBREINDEX operations
- DROP INDEX

Because this recovery model minimally logs these operations, they run fast. The transaction log marks only that the operations took place and tracks the *extents* (a group of eight data pages) affected by the bulk-logged operation. When the transaction log is backed up, the extents are copied to the transaction log in place of the bulk-logged marker.

The trade-off for bulk-logged operation performance is that the bulk-logged operation is not treated as a transaction. Although the transaction log itself stays small, copying all affected extents to the transaction-log backup can make the log-backup file large.

Because bulk-logged operations are minimally logged, if a failure should occur after the bulk-logged operation but before the transaction log is backed up, the bulk-logged operation is lost, and the restore must be made from the last transaction log. Therefore, if the database uses the bulk-logged recovery model, every bulk-logged operation should be immediately followed by a transaction-log backup.

This model is useful only when the database sees a large number of bulk-logged operations, and if it's important to increase their performance. If the database performs adequately during bulk-logged operations in the full recovery model, bypass the bulk-logged recovery model.

> **NOTE**
>
> A simple recovery model also minimally logs bulk-copy operations.

Using this setting is essentially the same as setting the `Select Into/Bulkcopy` database option to `true`.

Best Practice

You should minimally use a bulk-logged recovery model because you lose the ability to do point-in-time recovery to any point covered by a transaction log backup that contains even a single minimally logged operation. The best practice for production user databases is to use a full recovery model, take a transaction log backup before performing bulk operations, switch to a bulk-logged model, perform the bulk operations, and then immediately switch back to the full recovery model and take a transaction log backup. This allows point-in-time recovery and fully protects the data.

Setting the Recovery Model

The model system database's recovery model is applied to any newly created database. The full recovery model is the default for the Standard and Enterprise Editions. The Personal and Desktop editions use the simple recovery model as their default, but you can change the default by setting the recovery model for the model system database.

Using Management Studio, you can easily set the recovery model on the Options tab of the Database Properties dialog box. Select the database and right-click to get to the Database Properties dialog.

In code, the recovery model is set with the ALTER DATABASE DDL command:

```
ALTER DATABASE DatabaseName SET Recovery Option;
```

The valid recovery options are FULL, BULK_LOGGED, and SIMPLE. The following code sets the AdventureWorks2012 sample database to the full recovery model:

```
USE AdventureWorks2012;
ALTER DATABASE AdventureWorks2012 SET Recovery FULL;
```

You should explicitly set the recovery model in the code that creates the database.

TIP
You can determine the current recovery model for every database from the following query using the sys.databases catalog view:

```
SELECT name, recovery_model_desc
 FROM sys.databases;
```

Modifying Recovery Models

Although a production user database is typically set to a full recovery model, there's nothing to prevent you from switching between recovery models during an operation to optimize performance and suit the specific needs of the moment.

It's perfectly valid to run during the day with the full recovery model for transaction durability and then to switch to bulk-logged during data imports in the evening.

During recovery it's the full, differential, and transaction-log backups that count. The recovery operation doesn't care how they were made.

Because the simple recovery model does not permanently log the transactions, care must be taken in switching to or from the simple recovery model:

- If you switch to simple, the transaction log should be backed up prior to the switch.
- If you switch from simple, a full database backup should be performed immediately following the switch.
- Schedule regular transaction log backups and update your recovery plans.

Backing Up the Database

The actual process of performing a backup presents as many options as the underlying concepts present.

Backup Destination

A backup may copy the data to one of two possible destinations:

- **Disk subsystem:** You can perform a backup either to a local disk (preferably not the same disk subsystem as the database files) or to another server's disk drive by using the Universal Naming Convention (UNC). The SQL Server service account must have write privileges to the remote drive/share to save the backup file.

Best Practice

You should back up the databases to a local disk (not the same disk where databases are stored) and then copy the backup files to tape or DVD (for small databases) using the organization's preferred IT backup method. This method is the fastest for SQL Server, and it enables the IT shop to continue using a familiar single-tape backup-software technique.

- **Tape:** SQL Server can back up directly to most tape-backup devices.

NOTE

Several companies offer a third-party backup for SQL Server. Although you may find third-party backup useful, it is a good idea to become familiar with SQL Server's built-in recovery methods before making the decision to use it.

A disk- or tape-backup file is not limited to a single backup event. The file may contain multiple backups and multiple types of backups.

Backup Rotation

If the backup file is copied to tape, then *media retention* or *rotation*, and the off-site media-storage location, become important.

A common technique is to rotate a set of five tapes for the weekly backups and another set of six tapes for the remaining daily backups. The weekly tapes would be labeled Sunday1, Sunday2, and so on, and the daily tapes would be labeled Monday, Tuesday, Wednesday, Thursday, Friday, and Saturday.

Palindromes also represent a great method for rotating backup tapes. A *palindrome* is a word, phrase, or number that's the same backward or forward, such as "kayak" or "drab as a fool, aloof as a bard."

Using four tapes labeled A through D, a backup rotation might be ABCDCBA ABCDCBA....

Alternatively, you can implement the palindrome method so that each letter represents a larger interval, such as A for daily, B for weekly, C for monthly, and D for quarterly.

Rotating backup tapes off site is an important aspect of recovery planning. Ideally, a contract should support an off-site recovery site complete with server and workstations.

Performing Backup with Management Studio

The first backup must be a full database backup to begin the backup chain. You can perform a database backup from Management Studio, selecting the database to be backed up. From the database context menu, or from the database Summary Page, select Tasks ⇨ Back Up to open the Back Up Database form, as shown in Figure 21-3.

FIGURE 21-3

The General page of the Back Up Database form.

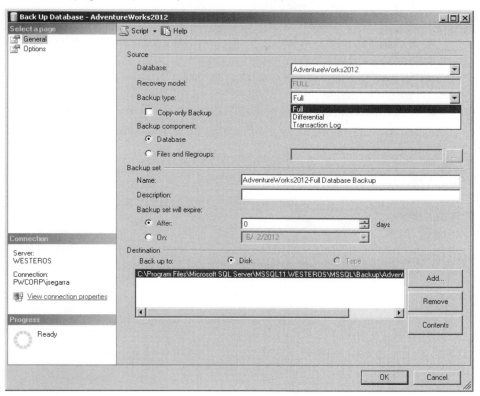

The backup source is configured in the General page:

- **Database:** The database to be backed up. By default this is the current database in Management Studio.

- **Backup Type:** The type of backup — Full, Differential, or Transaction Log. If the database is set to the simple recovery model, the transaction log will not be available. For full or differential backups, the whole database or selected files and filegroups can be backed up.

- **Copy Only Backup:** Enables you to copy only the backup. This backs up all the data without breaking the existing backup chain. Although this backup type was first introduced in SQL Server 2005, Management Studio in SQL Server 2005 did not support it.

- **Backup Component:** The database component to be backed up — Database or File and Filegroups. If the backup type selected is Transaction Log, the backup component is grayed out. Database indicates that the full database is backed up. File and Filegroups indicates that the specified files and filegroups are backed up.

The rest of the Back Up Database form specifies the destination:

- **Name:** The required name of the backup.

- **Description:** Optional additional information about the backup.

- **Backup Set Will Expire:** SQL Server prevents another backup from overwriting this backup until the expiration date.

- **Destination:** Sets the destination tape file or disk file. If the current destination is incorrect, delete it and add the correct destination.

- **Contents:** Displays the backups already in the selected destinations.

Figure 21-4 shows the Options page of the Back Up Database form.

FIGURE 21-4

The Options page of the Back Up Database form.

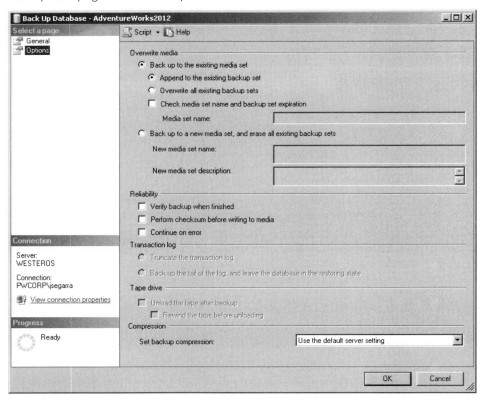

The Options page presents the following options:

- **Append to the Existing Backup Set or Overwrite All Existing Backup Sets**: Determines whether the current backup will be added to the backup file or whether the backup media should be initialized and a new series of backups placed in them.

- **Check Media Set Name and Backup Set Expiration**: Verifies the name and expiration date for the backup.

- **Verify Backup When Finished**: This verifies that the backup is complete and the file is readable. This option does not compare the data in the backup with the data in the database, nor does it verify the integrity of the backup.

- **Perform Checksum Before Writing to Media**: This verifies that the data read from the database is consistent with any checksum or torn-page detection on the database. It also calculates a checksum of the entire backup and saves it in the backup. This can help ensure that the database being backed up does not have any corruption due to the disk subsystem.

- **Continue on Error**: Enables backup to continue even after it encounters one or more errors.

- **Unload the Tape After Backup**: Directs the tape to eject, which helps prevent other backups from overwriting the backup file.

- **Rewind the Tape Before Unloading**: This is enabled only if you unload the tape after backup is selected. This rewinds the tape before ejecting it.

- **Truncate the Transaction Log**: Backs up the transaction log and truncates the inactive transactions to free log space. This is the default option for the Transaction Log backup. This option is available only when the Transaction Log is selected for Backup Type on the General page.

- **Back up the Tail of the Log, and Leave the Database in the Restoring State**: Backs up the transaction log that has not yet been backed up. This option is equivalent to using NO_TRUNCATE or NORECOVERY in the BACKUP statement. This option is available only when the Transaction Log is selected for Backup Type on the General page.

- **Set Backup Compression**: Enables you to choose the default server-level backup compression setting or ignore the server-level default and compress the backup or do not compress the backup. At installation, the default behavior is no backup compression. You can change this default by setting the default server-level backup compression setting in Management Studio by checking the Compress Backup check box in the Database Settings tab of Server Properties.

Backing Up the Database with Code

The BACKUP command offers a few more options than Management Studio, and using the BACKUP command directly is useful for assembling SQL Server Agent jobs by hand, rather than with the Maintenance Plan Back Up Database Task.

Without all the options and frills, the most basic BACKUP command is as follows:

```
BACKUP DATABASE Databasename
   TO DISK = 'file location'
   WITH
     NAME = 'backup name';
```

The following command backs up the AdventureWorks2012 database to a disk file and names the backup AdventureWorks2012Backup:

```
BACKUP DATABASE AdventureWorks2012
   TO DISK = 'e:\AdventureWorks2012Backup.bak'
   WITH
     NAME = 'AdventureWorks2012Backup';
```

Result:

```
Processed 17944 pages for database 'AdventureWorks2012', file
 'AdventureWorks2012_Data' on file 1.
Processed 2 pages for database 'AdventureWorks2012', file
 'AdventureWorks2012_Log' on file 1.
BACKUP DATABASE successfully processed 17946 pages in 7.954 seconds
 (17.625 MB/sec).
```

NOTE

In SQL Server 2012, the new Always On feature enables you to perform backups against availability replicas in the availability group as well. For more information on this, see Chapter 27, "Database Mirroring."

The backup command has a few important options that deserve to be mentioned first:

- **Backing up to a network share:** In the TO DISK option, you can use a network share as a target. Although this is an option, you must ensure that the SQL Server service account has proper rights on the target file share; otherwise you get an access denied error.

  ```
  TO DISK = ' \\FILESERVER\SQLbackups\AdventureWorks2012Backup.bak'
  ```

- **Tape (Backup To:):** To backup to tape instead of disk, use the TO TAPE option and specify the tape-drive location:

  ```
  TO TAPE = '\\.\TAPE0'
  ```

NOTE

Avoid using the Tape option because this feature will be removed in the future release of SQL Server.

- Differential: Causes the backup command to perform a differential backup instead of a full database backup. The following command performs a differential backup:

```
BACKUP DATABASE AdventureWorks2012
TO DISK = 'e:\AdventureWorks2012Backup.bak'
WITH
DIFFERENTIAL,
NAME = 'AdventureWorks2012Backup';
```

- To back up a file or filegroup, list it after the database name. This technique can help organize backups. For example, for backup purposes, you can design your database to place static tables in one filegroup and active tables in the primary filegroup.

- COMPRESSION/NO_COMPRESSION: Overrides the server-level default backup compression. COMPRESSION enables backup compression and performs checksums to detect media corruptions.

- CHECKSUM/NO_CHECKSUM: Identical to the Perform Checksum Before Writing to Media option within Management Studio.

- STOP_ON_ERROR/CONTINUE_AFTER_ERROR: Identical to Continue on Error option within Management Studio.

The backup command has numerous additional options:

- DESCRIPTION: Identical to the Description field within Management Studio.

- EXPIREDATE: Identical to Management Studio; prevents the backup from being overwritten before the expiration date.

- RETAINDAYS: The number of days, as an integer, before SQL Server overwrites the backup.

- STATS = *percentage*: Tells SQL Server to report the progress of the backup in the percentage increment specified; the default increment is 10 percent. This option is useful particularly while troubleshooting a failed backup. By using this option, it gives an idea when the backup is failing. Also, for huge databases this gives an idea of the percentage of backup completed and the amount remaining.

- BLOCKSIZE: Sets the physical block size in bytes. The default is 65536 bytes for tape devices and 512 otherwise. This option is usually not required because backup automatically selects the correct block size of the device. If a backup to disk will later be copied to a CD/RW, try a block size of 2048.

- MEDIANAME: Specifies the name of the media volume. This option serves as a safety check: If the backup is added to the media, the name must match.

- MEDIADESCRIPTION: Writes an optional media description.

- MediaPassword: Creates an optional media password that applies to the entire medium (disk file or tape). The first time the medium is created, the password can be set. If the password is specified when the medium is created, it must be specified every subsequent time the backup medium is accessed to add another backup or to restore.

> **NOTE**
>
> Avoid using the `MediaPassword` option because this feature will be removed in the future release of SQL Server.

- **INIT/NOINIT**: Initializes the tape or disk file, thus overwriting all existing backup sets in the medium. SQL Server can prevent initialization if any of the backups in the medium have not expired or still have the number of retaining days. `NOINIT` is the default.
- **NOSKIP/SKIP**: This option "skips" the backup-name and backup-date checking that normally prevents overwriting backups. `NOSKIP` is the default.
- **NOFORMAT/FORMAT**: `FORMAT` writes a new media header on media volumes used for backup and overwrites the existing backup sets; thereby the existing contents of the volume become unusable. `NOFORMAT` (default behavior) preserves the existing media header and backup sets. `FORMAT` automatically includes `SKIP` and `INIT`.

The last options apply only when backing up to tape:

- **REWIND/NOREWIND**: `REWIND` directs SQL Server to rewind the tape. The default is to `REWIND`.
- **UNLOAD/LOAD**: `UNLOAD` automatically rewinds and unloads the tape. This is the default until the user session specifies load.
- **RESTART**: This option has no effect. This is there for compatibility with previous versions of SQL Server.

Verifying the Backup with Code

Management Studio's backup includes an option to verify the backup, and the T-SQL `Backup` command does not. Management Studio actually calls the T-SQL `RESTORE VERIFYONLY` command after the backup to perform the verification:

```
RESTORE VERIFYONLY
    FROM DISK =  'e:\AdventureWorks2012Backup.bak'
```

Result:

```
The backup set is valid.
```

The verification has a few options, such as Eject Tape After Backup. Most of these verification options are for tapes and are self-explanatory.

> **NOTE**
>
> `RESTORE VERIFYONLY` does not actually restore the database. It checks only if the backup is complete and is readable. By default it checks the backup checksums if they are present and proceeds without verification if they are not present. Although this is a quick way to check if the backup set is complete and readable, it is *not* a replacement for actually performing a restore to see if the backup is valid because this check does not verify the structure of the data contained in the backup volumes. The only way to truly test and validate your backups is to perform a restore.

Working with the Transaction Log

Sometimes it seems that the transaction log has a life of its own. The space within the file seems to grow and shrink without rhyme or reason. If you've felt this way, you're not alone. This section should shed some light on why the transaction log behaves as it does.

Inside the Transaction Log

The transaction log contains all the transactions for a database. If the server crashes the transaction log, both transactions that have been written are used for recovery by rolling back uncommitted partial transactions and by completing any transactions that were committed but not written to the data file.

Virtually, the log can be imagined as a sequential list of transactions sorted by date and time. Physically, however, SQL Server writes to different parts of the physical log file in virtual blocks without a specific order. Some parts might be in use, making other parts available, so the log reuses itself in a loose round-robin fashion.

The Active and Inactive Divide

The transactions in the transaction log can be divided into two groups (see Figure 21-5):

- **Active transactions**: Uncommitted and not yet written to the data file
- **Inactive transactions**: All those transactions before the earliest active transaction

FIGURE 21-5

The inactive transactions are all those prior to the oldest active transaction.

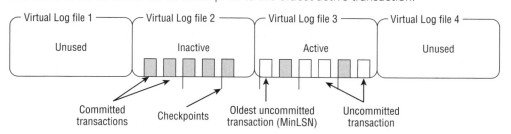

Because transactions are of varying duration, and are committed at different times, it's likely that committed transactions are in the active portion of the log. The active portion does not merely contain all uncommitted transactions, but all transactions since the start of the oldest uncommitted transaction. One old uncommitted transaction can make the active portion appear unusually large.

Understanding logging and how it relates to recovery functions is critical for a successful backup and recovery strategy. For an in-depth understanding of how logging works, check out an excellent article for TechNet magazine by Paul Randal titled "Understanding Logging and Recovery in SQL Server." The article can be found online at `http://technet.microsoft.com/en-us/magazine/2009.02.logging.aspx`

Transaction Checkpoints

Understanding how SQL Server uses checkpoints in the transaction log is important to understanding how the transaction log is backed up and emptied. Due to performance reasons, every time a database page is modified in memory, it is not written to disk immediately. SQL Server generates automatic checkpoints to write the dirty database pages from memory to disk. The time interval between automatic checkpoints is variable and depends on the amount of modifications made to the database and the `recovery interval` SQL Server configuration option. Checkpoints calculate the amount of work that must be done to recover the database during a system restart.

A checkpoint also occurs under any of the following conditions:

- When an ALTER DATABASE command is used.
- When the SQL Server is shut down.

> **NOTE**
> If you used the SHUTDOWN WITH NOWAIT command to shut down SQL Server, then SQL Server shuts down without performing checkpoints in any database.

- A minimally logged operation is performed in the database.
- A database backup is performed.
- When an activity requiring database shutdown or database restart is performed.
- When the number of log entries exceeds the estimated amount of work required by the SQL Server's `recovery interval` configuration option.
- If the database is in simple recovery model and the transaction log becomes 70 percent full.

Checkpoints may be manually initiated with a CHECKPOINT command. Checkpoints perform the following activities:

- Marks the checkpoint spot in the transaction log
- Writes a checkpoint-log record, including the following:
  - The oldest active transaction
  - The oldest replication transaction that has not been replicated

- A list of all active transactions
- Information about the minimum work required to roll back the database

- Marks the space before the oldest uncommitted transaction in a database with simple recovery for reuse
- Writes all dirty data and log pages to disk

Basically, a checkpoint gets everything up to date as best as it can and then records the current state of the dividing line between active and inactive in the log.

> **NOTE**
>
> In SQL Server 2012 there is a new type of checkpoint called an indirect checkpoint. This is actually a database-level setting in which you can manually specify a custom recovery point for a given database. By default the recovery interval is 0, which means SQL Server performs checkpoints on that database using the interval set by the recovery interval server option. For more information on Checkpoints see `http://msdn.microsoft.com/en-us/library/ms189573.aspx`.

Backing Up the Transaction Log

Performing a transaction log backup is similar to performing a full or differential backup, with a few notable differences.

The T-SQL command is as follows:

```
BACKUP LOG AdventureWorks2012
  TO DISK = 'e:\AdventureWorks2012Backup.bak'
  WITH
    NAME = 'AdventureWorks2012Backup';
```

Result:

```
Processed 2 pages for database 'AdventureWorks2012', file
'AdventureWorks2012_Log' on file 2.
BACKUP LOG successfully processed 2 pages in 0.118 seconds (0.095
MB/sec).
```

The same media options apply to the transaction log backup that apply to the database backup; in addition, two options are transaction-log specific.

- NO_TRUNCATE\CONTINUE_AFTER_ERROR: Used for backing up the tail of the log of a damaged database that is offline and does not start. If the data files of a user database are damaged, a tail log backup succeeds only if the transaction log files are not damaged, the state of database supports tail log backup, and the database does not contain any bulk logged operations.
- NORECOVERY: Used to back up the tail of the log of a database that is online, and you intend to perform RESTORE next.

If the data file of the user database and master database is damaged and the transaction log is not damaged, to minimize data loss you can still backup the tail of the transaction log as follows:

1. Rename the transaction log file. Do not delete this file as you will be using it again later in this procedure.

2. Rebuild the master database with the command line setup.

   For detailed instructions on how to do this see `http://msdn.microsoft.com/en-us/library/dd207003.aspx#RebuildProcedure`

3. Reapply any SQL Server updates or service packs that were previously applied.

4. Create a new user database. The number of data and log files need to match the files of the damaged database. The size of the files can be different.

5. Stop SQL Server.

6. Delete data files of the new database, and replace the log files with the original transaction log files.

7. Start SQL Server.

8. The new database will fail to recover because you deleted the data file. Run the following command to back up the tail of the log:

   ```
   BACKUP LOG Databasename
   TO DISK = 'file location'
   WITH NO_TRUNCATE;
   ```

> **NOTE**
>
> If only the data files of the user database are damaged and the master database and transaction log file of the user database are available, the tail of the log can be backed up directly by running the preceding BACKUP LOG command with the NO_TRUNCATE option.

The transaction log cannot be backed up if any of the following conditions exist:

- The database uses a simple recovery model.

- The database uses a bulk-logged recovery model, a bulk-logged operation has been executed, and the database files are damaged.

- Database files have been added or removed.

- The database uses bulk-logged or full recovery model, and a full database backup has not been performed yet.

In any of these cases, perform a full database backup instead.

Truncating the Log

Updates and deletes might not increase the size of a data file, but to the transaction log every transaction of any type is simply more data. Left to its own devices, the transaction log will continue to grow with every data modification.

The solution is to back up the inactive portion of the transaction log and then remove it. By default, backing up the transaction log also truncates the log (refer to Figure 21-3).

> **NOTE**
>
> BACKUP LOG WITH NO_LOG and BACKUP LOG WITH TRUNCATE_ONLY were discontinued in SQL Server 2008. To truncate the log, either take regular transaction log backups or put the database in simple recovery model.

The Transaction Log and Simple Recovery Model

When the database uses a simple recovery model, the transaction log ensures that each committed transaction is written to the data file, and that's it. When SQL Server performs a checkpoint and the transaction log is truncated, the free space of the transaction log fluctuates, but the minimum is the size of the active portion of the transaction log.

Under the simple recovery model, performing a manual checkpoint truncates the log and frees the log space.

> **NOTE**
>
> Truncating the log marks the inactive portion of the log for reuse and does not reduce the physical size of the transaction log. To reduce the physical size you need to run DBCC SHRINKFILE to manually shrink the log file. There are many DBAs that run the DBCC SHRINKFILE command to shrink the log file right after the log backup. This action is highly discouraged because DBCC SHRINKFILE can cause severe file-system fragmentation because the files will likely need to grow again after they have been shrunk and cause performance degradation. Instead, you must correctly size the transaction log at the time of creation and perform frequent log backups to keep the size in check.

> **TIP**
>
> To discover the operation preventing log truncation, use the log_reuse_wait_desc column of the sys .databases catalog view.

Recovery Operations

Many reasons exist to restore a database, including the following:

- A disk subsystem has failed.
- A sleepy programmer forgot a where clause in a SQL UPDATE statement and updated everyone's salary to minimum wage.
- Zombie apocalypse destroys your primary data center.
- A large import worked but with yesterday's data.

The best reason to restore a database is to practice the backup/restore cycle and prove that the recovery plan works. You must perform regular testing of your backup and restore strategy as a fire drill. Without confidence in the recovery, there's little point in doing backups. Remember this mantra: Backups are worthless; restores are priceless.

Detecting the Problem

If a database file is missing, clicking the database in Management Studio pops up a message saying that the database is unavailable. To further investigate a problem, check the SQL Server Errorlog. In Management Studio, you can view the log under Management ⇨ SQL Server Logs. SQL Server writes errors and events to an error log file in the \Log directory under the MSSQL directory. SQL Server creates a new file every time the SQL Server service starts. The six previous versions of the Errorlog file are saved in the same directory. Some errors may also be written to the Windows Application Event Log.

> **NOTE**
>
> To retain more than six Errorlogs, right-click SQL Server Logs in Management Studio, and select Configure.

> **TIP**
>
> You can also manually "roll the log" by using the stored procedure sp_cycle_errorlog. This can be helpful if you want to keep the error log's content limited to a certain time period. For example, you can schedule an agent job to execute the sp_cycle_errorlog command every day at midnight.
>
> In addition to rolling over the log on a scheduled basis, you probably want to increase the number of logs to retain from the default value, as stated in the previous Note. When configuring the number of logs to retain because the log rolls over with every service restart, you need to configure a number large enough for you to accommodate unexpected service restarts along with your scheduled ones.

Recovery Sequences

The two most important concepts about recovering a database are as follows:

- A recovery operation always begins by restoring a full backup and then restores any additional differential or transactional backups. The restore never copies only yesterday's work. It restores the entire database up to a certain point.

- There's a difference between restore and recover. A *restore* copies the data back into the database and leaves the transactions open. *Recovery* is the process of handling the transactions left open in the transaction log. If a database-recovery operation requires that four files be restored, only the last file is restored WITH RECOVERY.

Only logins who are members of the sysadmins fixed server role can restore a database that doesn't currently exist. sysadmins and db_owners can restore databases that do currently exist.

The actual recovery effort depends on the type of damage and the previous recovery plans. Table 21-2 is a comparative listing of recovery operations.

TABLE 21-2 Recovery Sequences

Recovery Model	Damaged Database File	Damaged Transaction Log
Simple	1) Restore full backup. 2) Restore latest differential backup (if needed).	It is likely there are unapplied transactions lost with the transaction log and the database is inconsistent. It is recommended to fall back on your backups and use the steps documented for "damaged database file."
Full or Bulk-Logged	1) Back up current transaction log with the NO_TRUNCATE option.* 2) Restore full backup. 3) Restore latest differential backup (if needed). 4) Restore all the transaction-log backups since the last differential or full backup. All committed transactions will be recovered.	1) Restore full backup. 2) Restore the latest differential backup (if needed). 3) Restore all the transaction-log backups since the last differential or full backup. Transactions made since the last log backup will be lost.

*If the database uses the bulk-logged recovery model and a bulk-insert operation occurred since the last transaction-log backup, the backup will fail. Transactions that occurred after the transaction-log backup are not recoverable.

Performing the Restore with Management Studio

As with the backup command, you can launch the restore from within Management Studio by following these steps:

1. Select the database to be restored.

2. From the context or Action menu, select Tasks ⟹ Restore ⟹ Database to open the SQL Server Restore database form.

The Restore Database form, as shown in Figure 21-6, does a great job of intelligently navigating the potential chaos of the backup sequences, and it always offers only legal restore options.

FIGURE 21-6

Only the correct sequence of restoring from multiple backup files is possible from Management Studio's Restore Database form.

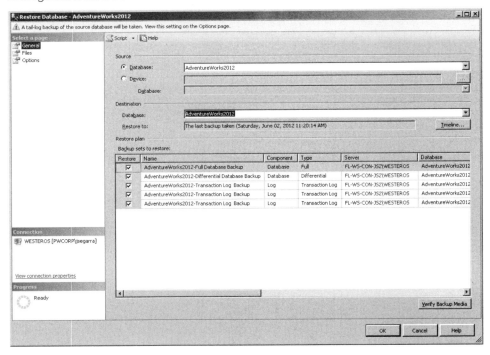

The selection you make at the top of the form is the name of the database after the restore.

The Restore Database form can restore database backups, file backups, or backups from a device (that is, a tape drive). The Restore Wizard presents a hierarchical tree of backups, whereas the filegroups or file restore lists the files and must be manually restored in the correct order.

The Backup Sets to Restore option displays the available backups. Management Studio uses the backup history in the msdb system database and creates a restore plan. For example, under the full recovery model, the restore plan selects the full database backup followed by the most recent differential database backup (if available) followed by subsequent log backups.

> **NOTE**
>
> If the database is in Full or Bulk-Logged recovery mode and you did not already take a tail-log backup, the Restore Database form will automatically select the option for you under the Options page to perform a tail-log backup.

If the backup history, stored in msdb, is not available — because the server is being rebuilt or the database is being restored to a different server — then use the Restore: From Device option to manually select the specific backup disk file and backup instance within the file.

The process of one full backup, the second differential backup, and the following 15 transaction-log backups can be correctly sequenced by selecting the final transaction log to be restored. Restoring the 17 backup files is performed with a single click of the OK button.

If one of the backup files being restored is a transaction log, the Point in Time Restore option becomes available because only a transaction log can restore some of the transactions. The point-in-time restore will restore all transactions committed before the time selected. A new option introduced in the Restore Database form SQL Server 2012 is the Backup Timeline form, as show in in Figure 21-7. You can access this dialog by clicking on the Timeline button on the Restore Database (General page) pane. This Backup Timeline dialog gives you an easy, visual indicator to help select which point-in-time you'd like to restore the current database to.

FIGURE 21-7

The Timeline.

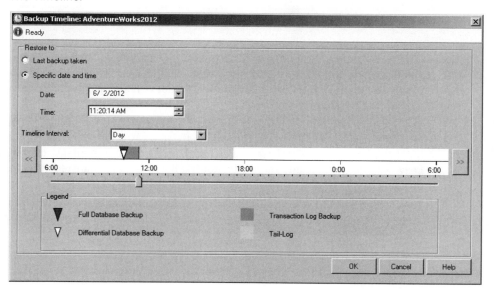

The Options page of the Restore Database form is shown in Figure 21-8.

FIGURE 21-8

The Options page of the Restore Database form.

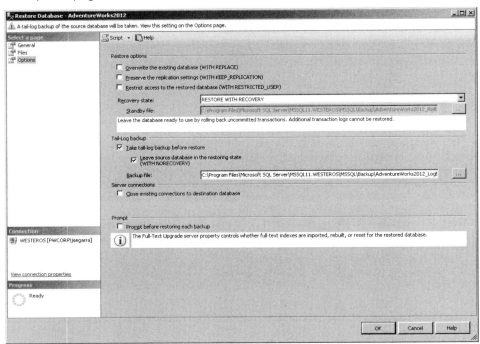

The Options tab of the Restore Database dialog box offers a few significant options:

- The Overwrite the Existing Database option disables a safety check that prevents Database A backup from being restored as Database B and accidentally overwriting an existing Database B.

- The Preserve the Replication Settings option preserves the replication settings when restoring a published database on a different SQL Server (other than the SQL Server where the database was created). This option is available only with the Leave the Database Ready for Use by Rolling Back the Uncommitted Transactions option.

- The Prompt Before Restoring Each Backup option prompts before continuing to restore the next backup in the restore sequence. This option is useful when you restore from tape backups and need to swap tapes.

- The Restrict Access to the Restored Database option restricts access to the restored database only to the members of db_owner, dbcreator, or sysadmin.

- Because it is possible that the database is restored to a different file location than the original backup, the Restore the Database Files As section in the Files page includes a way to assign new file locations.

- There are three Recovery state options to choose from when restoring a database:

  - Use the RESTORE WITH RECOVERY option to restore the final backup. This option recovers the database and does not allow additional transaction logs to be restored.

  - The RESTORE WITH NORECOVERY option leaves the database non-operational and enables you to restore additional backups. If you select this option, the Preserve Replication Settings option is unavailable.

  - The RESTORE WITH STANDBY option leaves the database in a standby mode in which the database is available for limited read-only access.

If only certain files or filegroups are restored, select Tasks ⇨ Restore ⇨ File or Filegroups to select the files or filegroups you want to restore.

Restoring Individual Pages

The ability to restore pages has been available since SQL Server 2005; however, up until now, you needed to use T-SQL code. In this release you can perform this type of restore through a native interface inside Management Studio.

What exactly does restoring a page allow you to do? You can restore one or more damaged pages without having to restore the entire database. Database pages that are suspect are specifically identified in the dbo.suspect_pages table inside the msdb system database.

To restore a page, select the database you want to restore the page to. From the context or Action menu, select Tasks ⇨ Restore ⇨ Page to open the SQL Server Restore page form. The Restore page is shown in Figure 21-9.

In the section marked Pages, SQL Server lists the pages identified as suspect in your selected database. If you want to run another check to make sure the suspected pages list is up to date, click the Check Database Pages button. This initiates a DBCC CHECKDB WITH PHYSICAL_ONLY check and then re-queries the msdb.dbo .suspect_pages table for any additional rows pertaining to your database.

In the Tail Log section, specify the location where you want the tail-log backup of the database stored. This is required because the restore process automatically initiates a tail-log backup. The default location selected is the default backup location for SQL Server. If you want to change this, click the Ellipsis button, and specify the new location.

FIGURE 21-9

The Restore Page interface lets you check and see which database pages are marked as suspect.

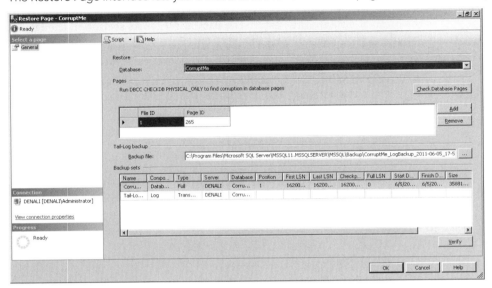

The database's backup chain is automatically loaded into the backup sets window. This is needed because the transaction log backups must be applied to all files that contain a page that is being recovered. If no existing transaction log backups exist, it uses the last full backup along with the latest differential backup, if there are any. It automatically adds the new tail-log backup that is created during this process. Clicking the Verify button performs a RESTORE WITH VERIFYONLY against the backup set to ensure that the backups are valid and readable.

After you verify that all options are valid, click OK. This initiates the restore process. You can see the progress of this activity at the top of the Restore Page window. When it is complete you see a pop-up message stating "Database '<database name>' Restored Successfully".

Restoring with T-SQL Code

A database backup is a regularly scheduled occurrence, so if SQL Server's built-in Maintenance Plan Wizard isn't to your liking, it makes sense to write some repeatable code to perform backups and set up your own SQL Server Agent jobs.

However, unless the backup plan is only a full backup, it's difficult to know how many differential backups or transaction-log backups need to be restored; and because each backup file requires a separate restore command, it's difficult to script the recovery effort beforehand without writing a lot of code to examine the msdb tables and determine the restore sequence properly.

NOTE

The `backupset` table in msdb database contains a row for each backup set. You can query this table to find information on all the successful backups.

The `RESTORE` command restores from a full, differential, or transaction-log backup:

```
RESTORE DATABASE (or LOG) DatabaseName
   Optional-File or Filegroup or Page
   FROM BackUpDevice
   WITH
     FILE = FileNumber,
   PARTIAL,

     NORECOVERY or RECOVERY or STANDBY = UnDoFileName,
     REPLACE,
     STOPAT datetime,
     STOPATMARK = 'markname'
     STOPBEFOREMARK = 'markname'
```

To restore a full or differential backup, use the `RESTORE DATABASE` command; otherwise, use the `RESTORE LOG` for a transaction log. To restore a specific file or filegroup, add its name after the database name. The `PARTIAL` option specifies a partial restore that restores the primary filegroup and any specified secondary filegroups.

A backup set often contains several backup instances. For example, a backup set might consist of the following:

1: Full backup

2: Differential backup

3, 4, 5, 6: Transaction-log backups

7: Differential backup

8, 9: Transaction-log backups

The `WITH FILE` option specifies the backup to restore. If it's left out of the command, the first backup instance is restored.

If a password were created with the backup, the `password` is required to perform restore from the backup.

NOTE

Avoid using the `password` option because this feature will be removed in the future release of SQL Server.

To restore one or more pages, use `PAGE = 'file:page[,...n]'` where `PAGE` indicates a list of one or more files and pages; `file` indicates the file ID containing the page to be restored; `page` indicates the page id of the page to be restored in the file; and `n` indicates multiple pages can be specified.

The RECOVERY/NORECOVERY option is vital to the restore command. Every time a SQL Server starts, it automatically checks the transaction log, rolling back any uncommitted transactions and completing any committed transactions. This process is called *recovery*, and it's a part of the ACID properties of the database.

Therefore, if the restore has the NORECOVERY option, SQL Server restores the log without handling any transactions. Conversely, RECOVERY instructs SQL Server to handle the transactions. In the sequence of the recovery operation, all the restores must have the NORECOVERY option enabled, except for the last restore, which must have the RECOVERY option enabled.

Deciding between RECOVERY and NORECOVERY is one of the complications involved in trying to write a script to handle any possible future recovery operation.

The STANDBY option enables the recovery effects to be undone.

If the recovery operation includes a transaction-log restore, the recovery can stop before the end of the transaction log. The options STOPAT and STOPATMARK leave the end of the transaction log unrestored. The STOPAT accepts a time, and the STOPATMARK restores only to a transaction that was created with a named mark. The STOPBEFOREMARK option restores everything up to the beginning of the marked transaction.

The REPLACE option creates the database and its related files even if another database already exists with the same name.

 Chapter 36, "Creating Triggers," details SQL Server transactions and how to create marked transactions.

The following script demonstrates an example of a restore sequence that includes a full backup and two transaction-log backups:

```
-- BackUp and recovery example

CREATE DATABASE Plan2Recover;
```

Result:

```
Command(s) completed successfully.
```

Continuing:

```
USE Plan2Recover;

CREATE TABLE T1 (
  PK INT Identity PRIMARY KEY,
  Name VARCHAR(15)
  );
```

```
Go
INSERT T1 VALUES ('Full');
go
BACKUP DATABASE Plan2Recover
  TO DISK = 'e:\P2R.bak'
  WITH
    NAME = 'P2R_Full',
    INIT;
```

Result:

```
(1 row(s) affected)
Processed 168 pages for database 'Plan2Recover', file 'Plan2Recover'
 on file 1.
Processed 6 pages for database 'Plan2Recover', file 'Plan2Recover_
 log' on file 1.
BACKUP DATABASE successfully processed 174 pages in 0.800 seconds
 (1.690 MB/sec).
```

Continuing:

```
INSERT T1 VALUES ('Log 1');
go
BACKUP Log Plan2Recover
  TO DISK = 'e:\P2R.bak'
  WITH
    NAME = 'P2R_Log';
```

Result:

```
(1 row(s) affected)
Processed 6 pages for database 'Plan2Recover', file 'Plan2Recover_
 log' on file 2.
BACKUP LOG successfully processed 6 pages in 0.113 seconds (0.393
 MB/sec).
```

Continuing:

```
INSERT T1 VALUES ('Log 2');
go
BACKUP Log Plan2Recover
  TO DISK = 'e:\P2R.bak'
  WITH
    NAME = 'P2R_Log';
```

Result:

```
(1 row(s) affected)
Processed 1 pages for database 'Plan2Recover', file 'Plan2Recover_
 log' on file 3.
```

```
BACKUP LOG successfully processed 1 pages in 0.082 seconds (0.005
MB/sec).
```

Continuing:

```
SELECT * FROM T1;
```

Result:

```
PK          Name
----------- ----------------
1           Full
2           Log 1
3           Log 2

(3 row(s) affected)
```

At this point the server is hit with a direct bolt of lightning, and all drives are fried, with the exception of the backup files. The following recovery operation goes through the full backup and the two transaction-log backups. Notice the NORECOVERY and RECOVERY options:

```
-- NOW PERFORM THE RESTORE
Use Master;
RESTORE DATABASE Plan2Recover
  FROM DISK = 'e:\P2R.bak'
  With FILE = 1, NORECOVERY;
```

Result:

```
Processed 168 pages for database 'Plan2Recover', file 'Plan2Recover'
  on file 1.
Processed 6 pages for database 'Plan2Recover', file 'Plan2Recover_
  log' on file 1.
RESTORE DATABASE successfully processed 174 pages in 0.168 seconds
(8.050 MB/sec).
```

Continuing:

```
RESTORE LOG Plan2Recover
  FROM DISK = 'e:\P2R.bak'
  With FILE = 2, NORECOVERY;
```

Result:

```
Processed 0 pages for database 'Plan2Recover', file 'Plan2Recover' on
  file 2.
Processed 6 pages for database 'Plan2Recover', file 'Plan2Recover_
  log' on file 2.
RESTORE LOG successfully processed 6 pages in 0.028 seconds (1.586
MB/sec).
```

Continuing:

```
RESTORE LOG Plan2Recover
  FROM DISK = 'e:\P2R.bak'
  With FILE = 3, RECOVERY;
```

Result:

```
Processed 0 pages for database 'Plan2Recover', file 'Plan2Recover' on
  file 3.
Processed 1 pages for database 'Plan2Recover', file 'Plan2Recover_
  log' on file 3.
RESTORE LOG successfully processed 1 pages in 0.004 seconds (0.122
  MB/sec).
```

To test the recovery operation:

```
USE Plan2Recover;
Select * from T1;
```

Result:

```
PK          Name
----------- ---------------
1           Full
2           Log 1
3           Log 2
(3 row(s) affected)
```

As this script shows, you can recover using T-SQL, but in this case Management Studio beats code as the best way to accomplish the task.

System Databases Recovery

So far, this chapter has dealt only with user databases, but the system databases are important to the recovery operation as well. The master database contains key database and security information, and the msdb database holds the schedules and jobs for SQL Server, as well as the backup history. A complete recovery plan must include the system databases.

Master Database

The master database, by default, uses the simple recovery model. Using only full backups for the master database is OK; it's not a transactional database.

Backing Up the Master Database

You back up the master database in the same manner as user databases.

Be sure to back up the master database when doing any of the following:

- Creating or deleting databases
- Modifying security by adding logins or changing roles
- Modifying any server or database-configuration options

Because the msdb database holds a record of all backups, back up the master database and then the msdb database.

Recovering the Master Database

If the master database is corrupted or damaged, SQL Server won't start. Attempting to start SQL Server will have no effect. Attempting to connect to the instance with Management Studio invokes a warning that the server does not exist or that access is denied. The only solution is to first rebuild the master database using the command line setup as shown next, reapply any SQL Server updates, start SQL Server in single-user mode, and restore the master database.

1. Rebuild the master database using the command line setup:

   ```
   setup /QUIET /ACTION=REBUILDDATABASE /INSTANCENAME="<instance name>"
   /SQLSYSADMINACCOUNTS="<DomainName\UserName >" /SAPWD="<password>"
   ```

   where

   - `setup.exe` is either from your original installation media or the "local" setup .exe as found in the 110\Setup Bootstrap\SQLServer2012 directory.
   - `/QUIET` switch suppresses all error messages.
   - `/ACTION=REBUILDDATABASE` switch rebuilds all the system databases.
   - `/INSTANCENAME` switch specifies the name of your SQL Server named instance. Use `MSSQLServer` for "<instance_name>" for default instance.
   - `/SQLSYSADMINACCOUNTS` switch corresponds to the currently-logged in domain user running this rebuild process. The user must be a member of the SQL instance's sysadmin server role.
   - `/SAPWD` switch is used to indicate a new SA password if you configured SQL Server for mixed authentication.

> **NOTE**
>
> A new feature was added to rebuilding the system databases in the last release. The system databases used for rebuilding the local system databases no longer come from the original installation media and are located locally in the `C:\Program Files\Microsoft SQL Server\MSSQL11.MSSQLSERVER\MSSQL\Binn\Templates\` folder, and setup.exe is located in the `C:\Program Files\Microsoft SQL Server\110\Setup Bootstrap\SQLServer2012SQLServer2012` folder. The switches have changed as compared to SQL Server 2005.

2. Run the following from the command prompt to start a default instance of SQL Server in single user mode:

```
sqlservr.exe -m
```

If the instance is a named instance of SQL Server in single user mode, run the following to start:

```
sqlservr.exe -m -s <instancename>
```

3. Reapply any SQL Server updates, service packs, and hotfixes previously applied to the SQL Server.

4. Restore the master database as you would a user database. If a master backup is not available, re-create all missing entries for your user databases, logins, endpoints, and so forth.

If the master database is accessible, start SQL Server in single-user mode, and then restore the master database as you would a user database.

> **NOTE**
> Rebuilding the master database also rebuilds the msdb and model databases. After rebuilding the databases, restore the system databases (master, msdb, and model) from the most recent good backup.
>
> Rebuilding the master database installs all system databases to their initial location. If initially one or more system databases were moved to a different location, a similar move is required again.

MSDB System Database

Like the master database, the msdb database, by default, uses the simple recovery model.

Because the msdb database contains information regarding the SQL Server Agent jobs and schedules, as well as the backup history, it should be backed up whenever you do the following:

- Perform backups.
- Save SSIS packages.
- Create new SQL Server Agent jobs.
- Configure SQL Server Agent mail or operators.
- Configure replication.
- Schedule tasks.
- Create or modify any policies created in Policy-Based Management.
- Configure or modify Management Data Warehouse.
- Add new registered servers (if an instance is set up as Central Management Server).

The msdb database is backed up in the same way that a user database is backed up.

To restore the msdb database, you do not need to put the server in single-user mode as you do with the master database. However, it's still not a normal restore because without a current msdb, Management Studio is not aware of the backup history. Therefore, the msdb backup can't be chosen as a backup database but must be selected as a backup device.

Use the Contents button to check the disk device for specific backups. If several backup instances are in the backup device, you can use the Contents dialog box to select the correct backup. It then fills in the file number in the restore form.

> **NOTE**
>
> Before restoring the msdb database, stop SQL Server Agent. This is to ensure that the msdb database is not accessed by the SQL Server Agent and allows the restore to complete.

Performing a Complete Recovery

If the server has completely failed and all the backups must be restored onto a new server, follow these steps:

1. Build the Windows server, and restore the domain logins to support Windows authentication.
2. Install SQL Server and any service-pack, cumulative updates, security upgrades, or hotfixes.
3. Start SQL Server in single-user mode, and restore the master database.
4. Verify that SQL Server Agent is stopped. Restore the msdb database.
5. If the model database was modified, restore it.
6. Restore the user databases.

> **Best Practice**
>
> Performing a flawless recovery is a "bet your career" skill. Take the time to work through a complete recovery of the production data to a backup server. The confidence you gain can serve you well as a SQL Server DBA.

Summary

The recovery cycle begins with the backup of the databases. The ability to survive hardware failure or human error is crucial to the ACID properties of a database. Without the transaction's durability, the database can't be fully trusted. Because of this, recovery planning and the transaction log provide durability to committed transactions. The recovery cycle transfers data from the past to the present.

They key take-away points from this chapter include the following:

- Invest the time to create a solid backup and recovery plan.

- Just performing regular backups is not enough. Because the only way to know that the backups are good is by restoring the backups, regularly restore the backups on a test server. This is a boring task but well worth it when a disaster occurs and you need to recover from the backups.

- A senior SQL DBA must create the backup and recovery plan to ensure that all aspects are taken care of. When the plan is ready, ascertain that the junior DBA can understand it and can perform all the steps in the plan because they will likely be the ones recovering from the backups in the middle of the night when a disaster occurs.

- Perform a complete recovery to simulate a server and disk subsystem failure at least every 6 months, and update your backup/recovery plan as required.

In the next chapter, you learn how to maintain the database.

Maintaining the Database

IN THIS CHAPTER

Using SQL Server's Database Console Commands (DBCC)

Creating Database Maintenance Plans

The previous chapter covered database recovery planning. This chapter explores various database maintenance tasks that need to be regularly performed, such as database backups, database integrity checks, and index maintenance. This chapter discusses database maintenance using Transact-SQL Database Console Commands (DBCC) and Maintenance Plans.

What's New in SQL Server Database Maintenance?

In earlier versions of SQL Server, DBCC stood for Database Consistency Checker— it has since been renamed Database Console Commands. The following deprecated DBCC commands are still in SQL Server 2012, but they will be removed in a future version of SQL Server. It is recommended to stop using the deprecated DBCC commands for new development work and plan to change existing applications using these commands.

- DBCC DBREINDEX
- DBCC INDEXDEFRAG
- DBCC SHOWCONTIG
- DBCC PINTABLE
- DBCC UNPINTABL

Although DBCC PINTABLE and DBCC UNPINTABLE commands are still in SQL Server 2012, they have no effect on SQL Server.

You can find a complete list of deprecated (outdated or no longer accessible) DBCC commands in Chapter 1, "The World of SQL Server," in Books Online, and at http://msdn.microsoft.com/en-US/library/ms143729(v=SQL.110).aspx.

DBCC Commands

Microsoft SQL Server Database Console Commands (DBCC) are used for checking database integrity; performing maintenance operations on databases, tables, indexes, and filegroups; and collecting and displaying information during troubleshooting issues.

The first DBCC command to become familiar with is the DBCC HELP command, which returns the syntax with all the options for any DBCC command. The following command returns the syntax for DBCC CHECKDB.

```
DBCC HELP ('CHECKDB');
```

Result:

```
dbcc CHECKDB
(
    { 'database_name' | database_id | 0 }
    [ , NOINDEX
    | { REPAIR_ALLOW_DATA_LOSS
    | REPAIR_FAST
    | REPAIR_REBUILD
    } ]
)
    [ WITH
        {
            [ ALL_ERRORMSGS ]
            [ , [ NO_INFOMSGS ] ]
            [ , [ TABLOCK ] ]
            [ , [ ESTIMATEONLY ] ]
            [ , [ PHYSICAL_ONLY ] ]
            [ , [ DATA_PURITY ] ]
            [ , [ EXTENDED_LOGICAL_CHECKS  ] ]
        }
    ]
DBCC execution completed. If DBCC printed error messages,
contact your system administrator.
```

The following command returns all DBCC commands for which help is available.

```
DBCC HELP ('?');
```

Result:

```
checkalloc

checkcatalog

checkconstraints

checkdb

checkfilegroup

checkident

checktable

cleantable

dbreindex

dropcleanbuffers

free

freeproccache

freesessioncache

freesystemcache

help

indexdefrag

inputbuffer

opentran

outputbuffer

pintable
```

22

```
proccache

show_statistics

showcontig

shrinkdatabase

shrinkfile

sqlperf

traceoff

traceon

tracestatus

unpintable

updateusage

useroptions
DBCC execution completed. If DBCC printed error messages,
contact your system administrator.
```

All DBCC commands report their activity or errors found, and then conclude with the standard DBCC execution completed statement, including any action that might be needed.

Database Integrity

DBCC CHECKDB performs several operations to check the logical and physical integrity of the database. It's critical for the health of the database that the physical structure is correct. DBCC CHECKDB checks things, such as index pointers, data-page offsets, the linking between data pages and index pages, and the structural content of the data and index pages. If a hardware hiccup has left a data page half written, DBCC CHECKDB is the best means of detecting the problem. The following command executes DBCC CHECKDB on the AdventureWorks2012 sample database.

```
DBCC CHECKDB ('AdventureWorks2012');
```

Result (abridged):

```
DBCC results for 'AdventureWorks2012'.
Service Broker Msg 9675, State 1: Message Types analyzed: 14.
Service Broker Msg 9676, State 1: Service Contracts analyzed: 6.
Service Broker Msg 9667, State 1: Services analyzed: 3.
Service Broker Msg 9668, State 1: Service Queues analyzed: 3
 .
 . . .
```

```
DBCC results for 'sys.sysrscols'.
There are 1406 rows in 14 pages for object "sys.sysrscols".
DBCC results for 'sys.sysrowsets'.
There are 263 rows in 3 pages for object "sys.sysrowsets".
DBCC results for 'sys.sysallocunits'.
. . .
DBCC results for 'Production.ProductModelProductDescriptionCulture'.
There are 762 rows in 4 pages for
object "Production.ProductModelProductDescriptionCulture".
DBCC results for 'Sales.Store'.
There are 701 rows in 101 pages for object "Sales.Store".
DBCC results for 'Production.ProductPhoto'.
There are 101 rows in 50 pages for object "Production.ProductPhoto".
CHECKDB found 0 allocation errors and 0 consistency errors
in database 'AdventureWorks2012'.
DBCC execution completed. If DBCC printed error messages,
contact your system administrator.
```

> **NOTE**
> The results you see could vary from those displayed in the book depending on your SQL Server configuration and any changes you have made to the database.

Two options simply determine which messages are reported, without altering the functionality of the integrity check: ALL_ERRORMSGS and NO_INFOMSGS. ALL_ERRORMSGS displays all the error messages; when it is not used, the default displays 200 errors per object. You can use the NO_INFOMSGS to suppress all informational messages.

The ESTIMATEONLY option returns the estimated size of the tempdb required by DBCC CHECKDB without actually running DBCC CHECKDB against the database.

If the database is large, you can use the NOINDEX option to skip checking the integrity of all user-table nonclustered indexes. For additional time-savings, the PHYSICAL_ONLY option performs only the most critical checks on the physical structure of the pages. Use these options only when time prevents a complete DBCC CHECKDB or when the indexes are about to be rebuilt.

If you want to perform logical consistency checks on indexed views, XML indexes, and spatial indexes, use the option EXTENDED_LOGICAL_CHECKS. This option increases the performance impact on the SQL Server, and currently its progress cannot be tracked. You should first run this on a similar database on a similar test SQL Server to get an estimate of the time it takes to run DBCC CHECKDB with this option and the performance impact on the SQL Server.

For databases upgraded from SQL Server 2000 or earlier, run DBCC CHECKDB WITH DATA_PURITY as a post-upgrade step to enable the column-value integrity checks because they are disabled by default on SQL Server 2000 and earlier. After successful completion, column-value integrity checks are enabled for the database, and you do not need to use the DATA_PURITY option for future DBCC CHECKDB executions. Column-value integrity checks are enabled by default starting from SQL Server 2005.

To reduce blocking and concurrency problems when integrity checks are done, DBCC CHECKDB uses an internal database snapshot to perform the checks. If a snapshot cannot be created or you use the TABLOCK option, DBCC CHECKDB uses locks, which include a short-term exclusive lock on the database. The TABLOCK option can reduce the time it takes for DBCC CHECKDB to run during peak usage, but it reduces the concurrency on the database. If you use the TABLOCK option, DBCC CHECKCATALOG is skipped and Service Broker data is not checked.

> **TIP**
>
> Review the percent_complete and command columns of sys.dm_exec_requests catalog view to display the progress and current phase of DBCC CHECKDB.

Repairing the Database

When an error is found and DBCC CHECKDB can fix it, DBCC CHECKDB indicates the repair level needed to repair the error. When an error is reported by DBCC CHECKDB, it is recommended to restore the database from a known good backup. Use the repair option with DBCC CHECKDB only when there is no known good backup. Repairing the database is a separate operation from the normal DBCC CHECKDB command because the database needs to be placed in single-user mode with the ALTER DATABASE command before a DBCC CHECKDB can be executed with the repair option. The following command places the AdventureWorks2012 sample database in single user mode.

```
ALTER DATABASE AdventureWorks2012 SET SINGLE_USER;
```

More on the Single User Mode

The previous command waits indefinitely if there is a lock on the database or if there are users connected to the database. You can use a termination clause WITH ROLLBACK AFTER integer [SECONDS] or WITH ROLLBACK IMMEDIATE to indicate to SQL Server to roll back incomplete transactions after the specified number of seconds or roll back immediately and close any active connections to the database. The following command places the AdventureWorks2012 sample database in single user mode and indicates SQL Server to roll back all incomplete transactions immediately and close any active connections to the database.

```
ALTER DATABASE AdventureWorks2012 SET SINGLE_USER WITH ROLLBACK IMMEDIATE;
```

If the AUTO_UPDATE_STATISTICS_AYSNC option for the database is set to ON, you can place the database in single-user mode but you cannot connect to the database because the background thread used to update the statistics takes a connection against the database. You can query the is_auto_update_stats_async_on column in the sys.databases catalog view to check if the AUTO_UPDATE_STATISTICS_ASYNC option is set to ON. If this option is set to ON, first set the AUTO_UPDATE_STATISTICS_AYSNC option for the database to OFF using the ALTER DATABASE command.

DBCC offers two repair modes:

- REPAIR_REBUILD: Performs a repair that does not lead to any data loss; however, this repairs only problems found in nonclustered indexes.
- REPAIR_ALLOW_DATA_LOSS: Performs the repairs and fixes corrupted database structures. As the name suggests, this mode can result in data loss.

NOTE

There used to be a third repair mode called REPAIR_FAST in earlier versions of SQL Server. This mode still exists in SQL Server 2012, but it does not perform any activity and is kept only for backward compatibility.

The following example places the AdventureWorks2012 sample database in single user mode and runs DBCC CHECKDB with the REPAIR_ALLOW_DATA_LOSS option. It then sets the database back to multiuser mode.

```
ALTER DATABASE AdventureWorks2012 SET SINGLE_USER
WITH ROLLBACK IMMEDIATE;
BEGIN TRANSACTION;
DBCC CheckDB ('AdventureWorks2012', REPAIR_ALLOW_DATA_LOSS);
--Check for any data loss
--ROLLBACK TRANSACTION if data
--loss is not acceptable else COMMIT TRANSACTION;
ALTER DATABASE AdventureWorks2012 SET MULTI_USER;
```

Result (abridged):

```
DBCC results for 'AdventureWorks2012'.
Service Broker Msg 9675, State 1: Message Types analyzed: 14.
Service Broker Msg 9676, State 1: Service Contracts analyzed: 6.
Service Broker Msg 9667, State 1: Services analyzed: 3.
. . .
DBCC results for 'sys.sysrowsets'.
There are 291 rows in 3 pages for object "sys.sysrowsets".
. . .
```

22

```
DBCC results for 'Production.TransactionHistoryArchive'.
There are 89253 rows in 620 pages for object
"Production.TransactionHistoryArchive".
CHECKDB found 0 allocation errors
and 0 consistency errors in database 'AdventureWorks2012'.
DBCC execution completed. If DBCC printed error messages, contact
your system administrator.
```

Best Practice

Since SQL Server 7.0, the storage engine quality has significantly improved, reducing the need for running DBCC CHECKDB frequently. However, a full proof recovery plan includes a full restore and a DBCC CHECKDB to make sure all the portions of the recovery plan work. The frequency to run a DBCC CHECKDB often depends on your comfort level, your environment, and the importance of your data. (The authors would never say that DBCC CHECKDB is not needed. It is recommended to run it now and then as well as restoring from backups.) You should also run DBCC CHECKDB after any hardware malfunction. If an error is detected, restore from a known good database backup. As mentioned, use the repair option only as the last option. If DBCC CHECKDB asks you to use REPAIR_ALLOW_DATA_LOSS, take a full database backup first, and then run DBCC CHECKDB with the repair option in a user transaction. That way you can verify the data loss after the command is executed and roll back the transaction if the data loss is not acceptable. After successfully repairing the database, take a full database backup.

As DBCC CHECKDB is a resource-intensive operation, run it during low peak hours.

Multi-User Concerns

DBCC CHECKDB without any repair option can be executed while users are in the database. However, DBCC CHECKDB is processor- and disk-intensive, so run it when the database has the fewest users. By default, DBCC CHECKDB can check objects in parallel across all CPUs in the box, which can boost the performance of DBCC CHECKDB and reduce the run times. The degree of parallelism is determined by the SQL Server query processor, and the algorithm used is similar to running parallel queries. Because running DBCC CHECKDB in parallel is processor-intensive, you may have environments or situations in which you want to disable parallel checking of objects by DBCC CHECKDB. SQL Server enables you to disable parallel checking of objects by DBCC CHECKDB by using the trace flag 2528.

Object-Level Validation

DBCC CHECKDB performs a host of database structural-integrity checks. You can run these checks individually. For example, if you have a large database (VLDB), it may not be possible to run DBCC CHECKDB on the entire database, but you may run individual checks on key database objects.

If the database requires repair, always use the full DBCC CHECKDB rather than one of the lesser versions:

- DBCC CHECKALLOC ('database'): A subset of DBCC CHECKDB that checks the allocation of all pages in the database. The report is detailed, listing the extent count (64KB or eight data pages) and data-page usage of every table and index in the database.

- DBCC CHECKFILEGROUP ('filegroup'): Similar to a DBCC CHECKDB but it is limited to the specified filegroup only.

- DBCC CHECKTABLE('table'): Performs physical and logical integrity checks on the table and all its nonclustered indexes (unless the NOINDEX option is used).

- DBCC CLEANTABLE ('database', "table"): Reclaims space from a varchar, nvarchar, text, or ntext column that was dropped from the table.

Data Integrity

Above the physical-structure layer of the database is the data layer, which can be verified by the following DBCC commands.

- DBCC CHECKCATALOG ('database'): Checks the integrity of the system tables within a database, ensuring referential integrity among tables, views, columns, and data types. Although it reports any errors, under normal conditions no detailed report is returned. This is also run as a part of DBCC CHECKDB.

- DBCC CHECKCONSTRAINTS ('table','constraint'): Examines the integrity of a specific constraint, or all the constraints for a table. It essentially generates and executes a query to verify each constraint and reports any errors found. As with DBCC CHECKCATALOG, if no issues are detected, nothing is reported.

- DBCC CHECKIDENT ('table'): Verifies the consistency of the current identity-column value and the identity column for a specific table. If a problem exists, the next value for the identity column is updated to correct any error. If the identity column is broken, the new identity value violates a primary key or unique constraint and new rows cannot be added to the table. You can also use this command to reseed the current identity value by using the RESEED option and a new_reseed_value.

    The following code demonstrates the use of the DBCC CHECKIDENT command. If it is needed, this command resets the current identity value of the Employee table in the AdventureWorks2012 sample database:

```
Use AdventureWorks2012;
DBCC CHECKIDENT ("HumanResources.Employee");
```

Result:

```
Checking identity information: current
identity value '290', current column value '290'.
DBCC execution completed. If DBCC printed error
messages, contact your system administrator.
```

Index Maintenance

Indexes provide the performance bridge between the data and SQL queries. Because of data inserts, updates, and deletes, indexes fragment, the data-distribution statistics become out of date, and the fill factor of the pages can be less than optimal. Index maintenance is required to combat these three results of normal wear and tear and to prevent performance reduction.

 Chapter 7, "Relational Database Design and Creating the Physical Database Schema," and Chapter 45, "Indexing Strategies," both contain more information on index creation.

Database Fragmentation

By default, as data is inserted into the data pages and index pages, the pages fill to 100 percent. At that point, SQL Server performs a page split, creating two new pages with about 50 percent page density each. Although this solves the individual page problem, the internal database structure can become fragmented.

To demonstrate the DBCC commands that affect fragmented tables and indexes, a table large enough to become fragmented is required. The following script builds a suitable table and a nonclustered index. The clustered primary key is a GUID, so row insertions can occur throughout the table, generating plenty of fragmentation:

```
USE Tempdb;

CREATE TABLE Frag (
  FragID UNIQUEIDENTIFIER NOT NULL DEFAULT NewID(),
  Col1 INT,
  Col2 CHAR(200),
  Created DATETIME DEFAULT GetDate(),
  Modified DATETIME DEFAULT GetDate()
  );

ALTER TABLE Frag
  ADD CONSTRAINT PK_Frag
  PRIMARY KEY CLUSTERED (FragID);

CREATE NONCLUSTERED INDEX ix_col
  ON Frag (Col1);
```

The following stored procedure adds 100,000 rows each time it's executed:

```
CREATE PROC Add100K
AS
SET nocount on;
DECLARE @X INT;
SET @X = 0;
  WHILE @X < 100000
    BEGIN
      INSERT Frag (Col1,Col2)
        VALUES (@X, 'sample data');
      SET @X = @X + 1;
    END
```

The following batch calls Add100K several times and populates the Frag table (be patient, the query can require several minutes to execute):

```
EXEC Add100K;
EXEC Add100K;
EXEC Add100K;
EXEC Add100K;
EXEC Add100K;
```

The dynamic management function sys.dm_db_index_physical_stats reports the fragmentation details and the density for a given table or index. With half a million rows, the Frag table is fragmented, and most pages are slightly more than half full, as the following command shows:

```
USE tempdb;
SELECT * FROM sys.dm_db_index_physical_stats ( db_id('tempdb'),
  object_id('Frag'), NULL, NULL, 'DETAILED');
```

In the following result (abridged), Index ID: 1 is the clustered primary-key index, so it's also reporting the data-page fragmentation. Index ID: 2 is the nonclustered index:

```
index_id: 1
index_type_desc: CLUSTERED INDEX
avg_fragmentation_in_percent: 99.1775717920756
page count: 22008
avg_page_space_used_in_percent: 68.744230294045

index_id: 2
index_type_desc: NONCLUSTERED INDEX
avg_fragmentation_in_percent: 98.1501632208923
page count: 2732
avg_page_space_used_in_percent: 58.2316654311836
```

> **NOTE**
>
> The sys.dm_db_index_physical_stats function requires an Intent-Shared (IS) table lock regardless of the mode it runs in. The DETAILED mode is the most rigorous of the scan levels that can be used with this function. There is another mode called LIMITED that can give a rough idea of the fragmentation in less time with less potential impact to the database.

ALTER INDEX REORGANIZE defragments the leaf level index pages of both clustered and nonclustered indexes. It reorders the leaf level index pages and compacts the index pages (based on the fill factor value in the sys.indexes catalog view) for faster index scanning performance:

```
ALTER INDEX IndexName ON TableName REORGANIZE;
```

Performing the ALTER INDEX REORGANIZE operation is similar to rebuilding an index (ALTER INDEX REBUILD, which is covered in the section, "Index density"), with the distinct advantage that defragmenting an index is performed in a series of small transactions that do not block users from performing inserts, updates, and deletes.

> **NOTE**
>
> ALTER INDEX REORGANIZE and ALTER INDEX REBUILD commands are equivalent to DBCC INDEXDEFRAG and DBCC DBREINDEX respectively. The sys.dm_db_index_physical_stats dynamic management function replaces DBCC SHOWCONTIG. It is recommended to stop using DBCC INDEXDEFRAG, DBCC DBREINDEX, and DBCC SHOWCONTIG because they will be removed in a future version of Microsoft SQL Server.

The following commands defrag both indexes:

```
USE tempdb;
ALTER INDEX PK_Frag ON Frag REORGANIZE;
ALTER INDEX ix_col ON Frag REORGANIZE;
```

A sys.dm_db_index_physical_stats dynamic management function examines the index structure after defragmenting the index. Both the logical-fragmentation and page-density problems created by the insertion of one-half million rows are resolved:

```
USE tempdb;
GO
SELECT * FROM sys.dm_db_index_physical_stats ( db_id('tempdb'),
object_id('Frag'), NULL, NULL, 'DETAILED');
GO
```

Result (abridged):

```
index_id: 1
index_type_desc: CLUSTERED INDEX
avg_fragmentation_in_percent: 0.559173738569831
page count: 15201
avg_page_space_used_in_percent: 99.538930071658

index_id: 2
index_type_desc: NONCLUSTERED INDEX
avg_fragmentation_in_percent: 1.23915737298637
page count: 1614
avg_page_space_used_in_percent: 99.487558685446
```

Index Statistics

The usefulness of an index is based on the data distribution within that index. For example, if 60 percent of the customers are in New York City, then selecting all customers in NYC will likely be faster with a table scan than with an index seek. However, to find the single customer from Delavan, Wisconsin, the query definitely needs the help of an index. The Query Optimizer depends on the index statistics to determine the usefulness of the index for a particular query.

DBCC SHOW_STATISTICS reports the last date the statistics were updated and basic information about the index statistics, including the usefulness of the index. A low density indicates that the index is selective. A high density indicates that a given index node points to several table rows and may be less useful than a low-density index.

To update the statistics for a specific table, use the UPDATE STATISTICS command. To update the statistics on all the tables in the current database, use the sp_updatestats system stored procedure. sp_updatestats procedure basically runs UPDATE STATISTICS on all the tables in the current database. sp_updatestats stored procedure does not unnecessarily update every statistics. It updates specific statistics only if enough data has changed based on rowmodctr information in the sys.sysindexes compatibility view. The following code updates the statistics for all the indexes on the Person.Contact table in the AdventureWorks2012 sample database.

```
USE AdventureWorks2012;
EXEC sp_help 'Person.Person;
UPDATE STATISTICS Person.Person;
```

The following code updates the statistics for all the tables in the AdventureWorks2012 sample database.

```
USE AdventureWorks2012;
EXEC sp_updatestats;
```

Index Density

Index density refers to what percentage of the index pages contains data. If the index density is low, SQL Server must read more pages from the disk to retrieve the index data. The index's *fill factor* refers to what percentage of the index page contains data when the index is created, but the index density slowly alters during inserts, updates, and deletes.

The `ALTER INDEX REBUILD` command completely rebuilds the index. Using this command is essentially the equivalent of dropping and creating the index with the added benefit to allow the user to set the fill factor as the index is re-created. In contrast, the `ALTER INDEX REORGANIZE` command repairs fragmentation to the index's fill factor but does not adjust the target fill factor.

The following code re-creates all the indexes on the `Frag` table and sets the fill factor to 98 percent:

```
USE tempdb;
ALTER INDEX ALL ON Frag REBUILD WITH (FILLFACTOR = 98);
```

At this point, you have a couple of objects in the `tempdb` database that you need to clean up. Use the following code to perform the task:

```
DROP TABLE Frag;
DROP PROCEDURE Add100K;
```

Database File Size

SQL Server 7.0 moved beyond SQL Server 6.5's method of allocated space with fixed-size files called *devices*. Since SQL Server 7.0, data and transaction logs can automatically grow as required. File size is still an area of database-maintenance concern. Without some intervention or monitoring, the data files could grow too large. The following commands and DBCC options deal with monitoring and controlling file sizes.

Monitoring Database File Sizes

Three factors of file size should be monitored: the size of the database files and their maximum growth size, the amount of free space within the files, and the amount of free space on the disk drives.

The current and maximum file sizes are stored within the `sys.database_files` database catalog view. The following code displays the name, size, and max size for the AdventureWorks2012 sample database:

```
USE AdventureWorks2012;
SELECT name, size, max_size from sys.database_files;
```

Result:

```
Name                         size     max_size
---------                    -------  ---------
AdventureWorks2012_Data      25080    -1
AdventureWorks2012_Log       256      268435456
```

where `size` is the current size and `max_size` is the maximum size of the file, in 8KB pages. A value of `-1` for max_size indicates that the file will grow until the disk is full, and `268435456` indicates that the maximum size of the log file will be 2TB.

To check the current and maximum file sizes for all the databases, use the `sys.master_files` catalog view.

To detect the percentage of the file that is actually used, use the `sp_spaceused` system stored procedure. Optionally, you can run the `DBCC UPDATEUSAGE` command to correct disk space usage inaccuracies or use the `@updateusage` optional parameter with the `sp_spaceused` command. The following command updates the space usage information of the AdventureWorks2012 sample database and then runs the `sp_spaceused` command.

```
USE AdventureWorks2012;
DBCC UPDATEUSAGE (AdventureWorks2012);
EXEC sp_spaceused;
```

Result:

```
database_name        database_size       unallocated space
-----------------    -----------------   -----------------
AdventureWorks2012 197.94 MB             15.62 MB

reserved             data                index_size          unused
-----------------    -----------------   -----------------   --------
184648 KB            96672 KB            81440 KB            6536 KB
```

To determine the size and percentage of used space within the transaction log, use the `DBCC SQLPERF (LOGSPACE)` command:

```
DBCC SQLPERF (LOGSPACE);
```

Result :

```
Database Name       Log Size(MB) Log Space Used(%) Status
-----------------   ------------ ----------------- ------
Master              0.9921875    41.73228          0
Tempdb              0.4921875    76.68651          0
Model               0.4921875    57.14286          0
Msdb                0.4921875    47.61905          0
AdventureWorks2012 1.992188      35.19608          0
DBCC execution completed. If DBCC printed error messages,
contact your system administrator.
```

To monitor the amount of free space on the server's disk drives, you can use the undocumented extended stored procedure `xp_fixeddrives`:

```
EXEC master..xp_fixeddrives;
```

Result:

```
drive MB Free
----- -------
C     429
F     60358
```

NOTE

Because `xp_fixeddrives` is an undocumented stored procedure, there is no support for this, and it can be removed from SQL Server at any time.

Shrinking the Database

Unless the database is configured to automatically shrink in the background, the file space freed by deleting unused objects and rows will not be returned to the disk operating system. Instead, the files remain at the largest size to which the data file may have grown. If data is regularly added and removed, constantly shrinking and growing the database would be a wasteful exercise. However, if disk space is at a premium, a large amount of data has been removed from the database, and the database is not configured to automatically shrink, then the following commands may be used to manually shrink the database. The database can be shrunk while transactions are working in the database.

> **NOTE**
>
> Using auto shrink is not a recommended practice and will definitely affect performance because this resource-intensive operation causes not only index fragmentation but file-system level fragmentation as well. For more detailed information, refer to Paul Randal's blog: Auto-Shrink - Turn It Off! at `http://www.sqlskills.com/blogs/paul/post/Auto-shrink-e28093-turn-it-OFF!.aspx`.

 For more information on @AutoShrink, see Chapter 20, "Policy Based Management."

DBCC SHRINKDATABASE can shrink the size of the database files by performing two basic steps:

1. Pack data to the front of the file, leaving the empty space at the end of the file.
2. Remove the empty space at the end of the file, reducing the size of the file.

You can control these two steps with the following options:

- The NOTRUNCATE option causes DBCC SHRINKDATABASE to perform only step 1, packing the database file but leaving the file size the same.
- The TRUNCATEONLY option eliminates the empty space at the end of the file but does not first pack the file.
- The target_percent option specifies the wanted percentage of free space after the file is shrunk. Because autogrowth can be an expensive operation, leaving some free space is a useful strategy. If the desired free space percentage is larger than the current amount of free space, this option does not increase the size of the file.

The following command shrinks the AdventureWorks2012 sample database and leaves 10 percent free space:

```
DBCC SHRINKDATABASE ('AdventureWorks2012', 10);
```

Result:

```
DBCC SHRINKDATABASE: File ID 1 of database ID 9 was skipped
   because the file does not have enough free space to reclaim. Cannot
shrink log file 2 (AdventureWorks2012_Log) because requested size
(568KB) is larger than the start of the last logical log file.

DbId    FileId      CurrentSize MinimumSize UsedPages   EstimatedPages
------  ----------- ----------- ----------- ----------- --------------
9       2           96          63          96          56

(1 row(s) affected)

DBCC execution completed. If DBCC printed error messages,
   contact your system administrator.
```

The results show that not all the files had space to reclaim. The command tells you which files it did change by displaying the old and new statistics. DBCC SHRINKDATABASE affects all the files for a database, whereas the DBCC SHRINKFILE command shrinks individual files.

Best Practice

DBCC SHRINKDATABASE causes massive index fragmentation and file-system fragmentation of the data files because they will likely need to grow again after you shrink all the space. This severely affects performance. As a best practice, if you do need to run DBCC SHRINKDATABASE, it's a good idea to rebuild all the indexes in your database to remove index fragmentation and boost performance.

For more information on the dangers of shrinking your data files, see Paul Randal's blog on Why You Should Not Shrink Your Data Files at www.sqlskills.com/BLOGS/PAUL/post/Why-you-should-not-shrink-your-data-files.aspx.

Shrinking the Transaction Log

When the database shrinks, the transaction log also shrinks. The NOTRUNCATE and TRUNCATEONLY options have no effect on the transaction log. If multiple log files exist, SQL Server shrinks them as if they were one large contiguous file.

A common problem is a transaction log that grows and refuses to shrink down to an expected minimum size. The most likely cause is an old open transaction. The transaction log is constructed of virtual log partitions. The success or failure of shrinking the transaction log depends on the aging of transactions within the virtual logs and log checkpoints. SQL Server can shrink only the transaction log by removing data older than the oldest transaction within the structure of the virtual logs, or in other words, it can remove only transactions marked as inactive.

To verify that an old transaction has a hold on the transaction log, use the DBCC OPENTRAN command. The following example detects open transaction information for the AdventureWorks2012 sample database.

```
USE AdventureWorks2012;
CREATE TABLE Test(Col1 int);
BEGIN TRAN;
INSERT INTO Test VALUES (1);
DBCC OPENTRAN;
```

Result:

```
(1 row(s) affected)
Transaction information for database 'AdventureWorks2012'.

Oldest active transaction:
    SPID (server process ID): 59
    UID (user ID) : -1
```

```
Name              : user_transaction
LSN               : (42:228:1)
Start time        : May 30 2012   7:31:53:077PM
SID               :
0x01050000000000000515000000f619041ca1c7523210b246a2e8030000
DBCC execution completed. If DBCC printed error messages,
contact your system administrator.
```

Based on this information, the errant transaction can be tracked down, and the SPID (user connection) can be killed. SQL Server Management Studio's Processes node in Activity Monitor can provide more information about the SPID's activity. A more drastic option is to stop and restart the server and then shrink the database.

> The recovery model and transaction log backups both affect how the transaction log grows and automatically truncates. For more information on these critical issues, refer to Chapter 21, "Backup and Recovery Planning."

Now that you've seen an open transaction, close it. The following code rolls back the transaction and verifies that there aren't any other open transactions for the database:

```
ROLLBACK TRAN;
DROP TABLE Test;

DBCC OPENTRAN;
```

Result:

```
No active open transactions.
DBCC execution completed. If DBCC printed error messages,
    contact your system administrator.
```

Miscellaneous DBCC Commands

The remaining DBCC commands are used in troubleshooting during testing of stored procedures and triggers. The first five DBCC commands must be used with caution and should not be run against a production SQL Server instance because it may result in a sudden decrease in query performance.

- DBCC DROPCLEANBUFFERS: Cleans the memory of any buffered data so that it doesn't affect query performance during testing. This command is useful for testing queries without recycling SQL Server service.

- DBCC FREEPROCCACHE: This command can clear an entire plan cache, remove specific plans from the plan cache (by specifying a plan or SQL handle), or you can clear all cache entries associated with a specified resource pool.

- DBCC FLUSHPROCINDB(DBID): Clears out the stored procedure cache for a specific SQL Server database and not the entire SQL Server.

- DBCC FREESESSIONCACHE: Clears the cache used by the distributed queries.

- DBCC FREESYSTEMCACHE: Clears the unused cache entries from all caches. It also clears the plan cache. It also causes an unload of all AppDomains for SQLCLR and frees the CLR memory allocations in the Virtual Address Space/Memory To Leave areas. Additionally, with this command, you're able to manually remove unused entries from all caches or from a specified Resource Governor pool cache.

- DBCC INPUTBUFFER (SPID): Returns the last command executed by a client, as identified by the client's SPID. This command can be executed only by members of the sysadmin server group or those who have explicit VIEW SERVER STATE permission.

- DBCC OUTPUTBUFFER (SPID): Returns the results of the last command executed by a client in hexadecimal and ASCII format. Like the DBCC INPUTBUFFER command, this command can be executed only by members of the sysadmin group.

- DBCC PROCCACHE: Reports some basic statistics about the procedure cache as queries and procedures are compiled and stored in memory.

- DBCC PINTABLE: Has been deprecated and has no effect on the server.

- DBCC UNPINTABLE: Has been deprecated and has no effect on the server.

- DBCC dllname (FREE): Unloads the specified extended stored procedure dll from memory.

- DBCC MEMORYSTATUS: Provides a snapshot of the current memory status of SQL Server. This command is useful in troubleshooting issues that relate to SQL Server memory consumption.

- DBCC USEROPTIONS: Returns the active SET options for the current connections.

You can use the following three DBCC commands with trace flags. Use trace flags to temporarily set certain specific SQL Server characteristics or turn off some behavior. For example, use trace flag 1204 to enable deadlock reporting to SQL Server Errorlog.

- DBCC TRACEON: Turns on the specified trace flags

- DBCC TRACEOFF: Turns off the specified trace flags

- DBCC TRACESTATUS: Displays the active trace flags

Managing Database Maintenance

SQL Server provides a host of database maintenance commands. Fortunately, it also provides the DBA with ways to schedule maintenance tasks.

Planning Database Maintenance

Database maintenance plans include the following routine tasks:

- Check database integrity.
- Perform index maintenance.
- Update database statistics.
- Perform database backups.

These maintenance tasks can be automated and scheduled using SQL Server Agent service. Once created, the maintenance plans (and subplans) are scheduled in SQL Server Agent as jobs.

Maintenance Plan

Following are two ways to create a Maintenance Plan:

- **Maintenance Plan Wizard**: Used to quickly create a basic maintenance plan. This enables you to choose one of the predefined typical maintenance tasks, such as performing database backup, rebuilding indexes, updating statistics, checking data integrity and cleaning up history and backup files.. It does not enable you to add any custom tasks.
- **Maintenance Plan Design Surface**: Used to design maintenance plans with more flexibility. This enables you to create a workflow of typical maintenance tasks and create custom maintenance tasks using T-SQL scripts. It also enables extended logging, which can prove to be useful for troubleshooting purposes.

All the maintenance plans appear in the Management\Maintenance Plans folder of SQL Server Management Studio. To launch the Maintenance Plan Wizard, right-click the Maintenance Plans folder, and choose Maintenance Plan Wizard. Follow the simple step-by-step wizard to create the maintenance plan.

To launch the Maintenance Plan Design Surface, right-click the Maintenance Plans folder, and choose New Maintenance Plan from the context menu. Type a name for the maintenance plan in the New Maintenance Plan dialog box, and click OK.

After you assign a name to your maintenance plan, Management Studio opens a new center window that includes the maintenance plan name, a description, the time you want to schedule the maintenance plan, and a list of tasks to perform. Figure 22-1 shows a sample maintenance plan with some tasks already entered.

22

Adding a Task

A maintenance plan must contain at least one task. Fortunately, it isn't hard to add one to your maintenance plan. Simply drag and drop the appropriate task from the Toolbox, as shown in Figure 22-2, to the design area of the maintenance plan. The resulting task appears as a square, as shown in Figure 22-1.

FIGURE 22-1

Create a maintenance plan by adding some tasks and scheduling a time to perform the tasks.

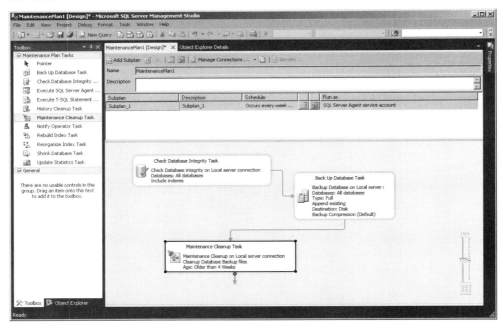

The task isn't configured yet. Use the Properties window, as shown in Figure 22-3, to configure the task. The content of the Properties window varies by task. For example, when you select a Back Up Database Task, you see properties to choose the kind of database, the backup device type, and other information associated with backing up the database. The upper portion of the Properties window contains the name of the selected task. You can choose other tasks using the drop-down list box. The middle of the Properties window contains a list of properties for the selected task. You can organize the properties by category or in alphabetical order. The lower part of the Properties window contains a description for the selected property. After you work with tasks for a while, the description usually provides enough information to help you remember how to use the selected property.

FIGURE 22-2

Use the Toolbox to add new tasks to your maintenance plan.

FIGURE 22-3

Define the task specifics using the Properties window.

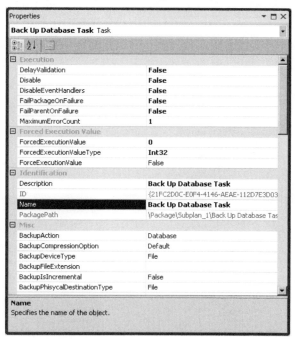

Sometimes you may not want to use the Properties window. For example, you might be working with a new task. In this case, you can bypass the Properties window by double-clicking the task. A task-specific window for a backup task appears, as shown in Figure 22-4. Unlike the Properties window, this dialog box displays the task properties in context. In addition, it grays out task elements until you define the correct functionality. For example, when you choose to back up specific databases, the dialog box won't let you perform any other configuration task until you choose one or more databases for the backup.

FIGURE 22-4

In addition to the Properties window, you can use the task-related dialog box for configuration.

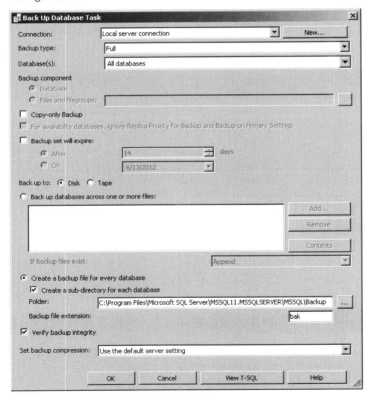

It's interesting to click View T-SQL when you finish configuring the task. The resulting window like the one shown in Figure 22-5, displays the T-SQL that the task uses. The Transact-SQL (Task Generated) window won't let you edit the command, but seeing how the Maintenance Plan Wizard generates the code can prove helpful when you need to create T-SQL commands of your own.

You know when a task is complete by the appearance of the square in the design area. Incomplete tasks, those that won't correctly execute, have a red circle with an X through it on the right side of the display.

After you define a task, add the next task in your list. You can add the tasks in any order and place them in any order on screen. Connect the tasks in the order in which you want SQL Server to execute them. Figure 22-1 showed two tasks with one task connected to the next task in the list. The example checks the integrity of the AdventureWorks2012 database first and then backs it up.

FIGURE 22-5

View T-SQL button enables you to see the Transact-SQL command.

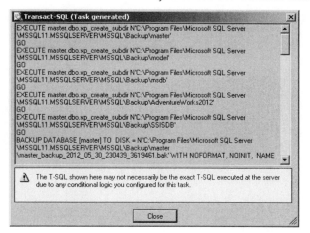

> **NOTE**
>
> There is a shrink database task available in the maintenance plan toolbox; however, it is highly recommended you AVOID using this in any regular maintenance plan. Shrinking databases, as mentioned earlier in this chapter, causes index and file-level fragmentation, which leads to degraded performance. If you currently are using this in your maintenance plans, it is highly recommended you re-evaluate your use for it and remove it from your plans if possible. This task leads to more harm than good.

Defining the Schedule

You can perform tasks on demand or schedule them to automatically run. Generally, it's a good idea to set standard tasks such as backup to run automatically. Click the calendar icon next to the Schedule field to display the Job Schedule Properties dialog box, as shown in Figure 22-6, when you want to change the task schedule.

Select the scheduling requirements for the task. For example, you can set a task to run daily, weekly, or monthly. The dialog box also enables you to select a specific starting time for the task and determine when the scheduling begins and ends. The one form of scheduling that this dialog box doesn't provide is on demand. To set the maintenance task to run on demand, uncheck the enabled box and click OK to save the changes.

FIGURE 22-6

Define a schedule that meets the task requirements; use off-hours scheduling for tasks that require many resources.

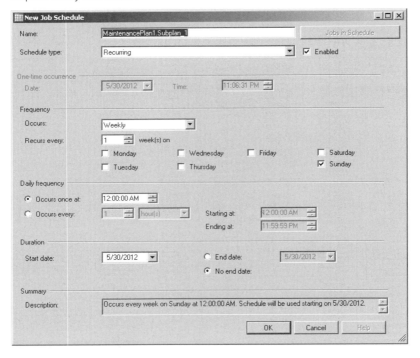

Creating New Connections

Depending on your database setup, you might need to create multiple connections to perform a particular task. The Maintenance Plan always provides a connection to the default instance of the local database.

1. Click Manage Connections to add more connections to the current maintenance plan. (Any additions won't affect other maintenance plans you create.) You see the Manage Connections dialog box, as shown in Figure 22-7.
2. Click Add in the Manage Connections dialog box to add a new connection. You see a New Connection dialog box. A connection consists of three elements: connection name, server name, and server security.

3. Choose a connection name that reflects the server and instance. Using a name such as My Connection isn't particularly helpful when you need to troubleshoot the maintenance task later. You can either type the server and instance name or select it from a list that the Maintenance Plan provides when you click the ellipses next to the Select or Enter a Server Name field.

4. Finally, choose between Windows integrated or SQL Server security.

5. Click OK to add the new connection to the list.

FIGURE 22-7

Add new connections as needed to perform maintenance tasks.

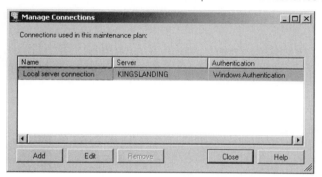

The Manage Connections dialog box also enables you to edit existing connections or remove old connections. When you edit an existing connection, you see a New Connection dialog box in which you can change the logon arguments or the server name for the connection. The dialog box grays out the other fields. Simply click Remove to delete a connection you no longer need from the list.

CAUTION

Connection deletion is a one-way process, and it happens quite quickly. Make sure you have the correct connection selected before you click Remove because the Maintenance Plan won't ask for confirmation before deleting the connection.

Logging the Maintenance Progress

Many of the maintenance tasks that you automate execute during off hours, when you're unlikely to be around to monitor the system. Fortunately, you can set maintenance tasks to log and report their actions so that you don't need to watch them every moment. To use this feature, click the Reporting and Logging icon next to the Manage Connections icon. You see the Reporting and Logging dialog box, as shown in Figure 22-8.

FIGURE 22-8

Add new connections as needed to perform maintenance tasks.

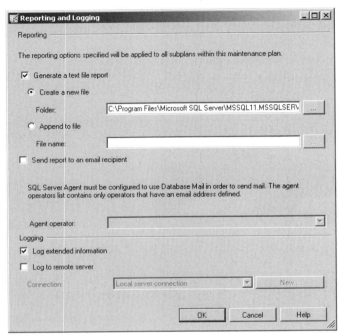

The features of the Reporting and Logging dialog box enable you to send the report to a file or to your e-mail. The e-mail feature works quite well and saves you the time of searching for the file on the hard drive. However, the text file provides an archive that could prove helpful long after you delete the e-mail from your inbox. Additionally you can choose to centralize your logging by selecting the Log to remote server option. After you configure the reporting options, click OK, and the maintenance plan records its actions for you.

Best Practice

You normally want to provide extended information about all maintenance tasks that the system performs without your supervision. Even the smallest piece of information can help you determine where a particular maintenance action went awry.

Command-Line Maintenance

Database maintenance is normally performed within SQL Server Management Studio or automated with SQL Server Agent. However, maintenance can be performed from the DOS command prompt by means of SQLMaint utility. This utility has numerous options that can perform backups, update statistics, and run DBCC.

> **NOTE**
>
> This feature will be removed in the next version of SQL Server. Do not use this feature in new development work and plan to change applications that use this feature. To run SQL Server maintenance plans from the command line, use the dtexec utility.

You can find specific information on SQLMaint and dtexec in SQL Server 2012 Books Online.

Monitoring Database Maintenance

It's not enough to simply schedule the tasks; they must be monitored as well. In larger installations with dozens of SQL Servers spread around the globe, just monitoring the health of SQL Server and the databases becomes a full-time job. Table 22-1 provides a sample DBA daily checklist that you can use as a starting point to develop a database monitoring plan.

TABLE 22-1 **DBA Daily Checklist**

Item	S	M	T	W	T	F	S
System Databases Backup							
Production User Databases Backup							
SQL Agent, SQL Maint, & DTC running							
Database Size, Growth, Disk Free Space							
Batch Jobs Execute OK							
DBCC Jobs Execute OK							
SQL Log Errors							
Replication Log Agent Running							
Replication Distribution Cleanup Job Execute OK							
SQL Server Last Reboot							

Depending on the complexity and the number of servers, you can manually maintain the DBA daily checklist with an Excel spreadsheet or track it in a SQL Server table.

Summary

This chapter covered database maintenance in detail. SQL Server offers a rich set of commands and utilities that you can use to monitor the health of, and perform maintenance on, SQL Server. The Maintenance Plan Wizard is also available to streamline database maintenance. All installations of SQL Server should also include a database maintenance schedule to assist the DBA in keeping track of maintenance performed.

The next chapter explains how to use SQL Agent, which you can use to schedule jobs and create custom maintenance jobs and Database Mail to send e-mails from SQL Server.

Transferring Databases

Transferring data may be a mundane task, but SQL Server databases are often developed on one server and deployed on other servers. Without a reliable and efficient method to move database schemas and whole databases, the project can't go far.

What's New in SQL Server Configuration?

sp_attach_db is a deprecated feature and will be removed in future versions of SQL Server. It is recommended to use CREATE DATABASE database_name FOR ATTACH instead.

For a full detailed listing of all features being deprecated in this, and future, releases of SQL Server see http://msdn.microsoft.com/en-us/library/ms143729.aspx.

SQL Server enables multiple means to move databases. As a database developer or database administrator (DBA), you should have basic skills in the following topics, four of which are covered in this chapter:

- Copy Database Wizard
- SQL scripts
- Detach/Attach
- Backup/Restore (covered in Chapter 21, "Backup and Recovery Planning")
- Data-Tier Application

The keys to determining the best way to move a database are knowing how much of it needs to be moved and whether the servers are directly connected by a fast network. Table 23-1 lists the copy requirements and the various methods to move a database.

TABLE 23-1 **Database Transfer Methods**

Requirement	Copy Database Wizard	SQL Scripts	Detaching Attaching	Backup Restore
Exclusive Access to the Database	Yes	No	Yes	No
Copies Between Disconnected Servers	No	Yes	Yes	Yes
Copies Database Schema	Yes	Yes	Yes	Yes
Copies Data	Yes	Depends on the script	Yes	Yes
Copies Security	Server logins, database users, security roles, and permissions	Depends on the script	Database users, security roles, and permissions	Database users, security roles, and permissions
Copies Jobs/User-Defined Error Messages	Yes	Depends on the script	Yes	Yes

The preceding four methods are good for moving databases from one SQL Server to another. But on many occasions a DBA needs to quickly move a few tables from one database to another or copy data from a non-SQL Server database (for example, Microsoft Office Excel or a flat file) to SQL Server or vice versa. To accomplish this, Microsoft provides the Import and Export Wizard to quickly copy data from one source to another.

Copy Database Wizard

The Copy Database Wizard generates a SQL Server Integration Services (SSIS) package that can copy or move one or more databases from one server to another. If the database is moved to a server on the same network server, this is the premiere method. This method won't work to copy a database from SQL Server 2012 to an older version of SQL Server. In addition, destination server must have the SQL Server Agent running. If the destination server's SQL Server Agent is not running, the wizard will prompt you to start it. The Copy Database Wizard offers the most flexibility and capability. The wizard offers you one of two choices: The detach and attach method or the SQL Management Object (SMO) method.

> **WARNING**
>
> The detach and attach method may be faster but requires the database to go offline because the database is being removed from the existing instance. You should be extremely careful with this method for upgrade purposes because this method is a "one-way" process. If you detach a database from a lower version of SQL Server (e.g. 2008 R2) and attach it to a higher level such as SQL Server 2012, upon attachment to the new instance, the database gets internally upgraded to be compatible with the new version. Due to this automatic upgrade process, the database files can no longer be attached to a lower-level version. Before you complete *any* upgrade or migration process make sure you get good full backups of your databases so you can roll back in case there are any issues.

You access the Copy Database Wizard by right-clicking the database you want to copy and choosing Tasks ➪ Copy Database from the context menu. Skip past the Welcome to the Copy Database Wizard page by clicking Next.

 For more information about starting and stopping SQL Server Agent, refer to Chapter 3, "Installing SQL Server."

On the first screen (Select a Source Server) and second screen (Select a Destination Server) the Copy Database Wizard begins by gathering the name of the source and destination servers and the required security information to log into the server.

On the third screen (Select the Transfer Method), as shown in Figure 23-1, the wizard asks how you want to transfer the database. Using the detach and attach method is faster, but it requires that SQL Server have additional rights to both source and destination databases, and you must allow exclusive access to both. The detach and attach method works best for large databases. The SQL Management Object (SMO) method doesn't require any special access, and users can continue using the source database, but the user can still have issues with rights so be sure you have sufficient rights to access all objects from the source database. However, this method is significantly slower and is not recommended for large databases.

On the Select Databases, screen, as shown in Figure 23-2, the wizard enables you to select the databases you want to move or copy. The status column lets you know if it is OK to move the database and explains if the database cannot be moved. For example, system databases (master, msdb, model and tempdb) cannot be moved or copied.

FIGURE 23-1

Select your preferred choice of transfer.

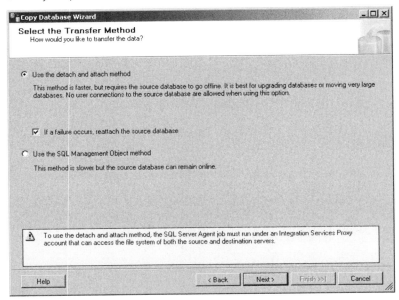

FIGURE 23-2

Select the databases you want to copy or move.

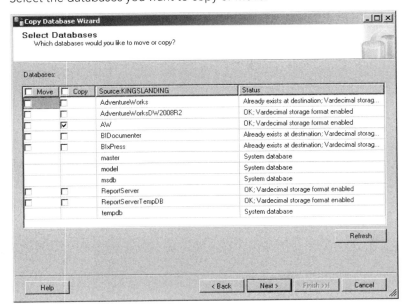

On the Configure Destination Database screen the wizard asks you to configure the destination database. You modify the destination database name and modify the default locations for the database files on the destination server. You also specify how the Copy Database Wizard reacts when a database with the requested name already exists on the destination. The options are either stopping the transfer or dropping the existing database and creating a new database with the same name. The wizard moves all the objects and data.

At the Select Server Objects screen you can optionally direct the wizard to move the following:

- All logins or only those that have access to the database
- All or selected nonsystem stored procedures in the Master database used by the database
- All or selected SQL Agent jobs (automated and optionally scheduled tasks)
- All or selected endpoints
- All or selected SSIS packages
- All or selected user-defined error messages (used by the `raiserror` T-SQL command)

Click the ellipsis button next to each selected option and choose individual objects you want to transfer. If you do not choose individual objects, all the objects of each selection option are transferred by default.

The Configure the Package screen shows the location of the Integration Services package generated by this process. You can also provide a name for the package and choose a method for logging errors. The default method uses the Windows event log. You can also send a list of errors to a text file. The wizard requests a filename when you choose this option.

The Schedule the Package directs the wizard to either run the Integration Services package once upon completion of the wizard, run it once later, or set it up on a regular schedule.

The final screen   shows a summary of choices that were made so far. If you want to change something, you can click the Back button to revisit your selections. If you are satisfied with all the choices, click Finish.

When finished, the wizard generates and runs (if you selected the option to run immediately) the Integration Services package on the destination server. If you selected the option to schedule the package, it is saved and scheduled on the destination server.

You can open the generated Integration Services job by selecting the Jobs node under SQL Server Agent (of destination SQL Server) in the console tree and then double-clicking on the package. If the name was not edited in the wizard's schedule page, the name should be CDW followed by the two server names and an integer. The creation date is also listed.

Working with SQL Script

Sometimes when you want to move a database, it is important to know that all the objects created on the destination are new and are exactly as you dictated them rather than potentially mix old and new objects/data together. This is where the option of scripting excels; it gives the administrator granular control over exactly what objects get created and when.

Scripts are smaller than databases. They often fit on a portable media, and they can be edited with simple tools such as Notepad. As an example, the sample databases for this book are distributed by means of scripts.

Scripts are useful for distributing the following:

- Database schema (databases, tables, views, stored procedures, functions, and so on)
- Security roles
- Database jobs
- Limited sample data or priming data

Although you could, it isn't recommended to create a script to move the following:

- **Data:** A script can insert rows, but this is a difficult method to move data.
- **Server logins:** A script can easily create server logins, but server logins tend to be domain-specific, so this option is useful only within a single domain.
- **Server jobs:** Server-specific jobs generally require individualized tweaking. Although a script may be useful to copy jobs, they likely require editing prior to execution.

You can also use scripts to implement a change to a database. The easiest way to modify a client database is to write a script. The change script can be tested on a backup of the database.

You can generate scripts in several ways:

- You can initially develop the database in Management Studio or SQL Server Data Tools using a handwritten DDL script. Chapter 7, "Relational Database Design and Creating the Physical Database Schema," explains how to create such a script. In addition, the sample databases on the website are all created using a DDL script.
- Management Studio can generate a script to create the entire database or a change script for schema changes made with the Table Designer or the Database Designer.
- Most third-party database-design tools generate scripts to create the database or apply changes.

With a focus on generating scripts with Management Studio, open the Management Studio script generator; select the database you wish to script out in the console tree, right-click, and select Tasks ➪ Generate Scripts.

Skip the Welcome to the Generate SQL Server Scripts screen by clicking Next. At the Choose Objects screen, as shown in Figure 23-3, you have the option of scripting out the entire database and all of the database objects together. Alternatively you can select to script out only specific database objects such as tables, views, stored procedures, etc.

FIGURE 23-3

Management Studio can generate scripts for any objects within the database.

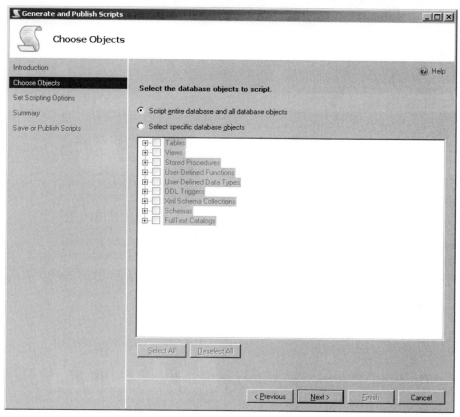

The Set Scripting Options screen, as shown in Figure 23-4, contains several options for saving the script. You can either save the scripts to a location of your choice or publish the objects directly to a remote web hosting provider. In order to be able to publish to a web service, you must have access to that service via the Database Publishing Services Web service.

In addition to saving to custom locations, you are given other options, such as generating a single script file for all objects or generating a script file per object. You can also choose to either save the generated script directly to the Windows clipboard or save to a new query window in SSMS.

FIGURE 23-4

Select your options for how your script should be saved or published.

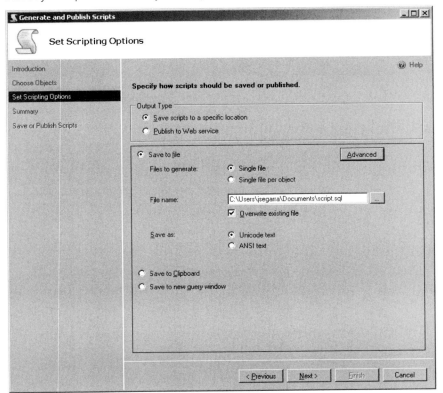

If you wish to have more granular options for your generated scripts, you can click the Advanced button to display the Advanced Scripting Options screen as shown in Figure 23-5. From there you specify advanced options, such as generating a script aimed at a specific version of SQL Server (which causes the scripted out options to be compatible with the selected target version), check for existing objects' existence, script for dependent objects, and much more.

FIGURE 23-5

Advanced Scripting Options.

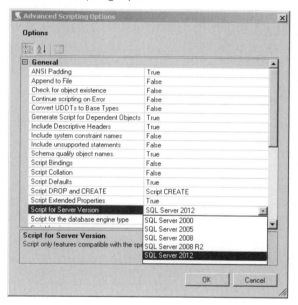

The Summary screen shows a summary of choices that were made so far. If you want to change something, you can click Previous and modify your selections. If you are satisfied with all the choices, click Next. Once you have clicked Next, the wizard will generate the scripts according to the options you selected. The Save or Publish Scripts screen shows a detailed breakdown of the status of each step of the process, as shown in Figure 23-6. If there are any errors, or if you simply wish to save results, you can click Save Report to save the output to HTML and review the report. Click Finish to complete the process.

FIGURE 23-6

Results of the script generation process.

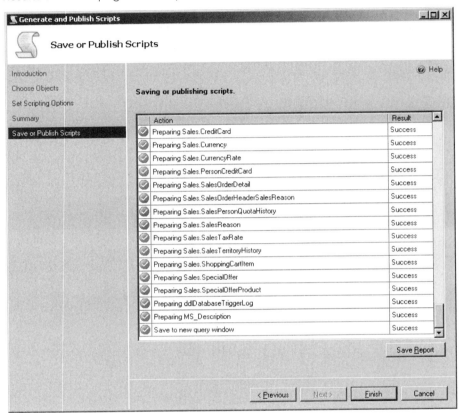

Detaching and Attaching

Although it is often overlooked, one of the easiest ways to move a database from one computer to another is to detach the database, copy the files, and attach the database to SQL Server on the destination computer.

For developers who frequently move databases between notebooks and servers, this is the recommended method. Detaching a database effectively deletes the database from SQL Server's awareness but leaves the files intact. The database must have no current connections, no snapshots, and not be replicated or mirrored if it is to be detached. Additionally, system databases or databases that are listed as being suspect may not be detached. In order to attach a database, you need at least CREATE DATABASE, CREATE ANY DATABASE, or ALTER ANY DATABASE permissions on the instance. To be able to detach a database, membership in the db_owner fixed database role is required.

> **WARNING**
>
> If you detach a database from a lower level of SQL Server and attach it to a higher level one (for example, 2005 to 2012), the database automatically upgrades. After you attach a database to a higher-level version, you cannot detach and reattach to a lower level version.

 For more details on the security roles, refer to Chapter 33, "Authorizing Securables."

Detaching and attaching the database can carry with it any database users, security roles, and permissions, but it cannot replicate server logins. These need to be resolved manually on the destination server. It's best to coordinate security with the network administration folks and leverage their security groups. If the source and destination servers have access to the same network security groups, this can alleviate the security login issues for most installations.

Using Management Studio, right-click the database to be copied, and select Tasks ➪ Detach. The Detach Database dialog box, as shown in Figure 23-7, appears.

FIGURE 23-7

The Detach Database feature removes the database from SQL Server's list of databases and frees the files for copying.

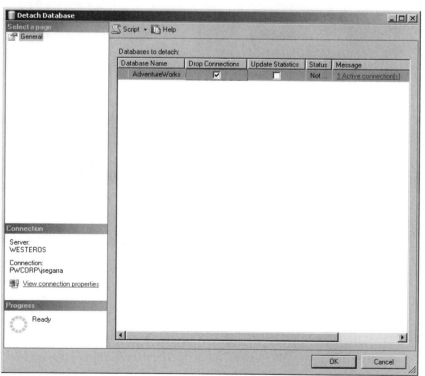

After the file is detached, the database disappears from the list of databases in Management Studio. The files may then be copied or moved like regular files.

To reattach the database file, select Databases in the Management Studio console tree and Tasks ➪ Attach from the action menu or context menu. The Attach Database dialog box, as shown in Figure 23-8, simply offers a place to select the file and verify the file locations and names.

FIGURE 23-8

The database may be reattached by means of Management Studio's Attach Database tool.

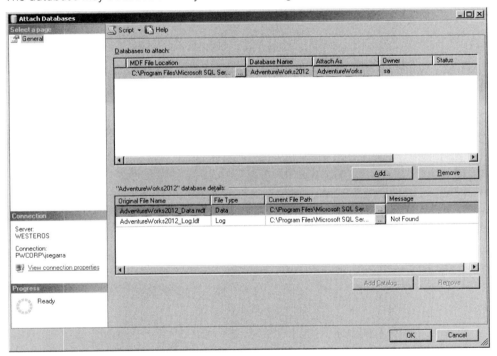

In code, the database is detached by running the sp_detach_db system stored procedure. The first parameter is the database to be detached. A second optional parameter simply turns off automatic updating of the index statistics. The following command detaches the AdventureWorks sample database:

```
sp_detach_db 'AdventureWorks'
```

If you want to reattach a database with code, the counterpart to sp_detach_db is the sp_attach_db system stored procedure. Attaching a database requires specifying the files' locations as well as the database name, as follows:

```
EXEC sp_attach_db @dbname = 'AdventureWorks2012',
    @filename1 = ' D:\MSSQL11.MSSQLSERVER\MSSQL\
Data\AdventureWorks2012_Data.mdf',
    @filename2 = 'E:\MSSQL11.MSSQLSERVER\MSSQL\
LOG\AdventureWorks2012_Log.ldf'
```

Best Practice

Use CREATE DATABASE database_name FOR ATTACH instead of sp_attach_db stored procedure because it will be removed in the future version of SQL Server. Following is an example:

```
CREATE DATABASE AdventureWorks2012 ON
    (FILENAME = ' G:\MSSQL10.INST1\MSSQL\Data\AdventureWorks2012_
Data.mdf'),

    (FILENAME = 'H:\MSSQL10.INST1\MSSQL\LOG\AdventureWorks2012_Log.ldf')
FOR ATTACH;
```

Special Instructions for Moving System Databases

Detaching and attaching system databases result in error by default. To move system databases, you must follow a strict set of procedures outlined at http://msdn.microsoft.com/en-us/library/ms345408.aspx.

Import and Export Wizard

On many occasions SQL DBAs need to do the following:

- Copy only a few tables from one SQL Server database to another SQL Server database.
- Import data from a flat file or a Microsoft Office Excel file.
- Copy data from one table to another with different collations.

To easily and quickly achieve these DBA tasks, Microsoft has provided another powerful wizard: called SQL Server Import and Export Wizard. This wizard enables copying data to and from any data source for which a managed .NET Framework data provider or a native OLE DB provider is available.

You can access the Import and Export Wizard from various locations:

- Choose Import and Export Data from Start ⇨ Programs ⇨ Microsoft SQL Server 2012.
- Open Management Studio, right-click a database and choose Task ⇨ Import Data or Export Data from the context menu.
- Open SQL Server Data Tools (SSDT) from Start ⇨ Programs ⇨ Microsoft SQL Server 2012. Open an SSIS solution, select SSIS Import and Export Wizard from the Project menu, or right-click the SSIS Packages folder.
- Run `DTSWizard.exe` (C:\Program Files\Microsoft SQL Server\110\DTS\Binn) from the command prompt.

To move data with the Import and Export Wizard, follow these steps:

1. Launch the Import and Export Wizard using one of the preceding methods.

2. Skip past the Welcome to SQL Server Import and Export Wizard by clicking Next.

3. On the Choose a Data Source screen, select the source data. If you launch the wizard from Management Studio by right-clicking the database and choose Task ⇨ Export Data, the source information is already preconfigured with the server and database name. Based on the source data, the other options on this screen can vary. For example, selecting SQL Server Native Client 11.0 enables you to specify the SQL Server, authentication, and database.

4. On the Choose a Destination screen, select the destination source. If you launch the wizard from Management Studio by right-clicking the database and choosing Task ⇨ Import Data, the destination information is already preconfigured with the server and database name. This screen also enables you to create a new destination database by clicking the New option.

5. Specify Table or Query page enable you to either copy all the data from existing source tables or views or write a T-SQL query to limit the data to copy.

6. On the Select Source Tables and Views screen, select all the tables and views you want to copy. If you opted to write a query on the previous screen, you can just select the query on this screen. Click Preview to preview up to 100 rows of source data. Click Edit Mappings to change the destination column names, data types, nullability, and size, as shown in Figure 23-9. If the destination table

exists, it enables you to either delete or append rows to the destination table. If no destination table exists, it enables creation of a new destination table.

FIGURE 23-9

Configuring the destination table and column mappings.

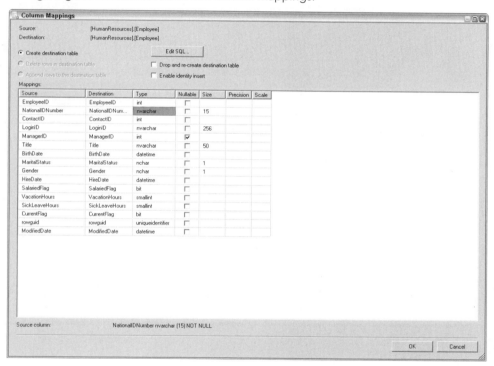

7. Depending on how you launch the Import and Export Wizard, the wizard works differently. For example, if you launch the wizard from SSDT, in the last step you cannot run the resulting package; instead the package is saved as part of the SSIS solution. On the other hand, if you launch the wizard from any other method (for example, Management Studio), the wizard enables running the package in the last step, as shown in Figure 23-10.

FIGURE 23-10

Indicating to run the package immediately and saving the package with encryption.

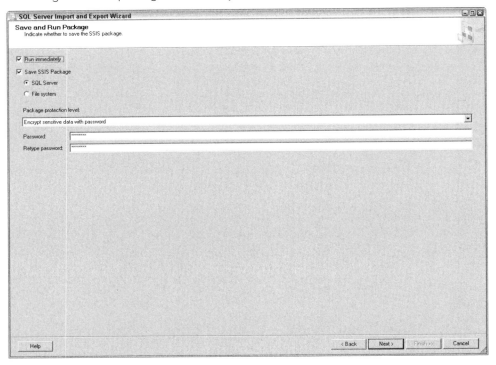

Best Practice

To copy the full database or multiple databases, use the Copy Database Wizard instead of the Import and Export Wizard.

Data-Tier Application (DAC)

Data-Tier Applications (DAC) were first introduced in SQL Server 2008 R2. A DAC defines all the database objects (such as tables and views) as well as instance objects associated with a database (such as logins).

This feature enables developers to build their database projects and encapsulates all the necessary database resources into a DAC package deployment file. The DAC file can then be deployed by administrators.

To begin creating and deploying DACs, you must first register a database as a DAC and then register that DAC definition to the instance. Follow these steps to register a database as a DAC:

1. Right-click the database, and from the context menu, choose Tasks ➪ Register as Data-Tier Application.

2. At the Introduction menu, click Next.

3. The DAC instance name is automatically the name of the database you register.

4. You can customize the Application name. If the database is associated with a particular application, you may want to use that name here so you can easily refer to it for a particular application.

5. Version level is set to 1.0.0.0 by default but can be manually incremented as needed.

6. In the description field, supply a quick description of what the database is and what application is associated with it. Click Next to proceed.

7. The DAC Wizard then validates all the objects in the database. When complete, you see a summary of your options selected as well as the validation checks. Click Next to proceed.

8. The DAC is then registered to the instance. Click Finish.

Now that you've registered your database as a DAC application, it's time to define its contents.

1. Right-click the database you registered in previous steps, and from the context menu, select Tasks ➪ Extract Data-Tier Application.

2. At the Introduction menu, click Next.

3. Here you supply the properties of the DAC. Give the Application a name and version number.

> **NOTE**
> Properly versioning your DAC application is important because this lets those who deploy the DACs in other environments know which revision level they are upgrading to.

4. Select a location to save the DAC package file (.dacpac) to by clicking the Browse button and navigating to your wanted location on your file system. If you want to overwrite an existing DAC package file, check the box for Overwrite existing file.

5. Click Next to proceed to Validation and Summary.

6. Click Next to proceed and build your DAC package.

7. Click Finish when complete.

Now that your application is encapsulated in a DAC package, you need to deploy it. Connect to the instance to which you want to deploy the DAC in Management Studio and follow these steps:

1. Right-click the databases node, and from the context menu, select Deploy Data-tier Application.

2. Click Next to advance the Introduction screen.

3. Click the Browse button, navigate to the file system location of your DAC package file. Select it and click Open.

4. At the Update Configuration screen you can customize the name of the deployed database. Click Next to proceed to the Summary screen.

5. After you verify your selections on the Summary screen, click Next to deploy the DAC application and database.

6. After deployment is complete, you can save a copy of the deployment by clicking the Save Report button.

7. Click Finish to complete.

Once you are done, you'll see your new database listed under the databases node on the target instance. One thing to note is that this process only encapsulates and deploys the database objects, the data itself is not transferred through DACPACs.

In order to move a Data-Tier Application, including its data, to another server you can instead choose to export the DAC rather than extract. Exporting a DAC creates another type of file, very similar to a DACPAC, called a BACPAC. This BACPAC file contains not only the database schema and objects but it also includes the data stored in the database.

Support for exporting a DAC or database can only be exported from a database in Azure SQL Database or SQL Server 2005 Service 4 (SP4) or later. Another limitation in exporting a DAC is that the database objects you are trying to export must also be supported in a DAC. For a full listing of supported objects and versions in a DAC refer to http://msdn.microsoft.com/en-us/library/ee210549.

Summary

When you need to move a database, backing up and restoring may not necessarily be the first or best option. Choose the right transfer method based on network proximity of the servers and the objects and data to be moved. Some key points to remember follow:

- Use the Detach/Attach method to quickly and easily move or copy a database from one server to another.

- If you cannot afford to detach a database, use the good old Backup/Restore method to copy a database from one server to another.

- The Copy Database Wizard is useful for copying or moving one or more databases from one server to another on the same network.

- To copy only a few tables from one server to another or copy data to and from any data source for which a managed .NET Framework data provider or a native OLE DB provider is available, use the Import and Export Wizard.

- Use Management Studio to quickly generate scripts to distribute database schemas, security, jobs, and limited data.

- Use Data-Tier Applications (DAC) to quickly encapsulate database projects for easy deployment and upgrades. Use DACPAC to encapsulate both schema and data, if your database objects are supported.

23

Database Snapshots

IN THIS CHAPTER

Understanding How Database Snapshots Work

Creating, Querying, and Dropping a Database Snapshot

Rolling Back a Database Snapshot

The Database Snapshot feature, originally introduced in SQL Server 2005, enables a point-in-time, read-only, consistent view of your user databases to use for reporting, auditing, or recovering purposes. Before database snapshots, this functionality was achieved by running a backup and restoring it to another database. The big advantages provided by database snapshots are the speed at which you create them and the capability to create multiple database snapshots of the same source database, providing you with snapshots of the database at different points in times.

> **NOTE**
> The Database Snapshot feature is an Enterprise Edition feature supported by all database recovery models.

The Database Snapshot feature was primarily designed to:

- Generate reports without blocking the production/source database.
- Perform reporting on a database mirror.
- Recover from user or administrator errors.
- Revert the source database to an earlier point in time.
- Report on historical and point-in-time data.
- Manage a test database.

Database snapshots are similar to databases in many ways but they do have some limitations of which you should be aware:

- Database snapshots are read-only static copies of the source database.
- You cannot create database snapshots for system databases (master, model, and tempdb).
- You can create database snapshots only on NTFS file system.

- You can create database snapshots only on the same SQL Server instance where the source database exists.
- Database snapshots depend on the source database, so if the source database is unavailable for any reason, all its database snapshots also become unavailable.
- The source database cannot be dropped, detached, or restored as long as it has any database snapshots. But source database backups are not affected by database snapshots.
- You cannot backup or restore a database snapshot. Nor can you attach or detach a database snapshot.
- You cannot revert to the database snapshot if you have multiple database snapshots. You need to drop all the database snapshots except the one that you want to revert to.
- Database snapshots do not support FILESTREAM.
- Full-text indexing is not supported on database snapshots and full-text catalogs are not propagated from the source database.
- In a log shipping configuration, database snapshots are allowed only on the primary database and not on the secondary or warm-standby database.
- Database snapshots are IO-intensive and may impact the performance of the system.

If these limitations are acceptable, the Database Snapshot feature can be an excellent way to create point-in-time, read-only copies of your production databases.

What's New with Database Snapshots in SQL 2012?

The new AlwaysOn feature in SQL 2012 supports database snapshots on the primary or secondary database in an availability group. For more information on database snapshots in availability groups refer to http://technet.microsoft.com/en-us/library/hh213414.aspx.

How Do Database Snapshots Work?

As discussed earlier, a database snapshot is a point-in-time, read-only, static view of the source database as it existed at the time of the database snapshot creation. Understanding the mechanics and technology behind database snapshots can help you understand how it all works.

Mechanics of Snapshots

When you create a database snapshot, SQL Server runs recovery on the database snapshot and rolls back uncommitted transactions to make the database snapshot transactionally consistent. The transactions in the source database are not affected.

A database snapshot is not the same as the source database. It is a different database and has the same number of data files as the source database, but it does not have any transaction log file. When it is initially created, the data files in the snapshot database do not contain any user data and are almost empty. That is why creating a database snapshot does not take a long time.

Copy on First Write

Database snapshots use a copy-on-first-write method for each source database page updated for the first time after you create the database snapshot . For every database snapshot, SQL Server creates an in-memory bitmap. It has a bit for each data page indicating if the page is copied to the snapshot.

Every time you make an update to the source database, SQL Server checks the bitmap to see if it has been copied to the snapshot. If it is not copied, SQL Server copies the data page from the source database to the database snapshot and then makes the update. Next time if the same page is updated, it is not copied because the database snapshot just contains the data as it existed on the source database when you created the snapshot.

This is referred to as copy-on-first-write technology, as shown in Figure 24-1. If a data page on the source database is never updated, it is never copied to the database snapshot.

FIGURE 24-1

Database snapshot using copy-on-first-write Technology.

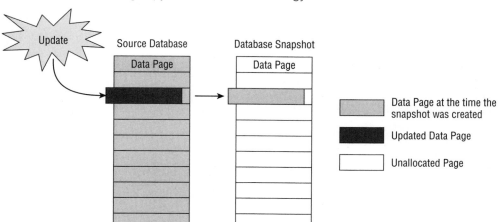

Using Database Snapshots

You can create, query, or drop database snapshots just as with regular databases. The main difference is that you can create them only from an existing database as a point-in-time, read-only database. After you create a snapshot, it can be queried the same way as regular databases. You cannot perform updates, inserts, or deletions on the data or make schema changes (adding or removing tables and columns).

You can use snapshots to revert a database to a specific point in time using similar syntax to what you would use to RESTORE the database from a database backup.

The following sections describe database snapshot operations in more detail.

Creating a Database Snapshot

You can create database snapshots only using the Transact-SQL command
CREATE DATABASE <...> ON <...> AS SNAPSHOT OF <...>.

NOTE

SQL Server Management Studio does not have any graphical interface to create database snapshots. You must use Transact-SQL.

Following are the step-by-step instructions to create a database snapshot of the AdventureWorks2012 sample database:

1. Find the information about the files in the source database. Use the following command to find the information about the files in the AdventureWorks2012 database.

```
USE AdventureWorks2012;
GO
EXECUTE sp_helpfile;
GO
```

The results of this query are shown in Figure 24-2.

FIGURE 24-2

Database file information.

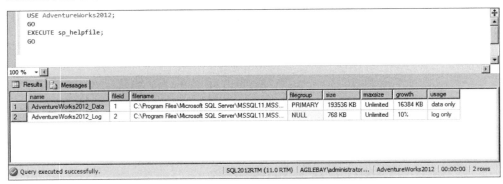

The logical name of the data files appears under the name column and their current file size under the size column. The preceding example has only one data file with the logical name AdventureWorks2012_Data and size 188160KB (or 183MB).

For each data file in the source database, a data file in the database snapshot exists. The data files in the database snapshot are different as compared to the source database data files. The data files in the database snapshot are NTFS sparse files. When you create the database snapshot, the sparse files are empty and do not contain any user data. The sparse files can potentially grow to the size of the data file of the source database at the time of the creation of the database snapshot. Therefore, you must verify that the volume where you want to place the database snapshot has enough free space.

NOTE

Even though you can create the database snapshot on a volume with little space, ensure that the volume has enough free space (at least the space of the source database when the database snapshot is created). If the volume runs out of space, the database snapshot is marked suspect, becomes unusable, and needs to be dropped.

2. Execute the CREATE DATABASE Transact-SQL command to create the database snapshot of the AdventureWorks2012 database:

```
CREATE DATABASE AdventureWorks2012_Snapshot ON
(NAME = AdventureWorks2012_Data, FILENAME =
'D:\DATABASE SNAPSHOTS\AdventureWorks2012_Snapshot.snap' )
AS SNAPSHOT OF AdventureWorks2012;
GO
```

NOTE

The FILENAME appears to wrap in the preceding code. In actual code, it should not wrap around or you get the error shown here:

```
Msg 5133, Level 16, State 1, Line 1
Directory lookup for the file "'D:\ DATABASE
    SNAPSHOTS\AdventureWorks2012_Snapshot.snap " failed with the
operating system error 123(The filename, directory name, or volume
label syntax is incorrect.).
```

24

Best Practice

To make it easier to use the database snapshot, think about how you want to name it before you start. One method is to include the source database name, some indication that it is a snapshot, the time it was created and a meaningful extension. The previous example uses the name AdventureWorks2012_Snapshot as the name and .snap as the extension to differentiate the database snapshot files from regular database files. The previous example creates the database snapshot on a different volume as the source database. Placing the database snapshot on a physically separate volume is best practice because this avoids disk contention and gives better performance.

After you create the database snapshot, you can view it using Management Studio. Using Object Explorer in Management Studio, connect to the SQL Server instance. Expand Databases and then Database Snapshots to see all the database snapshots, as shown in Figure 24-3.

FIGURE 24-3

Viewing database snapshots in Object Explorer.

> **TIP**
>
> Query the `sys.databases` catalog view, and review the `source_database_id` column. If this column is Null, then it is a regular database; if it is Non-Null, it represents the source database ID for the database snapshot.

To find out the space used by the database snapshot, open Windows Explorer, right-click the data file of the database snapshot, and select properties, as shown in Figure 24-4. The Size value (183MB in Figure 24-4) is not the actual size of the file. It is the maximum size of the file and should be approximately the same size of the source database when the database snapshot was created. The Size on Disk value 2.81MB (2,949,120 bytes), as shown in Figure 24-4, is the actual size of the database snapshot data file.

Alternatively, you can also find the size using the dynamic management view sys.dm_io_virtual_file_stats as shown here:

```
SELECT size_on_disk_bytes FROM
sys.dm_io_virtual_file_stats(DB_ID(N'AdventureWorks2012_Snapshot'),
1);
GO
```

Results:

```
2949120
```

FIGURE 24-4

Viewing the size of the database snapshot data file.

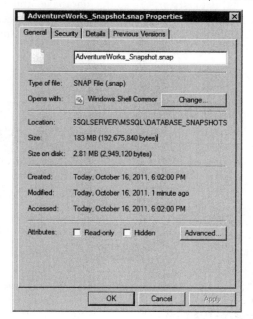

Querying Your Database Snapshots

After you create a database snapshot, users can query the database snapshot as if it were a regular database. For example, the following query retrieves the Name, ProductNumber, and ListPrice from the Product table in the AdventureWorks2012_Snapshot database snapshot.

```
USE AdventureWorks2012_Snapshot;
GO
SELECT Name, ProductNumber, ListPrice
FROM Production.Product
ORDER BY Name ASC;
GO
```

The main difference is that users cannot make any updates to the database snapshot because it is read-only. If users try to update the database snapshot, they receive error 3906 as shown here:

```
Msg 3906, Level 16, State 1, Line 1
Failed to update database "AdventureWorks2012_Snapshot" because the
database is read-only.
```

When a user reads from the database snapshot, SQL Server accesses the in-memory bitmap and finds out if the data it needs exists on the source database or database snapshot. If the data page was not updated, it exists on the source database, and SQL Server reads it from the source database. Figure 24-5 shows the read operation accessing the updated page from the database snapshot and the remaining pages from the source database.

FIGURE 24-5

Users querying the database snapshot, accessing the updated pages from the database snapshot, and unchanged pages from the source database.

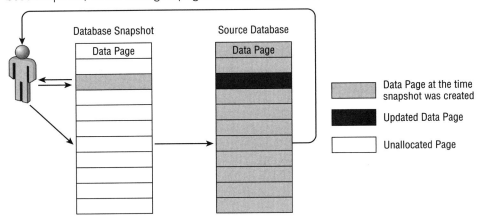

As discussed earlier, you cannot backup or restore database snapshots, nor can you attach or detach database snapshots. You can run reports against the database snapshot and can drop it when you no longer need it, it becomes too big, or the disk on which the database snapshot is located runs out of space and the database snapshot becomes suspect.

One of the great things about the implementation of database snapshots within Microsoft SQL Server is that even though a mirrored database cannot be read, a database snapshot can be taken of the mirrored database, and that snapshot can be read. This leads to some great options when it comes to moving all nightly and point-in-time reporting from a production database to another server. Simply set up database mirroring between the two servers (see Chapter 27, "Database Mirroring," for more information about database mirroring); then create a database snapshot on the mirrored database. Users can connect to the snapshot of the mirrored database and run reports from a point-in-time copy. You can refresh a snapshot of a mirrored database by deleting the original snapshot and creating a new one.

Dropping a Database Snapshot

Dropping a database snapshot is similar to dropping a regular database. The only thing different is that the users do not need to be terminated before dropping a database snapshot. They will be automatically terminated when you drop the snapshot.

The following example drops the database snapshot named AdventureWorks2012_Snapshot.

```
DROP DATABASE AdventureWorks2012_Snapshot;
```

The preceding Transact-SQL command drops the database snapshot and deletes the files in the database snapshot. You can also drop the database snapshot from Management Studio by right-clicking the database snapshot and selecting Delete.

Rolling Back a Database Snapshot

Database snapshots come in handy when testing code releases to ensure that a consistent database is available if a rollback is needed. Rolling back a database snapshot is done via the RESTORE DATABASE statement; however, instead of specifying a disk or tape to restore, a DATABASE_SNAPSHOT is specified instead. The following example reverts the AdventureWorks2012 database to the AdventureWorks2012_Snapshot database snapshot.

```
USE master;
GO
RESTORE DATABASE AdventureWorks2012
FROM DATABASE_SNAPSHOT = 'AdventureWorks2012_Snapshot';
GO
```

> **NOTE**
>
> Reverting to a database snapshot rebuilds the transaction log and breaks the log backup chain. This means that you cannot perform point-in-time restores in the period from the last log backup to the time when you reverted to the database snapshot. If you want to perform point-in-time restores in the future, take a full or differential backup and then start taking log backups again.

If the source database has multiple database snapshots and you attempt to revert the database to one of the snapshots, you receive error 3137 as shown here:

```
Msg 3137, Level 16, State 4, Line 1
Database cannot be reverted. Either the primary or the snapshot names
are improperly specified, all other snapshots have not been dropped,
or there are missing files.
Msg 3013, Level 16, State 1, Line 1
RESTORE DATABASE is terminating abnormally.
```

As per the error message, you must drop all the database snapshots except the one that you want to revert to.

NOTE

Using a database snapshot is not a replacement for your regular backup and restore strategy. For example, if there is a disk failure that results in the loss of the source database, you cannot use a database snapshot to recover. You need good backups. You can use database snapshots to supplement your restore strategy only if you need to quickly restore a table that has been accidentally dropped or some rows have been deleted. It's good practice to continue to take regular backups and restore them to test the backups to protect your data and minimize data loss when a disaster occurs.

After a database has been rolled back to a database snapshot, the snapshot still exists at the same point in time that it existed before the database was rolled back. This enables the database to continue to function and changes to be accepted while retaining the point-in-time state as part of the database snapshot. This can be extremely useful when performing load testing against a test instance because changes can be made, tested, rolled back, and tried again over and over without having to restore the entire database.

Anyone who has rights to restore a database on the SQL Server also has the ability to restore a database from a database snapshot. If database snapshots are in use on a production system, great care should be given as to who should have rights to the `RESTORE DATABASE` statement.

Rolling back a database to a prior point using a snapshot is not an operation that should be taken lightly. It requires that no users use the database and that the administrator is sure that all objects should be rolled back. If only a subset of the database needs to be rolled back, the database should not be restored from a database snapshot. Following is a partial list of things that are rolled back:

- Changes to data in tables
- Index creation and removal
- Table schema changes
- View schema changes
- Procedure code changes
- Messages in SQL Service Broker queues
- Any transactions that were not complete when the snapshot was taken
- Object permissions' changes
- FILESTREAM data
- File Table objects

Any data stored outside the application will not be rolled back when the database snapshot is rolled back. If there are files created and stored on the file system outside of the database (not using FILESTREAM and File Table) or somewhere on the network, these files will not be removed or updated when the database is rolled back.

Summary

Database snapshots enable you to create point-in-time, read-only versions of a database. You can use them for reporting, recovery, and comparison functionality. Some key takeaways from this chapter follow:

- Database snapshots enable maintaining readable point-in-time versions of a production database for reporting and recovery purposes.

- Database snapshots enable reporting on the mirror database that is not otherwise possible.

- Database snapshots enable you to restore the database to a specific point in time.

- Although database snapshots are powerful and flexible, they are I/O-intensive. If multiple database snapshots are created on a source database that is heavily updated, the I/O load increases and may impact the performance of the system.

Like any other feature, it is highly recommended you get a performance baseline of the environment before and after creating database snapshots and let your performance data help you decide whether or not you should use database snapshots.

24

Asynchronous Messaging with Service Broker

Service Broker is one of the most powerful features of SQL Server. This feature is essential in any Service-Oriented Architecture (SOA) data store architecture because it enables you to send asynchronous messaging and add work queues to a database to provide high flexibility, extensibility, and scalability.

If you've ever built a table to hold pending work, such as orders to be processed by a Material Resource Planning (MRP) system, then you've built a work queue. In one application, Service Broker is just that — a high-performance, wide-payload work queue manager integrated into SQL Server with DDL and monitoring capabilities, all rolled into one application.

For example, suppose that you want to pass sales order data to another database application that notifies customers that their order has been shipped. You can use Service Broker to send this message to another database where an e-mail message is queued to be sent out. The outgoing e-mails may have some sort of delay due to restrictions imposed by the e-mail provider. An independent process can manage e-mail transmissions without affecting the main sales database. You might also have a loosely coupled application in which communications cannot be guaranteed at all times. If data goes to a queue, it can be sent whenever the communications pipeline is open. Figure 25-1 illustrates an asynchronous shipping notification example using Service Broker.

FIGURE 25-1

Asynchronous Shipping Notification with Service Broker.

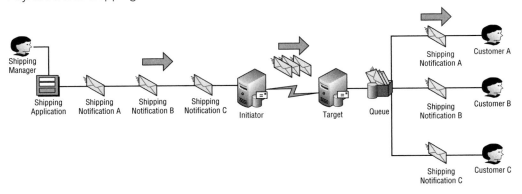

You can also use Service Broker to pass messages with guaranteed secure delivery between work queues, which opens a world of possibilities. Delivery of messages can occur within the same database, between databases hosted on the same instance, or within databases hosted on different instances. Asynchronous messaging between databases located in different geographical locations is extremely useful especially when they are at different time zones and work needs to be queued up during maintenance hours.

Because Service Broker is a SQL Server table managed internally, it includes all the cool transactional and back-up capabilities inherent to SQL Server. This is what sets Service Broker apart from other queuing technologies, such as MSMQ.

The queue contains a single column for the message body, which is fine because the message typically contains a single XML file or fragment or SOAP message as the payload. The queue will have other columns of its own that it manages.

Service Broker is not enabled by default, so the first step to working with Service Broker is to turn it on using the ALTER DATABASE command:

```
ALTER DATABASE AdventureWorks2012 SET ENABLE_BROKER;
```

Each database contains a Service Broker identifier that distinguishes it from all other databases in the network. The service_broker_guid column of the sys.databases catalog view shows the Service Broker identifier for each database in the instance. Service Broker systems can be designed to run multiple copies of a service. Each copy of the service runs in a separate database. In a system that has multiple copies of a service, use the BROKER_INSTANCE clause of the CREATE ROUTE statement to create a route to a specific copy of the service.

Service Broker routing uses the Service Broker identifier to ensure that all messages for a conversation are delivered to the same database. The BEGIN DIALOG CONVERSATION statement opens a conversation with a destination service. If a conversation is successfully opened, the acknowledgment message from the destination service contains the Service Broker identifier for the destination database. Service Broker then routes all messages for the conversation to the specified database.

Configuring a Message Queue

Service Broker uses a messaging or dialog metaphor, but there's much more to Service Broker than just the messages. The Service Broker uses the following objects, which must be defined in the following order:

1. Message types define the format and structure of a message.

2. Contracts define the agreement between the initiating service and the target, including the message type(s). Queues hold the messages for one or more services.

3. Services store messages in a queue and either send or receive messages as the *initiating service* or the *target service*, respectively.

Other than defining the message type as XML and naming the objects, there isn't much complexity to setting up a Service Broker database. Although the messages don't have to be XML, they almost always will be. That's because the data definition language, or DDL, does all the work; and Service Broker is a message-agnostic work queue that serves as an infrastructure for the messages. There's more work in placing messages on and taking messages off the queue.

The first step to is to enable Service Broker on the database. Then create a Service Broker queue by defining a message type and a contract that uses that message type:

```
ALTER DATABASE AdventureWorks2012 SET ENABLE_BROKER;
GO
CREATE MESSAGE TYPE HelloWorldMessage
  VALIDATION = WELL_FORMED_XML ;
GO
CREATE CONTRACT HelloWorldContract
  ( HelloWorldMessage SENT BY INITIATOR);
GO
```

The initiator and target queues are created using the CREATE QUEUE commands:

```
CREATE QUEUE [dbo].[TargetQueue] ;
GO
CREATE QUEUE [dbo].[InitiatorQueue] ;
GO
```

The initiator and target services are defined using the CREATE SERVICE command. Both services are associated with a queue, and the target, or receiving, service specifies that it can receive messages from a contract:

25

```
CREATE SERVICE InitiatorService
    ON QUEUE [dbo].[InitiatorQueue];
GO

CREATE SERVICE TargetService
    ON QUEUE [dbo].[TargetQueue]
    (HelloWorldContract);
GO
```

After the Service Broker objects are created, you can see them listed under the Object Explorer Service Broker node, as shown in Figure 25-2.

FIGURE 25-2

After the objects are created, they can be seen in Object Explorer.

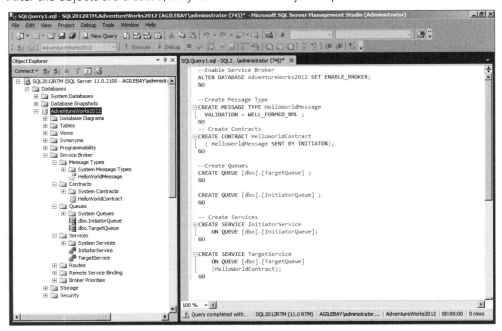

Additionally, you can query the Service Broker Catalog Views to list all Service Broker objects created as follows:

```
USE AdventureWorks2012
GO

--Query the sys.service_message_type catalog view
SELECT * FROM sys.service_message_types
```

```
WHERE name='HelloWorldMessage';
GO

--Query the sys.service_contracts catalog view
SELECT * FROM sys.service_contracts
WHERE name='HelloWorldContract'
GO

--Query the sys.service_queues_type catalog view
SELECT * FROM sys.service_queues
WHERE name in ('TargetQueue','InitiatorQueue');
GO

--Query the sys.services catalog view
SELECT * FROM sys.services
WHERE name in ('InitiatorService','TargetService');
GO
```

For a complete description of all Catalog Views available for Service Broker visit http://msdn.microsoft.com/en-us/library/ms173780.aspx

Working with Dialogs

With the Service Broker infrastructure created, messages can be sent between services and received from the queue. Messages exist as part of a conversation, and multiple conversations can be contained in a conversation group.

Service Broker makes multiple queue readers possible by locking the conversation group; however, locking the conversation group with normal database commands is almost impossible to accomplish efficiently. Service Broker accordingly uses a new kind of database lock, and only Service Broker commands understand this lock type.

Sending a Message to the Queue

The following code creates a conversation that is identified by a conversationhandle GUID. SEND places a single message onto a queue within a transaction. The BEGIN CONVERSATION command opens the conversation, and the SEND command actually places the message into the queue:

```
BEGIN TRANSACTION ;

DECLARE @message XML ;
SET @message = N'<message>Hello, World!</message>' ;

DECLARE @conversationHandle UNIQUEIDENTIFIER ;

BEGIN DIALOG CONVERSATION @conversationHandle
```

25

```
FROM SERVICE [InitiatorService]
TO SERVICE 'TargetService'
ON CONTRACT [HelloWorldContract]
WITH ENCRYPTION = OFF, LIFETIME = 1000 ;

SEND ON CONVERSATION @conversationHandle
  MESSAGE TYPE [HelloWorldMessage]
  (@message) ;

END CONVERSATION @conversationHandle ;

COMMIT TRANSACTION ;
```

A queue is an internal table, but all you can do is SELECT or RECEIVE. You can't use any other command such as UPDATE or DELETE. To view the messages in the target queue, select from the queue as if it were a normal relational table:

```
USE AdventureWorks2012
GO

SELECT * FROM [TargetQueue] WITH(NOLOCK);
GO
```

Figure 25-3 shows the result of the query.

FIGURE 25-3

Query results of the TargetQueue table.

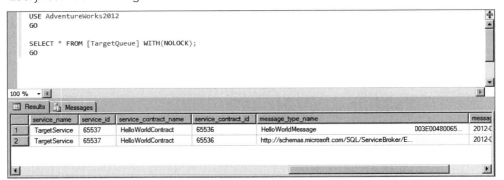

Receiving a Message

The receive command retrieves and removes the oldest message from the queue. Use receive within a transaction so that if something goes wrong, the receive action can be rolled back, and the message is still in the queue.

Service Broker is not a trigger that can code when a message is placed on the queue; some code must run to extract the message. To accomplish this, you use the waitfor command, enabling it to wait for a message to be placed in the queue. Without this option, the code would need to run a loop to continuously check for a new message.

You may want to wait for messages with the waitfor command. The following examples show how to wait for a specific time, a specific time period, and a specific queue:

```
--Wait until 9:00 PM
WAITFOR TIME '21:00'

--Wait for 22 Minutes to pass
WAITFOR DELAY '00:22:00'

--Wait for a message to be received from a Service Broker messaging
queue
WAITFOR (RECEIVE * FROMTargetQueue)
```

The following routine within a stored procedure waits for a message and then receives the top message from the queue:

```
USE AdventureWorks2012 ;
GO

-- Process all conversation groups.
WHILE (1 = 1)
  BEGIN

  DECLARE @conversation_handle UNIQUEIDENTIFIER,
       @conversation_group_id  UNIQUEIDENTIFIER,
       @message_body XML,
       @message_type_name NVARCHAR(128);

  BEGIN TRANSACTION ;

-- Get next conversation group.

  WAITFOR(
    GET CONVERSATION GROUP @conversation_group_id
FROM [dbo].[TargetQueue]),
    TIMEOUT 500 ;

  -- If there are no more conversation groups, roll back the
  -- transaction and break out of the outermost WHILE loop.

  IF @conversation_group_id IS NULL
  BEGIN
      ROLLBACK TRANSACTION ;
```

```
        BREAK ;
END ;

    -- Process all messages in the conversation group. Notice
    -- that all processing occurs in the same transaction.

    WHILE 1 = 1
    BEGIN

        -- Receive the next message for the conversation group.
        -- Notice that the receive statement includes a WHERE
        -- clause to ensure that the messages received belong to
        -- the same conversation group.

        RECEIVE
          TOP(1)
          @conversation_handle = conversation_handle,
          @message_type_name = message_type_name,
          @message_body =
          CASE
              WHEN validation = 'X' THEN CAST(message_body AS XML)
              ELSE CAST(N'<none/>' AS XML)
          END
        FROM [dbo].[TargetQueue]
        WHERE conversation_group_id = @conversation_group_id ;

        -- If there are no more messages, or an error occurred,
        -- stop processing this conversation group.

        IF @@ROWCOUNT = 0 OR @@ERROR <> 0 BREAK;

        -- Show the information received.

        SELECT 'Conversation Group Id' = @conversation_group_id,
               'Conversation Handle' = @conversation_handle,
               'Message Type Name' = @message_type_name,
               'Message Body' = @message_body ;


        -- If the message_type_name indicates that the message is
an error or an end dialog message, end the conversation.

        IF @message_type_name =
'http://schemas.microsoft.com/SQL/ServiceBroker/EndDialog'
           OR @message_type_name =
'http://schemas.microsoft.com/SQL/ServiceBroker/Error'
           BEGIN
               END CONVERSATION @conversation_handle ;
```

```
        END ;

      END; -- Process all messages in conversation group.

  -- Commit the RECEIVE and the END conversation statement.

      COMMIT TRANSACTION ;

  END ; -- Process all conversation groups.
```

Service Broker can handle complex message groups, such as multiple line items of an order that may not appear consecutively in the queue due to other messages being received simultaneously. The conversation group can be used to select out the related messages.

What's New in Service Broker for SQL Server 2012?

SQL Server 2012 adds several enhancements to Service Broker functionality and informational columns. The following sections describe each of these enhancements in more detail.

Message Multicast

Messages can now be sent to multiple target services using a single SEND statement. The ability to multicast the same message is possible by initiating multiple conversation handles and including them as a comma separated list after the ON CONVERSATON clause.

The caveat with message multicast is that if the SEND statement encounters an error with one or more of the conversations, the whole statement fails, and no messages are stored in the transmission queue or are received in any target service queue.

This means that all target services included in a message multicast must be in a valid state for the SEND statement to be successful.

AlwaysOn Support

AlwaysOn Availability Groups is the new high availability and disaster recovery solution introduced in SQL Server 2012. This new feature is discussed in detail in Chapter 27, "Database Mirroring."

Service Broker is supported in the AlwaysOn Availability Group but several requirements need to be met to successfully receive asynchronous messages. For a service in an Availability Group to receive remote messages, there are four main requirements as follows:

1. Create and configure a listener in the Availability Group.
2. Create and configure a Service Broker endpoint.

25

3. Grant CONNECT permission on the Service Broker endpoint to PUBLIC or to a login.

4. Ensure that the msdb system database contains the AutoCreatedLocal route or a route to the specified service.

For a service in an Availability Group to send remote messages, there are two main requirements as follows:

1. Create a route to the target service.

2. Ensure that the msdb system database contains the AutoCreatedLocal route or a route to the specified service.

For more information on the requirements for AlwaysOn support in Service Broker refer to http://msdn.microsoft.com/en-us/library/hh710058.aspx.

Poison Message Handling

A *poison message* is a message that has exceeded the maximum number of delivery attempts to a target service. A message is considered a poison message when it is continuously being added back to the message queue, after the transaction that it is part of is rolled back due to an error. Service Broker provides automatic poison detection and handling. By default, it will disable all queues from where messages were received by a transaction that is rolled back five times.

Poison message handling can now be controlled by enabling or disabling it via CREATE QUEUE and ALTER QUEUE statement using the POISON_MESSAGE_ HANDLING (STATUS = ON | OFF) clause.

A new column named is_poison_message_handling_enabled has been added to sys.service_ queues to indicate whether poison message handling is enabled or disabled.

When poison handling is set to OFF, message queues are not disabled automatically when they are involved in a poison message transaction.

Message Enqueued Time

A new column named message_enqueue_time has been added to the Queues to show how long a message has been in the queue.

Monitoring and Troubleshooting Service Broker

SQL Server has no user interface to monitor Service Broker activity. You can however make use of one or more of the following resources described in Table 25-1.

TABLE 25-1 Resources to Monitor Service Broker Activity

Resource	Description
SQL Profiler	SQL Profiler provides the same 13 trace events available since SQL Server 2005.
Extended Events	Extended Events is the preferred method for troubleshooting and monitoring Service Broker activity. For a complete list and description of the Service Broker events available in SQL Server 2012, refer to http://technet .microsoft.com/en-us/library/ms186347.aspx.
ssbdiagnose Utility	The ssbdiagnose utility introduced in SQL Server 2008R2 is still supported and is a great way to easily report issues in Service Broker conversations or service configuration issues. For more information on the ssbdiagnose utility, refer to http://msdn.microsoft.com/en-us/library/bb934450.aspx.
Catalog Views	SQL Server 2012 provides 12 catalog views for Service Broker. Table 25-2 lists and describes each of these Catalog Views.
Dynamic Management Views (DMVs)	SQL Server 2012 provides four basic DMVs to monitor tasks, messages, queues, and connections. Table 25-3 lists and describes each of these DMVs.

Table 25-2 describes the Service Broker Catalog Views available in SQL Server 2012.

TABLE 25-2 Service Broker Catalog Views

Catalog View	Description
sys.conversation_endpoints	This catalog view contains a row per conversation endpoint in the database.
sys.conversation_groups	This catalog view contains a row for each conversation group.
sys.conversation_priorities	Contains a row for each conversation priority created in the current database.
sys.remote_service_bindings	This catalog view contains a row per remote service binding.
sys.routes	This catalog views contains one row per route. Service Broker uses routes to locate the network address for a service.
sys.service_contracts	This catalog view contains a row for each contract in the database.
sys.service_contract_message_usages	This catalog view contains a row per (contract, message type) pair.

Continues

25

TABLE 25-2   *(continued)*

Catalog View	Description
sys.service_contract_usages	This catalog view contains a row per (service, contract) pair.
sys.service_message_types	This catalog view contains a row per message type registered in the service broker.
sys.service_queue_usages	This catalog view returns a row for each reference between service and service queue. A service can only be associated with one queue. A queue can be associated with multiple services.
sys.services	This catalog view contains a row for each service in the database.
sys.transmission_queue	This catalog view contains a row for each message in the transmission queue.

For a detailed description of each of these catalog views, refer to `http://msdn .microsoft.com/en-us/library/ms173780.aspx`.

Table 25-3 describes the Service Broker Dynamic Management Views available for SQL Server 2012.

TABLE 25-3   **Service Broker Dynamic Management Views**

DMV	Description
sys.dm_broker_activated_tasks	Returns a row for each stored procedure activated by Service Broker
sys.dm_broker_forwarded_messages	Returns a row for each Service Broker message that an instance of SQL Server is in the process of forwarding
sys.dm_broker_connections	Returns a row for each Service Broker network connection
sys.dm_broker_queue_monitors	Returns a row for each queue monitor in the instance

For a detailed description of each of these DMVs refer to `http://msdn.microsoft.com/ en-us/library/ms176110.aspx`.

As an alternative you can also query the queues directly using T-SQL. You can browse the different queues available using SQL Server Management Studio by expanding Service Broker ➪ Queues.

Summary

Service Broker is one of those technologies that provide no benefit out-of-the-box, meaning that unless you take the effort to architect the database using Service Broker, there's no inherent benefit. However, if you do take the time to design the database using Service Broker, then you'll see significant scalability benefits as Service Broker queues workloads.

Service Broker can reduce the amount of work required to create distributed applications by handling all the internal notification and queuing logic between databases. In SQL Server 2012 Service Broker also supports sending and receiving remote messages between services in the new HA/DR solution named AlwaysOn Availability Groups.

25

Log Shipping

IN THIS CHAPTER

Configuring a Warm Standby Server Using Management Studio and Transact-SQL

Monitoring Log Shipping

Modifying or Removing Log Shipping

Switching Roles

Returning to the Original Primary Server

T he *availability* of a database refers to the overall reliability of the system. The Information Architecture Principle, discussed in Chapter 2, "Data Architecture," lays the foundation for availability in the phrase *readily available*. The definition of readily available varies by the organization and the data. A database that's highly available is one that rarely goes down. For some databases, being down for an hour is not a problem; for others, 30 seconds of downtime is a catastrophe. Organization requirements, budget constraints, and other resources dictate the proper solution.

Of course, availability involves more than just the database; there are several technologies involved outside of the database: the instance, the server OS, the physical server, the organization's infra-structure, and so on. The quality and redundancy of the hardware, quality of the electrical power, preventive maintenance of the machines and replacement of the hard drives, security of the server room — all these contribute to the availability of the primary database. An IT organization that intends to reach any level of high availability must also have the right people, training, policies, and service-level agreements (SLAs) in place.

NOTE

This chapter is the first of a series of chapters dealing with high-availability technologies: Log Shipping, Database Mirroring, AlwaysOn Availability Groups and Clustering. Backup and Recovery, along with Replication; and even Azure SQL Database (SQL Server in the cloud) with Azure SQL Database Data Sync are also part of the availability options. A well-planned availability solution considers every option and then implements the technologies that best fit the organization's budget and availability requirements. Log shipping has not changed much since SQL Server 2008 R2 so if you're familiar with this feature this chapter should be more of a review for you.

A complete plan for high availability also includes a plan to handle true disasters. If the entire data center is suddenly gone, is there another off-site disaster recovery site prepared to come online?

Best Practice

Before implementing an advanced availability solution, ensure that the primary server is well thought out and provides sufficient redundancy. The most common issue won't be the data center melting but a hard drive failure or a bad NIC card.

Log shipping is perhaps the most common method to provide high availability. The basic idea is that the transaction log, with its record of the most recent transactions, is regularly backed up and then sent, or shipped, to another server where the log backup is applied so that the server has a fresh copy of all the data from the primary server. Log Shipping doesn't require any special hardware or magic. It's relatively easy to set up and administer.

There are three obstacles to overcome before log shipping will work smoothly. First, the policies and procedures must be established, implemented, and then regularly tested. The second one is a bit trickier: The client applications need a way to detect that the primary server is down and then switch over to the standby server. The third obstacle is a procedure to switch back to the primary server after it's repaired and ready to step back into the spotlight.

Upgrading Log Shipping to AlwaysOn Availability Groups

Prior to SQL Server 2012, if you wanted the option to have a warm standby copy of a database that you could query from, you were mainly limited to setting up log shipping. With the introduction of AlwaysOn Availability Groups you have another fantastic high-availability solution option. With AlwaysOn Availability Groups you can not only have up-to-date, queryable copies of your database, but you can also take advantage of other features such as multiple failover options (automatic, planned manual, and forced manual), multiple database grouping, alternative availability modes (asynchronous-commit, synchronous-commit), and much more. For more information on AlwaysOn Availability Groups, see Chapter 27 Database Mirroring."

Availability Testing

A database that's unavailable isn't useful. The availability test is a simulation of the database restore process assuming the worst. The measurement is the time required to restore the most current production data to a test server and prove that the client applications work. This measure of time is normally referred to in the business as a recovery time objective (RTO). As an administrator it's important to establish with the business what the expected RTO is, that way in the case of disaster there is an established expectation for getting data systems accessible again. This agreement is typically formalized in the form of a service level agreement (SLA), which is a written agreement between the business and technical units.

Warm Standby Availability

Warm standby refers to a database that has a copy set up on separate hardware. A warm standby solution can be achieved with log shipping. Log shipping involves periodically restoring a transaction log backup from the primary server to a warm standby server, making that server ready to recover at a moment's notice. In case of a failure, the warm standby server and the most recent transaction-log backups are ready to go. Apart from this, log shipping has the following benefits:

- It can be implemented without exotic hardware and may be significantly cheaper.
- It has been used for many years and is a robust and reliable technology.
- It can be used for disaster recovery, high availability and reporting scenarios.
- Implementing log shipping is simple because Microsoft has a user-friendly wizard, and when implemented it is easy to maintain and troubleshoot.
- The primary server and the warm standby server do not have to be in the same domain or same subnet. As long as they can talk to each other, log shipping works.
- There is no real distance limitation between the primary and warm standby servers, and log shipping can be done over the Internet.
- Log shipping allows shipping the transaction log from one primary server to multiple warm standby servers. It also allows having different copy and restore times for each warm standby server. This can be useful to set up one secondary server as a standby for disaster recovery purposes and use another secondary for reporting purposes.
- Log shipping can be implemented between different editions of SQL Server (Enterprise Edition to Standard Edition) and between different hardware platforms (x86 or x64-based SQL Server instance; if you're using an older version of SQL Server, IA64 also applies).

However, log shipping has a few drawbacks:

- Only user databases in full or bulk-logged recovery model can be log shipped. A simple recovery model cannot be used because it does not allow transaction log backup. This also means that log shipping can break if the recovery model for a log shipping database is changed from full/bulk-logged to a simple recovery model.
- System databases (master, model, msdb, and tempdb) cannot be log shipped.

- Log shipping provides redundancy at the database level and not at the SQL Server instance level like SQL Server failover clustering. Log shipping applies only the changes that are either captured in the transaction log or the initial full backup of the log shipping database. Any database objects such as logins, jobs, maintenance plans, SSIS packages and linked servers that reside outside the log shipping database need to be manually created on the warm standby server.

- When the primary server fails, any transactions made since the last time the transaction log backup was shipped to the warm standby server may be lost and result in data loss. For this reason, log shipping is usually set to occur every few minutes.

- The switch between primary and warm standby server is not transparent. A series of steps must be manually executed by the DBA on the warm standby server, and front-end application connections must redirect the data source and reconnect to the warm standby server.

- After the primary server is repaired, returning to the original configuration may require manual DBA intervention.

If these issues are acceptable, log shipping to a warm standby server can be an excellent safeguard against downtime.

Best Practice

Ideally, the primary server and the warm standby server should be in different locations so that a disaster in one location cannot affect the other. In addition, log shipping can place a large demand on a network every few minutes while the transaction logs are being moved. If the two servers can be connected with a private high-speed network, log shipping can take place without affecting other network users and the bandwidth they require.

Defining Log Shipping

In SQL Server 2000, log shipping was available only in Developer and Enterprise Editions. Starting with SQL Server 2005, log shipping was made available in Workgroup, Standard, Developer, and Enterprise Editions. Now, in SQL Server 2012, log shipping is available in Enterprise, Standard, Business Intelligence and Web editions. Developer Edition can be used only for development purposes and not for production.

Microsoft provides a simple-to-use Log Shipping Wizard to create a maintenance plan to back up, copy, and restore the transaction log from the primary server to the warm standby server every few minutes. Log shipping has built-in monitoring that makes it easy to maintain and troubleshoot.

Log Shipping normally involves three SQL Servers: a primary server, a warm standby server, and a monitor server, as shown in Figure 26-1.

FIGURE 26-1

Typical log shipping configuration.

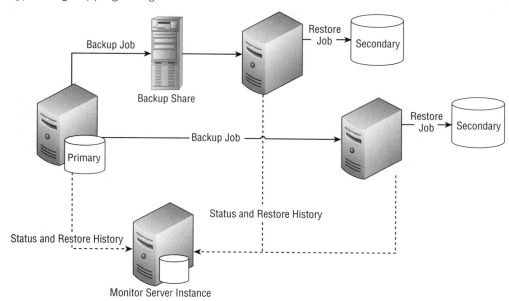

- The *primary server* or *source server* is the main production SQL Server to which clients connect. This server contains the log shipping database. The initial full database backup and subsequent transaction log backups are taken on this server. This server should be a high-quality server with redundant disk drives.

- The *warm standby server* is the backup SQL Server, otherwise known as the *secondary server*. If the source server fails, it becomes the primary server. This server should be capable of meeting the minimum performance requirements during a short-term crisis. If your business does not allow any performance degradation, then the warm standby server should be similar to the primary server. In the case of an offsite disaster recovery solution, network latency should also be considered.

- The *monitor server* polls both the primary server and the warm standby server by keeping track of what files have been sent where, generating an alert when the two are out of sync. A single monitor server can monitor multiple log shipping configurations. The monitor server is optional. If a monitor server is not used, the primary and warm standby servers store the monitoring information.

Best Practice

The monitor server can be an instance on the destination server, but locating the monitor server on the source server would be a self-defeating plan. If the source server physically failed, the monitor server would also fail. The best practice is to assign a monitor server to its own hardware to avoid disrupting monitoring in the event the primary or warm standby server is lost.

Each primary server database can have only one log shipping plan, and each plan can ship only one database. However, a plan may ship to multiple secondary servers.

Log Shipping Architecture

Log shipping can be configured by using one of two methods: either by using SQL Server Management Studio or by using system stored procedures.

Pre-Log Shipping Configuration

With either method of configuration, the following prerequisites need to be completed before configuring log shipping:

- Disk space needs to be created and shared. This network share is used by the backup job on the primary server to store the transaction log backups. Grant read and write permissions on the network share to the SQL Server service account on the primary server and read permissions to the proxy account for the copy job (usually the SQL Server Agent service account) on the secondary server.

- Destination folder needs to be created on the secondary servers. The copy job on the secondary server copies the transaction log backups from the network share to the destination folder on the secondary server. The load job then restores these transaction log backups from the destination folder. The SQL Server service accounts on the secondary server need to have read and write permissions on this folder.

- The recovery model of the log shipping database must be set to full or bulk-logged.

- The edition of the SQL Server 2012 participating in log shipping needs to be the Enterprise, Standard, or Workgroup Edition.

- If the primary and secondary servers are on different domains, then set up two-way trusts between the domains. If this is not possible, you can also use network pass-through security. With network pass-through security the SQL Service accounts for all the SQL Servers participating in log shipping use the same network account and the same password and enough permission to complete the log shipping tasks.

- If you have a large database, then it is recommended to take a full database backup, copy it to the secondary server, and restore it on the secondary server with NORECOVERY or STANDBY to put it into a state that allows restoring the transaction logs. NORECOVERY mode does not allow any database access to the secondary database, whereas STANDBY mode allows read-only access to the secondary database.

Configuring Log Shipping Using Management Studio

The following steps create a log shipping configuration using SQL Server Management Studio:

1. In the Object Explorer on the primary server in SQL Server Management Studio, right-click the database that will be log shipped and review the database properties.

2. On the Options page, verify that the recovery model is either Full or Bulk-logged and not Simple.

3. On the Transaction Log Shipping page, as shown in Figure 26-2, check the box that enables log shipping configuration.

FIGURE 26-2

Enabling the primary database for log shipping.

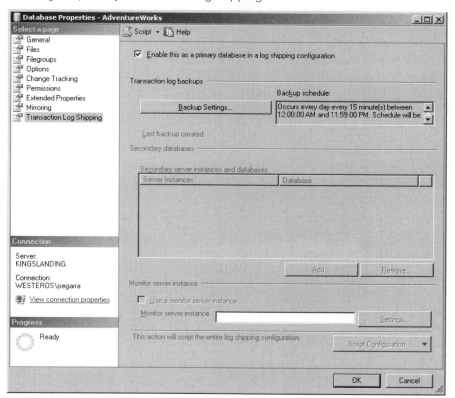

4. Configure the backup settings, as shown in Figure 26-3, by clicking the Backup Setting button. Enter the network share where the transaction log backups will be stored before being copied to the secondary server. If the backup folder is local to the primary server, also enter the local folder path.

TIP

A network share that is not located on the primary server will better protect the transaction logs in case of a hardware failure on the primary server.

FIGURE 26-3

Configuring transaction log backup settings for log shipping.

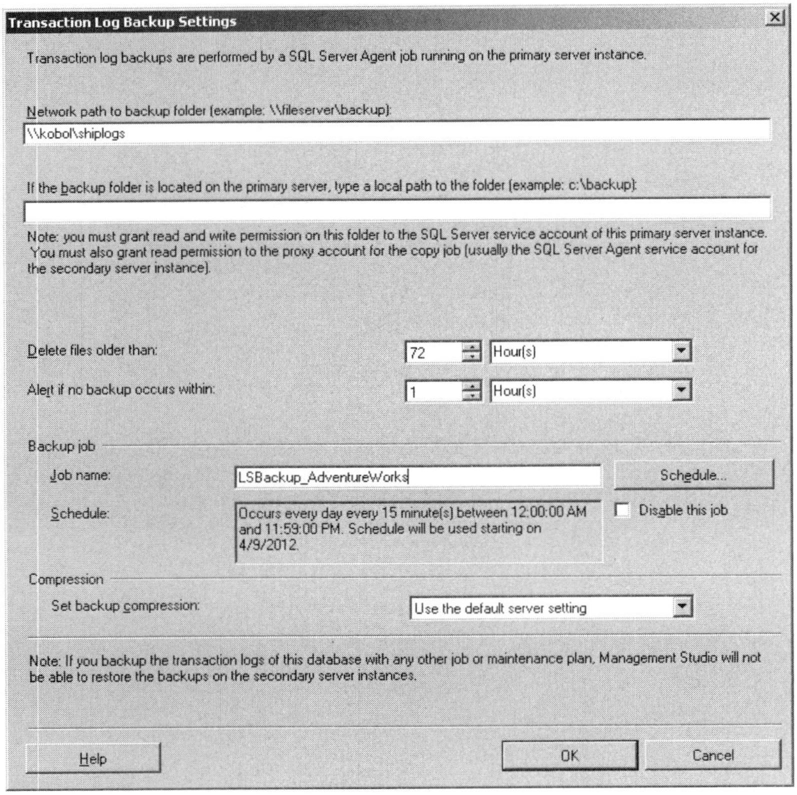

5. Enter an amount of time after which the transaction log backup files should be deleted. For example, if the files should be deleted after one day, then the Delete Files Older Than option should equal one day.

6. Enter an amount of time that the server should wait to send an alert if no new transaction log files are found. For example, if the server has not seen a transaction log backup in the past 1 hour, then the Alert If No Backup Occurs Within option should be set to 1 hour.

NOTE

The longer the length of the alert time, the higher is the risk. With a long alert setting, a transaction log backup failure results in a larger amount of data loss.

7. Schedule the job that will back up the transaction log by setting the job's name, time, and frequency by clicking the Schedule button. A shorter duration between transaction log backups minimizes the amount of data that could be lost. By default, the transaction log is backed up every 15 minutes. The default works for most environments, but for some environments, setting the duration to 5 minutes is needed to minimize data loss. The frequency of transaction log backups usually is determined by a lot of factors such as SLAs, speed of your disk subsystem, and transaction log size.

TIP

Make sure that the only transaction log backup that occurs is scheduled through the Transaction Log Shipping page. Otherwise, all the data changes will not be propagated to the secondary servers and log shipping will break.

If you have a powerful server with plenty of resources, you may be tempted to change the transaction log backup frequency to every 1 minute or less. SQL Server 2012 lets you schedule the frequency to as little as every 10 seconds. You may need this in your environment, but remember that this can create hundreds of transaction log backups. If you have to restore your database using backups, then you have to restore the full database backup followed by all the transaction log backups in order, and if one of the transaction log backups is bad, then the restore stops at that point.

8. SQL Server 2012 Enterprise Edition supports backup compression. You can control the backup compression by clicking the Set Backup Compression drop-down box on the Transaction Log Backup Settings page. By default, Use the Default Server Setting option is selected. This uses the default server level compression. You can bypass the server level default by selecting the Compress Backup option, or you can choose not to compress the backup by selecting the Do Not Compress Backup option.

NOTE

The performance increase achieved from backup compression comes at the expense of CPU usage. If you have a CPU bound SQL Server, then you may not want to compress the backup. It is recommended to do thorough testing to see the impact of the backup compression because the CPU increase can impact other operations.

9. Add the secondary servers to the transaction log configuration by clicking the Add button under the secondary instance's window. Multiple secondary instances can be added here by repeating steps 9 through 16.

10. On the secondary database screen, as shown in Figure 26-4, connect to the server that will be the secondary server, and enter the database name for the secondary database. If the database is not there, it will be created.

FIGURE 26-4

Configuring the secondary server database for log shipping.

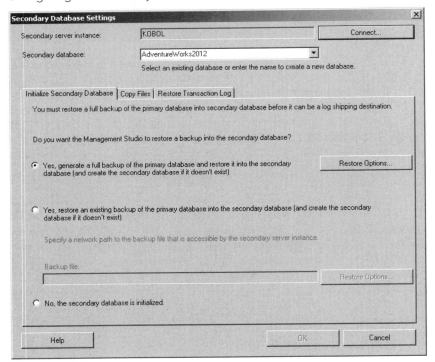

11. Initialize the secondary database by selecting either the option to have log shipping create a full database backup and restore it on the secondary server or the option to have it use the last known backup. If you select to use the last backup that was created, the name of the directory in which the backup is located needs to be supplied. To create the data and log files on nondefault folder locations on the secondary server, click Restore Options, and enter the local folder path on the secondary server where you want the data and log files to exist. The previous two options are best suited for smaller databases. If you have a large database, it is recommended to bypass the wizard by manually taking a backup of the database, copying it to the secondary database, and restoring it. If you take this approach, select the third option No, the Secondary Database Is Initialized.

12. The Copy Files tab, as shown in Figure 26-5, configures the copy job on the secondary server that copies the transaction log backups from the network share to the

destination local folder on the secondary server. This tab also has a setting that enables files to be deleted after a designated time.

FIGURE 26-5

Configuring the copy job on the secondary server.

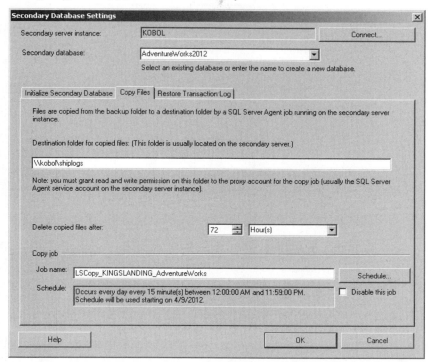

13. On the Copy Files tab, enter the local folder on the secondary server to which the transaction log files will be copied. The proxy account for the copy job (usually the SQL Server Agent service) on the secondary server must have read and write permissions on this folder.

14. On the Restore Transaction Logs tab, as shown in Figure 26-6, choose either No Recovery Mode or Standby Mode. Standby mode enables access to the secondary server for read-only operations. Select this mode if you want to use log shipping for reporting. If the standby mode is selected, the option to have the user connection killed during the transaction log restore is available. If you do not choose to disconnect the users, the transaction log backups fails, and the secondary server lags behind. The No Recovery Mode option will not allow any database access to the secondary database. This option is usually selected when log shipping is used for disaster recovery or high availability scenarios.

FIGURE 26-6

Configuring the restore transaction log job on the secondary server.

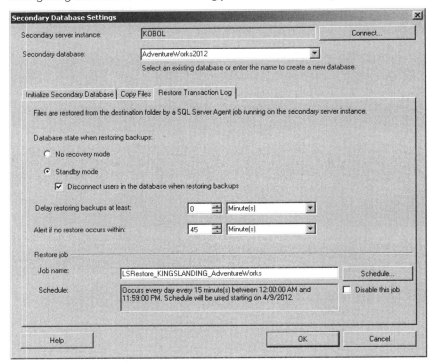

15. On the Restore Transaction Log tab, the option for delaying a restore and alerting is available as well. This configuration option enables all the transaction log backups to be held until the end of the business day or to apply the transaction logs as soon as they are received.

> **TIP**
>
> Delaying restores on secondary database can be extremely useful in case there is an unexpected data change on the primary database that you wish to recover. For example, say a user executes a delete statement and forgets a `WHERE` clause in their query and accidently deletes all the data from a table. If you delay log restores up to an hour on the secondary server, you'd be able to recover data that was accidently deleted on the primary from the secondary by querying or copying those rows out from the secondary, for up to an hour after the initial transaction occurred on the primary database. After that delay period, however, you'll need to rely on your backups in order to recover your data.

16. The option for more granularities on restores and when they are applied are set in the Restore job by clicking the Schedule button. By default, transaction log backups are restored every 15 minutes on the secondary server.

17. Click OK to complete the secondary database setup, and return to the database's Properties tab.

18. After the secondary database configuration has been completed, a monitor server can be configured on the primary database's Properties page by checking Use a Monitor Server Instance and clicking the Settings button. The Log Shipping Monitor settings page is shown in Figure 26-7.

FIGURE 26-7

Configuring the monitor server for log shipping.

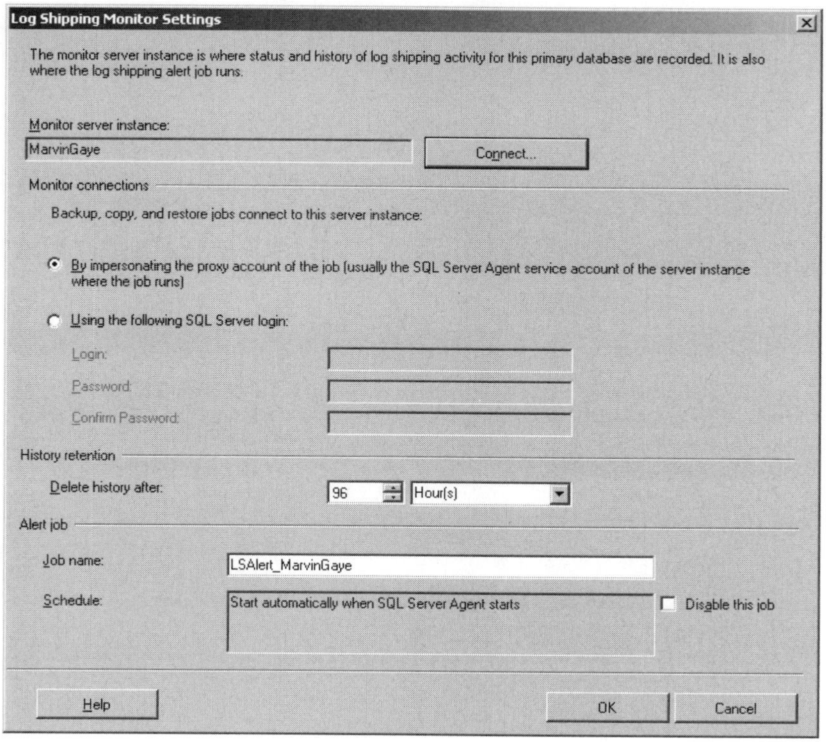

NOTE

As noted previously, adding a monitor server is optional. But if you do not add a monitor server now, you cannot add it later. And if you add a monitor server now, it cannot be changed without removing log shipping first.

19. After you finish configuring log shipping, you see a page similar to Figure 26-8. Notice that it also has the option of scripting the log shipping configuration.

TIP

If your log shipping has a number of nondefault options, scripting your changes makes it easier to ensure that each time it is done the configuration stays the same.

FIGURE 26-8

Finished configuring log shipping.

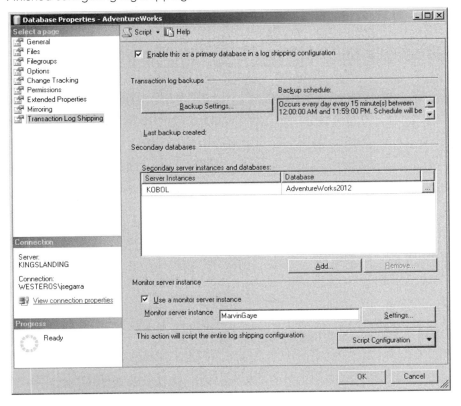

20. After you click OK, the Save Log Shipping Configuration dialog box sets up the log shipping, as shown in Figure 26-9.

FIGURE 26-9

Successful completion of Log Shipping Configuration.

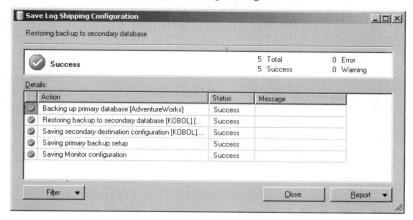

Configuring Log Shipping Using Transact-SQL

Like most other configurations, log shipping can also be configured using Transact-SQL. The easiest way to configure log shipping using Transact-SQL is to configure it once using SQL Server Management Studio and click Script Configuration as explained earlier (refer to Figure 26-8). The following system stored procedures need to be executed to configure log shipping:

On the primary server, execute the following system stored procedures:

- `master.dbo.sp_add_log_shipping_primary_database`: Configures the primary database and creates the transaction log backup job

- `msdb.dbo.sp_add_schedule`: Creates the schedule for the backup job

- `msdb.dbo.sp_attach_schedule`: Links the backup job to the schedule

- `msdb.dbo.sp_update_job`: Enables the backup job

- `master.dbo.sp_add_log_shipping_primary_secondary`: Adds an entry for a secondary database on the primary server

On the secondary server, execute the following system stored procedures:

- `master.dbo.sp_add_log_shipping_secondary_primary`: Configures the primary server information and creates the copy and restore jobs

- `msdb.dbo.sp_add_schedule`: Creates the schedule for the copy job

- `msdb.dbo.sp_attach_schedule`: Links the copy job to the schedule

- `msdb.dbo.sp_add_schedule`: Creates the schedule for the restore job

- `msdb.dbo.sp_attach_schedule`: Links the restore job to the schedule
- `master.dbo.sp_add_log_shipping_secondary_database`: Configures the secondary database
- `msdb.dbo.sp_update_job`: Enables the copy job
- `msdb.dbo.sp_update_job`: Enables the restore job

On the monitor server, execute the following system stored procedure:

- `master.dbo.sp_add_log_shipping_alert_job`: Creates the alert job and adds the job id to the `log_shipping_monitor_alert` table.

Post-Log Shipping Configuration

As mentioned earlier, log shipping applies only the changes that are either captured in the transaction log or the initial full backup of the log shipping database. Any database objects, such as logins, jobs, maintenance plans, SSIS packages, and linked servers that reside outside the log shipping database, need to be manually created on the warm standby server. After configuring log shipping, it is important to synchronize the warm standby servers with all objects that live outside the log shipping database. Most of these objects can be easily scripted using Management Studio and can be applied on the warm standby servers. The frequency of applying the changes must meet the rate of changes in your environment.

One of the ways to synchronize the logins is to create an Integration Services (SSIS) job that connects to each server and transfers the logins. The frequency of this job depends on how often new logins are added to your primary server.

Checking Log Shipping Configuration

After Log Shipping is configured, review the following checklist to verify the log shipping setup.

- **On the primary server:**
    1. Right-click the log shipping database and look at the database properties. On the Transaction Log Shipping page, note that the database is enabled as the primary database in the log shipping configuration. On this page you can review other log shipping details like the backup job schedule on the primary server, secondary server details, the copy and restore job schedule on the secondary server, and monitor server details and if backup compression is being used.
    2. Expand SQL Server Agent and review the backup transaction log job.

- **On the secondary server:**
    1. Expand SQL Server Agent and review the copy and restore transaction log backup jobs.

- **On the monitor server:**

    1. Expand SQL Server Agent and review the Alert job, log shipping primary server alert, and log shipping secondary server alert.

Monitoring Log Shipping

To monitor log shipping from SQL Server Management Studio, Microsoft provides a Transaction Log Shipping Status report. This report can be run on any SQL Server participating in the log shipping configuration. To run the Transaction Log Shipping Status report, execute the following steps:

1. Connect to the primary, secondary, or monitor server using Object Explorer in SQL Server Management Studio.

2. Right click the SQL Server instance; click Reports.

3. Click Standard Reports.

4. Click Transaction Log Shipping Status.

For a complete picture of the Log Shipping configuration, run this report on the monitor server, as shown in Figure 26-10.

FIGURE 26-10

Executing the Transaction Log Shipping Status report on monitor server.

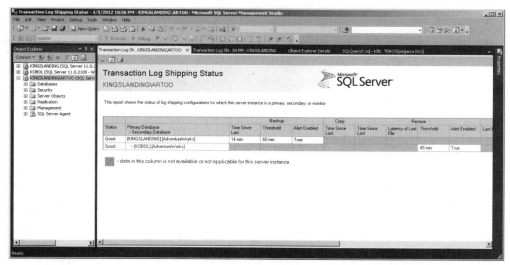

Another method to monitor log shipping is to directly review the status of the log shipping jobs. You can review the history of the transaction log backup job on the primary server and the history of the copy and restore jobs on the secondary server.

Log shipping can also be monitored using several monitoring tables and stored procedures. The information that can be retrieved from these sources includes the database name, last backup, last restore, time since last restore, and whether the alerts are enabled.

The following is a list of the tables that can be used to monitor log shipping. These tables exist in the MSDB database (because log shipping is mainly executed by a collection of jobs) on all the servers involved in the log shipping configuration.

- `msdb.dbo.log_shipping_monitor_alert`
- `msdb.dbo.log_shipping_monitor_error_detail`
- `msdb.dbo.log_shipping_monitor_history_detail`
- `msdb.dbo.log_shipping_monitor_primary`
- `msdb.dbo.log_shipping_monitor_secondary`
- `msdb.dbo.log_shipping_primary_databases`
- `msdb.dbo.log_shipping_secondary_databases`

The following is a list of stored procedures that can be used to monitor Log Shipping. They exist on all the servers in the master database involved in the log shipping:

- `master.sys.sp_help_log_shipping_monitor_primary`
- `master.sys.sp_help_log_shipping_monitor_secondary`
- `master.sys.sp_help_log_shipping_alert_job`
- `master.sys.sp_help_log_shipping_primary_database`
- `master.sys.sp_help_log_shipping_primary_secondary`
- `master.sys.sp_help_log_shipping_secondary_database`
- `master.sys.sp_help_log_shipping_secondary_primary`

Modifying or Removing Log Shipping

After configuring log shipping you can edit, add, or remove a log shipping configuration. For example, you can add another secondary server to the log shipping configuration. Or you may want to change the schedule of the backup, copy, or restore jobs. At some times you may need to remove a secondary server from the log shipping configuration or remove log shipping completely from all the participating servers.

To modify or remove log shipping, follow these steps:

1. In the Object Explorer on the primary server in SQL Server Management Studio, right-click the log shipping database, and look at the database properties.

2. Under Select a Page, click Transaction Log Shipping page, (refer to Figure 26-8).

3. To modify the parameters of the copy or restore jobs on the secondary server, highlight the secondary server under Secondary Server instances and databases and click the ellipsis (...).

4. To add a new secondary server, click Add under Secondary Server Instances and Databases. Follow steps 9 through 16 in the section "Configuring Log Shipping Using Management Studio."

5. To remove a secondary server, highlight the secondary server under Secondary Server Instances and Databases; click Remove. Log shipping can verify if you want to remove the secondary server, as shown in Figure 26-11. If you are sure, click Yes.

FIGURE 26-11

Removing a secondary server from the log shipping configuration.

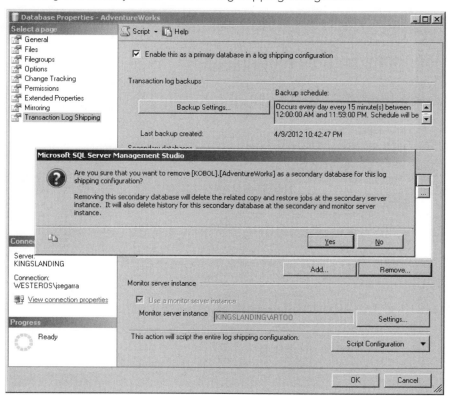

When Yes is clicked, log shipping deletes the secondary database entry on the primary server, as shown in Figure 26-12. You can also notice that the copy and restore jobs on the secondary server are deleted.

FIGURE 26-12

Deleting the secondary server from the log shipping configuration.

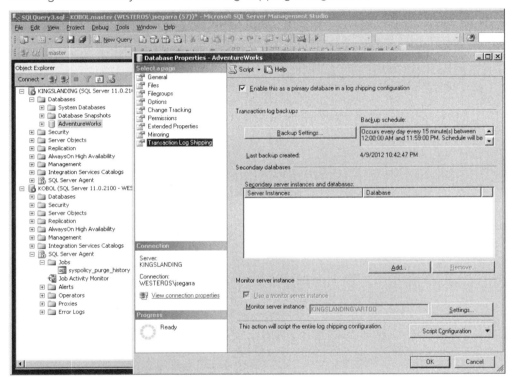

6. To completely remove log shipping, clear the Enable This as a Primary Database in a Log Shipping Configuration check box. Log shipping verifies if you actually want to remove log shipping as shown in Figure 26-13.

FIGURE 26-13

Checking if you want to completely remove log shipping.

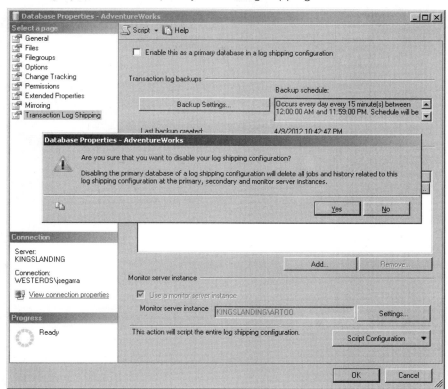

This action deletes all jobs and history related to this log shipping configuration on all the servers involved in this log shipping configuration. If you are sure, then click Yes. After it completely removes log shipping, Figure 26-14 displays.

FIGURE 26-14

Completely removed log shipping configuration.

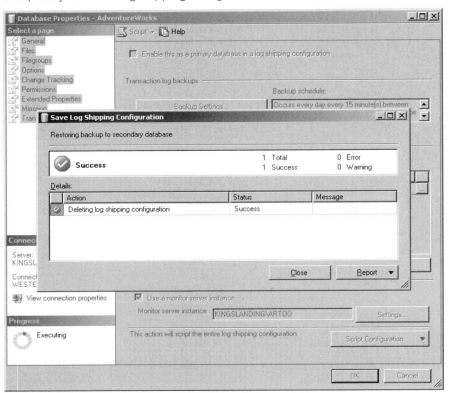

Switching Roles

Log shipping enables the capability to manually switch roles. This action can be performed for maintenance or in the case of a disaster. Depending on the cause of the disaster and its severity, the likely first step is to make a backup of the active transaction log, or tail of the log, on the primary server (if it is still accessible) with the NORECOVERY option.

The next step is to transfer all the transaction log backups to the secondary server either using a SQL Server Agent job or copying them manually. After copying, the transaction log backups need to be restored in sequential order to the secondary server using the WITH NORECOVERY or WITH STANDBY option for all transaction logs except the last one. The last transaction log is restored using the WITH RECOVERY option to close any open transactions and bring the secondary database up in an online state. If all the transaction log backups have been restored using the WITH NORECOVERY or WITH STANDBY option, there is no need to panic. You can still recover the database using the RESTORE DATABASE <database_name> WITH RECOVERY command. Then disable the log shipping jobs and alerts on the servers participating in the log shipping configuration.

Next verify that any database objects such as logins, jobs, maintenance plans, SSIS packages, and linked servers that reside outside the log shipping database are created on the warm standby server. For example, if the logins are not created on the warm standby server, then the users cannot connect, and you still have a server down situation.

Finally, manually redirect the applications and users to the new primary server.

Best Practice

It is highly recommended that you thoroughly execute the role reversal steps and document them prior to needing to failover to the warm standby server. Failure to do this can significantly increase the downtime and complexity when you actually need to failover to the warm standby server.

Returning to the Original Primary Server

Once the primary server has been repaired and is ready to return to service, the following steps reinitialize the primary server during a period when users are not connected:

1. Use Integration Services job to move all the user logins from the warm standby server to the primary server.

2. Transfer the database from the warm standby server to the primary server using either a full database backup and restore method or a detach and attach method. If you had failed over to the warm standby server in a controlled environment, you may be able to avoid taking a complete backup and restore of the database by applying the transaction log backups from the warm standby server to the original primary server.

3. Redirect the applications and users to the original primary server.

Summary

Availability is paramount to the success of most database projects and is becoming increasingly important for business requirements. Log shipping, failover clustering, database mirroring, AlwaysOn, and replication are all high-end features to provide a stable database environment for the users.

Log shipping is a robust and reliable high-availability, disaster recovery and reporting solution that can be implemented easily with the hardware that you already have, and there is no need to purchase any new, costly hardware. Log shipping backs up the transaction log on the primary server every few minutes and restores it on the warm standby servers. If the primary server stops working, you can make one of the warm standby servers your new primary server. The main problem with log shipping is that the role change is a manual process, and the DBA needs to be present to execute the role change. It is possible to automate most of the role change process using SQL Server Agent jobs, but still there is some manual intervention required, and the clients must be manually redirected to the new primary server.

The next chapter discusses database mirroring, which also provides per database protection like log shipping and provides an automatic failover option.

Database Mirroring

Achieving high database availability is one of the most important goals for critical business applications. Database mirroring is a software solution offered by Microsoft SQL Server 2012 to achieve high database availability. Database mirroring enables you to maintain a copy of your production database that could potentially be completely synchronized on a separate server for failover if a failed production server or database occurs. Like log shipping, database mirroring provides high availability at the database level, but unlike log shipping, you can configure database mirroring to provide no data loss and automatic failover.

What's New in SQL Server Database Mirroring?

One of the most exciting new enhancements in SQL Server 2012 is the AlwaysOn Availability Groups feature, which is the next evolution of the existing mirroring technology. With AlwaysOn Availability Groups, SQL Server 2012 enables you to have multiple, readable secondary databases. AlwaysOn Availability Groups also allows you to group databases together so that in the event of failure they will fail over together.

Another important thing to note is that as of the release of SQL Server 2012, the Database Mirroring feature is being listed as a deprecated feature. What this means is Database Mirroring will be supported in the next release of SQL Server but will be removed in a later version. Microsoft recommends you use AlwaysOn Availability Groups to replace your current mirroring configurations. If your edition of SQL Server does not support AlwaysOn Availability Groups it is suggested you that you use log shipping instead.

> **NOTE**
>
> Database mirroring has a log compression feature that is available in SQL Server 2012 Enterprise, Developer, Business Intelligence and Standard Editions. It is on by default, and there is no special configuration or switches to turn it on. However, if the extra CPU usage due to log compression is not desirable in your environment, you can turn off log compression by turning on the trace flag `1462`.
>
> The automatic page repair feature is not available in SQL Server 2012 Standard or Business Intelligence editions and is available only in SQL Server 2012 Enterprise and Developer Editions.

Database Mirroring Overview

Database mirroring was first officially supported with SQL Server 2005 SP1. Database mirroring is available in Enterprise and Developer Editions and with some restrictions in Standard and Business Intelligence Editions. Developer Edition can be used only for development purposes and not for production.

The basic concept of database mirroring is simple. Database mirroring maintains a hot standby database (mirror database) kept in sync with the production database (principal database) by transferring transaction log records from the principal database to a mirror database over the network, either synchronously or asynchronously. In case of a failure, the mirror database can be quickly accessed by the clients. Database mirroring has the following benefits:

- It increases database protection by maintaining a mirror copy of your database.

- It enables you to choose only the databases that you want to mirror from one SQL Server instance to another. There is a 1:1 ratio from the principal to mirror SQL Server. Multiple databases in a SQL Server instance can be mirrored together using AlwaysOn Availability Groups, which are covered later in the section "High Availability/AlwaysOn."

- By default, it compresses and encrypts the data between the principal and mirror server.

- It improves the availability of your databases during hardware or software upgrades.

- It can be used for high database availability and disaster recovery purposes. To achieve high database availability, place the principal and mirror SQL Servers in the same data center. For disaster recovery, place the principal and mirror SQL Servers in different data centers so that a disaster in one data center does not affect the other data center.

- It offers automatic page repair. If a page is marked as suspect due to corruption, SQL Server automatically attempts to recover the page from a database mirroring partner (principal or mirror) or an availability replica (primary or secondary).

- By default, it does not support reporting. If you want to use the mirror database for reporting purposes, you can create a database snapshot (refer to Chapter 24, "Database Snapshots," for details) on the mirror database and use the database snapshot for reporting purposes. Alternatively, you can use AlwaysOn Availability Groups to create read-only Secondary Replicas. See the "High Availability/lwaysOn" section for more details.

> **NOTE**
>
> If you use the mirror database for reporting purposes, you need to fully license the mirror server. On the other hand, if the mirror server is used as a hot standby or passive server, (as per Microsoft SQL Server 2012 Pricing and Licensing guide) a license is not required, provided that the number of processors in the passive server is equal to or less than those of the active server. The passive server can take the duties of the active server for 30 days. Afterward, it must be licensed accordingly.

- It provides options for no data loss for committed transactions.

- It can provide an almost instantaneous database failover solution by using an optional server called a witness.

- There is no real distance limitation between the principal and mirror servers.

- It can be implemented without exotic hardware and may be significantly cheaper than other high availability solutions such as SQL Server failover clustering. SQL Server failover clustering provides high availability for the entire SQL Server instance, whereas database mirroring provides high availability only at the database level. If you plan to use AlwaysOn Availability Groups, Windows Server Failover Clustering (WSFC) is required.

- It can complement existing log shipping and failover clustering implementations.

- If your applications use ADO.NET or the SQL Server Native Client to connect to a database, if a failure occurs, the applications can automatically redirect the clients to the mirror database.

However, database mirroring has a few drawbacks:

- Only user databases in `full` recovery model can be used for database mirroring. The `Simple` or `bulk-logged` recovery model cannot be used. This also means that database mirroring can break if the recovery model for a mirrored database is changed from the `full` to `simple` or `bulk-logged` recovery model.

- System databases (`master`, `model`, `msdb`, and `tempdb`) cannot be mirrored.

- Database mirroring does not support `FILESTEAM`. This means that databases with `FILESTREAM` filegroup cannot be mirrored, nor can you create a `FILESTREAM` filegroup on a principal database.

- Database mirroring does not support cross-database transactions or distributed transactions.

- Like log shipping, database mirroring provides redundancy at the database level and not at the entire SQL Server instance level, such as SQL Server failover clustering.

- Like log shipping, database mirroring applies changes that are captured only in the transaction log or the initial full backup of the principal database. Any database objects such as logins, jobs, maintenance plans, SSIS packages, and linked servers that reside outside the mirrored database need to be manually created on the mirror server.

- Unlike log shipping, database mirroring does not support having multiple copies for the same principal database. This means you can have only one mirror database for each principal database. If you want multiple copies of the principle database mirrored, you need to set up the AlwaysOn feature to create multiple Secondary Replicas.

- The mirror database name needs to be the same as the principal database name.

- If the mirror database fails, the transaction log space on the principal database cannot be reused even if you are taking transaction log backups. This means you either need to have enough space for the transaction log to grow and bring back the mirror database online before the log fills up the available disk space and brings the principal database to a halt, or break the database mirroring.

- Depending on the workload, your environment, and database mirroring configuration, database mirroring may impact application performance. Also, it can place a large demand on the network while the transaction log records are sent.

If these drawbacks are acceptable, database mirroring can be an excellent choice for high database availability, disaster recovery and reporting. It is highly recommended to thoroughly test database mirroring with your application and hardware and validate your service-level agreements (SLAs) before implementing it in production.

Defining and Configuring Database Mirroring

Although database mirroring appears to be similar to log shipping, it is different from log shipping. As explained in Chapter 26, "Log Shipping," log shipping involves periodically restoring a transaction log backup from the primary server to a warm standby server, making that server ready to recover at a moment's notice. Database mirroring continuously transfers the transaction log records, and not the transaction log backups, from the principal database and applies it to the mirror database.

Database mirroring normally involves three SQL Servers: a principal server, a mirror server, and an optional witness server.

- The *principal server* is the main production SQL Server to which clients connect. This server contains the database that you want to create as a duplicate, hot standby, or mirror copy. The initial full database backup is taken on this server.

- The *mirror server* is the hot standby SQL Server. If the principal server fails, the mirror server becomes the new principal server. This server must meet the minimum performance requirements during a short-term crisis. If your business does not allow any performance degradation, the mirror server should be similar (same CPU and memory configuration) to the principal server.

  The principal server and mirror server are often referred to as *partners* in a database mirroring session.

- The *witness server* is an optional separate SQL Server and is required only when automatic failover is required. The witness server helps create a quorum to ensure that only one SQL Server (either the principal server or the mirror server) owns the database accessible by the clients. The witness controls automatic failure to the mirror if the principal becomes unavailable.

27

> **NOTE**
> One witness server can be used for multiple database mirroring sessions, each for different databases and different partners.

Transaction log records are synchronously or asynchronously transferred from the principal server to the mirror server, based on the transaction safety level that you select for the database mirroring session. Database Mirroring has two transaction safety levels: `safety full` and `safety off`, as detailed in Table 27-1. The failover options are described in the "Role Switching" section later in this chapter.

TABLE 27-1 Database Mirroring Safety Levels and Failover Options

Safety Level	Operating Mode	Failover Mode	Witness Server Required
FULL	Synchronous Database Mirroring	Automatic and Manual	Yes
FULL	Synchronous Database Mirroring	Manual and Forced	No
OFF	Asynchronous Database Mirroring	Forced	N/A

`Safety full` is often referred to as *synchronous database mirroring or high-safety mode*. In this mode, the mirror database is in sync with the principal database all the time, and it provides full data safety. The sequence of events when you choose `safety full` is described here and shown in Figure 27-1.

1. The client submits a transaction to the principal database. The principal server writes the transaction log records to the transaction log buffer.

2. The transaction log buffer is written to disk (also referred to as hardening of the log) and simultaneously transfers the transaction log records from the buffer to the mirror server. The principal server waits for a confirmation from the mirror. Because the principal waits for an acknowledgment from the mirror, the application response time increases and transaction throughput slightly reduces. The actual performance impact depends on various factors such as your network latency, disk subsystem, application, and more.

> **NOTE**
> There are no specific restrictions on the network for database mirroring, but the network connection between the servers is critical. The process to determine a failover in synchronous database mirroring is based on the network connection. If a problem exists with the network, mirroring fails over or denies access to the database because of the quorum requirement. Although mirroring works as designed, this behavior may come as a surprise to new database mirroring users because with a regular stand-alone server, the database is still available. It is recommended to have a dedicated network of high quality and high bandwidth. As a rule, the network bandwidth should be three times the maximum log generation rate.

3. The mirror server writes the transaction log records to the transaction log buffer. The transaction log buffer is then written to disk.

4. The mirror server acknowledges that the transaction has been written.

5. The commit is reported to the client.

If you choose `safety full` and have a witness server in the database mirroring configuration, you can achieve automatic failover. This means if the principal database has a failure or is unavailable, the witness server and the mirror server form a quorum, and the mirror server performs an automatic failover. The mirror server becomes the new principal server and recovers the database and starts servicing the clients. This operating mode is also referred to as *high-safety mode with automatic failover*.

If you choose `safety full` and you do not have a witness server in the database mirroring configuration, you cannot achieve automatic failover because if the principal database fails, the mirror server cannot form a quorum because there is no witness server. In this configuration, you need to perform a manual failover. This operating mode is also referred to as *high-safety mode without automatic failover*.

FIGURE 27-1

Synchronous database mirroring mode.

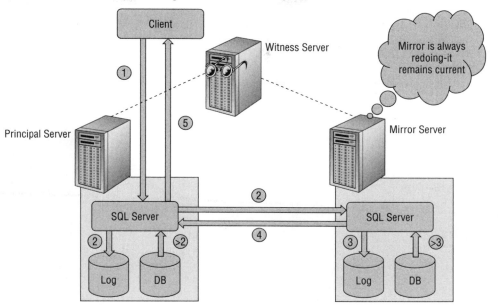

> **NOTE**
>
> Synchronous database mirroring (high-safety mode) is supported by SQL Server 2012 Enterprise, Business Intelligence, Developer, and Standard Editions. If you implement synchronous database mirroring using SQL Server 2012 Standard Edition, you cannot create database snapshots on the mirror database for reporting purposes because database snapshots are not supported by the SQL Server 2012 Standard Edition.

`Safety off` is often referred to as *asynchronous database mirroring* or *high-performance mode*. This safety level provides high performance with possible data loss. In this mode, the communication between the principal and mirror databases is asynchronous. The sequence of events when you choose `safety off` is shown in Figure 27-2. The transaction log records are written to the principal database transaction log and sent to the mirrored database transaction log in the same way as in synchronous mirroring mode. The main difference is that the principal does not wait for the mirror to acknowledge that the transaction has been written to disk. The transactions on the principal database commit as soon as it is written on the principal database transaction log. This increases the application performance, but a heavy load on the principal database or a network delay could cause the principal database transaction log waiting to be sent to the mirror database to grow. In the event of a failure of the principal, the unsent transaction log records may be lost. Automatic and manual failover is not enabled in high-performance mode due to possible data loss. Only a forced failover is allowed in this mode.

FIGURE 27-2

Asynchronous database mirroring mode.

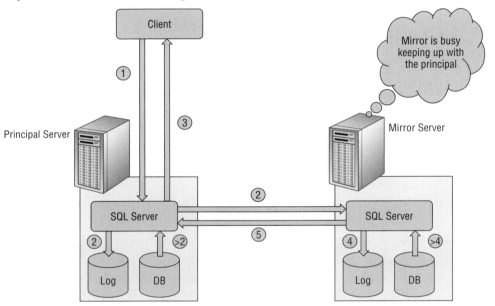

> **NOTE**
>
> Asynchronous database mirroring (high-performance mode) is only supported by SQL Server 2012 Enterprise or Developer Editions.

Best Practice

Do not configure a witness server in high-performance operating mode because there is no use of a witness server. If you use a witness server and for some reason the witness server and mirror server both become unavailable, the principal server cannot form a quorum, and the principal database is not accessible to the clients, even though the principal server is available and does not have any issues.

Configuring Database Mirroring

You can configure database mirroring using one of two methods: SQL Server Management Studio or system stored procedures.

Pre-Database Mirroring Configuration

With either method of configuration, the following prerequisites need to be completed before configuring database mirroring:

- The principal, mirror, and witness servers all must have the same version of SQL Server (SQL Server 2005,2008, 2008 R2, or 2012).

- The principal and the mirror server must have the same edition of SQL Server (Enterprise, Business Intelligence, or Standard Edition).

- The edition of witness server (if you configure high-safety mode with automatic failover) can be SQL Server Express, Web, Standard, Business Intelligence, or Enterprise Edition.

- The recovery model of the principal database must be set to `full`.

- Ensure that there is enough disk space for the mirror database on the mirror server.

- Create the mirror database. To do this, take a full database backup of the principal database and subsequent transaction log backups; copy the backups to the mirror server; and restore it on the mirror server `with norecovery` to put it into a state that allows inserting transaction log records. The name of the mirror database should be the same as the principal database. Before you start mirroring, take the transaction log backup on the principal database and restore it on the mirror database `with norecovery`. Do not restore the transaction log backups `with standby` because even though it's a loading state, database mirroring does not work.

Best Practice

Although not required, the mirror database should have the same directory structure as the principal database. If the directory structure is different, adding and removing file operations on the principal database cannot be allowed without suspending database mirroring.

 For more information about backup and restore, refer to Chapter 21, "Backup and Recovery Planning."

- Communication between the SQL Servers in database mirroring configuration is accomplished over Transmission Control Protocol (TCP) *endpoints*. Each server participating in database mirroring requires its own dedicated database mirroring endpoint. Each endpoint listens on a unique TCP/IP port.

- All the SQL Servers in database mirroring configuration need to trust each other. If they are on the same domain, you need to ensure that each SQL Server login can connect to the other mirroring SQL Server and have CONNECT permission on the endpoints. If the SQL Servers do not trust each other, you need to use certificates for the communication between the servers.

Best Practice

Use a private high-speed network between the principal and mirror servers to reduce the network bandwidth and impact on other users. SQL Server 2012 helps reduce the network bandwidth with the log compression feature.

Configuring Database Mirroring Using Management Studio

The following steps configure database mirroring using SQL Server Management Studio:

1. In the Object Explorer on the principal server in SQL Server Management Studio, right-click the principal database, and select Properties.

2. On the Options page, verify that the recovery model is full.

3. On the Mirroring page, click the Configure Security button to launch the Configure Database Mirroring Security Wizard. Click Next to begin the wizard. This wizard enables you to configure the security of the principal, mirror, and witness (optional) servers.

4. On the Include Witness Server page, click Yes if you want to operate database mirroring in synchronous (high-safety) mode with automatic failover. For other operating modes (high-safety without automatic failover and high-performance mode), click No.

5. On the Choose Servers to Configure page, as shown in Figure 27-3, ensure that the Witness server instance check box is checked. Click Next to continue. If you selected No in the previous step, you will not see this page.

6. The next page is the Principal Server Instance page, as shown in Figure 27-4. As discussed earlier, communication between the servers participating in database mirroring is accomplished over TCP endpoints. Each server requires its own, dedicated database mirroring endpoint. Each endpoint listens on a unique TCP/IP port. The default port is 5022, as shown in Figure 27-4 is 5022. For security reasons, it is recommended to use a nondefault port. You cannot change the port number from here, but it is configurable using the alter endpoint syntax later. Also, by default, the check box for Encrypt data sent through this endpoint is selected. Have this check box selected to ensure that the data transferred across the network is encrypted. If for any reason you do not need encryption, uncheck this box. You can also change the endpoint name on this page. Click Next to continue.

FIGURE 27-3

Selecting the witness server to save the security configuration.

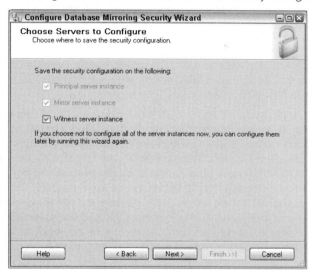

FIGURE 27-4

Configuring the Principal Server.

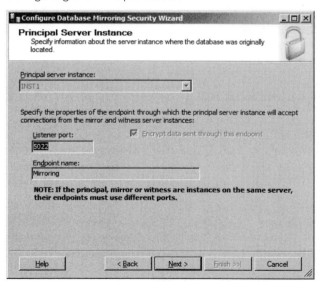

7. On the Mirror Server Instance page, click the Connect button to display the Connect to Server dialog box. Type the connection properties of the mirror server, and click Connect. This brings you back to the Mirror Server Instance page. Type the TCP/IP port for the endpoint on the mirror server. The default port is 5023, and again you should use a nondefault port for security reasons. Also, by default the check box for Encrypt data sent through this endpoint is selected. Have this check box selected to ensure that the data transferred across the network is encrypted. If for any reason you do not need encryption, uncheck this box. You can also change the endpoint name on this page. Click Next to continue.

8. The Witness Server Instance page, as shown in Figure 27-5, displays if you select Witness Server in the Include Witness Server page. Click the Connect button to display the Connect to Server dialog box. Type the connection properties of the witness server, and click Connect. This brings you back to the Witness Server Instance page. Type the TCP/IP port for the endpoint on the witness server. Also, if your witness server is on the same physical server as the mirror server, use a different port. Don't have the witness server on the same physical server as the principal server because the loss of the physical server can make both the principal and witness server unavailable, and automatic failover cannot be achieved. Also, by default the check box for Encrypt data sent through this endpoint is selected. Have this check box selected to ensure that the data transferred across the network is encrypted. If for any reason you do not need encryption, uncheck this box. You can also change the endpoint name on this page. Click Next to continue.

FIGURE 27-5

Configuring the Witness Server.

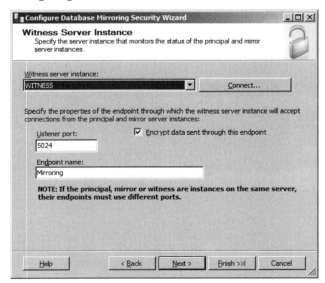

9. On the Service Accounts page type the service accounts for all the SQL Server instances (principal, mirror, and witness). After you specify the service accounts, logins are created for each account, if necessary, and will be granted `connect` permission on the endpoints. You do not need to create the logins if all the SQL Server instances use the same domain account or if you use certificate-based authentication. Similarly, if all the SQL Server instances are in a workgroup and all the SQL Server service accounts use the same login and password, you do not need to create the logins and can leave the fields empty on this page.

10. On the Complete the Wizard page, verify the choices made in the wizard, and click Finish.

11. On the Configuring Endpoints page, review the status of each endpoint. A successful configuration of the endpoints is shown in Figure 27-6. Click Close to exit the Configure Database Mirroring Security Wizard.

FIGURE 27-6

Configuring endpoints.

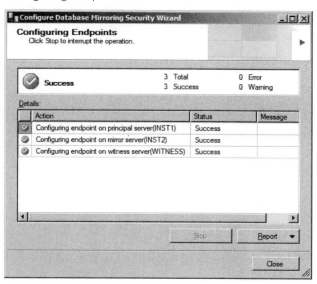

12. On the Database Properties dialog, as shown in Figure 27-7, do not select anything and leave it displayed. Before you start mirroring, verify that the mirror database is up-to-date. If required, take a full backup of the database and a transaction log backup of the principal database and restore it on the mirror database `with norecovery`. After the transaction log is restored, return to the Database Properties dialog box (Figure 27-7) and click the Start Mirroring button. You see a page similar to Figure 27-8. Click OK to exit.

FIGURE 27-7

Start database mirroring.

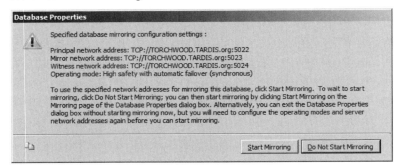

FIGURE 27-8

Database mirroring started.

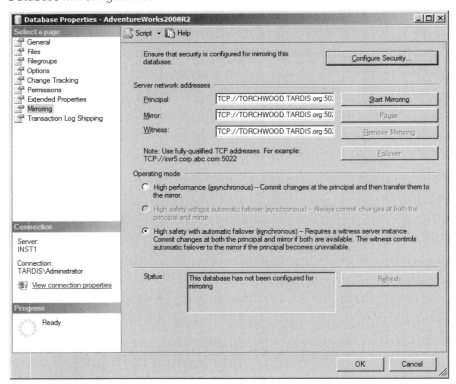

Configuring Database Mirroring Using Transact-SQL

Like most other configurations, you can also configure database mirroring using Transact-SQL. The following example shows the basic steps to configure a database mirroring session for the AdventureWorks sample database using Transact-SQL and Windows Authentication. The assumption is that both the partners and witness run under the same Windows domain service account. This means that you do not need to create a login for each partner because it already exists. If the partners and witness use different domain user accounts for their service, startup accounts create a login for the account of the server using the create login statement and grant connect permissions on the endpoint to the login using the grant connect on endpoint command.

1. Connect to the principal server and execute the following code to create an endpoint for the principal. In this example, the principal uses the TCP port 5091 for its endpoint:

```
CREATE ENDPOINT Endpoint_Mirroring
  STATE=STARTED
  AS TCP (LISTENER_PORT=5091)
  FOR DATABASE_MIRRORING (ROLE=PARTNER);
```

2. Connect to the mirror server, and execute the preceding code.

3. If you use a witness, connect to the witness server, and execute the following code:

```
CREATE ENDPOINT Endpoint_Mirroring
  STATE=STARTED
  AS TCP (LISTENER_PORT=5091)
  FOR DATABASE_MIRRORING (ROLE=WITNESS);
```

4. Execute the following code on the principal server to take a full database backup of the AdventureWorks database:

```
BACKUP DATABASE AdventureWorks
  TO DISK = 'C:\AdventureWorks.bak';
```

5. Copy the AdventureWorks.bak on the mirror server and execute the following code on the mirror server to restore the AdventureWorks database in restoring mode:

```
RESTORE DATABASE AdventureWorks
  FROM DISK = 'C:\AdventureWorks.bak'
  WITH NORECOVERY;
```

6. Execute the following code on the principal server to take a log backup of the AdventureWorks database:

```
BACKUP LOG AdventureWorks
  TO DISK = 'C:\AdventureWorksLog.bak';
```

7. Copy the AdventureWorksLog.bak on the mirror server and execute the following code on the mirror server to restore the AdventureWorks database in restoring mode:

```
RESTORE LOG AdventureWorks
```

27

```
FROM DISK = 'C:\AdventureWorksLog.bak'
WITH NORECOVERY;
```

8. Execute the following code on the mirror server to set the principal server as partner on the mirror database.

```
ALTER DATABASE AdventureWorks
    SET PARTNER =
    'TCP://principal.hol169.local:5091';
```

9. Execute the following code on the principal server to set the mirror server as a partner on the principal database. Executing this statement begins the database mirroring session.

```
ALTER DATABASE AdventureWorks
    SET PARTNER =
    'TCP://mirror.hol169.local:5091';
```

10. If you use a witness, set the witness server as follows on the principal server:

```
ALTER DATABASE AdventureWorks
    SET WITNESS =
    'TCP://witness.hol169.local:5091';
```

> **NOTE**
>
> By default, the database mirroring session is set to run in synchronous mode (`safety full`) without automatic failover. To change the transactions safety level to `OFF` (asynchronous database mirroring), execute the following command on the principal server:
>
> `ALTER DATABASE AdventureWorks SET PARTNER SAFETY OFF;`

 For configuring a database mirroring session using certificates, refer to SQL Server 2012 Books Online topic "Using Certificates for a Database Mirroring Endpoint." `http://msdn.microsoft.com/en-us/library/ms191477.aspx`

Post-Database Mirroring Configuration

As mentioned earlier, database mirroring applies only the changes that are either captured in the transaction log or the initial full backup of the principal database. Any database objects such as logins, jobs, maintenance plans, SSIS packages, and linked servers that reside outside the principal database need to be manually created on the mirror server. After configuring database mirroring, you need to synchronize the mirror server with all objects that live outside the mirrored database. Most of these objects can be easily scripted using Management Studio and can be applied on the mirror server. The frequency of applying the changes must meet the rate of changes in your environment.

One of the ways to synchronize the logins is to create an Integration Services (SSIS) job that connects to each server and transfers the logins. The frequency of this job depends on how often new logins are added to your principal server.

Checking Database Mirroring Configuration

After database mirroring is configured, you can verify the database mirroring setup in several ways.

- View the status of the principal and mirror databases.

- Expand Databases in Management Studio to view the status of the principal and mirror databases. Figure 27-9 shows an example for the principal database.

FIGURE 27-9

Status of principal database,

- Query the `sys.database_mirroring` catalog view to view the database mirroring metadata for each mirrored database. For example, executing the following T-SQL command against the principal and mirror server displays the results in Table 27-2.

```
SELECT DB_NAME(database_id) AS Database_Name,
mirroring_state_desc,
mirroring_role_desc,
mirroring_safety_level_desc,
mirroring_partner_name,
mirroring_witness_name,
mirroring_witness_state_desc,
mirroring_failover_lsn
FROM sys.database_mirroring
WHERE mirroring_state IS NOT NULL;
```

TABLE 27-2 **Querying the sys.database_mirroring Catalog View**

Column Name	Principal Server Results	Mirror Server Results
Database_Name	AdventureWorks	AdventureWorks
mirroring_state_desc	SYNCHRONIZED	SYNCHRONIZED
mirroring_role_desc	PRINCIPAL	MIRROR
mirroring_safety_level_desc	FULL	FULL
mirroring_partner_name	TCP://sql2008ni2.hol169.local:5022	TCP://sql2008ni1.hol169.local:5022
mirroring_witness_name	TCP://witness.hol169.local:5023	TCP://witness.hol169.local:5023
mirroring_witness_state_desc	CONNECTED	CONNECTED
mirroring_failover_lsn	1120000000012600001	1120000000012600001

The mirroring state result is SYNCHRONIZED. This state indicates that the mirror database has sufficiently caught up with the principal database. If you chose SAFETY FULL, there will be no data loss. If you chose SAFETY OFF, there is a potential for data loss. Other possible mirroring states are as follows:

- Synchronizing: Indicates that the mirror database is trying to catch up with the principal database. This is typically seen when you just start database mirroring or are in high-performance mode.

- SUSPENDED: Indicates that the mirror database is not available. During this time the principal is referred to as *running exposed* because it is processing transactions but not sending any transaction log records to the mirror.

- PENDING_FAILOVER: Indicates the state that the principal goes through before transitioning to the mirror role.

- DISCONNECTED: Indicates the partners are unable to communicate with each other.

The mirroring_failover_lsn indicates the log sequence number (lsn) of the latest transaction log record that is written to disk. When there is heavy load on the principal database and the mirror tries to catch up with the principal, you see that the mirroring_failover_lsn on the principal is ahead of the mirror.

- Query the sys.database_mirroring_witnesses catalog view to review database mirroring session information. For example, executing the following T-SQL command against the witness server displays the results in Table 27-3.

```
SELECT database_name,
principal_server_name,
mirror_server_name,
safety_level_desc,
```

```
partner_sync_state_desc
FROM sys.database_mirroring_witnesses;
```

TABLE 27-3   Querying the sys.database_mirroring_witnesses Catalog View

Column Name	Witness Server Results
database_name	AdventureWorks
principal_server_name	TCP://sql2008ni1.hol169.local:5022
mirror_server_name	TCP://sql2008ni2.hol169.local:5022
saftey_level_desc	FULL
partner_sync_state_desc	IN_SYNC

27

- Query the `sys.database_mirroring_endpoints` catalog view to review database mirroring endpoints information. For example, to check that the endpoints are started (STATE=STARTED), execute the following code on each server participating in the database mirroring session

```
SELECT state_desc FROM sys.database_mirroring_endpoints;
```

Monitoring Database Mirroring

You can monitor database mirroring in many ways. The simplest way to monitor database mirroring is to launch the Database Mirroring Monitor. To monitor database mirroring performance, you can use System Monitor performance counters on the mirroring partners. You can also use the SQL Server Profiler tool to capture the time taken for database mirroring failover.

Monitoring Using Database Mirroring Monitor

Microsoft provides a useful tool called *Database Mirroring Monitor* to monitor database mirroring. You can launch the Database Mirroring Monitor tool from SQL Server Management Studio as follows:

1. Open Management Studio, and connect to the principal or mirror server.
2. Expand Databases, and right-click the principal database.
3. Select Tasks, and then click Launch Database Mirroring Monitor.
4. Click Action menu, and select Register Mirrored Database.
5. On the Register Mirrored Database dialog box, click the Connect button to display the Connect to Server dialog box. Type the connection properties of the principal or

the mirror server, and click Connect. This brings you back to the Register Mirrored Database dialog box. Click Register. Database Mirroring Monitor registers the database and both partner servers. To modify the credentials used to connect to the partners, click the Show the Manage Server Connections Dialog Box When I Click OK check box. Click OK to continue.

6. The Database Mirroring Monitor should now show you the principal and mirror server status, the amount of database mirroring traffic and latency, and the operating mode, as shown in Figure 27-10.

FIGURE 27-10

Monitoring the database mirroring session.

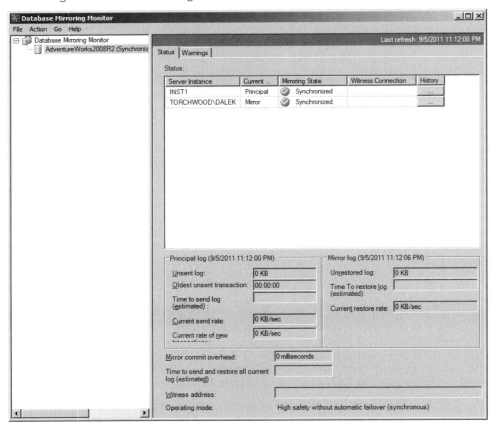

> **NOTE**
> If there is no traffic produced from the principal to the mirror, the Database Mirroring Monitor reflects that (refer to Figure 27-10).

7. Click the History button to see the database mirroring history, as shown in Figure 27-11.

8. The Database Mirroring Monitor also enables you to set warning thresholds. Click the Warnings tab. By default, thresholds are not enabled. To set the thresholds, click Set Thresholds. On the Set Warning Thresholds dialog box, as shown in Figure 27-12, check the warning for the principal and mirror server and type the value. Click OK to continue. The Warning tab, as shown in Figure 27-13, can now have the thresholds. When a threshold is exceeded, an event logs to the Application Event log. To automatically monitor these events, you can either configure an alert on the event using SQL Server Management Studio or Microsoft System Center Operations Manager.

FIGURE 27-11

Database Mirroring History.

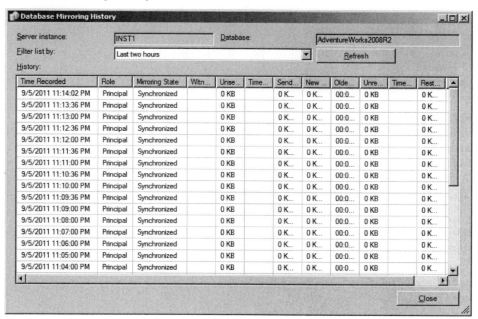

27

705

FIGURE 27-12

Setting warning thresholds.

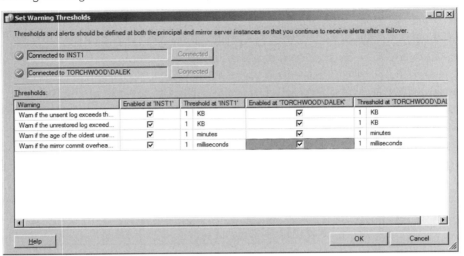

FIGURE 27-13

Database mirroring warnings.

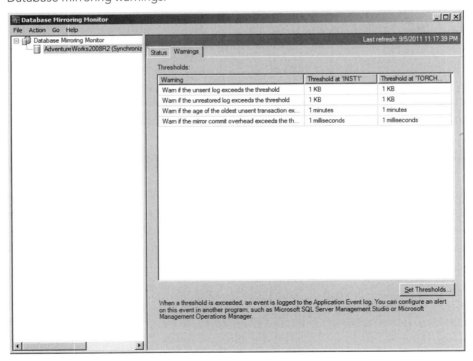

Monitoring Using System Monitor

Apart from using the Database Mirroring Monitor, you can also use System Monitor (previously referred to as Performance Monitor) to monitor database mirroring performance. The *SQLServer:Database Mirroring* object contains the database mirroring performance counters. Following are some of the key counters:

Key principal server counters:

- **Log Bytes Sent/sec:** Indicates the rate at which the principal transfers transaction log records to the mirror.
- **Log Send Queue KB:** Indicates the total number of kilobytes of the transaction log that has not been sent to the mirror yet.
- **Transaction Delay:** Indicates the delay in milliseconds spent in waiting for the commit acknowledgment from the mirror. This counter is useful to see if database mirroring is impacting performance on the principal server.
- **Log Compressed Bytes Sent/sec:** Indicates the number of compressed bytes of the transaction log sent in the last second. To find the factor by which the transaction log stream has been compressed, also referred to as the log compression ratio, divide the *Log Bytes Sent/sec* by *Log Compressed Bytes Sent/sec*.
- **Log Bytes Sent from Cache/sec:** Indicates how much of the transaction log bytes are sent from the principal to the mirror and is read from the principal's in-memory transaction log cache.

Key mirror server counters:

- **Redo Bytes/sec:** Indicates the rate at which log bytes are rolled forward on the mirror database.
- **Redo Queue KB:** Indicates the total number of kilobytes of the transaction log that has not been rolled forward to the mirror database yet. To estimate the time it takes the mirror to redo the log, divide *Redo Queue KB* by *Redo Bytes/sec*.
- **Log Bytes Received/sec:** Indicates the rate at which the log bytes are received from the principal. To estimate the time it takes the mirror to catch up with the principal, divide *Log Send Queue KB* by *Log Bytes Received/sec*.
- **Log Compressed Bytes Received/sec:** Indicates the number of compressed bytes of the transaction log received in the last second.
- **Log Bytes Redone from Cache/sec:** Indicates the number of redone transaction log bytes that were read from the mirror's in-memory transaction log cache.

 For more information on all the performance counters available for database mirroring refer to SQL Server, Database Mirroring Object at `http://msdn.microsoft.com/en-us/library/ms189931.aspx`.

Monitoring Using SQL Server Profiler

To capture the time taken for database mirroring failover, launch the SQL Server Profiler tool as follows:

1. Select Start ⇨ Programs ⇨ Microsoft SQL Server 2012 ⇨ Performance Tools ⇨ SQL Server Profiler.
2. From the File menu, select New Trace.
3. This brings up the Connect to Server dialog box. Enter the principal server information, and click Connect.
4. On the Trace Properties dialog box, enter the trace name in the General tab.
5. On the Trace Properties dialog box, click the Events Selection tab. Select the Show All Events check box. Expand the Database event, and select the Database Mirroring State Change check box. Select the columns *TextData* (gives a description of the database mirroring state change) and *StartTime* (tells you the time at which the event started).
6. Click Run to start the capture.

Pausing or Removing Database Mirroring

After configuring database mirroring, you can pause, resume, or remove database mirroring. If database mirroring impacts your applications performance, you may want to pause a database mirroring session and improve the performance. Pausing a database mirroring session causes the mirroring state to change to suspended. During this time the principal does not send any transactions to the mirror, and its principal database's transaction log keep growing, even if you schedule transaction log backups. The transaction log is not be truncated because it has to send the transactions to the mirror after the database mirroring session resumes.

To pause a database mirroring session using SQL Server Management Studio, follow these steps:

1. In the Object Explorer on the principal server in SQL Server Management Studio, right-click the principal database, and select Properties.
2. On the Mirroring page, as shown in Figure 27-8, click the Pause button.
3. You will be prompted for confirmation. Click Yes to confirm. This pauses the database mirroring session and changes the Pause button to Resume.
4. Click the Resume button to resume the database mirroring session.

To pause the database mirroring session for the AdventureWorks database in code, connect to either the principal or mirror server and execute the following:

```
ALTER DATABASE AdventureWorks SET PARTNER SUSPEND;
```

To resume the database mirroring session for the AdventureWorks database in code, connect to either the principal or mirror server and execute the following:

```
ALTER DATABASE AdventureWorks SET PARTNER RESUME;
```

To remove a database mirroring session using SQL Server Management Studio, follow these steps:

1. In the Object Explorer on the principal server in SQL Server Management Studio, right-click the principal database, and select Properties.

2. On the Mirroring page, as shown in Figure 27-8, click the Remove Mirroring button.

3. You will be prompted for confirmation. Click Yes to confirm. This removes the database mirroring session. This means that the relationship between the partners and witness is removed, and each partner is left with a separate copy of the database. The mirroring database will be left in the RESTORING state because the database was created using the restore with norecovery command.

4. To resume the database mirroring session after removing it, you need to configure a new database mirroring session, as explained earlier in this chapter.

To remove the database mirroring session for the AdventureWorks database in code, connect to either the principal or mirror server and execute the following:

```
ALTER DATABASE AdventureWorks SET PARTNER OFF;
```

Role Switching

Role switching in database mirroring is a process to change the principal and mirror roles. Three types of role switching exist based on the database mirroring operating mode: automatic failover, manual failover, and forced failover.

Automatic failover is available only in synchronous mode with failover. In this mode, if the principal database becomes unavailable due to any failure and the mirror and witness servers are still connected and the mirroring state is SYNCHRONIZED, automatic failover occurs. Here is a high-level sequence of events that occur in an automatic failover scenario:

1. The principal database becomes unavailable due to some failure.

2. If the principal server is still available, the state of the principal database is changed to DISCONNECTED and all the clients are disconnected from the principal database.

3. The mirror and the witness server detect the failure.

> **NOTE**
>
> The default timeout for communication between the principal, mirror, and witness servers is 10 seconds. If the principal does not respond within the timeout period, it is considered to be down. If you use high-safety mode, you can change the timeout period using the `ALTER DATABASE SET PARTNER TIMEOUT` command. The default timeout of 10 seconds works well for most environments. If you do want to change the timeout period, do not set it below 10 seconds because this may cause false failures.

4. The mirror server recovers the mirror database.

5. The mirror server forms a quorum with the witness server.

6. The mirror server becomes the new principal server and brings the mirror database online as the new principal database.

7. The old principal server, when it is back online, takes the mirror role, and the old principal database becomes the new mirror database and starts synchronizing with the new principal database.

Manual Failover is available only in synchronous mode with and without failover. As the name suggests, you decide to switch the roles of the servers and manually failover the database. Manual failover is used for planned downtime (for example, during hardware or software upgrades). Manual failover is allowed only when the partners connect and the mirroring state is SYNCHRONIZED. During a manual failover, the clients are disconnected from the principal database and the roles of the partners are switched.

To perform a manual failover using SQL Server Management Studio, follow these steps:

1. In the Object Explorer on the principal server in SQL Server Management Studio, right-click the principal database, and select Properties.

2. On the Mirroring page, as shown in Figure 27-8, click the Failover button.

3. You are prompted for confirmation. Click Yes to confirm. This performs a manual failover.

To perform a manual failover for the AdventureWorks database in code, connect to the principal server and execute the following:

```
ALTER DATABASE AdventureWorks SET PARTNER FAILOVER;
```

Forced Failover also referred to as *forced service (with possible data loss)* is available only in synchronous mode without failover and asynchronous mode. If the principal server is lost, the principal database is unavailable to the clients. You can make the database available by manually forcing service on the mirror server by executing the following command on the mirror server:

```
ALTER DATABASE AdventureWorks SET PARTNER FORCE_SERVICE_ALLOW_DATA_LOSS;
```

This brings the database online on the mirror server, which becomes the new principal server. When the old principal server becomes available, it automatically assumes the mirror role but the database mirroring session is suspended. To resume the database mirroring session, follow the steps discussed earlier in the chapter.

After any type of failover, clients must reconnect to the new principal database. If your applications use Microsoft ADO.NET or SQL Native Client to connect to a database, then if a database mirroring failover occurs, the applications can automatically redirect the clients to the current principal database. You must specify the initial principal server and database and failover partner server in the connection string. The failover partner in the connection string is used as an alternative server name if the connection to the initial principal server fails. If your applications do not use Microsoft ADO.NET or SQL Native Client automatic redirection, you need to use other methods such as using network load balancing (NLB), Domain Name System (DNS) alias, or custom code that can enable your application to failover.

After the role switching process is completed, verify that any database objects such as logins, jobs, maintenance plans, SSIS packages, and linked servers that reside outside the mirror database are created on the mirror server. For example, if the logins are not created on the mirror server, the users cannot connect, and you still have a server down situation.

Best Practice

Thoroughly execute the role-switching steps and document them prior to needing to failover to the mirror server. Failure to do this can significantly increase downtime and complexity when you actually need to failover to the mirror server.

High Availability/AlwaysOn

AlwaysOn Availability Groups are the next evolution of mirroring technologies in SQL Server. As reviewed in the first half of this chapter, mirroring allows you to mirror only on a per-database (1:1 ratio). With SQL Server 2012, you can define multiple databases together in a logical container called an availability group that enables the databases to fail over together as a single unit.

In addition to grouping databases together, you now get up to four readable secondary copies of your database. This gives you the flexibility to offload reporting from your primary transactional databases or even take backups from your secondaries! AlwaysOn Availability Groups offers the following benefits:

- Multiple secondary replicas (one primary and up to four secondary replicas).
- Readable secondary replicas.
- Flexible failover policies, for more granular control over conditions that cause automatic failovers for an availability group.

- No requirement for a witness server to achieve high-availability/automatic failover for your databases.

- Multiple availability modes, including Asynchronous-commit mode and Synchronous-commit mode. Asynchronous is a disaster-recovery solution recommended when secondary replicas are distributed over large distances (for example across a WAN). In Asynchronous mode, the primary does not wait for any of the secondary replicas to harden their logs; instead, after writing the log record locally to its log file, it then sends the transaction confirmation back to the client. In Synchronous-commit mode, the primary and secondary are always fully synchronized. This means that the primary replica must wait until all the secondary replicas harden their logs to disk before returning a transaction confirmation back to the client.

- Multiple failover modes, including automatic failover (without data loss), planned manual failover (without data loss), and forced manual failover (with possible data loss).

- Availability group listeners, which are virtual network names (VNN) for the availability group, which applications can connect to. For those familiar with clustering, this is the same as using a cluster name rather than using individual node names. This provides applications a way to quickly failover seamlessly after an availability group fails over. Listeners are also the vehicles that provide support for multisubnet failover.

- Automatic page repair. If a page is marked as suspect due to corruption, SQL Server automatically attempts to recover the page from a database mirroring partner (principal or mirror) or an availability replica (primary or secondary).

- By default, data is compressed and encrypted between primary and secondary replicas.

- Ability to force Windows Server Failover Cluster (WSFC) quorum.

Requirements and Prerequisites

To set up an AlwaysOn Availability Group, you must take many considerations into account, including the host servers, Windows Server Failover Cluster (WSFC) cluster, server instances, and availability group configurations. The following list gives you some of the high-level prerequisites to take into account when setting up AlwaysOn Availability Groups. For a fully detailed list see http://msdn.microsoft.com/en-us/library/ff878487.

- The systems that are members of the availability group are not domain controllers. Availability groups are not supported on domain controllers.

- Each computer in the availability group must run either x86 (non-WOW64) or x64 Windows Server 2008 or later. In addition, it must use the Enterprise Edition of the Windows Server software.

- Each computer in the availability group must be joined to the same domain.

- Each computer participating in an availability group must be part of the same Windows Server Failover Clustering (WSFC) cluster. Availability replicas must be hosted by different nodes of the same WSFC cluster.

- The host server must be a Windows Server Failover Cluster node. Each instance of SQL Server that hosts availability replicas for a given availability group must reside on separate nodes within a single WSFC cluster.

- Each instance of SQL Server 2012 in the availability group must run Enterprise Edition. Core editions of SQL Server are supported; however, you cannot mix modes (that is, Windows Server Core and Windows Server full UI in the same WSFC supporting an availability group).

- Each instance in an availability group must use the same SQL Server collation.

- Databases in an availability group must be in Full recovery model.

- Only user databases may belong to an availability group.

- If you use contained databases in an availability group, the server option for contained database authentication must be set to 1 on every instance that hosts an availability replica for the availability group.

> **NOTE**
> AlwaysOn Availability Groups, while being a powerful new addition to the SQL Server 2012 feature set, can be complex and confusing. A great resource to help clarify many of the questions that come up for AlwaysOn Availability Groups is an FAQ page maintained by Clustering MVP Allan Hirt. You can find his AlwaysOn Availability Groups FAQ page at http://www.sqlha.com/2012/04/13/allans-alwayson-availability-groups-faq/.

Configuring AlwaysOn Availability Groups

To deploy AlwaysOn Availability Groups, you must first set up a Windows Server Failover Clustering (WSFC) cluster. Each availability replica within an availability group must be on its own node in the same WSFC cluster. Figure 27-14 shows this setup.

1. Ensure all nodes participating in the cluster group have the .NET Framework 3.5.1 and the Failover Clustering features enabled. To enable these features, from the Server Manager click the Features node. From the Features page click the Add Features link on the right side.

2. When the .NET and Clustering features are enabled, you can configure the cluster. To configure the cluster go to Control Panel ⇨ Administrative Tools ⇨ Failover Cluster Manager, and click Validate a Configuration.

3. In the Validate a Configuration Wizard, provide the names of the SQL Servers that need to be configured. After you provide the server names, select the Run All Tests (Recommended) option. When the tests finish, the Failover Cluster Validation Report, as shown in Figure 27-15, shows any issues with your configuration. Click Finish to complete validation.

FIGURE 27-14

Overview of a WSFC cluster with an AlwaysOn Availability Group.

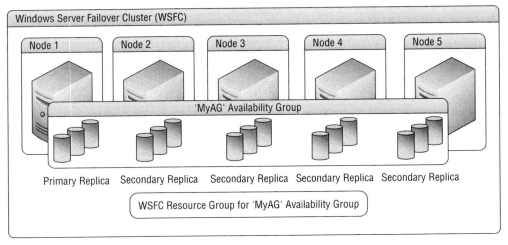

FIGURE 27-15

Failover Cluster Validation Wizard displays if any issues exist with creating your cluster.

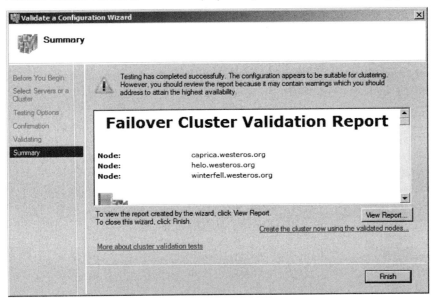

Failover Cluster Validation Report

The validation checks can complete successfully; however, your results may complete with warnings, as shown in Figure 27-15. If there are issues invalidating your setup, review the errors and remediate as needed. Warnings will not stop you from configuring clustering, but you may want to review those warnings. To see more detail on the results, you can click the View Report button.

4. When you return to the Failover Cluster Manager screen, click Create a Cluster.

5. On the Create Cluster Wizard screen, click Next. On the Select Servers screen, supply the names of the servers that will be part of the WFSC cluster (the same servers you validated in step 3), and click Next.

6. On the Access Point for Administrating the Cluster screen, supply a unique name for the cluster. This is a virtual name that clients can use for connectivity. If you already have a static IP address assigned for the cluster, you can supply it here, as shown in Figure 27-16. If you don't supply an IP address, DHCP can supply one for you, but this is not recommended. Click Next to proceed.

27

> **WARNING**
>
> If your server has multiple network cards configured on multiple networks, there will be an entry option for each on the Access Point for Administering the Cluster screen. You need to check only the box next to the network that the cluster is configured to be on. If you're not sure which network to use, contact your local network administrators and they can tell you the correct one.

FIGURE 27-16

Configuring the cluster name and IP address.

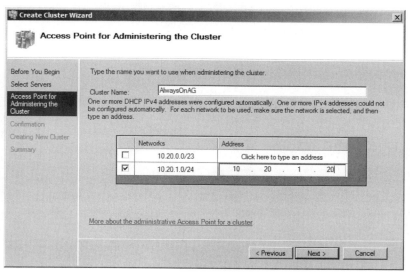

7. Next, the wizard validates your selections and presents you with a confirmation screen with a summary of your configuration. Click Next to proceed with the creation of your cluster. This step may take a few minutes to complete.

8. When the cluster creation is completed successfully, a Summary screen displays, as shown in Figure 27-17. Click Finish to complete cluster creation.

FIGURE 27-17

Summary screen of a successfully created cluster.

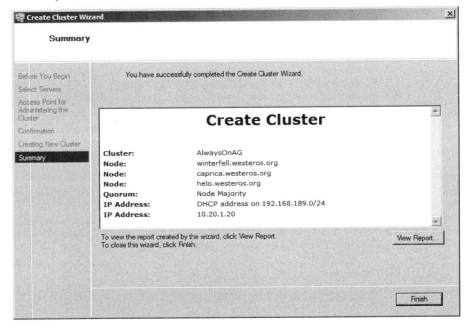

Now that you created your WSFC cluster, you must set up your availability group in SQL Server. To begin, you first need to enable AlwaysOn on each node.

1. Open SQL Server Configuration Manager, and go to SQL Server Services node.

2. Right-click the service for the SQL Server 2012 instance, and from the context menu select Properties.

3. Click the AlwaysOn High Availability tab. The name of the Windows failover cluster name is automatically populated for you. Check the box for Enable AlwaysOn Availability Groups, as shown in Figure 27-18, and click OK. To take effect, this requires a service restart.

FIGURE 27-18

Enabling AlwaysOn Availability Groups.

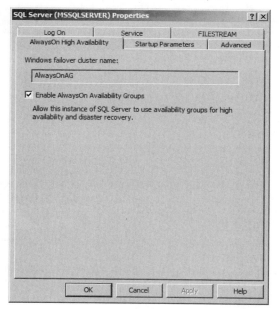

4. Open Management Studio, and connect to the instance you want to use as your primary replica. Under the instance, expand the AlwaysOn High Availability node, right-click the Availability Groups folder, and select New Availability Group Wizard. Click Next at the Introduction screen.

5. Provide a unique name (not the cluster name) for your availability group, and click Next.

6. From the Select Databases screen, select the databases you want to be in the availability group. Under the Status column, as shown in Figure 27-19, it tells you if the

database meets the prerequisites to be a member of the availability group. If there are actions that need to be taken on a database to qualify, you can click the status link to get more detail on the status. After you make your selections by checking the boxes next to the wanted databases, click Next.

FIGURE 27-19

Selecting databases to be in the availability group.

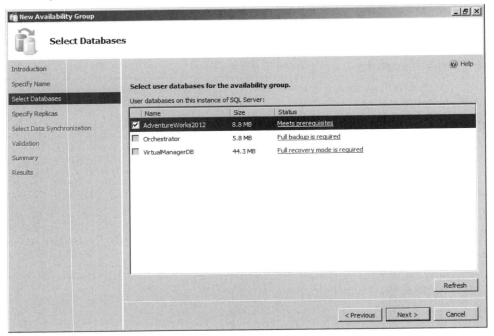

7. At the Specify Replicas screen, configure your secondary replicas in your availability group. On the Replicas tab, the primary replica is automatically populated for you. To add additional secondary replicas, click the Add Replica button. In the Connect to Server dialog, enter the name of your secondary server and connect. Repeat for any additional replicas you want to add. As shown in the figure, all the replicas you added are automatically given the role of Secondary under the Initial Role column.

You can also specify other options such as the failover mode, which specifies if the replica supports Automatic Failover (supports up to two replicas in a group) and Synchronous

Commit (supports up to three replicas in a group). You can also specify if the replica is a readable secondary. You have three options for this:

- **No:** The replica will not allow any connections.

- **Yes:** The replica will allow all connections for read access, including connections with older clients.

- **Read-Intent Only:** The replica will allow only connections with read-intent connections.

> **TIP**
>
> As you check and uncheck options for your various replicas, you may notice the area below the replicas updates based on your selections. This summary area provides a quick description of what the various replica modes are, as well as the readable secondary options.

8. Click the Endpoints tab. Here you can configure port numbers for your secondary endpoints. The default port for endpoints is 5022. In addition, you can specify if you want your endpoint connections encrypted (on by default).

Service Accounts and Endpoints

If your instance runs under a default local system account, you may encounter errors later in this process when the availability group attempts to create logins on the secondary replicas. It is highly recommended you run SQL Server service under a dedicated Windows service account.

9. Click the Backup Preferences tab. Here you configure where your backups should occur, as shown in Figure 27-20. You have several options to choose from:

- **Prefer Secondary:** Automated backups should occur against secondary replicas. If no secondary replicas are available, backups occur against the primary replica.

- **Secondary Only:** All automated backups must occur against a secondary replica.

- **Primary:** All automated backups must occur against a primary replica.

- **Any Replica:** Backups can occur on any replica in the availability group.

In addition, you can also set backup priorities for your various replicas. You can also select to explicitly exclude replicas from being used for backups as well.

FIGURE 27-20

Specifying backup preferences for your replicas.

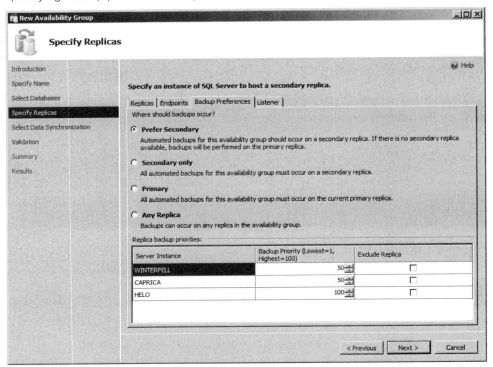

10. Click the Listener tab. Here you can specify an availability group listener that provides clients with a connection point. You can either choose to create an availability group listener in this screen, or you can configure one later using the Add Availability Group Listener dialog.

    If you choose to set one up at this point, you are given a few options as seen in Figure 27-21. You can specify the listener's DNS name (maximum 15 characters). You can also specify a custom port and IP address. For the IP address you can choose either to use a static IP address (recommended) or use DHCP to automatically allocate an address from the available subnet. When you finish configuring, click Next.

11. On the Select Initial Data Synchronization screen, as shown in Figure 27-22, you are presented with a few options to get your databases initialized in the availability group:

    ■ **Full:** Performs a full database and log backup against your selected databases. Those databases are then restored to each secondary replica joined to your availability group. If you select this option, you must also specify a file share on the network that all the replicas have access to. This is where the database and log backups will be sent to begin synchronization.

- **Join Only:** Assumes you have already restored a copy of the database on the secondary replicas and begins data synchronization to them. The selected databases are then joined to the availability group.

- **Skip Initial Data Synchronization:** Select this option if you want to manually perform a database and log a backup of each primary database.

12. After you choose your synchronization options and click Next, the Validation Wizard validates that all options specified are correct and working. If there are any issues in your configuration, click the result link for more details. Click Next to proceed to the Summary screen.

13. At the Summary screen, you can review all the options you've specified to this point. In addition, you can choose to generate a script of this process, as shown in Figure 27-23, by clicking the Script button. When you finish reviewing, click Finish to initiate the creation and initialization of the availability group.

FIGURE 27-21

Configuring the availability group listener.

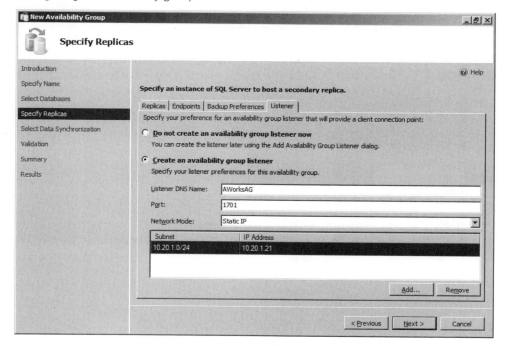

FIGURE 27-22

Setting up initial synchronization of databases.

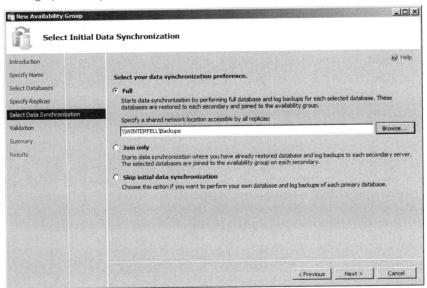

FIGURE 27-23

Scripting Out the Availability Group Setup.

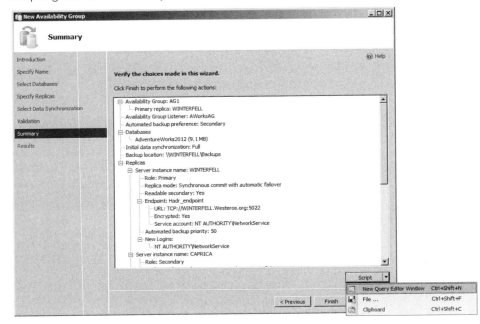

When completed, you can see your newly configured availability group in Management Studio, as shown in Figure 27-24.

FIGURE 27-24

Fully configured AlwaysOn Availability Group.

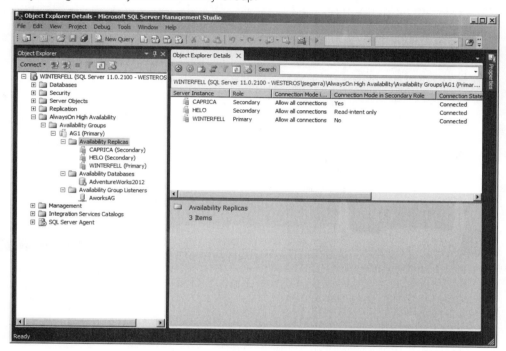

Monitoring AlwaysOn Availability Groups

Now that you have your availability group up and running, you need a way to monitor the health state of the availability group and its availability replicas. To accomplish this use the AlwaysOn Dashboard. To start the dashboard, in Object Explorer expand the AlwaysOn High Availability node, right-click the Availability Groups node, and then click Show Dashboard.

The dashboard displays the availability group summary screen that displays a summary line of all the availability groups configured on the connected instance. Clicking an availability group name launches the availability group details page, as shown in Figure 27-25.

FIGURE 27-25

Availability group details page.

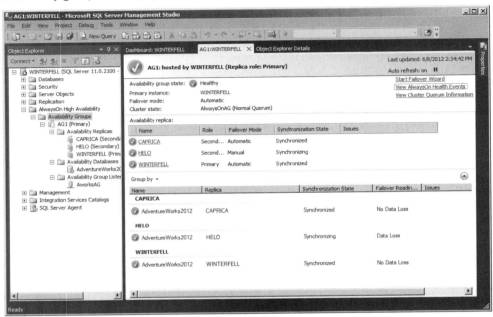

The availability replica details pane has tons of useful information such as the following:

- Failover mode for each replica in the group.
- Synchronization state of the replica and its associated databases.
- Any issues associated with groups or databases. These issues are determined via policy-based management policies. For more information on those policies, see http://msdn.microsoft.com/en-us/library/hh510235.aspx.
- Availability mode of the replica (hidden by default).

TIP

You can customize the properties you see in the availability group details pane by right-clicking the header and selecting your properties from the context menu. Properties hidden by default include Availability Mode, Connection State, and Quorum Votes. For a full detailed listed of available properties see http://msdn.microsoft.com/en-us/library/hh213474.aspx.

Also from this page you can access the following from the links in the top-right side of the page:

- **Start Failover Wizard:** Opens the Failover Wizard that enables you to manually failover your groups to make an existing secondary replica a primary replica in the availability group.
- **View AlwaysOn Health States:** Opens the Extended Events viewer. Here you can review the AlwaysOn-related events fired by the server.
- **View Cluster Quorum Information:** Opens the Cluster Quorum Information screen. This screen shows you members of the cluster, member type, member state, and quorum vote counts.

Summary

Database mirroring is an inexpensive software-based solution to achieve high database availability. Database mirroring works by transferring transaction log records from the production database on one SQL Server to a mirror database on another SQL Server over the network, either synchronously or asynchronously. Asynchronous database mirroring provides the best performance but has potential for data loss and does not support automatic failover. Synchronous database mirroring provides a higher level of data protection than asynchronous mode and provides automatic and manual failover options at the cost of reduced application performance.

AlwaysOn Availability Groups is a robust high-availability solution that offers a scalable and flexible architecture for your databases. Availability groups work much like mirroring; however, you can transfer and failover one or more databases together in a group. Through the use of Windows Failover Cluster Service (WSFC), AlwaysOn Availability Groups can maintain high availability and scalability across your network.

At first glance, database mirroring or AlwaysOn Availability Groups may appear to be better than log shipping, but it is not a replacement for log shipping. Each solution has unique features, and depending on your business requirements, you may require selecting one or both the solutions. For example, log shipping supports multiple copies of the production databases, but database mirroring allows only one copy of the production database. If you need multiple copies of the production database and the features of database mirroring, you can implement database mirroring and log shipping, or you can set up AlwaysOn Availability Groups. Database mirroring also complements existing failover clustering implementations.

As with any other solution, you should take a performance baseline of your environment before and after configuring database mirroring, and use your performance data to help you determine whether you should use database mirroring or whether you should use synchronous mode or asynchronous mode in your production environment.

Replicating Data

Replication is a native group of technologies in SQL Server 2012 that you can use to copy and distribute database objects and data from one database to another. In addition, replication synchronizes the databases to maintain consistency.

You can use replication for many purposes, listed here in order from most popular to rarely used:

- Offloading reporting from an OLTP server to a reporting server.
- Data consolidation; for example, consolidating branch office data to a central server.
- Data distribution; for example, distributing data from a central server to a set of member servers to improve read performance.
- Disaster recovery — replication can be used to keep a DR (disaster recovery) server synchronized with the main server, and clients can be manually redirected to the DR with minimal interruption.
- Synchronizing data with a central server and a mobile sales force.
- Synchronizing data with handheld devices (such as PDAs and smartphones).

You can make replication processes highly scalable, which typically can synchronize data between servers or databases with acceptable latency. *Latency* reflects the lag of time between when data is sent (replicated) from the source server and received at the destination server.

Moving Data Between Servers

Replication is not the only way to move data between servers. Following are several alternatives, each with its own pros and cons:

- bcp utility
- SSIS
- Distributed transactions

- Triggers
- Copy Database Wizard
- Backup and restore
- Log shipping and database mirroring

The following sections describe these options in more detail.

Bulk Copy Program

Bulk copy program (bcp) is a command-line tool that you can use to send tabular data to the file system and from there to a remote server. Although it can be scripted, it is slower than replication processes, requires significant work to set up, and the DBA/developer needs to ensure that all objects are in place on the destination server. For example, all tables, views, stored procedures, and functions must be on the destination server. There is no provision for change tracking. In other words, bcp can't tell what has changed in the data and sends only the changes to the destination server. The solution requires change tracking — a way to determine what has been inserted/updated/deleted on the source server. These may involve using Change Data Capture or the Change Tracking features.

SSIS

Think of SSIS as a programmatic interface to a high-performance bcp utility. It can be faster than bcp. As with bcp, it requires that the DBA/developer place all objects on the destination server, and there is no provision for change tracking.

Distributed Transactions

Distributed transactions normally involve using Microsoft Distributed Transaction Coordinator (MS DTC). With a distributed transaction, the transaction is committed on the source server and then on the destination server, and then the application can do the next unit of work. (This is sometimes called a *split write*.) The application must be configured to use distributed transactions, and the network connection must be stable and have ample bandwidth; otherwise, the transactions fails. With distributed transactions, only changes are "replicated." The DBA/developer needs to place all tables (along with the initial data), stored procedures, views, and functions on the destination server.

Triggers

Triggers are similar to distributed transactions. With distributed transactions, all application code (for example, stored procedures, and sometimes ADO.NET code) must be rewritten for the distributed transactions. With triggers, the replication logic is incorporated on the trigger. And like distributed transactions, only changes are replicated. The DBA/developer needs to place all tables (along with the initial data), stored procedures, views, and functions on the destination server. There is also overhead with using triggers, especially over a network.

Copy Database Wizard

The Copy Database Wizard can move or copy a database from one server to another. It is intended for a single use move or copy. In the move mode, you can move only the database one time. In the copy mode, the database can be copied multiple times if you specify the options to delete the database and the database files that might exist on the destination server.

Backup and Restore

Backup and restore copies the entire database to the destination server. The level of granularity possible for the preceding options are tables (bcp and SSIS) and transactions (triggers and distributed transactions).

Backup and restore, log shipping, database mirroring, and the Copy Database Wizard replicate entire databases. As the name suggests, backup and restore involves backing up the database on the source server and restoring it on the destination server. This option is not scalable for large databases, and the database must go offline while the database is restored. It is not a good option in environments with real-time data requirements because the data becomes progressively out-of-date until the latest backup is restored on the destination server.

Log Shipping

Log shipping is continuous backup and restore. The log is backed up on the source server and applied to a previously restored database backup on the destination server. Log shipping is not considered to be scalable, especially for large databases or large numbers of databases. The database on the destination server is not accessible with log shipping. There are options to make it accessible, but it will be in read-only mode, and users need to be kicked off when the next log is ready to be applied.

Database Mirroring

Database mirroring is continuous log shipping. Changes to the database transaction log are continually shipped from the source server to the destination server. The database on the destination server is inaccessible while being mirrored. There are two modes of database mirroring: high safety and high performance.

With high safety, application writes on the source server are not committed on the source server until they are also committed on the destination server. This can cause increased latency for all writes on the destination server, which may make database mirroring not a good fit for your particular requirements.

High-performance mode does not have this problem because changes occurring on the source server are applied to the destination server asynchronously. However, the high-performance option is only available on the Enterprise Edition of SQL Server 2005 and SQL Server 2008.

28

What's New with Replication in SQL 2012?

There are two new features in SQL Server 2012 replication:

- Supports up to 15,000 partitions
- Supports AlwaysOn publisher Failover Support

Replication Concepts

SQL Server replication uses a publish-subscriber mode that may include a separate distribution server. It enables you to copy or move data and database objects to another database. Consistency is maintained by a synchronizing process executed by replication. There can be three types of servers in a replication topology:

- **Publisher:** The source server.
- **Distributor:** For transactional replication and peer-to-peer replication, the distributor is where the changes are stored until they are replicated to the destination server. For merge replication, the distributor is merely a repository for replication process history. Changes and historical information are stored in a database called the *distribution database*.
- **Subscriber:** The destination server.

Types of Replication

SQL Server 2012 offers five basic types of replication, each serving a different purpose:

- **Snapshot replication:** A point-in-time image of database objects (a snapshot) is copied from the source server to the destination server. This image generation and deployment can be scheduled at whatever interval makes sense for your requirements; however, it is best used when the majority of your data seldom changes, and when it does, it changes at the same time.
- **Transactional replication:** Transactions occurring on the source server are asynchronously captured and stored in a repository (called a *distribution database*) and then applied, again asynchronously, on the destination server.
- **Oracle publishing:** This is a variant of transactional replication. Instead of SQL Server being the source server, an Oracle server is the source server, and changes are replicated from the Oracle server to SQL Server. This SQL Server can be the final destination for the Oracle server's data, or it can act as a gateway, and changes can be replicated downstream to other SQL Servers, or other RDBMs. Oracle publishing is only available on SQL Server Enterprise Edition and above.

- **Peer-to-peer replication**: Another variant of transactional replication used to replicate data to one or more nodes. Each node can publish data to member nodes in a peer-to-peer replication topology. Should one node go offline, changes occurring on the offline node, and the other member servers will be synchronized when that node comes back online. Changes are replicated bidirectionally, so a change occurring on Node A replicates to Node B, and changes occurring on Node B replicate to Node A. Peer-to-peer replication is an Enterprise Edition–only feature scalable to approximately 10 nodes, but your results may vary depending on your replicated workload, your hardware, and your available bandwidth.

- **Merge replication**: As the name indicates, merge replication is used to merge changes occurring on the destination server with changes occurring on the source server, and vice versa. It is highly scalable to hundreds if not thousands of destination servers. With merge replication, there is a central clearinghouse for changes that determines which changes go where. With peer-to-peer replication, any member node in the topology can assume the clearinghouse role.

Replication Agents

As you might imagine, a lot of work is required to move data between the various servers that are part of your replication environment. To do so, SQL Server replication makes use of three agents:

- **Snapshot agent**: Generates the tabular and schema data or schemas for the objects you want to replicate. The tables and schema data, and related replication metadata, is frequently referred to as the snapshot. The snapshot agent is used by all replication types. The snapshot agent writes the tabular/schema data to the file system. Snapshot and transactional replication can publish data to an ftp server. Although this topology is not commonly used, it is a viable option for those that need data replicated between different businesses and industries.

- **Distribution agent**: Used by snapshot replication to apply the snapshot on the subscribers, and used by transactional replication to apply the snapshot on the subscriber and to replicate subsequent changes occurring on the publisher to the subscriber. These changes can include both data and schema changes.

- **Merge agent**: Detects changes that have occurred on the publisher and the subscriber since the last time these agents ran and merges them together to form a consistent set on both the publisher and the subscriber. In some cases, the same primary key value will be assigned on the publisher and one or more subscribers between runs of the merge agent (called a *sync*). When the merge agent runs, it detects this conflict and logs it to conflict tables that can be viewed using the conflict viewer. With merge replication, the data in conflict persists on the publisher and the subscriber by default. For example, if a primary key value of 1,000 for a table is assigned on the publisher, and then the same value is assigned on the same table on the subscriber, when the merge agent runs, it logs the conflict but keeps the publisher's values for the row with a primary key (PK) of 1,000 on the publisher and keep the subscriber's values for the row with a PK of 1,000 on the subscriber.

Merge replication has a rich set of features to handle conflicts, including one that skips changes to different columns occurring on the same row between publisher and subscriber. This is termed *column-level conflict tracking*. For example, a change to John Smith's home phone number occurring on the publisher and his cell phone number occurring on the subscriber would be merged to have both changes persisting on both the publisher and subscriber. By default, merge replication uses row-level conflict tracking that might result in the change to John Smith's home phone number updating on both the publisher and the subscriber, but his cell phone change rolling back, with this conflict and the conflicting values logging to the conflict tables.

Best Practice

A single server can serve as both the publisher and distributor, and even as the subscriber. An excellent configuration for experimenting with replication is a server with multiple SQL Server instances. However, when performance is an issue, a dedicated distributor server is the best plan. This remote distributor can act as a distributor for multiple publishers; you can configure this remote distributor to have a separate distribution database for each publisher.

The publisher server organizes multiple articles (an article is a data source: a single table, view, function, or stored procedure) into a publication. You may find that you get better performance by grouping large or highly transactional articles (tables) into their own publication. The distributor server manages the replication process. The publisher can initiate the subscription and push data to the subscriber server, or the subscriber can set up the subscription and pull the subscription from the publisher.

Transactional Consistency

The measure of *transactional consistency* is the degree of synchronization between two replicated servers. As the lag time between synchronizations increases, transactional consistency decreases. If the data is identical on both servers most of the time, transactional consistency is said to be high. Conversely, a replication system that passes changes every two weeks by e-mail has low transactional consistency.

Configuring Replication

Using wizards is the simplest way to implement replication. Developers and DBAs generally avoid wizards because they have limited features, but implementing replication without wizards requires numerous calls to arcane stored procedures and is a tedious and painful process prone to user errors. However, in some cases it is necessary to use the replication stored procedures, for example, if you develop and test replication in several environments.

The task to use the wizard to configure it across the environments could be just as painful as running the scripts. Fortunately, during the wizard configuration process, you have the option to generate a script of all user actions. This script can come in handy during various stages of deployment and in some disaster recovery scenarios.

Before configuring replication, you must understand the limitations of various SQL Server editions. For example, SQL Server Express can act only as a subscriber, and the number of subscribers each edition can have is limited. Merge replication can be used to replicate only to subscribers with the same version or lower. For example, you can't have a SQL Server 2008 R2 publisher merge replicating to SQL Server 2012 subscribers; however, a SQL Server 2012 publisher can replicate to a SQL Server 2008 R2 subscriber. Merge replication is the only replication type that can replicate to SQL Server CE subscribers.

Creating a Publisher and Distributor

To enable a server as a publisher you must first configure it as a subscriber. Although you can configure the publisher with a local or remote distributor, it is recommended that you configure the distributor first before creating your first publication. This way, if a problem exists, it will be easier to troubleshoot.

The following steps walk you through the process to create your first distributor:

1. Connect to the server that will act as your publisher/distributor or remote distributor using SQL Server Management Studio. You need to use the SQL Server 2012 version of SQL Server Management Studio for this.

2. After you connect, right-click the replication folder, and select the menu option Configure Distribution.

> **NOTE**
> If you do not see the Configure Distribution option, either your SQL Server edition is SQL Server Web or Express, or you do not have the replication components installed. To install the replication components, you need to run Setup again.

3. After clicking through the initial splash screen, you have the option to select which server you should use as your distributor: either the local server or a remote server. If you use a remote server, you need to ensure that the remote server is already configured as a distributor. Because this is a local distributor, select the default option, and click Next.

4. You are prompted for a folder to serve as the default location where the snapshot agent deposits the snapshot. Select a different location if the default folder does not have adequate space for your snapshots, or if you want to minimize I/O contention. The snapshot generation process is an I/O-intensive process during snapshot generation. You do have the option to select a snapshot folder or share for each publication when you create it, so the snapshot folder location is not of critical

importance. There is a warning on this screen simply stating that the default location could not be accessed by pull subscriptions because it is not a network path.

5. After you select the location for your snapshot folder or snapshot share, click Next. The Distribution Database dialog enables you to name your distribution database and select folders where the database data and log files will reside.

Best Practice

If you have a large number of subscribers, or you replicate over a WAN, you should use a share for your snapshot folder, or use FTP along with pull subscribers. (You can configure FTP server details when you create your publication.) With pull subscribers, the merge or distribution agent or process runs on the subscriber. With push subscribers, the distribution and merge agents run on the publisher/distributor or distributor. If you use push subscribers with a remote distributor, your snapshot folder must also be configured as a snapshot share. It is not a good security practice to use the Admin shares (that is, C$), but rather a share name that hides the path of the actual physical snapshot folder location and does not require the distribution or merge agents to run under an account that has rights to access the snapshot share.

Best Practice

Optimal configuration of a distributor or a distribution server is on a 64-bit server with ample RAM and RAID 10 drives. The distributor server will be I/O and network bound, so the more RAM available for caching and the greater the available network bandwidth, the greater the throughput of your transactional replication solution. Merge replication is CPU- and network-bound, so these best practices do not apply for it.

6. Click Next to allow the publishers that you want to use this distributor. If this is a local publisher/distributor, your publisher is already selected. If not, you need to click the Add button if you want to allow other publishers to use this distributor.

7. Click Next to assign a distributor password. This allows remote publishers to use this distributor as their distributor.

8. Click Next, Next again, and Finish to complete the creation of your distributor. You also have the option to generate a script that allows you to manually create the distributor database using T-SQL. If you are adventurous, script it out, and run it on another server.

Using a Remote Distributor

To configure a publisher to use a remote distributor, follow these steps:

1. Connect to the publisher using SQL Server Management Studio, right-click the Replication folder, and select Configure Distribution.

2. When you get to the option to select which server you want to use as your distributor, select the Use the Following Server as the Distributor option.

3. Click the Add button, and enter the connection information to connect to the remote distributor. You are prompted for the password you configured to access the remote distributor.

4. Click Next, Next again, and Finish.

Your remote distributor is now ready to use.

Creating a Snapshot/Transactional Publication

After a distributor is set up for your server, you can create your publications. A publication is defined as a collection of articles, where an article is an item to be published. An article in SQL Server can be a table, a view, an indexed view, a user-defined function, or even a stored procedure or its execution. If you choose to replicate the execution of a stored procedure, the stored procedure call is executed on the subscriber.

For example, if you fire a stored procedure that updates 10,000 rows on a table, this table is replicated, and the execution of the stored procedure is executed; only the stored procedure call will be executed. If the replication of the stored procedure execution were not replicated, 10,000 update statements would need to be replicated by the publisher through the distributor to the subscriber. As you can imagine, there are considerable benefits to doing this.

Typically tables are published, but views can also be published. You just need to ensure that the base tables referenced by the views are also published.

To create a publication, execute the following steps:

1. Connect to your publisher using SQL Server Management Studio, and expand the Replication folder; then right-click the local publication folder, and select New Publication.

2. After clicking through the initial splash screen, select the database you want to replicate from the Publication Databases section.

3. Click Next. In the Replication Types dialog that appears, select the replication type you want to use. You then get an Articles dialog, from which you can select the type of objects you want to replicate.

4. Expand each object type tree, and select the articles you want to replicate. For example, if you want to replicate tables, expand the table tree, and select the individual tables you want to replicate. You can elect to replicate all tables by selecting the check box next to the table tree. You also have the option to replicate only a subset of the columns in tables you replicate.

> **NOTE**
> If you see a table with what appears to be a red circle with a slash through it next to the table, this table does not have a primary key, and you cannot replicate it in a transactional publication. Snapshot and merge replication enables you to replicate tables without primary keys.

If you highlight a table and then click the Article Properties drop-down box, you can configure options for how the table replicates to the subscriber. For example, you can replicate user triggers, include foreign key dependencies, and determine what happens if a table with the same name already exists on the subscriber. The options are as follows:

- Drop the subscriber table.

- Do nothing.

- Keep the table, but delete all of its data.

- Keep the table, but delete all the data that meets your filtering criteria (covered in the next step).

5. After you select the objects you want to replicate, click Next. The Filter Table Rows dialog appears. From here, you can configure filtering criteria that sends only a subset of the rows to the subscriber. For example, if you were replicating a table with a state column, you may decide that the subscriber should have only rows from California. To enable that, you would click the Add button, select the table in the drop-down box in the Select Table to Filter Option, click the State column in the Complete the Filter Statement section, and then add the state value. In code, it might look like this:

```
SELECT <published_columns> FROM [dbo].[SalesStaff] WHERE [State]='CA'
```

This would ensure that the subscriber receives only data and changes from sales staff when the value of State is CA.

6. After you enabled your filters, click Next. The next dialog is Snapshot Agent, which controls two snapshot options:

- Create a snapshot immediately, and keep the snapshot available to initialize subscriptions.

- Schedule the Snapshot Agent to run at the following times.

The first option generates the snapshot immediately; every replicated change that occurs in the publication is not only replicated to the subscriber, but also added to the snapshot files. This is a great option when you must deploy a lot of snapshots frequently, but it does add a constant load to your publisher. The second option to schedule the snapshot agent generates a snapshot on a schedule, so the snapshot files are updated each time you run the snapshot agent. Changes not in the snapshot must be stored in the distribution agent, which may mean extra storage requirements on the distributor. For most DBAs/developers, it is not a good practice to enable these options.

7. Click Next to configure Agent Security. This option enables you to select the security context you want your replication agents to run under. By default, SQL Server runs the replication agents under the same account under which the SQL Server agent account runs.

CAUTION

Using the SQL Server Agent account is not considered to be a good security practice because buffer overflow, worm attacks, or Trojan attacks might hijack the replication agent and run commands with the same security context as the SQL Server Agent on the publisher, distributor, or subscriber. This dialog enables you to control which account the replication agent is going to run under; ideally, this will be an account with as few rights as possible on the publisher, distributor, or subscriber. Figure 28-1 illustrates this dialog.

8. Click the Security Settings button to display the Snapshot Agent Security dialog, as shown in Figure 28-2. From here, you can enter the Windows or SQL Server Agent account under which you want the snapshot agent to run. If you choose a Windows account, it needs to be added using the following syntax: *DomainName/ AccountName*.

9. After you select the agents you want to use, click OK, and then click Next to exit the Agent Security dialog.

10. The Wizard Actions dialog displays. This enables you to create the publication immediately, create a script to create the publication, or both. After you make your selection, click Next. In the Complete the Wizard dialog that appears, you can name your publication.

11. After you give your publication a name, click Finish to create it.

FIGURE 28-1

The Agent Security dialog.

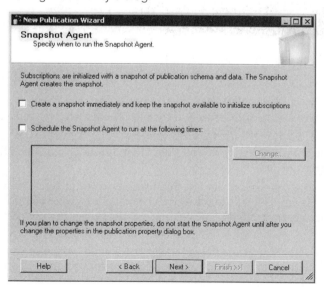

28

FIGURE 28-2

The Snapshot Agent Security dialog.

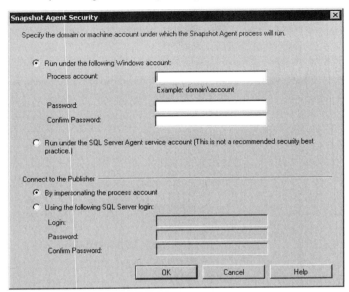

After you create your publication, you can now create one or more subscriptions to it.

Creating a Push Subscription to a Transactional/Snapshot Publication

The previous two sections discussed the two ways of replicating data: push and pull. This section focuses on how to create push subscriptions to transactional and snapshot publications:

1. Connect to your publisher in SQL Server Management Studio, and expand the Replication folder and the Local Publications folder.

2. Locate your publication, right-click it, and select New Subscriptions. Click Next to exit the splash screen.

3. In the Publication dialog, ensure that the publication you want to create a subscription to is highlighted. If it is not already selected, do so now; you may need to expand other databases to find it. When your publication is highlighted, click Next.

4. In the distribution Agent Location dialog, accept the default, which is Run All Agents on the Distributor, *MySQLServerName* (push subscriptions), where *MySQLServerName* is the name of your publisher.

5. Click Next to advance to the Subscribers dialog. All subscribers currently enabled appear in this dialog. If your subscriber does not appear, click the Add Subscriber button. This button is a drop-down button that enables you to create SQL Server and Non-SQL Server Subscribers. You can create subscriptions to SQL Servers as well as Oracle and DB2 subscribers using this wizard.

 For more information on how to replicate to Oracle and DB2 subscribers, refer to this link: `http://msdn.microsoft.com/en-us/library/ms151864.aspx`

6. After clicking the Add Subscriber button, you are prompted to connect to your Subscriber. This dialog looks similar to the Connect to SQL Server dialogs you are familiar with from connecting to SQL Server. After you add the subscriber, you can select the subscription database. Select it in the drop-down box, and then click Next.

7. The Distribution Agent Security dialog appears. This is similar to the Snapshot Agent Security dialog. Enter the account under which you want the distribution agent to run. You can also specify the accounts you want to use to connect to the distributor and subscriber here.

8. Click OK when you have completed the setup of these accounts.

9. Click Next to advance to the Synchronization Schedule dialog. From here, you can set a schedule. The default is Run Continuously, which means that the agent always runs in the case of transactional replication. (This setting has no effect on snapshot publications.) If you want to run your distribution agent on a schedule, click the drop-down button and define a schedule, or have the agent run on demand. If you select the option to run the agent on demand, you must run the agent either through the Replication Monitor, by running the job for the distribution agent, or by expanding the publication, locating the subscriber, right-clicking it, and selecting View Synchronization Status and then clicking the Start button.

10. Click Next to advance to the Initialize Subscriptions dialog. The options are to initialize, which means the snapshot will be applied at the subscriber, or not to initialize, which means that you need to put all the required objects in place. This includes all tables, the data, stored procedures, functions, and views, as well as replication stored procedures.

    a. To create the replication stored procedures, use the command `sp_scriptpublicationcustomprocs 'PublicationName'` in your publication database. The stored procedures appear in the results pane. Copy them into the query window, and run them in your subscription database. Under most circumstances the best choice is to select the initialize option.

    b. If you do select the initialize option, two selections are available in the drop-down list: At First Synchronization and Immediately. At First Synchronization means the snapshot will be generated when the distribution agent runs. Immediately means the snapshot will be generated and applied on the subscriber when you complete the dialog.

11. Click Next to advance to the Wizard options. Here you can specify whether you want the snapshot created immediately, scripted, or both.

12. Click Finish to complete the dialog and create your subscription.

Creating a Pull Subscription to a Transactional/Snapshot Publication

Creating a pull subscription is similar to creating a push subscription. The following steps show you how:

1. Connect to your subscriber using SQL Server Management Studio, expand the Replication folder, and then right-click the Local Subscriptions folder.

2. Select New Subscriptions, and click Next at the splash screen. In the drop-down box, select your publisher, and then expand your publication database and select your publication.

3. Click Next. In the Distribution Agent location dialog, select Run Each Agent at Its Subscriber (Pull Subscriptions) and click Next.

4. Click the check box next to your subscriber, and select your subscription database on the right side of the screen. Click Next to advance to the Distribution Agent Security dialog.

5. Select the security context you want the binary to run under, and choose the account you want to use to connect to the subscriber. This account should be in the dbo_owner role on the subscriber.

6. Click Next. In the Synchronization Schedule dialog, choose how frequently you want the subscriber to connect. The options are to run continuously, run on demand, or run on a schedule.

7. Click Next to continue to the Initialize Subscriptions dialog. The options are to initialize your subscription immediately, at first synchronization, or not to initialize your subscription at all (by not selecting the initialize check box). Follow the notes in Creating a Push Subscription for more details on this option.

8. Click Next to advance to the Wizard options. Here you can specify whether you want the snapshot created immediately, scripted, or both.

9. Click Finish to complete the dialog and create your subscription.

Creating a Peer-to-Peer Topology

To create a peer-to-peer topology you must run the Enterprise Edition of SQL Server. Create a transactional replication publication, and after you complete the publication creation, right-click the publication in the Local Publications folder. In the Subscription Options tab, ensure that Allow Peer-to-Peer Subscriptions is set to true. Click OK.

When this is done, follow these steps to set up a peer-to-peer topology:

1. Return to the publication, right-click the publication again, and this time select Configure Peer-to-Peer Topology. Click Next at the splash screen.

2. In the Publication dialog that appears, select your publication database and publication. These should be highlighted.

3. Click Next to launch the Configure Topology dialog. Right-click and select Add a New Peer Node.

4. Enter your subscriber name, select the appropriate authentication type, and click Next. You are then prompted for a database and Peer Originator ID. Choose 2 for the Originator ID; the publisher will have an Originator ID of 1.

5. Right-click the database icon in the center of the Configure Topology dialog, and select Connect to All Displayed Nodes. Click Next. This launches the Log Agent Security dialog.

6. Select a security context under which the Log Reader Agent runs, and click Next. This launches the Distributor Security dialog.

7. Select an account under which the Distribution Agent should run and how the Distribution Agent should connect to the Subscriber. You need to repeat this for each node in the topology. Click Next. This launches the New Peer Initialization dialog. You need to restore the publication database on each of the peers or place the tables and related replication metadata in place.

8. Click Next and then Finish to complete the peer-to-peer topology configuration.

Creating a Merge Publication

Creating merge publications is similar to creating transactional or snapshot publications. Follow these steps to create a merge publication:

1. Connect to your publisher in SQL Server Management Studio, expand the Replication folder, and right-click the Local Publications folder. Select New Publication and click Next.

2. Select the database you want to merge replicate, and click Next in the Publication Database dialog.

3. For Publication Type, select Merge publication, and click Next.

4. For Subscriber types, select the type of SQL Server to which you are replicating. You can select multiple subscriber types; for example, you can replicate to SQL 2005 and SQL 2008 publishers.

5. Click Next to Advance to the Articles dialog. From here, you can choose what you want to replicate — for example, tables, views, stored procedures, or functions. If you expand a table, you can notice that you have the option to select or deselect

columns that you want to replicate. The Article Properties button enables you to control how tables will be replicated. (For example, you can choose to replicate user indexes.) Click Next. The Article Issues dialog then warns you that a unique identifier (GUID) column will be added to all tables you are indexing.

6. Click Next to advance to the Filter Rows dialog. Merge replication is designed to replicate only a subset of the data to the subscriber. Part of the reason for this is because merge replication is frequently used over low bandwidth lines, such as over a phone line or the Internet. By filtering rows you can minimize the amount of data sent to your subscriber. You can also use join filters. Basically, join filters extend a filter you place on a table to all the other tables that have foreign key relationships on the filtered column. Consider the `SalesTerritory` table in the `AdventureWorks` database. It is joined to the `SalesOrderHeader` table by `TerritoryID`, and the `SalesOrderHeaderTable` is joined to the `SalesOrderDetail` table by the `SalesOrderID` column. If you filter on the `TerritoryID`, subscribers would get only the related data for a particular `TerritoryID`.

To use join filters, click the Add button in the Filter Table Rows dialog, and select Automatically Generate Filters, or click the Add Filter button, and select the tables and rows you want to filter on. You then have the option to click the Add Button again and select Add Join to Extend the Selected Filter. You can also filter on Host_Name() and USER_NAME(), both of which can be overridden by the Merge Agent (HostName and PublisherLogin, respectively).

7. After you create your filters, click Next to launch the Snapshot Agent dialog; in most cases you want to accept the default. Click Next to launch the Snapshot Security Agent dialog and set the appropriate accounts for your Snapshot Agent.

8. Click Next to advance to the Snapshot Options dialog, where you can either generate your publication or script it out. Click Next to name your publication, and then click Finish. When your publication has been created, click Close.

Creating merge replication subscriptions is almost identical to creating subscriptions to transactional and snapshot publications. There are two differences:

- The first is that there is a Subscription Type dialog. This controls conflicts. Conflicts arise when an attempt is made to update a row that has been deleted on the subscriber between syncs, or the same primary key value is assigned on the publisher and subscriber between syncs. The Subscription Type dialog controls how conflicts are resolved. For example, you can assign a value of 75 percent to your subscriber. This means that the subscriber change remains on the publisher unless another subscriber with a higher priority syncs that row at a later point in time. In this case, the subscriber with a higher priority replaces the value that came from the lower priority subscriber. The other subscription type is Client, which means that the first value to the publisher wins any conflicts.

- The other difference is that you can add a value for hostname that supplies a value to your filter.

Web Synchronization

One other feature of merge replication is web synchronization. Merge replication is frequently used to replicate to servers in branch offices over WANs or the Internet. To reduce the exposure of SQL Servers to viruses, worms, Trojan horses, and hackers, Microsoft created web synchronization, whereby the subscriber connects to a web server over port 80 or port 443, and an ISAPI filter redirects traffic to a SQL Server. Although most firewall administrators are reluctant to open port 1433 (the TCP/IP port that SQL Server listens on), they have no problem leaving port 80 or 443 open.

To configure web synchronization, execute the following steps:

1. Connect to your publisher using SQL Server Management Studio, and expand the Replication and Local Publications folders.
2. Right-click your publication, and select Configure Web Synchronization. Click Next.
3. Specify whether your subscribers run SQL Server or SQL CE, and select Next.
4. Enter the name of the web server, and choose to either create a new virtual directory or use an existing one. You receive a prompt to accept the copying of an ISAPI extension that can process your web synchronization. Click Yes, and then click Next to launch a dialog for Authentication Access. It is recommended that you use Basic Authentication.
5. For the domain, enter the name of the domain as it appears on the certificate; for the realm, enter the name of your fully qualified domain name as it appears on your certificate. After clicking Next, the Directory Access dialog appears.
6. Select an account or a group here that will be used to connect to your snapshot share. This group should have read rights to access the snapshot share.
7. Click Next to advance to the Snapshot Share Access dialog. Enter the name of the snapshot share as a UNC:\\MyServerName\ShareName. The share must pre-exist.
8. Click Next. If you have not already configured a publication to use this share as its snapshot folder, you get a prompt telling you that the share is empty. Ensure that this is the share you want to use, and click Next to continue to the Complete the Wizard dialog.
9. Confirm your choices and click Finish.

After the Web Configuration Wizard completes, you get a success or failure report. The latter report enables you to determine which component failed and to rerun the wizard to correct those portions.

28

Summary

Replication is a complex and powerful feature of SQL Server, and fully describing it could easily take a book by itself. Using the wizards and dialogs that Microsoft has written into Management Studio greatly simplifies the process to configure and deploy replication.

Key points from this chapter include the following:

- Replication can be a good fit for your data distribution needs.
- Replication uses a publisher-distributor-subscriber metaphor.
- Transactional replication is one-way replication by default and the fastest and most popular replication method.
- Peer-to-peer replication is bidirectional transactional replication and an Enterprise Edition–only feature.
- Merge replication is a best fit for bidirectional replication, especially when the publisher and subscribers are occasionally or frequently offline.

Clustering

IN THIS CHAPTER

Understanding High Availability vs. Scale Out

Understanding Clustering

Installing SQL Server 2012 as a Clustered Instance

Testing Failover on a Clustered Instance of SQL Server 2012

Databases are the backbone of almost every type of business application, whether it is an e-commerce website, loan processing system, or a patient monitoring application. Almost all mission-critical business processes such as sales, shipment, and supply chain management rely on database systems. A disruption in any of these processes affects an organization's capability to generate revenue, remain productive, and maintain customer satisfaction. For this reason businesses require that databases are always up and running. High availability of database systems can be achieved by a well-designed solution that includes SQL Server failover clustering.

What's New with Clustering in SQL 2012

SQL Server Failover Clustering is now considered as part of the SQL Server 2012 AlwaysOn implementation suite. Enhancements were made to the multi-site failover clustering technology:

- Automatic detection of multi-subnet environment.
- Automatic setting of IP address resource dependency to **OR**.
- SQL Server Engine startup logic skips binding to any IP address that is not in an online state, when bringing the SQL Server resource online.

What Does Clustering Do?

Clustering is a way to provide high availability to your SQL Server instance and its databases. It does this by providing a level of fault tolerance on the physical server hardware upon which SQL Server resides.

High Availability versus Scale Out

Clustering in Windows and with SQL Server 2012 is primarily designed around high availability rather than scalability. (Although you can get some scalability from the use of Read Only AlwaysOn, which is built on top of Windows Clustering.) So what is high availability and what is scalability?

High availability provides you with levels of redundancy to increase SQL Server's uptime. Although uptime of 100% is highly desirable, this is virtually impossible. Some level of downtime is required to perform certain tasks such as server or database patching, and there is always the chance of hardware problems that would impact that uptime number. A high number uptime number would be the oft quoted "five nines." This is an actual uptime of 99.999% over the course of a year. That means your SQL Server would need a total downtime not exceeding 5.26 minutes. Only having downtime of five minutes in a year is a huge challenge. Frequently, larger servers with a lot of memory can take that amount of time just to reboot once. If you had regular patching that required reboots, there is no way to achieve that number. This is where clusters can assist in greatly reducing that downtime.

In a simple cluster you may have only two physical servers (nodes) that host a single-clustered SQL Server 2012 instance. This instance has the facility to freely move between the two nodes and be available on either one. (An instance may only be up and running on a single node within a cluster at any given time.) This provides you with a level of redundancy and fault tolerance from a hardware perspective that you would not have otherwise. You may think of a cluster as providing you with a hot-standby physical server that you can go to if another one goes down. As a bonus with clusters, you get automated failover and invisible client redirection (with no special options required within application configuration strings).

With the Enterprise Edition of SQL Server 2012, you can have as many as 50 instances running on up to 16 nodes. You can only deploy 50 instances on a cluster when installing to SMB shares, otherwise you will run into a 25 instance limit (one instance per available drive letter in Windows).

The same clustered instance limit also applies to the Business Intelligence and Standard Editions of SQL Server 2012; however, you are limited to only two node failover clusters.

> **NOTE**
>
> With clustering at this level, you still have a single point of failure in your disk infrastructure because it is a shared resource. Multisite geographically diverse clusters can be built, but they generally require the use of specialized SAN replication techniques and third-party vendor tools.

Scalability is provided when you have data on multiple individual SQL Server 2012 instances. In this situation you may have an application that uses internal logic to write data to a particular server and then have some kind of data replication techniques to ensure that the data is pushed out to the other nodes. Alternatively, you could have a farm of SQL Server 2012 instances that are used for reporting purposes. You would replicate your data out from a single SQL Server 2012 instance to multiple servers that reside behind some kind of hardware or software load-balanced solution. This would provide you with a great deal of computing power to handle users' queries while providing you with a level of reporting redundancy (where individual machines behind the load balancer could go down and others would still be available to handle traffic).

What Does Online Mean?

SQL Server 2012 is considered as being online when the service is up and running and you can connect. For the SQL Server services to come up and remain online, there are several resources also required to be online. A failure in any one of these dependencies would cause SQL Server to go offline and the cluster to failover to another node. These critical resources include:

- Network name
- IP address
- Shared disk storage

If for any reason any of the required resources fail and cannot be brought up, SQL Server shows as offline in the Failover Cluster Manager, and you cannot connect:

How Does Clustering Work?

Clustering functions by performing constant checks to ensure that nodes, drives, IP address, network names, and many more items are up and available. This constant check of both the Windows and SQL Server resources serves to ensure that SQL Server remains available.

By default, Windows 2008 Failover Clustering performs a basic health check on each of these resources every 5 seconds and a more thorough check every 60 seconds. Both of these values are configurable from within the Failover Cluster Manager.

When the health check runs again SQL Server, resources also query the `sp_server_diagnostics` stored procedure. By default, the health check expects results within 60 seconds. (Although this can be configured and set as low as 15 seconds.) If no results are returned, by default, the cluster initiates a failover of the SQL Server instance to another node in the cluster. This action is also configured by adjusting the value of FailureConditionLevel for the SQL Server resource. There are six levels from which you can choose:

- **0**: No automatic failover or restart
- **1**: Failover or restart on server down
    - Triggered if the SQL Server service is down
- **2**: Failover or restart on server unresponsive
    - Triggered on level 1 error **OR**
    - Timeout from sp_server_diagnostics

- **3**: Failover or restart on critical server errors
  - Triggered level 1 or level 2 error **OR**
  - Sp_server_diagnostics returns "system error"
- **4**: Failover or restart on moderate server errors
  - Triggered level 1, 2 or 3 error **OR**
  - Sp_server_diagnostics returns "resource error"
- **5**: Failover or restart on any qualified failure condition
  - Triggered level 1, 2, 3, or 4 **OR**
  - Sp_servier_diagnostics returns "query_processing error"

By default, FailureConditionLevel 3 is used meaning that if the SQL Server service does not respond, sp_server_diagnostics times out or sp_server_diagnostics returns a system error; then a failover or restart will occur.

> **NOTE**
> Default values used to perform health checks and take actions should be changed only to resolve specific problems, and you should be fully aware of any potential impact.

Configuring Clustering

Although clustering Windows would normally be undertaken by the Systems Administration team, you may have to do this if you work in a small shop. It is also good to have an awareness of how to cluster Windows Server because it can help you with troubleshooting efforts in the event of an issue.

Configuring Windows Server 2008/2008R2 for Clustering

The process to configure Windows Server 2008/2008R2 clustering involves initial preparation steps such as setting up the right network configuration, installing required server roles and role services, and installing necessary server features.

Network Configuration

To ensure that cluster communications are not interrupted, you configure two networks. One network will be used for all public traffic and the other network for private internal communications. The private network should be configured to be nonroutable and have a unique IP address. If your domain network is not the first bound network on your server you may get a warning during setup. If this happens refer to http://technet.microsoft.com/en-us/library/dd391967(WS.10).aspx for adjusting the network binding order.

Server Role and Services Installation

To configure Windows Server 2008 and Windows Server 2008R2 for Clustering, first, you need to add the Application Server Role and required Server Role Services by following these steps:

1. Open Server Manager. Right-click Roles section, and select Add Roles. The Add Roles Wizard screen opens. Click Next.

2. On the next screen, click the check box next to Application Server to install the Application Server Role. A pop-up window opens prompting you to install additional required features. Click the Add Required Features button to install them. These additional required features may include the .NET Framework 3.5.1, the Windows Process Activation Service, and the Distributed Transactions components if they are not installed yet.

3. Click Next. The Select Role Services screen opens. Make sure that .Net 3.5.1 is checked. Check the check box next to Distributed Transactions along with Incoming Remote Transactions, Outgoing Remote Transactions, and WS-Atomic Transactions. Figure 29-1 shows the Select Role Services screen.

FIGURE 29-1

Select Role Services screen.

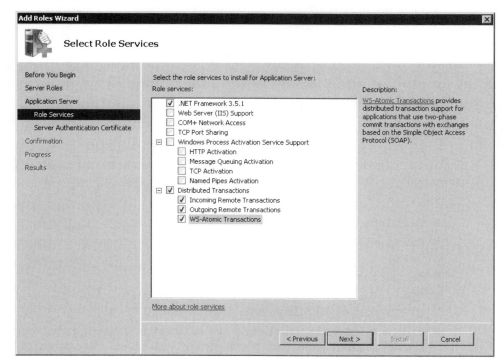

4. Click Next. The Choose a Server Authentication Certificate for SSL encryption screen opens. WS-Atomic transactions use SSL to encrypt traffic. In this screen you are provided with the option to choose an existing certificate, create a new self-signed certificate, or choose one later. For the purposes of this example, select the option to choose a certificate for SSL encryption later.

5. Click Next. The final screen gives you the ability to confirm your installation selections and go back should you want to change anything.

When the Application Server Role configuration is complete, you are ready to configure the Windows Server 2008/2008R2 Failover Clustering Feature described in the next section.

Server Feature Installation

To configure the Failover Clustering feature, follow the next steps:

1. Open Server Manager. Right-click the Features section, and select Add Features. The Add Features Wizard opens. In this screen, check the check box next to Failover Clustering.

2. Click Next. The Confirm Installation Selections screen opens. At this point you are not performing any configuration for the failover cluster, rather, just installing the feature so that it can be configured under Server Manager.

3. Click Install to complete the Failover Clustering feature installation.

When the Failover Clustering feature installation completes, you see the Failover Cluster Manager feature in Server Manager. From here you can perform all cluster-related tasks including creating and removing clusters, adding clustered services and performing all the configuration tasks. Figure 29-2 shows the Failover Cluster Manager option under the Features section in the Server Manager screen.

Validating a Cluster Configuration

Before actually creating a cluster, you should perform a cluster validation. The validation process goes through a series of tests against the servers that are part of the failover cluster. This configuration validation checks many options that can cause cluster problems including:

- Validating cluster resource status.
- Pulling BIOS, memory, service, and software update settings and comparing across nodes.
- Network configuration.
- Disk configurations including the file system and latency as well as disk failover when validating multiple servers.
- Performing the validation can help to identify potential issues early. Any warnings should be looked at and their possible impact considered. Any errors need to be resolved to continue building the cluster and installing SQL Server.

FIGURE 29-2

Failover Cluster Manager option.

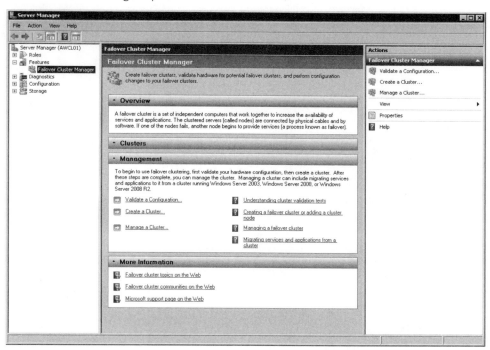

To validate a cluster configuration follow the next steps:

1. Open Server Manager. Expand the Features section, and right click on Failover Cluster Manager. Select the Validate a Configuration option. The Validate a Configuration Wizard screen opens.

2. Click Next. The Select Servers or a Cluster screen opens. Add the Windows Server 2008/2008R2 node(s) that you want to validate. If you have two nodes up and running, it is recommended to add them both, that way the validation tool can perform disk arbitration to ensure smooth storage failover. Figure 29-3 shows the Select Servers or a Cluster screen.

3. Click Next. The Testing Options screen opens. You can choose to run some or all tests. Running a smaller set of tests is useful when you want to check only certain parts of your configuration; however, to be sure that you maintain full supportability of your cluster, you should run all tests. Choose the Run All Tests option, and click Next.

4. The confirmation page screen shows you the list of servers to be tested along with a list of all tests that will be performed. Depending upon the number of nodes you selected to check and the number of configured disks, these tests could take quite some time. While the tests are running, you can track progress in the progress window. Figure 29-4 shows the validation progress window.

29

FIGURE 29-3

Select Servers or a Cluster screen.

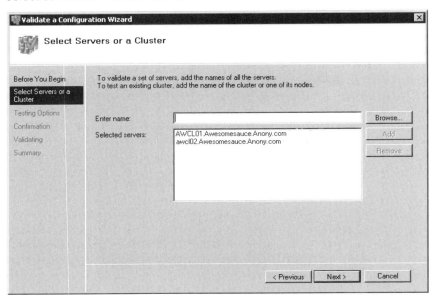

FIGURE 29-4

Validation progress window.

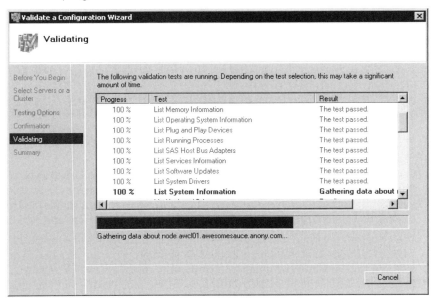

When the validation is complete, the summary screen displays. In this screen you can review the Cluster Validation Report. This report should be reviewed for warnings and errors. Validation reports are saved in the C:\Windows\Cluster\Reports folder and can be accessed at any time. This includes older reports, so you can easily perform comparisons as things change or you resolve issues.

If the Cluster Validation report came back clean, then you are ready to create your cluster. To do so you need the following items:

- Storage visible by all servers that are going to make up the cluster.
- Select one server to work with; initialize and format your storage plus assign drive letters.
- Do not touch this storage on the other servers because you can easily cause corruption on the file system.
- A unique IP address to be used for the cluster.
- An account that has the capability to write a new computer object in Active Directory (AD) for the network name. (Or have the computer account pre-created and disabled with full permissions on the object granted to the user installing the cluster.)

Creating a New Cluster

To create a new cluster, follow the next steps:

1. Open Server Manager. Expand the Features section, and right-click Failover Cluster Manager. Select the Create a Cluster option. The Create a Cluster Wizard screen opens.

2. Click Next. The Access Point for Administering the Cluster screen opens. Type the cluster name and a unique IP Address. The name and IP Address provided will be used to administer the failover cluster or communicate with a service application in the cluster. Figure 29-5 shows the Access Point for Administering the Cluster screen.

3. Click Next. On the next screen confirm the settings you entered, and click next to start the cluster creation process.

4. When the cluster creation process completes, a summary screen displays with a completion success message. In this screen, you can review a report of the actions performed by clicking the View Report button.

5. Click Finish. To confirm that the cluster has been created, open Server Manager, expand the Features section, and expand the Failover Cluster Manager. The newly created cluster is listed under the Failover Cluster Manager.

This completes the Cluster Creation process. You can drill further down into the newly created cluster to show details such as nodes, networks, and storage, as shown in Figure 29-6.

29

FIGURE 29-5

Access Point for Administering the Cluster screen.

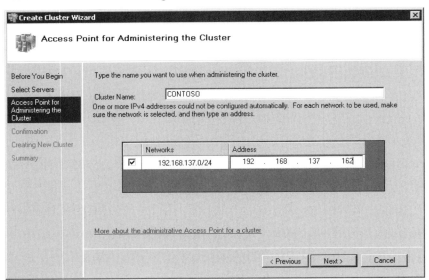

FIGURE 29-6

Newly created cluster details.

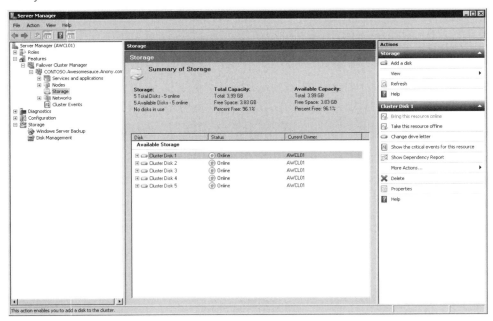

While you have the list of cluster disks opened, it is highly recommended to change the name property of each disk to more accurately reflect the usage and type of files to be placed on that disk. This can help a great deal later when installing SQL Server as well as for troubleshooting purposes.

Provide friendly names to every disk. The disk names should follow an intuitive naming convention for easy troubleshooting. Figure 29-7 shows the complete list of disks with friendly names.

FIGURE 29-7

Cluster disks with friendly names.

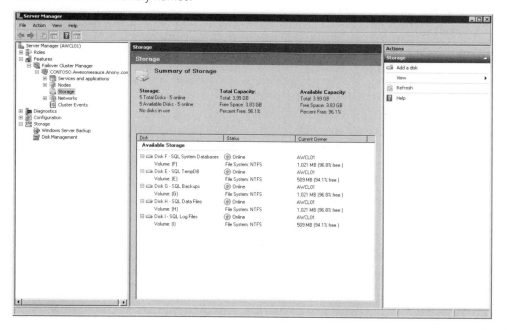

In addition, you should also provide friendly names to each network profile. For example, you can set the network profile names as Public and Private so that they are clearly identifiable. You should also change the private network so that clients are not allowed to communicate through it.

This completes the configuration of the Windows Server Clustering process. Now you are ready to install SQL Server 2012 as a clustered instance.

Installing SQL Server 2012 as a Clustered Instance

Prior to performing the install of SQL Server 2012, you need the following:

- Network name for the SQL Server instance
- Unique IP Address for the SQL Server instance
- Your Windows cluster configured and validated
- A service account for the SQL Server engine (and as a best practice a separate service account for SQL Server Agent)

With all of this in hand you are ready to start installing a SQL Server 2012 clustered instance. This begins with a single node. Once this first installation is complete you will have SQL Server up and running (and fully usable); however, you will not have failover capabilities until such time as you perform the installation on another node in the cluster.

To install SQL Server 2012 as a clustered instance, follow the next steps:

1. Open your SQL Server 2012 installation media, and run Setup.exe. The SQL Server 2012 Installation Center opens.

2. On the left side of the SQL Server Installation Center, click the Installation section; then click the New SQL Server failover cluster installation option on the right to launch the wizard to install a single-node SQL Server 2012 failover cluster.

3. On the next screen enter the SQL Server 2012 product key that was provided to you on your licensing package. Click next.

4. The license terms screen opens. Click Accept to continue the installation process.

5. The Setup Support Rules screen opens. The progress window displays the setup support rules that are checked. These setup support rules include checks to see if:

   - The server needs a restart.
   - The WMI Service is running.
   - There are no compatibility issues with the installed Windows version.

The required .NET versions are installed. You need to address any errors that show up before continuing. If no errors display, click OK.

6. The Install Setup Files screen opens. Click Install to initiate the SQL Server Setup files installation.

7. Click Next. The Setup Support Rules screen opens. A series of additional checks is performed to verify that there are no issues that might prevent a successful installation process. When these checks complete, you need to fix any errors before you continue.

You may see warnings regarding Microsoft Distributed Transaction Coordinator (MSDTC) not being installed or configured. You do have the option of not using MSDTC; however, if you want to use distributed transactions with SQL Server, you need MSDTC installed. There are two ways to configure MSDTC. Refer to `http://blogs.msdn.com/b /cindygross/archive/2009/02/22/how-to-configure-dtc-for-sql-server- in-a-windows-2008-cluster.aspx` for a complete reference on how to configure MSDTC for SQL Server in a Windows 2008/2008R2 cluster and the pros and cons of each method. It is recommended to have a clustered version of MSDTC with each SQL Server instance. This means you must install and configure it after the SQL Server installation completes. Figure 29-8 shows the Setup Support Rules screen with MSDTC warnings.

FIGURE 29-8

Setup Support Rules screen.

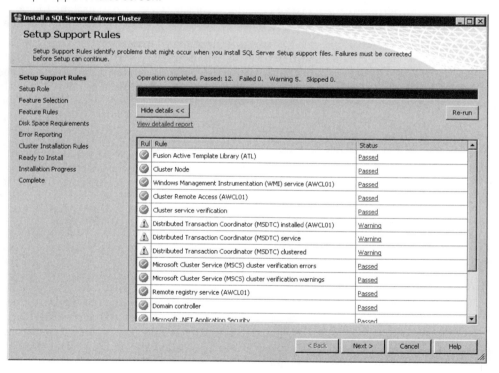

8. Click Next. The Feature Selection screen opens. In this screen you select the SQL Server 2012 features you want to install. Only the Database Engine Services and Analysis Services features support failover clustering. The other features are standalone and therefore run only on the current node. Select the features to install. The shared features install directory should not be on a clustered drive. Install the shared features to a drive that will not be included in the cluster.

9. Click Next. The Feature Rules screen opens. A third series of checks is performed to verify that there are no issues that might prevent a successful installation based on the features selected. These checks verify that the cluster setup is supported for the version of SQL Server 2012 that you want to install, that there are no previous versions of Visual Studio 2008 deployed on your server, and that Service Pack 1 for .NET Framework 3.5 is installed.

10. Click Next. The Instance Configuration screen opens. In this screen any SQL Server instances running on the current cluster node displays. In this step you need to provide the following information for the new install:

   - **SQL Server Network Name:** This is the name that your clients use to connect to the SQL Server instance. This needs to be unique in the network. If the user performing the install does not have the relevant permissions to create the computer object for the name in AD, then you need to have it created and have full control on the object granted to the cluster computer account.

   - **Default or Named instance:** To install a default instance, select the relevant radio button. You can have only a single default instance installed on your cluster, so if this option is grayed out, it is because a default instance has already been installed. To use a named instance, select the appropriate button, and type in the name that you want to use for your instance. For clients to connect to a named instance on the cluster they would need to use the NetworkName\ InstanceName. The instance name needs to be unique only to the cluster; it does need to be unique on your network.

   - **Instance ID:** The instance ID is used to identify the particular directories and Registry entries used for the SQL Server instance. By default this value is the same as the Named instance value.

   - **Instance root directory:** This is the directory used to install the SQL Server binary files. This defaults to C:\Program Files\Microsoft SQL Server but can be changed. This root directory must exist on local disk and cannot be configured on any shared cluster drive.

11. Click Next. The Cluster Resource Group screen opens. The setup wizard checks that you have sufficient disk space on the drives you selected for the install of the instance root and the shared features. If you have preconfigured your storage to a particular cluster group prior to starting the install, you can select that group on the Cluster Resource Group page. Otherwise leave the default group name to create a new cluster resource group.

12. Click Next. The Cluster Disk Selection screen opens. The Cluster Disk Selection screen provides you with the option to select which shared cluster disks you want to use for the new SQL Server 2012 instance. Select the disks that you want to use for this instance from the list of available shared disks. Figure 29-9 shows the Cluster Disk Selection screen.

13. Click Next. The Cluster Network Configuration screen opens. In this screen enter the unique IP Address that will be used by the new SQL Server 2012 Failover Cluster

instance. You do have the option to use DHCP; however, it is highly recommended specifying a reserved static IP Address.

FIGURE 29-9

Cluster Disk Selection screen.

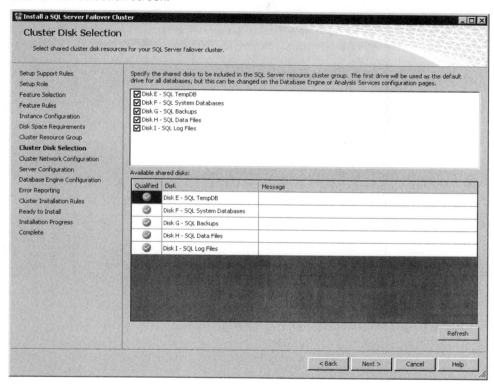

14. Click Next. The Server Configuration screen opens. The Server Configuration screen has two tabs: Service Accounts and Collation. On the Service Accounts tab enter the service account name and password for each of your services.

The Collation tab allows you to change the SQL Server and Analysis Services collation. For more information about Collation and Unicode support refer to `http://msdn` `.microsoft.com/en-us/library/ms143726.aspx`.

> **NOTE**
>
> As a best practice you should use different accounts for the SQL Server Database Engine and SQL Server Agent accounts to maintain the highest level of security. The startup type for the clustered services is always set to Manual by default. This setting cannot be changed by design because the Cluster decides which node owns the resources and therefore which instance should run the services.

15. Click Next. The Database Engine Configuration screen opens. The Database Engine Configuration screen has three tabs:

- **Server Configuration:** This is where you specify the initial authentication mode (Windows Authentication or Mixed Mode) and specify SQL Server administrators. As a security measure the BUILTIN\Administrators group is not added to the SQL Server sysadmin group by default, so you need to specify at least one domain account that can be used as a sysadmin. Pressing the Add Current User button adds the account of the person performing the install to the sysadmin group. If you choose Mixed Mode, you are required to enter a password that conforms to your organization's current Active Directory password policy.

- **Data Directories:** Here you can specify the default locations that you want to use for you data; user database and logs; and tempdb and backup directories. All of the location must be on shared cluster disk and would have had to be chosen as a part of the Cluster Disk Selection.

- **FILESTREAM:** This tab is used for enabling and performing configuration of FILESTREAM for T-SQL and I/O streaming access.

Figure 29-10 shows the Database Engine Configuration screen and the Data Directories tab options.

If you select Analysis Services to be installed, the Analysis Services Configuration page displays to set its Server Configuration and Data Directories as well.

16. Click Next. The Error Reporting screen opens. On the Error Reporting screen, select whether you want to automatically send error messages to Microsoft. This is optional.

17. Click Next. The Cluster Installation Rules screen opens. Cluster Installation Rules performs a final check to be sure that you are not running on a FAT32 file system and that there are no reboots pending that could prevent the install from completing successfully.

18. Click Next. The Ready to Install screen opens. The SQL Server 2012 Setup Wizard now has sufficient information to perform your install. The Ready to Install screen displays all features and configuration options that have been set. This screen also provides the path to the configuration file that will be used for the install.

19. Click Install. The Installation Progress screen opens and the installation process starts. During installation you can track progress on the installation progress bar. The install may take some time depending upon your configuration options.

FIGURE 29-10

Database Engine Configuration Screen.

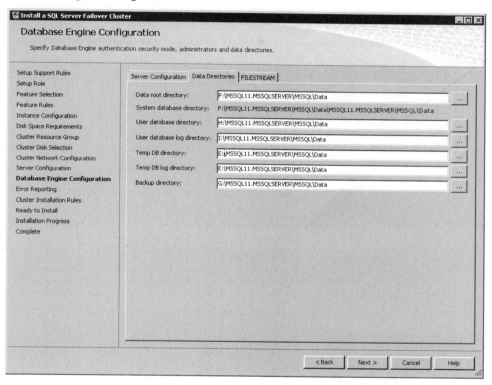

Upon successful completion of the install process, the Complete screen displays with a status for each component and a link to the installation summary log file.

With the installation now complete on this single node, SQL Server 2012 is now fully functional and can accept client connections. All the clustered resources for this instance have been created and can be seen within the Failover Cluster Manager console, as shown in Figure 29-11.

FIGURE 29-11

SQL Server clustered resources.

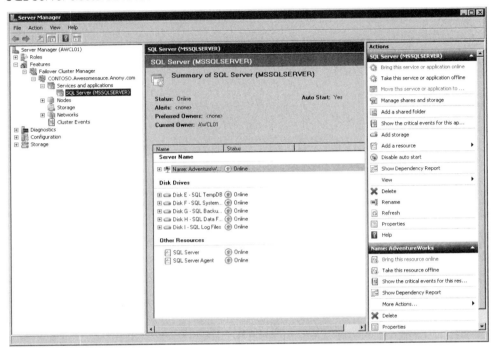

Configuring Microsoft Distributed Transaction Coordinator (MSDTC)

To configure MSDTC for this SQL Server 2012 instance as a clustered resource, follow the next steps:

1. Open Server Manager. Expand the Features section and right-click Failover Cluster Manager. Select the Add a Resource option. From the pop-up menu select the More Resources option; then select the Add Distributed Transaction Coordinator option. This adds a new MSDTC resource in an offline state. To configure and bring MSDTC online, open the resource properties window and add dependencies for:

   - **Name:** This is the network name of the install.

   - **AND Disk:** This needs to be one of your shared cluster disks. An MSDTC directory will be created on the root of this disk.

> **NOTE**
> MSDTC will not work if you attempt to use storage configured as a mount point.

Figure 29-12 shows the Dependencies tab that will be brought online before MSDTC comes online.

FIGURE 29-12

MSDTC Dependencies tab.

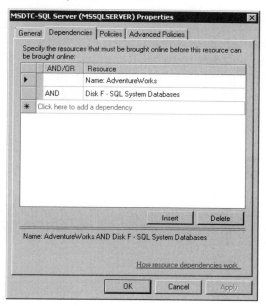

With the dependencies added you can bring the MSDTC service online. For this service to failover correctly when you add additional nodes, you must also map MSDTC to a service. This is done from the command line.

To map MSDTC as a service, follow the next steps:

1. Open an elevated command prompt, and run MSDTC with the following switches:

   - -tmMappingSet
   - -name: "<any unique name is fine here, recommend DTC_SQLNetworkName>"
   - -service: "<the actual service, for a default install this would be MSSQLSERVER; otherwise it would be MSSQL$INSTANCENAME>"
   - -ClusterResourceName: "<This is the name of the MSDTC resource in the cluster>"

   If the mapping is successful, another screen pops up stating Operation Succeeded. Figure 29-13 illustrates the command line syntax and the result screen.

29

> **NOTE**
>
> When you add the MSDTC resource, you add it to the same cluster group as SQL; it will be in the same group as the dependency disk.

FIGURE 29-13

MSDTC mapped as the service syntax and result.

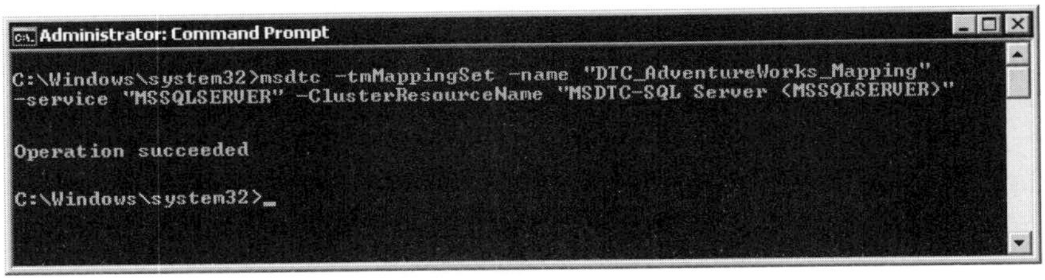

2. Close the command prompt windows. MSDTC is now mapped as a service.

To confirm that MSDTC was mapped correctly, open up another elevated command prompt, and type MSDTC -tmMappingView *. This provides you with a list of all the MSDTC mapped resources on the current server, as shown in Figure 29-14.

FIGURE 29-14

MSDTC mapping verification and result.

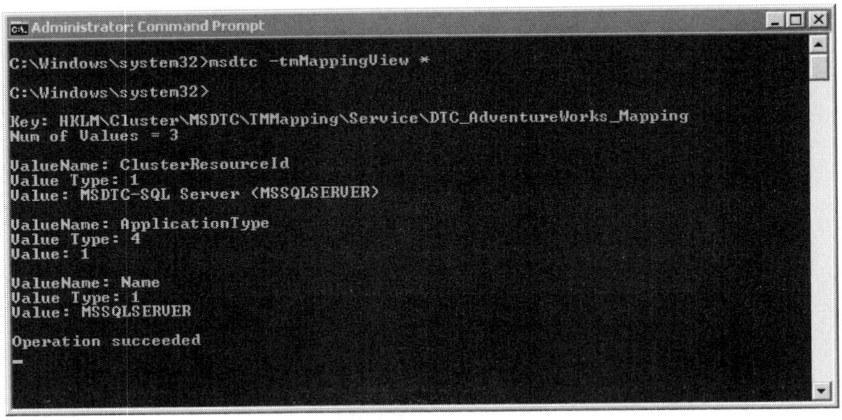

Adding a Node to an Existing SQL Server 2012 Failover Cluster

Because the whole point of clustering is to provide high availability, you now need to install SQL Server 2012 to another node in the cluster so that it can failover in the event of problems. You'll follow these steps for every additional node that you have in your cluster.

Before performing an install to add a new node to an existing SQL Server 2012 failover cluster, you need to ensure that the node is part of the Windows Cluster and that all the storage is viewable. You should also run a validation check to be sure that there are no errors that may impact availability.

Installing SQL Server 2012 on additional nodes requires a lot less user interaction because the vast majority of the information was provided when the original install took place.

To add a node to an existing SQL Server 2012 failover cluster, follow the next steps:

1. Open your SQL Server 2012 installation media and run Setup.exe. The SQL Server 2012 Installation Center screen opens.

2. Select Installation on the left side, and then click Add Node to a SQL Server Failover Cluster from the options on the right.

   The Cluster Node Configuration screen opens. On this screen all currently installed SQL Server 2012 instances on the cluster along with the possible owning nodes are listed.

3. From the drop-down select the instance that you want to add this node for.

4. Click Next. The Cluster Network Configuration screen opens. On this screen the existing network settings for the instance that you work with are listed. You cannot make changes on this screen.

5. Click Next. The Service Accounts screen opens. As a security measure on the Service Accounts screen, you are required to re-enter the passwords for the SQL Server Database Engine and SQL Server Agent accounts that the services are currently running under

6. Click Next. The Add Node Rules screen opens. The Setup Wizard performs a series of checks to confirm that you are not trying to exceed the maximum number of nodes permitted for the SQL Server 2012 edition, and that the node you are trying to add is ready for the install.

7. Click Next. The Ready to Add Node screen opens. This final screen shows a summary of the install actions to be performed and displays the path to the configuration file that will be used to add the node.

> **NOTE**
> The configuration file that is generated can be copied to another node to quickly add that node as an owner for this SQL Server 2012 instance using an elevated command prompt and running the following command:
> `setup.exe / ConfigurationFile=Myconfigurationfile.ini`

29

8. Click Install. The Installation Wizard installs and adds the new node. When the install is complete, you are presented with a final screen that shows the success status of each component as well as a link to the summary log file.

Testing Failover

After you have SQL Server 2012 installed on multiple nodes, you should take some time to perform some failover testing scenarios.

To do a manual failover test of SQL Server 2012, follow the next steps:

1. Open Server Manager. Expand the Features section, and right-click Failover Cluster Manager. Right-click the SQL Server instance in the tree view. Select the Move This Service or Application to Another Node option, and select the node that you want to move to. Figure 29-15 shows the manual failover options.

FIGURE 29-15

Manual failover options.

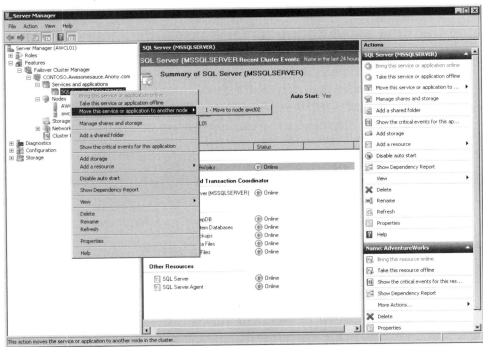

A confirmation window pop-up requesting you to confirm that you want to move SQL Server to another node is shown in Figure 29-16.

FIGURE 29-16

Confirm action pop-up window.

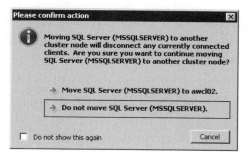

2. Click the Move SQL Server option to complete the manual failover. The following resources will be taken offline in the following order:

- MSDTC
- SQL Server Agent
- SQL Server
- Shared Disk & Network Name
- IP Address

The following resources will then be moved over to the node you selected and brought back online in the following order:

- IP Address & Shared Disk
- Network Name
- MSDTC
- SQL Server
- SQL Server Agent

The length of time that it takes for the failover process to complete and for SQL Server to be fully available on the other node depends on the time it takes the resources to go offline, move them, bring them back online again, and for SQL Server 2012 to perform database recovery.

After you perform manual failover testing, it is recommended to test automatic failover to ensure that you get the expected behavior. This can be accomplished by forcing failures such as:

- Pulling out network cables
- Powering down servers
- Unplugging cables to your storage

These things can be done to simulate real-world problems and should be performed prior to your clusters going online in production.

29

Summary

In this chapter, you learned that High Availability of a SQL Server 2012 instance is achieved through Clustering. Although achieving 100% uptime is virtually impossible, Clustering allows you to maintain a consistent service level guarantee close to 100% uptime, sometimes expressed as "five 9s" or 99.999%.

Clustering works by constantly checking for responsiveness of clustered nodes, drives, IP addresses, network names and other objects. If no response is detected within the default or configured thresholds, failover of SQL Server instance to another clustered node initiates.

To install SQL Server 2012 as a Clustered instance you first configure Windows Server for Clustering by setting up network configurations for public and private communications, adding necessary server roles and services to support the Failover Clustering feature. A Windows Cluster is created using the Failover Cluster Manager and following the Cluster Wizard.

After Windows Server is configured for Clustering, you install SQL Server 2012 as a Clustered instance from the SQL Server 2012 Installation Center option Add Node to a SQL Server Failover Cluster.

Configuring and Managing SQL Server with PowerShell

P owerShell is the new scripting environment for the Microsoft Windows platform. For administrators who don't have access to the Visual Studio environment, or for the IT professional who prefers scripting to compiled code, PowerShell provides access to the .NET Framework and the objects available within it. PowerShell is part of the operating system for Windows Server 2008, Windows Server 2008 R2, and Windows Server 2012. It's also available as a free download from Microsoft at www.microsoft.com/powershell/. SQL Server 2012 comes with a Provider and 40 cmdlets automatically installed when SQL Server Management Studio 2012 is installed. PowerShell is included with the Windows Server 2008 and later operating systems but must be installed on Windows 2003, Windows XP (SP2 or later), and Windows Vista. It cannot run on operating systems earlier than those mentioned here.

PowerShell was introduced in late 2006 to enable administrators to develop scripts for automating processes they did regularly. Prior to the introduction of PowerShell, most administrators used command-line batch files, VBScript, or some third-party proprietary application designed for this function.

Batch files had somewhat limited functionality and significant security problems. It was easy using batch files to "hijack" actual operating system commands by creating a batch file with the same name and placing it in a directory in the PATH environment variable or in the current directory. Batch files also suffer significant limitations for iterative processes.

PowerShell addresses these limitations through a strong security foundation that prevents command-line hijacking by allowing only the user (by default) to run digitally signed scripts, and by forcing the user to specify the directory for each command run from the script environment. It also supports the .NET Framework (2.0 and later), so the functionality built in the framework is available in this scripting environment.

Why Use PowerShell?

In today's business world it's important to get as much done in as little time as possible. The most successful people find ways to automate every repetitive task for which they're responsible. Consistency is important when automating tasks so that every administrator on the team is equally capable of stepping in to help other team members when necessary.

Microsoft has designated PowerShell as part of its *common engineering criteria (CEC)* for all server products. This means that an administrator who's responsible for Exchange or Active Directory probably has spent time learning PowerShell, and scripts written to manage SQL Server using PowerShell can be understood by administrators without specific SQL Server knowledge. Companies can run more efficiently with this common scripting language, and administrators with skills in PowerShell are more valuable to their companies.

What's New with PowerShell in SQL Server 2012

SQL Server 2012 brings not only improvements for SQL Server; it also brings an upgraded experience inside PowerShell 2.0. You no longer have to deal with multiple snap-ins to load all of the functionality for working with the relational database engine.

- Single Module for SQL Server
- A new Module for SSAS
- Ability to browse SSIS & Extended Events

Basic PowerShell

PowerShell, like any language, consists of commands, variables, functions, flow control methods, and other features necessary to enable work to be done. Because it is an interpreted language, the scripts don't have to be compiled into an executable form to be run.

Language Features

A *cmdlet* (pronounced "command-let") is a command-line utility built into PowerShell to provide some functionality. These cmdlets use a verb-noun naming convention, so it's easy to understand what they're doing. Microsoft has provided approximately 236 built-in cmdlets with the default installation of PowerShell (2.0), and additional cmdlets are installed depending on various server products that may be running. PowerShell 3.0 will be available in late 2012, but because it wasn't ready for release when SQL Server 2012 was shipped, the focus of this chapter is on PowerShell 2.0. (Version 3.0 expands the PowerShell language and introduces a more powerful integrated scripting environment, similar to Visual Studio.) All future development should take place inside the PowerShell 3.0 ISE if you have access to it. Its many built-in features are far superior to the simple console window.

Cmdlets are frequently aliased. In other words, a different command can be entered to run the cmdlet, rather than using its own name. For example, when browsing a directory, the PowerShell cmdlet to view the contents of the current directory is Get-ChildItem. Users of the DOS operating system (or cmd.exe on current windows systems) are familiar with the dir command, and UNIX users are familiar with the ls command. These three commands do the same thing, and both dir and ls are included with PowerShell as aliases of the Get-ChildItem cmdlet.

A feature of UNIX shell scripting environments is the capability to "pipe" the results of one command into another command's input buffer. This is a feature of shell scripting that makes it powerful — the ability to string multiple commands together to provide information quickly. PowerShell provides this ability, but differs from UNIX shell scripting in that the UNIX pipe sends text from one command to another, whereas PowerShell pipes objects from one cmdlet to another. UNIX scripts must parse the text from one command using commands such as grep, awk, and sed to format the text in a form that the next command expects. PowerShell's objects are understood by the receiving cmdlet, and no such parsing is required.

You can start the PowerShell environment in a number of different ways:

- Select the Start button ⇨ type **PowerShell**, and then select the Windows PowerShell ISE.

- From the cmd.exe command line, the powershell_ise command launches the ISE environment as well.

- There's also the old SQL Server wrapper called sqlps.exe, which should basically be avoided.

The examples here are based on the standard powershell_ise.exe environment. Normally, in the PowerShell environment, the user is informed of this by the prompt PS> at the beginning of the line where the next command is to be entered.

Here's an example using a series of cmdlets, piping the results of one to the next, and then filtering the results to get useful information. In this set of commands, the get-process command is used to return a set of all processes on the system, pipe the results into a sort on the size of the workingset (or the amount of memory each process is using), in descending order. Then select only the first 10, returning the biggest memory hogs on the system:

```
get-process | sort-object workingset -descending |
select-object -first 10
```

PowerShell is not case-sensitive. In addition, the alias sort could have been used instead of the proper name of sort-object, and select could have been used instead of select-object. This set of commands produces results like this:

Handles	NPM(K)	PM(K)	WS(K)	VM(M)	CPU(s)	Id	ProcessName
637	82	163668	157312	1228	232.92	2132	sqlservr
535	80	120208	117256	1225	261.53	1344	sqlservr

```
562      18    99972   77364    357   457.14   3580 Ssms
598      11    52048   50352    179    57.86   4012 powershell
308      73    61612   45740   1155   156.54    728 sqlservr
602      17    57452   37956    255   298.60   1400 Reporting
                                                   ServicesService
494      10    26636   33144    155     5.93   3308 SQLPS
713      46    36704   27984    210   241.31   1264 msmdsrv
1011     42    12872   19556     80   144.29    808 svchost
158       4    12248   13272    104     2.22   1204 MsDtsSrvr
```

PowerShell variables are declared by preceding the variable name with the dollar sign ($) character. Variables are actually objects of a particular type, and that data type can be created by preceding the variable name with the data type in brackets ([]). For example, a variable called $counter that's an integer object can be created and set to a value of 7 as follows:

```
PS> $counter = 7
```

However, a string object variable with the value of '7' can be created as follows:

```
PS> [string] $counter = '7'
```

Variables can also contain objects or collections. Collections are just a group of objects, such as an array. It's easy to create a collection just by assigning a list of values to a variable, like this:

```
PS> $stuff = 1,2,4,6,8
```

The list of numbers is grouped into a collection of integer objects and placed in the variable $stuff. Individual elements within the collection can be accessed by using their ordinal number:

```
PS> $stuff[2]
4
PS>
```

Addressing individual elements of an array is nice, but the power of collections is realized by iterating through the members of the collection. PowerShell offers two versions of foreach logic; the first is a cmdlet to which a collection is piped, like this:

```
PS> $stuff | foreach-object {write-output $_}
1
2
4
6
8
```

The variable $_ is defined as the current object in the set of objects the cmdlet is iterating through. The other version is the foreach language element, which enables naming of the member:

```
PS> foreach ($thing in $stuff) {write-output $thing}
1
```

```
2
4
6
8
```

Now, within the script block operating on the members of the collection, conditions can be checked. For example, if the script should operate only on elements with a value not greater than 4, the script would read as follows:

```
PS> $stuff | foreach-object { if ($_ -gt 4) {break}
else {write-output $_}}
1
2
4
```

The following list shows most of the comparison operators within PowerShell.

- **-lt**: Less than
- **-le**: Less than or equal to
- **-gt**: Greater than
- **-ge**: Greater than or equal to
- **-eq**: Equal to
- **-ne**: Not equal to
- **-like**: Like wildcard pattern matching

Suppose you have a text file called servers.txt that contains a list of servers, one server name per line. The file might resemble something like this:

```
SQLTWSS
SQLTBXP
SQLTBW7
SQLPROD1
SQLPROD2
```

By using the Get-Content cmdlet, this list of servers can easily be brought into a PowerShell variable as a collection by issuing the following command:

```
$servers = Get-Content 'servers.txt'
```

Each element in the collection can be addressed by its ordinal number, so the first item is referenced by $servers[0], the second item by $servers[1], and so on. This ability to create collections can come in handy later in this discussion.

Comments, always good in any language, are specified in PowerShell 1.0 by using the pound (#) character, with the comments following that character on the line. (PowerShell 2.0 can support an additional comment operator, enabling multiline comments, for example, <# Multi-Line Comment #>.)

30

Referencing the $servers collection, each element in the collection is a string object, and string objects have a Length property, so the element can be tested to determine whether it has a value using the following commands:

```
if ($servers[0].Length -gt 0) {
   #work
   }
```

Control flow is handled by the commands shown in Table 30-1.

TABLE 30-1   Control Flow Commands

Command	Example

If	if ($val -eq "target") {
	
	#work
	
	}

For	For ($i=0; $i -lt 10; $i++) {
	
	#work
	
	}

Switch	Switch ($val) {
	
	"Val1" {
	
	#work
	
	}
	
	"Val2" {
	
	#work
	
	}
	
	}

Do Until	Do {
	
	#work
	
	}
	Until ($val -eq "target")

Do While	Do {
	
	#work
	
	}
	While ($val -eq "target")

While	While ($val -eq "target") {
	
	#work
	
	}

To help with logic flow, PowerShell provides a group of "object" cmdlets, as shown in Table 30-2.

TABLE 30-2 Object Cmdlets in PowerShell

Cmdlet	Alias	Description
ForEach-Object	%	Executes once for each member in the collection
Where-Object	?	Filters objects based on conditions
Select-Object	select	Pipes only the specified properties
Sort-Object	sort	Sorts the objects
Tee-Object	tee	Sends the objects in two directions

In the earlier example of the $servers collection, the collection can be iterated through using the following commands:

```
$servers | Foreach-Object {
    Write-Output $_
    }
```

These cmdlets are useful when scripting. For example, they enable iteration through a collection of properties in objects, as shown here:

```
get-service | where-object {$_.Status -eq "Running"}
```

The preceding produced the following results:

```
Status    Name                 DisplayName
------    ----                 -----------
Running   1-vmsrvc             Virtual Machine Additions Services ...
Running   AeLookupSvc          Application Experience Lookup Service
Running   Browser              Computer Browser
Running   CryptSvc             Cryptographic Services
Running   DcomLaunch           DCOM Server Process Launcher
Running   Dhcp                 DHCP Client
Running   dmserver             Logical Disk Manager
Running   Dnscache             DNS Client
Running   ERSvc                Error Reporting Service
Running   Eventlog             Event Log
Running   EventSystem          COM+ Event System
Running   helpsvc              Help and Support
Running   HTTPFilter           HTTP SSL
Running   lanmanserver         Server
Running   lanmanworkstation    Workstation
Running   LmHosts              TCP/IP NetBIOS Helper
Running   MSDTC                Distributed Transaction Coordinator
Running   MsDtsServer100       SQL Server Integration Services 10.0
Running   MSOLAP$INST01        SQL Server Analysis Services (INST01)
```

30

```
Running   MSSQL$INST01        SQL Server (INST01)
Running   MSSQL$INST02        SQL Server (INST02)
```

In this example, PowerShell sifts through the current services on the system and returns only those services currently running. The braces ({}) delimit the operation of the `where-object` cmdlet. These braces allow embedded operations within loop-type structures; and together with the script content between them, are referred to as a *script block*.

> **NOTE**
>
> Most important, help is always available using the `Get-Help` cmdlet. It can also be called using the `help` or `man` aliases. Either way, help can be obtained for any cmdlet; it returns the syntax, description, and related links. `Get-Help` has options to return normal, full, detailed, or examples.

To get help on any cmdlet, type **Get-Help** followed by the cmdlet. To get help on `Get-Help`, type the following:

```
PS> Get-Help Get-Help
NAME
    Get-Help

SYNOPSIS
    Displays information about Windows PowerShell cmdlets and concepts.


SYNTAX
    Get-Help [[-name] <string>] [-component <string[]>]
[-functionality <string[]>] [-role <string[]>] [-category <stri
    ng[]>] [-full] [<CommonParameters>]

    Get-Help [[-name] <string>] [-component <string[]>]
[-functionality <string[]>] [-role <string[]>] [-category <stri
    ng[]>] [-detailed] [<CommonParameters>]

    Get-Help [[-name] <string>] [-component <string[]>]
[-functionality <string[]>] [-role <string[]>] [-category <stri
    ng[]>] [-examples] [<CommonParameters>]

    Get-Help [[-name] <string>] [-component <string[]>]
[-functionality <string[]>] [-role <string[]>] [-category <stri
    ng[]>] [-parameter <string>] [<CommonParameters>]


DETAILED DESCRIPTION
    The Get-Help cmdlet displays information about Windows PowerShell
cmdlets and concepts. You can also use "Help {<cm
    dlet name> | <topic-name>" or "<cmdlet-name> /?".
"Help" displays the help topics one page at a time. The "/?" disp
```

```
lays help for cmdlets on a single page.


RELATED LINKS
    Get-Command
    Get-PSDrive
    Get-Member

REMARKS
    For more information, type: "get-help Get-Help -detailed".
    For technical information, type: "get-help Get-Help -full".
```

Creating Scripts

Although it's sometimes useful to enter ad hoc commands into PowerShell to evaluate system state or other information, the real power of PowerShell comes with writing scripts. A good collection of scripts to perform normal administrative functions is a sign of an effective administrator.

For example, it's a good idea to have information about the physical servers on which SQL Server runs. Windows Management Instrumentation (WMI) provides this information through simple queries, available to PowerShell through the Get-WMIObject cmdlet (aliased as gwmi). A simple script to gather this information is shown in Listing 30-1. In this script, four different WMI classes are polled, and their results are piped into the select-object cmdlet (aliased as select), where the specific properties needed are retrieved. Those results are then piped into the format-list cmdlet for presentation.

LISTING 30-1   Get System Info

```
#getsysinfo.ps1
# Use WMI queries to retrieve information about the computer, operating
# system and disk devices

gwmi -query "select * from Win32_ComputerSystem" | select Name, Model,
    Manufacturer, Description, DNSHostName, Domain, DomainRole,
    PartOfDomain, NumberOfProcessors, SystemType, TotalPhysicalMemory,
    UserName, Workgroup | format-list

gwmi -query "select * from Win32_OperatingSystem" | select Name,
    Version, FreePhysicalMemory, OSLanguage, OSProductSuite, OSType,
    ServicePackMajorVersion, ServicePackMinorVersion | format-list

gwmi -query "select * from Win32_PhysicalMemory" | select Name,
    Capacity, DeviceLocator, Tag | format-table -Autosize

gwmi -query "select * from Win32_LogicalDisk where
    DriveType=3" | select Name, FreeSpace, Size | format-table -Autosize
```

30

When this script is run on a server, it returns results such as this:

```
Name                     : POSHSQL
Model                    : 43192PU
Manufacturer             : LENOVO
Description              : AT/AT COMPATIBLE
DNSHostName              : POSHSQL
Domain                   : WORKGROUP
DomainRole               : 0
PartOfDomain             : False
NumberOfProcessors       : 1
SystemType               : x64-based PC
TotalPhysicalMemory      : 17108058112
UserName                 : POSHSQL\Aaron.Nelson
Workgroup                : WORKGROUP

Name                         : Microsoft Windows 7 Ultimate
|C:\Windows|\Device\Harddisk0\Partition2
Version                  : 6.1.7601
FreePhysicalMemory       : 11955708
OSLanguage               : 1033
OSProductSuite           : 256
OSType                   : 18
ServicePackMajorVersion  : 1
ServicePackMinorVersion  : 0

Name               Capacity DeviceLocator Tag
----               -------- ------------- ---
Physical Memory  4294967296 DIMM 1        Physical Memory 0
Physical Memory  4294967296 DIMM 2        Physical Memory 1
Physical Memory  4294967296 DIMM 3        Physical Memory 2
Physical Memory  4294967296 DIMM 4        Physical Memory

Name   FreeSpace          Size
----   ---------          ----
C:     11414634496 119926681600
E:     49521369088 240054693888
```

Anytime a set of commands is used repeatedly, it's useful to encapsulate those commands in a function. Functions must be defined before they can be used because PowerShell is an interpretive language and doesn't "read ahead" to see what functions might be defined later.

Best Practice

Avoid scripting. This means you should write your chunks of code into modular, repeatable code and place that inside of functions. After you create a number of custom functions, place those functions into a PowerShell Module; then import the whole Module when you need it. For more information on not scripting, see http://blogs.technet.com/b/heyscriptingguy/archive/2011/06/26/dont-write-scripts-write-powershell-functions.aspx

The basic format of a function is as follows:

```
Function MyFunction {
    #work
    }
```

This, of course, doesn't do anything. Between the braces the real work needs to be coded, but most often functions need parameters. You can add functions in a number of ways, but two ways are most commonly used. The first, most obvious, format is like this:

```
Function MyFunction ($param) {
    #work
    }
```

This works fine, but the recommended method is to use a `param` block within the function, which enables the specification of multiple parameters, the specification of the data type for each parameter, and default values for each parameter:

```
Function MyFunction {
    param (
            [int]$x = 7,
            [int]$y = 9
            )
    #work
    }
```

The GetSysInfo.ps1 script (refer to Listing 30-1) is useful when run on an individual server but would be even more so if it could be run against all servers in the data center. By putting the working code from GetSysInfo.ps1 into a function (and adding the −computername parameter to each Get-WMIObject command within the function to specify which server to run the command against), it's possible to iterate through the set of servers in the $servers collection discussed earlier.

Listing 30-2 shows exactly how to do this. The function with the calls to the four WMI classes is defined first, followed by the main part of the script. Note that before attempting to get the server information, the main part of the script uses the WMI class Win32_PingStatus to determine whether the computer is reachable through the network. This saves time because the script doesn't attempt to run the four main queries against a server that doesn't respond.

LISTING 30-2   ServerStatus.ps1

```
function getwmiinfo ($svr) {
    gwmi -query "select * from
        Win32_ComputerSystem" -computername $svr | select Name,
        Model, Manufacturer, Description, DNSHostName,
        Domain, DomainRole, PartOfDomain, NumberOfProcessors,
        SystemType, TotalPhysicalMemory, UserName,
```

Continues

LISTING 30-2 *(continued)*

```
            Workgroup | format-list

        gwmi -query "select * from
            Win32_OperatingSystem" -computername $svr | select Name,
            Version, FreePhysicalMemory, OSLanguage, OSProductSuite,
            OSType, ServicePackMajorVersion,
            ServicePackMinorVersion | format-list

        gwmi -query "select * from
            Win32_PhysicalMemory" -computername $svr | select Name,
            Capacity, DeviceLocator, Tag | format-table -Autosize

        gwmi -query "select * from Win32_LogicalDisk
            where DriveType=3" -computername $svr | select Name, FreeSpace,
            Size | format-table -Autosize
    }

$servers = get-content 'servers.txt'

foreach ($server in $servers) {
    $results = gwmi -query "select StatusCode from Win32_PingStatus
        where Address = '$server'"
    $responds = $false
    foreach ($result in $results) {
        if ($result.statuscode -eq 0) {
            $responds = $true
            break
        }
    }

    if ($responds) {
        getwmiinfo $server
    } else {
        Write-Output "$server does not respond"
    }
}
```

The results of this script look like this:

```
Name           : POSHSQL
Model          : 43192PU
Manufacturer   : LENOVO
Description    : AT/AT COMPATIBLE
DNSHostName    : POSHSQL
```

```
Domain               : WORKGROUP
DomainRole           : 0
PartOfDomain         : False
NumberOfProcessors   : 1
SystemType           : x64-based PC
TotalPhysicalMemory  : 17108058112
UserName             : POSHSQL\Aaron.Nelson
Workgroup            : WORKGROUP


Name                        : Microsoft Windows 7 Ultimate
|C:\Windows|\Device\Harddisk0\Partition2
Version                     : 6.1.7601
FreePhysicalMemory          : 11955708
OSLanguage                  : 1033
OSProductSuite              : 256
OSType                      : 18
ServicePackMajorVersion     : 1
ServicePackMinorVersion     : 0


Name               Capacity DeviceLocator Tag
----               -------- ------------- ---
Physical Memory 4294967296 DIMM 1         Physical Memory 0
Physical Memory 4294967296 DIMM 2         Physical Memory 1
Physical Memory 4294967296 DIMM 3         Physical Memory 2
Physical Memory 4294967296 DIMM 4         Physical Memory 3


Name   FreeSpace          Size
----   ---------          ----
C:     11414634496 119926681600
E:     49521369088 240054693888


SQLTBXP does not respond
SQLTBW7 does not respond
SQLPROD1 does not respond
SQLPROD2 does not respond
```

SQL Server PowerShell Extensions

There are several different approaches to working with SQL Server from PowerShell; among them are WMI, the Provider; cmdlets, SMO, and ADO.NET. The SQL Server Provider and its resulting PSDrive provide some easy ways to get to information inside of your SQL Server instance. The SQL Server cmdlets that come with SSMS 2012 enable you to do some basic tasks such as running queries and backing up databases. On the other end of the spectrum (for the vast majority of DBAs) is the need to learn and leverage the SMO.

The easiest way to get comprehensive abilities to work with SQL Server from PowerShell is to download the SQL Server PowerShell Extensions project from CodePlex (http:// sqlpsx.codeplex.com). As of this writing SQLPSX comes with 163 advanced functions, 2 cmdlets, and 7 scripts. The download includes an installer to streamline the process. If you want to (or need to for security reasons) you can download just the source code, which is simply a bunch of text files.

Importing Modules

Starting with PowerShell 2.0 you can extend the native capabilities of PowerShell by importing modules. With SSMS 2012 the PowerShell functionality of SQL Server is finally available in module form. When working with the relational engine and its various components, you use the command IMPORT-MODULE SQLPS. When working with SSAS you use IMPORT-MODULE SQLASCMDLETS.

You need to import only a module once per PowerShell session; however, if you do accidentally import a module a second time, it won't throw an error like Snapins did. To see a list of all modules available on your machine, run Get-Module -ListAvailable.

The SQL PSDrive — SQLSERVER

The SQLSERVER PSDrive provides a wonderful way to programmatically access information from your SQL Server instances. The great thing is that you are already familiar with much of the hierarchy within the SQLSERVER PSDrive because it uses the same SMO tree that you use in Object Explorer in SSMS.

Native PowerShell provides the ability to navigate not only the disk file system, but also the system Registry as though it were a file system. The SQL Server provider adds a new PowerShell drive, also referred to as a PSDrive, called SQLSERVER:. Use of the Set-Location cmdlet (usually aliased as cd) can be used to change to the SQLSERVER: drive, and then SQL Server can be navigated like the file system. However, due to severe performance limitations, this approach should be avoided if possible. Instead keep your directory set to something basic such as C:\temp and run commands specifying the path of the database object in question.

There are nine main directories under SQLSERVER: DAC, DataCollection, SQL, SQLAS, SQLPolicy, SQLRegistration, SSIS, Utility, andXEvent:

- The SQL folder provides access to the database engine, SQL Server Agent, Service Broker, and Database Mail, all using the various SMO DLLs.

- The SQLRegistration folder enables access to the Registered Servers and Central Management Server.

- The SSIS folder enables you to see the SSIS PackageStore. This feature works only with SSIS 2012.

- SQLAS enables you to traverse any SSAS instances you may want to connect to.

- XEvent enables you to see your Extended Events.

- The SQLPolicy folder provides access to policy-based management using the DMF and Facets DLLs.

- The DataCollection folder enables access to the Data Collector objects provided with the Management Data Warehouse feature of SQL Server 2008 and above.

- Utility enables you to connect to Utility Control Point.

- DAC. The authors have nothing good to say about this product.

You can browse the SQLSERVER file system just like a disk file system. Issuing the command `cd SQL` (or `Set-Location SQL`) and running the `Get-ChildItem` cmdlet returns the local server and any other servers that may have been recently accessed from the PowerShell session. Changing to the local server and running `Get-ChildItem` returns the names of the SQL Server instances installed on that server. Changing to one of the instances and running `Get-ChildItem` returns the collections of objects available to that server, such as BackupDevices, Databases, Logins, and so on. Changing to the Databases collection and running `Get-ChildItem` returns the list of user databases, along with some of the database properties. The results look something like Figure 30-1.

FIGURE 30-1

Navigating the SQL Server file system.

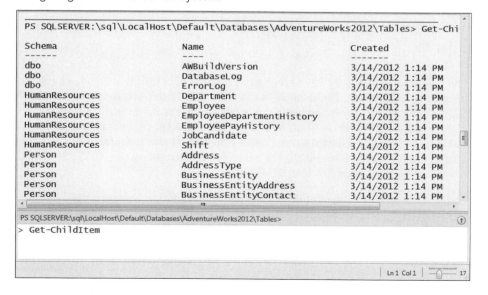

SQL Cmdlets

The SQL Server PowerShell module also provides 24 new (in addition to the previous 5) cmdlets specific for use with SQL Server. Although this is obviously more than SQL Server 2008 offered, the majority of administrative functions are managed using SMO, and data access is managed using ADO.NET, as mentioned before, which is why the SQLPSX CodePlex project is so vital to everyday DBA tasks.

To see a list of all cmdlets the SQL Server 2012 provides, first import the SQLPS module and then run `Get-Command -Module SQLPS`.

The most useful cmdlet, `Invoke-Sqlcmd`, takes query text and sends it to SQL Server for processing. Rather than set up the structures in ADO.NET to execute queries, the `Invoke-Sqlcmd` cmdlet returns results from a query passed in as a parameter or from a text file, which provides an easy way to get data out of SQL Server. It can perform either a standard Transact-SQL query or an XQuery statement, which provides additional flexibility.

Two new cmdlets introduced with SQL Server 2012 are `Backup-SqlDatabase` and `Restore-SqlDatabase`. These are a great alternative to the arduous task to back up a database when you must use the SMO directly. They also have the capability to produce a T-SQL script instead of actually backing up the databases. In general, these cmdlets are only useful when combined as a single step in a larger process that originates from PowerShell. (The authors don't use PowerShell for nightly backups.)

The `Invoke-PolicyEvaluation` cmdlet uses the Policy-based Management feature of SQL Server. It evaluates a set of objects against a policy defined for one or more servers to determine whether the objects comply with the conditions defined in the policy. It can also be used to reset object settings to comply with the policy, if that is needed. Lara Rubbelke has a set of blog posts on using this cmdlet at `http://sqlblog.com/blogs/lara_rubbelke/archive/2008/06/19/evaluating-policies-on-demand-through-powershell.aspx`.

The character set used by SQL Server has a number of conflicts with the character set allowed by PowerShell. For example, a standard SQL Server instance name is SQLTWSS\INST01. The backslash embedded in the name can cause PowerShell to infer a file system directory and subdirectory because it uses that character to separate the elements of the file system. The `Encode-SqlName` cmdlet converts strings acceptable to SQL Server into strings acceptable by PowerShell. For example, the instance name SQLTWSS\INST01 would be converted by this cmdlet into SQLTWSS%5CINST01.

The `Decode-SqlName` cmdlet does the exact opposite of `Encode-SqlName`: It converts the PowerShell-acceptable string of SQLTWSS%5CINST01 back to SQLTWSS\INST01.

Because SMO uses Uniform Resource Names (URN) for its objects, a cmdlet is provided to convert those URN values to path names, which can be used in a `Set-Location` cmdlet — for

example, to navigate through the SQL Server objects. The URN for the `HumanResources`
`.Employee` table in `AdventureWorks2012` on SQLTWSS\INST01 is as follows:

```
Server[@Name='SQLTWSS\INST01']\Database[@Name='AdventureWorks2012']\
Table[@Name='Employee' and @Schema='HumanResources']
```

Converting that to a path using `Convert-UrnToPath` would yield the following:

```
SQLSERVER:\SQL\SQLTWSS\INST01\Databases\AdventureWorks2012\
Tables\HumanResources.Employee
```

Don't Use SQLPS.exe

SQL Server 2008 incorporated PowerShell into its management toolset. Microsoft created a special version of PowerShell (1.0) called `sqlps.exe` that includes the provider and preloads all the DLLs that the provider requires, including the DLLs for SMO. Another difference between standard PowerShell and `sqlps.exe` is that the execution policy of PowerShell in `sqlps.exe` is set to RemoteSigned. This means that as soon as SQL Server 2008 is installed, `sqlps.exe` is ready to run scripts (on the local system, at least). Unfortunately, this closed shell approach has already been deprecated and is continuing to be provided only for backward compatibility.

Communicating with SQL Server via SMO

The two main reasons for communicating with SQL Server are to manage the server and to use the data contained on the server in some way. Not only are administrators expected to manage the server efficiently, but they're also frequently asked to extract some corporate data to send to another application, to make quick updates to correct a problem, or to respond to other such requests. SQL Server management can be done from PowerShell or any other .NET language using the Server Management Objects library, and the data can be accessed using ADO.NET.

SQL Server Management Objects

SQL Server Management Objects (SMO) and its related sisters (RMO for Replication Management Objects and AMO for Analysis Services Management Objects) are object libraries that provide a programmatic way to manage Microsoft SQL Server. SMO can be used to manage SQL Server 2005, 2008, 2008 R2, and 2012. It was introduced with SQL Server 2005 but supports the management of SQL Server 2000 instances as well. SMO was built using the .NET Framework, so the objects it exposes are available in PowerShell.

30

You work with the SMO every time that you navigate Object Explorer in SSMS, so you're already somewhat familiar with its use, some of its capabilities, and its hierarchy. In addition to Object Explorer, the Object Explorer Details view (press F7) inside of SSMS is great for getting more familiar with SQL Server objects and their properties.

Before using SMO within PowerShell, the SMO assembly must be loaded into the environment. If PowerShell is started from within SQL Server Management Studio or from SQL Server Agent, the `sqlps.exe` program is run, not full blown PowerShell. When running the native PowerShell environment interactively, the following commands are required:

```
[System.Reflection.Assembly]::LoadWithPartialName('Microsoft
.SqlServer.SMO')  | out-null
[System.Reflection.Assembly]::LoadWithPartialName('Microsoft
.SqlServer.SMOExtended')  | out-null
```

If SMO objects are going to be loaded on a regular basis, these commands can be loaded into a profile file. User profiles are generally loaded into `$PSHome\ Documents\ WindowsPowerShell\Microsoft.PowerShell_profile.ps1`, where `$PSHome` returns the current user's file path like `c:\Users\username`. The easiest way to open the current user's profile is to type **notepad $profile** inside of PowerShell.

The results of the command are piped to the `out-null` device because the version number of the library is generally not needed.

After loading the SMO libraries, it's easy to connect to a server (using Windows Authentication) by issuing the following command:

```
$sqlsvr = new-object ('Microsoft.SqlServer.Management.Smo.Server') 'MyServer'
```

The `$sqlsvr` variable now contains a `Server` object for the `MyServer` instance of SQL Server. The properties and methods of the `Server` object can be seen by piping the variable into the `Get-Member` cmdlet:

```
$sqlsvr | Get-Member
```

The SMO object library is best represented in a chart for ease in understanding. The basic object is the `Server` object, and managing the server starts with connecting to that object. For example, the SMO objects used in managing user databases are shown in Figure 30-2.

Creating databases and database objects using SMO may seem counterintuitive because usually these objects are created using Transact-SQL scripts, but automating the processes that create the objects can provide consistency in an area that is usually quite inconsistent.

FIGURE 30-2

Database objects.

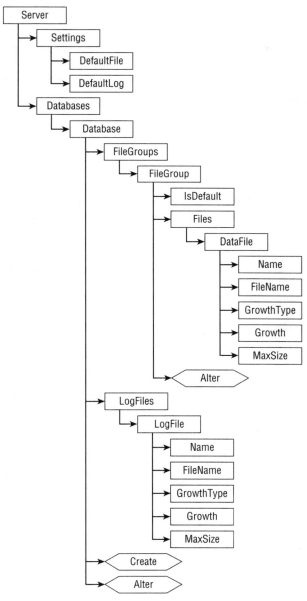

SQL Server requires that a database have a PRIMARY filegroup and that the system tables (the database metadata) reside in that filegroup. It is recommended that you keep your application data out of the PRIMARY filegroup, both from a manageability perspective and a performance perspective. When creating a database using SQL Server Management Studio (SSMS), it can be tedious to create a database with the wanted size and file location and with a separate, default filegroup to hold the application data. This is a relatively simple process using SMO.

Best Practice

Don't place application data in the primary filegroup because the size and location of application file groups are easier to control and manage, especially as the size of the database grows. The database metadata must exist in the primary filegroup, and after the primary filegroup is online, the database is considered available. As each additional filegroup becomes available, the data within it is usable by applications, but smaller, discrete filegroups can improve the overall uptime for the application data.

Listing 30-3 shows the script to create a database. The example database is a database called MyAppDB, which has a 5MB file in the primary filegroup to hold the database metadata. This file grows by 25 percent when required, but it shouldn't be required. The percentage or fixed growth size chosen depends on the actual usage history for the application, but a growth size too small can cause excessive fragmentation, and a growth size too large can take too much time when the autogrow event occurs. The logical name MyAppDB_SysData is used for this file and placed in the default data path for the server.

The application data is located in a second filegroup called AppFG, which is then set to be the default filegroup for the database. The filegroup contains one file with a logical name of MyAppDB_AppData and also is housed in the default data path for the server. The initial size is set to 25MB and allowed to grow by 25 percent each time it is required, but it is set to a maximum size of 100MB.

Log files in SQL Server do not use filegroups, so a log file named MyAppDB_Log is added to the LogFiles collection of the database and housed in the default log file path for the server. Its initial size is set to 10MB and allowed to grow by 25 percent each time it is required, but you won't set a maximum size for the log file.

After the structural objects have been created for the database, the Create() method is executed, but SQL Server automatically sets the default filegroup to primary when a database is created. After it has been created, the script sets the default filegroup to AppFG using the Alter() method at both the FileGroup and Database levels. Because of a bug in SMO, the DefaultFile and DefaultLog properties in the Server object's Settings collection don't properly initialize. Therefore, the script places the files in the same location as the master database data and log files, as defined in the MasterDBPath and MasterDBLogPath properties in the Server object's Information collection.

LISTING 30-3   CreateDB.ps1

```
#createdb.ps1
#Creates a new database using our specifications
[System.Reflection.Assembly]::LoadWithPartialName('Microsoft.SqlServer.SMO')
| out-null

# Instantiate a new SMO Server object and connect to server SQLTWSS\INST01
$s =
  new-object ('Microsoft.SqlServer.Management.Smo.Server') 'SQLTWSS\INST01'
$dbname = 'SMO_DB'

# Set the database logical and physical names
$syslogname = $dbname + '_SysData'
$applogname = $dbname + '_AppData'
$loglogname = $dbname + '_Log'

# An SMO bug in SQL 2005 and SQL 2008 cause the default locations to
possibly be null
$fileloc = $s.Settings.DefaultFile
$logloc = $s.Settings.DefaultLog
if ($fileloc.Length = 0) {
    $fileloc = $s.Information.MasterDBPath
    }
if ($logloc.Length = 0) {
    $logloc = $s.Information.MasterDBLogPath
    }

# Place the files in the same location as the master database
$dbsysfile = $fileloc + '\' + $syslogname + '.mdf'
$dbappfile = $fileloc + '\' + $applogname + '.ndf'
$dblogfile = $logloc + '\' + $loglogname + '.ldf'


# Instantiate the database object and add the filegroups
$db =
 new-object ('Microsoft.SqlServer.Management.Smo.Database') ($s, $dbname)
$sysfg =
 new-object ('Microsoft.SqlServer.Management.Smo.FileGroup') ($db, 'PRIMARY')
$db.FileGroups.Add($sysfg)
$appfg = new-object ('Microsoft.SqlServer.Management.Smo.FileGroup') ($db,
'AppFG')
$db.FileGroups.Add($appfg)

# Create the file for the system tables
$dbdsysfile = new-object ('Microsoft.SqlServer.Management.Smo.DataFile')
($sysfg, $syslogname)
$sysfg.Files.Add($dbdsysfile)
$dbdsysfile.FileName = $dbsysfile
$dbdsysfile.Size = [double](5.0 * 1024.0)
```

Continues

LISTING 30-3 *(continued)*

```
$dbdsysfile.GrowthType = 'None'
$dbdsysfile.IsPrimaryFile = 'True'

# Create the file for the Application tables
$dbdappfile = new-object ('Microsoft.SqlServer.Management.Smo.DataFile')
($appfg, $applogname)
$appfg.Files.Add($dbdappfile)
$dbdappfile.FileName = $dbappfile
$dbdappfile.Size = [double](25.0 * 1024.0)
$dbdappfile.GrowthType = 'Percent'
$dbdappfile.Growth = 25.0
$dbdappfile.MaxSize = [double](100.0 * 1024.0)

# Create the file for the log
$dblfile = new-object ('Microsoft.SqlServer.Management.Smo.LogFile') ($db,
$loglogname)
$db.LogFiles.Add($dblfile)
$dblfile.FileName = $dblogfile
$dblfile.Size = [double](10.0 * 1024.0)
$dblfile.GrowthType = 'Percent'
$dblfile.Growth = 25.0

# Create the database
$db.Create()

# Set the default filegroup to AppFG
$appfg = $db.FileGroups['AppFG']
$appfg.IsDefault = $true
$appfg.Alter()
$db.Alter()
```

ADO.NET

ADO.NET consists of a set of object libraries that enable communication between client programs and the source of the data, in this case SQL Server. Two groups of objects are defined within ADO.NET: a set of *connected objects*, which enables the client to communicate with the server using an active connection, and a set of *disconnected objects*, which acts as an offline data cache, enabling the client application to work with the data independently of the server. These two groups of objects are listed here:

Connected objects are as follows:

- **Connection object:** A connection to the data source.
- **Command object:** Can represent a query against a database, a call to a stored procedure, or a direct request to return the contents of a specific table.

- **DataReader object:** Designed to return query results as quickly as possible.

- **Transaction object:** Groups a number of changes to a database and treats them as a single unit of work. The Connection object has a BeginTransaction method that can be used to create Transaction objects.

- **Parameter object:** Enables the specification of parameters for stored procedures or parameterized queries.

- **DataAdapter object:** Acts as a bridge between the database and the disconnected objects in the ADO.NET object model.

Disconnected Objects are as follows:

- **DataTable object:** Enables the examination of data through collections of rows and columns

- **DataColumn object:** Corresponds to a column in a table

- **Constraint object:** Defines and enforces column constraints

- **DataRow object:** Provides access to the DataTable's Rows collection

- **DataSet object:** The container for a number of DataTable objects

- **DataRelation object:** Defines the relations between DataTables in the DataSet object

- **DataView object:** Enables the examination of DataTable data in different ways

The first thing needed for a session using ADO.NET is a connection to the database. The SqlConnection object is initialized using the following commands:

```
$connstring = "Data Source=myServerAddress;Initial
Catalog=myDataBase;Integrated Security=SSPI;"
# or its equivalent
$connstring = "Server=myServerAddress;
Database=myDataBase;Trusted_Connection=True;"
$cn = new-object system.data.SqlClient.SqlConnection($connstring)
```

Many options are available for configuring connection strings, most of which are available at www.connectionstrings.com/sql-server-2008.

After the connection object is initialized, the connection can be used to send queries to SQL Server. Alternatively, you can download Out-DataTable from the TechNet Script Center Repository (http://gallery.technet.microsoft.com/scriptcenter/4208a159-a52e-4b99-83d4-8048468d29dd) and pipe the results of Invoke-Sqlcmd to it. Doing so returns results in an ADO.NET datatable instead of an array.

Listing 30-4 shows an example using the AdventureWorks2012 sample database, returning query results to a DataTable object. Simply call the $Results variable one more time to present the results to the user.

30

LISTING 30-4   EmployeeExtract.ps1

```
#employeeextract.ps1
#This script pulls info from the Person.Contact table in AdventureWorks2012
and presents it to the user

$Results = Invoke-Sqlcmd -ServerInstance SQLTWSS\INST01 -Database AdventureWorks2012 -Query "
SELECT TOP 25 [ContactID]
      ,[FirstName]
      ,[LastName]
      ,[EmailAddress]
      ,[Phone]
   FROM [AdventureWorks2012].[Person].[Contact]" | Out-DataTable
```

The script first connects with the database server and then executes a query. That query and the connection object are supplied as parameters to the `Invoke-SQLCmd` cmdlet. The results are then passed to `Out-DataTable` and that function converts the results into a `DataTable` object. This `DataTable` is then stored in the `$Results` variable. Running this script produces these results:

```
 1: Gustavo, Achong, gustavo0@adventure-works.com, 398-555-0132
 2: Catherine, Abel, catherine0@adventure-works.com, 747-555-0171
 3: Kim, Abercrombie, kim2@adventure-works.com, 334-555-0137
 4: Humberto, Acevedo, humberto0@adventure-works.com, 599-555-0127
 5: Pilar, Ackerman, pilar1@adventure-works.com, 1 (11) 500 555-0132
 6: Frances, Adams, frances0@adventure-works.com, 991-555-0183
 7: Margaret, Smith, margaret0@adventure-works.com, 959-555-0151
 8: Carla, Adams, carla0@adventure-works.com, 107-555-0138
 9: Jay, Adams, jay1@adventure-works.com, 158-555-0142
10: Ronald, Adina, ronald0@adventure-works.com, 453-555-0165
11: Samuel, Agcaoili, samuel0@adventure-works.com, 554-555-0110
12: James, Aguilar, james2@adventure-works.com, 1 (11) 500 555-0198
13: Robert, Ahlering, robert1@adventure-works.com, 678-555-0175
14: François, Ferrier, françois1@adventure-works.com, 571-555-0128
15: Kim, Akers, kim3@adventure-works.com, 440-555-0166
16: Lili, Alameda, lili0@adventure-works.com, 1 (11) 500 555-0150
17: Amy, Alberts, amy1@adventure-works.com, 727-555-0115
18: Anna, Albright, anna0@adventure-works.com, 197-555-0143
19: Milton, Albury, milton0@adventure-works.com, 492-555-0189
20: Paul, Alcorn, paul2@adventure-works.com, 331-555-0162
21: Gregory, Alderson, gregory0@adventure-works.com, 968-555-0153
22: J. Phillip, Alexander, jphillip0@adventure-works.com, 845-555-0187
23: Michelle, Alexander, michelle0@adventure-works.com, 115-555-0175
24: Sean, Jacobson, sean2@adventure-works.com, 555-555-0162
25: Phyllis, Allen, phyllis0@adventure-works.com, 695-555-0111
```

Scripting SQL Server Tasks

Although using PowerShell interactively to perform maintenance tasks may be fun and interesting, it doesn't save much time. Scripting enables administrators to perform the same function the same way every time, saving the time it might take to remember how to solve a problem and enabling the administrator to focus on new problems as they occur. Typically, administrators create scripts for two basic categories of tasks: *administrative tasks*, those that perform normal administrative functions; and *data-based tasks*.

Administrative Tasks

Listing 30-5 shows a script to create a database, but nearly every administrative activity required of a SQL Server DBA can be scripted using PowerShell and SMO. One task that you can completely avoid having to write script against the SMO in SQL Server 2012 is backing up databases.

LISTING 30-5   Backup.ps1

```
Backup-SqlDatabase -Database AdventureWorks2012 -ServerInstance localhost
```

To back up all the databases on an instance, it's as simple as querying the instance for a list of databases and then piping that information to the `Backup-SQLDatabase` cmdlet. When you pipe the list to the backup cmdlet you must wrap the command in a `foreach` loop because the `Backup-SQLDatabase` cmdlet accepts only one database name at a time.

```
Dir SQLSERVER:\SQL\localhost\default\Databases\ |
foreach{
    Backup-SqlDatabase -Database $_.name -ServerInstance localhost
}
```

One of the great improvements in SMO over its predecessor, DMO, is in the area of scripting. With SMO, Transact-SQL scripts can be created from objects even if they don't yet exist. Almost all maintenance dialogs in SQL Server Management Studio include a button that enables a script to be generated from the changes made in that dialog. That way, the script can be executed, rather than making the changes from the dialog, and the script can be saved for future use.

Another useful feature of scripting existing objects is the capability to generate scripts of all database objects for documentation or to put into source code control. This enables administrators to rebuild a database in the form it existed at the time the script was created, should some problem arise requiring that effort.

At any time while creating or working with objects in SMO, those objects can be scripted for archival or later use (see Figure 30-3).

30

FIGURE 30-3

SMO scripting objects.

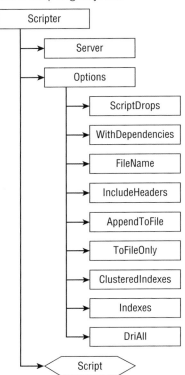

The `Server` property enables the `Scripter` object to connect to the server. The remaining properties needing to be set are in the Scripter Options collection.

The `ScriptDrops` property specifies whether the script consists of drops for the objects or creates for the objects. If this property is set to `True`, the script contains a DROP statement for each object (within an `IF` condition to ensure that it exists), but a `False` value causes the scripter to generate the CREATE statement for each object. The `WithDependencies` property, if `True`, causes the objects to be scripted in an order that respects the dependency of one scripted object on another. The `FileName` property contains the full path of the resultant script file. The `IncludeHeaders` property, when `True`, includes a comment indicating the name of the object and when the object was created in the script. The `AppendToFile` property appends the script to the end of an existing file if `True`, and overwrites the file if `False`.

By default, the scripting process sends the results to the console, so setting the `ToFileOnly` property to `True` causes the scripter to send the script only to the file specified. Setting the `ClusteredIndexes` property to `True` causes the clustered index for a table to be included in the script, and setting the `Indexes` property to `True` causes the nonclustered indexes to be included in the script. The `DriAll` property, when set to `True`, causes all objects with enforced declarative referential integrity to be included in the script.

The objects to be scripted need to be added to an array of type `SqlSmoObject`. After the array has been populated with all the objects to be scripted, invoke the `Script` method and the script will be created. Listing 30-6 shows the script to create a T-SQL script of all tables in the AdventureWorks2012 database.

LISTING 30-6   Scripting.ps1

```
function Export-DBObjectsIntoFolders(
[string]$dbname, [string]$server, [String]$Path,
    [string]$outputFilename=""){
   [System.Reflection.Assembly]::LoadWithPartialName("Microsoft.SqlServer.SMO") | out-null
    $SMOserver = New-Object ('Microsoft.SqlServer.Management.Smo.Server') -argumentlist $server
$db = $SMOserver.databases[$dbname]

<#Build this portion of the directory structure out here in case
scripting takes more than one minute.#>
$SavePath = "C:\TEMP\Databases\" + $($dbname)
$DateFolder = get-date -format yyyyMMddHHmm
if (!$Path) {$Path="$SavePath\$DateFolder"}
else {
if ((Test-Path -Path "$Path") -eq "true") `
        {"Scripting Out to $Path $DateFolder"} `
    else {new-item -type directory -name "$DateFolder"-path "$SavePath"}
    }

$Objects = $db.Tables
foreach ($ScriptThis in $Objects | where {!($_.IsSystemObject)}) {
<#Script the DRI too#>
$ScriptDrop = new-object ('Microsoft.SqlServer.Management.Smo.Scripter')
    ($SMOserver)
$ScriptDrop.Options.AppendToFile = $True
$ScriptDrop.Options.AllowSystemObjects = $False
$ScriptDrop.Options.ClusteredIndexes = $False
$ScriptDrop.Options.DriAll = $False
$ScriptDrop.Options.ScriptDrops = $False
$ScriptDrop.Options.IncludeHeaders = $True
$ScriptDrop.Options.ToFileOnly = $True
$ScriptDrop.Options.Indexes = $False
```

Continues

30

LISTING 30-6 *(continued)*

```
$ScriptDrop.Options.WithDependencies = $False
$ScriptDrop.Options.Default = $False
$ScriptDrop.Options.DriPrimaryKey = $False
$ScriptDrop.Options.DriForeignKeys = $True

$TypeFolder=$ScriptThis.GetType().Name
if ((Test-Path -Path "$Path\$TypeFolder\Constraint") -eq "true") `
        {"Scripting Out Constraint $ScriptThis"} `
    else {
new-item -type directory -name "Constraint" -path "$Path\$TypeFolder"}
$ScriptFile = $ScriptThis -replace "\[|\]"
$ScriptDrop.Options.FileName = "" + $($Path) + "\" + $($TypeFolder) + "\
    Constraint\" + $($ScriptFile) + ".SQL"

$ScriptDrop.Script($ScriptThis)
}

$Objects += $db.Schemas
$Objects += $db.Views
$Objects += $db.StoredProcedures
$Objects += $db.UserDefinedFunctions

foreach ($ScriptThis in $Objects | where {!($_.IsSystemObject)}) {
#Need to Add Some mkDirs for the different $Fldr=$ScriptThis.GetType().Name
$scriptr = new-object ('Microsoft.SqlServer.Management.Smo.Scripter')
    ($SMOserver)
$scriptr.Options.AppendToFile = $True
$scriptr.Options.AllowSystemObjects = $False
$scriptr.Options.ClusteredIndexes = $True
$scriptr.Options.DriAll = $False
$scriptr.Options.ScriptDrops = $False
$scriptr.Options.IncludeHeaders = $True
$scriptr.Options.ToFileOnly = $True
$scriptr.Options.Indexes = $True
$scriptr.Options.Permissions = $True
$scriptr.Options.WithDependencies = $False

<#This section builds folder structures.
Remove the date folder if you want to overwrite#>
$TypeFolder=$ScriptThis.GetType().Name
if ((Test-Path -Path "$Path\$TypeFolder") -eq "true") `
        {"Scripting Out $TypeFolder $ScriptThis"} `
    else {new-item -type directory -name "$TypeFolder"-path "$Path"}
$ScriptFile = $ScriptThis -replace "\[|\]"
$scriptr.Options.FileName = "$Path\$TypeFolder\$ScriptFile.SQL"

#This is where each object actually gets scripted one at a time.
```

```
$ScriptDrop.Script($ScriptThis)
$scriptr.Script($ScriptThis)
} #This ends the loop
} #This completes the function
```

The best method for creating and modifying tables in SQL Server is to use Transact-SQL scripts.

After scripting out the database objects, as shown in Listing 30-6, at some point you likely need to load them into a database. One of the easiest ways to do that is by simply pointing the `Get-ChildItem` cmdlet at the directory that contains the files for the table definition, and then streaming that list of files to the `-InputFile` parameter of the `Invoke-SQLCmd` cmdlet (see Listing 30-7).

LISTING 30-7   CreateTable.ps1

```
dir -recurse -Path C:\TEMP\Databases\AdventureWorksLT\201203041924\Tables |
where{ Test-Path $_.fullname -pathtype leaf} |
%{
Invoke-Sqlcmd -ServerInstance LocalHost -Database BlankDB -InputFile "$($_.FullName)"
}
```

Data-Based Tasks

In the section on ADO.NET, you saw an example that returned the results from a query to the user, using a `Invoke-SQLCmd` cmdlet to fill a `DataTable` by passing the results through the `Out-DataTable` function. This method is fine as long as there's enough memory to hold all the results of the query. If the result set is large, though, it is better to use the `ExecuteReader` method of the `SqlCommand` object.

The following example, as shown in Listing 30-8, uses the `AdventureWorks2012` database to extract department employee information by `DepartmentID` and creates a separate physical file for each department. The files are text files with commas separating the columns returned. This format is easily understood by most programs that import data. The `ExecuteReader` method returns a `DataReader` object, and the columns must be retrieved from the object using the `GetValue` method of the `DataReader`, supplying the column index number to `GetValue`. The script sets a local variable for each of the columns retrieved for each row. After those have been set, the script tests whether the `DepartmentID` value has changed. If so, a "header" row is created in a string variable (`$r`) and written to a file with the name of the department `Name` value and a `.txt` extension. After the header is written, the data row just read is written to the file.

30

LISTING 30-8 **dept_birthdays.ps1**

```
#dept_birthdays.ps1
#This script will extract information for employees by Department
#and write the results into text files named with the department name.

$cn = new-object System.Data.SqlClient.SqlConnection("Data Source=MyServer\
MyInstance;Integrated Security=SSPI;Initial Catalog=AdventureWorks2008");
$cn.Open()
$q = "SELECT d.[DepartmentID]"
$q = $q + "        ,d.[Name]"
$q = $q + "        ,p.[FirstName]"
$q = $q + "        ,p.[LastName]"
$q = $q + "        ,e.[JobTitle]"
$q = $q + "        ,e.[BirthDate]"
$q = $q + "        ,e.[SalariedFlag]"
$q = $q + "  FROM [AdventureWorks2008].[Person].[Person] p"
$q = $q + "  INNER JOIN [AdventureWorks2008].[HumanResources].[Employee] e"
$q = $q + "  ON p.[BusinessEntityID] = e.[BusinessEntityID]"
$q = $q + "  INNER JOIN [AdventureWorks2008]
.[HumanResources].[EmployeeDepartmentHistory] dh"
$q = $q + "  ON p.[BusinessEntityID] = dh.[BusinessEntityID]"
$q = $q + "  INNER JOIN [AdventureWorks2008].[HumanResources].[Department] d"
$q = $q + "  ON dh.[DepartmentID] = d. [DepartmentID]"
$q = $q + "  WHERE p.[PersonType] = 'EM'"
$q = $q + "  AND dh.[EndDate] IS NULL"
$q = $q + "  ORDER BY d.DepartmentID, p.LastName"

$cmd = new-object "System.Data.SqlClient.SqlCommand" ($q, $cn)
$cmd.CommandTimeout = 0

$dr = $cmd.ExecuteReader()
$did = ""

while ($dr.Read()) {
      $DepartmentID = $dr.GetValue(0)
      $Name = $dr.GetValue(1)
      $FirstName = $dr.GetValue(2)
      $LastName = $dr.GetValue(3)
      $JobTitle = $dr.GetValue(4)
      $BirthDate = $dr.GetValue(5)
      $SalariedFlag = $dr.GetValue(6)
if ($DepartmentID -ne $did) {
          $r = """DepartmentID"","""Name"","""FirstName"","""LastName"""
          $r = $r + """,""JobTitle"","""BirthDate"","""SalariedFlag"""

          $f = $Name + ".txt"
          $r | out-file $f -append -encoding ASCII
```

```
            $did = $DepartmentID
            }
        $r = """" + $DepartmentID + ""","""" + $Name + ""","""
        $r = $r + $FirstName + """,""" + $LastName + ""","""
        $r = $r + $JobTitle + """,""" + $BirthDate + """,""" + $SalariedFlag +
""""

        $f = $Name + ".txt"
        $r | out-file $f -append -encoding ASCII
        }
$dr.Close()
$cn.Close()
```

Summary

After looking at the basics of PowerShell and exploring a few ways to get some interesting information about servers, this chapter reviewed a script to provide information about each server you manage. Then it examined some of the structures in SQL Server Management Objects (SMO) and some scripts to perform basic administrative tasks. This chapter also looked at a couple scripts to extract data from SQL Server because that's a common request from business people. Finally, this chapter took a quick look at the features in SQL Server 2012 to make PowerShell an integral part of the SQL Server toolset.

Much more can be explored with PowerShell, but this provides a starting point. Automation enables administrators to do more in less time and provide more value to the companies that employ them. PowerShell is a powerful way to automate almost everything an administrator needs to do with SQL Server.

30

Managing Data in Windows Azure SQL Database

W ith all the talk in this book about the next version of SQL Server, SQL Server 2012, you can't ignore the "other" version of SQL Server that has been taking the world by storm.

Microsoft has put a lot of focus and energy into its cloud initiative, and this movement is not complete without providing a relational database platform in the offering; thus, Windows Azure SQL Database. This chapter focuses on managing data with Azure SQL Database, including performance and data migration.

Overview of Azure SQL Database

Azure SQL Database is Microsoft's transactional database offering for Cloud Computing based on SQL Server 2012. SQL Database extends SQL Server capabilities to the cloud by offering relational data services called Microsoft SQL database. With SQL Database you can easily create, deploy, and manage relational database solutions in the cloud.

SQL Database is one of the main components of the Windows Azure Platform and as such includes many of the benefits provided by the Azure platform, including manageability, high availability, scalability, and the well-known relational data model.

Entire books have been written on SQL Database, and it is difficult to cover all the great aspects of SQL Database. This chapter covers some of the aspects of managing SQL Database and migrating data to SQL Database, and some of the benefits of SQL Database, such as high availability and scalability.

This chapter is going to make certain assumptions, including the assumption that you have provisioned a SQL Database server and are somewhat familiar with the Windows Azure Management Portal.

Managing Windows Azure SQL Database

One of the great benefits of SQL Database, on top of its high availability, scalability, and familiar development model, is that SQL Database provides the great, same familiar development model that you know and love with SQL Server. This section looks at a couple of tools that help with the management of SQL Database.

SQL Server Management Studio

The first tool is the familiar SQL Server Management Studio. SQL Server Management Studio from SQL Server 2008, SQL Server 2008 R2, and SQL Server 2012 can be used to access, configure, manage, and administer your SQL Database instances.

The key to using SQL Server Management Studio is supplying the proper login and server information. The server name is in the following format:

```
server.database.windows.net
```

The server name is a fully qualified name that you use every time you connect to SQL Database, including connection strings. SQL Database supports only SQL Authentication, so your username is in the following format:

```
username@server
```

When logged in, SQL Server Management Studio provides the same great tool for working with your SQL Database environment that you are used to when working with SQL Server, as shown in Figure 31-1. In the Object Explorer windows, several of the nodes you typically use when working with SQL Server are not present when working with SQL Database, such as the Server Objects node and the Replication Node.

These nodes are not included in the Object Explorer because the specific functionality just isn't needed or is soon to be coming. For example, Replication will probably not be included simply because of the functionality SQL Database provides, such as how it provides high availability with multiple redundant copies and using sync services to keep those copies in sync. Plus, SQL Data Sync provides equivalent functionality without the headache of setting up and configuring Replication.

The key here is that after you connect to SQL Database via SQL Server Management Studio (SSMS), you have all the capabilities to manage and administer your SQL Database environment using a familiar tool.

One of the things that you also notice as you work with your Azure databases and other objects via SQL Server Management Studio is that the nice GUI you are used to isn't there (yet). For example, after you connect to an Azure database, expand the Databases node, and then right-click the Tables node and select New Table. Instead of the nice interface to design the table, a query window opens with the code template to create a new table. The same thing applies for creating a database and other objects. The GUI interface for creating SQL Database objects is missing. Is this coming? Certainly, but it is not known when.

FIGURE 31-1

SQL Server Management Studio Connected to SQL Database.

Windows Azure SQL Database Manager

A new tool to the playground is the SQL Database Manager (sometimes called SQL Database Manager), a web-based and lightweight database management tool specifically designed to enable a quick solution for developing, deploying, and managing their SQL Database instances. This tool is available via the Windows Azure Platform Management Portal.

The great thing about the SQL Database Manager is that it provides a GUI-driven mechanism for creating and managing tables, views, and stored procedures in a SQL database. This is a welcome tool because even though you can connect to SQL Database with SSMS, the wizard-driven interfaces for creating objects such as tables and views are missing. In SSMS if you right-click the Tables node for a given database and select the New Table option, you don't get the New Table dialog that you get when working with SQL Database. What you get is a new query window with the syntax for creating a new table.

SQL Database Manager fixes this, providing a nice web-based and GUI-driven mechanism for creating the SQL objects you frequently work with. Figure 31-2 shows the main page for the SQL Database Manager.

FIGURE 31-2

SQL Database Manager.

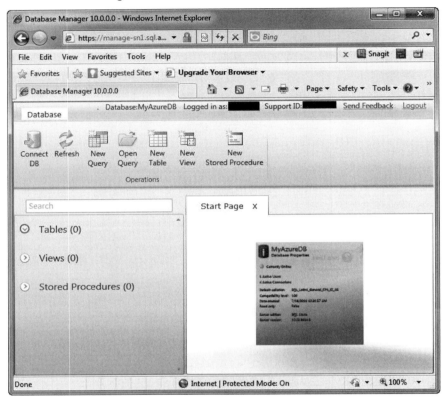

Another benefit of this tool is that you can also author and execute queries directly within the SQL Database Manager. Actually, you can do nearly everything in SQL Database Manager and not need Management Studio. Awesome.

Creating a Database in SQL Database

In this section you'll create a database using SQL Server Management Studio because you'll need it later in the chapter. Creating a database is pretty easy even though there isn't a wizard or dialog to help. So, open up SQL Server Management Studio in SQL Server 2012 and in the Server Connection dialog, enter the Fully Qualified Server Name of the SQL Database server and your username and password.

Once connected to SQL Database, open a new query window and type the following:

```
CREATE DATABASE AWMini
```

For those of you who are somewhat new to SQL Database, you are probably looking at that statement and thinking "There's more to a `create database` statement than that!" Well, in SQL Database, not really.

Truth be told, there *can* be more, but if you execute that statement as is against SQL Database, it will work. I'll briefly explain. SQL Database abstracts the logical administration from the physical administration. In SQL Database, you continue to administer databases, logins, users, and roles, but Microsoft administers the physical aspects of SQL Database, including hardware, hard drives, storage, etc.

Thus, when creating a database, Microsoft will determine the physical aspects of that database, including its physical location in the Windows Azure data center you choose. As such, your `create database` statement becomes much easier since you don't need to specify all the parameters of the `create` statement, such as drive and path.

There are two editions of SQL Database instances; Web and Business. Functionally, there are no differences between them, but they do differ in the sizes you can select. When creating a database in SQL Database, you need to specify the edition and size of the database. For the Web edition, you can select 1GB and 5GB database sizes. For the Business edition, you can select 10, 20, 30, 40, 50, 100, and 150GB sizes.

If you don't specify an edition and size, a 1GB Web edition will be created. If you want a 50GB database, for example, your statement will look like this:

```
CREATE DATABASE AWMini (Edition= 'Business', MaxSize=50 GB)
```

> **NOTE**
> A few words on cost and sizing. When you create a 50GB database, for example, you are paying for that 50GB, regardless of whether you have 5GB or 40GB of data in the database. That is because when you create the database, SQL Database allocates 50GB of space. You can programmatically change the size larger or smaller, but in SQL Database, you pay for the size you specify.

One last note; unlike on-premises databases where you can specify auto-grow options, SQL Database does not have this option. If you create a 50GB database and you fill it up, it will not auto-grow to the next size. The database will go into read-only mode and reject all inserts. Like I said, you can programmatically change the size via the `alter database` statement, but you will need to monitor database growth, either manually or programmatically, to prevent the database from filling up.

If you haven't, execute the first `create database` statement above to create your database as we will be using it during the data migration section.

High Availability and Scalability

The goal of SQL Database is to provide a highly available and scalable cloud database service built on SQL Server technologies. This database service is designed to include built-in high availability and fault tolerance with zero physical administration.

Think about this for a minute. How would you like to spend less time worrying about the physical aspects of your SQL Server and more time focusing on the things you really like to do, such as database development? This is exactly what SQL Database provides. The following sections discuss how SQL Database provides a managed service that has a 99.9 percent monthly SLA with high availability and scalability.

High Availability

SQL Database strives to maintain 99.9 percent availability, achieved by using commodity hardware that can be quickly replaced if hardware or drive failure occurs. However, more important, when you create a database in SQL Database, you actually get three databases: one primary and two replicas. These three databases are always in sync. If the primary fails, it is taken offline and one of the two replicas is designated as the new primary and another replica created. This automatic failover exists to optimize availability for your application.

Microsoft currently has six data centers world-wide dedicated to supporting the Windows Azure platform. Two data centers are located in the United States, two are located in Europe, and two are located in Asia.

Scalability

A huge benefit of using SQL Database is that of automatic and built-in scalability. This wonderful functionality comes free with the cost of your database. Two components within SQL Database help provide the built-in scalability and performance by constantly monitoring each SQL Database node: Engine Throttling and Load Balancing. These two components exist solely to ensure that each server is running at its optimum.

Throttling

The Azure platform, including SQL Database, is a shared resource environment. Meaning, when you create your database it is not the only database on the disk. You are sharing that disk and server with others. As such, SQL Database needs to ensure that you "play nice in the sandbox." Thus, throttling in SQL Database exists to ensure that critical resources are not robbed from others using the box, and more important, from the server itself. *Throttling* is simply the act of scaling back resource usage that is adversely impacting the overall health of the system.

What SQL Database wants to prevent is a situation in which one subscriber's application or process negatively affects the instance of SQL Server by doing something it shouldn't, such as imposing a heavy load or filling up the transaction logs (don't overburden IOPS or CPU cycles, for instance).

Thus, resources are monitored, including yours. The entire health of the machine is always monitored by the throttling engine. Things such as log size, log write duration, CPU usage, and database size (among others) are continuously monitored. If SQL Database determines that limits are exceeded, SQL Database may reject your connection for 10 seconds at a time. Continuous violations may result in the permanent rejection of read and writes. So play nice.

Load Balancing

Load balancing is another area where SQL Database shines. *Load balancing* in SQL Database is achieved by moving the databases within the physical machines, or across machines, based on periodic audits of system usage. However, you need to remember that SQL Database is a shared environment, and as such is it impossible to predict workloads of each subscriber. There are no performance guarantees, but performance is still crucial and important to SQL Database. Thus, when a new database is added to SQL Database, the Load Balancer determines the location of the primary and secondary replicas based on the current load of the machines in the data center.

However, the database may not remain there. SQL Database is continuously monitoring the loads of the servers and may move a primary to a machine with less load to ensure a properly performing database.

Migrating Data to SQL Database

So you want to move one or more of your applications and their databases to the cloud. It's a noble idea. More than likely, you're in the same category as countless others who are looking into moving applications into the cloud: You don't want to start from scratch. You'd rather migrate an existing application to the cloud, but you aren't sure about the steps necessary to do so, or the technologies available to help in the process. This section discusses three tools from Microsoft that come with SQL Server to help with your database migration needs:

- Generate and Publish Scripts Wizard
- SQL Server Integration Services (SSIS)
- Bcp utility

In addition to these three tools, a free utility found on CodePlex called the SQL Database Migration Wizard, which provides a wizard-driven interface to walk you through migrating your database and data to SQL Database, is briefly covered.

The examples in this chapter use SQL Server 2012. These examples also work with SQL Server 2008 R2.

NOTE
You may wonder why the SQL Server Import and Export Wizard isn't listed here. The answer is that the SQL Server Import and Export Wizard isn't supported for SQL Database yet. Microsoft is working on it. No timeframe has been given as to when the Import/Export Wizard will support SQL Database, but support is definitely in the works.

The database you will use in these examples is from a scaled-down version of the AdventureWorks database, which you can download from the website for this book.

Generate Scripts Wizard

You can use the Generate and Publish Scripts Wizard to create T-SQL scripts for SQL Server databases and related objects within the selected database. You have probably used this wizard, so this section doesn't walk through it step-by-step; instead, the section briefly highlights a few steps in the wizard and points out the necessary options to effectively work with SQL Database.

One of the differences between SQL Server 2012, SQL Server 2008 R2 and SQL Server 2008 (pertaining to object scripting) is a setting in the Advanced Scripting Options dialog as you go through the wizard. This dialog includes two properties you can set regarding the version of SQL Server for which you script database objects: Script for Server Version and Script for the Database Engine Type. The Script for Server Version option lists the version of SQL Server that the Generate and Publish Scripts wizard supports, which ranges from SQL Server 2000 to SQL Server 2012.

The Script for the Database Engine Type property has two options you can choose from: Stand-Alone Instance and SQL Database. The SQL database option works only with the SQL Server 2008 R2 Server and SQL Server 2008 R2 versions. For example, if you are using SQL Server Management Studio for 2008 R2 and set the Script for Server version to SQL Server 2008 (non-R2) and then set the Script for the Database Engine Type property to SQL database instance, the Script for Server version property value automatically changes to SQL Server 2008 R2. In SQL Server Management Studio for SQL Server 2012, the "Script for Server Version" will default to SQL Server 2012 if you script for engine type "SQL Database."

The Generate and Publish Scripts Wizard does a nice job of appropriately scripting objects for SQL Database. The wizard checks for unsupported syntax and data types, and checks for primary keys on each table. Thus, the following example sets SQL for Server Version to SQL Server 2008 (non-R2) for several reasons. First, many people aren't using SQL Server 2008 R2 or SQL Server 2012 and therefore don't have the option to script for SQL Database. Second, this exercise shows you the needed steps to get a script ready to run in SQL Database.

The examples in this chapter will use the Generate Scripts Wizard in SQL Server 2012, but the steps in SQL Server 2008 R2 are similar. To start the Generate and Publish Scripts Wizard in SQL Server Management Studio (SSMS), open Object Explorer, and expand the Databases node. Select a database, right-mouse click on it, and then select Tasks ⇨ Generate Scripts from the context menu.

You must follow four steps to complete this wizard, as shown on the Introduction page:

1. Select database objects.
2. Specify scripting or publishing objects.
3. Review selections.
4. Generate scripts.

The following sections work through these steps.

Choosing Target Objects

To select your target database objects, follow these steps:

1. On the Introduction page of the Generate and Publish Scripts Wizard, click Next.
2. On the Choose Objects page (see Figure 31-3), select the Select Specific Database Objects option because for the purposes of this example, you simply want to select a few objects to migrate.

FIGURE 31-3

Select the database objects to script.

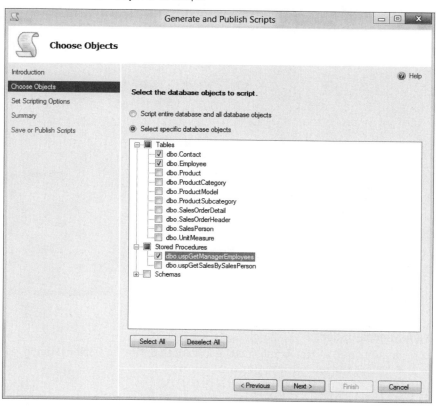

3. In the list of objects in Figure 31-3, expand the Tables and Stored Procedures nodes, and select the following objects:

- Tables: `Contact, Employee`
- Stored procedures: `uspGetManagerEmployees`

4. Click Next on the Choose Objects page.

5. On the Set Scripting Objects page, select the Save to New Query Window option, as shown in Figure 31-4, and then click the Advanced button.

FIGURE 31-4

Set Scripting Options.

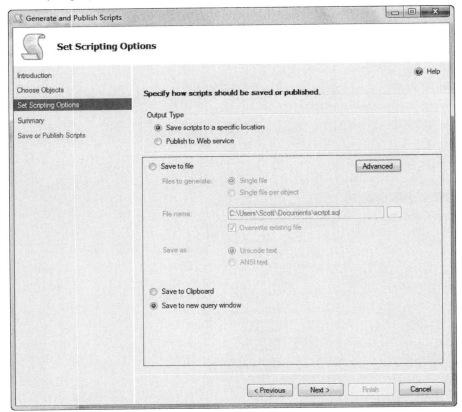

Setting Advanced Options

Clicking the Advanced button brings up the Advanced Scripting Options dialog, as shown in Figure 31-5. Select the following options:

31

- Check for Object Existence = True
- Script Extended Properties = False
- Script for Server Version = SQL Server 2012
- Script for the database engine type = Stand-alone instance
- Script Logins = False
- Script USE DATABASE = False
- Types of data to script = Schema and data
- Script Indexes = True

FIGURE 31-5

Advanced Scripting Options.

This example really doesn't need the extended properties, so those can be excluded. Same thing with the logins; those aren't needed. The use statement is not supported in SQL Database, thus the Script USE DATABASE property needs to be set to False. For this example, the data is also needed so you will want to script both the schema and the data. Lastly, the table indexes are also needed. Script those as well because, as you will learn later, tables without Primary Keys are not supported in SQL Database.

You can also set the Script DROP and CREATE option to Script DROP and CREATE (refer to Figure 31-5), but that option isn't required for SQL Database. Click OK in the Advanced Scripting Options dialog, and then click Next in the Generate Scripts Wizard.

Saving and Publishing

Complete the wizard with these steps:

1. On the wizard's Summary page, review your selections that you made in the previous wizard steps, and then click Next. The T-SQL script is generated, and you're taken to the Save or Publish Scripts page (see Figure 31-6).

FIGURE 31-6

Save or Publish Scripts.

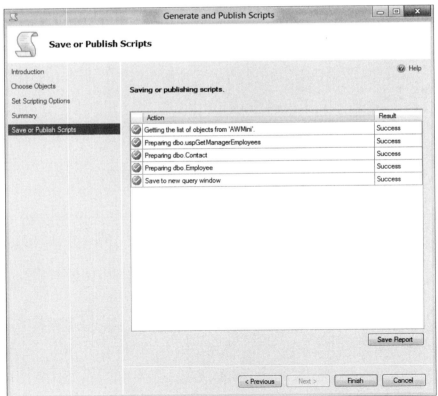

2. Click Finish. At this point your script is finished and displays in a query window in SSMS.

Reviewing the Generated Script

The following snippet is a create table statement from the results of the Generate Script wizard. Except for the things you told the Script-Generation Wizard to ignore, the following T-SQL looks like all other object creation T-SQL you typically deal with on a daily basis:

```
/******Object:  Table [dbo].[Contact]    Script Date: 04/07/2012 10:31:32******/
SET ANSI_NULLS ON
GO
SET QUOTED_IDENTIFIER ON
GO
SET ANSI_PADDING ON
GO
CREATE TABLE [dbo].[Contact](
    [ContactID] [int] IDENTITY(1,1) NOT FOR REPLICATION NOT NULL,
    [NameStyle] [bit] NOT NULL,
    [Title] [nvarchar](8) NULL,
    [FirstName] [nvarchar](50) NOT NULL,
    [MiddleName] [nvarchar](50) NULL,
    [LastName] [nvarchar](50) NOT NULL,
    [Suffix] [nvarchar](10) NULL,
    [EmailAddress] [nvarchar](50) NULL,
    [EmailPromotion] [int] NOT NULL,
    [Phone] [nvarchar](25) NULL,
    [PasswordHash] [varchar](128) NOT NULL,
    [PasswordSalt] [varchar](10) NOT NULL,
    [rowguid] [uniqueidentifier] ROWGUIDCOL  NOT NULL,
    [ModifiedDate] [datetime] NOT NULL,
 CONSTRAINT [PK_Contact_ContactID] PRIMARY KEY CLUSTERED
(
    [ContactID] ASC
)WITH (PAD_INDEX  = OFF, STATISTICS_NORECOMPUTE  = OFF, IGNORE_DUP_KEY = OFF,
ALLOW_ROW_LOCKS  = ON, ALLOW_PAGE_LOCKS  = ON) ON [PRIMARY]
) ON [PRIMARY]
GO
```

The script first enables several options, such as ANSI_NULL and ANSI_PADDING. Then, the script creates the Contact table. This table has an identity column that applies the not for replication clause, which means that this column cannot be used in SQL Server Replication. The Contact table also has a rowguid column that uses the uniqueidentifier data type. Also notice in the resulting script that the rowguid column also has a default on it, which uses the newsequentialid() function to automatically generate new GUIDs. Lastly, this table is created on the primary file group, followed by the setting of several table options via the with clause.

Further down in the script, a stored procedure is created, uspGetManagerEmployees. This stored procedure is a standard stored procedure that accepts single input parameters and uses the `with` option to specify procedure options: in this case, `recompile` (to indicate that the database engine doesn't need to cache a plan for this procedure and to compile the procedure at run time).

Fixing the Script

Because you selected to script for a Stand-alone instance and not for SQL Database, the script includes some syntax and statements that aren't supported in SQL Database. Figure 31-7 shows some of the errors you see if you try to run the script as generated.

FIGURE 31-7

Script execution errors.

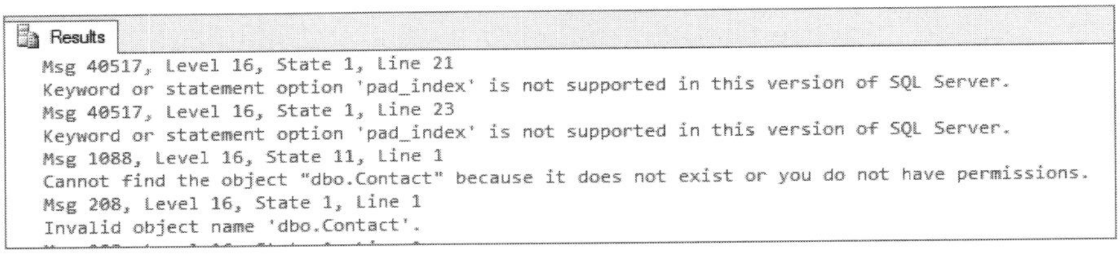

```
Results
Msg 40517, Level 16, State 1, Line 21
Keyword or statement option 'pad_index' is not supported in this version of SQL Server.
Msg 40517, Level 16, State 1, Line 23
Keyword or statement option 'pad_index' is not supported in this version of SQL Server.
Msg 1088, Level 16, State 11, Line 1
Cannot find the object "dbo.Contact" because it does not exist or you do not have permissions.
Msg 208, Level 16, State 1, Line 1
Invalid object name 'dbo.Contact'.
```

Another problem is that SQL Database doesn't support *heap tables*. A heap table is one without a clustered index. SQL Database currently supports only clustered tables.

You need to make some changes for your script to run under SQL Database. Follow these steps:

1. Delete all instances of `SET ANSI_NULLS ON`.
2. Delete all instances of `ON [PRIMARY]`.
3. Delete all instance of `PAD_INDEX = OFF` as well as `ALLOW_ROW_LOCKS = ON` and `ALLOW_PAGE_LOCKS = ON`.
4. In the Users table, modify the `rowguid` column, changing `DEFAULT NEWSEQUENTIALID()` to NULL.
5. In the stored procedure, remove the `encryption` clause.
6. Add a clustered index to any heap tables.

Following is a quick explanation of the reason for the changes you previously made:

- ON [PRIMARY] isn't needed because, as you learned in Chapter 1, "The World of SQL Server," and Chapter 2, "Data Architecture," SQL Database hides all hardware-specific access and information. There is no concept of primary or file groups because disk space is handled by Microsoft, so this option isn't required.
- According to SQL Server Books Online (BOL) you can remove the entire WITH clause that contains the table options. However, the only table options you need

to remove are those listed in step 3 (PAD_INDEX, ALLOW_ROW_LOCKS, and ALLOW_PAGE_LOCKS).

- The newsequentialid() function isn't supported in SQL Database because there is no CLR support in SQL Database, and thus all CLR-based types aren't supported. The newsequentialid() return value is one of those types. Also, the encryption option isn't supported because SQL Database as a whole doesn't yet support encryption.

- SQL Database doesn't support heap tables. Thus, you need to change any heap table into a clustered table by adding a clustered index. (Interestingly, if you execute one statement at a time, you can *create* a heap table. However, any inserts into that table fail.)

A word about the final item in the list. The syntax for defining a clustered index looks like this:

```
CREATE TABLE [dbo].[Contact]
(
    [ContactID] [int] NOT NULL,
    [Name] [nvarchar](25) NOT NULL
PRIMARY KEY CLUSTERED
(
    [ContactID] ASC
)
)
```

After you make the changes just described to your SQL script, it should look like the following:

```
/******Object:  Table [dbo].[Users]    Script Date: 03/31/2010 23:39:20******/

SET QUOTED_IDENTIFIER ON
GO
SET ANSI_PADDING ON
GO
CREATE TABLE [dbo].[Contact](
    [ContactID] [int] IDENTITY(1,1) NOT NULL,
    [NameStyle] [bit] NOT NULL,
    [Title] [nvarchar](8) NULL,
    [FirstName] [nvarchar](50) NOT NULL,
    [MiddleName] [nvarchar](50) NULL,
    [LastName] [nvarchar](50) NOT NULL,
    [Suffix] [nvarchar](10) NULL,
    [EmailAddress] [nvarchar](50) NULL,
    [EmailPromotion] [int] NOT NULL,
    [Phone] [nvarchar](25) NULL,
    [PasswordHash] [varchar](128) NOT NULL,
    [PasswordSalt] [varchar](10) NOT NULL,
    [rowguid] [uniqueidentifier] NOT NULL,
    [ModifiedDate] [datetime] NOT NULL,
```

```
CONSTRAINT [PK_Contact_ContactID] PRIMARY KEY CLUSTERED
(
[ContactID] ASC
)WITH (STATISTICS_NORECOMPUTE  = OFF, IGNORE_DUP_KEY = OFF)
)
GO
```

Now that you've made the necessary corrections, you're ready to create your objects in a SQL database.

Executing a Script Against an Azure SQL Database Instance

In this section you will use the database you created at the beginning of this chapter called AWMini. The following steps will walk you through executing the recently generated script from the Generate Scripts wizard against that database.

1. The query window from the results from the Generate Scripts wizard is currently connected to your local SQL instance, so you need to change it to your SQL Azure Database instance and the database you just created. Right-click anywhere in the script, and select Connection Change Connection from the context menu.

2. In the Connect to Database Engine dialog, enter the information for your SQL Azure Database instance, and enter the name of the database you created earlier on the Connection Properties tab.

3. Click Connect.

You now have your script and a connection to your SQL Azure database instance. Click the Execute button. Your script should run and create the tables, procedures, and data in your SQL Azure Database instance.

The SQL Server Generate and Publish Script Wizard is a great way to start understanding the required changes that you need to make when migrating to SQL Database. With this foundation, consider one of the other options, SQL Server Integration Services.

SQL Server Integration Services

SQL Server Integration Services (SSIS) is a data-integration and workflow-solutions platform, providing Extract, Transformation, Load (ETL) solutions for data warehousing, as well as extractions and transformations. With its graphical tools and wizards, developers often find that SSIS is a quick solution for moving data between a source and destination. As such, it's a great choice for migrating data between a local database and a SQL Azure database instance. Notice, however, that the previous sentence says *data*. When you use SSIS, the database and tables must already exist in SQL Database. If you're familiar at any level with SSIS, you're probably wondering why it has the limitation of moving only data. Several SSIS tasks can provide the functionality of moving objects as well as data, such as the Transfer SQL Server Objects task. When asked about this task, Microsoft replied that SSIS relies on SQL Server Management Objects (SMO) for this task, and SMO currently support a limited subset of SMO functionality in SQL Database. In addition, some of the SSIS connection managers use SMO and therefore are limited when dealing with objects. Thus, the current solution is to create databases and tables using straight SQL and then use SSIS to do the actual data transfer. The following section illustrates how to use SSIS to migrate your data from on-premise SQL to SQL Database.

> **NOTE**
>
> As with the rest of the items in this chapter, you'll be using SQL Server 2012 features, and in SQL Server 2012, Business Intelligence Development Studio (BIDS) has been renamed to SQL Server Data Tools (SSDT).

Creating an Integration Services Project

To create your project, follow these steps:

1. Fire up SQL Server Data Tools by choosing Programs ➪ Microsoft SQL Server 2012 ➪ SQL Server Data Tools.

2. When SSDT opens and the New Project dialog displays, expand the Business Intelligence node and the list of installed templates, select the Integration Services template type, and then select Integration Services Project, as shown in Figure 31-8. Click OK.

FIGURE 31-8

Creating an Integration Services Project.

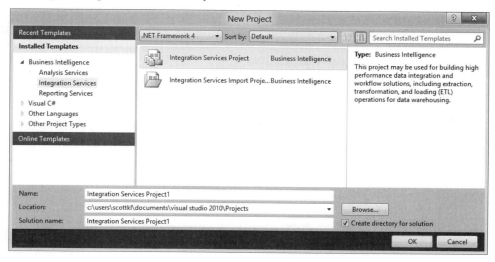

You now see an SSIS package designer surface. This surface has several tabs along the top: Control Flow, Data Flow, Parameters, Event Handlers, and Package Explorer, as shown in Figure 31-9. This example uses the Control Flow and Data Flow tabs.

FIGURE 31-9

SSIS Package Control Flow Surface.

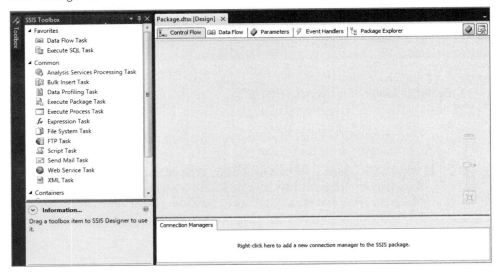

In SSDT, select View ➪ Toolbox. The Toolbox contains a plethora of what are called *tasks*, which are control and data-flow elements that define units of work contained and preformed within a package. You use a few of these tasks to migrate the data from your local database to your SQL Database instance.

Clearing Any Preexisting Data

Clear any data that exists in the SQL database so that you can start with a clean slate. In SSMS, open a new query connecting to the AWMini database, and delete the data from the Contact and Employee tables by executing the following delete statements:

```
DELETE FROM Employee
DELETE FROM Contact
```

All three of those tables should now be empty, as shown in Figure 31-10.

FIGURE 31-10

Verifying Empty Contact and Employee Tables.

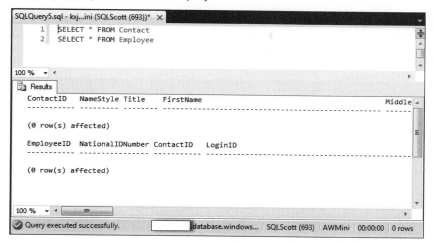

Building a Migration Package

Now it's time to start building an SSIS package to migrate your data. Follow these steps:

1. In the SSIS package designer, select the Control Flow tab, and drag an Execute SQL task and two data flow tasks from the Toolbox onto the Control Flow Designer.

2. Right-click Execute SQL task, and from the context menu, select Edit. The Execute SQL Task Editor opens.

3. Change the task name to **Clear Data**, leave the Connection Type as OLE DB, and leave the SQLSourceType as Direct Input.

4. In the Connection property, select <New connection>, as shown in Figure 31-11. The Configure OLE DB Connection Manager dialog opens, which lists the current connections defined for the package. This list will be empty because there are no defined connections; thus, you need to define a new connection by clicking the New button to open the Connection Manager dialog (see Figure 31-12).

FIGURE 31-11

Creating a New Connection.

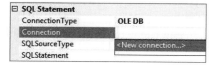

FIGURE 31-12

Defining a New Connection in the Connection Manager for SQL Database.

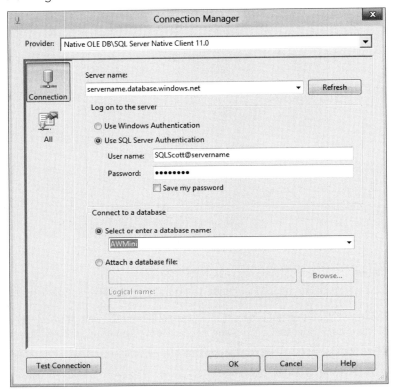

5. In the Connection Manager dialog, enter the server name of your SQL Database server, select Use SQL Authentication, and enter your SQL Database username and password. The username must be in the format *username@server* where *username* is your Administrator username or a valid SQL Database username and *server* is the first part of the server name (the piece prior to `.database.windows.net`).

6. In the Select or Enter a Database Name field, select the AWMini database from the list of databases.

7. Click the Test Connection button. If you correctly entered everything and your firewall is set up, your test connection succeeds.

8. Click OK in the Connection Manager dialog and then click OK on the OLE DB Connection Manager dialog.

9. Back in the Execute SQL Task Editor, click the Ellipsis button in the SQLStatement property to display a small Enter SQL Query dialog in which to enter one or more T-SQL statements. Enter the following DELETE statements, which clear out the data from the previous example. (This isn't critical, but it gives you a clean slate to start with.)

```
DELETE FROM Employee
DELETE FROM Contact
```

10. In the Enter SQL Query dialog, Click OK. The Execute SQL Task Editor dialog should look like Figure 31-13. Click OK.

FIGURE 31-13

Configured Execute SQL Task.

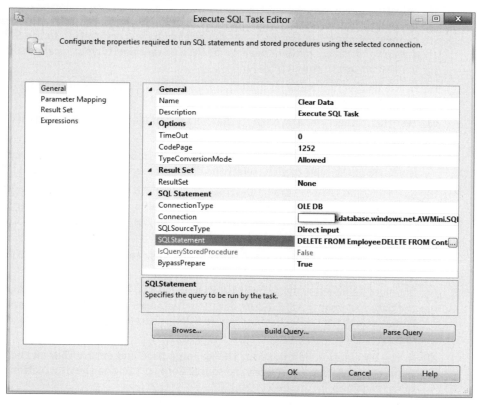

11. Back on the Control Flow tab in the SSIS package designer, make sure the Clear Data task is highlighted. Notice the green arrow coming from the bottom of the

Clear Data task: Click anywhere on this green arrow, and drag it to the first data flow task. Doing so creates a connection from the Clear Data task to the first data flow task, signifying the flow of execution. When the Clear Data task has completed executing, the first data flow task then executes.

12. Now you need to add logic to the first data flow task. Double-click the linked data flow task. (Or right-click and select Edit.) Doing so takes you to the Data Flow tab.

13. From the Toolbox, drag a Source Assistant task onto the designer. This will open the Add New Source dialog, which asks you to define a new data source. This is where the actions of pulling data from the source database (the local DB) and copying it to the destination database (SQL Database) take place. You have several options for data sources to choose from, such as Excel and SQL Server. Select SQL Server and then double-click New from the list of connection managers.

14. Selecting a New connection manager on the Add New Source dialog opens the OLE DB Source Editor, where you define a connection to your local database, such as the connection shown in Figure 31-12. You already have a connection to the SQL Azure database instance, but you need to create a connection to your local database that your tasks use to copy the data.

15. In the Connection Manager dialog, enter the information to connect to your local copy of the AWMini database.

16. Test the connection, and then in the Connection Manager dialog, click OK. This will also close the Source Assistant dialog.

17. Next, right mouse click on the Source task and select Edit from the context menu. In the Name of the table or view, select the Contact table from the list of tables. Click OK.

18. Now from the Toolbox, drag a Destination Task onto the Designer. The Add New Destination dialog will appear, and from this dialog select the SQL Server destination type. You will notice the connection to SQL Database in the list of connections, so select that connection and click OK.

19. Drag the green arrow from the OLE DB Source task to the OLE DB Destination task, as you did for the control flow task.

20. Double-click the OLE DB Source task to edit the task properties, which is where the data is going: the SQL Azure database instance. In the OLE DB Destination Editor, select the Contact table from the drop-down list of tables and click the Keep Identity option.

21. In the Destination Editor, select the Mapping page and ensure that all the columns are appropriately mapped from the source Contact table to the destination Contact table, shown in Figure 31-14. Click OK.

If you're new to SSIS, congratulations: You've just configured your first SSIS data flow. Your data flow should look like Figure 31-15 — not that exciting but useful nonetheless. If you aren't new to SSIS, you still deserve congratulations, because you've successfully configured a data flow to migrate data to the cloud.

FIGURE 31-14

Source to Destination Mapping.

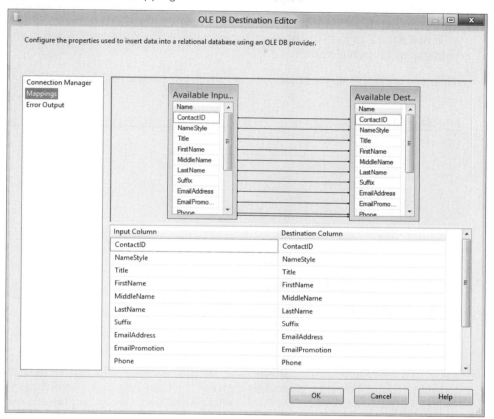

FIGURE 31-15

Completed Data Flow.

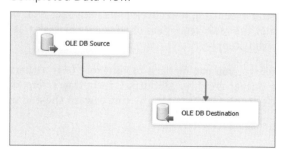

Put down the root beer, though, because you aren't quite done. You still need to configure the second data flow task to copy the data for the Employee table. Go back to the Control Flow designer, connect the first Data Flow task to the second Data Flow task, then configure the second Data Flow task to pull data from the Employee table from the on-premises AWMini database to the SQL Database Employee table. You don't need to define any new connections so it should be quick.

When you are finished, your Control Flow should look similar to Figure 31-16.

FIGURE 31-16

Completed Control Flow.

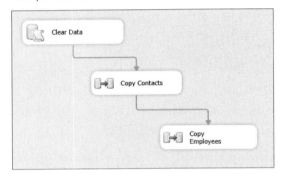

Executing Your Migration Package

You're now ready to test your SSIS package. In SSDT, click the green arrow on the toolbar to begin package execution. Execution starts at the Clear Data task — which, as you recall, deletes all the data from first the Employee table and then the Contact table. Execution next goes to the first data flow, which queries data from the local Contact table (source) and copies it to the AWMini database in the Contact table in SQL Database (destination). Execution then goes to the second data flow task.

When execution is complete, all the tasks show a green check mark, as shown (albeit not in green) in Figure 31-17, letting you know that they successfully executed. Any tasks that have a yellow check mark are currently executing. Red check marks are bad: That means an error occurred during the execution of the task, regardless of whether the task was in the control flow or data flow, and execution stops.

If your tasks have all green check marks, you can go back to your root beer. Otherwise, the best place to start debugging is the Output window. All output, including errors, is written to this window. You can easily find errors by looking for any line toward the end of the list that starts with Error:.

FIGURE 31-17

Successfully executed SSIS Package.

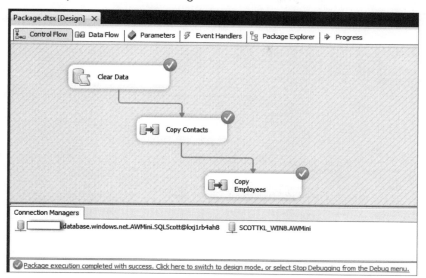

Errors you receive may be SSIS-specific or SQL Database specific. For example, did you correctly define your connections? Microsoft makes testing connections simple, and this doesn't mean the Test Connection button. The Source Editors dialog — regardless whether it's an OLE DB or ADO.NET Editor — includes a Preview button that provides a small preview of your data, up to 200 rows. This ensures that at least your source connection correctly works.

Verifying the Migration

When you have everything working and executing smoothly, go back to SSMS, and query the two tables in your your SQL Database instance. instance to verify that data indeed successfully copied. As shown in Figure 31-18, you should see over 20,000 rows between the two tables.

Other Cases to Consider

This example was simple; the source and destination tables were mirrors of each other, including column names and data types. This made data migration easy. However, in some cases the source and destination tables differ in column names and data types. There are tasks that help with this, such as the `Derived Column`, `Data Conversion`, and `Lookup` tasks. If you use these tasks and get errors, start by looking at these tasks to make sure they aren't the source of data-truncation or data-conversion errors.

FIGURE 31-18

Viewing the Migrated Data.

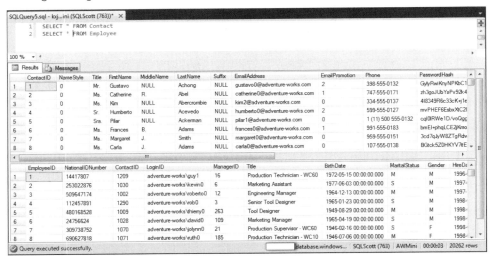

So far, this chapter has covered SSIS and the SQL Server Generate and Publish Scripts Wizard, which both offer viable but different options for migrating your data. For example, SSIS doesn't migrate schema while the Scripts Wizard does. The third tool, bcp, also provides a method for migrating data to SQL Database.

Using bcp Utility

The bcp utility provides bulk copying of data between instances of Microsoft SQL Server. This utility is installed with SQL Server and requires no knowledge or understanding of T-SQL syntax. If you aren't familiar with the bcp utility, don't confuse or associate its functionality with that of the Import/Export Wizard in SQL Server. Although the bcp documentation refers to what bcp does as a "bulk copy," be aware that you can't bcp data from a source into a destination with a single statement. You must first bcp the data out of the source; then, you can bcp the data into the destination.

## 31

> **NOTE**
>
> The bcp utility is flexible and powerful, and you can apply a lot of options to it. This section doesn't go into the entire range of bcp options or dive deep into the many uses of the utility. You can find that information in the SQL Server Books Online or on the Microsoft MSDN web site at `http://msdn.microsoft.com/en-us/library/ms162802.aspx`.

This section describes how to use the bcp utility to export data from a local database and import the data into your Azure SQL Database. It also discusses some things you should watch out for when using the bcp utility for SQL Database.

Invoking BCP

The bcp utility has no GUI; it's a command prompt–driven utility. But don't let that intimidate you, especially given what you're using it for. It's flexible and can seem a bit overwhelming, but it's quite simple. The basic syntax for the bcp utility is as follows:

```
bcp table direction filename -servername -username -password
```
where:

- *table* is the source or destination table based on the direction parameter.
- *direction* is in or out, depending on whether you copy data into the database or out of the database.
- *filename* is the filename you copy data to or from.
- *servername* is the name of the server you copy data to or from.
- *username* is the username used to connect to either the local or SQL Azure database instance.
- *password* is the password associated with the username.

Now start by exporting the data from your source database.

Exporting the Data

Begin by copying data out of your local SQL instance. Open a command prompt, and type the command, as shown in Figure 31-19. Enter your own values for the server name, the target directory, and the username and password for your local server. (The password is blanked out in Figure 31-19.)

In this example you use the out keyword for the direction parameter. That's because you copy data *out* of SQL Server.

The -n parameter performs the bulk-copy operation using the native database data types of the data. The -q parameter executes the set quoted_identifiers on statement in the connection between the bcp utility and your SQL Server instance.

FIGURE 31-19

FIGURE 31-19

Using bcp to export data from the on-premises Contact table.

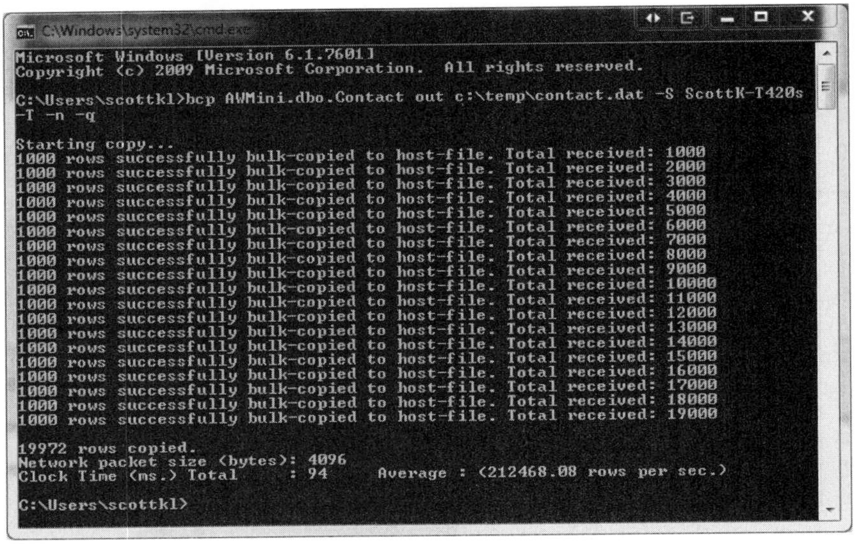

After you type in the command, press the Enter key to execute the bcp utility. In mere milliseconds, nearly 20,000 rows are exported and copied to the `contact.dat` file. Now, do the same for the Employee table.

Importing the Data

The next step is to copy the data into the cloud — specifically, to your SQL Database AWMini database. The syntax for copying *into* a database is similar to the syntax for copying data *out*. You use the `in` keyword and specify the server name and credentials for your SQL Azure database instance, as shown in Figure 31-20.

After you type in the command, press Enter to execute the bcp utility. You can see in Figure 31-20 that nearly 20,000 rows were imported into SQL Database within a matter of seconds. You can use the same process now to import the Employee data.

A word of caution. If you are expecting a large number of rows to be imported but the output states that only a single row was imported, with an unexpected end-of-file (EOF) encountered, this error isn't specific to SQL Database; the bcp utility has issues with columns of the `uniqueidentifier` data type. You can find posts and blogs all over the Internet about this problem.

The solution is to execute the following T-SQL against the table in question in your SQL Azure database instance:

```
alter table tablename
drop column rowguid
```

FIGURE 31-20

Using bcp to import data into SQL Database.

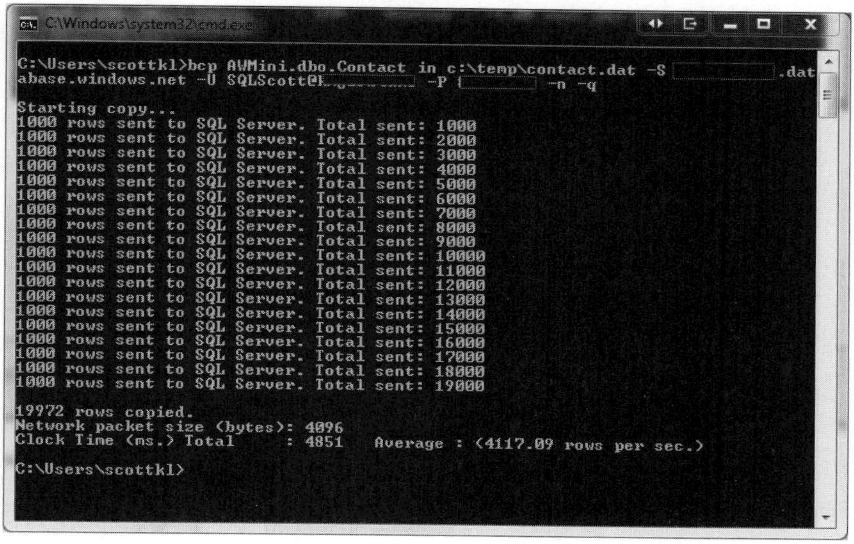

The cool thing is that you don't need to re-export the data. You can re-execute the bcp import command.

Don't forget to put the rowguid column back on the Users table. You can do this by using the same syntax as before:

```
ALTER TABLE tablename
ADD rowguid uniqeidentifier
```

Summary

SQL Database is a big topic; this chapter was not intended to provide a deep examination of SQL Database, but to provide a quick primer into subject, with a focus on data management and the great benefits surrounding this great relational database hosted as a Platform as a Service (PaaS) service.

This chapter began by providing an overview of what SQL Database is and why it exists, as well as the great benefits that come with it, including high-availability and scalability, which are offered as free functionality for the low cost of your database; hard to do in an on-premise environment.

Yet, the majority of this chapter spent some time discussing migration options. Understanding how to migrate your on-premise database to SQL Database becomes all too important. There are a number of options and this chapter highlighted a couple, primarily focusing on the Generate Scripts wizard to provide a method of helping you understand what is supported in SQL Database and better understand the other migration options.

Part VI

Securing Your SQL Server

Authentication Types in SQL Server

IN THIS CHAPTER

Understanding SQL Server Authentication Types

Understanding Advantages, Disadvantages, and Differences between SQL and Windows Authentication

Understanding Kerberos and Windows Authentication Delegation

One of the most important considerations in any deployment of SQL Server 2012 is the authentication type that users and applications use to connect to SQL Server databases. The two authentication types supported in SQL Server 2012 follow:

1. Windows

2. SQL Server

Windows authentication is always enabled and cannot be disabled. SQL Server authentication must be explicitly allowed during setup by choosing Mixed Mode or after setup by modifying SQL Server properties and enabling SQL and Windows Authentication mode. To verify if an instance supports SQL Server Authentication, you may use the SERVERPROPERTY function as shown in following script:

```
SELECT
CASE
        WHEN SERVERPROPERTY('IsIntegratedSecurityOnly') = 1
        THEN 'Windows Authentication Only'
        WHEN SERVERPROPERTY('IsIntegratedSecurityOnly') = 0
        THEN 'SQL and Windows Authentication'
        ELSE 'Configuration Error'
END
```

A value of 1 means the SQL Server instance is configured for only Windows Authentication. A value of 2 means the SQL Server instance is configured for both SQL and Windows authentication. Any other value or a value of NULL means there is an error in the configuration.

You may also check the Authentication mode under the SQL Server properties in SQL Server Management Studio under the Security tab, as shown in Figure 32-1.

FIGURE 32-1

SQL Server authentication in properties.

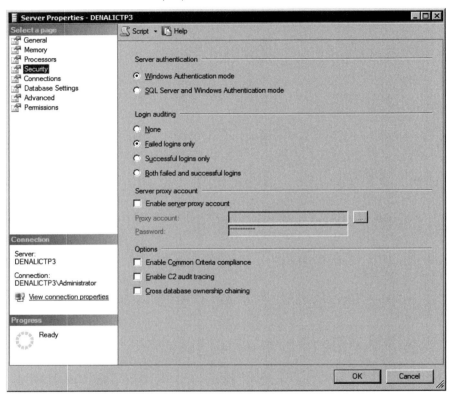

You can change the Authentication mode in SQL Server Management Studio (refer to Figure 32-1) or by modifying the *LoginMode* registry key found under Computer\HKEY_LOCAL_MACHINE\SOFTWARE\Microsoft\Microsoft SQL Server\MSSQL11.MSSQLServer\MSSQLServer\ where MSSQLServer is the instance name. Figure 32-2 shows the LoginMode registry key in the Registry Editor.

You can manually change the LoginMode registry key in the Registry Editor or with the following T-SQL script:

```
EXEC xp_instance_regwrite
N'HKEY_LOCAL_MACHINE',
N'Software\Microsoft\MSSQLServer\MSSQLServer',
N'LoginMode', REG_DWORD, 1
```

FIGURE 32-2

SQL Server LoginMode registry key.

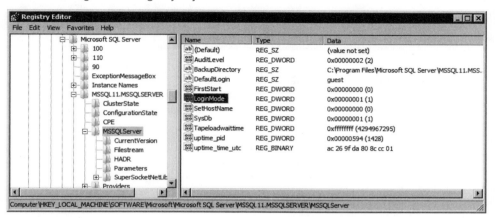

Additionally, you can use PowerShell to change the Authentication mode using the SQL Server Management Objects (SMO) as follows:

```
$srv = new-object Microsoft.SqlServer.Management.Smo.Server
("MySQLServerInstance")
$srv.Settings.LoginMode = [Microsoft.SqlServer.Management.Smo.
ServerLoginMode]::Integrated
$srv.Alter()
```

The next sections provide an overview of both Windows and SQL authentication in more detail.

Windows Authentication

You can use Windows authentication only where Windows Active Directory is used for network and user authentication. SQL Server permits or denies access to a user after its network logon credentials have been validated by a Windows Domain Controller, without requiring a separate login name and password. This authentication type is often referred to as *Windows Integrated Mode* and is considered a Trusted Authentication because SQL Server trusts the credentials provided by Windows.

In Windows authentication, all logins are created, stored, and managed by Active Directory. Active Directory enables central management and enforcement of strong and complex password policies, lockout, and expiration.

When an instance is configured for Windows Authentication mode, SQL authentication is disabled. The default sa (system administrator) account is still created but is disabled.

Best Practice

When changing to SQL authentication and Windows Authentication mode, always remember to create a strong password for the sa account.

Windows authentication has several advantages:

- Central account management and account policy enforcement through Active Directory.
- Support for Active Directory groups.
- Single sign-on experience by Windows authenticated users. You do not need to enter login name and password to connect to SQL Server.
- Less surface area, making it more secure against additional vulnerabilities and exploits.

Windows authentication has several disadvantages as well:

- Non-Windows domain account authentication is not supported.
- No support exists for legacy applications that require a SQL authentication.

SQL Authentication

SQL Server authentication enables users to specify a login name and password to connect to a SQL Server database. The login name and password are created, stored, and managed in SQL Server.

When an instance is configured for SQL Authentication mode, SQL authentication is enabled alongside with Windows authentication. Both Windows and SQL logins are supported.

SQL Authentication mode enables the default sa account. It is important to assign a strong password to the sa account.

Best Practice

If no requirement exists for the sa account to be active, you should always assign a strong password and disable it to prevent malicious attacks that target the sa account.

SQL authentication has several advantages:

- Backward compatibility for applications that require SQL logins and passwords
- Support for environments with mixed operating systems, where not all users are authenticated by a Windows domain
- Ability to deploy SQL Server databases as part of applications that require preset SQL Server logins

SQL authentication has several disadvantages:

- Increased surface area, making it more vulnerable to attacks and exploits
- Additional login name and password required for users to remember
- Limited amount of available password policies
- Additional overhead maintaining and synchronizing SQL logins and passwords across multiple SQL Servers

Differences Between SQL and Windows Authentication

Windows authentication is the recommended authentication method for SQL Server because it is superior to Mixed mode because the user does not need to learn yet another password, and because it leverages the security design of the network.

Using Windows authentication means that users must exist as Windows users to be recognized by SQL Server. The Windows security identifier (SID) is passed from Windows to SQL Server.

Windows authentication is robust in that it authenticates not only Windows users, but also users within Windows user groups.

When a Windows group is accepted as a SQL Server login, any Windows user who is a member of the group can be authenticated by SQL Server. Access, roles, and permissions can be assigned for the Windows group, and they apply to any Windows user in the group.

Best Practice

If the Windows users are already organized into groups by function and security level, using those groups as SQL Server users provides consistency and reduces administrative overhead.

SQL authentication is available only for backward compatibility and should be used only if legacy applications require it or when deploying SQL Server in non-Windows domain environments.

Kerberos and Windows Authentication Delegation

In an enterprise network with multiple servers and IIS, logins can become a problem because a user may be logged in to one server that is accessing another server. This problem arises because each server must have a trust relationship with the others. For internal company servers, this may not be a problem, but when one of those servers sits in an internal network exposed to untrusted networks such as the case of a perimeter network or DMZ (de-militarized network zone) on the Internet for example, you may not want to establish that trust because it presents a security hole.

Security delegation is a Windows feature that uses Kerberos to pass security information among trusted servers.

For example, a user can access IIS, which can access a SQL Server, and the SQL Server sees the user as the username even though the connection came from IIS.

A few conditions must be met for Kerberos to work:

- All servers must run Windows 2000 or later and run Active Directory in the same domain or within the same trust tree.
- Do not select the Account Is Sensitive and Cannot Be Delegated option for the user account.
- Select the Account Is Trusted for Delegation option for the SQL Server service account.
- Select the Computer Is Trusted for Delegation option for the server running SQL Server.
- SQL Server must have a Service Principal Name (SPN), created by setspn.exe, available in the Windows 2000 Resource Kit.

Security delegation is somewhat difficult to set up and may require the assistance of your network-domain administrator. However, the capability to recognize users going through IIS is a powerful security feature. Executing SETSPN to add or delete an SPN does require domain admin rights.

SPN is a powerful security feature, but it does weaken security because the user is impersonated. Therefore, the general warning of its use should be restricted to those cases in which it's absolutely necessary.

Best Practice

If Kerberos implementation is necessary, avoid the use of unconstrained delegation at all costs.

Summary

SQL Server 2012 supports both Windows-only authentication and SQL and Windows authentication. Windows-only authentication is the preferred authentication type because it provides additional security and management advantages. Use SQL authentication for backward compatibility reasons only or in non-Windows domain environments.

32

Authorizing Securables

T his chapter adds another important piece to the SQL Server security puzzle — securables. They include server and objects including databases, tables, and views that you can secure to prevent unauthorized access.

You can perform most security management in SQL Server Management Studio using T-SQL code to grant, revoke, and deny access, through the Data Control Language (DCL) commands and several system-stored procedures.

Permission Chains

In SQL Server databases, users often access data by going through one or several objects. Ownership chains apply to views, stored procedures, and user-defined functions, for example:

- A program might call a stored procedure that then selects data from a table.
- A report might select from a view, which then selects from a table.
- A complex stored procedure might call several other stored procedures.

In these cases, the user must have permission to execute the stored procedure or select from the view. Whether the user also needs permission to select from the underlying tables depends on the ownership chain from the object the user called to the underlying tables.

If the ownership chain is unbroken from the stored procedure to the underlying tables, the stored procedure can execute using the permission of its owner. The user needs permission only to execute the stored procedure. The stored procedure can use its owner's permission to access the underlying tables. The user doesn't require permission to the underlying tables.

Ownership chains are great for developing tight security in which users execute stored procedures but aren't granted direct permission to any tables.

If the ownership chain is broken, meaning that there's a different owner between an object and the next lower object, then SQL Server checks the user's permission for every object accessed.

The EXECUTE AS clause, added in SQL Server 2005, adds flexibility to control effective permissions under which SQL Server objects are accessed in queries, stored procedures, functions, and triggers. While EXECUTE AS provides additional control capabilities, it breaks ownership chaining because the user executing the query, stored procedure, or function impersonates the specified user in the EXECUTE AS clause.

When the chain is broken, the following happens:

- The ownership chain from dbo.A to dbo.B to dbo.Person is unbroken, so dbo.A can call dbo.B and access dbo.Person as dbo.
- The ownership chain from dbo.A to Sue.C to Jose.Purchase is broken because different owners are present. Therefore, dbo.A calls Sue.C using Jose's permissions, and Sue.C accesses Jose.Purchase using Jose's permissions.
- The ownership chain from dbo.A through dbo.B to Jose.Person is also broken, so dbo.A calls dbo.B using dbo's permissions, but dbo.B must access Jose.Purchase using Jose's permissions.
- It is possible for dbo, Sue, and Jose to all have the same owner. In that case, the ownership chain works.

Object Ownership

An important aspect of SQL Server's security model involves object ownership. Every object is contained by a schema. The default schema is dbo — not to be confused with the dbo role.

Ownership becomes critical when permission is granted to a user to run a stored procedure when the user doesn't have permission to the underlying tables. If the ownership chain from the tables to the stored procedure is consistent, then the user can access the stored procedure and the stored procedure can access the tables as its owner. However, if the ownership chain is broken, meaning there's a different owner somewhere between the stored procedure and the table, the user must have rights to the stored procedure, the underlying tables, and every other object in between.

There is a fine point in the details: A schema is owned. And because a schema is owned, anything contained by it has the same owner.

Securables Permissions

The database user can be granted granular permission to specific securable objects using the Securables page of the Database Role Properties form, as shown in Figure 33-1.

FIGURE 33-1

The Securables page is used to grant specific permission to individual objects.

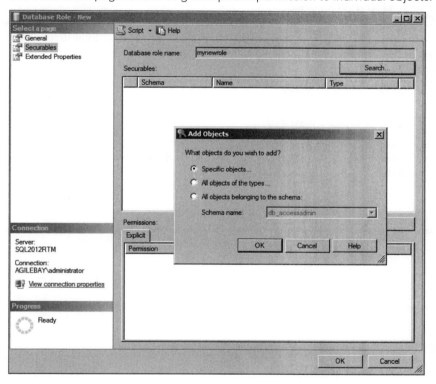

The permissions that can be granted depend on the type of object. Even databases and servers are included as a securable object, which presents several database-specific permissions.

Here is why servers need to be a securable themselves. Having server control is effectively the same as being a member of sysadmin. But if you're auditing only for membership in the sysadmin role and you're not auditing for server-level permissions, you'll never catch when a login is granted such rights. As a result, this is a prime way that attackers would seek to secure elevated access to SQL Server and attempt to keep their tracks a bit more hidden.

Unless you have a compelling reason to manage the permissions on an individual-statement level as with CREATE LOGIN or CREATE USER, it's easier to manage the database administrative tasks using the fixed database roles.

The grant, revoke, and deny commands are detailed in the next section.

Object Security

If the user has access to the database, permission to the individual database objects may be granted. Permission may be granted either directly to the user or to a user-defined role and the user assigned to the role. Users may be assigned to multiple roles, so multiple security paths from a user to an object may exist.

User-Defined Database Roles

User-defined database roles, sometimes called user-defined roles, can be created by any user in the server sysadmin, database db_owner, or database security admin role. These roles are similar to those in user groups in Windows. Permissions, and other role memberships, can be assigned to a user-defined database role, and users can then be assigned to the role.

Best Practice

The cleanest SQL Server security plan is to assign object permissions to user-defined database roles and then to assign users to the roles.

Object Permissions

Several specific types of permissions exist:

- **Select**: The right to select data. Select permission can be applied to specific columns.
- **Insert**: The right to insert data.
- **Update**: The right to modify existing data. Update rights for which a WHERE clause is used require select rights as well. Update permission can be set on specific columns.
- **Delete**: The right to delete existing data.

- **DRI (References):** The right to create foreign keys with DRI.
- **Execute:** The right to execute stored procedures or user-defined functions.

Object permissions are assigned with the SQL DCL commands GRANT, REVOKE, and DENY. The permissions in SQL Server work like they do in the operating system. SQL Server aggregates all the permissions a given user might have whether directly assigned against the user or through the roles. Then SQL Server gives the MAXIMUM of what has been granted. DENY is an exception. DENY functions as a trump. If anywhere a DENY has been issued, then just like in Windows, the user is blocked. For instance, if a user can SELECT against a table directly assigned but a role the user is a member of has a DENY for SELECT, the user is blocked from issuing a SELECT against the table. Whether security is managed from Management Studio or from code, you must understand these three commands.

Granting object permission interacts with the server and database roles. Here's the overall hierarchy of roles and grants, with 1 overriding 2, and so on:

1. The sysadmin server role. (A Windows login that owns a database will be mapped to dbo; because it maps to dbo, it ignores all security on the database.)
2. Deny object permission, the db_denydatareader database role, or the db_denydatawriter database role.
3. Grant object permission or object ownership, the db_datareader database role, or the db_datewriter database role.

Best Practice

An easy way to test security is to configure the server for Mixed mode and create a SQL Server Login test user. Using Management Studio, it's easy to create additional connections as different users — much easier than it is to change the server registration and log in to Management Studio as someone else.

Since SQL Server 2005, it has been possible to create a database principal that does not map to a server principal using the CREATE USER command and specifying WITHOUT LOGIN. Then, using EXECUTE AS USER = '<USERNAME>' to switch security contexts, the security can be tested. REVERT, of course, switches the context back.

If your environment prohibits Mixed-mode security, the easiest way to check security is to right-click Management Studio or Query Analyzer and use the Run As command to run as a different user. But this entails creating dummy users in the Windows domain. Generally speaking, in a "production" Windows domain, most auditors would flag dummy users as an audit point. Because workstations belonging to DBAs tend to belong in production domains, this recommendation wouldn't work where the auditors are diligent.

Granting Object Permissions with Code

Setting an object's permission is the only security command that can be executed without a system stored procedure being called:

```
GRANT [Permission]  ON [Securable]
   TO [User|Role]  [WITH GRANT OPTION]
```

The permission options available for each securable are listed in Table 33-1.

TABLE 33-1 Permission Options by Securable

Securable	Permission Options
Database	BACKUP DATABASE BACKUP LOG CREATE DATABASE CREATE DEFAULT CREATE FUNCTION CREATE PROCEDURE CREATE RULE CREATE TABLE CREATE VIEW
Scalar Function	EXECUTE REFERENCES
Table Table-Valued Function View	SELECT INSERT DELETE UPDATE REFERENCES
Stored Procedure	EXECUTE

The ALL permission option has been deprecated but is still available for backward compatibility reasons.

The User or Role refers to the database username, any user-defined public role, or the public role. For example, the following code grants SELECT permissions to Jose for the Person .Person table of the AdventureWorks2012 database:

```
USE AdventureWorks2012;
GO
GRANT SELECT ON Person.Person TO [AgileBay\Jose];
GO
```

The next example grants UPDATE permissions to the public role for the SalesOrderHeader table:

```
USE AdventureWorks2012;
GO
```

```
GRANT UPDATE ON Sales.SalesHeader TO Data_Analyst;
GO
```

Multiple users or roles, and multiple permissions, may be listed in the command. The following code grants select and update permission to the Developer user and to the DBATeam Windows Group:

```
GRANT SELECT, UPDATE ON Sales.SalesHeader to Developer, Data_Analyst;
```

The WITH GRANT option provides the ability to grant permissions to others for the object specified. For example, the following command grants Jose the permission to select from the SalesHeader table and grants select permission to others:

```
GRANT SELECT ON Sales.SalesHeader TO [AgileBay\Jose] WITH GRANT OPTION;
```

Revoking and Denying Object Permission with Code

Revoking and denying object permissions uses essentially the same syntax as granting permission. The following statement revokes select permissions from Jose on the Sales .SalesHeader table:

```
REVOKE All ON Sales.SalesHeader TO [AgileBay\Jose];
```

If the permission included the WITH GRANT option, then the permission must be revoked or denied with the CASCADE option so that the WITH GRANT OPTION will be removed. The following command denies select permissions from Jose on the Person table:

```
DENY SELECT ON Person.Person TO [AgileBay\Jose]CASCADE
```

Because using CASCADE can revoke not only the WITH GRANT OPTION permission, the DBA can also get rid of the ability to GRANT but must first get rid of the permission including WITH GRANT OPTION and then re-grant the original permission, but this time without specifying the WITH GRANT OPTION.

The Public Role

The public role is a fixed role, but it can have object permissions like a user-defined role. Every user is automatically a member of the public role and cannot be removed, so the public role serves as a baseline or minimum permission level.

> **CAUTION**
>
> Be careful when applying permissions to the public role because it affects everyone except members of the sysadmin role. Denying access to the public role blocks all users, even object owners, from accessing the data. Most importantly, remember that granting access to the public role allows all users to access the data. The exception is any login that maps to dbo and members of the sysadmin fixed server role because they bypass all security permissions.

Managing Roles with Code

Creating user-defined roles with code involves using the sp_addrole system stored procedure. The name can be up to 128 characters and cannot include a backslash, be Null, or be an empty string. By default, the roles will be owned by the dbo user. However, you can assign the role an owner by adding a second parameter. The following code creates the Manager role:

```
CREATE ROLE [Manager]
```

Result:

```
New Manager role added.
```

The counterpart of creating a role is removing it. A role may not be dropped if any users are currently assigned to it. The DROP ROLE command removes the role from the database:

```
DROP ROLE [Manager]
```

Result:

```
Manager role dropped.
```

> **NOTE**
>
> sp_addRoleMember and sp_dropRoleMember are deprecated features. Microsoft advises using ALTER instead.

After a role has been created, users may be assigned to the role by means of the ALTER ROLE command. The following code assigns the Windows login for Jose to the Manager role:

```
ALTER ROLE [Manager] ADD MEMBER [AgileBay\Jose]
```

Result:

```
The Windows login [AgileBay\Jose] added to the Manager role.
```

The ALTER ROLE command is also used to remove a user from an assigned role. The following code removed Jose from the Manager role:

```
ALTER ROLE [Manager] DROP MEMBER [AgileBay\Jose];Result:
```

The Windows login [AgileBay\Jose] removed from the Manager role.

Hierarchical Role Structures

If the security structure is complex, then a powerful permission-organization technique is to design a hierarchical structure of user-defined database roles. In other words, you can nest user-defined database roles.

- The worker role may have limited access.

- The manager role may have all worker rights plus additional rights to look up tables.

- The administrator role may have all manager rights plus the right to perform other database-administration tasks.

To accomplish this type of design, follow these steps:

1. Create the worker role and set its permissions.

2. Create the manager role and set its permissions. Add the manager role as a user to the worker role.

3. Create the admin role. Add the admin role as a user to the manager role.

The advantage of this type of security organization is that a change in the lower level affects all upper levels. As a result, administration is required in one location, rather than dozens of locations.

Object Security and Management Studio

Because object permissions involve users, roles, and objects, they can be set from numerous places within Management Studio. It's almost a maze.

From the Object List

Follow these steps to modify an object's permissions:

1. From an object node (tables, views, stored procedures, or user-defined functions) in the Object Browser, from the context menu select Properties to open the Properties dialog for that object type.

2. Click the Permissions page to open the Object Properties dialog.

As with setting statement permissions on the Database Properties Security tab, you can select grant, with grant, or deny. The object list at the top of the dialog lists all the objects in the database. This list can be used to quickly switch to other objects without backing out of the form to the console and selecting a different object.

The Columns button at the bottom opens the Column Permissions dialog. Select the user, and then click the button to set the columns permission for that user. Only select and update permissions can be set at the column level because inserts and deletes affect the entire row.

From the User List

From the list of database users in Management Studio, select a user and double-click, or select Properties from the right-click context menu. The Database User Properties dialog is used to assign users to roles.

Clicking the Properties button opens the properties of the selected role.

Clicking the Permissions button opens the Permissions tab of the Database User Properties dialog. This dialog is similar to the Permissions tab of the Database Object Properties dialog.

Unfortunately, the list of objects appears to be unsorted, or only partially sorted, and the grid headers don't re-sort the list of objects. This dialog also desperately needs a select all functions and other features, such as those in Access's permissions forms.

From the Role List

The third way to control object permissions is from the database role. To open the Database Role Properties dialog, double-click a role in the list of roles, or select Properties from the right-click context menu. You can use the Database Role Properties dialog to assign users or other roles to the role, and to remove them from the role.

The Permissions button opens the Permissions dialog box for the role. This form operates like the other permission forms except that it is organized from the role's perspective.

A Sample Security Model

The simplest way to assign permissions when more granularity is needed is to create user-defined roles and select effective permissions. Tables 33-2 and 33-3 list sample user-defined roles and user permission settings of the user-defined database roles. Table 33-3 lists a few of the users and their roles.

TABLE 33-2   Sample User-Defined Role Permission Assignment

User-Defined Role	Hierarchical Role Structures	Primary Filegroup Tables	Static Filegroup Tables	Other Permissions
DBTeam	sysadmin server role	-	-	-
DataEntry	-	-	-	Executes permissions for several stored procedures that read from and update required day-to-day tables
Admin	db_owner database fixed role	-	-	-
Customer	-	Select permissions	-	-

TABLE 33-3 **Sample User and Windows Group Role Assignments**

User / Windows Group	Database Roles
Sam	Admin
John	Public
Larry	DBTeam
Clerks (Betty, Tom, Martha, and Mary)	DataEntry

From this security model, the following users can perform the following tasks:

- Betty, as a member of the Clerks Windows group assigned to the DataEntry user-defined role, can execute the application that executes stored procedures to retrieve and update data. Betty can run select queries as a member of the Public role.

- Larry, as part of the DBTeam user-defined role, can perform any task in the database as a member of the sysadmin server role.

- John cannot connect, read, or write data to any database by default as a member of the public role.

- As a member of the Admin role, Sam can execute all stored procedures. He can also manually modify any table using queries.

- Only Larry has unrestricted access to the database server, which includes the ability to modify server and database roles and permission assignments.

Views and Security

A popular, but controversial, method to design security is to create a view that exposes only certain columns, or that restricts the rows with a WHERE clause and a WITH Check Option, and then grants permission to the view to allow users limited access to data. Some IT shops require that all access goes through such a view.

Those opposed to using views for a point of security have several good reasons:

- Views are not compiled or optimized.

- Column-level security can be applied with user-defined SQL Server security.

- Using views for row-level security means that the WITH CHECK OPTION must be manually created with each view. As the number of row-level categories grows, it can become cumbersome to do this type of manual maintenance.

Summary

It's essential to secure the database objects to prevent unauthorized access that may compromise data. SQL Server 2012 provides the ability to create user-defined roles for easier security management. Role-based security enables database administrators to standardize access control over databases and provide a higher degree of granularity of object permissions.

Role-based security is an integral part of the SQL Server security model. This chapter covered securables, and by now you can design, implement, and maintain a robust security model that satisfies your organization's security requirements.

Data Encryption

S ecuring access to the table is usually sufficient (commonly called data protection in motion); if not, securing the column suffices (commonly called data protection at rest). However, for some information, such as Social Security numbers or secret government data, the information's sensitivity warrants further security by encrypting the data stored in the database.

SQL Server 2012 can encrypt data inside SQL Server with passwords, keys, certificates, or transparent data encryption in the Enterprise edition. All editions of SQL Server support data encryption.

What's New with Encryption in SQL Server 2012

■ Transparent Data Encryption (in Enterprise only)

Introducing Data Encryption

Data encryption is the process to transform information using a process that basically makes text unreadable. The data is unreadable to anyone except those who have a special key to decrypt the data. Without the key, the data is impossible to unscramble.

Symmetric encryption uses one key to both encrypt and decrypt the sensitive data in the database.

The same key can encrypt and decrypt the messages, which is considered riskier because of the encryption algorithm. This may not be a problem when encrypting and decrypting data inside SQL Server.

Asymmetric is considered more secure because the decryption key does not need to be known to encrypt. This type of encryption has two keys, one being a private key, which is paired with a second public key. In other words, if I encrypt some data using my public key and you already have my private key, then you can decrypt the data.

Transparent Data Encryption (TDE) is a special kind of encryption using a symmetric key. This type encrypts the entire database using a symmetric key, which is called a database encryption key. Other keys protect the database encryption key or certificates, which are a protected database master key or an asymmetric key stored in an extensive key management module. TDE protects the data at rest, meaning the data and log files. It also enables the ability to comply with many guidelines and regulations established by many different industries.

> **NOTE**
> You should immediately back up the certificates and the private key associated with the certificates when using TDE. If you don't have them backed up you cannot restore or attach the database to another server.

A certificate is a digitally signed security object that is used for containers for keys because they can hold information like an expiration date and issuers. Asymmetric keys are used to secure the symmetric keys and are used for limited data encryption and digitally signed database objects. Certificates are similar to asymmetric keys but are generally issued by an organization, such as VeriSign to certify that the organization associated with the certificate is legitimate. It's possible, and recommended, to generate local certificates within SQL Server for your database encryption and decryption requirements. SQL Server 2012 also enables external key management and hardware security modules to be used by SQL Server internal key and certificate generation algorithms.

The SQL Server Crypto Hierarchy

SQL Server encryption is based on a hierarchy of keys. At the top of the hierarchy is a unique service master key generated by SQL Server for encryption the first time it's needed.

At the next level is the database master key, which is a symmetric key SQL Server uses to encrypt private certificates and asymmetric keys. You create a database master key using the `create master key` DDL command. SQL Server then encrypts the database master using the service master key and stores it in both the user database and the master database:

```
CREATE MASTER KEY
    ENCRYPTION BY PASSWORD = 'P@$rw0rD';
```

The password must meet Windows' strong password requirements.

> **TIP**
> To view information about the master keys, use the `sys.symmetric_keys` catalog view.

Within the database, and below the database master key in SQL Server's cryptographic hierarchy, are certificates and private keys.

To actually encrypt data, SQL Server provides five methods:

- Transact-SQL functions
- Symmetric key
- Asymmetric key
- Certificate
- Transparent Data Encryption

Encrypting with Transact-SQL

The first method to encrypt data is to use T-SQL, similar to a password but without the strong password requirements. The encrypted data is binary so the example code uses a varbinary data type for the membershipcardnumber column. You should test your situation to determine the required binary length.

The actual encryption is accomplished using the `EncryptbyPassPhrase` function. The first parameter is the passphrase, followed by the data to be encrypted. This example demonstrates encrypting data using the `insert` DML command:

```
CREATE TABLE GYM_Membership (
  MembershipCardID INT IDENTITY PRIMARY KEY NOT NULL,
  CustomerID INT NOT NULL,
  MembershipCardNumber VARBINARY(128),
  MembershipExpires CHAR(4)
  );
INSERT GYM_Membership(CustomerID, MembershipCardNumber, MembershipExpires)
  VALUES(1,EncryptByPassPhrase('Passphrase', '99999991111'), '0413');
```

A normal select query views the encrypted value actually stored in the database:

```
SELECT *
  FROM GYM_Membership
  WHERE CustomerID = 1;
```

Result (binary value abridged):

```
MembershipCardID CustomerID  MembershipCardNumber MembershipExpires
---------------- ----------  -------------------- -----------------
2                1           0x010000005FDB9A     0413
```

To decrypt the membership card data into readable text, use the `DecryptByPassPhrase` function and convert the binary result back to a readable format:

```
SELECT MembershipCardID, CustomerID,
  CONVERT(VARCHAR(20), DecryptByPassPhrase('Passphrase', MembershipCardNumber)),
      MembershipExpires
  FROM GYM_Membership
  WHERE CustomerID = 1;
```

Result:

```
MembershipCardID  CustomerID  MembersCardNumber  MembershipExpires
----------------  ----------  -----------------  -----------------
2                 1           99999991111        0413
```

Sure enough, the data decrypted to the same value previously inserted. If the passphrase were incorrect, then the result would have been null.

There is one other option to the passphrase encryption method. An authenticator may be added to the encryption to further enhance it. Typically, some internal hard-coded value unknown by the user is used as the authenticator to make it more difficult to decrypt the data if it's removed from the database.

An example of the importance of using the authenticator option is that if you look at a list of employees where you can read the names of the employees but the salaries are encrypted, you can then update your salary to have the same encrypted value of your CEO and give yourself a nice pay raise. If the company uses the authenticator option, it ensures that it can decrypt and encrypt the data before updating it. If your data is encrypted and you try to update you salary with the CEO's salary value but you can't decrypt or encrypt the data, then you end up with a salary of null!

The following code sample adds the authenticator to the passphrase encryption. The code, 1, enables the authenticator, and the last parameter is the authenticator phrase:

```
INSERT GYM_Membership (CustomerID, MembershipCardNumber, MembershipExpires)
    VALUES(3,EncryptbyPassPhrase('Passphrase','99999992222',
        1, 'hardCoded Authenticator'), '0413');

SELECT MembershipCardID, CustomerID,
    CONVERT(VARCHAR(20),DecryptByPassPhrase('Passphrase', MembershipCardNumber,
        1, 'hardCoded Authenticator')),
    FROM GYM_Membership
    WHERE CustomerID = 3;
```

Result:

```
MembershipCardID  CustomerID  MembersCardNumber  MembershipExpires
----------------  ----------  -----------------  -----------------
3                 3           99999992222        0413
```

Encrypting with a Symmetric Key

Using a symmetric key provides an actual object for the encryption, rather than just a human-readable passphrase. Symmetric keys can be created within SQL Server using the create DDL command:

```
CREATE SYMMETRIC KEY MembershipCardKey
WITH ALGORITHM = TRIPLE_DES
ENCRYPTION BY PASSWORD = 'P@s$wOrD';
```

After the keys are created, they are listed in Management Studio's Object Explorer under the database's Security ⇨ Symmetric Keys node.

Keys are objects and can be altered or dropped like any other SQL Server object.

Encryption Algorithms

The algorithm defines how the data will be encrypted using this key. There are ten possible algorithms: DES, TRIPLE_DES, TRIPLE_DES_3KEY, RC2, RC4, RC4_128, DESX, AES_128, AES_192, and AES_256. They differ in speed and strength.

The Data Encryption Standard (DES) algorithm was selected as the official data encryption method for the U.S. government in 1976, but it can be broken by brute force using today's computers in as little as 24 hours. DESX was incorrectly named and won't be used in future versions of SQL Server. When you would use a Symmetric key created with ALGORITHM = DESX, it actually would use the TRIPLE DES cipher with a 192-bit key. The triple DES (TRIPLE_DES) algorithm uses a longer key and is considerably stronger.

The RC algorithms (such as RC2 and RC4) are a set of symmetric-key encryption algorithms invented by Ron Rivest. They are older, dating back to the mid-'80s, and are fairly easy to break. These will also be removed in future versions of SQL Server like the DESX. So when doing new development, do not use the RC and DESX algorithms. Also make the appropriate modifications to older applications that use those two algorithms.

The National Institute of Standards and Technology (NIST) approved the Advanced Encryption Standard (AES), also known as Rijndael (pronounced "Rhine-dahl"), in November 2001. The 128, 192, or 256 in the algorithm name identifies the bit size of the key. The strongest algorithm in SQL Server's toolbox is the AES_256.

Because the symmetric key might be transported in the open to the client, the key itself can also be encrypted. SQL Server can encrypt the key using one or multiple passwords, other keys, or certificates. A `key_phrase` can be used to seed the generation of the key.

A temporary key is valid only for the current session and should be identified with a pound sign (#), similar to temporary tables. Temporary keys can use a GUID to help identify the encrypted data using the `indentity_value = 'passphrase'` option.

Using the Symmetric Key

To use the symmetric key, the first step is to open the key. This decrypts the key and makes it available for use by SQL Server:

```
OPEN SYMMETRIC KEY MembershipCardKey
    DECRYPTION BY PASSWORD = 'P@s$wOrD';
```

Using the same `gym_membership` table created previously, the next code snippet encrypts the data using the `MembershipCardKey` key. The `EncryptByKey` function accepts the GUID identifier of the key, which can be found using the `key_guid()` function, and the actual data to be encrypted:

```
INSERT gym_membership(CustomerID, MembershipCardNumber, MembershipExpires)
    VALUES(7,EncryptByKey(Key_GUID('MembershipCardKey'),'99999993333'), '0413');
```

To decrypt the data the key must be open. The `decryptbykey` function identifies the correct key from the data and performs the decryption:

```
SELECT MembershipCardID, CustomerID,
    CONVERT(varchar(20), DecryptByKey(MembershipCardNumber)) as MembershipCardNumber,
      MembershipExpires
    FROM gym_membership
    WHERE CustomerID = 7;
```

Result:

```
MembershipCardID   CustomerID   MembershipCardNumber   MembershipExpires
----------------   ----------   --------------------   -----------------
3                  7            99999993333            0413
```

It's a good practice to close the key after the transaction:

```
CLOSE SYMMETRIC KEY MembershipCardKey
```

For most applications, you want to encrypt the data as it goes into the database and decrypt it as it is selected. If you want to move the data to another server and decrypt it there, then both servers must have identical keys. To generate the same key on two servers, the key must be created with the same algorithm, `identity_value`, and `key_phrase`.

Using Asymmetric Keys

Using asymmetric keys involves encrypting and decrypting with matching private and public keys. Generating an asymmetric key is similar to generating a symmetric key:

```
CREATE ASYMMETRIC KEY GymMembershipKey
    WITH ALGORITHM = RSA_512
    ENCRYPTION BY PASSWORD = 'P@s$wOrD';
```

SQL Server supports RSA_512, RSA_1024, and RSA_2048 as possible asymmetric algorithms. The difference is the bit length of the private key.

RSA is an algorithm for public-key cryptography. It is the first algorithm known to be suitable for signing as well as encryption, and one of the first great advances in public key cryptography. Until recently, RSA had not been compromised. In most cases it is still considered secure.

Asymmetric keys can also be generated from existing key files:

```
CREATE ASYMMETRIC KEY GymMembershipKey
   FROM FILE  = ' C:\SQLServerBible2012\ GymMembershipKey.key'
   ENCRYPTION BY PASSWORD = 'P@s$w0rD';
```

Encrypting and decrypting data with an asymmetric key is similar to using symmetric keys except that the key doesn't need to be open to be used.

Using Certificates

Certificates are typically used to encrypt data over the web for HTTPS endpoints. SQL Server includes certificates as they fit into some companies' security standards. Certificates are typically obtained from a certificate authority.

To obtain a certificate from a certificate authority, you must contact them and provide information proving your identity. The information usually includes proof of a business license and proof of ownership of the domain. The most common certificate authorities include Thawte, VeriSign, and GoDaddy.

Summary

Data encryption can provide another level of security beyond authentication. It converts normal data that can be understood to data that cannot be understood. In this way, the wrong parties cannot use the data. SQL Server 2012 gives you many options for data encryption and makes it easy to use.

The next chapter continues the discussion of security. It talks about row level security, which is another necessary tool to keep data safe.

34

Row-Level Security

IN THIS CHAPTER

Extending The Abstraction Layer For Custom Row- Level Security

Implementing The Custom Cell-Level Security

SQL Server is excellent at vertical security (tables and columns), but it lacks the capability to dynamically enforce row-level security. Views, using `with check option`, can provide a hard-coded form of row-level security, but developing a row-based security schema for an entire database using dozens or hundreds of views would create a maintenance headache.

Enterprise databases often include data that is sensitive on a row level. Consider these four real-life business-security rules:

- Material data, inventory-cost data, and production scheduling are owned by a department and should not be available to those outside that department. However, the MRP system contains materials and inventory tracking for all locations and all departments in the entire company.

- HR data for each employee must be available to only the HR department and an employee's direct supervisors.

- A companywide purchasing system permits only lumber buyers to purchase lumber, and only hardware buyers to purchase hardware.

- Each bank branch should read any customer's data but only edit those customers who frequent that branch.

The best possible solution for these requirements is to build the security into the abstraction layer.

Chapter 2, "Data Architecture," made the case for database encapsulation and a strong abstraction layer as a means toward database extensibility. But a strong abstraction layer also enables the security objective.

Implementing a server-side code version of row-level security requires four components:

- **Security table:** Can contain the list of users and their departments, or branches, with their appropriate read-and-write rights

- **Security procedure:** Checks the user's rights against the data requested and returns a status of approved or denied

■ **Fetch procedure:** Checks the security procedure for permission to return the data

■ **Triggers:** Call the security procedure to check the user's right to perform the DML statement on the requested rows

To demonstrate this design, the following topics implement row-level security in the AdventureWorks2012 database. Each person in the `Person` table can be granted read, write, or administer privileges for each location's inventory and sales data. With this row-based security scheme, security can be checked by means of a stored procedure, function, Windows login, and trigger.

Although this is only an example of how to construct row-level security, the concepts here should help you design and develop your own custom row-level security solution.

The Security Table

The `Security` table serves as a many-to-many associative table (junction table) between the `Person` and `Address` tables. The security levels determine the level of access:

0 or no row: 0 access

1: Read access

2: Write access

3: Admin access

Alternatively, three-bit columns could be used for read, write, and administer rights, but the privileges are cumulative, so an integer column seems appropriate.

The `security` table has two logical foreign keys. The foreign key to the `address` table is handled by a standard foreign-key constraint; however, the reference to the `person` table should allow only contacts who are flagged as employees, so a trigger is used to enforce that complex referential-integrity requirement. The security assignment is meaningless without its contact or location, so both foreign keys are cascading deletes. A constraint is applied to the security-level column to restrict any entry to the valid security codes (0–3), and a unique constraint ensures that a person may have only one security code per address:

```
USE Adventureworks2012;


CREATE TABLE dbo.Security (
SecurityID INT IDENTITY(1,1) NOT NULL
    PRIMARY KEY NONCLUSTERED,
PersonID INT NOT NULL
    REFERENCES Person.Person(BusinessEntityID) ON DELETE CASCADE,
AddressID INT NOT NULL
    REFERENCES Person.Address(AddressID) ON DELETE CASCADE,
SecurityLevel INT NOT NULL DEFAULT 0
  );
```

The following three commands add the constraints to the Security table:

```
CREATE TRIGGER PersonID_RI ON dbo.Security

AFTER INSERT, UPDATE
AS
SET NOCOUNT ON;
IF EXISTS(SELECT *
             FROM Inserted
Left JOIN   Person.Person
               ON Inserted.PersonID = BusinessEntityID
             WHERE BusinessEntityID IS NULL
OR Person.Type NOT IN ('EM','SP')
  BEGIN
    RAISERROR
      ('Foreign Key Constraint: Security.PersonID', 16, 1);
    ROLLBACK TRANSACTION;
    RETURN
  END;
GO
ALTER TABLE dbo.Security
  ADD CONSTRAINT ValidSecurityCode CHECK
    (SecurityLevel IN (0,1,2,3));

ALTER TABLE dbo.Security
  ADD CONSTRAINT PersonAddress UNIQUE
    (PersonID, AddressID);
```

Assigning Permissions

Implementing row-level security requires a set of basic admin procedures to set up and maintain the security settings. These procedures handle assigning security levels to users.

Assigning Security

For the Security table to be viewed, the first procedure created is pSecurity_Fetch. This procedure returns all the row-based security permissions, or it can be restricted to return those permissions for a single person or a single address:

```
CREATE PROCEDURE pSecurity_Fetch
  @AddressCode VARCHAR(15) = NULL,
  @PersonCode VARCHAR(15) = NULL
AS
SET NOCOUNT ON;
SELECT p.BusinessEntityID,
a.AddressID,
```

```
    s.SecurityLevel
      FROM dbo.Security AS s
        INNER JOIN Person.Person AS p
          ON s.PersonID = p.BusinessEntityID
        INNER JOIN Person.Address AS a
          ON s.AddressID = a.AddressID
            WHERE (a.AddressID = @AddressCode
                        OR @AddressCode IS NULL)
              AND (p.BusinessEntityID = @PersonCode
                        OR @PersonCode IS NULL);
```

Adding or altering rows in the Security table, which serves as a junction between person and location, in keeping with the theme of server-side code, the pSecurity_Assign stored procedure assigns a security level to the person/address combination. There's nothing new about this procedure. It accepts a person code and address code, and then performs the insert:

```
CREATE PROCEDURE pSecurity_Assign
  @PersonCode VARCHAR(15),
  @AddressCode VARCHAR(15),
  @SecurityLevel INT
AS
  SET NOCOUNT ON;
  DECLARE
    @PersonID int,
    @AddressID int;

  -- Get PersonID
  SELECT @PersonID = BusinessEntityID
    FROM Person.Person
    WHERE BusinessEntityID = @PersonCode;
  IF @@ERROR <> 0 RETURN -100
  IF @PersonID IS NULL
    BEGIN;
      RAISERROR
        ('Person: ''%s'' not found', 15,1,@PersonCode);
      RETURN -100;
    END;

  -- Get AddressID
  SELECT @AddressID = AddressID
    FROM Person.Address
    WHERE AddressID = @AddressCode;
  IF @@ERROR <> 0 RETURN -100;
  IF @AddressID IS NULL
    BEGIN;
      RAISERROR
```

```
            ('Address: ''%s'' not found', 15,1,@AddressCode);
        RETURN -100;
    END;

    -- Insert
    INSERT dbo.Security (PersonID,AddressID, SecurityLevel)
      VALUES (@PersonID, @AddressID, @SecurityLevel);
    IF @@ERROR <> 0 RETURN -100;
    RETURN;
```

With the pSecurity_Fetch and pSecurity_Assign stored procedures created, the following batch adds some test data. The first two queries return some valid data for the test:

```
SELECT BusinessEntityID
  FROM [AdventureWorks2012].Person.Person
  WHERE PersonType IN ('EM','SP')
```

Result:

```
BusinessEntityID
---------------
1
2
```

The next query returns valid locations:

```
SELECT AddressID FROM Person.Address ;
```

Result:

```
AddressID
---------------
33
451
466
467
475
```

Based on this data, the next four procedure calls assign security:

```
EXEC pSecurity_Assign
  @PersonCode = '118',
  @AddressCode = '1',
  @SecurityLevel = 3;

EXEC pSecurity_Assign
  @PersonCode = '119',
  @AddressCode = '1',
  @SecurityLevel = 2;
```

```
EXEC pSecurity_Assign
  @PersonCode = '118',
  @AddressCode = '2',
  @SecurityLevel = 1;

EXEC pSecurity_Assign
  @PersonCode = '120',
  @AddressCode = '5',
  @SecurityLevel = 2;
```

The following two commands test the data inserts using the pSecurity_Fetch procedure. The first test examines the security settings for the '5' location:

```
EXEC pSecurity_Fetch @AddressCode = '5';
```

Result:

```
PersonCode      AddressCode     SecurityLevel
--------------- --------------- -------------
120             5               2
```

The next batch examines the security setting for "Don Hall" (contact code 118):

```
EXEC pSecurity_Fetch @PersonCode = '118';
```

Result:

```
ContactCode     LocationCode    SecurityLevel
--------------- --------------- -------------
118             1               3
118             2               1
```

The row-based security schema includes several constraints. The following commands test those constraints using the stored procedures:

Testing the unique constraint:

```
EXEC pSecurity_Assign
  @PersonCode = '120',
  @AddressCode = '5',
  @SecurityLevel = 2;
```

Result:

```
Server: Msg 2627, Level 14, State 2,
  Procedure pSecurity_Assign, Line 35
Violation of UNIQUE KEY constraint 'PersonAddress'.
Cannot insert duplicate key in object 'Security'.
The statement has been terminated.
```

Testing the valid security-code check constraint:

```
EXEC pSecurity_Assign
  @PersonCode = '118',
  @AddressCode = '5',
  @SecurityLevel = 5;
```

Result:

```
Server: Msg 547, Level 16, State 1,
  Procedure pSecurity_Assign, Line 35
INSERT statement conflicted with COLUMN CHECK constraint
'ValidSecurityCode'. The conflict occurred in database
'AdventureWorks2012', table 'Security', column 'SecurityLevel'.
The statement has been terminated.
```

Testing the employees-only complex-business-rule trigger:

```
SELECT BusinessEntityID
FROM Person.Person
WHERE PersonType NOT IN ('EM','SP')

EXEC pSecurity_Assign
  @PersonCode = '291',
  @AddressCode = '3',
  @SecurityLevel = 3;
```

Result:

```
Foreign Key Constraint: Security.PersonID
```

The next execution of the stored procedure tests the person foreign-key constraint and generates an error because 99999 is an invalid contact.

```
EXEC pSecurity_Assign
  @PersonCode = '99999',
  @AddressCode = '1',
  @SecurityLevel = 3;
```

Result:

```
Server: Msg 50000, Level 15, State 1, Procedure pSecurity_Assign, Line 19
Person: '99999' not found
```

Testing the location-code foreign-key constraint, it's also checked within the stored procedure:

```
EXEC pSecurity_Assign
  @PersonCode = '118',
  @AddressCode = '99999',
  @SecurityLevel = 3;
```

Result:

35

```
Server: Msg 50000, Level 15, State 1, Procedure pSecurity_Assign, Line 30
Address: '99999' not found
```

Handling Security-Level Updates

The pSecurity_Assign procedure used in the previous examples handles new security assignments but fails to accept adjustments to an existing security setting.

The following alteration to the procedure checks whether the security combination of person and address is already in the Security table, and then performs the appropriate insert or update. Security permissions may be created or adjusted with the new version of the procedure and the same parameters. Here's the improved procedure:

```
ALTER PROCEDURE pSecurity_Assign(
  @PersonCode VARCHAR(15),
  @AddressCode VARCHAR(15),
  @SecurityLevel INT
  )
AS
  SET NOCOUNT ON;
  DECLARE
    @PersonID INT,
    @AddressID INT;
  -- Get PersonID
  SELECT @PersonID = BusinessEntityID
    FROM Person.Person
    WHERE BusinessEntityID = @PersonCode;
  IF @PersonID IS NULL
    BEGIN;
      RAISERROR
        ('Person: ''%s'' not found', 15,1,@PersonCode);
      RETURN -100;
    END;
  -- Get AddressID
  SELECT @AddressID = AddressID
    FROM Person.Address
    WHERE AddressID = @AddressCode;
  IF @AddressID IS NULL
    BEGIN;
      RAISERROR
        ('Address: ''%s'' not found', 15,1,@AddressCode);
      RETURN -100;
    END;
  -- IS Update or Insert?
  IF EXISTS(SELECT *
            FROM dbo.Security
            WHERE PersonID = @PersonID
              AND AddressID = @AddressID)
  -- Update
    BEGIN;
```

```
      UPDATE dbo.Security
        SET SecurityLevel = @SecurityLevel
        WHERE PersonID = @PersonID
          AND PersonID = @PersonID;
      IF @@ERROR <> 0 RETURN -100;
    END;

  -- Insert
  ELSE
    BEGIN;
      INSERT dbo.Security
          (PersonID,AddressID, SecurityLevel)
          VALUES (@PersonID, @AddressID, @SecurityLevel);
      IF @@ERROR <> 0 RETURN -100;
    END;
  RETURN;
```

The following script tests the new procedure's capability to modify security permission for a person/address combination. The first command adds security for person 120:

```
EXEC pSecurity_Assign
  @PersonCode = '120',
  @AddressCode = '1',
  @SecurityLevel = 2;

EXEC pSecurity_Fetch
  @PersonCode = '120';
```

Result:

```
PersonCode        AddressCode       SecurityLevel
---------------   ---------------   -------------
120               1                 2
```

The following two commands issue new security permissions and edit existing security permissions. The third command fetches the security permissions for person code 120:

```
EXEC pSecurity_Assign
  @PersonCode = '120',
  @AddressCode = '2',
  @SecurityLevel = 1;

EXEC pSecurity_Assign
  @PersonCode = '120',
  @AddressCode = '1',
  @SecurityLevel = 3;

EXEC pSecurity_Fetch
  @PersonCode = '120';
```

Result:

```
PersonCode        AddressCode       SecurityLevel
```

35

```
-------------   ---------------   -------------
120             1                 3
120             2                 1
```

Checking Permissions

The value of row-level security is actually allowing or blocking reads and writes. These procedures, functions, and triggers are examples of how to build row-level read/write validation.

The Security-Check Stored Procedure

The security-check stored procedure, p_SecurityCheck, is central to the row-based security system. It's designed to return a true or false for a security request for a person, an address, and a requested security level.

The procedure selects the security level of the person for the given location and then compares that value with the value of the requested security level. If the person's permission level is sufficient, then a 1 (indicating true) is returned; otherwise, a 0 (for false) is returned:

```
CREATE PROCEDURE p_SecurityCheck
  @PersonCode VARCHAR(15),
  @AddressCode VARCHAR(15),
  @SecurityLevel INT,
  @Approved BIT OUTPUT
AS
SET NOCOUNT ON;
DECLARE @ActualLevel INT = 0;
SELECT @ActualLevel = s.SecurityLevel
  FROM dbo.Security AS s
    INNER JOIN Person.Person AS p
      ON s.PersonID = p.BusinessEntityID
    INNER JOIN Person.Address AS a
      ON s.AddressID = a.AddressID
  WHERE p.BusinessEntityID = @PersonCode
    AND a.AddressID = @AddressCode;

IF    @ActualLevel < @SecurityLevel
  SET @Approved = CAST(0 AS bit);
ELSE
  SET @Approved = CAST(1 AS bit);

RETURN 0;
```

The following batch calls the p_SecurityCheck procedure and uses the @OK local variable to capture the output parameter. When testing this from the script on the web, try several different values. Use the p_Security_Fetch procedure to determine possible parameters. The following code checks whether person code 118 has administrative privileges at the Charlotte warehouse:

```
DECLARE @OK BIT;
EXEC p_SecurityCheck
  @PersonCode = '118',
  @AddressCode = '2',
  @SecurityLevel = 3,
  @Approved   = @OK OUTPUT;
SELECT @OK;
```

Result:

```
0
```

The Security-Check Function

The security-check function, fSecurityCheck, includes the same logic as the p_Security_Check stored procedure. The advantage of a function is that it can be used directly within an if command without a local variable being used to store the output parameter. The function uses the same three input parameters as the stored-procedure version and the same internal logic, but it returns the approved bit as the return of the function, rather than as an output parameter. Here's the function's code:

```
CREATE FUNCTION dbo.fSecurityCheck (
  @PersonCode VARCHAR(15),
  @AddressCode VARCHAR(15),
  @SecurityLevel INT)
RETURNS BIT
AS
BEGIN;
DECLARE @Approved BIT = CAST(0 AS bit);

IF (SELECT s.SecurityLevel
  FROM dbo.Security AS s
    INNER JOIN Person.Person AS p
      ON s.PersonID = p.BusinessEntityID
    INNER JOIN Person.Address AS a
      ON s.AddressID = a.AddressID
  WHERE p.BusinessEntityID = @PersonCode
    AND a.AddressID = @AddressCode) >= @SecurityLevel
  BEGIN;
  SET @Approved = CAST(1 AS bit);
  END;
```

35

```
RETURN @Approved;
END;
```

The next code fragment demonstrates how to call the function to test security within a stored procedure. If the function returns a 0, then the person does not have sufficient security, and the procedure terminates:

```
-- Check within a Procedure
IF dbo.fSecurityCheck( '118', '2', 3) = CAST(0 AS bit)
  BEGIN;
    RAISERROR('Security Violation', 16,1);
    ROLLBACK TRANSACTION;
    RETURN -100;
  END;
```

Using the Windows Login

Some applications are designed so that the user logs in with the application, and, so far, the row-based security code has assumed that the username is supplied to the procedures. However, if the SQL Server instance is using Windows authentication, then the security routines can use that identification.

Rather than request the contact code as a parameter, the security procedure or function can automatically use suser_sname(), the Windows login, to identify the current user. The login name (domain and username) must be added to the Person table. Alternatively, a secondary table could be created to hold multiple logins per user. Some wide area networks require users to log in with different domain names according to location, so a PersonLogin table is a good idea.

The following function is modified to check the user's security based on her Windows login and a PersonLogin table. The first query demonstrates retrieving the login within T-SQL code:

```
SELECT suser_sname();
```

Result:

```
--------------
SHARK\David
```

The following code creates the secondary table to store the logins:

```
CREATE TABLE dbo.PersonLogin(
PersonLogin UNIQUEIDENTIFIER
    PRIMARY KEY NONCLUSTERED DEFAULT NewId(),
PersonID INT NOT NULL
    REFERENCES Person.Person(BusinessEntityID) ON DELETE CASCADE,
NTLogin NVARCHAR(128) UNIQUE CLUSTERED);
```

With the table in place, a simple insert can populate a single row using my login so that the code can be tested:

```
INSERT dbo.PersonLogin (PersonID, NTLogin)
  SELECT BusinessEntityID, 'SHARK\David'
    FROM Person.Person
    WHERE BusinessEntityID = 118;
```

Check the data:

```
SELECT p.BusinessEntityID, cl.NTLogin
  FROM Person.Person  AS p
    INNER JOIN PersonLogin AS pl
      ON p.BusinessEntityID = pl.PersonID;
```

Result:

```
PersonCode       NTLogin
---------------  --------------
118              SHARK\David
```

The new function you are creating is to join the `PersonLogin` table and to restrict the rows returned to those that match the Windows login name. Because the person code is no longer required, this `select` can skip the person table and join the `Security` table directly with the `PersonLogin` table:

```
CREATE FUNCTION dbo.fSecurityCheckNT (
  @AddressCode VARCHAR(15),
  @SecurityLevel INT)
RETURNS BIT
AS
BEGIN;
DECLARE @Approved BIT = CAST(0 AS bit);

IF (SELECT s.SecurityLevel
  FROM dbo.Security AS s
    INNER JOIN Person.Address AS a
      ON s.AddressID = a.AddressID
    INNER JOIN dbo.PersonLogin AS pl
      ON s.PersonID = pl.PersonID
  WHERE pl.NTLogin = suser_sname()
    AND a.AddressID = @AddressCode) >= @SecurityLevel
  BEGIN;
  SET @Approved = CAST(1 AS bit);
  END;

RETURN @Approved;
  END;
```

To test the new function, the following code fragment repeats the security check performed in the last section, but this time the user will be captured from the Windows login instead of being passed to the function:

```
IF dbo.fSecurityCheckNT('2', 3) = 0
  BEGIN;
    RAISERROR('Security Violation', 16,1);
    ROLLBACK TRANSACTION;
    RETURN;
  END;
```

The function did not return an error, so you can complete the transaction.

The Security-Check Trigger

The security-check stored procedure and function both work well when included within a stored procedure, such as the fetch, addnew, update, or delete procedures mentioned in the beginning of this chapter; but to implement row-based security in a database that allows access from views, ad hoc queries, or direct table DML statements, you must handle the row-based security with a trigger. The trigger can prevent updates, however, it cannot check data reads. If row-based security is a requirement for reads, then all reads must go through a stored procedure or a view.

The following trigger is similar to the security-check function. It differs in that the trigger must allow for multiple orders with potential multiple addresses. The joins must match up [SalesOrderHeader] rows and their address with the user's security level for each location. The join can go directly from the PersonLogin table to the Security table. Because this is an insert and update trigger, any security level below 2 for any order being written will be rejected and a security-violation error will be raised. The rollback transaction command will undo the original DML command that fired the trigger and all other modifications made as part of the same transaction:

```
CREATE TRIGGER OrderSecurity ON Sales.SalesOrderHeader
AFTER INSERT, UPDATE
AS
IF @@ROWCOUNT = 0 RETURN;
IF EXISTS (
SELECT *
  FROM dbo.Security AS s
    INNER JOIN dbo.PersonLogin  AS pl
      ON s.PersonID = pl.PersonID
    INNER JOIN Inserted AS i
      ON i.BillToAddressID = s.AddressID
  WHERE pl.NTLogin = suser_sname()
    AND s.SecurityLevel < 2 )
  BEGIN;
    RAISERROR('Security Violation', 16,1);
    ROLLBACK TRANSACTION;
  END;
```

Summary

SQL Server has a solid reputation for security, but it lacks row-based security. If the database is well architected with a carefully implemented abstraction layer, then adding a custom row-based security schema is not difficult.

This concludes Part VI, "Securing Your SQL Server," which is so critical for production databases. SQL Server security is based on matching privileges between principals and securables, and a chapter was devoted to each side of the equation.

35

Part VII

Monitoring and Auditing

IN THIS PART

Creating Triggers

SQL Server triggers are special stored procedures attached to table events. They can't be executed directly, but fire only in response to an INSERT, UPDATE, or DELETE event on a table. Users can't bypass a trigger; and unless the trigger sends a message to the client, the end user is unaware of its actions.

Developing well-behaved triggers involves understanding transaction flow, locking, T-SQL, and stored procedures. Triggers have a few unique elements that require careful planning, but they provide execution of complex business rules and data validation.

Trigger Basics

SQL Server triggers fire once per data-modification operation, not once per affected row. This may seem to be a limitation, but developing set-based triggers actually helps ensure clean logic and fast performance.

Triggers may be created for the three data-modification commands: INSERT, UPDATE, and DELETE.

Best Practice

For data integrity, sometimes a trigger is the best solution, but be aware of the potential performance impact. You should consider having business rules enforced by application code instead and only use triggers when this is not feasible.

SQL Server has two kinds of transaction triggers: *instead of triggers* and *after triggers*. They differ in their purpose, timing, and effect, as detailed in Table 36-1.

TABLE 36-1 Trigger Type Comparison

	Instead of Trigger	After Trigger
DML statement	Simulated but not executed	Executed, but can be rolled back in the trigger
Timing	Before PK and FK constraints	After the transaction is complete, but before it is committed
Number per table event	One	Multiple
May be applied to views?	Yes	No
Nested?	Depends on server option; however, Nested INSTEAD OF Triggers will always fire.	Depends on server option
Recursive?	Only for INSTEAD OF Triggers	Depends on database option

Transaction Flow

Triggers affect the transactional state in which they're fired. Knowing these effects can prevent conflicts with constraints, locking, and blocking on the affected tables.

Every transaction invokes various checks in the following order:

1. IDENTITY INSERT check.

2. Nullability constraint.

3. Data-type check.

4. INSTEAD OF trigger execution. If an INSTEAD OF trigger exists, then execution of the DML stops here. INSTEAD OF triggers are not recursive. (Recursive triggers are covered later .)

5. Primary-key constraint.

6. Check constraints.

7. Foreign-key constraints.

8. DML execution and update to the transaction log.

9. AFTER trigger execution.

10. Commit transaction.

Based on SQL Server's transaction flow, keep the following points in mind:

- An AFTER trigger occurs after all constraints are enforced. If a constraint is violated, then AFTER triggers are not fired.

- An INSTEAD OF trigger can circumvent foreign-key violations but not nullability, data-type, or identity-column violations.

- The AFTER trigger occurs before the DML transaction is committed, so it can roll back the transaction if the data is unacceptable.

Creating Triggers

A trigger can be fired for any combination of insert, update, or delete events. Triggers are created and modified with the standard DDL commands, CREATE, ALTER, and DROP, as follows:

```
CREATE TRIGGER Schema.TriggerName ON Schema.TableName
AFTER | INSTEAD OF [Insert, Update, (and or) Delete]
AS
Trigger Code;
```

You can also create, view and modify triggers using Management Studio's Object Explorer, as shown in Figure 36-1.

After Triggers

A table may have one or more AFTER triggers on each of the DML events. AFTER triggers cannot be applied to views.

AFTER triggers are useful for the following:

- Complex data validation or business rules
- Writing data-audit trails
- Maintaining modification tracking columns
- Enforcing custom referential-integrity or cascading actions

FIGURE 36-1

Object Explorer lists all triggers for any table and may be used to modify the trigger using the context menu.

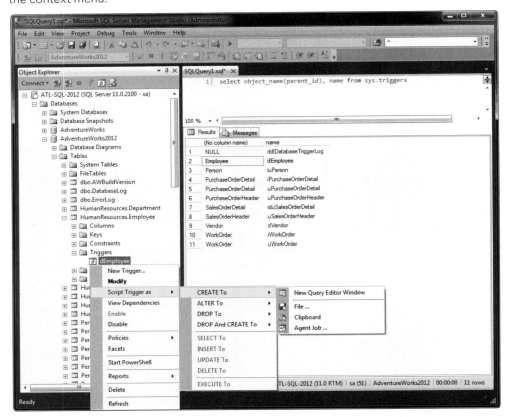

Best Practice

When planning triggers, consider the most likely path. If the trigger verifies data that will nearly always be accepted, then an AFTER trigger is optimal. In this case the trigger is merely a check.

For inserts, updates, or deletes that are rarely accepted, use an INSTEAD OF trigger, which substitutes the DML statement's work.

The following AFTER trigger simply prints 'In the After Trigger' when the trigger executes:

```
USE AdventureWorks2012;

CREATE TRIGGER HumanResources.TriggerOne ON
[HumanResources].[Department]

AFTER INSERT
AS
PRINT 'In the After Trigger';
```

With the AFTER trigger enforced, the following code inserts a sample row:

```
INSERT [HumanResources].[Department](Name, GroupName)
  VALUES ('Data Management', 'Hording & Forecasting');
```

Result:

In the After Trigger

```
(1 row(s) affected)
```

The INSERT worked and the trigger printed the message.

Instead of Triggers

INSTEAD OF triggers execute "instead of" (as a substitute for) the submitted DML statement. This is why such triggers are not classified as BEFORE triggers because they preempt the statement's normal execution.

As a substitution procedure, each table is limited to only one INSTEAD OF trigger per table event. In addition, INSTEAD OF triggers may be applied to views as well as tables.

INSTEAD OF triggers are useful when the DML statement firing the trigger will always be rolled back and some other logic will be executed *instead of* the DML statement, for example:

- When the DML statement attempts to update a nonupdatable view, the INSTEAD OF trigger updates the underlying tables instead.
- When the DML statement attempts to directly update an inventory table, an INSTEAD OF trigger updates the inventory transaction table instead.
- When deleting rows, an INSTEAD OF trigger moves them to an archive table instead.

The following code creates a test INSTEAD OF trigger and then attempts to INSERT a row:

```
CREATE TRIGGER HumanResources.TriggerTwo ON
[HumanResources].[Department]

INSTEAD OF INSERT
AS
PRINT
'In the Instead of Trigger';
go

INSERT [HumanResources].[Department](Name, GroupName)
  VALUES ('Datum Management', 'Hording & Forecasting');
```

Result:

```
In the Instead of Trigger

(1 row(s) affected)
```

The result includes the INSTEAD OF trigger's message and a report that one row was affected. However, selecting Name = 'Datum Management' can prove that no rows were inserted:

```
SELECT
[GroupName]

  FROM
[HumanResources].[Department]

  WHERE
[Name]
=
'Datum Management'
;
Result:
GroupName
---------------

(0 row(s) affected)
```

The INSERT statement worked as if one row were affected; although the effect of the INSERT statement was preempted by the INSTEAD OF trigger. The PRINT command was executed instead of the rows being inserted. In addition, the AFTER trigger is still in effect, but its PRINT message failed to print.

Trigger Limitations

Given their nature (code attached to tables), DML triggers have a few limitations. The following SQL commands are not permitted within a trigger:

- CREATE, ALTER, or DROP database
- RECONFIGURE
- RESTORE database or log

Disabling Triggers

DML statements cannot bypass a trigger, but a system administrator, database owner, or table owner can temporarily disable it.

> **WARNING**
>
> Disabling a trigger occurs on the table, not just the current connection or the current user. This could have unintended consequences and should not be undertaken lightly.

To temporarily turn off a trigger, use the ALTER TABLE DDL command with the ENABLE TRIGGER or DISABLE TRIGGER option:

```
ALTER TABLE schema.TableName ENABLE or DISABLE TRIGGER
    schema.TriggerName;
```

For example, the following code disables the INSTEAD OF trigger (TriggerOne on the Person table):

```
ALTER TABLE HumanResources.Department

DISABLE TRIGGER TriggerOne;
```

To view the enabled status of a trigger, use the OBJECTPROPERTY() function, passing to it the object ID of the trigger and the ExecIsTriggerDisabled option:

```
SELECT OBJECTPROPERTY(
    OBJECT_ID(' HumanResources.TriggerOne'), 'ExecIsTriggerDisabled');
```

Listing Triggers

The following query lists all the triggers in the database based on the sys.triggers catalog view:

```
USE AdventureWorks2012
GO

SELECT Sc.name + '.'' + Ob.name as [table],
  Tr.name as [trigger],
    CASE (Tr.is_instead_of_trigger )
    WHEN 0 THEN 'after'
    WHEN 1 THEN 'instead of'
  END AS type,
  CASE (Tr.is_disabled)
    WHEN 0 THEN 'enabled'
```

```
            WHEN 1 THEN 'disabled'
       END AS status
    FROM sys.triggers Tr
       JOIN sys.objects Ob
         ON Tr.parent_id = Ob.object_id
       JOIN sys.schemas Sc
         ON Ob.schema_id = Sc.schema_id
      WHERE Tr.type = 'TR' and Tr.parent_class = 1
      ORDER BY Sc.name + '.' + Ob.name, Tr.name
```

Result:

```
table                            trigger               type        status
-----------------------------    --------------------  ----------  -------
HumanResources.Employee          dEmployee             instead of  enabled
Person.Person                    iuPerson              after       enabled
Production.WorkOrder             iWorkOrder            after       enabled
Production.WorkOrder             uWorkOrder            after       enabled
Purchasing.PurchaseOrderDetail   iPurchaseOrderDetail  after       enabled
Purchasing.PurchaseOrderDetail   uPurchaseOrderDetail  after       enabled
Purchasing.PurchaseOrderHeader   uPurchaseOrderHeader  after       enabled
Purchasing.Vendor                dVendor               instead of  enabled
Sales.SalesOrderDetail           iduSalesOrderDetail   after       enabled
Sales.SalesOrderHeader           uSalesOrderHeader     after       enabled
```

Triggers and Security

Only the table or view owner, members of the sysadmin fixed server role, or the dbowner or ddldmin fixed database roles have permission to create, alter, drop, enable, or disable triggers.

A trigger executes under the security context of the owner of their parent object unless modified with the EXECUTE AS clause when the trigger is created or altered.

Working with the Transaction

SQL Server provides several ways for the trigger to determine the effects of the DML statement. The first two methods are the UPDATE() and columns_updated() functions, which are used to determine which columns were potentially affected by the DML statement. The other methods use deleted and inserted images, which contain the before and after data sets.

Determining the Updated Columns

SQL Server provides the UPDATE() function to test if a single column is affected by the DML transaction:

```
IF UPDATE(ColumnName)
```

Because an INSERT affects all columns, the UPDATE() function returns true for any column you pass. Conversely, UPDATE() always returns false for a DELETE. The following example demonstrates the UPDATE() function:

```
ALTER TRIGGER HumanResources.TriggerOne ON
HumanResources.Department

AFTER INSERT, UPDATE
AS
IF Update(GroupName)
  BEGIN;
  PRINT 'You might have modified the GroupName column';
  END;
ELSE
  BEGIN;
  PRINT 'The GroupName column is untouched.';
  END;
```

With the trigger looking for changes to the LastName column, the following DML statement tests the trigger:

```
UPDATE
HumanResources.Department

  SET GroupName = 'Forecasting & Analytics
'
  WHERE
Name =
'Data Management';
```

Result:

```
You might have modified the GroupName column
```

Note that the UPDATE() function returns true even if the column is updated with the same value, for example, from 'abc' to 'abc'.

The columns_updated() function returns a bitmapped varbinary data type representation of the columns updated. If the bit is true, then the column is updated. The result of columns_updated() can be compared with integer or binary data by means of the bitwise operators to determine whether a given column is updated.

The columns are represented by right-to-left bits within left-to-right bytes. A further complication is that the size of the varbinary data returned by columns_updated() depends on the number of columns in the table.

The following function simulates the actual behavior of the columns_updated() function. Passing the column to be tested and the total number of columns in the table returns the column bitmask for that column:

```
CREATE FUNCTION dbo.GenColUpdated
  (@Col INT, @ColTotal INT)
RETURNS INT
AS
BEGIN;
-- Copyright 2001 Paul Nielsen
-- This function simulates the Columns_Updated() behavior
DECLARE
  @ColByte INT,
  @ColTotalByte INT,
  @ColBit INT;

  -- Calculate Byte Positions
SET @ColTotalByte =     1 + ((@ColTotal-1) /8);
SET @ColByte = 1 + ((@Col-1)/8);
SET @ColBit = @Col - ((@ColByte-1) * 8);

  RETURN Power(2, @ColBit + ((@ColTotalByte-@ColByte) * 8)-1);
END;
```

To use this function, perform a bitwise AND (&) between columns_updated() and
GenColUpdated(). If the bitwise and is equal to GenColUpdated(), then the column in
question is indeed updated:

```
. . .
If COLUMNS_UPDATED() & dbo.GenColUpdated(@ColCounter,@ColTotal) =
@ColUpdatedTemp
```

Inserted and Deleted Logical Tables

SQL Server provides the inserted and deleted logical tables as read-only images of the
data affected by the DML statement. The deleted table contains the version of the rows
before and the inserted table version after the effects of the DML statement, as shown in
Table 36-2.

TABLE 36-2 **Inserted and Deleted Tables**

DML Statement	Inserted Table	Deleted Table
Insert	Rows being inserted	Empty
Update	Row versions after update	Rows versions before update
Delete	Empty	Rows being deleted

The scope of the `inserted` and `deleted` tables is limited to the trigger. Stored procedures called by the trigger will not see these tables. The DML statement that fired the trigger can output the `inserted` and `deleted` tables using the OUTPUT clause.

 For more details on the OUTPUT clause, refer to Chapter 12, "Modifying Data in SQL Server."

The following example uses the `inserted` table to report the new values for the `GroupName` column:

```
ALTER TRIGGER HumanResources.TriggerOne ON
HumanResources.Department

AFTER UPDATE
AS
SET NOCOUNT ON;

IF Update(GroupName)
   SELECT 'You modified the GroupName column to '
   + Inserted.GroupName
   FROM Inserted;
```

With `TriggerOne` implemented on the `Person` table, the following update modifies a `GroupName` value:

```
UPDATE
HumanResources.Department

  SET GroupName = '
Analytics & Guessing
'
  WHERE Name =
'Data Management';
```

Result:

```
----------------------------------------------------
You modified the GroupName column to
Analytics & Guessing

 (1 row(s) affected)
```

Developing Multiple Row-Enabled Triggers

Many people do not write triggers to handle multiple-row INSERT, UPDATE, or DELETE operations. They take a value from the `inserted` or `deleted` table and store it in a local variable for processing. This technique checks only one of the rows affected by the DML statement — a serious data integrity flaw. They'll even use cursors to step through each affected row. This is the type of slow code that gives triggers a bad name.

Best Practice

The best way to deal with multiple rows is to work with the `inserted` and `deleted` tables via set-oriented operations.

A join between the `inserted` table and the `deleted` or underlying table returns a complete set of the rows affected by the DML statement. Table 36-3 lists the correct join combinations for creating multirow-enabled triggers.

TABLE 36-3 **Multirow-Enabled FROM Clauses**

DML Type	FROM Clause
Insert	FROM Inserted
Update	FROM Inserted
	INNER JOIN Deleted
	ON Inserted.PK = Deleted.PK
Delete	FROM Deleted

The following trigger sample alters `TriggerOne` to look at the `inserted` and `deleted` tables:

```
ALTER TRIGGER HumanResources.TriggerOne ON
HumanResources.Department

AFTER UPDATE
AS
SELECT D.GroupName + ' changed to ' + I.GroupName
  FROM Inserted AS I
    INNER JOIN Deleted AS D
      ON I.DepartmentID = D.DepartmentID
GO

UPDATE
HumanResources.Department

  SET GroupName = '
Guessing & PowerPoints
'
  WHERE GroupName = '
```

```
    Analytics & Guessing
    ';
```

Result:

```
    ------------------------------------------
    Analytics & Guessing
     changed to
    Guessing & PowerPoints

    (1 row(s) affected)
```

The following AFTER trigger in the Family sample database enforces a rule that the FatherID points to a valid person (covered by the foreign key)and who also must be male:

```
CREATE TRIGGER HumanResources.Empolyee_OrgNode
ON HumanResources.Employee
AFTER INSERT, UPDATE
AS
IF UPDATE(OrganizationNode)
  BEGIN;
    -- Incorrect Father Gender
    IF EXISTS(
        SELECT *
          FROM HumanResources.Employee emp
            INNER JOIN Inserted
              ON Inserted.OrganizationNode = emp.OrganizationNode
          WHERE emp.OrganizationLevel = 0x)
      BEGIN;
        ROLLBACK;
        RAISERROR('Incorrect OrganizationNode for Chief Executive
          Officer',14,1);
        RETURN;
      END;
  END;
```

Multiple-Trigger Interaction

Multiple triggers can become disorganized and extremely difficult to troubleshoot unless they are carefully planned and their effects understood.

Trigger Organization

It is recommended that triggers be organized not by table event, but by the trigger's task, including the following:

- Data validation
- Complex business rules

- Audit trail
- Modified date
- Complex security

Nested Triggers

Trigger nesting refers to whether a DML trigger can cause another trigger to fire. For example, if the Nested Triggers server option is enabled, and a trigger updates `TableA`, and `TableA` also has a trigger, then any triggers on `TableA` can also fire, as shown in Figure 36-2.

FIGURE 36-2

The Nested Triggers configuration option enables a DML statement within a trigger to fire additional triggers.

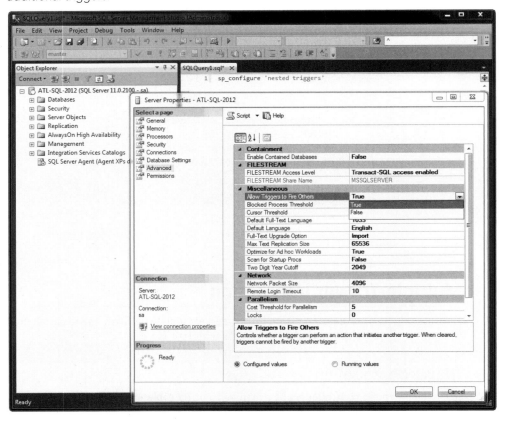

By default, the Nested Triggers option is enabled. Use the following configuration command to disable trigger nesting:

```
EXEC sp_configure 'Nested Triggers', 0;
RECONFIGURE;
```

SQL Server triggers have a limit of 32 levels of recursion and generate a fatal error when exceeded. You can test the trigger's nesting level with the `Trigger_NestLevel()` function to avoid this condition.

Recursive Triggers

A recursive trigger is a unique type of nested `AFTER` trigger. If a trigger executes a DML statement that causes itself to fire, then it's a recursive trigger (see Figure 36-3). If the database recursive triggers option is off, then the recursive iteration of the trigger won't fire. (Note that nested triggers is a server option, whereas recursive triggers is a database option.)

FIGURE 36-3

A recursive trigger is a self-referencing trigger — one that executes a DML statement that causes itself to be fired again.

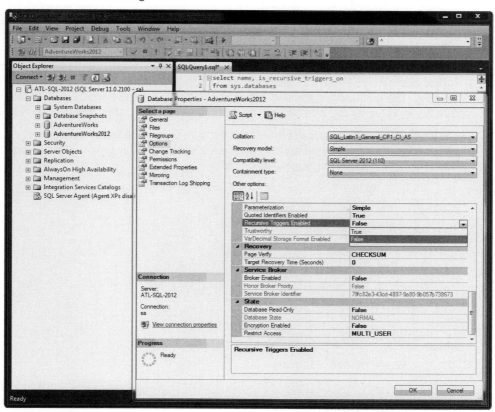

A trigger is considered recursive only if it directly fires itself. If the trigger executes a stored procedure that then updates the trigger's table, then that is an indirect recursive call, which is not covered by the recursive-trigger database option.

Recursive triggers are enabled with ALTER DATABASE:

```
ALTER DATABASE DatabaseName SET RECURSIVE_TRIGGERS ON | OFF ;
```

Practically speaking, recursive triggers are rare.

One example that involves recursion is a ModifiedDate trigger. This trigger writes the current date and time to the modified column for any row that's updated. Using the AdventureWorks2012sample database, this script first adds a Created and Modified column to the department table:

```
USE AdventureWorks2012;

ALTER TABLE [HumanResources].[Department]
  ADD
    Created SmallDateTime NOT NULL DEFAULT CURRENT_TIMESTAMP,
    Modified SmallDateTime NOT NULL DEFAULT CURRENT_TIMESTAMP;
```

If recursive triggers are enabled, then this trigger might become a runaway trigger, and after 32 levels of recursion will error out.

The trigger in the following example prints the Trigger_NestLevel() level. This is helpful for debugging nested or recursive triggers, but it should be removed when testing has finished. The second if statement prevents the Created and Modified date from being directly updated by the user. If the trigger is fired by a user, then the nest level is 1.

The first time the trigger is executed, the UPDATE is executed. Any subsequent executions of the trigger RETURN because the trigger nest level is greater than 1. This prevents runaway recursion. Here's the trigger DDL code:

```
CREATE TRIGGER Products_ModifiedDate ON Production.Product
AFTER UPDATE
AS
IF @@ROWCOUNT = 0
  RETURN;

If Trigger_NestLevel() > 1
Return;

SET NOCOUNT ON;

PRINT TRIGGER_NESTLEVEL();

If (UPDATE(ModifiedDate))

Begin;
```

```
    Raiserror('Update failed.', 16, 1);
    ROLLBACK;
    Return;
  End;

  -- Update the Modified date
  UPDATE Production.Product
    SET ModifiedDate = CURRENT_TIMESTAMP
    WHERE EXISTS
      (SELECT *
       FROM Inserted AS i
       WHERE i.ProductID = Product.ProductID);
```

To test the trigger, the next INSERT command causes the trigger to print out a message after a row has been inserted:

```
UPDATE Production.Product
  SET [Name] = 'ModifiedDate Trigger'
  WHERE ProductID = 999;

SELECT ProductID, ModifiedDate
  FROM Production.Product
 WHERE ProductID = 999;
```

Result:

```
ProductID     ModifiedDate
999           2012-03-04 15:52:23.800
```

Instead Of and After Triggers Used Together

If a table has both an INSTEAD OF trigger and an AFTER trigger for the same event, then the following sequence is possible:

1. The DML statement initiates a transaction.

2. The INSTEAD OF trigger fires in place of the DML.

3. If the INSTEAD OF trigger executes DML against the same table event, then the process continues.

4. The AFTER trigger fires.

Multiple After Triggers

If the same table event has multiple AFTER triggers, then they all execute. The order of the triggers is less important than it may at first seem.

Every trigger has the opportunity to ROLLBACK the transaction. If the transaction is rolled back, then all the work done by the initial transaction and all the triggers are rolled back. Any triggers that had not yet fired won't fire because the original DML is aborted by the ROLLBACK.

Nevertheless, it is possible to designate an AFTER trigger to fire first or last in the list of triggers. Do this only if one trigger is likely to roll back the transaction and, for performance reasons, you want that trigger to execute before other demanding triggers. Logically, however, the order of the triggers has no effect.

The sp_settriggerorder system stored procedure is used to assign the trigger order using the following syntax:

```
sp_settriggerorder
  @triggername = 'TriggerName',
  @order = 'first' or 'last' or 'none',
  @stmttype = 'INSERT' or 'UPDATE' or 'DELETE'
```

The effect of setting the trigger order is not cumulative if they are both for the same action. For example, setting TriggerOne to first and then setting TriggerTwo to first does not place TriggerOne in second place. In this case, TriggerOne returns to being unordered.

Transaction-Aggregation Handling

Triggers can maintain denormalized aggregate data.

A common example of this is an inventory system that records every individual transaction in an InventoryTransaction table, calculates the inventory quantity on hand, and stores the calculated quantity-on-hand in the Inventory table for performance.

 Index views are another excellent solution to consider for maintaining aggregate data. They're documented in Chapter 45, "Indexing Strategies."

To protect the integrity of the Inventory table, implement the following logic rules when using triggers:

- The quantity on hand in the Inventory table should not be updatable by any process other than the inventory transaction table triggers. Any attempt to directly update the Inventory table's quantity should be recorded as a manual adjustment in the InventoryTransaction table.

- Inserts in the InventoryTransaction table should write the current on-hand value to the Inventory table.

- The InventoryTransaction table should not allow updates. If an error is inserted into the InventoryTransaction table, an adjusting entry should be made to correct the error.

The AdventureWorks2012 database includes a simplified inventory system. To demonstrate transaction-aggregation handling, the following triggers implement the required rules. The first script creates a sample valid inventory item for test purposes:

```
USE AdventureWorks2012;

DECLARE
  @ProdID INT,
  @LocationID INT;

SELECT @ProdID  = ProductID
  FROM Production.Product
  WHERE ProductID = 998;
SELECT @LocationID = LocationID
  FROM Production.Location
  WHERE LocationID = 50;

INSERT Production.ProductInventory (ProductID, Shelf, Bin, LocationID)
  VALUES (@ProdID, 'A', 0, @LocationID);

SELECT P.ProductID, I.Shelf, I.Quantity, I.LocationID
  FROM Production.ProductInventory AS I
  INNER JOIN Production.Product AS P
    ON I.ProductID = P.ProductID
  WHERE P.ProductID = 998;
```

Result:

ProductID	Shelf	Quantity	LocationID
998	N/A	99	7
998	A	0	50
998	N/A	56	60

The Inventory-Transaction Trigger

The inventory-transaction trigger performs the aggregate function of maintaining the current quantity-on-hand value in the Inventory table. With each row inserted into the InventoryTransaction table, the trigger updates the Inventory table. The JOIN between the Inserted image table and the Inventory table enables the trigger to handle multiple-row inserts:

```
CREATE TABLE Production.InventoryTransaction
(InventoryID INT,
VALUE INT);
GO

CREATE TRIGGER InvTrans_Aggregate
ON Production.InventoryTransaction
AFTER Insert
```

```
AS

UPDATE Production.ProductInventory
   SET Quantity += i.Value
  FROM Production.ProductInventory AS Inv
 INNER JOIN Inserted AS i
    ON Inv.ProductID = i.InventoryID;

Return;
```

The next batch tests the InvTrans_Aggregate trigger by inserting a transaction and observing the InventoryTransaction and Inventory tables:

```
INSERT Production.InventoryTransaction (InventoryID, Value)
SELECT ProductID, 5
  FROM Production.ProductInventory
 WHERE ProductID = 707;

INSERT Production.InventoryTransaction (InventoryID, Value)
SELECT ProductID, -3
  FROM Production.ProductInventory
 WHERE ProductID = 707;

INSERT Production.InventoryTransaction (InventoryID, Value)
SELECT ProductID, 7
  FROM Production.ProductInventory
 WHERE ProductID = 707;
```

The following query views the data within the InventoryTransaction table:

```
SELECT i.ProductID, it.Value
  FROM Production.InventoryTransaction AS it
 INNER JOIN Production.ProductInventory AS i
    ON i.ProductID = it.InventoryID;
```

Result:

```
InventoryCode   Value
--------------- ------
A1              5
A1              -3
A1              7
```

The InvTrans_Aggregate trigger should have maintained a correct quantity-on-hand value through the inserts to the InventoryTransaction table. Indeed, the next query proves the trigger functioned correctly:

```
SELECT P.ProductID, I.Shelf, I.Quantity, I.LocationID
  FROM Production.ProductInventory AS I
 INNER JOIN Production.Product AS P
    ON I.ProductID = P.ProductID
 WHERE P.ProductID = 707;
```

Result:

```
ProductID   Shelf   Quantity   LocationID
707         N/A     297        7
```

The Inventory Trigger

The quantity values in the `Inventory` table should never be directly manipulated. Every quantity adjustment must go through the `InventoryTransaction` table. However, some users will want to make manual adjustments to the `Inventory` table. The gentlest solution to the problem is to use server-side code to perform the correct operations regardless of the user's method:

1. An inventory `INSTEAD OF` trigger must redirect direct updates intended for the `Inventory` table, converting them into inserts in the `InventoryTransaction` table, while permitting the `InvTrans_Aggregate` trigger to update the `Inventory` table.

2. The inserts into the `InventoryTransaction` table then update the `Inventory` table, leaving the correct audit trail of inventory transactions.

As a best practice, the trigger must accept multiple-row updates. The goal is to undo the original DML `UPDATE` command while keeping enough of the data to write the change as an `INSERT` to the `InventoryTransaction` table:

```
CREATE TRIGGER Inventory_Aggregate
ON Production.ProductInventory
INSTEAD OF UPDATE
AS
-- Redirect direct updates
If Update(Quantity)
  BEGIN;
UPDATE Production.ProductInventory
      SET Quantity = d.Quantity
      FROM Deleted AS d
        INNER JOIN Production.ProductInventory AS i
          ON i.ProductID = d.ProductID;

      INSERT Production.InventoryTransaction
        (Value, InventoryID)
        SELECT
          i.Quantity - Inv.Quantity,
        Inv.ProductID
          FROM Production.ProductInventory AS Inv
            INNER JOIN Inserted AS i
              ON Inv.ProductID = i.ProductID;
  END;
```

To demonstrate the trigger, the following UPDATE attempts to change the quantity on hand from 9 to 10. The new Inventory_Aggregate trigger traps the UPDATE and resets the quantity on hand back to 9, but it also writes a transaction of +1 to the InventoryTransaction table. (If the InventoryTransaction table had transaction type and comment columns, then the transaction would be recorded as a manual adjustment by user X.) The InventoryTransaction table's InvTrans_Aggregate trigger sees the INSERT and properly adjusts the Inventory.QuantityOnHand to 10:

```
-- Trigger Test
UPDATE Production.ProductInventory
   SET Quantity = 10
   WHERE ProductID = 707;
```

Having performed the manual adjustment, the following query examines the InventoryTransaction table:

```
SELECT i.ProductID, it.Value
   FROM Production.InventoryTransaction AS it
     INNER JOIN Production.ProductInventory AS i
       ON i.ProductID = it.InventoryID;
```

Sure enough, the manual adjustment of 1 has been written to the InventoryTransaction table:

```
InventoryCode   Value
--------------- ---------------------------------
A1               5
A1              -3
707              7
707              1
```

As the adjustment was being inserted into the InventoryTransaction table, the InvTrans_Aggregate trigger posted the transaction to the Inventory table. The following query double-checks the QuantityOnHand for inventory item 'A1':

```
SELECT p.ProductID, i.ProductID, i.Quantity
   FROM Production.ProductInventory AS i
     INNER JOIN Production.Product AS p
       ON i.ProductID = p.ProductID
     WHERE p.ProductID = 707;
```

Result:

```
ProductID       ProductID       Quantity
--------------- --------------- --------------
707             707             298
```

DDL Triggers

DDL triggers are useful for auditing server-level and database changes. They can easily pinpoint which objects were changed, who changed them, and even undo unauthorized changes.

DDL triggers fire as the result of some server-level or database schema–level event — typically data definition language (DDL) code — a CREATE, ALTER, or DROP statement. Where DML triggers respond to data changes, DDL triggers respond to schema changes.

Just like DML triggers, DDL triggers can execute T-SQL code and can rollback the event. Because DDL triggers can respond to so many types of events and commands, the information about the event is passed to the trigger in XML using the EventData() function.

Managing DDL Triggers

DDL triggers are easy to manage using normal DDL. The most significant factor when developing a DDL trigger is the scope of the trigger — deciding which server- or database-level events will fire a trigger.

Creating and Altering DDL Triggers

DDL triggers are created or altered using syntax similar to working with DML triggers. The location of the trigger, specified by the ON clause, is either ALL SERVER or DATABASE. The following code creates a database-level DDL trigger:

```
CREATE TRIGGER SchemaAudit
ON DATABASE
FOR DDL_Database_Level
AS
code
```

Server-level events are a superset of database-level events. They include all database level events. The next example shows a server-level DDL trigger:

```
CREATE TRIGGER SchemaAudit
ON ALL SERVER
FOR DDL_Server_Level
WITH Options
AS
code
```

Using Management Studio, database triggers are listed under the database's Programmability node in Object Explorer. Server triggers are listed under Server Objects in Object Explorer. Database triggers can be scripted using Object Explorer but not modified as easily as other programmability objects such as stored procedures. The context menu for DDL triggers does not offer the modify or script to alter options that a stored procedure's context menu includes.

To list the database DDL triggers using code, query the `sys.triggers` and `sys.events` catalog views. Server triggers are found at `sys.server_triggers` and `sys.server_trigger_events`.

Trigger Scope

There are dozens of events that can potentially fire a DDL trigger — one for every DDL type of action that can be executed on the server or database. These events are categorized into a hierarchy using event groups. Creating a DDL trigger for an event group causes the DDL trigger to fire for every event in that group. The DDL Event Groups page in Books Online details the whole hierarchy.

The top, or root, of the hierarchy is the `ddl_events` group, which includes every possible event. The next level has the `ddl_server_level_events` and `ddl_database_level_events` groups. Each of these groups includes several subgroups and events. Chances are there's a group that matches exactly with the types of events you want to handle.

DDL triggers can also be fired by specific events, such as `create_table`, `create_login`, or `alter_view`. The full list is in Books Online under "DDL Events."

The following code creates three DDL triggers to demonstrate DDL trigger scope. The first DDL trigger handles all server-level events:

```
CREATE TRIGGER DDL_Server_Level_Sample
ON ALL SERVER
FOR DDL_SERVER_LEVEL_EVENTS
AS
Set NoCount ON
Print 'DDL_Server_Level_Sample DDL Trigger'
```

The second DDL trigger fires for all database-level events:

```
USE tempdb
GO
CREATE TRIGGER DDL_Database_Sample
ON DATABASE
FOR DDL_DATABASE_LEVEL_EVENTS
AS
Set NoCount ON
Print 'DDL_Database_Sample DDL Trigger'
```

The third DDL trigger traps only create table commands:

```
CREATE TRIGGER DDL_Create_Table_Sample
ON DATABASE
FOR Create_Table
AS
Set NoCount ON
Print 'DDL_Create_Table_Sample DDL Trigger'
```

With these three DDL triggers installed, the next few DDL commands demonstrate DDL trigger scope. Creating a new database is a server-level event:

```
Create database Testdb
```

Result:

```
DDL_Server_Level_Sample DDL Trigger
```

Creating a new table fires the create table DDL trigger as well as the general database DDL events trigger:

```
create table Test (col1 INT)
```

Result:

```
DDL_Database_Sample DDL Trigger
DDL_Create_Table_Sample DDL Trigger
```

Dropping the table fires the general database DDL event trigger, but not the specific create table event trigger:

```
drop table Test
```

Result:

```
DDL_Database_Sample DDL Trigger
```

DDL Triggers and Security

The DDL trigger creation options, ENCRYPTION and EXECUTE AS, both ensure the security of system-level auditing triggers. The following DDL trigger will be encrypted when stored:

```
CREATE TRIGGER DDL_DDL_Level_Sample
ON ALL SERVER
WITH ENCRYPTION
FOR DDL_EVENTS
AS
code
```

As with stored procedures, triggers can be executed under a different security context. Instead of the user who issued the DDL command that caused the DDL trigger to fire, the trigger can execute as one of the following security contexts:

- **Caller**: Executes as the person executing the DDL command that fires the DDL trigger
- **Self**: Executes as the person who created the DDL trigger
- **login_name**: Executes as a specific login

Enabling and Disabling DDL Triggers

DDL triggers can be enabled or disabled. This is good because DBAs need an easy way to disable DDL triggers that roll back any schema changes. The following code disables and then enables the DDL_Create_Table_Sample trigger:

```
DISABLE TRIGGER DDL_Create_Table_Sample
ON DATABASE;

ENABLE TRIGGER DDL_Create_Table_Sample
ON DATABASE;
```

Removing DDL Triggers

DDL triggers aren't listed in sys.objects, nor can their presence be detected using object_id(). DDL triggers are listed in sys.server_triggers and sys.triggers DMVs. Because DDL triggers can exist on either the database or server level, dropping them requires a slightly different syntax:

```
IF EXISTS (SELECT *
             FROM sys.server_triggers
             WHERE Name = 'DDL_Server_Level_Sample')
   DROP TRIGGER DDL_Server_Level_Sample ON ALL SERVER

IF EXISTS (SELECT *
             FROM sys.triggers
             WHERE Name = 'DDL_Database_Sample')
   DROP TRIGGER DDL_Database_Sample ON DATABASE
```

Developing DDL Triggers

In some way, a DDL trigger is easier to write than a DML trigger. Because DDL triggers always fire for a single event, they avoid dealing with multiple rows involving the base table the inserted and deleted virtual tables exposed in DML triggers. The complexity of the DDL trigger results from the fact that the data about the event is in XML.

EventData()

DDL triggers can respond to so many different events that they need some method of capturing data about the event that caused them to fire. DML triggers have the inserted and `deleted` virtual tables; DDL triggers have the `EventData()` function. This function returns XML-formatted data about the event. The XML schema varies according to the type of event captured. Note that parts of the XML schema are case-sensitive.

Using the `EventData()` function to populate an XML variable, the trigger can use XQuery to investigate the values. Use the XQuery `Value()` method to extract the data from the XML.

The XML schema for event data is published at `http://schemas.microsoft.com/sqlserver`.

The following code example creates a DDL trigger that populates `EventData()` into an XML variable and then selects from the variable to display the data:

```
CREATE TRIGGER DDLTrigger
ON DATABASE
FOR CREATE_TABLE
AS
Set NoCount ON

    DECLARE @EventData XML =
EventData()

    SELECT
      @EventData.value
        ('data(/EVENT_INSTANCE/SchemaName)[1]','VARCHAR(50)') as
        'Schema',
      @EventData.value
        ('data(/EVENT_INSTANCE/ObjectName)[1]', 'VARCHAR(50)') as
        'Object',
      @EventData.value
        ('data(/EVENT_INSTANCE/EventType)[1]', 'VARCHAR(50)') as
        'EventType'
```

With the DDL triggers in place, the next command creates a table, which fires the trigger, which examines `EventData`'s XML, and returns the values to the client:

```
CREATE TABLE Test (Col1 INT)
```

Result:

```
Schema                Object       EventType
------------------    ----------   --------------------
dbo                   Test         CREATE_TABLE
```

 For more on XML and working with XQuery, see Chapter 14, "Using XML Data."

Preventing Database Object Changes

DDL triggers can execute code, including a transaction rollback. This could prohibit anyone from making server- or database-level changes.

The following code is a simple example of a rollback DDL trigger blocking any stored procedures from being altered in the database:

```
CREATE TRIGGER WonderfulProc
ON DATABASE
FOR ALTER_PROCEDURE, DROP_PROCEDURE
AS
Set NoCount ON
Raiserror ('These Procs may not be altered or dropped!',16,1)
Rollback
```

To test the DDL trigger, the next few commands attempt to modify the procedure so it won't print "SQL Rocks!":

```
DROP PROC dbo.uspGetBillOfMaterials
```

Result:

```
Msg 50000, Level 16, State 1, Procedure WonderfulProc, Line 6
These Procs may not be altered or dropped!
Msg 3609, Level 16, State 2, Procedure QuickProc, Line 3
   The transaction ended in the trigger. The batch has been aborted.
```

And

```
ALTER PROC dbo.uspGetBillOfMaterials
AS
Print 'Oracle Rocks!'
```

Result:

```
Msg 50000, Level 16, State 1, Procedure WonderfulProc, Line 6
These Procs may not be altered or dropped!
Msg 3609, Level 16, State 2, Procedure QuickProc, Line 3
The transaction ended in the trigger. The batch has been aborted.
```

With DDL triggers, you can write your own system to prevent object changes that disagree with your shop's policies, but a more strategic solution might be to use policy-based management, documented in Chapter 20, "Policy Based Management."

Summary

DDL triggers provide a safety net — a way to track every change to the schema. The event model that can be tracked is comprehensive, and the data available to the trigger using the EventData() function and XML is dynamic and complete. Because DDL triggers can fire for such a broad range of events, the EventData() function returns XML data about the event.

DDL triggers are well suited to the following scenarios:

- Server-level DDL triggers can trap any event and are seen in Object Explorer under the Server Objects ⇨ Triggers node.

- Database-level DDL triggers exist in the user database, can only fire for database-level events, and are listed in Object Explorer in the [Database] ⇨ Programmability ⇨ Database Triggers node.

- DDL Triggers can fire for any specific DDL event, or for DDL Event Groups — a hierarchy of DDL events.

Triggers are a key feature of client/server databases. It is the trigger that enables the developer to create complex custom business rules that are strongly enforced at the Database Engine level. SQL Server has two types of triggers: INSTEAD OF triggers and AFTER triggers.

- Triggers enable the developer to create complex custom business rules that are strongly enforced at the Database Engine level. SQL Server has two types of DML triggers: INSTEAD OF triggers and AFTER triggers.

- INSTEAD OF triggers cancel the firing DML statement and do something else instead of the original DML statement.

- Triggers extend the lock duration, so try to place the code in the abstraction layer before it goes into the trigger.

- Triggers fire once per DML statement, not once per row, so be certain the trigger is set-based and can handle multiple rows well.

- Use the inserted and deleted virtual tables to access the data being modified by the DML statement.

Trigger logic can easily become complex and cause significant performance issues if care is not taken to avoid this. This type of system is expensive to maintain or refactor.

Performance Monitor and PAL

A s a Database Professional, using and interpreting performance counters is one of the most important skill sets you can develop. When server performance starts to go sideways, jumping in and "reading" what's happening on the server based on a set of counters allows you to quickly identify and attack trouble areas.

Performance Monitor, or PerfMon, has been around for quite a while and isn't going anywhere. Anyone working with Windows as an IT platform is probably familiar with PerfMon. These are the first tools used for high-level diagnostics and the health of any server.

SQL Server extends PerfMon by adding hundreds of SQL Server–specific counters. Although PerfMon alone doesn't provide enough detail to fully diagnose SQL Server, it does a great job to illustrate the overall server performance issues and highlighting SQL Server themes.

PerfMon is more than just a pretty face. PerfMon's counter logs can write data to a binary perflog (*.blg) file or to a comma-delimited file (universal across Windows versions).

Perflogs can be integrated into SQL Server Profiler for review and analysis. However, SQL Server Profiler will be deprecated in a future version of SQL Server. If you want to get up to speed on what's replacing Profiler, check out Chapter 40, "Extended Events."

Using PerfMon

PerfMon includes a couple of important features: System Monitor and Data Collector Sets. Some servers have it installed in the Administrative Tools menu. It's also found at Control Panel ➪ Administrative Tools ➪ Performance Monitor, and it can be launched from SQL Server Profiler's Tools ➪ Performance Monitor menu command.

System Monitor

System Monitor, or SysMon, is familiar to anyone with experience with Windows server administration. System Monitor graphically displays multiple counters, aggregate and detailed data from the server internals. It looks a bit like a heart EKG monitor for Windows and SQL Server, as shown in Figure 37-1.

FIGURE 37-1

System Monitor is useful for watching the overall activity within SQL Server.

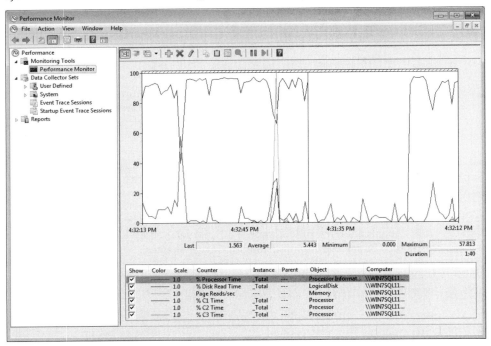

A performance counter can watch the local server or a remote server, so it isn't necessary to run System Monitor at the SQL Server machine. The counters can be watched as a timed line graph, a histogram bar graph, or a real-time report.

Counters are organized by object and, sometimes, instance. For example, (refer to Figure 37-1), the SQL Server: Databases object exposes many counters, including the Transactions/sec counter. This counter can be watched for All Instances (all databases on all instances on the selected server) or for a selected database.

NOTE

The SQL Server Database Engine isn't the only server to expose counters to System Monitor. Analysis Services, Reporting Services, .NET, ASP, BizTalk, and other servers all add counters to System Monitor.

If a new counter displays a line at the top or bottom of the graph, you can get more meaningful results by adjusting the scale. Using the System Monitor Properties dialog, available from the context menu, you can adjust the scale of the graph, the scale of each counter, and the presentation of each counter.

Although there are hundreds of possible System Monitor counters, Table 37-1 describes some counters commonly used when investigating a SQL Server installation.

TABLE 37-1   Key Performance Monitor Counters

Object	Counter	Description	Usefulness
SQL Server Buffer Manager	Page life expectancy	Number of seconds a page stays in the buffer pool without references.	Monitoring page life expectancy in an OLTP environment can provide a preliminary predictor of server slowdowns.
Processor	Percentage of processor time	Total percentage of processor activity for physical servers; not a reliable counter for virtual servers.	If CPUs are regularly more than 60 percent active, additional CPU cores or a faster server increases performance.
SQLServer: SQL Statistics	Batch requests per second	SQL batch activity.	A good indicator of user activity.
Physical Disk	Bytes received per second	Measures bytes received by the physical disk per second.	Disk throughput is a key hardware performance factor. Carefully splitting the database across multiple disk subsystems probably improves performance.
SQLServer: SQL Statistics	Failed auto-params per second	Number of queries for which SQL Server could not cache the query execution plan in memory; an indication of poorly written queries. (Check the scale when applying.)	Locating and correcting the queries improves performance.

Continues

911

TABLE 37-1   *(continued)*

Object	Counter	Description	Usefulness
SQLServer: Locks	Average wait time (in milliseconds), lock waits, and lock timeouts per second	A cause of serious performance problems; lock waits, the length of the wait, and the number of lock timeouts are all good indicators of the level of locking contention within a database.	If locking issues are detected, the indexing structure and transaction code should be examined.
SQLServer: User Connections	User connections	Number of current connections.	Indicates potential database activity.
SQLServer: Databases	Transactions per second	Number of current transactions within a database.	A good indicator of database activity.

The "best counter" list seems to change with every new article Paul Randal writes. Read the blogs, experiment, and keep track of the ones you find meaningful. To get your research off on the right foot, you can find a great article at SQLSkills.com by Paul Randal about performance tuning considerations at `www.sqlskills.com/BLOGS/PAUL/post/Important-considerations-when-performance-tuning.aspx`.

In addition, the `SQL Server: Wait Statistics` counters are useful windows into potential SQL Server bottlenecks; a number of interesting memory counters are in `SQL Server: Resource Pool Stats`.

> **TIP**
>
> A complete list of SQL Server counters and their current values can be queried from the `sys.dm_os_performance_counters` dynamic management view. This is cool, because you can get the counter data using Transact-SQL code. If you want to make retrieving this information even cooler, check out the section "Accessing Performance Counters with PowerShell" later in this chapter.

You can create custom counters using stored procedures `sp_user_counter1` through `sp_user_counter10` to pass data from your database code to System Monitor. This can be useful to show the number of transactions processed by a performance test or the number of rows inserted by a data generator. There are ten possible user counters. The following trivial example increments one of the counters:

```
DECLARE @Counter int
SET @Counter = 0
While @Counter < 100
```

```
BEGIN
  SET @Counter = @Counter + 1
  EXEC sp_user_counter1 @Counter
  WAITFOR Delay '00:00:02'
END
```

Best Practice

Use System Monitor to get an overall picture of the health of the server and to get an idea of the types of issues that might be occurring within SQL Server. Then, armed with this information, move to SQL Server Profiler or Extended Events to target the specific problem.

The configuration of System Monitor, including every counter, can be saved to a configuration file using File ⇨ Save As, and later restored using File ⇨ Open. Using this technique, you can export a System Monitor configuration to other servers.

There is one catch: The counter must be monitoring the local server to move from server to server. However, if the counters monitor a remote server, the configuration monitors that remote server regardless of where the System Monitor configuration file is opened. Because DBAs are seldom physically at the SQL Server being monitored, this is a problem. (If this bothers you, e-mail the author, Aaron Nelson, at Aaron@SQLvariant.com; one of these days I'm going to write a custom system monitor, probably using PowerShell, to fix this and other problems.)

Data Collector Sets

In Windows 2008, Performance introduces Data Collector Sets, which encompasses the functionality formerly known as counter logs. Data Collector Sets use the same server counters as System Monitor, but in addition to graphically displaying the data in real time, the Data Collector Sets also enable you to write the counter data to a log file. This means the data can be analyzed after the fact or even replayed within Performance Monitor.

Data Collector Sets are accessed via Performance Monitor and include User Defined, System, Event Trace Sessions, and Startup Event Trace Sessions subfolders. To see and configure where the log files will be stored, right-click a Data Collector Set, and choose Properties. Navigate to the Directory tab, and examine the Root Directory, Subdirectory, and Subdirectory name format areas. An example of the file format and location is shown in the Example directory area.

If you are ready to create a new Data Collector Set, follow these steps:

1. Right-click the User Defined subfolder, and mouse-over New.
2. From the context menu, select Data Collector Set.

3. After naming the log and choosing the Advanced radio button, select Next.

4. Check Performance Counters, and select Next.

5. Select the Add button, and choose the counters to write to the log. Adding an object adds every counter for the object, whereas adding counters provides a more granular capability to select counters similarly to System Monitor.

6. Select Finish.

The Figure 37-2 will help in case you get lost in the steps with all the windows that end up popping-up.

FIGURE 37-2

The Data Collector Set is configured to write server performance counter data.

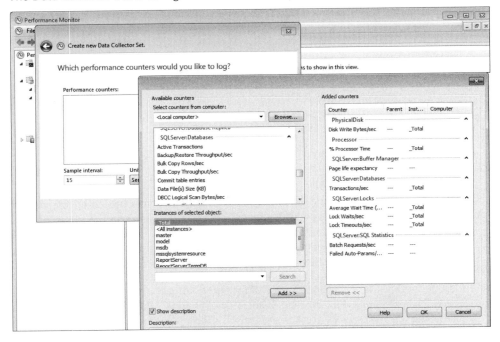

Data Collector Sets can be scheduled to run in the Data Collector Set Property dialog, or manually started and stopped using the log's context menu or the Start and Stop toolbar buttons.

If the Data Collector Set file was defined as a text file (comma-delimited or tab-delimited), you can open it using Excel. Each column is a counter value, and each row is a sample interval.

Performance Analysis for Logs Tool (PAL)

PAL is a CodePlex tool that helps you along your performance monitoring path by reading in performance monitor counter logs and analyzing them using known thresholds. This is a great option for both novice and experienced administrators. You can download and learn more about the Performance Analysis for Logs Tool at: `http://pal.codeplex.com/`.

Accessing Performance Counters with PowerShell

PowerShell enables you to easily discover and collect all performance counters from the Operating System. After they are converted to a datatable, they are easily stored in a CSV, Excel Spreadsheet, or a table inside of SQL Server. First, you need to know how to discover what counters are available. After you know which counters you want to monitor, you can grab large blocks of them using a hashtable. With PowerShell the easiest way to discover them is to run the following code:

```
Get-Counter -ListSet SQLSERVER* | ForEach-Object {$_.CounterSetName,
   $_.Paths} | Format-Table -Auto
```

To pick a list of performance counters, you simply create a hashtable. To explain what a hashtable is to SQL people is easy: You know how you can't have a comma separated list of values passed into a query as a variable — unless you resort to XML. A hashtable is precisely that thing that you don't have! To create a hashtable in PowerShell, just start with "@(" then place your CSV list of counters inside of here; then close it with ")."

Following is a sample list of SQL Server performance counters:

```
$CountersList = @('\SQLServer:Plan Cache(*)\Cache Pages',
'\SQLServer:Buffer Manager\Buffer cache hit ratio',
'\SQLServer:Buffer Manager\Page lookups/sec',
'\SQLServer:Buffer Manager\Free list stalls/sec',
'\SQLServer:Buffer Manager\Free pages',
'\SQLServer:Buffer Manager\Database pages',
'\SQLServer:Buffer Manager\Reserved pages',
'\SQLServer:Buffer Manager\Stolen pages',
'\SQLServer:Buffer Manager\Lazy writes/sec',
'\SQLServer:Buffer Manager\Readahead pages/sec',
'\SQLServer:Buffer Manager\Page reads/sec',
'\SQLServer:Buffer Manager\Page writes/sec',
'\SQLServer:Buffer Manager\Checkpoint pages/sec',
'\SQLServer:Buffer Manager\Page life expectancy',
'\SQLServer:Wait Statistics(*)\Lock waits',
'\SQLServer:Latches\Average Latch Wait Time (ms)',
'\SQLServer:Access Methods\Failed tree page cookie',
'\SQLServer:General Statistics\User Connections')
```

After you have your list of counters, you can start grabbing them using

```
Get-Counter -Counter $CountersList
```

When that is accomplished, you suddenly have become the dog that finally caught the bus. The counters come back in a format that is not readable by the average person. The counters look nothing like you would expect. That's because they need to be transformed into a DataTable to format properly on the screen or to save off to a file. Until you do, Figure 37-3 shows what those results look like by default:

FIGURE 37-3

Unformatted Performance Counter Output.

```
Timestamp                CounterSamples
---------                --------------
6/1/2011 10:12:33 PM     \\win7w510\sqlserver:buffer manager\page lookups/sec :
                         0

                         \\win7w510\sqlserver:buffer manager\free list stalls/sec :
                         0

                         \\win7w510\sqlserver:buffer manager\free pages :
                         0

                         \\win7w510\sqlserver:buffer manager\page life expectancy :
                         0

                         \\win7w510\sqlserver:latches\average latch wait time (ms) :
                         0

                         \\win7w510\sqlserver:general statistics\user connections :
                         0
```

With this bit of code, you can at least make the results (see Figure 37-4) display more presentably:

```
$CounterResults.CounterSamples | Format-Table -Auto
```

FIGURE 37-4

Formatted performance counter results.

```
PS C:\temp> $CounterResults.CounterSamples | Format-Table -auto

Path                                                         InstanceName CookedValue
----                                                         ------------ -----------
\\win7w510\sqlserver:buffer manager\buffer cache hit ratio                          0
\\win7w510\sqlserver:buffer manager\page lookups/sec                                0
\\win7w510\sqlserver:buffer manager\free list stalls/sec                            0
\\win7w510\sqlserver:buffer manager\free pages                                      0
\\win7w510\sqlserver:buffer manager\database pages                                  0
\\win7w510\sqlserver:buffer manager\reserved pages                                  0
\\win7w510\sqlserver:buffer manager\stolen pages                                    0
\\win7w510\sqlserver:buffer manager\lazy writes/sec                                 0
\\win7w510\sqlserver:buffer manager\readahead pages/sec                             0
\\win7w510\sqlserver:buffer manager\page reads/sec                                  0
\\win7w510\sqlserver:buffer manager\page writes/sec                                 0
\\win7w510\sqlserver:buffer manager\checkpoint pages/sec                            0
\\win7w510\sqlserver:buffer manager\page life expectancy                            0
\\win7w510\sqlserver:latches\average latch wait time (ms)                           0
\\win7w510\sqlserver:general statistics\user connections                            0
```

While the code above is useful for outputting results to the screen, in the long run you are going to ultimately want to convert the results into a datatable so that you can save the results into a database

```
$CounterResults = Get-Counter -Counter $CountersList
$CounterRecords = $CounterResults.CounterSamples | Out-DataTable
$CounterRecords | Format-Table -Auto
```

Finally, as an alternate option you may need to save off your results to a CSV file. You use the built in PowerShell cmdlet to do that for you.

```
$CounterResults = Get-Counter -Counter $CountersList
$CounterRecords = $CounterResults.CounterSamples | Out-DataTable|
Export-Csv "C:\Temp\MySQLCounters.csv" -NoTypeInformation
```

Summary

PerfMon is a powerful tool in any DBA's toolbox. Used alone, it provides a comprehensive overview of the server's status — both Windows and SQL Server. The key to PerfMon is understanding the overwhelming number of counters. If you know which counters to focus on, you'll find that PerfMon can be efficient.

The next chapter looks at Profiler, a SQL Server monitoring tool that you can use with PerfMon to produce thorough performance monitoring.

Using Profiler and SQL Trace

I f you've been working with SQL Server for any length of time, you've probably used SQL Server Profiler. If you haven't had the opportunity to use it, no big deal. With the exception of Profiler for Analysis Services (SSAS) it's being replaced by Extended Events. However, Profiler is still available in SQL Server 2012 and is still a vital tool to have available for any earlier versions of SQL Server that you may work with. This chapter covers the high-level features and functionality of Profiler. Your best bet is to be ready and able to capture performance data with either Profiler or Extended Events.

Features of SQL Server Profiler

- SQL Server Profiler is the optional front-end user interface for SQL Trace. The two are different components and technologies. SQL Trace runs on the server, is lightweight, and collects data points to be passed to Profiler or written to a file. Collectively, they have the following features and benefits: SQL Trace is a lightweight, but powerful, technology that can run on SQL Server; it collects performance data selected from hundreds of possible performance data points ranging from locks, to connections, to SQL DML statements, to recompiles.

- SQL Server Profiler is a separate application that can configure, start, and stop SQL Trace as well as capture and display data from SQL Trace.

- Profiler data can scroll on the screen or be saved to a file or table for further analysis.

- Data can be filtered in numerous ways, including viewing only events related to a specific database, excluding events from a specific application, or capturing only the queries that exceed a specified duration.

- Profile configurations can be saved and reused later.

- Profile event data can be merged with server counter data collected by Perfmon/SysMon for a great visual representation of what's happening on the server.

Running Profiler

SQL Server Profiler can be opened from several locations:

- From the Start menu, Profiler is under the SQL Server 2012 ⇨ Performance Tools menu.
- In Management Studio, Profiler is in the Tools menu.
- Within Management Studio's Query Editor, the context menu includes the option to Trace Query in SQL Server Profiler. This option opens Profiler filtered to the current connection.

Defining a New Trace

When a new trace is created (with the New Trace toolbar button or File ⇨ New Trace), a connection is created to a SQL Server, and the Trace Properties dialog (see Figure 38-1) displays. The Trace Properties General tab sets up the trace (name, file destination, and so on), and the Events Selection tab defines the events and data columns to be recorded, as well as the filter. If the trace is running, the properties may be viewed but not changed. You can save a trace configuration as a template to make creating new traces easier.

FIGURE 38-1

This SQL Server Profiler uses the T-SQL Duration template and can write information to a file.

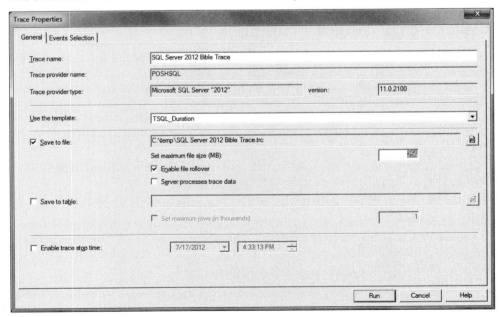

A Profiler trace is primarily viewed interactively (because otherwise you should be running a scripted server-side trace), but the data can also be written to a file or a SQL Server table. This is useful for further manual analysis, viewing alongside System Monitor counter data, or importing into the Database Engine Tuning Advisor.

When Profiler data is written to a file, SQL Server writes 128KB chunks of data at a time for performance. Conversely, writing data to a table involves a series of row inserts that doubles the transaction log workload and seriously hinders SQL Server's performance. Avoid tracing directly to a table on the server being traced; although, writing to a different server is OK.

Best Practice

To save Profiler data for further analysis, use the high-performance file method and a server-side trace (discussed later). If you want to analyze the data using T-SQL (and analyzing trace data with SQL aggregate queries and WHERE...LIKE clauses is extremely useful), save the trace to a file. After the trace is complete, open the trace file using Profiler and select File ⇨ Save As ⇨ Table.

Selecting Events and Data Columns

The Events Selection tab (see Figure 38-2) determines the data points that SQL Trace captures. SQL Trace can monitor more than 175 key SQL Server events. The default templates configure a trace with a few preselected events, but there's so much more.

Two important details of the interface are easily overlooked: The Show all events and Show all columns check boxes in the lower-right side of the Events Selection tab enable viewing and selecting from the complete set of events and columns. Without those options checked, the form displays only the currently selected events and columns. Although this can be useful to filter out noise, you must enable these options to select additional events or add columns to existing events.

The following list shows the event categories, along with the number of events in each category and a comment:

- **Broker (13):** The first category covers events related to Service Broker activity.
- **CLR (1):** Only CLR assembly loads can be traced.
- **Cursors (7):** These events are not related to T-SQL server-side cursors. They track ADO client-side cursor activity.
- **Database (6):** Tracks database file activity, such as autogrowth and mirror connections.
- **Deprecation (2):** A useful set of events. You can run these events when exercising code or running unit tests to highlight any deprecated features used in the code.

- **Errors and Warnings (16):** Any abnormal event or error can trigger these events; useful when watching for errors in an active system.

- **Full text (3):** The Full text events track only Full-Text Search crawl activity. There are no events for Full-Text Search configuration changes. More information about Full-Text Search queries is hidden in the Performance: FullTextQuery events.

- **Locks (9):** Although enabling lock events can be great for learning about locks in a controlled setting, using these events in a production environment can instantly fill Profiler with thousands of events, so be careful with this category. A noteworthy exception is the Deadlock Graph event, which captures a full set of data about the deadlock and even displays a graph.

- **OLEDB (5):** These events track OLE-DB distributed query calls made by SQL Server to other providers.

- **Objects (3):** DDL events (CREATE, ALTER, DROP) can be tracked with these events.

- **Performance (14):** These events track data about query plans and plan guides. A notable event is the ShowPlan XML event, which can display the query execution plan.

- **Progress Report (1):** This event category tracks the progress of online reindexing.

- **Query Notifications (4):** These show information about query notification activity, including subscriptions activity.

- **Scans (2):** When watching for performance issues, this category can trace index scans and table scans.

- **Security Audit (42):** With a nod to the *Hitchhiker's Guide to the Galaxy*, the Security Audit category includes numerous events to support C2 and Common Criteria compliance.

- **Server (3):** This odd category includes mount tape, memory change, and trace stop events.

- **Sessions (1):** This event fires when a trace is started and returns an event for every existing connection, including its properties.

- **Stored Procedures (15):** This rich category includes a number of events related to stored procedure execution, compilation, and cache hits.

- **TSQL (9):** These events fire for individual T-SQL statements.

- **Transactions (13):** SQL transactions events at the level of begin transaction, commit transaction, and rollback transactions are traced with this category. Playing with this event reveals how much activity actually happens with SQL Server. Unfortunately, there's no event to capture changing the transaction isolation level.

- **User Configurable (10):** To gather custom data about the environment or application's activity, the application can call the sp_trace_generateevent system stored procedure to fire an event and pass custom data to SQL Trace.

FIGURE 38-2

The Trace Properties Events Selection page enables you to select the events tracked by Profiler.

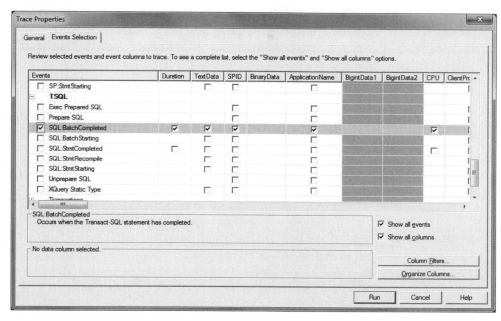

Depending on the events, different data becomes relevant to the trace. The data columns automatically offer the appropriate data. Although the SPID data column appears optional, it's only fooling you — it's mandatory. A useful data column to capture is StartDate, which is required if the trace will be correlated with Perfmon data later (explained in the "Integrating Performance Monitor Data" section).

Filtering Events

Profiler can capture so much information that it can fill a drive with data. Fortunately, the Profiler Trace Filter can narrow the scope of your search to the data of interest.

The filter uses a combination of `equal` and `like` operators, depending on the data types captured. A frustrating aspect of the filter is that it works only against collected data, and the data collected for some columns may not be what was expected. For example, if you want to filter the trace to only those batches that reference a specific table or column, filtering by object name won't work. Defining a `like` filter using wildcards on the `text data` column, however, causes Profiler to select only those batches that include that column name.

The Exclude system IDs check box sets the filter to select only user objects.

Best Practice

By default, SQL Server Profiler filters out the calls made by SQL Server Profiler, but it's a good idea to regularly also filter out the Reporting Services and SQL Agent applications to avoid any unnecessary event clutter.

Organizing Columns

To change columns to GROUP BY status, click on the Organizing Columns button (see bottom right of Figure 38-3) on the Events Selection tab inside Trace Profiler. Choose a column name and move it via the Up button (also in Figure 38-3) into the Groups section. Any GROUP BY columns become the first columns in the trace window; and as new events are added to the trace window, those events are automatically added within their group.

FIGURE 38-3

Moving columns into GROUP BY status.

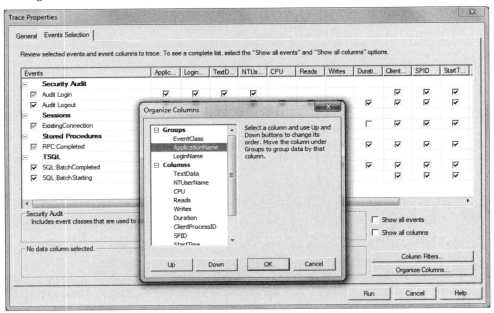

Running the Trace

Although Profiler is just a UI that consumes data generated by SQL Trace, it's quite good at controlling live traces. Profiler can start, pause, and stop the trace using the typical icons in the toolbar.

Following are a few details worth pointing out:

- The eraser toolbar button clears the results in Profiler.
- If the trace flies by too fast to view but you don't want to pause or stop the trace, the Auto Scroll Window toolbar button enables Profiler to continue to add new events at the bottom of the list without scrolling the window.
- While a trace is stopped, its events and data columns may be changed using the Properties button.

Using the Trace File

When the trace is captured, it can be browsed through using the Profiler trace window, and a Find toolbar button can help navigate the data. However, the trace is likely to be so large that it will be difficult to manually use the data.

The solution is to save the trace file to a SQL table using File ⇨ Save As; the data can then be analyzed and manipulated as in any other SQL table.

SQL Server Profiler has the capability to replay traces. If the trace is to be replayed, certain events must be captured. For example, the SQL Batch Start event can be replayed, but SQL Batch Complete cannot. Also, if data inserts are replayed, you need to reset the database to the same state as the beginning of the trace; otherwise, you'll likely have unique data conflicts and issues with identity column values.

In addition, the entire trace file can be submitted as a workload to the Database Engine Tuning Advisor so that it can tune for multiple queries. However, the authors of this book are not big fans of the Database Engine Tuning Advisor, as explained in Chapter 45, "Indexing Strategies."

Integrating Performance Monitor Data

Both System Monitor and Profiler present their own unique perspective on the state of the server. The two sets of information can be merged to produce a synchronized walk-through scenario viewing both perspectives using SQL Server Profiler.

To set up the dual-perspective experience, simultaneously capture server performance logs using both Performance Monitor's Counter Logs and SQL Server Profiler. These steps are specific:

1. Configure System Monitor with the exact counters you want to view later. Be sure to get the scale and everything right. Set up the Counter Log to the same configuration.

38

2. Configure Profiler with the right set of trace events. They must include the start and end time data columns so that Profiler can integrate the two logs later. Script the trace to T-SQL code. Close Profiler.

3. Manually start the Counter Log. Execute the T-SQL trace code to start the server-side trace.

4. Exercise the server with the code and load you want to analyze.

5. When the test is complete, stop both the Counter Log and the server-side trace.

6. Open Profiler, and then open the saved trace file.

7. Use the File ⇨ Import Performance Data menu command to import the Counter Log.

Profiler responds to the import by adding a pane that displays the System Monitor graph, as shown in Figure 38-4. Select a Profiler event or a time in the System Monitor graph; the two stay in sync.

FIGURE 38-4

SQL Server Profiler can integrate Performance Monitor data and move through the events in sync.

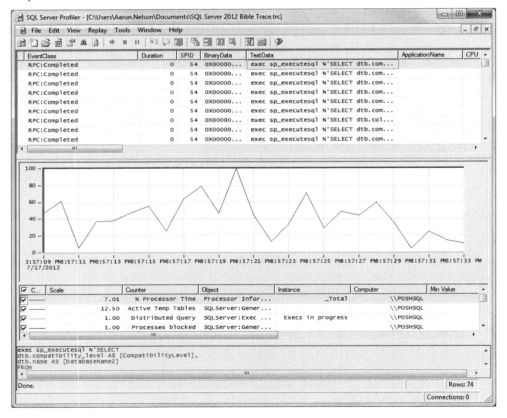

Using SQL Trace

SQL Server Profiler is usually used interactively, and for ad hoc data gathering, this is probably sufficient. However, running Profiler on a heavy transaction server can lead to problems:

- If Profiler can't keep up, some events will be dropped. This frequently happens on heavy transaction servers with Profiler.

- There's a measurable performance impact on the server when running Profiler. The heavier the transaction traffic on the server, the greater the percentage of performance impact from Profiler.

- The workstation gathering the events may run out of memory.

The solution is to run the SQL Trace directly on the server without collecting the data using the Profiler UI.

SQL Traces are started by the `sp_trace_create` system stored procedure. When the trace exists, events are added to it using `sp_tracesetevent`.

Although you can code stored procedures to configure SQL Traces, the most common method is to define the trace in Profiler and then script the trace to run on the server. After the trace is set up and tested in SQL Server Profiler, select File ⇨ Export ⇨ Script Trace Definition ⇨ For SQL Server 2005–2012 to generate a T-SQL script that launches the server-side trace.

Best Practice

For production systems running server-side traces, writing to a file is the best way to collect performance data with the least overhead to the server.

To view all the traces currently running in the server, query `sys.traces`:

```
SELECT id, path, start_time, last_event_time,
  event_count, dropped_event_count
  FROM sys.traces t
```

Result (abbreviated to fit):

```
id start_time          last_event_time     event_count dropped_event_count
-- ------------------- ------------------- ----------- -------------------
1  2011-08-27 03:07:49 2011-08-27 22:49:22 2770        NULL
2  2011-08-27 22:27:20 NULL                0           0
```

To programmatically view the events and data columns collected by a trace, use the following query (you need to modify the parameter for fn_trace_geteventinfo):

```
SELECT tcat.name +':' + te.name AS 'Event', tcol.NAME AS 'Column'
  FROM fn_trace_geteventinfo (2) tinfo
    JOIN sys.trace_events te
      ON tinfo.eventid = te.trace_event_id
    JOIN sys.trace_categories tcat
      ON te.category_id = tcat.category_id
    JOIN sys.trace_columns tcol
      ON tinfo.columnid = tcol.trace_column_id
```

Result:

```
Event                       Column
-------------------------   -----------------------
TSQL:SQL:StmtCompleted      TextData
TSQL:SQL:StmtCompleted      DatabaseID
TSQL:SQL:StmtCompleted      ApplicationName
TSQL:SQL:StmtCompleted      SPID
TSQL:SQL:StmtCompleted      Duration
TSQL:SQL:StmtCompleted      StartTime
TSQL:SQL:StmtCompleted      RowCounts
TSQL:SQL:StmtCompleted      IsSystem
TSQL:SQL:StmtCompleted      EndTime
TSQL:SQL:StmtCompleted      Reads
TSQL:SQL:StmtCompleted      Writes
TSQL:SQL:StmtCompleted      CPU
TSQL:SQL:StmtCompleted      DatabaseName
```

To stop a server-side trace, use the sp_trace_setstatus system stored procedure. The first parameter is the traceid, and the second parameter specifies the action: 0 = stop the trace, 1 = start the trace, and 2 = close and delete the trace. The sample code uses the trace as 2:

```
EXEC sp_trace_setstatus 2, 0
```

Another useful trace system stored procedure is fn_trace_gettable, which reads a trace file and returns the data in table form:

```
SELECT *
  FROM fn_trace_gettable
    ('C:\Program Files\Microsoft SQL Server
        \MSSQL11.MSSQLSERVER\MSSQL\Log\log_195.trc', 1)
```

Preconfigured Traces

SQL Server automatically runs a trace called the Default Trace that gathers basic events such as server start and stop, file growth, and creating or dropping objects. As the default trace, its trace ID is 1. Theoretically, it could be stopped without any ill effects, but there's no reason to do so.

Another preconfigured trace is the *blackbox* trace, which is used to diagnose server crashes. Starting a trace with `option = 8` starts this trace. Typically, this trace is not run unless there's a specific problem and Microsoft PSS has asked for data from the trace.

Common Criteria and the older C2 Audit security levels also involve running a specific trace that gathers login and other security data. Executing `sp_trace_create` with `option = 4` configures these traces.

Summary

SQL Server Profiler and SQL Trace are two technologies you need if you're interested in what's happening with your server. Profiler and SQL Trace may be venerable technologies compared to Change Tracking or Extended Events, but they're still two of the more useful tools in the DBA toolbox. Whereas some SQL Server technologies are optional — you can survive as a DBA without learning much about XML or SMO — PowerShell and Extended Events are mandatory.

Following are key points about SQL Trace and Profiler:

- Trace is a server-side technology that collects data that may be consumed by Profiler or written to a file.
- Profiler is a workable UI for Trace, but it may impact performance, so for heavy traces on a production server, it's best to use Profiler to configure the trace, generate a script, and then run the trace on the server.
- There are 179 SQL Trace events, and it's worth it to become familiar with them.
- Events can be filtered; typically, Reporting Services and SQL Agent are filtered out.
- SQL Trace can be completely configured and controlled by T-SQL code alone.
- SQL Trace events and Performance Monitor data can be integrated after the fact to produce a complete picture of what was happening on the server.

The next chapter stays in the mode of monitoring and auditing SQL Server. Similar to SQL Trace, but at a finer granularity, wait states track every process and every time it pauses for any reason.

38

Wait States

I magine there are three people in front of you in line at your favorite coffee shop. You eventually get to the front of the line and give the barista your order and patiently step aside. Two of the customers in front of you receive their orders quickly. The barista then hands you your coffee before the customer who was waiting directly in front of you because her request likely required more work to complete than yours.

This process is not unlike how SQL Server handles requests. SQL Server assigns requests (tasks) to worker threads, which wait in a queue to get their turn to run on the CPU (scheduler).

The SQL Server OS

To execute tasks, SQL Server uses its own custom operating system, referred to as the SQLOS, which serves as a thin layer between SQL Server and the Windows Operating System. SQLOS provides memory management, task scheduling, and IO completion, along with a number of functions for SQL Server.

The SQLOS is a nonpreemptive, or cooperative, operating system. This means that worker threads self-regulate the amount of time they use the scheduler. A worker can remove itself from the scheduler if its time slice is up. SQL Server operates this way because it has a better understanding as to how to most efficiently handle and schedule its work than the general Windows OS does.

To contrast, Windows is a preemptive operating system. This means that processes are taken on and off of the CPU at the decision of the OS (typically in a round-robin fashion).

As tasks run inside the database engine, they typically follow a circular pattern that jumps in and out of three main states:

- **Runnable:** Workers in a *runnable* status are waiting for time to execute on the scheduler. These can be workers that have previously been suspended, or workers executing new requests waiting to be executed. Time spent in the runnable queue is pure CPU wait time. This is also known as signal wait time because the tasks are waiting for their "signal" to run. Workers in the runnable queue eventually get to the scheduler so that they can execute.

- **Running:** Workers with a *running* status are currently executing a task. Only one worker thread can be running on a scheduler at any given time. The worker runs until it needs something that it must wait for, or until it removes itself from the scheduler. If the worker must wait on a resource, it is moved to the waiting list and is assigned the status of *suspended*. If it removes itself from the CPU, it is placed back on the runnable queue.

- **Suspended:** Workers waiting on something are flagged with a status of *suspended*. Suspended tasks are in the "waiting list" because they are waiting for something. As the resources that the process is waiting on become available, the process moves from the waiting list to the runnable queue.

When a worker must wait for a resource, such as CPU (signal wait time), IO, a lock, or memory, SQL server can track how long that process waits for that particular resource. You can use this data to see where SQL Server spends its time waiting and research to see if the root cause of the wait durations is a problem.

Examining Wait Statistics

You can retrieve wait statistic information in many ways. In this chapter, you examine three different dynamic management views (DMV) to use to gather this information.

Executing Requests

To view all tasks currently executing, use the DMV sys.dm_exec_requests (see Figure 39-1). This DMV includes information for all tasks that are currently executing (running), currently waiting on a resource (suspended), or currently waiting their turn to get on the scheduler to execute (runnable). Use this DMV for a high-level overview of all tasks currently executing on your SQL Server Instance.

Wait Stats

The DMV sys.dm_os_wait_stats (see Figure 39-2) returns the aggregated time waited, by wait type, since the last time SQL Server was restated or the last time the DMV was cleared. Use this DMV to see a holistic view of all the wait times on your system to see where SQL Server spends its time waiting. Many waits returned in this DMV are benign waits and should be ignored, even if they are high on the waiting list. Later in this chapter you review some common waits to watch if they represent a high percentage of wait time on your system.

FIGURE 39-1

Querying sys.dm_exec_requests for any request that has a status of running, suspended, or runnable. The query returns the current wait type of the request as well as the last wait type, and the total elapsed time for the request.

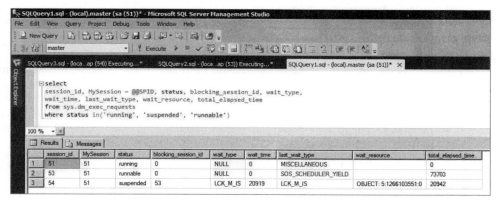

FIGURE 39-2

Returns all data from the sys.dm_wait_stats DMV ordered by the highest waits first. This DMV returns the number of waits by wait type, total elapsed time, highest wait time, and the total signal wait time for that wait.

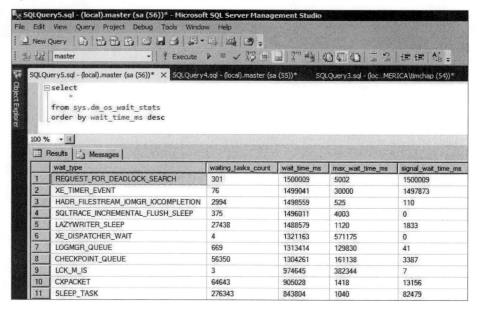

If can be useful to clear the values returned from this DMV for testing purposes. To do this, execute the following statement:

```
DBCC SQLPERF ('sys.dm_os_wait_stats', CLEAR);
GO
```

It's also a great idea to take regular snapshots of the contents of this DMV and store it in a table for reporting purposes. This allows you to trend over time where your SQL Server instance spends most of its time waiting.

Waiting Requests

The DMV sys.dm_os_waiting_tasks (see Figure 39-3) can reveal those sessions currently waiting for some resource. This DMV is a great place to start when you think you may have performance problems because you can quickly see the number of waiting tasks, the reason the task is waiting, and diagnose blocking issues, or view excessive parallelism. This DMV is also useful because it allows you to see wait patterns that you would not easily see with the DMV sys.dm_os_wait_stats.

FIGURE 39-3

This query returns all requests in the "waiting list" that are user processes. This query returns any session that may be blocking, the duration of the wait, and the reason the request is waiting.

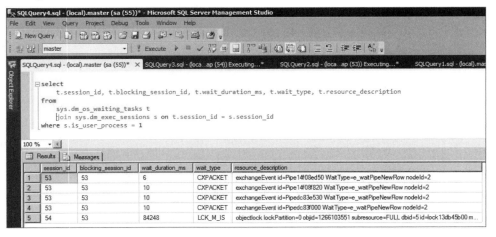

Common Red-Flag Wait Types

The following table lists common wait types that warrant investigation if they represent a high overall percentage of system waits.

Wait Name	Description
CXPACKET	Time spent waiting for thread synchronization to complete a parallel query. This often happens when one thread must perform more work than other threads to complete a single statement. High values here may be an indication that queries can be optimized for OLTP systems.
PAGEIOLATCH_x	Time spent waiting for a latch on a memory buffer for an IO request. High waits of this type may indicate a problem with the disk subsystem, large table scans, or not enough memory.
PAGELATCH_x	Time spent waiting for a latch that is not IO-related. This sometimes manifests itself as heavy inserts into the same page, which is often caused by heavy inserts on a table with a clustered index on an identity column. This is sometimes seen when there is a hot-spot on allocation pages within tempdb.
LCK_x	Time spent waiting for a lock to be acquired. High waits here could indicate poorly written queries that are taking locks and are long running, or potential problems with slow IO subsystems.
WRITELOG/LOGBUFFER	Time spent waiting for a log flush to complete, and time spent waiting for space to store a log record in a log buffer, respectively. Issues with either of these waits may indicate that your log file is not on the correct type of media or that your log is sharing IO with other files on its drive.
ASYNC_NETWORK_IO	Time SQL Server spends waiting for the client to process the data it has sent before it can send more. This typically occurs when a program runs a query that returns a large result set that it must consume.
SOS_SCHEDULER_YIELD	Time a worker spends waiting for its time-slice to be renewed. Occurs when a task removes itself from the scheduler so that other tasks can execute. High values here likely indicate CPU pressure.
RESOURCE_SEMAPHORE	Time spent waiting for a workspace memory request for a query to be granted. High values of this wait may indicate a large number of resource intensive queries, typically using hash-joins or sorts, or a potential memory bottleneck.

39

Other Ways to Gather Wait data

You can gather Wait data in other ways, including Extended Events, Management Data Warehouse, and the Activity Monitor.

Extended Events is a general event handling system in the database engine. You can use this feature to track waits as they occur in the database engine, such as tracking wait types at a given session level Use this tool when troubleshooting specific performance related issues. Chapter 40, "Extended Events," covers Extended Events.

MDW is a SQL Server database populated by the Data Collector that tracks wait stats along with many other pieces of performance data. Use this tool when taking a holistic approach to performance troubleshooting as it can capture a very wide range of performance related data. Chapter 43, "Management Data Warehouse," covers MDW.

Activity Monitor is a tool that you can launch through Management Studio that enables you to view performance information for your SQL instance. Through the Activity Monitor you can view active tasks, wait statistics, IO performance, and expensive queries. This tool provides a very nice snapshot view of the activity on a system at a given point in time.

Summary

Analyzing where SQL Server spends its time waiting should be one of the first steps you take for performance tuning. You need to realize that high wait values represent smoke, not fire. Use them as a compass to find where you may be experiencing performance problems on your SQL Server instance.

Extended Events

E xtended Events, which debuted in SQL Server 2008, is a general event-handling system that you can use to diagnose and troubleshoot issues inside the SQL Server database engine. The main design goals of the Extended Events engine are to ensure that the overhead it produces on the system is at a minimum and that it is as scalable and extensible as possible.

This chapter is an overview of the Extended Events object model as well as the many new features added to Extended Events in SQL Server 2012.

NOTE

SQL Trace is now deprecated in SQL Server 2012. Extended Events will be the tool of choice to use in the future versions of SQL Server for tracing and troubleshooting SQL Server events.

The Extended Events Object Model

The Extended Events engine is a collection of services and objects that enable and manage events and event processing inside of the SQL Server database engine. The Extended Events engine does not provide any of the events or the actions to take when events are fired. The information associated with the events and the objects associated with events lie in the object model shown in Figure 40-1.

FIGURE 40-1

This figure lists all objects in the Extended Events object model.

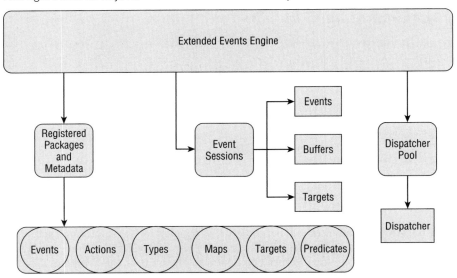

Packages

The Extended Events objects exist inside of modules called *Packages*. At the top level, Extended Events organizes its components into nine separate packages, not all of which you can interact with directly. Following are the three packages you're most likely to deal with:

- The Package0 package provides base functionality used by the other packages.
- The sqlos package works with the SQLOS events.
- The sqlserver package works with the rest of SQL Server. In SQL Server 2012 there are actually two different sqlserver packages.

Each of these packages contains several objects. To see the full list of objects within packages, use the following DMV query:

```
SELECT
PackageName = p.name, EventName = o.name,
EventDescription = o.description
FROM sys.dm_xe_objects o
JOIN sys.dm_xe_packages p ON o.package_guid = p.guid
ORDER BY p.name, o.object_type
```

Events

An Event is an interesting point in the SQL Server executable code. Events in Extended Events are similar in concept to SQL Trace events in that they represent specific data points that you want to capture. Everything in Extended Events centers on the Event object because it is the fulcrum on which all other Extended Events objects rely. Each Event has a default set of fields associated with the payload information the event delivers. Other information can be gathered for the Event through Actions.

Use the following query to find all available Extended Events and the Package they belong to:

```
SELECT
PackageName = p.name, EventName = o.name,
EventDescription = o.description
FROM sys.dm_xe_objects o
JOIN sys.dm_xe_packages p ON o.package_guid = p.guid
WHERE object_type = 'event'
```

Actions

An Action is the response to a captured Event. In most cases in Extended Events, you use Actions to acquire additional data not present in the default payload of the Event you capture. However, they can be used for other reasons, such as triggering a stack dump. Actions always occur synchronously, so capturing too many Actions may hinder the performance of Extended Events.

Use the following query to find all available Extended Events Actions and the Package they belong to:

```
SELECT
PackageName = p.name, ActionName = o.name,
ActionDescription = o.description
FROM sys.dm_xe_objects o
JOIN sys.dm_xe_packages p ON o.package_guid = p.guid
WHERE object_type = 'action'
```

Targets

A Target is the consumer of captured Extended Events data. The two formats for Targets are either a file destination or an in-memory destination, of which there are several formats. Targets can consume data synchronously or asynchronously depending on the type of the Target.

Use the following query to find all available Extended Events Targets and the Package they belong to:

```
SELECT
PackageName = p.name, TargetName = o.name,
TargetDescription = o.description
```

40

```
FROM sys.dm_xe_objects o
JOIN sys.dm_xe_packages p ON o.package_guid = p.guid
WHERE object_type = 'target'
```

Predicates

A Predicate is used to specify criteria on Events captured. There are a couple of things worth noting about Predicates. First, the criteria are evaluated in the order in which the Predicates are written, so it is important to place the most restrictive criteria first. Second, Predicates (pred_source values) are evaluated before additional Actions are captured. Because actions occur synchronously, the evaluation of Predicates before performing Actions leads to significant performance gains, which were previously not enjoyed in SQL Trace.

Use the following query to find all available Extended Events Predicate (global) fields and the Package they belong to:

```
SELECT
PackageName = p.name, PredicateName = o.name,
PredicateDescription = o.description
FROM sys.dm_xe_objects o
JOIN sys.dm_xe_packages p ON o.package_guid = p.guid
WHERE object_type = 'pred_source'
```

> **NOTE**
>
> There is an additional type of predicate that defines the rules in which values against predicate fields are compared. Sometimes known as comparators, these values can be found using the preceding query and searching for the object_type of pred_compare. In most cases, the usage of commonly known comparison operators, such as >, <, = will be overloaded and will work as expected.

Maps

A Map is similar to a lookup table in the database engine. Maps store detailed data that can be traced back to, typically, integer data stored in an Extended Events payload. This enables the engine to store less data for the Event, which aids performance.

One example you commonly see used with Maps is the lookup of different wait types for a SQL Server instance. You can use the following query to find the lookup values for all wait types available to Extended Events:

```
SELECT *
FROM sys.dm_xe_map_values
WHERE name = 'wait_types'
```

Sessions

A Session is the cohesive object that brings the rest of the Extended Events objects together and is similar to the concept of a Trace in SQL Trace. The Session is a collection of

Events and the associated Targets that consume the Event data. One significant feature of an Extended Events session is that it is defined in metadata and will persist a restart of SQL Server. This is an enhancement over a SQL Trace session, which would not survive a SQL Server reboot without administrative intervention.

To find all the Sessions defined on the SQL Server instance, use the following query:

```
select *
from sys.server_event_sessions.
```

To find all the Sessions defined and running on the SQL Server instance, use the following query:

```
select *
from sys.dm_xe_sessions
```

Channels

Although not an Extended Events object, a Channel provides useful Event association. A Channel is nothing more than a meta-data description that describes the typical audience for an event. In SQL Server 2008 and SQL Server 2012, four Channels associate with events:

- **Admin**: Events typically geared toward DBAs and end users. Often signals events with well-defined resolutions.
- **Analytic**: Events geared toward performance investigations. Typically high in volume and describe program operation.
- **Debug**: Events to assist product support and developers. Used to troubleshoot specific problems with working on a support ticket.
- **Operational**: Events geared toward DBAs and end users like Admin events, but include events that Operations may be interested in as well, such as when a database was detached.

Channels are useful when searching for types of events and are used heavily in the new Extended Events Profiler UI.

The system_health Session

The system_health session is a predefined Extended Events session that collects system data to help troubleshoot issues in the Database Engine. The session collections information associated with high-severity errors, deadlocks, nonyielding scheduler problems, and sessions that have had to wait a long time for locks or preemptive (OS) waits. This session starts when SQL Server starts and outputs data to a ring buffer as well as a file on the file system. You can disable or modify this session, but it is recommended that you do not because it can trap a lot of useful information that can be used to troubleshoot and fix SQL Server problems.

40

The Extended Events Profiler

The biggest change to Extended Events in SQL Server 2012 is the new user interface to create and modify Extended Events sessions. Extended Events now has a folder under the Management folder in Object Explorer (see Figure 40-2). From this folder you can create a new Extended Event session, modify existing sessions, view Target data for existing sessions, and Watch Live Data. If you choose the last option you're presented with an interface similar to the SQL Profiler you're familiar with, but one that captures Extended Events information as it is processed.

FIGURE 40-2

You can view the new Extended Events folder in Object Explorer. Users can now create and modify Event Sessions graphically using SQL Server Management Studio.

What's New with Extended Events in SQL Server 2012

There are several enhancements to Extended Events in SQL Server 2012. Although the largest improvement is the new Extended Events Profiler, there are new Actions and Targets, a new Extended Events event reader API, the ability to interact with Extended Events via PowerShell, and the new sp_server_diagnostics stored procedure. This system stored procedure uses Extended Events data to report on system components and is used heavily to capture system heartbeat information in the new AlwaysOn feature.

Finally, while there are no special commandlets in PS for interacting with XEvents, you can now use PS to traverse XE objects just like you would any other object in SQL.

Viewing the properties for a given session details the events for the session along with any predicates, actions, and targets associated with the session. You can modify the session as necessary using this user interface. See Figure 40-3.

FIGURE 40-3

You can use the Extended Events user interface in SQL Server 2012 to create new Event Sessions as well as modify existing Event Sessions.

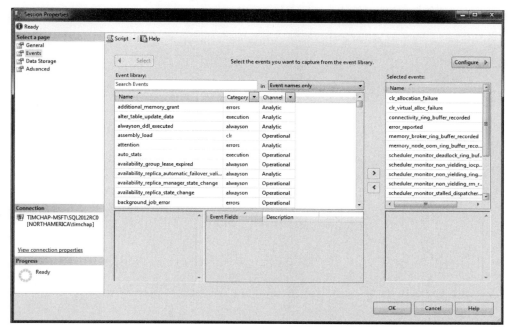

When creating a new session, you have the option to use the New Session Wizard or use the New Session dialog. The main difference between the two is that the wizard is more similar to the dialog you would see when you designed a Trace in SQL Server Profiler. With the wizard, you have two options for Targets: a file destination and a Ring Buffer. Also, Predicates are created session-wide. This is substantially different than the New Session Dialog where you can use any of the available Targets and can set Predicates at the Event level.

A useful option when defining an Extended Events Session is to use the built-in templates. Similar to the templates exposed in SQL Trace Profiler, the Extended Events templates are built with a specific purpose; such as finding high duration locking or exposing database file IO problems, etc. You can also define an Extended Events Session and save that definition as a template.

40

Summary

Extended Events is an extremely useful tool in troubleshooting SQL Server problems. In SQL Server 2008, the feature didn't have the graphical tools in place to create and modify event sessions, so it wasn't as widely adopted as was hoped. However, in SQL Server 2012, the new user-interface for Extended Events has provided a huge step forward in usability. With the new graphical user interface, users can easily create and modify event sessions without the need to know all the underlying DMVs, as was previously needed.

Data Change Tracking and Capture

All Change Tracking does is say to the world: "This row was changed; here's the PK." Clean and simple, no fuss, no muss. It's easy to configure and query.

Although Change Data Capture is limited to only the Enterprise Edition, Change Tracking is available in all the SQL Server editions, even SQL Server Express.

Change Tracking occurs synchronously within the transaction. It simply records in an internal table the primary key values of the rows that are modified. Although there's a performance cost to recording the changes within the transaction, it means that SQL Agent is not required.

Optionally, Change Tracking can store which columns were changed, using a bit-mapped method similar to how triggers know which column was included in the DML code.

The real purpose of Change Tracking is to support synchronization (not auditing). By easily and reliably recording the primary keys of which rows were inserted, updated, or deleted since the last synchronization, it becomes much simpler to perform the synchronization.

Change Tracking returns the net changes. If a row is inserted and updated since the last synchronization, then Change Tracking lists it as an insert and inserts the latest version of the row. If the row is inserted and deleted, then it won't even show in the Change Tracking results — which is perfect for applications that need synchronization.

Several applications can benefit from using Change Tracking:

- Microsoft Synch Framework
- Caching data in middle tiers for performance
- Synchronizing occasionally connected mobile applications

There is a small performance hit for using Change Tracking, but it's a lightweight feature with about the same performance hit as adding an index. The performance cost depends on the size of the primary key and the number of rows affected by the transaction. A single column integer primary will have less performance cost than a wide composite primary key. Adding column tracking also adds to the performance overhead.

Configuring Change Tracking

Compared to other optional SQL Server technologies, Change Tracking is relatively easy to turn on and configure. It's simply turned on for the database and then for each table.

Enabling the Database

Change Tracking may be enabled for the database in Object Explorer's Database Properties dialog, available from each database's context menu (as shown in Figure 41-1). Changing the values in the drop-down boxes immediately changes the database settings when you close the properties dialog.

FIGURE 41-1

The Database Properties' Change Tracking page displays the current settings and may be used to enable or disable Change Tracking.

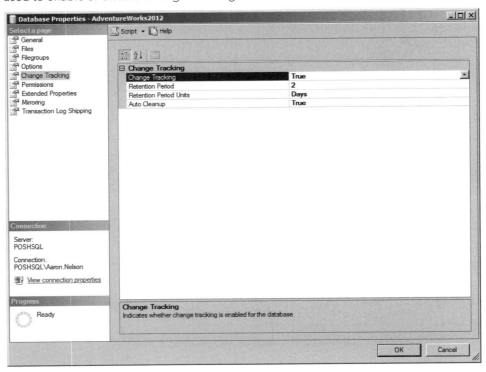

Change Tracking may also be configured with T-SQL using SQL ALTER SET:

```
ALTER DATABASE  AdventureWorks2012
SET Change_tracking = on
(change_retention = 24 hours,
auto_cleanup = on);
```

The current Change Tracking database configuration can be viewed in the Object Explorer Database Properties dialog, or by querying the sys.change_tracking_databases DMV:

```
SELECT d.name, ct.is_auto_cleanup_on, ct.retention_period,
   ct.retention_period_units, ct.retention_period_units_desc
  FROM sys.change_tracking_databases ct
    JOIN sys.databases d
      ON ct.database_id = d.database_id;
```

The database must be in 9.0 Compatibility Mode or higher, and at least db_owner role permission is required to enable the database for Change Tracking.

Auto Cleanup

Change Tracking can create a lengthy audit trail, but it can also optionally automatically clean up old Change Tracking data. The retention period can be set to any number of Days, Hours, or Minutes. The default is to retain the data for two days (which is probably too short for most applications).

Auto_cleanup and the retention period can be set when Change Tracking is initially enabled, or it can be modified later by reissuing the set Change_Tracking option with the new retention settings. In this situation, because Change Tracking is already enabled, re-enabling Change Tracking would generate an error. It's only necessary to change the option setting:

```
ALTER DATABASE [AdventureWorks2012]
SET change_tracking (change_retention = 7 days)
```

Change Tracking doesn't know when synchronizations occur. If the synchronization application doesn't run before the retention period expires, then the changes will not be seen by the synchronization. Meaning that by default, you'd have to re-sync everything if you had been disconnected for the weekend.

Best Practice

Estimate the longest possible period between synchronizations and then triple that time to set your retention time. Other than the disk space usage, there's no risk in a longer retention period, but there's considerable risk in a retention period that's too short.

Enabling Tables

The ease to configure Change Tracking continues with enabling Change Tracking of each table. Using Management Studio, table Change Tracking is viewed or enabled/disabled in the Table Properties dialog, on the Change Tracking page, as shown in Figure 41-2.

FIGURE 41-2

Use the Table Properties dialog to view the table's Change Tracking settings.

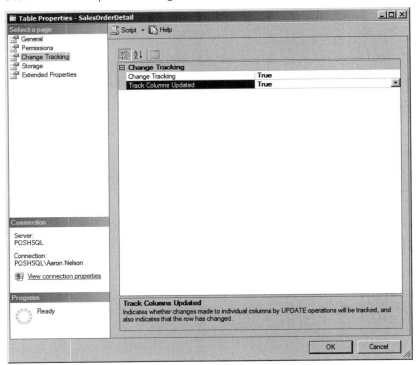

Like the database, Change Tracking is enabled using T-SQL for tables with an `alter` command:

```
ALTER TABLE HumanResources.Department
   Enable Change_tracking
   With (track_columns_updated = on);
```

The only option is to enable or disable whether Change Tracking tracks which columns were changed. By default, column tracking is disabled.

Enabling Change Tracking for a table can affect other tasks:

- The primary key constraint/index cannot be dropped while Change Tracking is enabled.

- If the table is dropped, then Change Tracking is first removed from the table.

- The table can't use a partitioned table's `alter table...switch partition` command.

- Change Tracking does not track changes made by the `truncate table` command. In this case, the synch target table should also be truncated.

To view the current tables with Change Tracking enabled, query the `sys.change_tracking_tables` DMV:

```
SELECT s.name + '.' + t.name as [table],
    ct.is_track_columns_updated_on,ct.min_valid_version,
    ct.begin_version, ct.cleanup_version
  FROM sys.change_tracking_tables ct
    JOIN sys.tables t
      ON ct.object_id = t.object_id
    JOIN sys.schemas s
      ON t.schema_id = s.schema_id
  ORDER BY [table];
```

Internal Tables

Change Tracking stores its data in internal tables. There's no reason to directly query these tables to use Change Tracking. However, it is useful to look at the space used by these tables when considering the cost to use Change Tracking and to estimate disk usage.

Query `sys.internal_tables` to find the internal tables. Of course, your Change Tracking table(s) will have a different name:

```
SELECT s.name + '.' + o.name as [table],
    i.name as [ChangeTracking],
    ct.is_track_columns_updated_on,
    ct.min_valid_version,
    ct.begin_version, ct.cleanup_version
  FROM sys.internal_tables i
    JOIN sys.objects o
      ON i.parent_id = o.object_id
    JOIN sys.schemas s
      ON o.schema_id = s.schema_id
    JOIN sys.change_tracking_tables ct
      ON o.object_id = ct.object_id
  WHERE i.name LIKE 'change_tracking%'
  ORDER BY [table]
```

Result (abbreviated):

```
table                       ChangeTracking
-----------------------      ----------------------------
HumanResources.Department    sys.change_tracking_757577737
```

Armed with the name, it's easy to find the disk space used. Because Change Tracking was just enabled in this database, the internal table is still empty:

```
EXEC sp_spaceused 'sys.change_tracking_757577737'
```

Result:

```
name                          rows reserved data index_size unused
-------------------------     ---- -------- ---- ---------- -------
change_tracking_757577737     0    0 KB     0 KB 0 KB       0 KB
```

Querying Change Tracking

When Change Tracking is enabled for a table, SQL Server begins to store information about which rows have changed. This data may be queried to select only the changed data from the source table — perfect for synchronization.

Version Numbers

Key to understanding Change Tracking is that Change Tracking numbers every transaction with a databasewide version number, which becomes important when working with the changed data. This version number may be viewed using a function:

```
SELECT Change_tracking_current_version();
```

Result:

```
0
```

The current version number is the number of the latest Change Tracking version stored by Change Tracking, so if the current version is 5, then there is a version 5 in the database, and the next transaction will be version 6.

The following code makes inserts and updates to the HumanResources.Department table while watching the Change Tracking version number:

```
INSERT HumanResources.Department (Name, GroupName)
   VALUES ('CT New Row', 'SQLPASS'),
          ('Test Two'  , 'SQLRally');

SELECT Change_tracking_current_version();
```

Result:

```
1
```

The inserts added two new rows, with primary key values of DepartmentID 17 and 18.

And now an update:

```
UPDATE HumanResources.Department
  SET Name = 'PASS Summit'
  WHERE Name = 'CT New Row';
```

The update affected row DepartmentID = 17.

Testing the Change Tracking version shows that it has been incremented to 2:

```
SELECT Change_tracking_current_version();
```

Result:

```
2
```

The version number is critical to querying ChangeTable (explained in the next section), and it must be within the range of the oldest possible version number for a given table and the current database version number. The old data is probably being cleaned up automatically, so the oldest possible version number will likely vary for each table.

The following query can report the valid version number range for any table. In this case, it returns the current valid queryable range for HumanResources.Department:

```
SELECT
  Change_tracking_min_valid_version
    (Object_id(N'HumanResources.Department')) as 'oldest',
  Change_tracking_current_version() as 'current';
```

Result:

```
oldest              current
------------------- -------------------
0                   2
```

Changes by the Row

Here's where Change Tracking shows results. The primary keys of the rows that have been modified after a given version number can be found by querying the ChangeTable table-valued function, passing to it the Change Tracking table and a beginning version number. For example, passing table XYZ and version number 10 to ChangeTable returns the changes for version 11 and versions following that were made to table XYZ. Think of the version number as the number of the last synchronization, so this synchronization needs all the changes after the last synchronization.

In this case, the Change Tracking table is `HumanResources.Department` and the beginning version is 0:

```
SELECT *
  FROM ChangeTable
    (Changes HumanResources.Department, 0) as CT;
```

Result:

SYS CHANGE VERSION	SYS CHANGE CREATION VERSION	SYS CHANGE OPERATION	SYS CHANGE COLUMNS	SYS CHANGE CONTEXT	DepartmentID
2	1	I	NULL	NULL	17
1	1	I	NULL	NULL	18

Since version number 0, two rows have been inserted. The update to row 17 is still reported as an insert because for the purposes of synchronization, row 17 must be inserted.

If version number 1 is passed to `ChangeTable`, then the result should show only change version 2:

```
SELECT *
  FROM ChangeTable
    (Changes HumanResources.Department, 1) as CT;
```

Result (formatted to include the `syschangecolumns` data):

SYS CHANGE VERSION	SYS CHANGE CREATION VERSION	SYS CHANGE OPERATION	SYS CHANGE COLUMNS	SYS CHANGE CONTEXT	DepartmentID
2	1	U	0x0000000002000000	NULL	17

This time row 17 shows up as an update because when version 2 occurred, row 17 already existed, and version 2 updated the row. A synchronization based on changes made since version 1 would need to update row 17.

Note that as a table-valued function, `ChangeTable` must have an alias.

Synchronizing requires joining with the source table. The following query reports the changed rows from `HumanResources.Department` since version 1. The left outer join is necessary to pick up any deleted rows which, by definition, no longer exist in the source table and would therefore be missed by an inner join:

```
SELECT CT.SYS_CHANGE_VERSION as Version,
    CT.DepartmentID, CT.SYS_CHANGE_OPERATION as Op,
    d.Name, d.GroupName
```

```
      FROM ChangeTable (Changes HumanResources.Department, 1) as CT
    LEFT OUTER JOIN HumanResources.Department d
        ON d.DepartmentID = CT.DepartmentID
    ORDER BY CT.SYS_CHANGE_VERSION;
```

Result:

```
Version  DepartmentID Op  Name           GroupName
-------  ------------ --- -------------  -------------
2        17           U   Changed Name   PASS Summit
```

As expected, the result shows row 17 being updated, so there's no data other than the primary key returned by the ChangeTable data source. The join pulls in the data from HumanResources.Department.

Removing Change Tracking

If you find that Change Tracking is causing performance problems or just not accomplishing what you want it to, it's as easy to remove Change Tracking as it is to enable it. All you have to do is disable it from every table, and then remove it from the database.

If the goal is to reduce Change Tracking by a single table, then the same ALTER command that enabled Change Tracking can disable it:

```
ALTER TABLE HumanResources.Department
    Disable Change_tracking;
```

When Change Tracking is disabled from a table, all stored ChangeTable data — the PKs and columns updated — are lost.

If the goal is to remove Change Tracking from the database, then Change Tracking must first be removed from every table in the database. One way to accomplish this is to leverage the sp_MSforeachtable stored procedure:

```
EXEC sp_MSforeachtable
    'ALTER TABLE ?
      Disable Change_tracking;';
```

However, after much testing, in many cases sp_msforeachtable often fails to remove Change Tracking from every table.

A less elegant, but more reliable, method to ensure that Change Tracking is completely removed from every table in the database is to actually cursor through the sys.change_tracking_tables table:

```
DECLARE @SQL NVARCHAR(MAX)='';
SELECT @SQL = @SQL + 'ALTER TABLE ' + s.name + '.' + t.name +
    ' Disable Change_tracking;'
FROM sys.change_tracking_tables ct
```

```
JOIN sys.tables t
  ON ct.object_id = t.object_id
JOIN sys.schemas s
  ON t.schema_id = s.schema_id;
PRINT @SQL;
EXEC sp_executesql @SQL;
```

Only after Change Tracking is disabled from every table can Change Tracking be removed from the database:

```
ALTER DATABASE AdventureWorks2012
  SET Change_tracking = off;
```

Even though Change Tracking is removed from the database, it doesn't reset the Change Tracking version number, so if Change Tracking is restarted it won't cause a synchronization nightmare. Although Change Tracking can be used with any edition, now take a look at a more feature-rich technology that is only available in Enterprise Edition: Change Data Capture.

Change Data Capture

Where change data capture shines is in gathering data for ETL from a high-traffic OLTP database to a data warehouse. Of the possible options, change data capture has the least performance hit and does a great job to provide the right set of data for the Business Intelligence ETL (extract-transform-load). When you think big-dollar BI, think CDC.

Any data written to the transaction log can be asynchronously captured using CDC from the transaction log after the transaction is complete, so it doesn't affect the original transaction's performance. CDC can track any data from the T-Log, including any DML insert, update, delete, and merge command, and DDL create, alter, and drop.

Changes are stored in change tables — tables created by CDC with the same columns as the tracked tables plus a few extra CDC-specific columns. All the changes are captured, so CDC can return all the intermediate values or just the net changes.

The new features (Considerations) for CDC introduced with SQL Server 2012 mostly fall into two main categories: AlwaysOn and External Drivers. When working with AlwaysOn Replicas there is only one way to collect the data properly. Some new third-party drivers have been developed for use with external data sources like Oracle.

For more information on the third-party drivers, see http://blogs.msdn.com/b/mattm/archive/2012/03/26/cdc-for-oracle-in-sql-server-2012.aspx.

Because CDC gathers its data by reading the log, the data in the change tables is organized the same way the transaction log is organized — by T-log log sequence numbers, known as LSNs.

There are only a few drawbacks to CDC:

- **Cost**: It requires Enterprise Edition.
- **T-Log I/O**: The transaction log experiences about twice as much I/O because CDC reads from the log.
- **Disk space**: Because CDC essentially stores copies of every transaction's data, without proper maintenance there's the potential that it can grow like a transaction log gone wild.
- **SSIS**: You will probably need to set up an SSIS package for the data.

New in SQL Server 2012

Although things haven't necessarily changed for CDC in SQL Server 2012, if you want to use CDC with the new AlwaysOn features, you need to know the ground rules. In short: CDC has to read the data from the Primary Replica. On failover, CDC can pick up on the new Primary where it left on the old Primary. However, if you haven't set up the SQL Agent Jobs on the failover machine, you need to do that on failover for everything to work properly. It might be advisable to set up the connection string to use the Primary Replica's Availability Group Listener name instead of the node name so that things continue to work on failover.

When reading from the CDC Change Tables, you can do so at the Primary or the Secondary. Obviously reading the data from the Secondary can help take the performance load off your Primary. If you decide to read the Change Table data at the Secondary, you must specify the connection with `readonly` intent. Optionally, you can connect to individual nodes of your Secondary, or you can specify the Availability Group name of the Secondary and have your query automatically routed to whichever Secondary is currently available.

For more information on AlwaysOn see Chapter 27, "Database Mirroring."

Enabling CDC

CDC is enabled at the database level first and then for every table that needs to be tracked. Because CDC reads from the transaction log, you might think that CDC requires the database to be set to full recovery model so that the transaction log is kept. However, SQL Server doesn't flush the log until after the transactions have been read by CDC, so CDC can work with any recovery model, even simple.

Also, and this is important, CDC uses SQL Agent jobs to capture and clean up the data, so SQL Agent must be running or data will not be captured.

Enabling the Database

To enable the database, execute the `sys.sp_cdc_enable_db` system stored procedure in the current database. It has no parameters:

```
EXEC sys.sp_cdc_enable_db
```

You can use the `is_cdc_enabled` column in `sys.databases` to determine which databases have CDC enabled on them:

```
SELECT *
FROM sys.databases
WHERE is_cdc_enabled = 1
```

This procedure creates six system tables in the current database:

- `cdc.captured_columns`: Stores metadata for tracked table's columns
- `cdc.change_tables`: Stores metadata for tracked tables
- `cdc.ddl_history`: Tracks DDL activity
- `cdc.index_columns`: Tracks table indexes
- `cdc.lsn_time_mapping`: Used for calculating clean-up time
- `dbo.systranschemas`: Tracks schema changes

These are listed in Object Explorer under the Database ➪ Tables ➪ System tables node.

Enabling Tables

After the database has been prepared for CDC, tables may be set up for CDC using the `sys.sp_cdc_enable_table` stored procedure, which has several options:

- `@source_schema`: The tracked table's schema
- `@source_name`: The name of the table to be tracked
- `@role_name`: The role with permission to view CDC data

The last six parameters are optional:

- `@capture_instance`: May be used to create multiple capture instances for the table. This is useful if the schema is changed.
- `@supports_net_changes`: Allows seeing just the net changes and requires a unique index or primary key. The default is `true`.
- `@index_name`: The name of the unique index, if there's no primary key for the table. (But you'd never do that, right?)
- `@captured_column_list`: Determines which columns are tracked. The default is to track all columns.

- ■ `@filegroup_name`: The filegroup the CDC will be stored on. If not specified, then the change table is created on the default filegroup.

- ■ `@allow_partition_switch`: Allows ALTER TABLE...SWITCH PARTITION on CDC table.

> **NOTE**
>
> If you were following along for the examples in the Change Tracking section of this chapter please note that you will need to drop and re-create your AdventureWorks database before attempting the examples here in the Change Data Capture section.

The following batch configures CDC to track changes made to the `HumanResources` `.Department` table:

```
EXEC sys.sp_cdc_enable_table
    @source_schema = 'HumanResources',
    @source_name = 'Department',
    @role_name = null;
```

With the first table that's enabled, SQL Server generates two SQL Agent jobs:

- ■ `cdc.dbname_capture`
- ■ `cdc.dbname_cleanup`

With every table that's enabled for CDC, SQL Server creates a change table. In addition, these three tables are created when CDC is enabled:

- ■ `cdc.change_tables`
- ■ `cdc.index_columns`
- ■ `cdc.captured_columns`

> **NOTE**
>
> For an excellent article on tuning the performance of CDC under various loads, see `http://msdn.microsoft` `.com/en-us/library/dd266396.aspx`.

Working with Change Data Capture

It isn't difficult to work with change data capture. The trick is to understand the transaction log's log sequence numbers.

Assuming `AdventureWorks2012` has been freshly installed, the following scripts make some data changes, so there will be some activity in the log for CDC to gather:

```
INSERT HumanResources.Department (Name, GroupName)
   VALUES ('CDC New Row', 'SQL Rocks'),
          ('Test Two'   , 'CDC Rocks ');

UPDATE HumanResources.Department
   SET Name = 'Changed Name'
   WHERE Name = 'CDC New Row';


INSERT HumanResources.Department (Name, GroupName)
   VALUES ('Row Three', 'PBM Rocks'),
          ('Row Four'  , 'TVP Rocks');

UPDATE HumanResources.Department
   SET GroupName = 'T-SQL Rocks'
   WHERE Name = 'Test Two';

DELETE FROM HumanResources.Department
   WHERE Name = 'Row Four';
```

With five transactions complete, there should be some activity in the log. The following DMVs can reveal information about the log:

```
SELECT *
   FROM sys.dm_cdc_log_scan_sessions

SELECT *
   FROM sys.dm_repl_traninfo

SELECT *
   FROM sys.dm_cdc_errors
```

Examining the Log Sequence Numbers

The data changes are organized in the change tables by log sequence number (LSN). Converting a given date time to LSN is essential to working with CDC. The `sys.fn_cdc_map_time_to_lsn` function is designed to do just that. The first parameter defines the LSN search (called *LSN boundary options*), and the second parameter is the point in time. Possible searches are as follows:

- Smallest greater than
- Smallest greater than or equal
- Largest less than
- Largest less than or equal

Each of the search options defines how the function can locate the nearest LSN in the change tables.

The following sample query defines a range beginning with Jan 20 and ending with Jan 24, and returns the LSNs that bound that range:

```
select
  sys.fn_cdc_map_time_to_lsn
     ('smallest greater than or equal', '20120101')
     as BeginLSN,
  sys.fn_cdc_map_time_to_lsn
     ('largest less than or equal', '20121231')
     as EndLSN;
```

Result:

```
BeginLSN                EndLSN
--------------------    ----------------------
0x0000002F000001330040  0x0000003B000002290001
```

The sys.fn_cdc_get_min_lsn() and sys.fn_cdc_get_max_lsn() functions serve as anchor points to begin the walk through the log. The min function requires a table and returns the oldest log entry. The max function has no parameters and returns the most recent LSN in the change tables:

```
DECLARE
  @BeginLSN VARBINARY(10) =
     sys.fn_cdc_get_min_lsn('HumanResources_Department');
SELECT @BeginLSN;

DECLARE
  @EndLSN VARBINARY(10) =
     sys.fn_cdc_get_max_lsn();
SELECT @EndLSN;
```

There's not much benefit to knowing the hexadecimal LSN values by themselves, but the LSNs can be passed to other functions to select data from the change tables.

Querying the Change Tables

Change tracking creates a function for each table being tracked using the name cdc .fn_cdc_get_all_changes concatenated with the schema and name of the table. The following script uses the sys.fn_cdc_map_time_to_lsn function to determine the LSN range values, store them in variables, and then pass the variables to the department tables' custom change data capture function:

```
-- with variables
DECLARE
  @BeginLSN VARBINARY(10) =
     sys.fn_cdc_map_time_to_lsn
        ('smallest greater than or equal', '20120101'),
  @EndLSN VARBINARY(10) =
```

```
sys.fn_cdc_map_time_to_lsn
    ('largest less than or equal', '20121231');
SELECT __$start_lsn, __$seqval, __$operation,
    __$update_mask, DepartmentID Name, GroupName, ModifiedDate
FROM cdc.fn_cdc_get_all_changes_HumanResources_Department
    (@BeginLSN, @EndLSN, 'all')
ORDER BY __$start_lsn
```

Result:

__$start_lsn	__$seqval	__$operation
0x0000005400001D6E0008	0x0000005400001D6E0003	2
0x0000005400001D6E0008	0x0000005400001D6E0006	2
0x0000005400001D700007	0x0000005400001D700002	4
0x0000005400001D7D0008	0x0000005400001D7D0003	2
0x0000005400001D7D0008	0x0000005400001D7D0006	2
0x0000005400001D7F0004	0x0000005400001D7F0002	4
0x0000005400001D810005	0x0000005400001D810003	1

__$update_mask	Name	GroupName	ModifiedDate
0x0F	17	SQL Rocks	2012-03-04 11:21:48.720
0x0F	18	CDC Rocks	2012-03-04 11:21:48.720
0x02	17	SQL Rocks	2012-03-04 11:21:48.720
0x0F	19	PBM Rocks	2012-03-04 11:21:55.387
0x0F	20	TVP Rocks	2012-03-04 11:21:55.387
0x04	18	T-SQL Rocks	2012-03-04 11:21:48.720
0x0F	20	TVP Rocks	2012-03-04 11:21:55.387

You can also pass the functions directly to the table's CDC function. This is essentially the same code as the previous query, but slightly simpler, which is usually a good thing:

```
SELECT *
FROM cdc.fn_cdc_get_all_changes_HumanResources_Department
    (sys.fn_cdc_map_time_to_lsn
        ('smallest greater than or equal', '20120101'),
    sys.fn_cdc_map_time_to_lsn
        ('largest less than or equal', '20121231'),
    'all') as CDC
ORDER BY __$start_lsn
```

You can also convert an LSN directly to a time using the fn_cdc_map_lsn_to_time() function. The next query extends the previous query by returning the time of the transaction:

```
-- with lsn converted to time
SELECT
sys.fn_cdc_map_lsn_to_time(__$start_lsn)
```

```
    as StartLSN, *
    FROM cdc.fn_cdc_get_all_changes_HumanResources_Department
      (sys.fn_cdc_map_time_to_lsn
          ('smallest greater than or equal', '20120101'),
       sys.fn_cdc_map_time_to_lsn
          ('largest less than or equal', '20121231'),
      'all') as CDC
    ORDER BY __$start_lsn
```

The __$Operation column returned by the CDC custom table functions identifies the type of DML that caused the data change. Similar to a DML trigger, the data can be the before (deleted table) or after (inserted table) image of an update.

The default 'all' parameter directs CDC to return only the after, or new, image from an update operation. The 'all update old' option, shown in the following example, tells CDC to return a row for both the before update image and the after update image.

This query uses a row constructor subquery to spell out the meaning of the operation:

```
SELECT
    sys.fn_cdc_map_lsn_to_time(__$start_lsn) as StartLSN,
    Operation.Description as 'Operation',
    DepartmentID, Name, GroupName
  FROM cdc.fn_cdc_get_all_changes_HumanResources_Department
    (sys.fn_cdc_map_time_to_lsn('smallest greater than or equal',
        '20120101'),
     sys.fn_cdc_map_time_to_lsn('largest less than or equal',
        '20121231'),
  'all update old') as CDC
    JOIN
      (VALUES
        (1, 'delete'),
        (2, 'insert'),
        (3, 'update/deleted'), -- 'all update old' option to view
        (4, 'update/inserted')
      ) as Operation(OperationID, Description)
      ON CDC.__$operation = Operation.OperationID
    ORDER BY __$start_lsn
```

Result:

StartLSN	Operation	DepartmentID	Name	GroupName
2012-06-04 23:06:35.753	insert	17	CDC New Row	SQL Rocks
2012-06-04 23:06:35.753	insert	18	Test Two	CDC Rocks
2012-06-04 23:06:47.580	update/deleted	17	CDC New Row	SQL Rocks
2012-06-04 23:06:47.580	update/inserted	17	Changed Name	SQL Rocks
2012-06-04 23:06:51.350	insert	19	Row Three	PBM Rocks

```
2012-06-04 23:06:51.350 insert          20          Row Four    TVP Rocks
2012-06-04 23:06:54.570 update/deleted  18          Test Two    CDC Rocks
2012-06-04 23:06:54.570 update/inserted 18          Test Two    T-SQL Rocks
2012-06-04 23:06:59.530 delete          20          Row Four    TVP Rocks
```

Querying Net Changes

All the previous queries returned all the changes within the requested time frame. But for many ETL operations or synchronizations, only the final net values are needed. Change data capture can automatically determine the net, or final, values. Use the cdc.fn_cdc_get_net_changes_schema_table function to return the net changes:

```
-- Querying Net Changes - 'all' option
SELECT
    sys.fn_cdc_map_lsn_to_time(___$start_lsn) as StartLSN,
    Operation.Description as 'Operation',
    DepartmentID, Name, GroupName
  FROM cdc.fn_cdc_get_net_changes_HumanResources_Department
 -- net changes
    (sys.fn_cdc_map_time_to_lsn('smallest greater than or equal',
        '20120101'),
      sys.fn_cdc_map_time_to_lsn('largest less than or equal',
        '20121231'),
      'all') as CDC
  JOIN
    (VALUES
      (1, 'delete'),
      (2, 'insert'),
      (3, 'update/deleted'), -- 'all update old' option to view
      (4, 'update/inserted')
    ) as Operation(OperationID, Description)
    ON CDC.___$operation = Operation.OperationID
  ORDER BY ___$start_lsn
```

Result:

```
StartLSN                Operation DepartmentID Name         GroupName
2012-06-04 23:06:47.580 insert    17           Changed Name SQL Rocks
2012-06-04 23:06:51.350 insert    19           Row Three    PBM Rocks
2012-06-04 23:06:54.570 insert    18           Test Two     T-SQL Rocks
```

When querying net changes using Change Data Capture, it's also possible to work with a column mask to determine whether a given column has changed. In the following query, the all with mask option and sys.fn_cdc_has_column_changed function are used together to test for changes in the GroupName column:

```
-- update the GroupName column
UPDATE HumanResources.Department
  SET GroupName = 'Updated 2'
```

```
    WHERE Name = 'Test Two';

-- Querying Net Changes - 'all with mask' option
SELECT
    Operation.Description as 'Operation',
    DepartmentID AS DeptID, GroupName,
    sys.fn_cdc_is_bit_set
        (sys.fn_cdc_get_column_ordinal
        ('HumanResources_Department',
        'GroupName') ,
        __$update_mask
        )
        as GroupNameUpdated,
    sys.fn_cdc_has_column_changed
        ('HumanResources_Department', -- wrong in BOL
        'GroupName',
        __$update_mask)
        as GroupNameHasChanged
FROM cdc.fn_cdc_get_net_changes_HumanResources_Department -- net
    changes
    (sys.fn_cdc_map_time_to_lsn('smallest greater than or equal',
      '20120307 8:40pm'), -- change datetime to pick up update as
    net change
    sys.fn_cdc_map_time_to_lsn('largest less than or equal',
      '20121231'),
    'all with mask') as CDC
JOIN
    (VALUES
      (1, 'delete'),
      (2, 'insert'),
      (3, 'update/deleted'), -- 'all update old' option to view
      (4, 'update/inserted')
    ) as Operation(OperationID, Description)
    ON CDC.__$operation = Operation.OperationID
    ORDER BY __$start_lsn
```

Result:

Operation	DeptID	GroupName	GroupNameUpdated	GroupNameHasChanged
Insert	17	SQL Rocks	0	NULL
Insert	19	PBM Rocks	0	NULL
Insert	18	Updated 2	0	NULL
1				

Walking Through the Change Tables

For most ETL and synchronization operations, selecting the data as a set is the best practice, but CDC also supports walking through the change table data iteratively. Think of these functions as CDC cursors.

The following script uses the sys.fn_cdc_get_min_lsn() function to identify a starting point in the change table and then iterates through the entries sequentially using the sys.fn_cdc_increment_lsn() function, which finds the next entry following the one passed in as a parameter:

```
DECLARE
  @BeginLSN VARBINARY(10) =
    sys.fn_cdc_get_min_lsn('HumanResources_Department');
SELECT @BeginLSN;

SET @BeginLSN = sys.fn_cdc_increment_lsn(@BeginLSN);
SELECT @BeginLSN;

SET @BeginLSN = sys.fn_cdc_increment_lsn(@BeginLSN);
SELECT @BeginLSN;
```

Result (obviously, your result will be different):

```
---------------------
0x000000420000136A003D
---------------------
0x000000420000136A003E
---------------------
0x000000420000136A003F
```

Likewise, CDC can move backward through the entries:

```
SET @BeginLSN = sys.fn_cdc_decrement_lsn(@BeginLSN);
SELECT @BeginLSN;
```

Result:

```
---------------------
0x000000420000136A003E
```

Removing Change Data Capture

Removing change data capture is a flexible and simple process, should you decide it isn't working or necessary. CDC can be disabled table by table, or for the whole database. When CDC is disabled for the database, it automatically disables all tables, removing the SQL Agent jobs, and dropping the custom tracked table functions. There's no need to remove CDC from each table individually before disabling CDC from the database:

```
EXEC sys.sp_cdc_disable_db;
```

To remove CDC from a specific table, use the following system stored procedure:

```
EXEC sys.sp_cdc_disable_table
  @source_schema = 'HumanResources',
```

```
        @source_name = 'Department',
        @capture_instance = 'all';
```

Summary

The need to track changes and synchronize changes with minimal performance impact to the base database (system) is requested in so many organizations that Microsoft developed multiple features to help you attack the problem.

For those of you on Standard Edition: Change Tracking does all the hard work of tracking the Primary Key ID of each row that has been updated; add auto cleanup, which is relatively easy to set up and use; and reliably return the net changes. Without question, using Change Tracking sets you up for success with ETL processes and mobile device synchronization.

For those of you running on Enterprise Edition: Change Data Capture (CDC) is Microsoft's high-end feature intended for heavy transaction OLTP systems to capture changes for ETL to the data warehouse.

Key points to remember about CDC:

- CDC uses the transaction log asynchronously to reduce the impact on OLTP transactions, but there will be some impact.
- Using CDC, you can query for all changes or net changes.
- CDC continues to be reliable even when used with a group of databases made highly available through the new AlwaysOn features.
- CDC continues to be enhanced to serve your data monitoring needs and can now capture changes from an Oracle database.

41

SQL Audit

SQL Audit was first introduced with SQL Server 2008. With the release of SQL Server 2012, several new and enhanced features to SQL Audit are available. This chapter explains what SQL Audit is and how to start using it, and points out the new features and updates from SQL Server 2008 to 2012.

SQL Audit is based on Extended Events technology; SQL Audit is both lightweight and powerful. Although you can create your own auditing solution from Extended Events, SQL Audit is an out-of-the-box solution to leverage Extended Events and collect server and database events. It is fast and easy to configure.

Although Extended Events is available for all editions of SQL Server 2008, SQL Audit is available only for the Enterprise (and Developer) Edition. Beginning with SQL Server 2012, server auditing is available for all editions of SQL Server; however, database audits are limited to Enterprise, Datacenter, Developer, and Evaluation editions.

SQL Audit Technology Overview

It takes several SQL Audit components working together to create a functioning Audit. A *SQL Server Audit* object is a bucket that collects the audit events defined by a *Server Audit Specification* and the *Database Audit Specification* and sends the audited events to a target. Following are the facts:

- A SQL Server Audit object can be written to by one Server Audit Specification and one Database Audit Specification per database.
- A SQL Server Audit can belong to only one SQL Server instance, but there may be several SQL Server Audits within an instance.
- A Server Audit Specification defines which server-level events will be captured and passed to the SQL Audit.
- A Database Audit Specification defines which database-level events are captured and passed to the SQL Audit.

- Both Server Audit Specifications and Database Audit Specifications can define sets of events or groups to be captured. Event groups encapsulate a number of related events. Database actions include select, insert, update, and delete, and they capture the user context and the entire DML query.

- The audited data includes user context information.

- The SQL Server Audit sends all the captured events to a single target: a file, the Windows Security event log (not in Windows XP), or the Windows Application event log. The Management Studio SQL Audit UI includes a tool for browsing the audit logs.

- SQL Server Audits, Server Audit Specifications, and Database Audit Specifications can all be created and managed either with Object Explorer or by using T-SQL.

- SQL Server Audits, Server Audit Specifications, and Database Audit Specifications can all be enabled or disabled. They may be modified only while disabled. All are disabled by default when they are first created because that's how Extended Events works.

- SQL Server Audits, Server Audit Specifications, and Database Audit Specifications can all be managed by Policy-Based Management.

- SQL Audits are serious. The SQL Server Audit object can be configured to shut down the server if the audit doesn't function properly.

Creating an Audit

The first step to working with SQL Audit is to create a SQL Server Audit object.

In Object Explorer, SQL Server Audit objects are listed under the server ⇨ Security ⇨ Audits node. The New Audit command in the Audits node context menu opens the Create Audit dialog, as shown in Figure 42-1.

The queue delay, which determines how long SQL Server can wait before processing the Extended Event, ranges from 1 second (1,000 milliseconds) to almost 25 days (2,147,483,647 milliseconds). The default (1 second) is reasonable for most situations. If the server is hit with heavy traffic, increasing the queue delay gives SQL Audit more flexibility.

Selecting Shut Down Server on Fail Operation ensures that the target file or the log receiving the events can be written to. If SQL Audit can't write to the target, then it writes a `msg_audit_forced_shutdown` event to the error log and shuts down the server. SQL Server Audit is much more resilient to failures in SQL Server 2012; if the target file or log receiving the events cannot be written to, SQL Server Audit can recover after the file or log comes back online. A new option has also been added, which enables you to fail database actions if they cause audited events to occur. Any action, which does not cause an audited event, continues but audited events do not. The audit continues attempting to log events and resumes when the condition that caused the failure is corrected. For additional information see the `fail_operation` for the `on_failure` event in `create server audit`.

FIGURE 42-1

Use the Create Audit dialog to define SLQ Server Audit objects, which collect events defined by the Server Audit Specification or the Database Audit Specification.

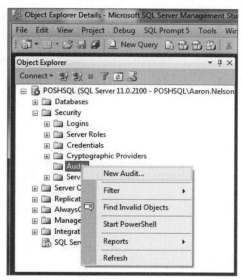

Fortunately, all the SQL Server Audit attributes may be changed after the object is created. Even the name can be changed; however, you must first disable the audit.

> **NOTE**
>
> If "audit is configured to shut down" is selected, and SQL Audit does indeed shut down the server, here's what to do: Start SQL Server with the minimal configuration option using the `-f` flag. This starts SQL Server in single-user mode and puts SQL Audit into `Auditing failure=continue` mode.

Defining the Target

The events can be sent to a file, the Windows Security event log (not available in Windows XP), or the Windows Application event log. If the target is the log, there are no other options.

If the target is a file, the receiving directory, the size of the file, and the number of roll-over files may be defined. SQL Server automatically names the files and places them in the specified directory. Beginning with SQL Server 2012, an option has been added to enable you to cap the number of audit files without rolling over. This allows users to control the amount of audit information and avoid risking losing audit records. When the `max_files` is reached and an action causes a new audit event to be recorded, the action that caused the event fails. To understand more about `max_files`, review `create server audit`.

If the target is the Windows Security Log, then there are special security permissions and configurations required. See `http://msdn.microsoft.com/en-us/library/cc645889.aspx` for detailed information.

SQL Server 2012 provides additional Transact-SQL stack frame information. Having this additional information can help auditors determine whether a query was called by an application or by a stored procedure.

Using T-SQL

You can create the SQL Server Audit object using the `CREATE SERVER AUDIT` command. The following example creates the same SQL Server Audit object (refer to Figure 42-1):

```
CREATE SERVER AUDIT [SQL Server 2012 Bible Audit]
   TO FILE (
      FILEPATH = N'C:\SQLData',
   MAXSIZE = 64 MB,
   MAX_ROLLOVER_FILES = 2147483647,
   RESERVE_DISK_SPACE = OFF
      )
   WITH (
      QUEUE_DELAY = 1000,
      ON_FAILURE = CONTINUE
      )
```

You can also modify the SQL Server Audit object using an `ALTER` command.

Beginning with SQL Server 2012, SQL Server Audit has the capability to filter audit events before being written to the audit log. You can accomplish this by including a `where` clause in the `create server audit` statement.

```
CREATE SERVER AUDIT [SQL Server 2012 Bible Audit]
   TO FILE (
      FILEPATH = N'C:\SQLData',
   MAXSIZE = 64 MB,
   MAX_ROLLOVER_FILES = 2147483647,
   RESERVE_DISK_SPACE = OFF
      )

   WITH (
      QUEUE_DELAY = 1000,
      ON_FAILURE = CONTINUE
      )
   WHERE Object_name = 'SensitiveData';
```

Enabling/Disabling the Audit

Object Explorer's SQL Server Audit node visually indicates whether the Audit is enabled or disabled with a red mark on the node if the item is currently turned off. The context menu includes commands to enable or disable the Audit.

Using T-SQL, the `alter` command has an additional parameter that enables or disables the SQL Server Audit. The following command enables the SQL Server 2012 Bible Audit:

```
ALTER SERVER AUDIT [SQL Server 2012 Bible Audit]
    WITH (State = ON)
```

Server Audit Specifications

A new Server Audit Specification may be created from Object Explorer using the Security ➪ Server Audit Specifications' context menu ➪ New Server Audit Specification command, which opens the Create Server Audit Specification dialog, as shown in Figure 42-2.

Each SQL Server Audit object may have only one Server Audit Specification, but there may be multiple Server Audits running, and each may have a Server Audit Specification.

The new Server Audit Specification can't be created unless it points to an existing SQL Server Audit object and that SQL Server Audit object currently does not have a Server Audit Specification connected to it.

With SQL Server 2012 Server-level audits are now able to be created on all editions of SQL Server.

Adding Actions

The most important part of defining the Server Audit Specification is adding actions to the specification. These actions aren't in a hierarchy like the DDL Triggers events and groups; each action group must be added individually.

Beginning with 2012, SQL Server audit specifications support a user defined audit group. You can use the `sp_audit_write` stored procedure to record audited events to the audit log. By using user-defined audit events, developers can code their applications to write custom information to the audit log.

The server-related events that can be audited are organized into 35 action groups. (Most are shown in the drop-down list in Figure 42-2.) Potentially, a Server Audit Specification could have all 35 action groups.

The Server Audit State Change Audit group, which audits whether SQL Audit is enabled or disabled, is automatically audited.

FIGURE 42-2

Creating a new Server Audit Specification using Management Studio.

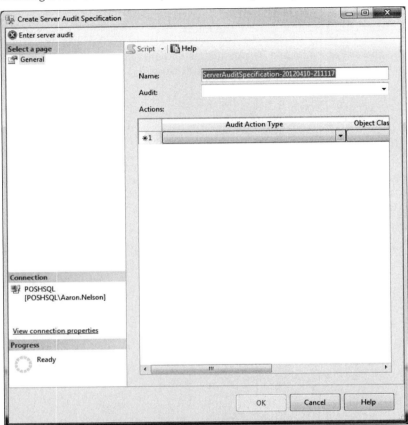

Creating with T-SQL

Using T-SQL's `create` command, it's easy to create a new Server Audit Specification. The principal parameter is the `add(action group)` option, which configures the Server Audit Specification with action groups. The following command creates a Server Audit Specification and assigns it to the SQL Server 2012 Bible Audit:

```
CREATE SERVER AUDIT SPECIFICATION
        [ServerAuditSpecification-20110801-212943]
    FOR SERVER AUDIT [SQL Server 2012 Bible Audit]
      ADD (DBCC_GROUP),
      ADD (FULLTEXT_GROUP),
      ADD (DATABASE_CHANGE_GROUP)
    WITH (STATE = ON)
```

Modifying Server Audit Specifications

You can add New Action Audit Types to the Server Audit Specification if the Server Audit Specification is disabled:

```
Alter Server Audit Specification name
    Add (Action Group)
```

To redirect a Server Audit Specification to a new SQL Server Audit, the Server Audit Specification must be disabled.

Database Audit Specifications

Database Audit Specifications are created using the same UI dialog as the Server Audit Specification. Like the Server Audit Specification, there may be only one Database Audit Specification per Database, per SQL Audit. To create multiple Database Audit Specifications, there must be multiple SQL Audits — one per Database Audit Specification.

The critical point is that Database Audit Specifications can audit DML events such as select, insert, update, and delete, as shown in Figure 42-3. You can also see the list of possible Database Audit Action Types in the drop-down list.

Beginning with SQL Server 2012, new audit groups exist that enable you to support the monitoring of contained database users.

FIGURE 42-3

This Database Audit Specification records every select statement executed by the dbo user in the AdventureWorks2012 database and passes the audit data to the SQL Server 2012 Bible SQL Audit bucket.

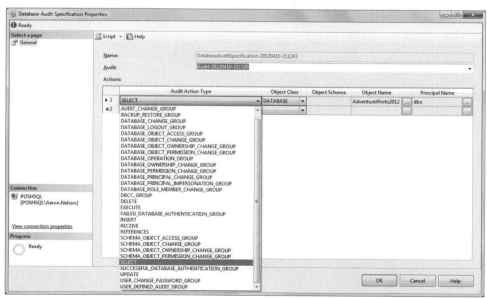

Viewing the Audit Trail

The easiest way to view the audit trail is to select the SQL Server Audit in Object Explorer and select View Logs in the context menu. This opens the Log File Viewer to the Audit Collection, as shown in Figure 42-4. The filter is useful to narrow the event viewed.

FIGURE 42-4

Viewing the audit history using Management Studio's Log File Viewer. Here, select statements issued in AdventureWorks2012 are audited on a per-table basis.

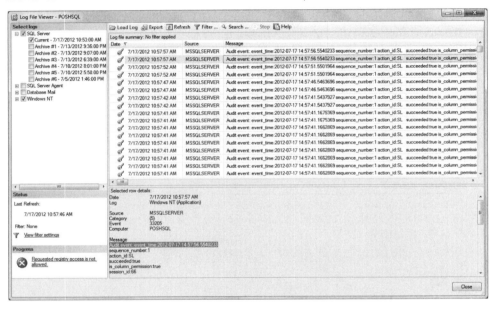

Using T-SQL, the logs can be read with the `fn_get_audit_file` function.

Enhancements have been made to Management Studio in SQL Server 2012 with the addition of new audit dialog boxes. These include the ability to manage the new filter audits feature. Additionally, you can now view the Windows NT logs; however, this feature is available in more than just SQL Audit.

Summary

Extended Events is a powerful, new auditing technology for Windows and SQL Server. By itself Extend Events take a lot of work to use. SQL Audit is a powerful collection of objects, easily configured, that extends and leverages Extended Events and makes it useful today. If your shop runs a version of SQL Server that supports SQL Server Audit, there is no reason to continue with other auditing technologies such as tracing or triggers for compliance and monitoring. SQL Audit is the future and will improve with each new version of SQL Server as is evident with the enhancements in SQL Server 2012.

Major highlights of this chapter include the following:

- Each instance may have multiple SQL Audits — collection buckets for audit data that can write to an audit file, application log, or security event log.

- Each SQL Audit can have one Server Database Specification and one Database Audit Specification per database writing to that SQL Audit. Each Server or Database Audit Specification may have multiple events or actions that it's auditing.

- Database Audit Specifications can audit DML statements: select, insert, update, and delete. In addition, the audit details include user context information.

This part covers another new monitoring technology targeted at enterprise servers. SQL Audit is a strategic tool, both for Microsoft and the IT shops that adopt it.

42

Management Data Warehouse

IN THIS CHAPTER

Using the MDW

Configuring MDW

Viewing MDW Reports Creating Custom Data Collections

M anagement Data Warehouse (MDW) is a resource and performance monitoring and reporting framework available in SQL Server 2012 Enterprise Edition. It was first introduced in SQL Server 2008 and continues to exist in SQL Server 2012.

MDW consists of a relational database, predefined data collectors, and reports. The relational database is used as a repository where performance statistics gathered by the data collectors are stored. A series of reports are provided out-of-the-box with the capability to drill down into more detailed reports about resource utilization, query performance, index utilization, and even suggestions to improve overall SQL Server performance. MDW can collect data from SQL Server 2008 and SQL Server 2012 but for no earlier versions.

Using the Management Data Warehouse

MDW provides you with detailed performance statistics that can help you with diagnosis, troubleshooting, trending, and reporting of key performance metrics. If some performance problem exists, you can use MDW to quickly diagnose and troubleshoot performance bottlenecks and analyze them over time. Examining the same time periods on different days gives you a way to find high-resource utilization patterns, performance bottlenecks, and expensive queries that cause performance degradation.

If performance suddenly decreases, you can immediately investigate and pinpoint the root cause of performance issues, such as high-memory utilization, an increase in data volume, or other processes that interfere with SQL Server operations. All potential performance problems can be isolated and dissected quickly, leading to a prompt solution.

In the past, it required a large effort to gather the necessary metrics and necessary statistics to pinpoint a performance issue. Database administrators would normally resort to third-party monitoring tools or spending a large amount of time profiling queries and consuming Dynamic Management Views (DMVs) to pinpoint a performance issue. MDW makes the process easier; it takes less time and provides an automated and simple way to report what is happening in real time, and also view performance patterns historically. It collects data, aggregates data, analyzes data, and reports on data. It does this with a minimal performance overhead to SQL Server.

The value of MDW can be more noticeable with the drill-down capability that allows looking at more detail data about a specific event, object, or a time period. For example, we can dig deep into the actual query execution plan and check for missing indexes or out-of-date statistics. You can also isolate and drill down into the processes running during high resource wait periods that might hint at resource contention issues.

The ability to collect all these data to do close to real-time analysis allows Database Administrators to quickly assess and implement corrective actions to guarantee and maintain performance service level agreements. Additionally, MDW is a valuable tool that helps in capturing and documenting server activity and resource utilization trends that can be used to do capacity planning.

Configuring MDW

This section demonstrates how to configure MDW. The first step is to make sure that SQL Agent is running and SQL Server Integration Services (SSIS) is installed and running as well. Assuming those two prerequisites have been met, follow these steps to configure MDW.

1. Launch SQL Server Management Studio, and connect to the SQL Server 2012 Database Engine where you want to configure MDW.

2. Expand the Management section, and right-click Data Collection.

3. From the context menu, select Configure Management Data Warehouse, as shown in Figure 43-1. The Configure Management Data Warehouse Wizard screen displays, as shown in Figure 43-2.

4. Click the Next button. The Select Configuration Task screen displays, as shown in Figure 43-3.

5. Select the Create or Upgrade a Management Data Warehouse option, and click Next. The Configure Management Data Warehouse Storage screen displays, as shown in Figure 43-4.

6. Select an existing database, or create a new database for MDW, and click Next. The Map Logins and Users screen displays, as shown in Figure 43-5.

FIGURE 43-1

Configure Management Data Warehouse context menu.

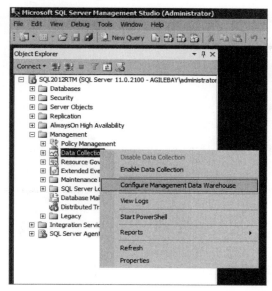

FIGURE 43-2

Configure Management Data Warehouse Wizard.

FIGURE 43-3

Select Configuration Task screen.

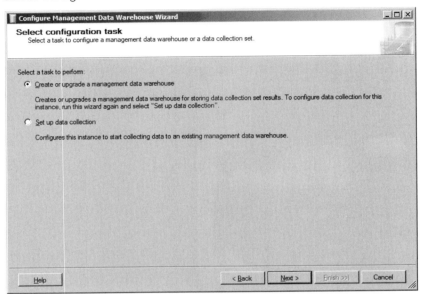

FIGURE 43-4

Configure Management Data Warehouse Storage screen.

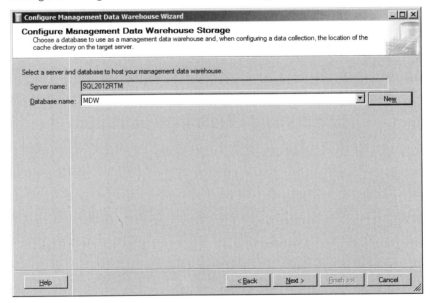

FIGURE 43-5

Map Logins and Users screen.

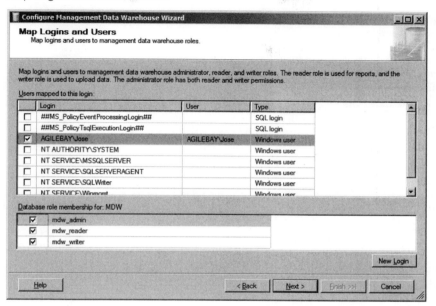

7. Select one or more logins, and assign the corresponding database role membership for the Management Data Warehouse database. The following roles are
   available:

   - **mdw_admin:** Full control, read, write, update, and delete access to the MDW and
     change schema

   - **mdw_reader:** Read-only access to the MDW

   - **mdw_writer:** Upload and write data to the MDW

8. After the proper logins map to the corresponding role, click Next to verify the
   installation. When installation options verify, click the Finish button, as shown in
   Figure 43-6.

9. When the installation successfully completes, a summary of actions performed
   displays. Click the Close button to finalize the configuration process, as shown in
   Figure 43-7.

FIGURE 43-6

Complete the Wizard screen.

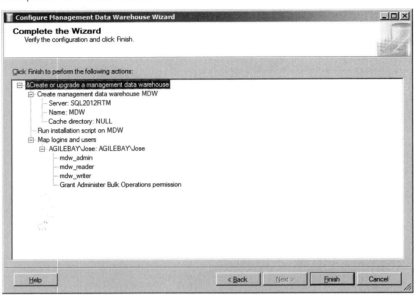

FIGURE 43-7

Configuration success.

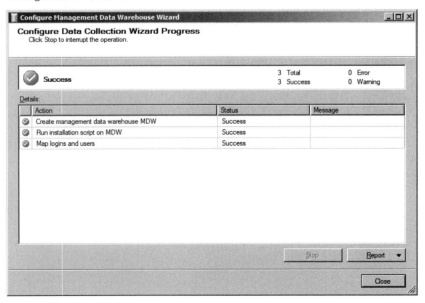

Setting Up Data Collection

After you configure the Management Data Warehouse collection database, you need to configure the instance to start collecting data from. To set up data collection, follow these steps:

1. Run the Configure Management Data Warehouse Wizard again. Refer to steps 1 and 2 from the previous section.

2. In the Task Selection screen, select Set Up Data Collection, and click Next, as shown in Figure 43-8.

FIGURE 43-8

Set Up Data Collection task option.

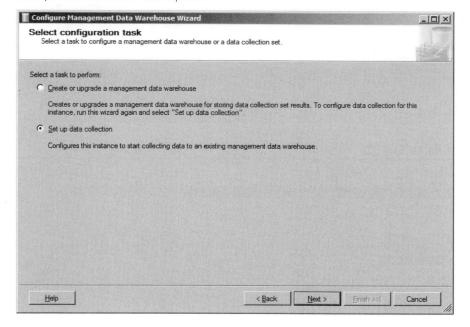

3. Select the server name and database to store the collected data. In this example, it should be the server and database configured in the previous section. In this screen, you can also select a folder to temporarily store collected data before it uploads to the MDW database. If no folder is selected, the TEMP folder will be used. Click Next. Figure 43-9 shows the MDW storage configuration screen.

4. Review the summary of actions to be performed, and click Finish, as shown in Figure 43-10.

FIGURE 43-9

Storage configuration screen.

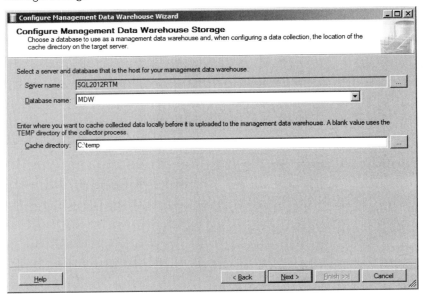

FIGURE 43-10

Configuration summary.

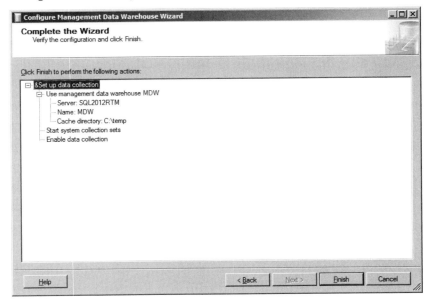

You have successfully completed configuring MDW and a Data Collection component.

Viewing MDW Reports

Now that MDW has been configured and Data Collection defined, you can see the System Data Collection Sets created under the Data Collection section, as shown in Figure 43-11.

FIGURE 43-11

Data Collection Sets.

In addition, several SQL Server Agent jobs are created and scheduled to collect and upload Disk Usage, Query Statistics, and Server Activity on a regular basis. The default upload schedule is 15 minutes but can be modified to upload data at a different interval.

After data is collected and uploaded, you can view the predefined reports for Disk Usage, Server Activity, and Query Statistic. To access these reports, follow these steps:

1. In SQL Server Management Studio, expand the management section.
2. Right-click Data Collection.
3. From the context menu, select Reports and then Management Data Warehouse.

Disk Usage Summary

The Disk Usage Summary report shows the starting size, current size, average growth and trend of your databases, and log files. Figure 43-12 shows the report for the development system.

FIGURE 43-12

The Disk Usage Summary report.

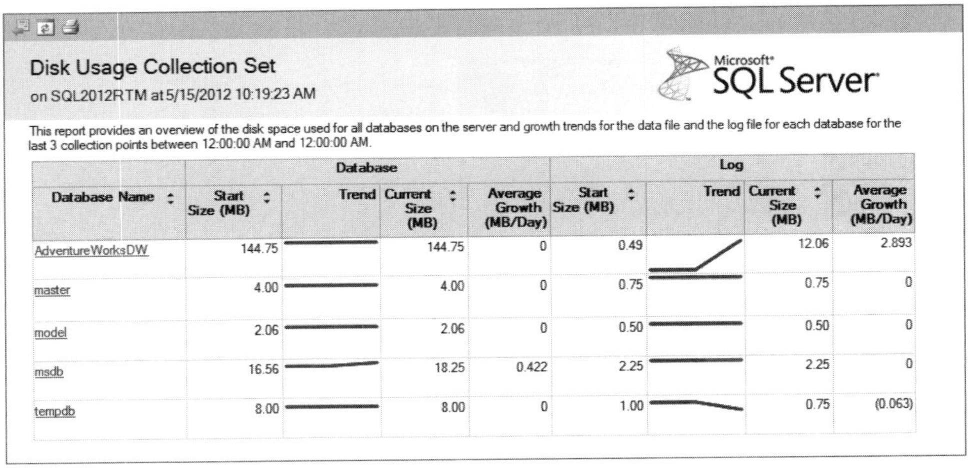

Disk Usage Collection Set
on SQL2012RTM at 5/15/2012 10:19:23 AM

This report provides an overview of the disk space used for all databases on the server and growth trends for the data file and the log file for each database for the last 3 collection points between 12:00:00 AM and 12:00:00 AM.

	Database				Log			
Database Name	Start Size (MB)	Trend	Current Size (MB)	Average Growth (MB/Day)	Start Size (MB)	Trend	Current Size (MB)	Average Growth (MB/Day)
AdventureWorksDW	144.75		144.75	0	0.49		12.06	2.893
master	4.00		4.00	0	0.75		0.75	0
model	2.06		2.06	0	0.50		0.50	0
msdb	16.56		18.25	0.422	2.25		2.25	0
tempdb	8.00		8.00	0	1.00		0.75	(0.063)

Server Activity History

The Server Activity History report shows information about resource utilization such as memory usage, percentage of CPU, disk I/O, and network usage. In addition, it shows information about operations that can impact the performance of the server including waits, locks, logging, compilations, transactions, connections, and more.. Figure 43-13 shows the Server Activity History Report.

Query Statistics

The Query Statistics report shows information about the queries that have been run and highlights the top queries by total CPU. It can identify queries that cause bottlenecks, or just consume too many resources. Figure 43-14 shows the report for the development system.

FIGURE 43-13

The Server Activity History report.

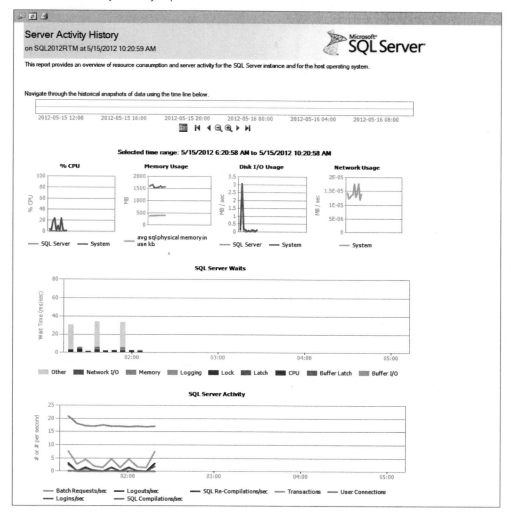

FIGURE 43-14

The Query Statistics report.

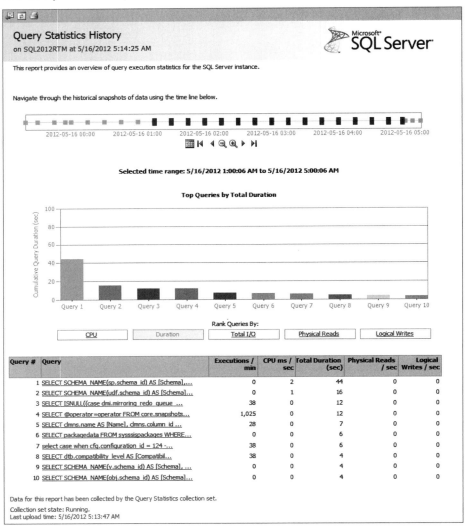

Creating Custom Data Collector Sets

The three system data collector sets discussed previously are pre-defined data collectors of some of the key metrics in SQL Server that every DBA should be familiar with. Additional data collectors can be created and scheduled to collect server activity and performance counters.

For example, a custom data collector could be created to capture clustered index fragmentation percentage levels of all databases in a SQL Server instance at different intervals throughout the day. This type of information can help database administrators to correlate and trend index fragmentation percentage levels with day-to-day data manipulation operations.

There is no user interface to create custom data collectors but one can be easily defined using T-SQL scripts and executing system stored procedures as follows:

1. Configure data collection parameters, including the instance name, database name, and cache directory. This step is necessary only if these parameters have not been set previously. These parameters were configured in the Management Data Warehouse Wizard under the section titled "Configuring MDW" earlier in this chapter.

   To configure data collection parameters you use the following T-SQL commands:

   ```
   USE msdb;
   EXEC sp_syscollector_set_warehouse_instance_name 'SQL2012RTM';
   EXEC sp_syscollector_set_warehouse_database_name 'MDW';
   EXEC sp_syscollector_set_cache_directory 'C:\temp';
   ```

2. Create the collection set using the sp_syscollector_create_collection_set system stored procedure as follows:

   ```
   USE msdb;
   DECLARE @collection_set_id int;
   DECLARE @collection_set_uid uniqueidentifier;
   EXEC sp_syscollector_create_collection_set
       @name=N'Clustered Index Fragmentation Pct',
       @collection_mode=1,
       @description=N'Collects fragmentation percentages of all Clustered Indexes
   over 10%',
       @logging_level=1,
       @days_until_expiration=14,
       @schedule_name=N'CollectorSchedule_Every_60min',
       @collection_set_id=@collection_set_id OUTPUT,
       @collection_set_uid=@collection_set_uid OUTPUT;
   SELECT @collection_set_id, @collection_set_uid;
   ```

3. Create the collection item using the sp_syscollector_create_collection_item system stored procedure as follows:

   ```
   DECLARE @collector_type_uid uniqueidentifier;
   ```

```
SELECT @collector_type_uid = collector_type_uid FROM syscollector_collector_
types
WHERE name = N'Generic T-SQL Query Collector Type';

DECLARE @collection_item_id int;
EXEC sp_syscollector_create_collection_item
@name= N'Clustered Index - Fragmentation Percentages',
@parameters=N'
<ns:TSQLQueryCollector xmlns:ns="DataCollectorType">
<Query>
<Value>DECLARE @DB_ID int
, @DB_Name varchar(100)
, @Query nvarchar(max) = ' '

DECLARE @TblOutput table (DBName varchar(100), TableName varchar(100),
IndexName varchar(100), AvgFragmentationPct real)

DECLARE DB_Cursor CURSOR FOR
SELECT database_id, name
FROM sys.databases where db_name(database_id) NOT IN ('master', 'tempdb',
'model', 'msdb')

OPEN DB_Cursor
FETCH NEXT FROM DB_Cursor INTO @DB_ID, @DB_Name;
WHILE @@FETCH_STATUS = 0
   BEGIN

  SET @Query=
    'SELECT
db_name('+convert(varchar(100),@DB_ID)+') DBName
,Object_Name(IPS.object_id, '+convert(varchar(100),@DB_ID)+') TableName
,IDX.name IndexName
,avg_fragmentation_in_percent AvgFragmentationPct
FROM

sys.dm_db_index_physical_stats('+convert(varchar(100),@DB_ID)+', NULL, NULL,
NULL, NULL) IPS
INNER JOIN '+'['+@DB_Name+']'+'.sys.indexes IDX
ON IDX.object_id=IPS.object_id AND IDX.index_id=IPS.index_id
WHERE
db_name(database_id) NOT IN (''master'', ''tempdb'', ''model'', ''msdb'')
AND index_type_desc = ''CLUSTERED INDEX''
AND avg_fragmentation_in_percent>10
AND database_id = '+convert(varchar(100),@DB_ID)+';'

INSERT INTO  @TblOutput
( DBName
 ,TableName
```

```
    ,IndexName
    ,AvgFragmentationPct
)
Execute sp_executesql @Query;

FETCH NEXT FROM DB_Cursor INTO @DB_ID, @DB_Name;
    END;
CLOSE DB_Cursor;
DEALLOCATE DB_Cursor;

SELECT * FROM @TblOutput</Value>
<OutputTable>clustered_index_fragmentation</OutputTable>
</Query>
</ns:TSQLQueryCollector>',
    @collection_item_id = @collection_item_id OUTPUT,
    @frequency = 5, -- This parameter is ignored in cached mode
    @collection_set_id = @collection_set_id,
    @collector_type_uid = @collector_type_uid;
SELECT @collection_item_id;
```

The new data collector named Clustered Index Fragmentation is listed under the Data
Collection section, as shown in Figure 43-15.

FIGURE 43-15

Custom Data Collector.

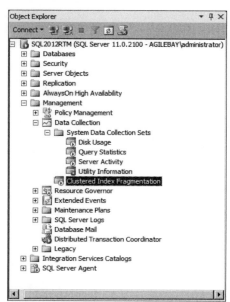

Summary

This chapter presented an overview of Management Data Warehouse and how to configure it. Management Data Warehouse helps collect and analyze resource utilization, activity, and trends on your server. MDW makes it easy to quickly identify server performance issues with minimal configuration efforts.

You can create custom data collectors to capture important metrics, such as index fragmentation levels, and schedule them to run at different intervals during the day. The collection of these data may allow database administrators to see trends in fragmentation levels throughout the day that could justify an index reorganize or index rebuild operation.

Part VIII

Performance Tuning and Optimization

IN THIS PART

Interpreting Query Execution Plans

A n execution plan is a set of instructions for how to process a SQL statement. Sounds easy, right? It's a relatively simple task to write a query to pull data from three different tables using INNER JOIN statements and summarize the data using a GROUP BY and a SUM() function. However, taking a query from its logical form, such as that SELECT statement, and devising a plan as to how to best execute that query is exponentially more complex. There are so many factors to consider that the Query Optimizer won't try to find the "best" plan — a "good enough" plan is often the best you can hope for.

This is where you come in. The SQL Server Query Optimizer is the best in the business at doing its job, but it is not always perfect because it relies heavily on a lot of factors outside of its control — statistics is one great example. Spotting these imperfections in plans is paramount to performance tuning a SQL Server system.

The ability to interpret and adjust execution plans is one of the base skills that all great performance-tuning artists possess. Yes, performance tuning is as much an art as it is a technical skill. Sure, it is not the ONLY skill you need to become great at performance tuning SQL Server; you need to understand the engine internals, how SQL Server uses memory and IO, along with a score of other things, but being great at reading execution plans and knowing how to adjust them is a great start.

What's New with Query Execution Plans?

There are several new execution plan features in SQL Server 2012. For me, one of the more exciting features is the graphical warnings in the execution plan that detail potential problems with implicit conversions and operators that can spill to tempdb.

- Management Studio's Query Editor can switch the graphical query execution plan into XML from the context menu.

- A saved query execution plan now includes the full query, so when it's re-opened, the original source query can be viewed in the Query Editor.

- The XML query execution plan is formatted better. The XML plan schema has also been greatly enhanced, which leads to many new operators in a query plan that will give additional insight into query tuning.

- The Query Editor can now open the XML query execution plan that's returned from the `sys.dm_exec_query_plan()` dynamic management function as a graphical plan with a single click.

Viewing Query Execution Plans

You have several options for viewing execution plans. This chapter looks at the options for viewing them graphically and as a result set in Management Studio, as well as viewing them via Dynamic Management Views and capturing them in SQL Server Profiler.

- Management Studio can display the estimated or actual query execution plan graphically, through XML, or via a result set.

- The Showplan directive can return the estimated query plan as a message or result set.

- The STATISTICS PROFILE directive can return the actual query plan as a message or result set.

- SQL Profiler can capture the query execution plan as plain text or as XML that can be viewed in graphic form.

- Execution plans in the plan cache may be viewed using dynamic management views (DMVs).

In addition, many of the preceding methods enable an execution plan to be saved as an XML file, which can be opened later using Management Studio.

Estimated versus Actual Execution Plans

SQL Server can return the estimated query execution plan before the query is executed, or it can return the actual query execution plan with the results of the query.

The difference between the estimated and the actual typically isn't the plan; the sequence of physical operations are often the same. The difference in the estimated versus actual plans are the number of rows returned by each operator. Before the query is executed, the

Query Optimizer can estimate the number of rows for each operator based on statistics and use that estimate in determining the plan.

This is a very important concept when it comes to performance tuning. The Query Optimizer relies heavily on statistics, and if the statistics are skewed, then a non-optimal plan may be chosen.

After the plan is executed, the query processor adds to the plan the actual number of rows processed by each operation.

The estimated query execution plan may be viewed by selecting the query in the Query Editor and either clicking the Display Estimated Execution Plan button on the toolbar, selecting Query ⇨ Display Estimated Execution Plan. The actual plan may be viewed in a similar fashion. To enable viewing the actual execution plan, choose Query ⇨ Include Actual Execution Plan.

Because the query isn't actually executed when viewing the estimated execution plan, the resulting plan should display in the Execution Plan tab rather quickly.

Reading the Execution Plan

The data flow of an execution plan is typically from right to left, top to bottom, as shown in Figure 44-1. Each operator is presented as an icon, otherwise known as a *plan operator or iterator*. The graphical execution plan is an interactive display, which enables you to hover the mouse over the operators and connections to discover the following:

- Mousing over the plan operators causes a dialog box to appear containing detailed information about the operator, including an operator description, different cost figures, number of estimated or actual rows involved, and the portion of the query handled by the operation.

- Mousing over a connector line presents detailed information about how much data is transferred between operators.

- The Property window also presents detailed information about any operator or connection between operators.

The display may be zoomed or sized to fit using the right-click context menu.

To walk through the query execution plan shown in the following Figure 44-1, follow these steps:

1. In the upper-right corner of the plan, the index seek operation finds every row with `ProductID = 757` using an index seek operation against the `WorkOrder`.`IX_WorkOrder_ProductID` nonclustered index.

2. The nested-loop operation receives every row from the index seek and asks for those same rows from the clustered index, calling the key lookup operation. You can ignore the compute scalar operation because it handles only a type conversion.

3. The nested-loop assembles, or joins, the data from the index seek and key lookup and passes the data to the select operation, which returns the correct columns to the client.

FIGURE 44-1

Execution plans show the operators SQL Server uses to satisfy a query.

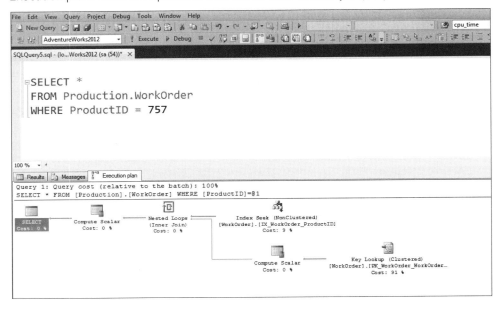

Key pieces of information on the query plan follow:

- The type of operation. Key operations are listed later in Table 44-1.
- The object, listed below the operator and in the pop-up information box, is the actual index hit by the operation.
- The estimated number of rows, because the query optimizer uses the estimated number of rows to choose the best query execution plan.
- The estimated operator cost and the estimated subtree cost are relative values used by the query optimizer. When tuning a query, these are critical values to watch. You can read the cost as cost times 1,000 — For example, .0051234 as 5, or .3255786 as 325, to make it easier to think through the plans.

You can also save plans to a plan file (.sqlplan) to be reexamined later. Re-opening a plan opens the graphical execution plan. The context menu has a new option to edit the SQL query, which opens the original SQL statement in a new Query Editor tab.

Using Showplan and STATISTICS PROFILE

In addition to the graphical execution plan, the Showplan and STATISTICS PROFILE directives reveal the execution plan with some additional detail. Similar to how you can view Estimated and Actual Execution plans graphically in Management Studio, these directives enable you to view the execution plans in different formats. Showplan is the estimated plan, whereas STATISTICS PROFILE is the actual plan.

Set Showplan must be the only statement in the batch.

Set Showplan comes is three flavors: all, text, and XML:

- Showplan_all displays the operators as a result set. It exposes the same information as the graphical execution plan. The executing statement is returned in the first row, and every operator is returned as subsequent rows. (This is a deprecated feature and will be eliminated in a future version.)

- Showplan_text is similar to showplan_all except that the executing statement and the operations are in separate result sets and only the stmt text (first column) displays.

  The showplan_text option, along with the set statistics options, may also be toggled graphically within Query Editor. Use the context menu's Query Options command to open the Query Properties, and you can find the Showplan options by selecting Execution ➪ Advanced.

- Showplan_xml displays more detail than any other method of viewing the execution plan, and it offers the benefit of storing and displaying unstructured data, so it can display additional information that may not pertain to all execution plans. For example, in the <Statement> element, Showplan_xml displays the Query Optimizer optimization level, or the reason why the Query Optimizer returned this execution plan.

  For the XML version of Showplan, the Include Actual Execution Query Editor option must be off. In addition, if the query results are set to grid, then the grid offers a link to open the XML using the browser.

SQL Profiler's Execution Plans

Within the Performance event category, SQL Server Profiler includes several Showplan events. The Showplan XML event includes the XML for the query execution plan, which SQL Profiler displays in a graphical form. It includes the same features as the Query Editor to mouse over the operation to see more properties and zoom the display.

You can save the plan with SQL Profiler, but it's well hidden: If you right-click anywhere in the upper pane on the line of a Showplan XML or Showplan XML Statistics Profile event, you can choose to Extract Event Data. This enables you to save the plan as a .sqlplan file. Cool add!

Examining Plans using Dynamic Management Views (DMVs) previously introduced with SQL Server 2005, provide an excellent window into SQL Server's internals. Three of the DMVs expose the query execution plans currently in the cache:

- sys.dm_exec_cached_plans: Returns the plan type, memory size, and usecounts.

- sys.dm_exec_query_stats: Returns several aggregate execution statistics (for example, last_execution_time, max_elapsed_time).

- sys.dm_exec_requests: Returns plans that are currently executing.

- `sys.dm_exec_procedure_stats`: Returns aggregated execution statistics for stored procedures.

Each of these previous DMVs returns a plan handle (binary identifier of the query execution plan in memory) that can be passed to one of the following dynamic management functions with a `cross apply` to extract the query text or the query execution plan:

- `sys.dm_exec_query_plan(plan_handle)`: Returns the query execution plan in XML. For some complex queries, if the XML nesting level is greater than 128, this method of extracting the query plan fails. Use the next method instead.

- `sys.dm_exec_text_query_plan(plan_handle)`: Returns the query execution plan as a text Showplan.

- `sys.dm_exec_sql_text(plan_handle)`: Returns the query SQL statement.

The code example in Figure 44-2 pulls together data from the DMVs to view the original SQL statements and query execution plans from the cache.

FIGURE 44-2

Using DMVs, you can view the SQL code and the query execution plan in the procedure cache. Clicking the XML in the right-most column would open another tab with the graphical view of the selected query execution plan.

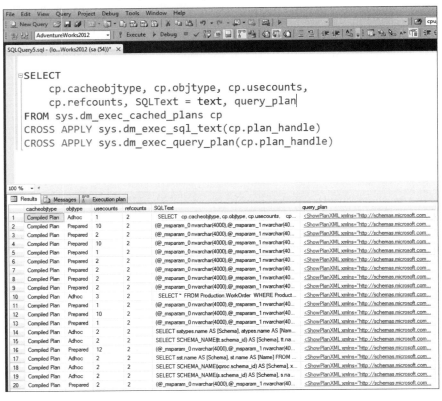

Understanding Execution Plan Operators

SQL server uses many different operators when creating execution plans. Some represent specific physical tasks, whereas most logically represent a collection of hidden tasks. Many of these operators are related to specific statements types — statements that you may rarely see. Others are much more common.

Table 44-1 lists the key operators regarding select queries and indexing.

TABLE 44-1   Query Execution Plan Operators

Icon	Definition	Description
	Clustered index scan	In a clustered index scan, SQL Server reads the entire clustered index — typically sequentially — but it can be otherwise depending on the isolation level and the fragmentation. SQL Server chooses this operation when the set of rows requested by the WHERE clause or JOIN condition is a large percentage of rows needed from the table or no index is available to select the range.
	Table scan	A table scan is similar to a clustered index scan but scans a heap.
	Clustered index seek	In a clustered index seek, SQL Server navigates the clustered index B-tree to retrieve specific rows. The benefit of the clustered index seek is that when the rows are determined, all the columns are immediately available.
	Hash match	A hash match is an join method that builds an in-memory hash table and iteratively matches with data from another table. A hash match is more efficient if one table is significantly larger than the other table.
	Merge join	The merge join is the fastest method of joining two tables if both tables are pre-sorted.
	Nested-loop	A nested-loop join iterates through an outer result set one record at a time and finds the matching rows in the inner result set (often a table) for each row from the first. Typically, nested-loop joins are best suited when a large index table is joined with a small table.
	Index scan (nonclustered)	In a nonclustered index scan, SQL Server reads through all the index sequentially looking for the data. This is typically must faster than a clustered index scan because the non-clustered data structure is much smaller.

Continues

44

TABLE 44-1   *(continued)*

Icon	Definition	Description
	Index seek (nonclustered)	A nonclustered index seek navigates the B-tree index from the root node, through the intermediate nodes, to the leaf node, and finally to the row. The benefit of a nonclustered index seek is that it tends to be narrow (have few columns), so more rows can fit on a page. When the correct row is identified, if all the required columns are found in the index, then the seek is complete because the index covers the needs of the query. If a range is required, an index seek operation can seek to the start of the range and then sequentially read to the end of the range.
	RID lookup	The RID lookup locates rows in the data pages of a heap (table without a clustered index). Typically, a RID lookup works with a nested-loop to locate the data pages following a nonclustered index seek or scan.
	Filter	In some situations, SQL Server retrieves all the data from a table and then uses filter operations to select the correct rows. Sometimes the Query Optimizer uses a Filter for performance reasons, but it's more often due to the lack of a useful index.
	Sort	In some situations SQL Server retrieves data and needs to sort it to prepare it for another operator. Such operations could involve sorting a result set such as in an ORDER BY clause or to prepare a result set to be received by a MERGE JOIN. Proper indexes can usually alleviate some or all of the overhead you see associated with a Sort operator. Sort operations also often involve a memory grant, which is a memory allocation that SQL Server must reserve to perform the operation.
	Spool	In a spool operation, SQL Server saves off a temporary set of data and revisits the data in later operations.

Summary

You can never become too good at performance tuning and optimization, and that skill is always in high demand because it requires a knowledge of so many different parts of the database engine.

SQL Server Management Studio does a good job at exposing execution plan internals, which allows you to dig deeply into the inner workings of the plan the Optimizer creates. Getting a feel for the logic behind the different tasks that an execution plan involves, coupled with the logic used behind these operations, is a huge step toward being a well-rounded PTO professional.

This chapter covered a small set of basics that you should be familiar with for tuning database systems. The more exposure you have, and the more frequently you work with execution plans and tuning queries, the better you prepare yourself for solving your company's performance problems when they crop up — and performance problems always happen.

The next chapter transitions into the whys and wherefores of query execution plans and how to manipulate them with indexes — an execution plan one-two punch.

44

Indexing Strategies

Over the years I've amassed a relatively large DVD collection. It's not a huge collection, but it can become somewhat painful when I have a movie I really want to watch and I need to find it among my other movies. What I should do is maintain my movie collection in a sorted order. This would make searching for a movie far less painful and much quicker. However, this approach is not without its own overhead. First, I'd have to perform one large sort of the movies (based on the movie title) and make sure I have them stored on my shelves based on a physical sorted order. This would be a relatively slow operation because I'd have to touch every DVD and move it around to make sure it is where it needs to be. There are, of course, numerous sorting algorithms I could use to perform this operation — but that is a story better discussed in a different book.

After I've performed my initial build of my sorted DVD collection, I then must maintain my list. Anytime I buy a new movie, I must make sure it is placed in the correct spot in the list. I must also make sure to remember to always insert movies that I've taken out into the proper spot on my shelf. This could be more overhead than I want to maintain in the long run, but it sure would make searching for a DVD when I want to watch it a lot easier.

This is similar to how indexes work inside a database engine. Indexes make searching and sorting so much faster because the data is maintained in a sorted order. Like in the DVD example, there is also overhead involved in maintaining the data in sorted order. Indexes are so absolutely crucial for database performance that a single missing or incorrectly defined index can bring a high-throughput system to its knees.

This chapter presents some things to consider for creating proper indexes inside SQL Server along with some common index operations that you should be aware of when performance tuning.

Zen and the Art of Indexing

Indexing and performance tuning are a mixture of art and science. The science portion includes knowing the details of how indexing works under the covers and when it makes sense to define indexes on the appropriate columns on a table. The art portion includes knowing when to stray away from what conventional wisdom tells you to do and designing a proper indexing strategy for what works best for *your* environment. There is no secret formula to define the correct indexes. An indexing strategy that works great for one system may perform poorly on another system.

Another aspect is that an indexing strategy is ever-evolving. Design and implement indexes for what your system needs at the present time. As your system evolves, so too must your indexes. Be careful defining indexes that your system does not currently use but may use later. This type of strategy often ends up in indexes not being used, but having to be constantly maintained.

What's New with Indexes?

New in SQL Server 2012 is the FORCESCAN query hint. Use this hint to ensure that a SCAN access method is used to retrieve rows from a table or an index.

One nugget of knowledge to take away is that a SCAN operation is not inherently evil. You may have heard colleagues talk about how evil scans are and how you should have only SEEK operations in query plans. Seek operations, although desireable for OLTP environments, are not without their perils. A seek operation coupled with a Bookmark Lookup operation can quickly become much more expensive than a SCAN operation. Always use query hints with caution.

Also new in SQL Server 2012 are Columnstore Indexes, which are reviewed in the section titled "The Columnstore Index," later in this chapter.

Indexing Basics

The following section presents an overview of the main indexes available in the SQL Server database engine. The rest of the chapter builds upon the ideas introduced in this section.

The B-Tree Index

The two main types of indexes in SQL Server are clustered and nonclustered indexes. Each index type is implemented via a balanced-tree (B-tree) data structure. A B-tree is a structure that stores data in a sorted order and enables fast access to the data it holds.

 Although technically not the only type of index present in the database engine, this chapter focuses exclusively on the clustered and nonclustered indexes. Other index types, such as Spatial and XML indexes, are outside of the scope of this chapter.

B-tree indexes exist on index pages and have a root level, one or more intermediate levels, and a leaf level. When you define an index, you specify one or more key columns. These columns are actually sorted in the index, as defined in Figure 45-1. The difference between clustered and nonclustered indexes is the way in which the data is stored at the leaf level of the index.

FIGURE 45-1

This figure illustrates a simplified view of a clustered index with an identity column as the clustered index key. The first name is the data column.

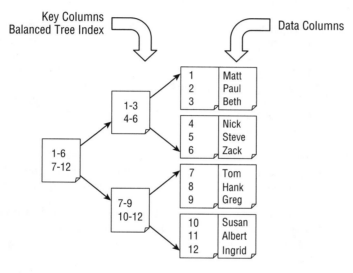

 Although this chapter discusses the strategies to design and optimize indexes and does include some code examples that demonstrate creating indexes, the sister Chapter 7, "Relational Database Design and Creating the Physical Database Schema," details the actual syntax and Management Studio methods to create indexes.

Over time, indexes will likely become fragmented, which can potentially impact performance. For more information on index maintenance, turn to Chapter 22 "Maintaining the Database."

Clustered Indexes

When a clustered index is created on a table, the index itself becomes the table. This is somewhat confusing at first. When you create a clustered index, under the covers the database engine sorts the data in the underlying table based on the index key(s) you define and stores the table in that order. The clustered index doesn't become a separate structure for the underlying table data like a nonclustered index does; the clustered index *is* the table. All the data for the table is stored in the leaf pages of the clustered index. Because you can sort a table only in one physical sorted order, you can have only one clustered index per table.

> **NOTE**
>
> The keys defined for a clustered index must always be unique. When you define a clustered index without using the UNIQUE keyword, a "uniquifier" is added to the clustered key to ensure the set of values is unique. This is an integer value that makes your key larger. Because the clustered key is always stored in nonclustered indexes, it makes these indexes larger as well. Keep this in mind when defining your clustered index keys.

Logically, the clustered index pages maintain the data in the clustered index sort order. However, physically those pages are connected via a linked list — each page links to the next page and previous page in the list, so it is not guaranteed that the data remains in a sorted physical order. Also, it is not guaranteed that the rows on a page are stored in sorted order. An offset array is used at the end of the page to indicate where in the page rows begin and end in a sorted fashion. In a perfect world the pages would be in the same order as the list, but in reality they are often moved around due to page splits and fragmentation (more on page splits later in this chapter).

A great example to illustrate a clustered index is a telephone book. A telephone book is always in sorted order, based on the last name of the individual followed by the first name. The sorted order makes it easy to find the phone number of the person you're looking for.

Assume you want to find my telephone number in the book. To do this, you'd base your search primarily on my last name, Chapman. You'd open the phone book approximately in the middle to gauge how close you were to the "Chapman" section. You'd then pick the side that contained C and split it again. You'd continue this operation until you find the page that contains the last name Chapman, and it would take you only a few operations to do this. When you find my last name, you could then perform a search for my first name (Tim) within the Chapman result set. When you find my full name, you'd then have access to my address information without needing to perform any additional searches. What you just performed to find my last name was a type of binary search operation. You split the problem in halves until you reached the solution.

This is similar to an index search operation. When searching for a value, you begin at the root page (approximately the "middle" of the values you're searching for) and continue down intermediate paths, choosing the proper path for the value you're searching for. Eventually you make it to the leaf level of the index, where you find the value you're looking for. For clustered indexes, after you make it to the leaf level, all the data you need is contained there, so there is no need to perform any additional searching on the data. All the data in the table is contained at the leaf level of the index; this means that the clustered index *is* the table.

Nonclustered Indexes

SQL Server nonclustered indexes are also implemented as a B-tree data structure. The difference between a clustered index and a nonclustered index is that the leaf level pages of the nonclustered index do not contain all the base table data like the clustered index does. Instead, the leaf level of the nonclustered index contains the index keys along with a pointer to the base table. If the nonclustered index is not unique, all levels of the index contain a pointer to the base table. If the base table is a clustered index, the clustered keys are stored in the nonclustered index. If the base table is a heap, the nonclustered index contains the row-identifier for the base table record.

For example, the nonclustered index shown in Figure 45-2 uses the first name column as its key column so that's the data sorted by the index. The nonclustered index points to the base table by including the clustered index key column. In Figure 45-2, the clustered index key column is the identity column used in Figure 45-1.

FIGURE 45-2

This simplified illustration of a nonclustered index has a B-tree index with a first name as the key column. The nonclustered index includes pointers to the clustered index key column.

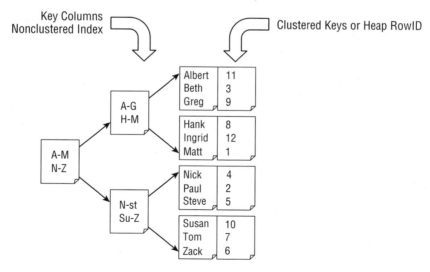

This is an important fact to consider when designing your nonclustered indexes. If your clustered key is large, such as a uniqueidentifier, that large data type will be included in the nonclustered index key for each row. So, a large clustered key can directly affect the size of your nonclustered indexes.

Since SQL Server 2005, additional unsorted columns can be *included* in the leaf level. The employee's title and department columns could be added to the previous index, which is extremely useful in designing covering indexes.

A SQL Server table may have up to 999 nonclustered indexes, but I've never seen a well-normalized table that required more than a dozen well-designed indexes.

Composite Indexes

A *composite index* is a clustered or nonclustered index that is defined on multiple columns. Consider the clustered index telephone book example; the keys of the composite index were based on the last name and first name of the individual, in that order. The ordering of the columns in a composite index is important. For a search to take advantage of a composite index, it must include the index columns from left to right. If the composite index is `lastname, firstname`, a search for only the `firstname` cannot seek the first name because it must first know the last name. The first name is not found independently in sorted order but is instead based on the lastname column. If you need to perform a search for `lastname`, or `lastname` and `firstname`, you can efficiently use the index.

 Various methods of indexing for multiple columns are examined in the section "The Path of the Query", later in this chapter.

Unique Indexes and Constraints

A Primary key and unique constraints are the method you use to uniquely identify a row. Indexes and primary keys are intertwined and a primary key must always be indexed. By default, creating a primary key automatically creates a unique clustered index, but it can optionally create a unique nonclustered index instead.

A unique index, as its name suggests, limits data to being unique. In other words, a unique index is constraining the data it indexes. A unique constraint builds a unique index to quickly check the data. A unique constraint and a unique index are the same thing — creating either one builds a unique constraint/index. The only difference between a unique constraint/index and a primary key is that a primary key cannot allow nulls, and a unique constraint/index can permit a single null value.

The Page Split Problem

Every index must maintain the key column data in the correct sort order. Inserts, updates, and deletes affect that data. As the data is inserted or modified, if the index page to which a value needs to be added is full, SQL Server must split the page into two less full pages so that it can insert the value in the correct position. Again using the telephone book example, if several new Chapmans moved into the area and the Cha page 515 had to now accommodate 20 additions, a simulated page split would take several steps:

1. Cut page 515 in half making two pages; call them 515a and 515b.
2. Print out and tape the new Chapman to page 515a.
3. Tape page 515b inside the back cover of the telephone book.
4. Make a note on page 515a that the Cha listing continues on page 515b located at the end of the book, and a note on page 515b that the listing continues on page 515a.

Page splits may cause several performance-related problems:

- The page split operation is expensive because it involves several steps and moving data.
- If after the page split there still isn't enough room, the page will be split again. This can occur again and again based on certain circumstances.
- The data structure is left fragmented and can no longer be read in a single contiguous pass.
- Page splits are also logged operations and can have a significant impact on the transaction log.

After the split, the page has more empty space. This means less data is read with every page read, and less data is stored in the buffer pool per page along with additional disk space required to store the data.

Index Selectivity

Another aspect of an indexing strategy is determining the selectivity of the index. An index that is selective has more distinct index values. A primary key or unique index has the highest possible selectivity, because every value in the constraint is defined as unique.

An index with only a few distinct values spread across a large table is less selective. Indexes that are less selective may not be useful for searching. A column with three values spread throughout the table is potentially a poor candidate for an index.

SQL Server uses its internal index statistics to track the selectivity of an index. DBCC SHOW_STATISTICS reports the last date on which the statistics were updated and the basic information about the index statistics, including the potential usefulness of the statistic (see Figure 45-3). A low density indicates that the index is highly selective, whereas a high density indicates low selectivity. The terms are the inverse of each other. A high density may be less useful, as shown in this code sample:

```
USE AdventureWorks2012
DBCC SHOW_STATISTICS ('Person.Person',
IX_Person_LastName_FirstName_MiddleName);
```

45

FIGURE 45-3

Use the output from DBCC SHOW_STATISTICS to determine the last time the statistics were updated and the sampling rate.

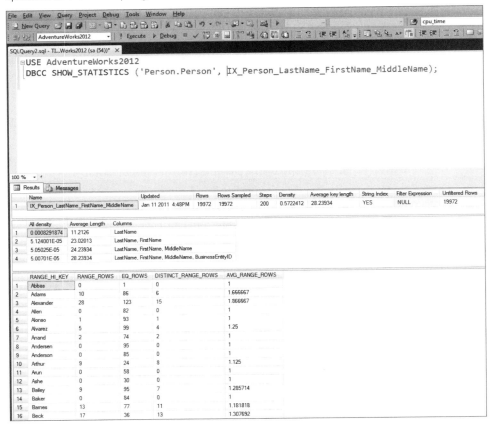

Changing the order of the key columns may improve the selectivity of an index and improve its performance for certain queries. Be careful however, because other queries may depend on the order for their performance.

Unordered Heaps

You can create a table without a clustered index, in which case the data is stored in a unordered *heap*. Instead of being stored in sorted order as defined by the clustered index key columns, the rows are identified internally using the heap's row identifier. The row identifier is an actual physical location composed of three values, FileID:PageNum:SlotNum, and cannot be directly queried. As mentioned earlier, all nonclustered indexes contain the clustered key if the base table is clustered. The clustered keys are used in the nonclustered index to navigate back to the clustered index; they're basically used as a pointer in the nonclustered index, so the base table can be used if additional columns are needed for a given query. If the base table is not clustered, then any nonclustered index can store the heap's row identifier in every level of the index, which is used to point back to the full row in the base table.

In a sense, you can think of SQL Server having two different types of tables: a clustered (index) table and a heap table, which are mutually exclusive. A table can never be a heap and a clustered table at the same time.

Query Operators

Although there are dozens of logical and physical query execution operations, SQL Server uses three primary operators to access data. These are also known as access methods.

- **Table Scan:** Reads the entire heap and, most likely, passes all the data to a secondary filter operation.

- **Index Scan:** Reads the entire leaf level (every row) of the clustered index or nonclustered index. The index scan operation might filter the rows and return only those rows that meet the criteria, or it might pass all the rows to another filter operation depending on the complexity of the criteria. The data may or may not be ordered.

- **Index Seek:** Locates specific row(s) of data using the B-tree and returns only the selected rows in an ordered list (see Figure 45-4).

FIGURE 45-4

An index seek operation navigates the B-tree index, selects a beginning row, and then scans all the required rows.

Clustered Index Seek

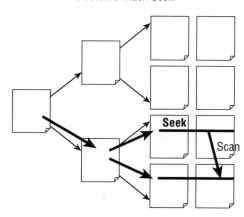

The query optimizer chooses the access method with the least overall cost. Sequentially reading the data is an efficient task, so an index scan and filter operation may actually be cheaper than an index seek with a bookmark lookup (see Query Path 5 in the next section) involving hundreds or thousands of random IO index seeks. SQL Server heavily uses statistics to determine the number of rows touched and returned by each operation in the query execution plan. If statistics are accurate, SQL Server has a great opportunity to choose the appropriate access method to most efficiently return the requested data. On the other hand, if statistics are skewed or out-of-date, the likelihood that SQL Server chooses the correct access method decreases significantly. I've seen hundreds of performance issues over the years caused by skewed statistics.

The Path of the Query

A good way to understand how to design efficient indexes is to observe and learn from the various possible paths' queries use to locate data using indexes.

The following section compares and contrasts ten different query paths. Not every query path is an efficient query path.

A good test table for observing the 10 query paths in the AdventureWorks2012 database is the Production.WorkOrder table. It has 72,591 rows, 10 columns, and a single-column clustered primary key. Here's the table definition:

```
CREATE TABLE [Production].[WorkOrder](
[WorkOrderID] [int] IDENTITY(1,1) NOT NULL,
[ProductID] [int] NOT NULL,
[OrderQty] [int] NOT NULL,
[StockedQty]  AS (isnull([OrderQty]-[ScrappedQty],(0))),
[ScrappedQty] [smallint] NOT NULL,
[StartDate] [datetime] NOT NULL,
[EndDate] [datetime] NULL,
[DueDate] [datetime] NOT NULL,
[ScrapReasonID] [smallint] NULL,
[ModifiedDate] [datetime] NOT NULL,
 CONSTRAINT [PK_WorkOrder_WorkOrderID] PRIMARY KEY CLUSTERED
  ([WorkOrderID] ASC)
    WITH (PAD_INDEX  = OFF, STATISTICS_NORECOMPUTE  = OFF,
    IGNORE_DUP_KEY = OFF, ALLOW_ROW_LOCKS  = ON,
    ALLOW_PAGE_LOCKS  = ON) ON [PRIMARY]
) ON [PRIMARY];
```

The WorkOrder table has three indexes, each with one column as identified in the index name:

- PK_WorkOrder_WorkOrderID (Clustered)

- IX_WorkOrder_ProductID (Nonunique, Nonclustered)

- IX_WorkOrder_ScrapReasonID (Nonunique, Nonclustered)

Performance data for each path, listed in Table 45-1, was captured by watching the T-SQL ⇨ SQL:StmtCompleted and Performance ⇨ Showplan XML Statistics Profile events in Profiler and examining the Query Execution Plan.

TABLE 45-1   Query Path Performance

Path No	Path Desc	Execution Plan	Rows	Cost	Reads	Missing Index	Duration (ms)	Rows per ms
1	Fetch All	C Ix Scan	72,591	.485	526		1,196	60.71
2	Clustered Index Seek	C Ix Seek	1	.003	2		7	.14
3	Range Seek Query (narrow)	C Ix Seek (Seek keys start-end)	11	.003	3		13	.85
	Range Seek Query (wide)	C Ix Seek (Seek keys start-end)	72,591	.485	526		1,257	57.73
4	Filter by Non-Key Column	C Ix Scan → filter (predicate)	85	.519	526	NC (include all columns)	170	.32
5	Bookmark Lookup (Select *)	NC Ix Seek → BML	9	.037	29		226	.04
	Bookmark Lookup (Select clustered key, non-key col)	NC Ix Seek → BML	9	.037	29		128	.07
6	Covering Index (narrow)	NC Ix Seek (Seek Predicate)	9	.003	2		30	.30
	Covering Index (wide)	NC Ix Seek (Seek Predicate)	1,105	.005	6		106	10.46
	NC Seek Selecting Clustered Key (narrow)	NC Ix Seek (Seek Predicate)	9	.003	2		46	.20
	NC Seek Selecting Clustered Key (wide)	NC Ix Seek (Seek Predicate)	1,105	.004	4		46	24.02

Continues

45

TABLE 45-1 *(continued)*

Path No	Path Desc	Execution Plan	Rows	Cost	Reads	Missing Index	Duration (ms)	Rows per ms
	Filter by Include Column	NC Ix Seek (Seek Predicate + Predicate)	1	.003	2		51	.02
7	Filter by 2 x NC Indexes	2 x NC Ix Seek (Predicate → Merge Join	1	.012	4		63	.02
8	Filter by Ordered NC Composite Index	NC Ix Seek (Seek Predicate w/ 2 prefixes)	1	.003	2		56	.02
9	Filter by Unordered NC Composite Index	NC Ix Scan	118	.209	173	NC by missing key, include C Key	72	1.64
10	Filter by Expression	NC Ix Scan	9	.209	173		111	.08

The key performance indicators are the query execution plan optimizer costs (Cost), and the number of logical reads (Reads).

For the duration column, each query path was executed multiple times with the results averaged. You should run the script on your own SQL Server instance, take your own performance measurements, and study the query execution plans.

The rows-per-ms column is calculated from the number of rows returned and the average duration. Before executing each query path, the following code clears the buffers:

```
DBCC FREEPROCCACHE;
DBCC DROPCLEANBUFFERS;
```

Query Path 1 — Fetch All

The first query path sets a baseline for performance by simply requesting all the data from the base table.

```
SELECT *
  FROM Production.WorkOrder;
```

Without a where clause and every column selected, the query must read every row from the clustered index. A clustered index scan (shown in Figure 45-5) sequentially reads every row.

FIGURE 45-5

The clustered index scan sequentially reads all the rows from the clustered index.

Clustered Index
PK_WorkOrder_WorkOrderID

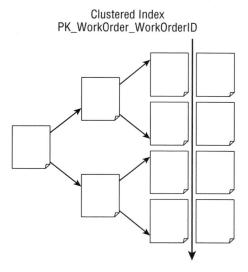

This query is the longest query of all the query paths, so it might seem to be a slow query, however, when comparing the number of rows returned per millisecond, the index scan returns the highest number of rows per millisecond of any query path.

Query Path 2 — Clustered Index Seek

The second query path adds a where clause to the first query and filters the result to a single row using a clustered key value:

```
SELECT *
  FROM Production.WorkOrder
  WHERE WorkOrderID = 1234;
```

The query optimizer has two clues that there's only one row that meets the where clause criteria: Statistics and that WorkOrderID is the primary key constraint, so it must be unique. WorkOrderID is also the clustered index key, so the query optimizer knows there's a great index available to locate a single row. The clustered index seek operation navigates the clustered index B-tree and quickly locates the desired row, as shown in Figure 45-6.

45

FIGURE 45-6

A clustered index seek navigates the B-tree index and locates the row efficiently.

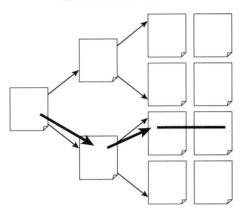

Clustered Index
PK_WorkOrder_WorkOrderID

Conventional wisdom holds that this is the fastest possible query path, and it is snappy when returning a single row; however, from rows returned on a per millisecond basis, it's one of the slowest query paths.

A common myth is that seeks can return only single rows, and that's why seeking multiple rows would be slow compared to scans. As the next two query paths indicate, that's not true.

Query Path 3 — Range Seek Query

The third query path selects a narrow range of consecutive values using a between operator in the where clause:

```
SELECT *
  FROM Production.WorkOrder
  WHERE WorkOrderID BETWEEN 10000 AND 10010;
```

The query optimizer must first determine if there's a suitable index to select the range. In this case it's the same key column in the clustered index as in the Query Path 2.

A range seek query has an interesting query execution plan. The seek predicate (listed in the index seek properties), which defines how the query is navigating the B-tree, has both a start and an end to the seek predicate, as shown in Figure 45-7. This means the operation is seeking the first row and then quickly scanning and returning every row to the end of the range (refer to Figure 45-8).

FIGURE 45-7

The clustered index seek's predicate has a start and an end, which indicates the range of rows searched for using the B-tree index.

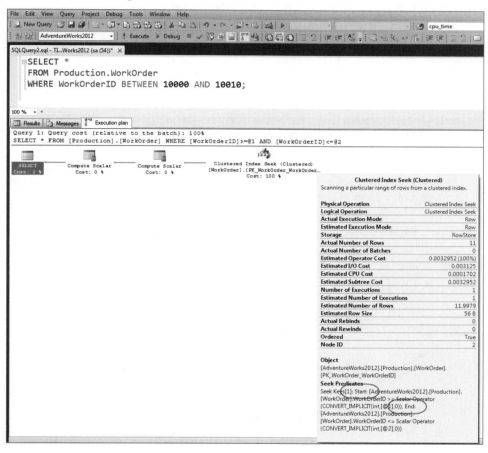

To further investigate the range seek query path, this next query pushes the range to the limit by selecting every row in the table. And both queries are tested just to prove that between is logically the same as >= with <=:

```
SELECT *
  FROM Production.WorkOrder
  WHERE WorkOrderID >= 1 and WorkOrderID <= 72591;

SELECT *
  FROM Production.WorkOrder
  WHERE WorkOrderID between 1 and 72591;
```

At first glance it would seem that this query should generate the same query execution plan as the first query path (`select * from table`), but just like the narrow range query, the `between` operator needs a consecutive range of rows, and this causes the query optimizer to select index seek to return ordered rows.

There's no guarantee that another row might be added after the query plan is generated and before it's executed. Therefore, for range queries, an index seek is the fastest possible way to ensure that only the correct rows are selected.

Index seeks and index scans both perform well when returning large sets of data. The minor difference between the two queries' durations listed in the performance chart (refer to Table 45-1) is more likely variances in my computer's performance. There were some iterations of the index seek that performed faster than some iterations of the index scan.

FIGURE 45-8

An index seek operation has the option of seeking to find the first row, and then sequentially scanning on a block of data.

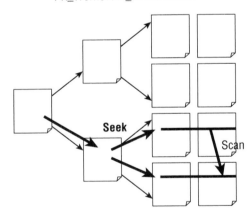

Query Path 4 — Filter by Nonkey Column

In the previous query paths, the clustered index key was used in the query predicate to find the rows. Because the query predicate matched the clustered index key column, all the data was available using a simple clustered key. But what if that isn't the case?

Consider this query:

```
SELECT *
FROM Production.WorkOrder
WHERE StartDate = '07/15/2007'
```

There's no index with a key column of StartDate. This means that the query optimizer can't choose an index to satisfy the query and must resort to scanning the entire table and then manually searching for rows that match the where clause. Without an index, this query path is 23 times slower than the clustered index seek query path.

The cost isn't the filter operation alone. (It's only 7 percent of the total query cost.) The real cost is having to scan in every row and pass 72,591 rows to the filter operation, as shown in the query execution plan in Figure 45-9.

FIGURE 45-9

Query Path 4 (filter by nonkey column) passes every row from an index scan to a filter operation to manually select the rows.

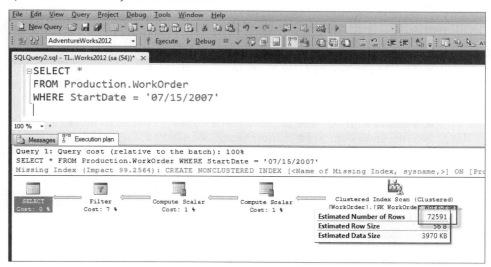

Management Studio suggests a missing index could potentially help this query execute faster. Management Studio can even generate the code to create the missing index using the context menu.

> **WARNING**
>
> Use care when considering implementing these suggested indexes. These index suggestions are suited specifically for the query being investigated and often proves to not be the best index for your overall indexing strategy. Too often the missing index is not the best index, and it often wants to build a nonclustered index that includes every column.

Query Path 5 — Bookmark Lookup

This bookmark lookup query path is a two-edged sword. For queries returning a small number of records, it's an acceptable query path, but for the queries that return a significant amount of records , this query path can significantly hinder performance.

To demonstrate a bookmark lookup query path, the following query filters by ProductID while returning all the base table's columns:

```
SELECT *
  FROM Production.WorkOrder
  WHERE ProductID = 757;
```

To rephrase the query in pseudo-code, find the rows for Product 757 and give me all the columns for those rows.

There is an index on the ProductID column, so the query optimizer has two possible options:

- Scan the entire clustered index to access all the columns, and then filter the results to find the right rows. Essentially, this would be the same as Query Path 4.

  Or:

- Perform an index seek on the IX_Workload_ProductID index to fetch the 11 rows. In the process it learns the WorkOrderID values for those 11 rows because the clustered index key columns are in the leaf level of the nonclustered index. Then it can index seek those 11 rows from the clustered index to fetch the other columns.

  This jump, from the nonclustered index used to find the rows to the clustered index to complete the columns needed for the query, is called a *bookmark lookup* as shown in Figure 45-10.

The real cost of the bookmark lookup is finding the rows that are typically scattered throughout the base table, which is a clustered index in this case. Locating the 11 rows in the nonclustered index was a single page hit, but those 11 rows might be on 11 different pages in the clustered index. With a larger number of selected rows, the problem intensifies. Selecting 1,000 rows with a bookmark lookup might mean reading three to four pages from the nonclustered index and then reading more than 1,000 pages from the clustered index and leaf level. Eventually, SQL Server decides that the bookmark lookup is more expensive than just scanning the clustered index.

The query execution plan for a bookmark lookup shows the two indexes as data sources for a nested loop join (as shown in Figure 45-11). For each row that comes from the seek of the nonclustered index, the nested loop join is requesting the matching rows from the clustered index by calling the key lookup.

FIGURE 45-10

The nonclustered index does not contain one or more columns that the query requests. To solve the query, SQL Server must perform a bookmark lookup (the dashed line) from the nonclustered index to the base table, which is a clustered index in this example. This illustration shows a single row. In reality it's often hundreds or thousands of rows scattered throughout the clustered index.

IX_WorkOrder_ProductID   PK_WorkOrder_WorkOrderID

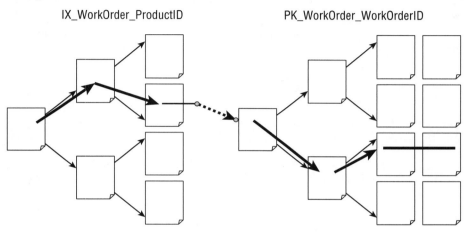

FIGURE 45-11

The query execution plan shows the bookmark lookup as an Index seek being joined with a key lookup.

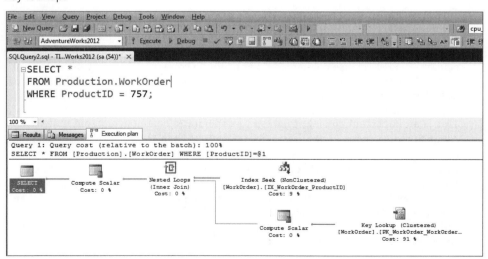

It's a common saying that Select * is a poor practice because it returns too many, and often unnecessary, columns in the result set — the extra data is considered wasteful if it is not needed. I agree that Select * is a poor practice, but often the reason isn't due to the extra network traffic; it's the bookmark lookup that is almost always generated by a Select *. However, the extra network traffic associated with bringing back more data than is needed can significantly hinder application throughput.

This query builds on the last bookmark lookup query and sheds a little more light on the bookmark lookup problem; the difference is that this query requests only one column that's not available from the nonclustered index.

```
SELECT WorkOrderID, StartDate
  FROM Production.WorkOrder
  WHERE ProductID = 757;
```

Consider the performance difference (again, refer to Table 45-1) between this query path and the select * bookmark lookup query path. Their performance is nearly identical.

It doesn't take many columns to force a bookmark lookup; a single column missing from the nonclustered index means SQL Server must also look to the clustered index to solve the query.

There are only two ways to avoid the bookmark lookup problem:

- Filter by the clustered index key columns, so the query can be satisfied using the clustered index (Query Path 2 or 3).
- Design a covering index (the next query path).

Query Path 6 — Covering Index

If a nonclustered index includes every column required by the query (and that means every column referenced by the query: select columns, join on condition columns, group by columns, where clause columns, and windowing columns), SQL Server's query optimizer can choose to execute the query using only that nonclustered index. When this occurs the index is said to cover the needs of the query, in other words, it's a *covering index*.

This is an important concept to grasp to understand how nonclustered indexes operate. A nonclustered index is a separate data structure than the base table. By default, non-clustered indexes have the same number of rows as the base table. In this aspect, you can think of a nonclustered index as a smaller sorted table — one that you can access quickly. When it makes sense, the query optimizer can choose to use *ONLY* this separate nonclus-tered index structure to satisfy a query. If this happens, the base table isn't even used in the query — only the nonclustered index.

A covering index is a concept that applies only to nonclustered indexes and only in the con-text of a query. There is no such thing as a covering index as a single entity; it is applicable only in the context of a query that uses the index.

Query Path 5's second query selected the StartDate column. Because StartDate isn't part of the IX_WorkOrder_ProductID index, SQL Server was forced to use a bookmark lookup. To solve the problem, the following code adds StartDate to the IX_WorkOrder_ProductID index so that the index can cover the query.

```
DROP INDEX Production.WorkOrder.IX_WorkOrder_ProductID

CREATE INDEX IX_WorkOrder_ProductID
  ON Production.WorkOrder (ProductID)
  INCLUDE (StartDate);
```

The include option (added in SQL Server 2005) adds the StartDate column to the leaf level of the IX_WorkOrder_ProductID index — but not to the list of keys of the index. This enables you to define additional columns that cover queries without hitting the index column or size limit. Included columns are stored at the leaf levels of the nonclustered index, but not at the intermediate levels. The query optimizer can now solve the queries with an index seek (as show in Figure 45-12):

```
SELECT WorkOrderID, StartDate
  FROM Production.WorkOrder
  WHERE ProductID = 757;   -- 9 rows

SELECT WorkOrderID, StartDate
  FROM Production.WorkOrder
  WHERE ProductID = 945; -- 1,105 rows
```

As mentioned earlier, when a nonclustered index is defined on a clustered base table, the clustered keys are stored in the nonclustered index to be used as a pointer back to the base table. Because of this, the nonclustered index can satisfy queries that include the clustered key columns. The following query filters by the nonclustered index key and returns the clustered index key value:

```
SELECT WorkOrderID
  FROM Production.WorkOrder
  WHERE ProductID = 757;
```

The Ix_WorkOrder_ProductID nonclustered index has the ProductID column as the key column, and the clustered index is defined on the WorkOrderID column which is available in the nonclustered index.

The next query is a rare example of a covering index. Compared to the previous query path, this query adds the StartDate column in the where clause. Conventional wisdom would say that this query requires an index scan because it filters by a nonkey column. (StartDate is an included column in the index and not a key column.)

```
SELECT WorkOrderID
  FROM Production.WorkOrder
  WHERE ProductID = 945
    AND StartDate = '2006-01-04';
```

45

FIGURE 45-12

With the StartDate column included in the index, the queries are solved with an index seek — a perfect covering index.

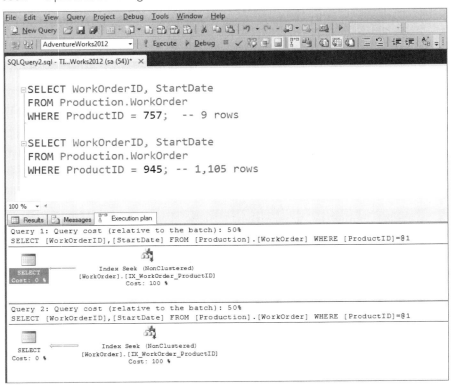

In this case the index seek operator uses the index (keyed by ProductID) to seek the rows matching ProductID = 945.

Then the index seek operator continues to select the correct rows by filtering the rows by the included column (AND StartDate = '2006-01-04'). In the index seek properties (see Figure 45-13), the *predicate* is filtering by the StartDate column.

The performance difference between the bookmark lookup solution and the covering index is dramatic. When comparing the query optimizer cost and the logical reads (refer to Table 45-1), the query paths that use a covering index are approximately 12 times more efficient. (The duration appears less in the figure due to my limited hardware.)

FIGURE 45-13

The index seek operator can have a seek predicate, which uses the B-tree; and a predicate, which functions as a nonindexed filter.

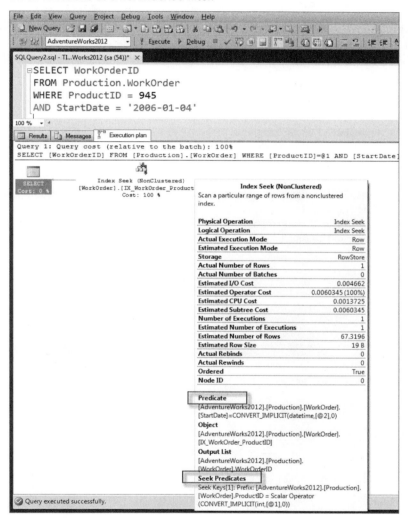

Query Path 7 — Filter by 2 x NC Indexes

A common indexing dilemma is how to index for multiple where clause criteria. Is it better to create one composite index that includes both key columns? Or do two single key column indexes perform better? Query Paths 7 through 9 evaluate the options.

The following code redefines the indexes: one index keyed on ProductID and one keyed on StartDate.

```
DROP INDEX Production.WorkOrder.IX_WorkOrder_ProductID;

CREATE INDEX IX_WorkOrder_ProductID
  ON Production.WorkOrder (ProductID);

CREATE INDEX IX_WorkOrder_StartDate
  ON Production.WorkOrder (StartDate);
```

With these indexes in place, this query filters by both key columns:

```
SELECT WorkOrderID, StartDate
  FROM Production.WorkOrder
 WHERE ProductID = 757
   AND StartDate = '01/04/2006';
```

To use both indexes, SQL Server uses a merge join to request rows from each index seek and then correlates the data to return the rows that meet both criteria, as shown in Figure 45-14. This is known as *index-intersection*. SQL Server makes use of both indexes via separate operations to serve the query.

FIGURE 45-14

Filtering by two indexes adds a merge join into the mix.

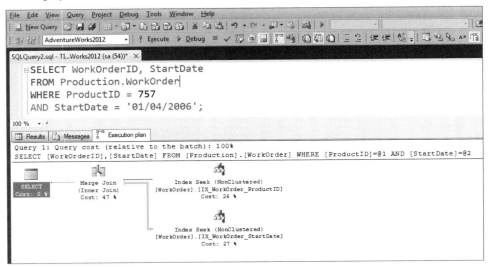

Examining the performance stat in Table 45-1, multiple indexes have a query optimizer cost of .12 and use four logical reads.

For infrequent queries, Query Path 7, with its multiple indexes, is more than adequate and much better than no index at all. However, for those few queries that run constantly, the next query path is a better solution for multiple criteria.

Query Path 8 — Filter by Ordered Composite Index

For the raw performance, the fastest solution to the multiple-where-clause-criteria problem is a single composite index as demonstrated in Query Path 8.

Creating a composite index with ProductID and StartDate as key columns sets up the test:

```
DROP INDEX Production.WorkOrder.IX_WorkOrder_ProductID
DROP INDEX Production.WorkOrder.IX_WorkOrder_StartDate

CREATE INDEX IX_WorkOrder_ProductID
  ON Production.WorkOrder (ProductID, StartDate);
```

Rerunning the same query,

```
SELECT WorkOrderID, StartDate
  FROM Production.WorkOrder
  WHERE ProductID = 757
    AND StartDate = '2006-01-04';
```

The query execution plan, as shown in Figure 45-15, is a simple single index seek operation, and it performs wonderfully.

FIGURE 45-15

Filtering two criteria using a composite index performs like greased lighting.

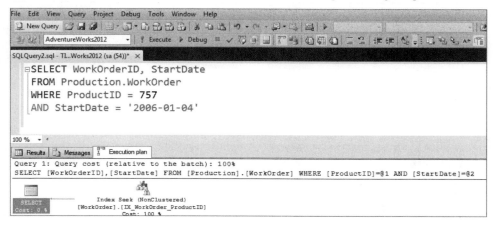

Query Path 9 — Filter by Unordered Composite Index

One common indexing myth is that the order of the index key columns doesn't matter, that is, SQL Server can use an index so long as the column is anywhere in the index. Like most myths, it's a half truth.

Searching an index requires the leading index key column to be present in the search predicate. Searching for col1, col2 works great when the index includes col1 as the leading index key with col2 following it. However, searching solely for col2 without col1 in the predicate requires scanning all the leaf level data if another suitable index is not present.

Query Path 9 demonstrates the inefficiency of filtering on an index column that is not the leading index key column.

StartDate is the second key in the composite index, so the data is there. Will the query use the index?

```
SELECT WorkOrderID
  FROM Production.WorkOrder
  WHERE StartDate = '2006-01-04';
```

The query optimizer uses the IX_WorkOrder_ProductID composite nonclustered index, as shown in Figure 45-16, because it's narrower than the clustered index, so more rows fit on a page. Because the filter is by the second column, it can't use the index; instead SQL Server is forced to scan every row and filter (in the scan operation) to select the correct rows. Essentially, it's doing the same operation as manually scanning a telephone book for everyone with a first name of Tim.

FIGURE 45-16

Filtering by the second key column of an index forces an index scan.

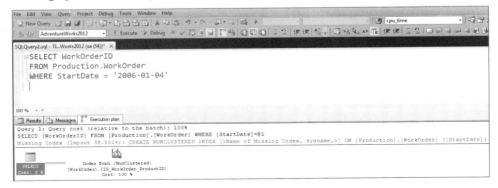

Query Path 10 — Non-SARG-Able Expressions

SQL Server's Query Optimizer examines the conditions within the query's predicates to determine which indexes are useful. If SQL Server can optimize the criteria statements, such as a WHERE clause, using an index, the condition is referred to as a *search argument (SARG)*. However, not every condition is a "SARG-able" search argument:

The final query path walks through a series of antipatterns, designing WHERE clauses with conditions that can't use index seek operations for one or more reasons. The result is an index scan, when an index seek is more advantageous. The following is a list of common types of "non-SARG-able" expressions:

- Including the table search column in an expression forces SQL Server to evaluate the outcome of the expression for every row before it can determine if the row passes the WHERE clause criteria:

```
SELECT WorkOrderID
  FROM Production.WorkOrder
  WHERE ProductID + 2 = 759;
```

- The solution to this non-SARG-able issue is to rewrite the query so that the expression is no longer dependent on the table column.

```
SELECT WorkOrderID
  FROM Production.WorkOrder
  WHERE ProductID = 759 - 2;
```

- Multiple inclusive criteria is typically SARG-able; however, the optimizer may have a more difficult time creating a seekable plan with criteria composed of OR logic.

```
SELECT WorkOrderID, StartDate
  FROM Production.WorkOrder
  WHERE ProductID = 757
    OR  StartDate = '2006-01-04';
```

- Negative search conditions (<>, !>, !<, Not Exists, Not In, Not Like) are not easily optimized. It's easy to prove that a row exists, but to prove it doesn't exist requires examining every row.

```
SELECT WorkOrderID, StartDate
  FROM Production.WorkOrder
  WHERE ProductID NOT IN (400,800, 950);
```

  It is possible that exclusive criteria can be SARG-able, so it's worth testing. Often, it's the number of rows returned that forces a scan, not the exclusive criteria.

- Search predicates that begin with wildcards aren't SARG-able. An index can quickly locate WorkOrderID = 757, but must scan every row to find any WorkOrderID's ending in 7:

```
SELECT WorkOrderID, StartDate
  FROM Production.WorkOrder
  WHERE WorkOrderID like '%7';
```

45

- If the `predicate` includes a function, such as a string function, a scan is required so that every row can be evaluated with the function before the final criteria is applied to the function output.

```
SELECT WorkOrderID, StartDate
  FROM Production.WorkOrder
  WHERE DateName(dw, StartDate) = 'Monday';
```

SQL Server 2008 does include some optimizations that can avoid the scan when working with the Date data type when conversions are included in the predicate

> **NOTE**
>
> The type of access (index scan versus index seek) not only impacts the performance of reading data from the single table, but it also impacts join performance. The type of join chosen by SQL Server depends on whether the data is ordered (among other things). Merge joins require ordered result sets as inputs. If the optimizer determines that a merge join is the most efficient join method to satisfy a query, a sort operation may be required to sort the inputs. In such a case, a memory grant is required and potentially tempdb space to store the intermediate result sets. This is another example of why indexing is important.

A Comprehensive Indexing Strategy

An index strategy deals with the overall application rather than fixing isolated problems to the detriment of the whole.

Identifying Key Queries

Analyzing a full query workload, which includes a couple of days of operations and nightly or weekend workloads, can likely reveal that although there may be a few hundred distinct queries, the majority of the CPU time is spent on the top handful of queries. I've tuned systems where 95 percent of the CPU time was spent on only five queries. Those top queries demand flat-out performance, whereas the other queries might afford a bookmark lookup.

To identify those top queries, follow these steps:

1. Create a profiler trace to capture all queries or stored procedures:

   Profiler Event: T-SQL `SQL:StmtCompleted` and `RPC:Completed`

   Profiler Columns: `TextData`, `ApplicationName`, `CPU`, `Reads`, `Writes`, `Duration`, `SPID`, `EndTime`, `DatabaseName`, and `RowCounts`.

   Do NOT filter the trace to capture only long-running queries. (A common suggestion is to set the filter to capture only queries with a duration > 1 sec.) Every query must be captured.

2. Test the trace definition using Profiler for a few moments; then stop the trace. Be sure to filter out applications or databases not being analyzed.

3. In the trace properties, add a stop time to the trace definition (so it can capture a full day's and night's workload), and set up the trace to write to a file.

4. Generate a trace script using File ⇨ Export ⇨ Script Trace Definition ⇨ for SQL Server 2005-SQL11.

5. Check the script. You may need to edit the script to supply a filename and path and double-check the start and stop times. Execute the trace script on the production server for 24 hours.

6. Pull the trace file into Profiler. This can be done through the Open ⇨ Trace File dialog in SQL Profiler. Then save it to a table using File ⇨ Save As ⇨ Trace Table.

7. Profiler exports the `TextData` column as `nText` data type, and that just won't do. The following code creates an `nVarChar(max)` column that is friendlier with string functions:

```
ALTER TABLE trace
  ALTER COLUMN textdata   NVARCHAR(MAX);
```

8. Run the following aggregate query to summarize the query load. This query assumes the trace data was saved to a table creatively named `trace`:

```
select substring(textdata, 1, CHARINDEX(' ',qtextdata, 6)),
    count(*) as 'count',
    sum(duration) as 'SumDuration',
    avg(duration) as 'AvgDuration',
    max(duration) as 'MaxDuration',
    cast(SUM(duration) as numeric(20,2))
      / (select sum(Duration) from trace) as 'Percentage',
    sum(rowcounts) as 'SumRows'
from trace
group by substring(textdata, 1, charindex(' ',textdata, 6))
order by sum(Duration) desc;
```

The top queries are obvious.

> **NOTE**
> The Database Engine Tuning Advisor is a SQL Server utility that can analyze a single query or a set of queries and recommend indexes and partitions to improve performance.

Selecting the Clustered Index

A clustered index can affect performance in several ways:

- When an index seek operation finds a row using a clustered index, the data is right there — no bookmark lookup is necessary. This makes the column used to select the row, probably the primary key, an ideal candidate for a clustered index.

- Clustered indexes gather rows with the same or similar values to the smallest possible number of data pages, thus reducing the number of data pages required to retrieve a set a rows. Clustered indexes are therefore excellent for columns that are often used to select a range of rows, such as secondary table foreign keys like `OrderDetail.OrderID`.

Creating Base Indexes

Even before tuning, the locations of a few key indexes are easy to determine. These indexes are the first step in building a solid set index foundation. Following are a few things to keep in mind when building these base indexes:

- As a rule of thumb, plan to create a clustered index for every table. There are a few exceptions to this rule, but as a general plan cluster your tables. In many cases, it makes sense to create the clustered index on the primary key of the table.

- Plan to create nonclustered indexes for each column belonging to a foreign key constraint. When data is entered that must adhere to a foreign key constraint, SQL Server must verify that the new values conform to the constraint. Nonclustered indexes prove critical to accomplish this lookup.

- Review the queries that you know will be executed often. This is where your relationship with the application developers is crucial. Everyone wins if the database supporting the application is indexed appropriately when the application rolls out.

Although this indexing plan is far from perfect, and it's definitely *not* a final indexing plan, it provides an initial compromise between no indexes and tuned indexes and can be a baseline performance measurement to compare against future index tuning.

Additional tuning can likely involve creating composite indexes and removing unnecessary indexes.

Best Practice

When planning indexes, there's a fine line between serving the needs of select queries versus update queries. Although an index may improve query performance, there's a performance cost because when a row is inserted, updated, or deleted, the indexes must be updated as well. Nonetheless, some indexing is necessary for write operations. The update or delete operation must locate the row prior to performing the write operation, and useful indexes facilitate locating that row, thereby speeding up write operations.

Therefore, when planning indexes, include the fewest number of indexes to accomplish the job.

TIP

SQL Server exposes index usage statistics via dynamic management views. Specifically, `sys.dm_db_index_operational_stats` and `sys.dm_db_index_usage_stats` uncover information about how indexes are used. In addition, four dynamic management views reveal indexes that the Query Optimizer looked for, but didn't find: `sys.dm_db_missing_index_groups`, `sys.dm_db_missing_index_group_stats`, `sys.dm_db_missing_index_columns`, and `sys.dm_db_missing_index_details`.

Specialty Indexes

Beyond the standard clustered and nonclustered indexes, SQL Server offers two type of indexes referred to as specialty indexes. Filtered indexes, which were new in SQL Server 2008, include less data; and indexed views, available since SQL Server 2000, build out custom sets of data. Both are considered high-end performance tuning indexes.

Filtered Indexes

A nonclustered index contains a record for every record in the base table on which it is defined. Historically, this has always been a 1-to-1 relationship. SQL Server 2008 introduced the concept of a filtered index. With a filtered index, you can set a predicate on your CREATE INDEX statement so that the index contains only rows that meet the criteria you set. This option is only available for nonclustered indexes because a clustered index *IS* the table, so it wouldn't make sense to allow you to filter on a clustered index. Because a filtered index can potentially have much fewer records than the traditionally nonclustered index, they tend to be much smaller in size. In addition, because the index has fewer records, the statistics on these indexes tend to be more accurate, which can lead to better execution plans.

An example of employing a filtered index in AdventureWorks2012 is the ScrappedReasonID column in the Production.WorkOrder table. Fortunately, for AdventureWorks, they scrapped only 612 (.8 percent) parts over the life of the database. The existing IX_WorkOrder_ScrapReasonID includes every row. The ScrapReasonID foreign key in the Production.WorkOrder table enables nulls for work orders that were not scrapped. The index includes all the null values with pointers to the workorder rows with null ScrapReasonIDs. The current index uses 109 pages.

The following script re-creates the index with a WHERE clause that excludes all the null values:

```
DROP INDEX Production.WorkOrder.IX_WorkOrder_ScrapReasonID

CREATE INDEX IX_WorkOrder_ScrapReasonID
  ON Production.WorkOrder(ScrapReasonID)
  WHERE ScrapReasonID IS NOT NULL
```

The new index uses only two pages. Interestingly, the difference isn't noticeable between using the filtered or nonfiltered index when selecting all the work orders with a scrap reason that's not null. This is because there aren't enough intermediate levels to make a significant difference. For a much larger table, the difference would be worth testing, and most likely the filtered index would provide a benefit.

Best Practice

When designing a covering index (see Query Path #6) to solve a specific query — probably one that is in the top handful of CPU duration according to the indexing strategy — if the covering index works with a relatively small subset of data, and the overall table is a large table, consider using a filtering covering index.

45

Another situation that might benefit from filtered indexes is building a unique index that includes multiple rows with null values. A normal unique index enables only a single row to include a null value in the key columns. However, building a unique index that excludes null in the WHERE clause creates a unique index that permits an unlimited number of null values.

In a sense, SQL Server has had filtered indexes since SQL Server 2000 with indexed views. There's no reason why an indexed view couldn't have included a WHERE clause and included data from a filtered set of rows. But filtered indexes are certainly easier to create than indexed views, and they function as normal nonclustered indexes — which is an excellent segue into the next topic, indexed views.

Indexed Views

When a denormalized and pre-aggregated data solution needs to be in real time, an excellent alternative to querying the base tables includes using indexed views. Indexed views are "materialized" in that when the base table is updated the index for the view is also updated. This stores pre-aggregated or deformalized data without using special programming methods to do so.

Instead of building tables to duplicate data and denormalize a join, a view can be created that can join the two original tables and include the two source primary keys and all the columns required to select the data. Building a clustered index on the view physically materializes every column in the select column list of the view.

 Although indexed views build on normal views, they should not be confused. A normal view is a saved SELECT statement—no data is physically stored, as explained on Chapter 11, "Projecting Data Through Views." Indexed views actually store the data on disk. An indexed view is Microsoft's terminology for a materialized view.

Numerous restrictions exist on indexed views, including the following:

- The ANSI null and quoted identifier must be enabled when the base tables are created, when the view is created, and when any connection attempts to modify any data in the base tables.
- The index must be a unique clustered index; therefore, the view must produce a unique set of rows without using distinct.
- The tables in the view must be tables (not nested views) in the local database and must be referenced by means of the two-part name (schema.table).
- The view must be created with the option with schema binding.

As an example of an indexed view used to denormalize a large query, the following view selects data from the Product, WorkOrder, and ScrapReason tables to produce a view of scrapped products:

```
USE AdventureWorks2012
SET ANSI_Nulls ON;
```

```
SET ANSI_Padding ON;
SET ANSI_Warnings ON;
SET ArithAbort ON;
SET Concat_Null_Yields_Null ON;
SET Quoted_Identifier ON;
SET Numeric_RoundAbort OFF;

GO

CREATE VIEW vScrap
WITH SCHEMABINDING
AS
   SELECT WorkOrderID, P.Name AS Product,
     P.ProductNumber,
      S.Name AS ScrappedReason, ScrappedQty
     FROM Production.WorkOrder W
       JOIN Production.Product P
         ON P.ProductID = W.ProductID
       JOIN Production.ScrapReason S
         ON W.ScrapReasonID = S.ScrapReasonID
```

With the view in place, the index can now be created on the view, resulting in an indexed view:

```
CREATE UNIQUE CLUSTERED INDEX ivScrap
   ON vScrap    (WorkOrderID, Product, ProductNumber,
      ScrappedReason, ScrappedQty) ;
```

Indexed views can also be listed and created in Management Studio under the Views ⇨ Indexes node.

To drop an indexed view, the drop statement must refer to the view instead of to a table:

```
DROP INDEX ivscrap ON dbo.vScrap
```

Dropping the view automatically drops the indexed view created from the view.

Indexed Views and Queries

When SQL Server's Query Optimizer develops the execution plan for a query, it includes the indexed view's clustered index as one of the indexes it can use for the query, even if the query doesn't explicitly reference the view. This happens only with the Enterprise Edition.

This means that the indexed view's clustered index can serve to speed up queries. When the Query Optimizer selects the indexed view's clustered index, the query execution plan indicates the index used. Both of the following queries use the indexed view:

```
SELECT WorkOrderID, P.Name AS Product,
  P.ProductNumber,
   S.Name AS ScrappedReason, ScrappedQty
```

```
FROM Production.WorkOrder W
  JOIN Production.Product P
    ON P.ProductID = W.ProductID
  JOIN Production.ScrapReason S
    ON W.ScrapReasonID = S.ScrapReasonID


SELECT * FROM vScrap
```

Although indexed views are essentially the same as they were in SQL Server 2000, the Query Optimizer can now use indexed views with more types of queries.

Updating Indexed Views

As with any denormalized copy of the data, the difficulty is keeping the data current. Indexed views have the same issue. As data in the underlying base tables is updated, the indexed view must be kept in sync. This process is completely transparent to the user and is more of a performance consideration than a programmatic issue.

The Columnstore Index

New to SQL Server 2012 is the Columnstore index, which is structured and behaves differently than traditional B-tree indexes. With B-tree indexes, column values are stored in rows in a page. However, with Columnstore indexes, the column values are stored together in segments, which allows for incredible data compression while dramatically increasing speed of processing for scanning huge amounts of data.

The major benefit for Columnstore indexes are for DataWarehouse style queries where a large Fact table is joined with smaller Dimension tables and data is scanned to produce the wanted result. When a Columnstore index is added to a table, it causes the table to be readonly until the index is dropped, which is also ideal for DataWarehouse tables because they are often updated infrequently and at defined intervals.

Consider the following script to create a Columnstore index on the dbo.FactFinance table in the AdventureWorks DataWarehouse sample database. The syntax should be familiar; it is practically the same as creating a nonclustered index. The only different is that in a traditional NC index, you only include the columns that you use in the index, and you need to be careful about the order in which you define those columns. However, in a Columnstore index the recommendation is to include every column in the table, the order in which you define the columns in the index does not matter.

```
CREATE NONCLUSTERED COLUMNSTORE INDEX idx_CS_Finance
ON dbo.FactFinance
(
FinanceKey, DateKey, OrganizationKey, DepartmentGroupKey,
ScenarioKey, AccountKey, Amount, Date
)
```

Summary

To intelligently create indexes you need to thoroughly understand not only the technologies — the Query Optimizer, index pages, and indexing options — but also both your schema and your queries. Indexing is essentially a bridge from the query to the data. Although indexes can't fully overcome a poor schema or poorly written queries, a database without good indexing is sure to perform poorly.

To highlight the key ideas about indexing:

- Clustered indexes store all the data of the base table, logically organized by the index keys.

- Nonclustered indexes are subsets of data with their own keys and optionally included columns.

- A nonclustered index that completely solves the query without having to jump over to the clustered index (using a bookmark lookup) is referred to as a covering index.

- Bookmark lookups are the tipping point of indexing - where scans vs seeks are decided. For the queries that consume the most CPU duration, avoid them with clustered indexes or covering indexes. For the other queries, bookmark lookups are the preferable method to reduce the number of indexes.

- Filtered nonclustered indexes include only a small subset of rows, are faster to maintain, and can make perfect covering indexes.

- Indexed views are custom indexes that actually materialize data and can pull from multiple base tables or pre-aggregate data.

The next chapter continues the theme of understanding SQL Server internals and pragmatically using that knowledge to leverage performance from the system.

Maximizing Query Plan Reuse

T he SQL language is a declarative language, meaning that the SQL statement describes the wanted result but does not specifically address how to best solve the query.

Often the best solution is to consider the available indexes and statistics on the objects involved in the query. The indexes, data distribution, and parameter values are likely to fluctuate, so generating a query execution plan (plan compilation) when you declare the statement doesn't make sense.

Also, the process to generate an execution plan can be expensive, sometimes more so than executing the statement, so it doesn't often make sense to generate the execution plan every time you execute the statement.

As a compromise, SQL Server generates an execution plan the first time the statement executes and then stores that execution plan in a portion of memory known as the Plan Cache. The next time the same statement needs to execute, SQL Server attempts to use the cached execution plan instead of generating a new plan.

Query Compiling

As previously noted, when SQL Server compiles a statement, it stores the execution plan in the Plan Cache, which stays there, ready to be used again, as long as the plan is useful and there is no memory pressure.

The Query Optimizer

The Query Optimizer is a component of the relational engine that creates execution plans. Think of the Query Optimizer as the brain of the engine because it is responsible for making your queries run as quickly and efficiently as possible. There are several components and stages to compiling a query.

First, the *Parser* dissects the T-SQL code, ensures that it is valid code, and generates a Parse Tree — a logical representation of the query.

Next, the *Algebrizer* attempts to simplify any arguments, resolves any object names and aliases, identifies any data type conversions required, and binds any aggregate functions (group by, count(*)). The result is a Query Processor Tree, which is a corrected version of the Parse Tree ready for the Query Optimizer.

Delayed Name Resolution means that SQL Server allows a stored procedure to be created even if the objects it references don't yet exist. The idea is that the object might be created by the time the code is executed. Objects aren't physically checked until the Algebrizer checks for them.

Best Practice

Delayed name resolution is one more reason why a simple parse check is insufficient when developing SQL code. Unit testing against sample data that exercises every use case, including dynamically creating objects, is the only way to fully test any SQL code.

The Query Optimizer will apply rules at three different optimization phases and evaluates several possible execution plans to satisfy the statement and evaluate their efficiency. During these phases many different types of rules identify potential plans, such as join ordering and physical join choice. At each phase of optimization, a cost figure evaluates to determine if the query plan is "fast enough." If it is, optimization ends, and the query is submitted to the relational engine. The cost figure isn't a value that correlates to actual execution time but a relative cost of CPU and IO used to choose the best operation for the given server. The cost per operation considers the amount of data involved, available indexes, and the statistics to determine the best method for accessing the data.

At the end of the day, the job of the query optimizer is to determine the amount of data required by and produced by each operation and then chooses the best operations for that amount of data.

After the query execution plan generates, SQL Server stores it in the Plan Cache — a portion of memory reserved for query plans — and informs the Query Processor that the plan is ready to be executed.

 Chapter 44, "Interpreting Query Execution Plans," has more details on reading and viewing the plans and interpreting the query operations within the plans.

Viewing the Plan Cache

Dynamic Management Views (DMVs) expose the contents of the Plan Cache. You can use these DMVs to query the plan cache to verify that the query plan actually caches. The plan cache can be large, and although it's not recommended in a production environment, clearing the cache can make checking for a specific query easier:

```
DBCC FREEPROCCACHE
```

You can also pass in a sql_handle or plan_handle into DBCC FREEPROCCACHE to remove specific plans. To remove all cached plans for a specific database, you can use the DBCC FLUSHPROCINDB(database_id) command.

To examine the procedure cache, use the sys.dm_exec_cached_plans DMV, which returns the plan handle. The plan handle is a hashed value which can be used to look up an execution plan that currently resides in memory. This handle can be passed to sys.dm_exec_sql_text(plan_handle) and sys.dm_exec_query_plan(plan_handle) to view the original SQL code and the Query Execution Plan, as shown in Figure 46-1.

FIGURE 46-1

Viewing the Plan Cache is easy with a few DMVs. You can view the query execution plan by clicking the XML in the query_plan column.

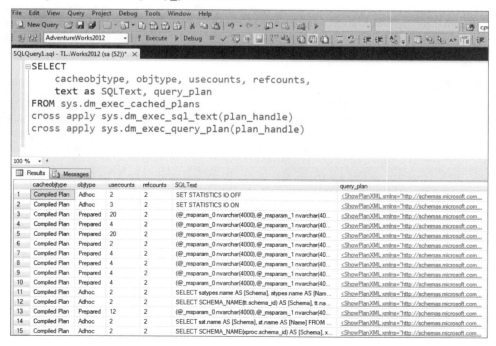

The DMV sys.dm_exec_query_stats provides a statement-level view of cached SQL statements. This DMV is a wonderful source of information as to how often statements execute, and how expensive they are. (This is one of the first DMVs I will look at when investigating performance problems.)

In addition to providing wonderful statement-level cached plan statistics, sys.dm_exec_query_stats provides two fields that enable you to determine statements and execution plans that are approximately the same. Use the query_hash column in this DMV to identity cached statements that are of a similar shape. If many statements have the same query_hash, consider parameterizing these statements if possible so that the usage of literal values in the queries do not bloat the plan cache and can be reused. Storing and keeping track of the query_plan_hash is useful because it enables you to see when a plan changes for a specific cached statement. Changes for well-known plans can be a cause for concern, which you should investigate.

Plan Lifetime

All the query plans in memory stay in the Plan Cache until SQL Server experiences memory pressure. SQL Server begins to age-out query plans based on how long it has been since they were last executed and how complex they are. A complex query plan with a high compilation cost stays in memory longer than a simple query with a lower compilation cost.

Query Plan Execution

When the Query Processor needs to execute a query, it first checks to see if the query can reuse an execution plan already in the Plan Cache. It's much faster to find and reuse a Query Execution Plan than to generate a new plan, even though that option is not always the best solution.

> **NOTE**
> You should always schema-qualify objects in your SQL statements. Doing so aids SQL Server to perform the initial object name to objectID lookup as well as prevent a second Plan Cache lookup with compile lock when checking to see if the cached procedure plan can be reused. Fully qualified objects provide more opportunities for plan reuse.

If the query qualifies for reuse, the Query Processor seeks the Plan Cache for an identical SQL statement (minus parameters). If the Query Processor finds a match, then an Execution Context holds the data and variables for that instance of the execution plan. This enables multiple users to simultaneously execute the same Query Execution Plan

Query Recompiles

Because the Execution Plan is based on a combination of the SQL statement, the indexes, and the data, a number of changes might cause SQL Server to decide that the execution plan is no longer valid, or no longer the optimal plan. SQL Server then marks the Execution Plan as invalid and generates a new Query Execution Plan the next time it executes.

Single statement query recompiles simply cause the query to recompile the next time it's executes. But stored procedures can recompile midstream.

Following are the most common causes of an automatic recompile:

- Updated Statistics. If statistics for data referenced by the query update, SQL Server blocks execution and recompiles based on the newer statistics. If asynchronous statistics updates occur, the update occurs in the background. The current query does not block, but it uses the out-of-date statistics for the current execution.

- Trivial plans. SQL Server cannot cache execution plans for reuse if the plan has a single best method for execution. An example is a SELECT * on a table that does not include a predicate.

- A large change in the number of rows in the base table referenced by the query (if AUTO_UPDATE of statistics is enabled), even rows inserted by a trigger.

- Mixing DML statements and DDL statements in a stored procedure can cause a recompile. For example, creating a temp table, running an update, and then creating another temp table forces a recompile of the stored procedure following the second temp table's creation.

- Some ALTER DATABASE commands force all plans out of the plan cache for a give database.

- A table, view, or index referenced by the query is altered. Therefore, if the stored procedure batch creates any temp tables, create them all at the beginning of the stored procedure or batch.

- Explicit recompile statements, such as using the OPTION(RECOMPILE) statement to force a recompile of a statement or stored procedure

Beginning with SQL Server 2005, individual statements recompile instead of whole batches. This means that recompiles are less costly, even if they occur more frequently.

The sp_recompile system stored procedure forces a recompile of any query plan stored that references that object (a stored procedure, table, or view) the next time the query executes. You can use the OPTION(RECOMPILE) hint at a statement level to force individual statements to recompile and forcibly not cache when included with a SQL statement.

You can monitor recompiles using SQL Profiler using the SQL:StmtRecompile event. You can also track recompiles using SQL Counters in Perfmon and with Extended Events.

> **CAUTION**
>
> Although plan reuse is typically a good thing, there are situations in which it is detrimental to performance. SQL Server creates execution plans based on the parameters passed in for the first execution of the parameterized statement. This is known as *parameter sniffing*. On subsequent executions, the cached plan will be reused regardless of the parameter values passed, which can cause performance problems if the stored plan is not well suited for the parameters.

Summary

The Query Optimizer is the technology that analyzes a query, the indexes available, and the data distribution, to compile a good-enough query execution plan for that query. The best way to optimize queries is to provide the Query Optimizer with good indexing and up-to-date statistics. From there, SQL Server usually does a great job of handling the rest.

The next chapter moves from single-user queries to multiuser contention and scalability — transactions — isolation — and the ACID properties. For some, the next topic is considered one of the harder topics in the database world, but it's foundational to developing SQL Server databases.

Managing Transactions, Locking, and Blocking

This chapter focuses on how contention occurs inside the database engine as data is read and modifications occur. Chapter 2, "Data Architecture," defines six database architecture design goals: usability, integrity, scalability, extensibility, availability, and security. Scalability is all about concurrency — multiple users simultaneously attempting to retrieve and modify data.

To ensure transactional integrity, SQL Server uses locks to protect transactions from affecting other transactions. A lock is a mechanism used by SQL Server to synchronize access by multiple users to the same piece of data at the same time. Specifically, transactions that are reading data may lock that data, which can prevent, or block, other transactions from writing the same data. Similarly, a transaction that's writing data can prevent other transactions from writing or reading the same data, depending on the isolation level of the transaction reading the locked data.

SQL Server uses locks to maintain the isolation property of a transaction. As more transactions occur inside the database, there is potential for more resources to acquire locks as data is modified. When more resources are locked, there is a good chance that other transactions also need to modify the data locked by other transactions. If this happens, the transactions needing to acquire locked resources are known as "blocked." Blocking occurs all the time inside the database and is not necessarily a cause for alarm. Excessive blocking, however, is a problem.

This chapter has four goals: to detail how transactions affect other transactions, explain the database theory behind transactions, illustrate how SQL Server maintains transactional integrity, and explain how to get the best performance from a high concurrency system.

What's New with Transactions?

SQL Server has always had transactional integrity, but Microsoft has improved it over the versions. SQL Server 7 introduced row locking, which eliminated the need to always create locks at the page level, which dramatically improved scalability. SQL Server 2000 improved how deadlocks are detected and rolled back. SQL Server 2005 introduced an entirely rewritten lock manager, which simplified lock escalation and improved performance. Beyond the ANSI standard isolation levels, SQL Server 2005 added *snapshot isolation*, which makes a copy of the data being updated in its own physical space, completely isolated from any other transactions, which enables readers to not block writers. Try-catch error handling, introduced in SQL Server 2005, can catch a 1205 deadlock error.

SQL Server 2008 continued the performance advances with the new ability to restrict lock escalation on a table, which forces row locks and can improve scalability.

New to SQL Server 2012 are the AlwaysOn read-only secondaries, which allow users to view data on a read-only copy of data. Read-only secondaries manage this through the use of the read-committed snapshot isolation level.

Transactions and locking in SQL Server can be complicated. So, this chapter explains the foundation of ACID transactions and SQL Server's default behavior first, followed by the potential problems and variations.

For the majority of SQL Server installations, the default Read Committed transaction isolation level works quite well for OLTP style environments. The section on transaction isolation level explains the exceptions.

The ACID Properties

Transactions must adhere to a set of requirements, known as the ACID properties. ACID is an acronym for four interdependent properties: Atomicity, Consistency, Isolation, and Durability. Much of the architecture of any modern relational database is founded on these properties. Understanding the ACID properties of a transaction is a prerequisite for understanding many facets of SQL Server.

Atomicity

A transaction must be *Atomic*, meaning all changes made by the transaction are completed as a single unit, or none of the changes are made. If a partial transaction were committed, the atomic property is violated, and the database is left in an inconsistent state. The ability to commit or roll back transactions is required for *Atomicity*.

Consistency

The transaction must preserve database *Consistency*, which means that the database must begin the transaction in a state of consistency and return to a state of consistency when the transaction is complete.

Consider the following example. Assume a foreign key constraint exists between a table named Orders and a table named OrderDetails based on a field named OrderID. This constraint ensures that before an OrderID exists in the OrderDetails table, the OrderID must first exist in the Orders table. If a transaction were to fail to write a record to the Orders table but successfully writes the record to the OrderDetails table, the database would no longer be in a consistent state.

Consistency allows for the database to be in an inconsistent state during the transaction. The key is that the database is consistent at the completion of the transaction. Like atomicity, the database must commit the whole transaction or roll back the whole transaction if modifications resulted in the database being inconsistent.

Isolation

Each transaction must be *isolated*, or separated, from the effects of other transactions. There are different levels of isolation, each level defining the rules for how transactions interact with each other. Some isolation levels, such as READ UNCOMMITTED enable transactions to read data that other transactions are modifying. More stringent isolation levels, such as SERIALIZABLE, are so strict that they lock ranges of rows (if those records aren't modified) to ensure that another transaction cannot read or modify the data involved in the transaction. SQL Server enforces the isolation levels between transactions through the use of locks and row versioning.

Durability

The *Durability* of a transaction ensures that after a transaction has been committed, it stays committed. This is accomplished by ensuring the transaction is written to stable media, which is typically thought of as writing to a disk drive, but it can also refer to a battery-backed memory cache. All SQL Server transactions must first be committed to the transaction log before they are written to the data file. This is known as write-ahead logging and will be explained in further detail in the section on the Transaction-Log Architecture later in this chapter.

Programming Transactions

A *transaction* is a sequence of tasks that together constitute a logical unit of work. All the tasks must complete or fail as a single unit, and the transaction must adhere to the ACID properties just outlined. For example, for an inventory movement transaction that reduces the inventory count from one bin and increases the inventory count in another bin, both updates must be committed together. If this did not occur, the reliability and usefulness of database management systems would be negligible.

In SQL Server, every DML operation (Select, Insert, Update, Delete, and Merge) is a transaction, whether or not it has been executed within a begin transaction. For example, a single `insert` command that inserts 25 rows is a logical unit of work. All the 25 rows must be inserted together or none of them are inserted. An `update` to a single row operates within a transaction so that the row in the clustered index (or heap) and the row's data in every nonclustered index are updated. Any partially competed transaction would violate transactional integrity.

Logical Transactions

If the logical unit of work involves multiple operations, some code is needed to define the bounds of the transaction: two statements — one at the *beginning* of the transaction and the other at its completion, at which time the transaction is *committed* to stable media. If the code detects an error, the entire transaction can be *rolled back*, or undone. The following three commands appear simple, but a volume of sophistication lies behind them:

- `begin transaction`
- `commit transaction`
- `rollback transaction`

(The text in bold is the required portion of the command.)

A transaction, once begun, should be either committed or rolled back as soon as possible. An open transaction continues to hold locks for the duration of the transaction, which likely leads to problems on a production system. Consider the following transaction. The first `update` statement decrements 100 units of quantity from the `ProductInventory` table for LocationID 6, whereas the next statement adds those 100 units of quantity to the LocationID of 50. You can see how both of these statements would need to commit together or not at all; otherwise you'd have Product quantity in the system that you'd have a hard time accounting for.

```
USE AdventureWorks2012
BEGIN TRY
  BEGIN TRANSACTION
    UPDATE Production.ProductInventory
      SET Quantity -= 100
      WHERE ProductID = 527
        AND LocationID = 6  -- misc storage
        AND Shelf = 'B'
        AND Bin = 4;
    UPDATE Production.ProductInventory
      SET Quantity += 100
      WHERE ProductID = 527
        AND LocationID = 50 -- subassembly area
        AND Shelf = 'F'
        AND Bin = 11;
```

```
    COMMIT TRANSACTION;
END TRY
BEGIN CATCH;
    ROLLBACK TRANSACTION;
    RAISERROR('Inventory Transaction Error', 16, 1);
    RETURN;
END CATCH;
```

 If you're not familiar with `Try...Catch`, the improved error handling code introduced in SQL Server 2005, it's covered in Chapter 16, "Programming with TSQL."

If all goes as expected, both updates are executed, the transaction is committed, and the `try` block completes execution. However, if either `update` operation fails, execution immediately transfers down to the `catch` block, the `commit` is never executed, and the `catch` block's `rollback transaction` will undo any work that had been done within the transaction.

Xact_State()

Every user connection is in one of three possible transaction states, which may be queried using the `Xact_State()` function, introduced in SQL Server 2005:

- **1**: Active, healthy transaction.
- **0**: No transaction.
- **−1**: Uncommittable transaction: You can begin a transaction, experience an error, and not commit that transaction. (Consider the consistency part of ACID.) In prior versions of SQL server, these were called doomed transactions.

Typically, the error handling catch block tests the `Xact_State()` function to see if the transaction can be committed or must be rolled back. The next `catch` block checks `Xact_State()` and decides if it can `commit` or `rollback` the transaction (using the catch block from the previous example):

```
BEGIN CATCH
    IF Xact_State() = 1 -- there's an active committable transaction
        COMMIT TRAN;
    IF Xact_State() = -1 -- there's an uncommittable transaction
        BEGIN
            ROLLBACK TRANSACTION;
            RAISERROR('Inventory Transaction Error', 16, 1);
        END
END CATCH;
```

Although the `XactState()` function is normally used within the error handling catch block, it's not restricted to the catch block and may be called at any time to see if the code is in a transaction.

Xact_Abort

A common SQL Server myth is that all error conditions roll back a transaction. Unless there's a try-catch error handling in place, a runtime error aborts only the statement causing the error. The batch continues and the transaction is completed even though an error occurred.

Turning on Xact_Abort solves some of these problems by ensuring that any runtime level error fails the entire batch and not just the statement that failed. So, Xact_Abort is a good thing and should often be set in code. Xact_Abort also triggers the try-catch code and sends execution into the catch block.

Nested Transactions

Nested transactions are a bit of a misnomer. Nested transactions behave as one large transaction: Changes made in one transaction can be read in a nested transaction, They do not behave as isolated transactions where actions of the nested transaction can be committed independently of a parent transaction.

When transactions are nested, a commit only marks the current nested transaction level as complete. However, and this is the important part, a Rollback at any level of nesting rolls back all pending and committed transactions that occurred inside the outermost transaction. The @@TranCount statement indicates the current nesting level. A commit when the trancount > 1 has no effect except to reduce trancount by 1. Only when the trancount is 1 are the actions within all levels of the nested transaction committed to disk. To prove this behavior, the next code sample examines the @@TranCount global variable, which returns the current transaction nesting level:

```
SELECT @@TRANCOUNT; -- 0
BEGIN TRAN;
  SELECT @@TRANCOUNT; -- 1
  BEGIN TRAN;
    SELECT @@TRANCOUNT; -- 2
    BEGIN TRAN;
      SELECT @@TRANCOUNT; -- 3
      ROLLBACK; -- undoes all nested transactions

SELECT @@TRANCOUNT; -- 0
```

Results:

```
0
1
2
```

```
3
0
```

If the code might have nested transactions, it's a good idea to examine @@TranCount (or XactState()) because attempting to commit or rollback a transaction if no pending transactions exist can raise a 3902 or 3903 error with a 16 severity code to the client.

Implicit Transactions

Although SQL Server requires an explicit begin transaction to initiate a logical transaction, this behavior can be modified so that every DML statement begins a transaction if one is not already started (so you don't end up with lots of nested transactions). This means that after a SQL DML command is issued, a commit or rollback is required.

To demo implicit transactions, the following code alone will not commit the update:

```
USE AdventureWorks2012
SET Implicit_Transactions ON;

UPDATE HumanResources.Department
  SET Name = 'Department of Redundant Departments'
  WHERE DepartmentID = 2;
```

Viewing the @@TranCount global variable does indeed show that there's one pending transaction level awaiting a commit or rollback:

```
SELECT @@TRANCOUNT;
```

Result:

```
1
```

Adding a commit transaction to the end of the batch commits the transaction, and the update is finalized:

```
COMMIT TRANSACTION;
```

Multiple DML commands or batches occur within a single logical transaction, so it doesn't create a bunch of nested transactions.

> **NOTE**
> Turning off implicit transactions affects only future batches. It does not commit any pending transactions. Be mindful if implicit transactions are turned on because if you do not explicitly commit the transaction, it remains open, potentially blocking other operations.

```
SET Implicit_Transactions OFF;
```

Save Points

You can also declare a *save point* within the sequence of tasks inside a transaction and then roll back to that save point. This gives you the flexibility to roll back sections of code without dooming the entire transaction.

Consider as an example a stored procedure called within a transaction. If you were to declare a save point at the beginning of the stored procedure, you could rollback any work accomplished inside that stored procedure without needing to roll back the outside transaction. Although this is not a best practice for coding standards, it does give you the flexibility to accomplish this task if needed.

Default Locking and Blocking Behavior

SQL Server uses locks, an internal memory structure, to provide transactional integrity between transactions.

There are different types of locks; among these are Shared (reading), Update (getting ready to write), Exclusive (writing), and many more. Some of these locks work well together, that is, two transactions can have Shared locks on a resource. However, when an exclusive lock has been acquired on a resource, no other transaction can acquire locks on that same resource. The locks used by the transactions are blocking other transaction from gaining access to the resource.

 The different types of locks and how compatible they are with each other is documented in BOL at: http://msdn.microsoft.com/en-us/library/ms186396(v=sql.105).aspx.

SQL Server's default transaction isolation is *read committed*, meaning that SQL Server ensures that only committed data is read. When a transaction updates a row, and the data is still yet uncommitted, SQL Server makes other transactions that want to read that data wait until the first transaction is committed.

To demonstrate SQL Server's default locking and blocking behavior, the following code walks through two transactions accessing the same row. Transaction 1 updates the row, whereas transaction 2 attempts to select the row. The best way to see these two transactions is with two query editor windows, as shown in Figure 47-1.

Transaction 1 opens a logical transaction and updates the department table:

```
-- Transaction 1
USE AdventureWorks2012
BEGIN TRANSACTION
  UPDATE HumanResources.Department
    SET Name = 'New Name'
    WHERE DepartmentID = 1;
```

FIGURE 47-1

Opening multiple Query Editor windows and sending the second tab into a New Vertical Tab Group (using the tab's context menu) is the best way to experiment with transactions.

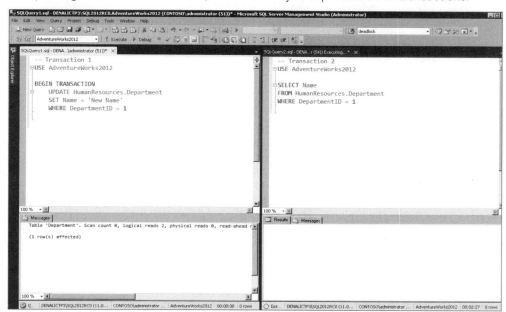

Transaction 1 (on my machine it's on session 54), now has an exclusive (X) write lock on the row being updated by locking the key of the record I'm updating. The locks can be viewed using the DMV sys.dm_tran_locks. (You can find the full query and more details about locks later in this chapter.)

Result:

```
Spid Object                            Type  Mode  Status
---- ------------------------------    ----- ----- ----------
51   HumanResources.Department         PAGE  IX    GRANT
51   HumanResources.Department         KEY   X     GRANT
```

Transaction 2 ensures the transaction isolation level is set to the default and then attempts to read the same row transaction 1 updates:

```
-- Transaction 2
USE AdventureWorks2012


SELECT Name
```

```
FROM HumanResources.Department
WHERE DepartmentID = 1;
```

There is no result yet for transaction 2. It's waiting for transaction 1 to complete, blocked by transaction 1's exclusive lock.

Requerying sys.dm_tran_locks reveals that the second transaction (spid 51) has an intent to Share (IS) read lock and is waiting for a Share (S) read lock.

Result:

```
Spid Object                       Type  Mode  Status
---- -------------------------    ----  ----  ----------
 51  HumanResources.Department     PAGE  IS    GRANT
 51  HumanResources.Department     PAGE  S     WAIT
 54  HumanResources.Department     KEY   X     GRANT
 54  HumanResources.Department     PAGE  IX    GRANT
 54  HumanResources.Department     PAGE  IX    GRANT
 54  HumanResources.Department     KEY   X     GRANT
 54  HumanResources.Department     KEY   X     GRANT
```

While transaction 1 is holding its exclusive lock, transaction 2 has to wait. In other words, transaction 1 blocks transaction 2.

Now, transaction 1 commits the transaction and releases the exclusive lock:

```
-- Transaction 1
COMMIT TRANSACTION
```

Immediately, transaction 1 completes and releases its locks. Transaction 2 springs to life and performs the select, reading the committed change.

Result:

```
Name
----------------------
New Name
```

The point of transaction isolation level read committed is to avoid reading uncommitted data. So what if the update doesn't change the data? If transaction 1 updates the data from "John" to "John" what's the harm of reading "John"?

SQL Server handles this situation by not respecting an exclusive lock if the page hasn't been changed, that is, if the page isn't flagged as dirty. This means that sometimes (because there's probably more data on the page than just the data in question) SQL Server avoids locking and blocking if the data isn't actually being changed.

You can prove this behavior by re-executing the previous locking and blocking sample code with the same update value.

Monitoring Locking and Blocking

SQL Server provides many different avenues for viewing and investigating locking problems. Locking may be investigated through sp_lock, sys.dm_tran_locks, SQL Profiler, PerfMon, and Extended Events, just to name a few.

Viewing Blocking with Management Studio Reports

With Management Studio, transaction information for a server or database may be seen using the Standard Reports, available from the server or database context menu, which pull data from the dynamic management views. The transaction-related reports include All Transactions, All Blocking Transactions (shown in Figure 47-2), Top Transactions by Age, Top Transactions by Blocked Transaction Count, Top Transactions by Lock Count, Resource Locking by Object, and User Statistics.

FIGURE 47-2

Management Studio's All Blocking Transactions Report is a quick way to view key transaction locking and blocking information.

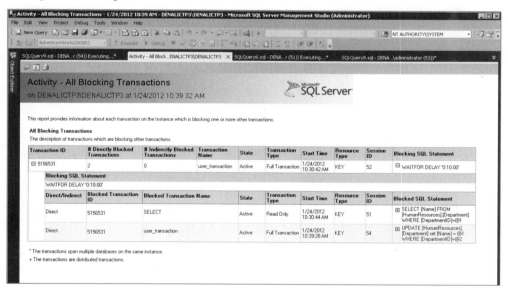

Viewing Blocking with Activity Monitor

Activity Monitor (see Figure 47-3) includes some useful bits of information that you can use to identify performance issues inside of SQL Server, including locking and blocking information. It's available on the toolbar and in the Object Explorer's server context menu.

FIGURE 47-3

Activity Monitor displays information about the current locks and any blocking going on. In this instance, spid 54 is blocked by spid 51, which is blocked by spid 52.

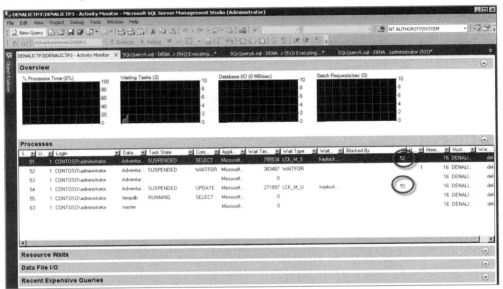

Using Profiler

You can also use SQL Server Profiler to watch blocked processes using the Error and Warnings: Blocked Process Report event (see Figure 47-4).

The catch to using Profiler is that by default the server is not configured to fire the blocked process event. To enable it, you must configure the
`blocked process threshold` setting. In addition, that's an advanced option, so you must first enable Show Advanced Options. The following snippet sets the blocking duration to 1 second.

```
sp_configure 'show advanced options', 1;
GO
RECONFIGURE;
GO
sp_configure 'blocked process threshold', 1;
GO
RECONFIGURE;
```

FIGURE 47-4

SQL Server Profiler can monitor and display the blocked and blocking code in XML.

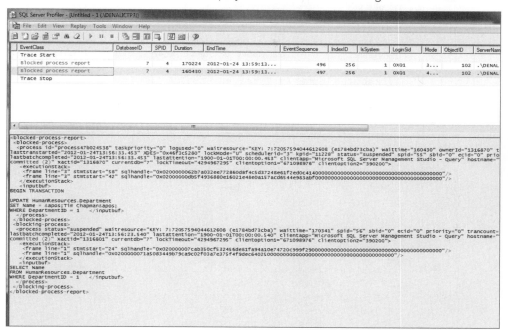

This means that the server checks every second for blocked statements, and for any statement that has been blocked for longer than 1 second, the blocked process report event fires. Due to when the last check was done, a statement may be blocked for more than the threshold value before it is reported. This can be seen by setting the threshold to a large value, say 10 seconds.

The result is a complete XML-formatted disclosure of the blocked and blocking process (refer to Figure 47-4). Saving this trace to a file and analyzing it in total is an excellent locking and blocking debugging technique.

Querying Locks with the DMVs

The dynamic management view sys.dm_exec_requests reports several interesting facts about current executing sessions, including the blocking session id:

```
SELECT session_id, blocking_session_id
  FROM sys.dm_exec_requests
  WHERE blocking_session_id > 0
```

Viewing all the locks is possible with the `sys.dm_tran_locks` DMV. The following query joins with other DMVs to provide a complete picture of the locks in a database:

```
SELECT
    request_session_id as Spid,
    Coalesce(s.name + '.' +  o.name + isnull('.' + i.name,''),
    s2.name + '.' +  o2.name COLLATE SQL_Latin1_General_CP1_CI_AS,
    db.name) AS Object,
    l.resource_type as Type,
    request_mode as Mode,
    request_status as Status
  FROM sys.dm_tran_locks l
    LEFT JOIN sys.partitions p
      ON l.resource_associated_entity_id = p.hobt_id
    LEFT JOIN sys.indexes i
      ON p.object_id = i.object_id
    AND p.index_id  = i.index_id
    LEFT JOIN sys.objects o
      ON p.object_id = o.object_id
    LEFT JOIN sys.schemas s
      ON o.schema_id = s.schema_id
    LEFT JOIN sys.objects o2
      ON l.resource_associated_entity_id = o2.object_id
    LEFT JOIN sys.schemas s2
      ON o2.schema_id = s2.schema_id
    LEFT JOIN sys.databases db
      ON l.resource_database_id = db.database_id
  WHERE resource_database_id = DB_ID()
  ORDER BY Spid, Object, CASE l.resource_type
                             When 'database' Then 1
                             when 'object' then 2
                             when 'page' then 3
                             when 'key' then 4
                             Else 5  end
```

Dealing with Deadlocks

A deadlock is a special situation that occurs when two or more processes are competing for the same set of resources; each prevents the other from obtaining the source it needs to complete its work.

Deadlocks are not a relational database specific problem; they can occur in any system where there is potential for resource contention, such as operating systems. However, because this is SQL Server-specific literature, you focus on the deadlock nuances inside the database engine.

Following is a simple example of a common deadlock scenario:

- Transaction 1 has a lock on data A and needs to lock data B to complete its transaction.

and

- Transaction 2 has a lock on data B and needs to lock data A to complete its transaction.

Each transaction is stuck waiting for the other to release its lock, and neither can complete until the other does, and each process will not release the resource it already has for the other process to use. This stalemate continues until the database engine chooses a victor.

Deadlocks do not always only include two transactions. It is completely possible that Process A can be waiting on a resource held by Process B, which is, in turn, waiting on a resource held by Process C. If C is waiting on a resource that Process A or Process B has locked, a deadlock is created.

Creating a Deadlock

It's easy to create a deadlock situation in SQL Server using two connections in Management Studio's Query Editor, as illustrated in Figure 47-5. Transaction 1 and transaction 2 simply try to update the same rows but in the opposite order. Use a third window to watch the locks using Activity Monitor or one of the DMV queries.

FIGURE 47-5

Creating a deadlock situation in Management Studio using two connections tiled vertically.

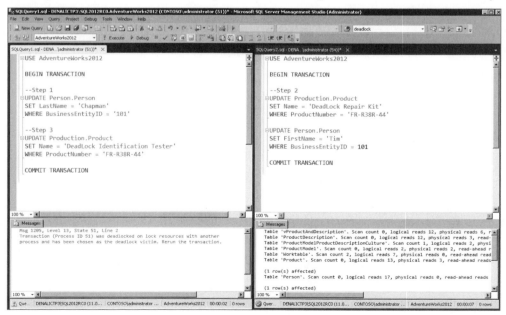

To execute the code, you need to do the following:

Create two Query windows.

In one paste the following:

```
USE AdventureWorks2012

BEGIN TRANSACTION

--Step 1
UPDATE Person.Person
SET LastName = 'Chapman'
WHERE BusinessEntityID = '101'

--Step 3
UPDATE Production.Product
SET Name = 'DeadLock Identification Tester'
WHERE ProductNumber = 'FR-R38R-44'

COMMIT TRANSACTION
```

In the second window paste:

```
USE AdventureWorks2012

BEGIN TRANSACTION

--Step 2
UPDATE Production.Product
SET Name = 'DeadLock Repair Kit'
WHERE ProductNumber = 'FR-R38R-44'

UPDATE Person.Person
SET FirstName = 'Tim'
WHERE BusinessEntityID = 101

COMMIT TRANSACTION
```

Executing step 1 in the first query window:

```
USE AdventureWorks2012

BEGIN TRANSACTION

--Step 1
UPDATE Person.Person
SET LastName = 'Chapman'
WHERE BusinessEntityID = '101'
```

Transaction 1 now has an exclusive lock on `BusinessEntityID` 101. Executing Step 2 in the second window:

```
USE AdventureWorks2012

BEGIN TRANSACTION

--Step 2
UPDATE Production.Product
SET Name = 'DeadLock Repair Kit'
WHERE ProductNumber = 'FR-R38R-44'

UPDATE Person.Person
SET FirstName = 'Tim'
WHERE BusinessEntityID = 101

COMMIT TRANSACTION
```

Transaction 2 gains an exclusive lock on `ProductNumber` "FR-R38R-44" and then tries to grab an exclusive lock on `BusinessEntityID` 101, but transaction 1 already has it locked.

It's not a deadlock yet, because although transaction 2 waits for transaction 1, transaction 1 is not waiting for transaction 2. At this point, if transaction 1 finished its work and issued a `commit transaction`, the data resource would be freed; transaction 2 could get its lock on the contact row and be on its way as well.

The trouble begins when transaction 1 tries to update `ProductNumber` "FR-R38R-44." It can't get an exclusive lock because transaction 2 already has an exclusive lock. So when this code is executed

```
-- Transaction 1
-- Step 3

UPDATE Production.Product
SET Name = 'DeadLock Identification Tester'
WHERE ProductNumber = 'FR-R38R-44'
```

Transaction 1 returns the following friendly error message in a few seconds:

```
Msg 1205, Level 13, State 51, Line 2
Transaction (Process ID 52) was deadlocked on lock resources with
another process and has been chosen as the deadlock victim.
Rerun the transaction.
```

The deadlock can also be viewed using SQL Server Profiler (as shown in Figure 47-6). Transaction 2 completes as if there's no problem.

FIGURE 47-6

SQL Server Profiler can monitor deadlocks using the Locks: Deadlock Graph event and can display the resource conflict that caused the deadlock.

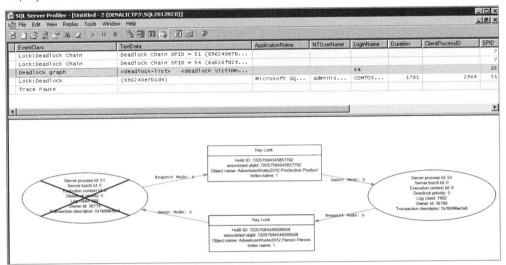

Automatic Deadlock Detection

As the previous deadlock code demonstrated, SQL Server uses an internal thread named the Deadlock Monitor, which automatically detects a deadlock situation by examining the waiting lock lists for cyclical locking and rolling back the transaction. By default, this thread checks for deadlocking characteristics every 5 seconds, but the database engine adjusts this threshold so that checks are made more often if deadlocks are detected frequently.

Typically, the transaction that has performed the least amount of work or is easiest to roll back is the victim, but this is not always true. As a database developer you do have a little bit of control in assigning deadlock priorities to your SQL batches.

Handling Deadlocks

Before SQL Server 2005, trapping a deadlock could occur only at the client, but fortunately a try-catch error handling code can trap a 1205 error, and deadlocks can now be handled in the catch block. If you catch the deadlock within the transaction, your only option is to roll back the transaction. However, you can then rerun your transaction using T-SQL logic.

```
USE AdventureWorks2012
DECLARE @retry INT
```

```
SET @retry = 1
WHILE @retry = 1
BEGIN
    BEGIN TRY
    SET  @retry  = 0

    BEGIN TRANSACTION

    UPDATE HumanResources.Department
    SET Name = 'Accounting'
    WHERE DepartmentID = 2;

    UPDATE HumanResources.Department
    SET Name = 'Development'
    WHERE DepartmentID = 1;
    COMMIT TRANSACTION

  END TRY
  BEGIN CATCH
  IF ERROR_NUMBER() = 1205
  BEGIN
    PRINT ERROR_MESSAGE()
    SET  @retry  = 1
    END
  ROLLBACK TRANSACTION
  END CATCH
END
```

Instead of letting SQL Server decide which transaction is the "deadlock victim," you can take control and assign priorities to your T-SQL code. The transaction with the lowest deadlock priority will be rolled back first. The priorities with the same priority fall back to the rollback cost to determine which to roll back. To set the priority, issue the following command before the beginning of the transaction:

```
SET DEADLOCK_PRIORITY LOW
```

The setting actually allows for a range of values from –10 to 10, or normal (0), low (–5), and high (5).

The System_Health Session

Starting in SQL Server 2008, an Extended Event session named the system_health session captures important diagnostic information for a given SQL Server instance, which includes deadlock information. Extended Events is greatly enhanced for SQL Server 2012. See Chapter 40, "Extended Events," for more information about the system_health session.

Minimizing Deadlocks

Even though deadlocks can be detected and handled, it's better to avoid them altogether. The following practices help prevent deadlocks:

- Keep a transaction short and to the point. Any code that doesn't need to be in the transaction should be left out of it.

- Never code a transaction to depend on user input.

- Try to write batches and procedures so that they obtain locks in the same order — for example, TableA, then TableB, and then TableC. This way, one procedure can wait for the next, and a deadlock can likely be avoided.

- Choose appropriate indexes to support your data usage. The quicker SQL Server can find the data that needs to be modified, the shorter the duration of the transaction.

- Don't increase the isolation level unless it's necessary. A stricter isolation level likely increases the duration of the transaction, which increases locks to be held longer and limit database concurrency.

Understanding SQL Server Locking

SQL Server implements the I (Isolation) portion of the ACID property via locks. Locks ensure that the data modified by one transaction is protected from data modified in a different transaction. There are a series of different levels for locking data. Before these locks can be controlled, they must be understood. SQL Server offers several methods to control locks.

Lock Granularity

A portion of the data controlled by a lock can vary from only a row to the entire database, as shown in Table 47-1. Several combinations of locks, depending on the lock granularity, can satisfy a locking requirement.

TABLE 47-1 **Lock Granularity**

Lock Size	Description
Row Lock	Locks a single row. This is the smallest lock available. SQL Server does not lock columns.
Page Lock	Locks a page, or 8KB. One or more rows may exist on a single page.
Extent Lock	Locks eight pages, or 64KB.
Table Lock	Locks the entire table.
Database Lock	Locks the entire database. This lock is used primarily during schema changes.
Key Lock	Locks nodes on an index.

For best performance, the SQL Server lock manager tries to balance the size of the lock against the number of locks. The struggle is between concurrency (smaller locks allow more transactions to access the data) and resource usage. (Fewer locks are faster because each lock requires memory in the system to hold the information about the lock.)

SQL Server automatically manages the granularity of locks by trying to keep the lock size small and escalating to a higher level only when it detects memory pressure.

Lock Mode

Locks not only have granularity, but also a mode that determines their purpose. SQL Server has a rich set of lock modes (such as shared, update, and exclusive). Understanding lock modes can dramatically aid in not only developing well-designed database applications, but can also assist you in troubleshooting locking problems.

Lock Contention

The interaction and compatibility of the locks plays a vital role in SQL Server's transactional integrity and performance. Certain lock modes block other lock modes, as detailed in Table 47-2. For example, if Transaction 1 has a shared lock (S), and transaction 2 requests an exclusive lock (X), then the request is denied because a shared lock blocks an exclusive lock.

TABLE 47-2 **Lock Compatibility**

| | T2 Requests | | | | | |
T1 Has	IS	S	U	IX	SIX	X
Intent shared (IS)	Yes	Yes	Yes	Yes	Yes	Yes
Shared (S)	Yes	Yes	Yes	No	No	No
Update (U)	Yes	Yes	No	No	No	No
Intent exclusive (IX)	Yes	No	No	Yes	No	No
Shared with intent exclusive (SIX)	Yes	No	No	No	No	No
Exclusive (X)	No	No	No	No	No	No

Exclusive locks are ignored unless the page in memory has been updated, that is, is dirty.

Shared Lock (S)

Shared locks are taken anytime data is in the database using the default isolation level, Read Committed, or with any pessimistic isolation level of lower concurrency. Assuming the default isolation level, two processes are allowed to read the same data by use of shared locks. However, because shared locks are not granted on resources that are intended to be, or currently are, locked, this is why you often see a read operation being blocked: Shared locks can never be taken on rows/pages/tables that are currently being modified.

Exclusive Lock (X)

An exclusive lock means that the transaction is performing a write to the data. As the name implies, an exclusive lock means that only one transaction may hold an exclusive lock at one time, and that no transaction can view the data during the exclusive lock.

Update Lock (U)

An update lock means that a transaction is getting ready to perform an exclusive lock and is currently scanning the data to determine the row(s) it wants for that lock. You can think of the update lock as a shared lock that can blossom into an exclusive lock after the data is found that needs to be modified.

To help prevent deadlocks, only one transaction may hold an update lock at a given time.

Intent Locks (various)

Intent locks serve to stake a claim for a shared or exclusive lock without actually being a shared or exclusive lock. In doing so they solve two performance problems: hierarchical locking and permanent lock block.

The primary purpose of an intent lock is to improve performance. Because an intent lock is used for all types of locks and for all lock granularities, SQL Server has many types of intent locks. The following is a sampling of the intent locks:

- Intent Shared Lock (IS)
- Shared with Intent Exclusive Lock (SIX)
- Intent Exclusive Lock (IX)

Without intent locks, if transaction 1 holds a shared lock on a row and transaction 2 wants to grab an exclusive lock on the table, then transaction 2 would need to check for table locks, extent locks, page locks, row locks, and key locks.

Instead, SQL Server uses intent locks to propagate a lock to higher levels of the data's hierarchical levels. When transaction 1 gains a row lock, it also places an intent lock on the row's page and table.

The intent locks move the overhead of locking from the transaction needing to check for a lock to the transaction placing the lock. The transaction placing the lock needs to place three or four locks, that is, Key, Page, Object, and Database. The transaction checking needs to check only for locks that contend with the three or four locks it needs to place. That one-time write of three locks potentially saves hundreds of searches later as other transactions check for locks.

The intent locks also prevent a serious shared-lock contention problem. As long as a transaction has a shared lock, another transaction can't gain an exclusive lock. What would happen if someone grabbed a shared lock every 5 seconds and held it for 10 seconds while a transaction was waiting for an exclusive lock? The update transaction could theoretically wait forever. However, when the transaction has an intent exclusive lock (IX), no other transaction can grab a shared lock. The intent exclusive lock isn't a full exclusive lock, but it lays claim to gaining an exclusive lock in the future.

Schema Lock (Sch-M, Sch-S)

Schema locks protect the database schema. SQL Server applies a schema stability (Sch-S) lock during any query to prevent a data definition language (DDL) command from modifying the structure that the statement is querying.

A schema modification lock (Sch-M) is applied only when SQL Server is adjusting the physical schema. If SQL Server is in the middle of adding a column to a table, the schema lock prevents any other transactions from viewing or modifying the data during the schema-modification operation.

Controlling Lock Timeouts

If a transaction is waiting for a lock, it continues to wait until the lock is available. By default no timeout exists — it can theoretically wait forever.

Fortunately, you can set the lock time using the `set lock_timeout` connection option. Set the option to a number of milliseconds or set it to infinity (the default) by setting it to `-1`. Setting the `lock_timeout` to `0` means that the transaction instantly gives up if any lock contention occurs. The application will be fast and ineffective.

The following query sets the lock timeout to 2 seconds (2,000 milliseconds):

```
SET Lock_Timeout 2000
```

When a transaction does time out while waiting to gain a lock, a 1222 error is raised.

Lock Duration

The third lock property, lock duration, is determined by the transaction isolation level of the transactions involved — the more stringent the isolation, the longer the locks will be held. SQL Server implements four transaction isolation levels. (Transaction isolation levels are detailed in the next section.)

Index-Level Locking Restrictions

Isolation levels and locking hints are applied from the connection and query perspective. The only way to control locks from the table perspective is to restrict the granularity of locks on a per-index basis. Using the `alter index` command, rowlocks and pagelocks may be disabled for a particular index, as follows:

```
ALTER INDEX AK_Department_Name
    ON HumanResources.Department
    SET (ALLOW_PAGE_LOCKS = OFF)
```

Disabling page level locks is useful for a couple of specific purposes. If a table frequently causes waiting because of page locks, setting `allowpagelocks` to `off` forces rowlocks. The decreased scope of the lock improves concurrency at the cost of requiring additional memory usage to keep track of row locks. This may also increase the number of lock escalation attempts you see. In addition, if a table is seldom updated but frequently read, row-level and page-level locks may be inappropriate. Allowing only table locks may be suitable during the majority of table accesses. For the infrequent update, a table-exclusive lock may not be a big issue.

`Sp_indexoption` is for fine-tuning the data schema; that's why it's on an index level. To restrict the locks on a table's primary key, use `sp_help tablename` to find the specific name for the primary-key index.

The following commands configure the `ProductCategory` table as an infrequently updated lookup table. First, `sp_help` reports the name of the primary key index:

```
sp_help ProductCategory
```

Result (abridged):

```
index                               index          index
name                                description    keys
-------------------------------     ------------   ----------------
PK__ProductCategory__79A81403       nonclustered,  ProductCategoryID
                                    unique,
                                    primary key
                                    located
                                    on PRIMARY
```

Having identified the actual name of the primary key, the `alter index` command can be set as shown previously.

Transaction Isolation Levels

Any study of how transactions impact performance must include *transactional integrity*, which refers to the quality, or fidelity, of the transaction. There are three types of side-effects of isolation levels that can violate transactional integrity: dirty reads, nonrepeatable reads, and phantom rows.

The level of isolation between transactions can be adjusted to control which transactional faults are permitted. The ANSI SQL-92 committee specified four isolation levels: Read Uncommitted, Read Committed, Repeatable Read, and Serializable.

SQL Server 2005 introduced two additional row versioning "SQL Server 2005 introduced row versioning, " which enables two levels of optimistic transaction isolation: Snapshot, and Read Committed Snapshot. All six transaction isolation levels are listed in Table 47-3 and then detailed in this section.

TABLE 47-3   ANSI-92 Isolation Levels

Isolation Level	Table Hint	Dirty Read	NonRepeatable Read	Phantom Row	Reader/ Writer Blocking
The Transaction isolation level is set for the connection.	Table Hints override the connection's transaction isolation level.	Seeing another transaction's non-committed changes.	The same query reading different data in a transaction.	Seeing additional rows selected by where clause as a result of another transaction.	A write transaction blocks a read transaction.
Read Uncommitted *(least restrictive)*	NoLock, ReadUncommitted	Possible	Possible	Possible	Yes
Read Committed *(SQL Server default; moderately restrictive)*	ReadCommitted	Prevented	Possible	Possible	Yes
Repeatable Read	RepeatableRead	Prevented	Prevented	Possible	Yes
Serializable *(most restrictive)*	Serializable	Prevented	Prevented	Prevented	Yes
Snapshot		Prevented	Prevented	Possible	No
Read Committed Snapshot		Prevented	Possible	Possible	No

47

Internally, SQL Server uses locks for isolation (locks are still used in snapshot-based isolation levels; the difference is that they typically do not block other operations)), and the transaction isolation levels determines the duration of the share lock or exclusive lock for the transaction, as listed in Table 47-4.

TABLE 47-4   Isolation Levels and Lock Duration

Isolation Level	Share-Lock Duration	Exclusive-Lock Duration
Read Uncommitted	None	Held only long enough to prevent physical corruption; otherwise, exclusive locks are neither applied nor honored.
Read Committed	Held while the transaction is reading the data	Held until transaction commit.
Repeatable Read	Held until the transaction is committed	Held until transaction commit.
Serializable	Held until transaction commit	Held until transaction commit. The exclusive lock also uses a keylock (also called a range lock) to prevent inserts.

Setting the Transaction Isolation Level

The transaction isolation level can be set at the connection level using the SET command. Setting the transaction isolation level affects all statements for the duration of the connection, or until the transaction isolation level is changed again. (You can't change the isolation level once you are in a transaction.)

```
SET TRANSACTION ISOLATION LEVEL
   READ COMMITTED;
```

To view the current connection transaction isolation level, use sys.dm_exec_sessions:

```
SELECT TIL.Description
   FROM sys.dm_exec_sessions dmv
     JOIN (VALUES(1, 'Read Uncommitted'),
                 (2, 'Read Committed'),
                 (3, 'Repeatable Read'),
                 (4, 'Serializable'))
              AS TIL(ID, Description)
        ON dmv.transaction_isolation_level = TIL.ID
     WHERE session_id = @@spid;
```

Result:

```
READ COMMITTED
```

Alternatively, the transaction isolation level for a single DML statement can be set by using table-lock hints in the `from` clause. These can be used to override the current connection transaction isolation level and apply the hint on a per table basis. For example, in the next code sample, the Department table is actually accessed using a read uncommitted transaction isolation level, not the connection's read committed transaction isolation level:

```
SET TRANSACTION ISOLATION LEVEL
   REPEATABLE READ;

SELECT Name
   FROM HumanResources.Department WITH (NOLOCK)
   WHERE DepartmentID = 1;
```

Level 1 — Read Uncommitted and the Dirty Read

The least stringent level of isolation, *Read Uncommitted*, does not take shared locks when reading data. (This applies ONLY when reading data.) As no shared locks are required, data x currently modified inside a transaction can be read in this isolation level. When this occurs, the data is said to be "dirty" because it has not yet been committed.

Figure 47-7 shows this type of dirty read.

FIGURE 47-7

A dirty read occurs when transaction 2 can see transaction 1's uncommitted changes.

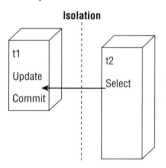

To demonstrate the Read Uncommitted Transaction Isolation level and the dirty read, it allows the following code to use two connections, creating two transactions. The second transaction sees the first transaction's update before that update is committed:

```
--Transaction 1
USE AdventureWorks2012
```

```
BEGIN TRANSACTION

UPDATE HumanResources.Department
SET Name = 'Transaction Fault'
WHERE DepartmentID = 1
```

In a separate Management Studio window, as shown in Figure 47-1, execute another transaction in its own connection window. This transaction sets its transaction isolation level to permit dirty reads. Only the second transaction needs to be set to read uncommitted for transaction 2 to experience a dirty read:

```
-- Transaction 2
USE AdventureWorks2012;
SET TRANSACTION ISOLATION LEVEL READ UNCOMMITTED;

SELECT Name
FROM HumanResources.Department
WHERE DepartmentID = 1;
```

Result:

```
Name
---------------------
Transaction Fault
```

Transaction 1 hasn't yet committed the transaction, but transaction 2 read "Transaction Fault." That's a dirty read side effect of the READ UNCOMMITTED isolation level..

To finish the task, the first transaction rolls back that transaction:

```
-- Transaction 1
ROLLBACK TRANSACTION
```

There are other issues about reading uncommitted data due to the way the SQL engine optimizes such a read that can result in your query reading the same data more than once.

Level 2 — Read Committed

SQL Server's default transaction isolation level, *read committed*, ensures that one transaction cannot read data that another transaction has altered but not yet committed. This is accomplished through shared locks, which are taken when data is read and released afterwards. Shared locks cannot be taken on data that is currently being modified. This prevents dirty reads, but it is susceptible to other types of isolation level side effects. These side effects (described in detail later in this chapter), although undesirable, require more stringent isolation levels to protect against them, which can drastically inhibit concurrency. That being said, the read committed isolation level works quite well for most SQL Server installations.

Level 3 — Repeatable Read

The third isolation level, repeatable read, is a more stringent isolation level than the previous two. In repeatable read, any shared lock acquired during the transaction is held until the transaction has been committed. This is different than the read committed isolation level, which holds only shared locks on data while it is being read. Holding shared locks for the duration of the transaction ensures that the transaction can read the same data set consistently for the duration of the transaction.

Nonrepeatable Read

A nonrepeatable read occurs when a transaction reads a set of data, performs additional operations, and reads the set of data again in the same transaction, retrieving a different result set the second time around, as shown in Figure 47-8. This type of isolation-level side effect is present in the read-uncommitted and read-committed isolation levels.

FIGURE 47-8

A nonrepeatable read side effect occurs when transaction 2 selects the same data twice and sees different values.

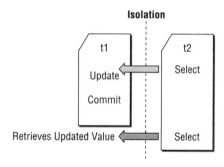

To demonstrate a nonrepeatable read, the following sequence sets up two concurrent transactions. Transaction 2, on the right side, is in the default read committed transaction isolation level, which allows the nonrepeatable read.

Assuming an unaltered copy of AdventureWorks2012, transaction 2 begins a logical transaction and then reads the department name as Engineering.

```
-- Transaction 2
```

```
USE AdventureWorks2012

SET TRANSACTION ISOLATION LEVEL
READ COMMITTED

BEGIN TRANSACTION
SELECT Name
FROM HumanResources.Department
WHERE DepartmentID = 1
```

Result:

```
Name
-----------------------
Engineering
```

Transaction 1 now updates the department name to Non-Repeatable Read:

```
-- Transaction 1
USE AdventureWorks2012;
UPDATE HumanResources.Department
SET Name = 'Non-Repeatable Read'
WHERE DepartmentID = 1;
```

Transaction 2 reads the row again. If it sees the value updated by transaction 2, it results in a nonrepeatable read:

```
SELECT Name
FROM HumanResources.Department
WHERE DepartmentID = 1

COMMIT TRANSACTION
```

Result:

```
Name
-----------------------
Non-Repeatable Read
```

Sure enough, transaction 2's read was not repeatable.

Preventing the Fault

Rerunning the same scripts with transaction 2's transaction isolation level to repeatable read will result in a different behavior (assuming an unaltered copy of AdventureWorks2012):

```
                        -- Transaction 2

USE AdventureWorks2012
SET TRANSACTION ISOLATION LEVEL
```

REPEATABLE READ

```
BEGIN TRANSACTION;
SELECT Name
FROM HumanResources.Department
WHERE DepartmentID = 1
```

Result:

```
Name
-----------------------
Engineering
```

Transaction 1 now updates the department name to Non-Repeatable Read:

```
-- Transaction 1
USE AdventureWorks2012
UPDATE HumanResources.Department
SET Name = 'Non-Repeatable Read'
WHERE DepartmentID = 1
```

Here's the first major difference: Transaction 1 is blocked because it tries to update a record still locked by transaction 2. Shared locks are still present on the records read from transaction 2, so transaction 1 cannot modify the data.

Transaction 2 reads the row again. If it sees the value updated by transaction 2, that's a nonrepeatable read:

```
SELECT Name
FROM HumanResources.Department
WHERE DepartmentID = 1
```

Result:

```
Name
-----------------------
Engineering
```

But the result is not the updated value from transaction 1. Instead the original value is still in place. The read was repeatable and the nonrepeatable read fault has been prevented.

When transaction 2 completes the transaction, it releases the share lock:

```
COMMIT TRANSACTION;
```

Immediately, transaction 1, is now free to complete its update and the "1 row(s) affected" message appears in the Messages pane.

Although repeatable read protects against the selected rows being updated, it doesn't protect against new rows being added to or deleted from the selected range. This is known as a phantom row, which means you could get a different value/set of results if new rows are added or deleted. To avoid this, use a Serializable transaction isolation level of protection.

Best Practice

Repeatable read has a significant concurrency overhead, but it's perfect for situations in which a transaction must read the data multiple times, perhaps performing calculations, and guarantees that no other transaction updates the data during these calculations.

Level 4 — Serializable

This most restrictive isolation level prevents all transaction isolation side effects; dirty reads, nonrepeatable reads, and phantom rows. Serializable prevents the previously described side-effects by ensuring that data can be modified in such a way so that it would be present in a range of rows previously read in a transaction. To ensure this happens, SQL Server locks a range of rows being read rather than only the rows that have been read.

This isolation level is useful for databases for which absolute transactional integrity is more important than performance. Banking, accounting, and high-contention sales databases, such as the stock market, typically use serialized isolation.

Phantom Rows

A phantom row occurs when a transaction's insert, update, or delete causes different rows to be returned in another transaction, as shown in Figure 47-9.

FIGURE 47-9

When the rows returned by a select are altered by another transaction, the phenomenon is called a *phantom row*.

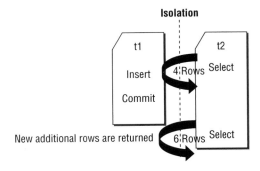

Beginning with a clean copy of AdventureWorks2012, transaction 2 selects all the rows in a specific range (Name BETWEEN 'A' AND 'G'):

Keep a Copy of Your AdventureWorks2012 Database

Many of the samples in this chapter assume an unmodified version of the AdventureWorks2012 database. Once you download the AdventureWorks2012 data file, keep a copy of it around so that you can attach it after running through the examples and start with a clean copy of the database.

```
-- Transaction 2
USE AdventureWorks2012
SET TRANSACTION ISOLATION LEVEL REPEATABLE READ

BEGIN TRANSACTION
SELECT DepartmentID as DeptID, Name
FROM HumanResources.Department
WHERE Name BETWEEN 'A' AND 'G'
```

Result:

```
DeptID      Name
----------  --------------------
12          Document Control
1           Engineering
16          Executive
14          Facilities and Maintenance
10          Finance
```

Transaction 1 now inserts a new row into the range selected by transaction 2:

```
-- Transaction 1
-- Insert a row in the range
INSERT HumanResources.Department (Name, GroupName)
VALUES ('ABC Dept', 'Test Dept')
```

When transaction 2 selects the same range again, if 'ABC Dept' is in the result list, then a phantom row transaction fault occurred:

```
-- Transaction 2
SELECT DepartmentID as DeptID, Name
FROM HumanResources.Department
WHERE Name BETWEEN 'A' AND 'G'
COMMIT TRANSACTION
```

Result:

```
DeptID      Name
----------  --------------------
17          ABC Dept
12          Document Control
```

```
DeptID      Name
------      ----
1           Engineering
16          Executive
14          Facilities and Maintenance
10          Finance
```

ABC Dept is in the result list, and that's the phantom row.

Serialized Transaction Isolation Level

The highest transaction isolation level can defend the transaction against the phantom row. Transaction 2 first inserts a sample row, "Amazing FX Dept," so transaction 1 has a row that can be deleted without worrying about referential integrity issues. It then sets the transaction isolation level, begins a transaction, and reads a range of data:

```
-- Transaction 2
USE AdventureWorks2012

-- insert test row for deletion
INSERT HumanResources.Department
(Name, GroupName)
VALUES ('Amazing FX Dept', 'Test Dept')

SET TRANSACTION ISOLATION LEVEL
SERIALIZABLE

BEGIN TRANSACTION

SELECT DepartmentID as DeptID, Name
FROM HumanResources.Department
WHERE Name BETWEEN 'A' AND 'G'
```

Result:

```
DeptID       Name
----------   --------------------
17           Amazing FX Dept
12           Document Control
1            Engineering
16           Executive
14           Facilities and Maintenance
10           Finance
```

Transaction 2's select returned six rows.

With transaction 2 in a transaction and serialized transaction isolation level protecting the range of names from "A" to "G", transaction 1 attempts to insert, update, and delete into and from that range:

```
-- Transaction 1
-- Insert a row in the range
INSERT HumanResources.Department (Name, GroupName)
VALUES ('ABC Dept', 'Test Dept')

-- Update Dept into the range
UPDATE HumanResources.Department
SET Name = 'ABC Test'
WHERE DepartmentID = 1 -- Engineering

-- Delete Dept from range
DELETE HumanResources.Department
WHERE DepartmentID = 17 -- Amazing FX Dept
```

The significant observation is that none of transaction 1's DML commands produced a
"1 row(s) affected" message; it is blocked on the first statement.

Transaction 2 now reselects the same range:

```
SELECT DepartmentID as DeptID, Name
FROM HumanResources.Department
WHERE Name BETWEEN 'A' AND 'G'
```

Result:

```
DeptID      Name
----------  --------------------
17          Amazing FX Dept
12          Document Control
1           Engineering
16          Executive
14          Facilities and Maintenance
10          Finance
```

The select returns the same six rows with the same values. Transactional integrity is
intact and the phantom row fault has been thwarted.

Transaction 1 is still on hold, waiting for transaction 2 to complete its transaction:

```
COMMIT TRANSACTION
```

As soon as transaction 2 issues a commit transaction and releases its locks, transaction 1 is
free to makes its changes and three "1 row(s) affected" messages appear in transaction 1's messages pane:

```
SELECT *
FROM HumanResources.Department
```

Result:

```
DeptID      Name
----------  --------------------
18          ABC Dept
1           ABC Test
12          Document Control
1           Engineering
16          Executive
14          Facilities and Maintenance
10          Finance
```

Selecting the range after the transaction 2 is committed, and transaction 1 has made its updates, reveals the inserted and updated rows added to the range. And the Amazing FX Dept disappeared.

Concurrency and serialized isolation levels do not play well together because to get the protection needed for the serialized isolation level requires additional locks. And worse, those locks have to be on key ranges to prevent someone else inserting rows. If you don't have the correct indexes, the only way SQL can prevent phantoms is to lock the table. Locking the table is obviously not good for concurrency. For this reason, if you need to use serialized transactions, you must make sure you have the correct indexes to avoid table locks occurring.

Snapshot Isolations

Traditionally, writers block readers, and readers block writers, but version-based isolations are a completely different twist. When version-based isolations are enabled if a transaction modifies (irrespective of the isolation level) data, a version of the data as it was before the modification is stored. This allows other transactions to read the original version of the data even while the original transaction is in an uncommitted state.

So snapshot isolation eliminates writer versus reader contention. Nevertheless, contention isn't completely gone — you still have writers conflicting with writers. If a second writer attempts to update a resource that's already being updated, the second resource is blocked.

There are two version based isolations: snapshot isolation and read committed snapshot isolation.

- Snapshot isolation operates like serializable isolation without the locking and blocking issues. The same SELECT within a transaction can see the same version of the before image of the data.

- Read Committed Snapshot Isolation sees any committed data similar to SQL Server's default isolation level of read committed. Most important, it doesn't place any shared locks on the data read.

Best Practice

Oracle's default transaction behavior is just like snapshot isolation, which is why some DBAs moving up to SQL Server like snapshot isolation, and why some assume snapshot isolation must be better somehow than traditional transaction isolation levels.

It's true that snapshot isolation can eliminate some locking and blocking issues and would therefore improve performance given the right hardware. However, and the best practice is this point, if you choose snapshot isolation, it should be an architecture issue, not a performance issue. If another transaction is updating the data, should the user wait for the new data, or should the user see the before image of the data? For many applications, returning the before image would paint a false picture.

Enabling Row Versioning

Snapshot actually leverages SQL Server's row versioning technology, which copies any row being updated into TempDB. Configuring snapshot isolation therefore require first enabling row versioning for the database. In addition to the TempDB load, row versioning also adds a 14-byte row identifier to each row. This extra data is added to the row when the row is modified if it hasn't been done previously. It is used to store the pointer to the versioned row.

CAUTION

Snapshot isolation uses row versioning, which writes copies of the rows to TempDB. This increases the load on TempDB. Use care enabling this feature if your tempdb is already stressed.

Row versioning alters the row structure so that a copy of the row can be sent to TempDB.

The following code enables snapshot isolation. To alter the database and turn on snapshot isolation, there can be no other connections to the database:

```
USE AdventureWorks2012
ALTER DATABASE AdventureWorks2012
SET ALLOW_SNAPSHOT_ISOLATION ON
-- check snapshot isolation
select name,
  snapshot_isolation_state,
  snapshot_isolation_state_desc,
  is_read_committed_snapshot_on
from sys.databases
where database_id = DB_ID()
```

Transaction 1 now begins a reading transaction, leaving the transaction open (uncommitted):

```
USE AdventureWorks2012
SET TRANSACTION ISOLATION LEVEL SNAPSHOT

BEGIN TRAN
SELECT LastName
FROM Person.Person
WHERE BusinessEntityID = 1
```

Result:

```
LastName
--------
Sánchez
```

A second transaction begins an update to the *same* row that the first transaction has open:

```
USE AdventureWorks2012;
SET TRANSACTION ISOLATION LEVEL SNAPSHOT

BEGIN TRAN

UPDATE Person.Person
SET LastName = 'Chapman'
WHERE BusinessEntityID = 1

SELECT LastName
FROM Person.Person
WHERE BusinessEntityID = 1
```

Result:

```
LastName
---------
Chapman
```

This is amazing. The second transaction updated the row even though the first transaction is still open. Going back to the first transaction, it can still see the original data:

```
SELECT LastName
FROM Person.Person
WHERE BusinessEntityID = 1
```

Result:

```
LastName
--------
Sánchez
```

Opening up a third or fourth transaction, they would all still see the original value, The Bald Knight.

Even after the second transaction committed the change, the first transaction would still see the original value "Sánchez" This is the same behavior as the serializable isolation, but there is not the blocking that there was with serializable isolation. Any new transactions would see update value 'Chapman'.

Using Read Committed Snapshot Isolation

Read committed snapshot isolation is enabled using a similar syntax:

```
ALTER DATABASE AdventureWorks2012
SET READ_COMMITTED_SNAPSHOT ON
```

Like snapshot isolation, read committed snapshot isolation uses row versioning to stave off locking and blocking issues. In the previous example, transaction 1 would see transaction 2's update after it was committed.

The difference to snapshot isolation is that you don't specify a new isolation level. This just changes the behavior of the standard read committed isolation level. This means you shouldn't need to change your application to benefit from it.

Handling Write Conflicts

Transactions that write to the data within a snapshot isolation can be blocked by a previous uncommitted write transaction. This blocking won't cause the new transaction to wait; instead, it generates an error. Be sure to use try...catch to handle these errors, wait a split second, and try again.

Using Locking Hints

Locking hints enable you to make minute adjustments in the locking strategy. Although the isolation level affects the entire connection, locking hints are specific to one table within one query (see Table 47-5). The with (locking hint) option is placed after the table in the from clause of the query. You can specify multiple locking hints by separating them with commas.

TABLE 47-5 **Locking Hints**

Locking Hint	Description
ReadUnCommitted	Isolation level. Shared locks are not taken as data is read.
ReadCommitted	Isolation level. Uses the default transaction-isolation level, Read Committed.
RepeatableRead	Isolation level. Holds share and exclusive locks until `commit transaction`.
Serializable	Isolation level. Applies the serializable transaction isolation–level durations to the table, which holds the shared lock on a necessary range of data until the transaction is complete.
ReadPast	Skips locked rows instead of waiting.
RowLock	Requests row-level locks be taken instead of page, extent, or table locks.
PagLock	Requests the use of page locks instead of row or table locks.
TabLock	Automatically escalates row, page, or extent locks to the table-lock granularity.
NoLock	Shared locks are not used to read data.. Same as ReadUnCommitted.
TablockX	Forces an exclusive lock on the table. This prevents any other transaction from working with the table.
HoldLock	Holds the share lock until the `commit transaction`. (Same as Serializable.)
Updlock	Uses an update lock instead of a shared lock and holds the lock. This blocks any other reads or writes of the data between the initial read and a write operation. This can be used to escalate locks used by a SELECT statement within a serializable isolation transaction from causing deadlocks.
XLock	Holds an exclusive lock on the data until the transaction is committed.

The following query uses a locking hint in the `from` clause of an `update` query to prevent the lock manager from escalating the granularity of the locks:

```
USE AdventureWorks2012
UPDATE Person.Person WITH(ROWLOCK)
SET LastName = 'Chapman'
WHERE BusinessEntityID = 1
```

If a query includes subqueries, don't forget that each query's table references can generate locks and can be controlled by a locking hint.

Application Locks

Application locks open up the whole world of SQL Server locks for custom uses within applications. Instead of using data as a locked resource, application locks use any named user resource declared in the `sp_GetAppLock` stored procedure.

Application locks must be obtained within a transaction. As with the locks the engine puts on the database resources, you can specify the lock mode (`Shared`, `Update`, `Exclusive`, `IntentExclusive`, or `IntentShared`). The return code indicates whether the procedure was successful in obtaining the lock, as follows:

- 0: Lock was obtained normally.
- 1: Lock was obtained after another procedure released it.
- -1: Lock request failed (timeout).
- -2: Lock request failed (canceled).
- -3: Lock request failed (deadlock).
- -999: Lock request failed (other error).

The `sp_ReleaseAppLock` stored procedure releases the lock. The following code shows how you can use the application lock in a batch or procedure:

```
BEGIN TRANSACTION
DECLARE @ShareOK INT
EXEC @ShareOK = sp_GetAppLock
                  @Resource = 'TimChapman',
                  @LockMode = 'Exclusive'
IF @ShareOK < 0
  --Error handling code

  --code
...
EXEC sp_ReleaseAppLock @Resource = 'TimChapman'
COMMIT TRANSACTION
Go
```

When the application locks are viewed using SQL Server Management Studio or `sp_Lock`, the lock appears as an "APP"-type lock. The following is an abbreviated listing of `sp_lock` executed at the same time as the previous code:

```
EXECUTE sp_Lock
```

Result:

```
spid   dbid   ObjId   IndId   Type   Resource         Mode   Status
-----  -----  ------  ------  ----   --------------   -----  ------
57     8      0       0       APP    Cab11f94c136     X      GRANT
```

Note two minor differences from the way application locks are handled by SQL Server:

- Deadlocks are not automatically detected.
- If a transaction gets a lock several times, it must release that lock the same number of times.

Application Locking Design

Aside from SQL Server locks, another locking issue deserves to be addressed. How the client application deals with multiuser contention is important to both the user's experience and the integrity of the data.

Implementing Optimistic Locking

The two basic means of dealing with multi-user access are optimistic locking and pessimistic locking. The one you use determines the coding methods of the application.

Optimistic locking assumes that no other process will attempt to modify data while it is currently being modified. The idea is that you should read data, and then any time in the future, update the data based on what you originally read. The disadvantage of optimistic locking is that its multiple users can read and write the data because they aren't blocked from doing so by locks, but this can result in lost updates.

Pessimistic locking takes a different approach: With pessimistic locking, it is assumed that processes contend to modify the same resources at the same time. When a process modifies data, a pessimistic locking scheme locks that data until the user has finished with it.

Lost Updates

A lost update occurs when two users edit the same row, complete their edits, and save the data, and the second user's update overwrites the first user's update. For example:

1. Tim opens ProductID 876 from the `Production.Product` table, a 4 Bike Hitch Rack, in the front-end application. SQL Server applies a shared lock while retrieving the data.
2. Tim's wife, Brittany, also opens ProductID 876 using the front-end application.
3. Tim and Brittany both make edits to the box-kite data. Tim rephrases the product description, and Brittany fixes the product category.
4. Tim saves the data in the application, which sends an update to SQL Server. The `update` command replaces the old product description with Tim's new description.

5. Brittany presses the Save and Close button, and her data is sent to SQL Server in another update statement. The product category is now fixed, but the old description was in Brittany's form, so Tim's new description was overwritten with the old description.

6. Tim discovers the error and complains to the IT vice president during the next round of golf about the unreliability of that new SQL Server–based database.

Minimizing Lost Updates

If the application uses an optimistic locking scheme, you can minimize the chance that a lost update can occur, as well as minimize the effects of a lost update, using the following methods:

- If the update statement is constructed by the front-end application, ensure it updates only those columns actually changed by the user. This technique alone would prevent the lost update in the previous example of Tim and Brittany's updates, and most lost updates in the real world. As an added benefit, it reduces client/server traffic and the workload on SQL Server.

- If an optimistic locking scheme is not an option, then the application uses a "he who writes last, wins" scheme. This is otherwise known as pessimistic locking, and was outlined in the section earlier on Isolation Levels. Although lost updates may occur, a data-audit trail can minimize the effect by exposing updates to the same row within minutes and tracking the data changes. This can allow you to identify those scenarios and potentially put additional safeguards in place in your application. One option for this would be to add application logic to superficially "lock" a row. The application could keep track of what is and isn't locked so that lost updates do not occur. In my experience, this is often very unnecessary. The isolation levels exposed in SQL Server are more than sufficient at providing segregation between data manipulation changes between transactions.

Transaction-Log Architecture

The ACID properties of a transaction are enforced in SQL Server through the Write-Ahead Logging (WAL) protocol. The WAL protocol ensures the Durability of a transaction by ensuring that all modifications are first written to the transaction log before they are written to the data file. Once a transaction has been hardened to the transaction log, it can be re-created (or rolled back) in the event of a server crash.

Transaction-Log Sequence

Every data-modification operation goes through the same sequence, in which it writes first to the transaction log and then to the data file

Database Beginning State

Before the transaction begins, the database is in a consistent state. All indexes are complete and point to the correct row. The data meets all the enforced rules for data integrity.

Some data pages are likely already cached in the buffer pool. Additional data pages or index pages are copied into memory as needed. Following are the steps of a transaction.

So the first step in a transaction is: The database is in a consistent state.

Data-Modification Command

The transaction is initiated by a submitted batch, as shown in Figure 47-10.

The second step in a transaction is: The code issues a begin transaction command. Even when the DML command is a standalone command without a begin transaction and commit transaction, it is still handled as a transaction.

FIGURE 47-10

The SQL DML commands are performed in memory as part of a transaction.

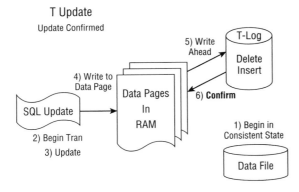

The third step in a transaction is: The code issues a single DML insert, update, or delete command, or a series of them.

To give you an example of the transaction log in action, the following code initiates a transaction and then submits two update commands:

```
USE AdventureWorks2012

BEGIN TRANSACTION

UPDATE Production.Product
  SET Name = 'Transaction Log Test A',
```

```
        SellEndDate = '12/31/2003'
    WHERE ProductID = '1001'

UPDATE Production.Product
    SET Name = 'Transaction Log Test B',
        SellEndDate = '4/1/2003'
    WHERE ProductID = '1002'
```

Notice that the transaction has not yet been committed.

This brings you to the fourth step in a transaction: The query execution plan is either generated or pulled from the plan cache. Any required locks are applied, and the data modifications, including index updates, page splits, and any other required system operation, are performed in memory. At this point the data pages in memory are different than those stored in the data file.

The following section continues the chronological walk through the process.

Transaction Log Recorded

The most important aspect of the transaction log is that all data modifications are written to it and confirmed prior to being written to the data file, as shown in Figure 47-10.

The fifth step in a transaction is: The data modifications are written to the transaction log.

The sixth step in a transaction is: The transaction-log DML entries are confirmed. This ensures that the log entries are written to the transaction log.

Transaction Commit

When the sequence of tasks is complete, the commit transaction closes the transaction. Even this task is written to the transaction log, as shown in Figure 47-11.

FIGURE 47-11

The commit transaction command launches another insert into the transaction log.

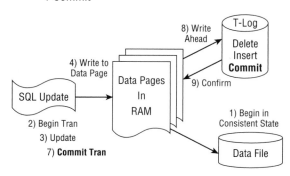

In the seventh step of a transaction, the code closes the transaction:

COMMIT TRANSACTION

Next, the commit entry is written to the transaction log and the transaction-log commit entry is confirmed.

Data-File Update

With the transaction safely stored in the transaction log, the last operation is to write the data modification to the data file, as shown in Figure 47-12.

FIGURE 47-12

As one of the last steps, the data modification is written to the data file.

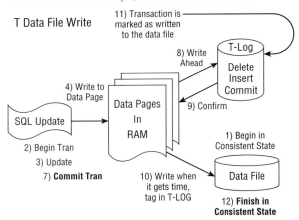

In the background, when a checkpoint occurs (a SQL Server internal event) the lazy writer runs, or a worker thread initiates the work, SQL Server writes any dirty (modified) data pages to the data file. It tries to find sequential pages to improve the performance of the write. Even though this is listed here as step 10, this can happen at nearly anytime during the transaction or after it depending on the amount of data changed and the memory pressure on the system. SQL Server receives a "write complete" message from Windows.

At the conclusion of the background write operation, SQL Server marks the oldest open transaction in the transaction log. All older, committed transactions have been confirmed in the data file and are now confirmed in the transaction log. The DBCC OpenTran command reports the oldest open transaction.

Transaction Complete

The sequence comes full circle and returns the database to a consistent state, which brings you to the final step in a transaction: The database finishes in a consistent state.

Transaction-Log Rollback

If the transaction is rolled back, the DML operations are reversed in memory, and a transaction-abort entry is made in the log.

Transaction-Log Recovery

The primary benefit of a write-ahead transaction log is that it maintains the durability transactional property in the case of system failure.

If SQL Server should cease functioning (perhaps due to a power failure or physical disaster), the transaction log is automatically examined when it recovers, as follows:

- Any transactions that have been committed but not yet written to the data file are "redone." This is the REDO portion of crash recovery.

- If any entries are in the log as DML operations but are not committed, they are rolled back. This is known as the UNDO phase of crash recovery.

- To test this feature, begin a transaction and shut down the SQL server before issuing a commit transaction (using the services applet). This does a shutdown nowait. Simply closing Management Studio won't do it; Management Studio requests permission to commit the pending transactions and rolls back the transaction if permission isn't given. If SQL Server is shut down normally (this varies greatly; there are many ways to stop; some gracefully shut down; others don't), it waits for any pending tasks to complete before stopping.

- If you have followed the steps outlined previously, and you disable the system just before step 7, the transaction-log entries will be identical to those shown later (refer to Figure 47-10).

- Start SQL Server and it recovers from the crash nicely and rolls back the unfinished transaction. This can be seen in the SQL Server error log.

- If any entries are in the log as DML operations and committed but not marked as written to the data file, they are written to the data file. This feature is nearly impossible to demonstrate.

Transaction Performance Strategies

Transaction integrity theory can seem daunting at first, and SQL Server has numerous tools to control transaction isolation. If the database is low usage or primarily read-only, transaction locking and blocking shouldn't be a problem. However for heavy-usage OLTP databases, you need to apply the theory and working knowledge from this chapter using these strategies. Also if you mix reporting and OLTP systems, you potentially face blocking issues because reporting systems generally place locks at page or table level, which isn't ideal for your OLTP system, which often requires more granular row level locks.

Make sure you consider the following points when designing your application for performance:

1. Begin with a well-designed database schema: Start with a clean, simplified schema to reduce the number of unnecessary joins and reduce the amount of code used to shuttle data from bucket to bucket.

2. Use efficient set-based code, rather than slow iterative cursors or loops. However, there is a tradeoff. Large set-based operations can cause locking and blocking, so there must be a fine line between large and small sets when modifying data.

3. Use a good indexing strategy to eliminate unnecessary table scans and to speed transactions.

To reduce the severity of a locking problem, do the following:

- Evaluate and test using the read committed snapshot isolation level. Depending on your error handling, application flexibility, and hardware capabilities, snapshot isolation can significantly reduce concurrency contention.

- Check the transaction-isolation level, and make sure it's not any higher than required.

- Make sure transactions begin and commit quickly. Move any code that isn't necessary to the transaction out of the transaction unless it is needed to ensure transactional consistency.

- If two procedures are deadlocking, make sure they lock the resource in the same order. Review the objects that the deadlock occurs on.

Evaluating Database Concurrency Performance

It's easy to build a database that doesn't exhibit lock contention and concurrency issues when tested with a handful of users. The real test is when several hundred users are all updating orders.

Best Practice

Multiuser concurrency should be tested during the development process several times. Do not allow your first tests to be the ones the real users put on your production system.

Concurrency testing requires a concerted effort. At one level, it can involve everyone available running the same front-end form concurrently. A program that constantly simulates a user viewing data and updating data is also useful. A good test is to run 20 instances of a script that constantly hits the database and then let the test crew use the application.

SQL Server 2012 Distributed Replay

New in SQL Server 2012 is Distributed Replay. This feature can be used on multiple computers to replay a SQL Profiler trace to simulate a mission-critical workload. This is a very useful tool for performance testing or capacity planning.

47

Summary

A transaction is a logical unit of work. Although the default SQL Server transaction isolation level works well for most applications, there are several means to manipulate and control the locks. To develop a serious SQL Server application, your understanding of the ACID database principles, SQL Server's transaction log, and locking contribute to the quality, performance, and reliability of the database.

Major points from this chapter include the following:

- Transactions must be ACID: atomic (all or nothing), consistent (before and after the transaction), isolated (not interfering with another transaction), and durable (once committed always committed).

- SQL Server transactions are durable because of the write-ahead transaction log.

- SQL Server transactions are isolated because of locks or snapshot isolation.

- Using traditional transaction isolation readers block writers, and writers block readers and other writers.

- SQL Server offers four traditional transaction isolation levels: read uncommitted, read committed, repeatable read, and serializable. Read committed, the default transaction isolation level, works well for most OLTP databases.

- Do not use read uncommitted (or the `nolock` hint) unless you are absolutely sure the side effects will not negatively affect your application data.

- Snapshot isolation involves reading the before image of the transaction instead of waiting for the transaction to commit. Using snapshot isolation, readers don't block writers; writers don't block readers; and only writers block other writers.

Data Compression

P ushing a database into the tens of thousands of transactions per second requires massive amounts of raw I/O performance. At those rates, today's servers can supply the CPU and memory, but I/O struggles. By reducing the raw size of the data, data compression trades I/O for CPU, improving performance.

SQL Server 2008 introduced data compression. Unfortunately, it was not as widely publicized as you might anticipate. This could be because it is only available in the Enterprise Edition of SQL Server. However, it is an important feature that offers tremendous benefits, and it's easy to enable.

In other words, data compression doesn't warrant an entire chapter because of its complexity or length, but because of its value. Its impact is such that it deserves center stage, at least for this chapter.

Understanding Data Compression

Every IT professional is familiar with data compression, such as zip files and .jpg compression, to name a couple of popular compression technologies.

But SQL Server data compression is specific to the SQL Server storage engine and has a few database-specific requirements. First, there must be zero risk of loss of data fidelity. Second, it must be completely transparent — enabled without any application code changes.

SQL Server data compression isn't like .jpg compression, where you can choose the level of compression and more compression means more data loss. With SQL Server data compression, the data is transparently compressed by the storage engine, and every compressed data page retains every data value when decompressed.

> **NOTE**
> Don't confuse data compression with backup compression — the two technologies are completely independent.

You can compress the following data objects:

- Entire heap
- Entire clustered index
- Entire nonclustered index
- Entire indexed view (specifically, the materialized clustered index of an indexed view)
- Single partition of partitioned table or index

> **NOTE**
> Although indexes can be compressed, they are not automatically compressed with the table's compression type. All objects, including indexes, must be individually, manually enabled for compression.

Following are data compression limitations:

- Heaps or clustered indexes with sparse data may not be compressed.
- File stream data or LOB data is not compressed.
- Tables with rows that potentially exceed 8,060 bytes and use row overflow cannot be compressed.
- Data compression does not overcome the row limit. The data must always be able to be stored uncompressed.

Data Compression Pros and Cons

Data compression offers several benefits and a few trade-offs, so although using data compression is probably a good thing, it's worth understanding the pros and cons.

The most obvious con is the financial cost. Data compression, as mentioned earlier, is only available with the Enterprise Edition. If you already use the Enterprise Edition, great; if not, then moving from Standard to Enterprise is a significant budget request.

Data compression uses CPU. If your server is CPU pressured, then turning on data compression will probably hurt performance. Depending on the data mix and the transaction rate, enabling data compression might slow down the application.

Not all tables and indexes compress well. Some objects can compress up to 70 percent, but many tables see little compression, or even grow in size when compressed. Therefore, you shouldn't simply enable compression for every object; it takes some study and analysis to choose compression wisely. More specifically, data that contains the following data patterns are not good candidates for compression:

- FILESTREAM data
- Data that has nonrepeating prefixes
- Data that does not have many repeatable values
- Fix-length character data types whose value consumes all the bytes available for the specified data type

With these possible drawbacks understood, plenty of reasons exist to enable data compression (assuming the data compresses well):

- Data compression significantly reduces the I/O bottleneck for a high-transaction database.
- Data compression significantly reduces the memory footprint of data because the data remains compressed in memory, thus increasing the amount of data that can cache in memory and probably improving overall performance.
- More rows on a page mean that scans and count(*) type operations are faster.
- Compressed data means SAN shadow copies are smaller.
- Database snapshots are smaller and more efficient with data compression.
- SANS and high-performance disks are expensive. Compressed data means less disk space is required, which means more money is left in the budget to attend a SQL Server conference in Maui.
- Compressed data means backup duration and restore duration is reduced, and less storage space is used for backups.

48

> **NOTE**
> Hardware-based data compression solutions compress data as it's written to disk. Although these can reduce disk space and off-load the CPU overhead of compression, they fail to reduce the I/O load on SQL Server, or reduce the data's memory footprint within SQL Server.

Two types, or levels, of data compression exist in SQL Server 2012: row level and page level. Each has a specific capability and purpose. So that you can best understand how and when to employ data compression, the following sections describe how they work.

Row Compression

Row compression converts the storage of every fixed-length data type column (both character and numeric data types) to a variable-length data type column. Row compression grew out of the vardecimal compression added with SQL Server 2005 SP2. Depending on the number of fixed-length columns and the actual length of the data, this level may, or may not, provide significant gain.

Although you still see the columns as fixed length when viewing the database, under the covers the storage engine is actually writing the values as if the columns were variable length. A `char(50)` column is treated as if it's a `varchar(50)` column. Therefore, if the value stored in the column requires less than that specified by the fixed length definition, the amount stored will be reduced to what is needed.

When row compression is enabled, SQL Server also uses a new variable-length row format that reduces the per-column metadata overhead from 2 bytes to 4 bits.

Row-level data compression is designed specifically for third-party databases that have several fixed-length columns but don't allow schema changes. In addition, you can use it on large look up tables in operational databases — more specifically, on tables that require few updates.

Page Compression

SQL Server page compression automatically includes row compression and takes compression two steps further, adding prefix compression and then dictionary compression. Page compression applies only to leaflevel pages (clustered or heaps) and not to the B-tree root or intermediate pages.

Prefix compression may appear complex at first, but it's actually simple and efficient. For prefix compression the storage engine follows these steps for each column:

1. The storage engine examines all the values and selects the most common prefix value for the data in the column.

2. The longest actual value beginning with the prefix is then stored in the compression information (CI) structure.

3. If the prefix is present at the beginning of the data values, a number is inserted at the beginning of the value to indicate n number of prefix characters of the prefix. The nonprefix portion of the value (the part to the right of the prefix) is left in place.

Prefix compression actually examines bytes, so it applies to both character and numeric data.

For example, assume the storage engine was applying prefix compression to the following data, as shown in Figure 48-1.

For the first column, the best prefix is ggghh. The longest value beginning with the prefix is ggghii, so that value is written to the CI structure, as shown in Figure 48-2. For the second column, the best prefix is gggg and the longest value is ggggii. The prefixes are written to an anchor row at the beginning of each page. This method is repeated for all subsequent columns in the table.

FIGURE 48-1

The sample data before page compression is enabled.

Page Header
ggghh
ggggh
ghik
ggghii
hhhh
ghik
gggiii
ggggii
hhhh

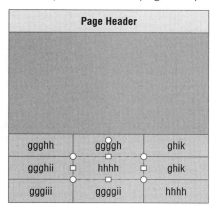

The values are then updated with the prefix (see Figure 48-2). The first value, `ggghh`, begins with four letters of the prefix, so `4h` is written, which saves space on the page. The compression ratio is much better for values that include more of the prefix — for example, `ggghii` is compressed into just the number `6` because it contains six characters of the prefix with nothing remaining.

FIGURE 48-2

Prefix compression identifies the best prefix for each column and then stores the prefix character count in each row instead of the prefix characters.

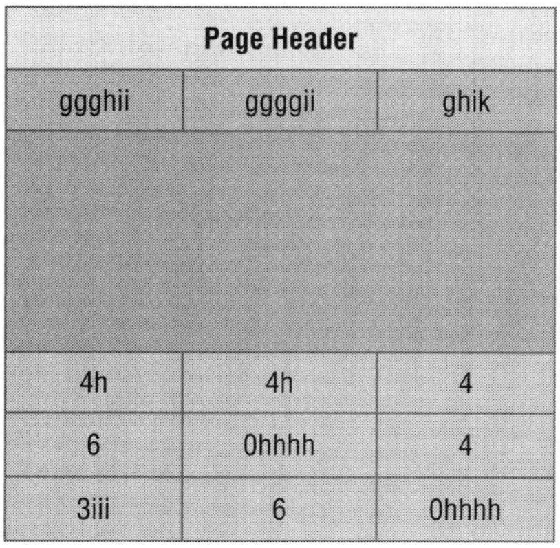

Page Header
ggghii
ggggii
ghik
4h
4h
4
6
0hhhh
4
3iii
6
0hhhh

As demonstrated, depending on the commonality of the data set, prefix compression can significantly compress the data without any loss of data fidelity.

In this example, one value in the second column, hhhh, doesn't match the prefix at all. It's stored as 0hhhh, which increases the length. If this is the case for most of the rows, and prefix compression offers no benefit for a given column, the storage engine leaves the anchor row null and does not use prefix compression for that column. This is one reason why sometimes tables actually grow when compressed.

After the data is prefix compressed, the storage engine applies *dictionary compression*. Every value is scanned and any common values are replaced with a token that is stored in the compression information area of the page. Prefix compression occurs on the column level, whereas dictionary compression occurs across all columns on the page level.

Data warehouses are good candidates for this level of compressions. Because the data in a warehouse is typically updated infrequently, the cost of decompressing it during updates is minimized. Therefore, you can apply page compression to the entire data warehouse — considering only those tables that are eight pages or larger. However, as with any new implementation, you should fully test this scenario before applying it to your production system.

Compression Sequence

The cool thing about data compression is that it's completely handled by the storage engine and transparent to every process outside of the storage engine. This means that the data is compressed on the disk and is still compressed when it's read into memory, as previously mentioned. The storage engine decompresses the data as it's passed from the storage engine to the query processor, as shown in Figure 48-3.

FIGURE 48-3

The storage engine compresses and decompresses data as it's written to and read from the buffer.

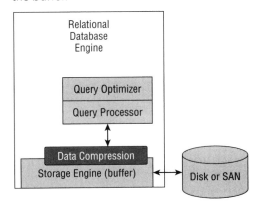

If the object is row compressed, or page compressed (which automatically includes row compression), then row compression is always enabled for every page of the object. Page compression, however, is a different story:

- The storage engine enables page compression on a page-by-page basis when there's a benefit for that page. When the storage engine creates a new page, it's initially uncompressed and remains uncompressed as rows are added to the page.

- When the page is full but SQL Server wants to add another row to it, the storage engine tests the page for compression. If the page compresses enough to add the new rows, then the page is compressed.

- When the page is a compressed page, any new rows will be inserted compressed. (But they won't trigger recalculation of the compression information, the prefix anchor row, or the dictionary tokens.)

- Pages might be recompressed (and the prefixes and dictionary tokens recalculated) when the row is updated, based on an algorithm that factors in the number of updates to a page, the number of rows on the page, the average row length, and the amount of space that can be saved by page compression for each page, or when the row would again need to be split.

- Heaps are recompressed only by an index rebuild or bulk load.

- In the case of a page split, both pages inherit the page compression information (compression status, prefixes, and dictionary tokens) of the old page.

- During an index rebuild of an object with page compression, the point at which the page is considered full still considers the fill factor setting, so the free space is still guaranteed.

- Row inserts, updates, and deletes are normally written to the transaction log in row compression, but not in page compression format. An exception is when page splits are logged. Because they are a physical operation, only the page compression values are logged.

Applying Data Compression

Although data compression is complicated, actually enabling data compression is a straightforward task using either the Data Compression Wizard or an ALTER command.

Determining the Current Compression Setting

When working with compression, the first task is to confirm the current compression setting. Using the Management Studio UI, you can view the compression type for any single object in two ways:

- The Table Properties or Index Properties Storage page displays the compression settings as a read-only value.

- The Data Compression Wizard, found in Object Explorer (Context menu ⇨ Storage ⇨ Manage Compression) opens with the current compression selected.

To see the current compression setting for every object in the database, run this query:

```
SELECT O.object_id, S.name AS [schema], O.name AS [Object],
    I.index_id AS Ix_id, I.name AS IxName, I.type_desc AS IxType,
    P.partition_number AS P_No, P.data_compression_desc AS Compression
FROM sys.schemas AS S
  JOIN sys.objects AS O
    ON S.schema_id = O.schema_id
  JOIN sys.indexes AS I
    ON O.object_id = I.object_id
  JOIN sys.partitions AS P
    ON I.object_id = P.object_id
      AND I.index_id = P.index_id
WHERE O.TYPE = 'U'
ORDER BY S.name, O.name, I.index_id ;
```

Abbreviated result when executed in the AdventureWorks database:

```
object_id   schema  Object ix_id ixName                ixType        P_No Comp
----------  ------  ------ ----- -------------------   ------------- ---- ----
1509580416  Person  Person 1     PK_Person_Busines...  CLUSTERED     1    NONE
1509580416  Person  Person 2     IX_Person_LastName... NONCLUSTERED  1    NONE
1509580416  Person  Person 3     AK_Person_rowguid     NONCLUSTERED  1    NONE
...
```

Estimating Data Compression

Because every object can yield a different compression ratio, you need to have some idea of how much compression is possible before actually performing the compression. Toward this end, SQL 2012 includes the ability to pre-estimate the potential data reduction of data compression using the sp_estimate_data_compression_savings system stored procedure.

Specifically, this system stored procedure can be used to copy 5 percent of the data to be compressed into tempdb and compress it. The 5 percent is not a random sample but every twentieth page, so it should give consistent results:

```
EXEC sp_estimate_data_compression_savings
  @schema_name = 'Production',
  @object_name = 'BillOfMaterials',
  @index_id = NULL,
  @partition_number = NULL,
  @data_compression = 'page';
```

The result displays the following columns for each object (base table and index):

```
object_name
schema_name
index_id
partition_number
size_with_current_compression_setting(KB)
size_with_requested_compression_setting(KB)
sample_size_with_current_compression_setting(KB)
sample_size_with_requested_compression_setting(KB)
```

The Data Compression Wizard, as shown in Figure 48-4, uses this same system stored procedure to estimate the compression. Select the type of compression to estimate, and press the Calculate button.

FIGURE 48-4

The Data Compression Wizard estimates the compression ratio and applies the selected type of data compression.

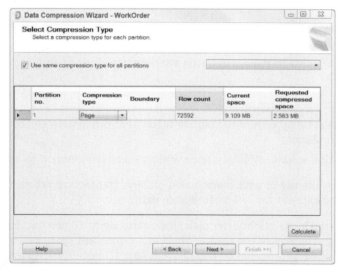

Enabling Data Compression

Data compression alters the structure of the data on the disk, so it makes sense that data compression is enabled using a CREATE or ALTER statement.

Using the UI, the only way to adjust an object's data compression is by using the same Data Compression Wizard used previously to estimate the compression gain.

With T-SQL, compression may be initially set when the object is created by adding the data compression setting to the CREATE statement with the following option:

```
WITH (DATA_COMPRESSION = [none, row, or page])
```

Use the following to create a new table with row compression:

```
CREATE TABLE CTest (col1 INT, Col2 CHAR(100))
WITH (Data_Compression = Row);
```

To change the compression setting for an existing object, use the ALTER statement:

```
ALTER object REBUILD
WITH (DATA_COMPRESSION = [none, row, or page])
```

For instance, the following code changes the BillOfMaterials table to page compression:

```
ALTER TABLE [Production].[BillOfMaterials]
Rebuild with (data_compression = Page);
```

Data Compression Strategies

Data compression is new to SQL Server and at this early stage, applying compression is more an art than a science. With this in mind, Following are recommendations on how to best use data compression:

1. Establish a performance baseline.
2. Use the estimate store procedure to identify tables that can benefit (space will be saved) from compression.
3. Analyze application workload to determine what level of compression to use.
4. Carefully monitor the use of data compression on high-transaction tables, in case the CPU overhead exceeds the I/O performance gains.

In practice row compression alone might offer disk space gains up to 50 percent, but sometimes it actually increases the size of the data. If there is a significant space savings and your server can accommodate approximately an 8 percent to a 12 percent increase in CPU usage, you should consider row compression as your compression method. Remember, you need to consider other factors prior to holistically compressing all tables in the database.

Page compression, on the other hand, can increase CPU usage significantly as compared to row compression. As a result, it is a little more difficult to decide what to page compress. If you don't have any CPU headroom, you should avoid any compression, especially page compression.

Typical data warehouse queries and workloads are scan-intensive. Scanning these large sets of data can be both physically and logically I/O intensive. Even though page compression may increase CPU cycles, this is often offset by the large reduction in I/O. Therefore, if sufficient CPU overhead is available on your system, you can holistically page compress your entire data warehouse.

Most of the references so far have been focused on data warehouses, but what about operational databases? Should you compress tables in these types of databases? This implementation requires a more detailed approach. An analysis of the tables, indexes, and their workload characteristics are required. This analysis is based on two basic metrics: updates and scans.

You can use the sys.dm_db_index_operational_stats dynamic management view to compute the metrics. Consider page compressing tables with high scan values. For those tables with high update values, you should avoid compression at any levels. However, as previously mentioned if the space savings can offset the CPU increase, you could consider row or page compression. Remember, as with any DMV, the values returned are cumulative since the last server restart. Therefore, ensure that your server has been running long enough before depending on the values in the DMV.

Coupling a few system objects with the aforementioned DMV helps to produce queries that provide enough information to determine the amount of updates and reads performed on an object. Use the following query to determine update percentages for each object:

```
SELECT
    o.name AS [Table_Name],
    ISNULL(x.name, 'HEAP') AS [Index_Name],
    x.type_desc AS [Index_Type],
    i.leaf_update_count * 100.0 /
    (i.range_scan_count + i.leaf_insert_count
    + i.leaf_delete_count + i.leaf_update_count
    + i.leaf_page_merge_count + i.singleton_lookup_count
    ) AS [Percent_Update]
FROM sys.dm_db_index_operational_stats (db_id(), NULL, NULL, NULL) i
JOIN sys.objects o ON o.object_id = i.object_id
JOIN sys.indexes x ON x.object_id = i.object_id AND x.index_id = i.index_id
WHERE (i.range_scan_count + i.leaf_insert_count
    + i.leaf_delete_count + leaf_update_count
    + i.leaf_page_merge_count + i.singleton_lookup_count) != 0 AND
    o.type = 'U'
ORDER BY [Percent_Update] ASC
```

Use the following query to determine scan percentages for each object:

```
SELECT o.name AS [Table_Name], ISNULL(x.name,'HEAP') AS [Index_Name],
    x.type_desc AS [Index_Type],
    i.range_scan_count * 100.0 /
        (i.range_scan_count + i.leaf_insert_count
        + i.leaf_delete_count + i.leaf_update_count
        + i.leaf_page_merge_count + i.singleton_lookup_count
        ) AS [Percent_Scan]
```

```
FROM sys.dm_db_index_operational_stats (db_id(), NULL, NULL, NULL) i
JOIN sys.objects o ON o.object_id = i.object_id
JOIN sys.indexes x ON x.object_id = i.object_id AND x.index_id = i.index_id
WHERE (i.range_scan_count + i.leaf_insert_count
        + i.leaf_delete_count + leaf_update_count
        + i.leaf_page_merge_count + i.singleton_lookup_count) != 0
AND o.type = 'U'
ORDER BY [Percent_Scan] DESC
```

After you execute these queries, use the returned values along with the estimated space savings to determine whether to page or row compress.

Summary

Data compression was the sleeper feature when it was introduced. With both row compression and page compression, including both prefix and dictionary compression, SQL Server offers the granularity to tune data compression. Using data compression carefully, you can push the envelope for an I/O bound, high-transaction database.

The next chapter continues the thread of technologies used for highly scalable database design with a look at several types of partitioning.

Partitioning

When working with large tables — in terabytes — you are often posed with several challenges. How can you mitigate those problems? Division.

Dividing data brings several benefits:

- It's significantly easier to maintain, back up, and defragment a divided data set.
- The divided data sets mean smaller indexes, fewer intermediate pages, and faster performance.
- The divided data sets can reside on separate physical servers, thus scaling out and lowering costs and improving performance.

However, dividing, or partitioning, data has its own set of problems to conquer. You can solve this problem in several ways. SQL Server offers a couple of technologies that handle partitioning: *partitioned views* and *partitioned tables*.

Partitioning Strategies

Partitions are most effective when the partition key is a column often used to select a range of data so that a query has a good chance to address only one of the segments, such as the following:

- A company partitions data by Sales Territory.
- A school partitions data by School Year.
- A manufacturing company partitions data by departments.

The common factor among each strategy is that each enables the querying of smaller sets of data. Instead of the queries searching the entire data set, only the necessary data are queried.

Best Practice

Large, frequently accessed tables, with data that can logically be divided horizontally for the most common queries, are the best candidates for partitioning. If the table doesn't meet this criteria, don't partition the table.

In the access of data, the greatest bottleneck is reading the data from the drive. The primary benefit of partitioning tables is that a smaller partitioned table can have a greater percentage of the table cached in memory.

You can consider partitioning from two perspectives:

- *Horizontal partitioning* means splitting the table by rows. For example, if you have a large 5,000-row spreadsheet and split it so that rows 1 through 2,500 remain in the original spreadsheet and move rows 2,501 to 5,000 to a new, additional spreadsheet, that move would illustrate horizontal partitioning.
- *Vertical partitioning* splits the table by columns, segmenting some columns into a different table. Sometimes this makes sense from a logical modeling point of view, if the vertical partitioning segments columns that belong only to certain subtypes. But strictly speaking, vertical partitioning is less common and not considered a best practice.

All the partitioning methods discussed in this chapter involve horizontal partitioning.

Partitioned Views

The concept of partitioned views was introduced with SQL Server 2000. You can partition a view locally, which means that all the underlying tables are stored on the same SQL Server instance. You can also base a view on tables distributed across multiple servers, which is known as a *distributed partitioned view*. The databases are said to be *federated*. You can use linked servers to union all the data through views.

With the data split into several member tables, of course, each individual table may be directly queried. A more sophisticated and flexible approach is to access the whole set of data by querying a view that unites all the member tables — this type of view is called a *partitioned view*.

The SQL Server query processor is designed specifically to handle such a partitioned view. If a query accesses the union of all the member tables, the query processor can retrieve data only from the required member tables.

A partitioned view not only handles selects, but also data can be inserted, updated, and deleted through the partitioned view. The query processor engages only the individual tables necessary.

Local-Partition Views

Local-partition views access only local tables. For a local-partition view to be configured, the following elements must be in place:

- The data must be segmented into multiple tables according to a single column, known as the *partition key*.
- Each partition table must have a check constraint restricting the partition-key data to a single value. SQL Server uses the check constraint to determine which tables are required by a query.
- The partition key must be part of the primary key.
- The partition view must include a union statement that pulls together data from all the partition tables.

Segmenting the Data

To implement a partitioned-view design for a database and segment the data in a logical fashion, the first step is to move the data into the member tables.

Using the SalesOrderHeader and SalesOrderDetail tables from the AdventureWorks database, the data is partitioned by Country. The data is broken down as follows:

```
SELECT st.CountryRegionCode Country, count(*) Count
FROM Sales.SalesOrderHeader soh
INNER JOIN Sales.SalesOrderDetail sod
   ON soh.SalesOrderID = sod.SalesOrderID
INNER JOIN Sales.SalesTerritory st
   ON soh.TerritoryID = st.TerritoryID
GROUP BY  st.CountryRegionCode
```

Result:

```
Country Count
------- -----------
DE      7528
GB      10426
AU      15058
CA      19064
FR      9088
US      60153
```

To partition the sales data, the SalesOrderHeader and SalesOrderDetail tables split into a table for each country. The first portion of the script creates the partition tables.

They differ from the original tables only in the primary-key definition, which becomes a composite primary key consisting of the original primary key and the CountryRegionCode. In the SalesOrderDetail table the CountryRegionCode column is added so that it can serve as the partition key, and the SalesOrderID column foreign-key constraint points to the partition table.

The script then progresses to populating the tables from the nonpartition tables. To select the correct SalesOrderDetail rows, the table needs to be joined with the SalesOrderHeaderUS)) table.

For brevity's sake, only the United States (US) region is shown here. The chapter's sample code script includes similar code for all the other regions.

```
IF(OBJECT_ID('dbo.SalesOrderDetailUS')) IS NOT NULL
   DROP TABLE dbo.SalesOrderDetailUS
GO
IF(OBJECT_ID('dbo.SalesOrderHeaderUS')) IS NOT NULL
   DROP TABLE dbo.SalesOrderHeaderUS
GO
--SalesOrderTable
CREATE TABLE dbo.SalesOrderHeaderUS
(
    CountryRegionCode varchar(5) NOT NULL,
    SalesOrderID int NOT NULL,
    SalesOrderNumber varchar(25) NOT NULL,
    CustomerID int NOT NULL,
    SalesPersonID int NOT NULL,
    OrderDate datetime NOT NULL
) ON [PRIMARY ]
GO
--PK
ALTER TABLE dbo.SalesOrderHeaderUS
   ADD CONSTRAINT PK_SalesOrderHeaderUS PRIMARY KEY NONCLUSTERED
       (CountryRegionCode, SalesOrderID)
GO
--Check Constraint
ALTER TABLE dbo.SalesOrderHeaderUS
   ADD CONSTRAINT SalesOrderHeaderUS_PartitionCheck CHECK
(CountryRegionCode = 'US')
GO

--SalesOrderDetail Table
CREATE TABLE dbo.SalesOrderDetailUS
(
    CountryRegionCode varchar(5) NOT NULL,
    SalesOrderDetailID int NOT NULL,
    SalesOrderID int NOT NULL,
    ProductID int NOT NULL,
```

```
    OrderQty int NOT NULL,
    UnitPrice money NOT NULL,
    CarrierTrackingNumber varchar(25) NOT NULL
)
ON [PRIMARY]
GO

ALTER TABLE dbo.SalesOrderDetailUS
    ADD CONSTRAINT FK_SalesOrderDetailUS_SalesOrderHeader
        FOREIGN KEY (CountryRegionCode, SalesOrderID)
        REFERENCES dbo.SalesOrderHeaderUS(CountryRegionCode,
        SalesOrderID)
         GO
ALTER TABLE dbo.SalesOrderDetailUS
    ADD CONSTRAINT PK_SalesOrderDetailUS PRIMARY KEY NONCLUSTERED
        (CountryRegionCode, SalesOrderDetailID)
        GO

ALTER TABLE dbo.SalesOrderDetailUS
    ADD CONSTRAINT
        SalesOrderDetailUS_PartitionCheck CHECK
        (CountryRegionCode = 'US')
GO

--move data
INSERT INTO dbo.SalesOrderHeaderUS(CountryRegionCode, SalesOrderID,
      SalesOrderNumber, CustomerID, SalesPersonID, OrderDate)
SELECT
    st.CountryRegionCode CountryRegionCode,
    SalesOrderID,
    SalesOrderNumber,
    CustomerID,
    SalesPersonID,
    OrderDate
FROM Sales.SalesOrderHeader soh
INNER JOIN Sales.SalesTerritory st
    ON soh.TerritoryID = st.TerritoryID
WHERE st.CountryRegionCode = 'US' AND SalesPersonID IS NOT NULL

INSERT INTO dbo.SalesOrderDetailUS(CountryRegionCode,
      SalesOrderDetailID, SalesOrderID, ProductID, OrderQty,
      UnitPrice, CarrierTrackingNumber)
SELECT
    'US',
    SalesOrderDetailID,
    soh.SalesOrderID,
    sod.ProductID,
    sod.OrderQty,
    sod.UnitPrice,
```

```
      sod.CarrierTrackingNumber
FROM Sales.SalesOrderDetail sod
INNER JOIN dbo.SalesOrderHeaderUS soh
   ON sod.SalesOrderID = soh.SalesOrderID
```

Creating the Partition View

With the data split into valid partition tables that include the correct primary keys and constraints, SQL Server can access the correct partition table through a partition view. The SalesOrderAll view uses a UNION ALL to vertically merge data from all three partition tables:

```
CREATE VIEW SalesOrderAll
AS
SELECT CountryRegionCode, SalesOrderID, SalesOrderNumber, CustomerID,
   SalesPersonID, OrderDate
FROM SalesOrderHeaderUS
UNION ALL
SELECT CountryRegionCode, SalesOrderID, SalesOrderNumber, CustomerID,
   SalesPersonID, OrderDate
FROM SalesOrderHeaderCA
UNION ALL
SELECT CountryRegionCode, SalesOrderID, SalesOrderNumber, CustomerID,
   SalesPersonID, OrderDate
FROM SalesOrderHeaderAU
```

Selecting Through the Partition View

When all the data is selected from the OrderAll partition view, the query plan, as shown in Figure 49-1, includes all three partition tables as expected:

```
SELECT CountryRegionCode, SalesOrderNumber
FROM SalesOrderAll
```

Result (abridged):

```
CountryRegionCode SalesOrderNumber
----------------- -------------------------
US                SO43659
...
CA                SO71916
CA                SO71921
FR                SO46623
FR                SO46626
```

What makes partition views useful for advanced scalability is that the SQL Server query processor can use the partition tables' check constraints to access only the required tables if the partition key is included in the WHERE clause of the query calling the partition view.

The following query selects on the United States sales orders from the partition view. The CountryRegionCode column is the partition key, so this query optimizes for scalability. Even though the view's union includes all three partition tables, the query execution plan, as shown in Figure 49-2, reveals that the query processor accesses only the SalesOrderHeadUS partition table:

```
SELECT OrderNumber
  FROM OrderAll
  WHERE LocationCode = 'KDH'
```

FIGURE 49-1

The partition table's query plan, when run without a WHERE clause restriction, includes all the partition tables as a standard union query.

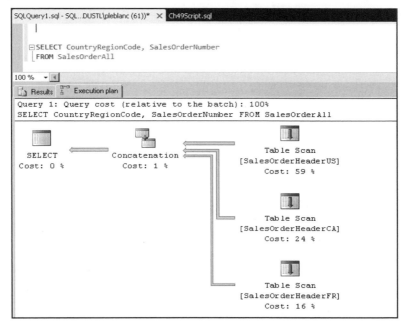

Updating Through the Partition View

Union queries are typically not updatable. Yet, the partition tables' check constraints enable a partition view based on a union query to be updated, as long as a few conditions are met:

- The partition view must include all the columns from the partition tables.
- The primary key must include the partition key.
- Partition table columns, including the primary key, must be identical.
- Columns and tables must not be duplicated within the partition view.

FIGURE 49-2

When a query with a `WHERE` clause restriction that includes the partition key retrieves data through the partition view, SQL Server's query processor accesses only the required tables.

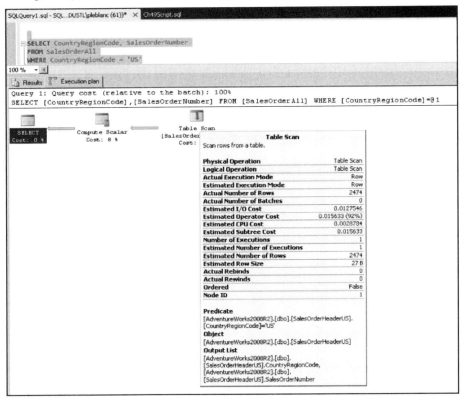

The following `UPDATE` query demonstrates updating through the `SalesOrderAll` view:

```
UPDATE SalesOrderAll
SET OrderDate = GETDATE()
WHERE SalesPersonID = 280
```

Unfortunately, an `UPDATE` does not benefit from query optimization to the extent that a `SELECT` does. For heavy transactional processing at the stored-procedure level, the code should access the correct partition table.

Partitioned Tables and Indexes

Partitioned tables are similar to partitioned views — both involve segmenting the data. However, whereas partitioned views store the data in separate tables and use a view to access the tables, partitioned tables store the data in a segmented clustered index and use the table to access the data. In SQL Server 2012 the number of partitions you can create on a table has been increased to 15,000. Care should be taken when implementing a partitioning strategy that has a large number of partitions. In this case a minimum of 16G of RAM should be used. If not, certain operations can fail due to insufficient memory.

Partitioning tables reduces the sheer size of the clustered and nonclustered B-tree indexes, which provide the following manageability and performance benefits:

- You can quickly and efficiently access data because you are accessing only subsets of data.

- Backing up part of a table using Backup Filegroups eases backups.

- A partition's index is significantly smaller; therefore, maintenance operations on one or more partitions take less time. As a result, you can reduce the performance cost of rebuilding or re-indexing.

- The selectiveness of a WHERE clause is often improved because a partition table can segment the data.

Best Practice

The performance benefit of partitioned tables doesn't kick in until the table is extremely large — billion-row tables in terabyte-size databases. In some testing, partitioned tables actually hurt performance on smaller tables with less than a million rows, so reserve this technology for the big problems. Maybe that's why table partitioning isn't included in the Standard Edition.

On the other hand, even for tables with fewer than one million rows, partitioning can be an effective part of archiving old data into one partition while keeping current data in another partition.

49

Creating SQL Server 2012 table partitions is a straightforward four-step process:

1. Create a filegroup or filegroups to store the partitions specified by the partition function.
2. Create the partition function that determines how the data is partitioned.

3. Create the partition scheme that assigns partitions to filegroups.

4. Create or modify a table or index by specifying the partition scheme.

Partition functions and partition schemes work together to segment the data, as shown in Figure 49-3.

FIGURE 49-3

The partition scheme uses the partition function to place the data in separate filegroups.

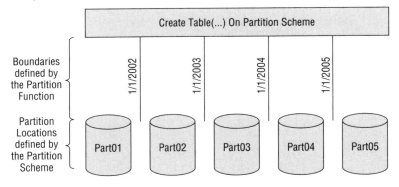

Create the Filegroups

A best practice when implementing a partitioning strategy is to create a filegroup for each partition. The partition scheme created later maps a partition to a specific filegroup. To start with your partition creation process, add four filegroups to the AdventureWorks database. The following script illustrates how to accomplish this:

```
USE master;
ALTER DATABASE AdventureWorks
ADD FILEGROUP AdventureWorks_SalesOrderDetail2005Partition
GO
ALTER DATABASE AdventureWorks
ADD FILE
(
    NAME = 'AdventureWorks_SalesOrderDetail2005Partition',
    FILENAME =
    'C:\SQLData\AdventureWorks_SalesOrderDetail2005Partition.ndf',
    SIZE = 10,
    MAXSIZE = 120,
    FILEGROWTH = 10
)
TO FILEGROUP AdventureWorks_SalesOrderDetail2005Partition
```

```
GO

ALTER DATABASE AdventureWorks
ADD FILEGROUP AdventureWorks_SalesOrderDetail2006Partition
GO
ALTER DATABASE AdventureWorks
ADD FILE
(
   NAME = 'AdventureWorks_SalesOrderDetail2006Partition',
   FILENAME = 'C:\SQLData\
   AdventureWorks2008R2_SalesOrderDetail2006Partition.ndf',
   SIZE = 10,
   MAXSIZE = 120,
   FILEGROWTH = 10
)
TO FILEGROUP AdventureWorks_SalesOrderDetail2006Partition
GO

ALTER DATABASE AdventureWorks
ADD FILEGROUP AdventureWorks_SalesOrderDetail2007Partition
GO
ALTER DATABASE AdventureWorks
ADD FILE
(
   NAME = 'AdventureWorks_SalesOrderDetail2007Partition',
   FILENAME = 'C:\SQLData\
   AdventureWorks2008R2_SalesOrderDetail2007Partition.ndf',
   SIZE = 10,
   MAXSIZE = 120,
   FILEGROWTH = 10
)
TO FILEGROUP AdventureWorks_SalesOrderDetail2007Partition
GO


ALTER DATABASE AdventureWorks
ADD FILEGROUP AdventureWorks_SalesOrderDetail2008Partition
GO
ALTER DATABASE AdventureWorks
ADD FILE
(
   NAME = 'AdventureWorks_SalesOrderDetail2008Partition',
   FILENAME = 'C:\SQLData\
   AdventureWork_SalesOrderDetail2008Partition.ndf',
   SIZE = 10,
   MAXSIZE = 120,
   FILEGROWTH = 10
)
TO FILEGROUP AdventureWorks_SalesOrderDetail2008Partition
```

49

```
GO

ALTER DATABASE AdventureWorks
ADD FILEGROUP AdventureWorks_SalesOrderDetail2009Partition
GO
ALTER DATABASE AdventureWorks
ADD FILE
(
    NAME = 'AdventureWorks_SalesOrderDetail2009Partition',
    FILENAME = 'C:\SQLData\
    AdventureWorks_SalesOrderDetail2009Partition.ndf',
    SIZE = 10,
    MAXSIZE = 120,
    FILEGROWTH = 10
)
TO FILEGROUP AdventureWorks_SalesOrderDetail2009Partition
GO
```

The file location specified in this script is specific to the author's machine. You must modify it before running the script. In the above script you should change the file path, which is bolded in the script, to a valid location on your machine.

Creating the Partition Function

A partition function simply specifies how the index or table is partitioned. The function creates a mapping of domains into a set of partitions. When creating a partition function, you define the number of partitions, the column that will be used to define the boundaries of partitions, and the range of partition column values for each partition.

In the following example, the function fnOrderYears takes a datetime value. The function defines the boundary values for the ranges of each partition. An important aspect of boundary values is that you specify only the boundary values between ranges; they don't define the upper or lower values for the whole table.

A boundary value can exist only in one partition. The ranges are defined as left or right. If a row has a partition column value that is the same as a boundary value, then SQL Server needs to know in which partition to put the row.

Left ranges mean that data equal to the boundary is included in the partition to the left of the boundary. A boundary of '12/31/2011' would create two partitions. The lower partition would include all data up to and including '12/31/2011', and the right partition would include any data greater than '12/31/2011'.

Right ranges mean that data equal to the boundary goes into the partition on the right of the boundary value. To separate at the new year starting 2012, a right range would set the boundary at '1/1/2012'. Any values less than the boundary go into the left, or lower, boundary. Any data with a date equal to or later than the boundary goes into the next partition. These two functions use left and right ranges to create the same result:

```
CREATE PARTITION FUNCTION fnOrderYears(DateTime)
AS RANGE LEFT FOR VALUES
('12/31/2005', '12/31/2006', '12/31/2007', '12/31/2008');
```

or

```
CREATE PARTITION FUNCTION fnOrderYears(DateTime)
AS RANGE RIGHT FOR VALUES
('1/1/2006', '1/1/2007', '1/1/2008', '1/1/2009');
```

These functions both create four defined boundaries and thus five partitions. This example uses the function that uses LEFT boundaries.

> **NOTE**
>
> Three catalog views expose information about partition function: `sys.partition_functions`, `sys.partition_range_values`, and `sys.partition_parameters`.

Creating Partition Schemes

The partition schema builds on the partition function to specify the physical locations for the partitions. As previously mentioned, the scheme maps the partitions to the database filegroups. The physical partition tables may all be located in the same filegroup or spread over several filegroups. The first example partition scheme, named `psOrderYearsAll`, uses the `fnOrderYears` partition function and places all the partitions in the `Primary` filegroup:

```
CREATE PARTITION SCHEME psYearsOrderAll
AS PARTITION fnOrderYears
  ALL TO ([PRIMARY]);
```

To place the table partitions in their own filegroup, omit the `ALL` keyword and list the filegroups individually. This creates five partitions to match the four boundary values specific in the function:

```
--Create Partition Scheme
CREATE PARTITION SCHEME psOrderYearsFiles
AS PARTITION pfyearsfnOrderYears
TO(
   AdventureWorks_SalesOrderDetail2005Partition,
   AdventureWorks_SalesOrderDetail2006Partition,
   AdventureWorks_SalesOrderDetail2007Partition,
   AdventureWorks_SalesOrderDetail2008Partition,
   AdventureWorks_SalesOrderDetail2009Partition
)
```

The partition functions and schemes must be created using T-SQL code, but after they've been created, you can view them in Management Studio's Object Explorer under the database Storage node.

49

TIP

For information about partition schemes programmatically, query `sys.partition_schemes`.

Creating the Partitioned Table

Now that all the required elements are in place, you can create the table and indexes that use them. First, create your table with a nonclustered primary key. Then add a clustered index, which partitions the table based on the partition scheme. Because partition functions and schemes don't have owners, you do not need to refer to the owners in the name.

The following table is similar to the AdventureWorks2012 SalesOrderDetail table in the sales scheme:

```
CREATE TABLE [dbo].[SalesOrderDetail]
(
    [SalesOrderID] [int] NOT NULL,
    [SalesOrderDetailID] [int]NOT NULL,
        CONSTRAINT SalesOrderDetailPK PRIMARY KEY
            NONCLUSTERED (SalesOrderDetailID),
    [CarrierTrackingNumber] [nvarchar](25) NULL,
    [OrderQty] [smallint] NOT NULL,
    [ProductID] [int] NOT NULL,
    [SpecialOfferID] [int] NOT NULL,
    [UnitPrice] [money] NOT NULL,
    [UnitPriceDiscount] [money] NOT NULL,
    [LineTotal]  money,
    [OrderDate] [datetime] NOT NULL
);
CREATE CLUSTERED INDEX CIX_SalesOrderDetail_OrderDate
ON dbo.SalesOrderDetail(OrderDate)
ON psOrderYearsFiles(OrderDate)
```

The next script inserts data from the Sales.SalesOrderDetail table into the newly created partitioned dbo.SalesOrderDetail table.

```
INSERT INTO dbo.SalesOrderDetail
(
SalesOrderID, SalesOrderDetailID, CarrierTrackingNumber,
OrderQty, ProductID, SpecialOfferID, UnitPrice, UnitPriceDiscount,
LineTotal,  OrderDate
)
SELECT
SalesOrderID, SalesOrderDetailID, CarrierTrackingNumber,
OrderQty, ProductID, SpecialOfferID, UnitPrice, UnitPriceDiscount,
```

```
LineTotal,  ModifiedDate
FROM Sales.SalesOrderDetail
```

Multiple partition schemes can share a single partition function. Architecturally, this might make sense if several tables should be partitioned using the same boundaries because this improves the consistency of the partitions. To verify which tables use which partition schemes, based on which partition functions, use the Object Dependencies dialog for the partition function or partition scheme. You can find it using the partition function's context menu.

> **TIP**
>
> For information about how the partitions are used, look at `sys.partitions` and `sys.dm_db_partition_stats`.

Querying Partition Tables

The nice thing about partition tables is that no special code is required to query either across multiple underlying partition tables or from only one partition table. The Query Optimizer automatically uses the right tables to retrieve the data.

The `$partition` operator can return the partition table's integer identifier when used with the partition function. The next code snippet counts the number of rows in each partition:

```
SELECT $PARTITION.pfyearsfnOrderYears(OrderDate) AS Partition,
    COUNT(*) AS Count
  FROM SalesOrderDetail
  GROUP BY $PARTITION.pfyearsfnOrderYears(OrderDate)
  ORDER BY Partition;
```

Result:

```
Partition   Count
----------- -----------
1           5151
2           19353
3           51237
4           45576
```

The next query selects data for one year, so the data should be located in only one partition. Examining the query execution plan (not shown here) reveals that the Query Optimizer used a high-speed clustered index scan on partition ID `PtnIds1005`:

```
SELECT *
FROM dbo.SalesOrderDetail
WHERE OrderDate BETWEEN '1/1/2005' AND '12/31/2005'
```

Altering Partition Tables

For partition tables to be updated to keep up with changing data, and to enable the performance testing of various partition schemes, they are easily modified. Even though the commands are simple, modifying the design of partition tables never executes quickly, as you can imagine.

Merging Partitions

Merge and split surgically modify the table partition design. The ALTER PARTITION...MERGE RANGE command effectively removes one of the boundaries from the partition function and merges two partitions. For example, to remove the boundary between 2007 and 2008 in the fnOrderYears partition function, and combine the data from 2007 and 2008 into a single partition, use the following ALTER command:

```
ALTER PARTITION FUNCTION pfyearsfnOrderYears()
    MERGE RANGE ('12/31/2007');
```

Following the merge operation, the previous count-rows-per-partition query now returns three partitions, and scripting the partition function from Object Explorer creates a script with three boundaries in the partition function code. The 2007 partition has been removed or merged with the 2008 partition.

> **NOTE**
>
> If multiple tables share the same partition scheme and partition function being modified, then multiple tables will be affected by these changes.

Splitting Partitions

To split an existing single partition, the first step is to designate the next filegroup to be used by the partition scheme. You can do this by using the ALTER PARTITION...NEXT USED command. If you specify too many filegroups when creating a scheme, you get a message that the next filegroup used is the extra file group you specified. Then you can modify the partition function to specify the new boundary using the ALTER PARTITION...SPLIT RANGE command to insert a new boundary into the partition function. The ALTER FUNCTION command actually performs the work.

This example segments the 2007–2008 sales order data into two partitions. The new partition includes only data for 2007:

```
ALTER PARTITION SCHEME psOrderYearsFiles
    NEXT USED [AdventureWorks_SalesOrderDetail2007Partition];

ALTER PARTITION FUNCTION pfyearsfnOrderYears()
    SPLIT RANGE ('12/31/2007');
```

Switching Tables

Switching tables is the cool capability to move an entire table into a partition within a partitioned table or to remove a single partition so that it becomes a standalone table. This is useful when importing new data, but following are a few restrictions:

- Every index for the partition table must be a partitioned index.
- The new table must have the same columns (excluding identity columns), indexes, and constraints (including foreign keys) as the partition table, except that the new table cannot be partitioned.
- The source partition table cannot be the target of a foreign key.
- Neither table can be published using replication or have schema-bound views.
- The new table must have check constraint restricting the data range to the new partition, so SQL Server doesn't need to reverify the data range. (And it needs to be validated; no point loading and then creating the constraint with nocheck.)
- Both the standalone table and the partition that receives the standalone table must be on the same filegroup.
- The receiving partition or table must be empty.

In essence, switching a partition is rearranging the database metadata to reassign the existing table as a partition. No data is actually moved, which makes table switching nearly instantaneous regardless of the table's size.

Prepping the New Table

You can create the `SalesOrderDetailNew` table to demonstrate switching. It holds all the 2009 data from the `AdventureWorks` database:

```
CREATE TABLE [dbo].[SalesOrderDetailNew]
(
    [SalesOrderID] [int] NOT NULL,
    [SalesOrderDetailID] [int] NOT NULL,
    [CarrierTrackingNumber] [nvarchar](25) NULL,
    [OrderQty] [smallint] NOT NULL,
    [ProductID] [int] NOT NULL,
    [SpecialOfferID] [int] NOT NULL,
    [UnitPrice] [money] NOT NULL,
    [UnitPriceDiscount] [money] NOT NULL,
    [LineTotal] money,
    [OrderDate] [datetime] NOT NULL
)
ON [AdventureWorks_SalesOrderDetail2009Partition];
```

You can create indexes identical to those on the preceding table on the partitioned table:

```
ALTER TABLE dbo.SalesOrderDetailNew
```

```
      ADD CONSTRAINT SalesOrderDetailNewPK
      PRIMARY KEY NONCLUSTERED (SalesOrderDetailID, OrderDate)
   GO
   CREATE CLUSTERED INDEX CIX_SalesOrderDetailNew_OrderDate
      ON dbo.SalesOrderDetailNew (OrderDate)
   GO
```

The following adds the mandatory constraint:

```
   ALTER TABLE dbo.SalesOrderDetailNew
      ADD CONSTRAINT SODNewPT
         CHECK (OrderDate BETWEEN '1/1/2009' AND '12/31/2009')
```

Now import the new data from `AdventureWorks`, reusing the 2008 data:

```
   INSERT INTO dbo.SalesOrderDetailNew
   (
      SalesOrderID, SalesOrderDetailID, CarrierTrackingNumber, OrderQty,
      ProductID, SpecialOfferID, UnitPrice, UnitPriceDiscount,
      LineTotal, OrderDate
   )
   SELECT
      SalesOrderID, SalesOrderDetailID, CarrierTrackingNumber, OrderQty,
      ProductID, SpecialOfferID, UnitPrice, UnitPriceDiscount,
      LineTotal, DATEADD(YEAR,1,ModifiedDate)
   FROM Sales.SalesOrderDetail
   WHERE ModifiedDate BETWEEN '1/1/2008' AND '12/31/2008'
```

The new table now has 45,576 rows.

Prepping the Partition Table

The original partition table, built earlier in this section, has a nonpartitioned, nonclustered primary key. Because one of the rules of switching into a partitioned table is that every index must be partitioned, the first task for this example is to drop and rebuild the `SalesOrderDetail` table's primary key so it will be partitioned:

```
   ALTER TABLE dbo.SalesOrderDetail
      DROP CONSTRAINT SalesOrderDetailPK
   GO

   ALTER TABLE dbo.SalesOrderDetail
      ADD CONSTRAINT SalesOrderDetailPK
      PRIMARY KEY NONCLUSTERED (SalesOrderDetailID, OrderDate)
         ON psOrderYearsFiles(OrderDate)
   GO
```

Next, the partition table needs an empty partition:

```
   ALTER PARTITION SCHEME psOrderYearsFiles
```

```
        NEXT USED [AdventureWorks_SalesOrderDetail2009Partition]
GO

ALTER PARTITION FUNCTION pfyearsfnOrderYears()
  SPLIT RANGE ('12/31/2009')
  GO
```

Performing the Switch

The ALTER TABLE...SWITCH TO command moves the new table into a specific partition.

```
ALTER TABLE SalesOrderDetailNew
  SWITCH TO SalesOrderDetail PARTITION 5
```

Switching Out

You can use the same technology to switch a partition out of the partition table so that it becomes a standalone table. Because no merge takes place, this is much easier than switching in. The following code takes the first partition out of the SalesOrderDetail partitioned table and reconfigures the database metadata so that it becomes its own table:

```
CREATE TABLE [dbo].[SalesOrderDetailArchive]
(
    [SalesOrderID] [int] NOT NULL,
    [SalesOrderDetailID] [int] NOT NULL,
    [CarrierTrackingNumber] [nvarchar](25) NULL,
    [OrderQty] [smallint] NOT NULL,
    [ProductID] [int] NOT NULL,
    [SpecialOfferID] [int] NOT NULL,
    [UnitPrice] [money] NOT NULL,
    [UnitPriceDiscount] [money] NOT NULL,
    [LineTotal] money,
    [OrderDate] [datetime] NOT NULL
)
ON [AdventureWorks_SalesOrderDetail2009Partition];

CREATE CLUSTERED INDEX CIX_SalesOrderDetailArchive_OrderDate
ON dbo.SalesOrderDetailArchive(OrderDate)
ON [AdventureWorks_SalesOrderDetail2009Partition];

ALTER TABLE SalesOrderDetail
  SWITCH PARTITION 5 to SalesOrderDetailArchive
```

Rolling Partitions

With a little imagination, you can use the technology to create and merge existing partitions to create rolling partition designs.

Rolling partitions are useful for time-based partition functions such as partitioning a year of data into months. Each month, the rolling partition expands for a new month. To build a 13-month rolling partition, perform these steps each month:

1. Add a new boundary.
2. Point the boundary to the next used filegroup.
3. Merge the oldest two partitions to keep all the data.

Switching tables into and out of partitions can enhance the rolling partition designs by switching in fully populated staging tables and switching out the tables into an archive location.

Indexing Partitioned Tables

Large tables mean large indexes, so nonclustered indexes can be optionally partitioned.

Creating Partitioned Indexes

Partitioned nonclustered indexes must include the column used by the partition function in the index and must be created using the same ON clause as the partitioned clustered index:

```
CREATE INDEX SalesOrderDetail_ProductID
  ON SalesOrderDetail (ProductID, OrderDate)ON  psOrderYearsFiles
  (OrderDate);
```

Maintaining Partitioned Indexes

One of the advantages of partitioned indexes is that they can be individually maintained. The following example rebuilds the newly added fifth partition:

```
ALTER INDEX SalesOrderDetail_ProductID
  ON dbo.SalesOrderDetail
  REBUILD
  PARTITION = 5
```

Removing Partitioning

To remove the partitioning of any table, drop the clustered index and add a new clustered index without the partitioning ON clause. When dropping the clustered index, you must add the MOVE TO option to actually consolidate the data onto the specified filegroup, thus removing the partitioning from the table:

```
DROP INDEX CIX_SalesOrderDetail_OrderDate  ON dbo.SalesOrderDetail
  WITH (MOVE TO [PRIMARY]);
```

Summary

Not every database needs to scale to higher magnitudes of capacity, but when a project does grow into the terabytes, SQL Server 2012 provides some advanced technologies to tackle the growth. However, even these advanced technologies are no substitute for smart database design.

Following are key points on partitioning:

- Partitioned views use a union to merge data from several user-created base tables. Each partition table must include the partition key and a constraint.

- The Query Processor can carefully choose the minimum number of underlying tables when selecting through a partitioned view but not when updating.

- Partitioned tables are a completely different technology than partitioned views and use a partition function, schema, and clustered index to partition a single table.

The next chapter wraps up this part covering optimization with features that are available in the Enterprise Edition of SQL Server 2012.

49

Resource Governor

I t's a DBA's nightmare. A query runs and eats up resources to the point that everything else slows to a crawl. The fault might belong to a software developer who didn't consider the resources that his queries chew up, but you get the call. And saying that you don't know what the problem is won't satisfy anyone.

You might get to the bottom of the problem, but what then? Do you sever the connection that the errant application comes in on? That could be a disaster for a mission-critical process. These issues challenged SQL Server DBAs in the past.

The 2008 release of SQL Server introduced the Resource Governor feature, which enables you to limit the CPU and memory usage by a specific application, hostname, user, or any other attribute of the connection session. Now you can stop having those nightmares because you can limit the resources for a query that might typically bring the server to a crawl.

Resource Governor is also an Enterprise Edition-only feature.

You can configure the Resource Governor in two ways. The first is through T-SQL commands. The second is via the Object Explorer from within SQL Server Management Studio.

OTE

ere is a difference between the Resource Governor and the Work Load Governor. The Workload Governor was part of earlier rsions of SQL Server and limited the performance of SQL Server as a whole. It was not granular so that it could limit parts of QL Server. Although this was useful, it was not nearly as useful as the Resource Governor.

e Resource Governor can't actually limit queries, but rather workloads. A *workload* is an identifiable process, identifiable by application name, a hostname, or a login.

Exploring the Fundamentals of the Resource Governor

The Resource Governor relies on resource pools, workload groups, and classifier functions. This section covers these concepts. You need to understand them before using the Resource Governor.

Understanding the Resource Pool

A resource pool collects physical resources together so that you can manage them. Under the covers, a resource pool acts as a virtual instance of SQL Server when accessed by an application. It has a number of parameters including the minimum and maximum values for the resource. This may include CPU utilization and memory usage. (File I/O is planned for a later version of SQL Server — most DBAs currently reduce I/O contention by separating databases, tables, or indexes onto different physical disks.) SQL Server 2012 can have up to 64 user-defined resource pools (64-bit versions only), up from the limit of 18 in the previous release. In addition, there are two built-in pools:

- **Internal**: Used solely by the Database Engine. This cannot be reconfigured by the user.
- **Default**: Used by all those workloads that have not been assigned to any specific resource pool.

SQL Server DBAs can also define their custom resource pools. The custom resource pools can define limits for each resource with minimum and maximum values. The sum of all resource pool minimum values can't exceed 100 percent. The maximum values for each resource pool can range from 0 to 100.

A resource pool cannot always operate at its maximum value. The reason for this in most cases is that the minimum values of all other resource pools can add up to a value that is too great to enable any given resource pool to operate at its maximum value. For instance, there might be five resource pools. If four of the resource pools have minimum values of 10 percent, the fifth resource pool can't possibly use more than 60 percent because that is all that remains with all other pools operating at their minimum. The actual maximum for any pool is the Effective Maximum Rate, which is equal to the difference between the maximum value of the said resource pool and the sum of the minimum values of all others.

> **NOTE**
>
> The internal resource pool has a higher priority than all other pools. For this reason it always has an Effective Maximum Rate of 100 percent. This happens even if the internal pool violates the resource requirements of all other pools.

Table 50-1 shows five resource pools with the minimum and maximum values for each resource pool. It also shows the Effective Maximum Rate along with the Shared percentage. The Shared percentage is the difference between the Effective Maximum Rate and the

Minimum Rate for any resource pool. This example illustrates how resources can share when no workload for any process is available.

TABLE 50-1 **Example Showing Resource Sharing Among Pools**

Resource Pool	Minimum Percentage	Maximum Percentage	Effective Maximum Percentage	Shared Percentage
Internal	0	100	100	100
Default	0	100	25	25
Custom Pool 1	10	100	35	25
Custom Pool 2	35	90	50	15
Custom Pool 3	30	80	35	5

For example, referring to Table 50-1, Custom Pool 1 has a minimum percentage of 10 percent and a maximum of 100 percent; subtract Custom Pools 2's and Custom Pool 3's minimums (100 – 35 – 30 = 35).

What's New with the Resource Governor in SQL Server 2012

There are a few subtle changes in the Resource Governor in SQL Server 2012. These changes give greater performance controls in multi-tenancy environments such as a private cloud:

- Support for up to 64 user-defined resource pools (64-bit editions only).

- Greater CPU usage control, namely the ability to now set affinity to a particular scheduler, group of schedulers, or a NUMA node.

- CPU Capping for predictable performance. You can now specify a hard cap on CPU bandwidth that all requests in the resource pool will receive, regardless of whether or not there are other workloads running on the instance. In the previous release, MAX_CPU_PERCENT was only enforced if there were other workloads competing for CPU resources. Specifically providing a hard cap allows for predictable resource allocations.

- Memory allocation controls now extend to all areas *except* for the buffer pool and column store cache. In previous versions this control only extended to query grant memory.

You can create and manage resource pools with T-SQL using CREATE, DROP, and ALTER statements. After you issue the T-SQL commands to the add, alter, and drop resource pools, you must get the Resource Governor to reconfigure with ALTER RESOURCE GOVERNOR RECONFIGURE. The following statement creates a resource pool named CustomPool1 that simply sets the maximum CPU value for this resource pool at 30 percent.

50

```
CREATE RESOURCE POOL CustomPool1
    WITH (MAX_CPU_PERCENT = 30);
GO
ALTER RESOURCE GOVERNOR RECONFIGURE;
GO
```

You can set the minimum and maximum CPU values as well as the minimum and maximum memory values with the CREATE RESOURCE POOL statement as shown here. You'll also set a hard cap of 40 percent and restrict this resource pool to only use NUMA node 0.

```
DROP RESOURCE POOL CustomPool1;
GO
ALTER RESOURCE GOVERNOR RECONFIGURE;
GO

CREATE RESOURCE POOL CustomPool1
    WITH( MIN_CPU_PERCENT = 5,
      MAX_CPU_PERCENT = 30,
CAP_CPU_PERCENT = 40,
AFFINITY NUMANODE = (0),
      MIN_MEMORY_PERCENT = 5,
      MAX_MEMORY_PERCENT = 30);
GO
ALTER RESOURCE GOVERNOR RECONFIGURE;
GO
```

You can increase the maximum CPU value to 35 with the following SQL statement.

```
ALTER RESOURCE POOL CustomPool1
    WITH( MIN_CPU_PERCENT = 5,
      MAX_CPU_PERCENT = 35,
      MIN_MEMORY_PERCENT = 5,
      MAX_MEMORY_PERCENT = 30);
GO
ALTER RESOURCE GOVERNOR RECONFIGURE;
GO
```

You can also create resource pools with SQL Server Management Studio. Even before creating resource pools, you must enable the Resource Governor. The following steps enable the Resource Governor and then add a resource pool named CustomPool2.

1. Open SQL Server Management Studio.

2. Open the instance in which you want to enable the Resource Governor.

3. Open the Management folder.

4. Right-click Resource Governor; a menu appears.

5. Click Enable.

6. Drill down on the Resource Governor, and open the Resource Pools folder.

7. Right-click the Resource Pools folder; a menu appears.

8. Select New Resource Pool; a dialog box appears.

9. Scroll to the bottom of the Resource Pools list until you see an empty slot, as shown in Figure 50-1.

FIGURE 50-1

The Resource Governor Properties dialog box enables you to set the new resource pool's values.

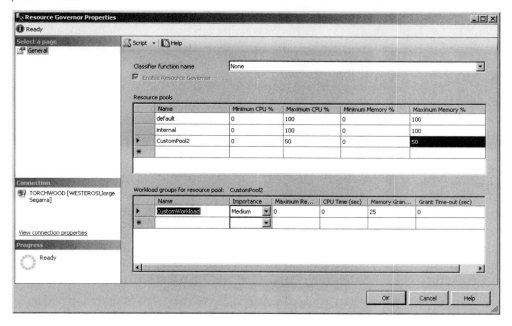

10. Enter a name for the new resource pool.

11. Set the minimum and maximum CPU and memory values for the new resource pool.

12. Enter a workload group name for the resource pool.

13. Click the OK button.

14. Your resource pool is now created, but until you create a `classifier` function, Resource Governor cannot use it.

Additionally, you can enable and disable the Resource Governor feature through script. You can use the following SQL Statements to disable or enable the Resource Governor:

```
ALTER RESOURCE GOVERNOR DISABLE; --Disables Resource Governor

ALTER RESOURCE GOVERNOR RECONFIGURE; --Enables Resource Governor
```

The next sections cover Workload Groups and the `classifier` function.

50

Workload Group

To keep the assignment of resource pools manageable and to allow for highly granular monitoring and juggling of workloads within a resource pool, SQL Server has workload groups. You can assign users to a workload group, and assign one or more Workload Group to a resource pool. This mechanism is loosely analogous to login groups that contain users.

There are two built-in workload groups:

- **Internal**: Assigned to the internal resource pool. Used by Database Engine.
- **Default**: All those sessions that do not classify to any other workload group are assigned to it.

You can easily create workload groups with T-SQL. The following statement creates a workload group named Workload2 and assigns it to CustomPool2.

```
CREATE WORKLOAD GROUP Workload2
    USING CustomPool2
```

You can also use ALTER and DROP statements to change and delete workload groups. Following are several examples that show you how to use ALTER statements to do useful things.

When SQL Server is first installed, the Resource Governor is disabled. The following example starts the Resource Governor. After the statement executes, the Resource Governor runs and can use the predefined workload groups and resource pools.

```
ALTER RESOURCE GOVERNOR RECONFIGURE;
```

The following example assigns all new sessions to the default workload group by removing any existing classifier function from the Resource Governor configuration. The classifier function is a user-defined function that uses properties such as IP address, Application Name, or User Name to assign a session to a workload group. Classifier functions will be explained in more detail in the next section.

If you do not designate a specific classifier function, all new sessions assign to the default workload group. This change applies to new sessions only. This does not affect existing sessions.

```
ALTER RESOURCE GOVERNOR WITH (CLASSIFIER_FUNCTION = NULL);
GO
ALTER RESOURCE GOVERNOR RECONFIGURE;
```

The following example creates a classifier function named dbo.rgclassifier_v1. The function classifies every new session based on either the username or application name and assigns the session requests and queries to a specific Workload group. If sessions do not map to the specified user or application names, the function assigns them to the default Workload group. The classifier function then registers and the configuration changes.

```
-- Store the classifier function in the master database.
USE master;
GO
SET ANSI_NULLS ON;
GO
SET QUOTED_IDENTIFIER ON;
GO
CREATE FUNCTION dbo.rgclassifier_v1() RETURNS sysname
WITH SCHEMABINDING
AS
BEGIN
-- Declare the variable to hold the value returned in sysname.
    DECLARE @grp_name AS sysname
-- If the user login is 'sa', map the connection to the groupAdmin
-- workload group.
    IF (SUSER_NAME() = 'sa')
        SET @grp_name = 'groupAdmin'
-- Use application information to map the
--connection to the groupAdhoc
-- workload group.
    ELSE IF (APP_NAME() LIKE '%MANAGEMENT STUDIO%')
        OR (APP_NAME() LIKE '%QUERY ANALYZER%')
            SET @grp_name = 'groupAdhoc'
-- If the application is for reporting, map the connection to
-- the groupReports workload group.
    ELSE IF (APP_NAME() LIKE '%REPORT SERVER%')
        SET @grp_name = 'groupReports'
-- If the connection does not map to any of the previous groups,
-- put the connection into the default workload group.
    ELSE
        SET @grp_name = 'default'
    RETURN @grp_name
END
GO
-- Register the classifier user-defined function and update the
-- the in-memory configuration.
ALTER RESOURCE GOVERNOR WITH
(CLASSIFIER_FUNCTION=dbo.rgclassifier_v1);
GO
ALTER RESOURCE GOVERNOR RECONFIGURE;
GO
```

The following example resets all workload group and pool statistics:

```
ALTER RESOURCE GOVERNOR RESET STATISTICS;
```

50

1137

Classifier Function

SQL Server sessions are assigned to workload groups, which in turn belong to resource pools. You must provide a way for SQL Server to assign sessions to the correct group, which you do with a `Classifier` function. These are user-defined functions, which can use properties such as IP Address, Application Name, or User Name to assign a session to a workload group. Once a session is assigned to a workload group, the sessions (and queries) are bound by the resource constraint rules of that workload group.

The following code is an example of a Classifier function.

```
CREATE FUNCTION MyClassifer()
RETURNS SYSNAME WITH SCHEMABINDING
BEGIN
 --workload definition based on login names
 DECLARE @WorkLoadName sysname
 IF SUSER_SNAME()= 'admin'
 BEGIN
 SET @WorkLoadName='AdminUsers';
 END

--workload definition based on application
 IF APP_NAME() = 'SuperApp'
 BEGIN
 SET @WorkLoadName='OurApps';
 END

 RETURN @WorkLoadName;
 END
```

After you create a Classifier function, you must let the Resource Governor know that you want to use it. Following is how you assign a Classifier function.

```
ALTER RESOURCE GOVERNOR
WITH (CLASSIFIER_FUNCTION = dbo.MyClassifer)
```

You can extend the classifier function, for example, to consult a lookup table. However, the classifier function executes with each login, and you must ensure that it performs optimally. Whenever there is a request for a connection, you can classify the request through the classifier function to identify a workload group that this session request should handle. Now you can assign a workload group to only a single resource pool. You can use this resource pool to assign and limit the resources required by the session.

Performance Monitoring of Resource Governor

You can check the performance through the Reliability and Performance Monitor. The two SQL Server performance monitors available are Resource Pool Stats (as shown in Figure 50-2).

FIGURE 50-2

Performance Monitor enables you to know how the resource pools function.

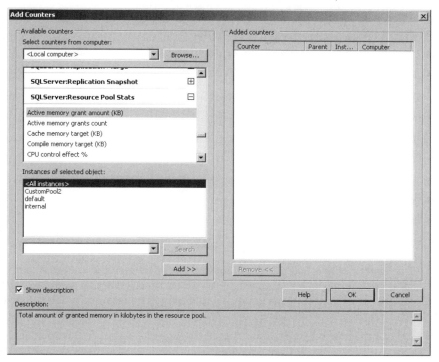

While using the Resource Governor, you must monitor the workloads inside each resource pool. You may find that a specific workload consumes all the resources of a resource pool. In that case you may want to place that workload in a different workload group in its own resource pool. Microsoft recommends that in planning for the Resource Governor you run all workloads in the default resource pool, each in their own workload group. This way you can determine the resource consumption characteristics of each workload and create appropriate resource pools for each workload, or place workload loads with similar resource consumption characteristics in their own workload group and resource pool.

For example, all reporting applications might be in a single resource pool, which limits their CPU consumption, and you can place all OLTP workloads into a different resource pool, which has a higher importance setting.

50

Views and Limitations

Following are three catalog views for the Resource governor:

- `sys.resource_governor_configuration`
- `sys.resource_governor_resource_pools`
- `sys.resource_governor_workload_groups`

These views enable you to view how the Resource Governor, your resource pools, and your Workload groups are configured.

Three Dynamic Management Views support the Resource Governor, which enable you to monitor it:

- `sys.dm_resource_governor_workload_groups`
- `sys.dm_resource_governor_configuration`
- `sys.dm_resource_governor_resource_pools`

The Resource Governor also has some limitations:

- It is limited only to the Database Engine. But some services are not a part of the Database Engine such as Analysis, Integration, and Reporting services. For these, you still must rely on other solutions to manage the resource problem (such as installing separate SQL Server instances).
- You can manage only a single instance through the Resource Governor. An organization may have more than a single instance but must manage each separately.
- The Resource Governor currently has only two resources: CPU and memory.

Summary

Resource Governor is an extremely useful tool to prevent run-away queries. In addition, it can prevent many DBA nightmares. Judicious use of the Resource Governor allows you to dynamically control resource CPU and memory allocations for queries, which allows you to control your environments proactively rather than reactively. This granular control of resource allocation becomes critical in consolidated environments, such as shared instances or private cloud.

Part IX

Business Intelligence

Business Intelligence Database Design

The majority of this book discusses Online Transactional Processing (OLTP) databases, which are typically used for operational purposes, such as Sales, Human Resource and Payroll management, Business Process Management, Student Information Systems, and so on. In recent years there has been a slow evolution by a large number of organizations to analyze their data for trends in an attempt to make more informed decisions about a company's direction, which is often referred to as *Business Intelligence (BI)*. When these queries and analytics are run directly against the OLTP database, often conflicts and contention occur that generally affect performance.

To mitigate these problems, organizations usually copy the OLTP database to another server and offload all the reporting to that database. Although this approach may solve some of the problems, it does not completely solve them all. This is because OLTP systems are not optimized for large summary queries that return large volumes of data. In addition, OLTP systems usually don't persist historical data values. Finally, OLTP systems usually have a primary focus as mentioned earlier. As a result, typically, a small population of individuals has a deep understanding of the data.

The next step that is usually taken is to create a database that summarizes the OLTP data into new tables. Again, this may solve some of the problems. However, because it is still a refined set of data, it is often insufficient in performing analytics that are holistic to the entire organization.

So how do you completely solve this problem? To solve the problem you must provide a data source that contains a centralized consistent view of the data available to the organization as a whole. Now users can perform OLAP without contending with the operations system. Over the years OLAP has become synonymous with data warehousing. OLAP provides business with the ability to quickly analyze large data sets in different ways. The data warehouse is typically the database structure that acts as the source for OLAP. The result of coupling these two is typically a cube, which Chapter 53, "Building Multidimensional Cubes in Analysis Services with MDX," discusses.

This chapter defines key concepts for data warehousing and techniques used to build and load a data warehouse.

Data Warehousing

A data warehouse is the structural foundation of most OLAP and BI solutions. Data warehouses, in most cases, are less normalized than the OLTP databases that act as its sources. A typical data warehouse contains two types of tables: facts and dimensions. Fact tables contain the measurable values, such as sales, number of sales, and count of items, to mention a few. The values are often referred to as measures; dimensions categorize or group those measurable values. As SQL Server has evolved, so has its capability to build OLAP solutions on database structures that are not data warehouses. However, using a data warehouse as the data source has several benefits and offers the developer a seamless process for design and data refresh.

Designing a Data Warehouse Using a Star Schema

Data warehouse design technique is referred to as a Star Schema. As mentioned earlier, a data warehouse is composed of facts and dimensions. The layout of these tables resembles a star, as shown in Figure 51-1.

You see from the diagram that the one fact is central to multiple dimensions. Each dimension is representative of a way that the measures in the fact can be grouped, aggregated, or categorized. For example, you could use the SalesAmount column from the FactInternetSales table and aggregate it by Customer to see the total sales for each customer.

A fact table usually consists of two types of columns: The surrogate key column, which is defined in the Surrogate Key section of this chapter, and the facts (or measures) column.

The dimension tables, on the other hand, contains a primary key (surrogate key), and alternate key, and one or more attributes. The alternate key is not always present in the dimension. It is, in most cases, the primary key for each row from the operational system. The attributes are the data that categorizes the dimensions. For example, a student dimension may include attributes for name, address, city, state, and e-mail address. Dimensions in many instances are denormalized versions of the data structures in the OLTP databases.

The most difficult decision that most organizations face is determining which dimensions and facts to use in their data warehouse. The information technology group often tries to make this decision without the involvement of the business, which is a critical mistake.

Because the business has an intimate relationship with the data and works with it on a daily basis, the decision as to what goes into a data warehouse should be made by it or with it. Not using its knowledge could result in a data warehouse that contains inaccurate or irrelevant data. As a result, time and money could be wasted building a solution that may never be used.

FIGURE 51-1

The diagram view of the AdventureWorks data warehouse database shows one fact table and several dimensions resembling a star.

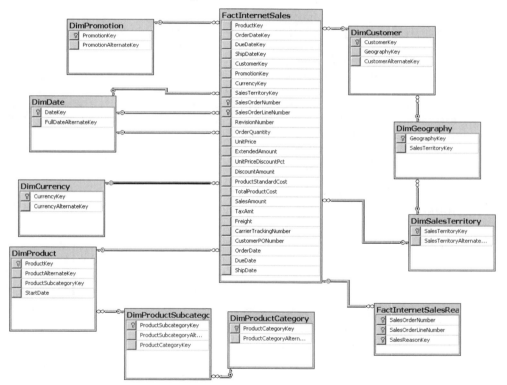

Surrogate Keys

The foundation of any star schema design is the foreign keys that exist between the fact and dimension tables. However, you should not use the primary and foreign keys that exist in the OLTP database or databases that act as the source for your data warehouse. Instead, when designing dimensions a new column, a surrogate key, will be added to each table. This column is usually an identity column, which is used to relate the fact to the dimensions.

Assume you are required to replace your current Student Information System and all StudentIDs will be changed. If you were using the primary key to relate your facts and dimensions, this could require several changes in your data warehouse to student dimensions, and the entire fact table needs to be updated. In addition, potential conflicts may be introduced if the new system reuses existing keys from the old system. By using surrogates you can avoid conflicts and correct the student dimension with a few updates.

Designing Your Data Warehouse Using a Snowflake Schema

In some cases it may be necessary to limit the amount of denormalization done when building your dimensions. This results in a slight modification to the star schema. Instead of the star schema, it may be referred to as a snowflake schema. This method is often effective for large complex dimensions. This approach becomes relevant when the loading process involves consistency or sequencing. Figure 51-2 shows a snowflaked product dimension.

FIGURE 51-2

Snowflake Dimension.

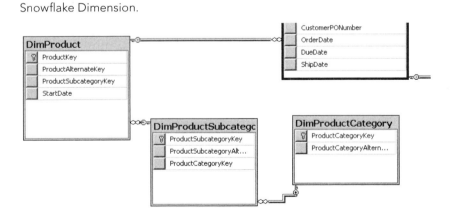

Instead of placing the product, productcategory, and productsubcategory into one dimension, each individual table was included in the data warehouse schema. This approach does add some slight complexities when building an OLAP cube. Therefore, careful consideration should be taken before implementing this modeling approach.

Ensuring Consistency within a Data Warehouse

Inconsistent data can quickly void any confidence that end users have garnered when working with any data system. Because one of the primary reasons for designing a star schema is to provide faster query response time when performing OLAP queries, it is pivotal that the results are accurate and consistent. To ensure this level of accuracy and consistency, data warehouse developers typically institute two basic design rules during the load process.

The first rule is to ensure that you are properly handling null or invalid values. This is usually accomplished by replacing these values with values that are more meaningful to an end user. The decision as to what these values are should not be determined by a single person or group. This is an effort that should be decided upon by the organization as a whole because the data warehouse will likely be used by a broad audience. This results in a consistent interpretation across the entire organization. A common practice is to insert rows into dimensions that satisfy as many inconsistent or invalid data scenarios. The values are usually replaced with values such as Unknown, NA, Internal, and so on.

The second rule relates to the fact table. After data has been inserted into the fact table, it should not be updated or deleted. This could lead to varying results from day to day. If this is a requirement, you should consider creating a separate table to maintain these transient transactions. You should also inform the users of the level of volatility of this data. This can establish user expectations about data and query results for particular data sets and reduce the likelihood of inconsistent data for other data sets.

Loading Data

When loading a data warehouse, it typically starts with loading the dimensions and then the facts. The obvious reason is to satisfy the fact tables' foreign key constraints. In the SQL Server world, the Extraction, Transformation and Loading (ETL) is accomplished using SQL Server Integration Services (SSIS). Chapter 52, "Building, Deploying, and Managing ETL Workflows in Integration Services," provides a detailed explanation of how to do this. Figure 51-3 shows a simple dimension load with SSIS, and Figure 51-4 illustrates a fact load. This chapter focuses on loading the data with pure Transact-SQL.

FIGURE 51-3

Simple Dimension Load from SSIS.

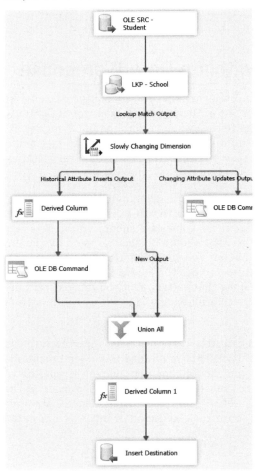

FIGURE 51-4

Fact load using SSIS.

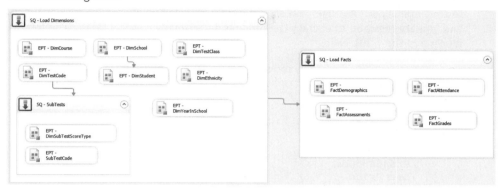

Loading Dimensions

The source data has a tremendous effect on which method will be used when loading the data into the data warehouse. If you encounter a situation in which all the fact and dimension data has relatable column, or more preferably foreign, keys, the process is straightforward. To load a dimension you would compare the rows in the dimension table to the rows that are contained in the incoming source data. As a best practice, you should copy the source data into staging tables instead of loading data directly from your source system. This should eliminate the possibility of contention during the loading of a dimension table. The following example illustrates the use of a LEFT OUTER JOIN to detect the new rows that will be inserted into the DimProduct table:

```
INSERT INTO Warehouse.dbo.DimProduct
(ProductAK, ProductName, ProductNumber, StandardCost, ListPrice)
SELECT
    ProductID,
    Name,
    ProductNumber,
    StandardCost,
    ListPrice
FROM Stage.dbo.DimProduct sp
LEFT OUTER JOIN Warehouse.dbo.DimProduct  p
    ON sp.ProductID = p.ProductID
WHERE
    sp.ProductID IS NULL
```

This is a simple approach. This assumes that you have imported the source data into a staging table and that you are not tracking history about data changes and focus only on new row additions. In this case your query needs to scan only the existing dimension table.

Unfortunately, this is not always the case. You may encounter a scenario in which you need to extract dimension data from a table that contains other data besides that data specific to that dimension. Assume your source data is mingled with product data and sales data, and you are required to extract the product data from the single table. The following query illustrates the T-SQL code:

```
INSERT INTO dbo.DimProduct(ProductAK, ProductName, ProductNumber,
StandardCost, ListPrice)
SELECT
    DISTINCT
    ProductID,
    Name,
    ProductNumber,
    StandardCost,
    ListPrice
FROM stage.Sales sp
LEFT OUTER JOIN DimProduct  p
    ON sp.ProductID = p.ProductID
WHERE
    sp.ProductID IS NULL
```

The primary difference is the use of the DISTINCT keyword to ensure that you pull a single row for each product.

Loading Fact Tables

The next stop in the data warehouse, after the dimensions are loaded, is to load the facts. As mentioned earlier, fact tables typically contain two types of columns: measures and surrogate keys. The following is a script that creates a fact table that references the customer and product dimensions via surrogate keys from those dimensions and one measure — TotalDue:

```
CREATE TABLE FastSales
(
    CustomerSK int
        CONSTRAINT UQ_FactSales_FactSalesID UNIQUE,

    CONSTRAINT FK_FactSales_To_DimCustomer_On_CusotmerSK
        FOREIGN KEY (CustomerSK)
            REFERENCES dbo.DimCustomer(CustomerSK),
    ProductSK int,
        Constraint FK_FactSales_To_DimProduct_On_ProductSK
    FOREIGN KEY (ProductSK)
    REFERENCES dbo.DimProduct(ProductSK),
    TotalDue money
)
```

As with the dimensions tables, you should copy the source data for the fact tables into a staging table. The source data for the facts should contain the measures that you want to load into the fact table and the primary keys for the dimensions related to the facts. The code to load the fact table looks like this:

```
INSERT INTO Warehouse.dbo.FactSales(CustomerSK, ProductSK, TotalDue)
SELECT
    ISNULL(CustomerSK, -1),
    ISNULL(ProductSK, -1),
    TotalDue
FROM Staging.dbo.Sales s
LEFT OUTER JOIN Warehouse.dbo.DimProduct p
    ON s.ProductID = p.ProductID
LEFT OUTER JOIN Warehouse.dbo.DimCustomer c
    ON s.CustomerID = c.CustomerID
```

You may wonder about the use of ISNULL in the SELECT and why LEFT OUTER JOIN is used. The purpose of LEFT OUTER JOIN is to identify any rows in the source data unrelated to any dimensions. Then in the SELECT if the value is NULL, it is set to –1. Why –1? As mentioned in the "Ensuring Consistency within a Data Warehouse" section, you should insert a row into each dimension in an attempt to establish and maintain consistency for invalid or missing data. This is where that row becomes valid. Instead of allowing the identity value of the surrogate key to set the value, when inserting the row you should set the value to a number that is consistent across all dimensions. In this case –1 was selected; therefore it is specified for missing rows.

Changing Data in Dimensions

In the "Loading Dimensions" section, a brief reference was given to loading historical data into dimensions. This is a common scenario encountered when building the ETL process for a data warehouse. When defining the requirements for your data warehouse, this is something that should definitely be addressed with your user population. The nomenclature that is used when defining dimensions can be somewhat confusing. Dimensions are often categorized into types: Type 0, Type 1, and Type 2. This is not an exhaustive list. However, for the sake of brevity, you can focus on the aforementioned list.

This typing of dimensions can be confusing because it is not the entire dimension that is typed, but instead each column (attribute) has a type of its own. During the initial load, a single row for each unique row is loaded into the dimension. The type of dimension can determine what, if any, operation will be performed on that row. The following is a brief description of the types:

- **Type 0**: History is not tracked and changes to any column are completely ignored. For example, you may have an Employee dimension that contains a Social Security number. This is a value that usually does not change. In this case if a change did occur you could define this column as Type 0, and if a change occurs, the update would be ignored in the ETL process.

- **Type 1**: Similar to type 0, history is not tracked. Therefore, if a change occurs to the source data, the column specified as Type 1 would be updated. For example, assume that your data warehouse contains a customer dimension that includes Last Name as one of the columns. If there were a case when a Last Name changed, like when a woman gets married, then the Last Name for that row would be updated.

- **Type 2**: Unlike the first two types, Type 2 does track history. Using that approach, every change that occurs in the source data for a particular column is tracked in the dimension table. Therefore, if an existing row changes, a new row will be inserted into the dimension table that reflects that value of the changed data. To accommodate this you need to modify the structure of the table so that you can identify the row that is active at the time of the fact load. In some cases a simple bit flag is added to the table. However, if you want a more robust solution, one that allows you to identify when a row is active, you need to add two columns to your table. One column, start date, defines when the row was modified; and the other column, end date, specifies when another change occurs. As the fact is loaded, the ETL process can either use the bit flag to identify which row to use, or it can use the start and end dates.

Accommodating the varying uses of these types presents certain challenges when loading dimensions and facts, unless every column in the dimension must be specified as Type 0. On the other hand, if one column is designated as Type 1 or Type 2, then the load process becomes complicated. The primary challenge with Type 2 attributes is creating a process that can detect changes to a given attribute. You can accomplish this with T-SQL by using the CHECKSUM or HASHBYTES functions. Although they both offer a certain level of confidence, neither guarantees 100 percent change detection.

With a Type 2 dimension, you must not detect only changes, but you must also incorporate a process that expires the old row and inserts the new row. The process must first detect if the row currently exists in the dimension. If it does not, then the process must simply insert a new row. Depending on whether you include the bit flag, the start and end date, or both, you must include them during the insertion. If you included only the bit flag, it would be set to on when a new row is added. When you include the start and end date, the start date is when the row is first inserted, and the end date is some date in the far future. Figure 51-5 illustrates the use of both methods. If it does exist, then the existing row must be expired, by turning the bit flag off and updating the end date, which is shown in Figure 51-6. Finally, a new row will be inserted reflecting the changed data, with the active flag on and setting the start and end dates.

FIGURE 51-5

When a new row is inserted into a type 2 dimension, the bit flag is set to on, and the start and end date are set.

EmployeeSK	FirstName	LastName	StartDate	EndDate	BitFlag
1	Jenny	Doe	5/25/2012	6/6/2079	1

FIGURE 51-6

When a row is inserted and a version of that row exists, the bit flag for the existing row is set to off, and the end date is set to the date and time of insertion of the new row.

EmployeeSK	FirstName	LastName	StartDate	EndDate	BitFlag
1	Jenny	Doe	5/25/2012	6/28/2012	0
2	Jenny	Smith	6/28/2012	6/6/2079	1

You can use several methods to accomplish the Type 1 and Type 2 changes. Using SSIS you can implement many frameworks, or you can use the built-in Slowly Changing Dimension task. More details on this task are explained in Chapter 52, "Building, Deploying, and Managing ETL Workflows in Integration Services." If you are not well versed with SSIS and prefer to use T-SQL, you can use the MERGE keyword.

Summary

BI provides a consistent view of the data across the entire organization. In addition, it relieves the contention possibilities and provides a means for historical reporting of your operations data. In the end, your organization has the capability to provide secure and accurate data without the complexities and dependencies on your OLTP system.

The concepts introduced in this chapter should provide a foundation that prepares you to leverage the Integration and Analysis Services chapters in this book.

Building, Deploying, and Managing ETL Workflows in Integration Services

IN THIS CHAPTER

ETL stands for Extract, Transform, and Load, and is most commonly associated with data warehousing; however, many businesses require ETL processes without ever moving into the realm of the data warehouse. For example, a call center that processes the insurance claims of hundreds of insurance companies must import each client companies' location and policy data. That data must live in both systems, and because both systems almost always have different data schemas, you must perform a constant transform process on the data to achieve proper data integrity and synchronization. Enter the ETL developer armed with SSIS.

Integration Services offers a lot of ETL bang for the buck in the world of Enterprise ETL tools. The multitude of new features offered in SSIS in SQL Server 2012 addresses many of the reported complaints about the steep learning curve and the difficulty of using configurations.

What's New in Integration Services for SQL Server 2012?

A lot. SSIS began with SQL Server 2005 as a dramatic rewrite of Data Transformation Services from SQL Server 2000. In addition to an entirely new design environment, SSIS introduced a suite of powerful functionality with the Data Flow Task, a task that merited its own tab in the SSIS Designer. There were a few changes made with the 2008 release; it used memory more efficiently, the scripting environment was changed to VSTA, and C# was added to the scripting environment, but the basics remained largely unchanged.

But for SQL Server 2012, Microsoft's SSIS Product Group spent much time and effort gathering feedback on the use (or lack of use) of SSIS. This feedback resulted in feature changes targeted at easing the learning curve for new users and encouraging adoption by previous reluctant users. Following are the three main categories of the changes:

1. **UI/Usability enhancements:** The "ramp" geared toward easing the SSIS learning curve for new users and slow adopters.

   - A modern look and feel — new icons, round edges. Connection managers have icons on them to indicate they use an expression.

   - A new custom and customizable SSIS toolbox SSIS no longer uses the Visual Studio toolbox, which makes installing Toolbox extensions much more streamlined.

   - Flexible order of authoring; the ability within the data flow designer to edit a component regardless of its connection state. It also enables previously configured components to retain their metadata and provides the Resolve References Editor to remap unresolved columns.

   - Undo and Redo capability.

   - Better copy and paste functionality.

   - Annotations are word-wrap–enabled. No more Control + Enter! They are also stored in plain text instead of binary.

   - Breakpoints are now available inside script components.

2. **SSIS Project Model:** SSIS Projects now contain related packages with the designed intent deployed, configured, and executed related packages as one unit. To this end, a new object called Parameters, which behave much like variables but that can be scoped to the Project level, has been introduced. There is much more on parameters later in this chapter.

3. **SSIS Server improvements:** These changes are geared to the DBA charged with executing ETL packages he/she did not write, and who may be in a locked down environment. There is the new SSISDB catalog, available in the database connection of SSMS; new execution tools inside SSMS to execute packages using the Project Deployment model; and new logging features in SSMS that can be viewed regardless of the logging features programmed in each package.

There are some other enhancements which don't fit neatly into the above three categories. ODBC sources and destinations have been added to the data flow to prepare for Microsoft's planned deprecation of OLE DB. Another recent addition is that Visual Studio configurations can now be used with SSIS.

With the enhancements of SSIS in SQL Server 2012, the changes do not change the core data flow design of SSIS. You apply business logic to ETLs in the same ways as with previous versions; the improvements remove unnecessary impediments, namely the steep learning curve of SSIS and Package Configurations.

Exploring the SSIS Environment in Brief

In order to get a high level view of Integration Services you are going to step through an example. This example will use the AdventureWorks database, available for free download at `www.codeplex.com`.

Imagine that you are a database developer for Adventureworks Bicycles. Business has been fantastic, and the company expanded its sales to an increasing number of outlets. Many websites now carry your bicycles so that you receive Product Reviews from multiple sources, which you must import via text files.

You are tasked with creating the SSIS Project that can load these reviews into the AdventureWorks database, specifically the Production.ProductReview table, as shown in Figure 52-2. You start with one Product Review site: BikesNSuch. The files you receive are named bikesnsuch.txt/. See Figure 52-1 for the file layout. The file contains the ProductNumber, which you must use to locate and load the actual ProductID in the Adventureworks database. The sample file can be downloaded from this book's website.

FIGURE 52-1

The source file. Notice the absence of a ProductID.

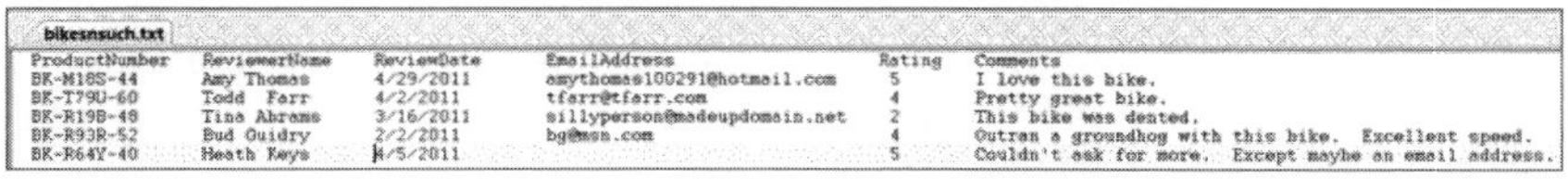

bikesnsuch.txt

ProductNumber	ReviewerName	ReviewDate	EmailAddress	Rating	Comments
BK-M18S-44	Amy Thomas	4/29/2011	amythomas100291@hotmail.com	5	I love this bike.
BK-T79U-60	Todd Farr	4/2/2011	tfarr@tfarr.com	4	Pretty great bike.
BK-R19B-48	Tina Abrams	3/16/2011	sillyperson@madeupdomain.net	2	This bike was dented.
BK-R93R-52	Bud Ouidry	2/2/2011	bg@msn.com	4	Outran a groundhog with this bike. Excellent speed.
BK-R64Y-40	Heath Keys	4/5/2011		5	Couldn't ask for more. Except maybe an email address.

You extract the source file's rows, transform the data to the proper specifications and format, and load it into the Adventureworks database. The transforms include finding the ProductID by ProductNumber and adding the Modified Date.

FIGURE 52-2

Target table in Adventureworks (two views, one including the foreign key reference to Product).

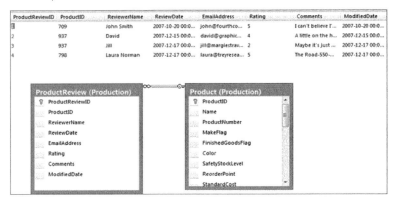

Creating a Basic SSIS Package Inside SQL Server Data Services

You can develop SSIS projects inside a shell of Microsoft Visual Studio called SQL Server Data Tools (SSDT). SSDT is the replacement for Business Intelligence Development Studio. It contains the new SSIS toolbox and other features like the zoom bar on the lower right corner.

1. Open SSDT by clicking Programs ⇨ Microsoft SQL Server 2012 ⇨ SQL Server Data Tools from the Start menu.

2. To start a new project, select File ⇨ New ⇨ Project. If SQL Server is all that you have installed on your machine rather than the entire Visual Studio suite, you see only the Business Intelligence templates as options for projects.

3. Select Integration Services Project from the list of available templates, navigate to the wanted file location in which to create the project, name it, and click OK. Figure 52-3 represents a newly created SSIS project.

On the upper-right side of your environment, you see the Solution Explorer. This is native to Visual Studio. You look at it because SSDT is a shell of Visual Studio. This is where packages are added, named, and deleted from your Project.

Deprecated Feature

The Data Source View has been deprecated in SSIS in SQL Server 2012. The need for Data Source Views has been eliminated by Shared Connection Managers.

The SSIS Designer

In the middle of the environment, you'll see the SSIS Designer, a pale blue area with four (five at run time) tabs:

- **The Control Flow tab**: Contains Containers, Tasks, and Precedence Constraints. The main workflow of a package is defined in the Control Flow. You can drag the Control Flow tab elements onto the designer from the Toolbox, which is explained shortly.

- **The Data Flow tab:** Born from a data flow task on the Control Flow, this tab contains data sources, transformations, and destinations used for moving data from source to target. Every data flow task on the control flow of a package has its own set of configurations available on the Data Flow tab.

  The Control Flow and Data Flow tabs are major players in the SSIS designer; other tabs are as follows:

  - **The Event Handler tab:** Designer for configuring behavior when events occur, for instance, OnError. Contains the same set of tools as available on the Control Flow tab. Event handlers are commonly used for auditing and error handling.

  - **The Package Explorer:** Shows a tree view of all configured elements of a package. Useful for troubleshooting.

  - **Progress/Execution Results tab:** (Not pictured until run time); shows the list of logging events occurring as the package executes in the SSIS Designer. When debugging has ended, the logging history remains as the Execution Results tab. Useful for debugging because error messages are reported here.

FIGURE 52-3

A new project and package.

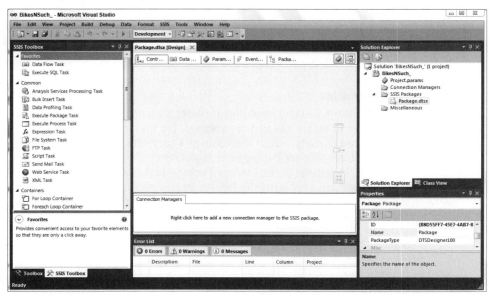

52

The Toolbox

To the left of your screen is the SSIS Toolbox, which is new in SSIS in SQL Server 2012 and native to SSIS. It is no longer the Visual Studio toolbox with SSIS options as in previous versions of SSIS. With the new toolbox, there is also a new button in the upper-right corner of the SSIS Designer that makes the toolbox appear if it is obscured (see Figure 52-4.) You can arrange the items on the toolbox by dragging tasks to different groupings now featured on the toolbox, such as the Favorites group at the top. The default favorites are the Execute SQL tasks and Data Flow tasks because these are indeed the two most commonly used tasks for performing ETL with SSIS.

FIGURE 52-4

The Toolbox button and the Variables button.

If you are not in the Control Flow tab, click there now. Now look at the toolbox. Now click the Data Flow tab beside the Control Flow tab. Now look at the toolbox again. Note the entire contents of the toolbox changed as you moved from the Control Flow tab to the Data Flow tab (see Figure 52-5 for comparing views of the Toolbox). The Control Flow is used to call one or many tasks, one of which can be a data flow task. Data flow tasks actually perform changes on data and move data from sources to destinations. Data flow tasks are comprised of components. The control flow can be thought of as the mechanism to implement an entire logical workflow, whereas the data flow is one task in a control flow.

You can use items from the toolbox by dragging items from the toolbox onto the appropriate design area and configuring them. The Control Flow toolbox is available to the Control Flow and Event Handler tabs, and the Data Flow toolbox is available to the Data Flow tab.

Parameters and Variables

SSIS has always included variables and now includes parameters; both are used throughout SSIS to assign values to properties inside packages. For instance, a variable has always been able to be used to dynamically assign the value of a connection manager based on a list of file names. Now with the Project Deployment Model, the value of that variable could also be passed to a Package Parameter in an Execute Package task. Parameters are the replacements for configurations and are used with the Project Deployment Model. Variables and parameters behave similarly and are configured in much the same manner. The differences are in scope, exposure to change, and properties.

Properties Window

Most objects inside SSIS have a properties window, with configurable properties specific to that element. You can determine Property values at run time through the evaluation of an

Expression. For example, the Connection String property of a Connection Manager can be evaluated by an Expression that includes a variable. The value of the variable can be evaluated at run time, thus changing the value of the connection string.

FIGURE 52-5

The Control Flow and Data Flow Toolboxes, side-by-side.

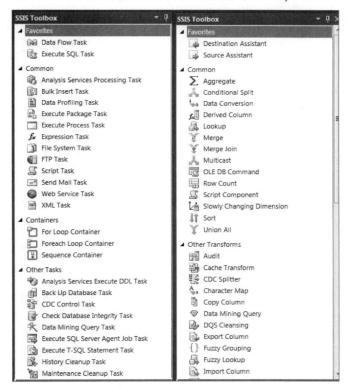

Expressions

You use expressions throughout Integration Services to make properties dynamic. Almost anything that can be hardcoded with a value can be populated in an SSIS package using an expression. The language used to define an expression is called the SSIS Expression Language and is native to SSIS, resembling a cross between C# and Transact-SQL. The Expression Builder editor is available in most places where an expression can be entered.

Connection Managers

In the bottom center of your screen is the area for Connection Managers, which are the wrappers for connection strings and properties required to make a connection at run time.

When the connection is defined by a Connection Manager, it can be referenced by other elements in the package without duplicating the connection definition. Connection managers provide the context for other tasks and components in SSIS. Connection Managers are now available at both the Project and Package level.

Using the UI Enhancements to Easily Configure Package Elements from One Data Flow Task

The following steps can be taken using the AdventureWorks ProductReview example to quickly configure a Data Flow Task, two connection managers, a data flow source, and a data flow destination. This example demonstrates the Usability enhancements in SSIS.

Adding a Data Flow Task to the Control Flow

To add a Data Flow Task to the package:

1. Drag a Data Flow Task from the Control Flow toolbox onto the Control Flow tab.

2. Move to the Data Flow tab by either double-clicking the Data Flow Task or clicking the Data Flow tab.

3. Double-click the Source Assistant, and from the Source Assistant dialog box, choose Flat file under Types; then click OK. The Flat File Connection Manager Editor appears.

4. Configure your General tab to match that in Figure 52-6, where the Filename is the file location you have saved bikesnsuch.txt.

5. On the Advanced tab of the editor, click each column and change it, as shown in Table 52-1 in the DataType and OutputColumnWidth boxes.

TABLE 52-1 **How to Configure Your Flat File (on the Advanced Tab)**

Column	DataType	OutputColumnWidth
ProdNo	Unicode string [DT_WSTR]	50
Name	Unicode string [DT_WSTR]	50
Date	database timestamp [DT_DBTIMESTAMP]	0
EmailAddress	Unicode string [DT_WSTR]	50
Grade	Single byte signed integer [DT_I1]	0
Comments	Unicode string [DT_WSTR]	3850

6. Click OK. A new Connection Manager appears in the Connection Managers pane, and a new Flat File Source appears on the data flow.

FIGURE 52-6

Flat File Connection Manager Editor.

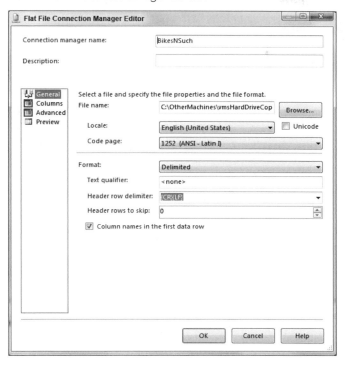

To create the Adventureworks Database destination along with its Connection Manager, execute the following steps:

1. Double-click the Destination Assistant.

2. Select SQL Server, and click OK. The Ole DB connection manager editor appears.

3. Configure it as shown in Figure 52-7, where JASHP is the name of your SQL Server.

4. Click OK.

> **NOTE**
>
> Although OLEDB is still the default connection type that SSIS uses when SQL Server is selected from the Destination Assistant, it should be noted that Microsoft intends to deprecate OLEDB in the future. ODBC is now the preferred connection type for SQL Server. There is now an ODBC Source and Destination available inside the SSIS Data Flow. For more information, see "Microsoft is Aligning with ODBC for Native Relational Data Access" at http://blogs .msdn.com/b/sqlnativeclient/archive/2011/08/29/ microsoft-is-aligning-with-odbc-for-native-relational-data-access.aspx.

FIGURE 52-7

An OLEDB Connection Manager Editor.

You have started with one Data flow task and by moving through a series of dialog boxes, you have easily configured two connection managers, a source in your data flow and a destination in your dataflow. If this were a simple data push where the source schema exactly matched the destination schema, then you could map your columns in the destination, and the package would be complete. But remember that you also have to add the current datetime for the ModifiedDate column, and that you need to look up the ProductID for these reviews based on the Product Number. For this you need Data Flow Transformations. Use a Derived Column to add the modified date and a Lookup transform to perform the "lookup" of the ProductID.

Finishing the Data Flow

To configure the derived column, follow these steps:

1. Drag a derived column transform from the data flow Toolbox onto the Data Flow tab under the Flat File Source.

2. Click the Flat File Source.

3. Drag the green data flow path from the Flat File Source to the Derived Column transform.

4. Double-click the Derived Column transform to open its editor.

5. Enter **ModifiedDate** in the Derived Column Name field.

6. In the Derived Column box, click the drop-down arrow, and select <add as a new column>.

7. Enter **GetDate**() in the Expression Box.

8. Click OK.

To configure the Lookup used to determine ProductID, follow these steps:

1. Drag a Lookup transform from the data flow toolbox onto the Data Flow tab under the Derived Column transform.

2. Click the Derived Column transform.

3. Drag the green data flow path from the Derived Column transform to the Lookup transform.

4. Double-click the Lookup transform to open its editor.

5. Click Connection in the editor.

6. Click the Use Results of a SQL Query button.

7. Click inside the Query Editor.

8. Type: `Select ProductID, ProductNumber from Production.Product.`

9. Click Columns.

10. Click and hold ProdNo from Available Input Columns.

11. Drag to ProductNumber from Available Lookup Columns so that a line connects the two.

12. Click the check box next to ProductID from available Lookup Columns.

13. Click OK.

You now added the ModifedDate and the ProductID columns to the Data Flow in this Data Flow Task. You are ready to map all the columns to the destination and run the package in debug mode.

To finish and map, follow these steps:

1. Click the Lookup transform.

2. Drag the green data flow path from the Lookup transform to the OLE Destination.

3. The Input Output Selection dialog box appears. Click inside the output box, and select Lookup Match Output from the drop-down menu.

4. Double-click the OLE DB Destination to bring up its editor.

5. If not already chosen, choose your AdventureWorks Connection Manager for the OLE DB Connection Manager.

6. Select Production.ProductReview for the Name of the Table or the View.

7. Click Mappings.

8. Either drag or select from the drop-downs in the input boxes for the mappings, as shown in Figure 52-8, and click OK.

FIGURE 52-8

The Destination Mappings tab.

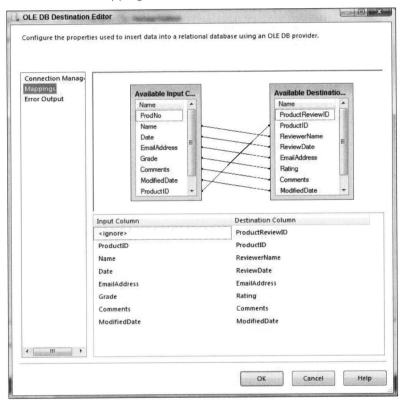

Finishing Touches and Executing Inside SSDT

You have almost completed the development of your first package. Perform these last few steps to complete and test.

1. Get in the habit of good formatting: Select all four of the components in the data flow by holding the control key and clicking them.

2. Click the Format menu. Select MakeSameSize ⇨ Both.

3. Click Format again. Select AutoLayout ⇨ Diagram.

4. To run, go to the solution Explorer and select the package.

5. Right-click and select Execute Package. You see a yellow circle appear in the upper right hand corner of a task to signify beginning, a green circle with a checkmark for success, and although you shouldn't see this for this example, a circle with a red "x" for failure.

6. Check the number of rows loaded by clicking the Data Flow tab.

The package has now been created with all the specified requirements met.

Exploring the SSIS Environment in More Detail

The first section of this chapter gave a quick overview of some basic elements of SSIS. The following section offers a more complete guide to the features of SSIS.

Using Connection Managers

Recall that a connection manager is a wrapper for the connection string and properties required to make a connection at run time. The following sections represent types available and configuration options to consider

What's New in SQL Server 2012

The keystone added feature of SSIS in SQL Server 2012 is the Project Deployment Model, where Projects are now the basic unit of SSIS. To this end, there is now the ability to create Connection Managers at the Project level. You create these once, read from all packages in the Project unlimited. The shared Connection Managers appear bolded inside the packages. Shared Connection Managers have a node under the Project in Solution Explorer. Right-click this node and select New. The Connection Manager Dialog boxes are the same whether you configure a Connection Manager at the project or package level.

Using Database Connection Managers

Defining database connections through one of the available connection managers requires setting a few key properties:

- **Provider:** The driver to be used in accessing the database
- **Server:** The server or filename containing the database to be accessed

- **Initial Catalog:** The default database in a multidatabase source
- **Security:** Database authentication method and any username/password required

The first choice for accessing databases has generally been an OLE DB connection manager using one of the many native providers, including SQL Server, Oracle, Jet (Access), and a long list of other source types. But with SQL Server 2012, Microsoft announced that OLE DB is deprecated. ODBC is now being touted as the preferred access method. Other database connection managers include the following:

- **ADO:** Provides ADO abstractions (such as command and recordset) on top of the OLE DB provider. ADO is not used by Integration Services built-in elements, but it could be required by custom tasks written to the ADO interface.
- **ADO.NET:** Provides ADO.NET abstractions (such as named parameters, data reader, and data set) for the selected database connection. Although not as fast as using OLE DB or ODBC, an ADO.NET connection can execute complex parameterized scripts, provide an in-memory recordset to a Foreach loop, or support custom tasks written using C# or VB.NET.
- **ODBC:** Enables a connection manager to be configured based on an ODBC DSN. This is useful when OLE DB or .NET providers are not available for a given source (for example, Paradox).
- **OLE DB:** The OLE DB connection manager was generally the preferred database connection due to its raw speed. It provides methods for basic parameter substitution but falls short of ADO.NET's flexibility.
- **Analysis Services:** When accessing an existing Analysis Services database, this connection manager is equivalent to an OLE DB connection using the Analysis Services 10.0 provider. Alternatively, an Analysis Services database in the same solution can be referenced — a useful feature for packages developed in support of a new database. If one of the older OLAP providers is needed for some reason, it can be accessed via the OLE DB connection manager.
- **Data Quality Services:** Connection to Data Quality Services, enabling the Data Cleansing task to cleanse columns in the data flow according to rules established in DQS.
- **SQL Server Mobile:** Enables a connection to mobile database .SDF files.

Using File Connection Managers

The following are the many file configuration managers:

- **Flat File:** Presents a text file as if it were a table, with locale and header options. Flat file connection managers can now handle unequal numbers of columns. The file can be in one of four formats:
  - **Delimited:** File data is separated by column (for example, comma) and row delimiters (for example,{CR}{LF}).
  - **Fixed Width:** File data has known sizes without column or row delimiters.

- **Ragged Right:** File data is interpreted using fixed width for all columns except the last, which is terminated by the row delimiter.
- **Multiple Flat Files:** Same as the Flat File connection manager, but it enables multiple files to be selected, either individually or using wildcards. Data then appears as a single large table to Integration Services elements.
- **File:** Identifies a file or folder in the file system without specifying content.
- **Multiple Files:** Same as the file connection manager, but it enables multiple files to be selected, either individually or using wildcards. This type of connection manager can greatly improve speed.
- **Excel:** Identifies a file containing a group of cells that can be interpreted as a table (0 or 1 header rows, data rows below without row, or column gaps).

Using Other Connection Managers

Beyond Database and File connection managers, several other types are provided:

- **Cache:** Defines a data cache location. The cache is first populated using the Cache transform and then used by Lookup transforms within Data Flow tasks. The cache is a write once, read many data store: All the data to be included in the cache must be written by a single Cache transform but can then be used by many Lookup transforms.
- **FTP:** Defines a connection to an FTP server. This is used with the FTP task to move and remove files or create and remove directories using FTP.
- **HTTP:** Defines a connection to a web service. Enter the URL of the WSDL (Web Service Definition) for the web service in question — for example, `http://MyServer/reportserver/reportservice.asmx?wsdl` points to the WSDL for Reporting Services on MyServer. Used with the Web Service task to access Web Service methods.
- **MSMQ:** Defines a connection to a Microsoft Message Queue; used with a Message Queue task to send or receive queued messages.
- **SMO:** Specifies the name and authentication method to be used with Database Transfer tasks (Transfer Objects, Transfer Logins, and so on).
- **SMTP:** Specifies the name of the Simple Mail Transfer Protocol Server for use with the Send Mail task. Older SMTP server versions may not support all the commands necessary to send e-mail from Integration Services.
- **WMI:** Defines a server connection for use with Windows Management Instrumentation tasks, which enable logged and current event data to be collected.

Using Control Flow Elements

The Control Flow tab provides an environment for defining the overall work flow of the package. The control consists of Containers, Tasks, and Precedence Constraints.

Using Containers

Containers provide important features for an Integration Services package, including iteration over a group of tasks and isolation for error and event handling.

The containers available are as follows:

- **TaskHost:** This container is not visible in a package but implicitly hosts any task that is not otherwise enclosed in a container. Understanding this default container helps you understand error and event handler behaviors.

- **Sequence:** This simply contains a number of tasks without any iteration features, but it provides a shared event and error-handling context, provides task grouping for control flow logic, and enables the entire container to be disabled at once during debugging.

- **For Loop:** This container provides the ability to iterate over the contained tasks until an evaluation property evaluates to `false`. It is the SSIS equivalent to programming For Loops.

- **Foreach Loop:** This container provides iteration over the contents of the container based on various lists, or enumerators of items:
    - **File:** Each file in a wildcarded directory command.
    - **Item:** Each item in a manually entered list.
    - **ADO:** Each row in a variable containing an ADO recordset or ADO.NET data set.
    - **ADO.NET Schema Rowset:** Each item in the schema rowset from an ADO connection manager.
    - **Foreach From Variable:** Each item in a variable containing an array. The array is populated programmatically, usually by a script task.
    - **Nodelist:** Each node in an XML XPath result set.
    - **SMO:** List of server objects (such as jobs, databases, file groups).

Choose the enumerator type to be iterated on the Collection page, and then map each item being iterated over to a corresponding variable on the Variable Mapping page.

In addition to containers, the Integration Services Designer also creates task Groups. Define a group by selecting a number of Control Flow items, right-clicking one of the selected items, and choosing Group. This encloses several tasks in a group box that can be collapsed into a single title bar. This group has no properties and cannot participate in the container hierarchy — in short, it is a handy visual device that has no effect on how the package executes.

Using Control Flow Tasks

Tasks that can be included in control flow are as follows:

- **Analysis Services Execute DDL:** Sends Analysis Services Scripting Language (ASSL) scripts to an Analysis Services server to create, alter, or process cube and data mining structures.

- **Analysis Services Processing:** Identifies an Analysis Services database, a list of objects to process, and processing options.

- **Bulk Insert:** Provides the fastest mechanism to load a flat file into a database table without transformations. Similar to the BCP function of SQL. Specify source file and destination table as a minimum configuration. If the source file is a simple delimited file, then specify the appropriate row and column delimiters; otherwise, create and specify a format file that describes the layout of the source file.

- **CDC Control:** Provides a comprehensive set of options for using Change Data Capture enabled tables in your SSIS packages. For more on using, see "CDC in SSIS for SQL Server 2012" at www.mattmasson.com/index.php/2011/12/cdc-in-ssis-for-sql-server-2012-2/?utm_source=rss&utm_medium=rss&utm_campaign=cdc-in-ssis-for-sql-server-2012-2

- **Data Flow:** Provides a flexible structure for loading, transforming, and storing data as configured on the Data Flow tab. See the section "Using Data Flow Components," later in this chapter for the components that you can configure in a Data Flow task. The Data Flow task represents the highest impact change between DTS and SSIS.

- **Data Profiling:** Builds an XML file to contain an analysis of selected tables. Available analyses include null ratio, column length for string columns, statistics for numeric columns, value distribution, candidate keys, and inter-column dependencies. Open the resulting file in the Data Profile Viewer to explore the results. Alternatively, the analysis results can be sent to an XML variable for programmatic inspection as part of a data validation regimen.

- **Data Mining Query:** Runs prediction queries against existing, trained data mining models.

- **Execute Package:** Executes the specified Integration Services package, enabling packages to perform smaller tasks, all controlled by parent packages in the Package Deployment Model, or by Entry point packages in the Project Deployment Model. Execute Package tasks now can choose between referring to an external source (File Connection Manager) or Project References (Parameters) depending on the mode of deployment model. Execute Package tasks using the Project Reference type can set the values of Package Parameters, but cannot set the values of Project Parameters.

- **Execute Process:** Executes an external program or batch file, including PowerShell scripts. Specify the program to be run in the `Executable` property, including the extension (for example, `MyApp.exe`), and the full path if the program is not included in the computer's `PATH` setting (for example, `C:\stuff\MyApp.exe`).

- **Execute SQL:** Runs a SQL script or query, optionally returning results into variables. On the General page of the editor, set the `ConnectionType` and

`Connection` properties to specify which database the query runs against. `SQLSourceType` specifies how to enter the query:

- **Direct Input:** Enter into the `SQLStatement` property by typing in the property page, pressing the ellipses to enter the query in a text box, pressing the Browse button to read the query from a file into the property, or pressing the Build Query button to invoke the Query Builder.

- **File connection:** Specify a file that the query will be read from at run time.

- **Variable:** Specify a variable that contains the query to be run.

A query can be made dynamic by using parameters. Parameter use is limited — only in the `WHERE` clause and, with the exception of ADO.NET connections, only for stored procedure executions or simple queries. If parameters are to be used, then the query is entered with a marker for each parameter to be replaced, and then each marker is mapped to a variable via the Parameter Mapping page. Parameter markers and mapping vary according to connection manager type:

- **OLE DB:** Write the query leaving a ? to mark each parameter location, and then refer to each parameter using its order of appearance in the query to determine a name: 0 for the first parameter, 1 for the second, and so on.

- **ODBC:** Same as OLE DB, except parameters are named starting at 1 instead of 0.

- **ADO:** Write the query using ? to mark each parameter location, and specify any non-numeric parameter name for each parameter. For ADO, it is the order in which the variables appear on the mapping page (and not the name) that determines which parameter they replace.

- **ADO.NET:** Write the query as if the parameters were variables declared in Transact-SQL (for example, `SELECT name FROM mytable WHERE id = @ID`), and then refer to the parameter by name for mapping.

The `ResultSet` property (General page) specifies how query results are returned to variables:

- **None:** Results are not captured.

- **Single row:** Results from a singleton query can be stored directly into variables. On the Result Set tab, map each result name returned by the query to the corresponding target variable. As with input parameters, result names vary according to connection manager type.

- **Full result set:** Multiple-row result sets are stored in a variable of type `Object` for later use with a Foreach loop container or other processing. On the Result Set tab, map a single result name of 0 (zero) to the object variable, with a result type of Full Result Set.

- **XML:** Results are stored in an XML DOM document for later use with a Foreach loop container or other processing. On the Result Set tab, map a single result name of 0 (zero) to the object variable, with a result type of Full Result Set.

- **Expression Task:** Provides a way to add a value into the package using an expression that is always evaluated at run time.

- **File System Task:** Provides a number of file (copy, delete, move, rename, and set attributes) and folder (copy, create, delete, delete content, and move) operations. Source and destination files/folders can be specified by either a File connection manager or a string variable that contains the path.

- **FTP:** Supports a commonly used subset of FTP functionality, including send/ receive/delete files and create/remove directories.

- **Message Queue:** Sends or receives queued messages via MSMQ. Specify the message connection, send or receive, and the message type.

- **Script:** This task enables either Visual Basic 2010 or Visual C# 2010 code to be embedded in a task. Properties include the following:

- **ScriptLanguage:** Choose which language to use to create the task.

- **ReadOnlyVsariables/ReadWriteVariables:** List the read and read/write variables to be accessed within the script, separated by commas, in these properties. Entries are case-sensitive, so myvar and MyVar are considered different variables.

- **EntryPoint:** Name of the class that contains the entry point for the script. There is normally no reason to change the default name.

See "Coding and Debugging the Script Task , Interacting with the Package in the Script Task" at http://msdn.microsoft.com/en-us/library/ms135952(v=sql.110).aspx in SQL Server 2012 Books Online for additional details.

- **Send Mail:** Sends a text-only SMTP e-mail message. Specify the SMTP configuration manager and all the normal e-mail fields (To, From, and so on). Separate multiple addresses by commas (not semicolons).

- **Transfer Database Objects Tasks:** All use SMO Connection Managers.

  - **Transfer Database:** Copies or moves an entire database between SQL Server instances

  - **Transfer Error Messages:** Transfers custom error messages (via sp_ addmessage) from one server to another

  - **Transfer Jobs:** Copies SQL Agent jobs from one SQL Server instance to another

  - **Transfer Logins:** Copies logins from one SQL Server instance to another

  - **Transfer Master Stored Procedures:** Copies any custom stored procedures from the master database on one server to the master database on another server

  - **Transfer Objects:** Copies any database-level object from one SQL Server instance to another

- **Web Service:** Executes a web service call, storing the output in either a file or a variable.

- **WMI Data Reader:** Executes a Windows Management Instrumentation (WQL) query against a server to retrieve event log, configuration, and other management information.

- **WMI Event Watcher:** Similar to a WMI data reader but instead of returning data, the task waits for a WQL specified event to occur. When the event occurs or the task times out, the SSIS task events `WMIEventWatcherEventOccurred` or `WMIEventWatcherEventTimeout` can fire, respectively.

- **XML:** Performs operations on XML documents, including comparing two documents (diff), merging two documents, applying diff output (diffgram) to a document, validating a document against a DTD, and performing XPath queries or XSLT transformations. Choose a source document as direct input, a file, or a string variable, and an output as a file or a string variable. Set other properties as appropriate for the selected `OperationType`.

Deprecated Features

ActiveX tasks and Execute DTS Package tasks were deprecated in SSIS in SQL Server 2012.

Using Control Flow Precedence

Precedence constraints determine the order in which tasks execute. Select any task or container to expose its precedence constraint arrow, and then drag that arrow to the task that should follow it, repeating until all items are appropriately related. Any unconstrained task can be run at the discretion of the runtime engine in an unpredictable and often parallel ordering. Each constraint defaults to an On Success constraint, which you can adjust by double-clicking the constraint to reveal the Precedence Constraint Editor, as shown in Figure 52-9.

The upper half of the editor, Constraint options, determines when the constraint should fire. It relies on two evaluation operation concepts:

- **Constraint:** How the previous item completed — Success, Failure, or Completion (Completion being any outcome, either success or failure)

- **Expression:** The evaluation of the entered expression, which must resolve to either `true` or `false`

These concepts are combined as four separate options — constraint, expression, expression and constraint, expression or constraint — enabling flexible constraint construction. For example, consider a task that processes a previously loaded table of data and counts the successfully processed rows. The processing task could have two outgoing paths: a success path indicating that the task was successful and that the processed rowcount matches the loaded rowcount, and a failure path indicating that either the task failed or the rowcounts don't match.

FIGURE 52-9

The Precedence Constraint Editor.

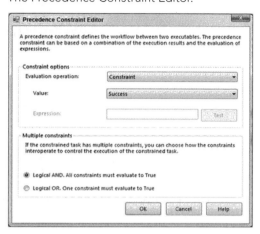

The lower half of the editor, labeled Multiple constraints, determines how the downstream tasks should deal with multiple incoming arrows. If logical AND is chosen (the default), then all the incoming constraints must fire before the task can execute. If logical OR is chosen, then any incoming constraint firing causes the task to execute. Logical AND is the most frequently used behavior, but logical OR is useful for work flows that split apart and then rejoin. For example, control can split when an upstream task has both success and failure branches, but the failure branch needs to rejoin the normal processing after the error has been resolved. Using a logical AND at the merge point would require both the success and the failure branches to execute before the next task could run, which cannot happen by definition. Logical AND constraints are presented visually as solid lines, whereas logical OR constraints are dotted lines.

The arrows that represent precedence constraints provide other visual clues as to the type of constraint. Green arrows denote a success constraint, red a failure constraint, and blue a completion constraint. Constraints that use an expression include an f(x) icon. There is no visual queue to distinguish between a Constraint AND expression versus a Constraint OR expression, so it is best to double-check the Precedence Constraint Editor when an f(x) displays. For example, a green arrow with an f(x) displayed could fire even if the preceding task had failed, given that the expression had been satisfied and the Constraint OR expression option was chosen.

Using Data Flow Components

This section describes the individual components that you can configure within a Data Flow task: sources of data for the flow, destinations that output the data, and optional transformations that can change the data in between.

Using the Data Flow to Move Your Data

Unlike other tasks that you can configure in the control flow, a Data Flow task does not show an Editor dialog in response to an edit request. Instead, it switches to the Data Flow tab to view/configure the task details. Each component appearing on the design surface can in turn be configured in the Properties pane, by a component-specific editor dialog, and, for many components, by an advanced editor as well.

Each data flow must begin with at least one Data Flow source, and generally ends with one or more Data Flow destinations, providing a source and sink for the data processed within the task. Between source and destination, any number of transformations may be configured to sort, convert, aggregate, or otherwise change the data.

Out of each source or transformation, a green Data Flow path arrow is available to connect to the next component. Place the next component on the design surface, and connect it to the path before attempting to configure the new component, as the path provides necessary meta-data for configuration. Follow a similar process for the red error flow for any component that has been configured to redirect error rows. Figure 52-10 shows the Data Flow created earlier.

FIGURE 52-10

The Data Flow from Product.ProductReview.

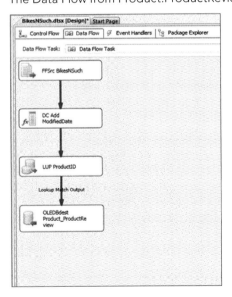

Use the Data Flow Path Editor to view/configure paths as necessary, double-clicking a path to invoke its editor. The editor has three pages:

- **General:** For name, description, and annotation options. Although the default annotations are usually adequate, consider enabling additional annotations for more complex flows with intertwined paths.
- **Metadata:** Displays metadata for each column in the Data Flow path, including data type and source component. This information is read-only, so adjust upstream components as necessary to make changes, or use a Data Conversion transformation to perform necessary conversions.
- **Data Viewers:** Enables different types of Data Viewers to be attached to the path for testing and debugging.

Understanding SSIS Sources

Data Flow sources supply the rows of data that flow through the Data Flow task. Each source has two different editing options: Edit (basic) and Show Advanced Editor; although in some cases the basic Edit option displays the Advanced Editor anyway. The common steps to configuring a source are represented by the pages of the basic editor:

- **Connection Manager:** Specify the particular table, files, view, or query that provides the data for this source.
- **Columns:** Choose which columns appear in the data flow. Optionally, change the default names of the columns in the data flow.
- **Error Output:** Specify what to do for each column should an error occur.

The advanced editor provides the same capabilities as the basic editor in a different format, plus much finer control over input and output columns, including names and data types. Table 52-2 outlines available Data Flow Sources.

TABLE 52-2 **Data Flow Sources**

Source	Definition
ADO Net	Uses an ADO.NET connection manager to read database data, either by identifying a database object or entering a query to execute.
CDC Source	Uses an ADO.NET connection manager to read database data from a SQL Server CDC enabled table.
Excel	Uses an Excel connection manager and either a worksheet or named ranges as tables. Data types are assigned to each column by sampling the first few rows but can be adjusted using the advanced editor.
Flat File	Requires a Flat File connection manager. Delimited files translate zero-length strings into null values for the data flow when the RetainNulls property is true.
Ole DB	Requires an OLE DB connection manager.
Raw File	Often used when data processed by one stage of a package needs to be stored and reused by a later stage.

Continues

1177

TABLE 52-2 *(continued)*

Source	Definition
XML	Reads a simple XML file and presents it to the data flow as a table, using either an inline schema (a header in the XML file that describes the column names and data types) or an XSD (XML Schema Definition) file. The XML source does not use a connection manager; instead, specify the input filename and then either specify an XSD file or indicate that the file contains an inline schema.
Script	A script component can act as a source, destination, or transformation of a data flow. Use a script as a source to generate test data or to format a complex external source of data. Search for the topic "Extending the Data Flow with the Script Component" in SQL Server Books Online for full code samples and related information.

Understanding SSIS Destinations

Data Flow destinations provide a place to write the data transformed by the Data Flow task. Configuring destinations is similar to configuring sources, including both basic and advanced editors, and the three common steps:

- **Connection Manager:** Specify the particular table, files, view, or query to which data will be written.

- **Columns:** Map the columns from the data flow (input) to the appropriate destination columns.

- **Error Output:** Specify what to do should a row fail to insert into the destination: Ignore the row, cause the component to fail (default), or redirect the problem row to error output.

Table 52-3 outlines available Data Flow Destinations.

TABLE 52-3 **Data Flow Destinations**

Destination	Definition
ADO Net	Uses an ADO.NET connection manager to write data to a selected table or view.
	New since R2, ADO.NET destinations now has option Use Bulk Insert When Possible, which mimics the OLE DB *fast load*.
DataReader	Makes the data flow available via an ADO.NET DataReader, which can be opened by other applications, notably Reporting Services, to read the output from the package.
Dimension Processing	Enables the population of Analysis Services dimensions without first populating the underlying relational data source.
	Identify the Analysis Services connection manager of interest, choose the desired dimension, and then select a processing mode.

Destination	Definition
Excel	Sends rows from the data flow to a sheet or range in a workbook using an Excel connection manager. Strings are required to be Unicode, so any DT_STR types need to be converted to DT_WSTR before reaching the Excel destination.
Flat File	Writes the data flow to a file specified by a Flat File connection manager. Choose whether to overwrite any existing file and provide file header text if wanted.
Ole DB	Writes rows to a table, view, or SQL command (ad hoc view) for which an OLE DB driver exists. Table/view names can be selected directly in the destination or read from a string variable, and each can be selected with or without fast load. Fast load can decrease run time by an order of magnitude or more depending on the particular data set and selected options.
Partition Processing	Enables the population of Analysis Services partitions without first populating the underlying relational data source.
Raw File	Writes rows from the data flow to an Integration Services format suitable for fast loads by a raw source component. It does not use a connection manager; instead, specify the AccessMode by choosing to supply a filename via direct input or a string variable. Useful for increasing performance.
Recordset	Writes the data flow to a variable. Stored as a recordset, the object variable is suitable for use as the source of a Foreach loop or other processing within the package.
Script	A script can also be used as a destination. Use a script as a destination to format output in a manner not allowed by one of the standard destinations. For example, a file suitable for input to a COBOL program could be generated from a standard data flow.
SQL Server	This destination uses the same fast-loading mechanism as the Bulk Insert task but is restricted in that the package must execute on the SQL Server that contains the target table/view. Speed can exceed OLE DB fast loading in some circumstances.
SQL Server Compact	Writes rows from the data flow into a SQL Mobile database table.

Understanding SSIS Transformations

Between the source and the destination, transformations provide functionality to change the data from what was read into what is needed. Each transformation requires one or more data flows as input and provides one or more data flows as output. Like sources and destinations, many transformations provide a way to configure error output for rows that fail the transformation. In addition, many transformations provide both a basic and an advanced editor to configure the component, with normal configurations offered by the basic editor when available.

> **TIP**
>
> You need to understand features of transforms when choosing them. Some transforms are fully blocking, which means that SSIS must read the entire data flow into memory before it can release any rows, greatly degrading performance. See "Integration Services: Performance Tuning Techniques" at `http://technet.microsoft.com/en-us/library/cc966529.aspx` for more information.

The standard transformations available in the Data Flow task are shown in Table 52-4.

TABLE 52-4 **Data Flow Transformations**

Transform	Definition/Use
Aggregate	Functions rather like a GROUP BY query in SQL, generating Min, Max, Average, and such on the input data flow. Due to the nature of this operation, Aggregate does not pass through the data flow but outputs only aggregated rows.
Audit	Adds execution context columns to the data flow, enabling data to be written with audit information about when it was written and where it came from. Available columns are ExecutionInstanceGUID, PackageID, PackageName, VersionID, ExecutionStartTime, MachineName, UserName, TaskName, and TaskID.
Cache	Places selected columns from a data flow into a cache for later use by a Lookup transform. Identify the Cache connection manager and then map the data flow columns into the cache columns as necessary. The cache is a write once, read many data store: All the data to be included in the cache must be written by a single Cache transform but can then be used by many Lookup transforms.
CDC Splitter	Splits data from a data flow into inserts, updates, or deletes based on info obtained from a CDC enabled table.
Character Map	Enables strings in the data flow to be transformed by a number of operations: Byte reversal, Full width, Half width, Hiragana, Katakana, Linguistic casing, Lowercase, Simplified Chinese, Traditional Chinese, and Uppercase.
Conditional Split	Enables rows of a data flow to be split between different outputs depending on the contents of the row. Configure by entering output names and expressions in the editor. When the transform receives a row, each expression is evaluated in order, and the first one that evaluates to true receives that row of data. When none of the expressions evaluate to true, the default output (named at the bottom of the editor) receives the row.
Copy Column	Adds a copy of an existing column to the data flow.

Transform	Definition/Use
Data Conversion	Adds a copy of an existing column to the data flow, enabling data type conversions in the process.
Data Cleansing	New with SQL Server 2012, this task cleanses data in the data flow by using a Data Quality Services Connection. Rows can be mapped to DQS Domains and either corrected according to rules or simply marked as violations of rules.
Data Mining Query	Runs a DMX query for each row of the data flow, enabling rows to be associated with predictions, such as the likelihood that a new customer makes a purchase or the probability that a transaction is fraudulent.
Derived Column	Uses expressions to generate values that can either be added to the data flow or replace existing columns.
Export Column	Writes large object data types (DT_TEXT, DT_NTEXT, or DT_IMAGE) to files specified by a filename contained in the data flow. For example, large text objects could be extracted into different files for inclusion in a website or text index.
Fuzzy Grouping	Identifies duplicate rows in the data flow using exact matching for any data type and fuzzy matching for string data types (DT_STR and DT_WSTR).
Fuzzy Lookup	Similar to the Lookup transform, except that when an exact lookup fails, a fuzzy lookup is attempted for any string columns (DT_STR and DT_WSTR).
Import Column	Reads large object data types (DT_TEXT, DT_NTEXT, or DT_IMAGE) from files specified by a filename contained in the data flow, adding the text or image objects as a new column in the data flow.
Lookup	Finds rows in a database table or cache that match the data flow and includes selected columns in the data flow, much like a join between the data flow and a table or cache. For example, a product ID could be added to the data flow by looking up the product name in the master table.
Merge	Combines the rows of two sorted data flows into a single data flow. For example, if some of the rows of a sorted data flow are split by an error output or Conditional Split transform, then they can be merged again. Rows in the data flow must be sorted, either by using advanced editor of ole db source or the sort component.
Merge Join	Provides SQL join functionality between data flows sorted on the join columns. Rows in the data flow must be sorted by using the method described for the merge transform.
Multi Cast	Copies every row of an input data flow to many different outputs.
Ole DB Command	Executes a SQL statement (such as UPDATE or DELETE) for every row in a data flow, row-by-row. Use with caution because this is a slow transform.

52

Continues

TABLE 52-4 *(continued)*

Transform	Definition/Use
Percentage Sampling	Splits a data flow by randomly sampling the rows for a given percentage. For example, this could be used to separate a data set into training and testing sets for data mining.
Pivot	Denormalizes a data flow, similar to the way an Excel pivot table operates, making attribute values into columns.
Row Count	Counts the number of rows in a data flow and places the result into a variable. Configure by populating the VariableName property.
Row Sampling	Nearly identical to the Percentage Sampling transform, except that the approximate number of rows to be sampled is entered, rather than the percentage of rows.
Script Component	Using a script as a transformation enables transformations with complex logic to act on a data flow.
Slowly Changing Dimension	Compares the data in a data flow to a dimension table, and, based on the roles assigned to particular columns, maintains the dimension. This component is unusual in that it does not have an editor; instead, a wizard guides you through the steps to define column roles and interactions with the dimension table. At the conclusion of the wizard, several components are placed on the design surface to accomplish the dimension maintenance task.
Sort	Sorts the rows in a data flow by selected columns. Configure by selecting the columns to sort by. Then, in the lower pane, choose the sort type, the sort order, and the comparison flags appropriate to the data being sorted. This is a fully blocking transform; it can adversely affect performance.
Term Extraction	Builds a new data flow based on terms it finds in a Unicode text column (DT_WSTR or DT_NTEXT). This is the training part of text mining, whereby strings of a particular type generate a list of commonly used terms, which is later used by the Term Lookup component to identify similar strings.
Term Lookup	Provides a "join" between a Unicode text column (DT_WSTR or DT_NTEXT) in the data flow and a reference table of terms built by the Term Extraction component.
Union All	Combines rows from multiple data flows into a single data flow, assuming the source columns are of compatible types. Configure by connecting as many data flows as needed to the component. Then, using the editor, ensure that the correct columns from each data flow are mapped to the appropriate output column.
Unpivot	Makes a data flow more normalized by turning columns into attribute values. For example, a data flow with one row for each quarter and a column for revenue by region could be turned into a three-column data flow: Quarter, Region, and Revenue.

What's New in SQL Server 2012

Flexible order of authoring and the Resolve References Window. SSIS in SQL Server 2012 is now more forgiving in situations where remapping the columns in a data flow is required. The new Flexible Order of Authoring enables configuring of data flow components even without metadata, and the Resolve References Editor, as shown in Figure 52-11, enables quick remapping of columns in the Data Flow.

FIGURE 52-11

The Resolve References editor.

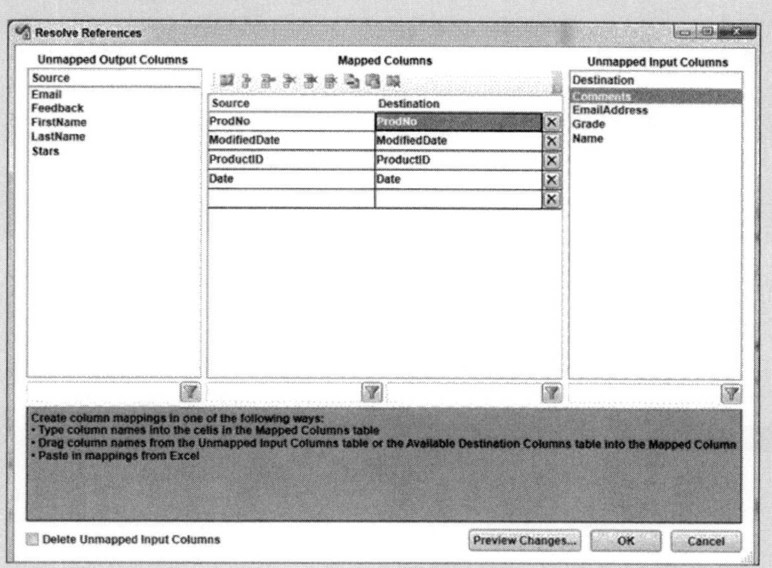

Using Parameters and Variables

Parameters and variables are configured in the Parameters and Variables window. For packages, this can be reached by clicking on the Parameters tab in the middle of the SSIS Designer.

For Project level parameters, click on the Project.params button directly below your project in the Solution Explorer window (see Figure 52-12).

Creating and Using Parameters to Set Values

Parameters and the Project Deployment Model represent the single biggest change to SSIS in SQL Server 2012. Parameters behave like read-only variables, they are the replacements for Configurations, and they are used to assign values to properties inside packages.

1183

Things to consider:

- Parameters can be used only with the Project Deployment model.
- Parameters are read-only at design time; their values can be set at deployment and execution. Package Parameter values can be set by Execute Package tasks.
- Parameters can be scoped to the Project level or the Package level.
- To distinguish them from Variables, Parameters are prefixed by a $, followed by either Project or Package to indicate the scope. Thus, if there were a Project Parameter, a Package Parameter, and a User Variable, each with the name Foo, then they appear as $Project::Foo , $Package::Foo, and User::Foo, respectively, under the variables node in the Expression Builder.

You create and configure project parameters in the Project Parameters Editor, shown in Figure 52-12. To open this, click the project.params button in Solution Explorer. It is located underneath the Miscellaneous folder.

To create Package level parameters, click on the third tab in the SSIS designer, between the Data Flow and the Event Handlers tabs. In both of these editors, click on Add Parameter button to add a new parameter.

FIGURE 52-12

The Project Parameters Editor.

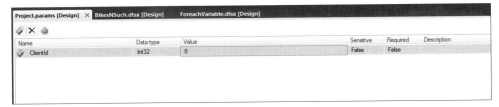

The options for configuring Parameters are as follows:

- **Name:** Give the parameter a meaningful name.
- **Datatype:** Assign the proper datatype.
- **Value:** Default Design time value.
- **SensitiveOnServer:** All SSIS Projects are deployed to the SSIS catalog. The SensitiveOnServer flag indicates whether the parameter receives special treatment to hide its value. If flagged yes, it is encrypted at the time of deployment and masked in UI, and its value is not available in logs.
- **Required:** This flag signifies whether the value of the Parameter must be changed from its Default design-time value at run time. This is a useful property, which is

aimed at preventing packages from running with default values, like accidentally running a production package in a test environment.

Parameters have types of values. Their significance is as follows:

- **Value:** Design time value.
- **Override Values:** Default value can be overridden at run time. You can flag a project to fail if this does not occur.

The methods to change the value of a Parameter are as follows:

- Through the Project Deployment process, a new value can be sent with the deployment to the server.
- In an Execution of a package using the Project Deployment model in SSMS.
- Using new Environments and Environment Variables inside the SSIS Server/Catalog.
- Through an Execute Package task using the Project reference type.

Variables

SSIS has variables just like most programming languages, and they are used throughout SSIS to assign values to properties inside packages. Variables and Parameters behave similarly and you configure them in much the same manner. The differences are in scope, exposure to change, and properties.type="general."

New System Variable: ServerExecutionID

New with SSIS in SQL Server 2012 is the system variable named ServerExecutionID. This variable will record the Execution ID of the project as it is being run from inside the SSIS catalog. It enables developers to synchronize their custom logging with the new logging features available through the catalog.

Variables have two namespaces, System and User. System Variables come predefined and are useful for standard metadata collection. For instance, the System Variable UserName captures the username at package run time. Variable names include the namespace; thus all system variables appear with the word System followed by two colons. User variables are defined using the Variables editor. Their name includes the word User; thus, the user-defined Variable Foo appears as User::Foo.

To create a new user variable, click on the variables button in the upper right corner of the SSIS designer, right beside the toolbox button. You may also select it from SSIS ⇨ Variables. Once the variables dialog box opens, click on the Add Variable button in the upper left corner.

The options for configuring User Variables are as follows:

- **Name:** The name assigned to your variable.
- **Scope:** Variable scope used to be determined by the selected object in the control flow at the moment of creation, but now all variables default to being at the Package level — an improvement. There is also now a Move Variable button that changes the scope of a variable if necessary.
- **Datatype:** The SSIS datatype. For a comprehensive look at SSIS datatypes as well as a discussion on equivalency between SSIS datatypes and SQL Server datatypes see `http://msdn.microsoft.com/en-us/library/ms141036.aspx`.
- **Value:** A default value that can easily be overwritten by a number of methods. Variables are read/write, whereas Parameters are read-only during package execution.

The other buttons available in the variables window include a Move Variable button used for changing a variable's scope (new with SQL Server 2012), a Delete Variable button and the Grid Options button, which enables you to see all the properties of the variables, including seeing all system variables.

Variables can and are used to determine values during a package's execution. The methods to change the value of a Variable are as follows:

- Through the result set of an Execute SQL task
- Through the configuration of For and ForEach Loop Containers
- Through Script Tasks and Components
- With an Expression, which can include a Parameter reference and often does
- With a package using Package Deployment Model, with the Set parameter in the DTEXEC command line interface

Using The SSIS Expression Language

You used a simple expression in the example to create the ModifiedDate column in the data flow. This expression was written using the SSIS Expression Language, which you can use throughout the SSIS environment anywhere a value must be formulaically evaluated. Some of the key characteristics of the SSIS Expression Language include the following:

- Parameters and Variables are referred to by prefixing them with an @, making `@[User::foo]` the fully qualified reference to the user variable `foo`, and `@[$Project::foo]` the reference to the Project Parameter `foo`. Columns are referred to by their name and can be qualified by their source name, making `[BikesNSuch].[Name]` the fully qualified reference to the `Name` column read from the `BikesNSuch` connection manager.
- Operators are C-like, including `==` (double equal signs) for equality tests, prefix of an exclamation mark for not (for example, `!>` and `!=`), `&&` for logical AND, `||` for logical OR, and `?` for conditional expressions (think `IIf()` function). For example,

@[User::foo] == 17 && CustomerID < 100 returns true if the variable foo equals 17 AND the CustomerID column is less than 100.

- String constants are enclosed in double quotes, and special characters are C-like backslash escape sequences, such as \n for new line and \t for tab.

- The cast operator works by describing the target type in parentheses immediately before the value to be converted. For example, (DT_I4)"193" will convert the string "193" to a four-byte integer. The cast operator is often used inside a Derived Column transform to achieve data conversions, often with other logic in the expression.

- Functions mostly come from the Transact-SQL world, including the familiar date (GETDATE(), DATEADD(), YEAR()), string (SUBSTRING(), REPLACE(), LEN()), and mathematical (CEILING(), SIGN()) entries. Newly added with this release is the familiar T-SQL ISNULL() expression. Details in syntax sometimes do differ from standard T-SQL, however, so use the Expression Builder, as shown in Figure 52-13, or Books Online to check availability and syntax.

FIGURE 52-13

The ever-helpful Expression Builder.

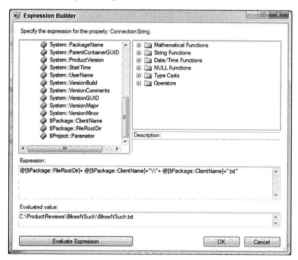

Using Package Logging

Because many packages are destined for unattended operation, generating an execution log is an excellent method for tracking operations and collecting debug information. To configure package level, customized logging for a package at its design time, right-click the package design surface; and choose Logging. On the Providers and Logs tab, add a provider for each output type that will be logged (multiple are allowed). On the Details tab, specify the events for which log entries will be written; the advanced view, also enables selecting which columns will be included in each event's log entry.

The tree view in the left pane represents the container hierarchy of the package. The check boxes correspond to each object's LoggingMode property: clear for Disabled, a black check for Enabled, and a gray check for UseParentSetting (logging settings inherited from the parent). By default, all objects inherit from the package settings. Highlighting an item in the tree displays the details for that object in the current tab. Providers can be configured only for the package, and any object with UseParentSetting will have its options grayed out in deference to its parents' settings.

The standard log providers are as follows:

- **Text File:** Writes a comma-separated-value text file. Configure with an appropriate File connection manager.
- **SQL Profiler:** Writes a .TRC file that can be viewed in the Profiler application.
- **SQL Server:** Writes log entries to the dbo.sysssislog table in the database indicated by the associated OLE DB connection manager. Any database can be chosen to host this table. If the table does not exist, then it will be created on first use.
- **Event Log:** Writes log entries to the Windows application event log on the computer that executes the package. No configuration is required.
- **XML File:** Writes an .XML file. Configure with an appropriate File connection manager.

After you construct a useful set of event/column combinations, save it as a template and reload on other packages.

Deploying and Executing Projects and Packages

Once a package is developed and working properly, it must be deployed to a server where it can be executed to perform its designated tasks. In this section the new Project Deployment Model is explained, as well as the Package Deployment Model (sometimes referred to as Legacy or File deployment).

Using the Package Deployment Model

Package Configurations used to be the only way to enable developers to quickly deploy packages between servers and environments, providing a way to set properties within the package based on environment-specific configurations. Although effective, the learning curve for this method of configuring packages proved to be one of the most challenging features to learn. There are, however, countless multipackage solutions deployed to production systems at this moment that utilize this deployment model, and therefore this method deserves careful consideration.

To access Package configurations, first make sure that your project is in Package Deployment Mode. The words (package deployment model) will be beside the project name in Solution Explorer. If it is not in package deployment mode, change it by right clicking on the project and selecting Convert to Package Deployment Model from the menu. Open the Configurations dialog box by going to the SSIS menu. Select SSIS ⇨ Package Configurations. Configurations are applied to the package in the order they are listed here. To add a new configuration, ensure that configurations are enabled by clicking the box beside Enable package configurations, and click Add to start the Package Configuration Wizard. Choose the desired Configuration Type (storage location). There are essentially three categories to consider:

- **Registry and Environment Variable:** These types can hold a single property only.
- **XML File and SQL Server Table:** Each of these configuration types can hold any number of property settings.
- **Parent Package Variable:** Enables access to the contents of a single variable from the calling package.

On Indirect Configurations

Although complicated, you can effectively use file configurations to make File Deployments to internal environments, such as Test, QA, and Production, seamless. At the beginning of development, you can set up an indirect File configuration to reference an Environment Variable on each server, with those environment variables having the same name. The Environment variable on each server contains the location of the XML File on that server, which in turn contains the rest of the configurations for that specific server. After you successfully implement the configurations, you can deploy packages to each environment without the developer needing to manually configure a connection manager again. See "Adding Package Configurations" at http://msdn.microsoft.com/en-us/library/ms365339 .aspx for more information.

Most configuration types enable the storage location to be identified either directly or via an environment variable. The environment variable approach can be useful when the storage location (such as file directory) must change between environments. When the configuration type and location are specified, the Select Properties to Export option enables the properties that change between environments to be chosen. Complete the wizard by reviewing the selections and giving the configuration a name.

You can reuse configurations between packages if the names of the objects containing the properties to be set are the same between packages. For example, packages that use the same names for their connection managers could share a configuration that sets server names or filenames. To share a configuration in a subsequent package, choose the same configuration type, and then specify the same storage location (for example, XML filename) as the initial package. When prompted by a dialog warning that the configuration already exists, select Reuse Existing.

Converting to the Project Model from the Package (Legacy) Model

Pre-SQL Server 2012 SSIS solutions often involved Parent Child Packages, which were deployed using Configurations and Parent Package Variables. To allow these solutions to take advantage of the new Project Model, there is a Project Conversion Wizard available to step through a conversion to the Project model. This wizard accepts a Project as input and converts all execute package tasks to use Project References, and all configurations to use Project or Package level Parameters. Note that after a project converts, it can no longer use Configurations.

Using the Project Deployment Model

SSIS developers have often created projects containing related packages. But at deployment time, the packages and their connection managers were atomic. Preserving any dependencies between packages at deployment had to be done manually. The new Project Deployment Model attempts to remedy this by treating an entire Project and all its Packages, Parameters, and connection managers as one unit throughout development, deployment, and executions.

Using the Build button in SSIS now actually compiles a new file, which has the extension .ispac. Create an .ispac file by clicking Project ➪ Build. An .ispac file is created, which is saved to the bin folder under your project. (You can change this location by going to project ➪ Project Properties ➪ ConfigurationProperties ➪ Build on the Right Outputs ➪ outputpath.)

Using the Project Deployment Model, SSIS Projects can be deployed only to SQL Servers, specifically to the new SSIS catalog, called SSISDB. (Packages using the package deployment model can still be deployed to the MSDB system database.)

> **NOTE**
> To successfully start and use the SSIS catalog, you must enable CLR on the SQL Server. You can do this via a prompt that appears while configuring the catalog, or you can enable it by executing:
>
> ```
> sp_configure 'clr enabled', 1;
> GO
> RECONFIGURE
> GO
> ```
>
> For more information on configuring the SSIS catalog for initial use, see "Create the SSISDB Catalog" at http://msdn.microsoft.com/en-us/library/gg471509(v=sql.110).aspx.

The steps for deploying a Project to the catalog from SSDT are as follows:

1. Click Project ⇨ Build.
2. Click Project ⇨ Deploy.
3. The Integration Services Deployment Wizard appears (Figure 52-14).

This wizard guides you through the following:

- Selecting the project (either .ispac file from a build or one already deployed from the catalog)
- Choosing on which SSIS Server to deploy
- Choosing in which Project folder in the SSIS Catalog to deploy
- Overriding the values of any Parameters with the deployment to be used at Execution

FIGURE 52-14

Deploying using the Integration Services Deployment Wizard.

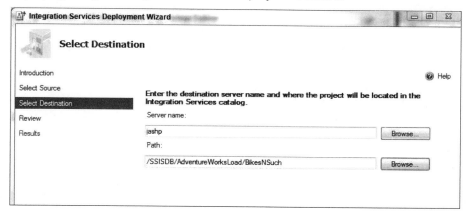

Projects are deployed to the SSIS Server, which is visible under the Database Engine Connections in SSMS. It is no longer necessary to connect to Integration Services from SSMS. After a project deploys, the project folder on the server contains a directory for the project and its packages and another subfolder for Environments, as shown in Figure 52-15. Environments are explained shortly.

Using the SSIS Server to Execute Projects and Packages

Now that you have read the steps required for deploying a project to the SSIS Server/ SSISDB Catalog, you can take a good look at the features inside it. These include:

- **Environments:** Containers for sets of a new type of variable. You create these new Environment Variables inside Environments.

- **Executions:** A configuration for the execution of a package, including the overridden values of Parameters, Connection Managers, and the Environment to run a package.

- **Encryption:** Of Parameters and Connection Managers.

- **Row Level Security:** Projects deploy to the server in Project folders; security can be administered much more granularly at this level or at the server level.

- **Logging:** Of package executions available on the server. A new dashboard is available after packages are executed on the SSIS Server. The log displays success and failure messages and warnings, as well as the values of parameters and has rich data visualizations.

FIGURE 52-15

SSMS folder with deployed project.

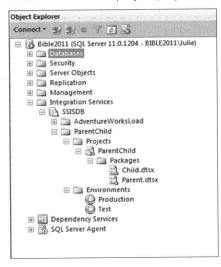

NOTE

Because an instance of SSIS is now tied to the SQL instance in SSMS, you no longer connect to SSIS to manage it.

Configuring a Project in the SSIS Server

Packages are run by creating an Execution. An Execution runs using the configured values set inside the SSIS Server. To configure an execution for a project, right-click the project from the project folder, and click Properties. The properties editor for the project appears.

This editor enables the overrides of Parameters and Connection Managers, as well as Environments (more on Environments in next section.) All parameters and their values from an Execution get logged at run time, so you have an audit trail.

Configuring and Using Environments

Inside the SSISDB catalog is a node named Environments. SSIS Catalog Environments give users the ability to create sets of variables specific to different environments. The best way to understand these new environments is to think of them as sets of connection values in stages of development. For instance, most organizations have a separate environment for QA and Production, with corresponding separate servers. You could easily create a QA Environment and a separate Production Environment on the SSIS Server and configure projects to use an Environment Reference. Inside each of these two Environments, you can create a variable called SQLServer (it's very important that the variable be named exactly the same in each environment) for the SQL Server, and configure the value to be the respective connection strings. From there, the environment variable you created in these environments could be used to populate the value of a connection manager for the Execution of a Package.

With the Environment Variables in place inside the Execution, at run time, the DBA simply chooses an Environment, and the package executes using the proper values for that Environment.

Executions of Packages Using Project Deployments

To run a package from the SSIS server, right-click the Package and click Run. The package runs using the last configured set of values.

Transact-SQL for Executions

SSIS in SQL Server 2012 includes a new set of Transact-SQL commands for creating and managing Executions:

- **catalog.create_execution:** Creates the execution object. Parameters to configure include the Project folder, the Project Name, the Package name, and optionally, the environments to use.
- **catalog.set_execution_parameter_value (optional):** Overrides a server default parameter value.
- **catalog.start_execution:** Starts the execution.

Scheduling Executions with SQL Server Agent

To create a job that runs a package from the SSIS Catalog, perform the following steps:

1. Click New Job, and give the job a meaningful name.
2. Click New Step, and give the step a meaningful name.
3. Select Integrations Services.
4. Select SSIS Catalog.

5. Choose the user to execute the job (either your credentials or proxy account).

6. Configure any overrides for parameters and connection managers in exactly the same manner in which you would if you were using the Execution method.

Summary

Integrations Services is a robust environment capable of easily moving large quantities of data efficiently. Its ETL-specific tools provide a framework where the developer can focus on applying business logic rather than such repeatable features such as manually mapping data with scripts. Moreover, the dataflow provides the ability to transform data in memory with Data Flow Transformations, giving SSIS packages major performance benefits over comparable transformations performed with Transact-SQL. Those features, with its built- in error handling and logging, and with the exciting makeover that SSIS received with the SQL Server 2012 release, make SSIS one of the most useful tools in the realm of SQL Server. If you happen to be a reluctant adopter of SSIS, give it one more try. A little bit of effort learning this great tool goes a long way toward improving the lives of most developers.

Building Multidimensional Cubes in Analysis Services with MDX

A nalysis Services is a tool for centralizing logic, relating disparate systems, and serving up answers fast. It summarizes billions of rows in a second — a task that would take relational queries several minutes or longer. And unlike summary tables in a relational database, you don't need to create a different data structure for each type of summary.

Analysis Services is all about simple access to clean, consistent data. You can easily construct complex calculations, even those involving period-over-period comparisons. It is the perfect tool to create a single version of the truth.

Analysis Services Quick Start

One quick way to start with both data warehousing and Analysis Services is to let the Business Intelligence Development Studio build the Analysis Services database and associated warehouse tables for you. Begin by identifying or creating a SQL Server warehouse (relational) database. Then open Business Intelligence Development Studio, and create a new Analysis Services project.

Right-click the Cubes node in the Solution Explorer, and choose New Cube to begin the Cube Wizard. On the Select Creation Method page of the wizard, choose Generate Tables in the Data Source, and choose the template from the list that corresponds to your edition of SQL Server. Work through the rest of the wizard choosing measures and dimensions that make sense in your business.

At the Completing the Wizard page, select the Generate Schema Now option to automatically start the Schema Generation Wizard. Work through the remaining wizard pages. At the end of the Schema Generation Wizard, all the Analysis Services and relational objects are created. Even if the generated system does not exactly meet a current need, it provides an interesting example. You can modify the resulting design and regenerate the schema by right-clicking the project within the Solution Explorer and choosing Generate Relational Schema at any time.

Analysis Services Architecture

Analysis Services builds on the concepts of the data warehouse to present data in a multidimensional format instead of the two-dimensional paradigm of the relational database. When selecting a set of relational data, the query identifies a value via row and column coordinates, whereas the multidimensional store relies on selecting one or more items from each dimension to identify the value to be returned. Likewise, you can organize a result set returned by the multidimensional database along many axes.

 Chapter 51, "Business Intelligence Database Design," presents the background on Business Intelligence and data warehousing. If you are unfamiliar with these areas, this background can help you understand Analysis Services.

Instead of the two-dimensional table, Analysis Services uses the multidimensional cube to hold data in the database. The cube thus presents an entity that can be queried via *multidimensional expressions (MDX)*, the Analysis Services equivalent of SQL.

Analysis Services uses a combination of caching and precalculation strategies, aggregations, and partitioning to deliver query performance that is dramatically better than queries against a data warehouse.

What's New with Cubes and Analysis Services in SQL 2012

Not much has changed with Analysis Services from a multidimensional perspective in this release. There are a couple of key things to note, however:

- New Tabular Model to provide for self-service model development.
- SQL Server Data Tools are now the default working platform for SSAS. This works in Visual Studio 2010.

Unified Dimensional Model

The Unified Dimensional Model (UDM) defines the structure of the multidimensional database including attributes presented to the client for query and how data relates and is stored, partitioned, calculated, and extracted from the source databases.

At the foundation of the UDM is a data source view that identifies which relational tables provide data to Analysis Services and the relations between those tables. Based on the data source view, measure groups (facts) and dimensions are defined. Cubes then define the relations between dimensions and measure groups, forming the basis for multidimensional queries.

Server

The UDM, or database definition, is hosted by the Analysis Services server. Data can be kept in a Multidimensional OLAP (MOLAP) store, which generally results in the fastest query times, but it requires preprocessing of source data. Processing normally takes the form of SQL queries derived from the UDM and sent to the relational database to retrieve underlying data. Alternatively, you can send data directly from the Integration Services pipeline to the MOLAP store.

In addition to storing measures at the detail level, Analysis Services can store precalculated summary data called *aggregations*. For example, if aggregations by month and product line are created as part of the processing cycle, queries that require that combination of values do not need to read and summarize the detailed data but can use the aggregations instead.

Data can also be left in the relational database, or ROLAP store, which generally results in the fastest processing times at the expense of query times. Without aggregations, queries against a ROLAP store cause the equivalent SQL to be executed as needed. Aggregations can be precalculated for ROLAP, but doing so requires processing all the detailed data, so MOLAP is the preferred option. A compromise between the speed of MOLAP storage and the need for preprocessing, called *proactive caching*, serves queries out of MOLAP storage when possible, but queries the relational database to retrieve the latest data not yet processed into the MOLAP store.

Client

Clients communicate with Analysis Services, like any other web service, via the Simple Object Access Protocol (SOAP) using an XML format called XMLA or XML for Analysis. Client applications can hide XMLA and SOAP details by using the provided data access interfaces to access Analysis Services:

- All .NET languages can use ADOMD.NET.
- Win32 applications (such as C++) can use the OLE DB for OLAP driver.
- Other COM-based applications (such as VB6, VBA, and scripting) can use ADOMD.

53

In addition to custom applications, you can access Analysis Services using several provided tools, including the following:

- SQL Server Data Tools, for defining database structure
- SQL Server Management Studio, for managing and querying the server
- Reporting Services, which can base report definitions on Analysis Services data
- Excel features and add-ins, for querying and analyzing data
- Performance Point 2010 for Visualizing Data in a dashboard

A wide variety of third-party tools are also available to exploit the features of Analysis Services.

Building a Database

You would build an Analysis Services database by identifying the data to include in the database, specifying the relationships between those data, defining dimension structures on those data, and finally building one or more cubes to combine the dimensions and measures.

SQL Server Data Tools

The process to build an Analysis Services database begins by opening a new Analysis Services project in the SQL Server Data Tools. Each project corresponds to a database created on the target server when the project deploys.

Best Practice

Along with opening an Analysis Services project, you can also directly open an existing database in Business Intelligence Development Studio. Although this is a useful feature for examining the configuration of a running server, you should make changes in a project, deployed first to a development server, and deployed to production only after testing. Keep the project and related files in source control.

Be sure to set the target server before attempting to deploy your new database, as shown in Figure 53-1. Right-click the project in the Solution Explorer, and choose Properties. Then set the target server in the deployment property page.

Data Sources

You can define a data source on any data for which an OLE DB provider exists, enabling Analysis Services to use many types of data beyond the traditional relational sources.

FIGURE 53-1

Project Properties.

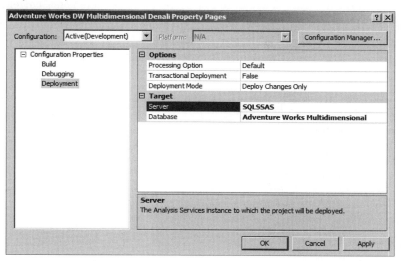

Start the New Data Source Wizard by right-clicking the Data Sources folder in the Solutions Explorer and selecting the New option. After you view the optional welcome screen, the Select How to Define a Connection screen appears and presents a list of connections. Select the appropriate connection if it exists.

If the appropriate connection does not exist, click the New button and add it. Choose an appropriate provider, giving preference to native OLE DB providers for best performance. Then enter the server name, authentication information, database name, and any other properties required by the chosen provider. Review entries on the All tab and test the connection before clicking OK.

Work through the remaining wizard screens, choosing the appropriate login (impersonation) information for the target environment and finally the name of the data source. The choice of impersonation method depends on how access is granted in your environment. Any method that provides access to the necessary tables is sufficient for development. You can modify this later under the Impersonation Information tab of the Data Source Designer, as shown in Figure 53-2.

- **Use a Specific Windows Username and Password:** Allows the entry of the credential to be used when connecting to the relational database.

- **Use the Service Account:** Uses the account that the Analysis Server service is logged in under to connect to the relational database.

- **Use the Credentials of the Current User:** Uses the current developer's login to read the relational database. This can be a good choice for development, but won't work when the database is deployed to a server because there is no "current user."
- **Inherit:** Uses the Analysis Services database impersonation method, which defaults to using the service account, but can be changed in database properties.

FIGURE 53-2

Choosing impersonation method for processing.

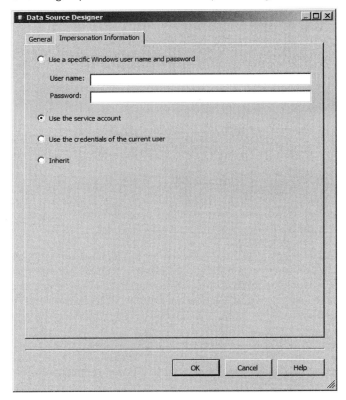

Data Source View

A data source describes where to look for tables of data, whereas the data source view specifies which tables to use and how they are related. The data source view also associates metadata, such as friendly names and calculations, with those tables and columns.

Creating the Data Source View

Use the following basic steps to create a data source view:

1. Add needed tables and named queries to a data source view.
2. Establish logical primary keys for tables without a primary key.
3. Establish relationships between related tables where necessary.
4. Change tables' or columns' friendly names and create named calculations.

Begin by creating the data source view via the wizard: Right-click the Data Source Views folder, and select the New option. There are several pages in the wizard:

- **Select a Data Source**: Choose a data source to add tables from. If more than one data source is to be included in the data source view, then the first data source must be a SQL Server data source.

- **Name Matching**: This page appears only when no foreign keys exist in the source database, providing the option to define relationships based on a selection of common naming conventions. Matching can also be enabled via the `NameMatchingCriteria` property after the data source view has been created, identifying matches as additional tables added to an existing view.

- **Select Tables and Views**: Move tables to be included from the left (available objects) to the right (included objects) pane. To narrow the list of available objects, enter any part of a table name in the Filter box, and press the Filter button. To add objects related to included objects, select one or more included objects, and press the Add Related Tables button.

- **Completing the Wizard**: Specify a name for the data source view.

After you create the data source view , you can add more tables by right-clicking in the diagram and choosing Add/Remove Tables. Use this method to include tables from additional data sources as well.

Similar to a SQL view, you can define named queries , which behave as if they were tables. Either right-click the diagram and choose New Named Query, or right-click a table and choose Replace Table/with New Named Query. This brings up a Query Designer to define the contents of the named query. Using named queries avoids the need to define views in the underlying data sources and allows all metadata to be centralized in a single model.

As you add tables to the data source view, primary keys and unique indexes in the underlying data source are imported as primary keys in the model. Foreign keys are automatically imported as relationships between tables. For cases in which primary keys or relationships are not imported, they must be manually defined.

For tables without primary keys, select one or more columns that define the primary key, right-click, and select Set Logical Primary Key. When primary keys are in place, you can

53

relate any tables without appropriate relationships by dragging and dropping the related columns between tables. If the new relationship is valid, the model shows the new relationship without additional prompting. If errors occur, the Edit Relationship dialog appears, as shown in Figure 53-3. A common issue when working with multiple data sources is different data types. For instance, tables from different databases containing the same key information could be a 16-bit integer in one table and 32-bit integer in another. You can address this situation by using a named query to cast the 16-bit integer as its 32-bit equivalent.

FIGURE 53-3

Editing relationships within your cube.

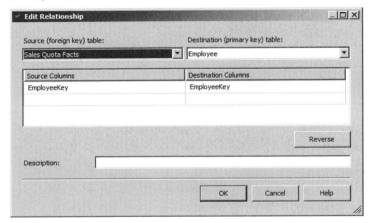

You can also access the Edit Relationship dialog by double-clicking an existing relationship, by right-clicking the diagram, and from the toolbar and menu selections. Be sure to define all relationships, including relationships between different columns of the fact table and the same dimension table (for example, OrderDate and ShipDate both relate to the Time dimension table), because this enables role-playing dimension functionality when you create a cube.

Refining the Data Source View

It is important to keep in mind the end user when designing your data source view. Table and column names should make sense to the person who browses the cube. Following are a few best practices:

- Set friendly names on tables and columns in the Properties pane.
- Use named queries to change codes such as M or F to Male and Female.
- Add descriptions for tables and columns for nonobvious notes.
- Do simple, single row and table-wide calculations in the DSV.

Best Practice

Make the data source view the place where metadata lives. If a column needs to be renamed to give it context at query time, give it a friendly name in the data source view, rather than rename a measure or dimension attribute — the two names display side-by-side in the data source view and help future modelers understand how data is used. Use description properties for nonobvious notes, capturing the results of research required in building and modifying the model.

When creating named queries, you must write the code so that the underlying data provider can interpret it. For instance, if SQL Server is the relational database behind the scenes, you must write the named query in T-SQL. Figure 53-4 shows a sample completed DSV.

FIGURE 53-4

A completed DSV in Analysis Services.

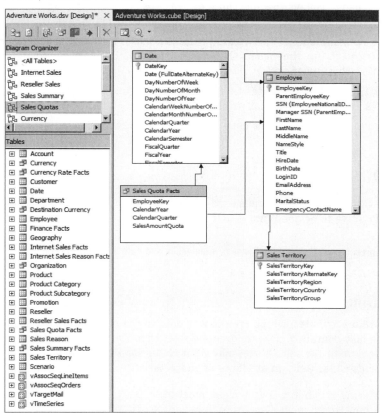

Creating a Cube

The data source view forms the basis for creating the cubes, which in turn present data to database users. Running the Cube Wizard generally provides a good first draft of a cube. Begin by right-clicking the Cubes folder and selecting New, and then work through these pages:

- **Select Build Method**: Choose Use Existing Tables. The Generate Tables in the Data Source option is outlined previously in the Quick Start section. The option Create an Empty Cube essentially bypasses the wizard.

- **Select Measure Group Tables**: Choose the appropriate data source view from the drop-down, and then indicate which tables to use as fact tables (measure groups). Pressing the Suggest button makes an educated guess at which tables to check but is not always accurate.

- **Select Measures**: Each numeric column is assumed to be a measure. Check/uncheck columns as appropriate; you can also add/remove/adjust measures later.

- **Select Existing Dimensions**: If the current project already has dimensions defined, then this page displays to allow those dimensions to be included in the new cube. Check/uncheck dimensions as appropriate for the cube being created.

- **Select New Dimensions**: The wizard presents a list of dimensions and associated tables. Deselect any dimensions that are not wanted or tables that should not be included in that dimension.

- **Completing the Wizard**: Enter a name for the new cube and optionally review the measures and dimensions that will be created.

Upon completion of the wizard, a new cube and associated dimensions will be created.

Dimensions

Dimensions are categories used to summarize the data of interest. Dimensions created by a wizard generally prove to be good first drafts but need refinement.

 Chapter 51 presents background on Business Intelligence and data warehousing concepts.

Creating a Dimension

Dimensions contain attributes, which are the way data in the cube will be sliced. For instance, a cube may contain a measure group of sales that stores the product sold, the sale amount, and the date of the sale. A user may want to see sales totals by year and would slice the data by calendar year, an attribute or characteristic of the date dimension.

In addition to storing attributes, a dimension must have exactly one key column. The key column denotes how to uniquely identify each record. A date dimension may have quarters, months, and years, but the data key uniquely identifies each record. In this case the date key could be the concatenation of month, day, and year.

If you do not create dimensions during the Cube Wizard process, you can manually create them independent of the cube. Before creating additional dimensions, be sure to add the tables required to build the dimension to the data source view. When all the required tables are in the DSV, right-click the Dimensions folder in the Solution Explorer, and select New Dimension to launch the Dimension Wizard.

- **Select Creation Method:** Click next to go past the welcome page, and select the Use an Existing Table option.

- **Specify Source Information**: Select the DSV that holds the source data, pick the primary table for the dimension, and set the key columns and the name column.

- **Select Dimension Attributes**: Select each attribute of the dimension by checking the box to the left of the column name.

- **Completing the Wizard**: Review and name the new dimension.

To modify an existing dimension, double-click it from inside the Solution Explorer. A window with several tabs and three panes labeled Attributes, Hierarchies, and Data Source View appear, as shown in Figure 53-5. The data source view displays all tables associated with the dimension. You can see additional tables by right-clicking in the blank area of this pane, choosing Show Tables, and selecting the tables to add.

FIGURE 53-5

Example dimension design screen.

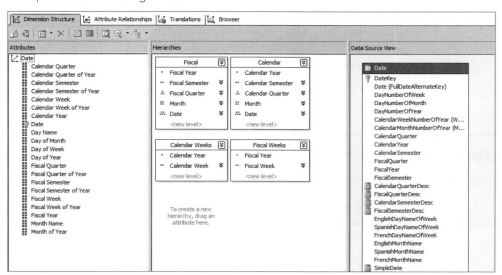

You can add additional attributes by dragging a column from the Data Source View pane onto the Attributes pane. In the center pane, you can create user hierarchies to give users the ability to drill-down through multiple attribute levels. Create these in the Hierarchies pane with the least granular level at the top and most granular at the bottom.

Hierarchies and Attribute Relationships

Each attribute not specifically disabled becomes an *attribute hierarchy* for browsing and querying. The attribute hierarchy generally consists of two levels: the All level and a level that individually lists each value. An important practice to optimize cube performance is to build out dimension attribute relationships; this helps analysis services in aggregating the data. Figure 53-6 shows an attribute relationship sample. Notice the more specific points to the less specific. For instance, a product (very specific) belongs in a subcategory (less specific).

FIGURE 53-6

Sample attribute relationships in a dimension.

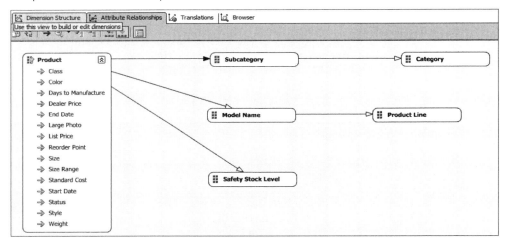

Best Practice

Although natural hierarchies are important for cube performance, user hierarchies provide drill-down paths for users who interactively browse the contents of a cube, so you need to define paths that make sense to the user of the cube as well.

Creating User Hierarchies

To start a new hierarchy, drag an attribute to an empty spot of the pane. Add new levels by dragging attributes onto an existing hierarchy. Remember to rename each hierarchy with a user friendly title.

The browser view is a good place to get a feel for how the user experiences the hierarchies as created. Right-click the dimension name in the Solution Explorer, and choose Process to update the server with the latest dimension definition. Then switch to the Browser tab of the dimension designer, choose the hierarchy to view in the toolbar, and explore the hierarchy in the pane. If the latest changes do not appear in the Browser tab, press the Reconnect button in the toolbar. Notice names, values, and ordering associated with each hierarchy, and adjust as needed. Note the differing icons to distinguish between user and attribute hierarchies while browsing.

Dimension Clean-Up

Not every attribute of a dimension needs to be included in the cube and not every included attribute needs to be shown to the user. Following are a few guidelines:

- Delete attributes that are not useful to users.
- Display attributes only in the hierarchy where applicable, such as individual days of the year. For these cases, build the appropriate user hierarchy and set the `AttributeHierarchyVisible` property to `False` for the Date attribute in this instance. You can fully disable attributes that will not be queried but are still needed, such as for calculations. Set `AttributeHierarchyEnabled` to `False`, `AttributeHierarchyOptimizedState` to `NotOptimized`, and `AttributeHierarchyOrdered` to `False`. For attributes that need to be modeled but are infrequently used, consider setting their `AttributeHierarchyVisible` property to `False`. The will not be visible but can still be referenced via MDX queries.
- On large dimensions use the `AttributeHierarchyDisplayFolder` to group related attributes and `DisplayFolder` for user hierarchies.

Best Practice

Well-organized dimensions using well-understood names are essential to gaining acceptance for interactive applications — most users will be overwhelmed by the amount of available attributes. Excluding unused attributes not only helps simplify the user's view of the data, it also can greatly speed performance — especially for cubes with substantial calculations because the more attributes, the larger the number of cells each calculation must consider.

Best Practice Warnings

SQL Server 2012 implements best practice warnings throughout the Analysis Services design environment. The warnings appear as blue underlines on the object in question, such as the dimension name as viewed in the dimension designer. Don't confuse these advisories with actual errors, which appear as red underlines and which prevent a design from operating. Best practice warnings flag designs that are valid but may not be optimal, depending on the application built. A list of best practice warnings also generates in the Error List windows whenever the cube deploys.

You can globally disable warnings that don't apply to a given project by right-clicking the project within the Solution Explorer and choosing Edit Database. Select the Warnings tab to see a list of all warning rules. Disabling a rule keeps a warning from being checked anywhere in the project.

Beyond Regular Dimensions

Dimension concepts described so far in this chapter focus on the basic functionality common to most types of dimensions. For clarity, the discussion is limited to standard, or nondata mining, dimensions. Other discussions may cover other definitions of the term dimension; the term has many meanings in the context of dimensional design.

Other Dimension Types

Analysis Services recognizes more than a dozen dimension types, including Customers, Accounts, and Products. Included templates can define a table similar to the process described for generating time dimensions. Start the Dimension Wizard, and choose Generate a Non-Time Table in the Data Source; then select a template. You can cast existing tables as a special type as well by assigning the Type property for the dimension (such as Account) and the Type property for the dimension's attributes (such as AccountNumber).

Parent-Child Dimensions

Most dimensions are organized into hierarchies that have a fixed number of levels, but certain business problems do not lend themselves to a fixed number of levels. Relational databases solve this problem with self-referential tables, which Analysis Services handles using parent-child dimensions.

A self-referential table involves two key columns — for example, an employee ID and a manager ID like the table in Figure 53-7. To build the organizational chart, start with the president and look for employees that she manages; then look for the employees they manage, and so on. Often this relationship is expressed as a foreign key between the employee ID (the primary key) and the manager ID. When such a relationship exists on the source table, the Dimension Wizard suggests the appropriate parent-child relationship. In the employee table example, the employee ID attribute will be configured with the Usage property set to `Key`, whereas the `manager ID` attribute will be configured with a `Usage` of `Parent`. Other important properties for configuring a parent-child dimension include the following:

- **RootMemberIf**: Used on the parent attribute to identify the top level. Values include `ParentIsBlank` (null or zero), `ParentIsSelf` (parent and key values are the same), `ParentIsMissing` (parent row not found). The default value is all three, `ParentIsBlankSelfOrMissing`.

- **MembersWithData**: As set on the parent attribute, this controls how nonleaf members with data display. Under the default setting, `NonLeafDataVisible`, Analysis Services repeat parent members at the leaf level to display their corresponding data. This would be a situation in which the manager is also listed as an employee. Sales for the employee will be included in the total but not in the details when setting the property to `NonLeafDataHidden`.

FIGURE 53-7

A self-referential table.

After you configure the parent-child relationship, the parent attribute presents a multilevel view of the data. All the other attributes of the dimension behave as normal.

Dimension Refinements

After you build a dimension, a large number of properties are available to refine its behavior and that of its attributes. This section details some of the more common and less obvious refinements possible.

Hierarchy (All) Level and Default Member

The (All) level is added to the top of each hierarchy by default, and represents every member in that hierarchy. At query time, the (All) level enables everything in a hierarchy to be included, without listing each member separately.

By default, the name of the (All) level will be All, which is quite practical and sufficient for most applications. Use the `AttributeAllMemberName` or the user hierarchy property `AllMemberName` to customize the All level name. Regardless of name, the (All) member is also the default member. You can change the default member by setting the dimension's `DefaultMember` property.

You can often set default members when data included in a cube is not commonly queried. Consider a cube populated with sales transactions that are mostly successful but sometimes fail due to customer credit or other problems. Nearly everyone that queries the cube will be interested in the volume and amount of successful transactions. Only someone doing failure analysis will want to view other than successful transactions.

Another option is to eliminate the (All) level entirely by setting an attribute's `IsAggregatable` property to `false`. When the (All) level is eliminated, either a `DefaultMember` must be specified or one will be chosen at random at query time. In addition, the attribute can participate in user hierarchies only at the top level because appearing in a lower level would require the attribute to be aggregated.

Grouping Dimension Members

The creation of member groups, or discretization, is the process to group the values of a many-valued attribute into discrete "buckets" of data. This is a useful approach for representing a large number of continuous values, such as annual income or commute distance. Enable the feature on an attribute by setting the `DiscretizationBucketCount` property to the number of groups to be created and by choosing a `DiscretizationMethod` from the list. Automatic results in reasonable groupings for most applications. Changes to the underlying data may cause new groupings to be calculated during cube processing.

Cubes

A cube brings the elements of the design process together and exposes them to the user, combining data sources, data source views, dimensions, measures, and calculations in a single container. A cube can contain data (measures) from many fact tables organized into measure groups.

Using the Cube Wizard has been covered in earlier sections, both from the top-down approach (see "Analysis Services Quick Start") and from the bottom-up approach (see "Creating a Cube"). After you create the cube structure, you can refine it using the Cube Designer.

Open any cube from the Solution Explorer to use the Cube Designer, as shown in Figure 53-8. The Cube Designer presents information in several tabbed views described in the remainder of this section.

FIGURE 53-8

Analysis Services cube designer in solution explorer.

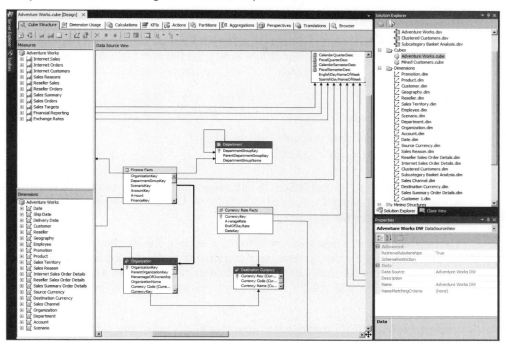

Cube Structure

The cube structure view is the primary design surface for defining a cube. Along with the ever-present Solution Explorer and Properties panes, three panes present the cube's structure:

- The Data Source View pane, located in the center of the view, shows a chosen portion of the data source view on which you can build the cube. Each table is color-coded: yellow for fact tables, blue for dimensions, and white for neither. A variety of options are available by right-clicking a table or the background, including hiding tables, showing tables, and showing related tables. The Measures pane, located in the upper-left corner of the view, lists all the cube's measures organized by measure group.

- The Dimensions pane, located in the lower-left section of the view, lists all dimensions associated with the cube. Not all dimensions from the project are required to be in this list, only those needed for the available measure groups.

Like the Dimension Designer, you must deploy changes to a cube before you can browse them.

Measures

Each measure is based on a column from the data source view and an aggregate function. The aggregate function determines how data from the fact table is summarized. A variety of aggregations are available including, but not limited to, the following:

- sum
- max and min
- counts of distinct records
- last non-empty

A common aggregate to use is Sum to add values such as order quantities or sales amounts, whereas last non-empty could be used for getting the latest inventory value from a measure that pre-aggregates the inventory daily.

The best way to add a new measure is to right-click in the Measures pane, choose New Measure, and specify the aggregation function and table/column combination. Measure groups are created for each fact table and folders can be defined as well. The measure `FormatString` should also be specified by choosing a provided format or entering a custom format.

Because you can create multiple measures in a single cube, you can set the `DefaultMeasure` property to choose a measure to be pulled for queries when no measure is specified.

Cube Dimensions

You can disable or make invisible the hierarchies and attributes for each dimension if appropriate for a particular cube context. Access these settings in the Dimensions pane, and then adjust the associated properties. These properties are specific to a dimension's role in the cube and do not change the underlying dimension design.

You can add dimensions to the cube by right-clicking the Dimensions pane and choosing New Dimension. After the dimension is added to the cube, review the dimension usage tab to ensure that the dimension appropriately relates to all measure groups.

Dimension Usage

The dimension usage tab, shown in Figure 53-9, displays a table showing how each dimension is related to each measure group. With dimensions and measure groups as row and column headers, respectively, each cell of the table defines the relationship.

FIGURE 53-9

Analysis Services dimension usage tab.

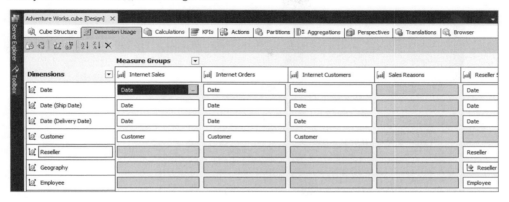

The Cube Designer creates default relationships based on the data source view relationships, which are accurate in most cases; although, any linked objects require special review because they are not derived from the data source view. Click the ellipsis in any table cell to launch the Define Relationship dialog, and choose the relationship type.

- **No Relationship**: Use this when a dimension does not relate to a fact table. This is common with more than one fact table present.

- **Regular**: This type appears when there is a direct relationship between the dimension and the fact table, for instance, a customer key in a dimension to a customer key column in a sales fact table.

- **Fact**: Fact dimensions are derived from fact tables, contain both fact and dimension data, and have a direct relationship to the fact table.

- **Referenced**: Used when a table connects to the fact table through another table with a regular relationship. This is useful for reusing a dimension, for instance, a geography dimension that relates to both the customer and store dimensions.

- **Many-to-Many**: All previous relationships are one-to-many; however, many-to-many would be authors to books, for instance. One author can write many books, and each book can have many authors. This relationship requires an intermediate fact table to list each pair of regular and many-to-many relationships.

Calculations

The Calculations tab, as shown in Figure 53-10, enables the definition of calculated measures, sets of dimension members, and dynamic control over cube properties. Although the Calculations tab offers forms to view many of the objects defined here, the underlying language is Multidimensional Expressions (MDX).

FIGURE 53-10

Cube calculations tab.

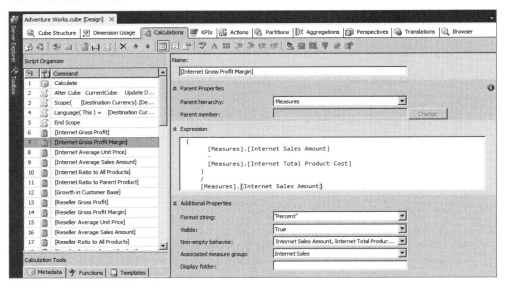

KPIs

A *Key Performance Indicator (KPI)* is a server-side calculation meant to define an organization's most important metrics. You frequently use these metrics, such as net profit, client utilization, or funnel conversion rate in dashboards or other reporting tools.

Within the KPI's view, an individual KPI consists of several components:

- The actual value of the metric
- The goal for the metric, for example, budget sales
- The status for the metric, comparing the actual and goal values, returning a value between –1 and 1
- The trend for the metric, showing which direction the metric is headed, also returning a value between –1 and 1

Actions

The Actions tab of the Cube Designer provides a way to define actions that a client can perform for a given context. For example, a drill-through action can show detailed rows behind a total, or a reporting action can launch a report based on a dimension attribute's value. Actions can be specific to any displayed data, including individual cells and dimension members, resulting in more detailed analysis or even integration of the analysis application into a larger data management framework.

Partitions

Partitions are the unit of storage in Analysis Services. Initially, the Cube Designer creates a single MOLAP partition for each measure group.

Partition Sizing

Cube development normally begins by using a small but representative slice of the data, yet production volumes are frequently quite large. You need a partitioning strategy to manage data, beginning with the amount of data to be kept online and the size of the partitions that hold that data.

The amount of data to be kept online is a trade-off between the desire for access to historical data and the cost of storing that data. You can partition data in many possible ways, but a time-based approach is widely used, usually keeping either a year's or a month's worth of data in a single partition. For partitions populated on the front end, the size of the partition is important for the time it takes to process. While partitions are deleted at the back end, the size of the partition is important for the amount of data it removes at one time.

Matching the partition size and retention between the relational database and Analysis Services is a simple and effective approach. As long as the aggregation design is consistent across partitions, Analysis Services enables smaller partitions to be merged, keeping the overall count at a manageable level.

Best Practice

Take time to consider retention, processing, and partitioning strategies before an application goes into production. When in place, changes may be expensive given the large quantities of data involved.

Creating Partitions

The key to accurate partitions is including every data row exactly once. Because it is the combination of all partitions that is reported by the cube, including rows multiple times inflates the results.

The partition view consists of one collapsible pane for each measure group, each pane containing a grid listing the currently defined partitions for that measure group.

Start the process to add a partition by clicking the New Partition link, which launches a series of Partition Wizard dialogs:

- **Specify Source Information**: Choose the appropriate Measure group and data source view to look in.

- **Restrict Rows**: If the source table contains exactly the rows to be included in the partition, then click Next. If the source table contains more rows than should be included in the partition, then select the Specify Query to Restrict Rows option, and the Query box populates. Supply the WHERE clause, and press the Check button to validate syntax.

- **Processing and Storage Locations**: The defaults suffice for most situations. If necessary, choose options to balance the load across disks and servers.

- **Completing the Wizard**: Supply a name for the partition — generally the same name as the measure group suffixed with the partition slice (for example, Internet_Orders_2004). If aggregations have not been defined, define them now or copy them from another partition.

When a partition has been added, you can edit the name and source by clicking in the appropriate cell in the partition grid.

Aggregation Design

The best trade-off between processing time, partition storage, and query performance is defining only aggregations that help answer queries commonly run against a cube. Analysis Services' usage-based optimization tracks queries run against the cube and then designs aggregations to meet that query load, but it requires a period of production use to gather sample data.

A good approach is to first create a modest number of aggregations using the Aggregation Design Wizard and assign that design to all active partitions. Then deploy the cube for use to collect a realistic query history, and run the Usage Based Optimization Wizard.

Aggregation Design Wizard

Aggregation Design Wizard creates aggregations based on intelligent guesses. Invoke the wizard from the toolbar on the Aggregations tab of the cube designer. The wizard steps through several pages:

- **Select Partitions to Modify**: The wizard runs based on the currently selected measure group. Check all the partitions that you want to update.

- **Review Aggregation Usage**: Here defaults generally suffice, but options include Full — include in every aggregation; None — don't include in any aggregation;

and Unrestricted — considers this attribute for inclusion in the design without restrictions.

- **Specify Object Counts**: Pressing the Count button provides current row counts. You can manually enter numbers if the current data source is different from the target design (for example, a small development data set).

- **Set Aggregation Options**: Options on the left tell the designer when to stop creating new aggregations. Press the Continue button to create an aggregation design before pressing the Next button.

  No strict rules exist, but some general guidelines may help:

  - Target an initial performance gain of 10–20 percent. On the most complex cubes, this is difficult to obtain with a reasonable number of aggregations. Keep the total number of aggregations under 200.

  - Look for a flattening of the curve in the storage/performance graph and stop there.

- **Completing the Wizard**: Give the new aggregation design a name and optionally process it.

Best Practice

The best aggregations are usage-based: Collect usage history in the query log and use it to periodically optimize each partition's aggregation design. Query logging must be enabled in Analysis Server's Server properties, in the Log\QueryLog section.

Aggregations Tab

The toolbar of this tab can launch the wizard and the Usage-Based Optimization Wizard. The pane toggles between standard and advanced views. Standard view lists all the measure groups and summarizes which aggregation designs are assigned to which partitions.

The advanced view, as shown in Figure 53-11, enables manual modification of an aggregation design. Manual updates to a design are generally not effective because usage-based optimization tends to be more accurate than individual judgment, but cases do arise in which problem queries can be addressed by a well-placed aggregation. Use the toolbar to copy an existing design to a new name, and then modify as needed.

Perspectives

A perspective is a view of a cube that hides items and functionality not relevant to a specific purpose. Perspectives appear as additional cubes to the end user, so each group within the company can have its own "cube," each just a targeted view of the same data.

FIGURE 53-11

Advanced view for designing aggregations in your cube.

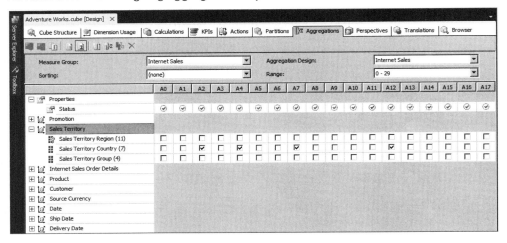

Add a perspective from the Perspectives tab of the cube designer by either right-clicking or using the toolbar, and a new column appears. Change the name at the top of the column to something meaningful, and then uncheck the items not relevant to the perspective. A default measure can be chosen for the perspective as well. Figure 53-12 shows a sample setup of perspectives.

FIGURE 53-12

Creating and setting perspectives in your cube.

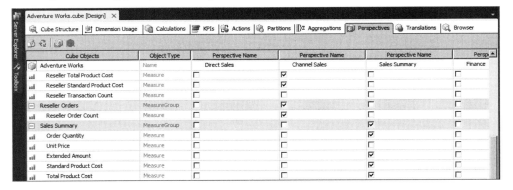

Data Storage

The data storage strategy chosen for a cube and its components determines not only how to store the cube , but also how to process it. You can set storage settings at three different levels, with parent settings determining defaults for the children:

- **Cube**: Begin by establishing storage settings at the cube level (sets defaults for dimensions, measure groups, and partitions). Access the Cube Storage Settings dialog by choosing a cube in the Cube Designer, and then clicking the ellipsis on the Proactive Caching property of the cube.

- **Measure Group**: Use when storage settings for a particular measure group differ from cube defaults. Access the Measure Group Storage Settings dialog by either clicking the ellipsis on the measure group's Proactive Caching property in the Cube Designer or by choosing the Storage Settings link in partition view without highlighting a specific partition.

- **Object level (specific partition or dimension)**: Sets the storage options for a single object. Access the Dimension Storage Settings dialog by clicking the ellipsis on the dimension's Proactive Caching property in the Dimension Designer. Access the Partition Storage Settings dialog by selecting a partition in the partition view and clicking the Storage Settings link.

Each of the storage settings dialogs are essentially the same, differing only in the scope of the setting's effect. The main page of the dialog contains a slider that selects preconfigured option settings — from the most real-time (far left) to the least real-time (far right).

By default, the pure MOLAP setting is chosen and works well for traditional data warehouse applications. However, if you build a partition based on frequently changing source data (for example, directly on OLTP tables), then proactive caching can automatically manage partition updates.

Cube Processing

Before browsing or querying the cube, you must refresh the data it contains by processing the cube. You generally accomplished this on a regular schedule through SQL Server Agent or an SSIS package after you update the data warehouse.

Processing Methods

You can process the cube as a whole or individual object such as the dimensions or a single partition. This is particularly useful so that you can process different partitions on different schedules. Several options are available when you process the cube and vary it based on the object chosen. Figure 53-13 shows the cube processing screen. Each option can cause different objects to process:

- **Process Default**: Processes only unprocessed objects.
- **Process Full**: Processes the structure, data, and aggregations.
- **Process Data**: Processes only data.
- **Process Structure**: Processes the cube definition, but not any data.
- **Unprocess**: Removes the data stored in the cube.
- **Process Index**: Processes only aggregations.
- **Process Incremental**: You must provide a query that contains the fact data for processing.

FIGURE 53-13

Setting processing options for your cube.

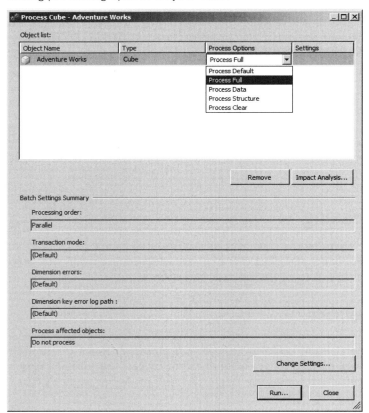

Other Considerations

Data integrity functionality in Analysis Services addresses inconsistencies that would otherwise cause improper data presentation. Analysis Services views these inconsistencies in two categories: Null Processing and Key Errors. Analysis Services also enables deep configuration on handling errors during processing.

Best Practice

A key strength of OLAP, in general, and the UDM, in particular, is consistent interpretation of data. Data integrity settings and centralized calculations are examples of the many ways that UDM centralizes data interpretation for downstream data consumers. Address these issues in the design of the warehouse and UDM to deliver the most useful product. Think of it as building a "data object" complete with information hiding and opportunities for reuse.

Null Processing

How you treat nulls depends on the NullProcessing property of the object in question. For measures, the property appears as part of the source definition. Options include changing Nulls to zeros, throwing an error, or keeping the value as Null.

A good way to choose among these settings is to consider how an average value should be calculated on the data for a given measure. If the best interpretation is averaging only the non-null values, then Preserve (keep as Null) yields that behavior. For dimensions, the NullProcessing property can take on an additional value called Unknown Member, where Null is interpreted as the unknown member. You can define null handling on each attribute's NameColumn as well as each dimension attribute's KeyColumn.

Unknown Member

Choosing an unknown member option, either as part of null processing or in response to an error, requires the unknown member to be configured for the affected dimension. After the unknown member is enabled for a dimension, the member is added to every attribute in the dimension. The UnknownMember dimension property can take on three possible settings:

- **None**: The unknown member is not enabled for this dimension, and any attempt to assign data to the unknown member results in an error. This is the default setting.
- **Visible**: The unknown member is enabled and is visible to queries.
- **Hidden**: The unknown member is enabled but not directly visible in queries but is accessible through MDX.

The default name of the unknown member is simply Unknown, which you can change by entering a value for the dimension's UnknownMemberName property.

Error Configuration

For data integrity errors as described and several others, the `ErrorConfiguration` property specifies how errors will be handled. Initially, the setting for this property is (default), but choose the (custom) setting from the list and eight properties appear. The `ErrorConfiguration` properties are available on several objects but are primarily set for dimensions and measure groups.

Some properties to take note of are:

- **KeyDuplicate**: Triggered when a duplicate key is seen while building the dimension. The default is `IgnoreError`; other settings are `ReportAndContinue` and `ReportAndStop`. `IgnoreError` causes all the attribute values to incorporate into the dimension, but Analysis Services randomly chooses which values to associate with the key

- **KeyErrorAction**: Triggered when a `KeyNotFound` error is encountered. This occurs when a key value cannot be located in its associated table. For measure groups, this happens when the fact table contains a dimension key not found in the dimension table.

- **KeyNotFound**: Determines how `KeyNotFound` errors interact with the `KeyErrorLimit`, such as reporting the error and stopping processing. There are other properties available to go deeper with error handling during processing as well. You can set these same properties as server properties to establish different defaults. You can also set them for a particular processing run to provide special handling for certain data.

Summary

Analysis Services provides the capability to build fast, consistent, and relevant repositories of data suitable for both end-user and application use. You easily can resolve simple problems by using default behaviors, and more complex problems with the flexibility provided by the breadth of this server and its design environment.

Configuring and Administering Analysis Services

The focus of this chapter is on deploying and administering a SQL Server Analysis Services Server. Key new SQL Server Analysis Services features require your attention, which are also discussed. Analysis Services provides a specialized storage and query engine optimized for handling queries that often require large result sets to be scanned and aggregated. An important enabler of these impressive data retrieval capabilities are Analysis Services storage engine optimizations, most notably Aggregations.

Installing Analysis Services

This section details the various ways in which Analysis Services may be installed along with key options available within the different modes supported.

Analysis Services, in this release, supports three different modes of operation. These modes include Multidimensional and Data Mining (the default mode), Tabular, and PowerPivot for SharePoint. As a result, ensuring the correct mode is selected during installation is important because the only available option to change the mode is to uninstall and reinstall Analysis Services selecting the wanted mode. These server modes ultimately determine which features will be installed for use, and as might be guessed, they each support different usage scenarios.

See the Microsoft Technet article Feature by Server Mode or Solution Type (SSAS) at `http://msdn .microsoft.com/en-us/library/hh212940.aspx` for details about the various features supported by each of the Analysis Services server modes.

As with other SQL Server Services, Analysis Services can install multiple instances on the same server, and often this is used to support multiple server modes. It is often best to install the Multidimensional and Data Mining server mode as the default instance for the server. Another option is to create instances for each server mode employing a naming convention that would assist in knowing the server mode of each instance.

The following steps outline how to install a Multidimensional and Data Mining mode (default mode) Analysis Services instance, while also pointing out how the other modes may be selected as part of the installation process.

1. On the left side of the main SQL Server Installation Center dialog, select the Installation option.

2. From the Installation options, select New SQL Server Stand-Alone Installation or Add Features to an Existing Installation option.

3. After the installation runs setup rules, on the Product Key dialog, enter a valid product key, and press next.

4. In the License Terms dialog, check I Accept the License Terms option, and press Next.

5. After the installation installs step files and runs setup support rules, on the Setup Support Rules dialog, press Next.

6. In the Setup Role dialog, select SQL Server Feature Installation, and press Next. (Note the SQL Server PowerPivot for SharePoint option; use this to setup an instance of Analysis Services in PowerPivotfor SharePoint mode.) See Figure 54-1 for an example of this.

7. In the Feature Selection dialog, select the wanted SQL Server features to install. Minimally, select Analysis Services, SQL Server Data Tools, Client Tools Connectivity, and Management Tools - Complete, and press Next.

8. After the installation completes the installation rules, on the Installation Rules dialog, press Next.

9. In the Instance Configuration dialog, select either Default Instance or Named Instance option, provide an instance name if Named Instance option is selected, change Instance ID and Instance root directory if wanted, and press Next.

10. In the Disk Space Requirements dialog, press Next.

11. In the Server Configuration dialog, review the Service Accounts and Collation tabs, make wanted modifications, and press Next.

12. If the Database Engine were selected for installation, on the Database Engine Configuration dialog, review the Server Configuration, Data Directories, and FILESTREAM tabs to make wanted modifications, and press Next.

FIGURE 54-1

The Setup Role dialog.

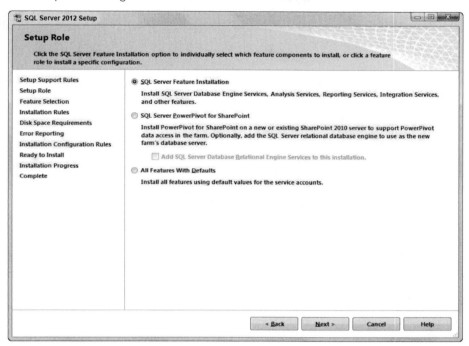

13. In the Analysis Services Configuration dialog, on the Server Configuration tab, within the Server Mode options, select Multidimensional and Data Mining Mode, and optionally specify the users to be assigned administrative permissions for the Analysis Services server. Note that the other option as seen in Figure 54-2, Tabular Mode, can be used to configure the Tabular Mode of Analysis Services.

14. In the Analysis Services Configuration dialog, on the Data Directories tab, specify the file path locations for storing Analysis Services data, log, temp, and backup files, and press Next.

15. If Reporting Services were selected for installation, in the Reporting Services Configuration dialog, review and make wanted changes to the options, and press Next.

16. In the Error Reporting dialog, review and make wanted selections, and press Next.

54

17. In the Installation Configuration Rules dialog, press Next.

18. In the Ready to Install dialog, review the listing of features to be included in the installation, especially noting the configuration file path because that contains information about the installation that may be helpful to resolve any installation problems, and press Install.

FIGURE 54-2

The Analysis Services Configuration dialog.

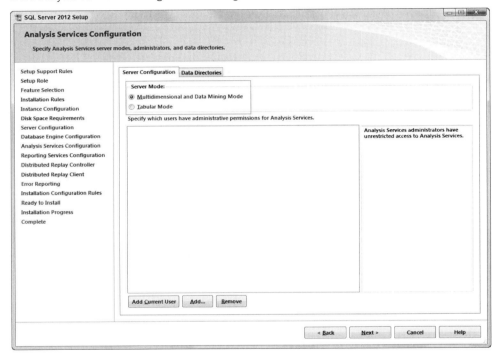

After these steps have been successfully completed, a new Multidimensional and Data Mining instance of SQL Server Analysis Services has been installed and is ready for use. You may confirm that the service has been installed and is successfully running by launching SQL Server Configuration Manager and selecting the SQL Server Services node from the options within the left pane. Within the right pane of SQL Server Configuration Manager, you should see SQL Server Analysis Services (2012) with the State set to Running and the Start Mode set to Automatic, as shown in Figure 54-3.

- You can use the Analysis Services Server icons within Object Explorer to determine the Server Mode, as shown in Figure 54-4.

- Multidimensional and Data Mining instances have a yellow cube.

- Tabular instances have a blue flat grid.

- PowerPivot for SharePoint instances have a set of three people blue, yellow, and red.

FIGURE 54-3

The SQL Server Configuration Manager showing Analysis Services running.

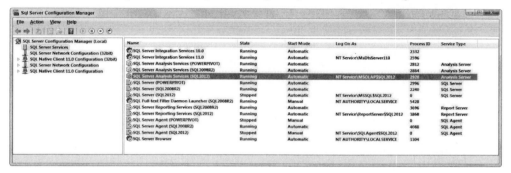

FIGURE 54-4

Object Explorer showing different Analysis Services instances.

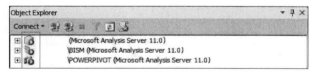

Configuring Basic Analysis Services Settings

After Analysis Services is installed and running, Analysis Services administrators may configure various settings that customize how Analysis Services performs. This section reviews common basic settings for Analysis Services. You can find a more thorough detailing of the Analysis Service settings in *Professional Microsoft SQL Server Analysis Services with MDX and DAX* (Harinath, et al Wrox, 2012)

To modify settings for Analysis Services, launch SQL Server Management Studio, and when prompted with the Connect to Server dialog, select the Server type as Analysis Services, and provide your Server and Instance Name, as shown in Figure 54-5.

54

FIGURE 54-5

The Connect to Server dialog.

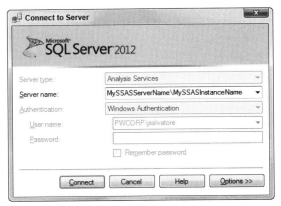

With a connection made to the Analysis Services Server, within the Object Explorer pane on the left, right-click the Server (topmost with yellow box and running green arrow indicator) node and select properties. The Analysis Services properties window displays, showing all the configurable settings for this server instance. Take note of the option at the bottom of the Analysis Server Properties window Show Advanced (All) Properties, as shown in Figure 54-6.

With the Analysis Server Properties, many different properties may be modified to suit the specific needs of a given environment. Some of the properties, such as `BackupDir` and `DataDir`, were actually configured as a result of the choices made during the installation. In addition, it is worth noting that the properties displayed for a given server instance of Analysis Services varies depending on the Server Mode selected. More specifically, the properties shown within the Analysis Server Properties will be different for a Multidimensional and Data Mining mode Analysis Services server instance than a Tabular mode Analysis Services server instance.

Commonly adjustedBasic and Advanced Analysis Server Properties for a Multidimensional and Data Mining mode Analysis Services server instance include the following:

- **AllowedBrowsingFolders**: Contains a listing of all file directories that may be used by Analysis Services for processes such as Backup and Restore and automatically contains those directories specified for Backup, Logs, and Data during installation
- **BackupDir**: Specifies the directory that will be used to store Analysis Services backup files and automatically contains a file directory that was specified during installation
- **Log \ FlightRecorder \ {Various}**: Can configure tracing of Analysis Server activity using FlightRecorded
- **Memory \ TotalMemoryLimit**: Places a cap on the amount of physical memory Analysis Services may use and is expressed in terms of a percentage of the total physical memory

- **Network \ Responses \ EnableCompression:** Can assist with reducing the IO size of Analysis Services query responses sent back to the requestors by compressing the results

- **OLAP \ LazyProcessing \ Enabled:** Instructs Analysis Services to process aggregations and indexes in the background after performing fast updates to dimensions

- **OLAP \ Process \ BufferMemoryLimit:** Used by Analysis Services to limit the system memory used when processing cubes and is valued as a percentage of total system physical memory

- **OLAP \ Query \ DefaultDrillthroughMaxRows:** Used to limit the total number of rows that is allowed to be returned when executing a drill-through query in Analysis Services

- **Security \ BuiltinAdminsAreServerAdmins:** Determines whether the local Administrators on the server are also permitted to be Analysis Services Server Administrators

- **Security \ RequireClientAuthentication:** Determines whether users can connect to Analysis Services using anonymous connections

FIGURE 54-6

Analysis Server Properties.

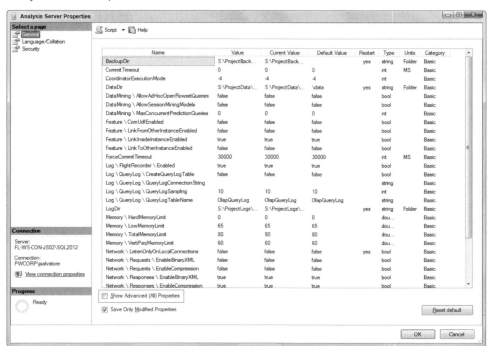

Although the General node properties are the main focus of the Analysis Server Properties, the Language/Collation and Security settings may also be changed using this properties dialog. Users or groups entered in the Security section will become Analysis Services Server administrators.

Advanced SSAS Deployments

Analysis Services supports quite a number of options to assist in meeting processing or querying goals. Key to the architecture of Analysis Services is that it natively supports server failover clustering.

Processing can be done on one instance of Analysis Services, and the processed data may then be copied to other instances used for querying. Many different ways to copy the data exist including but not limited to SAN Snapshots, Storage Mirrors, XCopy, and Analysis Services Cube Synchronization.

Querying can be managed through the use of several identical Analysis Services instances that are clustered and placed behind a Network Load Balancing (NLB). More details are available in the SQLCAT article Analysis Services Load Balancing Solution located at `http://sqlcat.com/sqlcat/b/technicalnotes/archive/2010/02/08/aslb-setup.aspx`.

Reviewing Query Performance with SQL Profiler

Efficient and fast queries are the cornerstone to a successful Analysis Services solution. Key for delivering the expected performance is ensuring that the system is optimized.

The main tool used to monitor the performance of Analysis Services is SQL Server Profiler. SQL Server Profiler contains a vast array of Analysis Services events that can be used to monitor performance, determine poorly performing MDX statements, step through MDX statements, replay events on another system, and audit activity. This section provides a brief introduction to using SQL Server Profiler for monitoring Analysis Services.

Event categories that can prove useful for tracing the Analysis Services server activity and investigating the performance of MDX queries submitted to the server to process user requests include:

- **Command events:** These provide insight into the actual types of statements issued to perform actions.
- **Discovery events:** These detail requests for metadata about server objects such as open connections.
- **Error and Warning events:** These events alert the developer to issues with building and deploying Analysis Services databases.
- **Notification events:** These events notify the user through tracing that certain query actions are taking place.

- **Query events:** These events notify the developer or administrator that query steps are taking place, for example, query begin, query end.

- **Query Processing:** These provide detailed insights into how a query was prepared and run by the query and storage engines

The following steps detail how to perform a SQL Server Profiler trace of Analysis Services:

1. From the Start menu, select All Programs ➪ Microsoft SQL Server 2012 ➪ Performance Tools ➪ SQL Server Profiler.

2. On SQL Server Profiler menu, select File ➪ New Trace or press Ctrl-N.

3. Within the Connect to Server dialog, provide the Server type of Analysis Services, and provide the wanted Server name for the server/instance that is to be traced.

4. In the Trace Properties dialog, on the General tab, configure the name of the trace and provide destination (file or table) and duration information. Only locations specified in the server property `AllowedBrowsingFolders` are allowed to be used.

5. In the Trace Properties dialog, on the Events Selection tab, check off the wanted events to be captured as part of the trace. For user queries it is best to capture the Audit Login event class, the Query Begin event class, and the Query End event class, as shown in Figure 54-7.

FIGURE 54-7

Trace Properties dialog Events Selection.

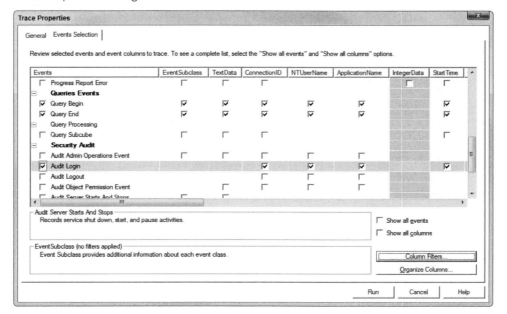

6. In SQL Server Management Studio, connect to an Analysis Services server instance, and browse a cube.

7. With a few measures and dimensions selected for browsing, return to SQL Server Profiler, and in the Trace Properties dialog, press Run to start the trace.

8. With the trace started, return to SQL Server Management Studio, and press Execute Query.

9. Having run an Analysis Services query, return to SQL Server Profiler, and stop the trace.

10. Trace results should display as shown in Figure 54-8.

FIGURE 54-8

Trace Results.

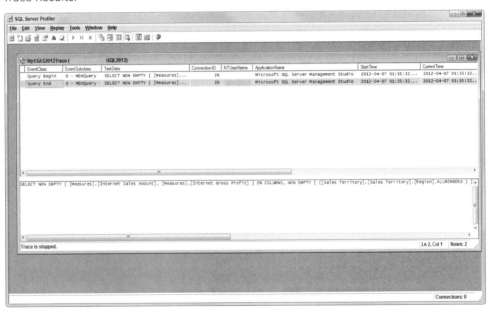

SQL Server Extended Events (XEvents) enables tracing events using a less-intrusive monitoring system that consumes fewer resources. In addition, performance counters can be monitored to get additional insights into the operation of an Analysis Services instance.

Summary

This chapter provided a general understanding of how to install and configure Analysis Services, provided details to aid in changing Analysis Server properties, reviewed various advanced Analysis Services deployments, and demonstrated how SQL Server Profiler traces may be used for monitoring Analysis Services performance.

Authoring Reports in Reporting Services

IN THIS CHAPTER

Creating Reports

Connecting a Report to Data Using Data Sources

Using Report Builder

Exploring Data Visualizations

Understanding the Report Gallery and Report Parts

P ractically all people with jobs consume data to perform them, usually via some sort of report. Looking at reports with this perspective, SQL Server Reporting Services (SSRS) becomes the most important element of the Microsoft BI Stack. A properly designed reporting solution quickly points decision makers to the information they need to solve critical business problems, whereas a cumbersome solution leads to frustration and disuse. Much like the proverbial tree falling in the forest, what good is the data in your warehouse if no one uses it?

To this end, SSRS continues to add tools that stack the deck in favor of successful data delivery. Whether it is through a weekly detailed report pushed to users via an e-mail subscription; an executive dashboard used to apprise the CEO of the overall health of a company viewed through SharePoint; or a completely interactive, ad hoc Power View report used to "wow" the Board of Directors during the annual meeting, SSRS gives end users both the data they need and the ability to quickly get it.

What's New in SSRS 2012

The features offered in SSRS 2012 follow:

- A new ad hoc report authoring tool called Power View.
- Self-Service Report alerts.
- Office 2007 and 2010 rendering for Excel and Word.
- Better integration with SharePoint.
    - Seamless SharePoint configurations and deployments.
    - Better performance in integrated mode: With a 30 percent to 60 percent increase in report rendering time than with 2008 R2.
    - SSRS in integrated mode now uses SharePoint backup and restore methods.
    - SSRS catalogs are now stored in SharePoint.

Report Authoring Environments

Standard Reports can be created and edited by your choice of two tools: Visual Studio's Report Designer or Report Builder. For instant ad hoc reporting, there is the exciting new Power View option, which renders inside a browser based on the Business Intelligence Semantic Model (BISM).

This chapter mainly covers the two modes of editing standard reports (RDLs), Report Designer inside Visual Studio and Report Builder. Chapter 59, "Creating and Deploying Power View Reports," covers that topic at length.

Throughout this chapter, data from the AdventureWorksDW sample relational database and the Adventure Works DW Analysis Services sample database are used to create sample reports. You can download copies of these databases from www.codeplex.com.

The Report Designer in SQL Server Data Tools (SSDT)

The Report Designer is the Visual Studio report authoring environment. It is launched when a reporting project is created inside SQL Server Data Tools or Visual Studio 2010. It provides the objects and controls necessary to create multiple reports and their data sources and sets. The advantage of using Report Designer is integration with source control such as Team Foundation Server and the ability to view source code. Report Designer also allows the developer to group similar reports into projects.

Report Builder

Released with SQL Server 2008 R2, this third iteration of Report Builder has matured dramatically since its first incarnation. You can access Report Builder via the Report Manager. It features the same objects and formatting options available in the Report Designer in a more Office-friendly context.

Because it was released as Report Builder 3.0, Report Builder also has the capability to use the Report Gallery, accessed through Report Manager. The Report Gallery enables Report Parts to be saved and published to the Report Server and used in Report Builder reports by other users, greatly increasing reusability within organizations.

Power View

Power View is the newest report authoring tool offered in Reporting Services, new with SSRS 2012. It is completely web-based; no installation is required to use it other than the web browser and Silverlight. Power View delivers an instant visual design experience that is always presentation-ready. Reports are built in Preview mode, meaning as objects are configured, the data is populated — no toggling between design and preview. Power View is only available in Reporting Services SharePoint Integrated mode. It can only use the Business Intelligence Semantic Model (BISM) as its data source.

 For more information on working with Power View reports, see Chapter 59.

The Basic Elements of a Report

Any report created inside SQL Server Data Tools has three main elements: the report data source, the report dataset, and the report definition language file. All three are essential for a report to work properly after it is deployed to the Report Server.

 See Chapter 56, "Configuring and Administering Reporting Services," for more information on deploying reporting elements to the Report Server.

Data Sources

The data source is the stored connection string to a data source of a report. For instance, if you report from a database inside SQL Server, the data source contains the server name, database name, and the credentials necessary for connecting to it. Data sources can be shared between reports in a project or embedded in a particular report. An embedded data source will not appear under the shared data sources node inside SSDT. It exists solely in the report in which it was created. In addition to being shareable inside a project, data

55

sources can now be published to the Report Server and used by other developers in their projects. Data sources created inside a Reporting Services project are deployed with the project to the Report Server. Data source files are suffixed with the .rds file extension.

Although you can extend Reporting Services by creating a custom data extension, several data source types are available out-of-the-box:

- Microsoft SQL Server
- Windows Azure SQL Database (introduced in SSRS 2008 RS as SQL Azure)
- Microsoft SQL Server Parallel Data Warehouse (offered since SSRS 2008 R2)
- OLE DB
- Microsoft SQL Server Analysis Services
- Oracle
- ODBC
- XML
- Report Server Model
- Microsoft SharePoint List (offered since SSRS 2008 R2)
- SAP NetWeaver BI
- Hyperion Essbase
- TERADATA

Datasets

The dataset represents a filtered subset of the data from the data source. Using the example of the data source being a SQL Server database, the dataset would be a query. New with SQL Server 2008 R2, datasets can also be shared inside a project and published to the Report Server for consumption by other reporting projects. Dataset files are denoted by the file extension .rsd. Defining or changing a dataset launches the Dataset Properties dialog, which includes several tabs:

- **Query:** Consists of most any string appropriate to the data source, including SQL statements, stored procedure calls, or XML queries.
- **Parameters:** Displays the parameters used in the query and the mapping to the report's parameters.
- **Fields:** Lists all fields returned by the query and the corresponding names used in the dataset. When the names of the fields can't be determined at design time, these names must be manually entered. Calculated fields may also be added here, which helps centralize expressions referred to frequently in the report. (For example, defining profit as [revenue] − [expenses] enables profit to be referred to throughout the report as if it came from the source data.)

- **Options**: Provides source-specific options such as collation.

- **Filters**: Enables the definition of filters on the data returned from the source. Filters are run in-memory after the entire dataset has been returned and are often used with report parameters to enable users to display a subset of the data without querying the source a second time.

Since SSRS 2008 R2, datasets have had the capability of being created as shared datasets and published as separate objects to the Report Manager. This enabled users, who might not create a query for a drop-down list in a parameter to consume shared datasets in their own reports, speeding development time.

Report Definition Language (RDL) Files

The report definition language files contain the layout of data fields, formatting, and other design elements that make up the actual report. They have the file extension of .rdl.

Building a Report with the Report Wizard

Reports vary in complexity and required design time; however, you can create a quick report by using the Report Wizard inside SSRS. it often speeds development time to get a report foundation by using the wizard, which can then be modified to any further requirements you have.

Imagine that you are the report writer for Adventureworks. You have been tasked with a simple report giving the contact information for all of the resellers of Adventureworks products. You have worked out the following query from the AdventureworksDW database to satisfy the requirements:

```
SELECT dsr.ResellerName , dsr.Phone
,dsr.AddressLine1, dsr.AddressLine2, dg.City,
dg.StateProvinceCode , dg.EnglishCountryRegionName ,
dsr.AnnualSales
FROM DimReseller dsr
JOIN DimGeography dg ON dsr.GeographyKey = dg.GeographyKey
```

FIGURE 55-1

Query result for reseller contact info.

	ResellerName	Phone	AddressLine1	AddressLine2	City	StateProvinceCode	EnglishCountryRegionName	AnnualSales
1	Volume Bike Sellers	1 (11) 500 555-0119	2565-175 Mitchell Road	NULL	Alexandria	NSW	Australia	3000000.00
2	Mass Market Bikes	1 (11) 500 555-0197	Level 59	NULL	Alexandria	NSW	Australia	300000.00
3	Twin Cycles	1 (11) 500 555-0190	2253-217 Palmer Street	NULL	Darlinghurst	NSW	Australia	800000.00
4	Rich Department Store	1 (11) 500 555-0118	99 - 6 Orion Road	NULL	Lane Cove	NSW	Australia	3000000.00
5	Rental Gallery	1 (11) 500 555-0176	2520b Underwood Street	NULL	Lavender Bay	NSW	Australia	1500000.00
6	Budget Toy Store	1 (11) 500 555-0140	25 Epping Road	NULL	Lavender Bay	NSW	Australia	3000000.00
7	Global Sports Outlet	1 (11) 500 555-0189	Circot Bus Pk/995-27 Paul St N	NULL	Lavender Bay	NSW	Australia	3000000.00
8	Online Bike Catalog	1 (11) 500 555-0113	65 Epping Rd	NULL	Lavender Bay	NSW	Australia	3000000.00

55

To create a basic report using the Report Wizard that displays the reseller contact information shown in Figure 55-1, first open the Report Designer in SSDT by going to Start ⇨ All Programs ⇨ Microsoft SQL Server 2012 ⇨ SQL Server Data Tools. SSDT opens. To create a Reporting Services Project, go to File ⇨ New ⇨ Project. From the New Project dialog box ensure that Business Intelligence is the selected project type, and then select Report Server Project Wizard from the choices of available templates. Name the project **AdventureworksReports** and select the file location for the project. Click OK.

Follow these steps to create and view the reseller report with the wizard:

1. If the Welcome screen appears with the Report Wizard dialog box, click Next.

2. Select the radio button for New Data Source.

3. Name the source **AWDW**.

4. Select Microsoft SQL Server under Type.

5. Click Edit.

6. In the Connection Properties window, type in the server name where your copy of AdventureworksDW is located.

7. Supply the credentials needed to connect to the server (Windows Authentication or SQL Server user and password).

8. From the drop-down menu for the database, select AdventureworksDW.

9. Click OK to finish configuring the Connection.

10. Returning to the Report Wizard, click the box to make this a Shared Data Source.

11. Click Next.

12. In the Query window, paste the query from your query editor:
    ```
    SELECT dsr.ResellerName , dsr.Phone
    ,dsr.AddressLine1, dsr.AddressLine2, dg.City,
    dg.StateProvinceCode , dg.EnglishCountryRegionName ,
     dsr.AnnualSales
    FROM DimReseller dsr
    JOIN DimGeography dg ON dsr.GeographyKey = dg.GeographyKey
    ```

13. To choose the report type, click Next.

14. Leave the radio button beside Tabular selected, and click Next.

15. To move fields from the Available Fields section to the report, click the Details button for every field until all fields have been moved to the Detail section. Click Next.

16. Select Corporate as a color scheme. Click Next

17. Select the Report Server and folder on which you wish to deploy the report.

18. Name the report **Reseller Contact**, and click Finish.

19. Click the Preview tab in the Report Designer to view the report.

FIGURE 55-2

The Reseller Contact Report, Preview mode.

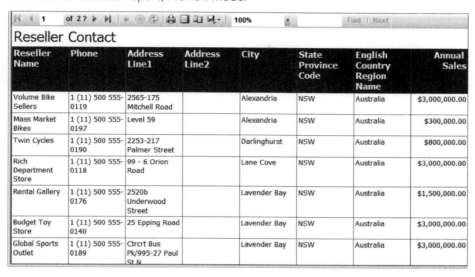

| | 1 | of 2 ? | | | 100% | | | Find | Next |

Reseller Contact

Reseller Name	Phone	Address Line1	Address Line2	City	State Province Code	English Country Region Name	Annual Sales
Volume Bike Sellers	1 (11) 500 555-0119	2565-175 Mitchell Road		Alexandria	NSW	Australia	$3,000,000.00
Mass Market Bikes	1 (11) 500 555-0197	Level 59		Alexandria	NSW	Australia	$300,000.00
Twin Cycles	1 (11) 500 555-0190	2253-217 Palmer Street		Darlinghurst	NSW	Australia	$800,000.00
Rich Department Store	1 (11) 500 555-0118	99 - 6 Orion Road		Lane Cove	NSW	Australia	$3,000,000.00
Rental Gallery	1 (11) 500 555-0176	2520b Underwood Street		Lavender Bay	NSW	Australia	$1,500,000.00
Budget Toy Store	1 (11) 500 555-0140	25 Epping Road		Lavender Bay	NSW	Australia	$3,000,000.00
Global Sports Outlet	1 (11) 500 555-0189	Ctrcrt Bus Pk/995-27 Paul St N		Lavender Bay	NSW	Australia	$3,000,000.00

You now have a report as a solid starting point. You learn the Report Designer environment and build on this report throughout the next few sections.

Authoring a Report from Scratch

You have just created a project in the Report Designer using the Report Wizard. You may also forego the wizard and create the same Reporting Services project by following similar steps. From the Report Designer, go to File ➪ New ➪ Project. From the New Project dialog box ensure that Business Intelligence is the selected project type, and then select Report Server Project from the choices of available templates. Name the project **AdventureworksReports** and select the file location for the project. Click OK.

To create the Reseller Contact inside a blank Report Server project, perform the following:

1. From the right side of the screen under Solution Explorer, select Reports.
2. Right click Reports, and select Add New Report.
3. If the Welcome screen appears with the Report Wizard dialog box, click Next.
4. Select the radio button for New Data Source.
5. Name the source **AWDW**.
6. Select Microsoft SQL Server under Type.

55

7. Click Edit.

8. In the Connection Properties window, type in the server name where your copy of AdventureworksDW is located.

9. Supply the credentials needed to connect to the server (Windows Authentication or SQL Server user and password).

10. From the drop-down menu for the database, select AdventureworksDW.

11. Click OK to finish configuring the Connection.

12. Returning to the Report Wizard, click the box to make this a Shared Data Source.

13. Click Next.

14. In the Query window, paste the query from your query editor:

```
SELECT dsr.ResellerName , dsr.Phone
,dsr.AddressLine1, dsr.AddressLine2, dg.City,
dg.StateProvinceCode , dg.EnglishCountryRegionName ,
 dsr.AnnualSales
FROM DimReseller dsr
JOIN DimGeography dg ON dsr.GeographyKey = dg.GeographyKey
```

15. To choose the report type, click Next.

16. Leave the radio button beside Tabular selected, and click Next.

17. To move fields from the Available Fields section to the report, click the Details button for every field until all fields have been moved to the Detail section. Click Next.

18. Select Corporate as a color scheme.

19. Name the report **Reseller Contact**, and click Finish.

20. Click the Preview tab to view the report.

Exploring the Report Designer

Now that you have a report created inside the Report Designer, it is a good time to take a look around to become familiar with this environment.

The Design Surface

Figure 55-3 shows the Report Designer with the report you just created open in Design mode. When working with Reporting Services, you see many toolbars at the top of the screen. These can prove useful as shortcuts when formatting the report. For instance, there is a button for background color that you easily can use instead of using the properties box for a row. The area in the middle of the screen is the configurable portion of the report and is referred to as the design surface. Here you can drag items onto the report and format the report objects. To toggle between Design view and preview, click the Preview and Design tabs to the top left of the design surface.

FIGURE 55-3

The Reseller Contact report in Design view.

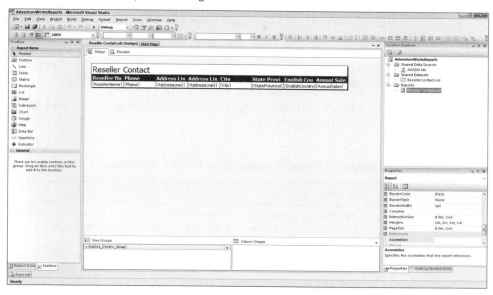

You can also add headers and footers to your report by going to the menu toolbar and selecting Report ⇨ Add Page Header or Report ⇨ Add Page Footer. Items in the header and footer sections appear on every page of the report.

Solution Explorer and Properties

On the right side of the screen is the Solution Explorer, which appears in any Visual Studio project. The items that are manipulated here in the context of a Reporting Services project are the Shared Data Sources, Shared Data Sets, and Reports. Under the Solution Explorer is the Properties Window, which changes in context to reveal the properties of the currently selected object. Changing the properties of objects affects both their behavior and appearance, as shown in the next section.

> **TIP**
>
> To be able to see the solution tick box in VS, go to Tools ⇨ Options ⇨ Projects and Solutions ⇨ Always show solution tick box in Visual Studio.

Report Data and Toolbox Panes

On the left side of the screen are two critical panes sharing the same space: the Report Data and the Toolbox panes. Toggle between these panes by clicking on the tabs at the bottom of the pane (refer to the bottom-left corner of Figure 52-3.)

The Report Data pane contains the elements necessary for working with the data in each report. In this pane you can find the Built-In Fields, Images, Parameters, Data Sources, and Datasets for the report. Dataset fields, which compose the data in the report, are found here and can be dragged from here onto the report. Built-In Fields are canned values, particularly useful when placed in the report header and footer. They are items, such as the page number, name of the report, and total number of pages. Parameters enable the report user to filter the results of a report by changing the values of configured fields.

The Report Items toolbox contains all the available objects that can be used on the report. Table 55-1 explains all the objects.

TABLE 55-1 Report Objects Available in the Toolbox

Report Item	Description
Textbox	Adds report content not located within a table or matrix. The textbox can contain static text or an expression, or can be bound to a data field.
Line, Rectangle	Adds visual separation and formatting to a report. Rectangles can also be used to group other items, enabling them to be treated as a group for placement and visibility. They also enable multiple controls to be placed where, by default, you can place only a textbox.
Image	Places an image in the report. The image source can be Embedded, Project, Database, or the web.
Table	Renders the dataset in a Tablix with a fixed set of columns. The item contains many options to control how the data is grouped, sorted, exported, and presented. A report can contain multiple tables, providing the capability to include data from multiple datasets and data sources in a single report. Begin with a Table instead of a Matrix if the data will be presented primarily as fixed columns.
Matrix	Renders a dataset as a crosstab. For example, the Matrix report item could show total sales by region as row headers, and periods as column headers, enabling the column headers to change over time based on the underlying dataset. Multiple column, row, and detail criteria can be added to the Matrix report item. Begin with a Matrix instead of a Table when the data will be presented primarily with variable column headers.
List	The list is bound to a dataset. The content of a list is repeated for each row in the dataset or for each grouped row if group criteria are specified. The body of the list represents the template for the report items to be displayed. The report author places items within the template, free-form, without the spatial constraints of a table.

Report Item	Description
Chart	This item includes a wide variety of charts and provides extensive control over the chart type and formatting.
Gauge	Similar to charts, gauges come in a wide variety of shapes and sizes. But unlike charts, which show many data points, gauges display a single data point. For example, a gauge might be used to display actual sales versus a planned sales goal.
Subreport	Use this item to render another report within the current report, usually displaying some details not available from the dataset driving the current report.
Map	Use to visualize and analyze spatial data.
Data Bar	Displays the value of one textbox in a detail line graphically as either a bar or a column.
Sparkline	Displays data in one row or group graphically as a tiny graph placed beside each row. Useful for showing trending of a report line.
Indicator	Displays data based on predetermined ranges and value as a state indicator. For instance, place an indicator object beside every row in a data grid. The indicator can be related to a sales figure: Green for over $1,000, yellow for $999 to $500, and red for $499 and under.

The Text Box Properties Window

After you complete the steps of the wizard, you usually do some more formatting to clean up the report. The width and height of the textboxes can be modified by placing your mouse on the lines of the textbox. After the mouse turns into an arrow, click and drag to change the size. Another thing you can easily accomplish is to change captions or labels. Simply click inside the textbox and change the text as wanted. These actions are changing the properties of the textbox. To get a full view of all the properties a textbox possesses, right-click one and select Text Box properties. You see the multi-tabbed Text Box properties window; the features are shown in Table 55-2.

TABLE 55-2   The Text Box Properties Window

Tab	Items Configured
General	Name, Value (this is the label), and tooltips. Autosizing options.
Number	The number tab contains several options with suboptions for configuring all number data types: Number enables formatting of numbers. Options are default (none), number (you can specify the decimal places shown, and commas. Currency shows decimals, comma placement, and the currency (Dollars, Euros, and so on). Date enables formatting of date, percentage, scientific, and custom.

Continues

TABLE 55-2 *(continued)*

Tab	Items Configured
Alignment	Horizontal options are Left, Center, and Right. Vertical options are Top, Center, and Bottom. Configure any padding here.
Font	Change the font of text inside the box. Standard formatting options are Font, Properties, Strikethrough.
Border	Border options. You can control which edges have a border, and the width, color, and pattern of the line edging the box.
Fill	Fill options are colors, patterns, images for display, or a watermark.
Visibility	Can hide objects in a report. This is also where drill-downs are configured.
Interactive Sorting	When a property is set, enables user to click a column header and interactively sort the report.
Action	When a property is set, enables drill-throughs to a URL or to another report after clicking the item.

Using Reporting Services Features to Visualize Your Data

So you have a basic report thanks to the wizard. Now you receive another few requirements. Your boss says, "This is great, but I'd like to know who my top clients are. Can you highlight clients who exceed $1,000,000 in sales?" You can accomplish this in several ways; two of them are covered next.

One way to achieve the goal would be add another field to the dataset, which would evaluate the annual sales and evaluate to `true` when they are more than $1,000,000. To create a calculated field on the dataset, perform the following steps:

1. Right-click the `ResellerContact` dataset.
2. Select Add Calculated Field.
3. In the last Field Name on the Fields tab, type **PremiumClient**.
4. Click the Fx button beside the Field Source box beside the Field Name.
5. In the Expression Dialog box, enter **=IIF(Fields!AnnualSales .Value>1000000,"True", Nothing)** and click OK twice.
6. Drag the PremiumClient Field onto the report surface beside the AnnualSales field. Let go of the field when the ibar appears.
7. Click Preview to see the results.

The previous method gives another literal value to answer the question "who are my best customers?" If space on the report is tight or your user prefers to see visualizations in color to highlight the data, you can achieve the same goal by conditionally formatting the AnnualSales field. To change the background color of the AnnualSales field to Yellow when the criteria are met, perform the following steps:

1. Right-click the text box for AnnualSales (the data, not the label).
2. Select Text Box Properties.
3. Select the Fill tab.
4. Click the Expression box Fx beside the drop-down menu for Fill color.
5. Type **=IIF(Fields!AnnualSales.Value>1000000,"Yellow", Nothing).**
6. Click OK twice.
7. Click on the preview tab to preview the report.

Creating a Matrix Report

Released with SSRS 2008, the matrix data region gives the utmost flexibility in configuring the data in a report and easily achieves what used to take custom expressions to accomplish. The matrix template enables reports to aggregate detail rows both horizontally and vertically and to drill both horizontally and vertically. Matrix reports often contain row and column groups, which are expandable in the report and enable data to be aggregated horizontally or vertically. To create a matrix report, proceed through the same steps outlined in the section "Authoring a Report from Scratch," with the exception of step 16. Instead of leaving the report type as Tabular, select Matrix.

Working with Cubes

SQL Server Analysis Services cubes are objects that contain measures aggregated by one or more dimensions. For instance a cube might contain sales data aggregated by date and region. You have just been introduced to matrix reports, which work beautifully with data from Analysis Services. You will now create a matrix report with the data from the Adventureworks cube inside the Adventure Works DW Analysis Services database. You create a report that details the Internet Sales by Geographical region and Product Category data. To create the report, perform the following:

1. In Solution Explorer, right-click Reports, and select Add ⇨ New Item.
2. In the Add New Item dialog box, select Report from templates, and type in **InternetSales** for the report name. Click Add.
3. From the Report Data pane, right-click data sources, and select Add Data Source.
4. In the Data Source Properties Dialog box, type **AWCube**.
5. For Type, click the drop-down, and select Microsoft SQL Server Analysis Services.

55

6. Click Edit to supply the connection string information to your copy of the Adventureworks AS database. Supply the connection to Adventure Works DW. Click OK.

7. Right-click the `Datasets` and click Add Dataset.

8. Enter **InternetSales** for the name.

9. Leave the Use a Dataset Embedded in My Report radio button selected.

10. Choose `AWCube` as the Data Source.

11. Click the Query Designer button to launch the query designer.

12. Under the measure group, click the drop-down arrow, and select `Internet Sales`.

13. Expand the measures under the Internet Sales measure group. Drag `Internet_ Sales_ Amount` to the center design surface.

14. Expand the product dimension. Expand the members of the `Product Categories` hierarchy by clicking the plus sign beside it.

15. Drag the `Subcategory` and `Category` attributes to the left of `Internet_Sales_ Amount`.

16. Expand the `Sales Territory` dimension. Expand the `Sales Territory` hierarchy underneath it.

17. Drag over the `Region` and `Country` attributes.

18. In the dimension filter columns above the data grid, select `Sales Territory` as the dimension. Then select `Sales Territory Group` as the hierarchy. Select `Equal` as the operator, and then select `North America` as the Filter Expression by clicking in the Filter Group box and then drilling through to the attribute.

19. Click OK to exit the query designer window, and OK to exit the dataset window.

20. Click the Toolbox pane beside the Report Data pane.

21. Drag a `Matrix Grid` onto the design surface.

22. Click the Report Data pane.

23. Drag the field `Internet_Sales_Amount` onto the date field (the lower-right corner of the matrix grid).

24. Drag the `Subcategory` field from the dataset to the immediate left of the `Internet_Sales_Amount` in the rows field.

25. Drag the `Category` to the immediate left of the `Subcategory`.

26. Drag the `Region` directly on top of the Internet Sales amount label in the columns field.

27. Drag `Country` directly above it.

28. Select all the label (nondata or Internet Sales) fields by clicking them with the mouse and the `Ctrl` key pressed.

29. Click the Background color button on the Formatting toolbar. (If the formatting toolbar is not present, you can make it so by clicking View ➪ Toolbars ➪ Formatting from the menu bar.) Select LightSteelBlue and click OK. Leaving the text boxes selected; click the B on the formatting toolbar to make the font of all the labels bold.

30. Select the Internet Sales Amount field on the report, and right-click. Select Text Box Properties.

31. Click the Numbers tab.

32. Select Currency, and then click the check box beside Use Thousands Separator. Click OK.

33. Under row groups in the bottom left of the design surface, right-click the Subcategory group. Select Group Properties. Click the Visibility tab.

34. Select hide.

35. Click the check box beside Display can be toggled by this report item.

36. Select Category for the report item to toggle by..

37. Under column groups in the bottom right of the design surface, right-click the Region grouping. Click the Visibility tab.

38. Select Hide.

39. Click the check box beside Display can be toggled by this report item.

40. Select Country for the field that is used to toggle the grouping. Click OK.

Click preview to see the results. Because the Subcategory group has been conditionally hidden and can be toggled with the Category group, there will be a plus sign beside the Category group on the report. The Subcategory data can be seen by clicking the plus sign beside the Category group, as shown in Figure 55-4. The same toggling can be performed on the Country column. This toggling is referred to as *drill-down*.

FIGURE 55-4

A matrix report with toggling enabled.

Category	Subcategory	□ United States				
		Central	Northeast	Northwest	Southeast	Southwest
		Internet Average Sales Amount	Internet Average Sales Amount	Internet Average Sales Amount	Internet Average Sales Amount	Internet Average Sales Amount
⊞ Accessories		$232.46	$381.42	$110,150.80	$531.97	$145,125.42
⊟ Bikes	Mountain Bikes	$2,071.42	$4,344.09	$1,333,561.55	$7,455.89	$2,070,024.79
	Road Bikes	$539.99	$1,700.99	$1,716,135.51	$1,565.98	$2,569,983.42
	Touring Bikes			$431,788.26	$2,384.07	$858,303.57
⊞ Clothing		$156.96	$105.97	$58,230.43	$300.94	$74,713.61

55

Working with Parameters

Most report users want to interact with the data in a report. For instance, a user may want to see the sales of a product for only one state, Pennsylvania, and then change the state filter to Florida and peruse that data. To accomplish this, parameters are used in Reporting Services. Not only do parameters help the user, they also aid in report rendering, by limiting the amount of data returned by a dataset. Parameters are added to the dataset through several methods. If the dataset connects to a SQL Server relational source, you can add a parameter by adding @ParameterName in the WHERE clause of the query text in the dataset, using the same structure as you would use to parameterize Transact-SQL.

In the case of the first query written in the ResellerContact report, if you want to add a parameter to filter by country, you could accomplish this by adding a line to the end of the query in the ResellerContact dataset, like this:

```
SELECT dsr.ResellerName , dsr.Phone
,dsr.AddressLine1, dsr.AddressLine2, dg.City,
dg.StateProvinceCode , dg.EnglishCountryRegionName ,
dsr.AnnualSales
FROM DimReseller dsr
JOIN DimGeography dg ON dsr.GeographyKey = dg.GeographyKey
where dg. EnglishCountryRegionName = @RegionCountryName
```

After the parameter has been added to the ResellerContact dataset, a parameter is available in the Report Data pane under the parameters node. A parameter can be further configured by right-clicking the parameter in the Report Data pane and selecting Parameter Properties, which opens the Report Parameter Properties window, as shown in Figure 55-5.

Located on the General tab of the Report Parameter Properties window, the Prompt box enables changing the text beside the parameter. The Available Values tab is quite important. The parameter as currently configured would take free form text and then enable the user to submit the parameter and view the report. A better way to choose the value of a parameter is to create another dataset of known available values and attach that dataset to the parameter. For instance, the parameter you just configured would return data only if one of the countries available in the table were typed into it, so wouldn't it be more efficient to configure a dataset of the distinct values available in the CountryRegionName column? To accomplish this, you can create a dataset named CountryRegionName in the report using the following query:

```
SELECT Distinct EnglishCountryRegionName  FROM DimGeography
```

Then attach the dataset to the @RegionCountryName parameter by configuring the values in its Available Values tab, as shown in Figure 55-6:

FIGURE 55-5

The Report Parameter Properties window.

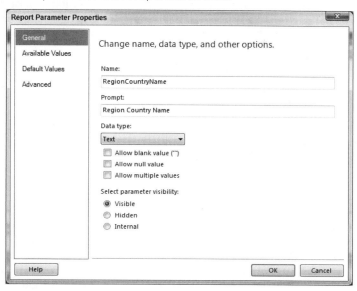

FIGURE 55-6

The Available Values tab configuration.

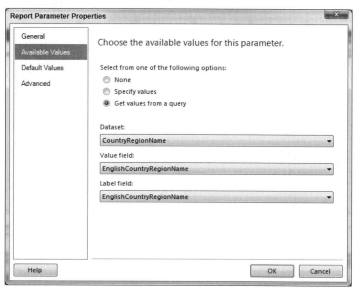

You can create parameters inside datasets built off of cubes as well. Going back to the matrix report you created off of the Adventure Works cube, you can check the parameter box inside the query designer as shown in Figure 55-7. This creates a hidden dataset that the report uses for the parameter. You can see existing hidden datasets inside a project by selecting Datasets in the Report Data pane, right clicking and selecting Show Hidden Datasets.

FIGURE 55-7

Parameterizing a dataset built off of a cube.

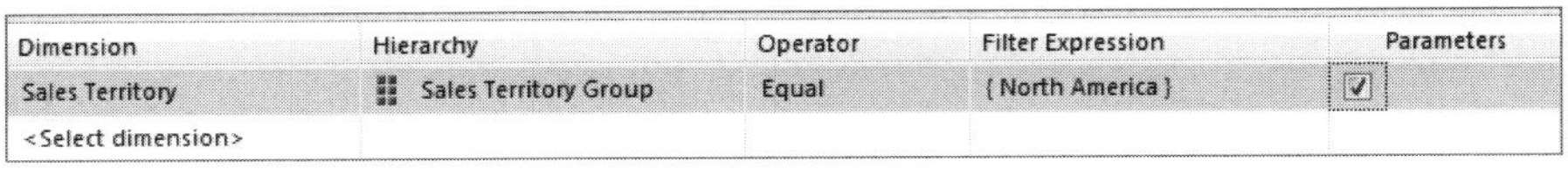

Dimension	Hierarchy	Operator	Filter Expression	Parameters
Sales Territory	Sales Territory Group	Equal	{ North America }	☑
<Select dimension>				

For more information on working with parameters inside the Report Designer, see `http://msdn.microsoft.com/en-us/library/aa337432.aspx`.

Working with RS Expressions

Anywhere inside the report designer you see a button with the Fx icon or a drop-down list with Expression indicates that you can perform modifications with an expression. Expressions in SSRS are visual basic code snippets that evaluate to a single value. Their dynamic evaluations are used to change the properties of report elements. The dynamic formatting accomplished at the beginning of this section was done with expressions. As you saw, they can be used to change values and change text box properties, formatting properties, and parameters; virtually any object inside a report can be configured using expressions. Using visual basic as its base language, they can be extremely simple or complex depending on your needs.

One common function used in reporting is the IIF statement, which accepts three parameters: an expression, a true part (meaning what to return when the expression evaluates to true) and a false part (what to return when the expression evaluates to false). For instance, to format the detail rows on a report to alternate in color between LightSteelBlue and no color, the following expression should be entered in the property box expression for Background Color of the row:

```
= IIf(RowNumber(Nothing) Mod 2 = 0, "LightSteelBlue", "Transparent")
```

The logic of the expression can be interpreted as "if the RowNumber divided by 2 = 0 (meaning it's an even numbered row), then the property (in this case the background color of the row) equals LightSteelBlue; if it does not equal 0, then the background color equals transparent. Nifty trick isn't it?

For more information on using SSRS Expressions inside both Report Designer and Report Builder 3.0 see Expression Uses in Reports (Report Builder 3.0 and SSRS) at `http://msdn.microsoft.com/en-us/library/ms345237(v=SQL.110).aspx`.

Designing the Report Layout

The Report Designer contains a rich feature set for designing reports. This section discusses the basics of report design and demonstrates creating a report design, grouping and sorting data, and adding data visualizations to a report.

The Design tab in the Report Designer contains rich features to make formatting even the most complicated reports possible. The page layout contains three sections: header, body, and footer. Table 55-3 summarizes the behavior and purpose of each section. Designing the report layout is similar to working with Windows Forms. Report items are added by dragging them from the Toolbox onto the report.

TABLE 55-3 Report Sections

Section	Description
Header	By default, content in the header appears on every page. This is a good place to include the report title to indicate why the report exists. The `PrintOnFirstPage` and `PrintOnLastPage` properties can be used to prevent the header from appearing on the first and last pages.
Body	If the report contains parameters, it's a good idea to add a section to the top or bottom of the body to show the value of the parameters used to execute the report, and perhaps a short description of what the report represents. Adding this detail at the top or bottom of the body ensures that the information is printed only once, rather than on every page.
Footer	Like the header, the footer also appears on every page by default and can be turned off for the first and last pages. This is a good place to include information specifying who ran the report, when he ran it, the report version, and page numbering.

Choosing a Report Type

The Tablix data region replaced Table, Matrix, and List regions, but Table, Matrix, and List are still available as templates from the toolbar. For instance, a List can be nested under a matrix region. In SSRS 2005, these would have been using separate schemas, but now they both use the Tablix schema, even though they affect the data layout differently.

A matrix report is sometimes referred to as a tablix, and you have developed a report using the matrix already in this chapter. Matrix reports enable grouping (and therefore aggregating) on columns and rows, and enable variable numbers of columns and rows. Tables are desirable for displaying data that would easily fit into an Excel workbook, as in a set number of columns and a variable number of rows. Lists are great for free-form visualization of data. Any item available can be dragged onto a list, such as images and charts. Lists are great for nesting forms, such as rows under other Report Parts.

Grouping and Sorting

Grouping is an integral part of the matrix report. Grouping within a matrix provides the power to organize data in many ways. Figure 55-8 shows a matrix item with groups. The row and column groups displayed at the bottom show the name and order of the groups of the currently selected report item. This grouping display is enabled by checking the Grouping option of the Report menu of the design environment. The scope of the grouping in the Tablix is indicated by the brace markings within the row and column handles, indicating which portions will be repeated for each group.

Groups can be created by dragging fields into the Row Groups or Column Groups areas, or by clicking the drop-down on each group. The drop-down also enables a group to be removed or totals to be added.

The drop-down is also a convenient way to access the Group Properties dialog, as shown in Figure 55-8, to control the details of a grouping. Although the ability to group data seems simple, the effect on report presentation can be stunning.

FIGURE 55-8

The Grouping Properties dialog box.

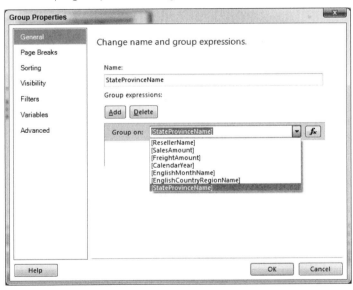

Because sort order can be specified at both the Tablix and group level, you need to understand that group sort definitions override Tablix definitions. This is in keeping with the Reporting Services theme of child property settings overriding the parent settings.

Interactive sorting can also be enabled in a variety of ways. Traditionally, this has been implemented by adding sort arrows to the column header of a table. Pressing the arrows on the rendered report causes the report to re-sort as wanted. Although column headers are the normal place to enable sorting, no real restrictions exist for how interactive sorting is enabled, and it can be used for detail rows, groups, or various combinations.

Working with Visualization Tools

Reporting Services has greatly enhanced graphics to present report data. Charts show proportion, trends, and comparisons of series of data. Drag a chart onto the design surface, and click to select the item. Three areas appear ready for data fields to be dragged onto them:

- **Series:** This is the field that separates the data into groups that appear in the legend.
- **Category:** This is the field that subdivides a series into distinct bars or points on a line.
- **Data:** These are the actual values to be charted.

Fields can be dragged directly from the Report Data pane where the dataset is defined to a chart. Titles, placement, and many formatting details can now be set by directly typing on or moving items within the chart. An exhaustive set of additional properties is available via the right-click menu to control nearly every detail of the chart.

To change the colors of elements inside a chart, right click the selected item. From the context menu, select its properties. Then select the `Fill` tab and select the color and pattern you desire. For instance, if you want to change the colors of the bars on a bar chart you would select the series in design mode, right click and then select `Series Properties`. From the properties window, select `Fill` and customize the colors as you wish.

Prior to SQL Server 2008 R2 Reporting Services, the only option for enhancing a report with data visualization was to add a chart. Now visualization options have been expanded to include Databars, Sparklines, Indicators, gauges, and maps.

A gauge is, conceptually speaking, a much simpler control. It displays how far a value falls on a scale, such as a gas gauge or thermometer. The dataset that drives the gauge needs to provide only a single value (or for some gauges a few), and, optionally, the minimum and maximum values for the scale. For example, a gauge could display how all salespeople perform against their sales quota.

Drag a gauge onto the design surface, and select it to see the data handle. Drop the field from the dataset to be displayed into this handle. Then right-click to access the scale properties to enter the minimum and maximum scale values, or choose the dataset fields to associate them with.

Databars, Sparklines, and Indicators are new chart types that are best used at the end of each line of data in a report. They provide a way to quickly assess the data in a detail or group line-by-line by providing a tiny visual representation of the data, which the mind can interpret much faster than it can read the data in the row. A Databar visually

55

represents one or more data points of the row, with each data point using one bar or column. It can be the literal value of a field, or the databar can indicate the result of an expression.

To provide the cell for one of these new chart types, select the furthermost right column handle in a report. Right-click and select Insert Column ➪ Right. To insert a databar, right-click the newly created text box, and select Insert ➪ Databar. The Select Databar Type dialog box appears where a databar or column can be selected. After the type is selected, you can configure the chart with data by double-clicking the bar in the Design view. You can add Data fields from the dataset to the Values by clicking the green plus sign, as shown in Figure 55-9.

FIGURE 55-9

Adding fields to values in a Databar.

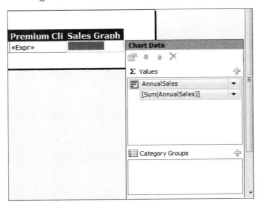

Another mini-chart, available since SSRS 2008 R2, is the Indicator. Indicators work by visualizing a value in a dataset as compared to a range of values. For instance, Figure 55-10 shows an Indicator setup that assesses the annual sales for the Adventureworks clients and breaks them evenly into three categories by percentage of sales. The bottom third is shown with the red diamond, midrange clients receive the yellow triangle, and the high sales clients achieve the green dot.

Sparklines are mini-charts which can represent multiple values for a line of a report. They differ from Databars and Indicators in that they can represent more than one value on the row. For instance, a client's sales over time can be represented on one line of a report, and a Sparkline can be applied at the end of the line to show the trending line chart of the sales values. Sparklines give instant visual representation of the data and the ability to quickly compare rows. As shown in Figure 55-11, they provide instant trending information.

FIGURE 55-10

Configuring an Indicator.

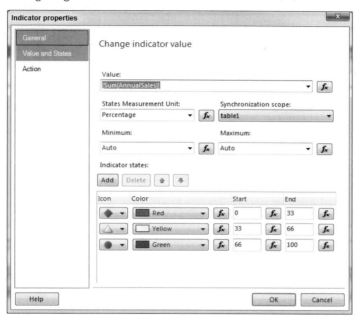

FIGURE 55-11

Using Sparklines to compare sales trends for products over time.

Building Reports with Report Builder

When Reporting Services first debuted with the 2005 release of SQL Server, an ad hoc tool called Report Builder 1.0 was released with it. This ad hoc tool had much promise but proved to be fairly limited in its reporting capabilities because it lacked many design-rendering elements available in Report Designer and was limited to being sourced from a report model. (Report Models were objects created in Busines Intelligence Development Studio that worked like a data view, specifically for the Report Builder.) It went through another iteration as Report Builder 2.0 in the 2008 version, but it was with the 2008 R2 release, when it was named Report Builder 3.0, that it achieved enough sophistication to be fully embraced by the report building world. Now it is simply called Report Builder and offers nearly all the same design elements that Report Designer does in a more Office-like interface.

Creating a Report with Report Builder

Report Builder can be launched as a standalone program from the Report Manager, or from inside SharePoint. Regardless of how it is launched, after it is opened, a Report Wizard is also opened, as shown in Figure 55-12. The Report Wizard guides the user through the creation of a report. Report Builder reports no longer require a report model as a data source; they use the same datasets and sources as reports created in the Report Designer; the interchangeability of pieces between Report Designer and Report Builder was one of the major improvements of the SQL Server 2008 release for SSRS.

Because you have created a shared dataset for the `ResellerContact` report, it will be easy to create a quick report from Report Builder. To create the following example, you need to make sure that you have deployed the `AdventureWorksReports` project created earlier in this chapter and that you have access to Report Manager on the server where you deployed it. If you need help with these tasks, see Chapter 56.

FIGURE 55-12

The Report Builder Wizard.

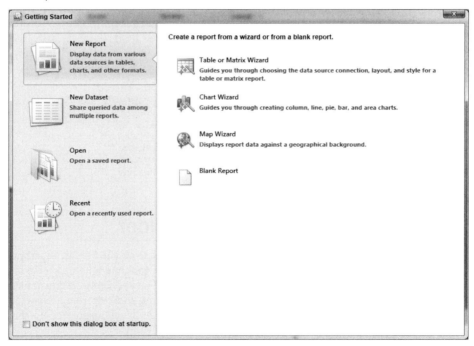

To create a simple tabular report in Report Builder using the `ResellerContact` shared dataset, perform the following steps:

1. Open Report Builder by clicking the Report Builder button from inside Report Manager.

2. Click New Report on the left of the wizard dialog box, and then select Table or Matrix Wizard from the center of the dialog box.

3. Leave the radio button for Choose an Existing Dataset in This Report or a Shared Dataset selected. Select the `ResellerContact` shared dataset from the available shared datasets. Click Next.

4. In the Arrange Fields window, drag the following fields from the Available Fields on the left to the Values box on the lower-right side of the window: `ResellerName`, `AddressLine1`, `City`, `StateProvinceCode`. Click Next.

5. Click Next again, leaving Layout options unchecked.

6. Click on `Slate` for the Style in the Choose a style window.

7. Click the title and type **Resellers**.

8. Click the table and hover between the ResellerName and AddressLine1 columns. Click and drag to the right to make the first column in the report wider. Adjust the other columns accordingly to allow a reasonable amount of room for the textboxes.

9. Click the `Run` button in the upper-left corner of Report Builder to preview the report, as shown in Figure 55-13. If the report no longer fits on the page, you can click the Page Setup button and change the orientation to landscape.

FIGURE 55-13

A report created in Report Builder.

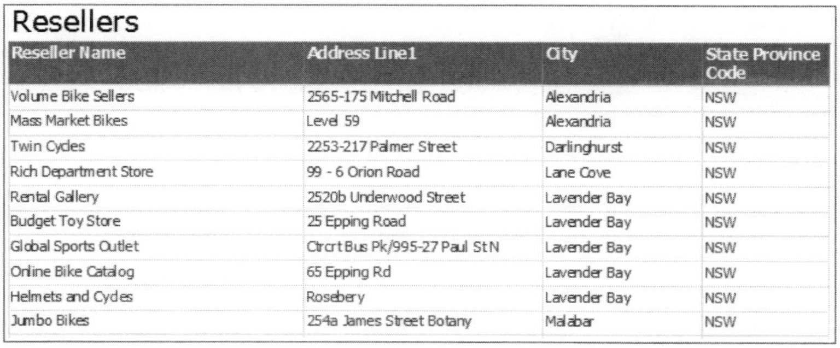

Reseller Name	Address Line1	City	State Province Code
Volume Bike Sellers	2565-175 Mitchell Road	Alexandria	NSW
Mass Market Bikes	Level 59	Alexandria	NSW
Twin Cycles	2253-217 Palmer Street	Darlinghurst	NSW
Rich Department Store	99 - 6 Orion Road	Lane Cove	NSW
Rental Gallery	2520b Underwood Street	Lavender Bay	NSW
Budget Toy Store	25 Epping Road	Lavender Bay	NSW
Global Sports Outlet	Ctrcrt Bus Pk/995-27 Paul St N	Lavender Bay	NSW
Online Bike Catalog	65 Epping Rd	Lavender Bay	NSW
Helmets and Cycles	Rosebery	Lavender Bay	NSW
Jumbo Bikes	254a James Street Botany	Malabar	NSW

The Report Data pane to the left of the design surface in Report Builder has identical functions as it does inside the Report Designer found in SSDT. A main difference between the two authoring tools, however, is the lack of a Toolbox in Report Builder. Charts, maps, Sparklines, and tables are added via the Insert Toolbar. Regardless of the toolbar used to access the objects, they have now been synchronized, and business users now have free access to the same robust features available in SSDT, without having to pay the license for SQL Server or Visual Studio.

Using the Report Gallery

The Report Gallery is the home in Report Manager for aptly named Report Parts. Report Parts are objects such as maps, charts, and tables that have been created as part of a report elsewhere and published to the Report Manager. One great feature of Report Parts is that when published, their datasets are also published as shared datasets. This enables a separation of duties in a business, enabling more tech savvy users to develop complex queries for consumption by all Report Builders. Although reports built inside the Report Designer cannot consume Report Parts, it is easy to publish objects as Report Parts from inside SSDT. From the Report menu inside Report Designer, you can select `Publish Report Parts`. A dialog box opens with all the available objects created inside the rdl. Ticking the box beside an object causes SSRS to publish that object to the Report Parts Gallery when the report is deployed.

To access a Report Part from Report Builder, click the Insert menu from the Ribbon. Click Report Parts, which brings up the Report Parts Pane on the right side of the Report Builder. Type in a search criteria, and click Search. Items that match your search should appear. Double-click the item you want to add to your report. It should appear in the design surface, along with its datasets and data sources. Figure 55-14 shows a report in Report Builder that includes a chart from the Report Gallery.

FIGURE 55-14

Using the Report Gallery.

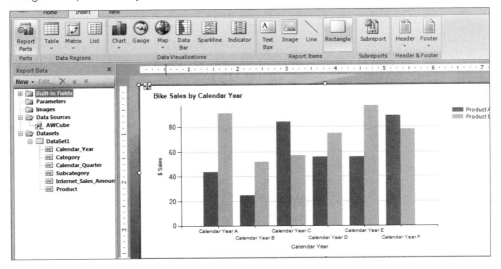

Summary

Reporting is the lifeblood of most organizations because good information leads to action. How do you know how your business is doing without sales data, and how else do you see your sales data other than through reports? The latest two releases of Reporting Services give more power to data consumers, enabling them to access data without an IT development bottleneck. The Report Builder now offers almost all the features available in the Report Designer, and the tool is familiar to anyone who uses Excel.

55

Configuring and Administering Reporting Services

A good administrator keeps an organization's reports secure, highly available, and easily recovered from disasters. Many decisions and skills are required to do this for Reporting Services, many of which are new with the changes in this new release. This chapter covers the essentials to keep your reports safe and performing well.

Installing Reporting Services

A primary component of a Reporting Services solution happens at the initial installation. This has never been truer than with this release, with the rapidly expanding suite of features available through SharePoint integrated mode. Although using Reporting Services in native mode still delivers a sophisticated set of functionality, the focus of the latest edition of SQL Server adds many new features to SharePoint integrated installations.

Native Mode

A Reporting Services native mode instance can run on the same hardware as the relational database but doesn't need to if the system load requires scale-out. For more information on scale-out reporting solutions, see http://sqlcat.com/sqlcat/b/technicalnotes/archive/2008/06/05/ reporting-services-scale-out-architecture.aspx. Installing the server in native mode creates one Windows service and installs two relational databases: one that contains deployed report definitions and other metadata, and a second for temporary objects used in processing. After installation, be sure to visit the Reporting Services Configuration Manager to adjust settings, back up the encryption keys, and save them in a safe place. Keeping all the metadata in the ReportServer database makes it simple to back up, but without the encryption key a restore is difficult.

If you have chosen native mode in the installation program of SQL Server, you should choose a service account under which Reporting Services will run. You also should install the following shared features:

- **SQL Server Data Tools:** Gives you the Report Designer, the Visual Studio tool used to develop reporting project objects
- **Client Tools connectivity:** Gives you access to OLE DB and ODBC connections
- **The Management Tools:** Provides you with SQL Server Management Studio, which provides administrative tools for Reporting Services

During installation you will also be prompted to choose the Service Account under which Reporting Services runs. Which account and what type of account (local, domain, separate accounts, same account for all SQL Server Services, and so on) depends greatly on whether the server is a development machine, production, or part of a scale out deployment. For guidance in selecting the best account to use, see Configuring the Report Server Service Account at http://msdn.microsoft.com/en-us/library/ms160340(v=SQL.110).aspx.

SharePoint Integrated Mode

The other option for hosting your reports is SharePoint integrated mode.
Previous to SQL Server 2012, Reporting Services Integration to SharePoint had been complex to configure, requiring the skillsets of both a database administrator and a SharePoint administrator. Now all configuration options for Reporting Services are available from the Central Administration page of SharePoint. All that is required from the SQL Server install is to click the radio buttons under Shared Services: Reporting Service - SharePoint and Reporting Services Add-In for SharePoint Products, as shown in Figure 56-1.

Some other improvements offered with 2012 integrated mode include the following:

- Reporting Services uses SharePoint's built-in scale and load balancer.
- The Reporting Services catalog is a SharePoint Service Database.
- Data Alerts are available for configuration. A user can configure e-mails to be sent when certain criteria are met in a report.
- SharePoint cross-farm access: If the farm is trusted, users on one farm can consume reports on the other.
- Ability to back up and restore Reporting Services catalog from inside Central Admin UI.

FIGURE 56-1

When installing Reporting Services during a SQL Server 2012 installation, you can install the necessary components for both native mode and SharePoint integrated mode. This figure shows installation of both modes.

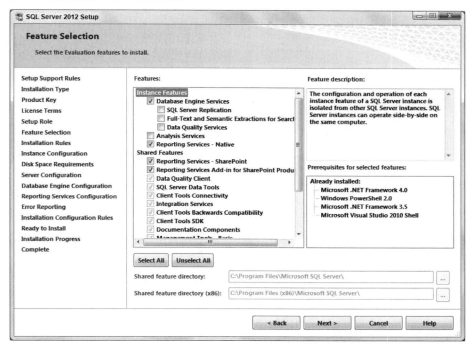

Reporting Services is now a service application in SharePoint. It is no longer a web service. There can now be more than one Reporting Services instance on a SharePoint server. New Reporting Services service applications are mapped to web applications inside SharePoint by performing the following steps:

1. From the Central Admin UI, under the Application Management section, select Manage Service Applications.

2. Click New ⇨ SQL Server Reporting Services Service Application.

3. Perform the outlined steps in the next screen's four sections (Name, Application Pool, SQL Server Reporting Services (SSRS) Service Database, and Web Application Association) as shown in Figure 56-2.

   1. Provide a name for your new Service application in the Name section.

   2. In the Application Pool section, assign the service application to an application pool. You can choose an existing application pool or create a new one here.

   3. Also in the Application Pool section, select the wanted security account.

4. In the SQL Server Reporting Services (SSRS) Service Database section, select the server. By default the database server that hosts the Content database for the SharePoint server is selected as the database server for the service app; this can be changed.

FIGURE 56-2

Mapping the Reporting Services Service Application inside SharePoint.

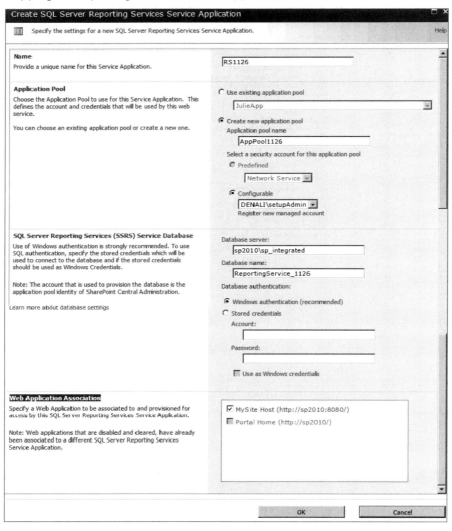

5. In the same section as step 4, type a name for the Reporting Service database. If you do not choose a name, the name will be ReportingServices followed by a GUID.

6. As the last step of this section, choose a database authentication method. Windows authentication is the recommended method.

7. In the final section, Web Application Association, click the radio button next to the web application to which you want to map this service application. The web application is now configured to host reports.

Deploying Reporting Services Reports

This section explores the options and strategies to deploy the reports to the report server. Deploying directly from the development environment, SQL Server Data Tools (SSDT) is the simplest method for the developer, but it may not always be possible or wanted depending on configuration and security constraints.

Deploying Reports Using SSDT

Deploying reports using SSDT requires some basic configuration of the Reporting Services project. When configured, reports (and other resources such as data sources and images) can be deployed individually or the entire project can be deployed.

To configure the deployment properties for a Reporting Services project, open the project's property page by right-clicking the Reporting Services project and selecting Properties. Figure 56-3 shows the property page for a Reporting Services project, and Table 56-1 summarizes the deployment properties available for a Reporting Services project. You can deploy to either the native mode Report Manager or a SharePoint integrated mode server using SSDT.

FIGURE 56-3

Use the settings on the property page of a Reporting Services project to configure the deployment options.

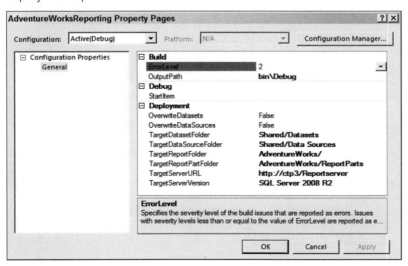

TABLE 56-1 Reporting Services Project Deployment Properties

Property	Description
OverwriteDataSets	Set this to true if you want to overwrite data sets on the report server with data sets in the report project.
OverwriteDataSources	Set this to true if you want to overwrite data sources on the report server with data sources in the report project.
TargetDataSetFolder	This is the path of the folder to which you want to deploy shared data sets.
TargetDataSourceFolder	This is the path of the folder to which you want to deploy shared data sources. Using this parameter enables the definition of a common data source that can be deployed to a common location and used by reports across multiple folders (or projects in development).
	For Integrated mode, use the `http://<servername>/sites/ssrs/data connections` address.
TargetReportFolder	This is the path of the folder to which you want to deploy reports. In SSDT, you must create a project for each folder (or subfolder) to which you want to deploy reports. For native mode, it is common to keep the default value from the project. For Integrated mode, enter the fully qualified name of your Reports Library `http://<servername>>/sites/ssrs/ReportsLibrary`.
TargetReportPartFolder	This is the path of the folder to which you want to deploy Report Parts.
TargetServerURL	This is the URL of the report server you want to deploy to. The default location of your local report server for native mode is `http://localhost/ReportServer`. If you named the instance SQL2012, the local report server would be `http://localhost/ReportServer$SQL2012`.
	For Integrated mode, the target server is `http://<servername>>/sites/ssrs/`.
TargetServerVersion	The version of SQL Server Reporting Services the project will be deployed to.

Deploying Reports Using Report Manager — Native Mode

Although SSDT provides an easy way to deploy reports to the report server, it is not required for report deployment. You can deploy and configure individual Reporting Services objects using the Report Manager. The Report Manager includes features that enable the creation of new folders and data sources, and it provides the capability to upload and update report definitions (.rdl files), report data sources (.rds files), and any other file type you want to make available on the report server (such as a PDF, Word document, PowerPoint presentation, Excel file, and so on).

To deploy a report using the Report Manager, follow these steps:

1. Open the Report Manager application in a web browser. The default location for the Report Manager is `http://localhost/reports`. This default url changes for a named instance to `http://localhost/reports_instancename`.

2. Navigate to the folder to which you want to deploy the report.

3. Click the Upload File button.

4. Enter the path to the file, or use the Browse button to find the file.

5. Enter the report name.

6. If you want to overwrite an existing report with the same name, check the option to Overwrite Item if it exists.

7. Click OK to upload the file and return to the contents of the folder. The new report now appears in the list.

It's a good idea to execute the report and verify that the data source is valid. Reports using shared data sources and shared datasets need to have the paths of the data source and dataset redirected. To access report properties, click the arrow next to the report, as shown in Figure 56-4, and select Manage. Use the Data Sources link on the Properties tab of the report to either select a shared data source or specify a custom data source for the report, as shown in Figure 56-5. Use the datasets link below the Data Sources link to update the references for any shared datasets the report uses. You should also review the other links available on the Properties tab to set parameter defaults and configure report execution, history, and security settings.

FIGURE 56-4

Accessing the properties of a report inside Report Manager.

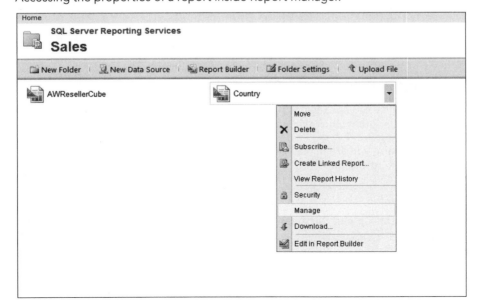

FIGURE 56-5

Updating the reference for a dataset is done from the Properties page.

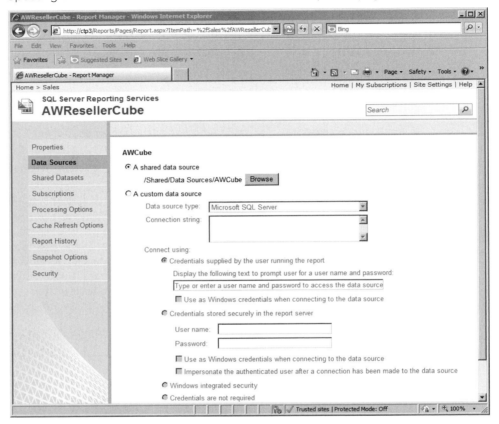

Deploying Reports Inside SharePoint

To upload directly to your reports library from SharePoint, navigate to the desired Library, and perform the following steps:

1. Make sure you are on the Documents tab under the Library Tools from the SharePoint toolbar.

2. Click the Upload Document button on the SharePoint toolbar as shown in Figure 56-6.

3. **From the Upload Document**: Your Library Name page, enter the address of the report, or browse to your wanted report .rdl file as shown in Figure 56-7. Click OK.

4. A SharePoint properties window will appear where you can fill in the Name, Owner, Description, and Category of the report, as seen in Figure 56-8. Click Save.

New Features of Reporting Services

Reporting Services contained a number of changes in the 2008 R2 release. The features in Report Manager included the following:

- A Robust, Office-like Report Builder 3.0. (Its name is now simply Report Builder.)
- A more modern look and feel to the Report Manager interface.
- More direct access to report properties inside Report Manager.
- Shared Datasets: Datasets can be published as objects to Report Manager the same way that data sources are, and consumed by other authors.

New in SQL Server 2012:

- Reporting Services uses SharePoint's built-in scale and load balancer.
- The Reporting Services catalog is a SharePoint Service Database.
- Data Alerts are available for configuration. A user can configure e-mails to be sent when certain criteria are met in a report.
- **SharePoint cross-farm access**: If the farm is trusted, users on one farm can consume reports on the other.
- Ability to back up and restore Reporting Services catalog from inside Central Admin UI.
- Microsoft Excel 2010 and Microsoft Word 2010 rendering capabilities.

FIGURE 56-6

Upload a report.

FIGURE 56-7

Find the Report.

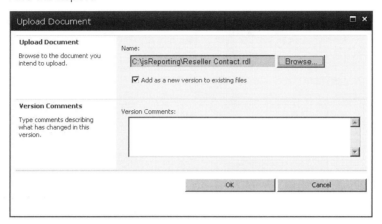

FIGURE 56-8

Enter any relevant descriptions in the properties tab.

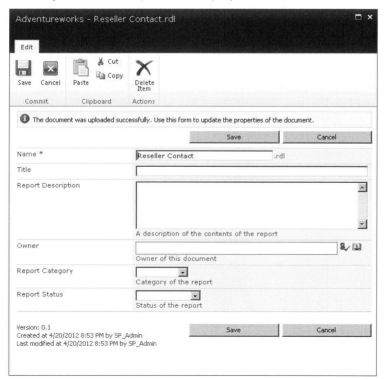

Just as in Report Manager, you need to update any references to shared datasets or shared Data Sources in SharePoint integrated mode.

Managing Security with Reporting Services

Security poses the greatest challenge for most reporting solutions. Sensitive data must be protected, and the SSRS administrator must leverage features of reporting services to do so.

In native mode, it is best to use Report Manager for all content-related management and permission assignments, and to use SQL Server Management Studio for management of server properties and role definitions. This is because since SQL Server 2008, those respective interfaces have been streamlined for these purposes.

Accessing Remote Data Sources in Reporting Services

A common infrastructure set up for Reporting Services involves a client consuming reports, a report server, and a data source, such as an SSAS cube, residing on a separate server. This requires that the user's credentials pass from the client to the Report Server and then to the Cube, often called the Double Hop. A common way to implement this is with Kerberos in Active Directory. Kerberos is a ticket-based computer network authentication protocol. Kerberos in BI can be explored in "Kerberos for Microsoft BI" located at http://social.technet.microsoft.com/wiki/contents/articles/1406.kerberos-for-microsoft-bi-en-us.aspx.

To avoid using Kerberos, the data source must be configured to specify the credentials to the remote data source. For more information, see "Specify Credential and Connection Information for Report Data Sources," located at http://msdn.microsoft.com/en-us/library/ms160330.aspx.

Managing Roles in Native Mode

The security model in Reporting Services leverages Active Directory to grant access to the Report Manager and to items (folders, reports, shared data sources and sets, and so on) within the report server. Security is administered by assigning users or groups to roles. Roles contain selected tasks that enable specific actions within the Report Manager application. Two types of predefined roles and tasks exist: system-level and item-level. Most Reporting Services installations do not actually require changes to the default roles, but rather focus on managing membership in those roles via Report Manager.

Since 2008 R2, roles can be created, deleted, and modified only inside Management Studio. Role assignment takes place inside of Report Manager for native mode.

56

System-Level Roles

System-level roles grant access to server functions that are not item-specific. Two system-level roles are created when the report server is installed: System Administrator and System User. Table 56-2 shows the tasks granted to these roles by default.

TABLE 56-2 **Default System Roles**

Task	System Administrator	System User
Execute report definitions	X	X
Generate events		
Manage jobs	X	
Manage report server properties	X	
Manage report server security	X	
Manage roles	X	
Manage shared schedules	X	
View report server properties		X
View shared schedules		X

You can change the default role definitions by expanding the System Roles folder in Object Explorer inside Management Studio, right-clicking the role to be changed, and selecting Properties. If necessary, you can create additional roles by right-clicking the System Roles folder and choosing New System Role. When defined in SSMS, managing the membership of these roles is handled by the Report Manager application, as described in the following section.

Best Practice

You need to be consistent in your approach to granting access to the Report Manager and to items within the Report Manager. Consider your environment when choosing how to manage and assign access and whether you grant access to Active Directory groups or to individual users. If you have already taken the time to create Active Directory groups in your organization, you can most likely leverage your existing groups to administer access to your report server.

For example, if you have an Active Directory group for accounting, you can simply create a new system role assignment for that group to grant all the accounting members access to the report server. Perhaps you have an Accounting folder with accounting reports to which only accounting employees should have access. When creating this folder, simply adjust the inherited role assignments to ensure that only the accounting group has access.

Regardless of which strategy you choose (user versus groups), maintain a consistent approach to minimize maintenance, research, and troubleshooting efforts in the future.

56

Item-Level Roles

Item-level roles manage permissions associated with the reports, folders, and so on stored in the report server. SSMS presents them in the Roles folder of the Object Explorer, with the same functionality (right-click the role to edit, and then right-click the folder to add) as used with system folders. Of course, the capabilities being granted differ as described in the next section.

Managing Access with Roles

Whether you use the default role definitions or custom definitions, as described earlier, the majority of security management occurs by assigning users to the proper role membership.

Granting System Access to Users and Groups

By default, the BUILTIN\Administrators group is assigned the System Administrator role. Follow these steps to grant system access to additional users or Active Directory groups:

1. Start the Report Manager application by entering the appropriate URL into a browser.
2. Click the Site Settings link in the upper-right corner, and then choose the Security tab. A list of current users assigned to system roles displays.
3. Click the New Role Assignment button on the System Role Assignments page.
4. Enter the Group or User name — for example, *myDomain*\jdoe or *myDomain*\ SRSAdminstrators.
5. Select one or more system roles to assign to the group or user.
6. Click OK to save.

Assigning Item-Level Permissions

Item-level roles are used to control the tasks available for managing folders, reports, shared data sources, shared datasets, models, and other resources in the Report Manager application. Table 56-3 describes the default item-level roles created when the report server is installed. You can use SQL Server Management Studio to modify or add to these roles, as described in the preceding section.

TABLE 56-3 **Default Item-Level Roles**

Task	Browser	Content Manager	My Reports	Publisher	Report Builder
Consume reports		X			X
Create linked reports		X	X	X	
Manage all subscriptions		X			
Manage data sources		X	X	X	

Continues

TABLE 56-3 *(continued)*

Task	Browser	Content Manager	My Reports	Publisher	Report Builder
Manage folders		X	X	X	
Manage individual subscriptions	X	X	X		X
Manage models		X		X	
Manage report history		X	X		
Manage reports		X	X	X	
Manage resources		X	X	X	
Set security for individual items		X			
View data sources		X	X		
View folders	X	X	X		X
View models	X	X			X
View reports	X	X	X		X
View resources	X	X	X		X

Controlling Item-Level Security

By default, every item-level resource inherits the security settings of its parent. If the security settings for an item have not been modified (they still inherit from their parent item), then the Security page for that item contains an Edit Item Security button. After modifying the security settings (and breaking the inheritance from the parent item), the Security page for the item contains item-level access to a user or group.

Best Practice

When inheritance has been broken, it can be complex to make broad changes to site-wide permissions. Because of this, planning ahead for the folder hierarchy can be a big win. Keep the structure simple so permissions can be granted on a few parent folders. For complex cases, it is sometimes easier to use linked reports to provide appropriate access, rather than break inheritance.

Reporting Services roles are bundles of rights that are applied to users or groups for each object. You must belong to a system role with the Set Security for Individual Items task to complete these tasks. To edit an item level role's security, perform the following steps:

1. Select the item for which you want to modify security settings.

2. Click the arrow next to the item, and from the drop-down menu, select Security.

3. If the item still inherits its security settings from its parent, click the Edit Item Security button. An alert displays indicating that the security is inherited, and that if you continue to edit the item's security, you will break the inheritance. Select OK to continue. You can also delete roles that were assigned to the parent.

4. Click the New Role Assignment button.

5. Enter the group or username, for example, *myDomain*\accounting.

6. Select one or more roles to assign to the group or user.

7. Click OK to save the new role assignment.

Remember that for users to access an item-level resource, they must also be granted system-level access. (See the previous section "Granting System Access to Users and Groups.")

In addition, modifying an item's security automatically applies the security to all child items that inherit that security. To restore the inherited security for an item that has been customized, click the Revert to Parent Security button. An alert displays prompting for confirmation before the security settings defined for that item are replaced by the security settings of its parent.

Managing Subscriptions

The capability to subscribe to reports represents an extremely valuable feature in Reporting Services to automate report delivery. Reporting Services supports both push-and-pull paradigms for report delivery. For example, upon scheduled report execution, a subscription can send an e-mail with an attachment containing the report content (push), with the report content in the body of the e-mail (push), or with a link to the report stored on the report server (pull). Alternatively, reports can be written to a file share or to SharePoint libraries where users or other systems can access the report or exported data.

Report subscriptions require that the SQL Server Agent service runs on the relational database hosting the `ReportServer` database. This service executes jobs, monitors SQL Server, fires alerts, and allows automation of some administrative tasks for the report server. Before creating a subscription, ensure that this service is started. In addition, to successfully creating a report subscription, the connection credentials for the report data source must be stored. For example, setting a data source to connect using user credentials does not work for reports running as subscriptions because there is no interactive user at the time the subscription runs.

To begin creating a subscription, select the report you want to subscribe to, and click the New Subscription button in the report control header. Figure 56-9 shows the options available for a file share subscription. You can configure options for report delivery, subscription processing and scheduling, and the report parameter values. More information about each of these options is detailed in the next section, which describes how to create data-driven subscriptions, which enables these options to be set using the results from a query.

FIGURE 56-9

Create a report subscription to be delivered to a windows file share by configuring these options.

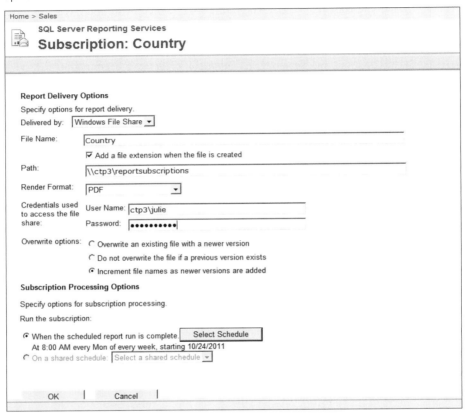

Creating a Data-Driven Subscription

A data-driven subscription enables delivery settings and report parameters to be set dynamically using the results of a query. This is an excellent way to deliver reports and to customize the content of the reports being delivered. (This feature is available only in the Enterprise Edition of SQL Server.) For example, instead of creating linked reports for each region as described earlier, a data-driven subscription could obtain the list of recipients and their corresponding region from a data source and automatically generate and deliver the reports with the content appropriate to each recipient.

To create a data-driven subscription, select the Subscriptions tab on the report you want to deliver, and click the New Data-Driven Subscription button. This guides you through the process to create a data-driven subscription. Data-driven subscriptions can be delivered by e-mail or written to a file share. In either case, you can specify a data source containing the dynamic data for the report and write a query to return the appropriate data.

Data Alerts in Integrated Mode

Data alerts give users the ability to configure an e-mail alert to be delivered when a data criteria is met in a report. The benefit of Data Alerts is that the report does not need to be rendered; the alert fires based on the underlying data. Thus, when something happens, for instance, sales plummet to below a threshold, an e-mail is sent to alert the Sales Manager to run the report and see what is wrong. To use Data Alerts, you must be in integrated mode. The steps to configure an alert are as follows:

1. From a Report in the Reports Library, select Actions ⇨ New Data Alert. The New Data Alert Window opens.

2. Let the alert keep the default name value (the name of the report) or change it to a more suitable name.

3. Click Add rule.

4. From the drop-down select a column from the report to which you want to add the rule.

5. Select the operator; for instance, for a column with a numeric datatype the choices are Is, Is Not, Is Less Than, Is Less Than or Equal To, Is Greater Than, Is Greater Than or Equal To. Type in the value that you want in the text box. For instance, **SalesAmountForMonth is less than or equal to $100,000**.

6. Select Schedule options, and select the frequency of the alert. The default value is once per day.

7. Type in e-mail addresses for the alert to be delivered to.

8. Type in a subject for the e-mail.

9. Type in an optional description.

10. Save the alert.

Disaster Recovery

Disasters happen. Servers crash or retire. To quickly and gracefully recover from an unexpected loss of a Reporting Services Server, a couple of objects must be accessible for restoring:

- The Reporting Catalog (ReportServer and ReportServerTempDB)
- The reporting services encryption key

It is also a good idea to back up all the configuration files for reporting services upon initial installation and thereafter when a change is made to them. For more information on working with SSRS configuration files, see http://msdn.microsoft.com/en-us/library/ms155866(v=SQL.110).aspx.

Backing Up the Catalog

The Reporting Services catalog consists of two SQL Server databases: ReportServer and ReportServertempdb. ReportServer is critical to backup because it contains your reports, metadata, and source — all your designed, permanent objects are stored here. ReportServertempdb contains report snapshots and user session information and can be re-created by re-creating the ReportServer database, but it is much better to restore the table structure from a backup. Because these members of the catalog are SQL Server databases, they can be backed up natively or using any third-party tool that supports SQL Server. SQL Server 2012 integrated mode introduces a third database to the catalog, the ReportServerAlerts database, which as the name implies, contains the metadata for data alerts.

 For more information on backing up and restoring SQL Server, see Chapter 21, "Backup and Recovery Planning."

When considering the frequency of backups, the key question is, "How much loss can my organization tolerate?" If mission critical reports are deployed every day, you should probably back up the ReportServer database daily, if not more frequently. If reports and other metadata change less frequently, you can adjust downward. Always remember to test your backups. Can you actually restore from them? Don't wait to find out they are corrupt the day your server suffers a disk failure.

Backing Up the Symmetric Encryption Key

Sensitive data inside Reporting Services is encrypted with three keys: the public and private keys (managed by the operating system) and a symmetric key, which can be backed up and restored. The only way to access your sensitive data should a migration or failure occur is to restore both the Reporting Services catalog and the symmetric key.

You can back up and restore the symmetric key in the Reporting Services Configuration manager, located under Start ⇨ All Programs ⇨ Microsoft SQL Server 2012 ⇨ Configuration Tools ⇨ Reporting Services Configuration Manager, as shown in Figure 56-10. You should create a backup of your Encryption key as part of the initial installation.

If you are in integrated mode, the encryption key can be backed up from the Key Management interface under Central Admin, as shown in Figure 56-11. To back up the encryption key in SharePoint perform the following from Central Admin:

1. Select Application Management ⇨ Manage Service Applications.

2. Select the particular Reporting Service Service Application with which you are working.

3. Select Key management ⇨ Backup Encryption Key.

4. Enter a password and verify that password.

5. Select Export. The encryption key will be saved to your download folder.

FIGURE 56-10

Backup and restore the Reporting Services encryption key on the Encryption Keys tab of Reporting Services Configuration Manager.

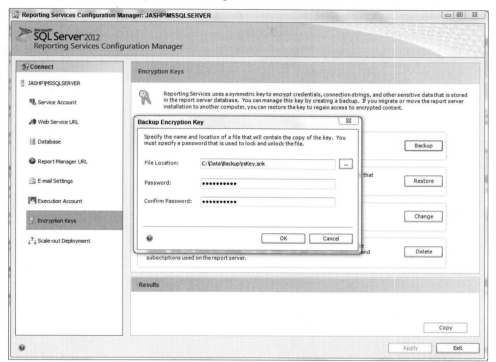

Restoring Reporting Services

Even with the best preventive measures, catastrophes still can bring down one or more of your servers. Very few high availability solutions are 100 percent perfect; nothing can give you absolute assurance that you won't have to perform a restore of your SSRS solution at some point in your career. In case of a disaster or a planned server migration, for native mode, perform the following steps:

1. Using either native SQL Server restore methods or with your supported backup application, perform a restore of the ReportingServer database from your backup file.

2. Do the same for the ReportServerTempDB database from your backup file.

3. Using Reporting Services Configuration manager, restore the symmetric encryption key from your .snk file.

It is likely that after the preceding steps have succeeded, you will need to step through configuring the server using Reporting Services Configuration Manager.

FIGURE 56-11

Key Management is located under Service Applications in integrated mode.

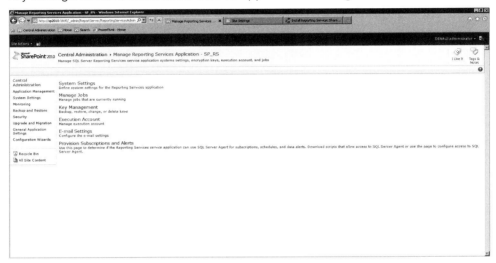

Summary

Reporting Services provides a robust suite of applications to administer a report server. SQL Server Management Studio configures the basic server features and defines roles, whereas Report Manager configures the application of those roles to individual objects. Reporting Services Integrated mode with SharePoint continues to improve in ease of use and additional features such as Data Alerts.

Given a well-thought-out configuration, these features combine to provide a robust and continually evolving platform that can be an effective tool for users, developers, and administrators alike.

Data Mining with Analysis Services

Many business questions can be easily answered by directly querying a database; for example, "What is the most popular page on our website?" or "Who are our top customers?" Other questions require deeper exploration — for example, the most popular paths through the website or common characteristics of top customers. Data mining provides the tools to analyze the answers to these questions.

Data mining is the algorithmic discovery of patterns from large quantities of data. You can create a variety of data mining algorithms within the Analysis Services environment.

Analysis Services implements algorithms to extract information addressing several categories of questions:

- **Segmentation:** Groups items with similar characteristics. For example, develop profiles of top customers.
- **Classification:** Places items into categories. For example, determine which e-mails are likely to be spam.
- **Association:** Sometimes called *market basket analysis,* this determines which items tend to occur together. For example, "Customers who bought this book also bought...."
- **Estimation:** Estimates a value. For example, estimate revenue from a customer.

- **Time Series or Forecasting**: Predicts what a time series looks like in the future. For example, what revenue do we expect in the upcoming quarter?

- **Sequence Analysis**: Determines what items tend to occur together in a specific order. In what order are products normally purchased?

These categories are helpful when you think about what you can use data mining for, but with increased comfort level and experience, many other applications are possible.

The Data Mining Process

A traditional practice in data mining is to train a data mining model using existing data for which an outcome is already known and then use that model to predict the outcome of new data. This requires several steps, only some of which happen within Analysis Services:

- **Business and data understanding**: Understand the important questions and the available data to answer those questions. Insights gained must be relevant to business goals to be of use. Data must be of acceptable quality and relevance to obtain reliable answers.

- **Prepare data**: Preparing data can be a simple or difficult task depending on the current state of the data. Some of the tasks to consider include the following:

  - Eliminate rows of low data quality. The measure of quality is domain-specific. Eliminate values outside of expected norms, or failing any test that proves the row describes an impossible or highly improbable case.

  - Eliminate duplicates, invalid values, or inconsistent values.

  - Denormalize data by creating views to create a single "case" table.

  - Erratic time series data may benefit from smoothing to remove dramatic variations.

  - Derived attributes, such as profit, can be useful in the modeling process.

- **Model**: You build Analysis Services models by first defining a data mining structure that specifies the tables to use as input. Then, add data mining models (different algorithms) to the structure. Use the training data to simultaneously train all the models within the structure.

- **Evaluate**: You can simplify evaluating the accuracy and usefulness of the candidate mining models by using the Analysis Services' Mining Accuracy Chart. Use the testing data set to understand the expected accuracy of each model and compare it to business needs.

- **Deploy**: Integrate prediction queries into applications to predict the outcomes of interest.

The process may just iterate between prepare/model/evaluate cycles. At the other end of the spectrum, an application may build, train, and query a model to accomplish a task, such as identifying outlier rows in a data set. Regardless of the situation, understanding this typical process can aid in building appropriate adaptations.

Modeling with Analysis Services

Create data mining structures within an existing Analysis Services project inside the Business Intelligence Development Studio. When deployed, the Analysis Services project creates an Analysis Services database on the target server. Often, data mining structures deploy with related cubes in the same database.

Begin the modeling process by telling Analysis Services where the training and testing data reside:

- Define data sources that reference the location of data to be used in modeling.
- Create data source views that include all training tables. When you use nested tables, the data source view must show the relationship between the case and nested tables.

 For information to create and manage data sources and data source views, see Chapter 53, "Building Multidimensional Cubes in Analysis Services with MDX."

Data Mining Wizard

The Data Mining Wizard steps through the process to define a new data mining structure and optionally the first model within that structure. Right-click the Mining Structures node within the Solution Explorer, and choose New Mining Model to start the wizard. The wizard consists of several pages:

- **Select the Definition Method**: Enables the choice of either relational (from existing relational database or data warehouse) or cube (from existing cube) source data. Choose relational.
- **Create the Data Mining Structure**: Choose the algorithm to use in the structure's first mining model. (See the "Algorithms" section in this chapter for common algorithm usage.) You can create a structure with no models and add a model later.
- **Select Data Source View**: Choose the data source view containing the source datatables.
- **Specify Table Types**: Choose the case table containing the source data and any associated nested tables. Nested tables always have one-to-many relationships with the case table.
- **Specify the Training Data**: Categorize columns by their use in the mining structure. When a column is not included in any category, it is omitted from the structure. Categories are as follows:

- **Key**: Choose the columns that uniquely identify a row in the training data.
- **Input**: Mark each column to use in a prediction — generally this includes the predictable columns as well. The Suggest button may aid in selection after the predictable columns have been identified. Avoid inputs with values that are unlikely to occur again as input to a trained model. For example, an address might be effective at training a model, but when the model is built to look for a specific address, it is unlikely new customers will ever match those values.
- **Predictable**: Identify all columns the model should predict.
- **Specify Columns' Content and Data Type**: Adjust the data type (Boolean, Date, Double, Long, and Text) as needed. The Detect button calculates continuous versus discrete content types for numeric data. Available content types include the following:
  - **Key**: Contains a value that, either alone or with other keys, uniquely identifies a row in the training table.
  - **Key Sequence**: Acts as a key and provides order to the rows in a table. It is used to order rows for the sequence clustering algorithm.
  - **Key Time**: Acts as a key and provides order to the rows in a table based on a time scale. It is used to order rows for the time series algorithm.
  - **Continuous**: Continuous numeric data — often the result of some calculation or measurement, such as age, height, or price.
  - **Discrete**: Data that can be thought of as a choice from a list, such as occupation, model, or shipping method.
  - **Discretized**: Analysis Services transforms a continuous column into a set of discrete buckets, such as ages 0–10, 11–20, and so on.
  - **Ordered**: Defines an ordering on the training data, but without assigning significance to the values used to order. For example, if values of 5 and 10 are used to order two rows, 10 simply comes after 5; it is not "twice as good" as 5.
  - **Cyclical**: Similar to ordered, but repeats values defined by a cycle in the data, such as day of month or month of quarter.
- **Create Testing Set**: In SQL Server 12, the mining structure can hold both the training and testing data directly, instead of using separate tables. Specify the percentage or number of rows to be held out for testing models.
- **Completing the Wizard**: Provide names for the overall mining structure and the first mining model within that structure. Select Allow Drill Thru to enable the direct examination of training cases from within the data mining viewers.

When the wizard finishes, the new mining structure with a single mining model is created, and the new structure opens in the Data Mining Designer where you can make changes, such as adding columns, to the model.

Mining Models

The Mining Models view of the Data Mining Designer enables you to configure different data mining algorithms on the data defined by the mining structure. Add new models by right-clicking in the structure/model matrix and selecting New Mining Model, as shown in Figure 57-1.

FIGURE 57-1

Adding a new mining model to your SSAS cube.

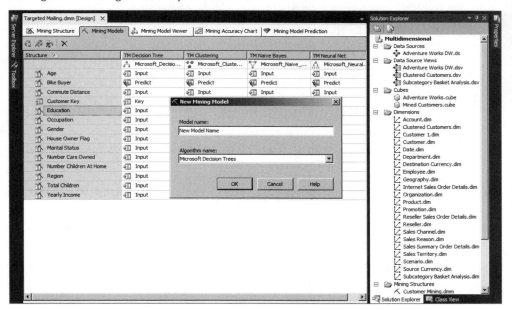

Depending on the structure definition, not all algorithms are available — for example, the Sequence Clustering algorithm requires that a Key Sequence column be defined, whereas the Time Series algorithm requires a Key Time column to be defined. In addition, not every algorithm uses each column in the same way — for example some algorithms ignore continuous input columns.

SQL Server 2012 enables you to place filters on models, which can be useful when training models specific to a subset of the source data. For example, you can target different customer groups by training filtered models in a single mining structure. Right-click a model, and choose Set Model Filter to apply a filter to a model. When set, you can see the current filter in the model's properties.

In addition to the optional model filter, each mining model has both properties and algorithm parameters. Select a model (column) to view and change the properties common to all algorithms including Name, Description, and AllowDrillThrough. Right-click a model, and choose Set Algorithm Parameters to change an algorithm's default settings.

When both the structure and model definitions are in place, you must deploy the structure to the target server to process and train the models. The process to deploy a model consists of two parts. First, the structure or changes are sent to the server in the build phase. Then Analysis Services caches data and trains the models using data not held back for testing.

For information on setting up an Analysis Services project for deployment, see Chapter 53.

After processing, the Mining Model Viewer tab contains processing results; here one or more viewers are available depending on which models are included in the structure. The algorithm-specific viewers assist in understanding the rules and relationships discovered by the models (see the "Algorithms" section in this chapter).

Model Evaluation

Evaluate the trained models to determine which model most reliably predicts the outcome and to decide whether the accuracy is adequate to meet business goals. The mining accuracy chart view provides tools for performing the evaluation.

You can enable the charts visible within this view by supplying data for testing under the Input Selection tab. Choose one of three sources:

- **Use mining model test cases**: Uses test data held out in the mining structure, but applies model filters.

- **Use mining structure test cases**: Uses test data held out in the mining structure, ignoring any model filters.

- **Specify a different data set**: Enables the selection and mapping of an external table to supply test data. After selecting this option, press the ellipsis to display the Specify Column Mapping dialog, and select the table with the test data by clicking Select Case Table.

If the value predicted is discrete, the Input Selection tab also enables choosing a particular outcome for evaluation; otherwise, all outcomes are evaluated.

Lift Charts and Scatter Plots

When the source data and any Predict Value have been specified, switch to the Lift Chart tab, and select Lift Chart from the Chart Type list, as shown in Figure 57-2. The lift chart can compare the predicted against the actual outcomes by showing the percentage of correct cases (Target Population percent) versus the percentage of cases tested (Overall Population percent). An Ideal Model and Random Guess line displays to plot the best possible and random outcomes, respectively.

FIGURE 57-2

Verifying accuracy with the accuracy chart tool.

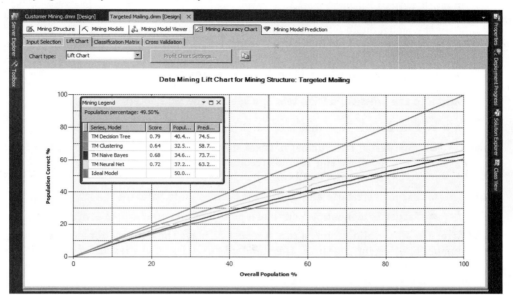

The profit chart extends the lift chart and aids in calculating the maximum return from efforts such as marketing campaigns. Select the Profit Chart from the Chart Type drop-down, and press the Settings button to specify the number of prospects, the fixed and per-case cost, and the expected return from a successfully identified case. The resulting chart describes profit versus Population percent included. This is useful in deciding how much of the population to include in the effort either by maximizing profit or by locating a point of diminishing returns.

Classification Matrix

The simplest view of model accuracy is offered by the Classification Matrix tab, which creates one table for each model, with predicted outcomes listed down the left side of the table and actual values across the top, similar to the example shown in Table 57-1. This is not available for continuous outcomes.

TABLE 57-1   Example Classification Matrix

Predicted	Red (Actual)	Blue (Actual)
Red	95	21
Blue	37	104

Cross Validation

Cross validation is useful for evaluating the stability of a model for unseen cases. The concept is to partition available data into some number of equal sized buckets called "folds," train the model on all but one fold, and test with the remaining fold. This will be repeated until each of the folds has been used for testing. For example, if three folds were selected, the model would be trained on 2 and 3 and tested with 1, then trained on 1 and 3 and tested on 2, and finally trained on 1 and 2 and tested on 3.

Switch to the Cross Validation tab, and specify the parameters for the evaluation:

- **Fold Count:** The number of partitions the data will be placed into.
- **Max Cases:** The number of cases that the folds will be constructed from. For example, 1000 cases and 10 folds result in approximately 100 cases per fold. Setting this value to 0 results in all cases being used.
- **Target Attribute and State:** The prediction to validate.
- **Target Threshold:** The minimum probability required before assuming a positive result.

After the cross-validation has run, a report displays the outcome for each fold across a number of different measures. The standard deviation of the results of each measure should be relatively small. If the variation is large between folds, then it is likely an indication that the model will not work well in actual use.

Troubleshooting Models

Models are rarely perfect in the real world, so you must assume an acceptable margin of error. Several common problems arise when creating models:

- A nonrandom split of data into training and test data sets.
- Input columns are too case-specific (for example IDs, Names, and so on). Adjust the mining structure to ignore data that occurs in training data but never for production data.
- Too few rows (cases) in the training data set to accurately characterize the population of cases. Add additional data sources or limit special cases included.
- If all models are closer to the Random Guess line than the Ideal Model line, then the input data does not correlate with the predicted outcome.

Some algorithms, such as Time_Series, do not support the mining accuracy chart view. Always evaluate the model and modify the data and model definition until it meets the business needs and margin of error.

Deploying

Several methods are available for interfacing applications with data mining functionality:

- Directly constructing XMLA, communicating with Analysis Services via SOAP. This exposes all functionality at the price of in-depth programming.

- Analysis Management Objects (AMO) provides an environment for creating and managing mining structures and other metadata, but not for prediction queries.

- The Data Mining Extensions (DMX) language supports most model creation and training tasks and has a robust prediction query capability. DMX can be sent to Analysis Services via the following:

  - ADOMD.NET for managed (.NET) languages

  - OLE DB for C++ code

  - ADO for other languages

DMX is a SQL-like language modified to accommodate mining structures and tasks. For purposes of performing prediction queries against a trained model, the primary language feature is the prediction join. Because the DMX query is issued against the Analysis Services database, the models can be directly referenced. DMX also adds a number of mining-specific functions such as the `Predict` and `PredictProbability` functions that return the most likely outcome and the probability of that outcome, respectively.

Another useful form of the prediction join is a singleton query, whereby data is provided directly by the application instead of read from a relational table. One example would be to return the probability that a particular case would perform an action, for instance, returning [Bike Buyer] = 1 to see if a customer is likely to buy a bike.

The Business Intelligence Development Studio aids in the construction of DMX queries via the Query Builder within the mining model prediction view. Like the Mining Accuracy chart, select the model and case table to be queried, or alternatively press the singleton button in the toolbar to specify values. Specify `SELECT` columns and prediction functions in the grid at the bottom. SQL Server Management Studio also offers a DMX query type with metadata panes for drag-and-drop access to mining structure column names and prediction functions.

Algorithms

When working with data mining, it is useful to understand mining algorithm basics and when to apply each algorithm. Table 57-2 summarizes common algorithms used for the problem categories presented in this chapter's introduction.

TABLE 57-2   Common Mining Algorithm Usage

Problem Type	Primary Algorithms
Segmentation	Clustering, Sequence Clustering
Classification	Decision Trees, Naive Bayes, Neural Network, Logistic Regression
Association	Association Rules, Decision Trees
Estimation	Decision Trees, Linear Regression, Logistic Regression, Neural Network

Continues

TABLE 57-2 *(continued)*

Problem Type	Primary Algorithms
Forecasting	Time Series
Sequence Analysis	Sequence Clustering

These are guidelines only because not every data mining problem falls into these categories. In addition, there may be other algorithms that you can apply to the listed problem types.

Decision Trees

The *decision trees algorithm* is the most accurate for many problems. It operates by building a decision tree beginning with the All node, corresponding to all the training cases, as shown in Figure 57-3. Then an attribute is chosen to split those cases into groups, which then separate based on another attribute, and so on. The goal is to generate leaf nodes with a single predictable outcome. For example, if the goal is to identify who will purchase a bike, then leaf nodes should contain cases that are either bike buyers or not bike buyers, but no combinations (or as close to that goal as possible).

FIGURE 57-3

This is a great example of the decision tree being implemented.

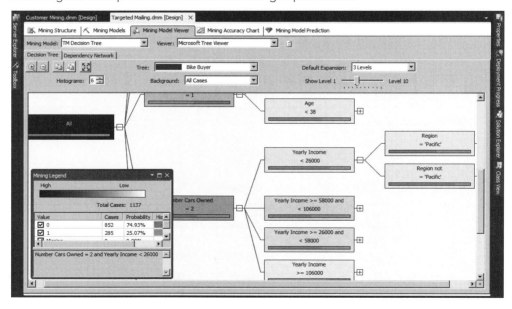

The Decision Tree Viewer, as shown in Figure 57-3, graphically displays the resulting tree for potential bike buyers. The Mining Legend pane displays the details of any selected node, including how the cases break out by the predictable variable. The Dependency Network Viewer is also available for decision trees, displaying both input and predictable columns as nodes with arrows indicating what predicts what. Move the slider to the bottom to see only the most significant predictions. Click a node to highlight its relationships.

Linear Regression

The *linear regression algorithm* is implemented as a variant of decision trees and is a good choice for continuous data that relates more or less linearly. The result of the regression is an equation in the following form

$$Y = B_0 + A_1{}^*(X_1+B_1) + A_2{}^*(X_2+B_2) + \ldots$$

where Y is the column predicted, X_i are the input columns, and A_i/B_i are constants determined by the regression. Because this algorithm is a special case of decision trees, it shares the same mining viewers. You can use the equation either directly or queried in the mining model via the Predict function.

Clustering

The *clustering algorithm* functions by gathering similar cases together into groups called clusters and then iteratively refining the cluster definition until no further improvement can be gained. This approach is good for profiling populations. Several viewers display data from the finished model:

- **Cluster Diagram:** This viewer displays each cluster as a shaded node with connecting lines between similar clusters — the darker the line, the more similar the cluster. You can use a slider at the bottom to show more similar clusters.

- **Cluster Profiles:** Unlike node shading in the Cluster Diagram Viewer, where you can examine one variable value at a time, the Cluster Profiles Viewer shows all variables and clusters in a single matrix. Each cell of the matrix is a graphical representation of that variable's distribution in the given cluster, as shown in Figure 57-4. Discrete variables are shown as stacked bars and continuous variables as diamond charts centered on the mean. The taller the diamond, the less uniform the values.

- **Cluster Characteristics:** This view displays the list of characteristics that make up a cluster and the probability that each characteristic appears.

- **Cluster Discrimination:** Similar to the Characteristics Viewer, this shows which characteristics favor one cluster versus another.

FIGURE 57-4

This is a good example of the cluster profile viewer.

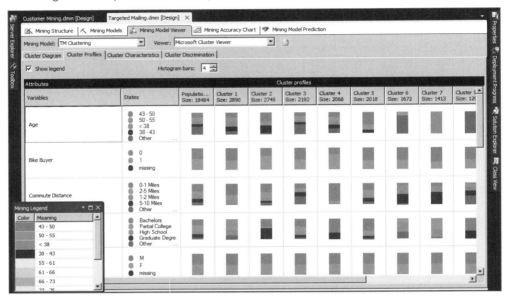

After you gain a better understanding of the clusters for a given model, it is often useful to rename each cluster to something more descriptive than the default "Cluster n." From within either the Diagram or Profiles Viewer, right-click a cluster, and choose Rename Cluster to give it a new name.

Sequence Clustering

As the name implies, the *sequence clustering algorithm* still gathers cases together into clusters, but based on a sequence of events or items rather than on case attributes. For example, you can use the sequence of web pages visited during user sessions to define the most common paths through that website.

The nature of this algorithm requires input data with a nested table, whereby the parent row is the session or order (for example, shopping cart ID), and the nested table contains the sequence of events during that session (for example, order line items). In addition, you must mark the nested table's key column as a Key Sequence content type in the mining structure.

After the model is trained, the same four cluster viewers previously described are available to describe the characteristics of each. In addition, the State Transition Viewer displays transitions between two items (for example, a pair of web pages), with its associated probability of that transition happening. Select a node to highlight the possible transitions from that item to its possible successors. The short arrows that don't connect to a second node denote a state that can be its own successor.

Neural Network

The *neural network algorithm* is generally slower than others but often handles more complex situations. You build the network using the output of each layer as the input of the next layer. Each layer accepts inputs that are combined using weighted functions that determine the output.

The Neural Network Viewer presents a list of characteristics (variable/value combinations) and how those characteristics favor given outcomes. Choose the two outcomes compared in the Output section at the upper right of Figure 57-5. Leaving the Input section in the upper-left blank compares characteristics for the entire population. Figure 57-5 displays the characteristics that affect the buying decisions of adults 32–38 years of age with no children.

FIGURE 57-5

This is a good example of the Neural Network Viewer.

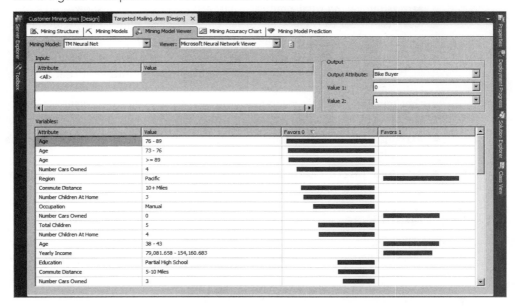

Logistic Regression

Logistic regression is a special case of the neural network algorithm. Although you can use logistic regression for many tasks, it is especially suited for estimation problems where linear regression would be a good fit. However, because the predicted value is discrete, the linear approach tends to predict values outside the allowed range — for example, predicting probabilities more than 100 percent for a certain combination of inputs.

Because it is derived from the neural network algorithm, logistic regression shares the same viewer.

Naive Bayes

Naive Bayes is a fast algorithm with accuracy adequate for many applications. It does not, however, operate on continuous variables. Every input is independent. For example, the probability of a married person purchasing a bike is computed from how often a married person and a bike buyer appear together in the training data without considering any other columns. The probability of a new case is just the normalized product of the individual probabilities.

Several viewers display data from the finished model:

- **Dependency Network**: Displays both input and predictable columns as nodes with arrows indicating what predicts what; a simple example is shown in Figure 57-6. Move the slider to the bottom to see only the most significant predictions. Click a node to highlight its relationships.

- **Attribute Profile**: This shows all variables and predictable outcomes in a single matrix. Each cell of the matrix is a graphical representation of that variable's distribution for a given outcome. Click a cell (chart) to see the full distribution for that outcome/variable combination in the Mining Legend, or hover over a cell for the same information in a tooltip.

- **Attribute Characteristics**: This viewer displays the list of characteristics associated with the selected outcome.

- **Attribute Discrimination**: This viewer is similar to the Characteristics Viewer, but it shows which characteristics favor one outcome versus another.

Association Rules

The *association rules algorithm* operates by finding attributes that appear together in cases with enough frequency to be significant. These attribute groupings are called *itemsets*, which are in turn used to build the rules used to generate predictions. Although you can use Association Rules for many tasks, it is specifically suited to market basket analysis. Generally, you can prepare data for market basket analysis using a nested table, whereby the parent row is the transaction (for example, Order) and the nested table contains the individual items. Three viewers provide insight into a trained model:

- **Itemsets**: Displays the list of itemsets discovered in the training data with the number of items in the set and number of training cases in which this set appears. Several controls for filtering the list are provided, including the Filter Itemset text box, which searches for any string entered and displays only itemsets that include that string.

- **Rules**: Similar in layout and controls to Itemsets but lists rules instead of itemsets. Each rule has the form A, B ≥ C, meaning that cases that contain A and B are likely to contain C; for example people who bought pasta and sauce also bought cheese. Each rule is listed with its probability and importance (usefulness in performing predictions).

- **Dependency Network**: Similar to the Dependency Network used for other algorithms, with nodes representing items in the market basket analysis. Nodes have a tendency to predict each other (displayed with dual-headed arrows). The slider hides the less probable (not the less important) associations. Selecting a node highlights related nodes.

FIGURE 57-6

Naive Bayes dependency viewer is shown here.

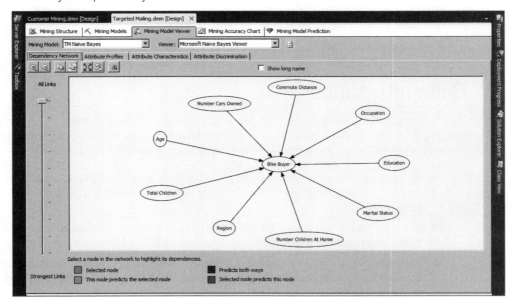

Time Series

The *time series algorithm* predicts the future values for a series of continuous data points (for example, web traffic for the next 6 months given traffic history). Unlike the algorithms already presented, prediction does not require new cases on which to base the prediction, just the number of steps to extend the series into the future. Input data must contain a *time key* to provide the algorithm's time attribute.

After the algorithm runs, it generates a decision tree for each series forecast. The decision tree defines one or more regions in the forecast and an equation for each region, which you can review using the Decision Tree Viewer. The Tree pull-down at the top of the viewer enables the models for different series to be examined. Each node also displays a diamond chart whose width denotes the variance of the predicted attribute at that node. In other words, the narrower the diamond chart, the more accurate the prediction.

The second Time Series Viewer, labeled Charts, plots the actual and predicted values of the selected series over time. Choose the series to be plotted from the drop-down list in the upper-right corner of the chart. Use the Abs button to toggle between absolute (series) units and relative (percentage change) values. The Show Deviations check box adds error bars to display expected variations on the predicted values, and the Prediction Steps control enables the number of predictions that display. Drag the mouse to highlight the horizontal portion of interest, and then click within the highlighted area to zoom into that region. Undo a zoom with the zoom controls on the toolbar.

Because prediction is not case-based, the Mining Accuracy Chart does not function for this algorithm.

Cube Integration

Data mining can use Analysis Services cube data as input instead of using a relational table (see the first page of the Data Mining Wizard section earlier in this chapter); cube data behaves much the same as relational tables, with some important differences:

- Although a relational table can be included from most any data source, the cube and the mining structure that references it must be defined within the same project.

- The case "table" is defined by a single dimension and its related measure groups. When additional data mining attributes are needed, add them via a nested table.

- Instead of choosing a primary key, choose mining structure keys from dimension data at the highest (least granular) level possible. For instance, choose the quarter as the key attribute for quarterly analysis rather than the date key.

- Data and content type defaults tend to be less reliable for cube data, so review and adjust type properties as needed.

- Some dimension attributes based on numeric or date data may appear to the data mining interface with a text data type. This is because data mining uses the Name column's data type instead of the Key column. If this causes an issue, remove the Name column property from the dimension attribute, or add the same column to the dimension a second time without using the Name column property.

- The portion of cube data to use for training is defined via the mining structure's cube slice.

- A Lift Chart cannot be run against cube test data, so model evaluation requires either test data in a relational table, or some strategy that does not rely on the tools of the Mining Accuracy Chart.

Using a cube as a mining data source can be effective, providing access to what is often large quantities of data for training and testing, and providing the ability to create a dimension or even an entire cube based on the trained model.

57

Summary

Data mining provides insights into data well beyond those provided by reporting, and Analysis Services streamlines the mining process. Although the data must still be prepared, mining models hide the statistical and algorithmic details of data mining, enabling focus on analysis and interpretation.

Beyond one-time insights, you can use trained models in applications to allocate scarce resources, forecast trends, and identify suspect data, and for a variety of other uses.

Creating and Deploying BI Semantic Models

SQL Server 2012 introduces a new Analysis Services engine based on the recently acquired columnar database known as the xVelocity in-memory analytics engine (formerly known as VertiPaq engine). This new engine provides the advantage of performing analysis over billions of rows with subsecond response times. High volumes of data are kept and analyzed in memory by this new engine due to its high data compression algorithms and its column-based storage. Compression ratios range from 10x to 100x based on Microsoft's benchmarks.

In SQL Server 2012, Analysis Services can be installed in either of two modes:

- Multidimensional and Data Mining Mode
- Tabular Mode

Multidimensional and Data Mining Mode supports the traditional UDM Model that you may have used in SQL Server 2005, 2008, and 2008R2. Tabular Mode runs the xVelocity engine and supports a new data model known as the BI Semantic Model, sometimes referred to as the Tabular Model. This new model does not replace the UDM Model. The UDM Model is still supported by SQL Server 2012 Analysis Services deployed in Multidimensional and Data Mining Mode. BI Semantic Models are supported only by SQL Server 2012 Analysis Services deployed in Tabular Model.

What Is a BI Semantic Model?

The Business Intelligence Semantic Model is defined by Microsoft as one model for all user experiences that includes reporting, analytics, scorecards, dashboards, and custom applications. It is a rich, scalable, and flexible model that can be viewed conceptually as a three-layer model.

- **Data Model**: The conceptual model that contains all the relationships between the different data entities in the organization. It supports both multidimensional and tabular data modeling.

- **Business Logic & Queries**: Represents the intelligence or semantics in the model. Calculations are embedded in the model using either MDX or DAX languages. Both languages are supported and can be used to extend basic business logic.

- **Data Access**: Where source data is integrated. Multiple data sources are supported natively including data coming from relational databases, flat files, OData feeds, and so on.

Figure 58-1 illustrates the three layers of the BI Semantic Model.

FIGURE 58-1

The three layers of the BI Semantic Model.

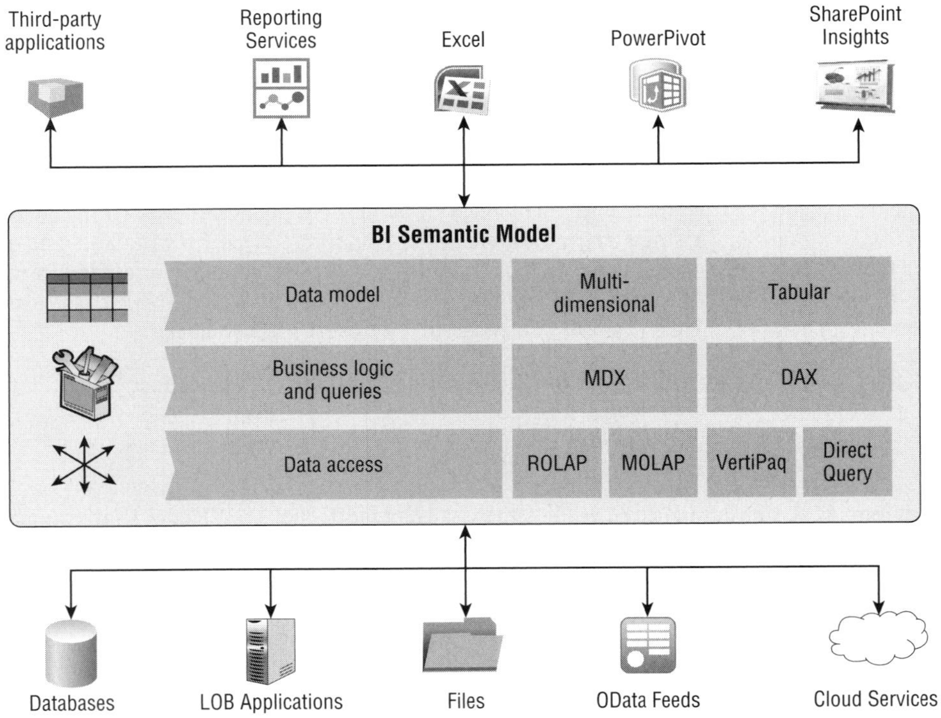

One of the objectives of the BI Semantic Model is to simplify development and querying. The development environment of BI Semantic Models resembles tables displayed as tabs related to one another and is the reason why it is sometimes called Tabular models. Querying is simplified because BI Semantic Models can be queried either by using

Multidimensional Expressions Language (MDX) or Data Analysis Expressions Language (DAX). MDX has a steeper learning curve than DAX. DAX is the new querying language that is much easier to learn because it is similar to Excel functions.

The Development Environment

BI Semantic Models were first introduced with PowerPivot as two offerings:

- PowerPivot add-in for Excel 2010
- SQL Server 2008R2 PowerPivot for SharePoint 2010

PowerPivot add-in for Excel leverages on the xVelocity engine to provide the ability to manipulate and create compelling analyses over billions of rows in a desktop environment. The development environment of BI Semantic Models in the PowerPivot add-in for Excel looks and feels just like Excel, as shown in Figure 58-2.

FIGURE 58-2

PowerPivot add-in for Excel 2010.

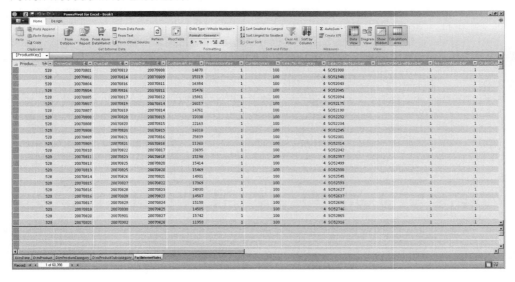

Alternatively, BI Semantic Models can also be developed using the SQL Server Data Tools environment. This tool is a rebranding of Business Intelligence Development Studio (BIDS) found in previous versions of SQL Server based on Visual Studio 2010. Figure 58-3 shows the SQL Server Data Tools development environment.

FIGURE 58-3

SQL Server Data Tools.

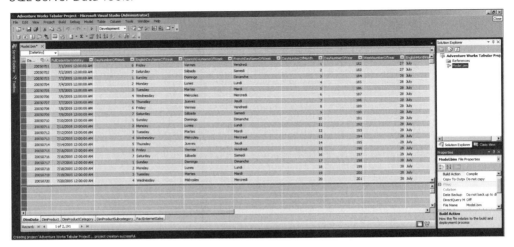

As you can see, both development environments look similar. The same concept of a model based on tables organized in tabs similar to worksheets in an Excel workbook is evident in both development environments. This similarity is designed to bridge the skillset gap between developers and business users. By simplifying and making the development environment similar, both developers and business users can "talk" the same language and deliver faster analytical solutions.

In the next sections you create and deploy BI Semantic models using PowerPivot and SQL Server Data Tools development environments. The examples provided to create BI Semantic Models uses the AdventureWorks Data Warehouse 2012 sample database available for download at Codeplex at `http://msftdbprodsamples.codeplex.com/releases/view/55330`.

What's New with BI Semantic Models in SQL 2012?

The majority of the enhancements of the Business Intelligence toolset in SQL Server 2012 focus around BI Semantic Models.

- BI Semantic Models can now be developed using SQL Server Data Tools (formerly BIDS).
- BI Semantic Models can be deployed to the new Tabular Mode of the Analysis Services Engine.
- BI Semantic Models support both In-Memory (cached) and Direct-Query (relational) query modes.
- BI Semantic Models support MDX and DAX query languages.
- KPIs, hierarchies, images, perspectives, and roles are now supported in BI Semantic Models.

Creating BI Semantic Models Using PowerPivot

The PowerPivot add-in for Excel is an intuitive and lightweight development environment of BI Semantic Models that you can download for free as part of the SQL Server 2012 Feature Pack from the Microsoft Download Center at www.microsoft.com/download/en/details.aspx?id=29074.

In the following example, you extract data from AdventureWorksDW2012.

To create a new BI Semantic Model using the PowerPivot add-in for Excel 2010, follow these steps:

1. Open Excel 2010.
2. Locate and click the PowerPivot tab.
3. Click the PowerPivot Window option. The PowerPivot development window opens.
4. In the Get External Data Ribbon section, click the From Database icon. Figure 58-4 shows the database source options available to extract external data.

FIGURE 58-4

External data database source options.

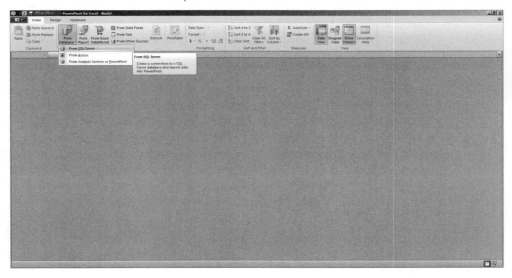

5. From the drop-down menu, select From SQL Server. The Table Import Wizard dialog window opens prompting for the SQL Server instance and database to connect to. Type the name of the SQL Server instance where the AdventureWorksDW2012 database is hosted. Select or type the **AdventureWorksDW2012** database under the database name.

6. Click Next. The Choose How to Import the Data dialog window opens. You are presented with two options:

   ■ Select from a list of tables and views to choose the Data to import.

   ■ Write a query that will specify the data to import.

   For the purposes of this example, select the first option, Select from a list of tables and views to choose the data to import.

7. Click Next. The Select Tables and Views dialog window opens. In this dialog window you select the tables and views to be included in the BI Semantic Model. You can choose to import the entire table or add a filter to import only a subset of the data.

8. Select the following tables to import:

   ■ DimProduct

   ■ DimProductSubcategory

   ■ DimProductCategory

   ■ DimReseller

   ■ FactResellerSales

   Figure 58-5 shows the Select Tables and View dialog window.

FIGURE 58-5

Select Tables and View screen.

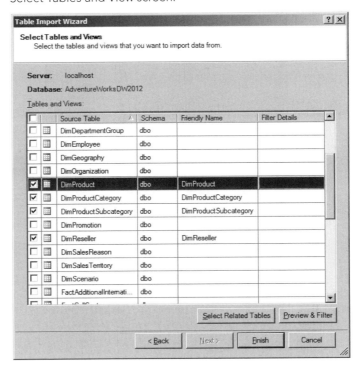

9. Click Finish. The import process dialog window opens. In this dialog window you can track the progress of the import process for each table selected. At the end of the import process, you can see a summary of each work item, status, row count, and messages.

10. Click Close. The data model opens in data view. The tables that were imported in the previous step display in separate tabs.

11. Click the Design menu option, and select Manage Relationships. The Manage Relationships window opens. This step is important because it ensures you have the correct relationships in your model to slice and dice the data. The existing relationships listed in the Manage Relationships window are relationships that have been defined in the SQL Server database. Click Close to close the Manage Relationships window.

12. Click the Home tab, and select Diagram View from the View section. The diagram view of the BI Semantic Model displays. The Diagram View shows the logical relationships between each table in the data model, as shown in Figure 58-6.

FIGURE 58-6

Diagram view.

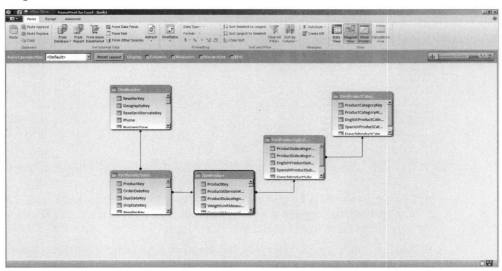

At this point you are ready to see the results of your PowerPivot analysis. To interact with the in-memory BI Semantic Model follow these steps:

1. Under the Home tab, click the PivotTable icon. A pop-up window opens prompting you to specify where you want to create the PivotTable.

2. Select New Worksheet and Click OK. A new worksheet opens in the Excel window with a PivotTable connected to the in-memory BI Semantic Model. The PivotTable Field list displays on the right with the four dimension tables and the single fact table selected. Notice that you are working in the Excel environment.

3. To interact with the data, expand FactResellerSales, and drag SalesAmount and OrderQuantity to the Values area in the PivotTable Field List. The aggregated SalesAmount and OrderQuantity displays.

4. To slice the data further, expand DimProduct, and drag EnglishProductName to the Row Labels of the PivotTable Field List. The data is instantaneously broken down by each product in the list, as shown in Figure 58-7.

FIGURE 58-7

Data sliced by products.

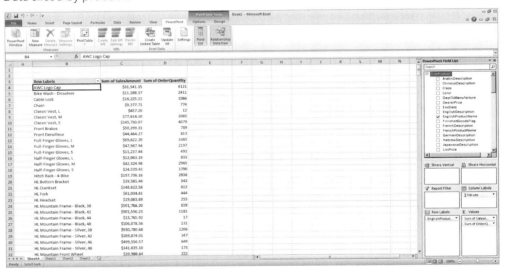

5. To analyze the data in an organized way, you can add filters and slicers. Expand DimProductCategory and drag EnglishProductCategoryName to the Slicers Vertical area in the PivotTable Field List.

6. Expand DimProductSubcategory and drag EnglishProductSubcategoryName to the Slicers Vertical area in the PivotTable Field List, below EnglishProductCategoryName.

7. Click Accessories in the EnglishProductCategoryName slicer. The product list is filtered and shows only products categorized as Accessories.

8. Click Helmets in the EnglishProductSubcategoryName slicer. The product list is filtered further and shows only products categorized as Accessories and subcategorized Helmets.

Figure 58-8 shows the filtered list of products.

FIGURE 58-8

Filtered list of products using slicers.

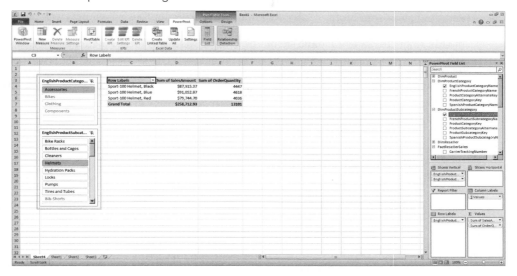

9. Expand DimReseller and drag ResellerName to the Report Filter area in the PivotTable Field List. ResellerName is added as a filter on the PivotTable area. Click the drop-down menu, and select the reseller named A Typical Bike Shop from the list. The product list, sales amount, and order quantity is filtered to reflect only the sum of the orders placed by this particular reseller.

10. You have just created your first BI Semantic Model using PowerPivot Excel add-in. To save your PowerPivot analysis, click File ⇨ Save and provide a name, for example **AWPowerPivot**. The PowerPivot analysis is saved as part of the Excel workbook and can be referred to as a PowerPivot workbook.

Extending a BI Semantic Model with PowerPivot

The SQL Server 2012 PowerPivot Excel add-in introduces new features to extend a basic BI Semantic Model created in a PowerPivot workbook. These new features include:

- Key Performance Indicators (KPI)
- Hierarchies
- Perspectives

Creating KPIs in PowerPivot

KPIs provide a quick and effective way to evaluate success of an organization's activity. For example, you can create a KPI that evaluates Reseller Sales Gross Profit from the AdventureWorksDW2012 database. The Reseller Sales Gross Profit formula is as follows:

Reseller Sales Gross Profit = Sales Amount – Total Product Cost

In this example, Sales Amount should be greater than the Total Product Cost to earn a profit. If Sales Amount is less than Total Product Cost than, the business loses money. You want to create a KPI that displays a green flag if there is a profit or a red flag if there is a loss on the reseller sales transactions. To create a KPI to track Reseller Sales Gross Profit, first create a calculated column named Gross Profit as follows:

1. Follow steps 1 to 10 from the section "Creating BI Semantic Models Using PowerPivot."

2. Click the FactResellerSales tab.

3. Scroll all the way to the right until you see a blank column with Add Column as header name.

4. Click on the Add Column header and position the mouse cursor inside the formula bar.

5. Type the following formula inside the formular bar

   =[Sales Amount]-[Total Product Cost] and press enter.

6. Right-click the header and select Rename to rename the column as Reseller Sales Gross Profit. Figure 58-9 shows the Reseller Sales Gross Profit calculated column.

7. Click the Reseller Sales Gross Profit header and create a measure by clicking the Autosum option from the Office Ribbon. The new measure name Sum of Reseller Sales Gross Profit displays below the Reseller Sales Gross Profit column.

8. Click the Sum of Reseller Sales Gross Profit measure and create a KPI by clicking the Create KPI option from the Office Ribbon. The Key Performance Indicator (KPI) window opens.

9. Check the option Absolute value under the Define target value section. Replace the value with the number zero and press the TAB key. The status thresholds recalculate the base on the new zero value.

10. Make sure that the first color band displaying the Green-Yellow-Red pattern is selected.

11. Click the solid circle icon group under the icon style section and Click OK.

Figure 58-10 shows the Key Performance Indicator (KPI) window with selected options for this example.

FIGURE 58-9

Reseller Sales Gross Profit.

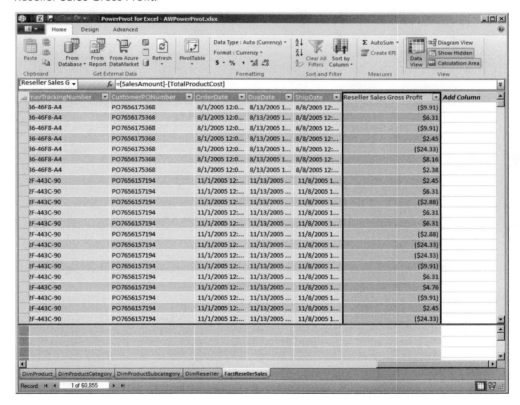

FIGURE 58-10

Key Peformance Indicator (KPI) window.

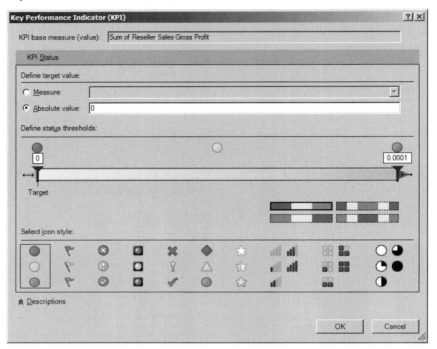

The KPI you just created can now be displayed by any application that supports BI Semantic Models and KPIs, including Excel and Performance Point. Reporting Services can consume the KPI data but does not automatically render the KPI status graphically as Excel or Performance Point does.

To view the KPI in Excel follow these steps:

1. Click the PivotTable option of the Office Ribbon. The Create PivotTable pop-up window opens.
2. Select New Worksheet and click OK.
3. From the PowerPivot field list, expand the DimProductCategory dimension and drag EnglishProductCategoryName to the Row Labels section.
4. Expand DimProductSubcategory and drag EnglishProductSubCategoryName to the Row Labels section below EnglishProductCategoryName.
5. Expand FactResellerSales and drag Sales Amount and TotalProductCost to the Values section.

6. Expand the Sum of Reseller Sales Gross Profit KPI. You will notice a Green-Yellow-Red icon next to it.

7. Drag Value and Target to the Values section. Figure 58-11 shows the Excel PivotTable with the KPI status icon.

FIGURE 58-11

Excel PivotTable with KPI status.

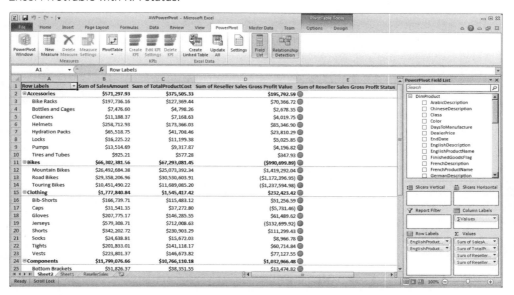

At this point you have successfully created and displayed a KPI using PowerPivot and Excel Pivot Tables.

Creating Hierarchies in PowerPivot

Hierarchies provide a better user experience by enabling users to drill-down from an aggregate top level down to more detail level data. Hierarchies also help users understand relationships between attributes.

One of the easiest to understand hierarchies is the Product Drilldown hierarchy. The AdventureWorksDW2012 database contains 606 products categorized under 37 subcategories and 4 main categories from which you can create a hierarchy to facilitate navigation and aggregation.

Each of these category levels are contained in normalized tables in a database table arrangement often referred to as a snowflake schema in the data warehousing industry.

This means that there are three tables, DimProduct, DimProductSubCategory, and DimProductCategory, that are related to each other by foreign key constraints as shown in the Diagram View in Figure 58-12

FIGURE 58-12

Product tables' relationships in the Diagram View.

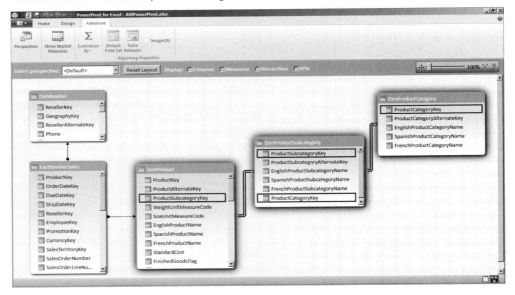

In order to create a hierarchy, you need to flatten these three tables, in one of the following ways:

1. Load a single Product table with all levels represented as columns.
2. Create a view that flattens all three tables with all levels represented as columns.
3. Import the three tables into the BI Semantic Model as a single flat table using a query.
4. Use the `related()` DAX function to look up the name values of the related tables and use them as hierarchy levels in the Product table.

In this example, we will work with option 4 to exemplify the use of the `related()` DAX function. To create the Product Drilldown hierarchy follow these steps:

1. Follow steps 1 to 10 from the section "Creating BI Semantic Models Using PowerPivot."
2. Click the DimProduct tab.

3. Scroll all the way to the right until you see a blank column with Add Column as the column header.

4. Click the header of the column named Add Column.

5. Position the mouse cursor inside the formula bar and type
=RELATED(DimProductSubcategory[EnglishProductSubcategoryName])
and press ENTER.

6. Rename the column to **ProductSubcategory.**

7. Click the new blank column that was added to the right.

8. Position the mouse cursor on the formula bar and type
=RELATED(DimProductCategory[EnglishProductCategoryName]) and
press ENTER.

9. Rename the column to **ProductCategory.**

So far you populated two new columns in the DimProduct table with the EnglishProductSubcategoryName of the DimProductSubcategory table and the EnglishProductCategoryName of the DimProductCategory table. As you can see, the related() DAX function works similar to the vlookup() Excel function.

Now that you have a flattened table with all levels of the hierarchy represented, you can proceed and create the Product Drilldown hierarchy from the DimProduct table by following these steps:

1. Click the Diagram View to switch to the graphical representation of your BI Semantic Model.

2. Select the DimProduct table and click on the Create Hierarchy option on the top right of the table as shown in Figure 58-13.

FIGURE 58-13

Create Hierarchy icon.

3. Rename the new user hierarchy to **Product Drilldown.**

4. Locate and right-click the ProductCategory attribute of the DimProduct table. Select Add to Hierarchy ⇨ Product Drilldown.

5. Locate and right-click the `ProductSubCategory` attribute of the `DimProduct` table. Select Add to Hierarchy ⇨ Product Drilldown.

6. Locate and right-click on the `EnglishProductName` attribute of the `DimProduct` table. Select Add to Hierarchy ⇨ Product Drilldown.

Figure 58-14 shows the Product Drilldown hierarchy in the `DimProduct` table.

FIGURE 58-14

Product Drilldown hierarchy.

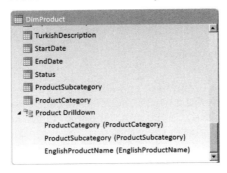

At this point you have successfully created a hierarchy that allows you to drill down from product categories, then to subcategories, and finally down to products. Optionally, you can hide the `DimProductSubcategory` and `DimProductCatetogory` tables by right-clicking on each table and selecting Hide from Client Tools.

To interact with the Product Drilldown hierarchy you just created follow these steps:

1. Click the PivotTable option on the Office Ribbon.

2. Select New Worksheet from the Create PivotTable pop-up window.

3. Expand `FactResellerSales` and drag `SalesAmount` to the Values section.

4. Expand `DimProduct` and drag the Product Drilldown hierarchy to the Row Labels section. Notice the + symbol next to Product Drilldown in the field list. Click the the + symbol to expand the hierarchy members as shown in Figure 58-15.

You have successfully created a hierarchy by utilizing the `related()` function to flatten the three product category tables.

FIGURE 58-15

Product Drilldown hierarchy.

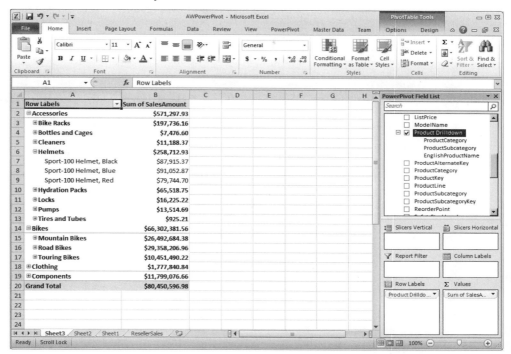

Creating Perspectives in PowerPivot

Perspectives are a subset of objects in a BI Semantic Model. Perspectives are created by selecting specific dimensions, attributes, hierarchies, measure groups, measures, or KPIs. These
subset of objects within the BI Semantic Model are typically defined for a particular audience
or analysis scenario. A smaller set of objects make it easier to navigate large data sets.

To create a new perspective follow these steps:

1. Follow steps 1 to 10 from the section "Creating BI Semantic Models Using
   PowerPivot."

2. Click the Office Ribbon options on the top left and select Switch to Advanced Mode. The Advanced tab displays in the Office Ribbon.

   Figure 58-16 shows the Office Ribbon options to enable the Advanced tab.

FIGURE 58-16

Office Ribbon options' menu and the Switch to Advanced Mode option.

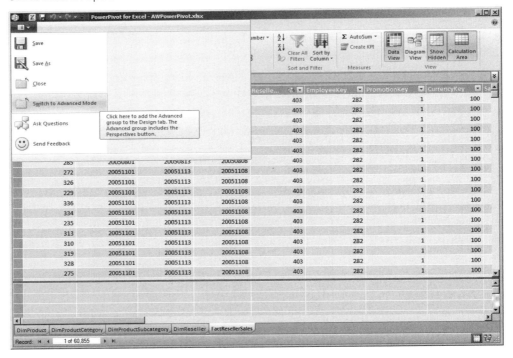

3. Click the Advanced tab.

4. Click the Perspectives option in the Office Ribbon. The Perspectives window opens.

5. Click the New Perspective button to create a new perspective.

6. Rename the perspective to **SalesOrderData**.

7. Select the following objects from the list:

   - English Product Name
   - SalesAmount
   - TaxAmount
   - DiscountAmount
   - Freight

8. Click OK.

9. Click on the PivotTable option in the Office Ribbon.

10. Select New Worksheet from the Create PivotTable pop-up window.

To interact with the SalesOrderData Perspective you just created, click on the drop-down menu in the field list on the top right and select SalesOrderData as shown in Figure 58-17.

FIGURE 58-17

SalesOrderData Perspective.

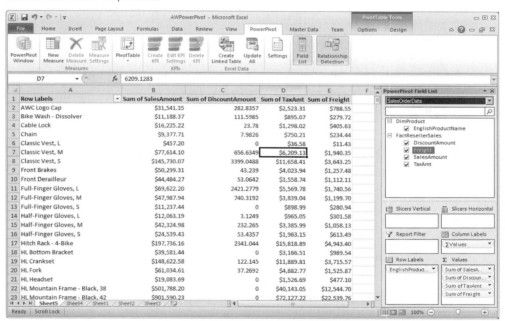

Notice that the BI Semantic Model has been simplified and is easier to navigate with the perspective you just created.

Deploying BI Semantic Models to SharePoint

After you create a PowerPivot analysis, you may want to share it with other colleagues in your organization. Typically, you would e-mail this workbook or save it in a network share. This way of sharing PowerPivot workbooks creates several challenges:

- Increased mailbox size due to potentially large files sent as an attachment.

- The workbook can be modified, creating the risk of multiple colleagues having different versions of the same workbook.

- The workbook's content is static unless the data is refreshed from the underlying data sources.

To overcome these and other challenges, Microsoft released a dedicated Analysis Services engine based on the xVelocity engine that integrates with SharePoint 2010 called SQL Server PowerPivot for SharePoint.

SQL Server PowerPivot for SharePoint enables you to deploy and manage PowerPivot workbooks in SharePoint to special libraries called the PowerPivot Gallery. The main benefits of deploying PowerPivot workbooks to a SharePoint PowerPivot Gallery include:

- Centralized and secure storage
- Less storage wasted by avoiding multiple copies of the same workbook sent out to user mailboxes
- Ability to generate workflows and alerts when a PowerPivot workbook is modified
- Scheduling of automatic data refresh

The scheduling of automatic data refresh is a nice feature because it enables you to keep the PowerPivot workbook up to date with no manual intervention. For example, you can schedule a data refresh every night so that users always see the previous end-of-business-day transactions.

To deploy a BI Semantic Model to SharePoint, you need to deploy the PowerPivot workbook to a PowerPivot Gallery by following these steps:

1. Open the PowerPivot workbook in Excel. In this example, use the PowerPivot workbook called AWPowerPivot.xlsx created in the previous section.

2. Click File ⇨ Save & Send; then click the Save to SharePoint option.

3. Click the Save As button, and type the full URL of the SharePoint PowerPivot Gallery along with the name of the workbook in the File Name section, For example, `http://sql2012rtm/PowerPivot Gallery/AWPowerPivot`.

4. Click the Save button. The PowerPivot workbook is now deployed to the SharePoint 2010 PowerPivot Gallery.

Managing Automatic Data Refresh of PowerPivot Workbooks in SharePoint 2010

As mentioned previously, one of the biggest advantages of deploying PowerPivot workbooks to a SharePoint 2010 PowerPivot Gallery is the ability to schedule automatic refresh of the data in the BI Semantic Model.

To schedule automatic data refresh of a PowerPivot workbook follow these steps:

1. Navigate to the SharePoint PowerPivot Gallery to which the PowerPivot workbook is deployed.

2. Open the Manage Data Refresh screen. Launch the Manage Data Refresh screen by clicking the Calendar icon on the top right of the workbook preview area in the Theater, Carousel, or Gallery view. Alternatively, you can also launch the Manage Data Refresh screen by selecting the option from the PowerPivot workbook options in the All Documents view.

3. In the Manage Data Refresh screen, click the Enable checkbox and configure the schedule settings such as the frequency, start time, e-mails for notifications, data source credentials and data source(s) to refresh.

4. Click OK.

The PowerPivot workbook's data will be refreshed automatically according to the schedule configured.

Creating BI Semantic Models Using SQL Server Data Tools

You can develop BI Semantic Models using the SQL Server Data Tools using a special type of project called the Analysis Services Tabular project. As mentioned earlier, the development environment and development process are similar to that of the PowerPivot add-in for the Excel 2010 environment. If you read the section "Creating BI Semantic Models Using PowerPivot," you can find a lot of similarities.

To create a new BI Semantic Model using SQL Server Data Tools, follow the next steps:

1. Launch SQL Server Data Tools. You can find the shortcut under the default install location located at Start ⇨ All Programs ⇨ Microsoft SQL Server 2012. The SQL Server Data Tools launches and displays the default Start Page.

2. On the Start Page, click the New Project option. You can also create a new project by clicking Start ⇨ New ⇨ Project. The New Project dialog window opens.

3. Select the Analysis Services Tabular project template option. Change the name of the project to **AWTabularProject**. Change the solution name to **AWTabularSolution**. You may also change the location to save the project.

4. Click OK. A blank model named Model.bim opens. At this point the model is an empty canvas. You need to create a table structure and import data.

5. Click Model menu option. From the menu list, select Import from Data Source,

6. The Table Import Wizard window opens. Select the Microsoft SQL Server option, as shown in Figure 58-18.

FIGURE 58-18

Table Import Wizard dialog window.

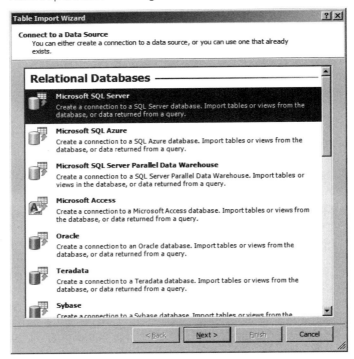

7. Click Next. The Connect to a Microsoft SQL Server Database dialog window opens. Type the SQL Server name, and select the AdventureWorksDW2012 database from the list.

8. Click Next. The Impersonation Information dialog window opens. In this window you specify the credentials that Analysis Services will use to connect to the data source when establishing a connection import and process data. You can choose a specific Windows username and password or use the credentials of the Analysis Services service account.

Best Practices

In high security environments, it is always recommended to use a separate Windows username and password to connect to the data sources in case the service account is compromised.

9. Click Next. The Choose How To Import Data dialog window opens. You can choose to select individual tables or write a query that specifies the data to open. For this example, click the Select from a List of Tables and Views to Choose the Data to Import option.

10. Click Next. The Select Tables and Views dialog window opens. Select the following tables:

  - DimReseller
  - DimProduct
  - DimProductSubcategory
  - DimProductCategory
  - FactResellerSales

11. Click Finish. The import process dialog window opens. In this dialog window, you can track the progress of the import process for each table selected. At the end of the import process, you can see a summary of each work item, status, row count, and messages.

12. Click Close. The data model opens in data view. The tables that were imported in the previous step display in separate tabs.

At this point you have created a basic Tabular project. An important step now is to manage relationships between the tables you imported so you can slice and dice our data with dimension attributes.

To manage table relationships click the Table menu option, and select Manage Relationships. The Manage Relationships window opens. This step is important, because it ensures you have the right relationships in your model that allow you to slice and dice the data. The existing relationships listed in the Manage Relationships window are relationships that have been defined in the SQL Server database.

To view a graphical representation of our table relationships, click the Model menu option, click Model View submenu, and select Diagram View. The diagram view of the BI Semantic model displays. The Diagram View shows the logical relationships between each table in the data model. Click OK to close the Diagram View.

In addition, you can extend your basic Tabular Project with measures that aggregate data across a column. For example, you can create a sum of order quantity and a sum of sales amount by following these steps:

1. Click the Model menu option, click Model View submenu, and select Data View to create measures. Click the FactResellerSales tab. Click the column header titled OrderQuantity. The entire column is highlighted.

2. Click the Column menu option, click the AutoSum submenu, and select Sum from the list. An aggregated column measure named Sum of OrderQuantity is created.

3. Click the column header titled SalesAmount. The entire column is highlighted.

4. Click the Column menu option, click the AutoSum submenu, and select Sum from the list. An aggregated column measure named Sum of SalesAmount is created.

At this point a basic BI Semantic Model is complete. In the next section, you deploy the Tabular Project to an Analysis Services Tabular Mode instance.

Extending a BI Semantic Model with SQL Server Data Tools

BI Semantic Models developed with SQL Server Data Tools support all the features available in the PowerPivot Excel Add-in. The steps to add these features with SQL Server Data Tools are very similar to the steps already covered earlier in this chapter under the section titled "Extending a BI Semantic Model with PowerPivot."

In addition, SQL Server Data Tools allows you to define security roles, a feature not available in the PowerPivot Excel add-in. The next sections describe the steps to add this functionality to a BI Semantic Model using the SQL Server Data Tools.

Creating Roles in SQL Server Data Tools

Roles provide the ability to limit access to Windows users by allowing specific rows that match the DAX . The permissions available include:

- None
- Read
- Read and Process
- Process
- Administrator

To create a new role in SQL Server Data Tools follow these steps:

1. Follow steps 1 to 12 of the section titled "Creating BI Semantic Models Using SQL Server Data Tools."

2. Click on the Model menu option and select Roles. The Role Manager window opens.

3. Click on New to add a new role.

4. Type **BicycleProductManagers** in the new role's name.

5. Select the Read option in the Permissions column.

6. In the description textbox, type **Read Access to Bicycle Category Product Managers**.

7. In the Row Filters section, click inside the DAX filter textbox next to
DimProductCategory and type the following formula:

=DimProductCategory[EnglishProductCategoryName] = "Bikes"

Figure 58-19 shows the Role Manager Window.

FIGURE 58-19

Role Manager Window.

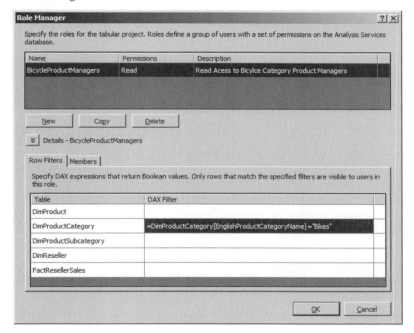

8. Click the Members tab.
9. Click the Add button. The Select Users, Service Accounts, or Groups window opens.
Type the Windows user or group you wish to add to the new role and click OK.
10. Click OK to close the Role Manager window.

At this point you have created a role that limits its members to see only rows associated
with the Bikes Product Category. To test the new role follow these steps:

1. Click on the Model menu option and select Analyze in Excel.
2. Select the Role option from the Analyze in Excel window.

3. Select the BicycleProductManagers role from the roles drop down list and click OK. An Excel worksheet opens with a PivotTable to browse the BI Semantic Model.

4. Drag Sum of SalesAmount from the field list to the Values section.

5. Drag EnglishProductCategoryName from DimProductCategory to the Row Labels section.

6. Drag English ProductSubcategoryName from DimProductSubcategory to the Row Labels section below EnglishProductCategoryName.

Notice that only sales data for the Bikes Product Category displays. The DAX filter specified in the BicycleProductManagers role effectively limits the data as expected.

Deploying BI Semantic Models to an Analysis Services Instance

Only BI Semantic Models defined as Tabular Projects can be deployed to an Analysis Services Tabular Mode instance. This does not mean that only projects originally developed in SQL Server Data Tools can be deployed. Microsoft has made it easy to convert a BI Semantic Model developed in PowerPivot add-in for Excel 2010 into a Tabular Project as well as UDM models from Analysis Services Multidimensional Mode.

To deploy a BI Semantic Model to an Analysis Services Instance, follow these steps:

1. In SQL Server Data Tools, open the Tabular Project.

2. Right-click the Tabular Project properties. The Tabular Project Property Pages dialog window opens. In this dialog window you need to provide information for:

   - Deployment Options
   - Deployment Server
   - DirectQuery Options

3. In the Server section, type the target Analysis Services server name, and in the Edition section, specify the Analysis Services server edition. You can leave the default values for the rest of the options for now.

4. Click Apply. To deploy, click the Build menu option, and select Deploy AWTabularProject. The Tabular project AWTabularProject used in this example is now deployed.

Deployment Options

The deployment options specify how the project and model is deployed. The processing option specifies whether Analysis Services objects should be processed using full processing or no processing when the project is deployed. The default option allows Analysis Services to determine the type of processing required.

The Transactional Deployment Option specifies whether deployment and processing should be part of the same transaction. This means that if deployment succeeds but processing fails, both operations will be rolled back. The default is `False`, meaning the operations are not part of the same transaction.

Query Mode specifies the source from which query results are returned. The options follow:

- **In-Memory:** Query results are returned from cache only.
- **Direct Query:** Query results are returned directly from the relational data source only. Only a single relational data source is supported. For additional limitations refer to `http://msdn.microsoft.com/en-us/library/hh230898.aspx`.
- **In-Memory with Direct Query:** Query results are returned from cache by default unless otherwise specified in the connection string from the client.
- **Direct Query with In-Memory:** Query results are returned from the relational data source by default unless otherwise specified in the connection string from the client.

Deployment Server Options

The deployment server options specify target server and database properties. The deployment server options include:

- **Server:** The target Analysis Services Tabular Mode instance name to deploy the project to.
- **Edition:** The SQL Server Edition of the Analysis Services Tabular Mode instance. Options are Business Intelligence, Enterprise, Enterprise Core Licensing, Evaluation, or Standard Edition.
- **Database:** The name of the in-memory column-store database that hosts the cube, dimensions, and measures.
- **Cube name:** The name of the cube that integrates the data model and business logic and to which users connect to do analysis.

DirectQuery Options

DirectQuery Options specify the credentials you need to use to connect to the relational data source when querying a model running in DirectQuery Mode. The Default Impersonation Setting specifies that the same credentials provided during the Data Import Wizard will be used. The ImpersonateCurrentUser setting specifies to use the credentials of the user trying to establish the connection.

58

Summary

BI Semantic Models is a rich, scalable, and flexible model that can be deployed as part of a PowerPivot workbook or as Tabular Project using SQL Server 2012 Analysis Services in Tabular Mode. The BI Semantic Model can be viewed conceptually as a three-layer model consisting of the Data Model, the Business Logic, and Data Access.

BI Semantic Models are developed using the PowerPivot Excel Add-in or SQL Server Data Tools. The user interface of these two applications is very similar. Almost all features of a BI Semantic Model can be developed with the PowerPivot Excel Add-in, with the exception of roles and partitions available only through the SQL Server Data Tools development environment.

BI Semantic Models developed in PowerPivot workbooks can be deployed to SharePoint2010 PowerPivot Galleries to manage automatic data refresh.

In addition, BI Semantic Model Tabular Projects developed using SQL Server Data Tools, can be deployed to SQL Server 2012 Analysis Services running in Tabular Mode. The deployment options include:

- In-Memory
- In-Memory with DirectQuery
- DirectQuery
- DirectQuery with In-Memory

Creating and Deploying Power View Reports

P ower View is the new ad-hoc reporting tool part of SQL Server 2012 Reporting Services add-in for SharePoint 2010. It is a browser-based Silverlight application available through SharePoint 2010 that provides end users with the ability to create rich and interactive reports through a true drag-and-drop experience, with no coding or report development experience necessary.

This new tool provides end users with the familiar Ribbon interface of Microsoft Office with the benefits of a WYSIWYG development environment. Power View launches directly from a BI Semantic Model found in a PowerPivot workbook or from an Analysis Services Tabular database.

Power View Requirements

You can categorize Power View requirements as server-side requirements and client-side requirements.

Server-Side Requirements

Power View server-side requirements include feature installations of SQL Server 2012 and SharePoint 2010. Power View is a SQL Server 2012 Reporting Services feature available in SharePoint mode only and as part of the following SQL Server 2012 Editions:

- Enterprise Edition
- Business Intelligence Edition
- Developer Edition
- Evaluation Edition

Power View requires a SQL Server 2012 Reporting Services server configured in SharePoint mode. Integration with SharePoint 2010 requires the Enterprise Edition of SharePoint.

Best Practices

Microsoft recommends applying Service Pack 1 to SharePoint 2010 if you will be integrating SQL Server 2012 BI features.

Client-Side Requirements

There are two main requirements on the client-side: A browser and the Silverlight version. Power View is supported by Silverlight 5 and above in Internet Explorer, Firefox, and Safari. Table 59-1 lists the browser versions supported by Power View.

TABLE 59-1   Power View Browser Support

Browser	Browser Version
Internet Explorer	v7, v8, v9 32-bit, and 64-bit
Firefox	v7 32-bit
Safari	v5 32-bit and 64-bit

NOTE

Power View does not support the InPrivate browser feature of Internet Explorer.

Creating and Deploying Reports with Power View

You can launch Power View from a data source containing a BI Semantic Model published to SharePoint 2010. There are five options to launch Power View:

1. Directly from a PowerPivot workbook (.xlsx file) in PowerPivot Gallery

2. From a Report Data Source (.rsds file) pointing to a PowerPivot workbook

3. From a Report Data Source (.rsds file) pointing to an Analysis Services Tabular database

4. From a BI Semantic Model connection (.bism file) pointing to a PowerPivot workbook

5. From a BI Semantic Model connection (.bism file) pointing to an Analysis Services Tabular database

The PowerPivot Gallery in SharePoint 2010 enables you to launch Power View directly from a PowerPivot workbook (.xlsx file), as shown on Figure 59-1.

FIGURE 59-1

Launching Power View from PowerPivot workbook in PowerPivot Gallery.

You can also launch Power View from a shared data source with a Microsoft Business Intelligence Semantic Model data source type, based either on a PowerPivot file or a tabular model database on an Analysis Services server from any library. Shared data sources have a file type extension of .rsds.

The next section walks you through the steps to create a document library that supports Semantic Model data source connection files. The sections that follow walk you through the steps to create Report Data Source files and BI Semantic Model Connection files based on a PowerPivot workbook and an Analysis Services tabular model database.

For more information on creating and deploying BI Semantic Models to SharePoint 2010 using PowerPivot or deploying Tabular Models to an Analysis Services Tabular mode instance, refer to Chapter 58, "Creating and Deploying BI Semantic Models,". The examples in the next two sections assume that a PowerPivot workbook has already been deployed to a SharePoint 2010 PowerPivot Gallery and that a Tabular Model has been deployed to an Analysis Services instance in Tabular Mode.

Creating a Connection File Library

Before creating Power View Reports, you need to create a document library that supports the type of connection files that Power View can use to connect to Semantic Model data sources. This is a very important step as the Report Data Source content type contains special fields to define data source connections.

To create a document library that supports connection files to Semantic Model data sources follow these steps:

1. Launch your browser and navigate to the SharePoint 2010 site for which you want to create the Connections File Library.

2. Click Site Actions and select New Document Library from the options. The Create screen opens.

3. Type a name for the new library, for example, **Connection Files**. Select None from the Document Template option and click on the Create button. The Connection File library is created and opens.

4. Click the Library option under the Library Tools tab of the SharePoint ribbon and click on Library Settings. The Library settings screen opens.

5. Click on Advanced settings. The Advanced settings screen opens.

6. Select the Yes radio button of the Content Types section to allow management of content types and click OK. The Document Library screen opens again.

7. Under Content Types, click Add from existing site content types. The Add Content Types screen opens.

8. From the available content types, select the BI Semantic Model Connection and Report Data Source content types to the add list, and click OK.

The Connection File document library that supports Semantic Model data source connection files is now created

Creating a Report Data Source File

To create a Report Data Source file based on a PowerPivot workbook, follow the next steps:

1. Launch your browser, and navigate to the SharePoint 2010 Connection File document library created in the previous section.

2. Under the Library Tools tab on the SharePoint Ribbon, click the Documents option. The Documents menu options display on the SharePoint Ribbon section.

3. Click the small downward pointing arrow in the right corner of the New Document menu option to display the drop-down menu, as shown in Figure 59-2.

FIGURE 59-2

New Document drop-down menu options.

4. From the list select the Report Data Source option. The data source properties screen opens.

5. Type a name for the shared data source file, for example **AWPowerPivotDS**.

6. From the Data Source Type drop-down list, select Microsoft BI Semantic Model for Power View.

7. In the Connection String textbox, type the URL to the PowerPivot workbook. For example: Data Source=http://sql2012rtm/PowerPivot%20Gallery/ AWPowerPivot.xlsx.

8. Click the Test Connection button. You should see a message in green below the Test Connection button displaying the message: Connection String Created Successfully. Figure 59-3 shows the data source properties screen with the entries used for this example.

9. Click OK. The Report Data Source file is created.

10. To launch Power View using the newly created Report Data Source file, click the file's drop-down menu options, and select Create Power View Report.

The next section walks you through the steps to create BI Semantic Model Connection files based on a PowerPivot workbook and an Analysis Services Tabular Model database.

FIGURE 59-3

Data Source Properties screen.

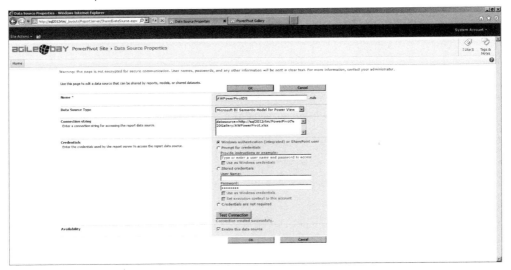

Creating a BI Semantic Model Connection File

To create a BI Semantic Model Connection file based on a PowerPivot workbook follow the next steps:

1. Launch your browser, and navigate to the SharePoint 2010 Connection Files document library created in the Creating a Connection File Library section.

2. Under the Library Tools tab on the SharePoint Ribbon click the Documents option. The Documents menu options display in the SharePoint Ribbon section.

3. Click the small downward pointing arrow in the right corner of the New Document menu option to display a drop-down menu.

4. Select the BI Semantic Model Connection option from the list. The New BI Semantic Model Connection screen opens.

5. Type a name for the shared data source file, for example, **AWPowerPivotBISMC**.

6. In the Workbook URL or Server Name textbox, type the URL of the PowerPivot workbook, for example, **http://sql2012rtm/PowerPivot%20Gallery/ AWPowerPivot.xlsx**.

7. Leave the Database textbox blank.

Figure 59-4 shows the BI Semantic Model Connection screen properties with the entries used for this example.

FIGURE 59-4

PowerPivot Workbook BI Semantic Model Connection properties.

8. Click OK. The BI Semantic Model Connection file is created.

9. To launch Power View using the newly created BI Semantic Model Connection file, click the file's drop-down menu options, and select Create Power View Report.

You can also create a BI Semantic Model Connection file based on an Analysis Services Tabular Model database by following the next steps:

1. Repeat steps 1 through 4 from the previous set of steps.

2. Type a name for the shared data source file, for example **AWTabularBISMC**.

3. In the Workbook URL or Server Name textbox, type the server name of the Analysis Services instance, for example, **localhost**.

4. In the Database textbox, type the name of the tabular model database, for example, **AWTabularProject** as shown in Figure 59-5

59

FIGURE 59-5

Analysis Services BI Semantic Model Connection file properties.

5. Click OK. The BI Semantic Model Connection file is created.

6. To launch Power View using the newly created BI Semantic Model Connection file, click the file's drop-down menu options and select Create Power View Report. You are now ready to create a Power View report

Creating Reports with Power View

Power View offers several visualization options to display data. The initial building block of all visualizations is a basic table. After the initial table is created, you can change the visualization type by simply clicking the visualization on the Ribbon menu.

In the examples, you create Power View reports based on the HelloWorldPicnicPowerViewRTM PowerPivot workbook. You can download the sample files from www.microsoft.com/download/en/details.aspx?id=26718.

In addition, you need to download the image files from www.microsoft.com/download/en/details.aspx?id=26719.

Also download and refer to the readme files for instructions on how to deploy the sample files and images. The readme file can be found at http://social.technet.microsoft.com/wiki/contents/articles/3735.sql-server-samples-readme-en-us.aspx.

> ### TIP
> The images need to be deployed to the HelloWorldPicnicImages subfolder under the HelloWorldPicnicSQL2012 folder in the Shared Documents Library.

Working with Charts and Slicers

In this example, you create a simple report that implements a Column Chart and a couple slicers. To create this Power View report, follow these steps:

1. Open your browser, and navigate to the PowerPivot Gallery in SharePoint 2010. The PowerPivot Gallery opens.

2. If it is not the current view, change the current view to the Gallery view. You may change the current view by clicking Library under the Library Tools tab in the SharePoint Ribbon, as shown in Figure 59-6.

FIGURE 59-6

Library view options of the PowerPivot Gallery.

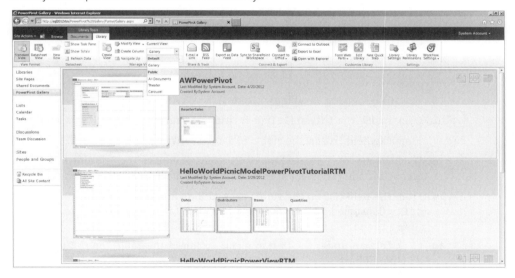

3. Scroll down to the PowerPivot workbook titled HelloWorldPicnicPowerView.

4. On the top-right corner, click the Create Power View Report icon to launch PowerView, as shown in Figure 59-7.

FIGURE 59-7

Create Power View Report option.

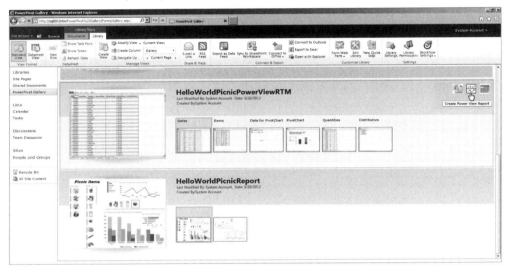

5. Power View opens as a blank canvas.

6. Click inside the title area. Type a title, for example, **Picnic Items Analysis**.

7. From the field list on the right, expand Quantities.

8. Drag the measure named Sum of Qty Consumed 2 to the left side of the Power View layout section. The Sum of Qty Consumed 2 measure displays as a table.

9. From the field list on the right, expand Date and drag MonthName next to the Sum of Qty Consumed 2 measure inside the same table. Make sure MonthName is placed inside the same table and not on a separate table.

10. Click Column under the Design menu option of the Table Tools. The table changes to a Column Chart.

11. Move the chart to the right. Expand the chart so that it occupies approximately 3/4 of the layout section's width below the title, as shown in Figure 59-8.

12. From the field list on the right, expand Items, and drag Category Drawing outside and to the left of the Column Chart.

13. Click Slicer from the Ribbon menu. The images act as slicers of the Column Chart on the right. The image slicers can be selected one-by-one or multi-selected by keeping the CTRL or SHIFT key pressed while clicking on the image.

FIGURE 59-8

Column Chart.

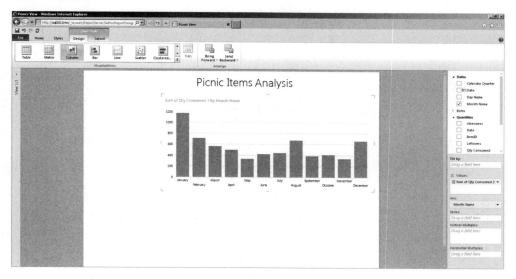

14. From the field list on the right, expand Items, and drag Drawing outside and to the right of the Category Drawing slicers. Click Slicer from the Ribbon menu. The new item Drawing slicer is also a slicer of the Column Chart. Notice that as you click the Category Drawing slicer images, the Drawing slicer is filtered to the item category or item categories selected. The same behavior displays in the Drawing Category slicer as individual images from the Drawing slicer are selected.

15. Resize and reposition the Drawing slicer between the Category Drawing slicer and the Column Chart, as shown in Figure 59-9.

16. From the field list on the right, expand Quantities and drag Sum of Leftovers outside and below the Column Chart.

17. Drag Sum of Qty Served next to Sum of Leftovers inside the same table.

18. Click Line under the Design menu option of the Table Tools. The table changes to a Line Chart.

19. From the field list on the right, expand Dates and drag and drop MonthName to the Axis box below the field list.

FIGURE 59-9

Image slicers with Column Chart.

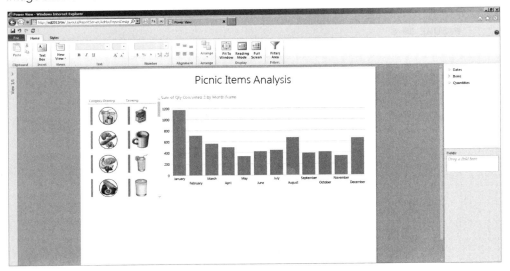

20. Click Layout in the Ribbon menu, and select Show Legend at the bottom from the Legend drop-down menu.

21. Resize the Line Chart to fill the bottom section.

22. Save the Power View report by clicking File ⇨ Save As. The Save As dialog box displays. Type a name, for example, **PicnicItemAnalysis**.

Working with Views

Power View views are like slides in Office PowerPoint. They help organize the report storyline.

To create an additional view follow the next steps:

1. Open the PicnicitemAnalysis report created in the previous set of steps.

2. Under the Home tab click New View on the Ribbon menu. A blank new view opens. You can also duplicate an existing view from the New View option. Notice that the view navigation pane on the left looks similar to the slide navigation pane in Office PowerPoint.

To delete an existing view, follow the next steps:

1. Hover over the view you want to delete on the slide navigation pane on the left.

2. Click the small downward facing arrow on the top-right corner of the view.

3. Select delete view.

Working with Horizontal and Vertical Multiples

Power View supports the ability to break down a chart into smaller multiples of the chart. For example, you can break down a single chart that spans a year into multiple, smaller charts broken down by each month of the year.

To create a chart with vertical multiples follow these steps.

1. Open the PicnicItemAnalysis Power View Report.
2. Create a new view.
3. Click inside the title area. Type a title, for example, **Leftover Versus Server Monthly Analysis**.
4. From the field list on the right, expand Quantities.
5. Drag the measure named Sum of Leftovers to the layout section. The Sum of Leftovers measure displays as a table.
6. Drag the Sum of Qty Served measure next to Sum of Leftovers inside the same table. Make sure Sum of Qty Served is placed inside the same table and not on a separate table.
7. Under the Design menu option of the Table Tools, expand the visualizations options on the Ribbon menu. Click Clustered Column. The table changes to a Clustered Column Chart.
8. From the field list on the right, expand Date.
9. Drag MonthName to the Vertical Multiples box below the field list section.
10. Click Grid on the Layout menu option on the Ribbon menu. Change the chart to a 6 x 2 chart.
11. Change the Legend to show Legend at Top.
12. Resize the chart to occupy all the area below the title, as shown in Figure 59-10.
13. Save the Power View report.

An example involving horizontal multiples may include an analysis where distributors can be compared on a quarterly basis broken down by the months in each quarter.

To create a chart with horizontal multiples follow these steps.

1. Open the PicnicItemAnalysis Power View Report.
2. Create a new view.
3. Click inside the title area. Type a title, for example, **Leftover Versus Server Distributors Quarterly Analysis**.
4. From the field list on the right, expand Quantities.
5. Drag the measure named Sum of Leftovers to the layout section. The Sum of Leftovers measure displays as a table.

59

FIGURE 59-10

Vertical multiples.

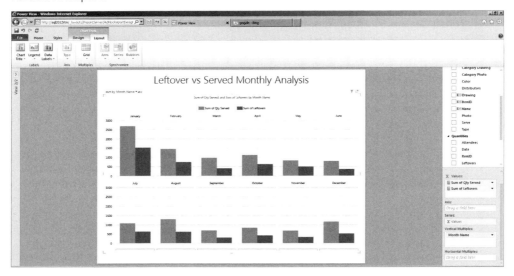

6. Drag the Sum of Qty Served measure next to Sum of Leftovers inside the same table. Make sure Sum of Qty Served is placed inside the same table and not on a separate table.

7. Under the Design menu option of the Table Tools, expand the visualizations options on the Ribbon menu. Click Clustered Bar. The table changes to a Clustered Bar Chart.

8. From the field list on the right, expand Date.

9. Drag MonthName to the Horizontal Multiples box below the field list section.

10. From the field list on the right, expand Items.

11. Drag Distributors to the Axis box below the field list section.

12. Click Grid on the Layout menu option on the Ribbon menu. Change the chart to a 3 x 1 chart.

13. Change the Legend to show Legend at Top.

14. Resize the chart to occupy all the area below the title, as shown in Figure 59-11.

15. Save the Power View report.

Working with Animated Scatter and Bubble Charts

Scatter charts and its variation, the Bubble chart, are great visualizations to see the relationships between data series. Combined with a date dimension, Power View supports animated playback of these relationships through a timeline.

FIGURE 59-11

Horizontal multiples.

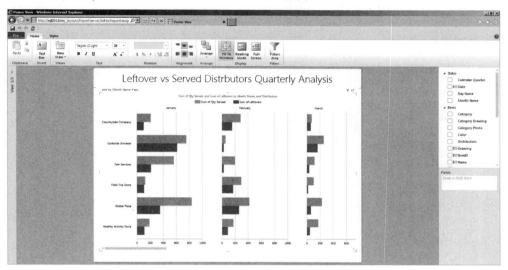

To create an interactive Bubble chart, we by creating a scatter chart by following the next steps:

1. Open the PicnicItemAnalysis Power View Report.

2. Create a new view.

3. Click inside the title area. Type a title, for example, **Attendance & Consumption Analysis**.

4. From the field list on the right, expand Quantities.

5. Drag the measure named Qty Served YTD to the layout section. The Qty Served YTD measure displays as a table.

6. Drag the Sum of Attendees measure next to Qty Served YTD inside the same table. Make sure Sum of Attendees is placed inside the same table and not on a separate table.

7. Expand the visualizations options on the Ribbon menu under the Design menu option of the Table Tools. Click Scatter. The table changes to a Scatter Chart.

8. Drag the Sum of Qty Consumed 2 measure to the Size box below the field list.

9. Expand Items and drag the Name to Details box below the field list.

10. Drag Category to the Color box below the field list.

11. Expand Date and drag MonthName to the Play Axis box below the field list.

12. Resize the chart to occupy all the area below the title, as shown in Figure 59-12.

59

FIGURE 59-12

Bubble chart.

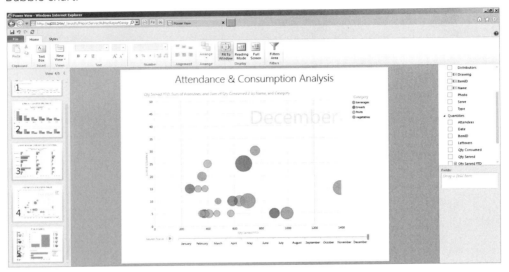

13. Notice the Play button to the left of Months axis (X-axis). Click the Play button and watch the animated rendering of the data through time.

14. Save the Power View report.

Working with Cards

Cards provide a way to display attribute data for dimension members. For example, it can be valuable for building a product catalog.

To create a product catalog using Cards in Power View, follow the next steps:

1. Open the PicnicItemAnalysis Power View Report.

2. Create a new view.

3. Click inside the title area. Type a title, for example, **Product Catalog**.

4. From the field list on the right, expand Items.

5. Drag Name to the layout section.

6. Expand the visualizations options on the Ribbon menu under the Design menu option of the Table Tools. Click Card. The table changes to a Card visualization.

7. Drag the Drawing inside the Card visualization next to Name. The image of the item displays below the item name.

8. Drag Category, Type, and Serve inside the card visualization.

9. Reduce the width of the Card to form two columns, as shown in Figure 59-13.

FIGURE 59-13

Two-column Power View Card.

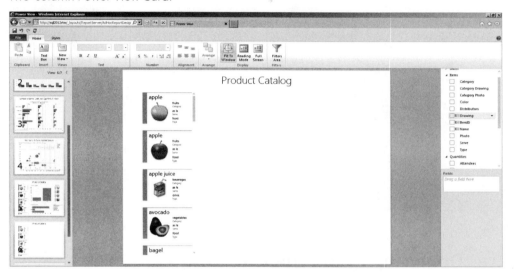

10. Click outside the Card visualization area on an empty area of the layout section.

11. Drag Type to the layout section to create a new table. Click the downward facing arrow next to Type in the field list, and select Add to Table as Count from the drop-down list.

12. Click Column under the Design menu option of the Table Tools. The table changes to a Column Chart.

13. Drag Serve to the layout section to create a new table. Click the downward-facing arrow next to Serve, and select Add to Table as Count from the drop-down list.

14. Click Bar under the Design menu option of the Table Tools. The table changes to a Bar Chart.

15. Drag Distributors to the layout section to create a new table.

16. Click Slicer on the Ribbon menu. The table becomes a slicer.

17. Drag Category Drawing outside and to the right of the Type Column Chart.

18. Click Slicer from the Ribbon menu.

19. Reorganize the data regions, as shown in Figure 59-14.

20. Save the Power View Report.

59

FIGURE 59-14

Product Catalog using a Card.

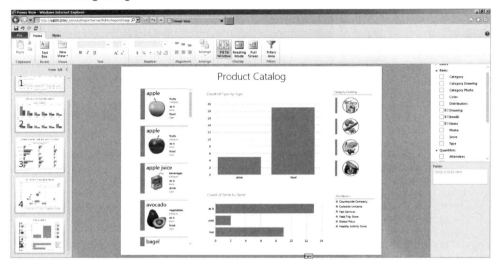

Deploying Power View Reports

Power View reports can be deployed two ways:

1. Uploading the report definition file (.rdlx) to a PowerPivot Gallery
2. Opening and saving the report to the target PowerPivot Gallery.

When deployed, the entity data source properties need to be modified to point to the corresponding Report Data Source.

In addition, Power View enables you to export the entire report into Office PowerPoint while conserving all data interactivity and animations. To export a Power View report to Office PowerPoint, follow these steps:

1. Open the Power View report titled PicnicItemAnalysis created in the previous section.
2. Click File ⇨ Export to PowerPoint.
3. When the export process completes, click Save and provide a name, for example, **PicnicItemAnalysisPPT**.

At this point an Office PowerPoint file has been created containing the controls necessary to provide the same interactivity as Power View. Open the PicnicItemAnalysisPPT file and start the Slide Show. To enable interactivity click the Click to Interact box in the lower-right section of the slide, as shown in Figure 59-15.

FIGURE 59-15

Interactive Power View Report exported to Office PowerPoint.

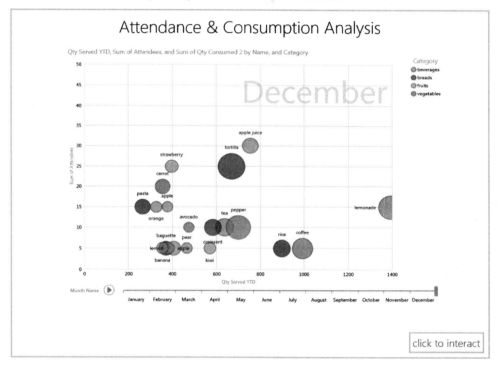

Summary

In this chapter you learned that SQL Server 2012 Reporting Services integration with SharePoint 2010 is required to enable Power View. The SQL Server 2012 edition required is Business Intelligence Edition or Enterprise Edition for production environments along with the SharePoint 2010 Enterprise Edition.

In addition, a browser that supports Silverlight 5 is required to create and view Power View reports.

In order to create Power View reports you first need to create a document library that supports Semantic Model connection file content types. The connection files supported to create Power View reports are the Report Data Source connection file and the BI Semantic Model connection file.

Power View allows you to create horizontal and vertical bar charts, horizontal and vertical multiples, and scatter and bubble charts. Slicers and cards are used to dynamically filter and slice the data.

A nice feature of Power View is the ability to export reports as PowerPoint slides, maintaining the same filtering, slicing, and time re-play interactivity.

Index

Symbols

, (comma)
  CTEs, 239, 240
  locking hints, 1085
; (semi-colon)
  IF, 399
  statements, 137
    termination, 392
*/, comments, 393
/*, comments, 393
$_, PowerShell, 772
& (ampersand)
  and, 179–180
  string concatenation operator,
    178
&& (ampersand/double), SSIS
    Expression Language
    operator, 1186
(angled brackets), nulls, 186
@ (at sign)
  parameters and variables, 1186
  stored procedures, 437
\ (backslash), PowerShell
    directories, 784
^ (caret), XOR, 180–181
{} (curly brackets), PowerShell
    script blocks, 776
$ (dollar sign), parameters, 1184
= (equals sign), nulls, 186
== (equals sign/double), SSIS
    Expression Language
    operator, 1186
! (exclamation mark), SSIS
    Expression Language
    operator, 1186
% (percent sign), modulo operator,
    178
| (pipe symbol), OR, 180
|| (pipe symbol/double), SSIS
    Expression Language
    operator, 1186
+ (plus sign), mathematical
    operator, 178
(pound sign)
  PowerShell comments, 773
  temporary keys, 857

? (question mark), SSIS Expression
    Language operator, 1186
"" (quotation marks-double), SSIS
    Expression Language
    operator, 1187
/ (slash), division operator, 178
[] (square brackets), PowerShell
    variables, 772
* (star), 128
` (tick mark), string values, 441
~ (tilde), NOT, 181

A

abstraction layer
  data integrity, 19
  database
    extensibility, 18
    usability, 17
Access, 376–377
ACID. *See* atomic, consistent,
    isolated, and durable
Action, 1244
/ACTION, 59
actions
  cubes, 1214–1215
  Extended Events, 939
  SQL Audit, 971
/ACTION=REBUILDDATABASE, 580
Active Directory (AD), 753
  installation, 55, 68
  Kerberos, 1271
  Report Manager, 1272
  wait states, 936
  Windows authentication, 836
active transactions, 563
ActiveX, SSIS, 1174
Activity Monitor
  deadlocks, 1061
  transaction blocks, 1057–1058
AD. *See* Active Directory
ad hoc queries, 377
ad hoc reports
  BISM, 1234
  Power View, 1327
add -nosplash, 85
Add Related Tables, 96

addnew, 874
Address Windowing Extensions
    (AWE), 487
Admin Channel, Extended Events,
    941
ADO.NET
  database mirroring, 687
  PowerShell
    module cmdlets, 784
    scripts, 790–792
  SNAC, 74
  SSIS
    Connection Managers, 1168
    container, 1170
    Control Flow, 1172
    Data Flow, 1177, 1178
Advanced Encryption Standard
    (AES), 857
advanced options
  configuration, 478–480
  WHERE, 478
advanced server configuration,
    504–509
  SSMS, 505
AES. *See* Advanced Encryption
    Standard
affinity I/O mask, 488–490
affinity mask, 488–490
AFTER
  columns, 881
  DML, 882
  INSERT, 883
  INSTEAD OF, 895
  RI, 881
  ROLLBACK, 896
  triggers, 880–883
    multiple, 895–896
    recursive, 893
Agent Security, 736–737
Aggregate, SSIS Data Flow, 1180
aggregate concatenation. *See*
    multiple assignment
    variables
aggregate functions
  data, 249–256
  expressions, 251
  GROUP BY, 283

Index

Index